S0-BAA-994

EJS: Discography of the Edward J. Smith Recordings

THE GOLDEN AGE OF OPERA

1. Africaine - O Paradis - Jean De Reszke
2. La Calasera - Adelina Patti
3. Herodiade - Adieu Donc - Francesco Tamagno
4. Titus - Parto - Ernestine Schumann - Heink
5. Martha - Porter Song - Edoard De Reszke

Side 1

33 ⅓ RPM LP
Microgroove

6. Prophete - Roi Du Ciel - Charles Dalmores
7. Prophete - Brindisi - Marianna Brandt
8. Tosca - E Lucevan Le Stelle - Riccardo Martin
9. Romeo - Waltz - Geraldine Farrar
10. Caid - Tambour Major - Pol Plancon

Private Record
Not For Sale

THE GOLDEN AGE OF OPERA

1 Tosca - Recondita Armonia - Ferdinand Ansseau
2. Walkure - Ein Schwert - Lauritz Melchoir
3. Boheme - Addio and Farewell Speech - Nellie Melba
4. Fanciulla Del West - or Son Sei Mesi - Edward Johnson

Side 2

33 ⅓ RPM LP
Microgroove

5. Tosca - Vissi D'Arte - Lotte Lehmann
6. Don Giovanni - Madamina - Feodor Chaliapin
7. Boheme - Vecchia Zimara - Enrico Caruso

Private Record
Not For Sale

"The Golden Age of Opera" - The first of the series' 479 issues, un-numbered except for the matrix number "EJS 100."

EJS: Discography of the Edward J. Smith Recordings

"The Golden Age of Opera," 1956–1971

William Shaman, William J. Collins, and Calvin M. Goodwin

Discographies, Number 54
Michael Gray, Series Editor

Greenwood Press
Westport, Connecticut • London

Library of Congress Cataloging-in-Publication Data

Shaman, William.
EJS, discography of the Edward J. Smith recordings : The golden age of opera, 1956-1971 / William Shaman, William J. Collins, and Calvin M. Goodwin.
p. cm.—(Discographies, ISSN 0192-334X ; no. 54)
Includes bibliographical references (p.) and indexes.
ISBN 0-313-27868-7 (alk. paper)
1. Operas—Discography. I. Smith, Edward J. (Edward Joseph), 1913-1984. II. Collins, William J. III. Goodwin, Calvin M. IV. Title. V. Title: Discography of the Edward J. Smith recordings. VI. Title: Golden age of opera, 1956-1971. VII. Series.
ML156.4.046S5 1994
016.7821'0266—dc20 93-21436

British Library Cataloguing in Publication Data is available.

Library of Congress Catalog Card Number: 93-21436
ISBN: 0-313-27868-7
ISSN: 0192-334X

First published in 1994

Greenwood Press, 88 Post Road West, Westport, CT 06881
An imprint of Greenwood Publishing Group, Inc.

Printed in the United States of America

The paper used in this book complies with the Permanent Paper Standard issued by the National Information Standards Organization (Z39.48-1984).

P

In order to keep this title in print and available to the academic community, this edition was produced using digital reprint technology in a relatively short print run. This would not have been attainable using traditional methods. Although the cover has been changed from its original appearance, the text remains the same and all materials and methods used still conform to the highest book-making standards.

To the memory of Edward J. Smith (1913-1984),
in appreciation of his remarkable legacy of recordings

Contents

Preface

WILLIAM SHAMAN

This is not a book about Edward J. Smith. Nor is it offered as a tribute to his work. Rather, it is an exhaustive discography of The Golden Age of Opera (1956-1971), one of three series of private long-playing reissues commonly referred to as the "EJS" recordings. A second volume will be needed to address the contents of the Unique Opera Record Corporation (UORC) issues (1972-1977), A.N.N.A. Record Company (1978-1981), and the many intervening special issues that completed Smith's private recordings. Not discounting his indefatigable activities as a producer of commercial LPs, the essence of Smith's legacy lay in the many private records compiled and issued under his auspices. By comparison, though the point might be disputed, little of widespread interest appeared in his commercial output of the 1950s and 1960s, whether on Top Artist Platters (TAP), the American Stereophonic Corporation (ASCO), or the myriad of Record Corporation of America labels with which he enjoyed varying degrees of involvement early in his days as a record producer. Clearly, from the standpoint of artistic and historical interest, the private labels emerge in retrospect as his most substantial contribution. Spanning a quarter century, they amounted to nearly a thousand individual releases and perhaps more than five thousand individual recordings.

Unlike my coauthors, I never met Eddie Smith. Nor was I a subscriber to any of the three series of private issues. In fact, my first awareness of them came in the midst of an earlier article that happened to involve the documentation of a solitary Golden Age of Opera (GAO) LP. At the time, William R. Moran, who would eventually come to initiate the "EJS Project," had to instruct me in citing the LP properly, explaining that it was part of a series entitled The Golden Age of Opera and that the catalog number should be preceded by the prefix "EJS," the initials of Edward J. Smith, its producer. I found this first encounter with the label less than fascinating, and thought nothing more of it until the project itself was suggested some three years later. When Bill presented his idea of a complete catalog of the various series, the task seemed an easy one. Notorious for their careless and often negligible documentation, the LPs have been prized collectors' puzzles for generations. Each issue would have to be scrutinized in order that the individual recordings contained might be accurately identified, something Smith never bothered to do himself. We would form a core group of interested "experts" and solicit information from collectors worldwide if necessary, all under my editorship. The project would be run in the English journal *The Record Collector*, edited at the time by the late Clifford Williams, who signed on wholeheartedly. The initial reaction was encouraging. Some of the most distinguished names in the collecting community pledged their immediate support, including coauthor Bill Collins. Early on, Calvin Goodwin wrote to tell me that he owned copies of many of the LPs, had met Smith many years ago, and was willing to assist in any way he could. I had been made aware of only one well-known collector who refused to cooperate at all: Smith's "bungling," this person argued, simply wasn't worth the effort.

Once I received the full set of GAO, UORC, and A.N.N.A. bulletins, I was astonished at the amount of work that needed to be done, but was still confident that it would all be wrapped up neatly within a year or two. More than anyone else, Bill Collins was the first to sober me up, sending me rough outlines of his own early research: dates for French, Belgian, and Mexican performances; grim reminders that certain of the artists were known to have performed the same arias and songs on at least five different broadcasts between 1935 and 1942, so that potpourris and the identification of certain individual items would inevitably present problems; a report that the original NBC acetate information might also be available to us; and notes to the effect that so-and-so had done a great deal of work on such-and-such, but that the manuscript was not yet accessible. From Cal Goodwin came constant mention, in torturous detail, of fluctuations in the playing speeds of the LPs (Bill Moran had warned me that Smith generally transferred all commercial recordings, regardless of their vintage, at 78.26 rpm). Goodwin sent a number of preliminary warnings: that fourteen measures of a *Walküre* Act II had been omitted from one of the LPs, probably for purposes of timing, but that the missing section *had* been recorded and issued on subsequent LPs; and that a certain section of a *Bohème* Act III sounded as if it had been patched in from another source. It then dawned on me that the puzzle might take a while to assemble.

By this time, most pledges of assistance simply disappeared without a trace, leaving the project with two sustaining informants (Collins and Goodwin), a small band of authorities who could always be approached when individual problems arose, and an already discouraged editor. However, it should be clear from the acknowledgments in the Introduction that the response was still very encouraging and remained so throughout the project. Many collectors from around the world sent suggestions, bits of information, and invaluable archival materials from their own research. Some were collectors whose enthusiasm was limited to a single, significant performer. Others were able to send an incredible array of facts and observations. Some were writing books and articles and were gracious enough to provide us with information gathered during their own investigation of EJS-related material. Many were approached for specific details and willingly combed their shelves for the required discs. Institutions and archives never let us down, nor did any of the record dealers we approached; my own bids having failed to purchase the required items at auction, dealers were always willing to furnish the information we needed before sending discs off to their new owners.

Gradually, over a period of three or four years, it became apparent that the collective expertise and spade work of both Bill Collins and Cal Goodwin deserved more than a starred acknowledgment in the beginning of what had already become a book-length discography. The project had long outgrown the serialized approach originally proposed, as well as the support of the magazine in which it began. I offered coauthorship to both Collins and Goodwin, with the understanding that I would actually do the writing, organizing, and assembling. They accepted, and what gradually emerged was a catalog fully compiled by the three of us. The notes and text are mine, for the most part, and I must take full and unhappy responsibility for their length and often peripheral relevance. All first-person references, therefore, designate my own views; Bill Collins's direct additions to the text will frequently be quoted when left to stand on their own. Our respective roles in the compilation of the discography reflect our own areas of interest and specialization: both Bill Collins and Cal Goodwin are truly multifaceted authorities on all matters operatic; I am not, so that much of the textual score analysis is their work. The lion's share of details prescribing correct playing speeds were provided by Cal Goodwin, and constitute one of the most significant additions to the discography. Live performances, especially from abroad, were the domain of Bill Collins, who has been compiling information on them from a host of contemporary and retrospective sources for many years, while the responsibility for documenting broadcasts, foreign and domestic, was shared. Commercial recordings were my own private obsession, and no effort has been spared to document those that appeared on the LPs in the greatest detail, whether from private collections or from company ledgers--the latter with the unfailing cooperation of William R. Bryant (Columbia), Alan Kelly (the Gramophone Company), and William R. Moran (Victor and miscellaneous labels).

One question has followed us throughout our seven years of researching the contents of these LPs: why EJS? Why bother cataloging their contents in the first place, considering their often primitive transfers, inaccurate playing speeds, noisy surfaces, and the many outrageous errors and falsehoods of documentation that have come to discredit them? Indeed, the current editor of a prominent collector's magazine once argued in correspondence that the EJS issues have become useless in the wake of a "new generation" of collectors' LPs. He named several well-known labels to support his case, and by implication, countless other pirate products currently available, most of them similar in their overall content to the EJS LPs.

Above all, there is pride of place. Edward J. Smith was not the first record pirate, nor was he the first, strictly speaking, to issue live historical performances. Rather, the sheer thrust of what he accomplished, as well as when and under what practical obstacles he accomplished it, made him a pioneer. The quantity of LPs he issued may eventually be matched or even exceeded by those who have followed, just as the quality of current and future private offerings will no doubt surpass Smith's--certainly the advent of the compact disc alone has already seen to that. Similarly, as more is discovered, even greater rarities will undoubtedly appear. But Smith's issues will always be there to mock any claims of pioneering efforts; while others may succeed in cleaning up the mess he often made, the fact remains that Smith was there before them.

Second, even more remarkable than their sheer quantity is the general quality of Smith's offerings. The routinely poor pressings notwithstanding, his instincts were always sharp and true; with few exceptions, the contents of his private LPs remain relevant even today, and of the utmost artistic and historical value, whether in the preservation of rare individual performances of significant vintage or in the obscure repertory they offer. The often poor quality of the source materials Smith used, like that of the transfers and the record surfaces, can be overcome to some extent through the use of modern equipment: for all of the abuse that his releases have sustained, it is significant that his original LPs have been used time and again by other major reissue labels as their source. With surprisingly few exceptions, the new crop of collectors' labels that emerged alongside and subsequent to Smith's activities have proven equally disappointing, imitating, for the most part, rather than learning from, their predecessors. Many have converted their catalogs recently to compact disc employing the same tapes used to prepare their earlier LPs, making it painfully obvious from the reissues just how poor the surfaces of the original LPs really were--matching in quality some of Smith's worst efforts.

Several of these labels, moreover, continue to offer recitals without any accompanying documentation and do so without explanation, one of several indictments traditionally tendered against Smith. Live performances often carry no dates or circumstances, and vintage studio recordings may appear without even so much as a catalog number! A prolific British label, for example, whose historical reissues now number in the hundreds, persists in offering liner notes as comically error ridden as any Smith ever produced. In other curious instances, a New York label issued a recital some years ago that included a stray aria by another singer, and instead of correcting the error on the original LP, simply added a note on the jacket testifying to the fact that the company was aware of the mistake; a Canadian label managed to include an aria incorrectly attributed to the singer in question, and though purged from later pressings, the error remained (with an explanation) on the LP jacket and in the enclosed notes. Major labels have had similar difficulties in reconciling the stated contents of an LP with what is actually included--Victor's various Caruso editions are a sobering case in point. Incorrect transfer speeds, another regrettable shortcoming in Smith's catalog of issues, have plagued LPs for decades, including those produced by the most prestigious major labels--the first volume of Electrical Musical Industries' (EMI) original "The Record of Singing" and "Sänger auf dem grünen Hügel" sets, and Danacord's multivolume Melchior Anthology are only a few of the more baffling examples. Like proud sleuths who have just broken the case, collectors, as authorities in such matters, delight in the detection of these kinds of "bloopers"--until cast themselves in the more vulnerable role of consumer. While the Smith LPs carried more than their fair share of sloppy documentation, tangled contents, and wild playing speeds, they were hardly unique in this respect. Even surveying the current scene, when the potential for documenting historical recordings from primary source materials has never been greater, a resolution to address these problems once and for all seems to be disappointingly slow in arriving.

The EJS LPs have become a permanent part of the landscape of recorded sound and the contemplation of historical performance. For all their perceived faults, they will be eagerly sought until each one of them has been replaced by something better. Even now, the Golden Age of Opera, UORC, and A.N.N.A. LPs command high prices on the collectors' market, with no indication that their value will decrease as the supply diminishes. For those who were fortunate enough to subscribe to the various series while they were still active, for those who continue to fill in the gaps in their holdings, and for those who are just now discovering the value of what Smith was able to produce, it is our hope that this discography will prove useful, revealing, and even entertaining, or at least lead to a thorough understanding of the contents of the LPs. To the discographical community at large, which may include those with few of Smith's LPs or perhaps none at all, we hope that it will provide an adequate means of dealing confidently with other important matters lying outside of one's ownership of the actual records. Considering the number of off-the-air, live, and privately recorded performances that are documented in the discography, there will no longer be any need to indulge in cursory entries dated from Smith's own labels and bulletins, or to ignore altogether the many extant noncommercial recordings released by Smith in the first place. We feel that the details given in the discography extend far beyond the mere fact that the material was issued by Smith. The Smith LPs give us the opportunity to marvel at the quantity and variety of musical performances that have survived from the adolescence--if not the infancy--of recorded sound through the 1970s, a period of nearly three quarters of a century. Taken with other sources, this first volume of *EJS: The Discography of the Edward J. Smith Recordings* chronicles far more than the contents of The Golden Age of Opera series, which is why we were so easily absorbed in the task of compiling it.

Our greatest hope is that the book gives some indication that there is little out there that cannot be documented if the facts are ruthlessly pursued, and that there is absolutely no excuse for assuming otherwise.

WILLIAM J. COLLINS

Some of the performances that Edward J. Smith presented on his thousand-odd LP releases can truly be honored by that much-overused word in record collecting and opera fandom, "legendary." In several subsidiary connections, it can as well be applied to the man himself. Whether Eddie Smith was describing his own background, his personal relationships with singers, or little-known "facts" concerning the history of recording, his rapt listeners (he was a remarkably talented raconteur) could never be sure whether he was recounting literal, though seemingly outlandish, truth; relaying some traditional fable, often esoteric; or relating a felicitous invention, something that should have been true, even if it wasn't. Nor was one sure that in the years of his retelling, the fables and inventions had not become true for him.

Notice that I do not, and will not, convict Eddie Smith of knowingly telling falsehoods (except, with some justification, on a very few of his many error-filled labels). Rather, I think that some of his stories, especially about himself, may have been wishes that would have been so "right," so worthy of being true, that by the time they became a portion of his repartee, he genuinely believed them. And then again, fabulous as some of them were, I hope they were true.

The legend of Eddie Smith himself, which he told me on our first meeting in 1960, and which I later heard almost word for word in the company of others just meeting him, begins in infancy. His mother, he would recount, had a box at the Metropolitan Opera House and, lacking a nanny, would often take the infant Smith with her to performances. Thus he heard Caruso some sixty times before the tenor's untimely death. Smith sometimes added that (as befit a future critic) when lesser singers displayed their art, he might be prone to crying, but Caruso's voice (according to his mother) always soothed him. Of course, Eddie would conclude wistfully that he had no conscious memory of this time, but he *had* heard Caruso!

Another memory, this of a nine-year-old Smith dragged away from his beloved baseball for a tour of France with his mother, involves him sitting in a hallway of a palatial home in Nice, slapping a ball into the mitt he'd insisted on bringing abroad, and being told sharply, as a voice welled from the adjoining room, to be quiet and listen! He'd never hear this sound again! Shortly thereafter his mother introduced him to the owner of the voice, just finished giving a lesson: the portly, courtly Polish emigré, Jean De Reszke, who in the course of the coaching session had momentarily, miraculously, recovered the voice of legend for a few moments. (From this French tour there was also a story of hearing, at a private concert, one of the last appearances of Mattia Battistini, but I don't remember the details.)

Baseball occupied the next Smith legend, that he had "a cup of coffee" with the Brooklyn Dodgers. The phrase, well known to American sports fans, is usually taken to refer to a brief appearance in a major league game or two, but no encyclopedia of baseball lists a "Smith, Edward J." in its complete roster of major league players. I once mentioned this to Eddie privately, at which point he elaborated that he had participated in spring training with the Dodgers (an annual month-long session in March, held in sunny Florida, at which regular players work off months of rust and promising minor leaguers are given an opportunity to show their skills in exhibition games) but hadn't been invited to join Brooklyn for its official schedule.

As baseball faded and music, in some form, became Eddie's profession, his stories became more involved with singers, both as participant in personal encounters and as recipient of their own, perhaps embroidered, tales. Certainly, Eddie and his family had close ties to the great Metropolitan Opera singers of the late 1920s and 1930s. His accounts of being dandled on the knee of "Uncle Giovanni" Martinelli ring true, given the close relationship he maintained with the great tenor from Smith's youth through Martinelli's death in 1969, and suggest he may have been recounting unwritten history rather than tall tales, no matter how outrageous.

From time to time, his stories were off-color. Eddie maintained a repertoire of "men only" stories, and would sometimes politely request "the ladies" to retire from the room for a while (then, on at least one occasion that I recall, telling the stories loudly enough that the banished females would be sure to hear, in the airiness of California-modern architecture). I, for one, believe Smith's veracity when he stated that Martinelli was born in 1881 rather than 1885, and that a friendly parish priest altered the birth register so that Martinelli could help his family until the next oldest brother could relieve him to do mandatory military service. According to Smith, Martinelli retained the later date in his official biography because, he quoted the tenor, "If I tell a young woman I'm 65, she'll only think I have one foot in the grave. If I say I'm 69, she'll think I have both feet there." I confess to having sanitized the quote to refer to "critics" rather than "a young woman" in my own 1979 biography of the tenor published in *The Record Collector*.

Martinelli's London debut in 1912 provided another favorite "men only" story. The tenor, recently married, had been observing the folk tale that a period of celibacy prior to performances enhanced the voice (a practice that many female singers, Tetrazzini among them, appear to have rejected). At any rate, according to Smith, Martinelli claimed that a Covent Garden female chorister hid in the tenor's dressing room on the night of his London debut, and seduced him. "I never sang better," Smith quoted Martinelli as saying.

If the story is true, an aftermath may have proved disastrous. In January 1938, Martinelli sang Radames in a Metropolitan Opera *Aïda* broadcast (preserved on UORC 262) in which he became ill during "Celeste Aïda" and was replaced by Frederick Jagel. The official press release stated that Martinelli had eaten some tainted fish, but according to Smith, he had spent the night before with a young French soprano.

Smith's "great moment" is somewhat more suspect. He would reminisce about his days as a cub reporter, especially one snowy afternoon when he was scheduled to interview Geraldine Farrar at her Connecticut home. By the time he reached her house, the roads had become impenetrable. The interview over, Farrar insisted that he stay the night, rather than risk his life in the blizzard. And yes, fairy tales do come true, according to Eddie, though personally I'd have less trouble believing that he really heard Jean De Reszke!

Only a few of Smith's favorite stories were off-color, though. He was more of a master at embroidering wonderful, sometimes demonstrably untrue, stories in which he played no part. For James Seaver's PBS-syndicated radio show from Lawrence, Kansas, he could, with a straight face, insist that in the 1908 Victor recording of the *Madama Butterfly* duet with Caruso and Farrar, Farrar noticed Caruso was drunk and, in place of the text's "Si per la vita," interpolated to the studio crew "He's had a highball" (Farrar did, in fact, pronounce "vita" as "vye-ta," a common practice among sopranos, the "ee" sound being difficult above the staff), and that Caruso, indignant, sang "Vieja, vieja" (in Spanish, "witch") instead of the written "Vieni, vieni." The story, which had circulated for decades, had been exploded long before. But it was a legend, and a treasured one.

Legends that can't be documented one way or another can be even more tantalizing. One such involved Beniamino Gigli. According to Eddie, on Christmas Eve, 1944, following the Allied conquest of Italy, a band of partisans kidnapped a pajama-clad Gigli, intent on executing him for his willing service to the fallen dictator, Benito Mussolini. Far out in the woods, snow falling, Gigli expected to be shot. But at the last moment, the partisan leader (obviously a true Italian) said, "The man deserves to die--but we have no right to kill the voice," and punished the tenor by making him walk back in the freezing cold in his slippers and thin clothing. Certainly Gigli never mentioned this incident in his ghostwritten autobiography, and one would search for it in vain in the sycophantic, almost useless biography by his daughter, Rina. But there is an Italian saying that applies to all of Eddie Smith's stories: "Se non e vero e ben trovato" (loosely, "If it's not true, it should be").

Having to some undetermined extent created a past involving incidents both in his own life and in the lives of others (at which he could not have been present) one can begin to understand how many of Eddie Smith's errors of documentation, as "exposed" in this volume, proceed from the same impulse, directed at recordings. He was often honest enough, as with the purported Jean De Reszke cylinder on The Golden Age of Opera 452, or the bogus "undiscovered" Mapleson cylinders on GAO 267, to caution prospective buyers as to the possibility--even probability--of their not being genuine. As probably the first private-label publisher to feature broadcast performances prominently on his reissues (a few broadcast fragments had appeared on such labels as The International Record Collectors' Club [IRCC] and the Peoria Record Collectors' Club, but those labels were composed overwhelmingly of rare commercial discs), Eddie was the first to feel the wrath of such giants as the Toscanini family, the Metropolitan Opera, and Universal Edition, publishers of, among other works, the operas of Richard Strauss. Thus, a few of his labels are intentionally misleading. In such cases he relied on either the closely knit fellowship of record collectors or plain common sense to separate fiction from fact. Is there any subscriber who corresponded with Eddie, or who had a collector friend in the New York area, who wasn't aware that in the Martucci *Canzone dei Ricordi* (GAO 384) the orchestra and conductor assisting Bruna Castagna was not the Teatro Colon Orchestra under Panizza, as labeled, but the NBC Symphony Orchestra conducted by Toscanini? Is there anyone who believed that a Mexican or Brazilian opera company would not only import Metropolitan Opera stars (which they often did) but also send thousands of miles for Thelma Votipka, John Dudley, or George Cehanovsky to sing comprimario roles? (At least one of Smith's vinyl descendants, ERR Records, on publishing the March 1960 Met *Andrea Chenier* with Tucker, Tebaldi, and Bastianini, disguised the fact by listing an undercast populated by such documented Mexican comprimarii as Concha de los Santos, Carlos Sagarminaga, and Francisco Alonso.)

Ironically, Smith need not have feared Universal Edition. As they demonstrated in licensing Strauss operas for limited-edition pressing by various companies headed by Fred Maroth (the Bruno Walter Society, Discocorp, and so forth) for fees often under three figures, the publishing company cared not a whit whether the actual performances were of dubious legality or not. But Eddie's sense of mystery at least once extended beyond recordings to an actual series of performances. By the time, in 1967, that he and Giovanni Martinelli had left New York for a series of lectures by Martinelli on the West Coast, every opera fanatic in New York knew that Smith had arranged the tenor's Seattle talk to coincide with the local opera company's performance of *Turandot*, and had further arranged for the tenor singing the Emperor Altoum to "become ill" at the last moment, whereupon the company's director would appeal to Martinelli, retired for 19 years, to tread the boards once more, in a role his now limited vocal resources could still handle. It is also not a coincidence that *Time Magazine*'s Seattle correspondent "happened" to be present at the otherwise undistinguished performance, to write of the event as the next week's major music article. Only Martinelli remained ignorant of the subterfuge.

But many, many of Eddie Smith's issues came with errors that have the justification of neither wishful thinking nor of legitimate prevarication, and the compilers of this volume have, collectively and individually, muttered endless imprecations in his direction for not having possessed the soul of a researcher, a reaction we undoubtedly share with many of his fortunate subscribers to the various labels he published. But then we collect ourselves, and recall that if he had not so prodigally and prolifically issued those truly legendary radio performances by the great singers of the 1920s and 1930s; if he had not filled in, in whatever semiacceptable sound and questionable speeds, the otherwise unrecorded operas of Meyerbeer, Rossini, Donizetti, and lesser lights, at least a decade before other private labels emerged to clothe them in better sound, better pressings, and (usually) better documentation, perhaps FWR, Penzance, BJR, MRF, and VOCE, to name only a few, would not have existed. Perhaps Philips would never have embarked on its early Verdi and complete Haydn series of the early 1970s. Perhaps Bongiovanni and Nuova Era would not have realized the potential audience for the works of Catalani, Gomes, Mercadante, Smareglia. They might still only be available in libraries, as forgotten scores. And though there are score readers who love opera, the true opera fan knows that a score only comes alive in performance--whether good, bad, or mediocre--that can be felt, at least aurally. Eddie Smith was the first to give us those aural thrills.

The various EJS labels predeceased Edward J. Smith by only a brief time. To this day, on his labels and those of his pirate successors, the only real way to assess forgotten composers is through out-of-print, rarely found recordings. The off-trail repertoire seems in safe hands via a number of European companies, but legal restrictions have ensured that many of the Metropolitan's fabled 1930s broadcasts remain retrievable only on Smith's labels. More important, among the thousands of vocal treasures published on the EJS potpourris and artist recital discs, except for a few artists such as Bjoerling and Ponselle, only a handful have been retrieved in CD form. If the present volume also serves to acquaint current CD publishers with what exists, it will have served a valuable purpose.

No, Eddie Smith was no scholar-discographer. He responded viscerally to great singing and great music, and felt an unselfish need to share that response with others. By his upbringing, his various professions, his second marriage (of three), which opened the doors of private Italian collections to him, he had an access afforded to few others to the vocal treasures he shared with us. The private transcription collections of old Met friends such as Martinelli, Tibbett, Ponselle, and Pinza; broadcast tapes and acetates from Europe, Mexico, and South America; in-house recordings made by fellow opera fanatics--all these he felt it his duty to share with those of us who lacked his background and his friendships.

Having been exposed, if we believe him, almost from birth to great singing, it should come as no surprise that in his later years he became impatient with what he considered the continually declining standards of vocal art. On a visit to his Weehawken home a few years before his death, I was told by his third wife, Anna, that she had seen the first acts of dozens of operas, but that she quickly became used to the signs: ill-concealed muttering and grumbling, increasing as the end of the first act of Whatever approached--culminating in his escorting her from the opera house, complaining that Flagstad or Leider and Melchior, Martinelli and Ponselle, Gigli and Caniglia, Tibbett, Schorr, Pinza, Lauri-Volpi had all done it so much better. The one performance she remembered managing to see all the way through was, ironically, an opera she found she disliked, Eve Queler's concert performance of Smetana's *Dalibor*, with Nicolai Gedda, which Eddie later issued on the A.N.N.A. label. In this respect, Eddie showed somewhat less forbearance than his grandmother, according to one of his least-related but most endearing stories. The grandmother, who lived several years beyond her centenary, had, according to a prelude to the main story, been so passionate about music that, at the age of six or seven, she had sneaked out of her convent school in Paris to hear Mendelssohn conduct his *Elijah*, and had maintained her love of music for 106 or so remarkably alert years. Just before her death, around 1945, Smith related that he decided to take her to a New York Philharmonic matinee, an all-Mozart program conducted by Bruno Walter. At intermission, though Walter had conducted beautifully and the orchestra had played at its best, Grandmother began putting on her wraps. Surprised and a bit alarmed, Eddie queried her. Was she feeling ill? No. Didn't she like the music? The performance? She responded, "Yes, dear, it's quite nice, but I've been listening to Mozart for a hundred years, and I'd like to hear something else now."

Ill health may have contributed to Smith's dissatisfaction with live performance, but almost to the end it could not dampen his enthusiasm for sharing significant performances with us. He left us thousands of hours of legend. The compilers of this book have spent many years in service to that legacy. Far more often than our periodic frustrations at having to comb the resources of three continents (or worse, having to discover them first), we have contemplated the immense debt that we--compilers (and the host of collectors who have assisted us), vocal connoisseurs, students of conducting and performance practice, repertoire completists--owe to him. Edward J. Smith left us a vocal and musical treasure the magnitude of which is immense--truly, like the man and his stories, legendary.

CALVIN M. GOODWIN

"For those who understand, no explanation is necessary; for those who do not, no explanation is possible." Like a Dante warning, this ought perhaps to be written at the entryway to the book that follows. The world of The Golden Age of Opera, as Edward J. Smith grandly titled his first series of private long-play releases, is a labyrinth of off-center pressings, off-pitch transfers, misattributions, incorrect dates, and grinding, hissing, crackling surface noise. Some might reasonably ask, why bother?

A long time ago, when I was young, I used to amuse myself by leafing through the pages of William Seltsam's *Metropolitan Opera Annals*. Yet, here I am being disingenuous; it was not amusement, it was passion. I dreamt of those performances of yesteryear, lost, as I supposed, forever--Ponselle's Violetta, Bori's Melisande, Martinelli's Enzo, and Tibbett in all those intriguing American creations. No voices are more enticing than those beyond recall.

Then, quite without fanfare or previous information, I discovered the Smith records. An older collector handed me a copy of EJS 404, Pacini's *Saffo*, the title role sung by Leyla Gencer. I accepted it without much enthusiasm. It was entirely unimpressive, a rough-looking pressing in plain white envelopes, no outer sleeve, no notes, no information of any kind beyond a cast listing on the white label. I had never heard of the opera and the soprano's name meant nothing to me, but the composer at least sounded familiar (actually, I was confusing him with Piccinni!). I played the records, listened to Leyla Gencer, and fell in love.

As if this weren't enough for a susceptible adolescent collector, I next acquired a Smith list. This was a catalog of previous releases that Smith issued in updated form at irregular intervals. Some of the record numbers were incorrect. Not all available titles were listed. Many listed recordings were unavailable. But still . . .

There was the Ponselle *Traviata*. I could not believe my eyes: my headiest fantasy come true! And Martinelli in *Aïda*--at Gina Cigna's Met debut! This was beyond belief. *Peter Ibbetson*, *Merry Mount*, *The Emperor Jones*, and a contemporary radio adaptation of *The King's Henchman*: practically a catalog of Tibbett's *creator* repertoire at the Met!

When I bought my first Smith recordings, they cost $3.25. Even for a kid in high school, with a high school kid's budget, this was cheap. Boring commercial records cost twice that. Here was treasure for the asking. And did I ask! Ultimately Mr. Smith got so sick of me asking for out-of-print items (and of course *all* the most desirable issues were out of print) that he finally said to me on the telephone one day, "Goodwin, if you can get yourself down to New Jersey, you can go through the odds and ends in my basement and see what you can find." I flew.

That was when I first met Ed Smith, about eight years after my encounter with *Saffo*. I'm not sure what I expected him to be like. In any event, I thought he looked like a gangster and talked like one. Jaded collectors will perhaps not be surprised to know this. In the cellar of his home in Weehawken were rows and rows of shelves from ceiling to floor, filled with Golden Age of Opera records in their paper sleeves. There must have been thousands of them. They were in no order whatsoever, and I mean *no* order: you might find one record of a two-disc set on one shelf and its partner several hundred records away. Or you might not find it at all. Some were without labels, and here Mr. Smith really did impress me because he could tell me what the records were just from the catalog numbers etched upon them. Now, after working on this book for all these years, the authors can probably do the same, but at the time I thought it quite a feat.

Mr. Smith could be a little abrupt in manner, but he was also a kind and generous man. When I presented my pile of a few hundred treasures gleaned from his abundant shelves (thinking that I'd never be able to afford them all and that I'd never be able to eliminate any of them either), he said, "O.K., a dollar if they're in good shape and fifty cents if the surface is poor." Of course his records almost always had poor surfaces, so I made out very well indeed.

That visit resulted in a substantial addition to my Smith collection, though I have added continuously since. Mr. Smith lived only a few years more, but he continued to issue records almost to the end, first on the Unique Opera Records label (he eschewed modest names for his labels: remember TAP, Top Artist Platters, and ASCO, the all-mono American Stereophonic Corporation?) and then on the A.N.N.A. label.

Those who are acquainted with the records will also be familiar with their limitations. Label information is often approximate and always incomplete. Spelling is casual. Almost everything was slapped onto the discs at one speed, and the fact that very few of the sources were correctly pitched seemed to be of little importance. Smith's penchant for squeezing maximum (sometimes beyond maximum!) amounts of music onto an LP side, so often to the detriment of the sound quality, is legendary. Moreover, he has frequently been accused of lack of discrimination in determining what should be issued, sometimes including items that were not flattering to an artist's reputation, last gasps of long-retired singers, and what J. B. Steane has called "jollifications at parties." Well, it's all true, and no one knows it better than the authors of this book.

But then history does not always come in neat, ideally preserved and annotated packages. When Smith began to make available often-extraordinary material to collectors, many were not even aware of its existence. How easy, in hindsight, to wish that he had been more careful in his presentation, accuracy, and technical niceties. Perhaps there were others, even in those early days, who might have done a better job. But it was Smith alone, for many years, who made it possible for historians, students, and music lovers to hear and examine whole segments of operatic history in our century. The fine tuning was indeed left to us, but the substance was there for study and delight. For this reason a thorough, serious examination of his voluminous output is warranted and needed.

Yet I must say, from the vantage of a collector, that it is the sheer delight in my experience of these recordings that has remained throughout the years: the delight in the chance to listen to Bori, Johnson, and Tibbett in Deems Taylor's faded yet fragrant *Peter Ibbetson*, the delight in meeting a range of otherwise unheard music that has given great pleasure--Mascagni's *Isabeau*, Bellini's *La Straniera*, Damrosch's *The Man Without a Country*--as well as many others decades before commercial companies got round to them: Korngold's *Die Tote Stadt*, Catalini's *Dejanice*, Richard Strauss's *Guntram*, and so many of the less well-known Verdi operas.

Over the years I have waded through so much, and so many varieties of surface noise that even the hurricane or tornado that seems to be going on during the 1934 *Pelléas* with Bori, Johnson, and Pinza doesn't really bother me: I'm too grateful for the opportunity to be there at all. It is true that for many of us collectors the marvel of recorded music in itself has never faded, but the opportunity to hear, at the touch of a switch, Ponselle, Schorr, Lehmann, Steber, Castagna, Pinza, and so many others in performances that are historic in every sense--well, Unique Opera Records, indeed!

The work that we have done to compile this book has taken a long time. In fact, the work is still incomplete. It has to be. There are mysteries that we simply could not solve; there is information that we could not recover. We can only say that we have done our best to give a full account of this extraordinary series of records. We hope that collectors will be able to supplement, complete, and correct our work where possible. Incredible as it may sound, considering the bulk of the volume at hand, I think that I can say that we regard it as a beginning more than anything else. We hope also that this book may serve as a tribute to a man who could be stubborn, cavalier, indiscriminate, and exasperating, and to whom we all owe a debt of gratitude that never, never can be repaid.

Acknowledgments

Thanks first to the colleagues listed below, who assisted most, going far beyond the call of duty in the time they spent researching, listening, and reporting details to one or more of the authors, sending original source information or helping in some way to see that this project came eventually to be published. Their contributions, sometimes direct, sometimes indirect, were of inestimable value.

Mr. William R. Bryant, Portland, Maine
Mr. Jim Cartwright, Austin, Texas
Mr. Robert Fazio, Long Island, New York
Mr. Victor Girard, Concord, California
Dr. Herbert Glass, Champaign, Illinois
Mr. Stanton Golding and the late Mimi Golding, San Francisco
Mr. David Hamilton, New York City
Mr. Alan Kelly, Sheffield, England
Dr. Deane A. Kishel, Bemidji, Minnesota
Mr. W.R. Moran, La Cañada, California
Mr. Marc Ricaldone, East Sussex, England
Mr. Charles R. Rose, Oakland, California
Mr. Desmond Shawe-Taylor, Wimborne, Dorset, England
Mr. Christopher Sullivan, Norwich, England
Mr. Ed Wilkinson, Oakland, California

Thanks also to the many others who have come to our aid at various stages, some bearing information, lists of corrections, or important editorial support, others bearing details essential to the project:

Peter Adamson, St. Andrews, Fife, Scotland
Linda Ashworth, Amsterdam
Brian Bailey, Bellingham, Washington
Manfred Bartolet, Merion Station, Pennsylvania
Loftus E. Becker, Jr., Hartford, Connecticut
David Breckbill, Lincoln, Nebraska
Jonathan Brown, Turner, A.C.T., Australia

Nathan Brown, San Pablo, California
Daniel Budinger, Arlington Heights, Illinois
J. Christjaans, Maastricht.
Frederick B. Crane, Iowa City, Iowa
César-Arturo Dillon, Buenos Aires
Juan Dzazopulos, Santiago, Chile
Henrik Engelbrecht, Copenhagen
Byron Erck, Royal, Arkansas
Edward C. Gordon, Kensington, California
Henry Hall, Sydney, Australia
Lawrence F. Holdridge, Amityville, New York
T. A. Hood, Vancouver, Canada
John T. Hughes, Orpington, Kent, England
A. H. Julian, Murrieta, California
John Kunish, Lake Mills, Wisconsin
Lim Lai, San Francisco
Hardy Laporte, San Francisco
George E. Laviolette (the late), Bridgeport, Connecticut
Derek Lewis, BBC, London
Ernst Lumpe, Soest, Germany
Carlo Marinelli, Rome
Gus Mollee, Secretary, *Leo Riemans Stichting*, Liderdorp, Holland
Susan K. Nelson, Bemidji, Minnesota
Dan Opperman, San Francisco
C.-P. Gerald Parker, Montreal
Emil Pinta, Worthington, Ohio
John B. Richards (the late), England
Leo Riemans (the late), Holland
Phillip Rochlin, Silver Springs, Maryland
Giorgio Sani, Genova, Italy
Ronald Seeliger, Austin, Texas
Donald M. Sileo, Norwalk, Connecticut
Clyde W. Smith, Melville, New York
James Sneddon, London
Alex Soto, San Francisco
Klaus Tobias (the late), London
Richard Warren, Jr., Yale University, New Haven, Connecticut
Milt Weiss, Hollywood, Florida
Raymond R. Wile, Flushing, New York
Clifford Williams (the late), Pontrhydyfen, Port Talbot, Wales
Dan Wolfert, Roslyn Heights, New York
Robert Ziering (the late), New York City

Libraries and Institutions

Biblioteca Nacional (Elaine Perez), Rio de Janeiro, Argentina
U. C. Berkeley Libraries, University of California, Berkeley
The DeBellis Collection (Mrs. Serena DeBellis), California State University, San Francisco
The Furtwängler Society of America, San Francisco
Peter J. Shields Library, University of California, Davis
Stanford University Archives of Recorded Sound, Palo Alto, California
United States Consulate (Janet Boggs), Montevideo, Uruguay
University of Illinois Libraries, Champaign-Urbana
Visual and Performing Arts Department, Harold Washington Library Center, Chicago

It is our sincere hope that none of our generous informants have been omitted. Thanks is tendered as well to the many authors who have published discographical research over the years, whether in standard sources or as appendices to book-length works. From this large body of work, much information has been taken.

Introduction

Edward J. Smith crowded many professions into a busy lifetime. He was at various times a journalist, music critic, publicist, and impresario, but the lion's share of his abundant energy, from the early 1950s until his death, was devoted to his work as a producer of commercial and noncommercial long-playing records, first for a number of small, New York-based labels, and eventually for several of his own. Few of the commercial records he produced were in any way distinguished. The best of them were compiled with collectors in mind and featured, like so many other labels in the 1950s and 1960s, compilations of old operatic recordings of limited appeal to anyone else. A few sought to preserve in high fidelity the voices of artists long retired but still capable of singing professionally, and these remain among his most substantial, if somewhat obscure, accomplishments. The others, for the most part, were operatic adaptations produced on a small budget with minor performers. Gradually, Smith must have come to realize that his audience was, and would remain, extremely limited, and that he could scarcely compete with the major labels for a share of a retail market already dominated by popular music. Even in the field of historical reissues, the major labels were offering formidable, if sporadic, competition. So, by the mid-1950s Smith adopted another, wisely conservative strategy that had served a number of eminent predecessors well: private issues sold by subscription.

Special edition recordings sold by subscription were already entrenched by the 1950s. In 1931 EMI inaugurated a variety of subscription editions on their HMV, Columbia, and Parlophone labels, devoted primarily to repertory scantily represented in the general catalogs. Distinctive performances by major artists made available hitherto unrecorded works of Bach, Beethoven, Brahms, Couperin, Delius, Haydn, Mahler, Mozart, Schubert, Sibelius, and Wolf to the gramophile. Christened "Society" issues, they were nonetheless sold in retail stores, the only restriction being that individual discs were not sold separately, but only in complete sets. These were contemporary recordings, not reissues, however, as were the chamber music recordings of the Chicago Gramophone Society and British National Gramophonic Society, the dominant concerns of which were repertory, not performance. New Music Quarterly, similarly, devoted itself to twentieth-century music, while the French *L'Anthologie Sonore* and *Éditions de l'Oiseau-Lyre* offered scholarly performances primarily of choral and chamber music.

The small market for historical material had previously been overseen by at least two major labels, Victor and HMV. Both courteously maintained special-order catalogs throughout the 1920s and 1930s, making available on demand a large number of their own out-of-print recordings, including, often unintentionally, a fair amount of previously released material. This could hardly have caused them any major hardship, as the machinery was already in place to produce these special pressings: using their own masters, they were simply keeping deleted issues on the market in the very limited quantities necessary to meet public demand. The Gramophone Company also sponsored a retail equivalent, the *Catalogue No. 2* ("Records of Unique and Historical Interest"), offering material no longer available in their general catalogs.

William Seltsam's International Record Collectors' Club (IRCC) of Bridgeport, Connecticut, appears to have been the first organization to offer historical recordings by subscription as the basis of operation--material aimed solely at enthusiasts, whose buying power had been severely reduced by a Depression economy. "I am convinced that there is a demand for the historical record," Seltsam declared in his initial prospectus of January 1932. "To test my theory more fully," he continued, "I am founding the INTERNATIONAL RECORD COLLECTORS' CLUB, the policy being to unearth and offer special editions of these rarities. The club will be run somewhat similarly to the record-of-the-month plan, with, however, the omission of the dues fee." The bargain rates IRCC was able to offer at the time were indicative of a desperate Depression economy that had already crippled the well-being of the recording industry. These were never brought into perspective as alarmingly as in the April 1934 IRCC bulletin, when Seltsam announced Victor's recent price increases for their single-sided special pressings: $5.50 and $6.50 for ten-inch and twelve-inch discs, respectively--enormous sums in 1934, especially considering that IRCC was peddling their two double-sided offerings that month at $3.50 for the pair!

If Seltsam was the first to sell historical recordings via subscription, he was certainly not the last. Within a few years, William Speckin began the Historic Record Society (HRS) in Chicago with an identical agenda, as did Jack Caidin with his Collectors Record Shop in New York. The more populous jazz fraternity began doing much the same thing in the mid and late 1930s with equal success, on labels that came to include the Hot Jazz Club of America, Hot Record Society, United Hot Clubs of America, British Rhythm Society, Jazz Classics, and Century. In demonstrating to the record industry that there was an appreciable market for these reissues, a number of major labels here and abroad were prompted to reissue pressings of their own classic jazz recordings of the 1920s and 1930s.

What made these early subscription clubs less than profitable was the cumbersome process of seeking out masters from those recording companies willing to cooperate (early on, IRCC and HRS were importing metals from Europe as well as availing themselves of material provided by Victor and Columbia, while the jazz clubs usually had to content themselves from the beginning with re-recordings), having them pressed to acceptable standards, and judging the quantity of copies adequately for a given run so as to avoid unsold back stock. Seltsam's bulletins frequently warned that press runs would be limited, often with little hope of reissue, which does much to explain the rarity of many of the earliest IRCC issues today. Eventually all of the clubs--classical and popular--began producing dubbings instead: rare recordings copied from private collections that could be pressed cheaply and made in larger quantities not governed entirely by subscription commitments.

The war made the process considerably more challenging because of the shortage of shellac. Seltsam issued a special bulletin in May 1942 announcing that the U.S. government had frozen 70 percent of the available stock needed to produce records and that RCA would no longer be able to press new IRCC editions "until further notice." This, after some three hundred issues. Only three IRCC bulletins appeared between November 1942 and May 1944, before the resumption of semiregular releases in July 1945. After the war, vinylite superseded shellac as the standard, which evidently made production even cheaper: throughout the 1950s, IRCC, HRS, and CRS were joined by a number of small-scale competitors who began pressing their own re-recordings.

With the advent of the long-playing record, the process of producing limited-edition records in modest runs became easier and cheaper still. The contents could be assembled on tape, master lacquers could be prepared quickly, and pressings could be produced inexpensively in virtually any desired quantity. It was a watershed era for the record collector, and specialized labels quickly began popping up everywhere, some establishing a successful corner in the market that would last decades. IRCC issued its first long-playing collection in December 1953, though regular vinylite 78s were still being produced through June 1954. HRS issued a first batch of ten-inch LPs at about the same time, followed by Jack Caidin, who began reissuing some of his own CRS releases on the Famous Records of the Past label in 1955. Unfortunately, these LPs jeopardized the continuing prosperity of repressings. The last prominent series of 78 rpm repressings were issued by Addison Foster's American Gramophone Society and by the Gramophone Company, whose VA and VB "Archive" series was initiated in October 1951. It wasn't until the late 1960s and early 1970s that the practice resumed commercially, with the first issues of vinyl repressings by Rubini and Historic Masters, the latter a joint venture of the British Institute of Recorded Sound and EMI. Historic Masters continues to manufacture vinyl pressings to the present day, along with Symposium Records and several private concerns. But just as the LP threatened the prosperity of the 78 rpm disc as a format in the 1950s, so the compact disc has endangered the production of vinyl itself, all but prohibiting the long-term viability of repressings, even on the subscription level.

Into this honorable tradition came Edward J. Smith, who, as it would turn out, brought some remarkable innovations of his own to the formula. He was born Edward Joseph Smith in Brooklyn on 17 June, 1913. His father, Joseph Smith, the first president of the Brooklyn Neurological Society, was a physician attached to the staffs of both the Brooklyn State and Kings County Hospitals. His mother, Sophia Sagere, was a concert pianist, a pupil of the Hungarian pianist Rafael Joseffy (1852-1915), himself a pupil of Franz Liszt, Karl Tausig, and Josef Hofmann. Touring the world with his mother between the ages of eight and seventeen, Smith claimed to have met many of the legendary artists who would later figure prominently on his LPs--Jean De Reszke, Battistini, and Ruffo among them--and in later years he was rarely without a ready anecdote about any of them. His early adulthood was occupied as a professional baseball player (a catcher), although his claims to have to have made the major leagues were apparently untrue. He also managed to take a B.A. (1933) and an M.A. (1934) in journalism from Columbia University, where he pursued a minor in music. Landing his first professional job as a journalist with the New York bureau of the

Hollywood Reporter, he served as a film reviewer and general staffer between 1934 and 1938. He became *Variety*'s concert and opera critic in 1938 and served in the U.S. Army between 1942 and 1945, as a member of the 265th Coast Artillery, Special Services. After the war he became a publicist for the Earl Ferris and Muriel Francis Publicity Agency in New York, writing publicity releases for a number of artists who, like those he claimed to have met as a child, would remain objects of his unswerving artistic admiration, and ultimately would become mainstays of his LPs. Many, like Martinelli, Bjoerling, Pinza, and Melchior, became his close, personal friends. Between 1946 and 1949 he served variously as the associate editor of the *Musical Digest* and as editor-in-chief of the *World Wide Music Syndicate*. For the latter, he wrote weekly music columns syndicated in over one-hundred American newspapers.

Smith's maiden voyage as a record producer was in arranging an inexpensive studio session for Enrico Caruso, Jr., accompanied by J. Konstantin, at Victor's 24th Street studio in March 1938. The recordings were produced in league with Jack Caidin, proprietor of the Collectors Record Shop, 71 West 48th Street, New York City. Only two of the four titles recorded were eventually issued, and only in one-thousand copies (each is numbered): a *Rigoletto* "Questa o quella" (BS-018893-1) and *Tosca* "Recondita armonia" (BS-021165-1), recorded 1 and 14 March, 1938, respectively, and released on Caidin's CRS label. A "Core 'ngrato" from 1 March and a *Trovatore* "Deserto sulla terra" from 14 March remained unissued on shellac. In 1939 (according to Smith), four more records were made at a private recording studio--Tosti's "L'Alba separa dalla luce l'ombra" and the "Nessun dorma" from *Turandot* on 25 June, and the *Fedora* "Amor ti vieta" and *Bohème* "Che gelida manina" on 27 September, none of them issued commercially on shellac. Smith became Enrico Jr.'s friend and promoter, working tirelessly on his behalf for several years.

It was only after the war, in 1949, that Smith was able to become more persistently involved in the recording industry, first in initiating classical issues on the Continental and Remington labels as a producer and author of liner notes. For Continental he appears to have been responsible for at least two remarkable studio recitals, one by baritone Giuseppe De Luca (CLP-102), the other by tenor Giovanni Martinelli (CLP-103), both made in early 1950. For Remington there were a number of abridged operas and recitals, some featuring his first wife, contralto Elizabeth Wysor. He was also involved with the Record Corporation of America, Union City, New Jersey, in the early and mid-1950s, whose stable of inexpensive commercial labels--Allegro, Royale, and Allegro-Royale--often availed themselves of performances actually mounted by Smith in European (primarily Italian and German) studios during his four-year stay in Italy, 1951-1954, or materials appropriated with the help of friends and confederates throughout the world. Most were complete or abridged operatic performances of varying quality, although a good many orchestral performances appeared on Allegro-Royale. Some of this commercially issued material derived from live broadcast performances subsequently peddled in the United States pseudonymously to hide their origin. He also produced modest piano- and harmonium-accompanied studio sessions in New York, some featuring major artists, and sent the tapes abroad to be dubbed with added orchestral accompaniments (at least one of these, a circa 1955 Tibbett song recital, was reissued on other obscure labels such as Hudson--the Hudson Record Company of West New York, New Jersey, possibly a Smith venture--as late as 1960).

His childless marriage to Elizabeth Wysor ended in divorce, but he married twice again: in 1946 to Roman countess Concetta ("Tina") Chiodo, whom he met during the war and who eventually bore him two children, a son and a daughter, and in 1971, to his nurse, Anna Perez, nearly thirty years his junior. Tina's connections in Rome were largely responsible for Smith's success in mounting the large-scale recorded productions that appeared on Remington and Allegro in the mid-1950s, and are said to have paved the way for his seemingly inexhaustible access to Italian radio broadcasts, especially those of Radio Audizioni Italiana (RAI), during the heyday of his private labels. Smith is also rumored to have contracted GIs stationed in Europe to tape German performances for issue on Allegro-Royale.

Between 1956 and November 1971, Smith compiled, released, and sold through subscription his first series of private long-playing records. Issued collectively under the series title The Golden Age of Opera, there were 479 entries in all, numbered, using his own initials, EJS 100 through EJS 578. The series was continued in much the same vein beginning in February 1972 with a new label, Unique Opera Record(s) Corporation (Company)--the title varying according to the vintage of the labels or bulletins consulted. UORC ceased production in December 1977 with the 279th issue and was, in turn, superseded in May 1978 by the A.N.N.A. Record Company label, taking the punctuated forename of his third wife as its namesake. A.N.N.A., Smith's private last venture, consisted of seventy-two long-playing issues. The content of all three labels, which bore the legend "Private Record / Not For Sale," was overwhelmingly operatic, compiled from a variety of sources. Although sold only by subscription, they managed somehow to find their way into big-city record stores in limited quantities, and through Smith's intervention, into libraries, where they were received gratis.

Smith issued a number of other private labels between the mid-1950s and early 1970s--ABC, Celebrity Record Company, Great French Opera Performances of the Century, Great Mozart Recordings [of the Century], Great Performances of the Past, MOP (thought to be an acronym for "Metropolitan Opera Performances"), Recorded Treasure Production, and Richard Strauss, as well as a limited series of releases with the improbable foreign names Die Goldene Aera Richard Wagners and Voix Illustres Belges. Other limited-edition compilations bore no label name at all, and were titled simply to reflect their contents. Supplementing the limited income these records brought him were clandestine sales of ancient Roman and Etruscan artifacts!

The commercially produced Smith labels were similar in their operatic thrust but were legally a bit less precarious, generally using older, commercial recordings as the basis of their content. As a long-time friend of his once quipped, Smith could come up with a new label in an instant when the task confronted him. His two best-known commercial labels were the American Stereophonic Corporation (ASCO) of 17 West 60th Street, New York City, which never once carried a *stereophonic* release, and Top Artists Platters (TAP), a frank imitation, at least in name, of Famous Artists of the Past (FRP), Jack Caidin's earlier LP series compiled in part from his own Collectors' Record Shop 78s. TAP was widely criticized for its poor transfers, skimpy documentation, almost unplayable groove pitch, and even its name--arguably one of the worst, least-appropriate appellations ever conceived. Indeed, in a March 1959 letter to a close friend who had protested this unattractive and misrepresentative moniker, Smith agreed, exclaiming "I . . . think it ["TAP"] stinks--but I had nothing to do with [the] choice and can't change it now." ASCO and TAP both produced a number of memorable releases, more remarkable for their offerings than for their indifferent quality. On ASCO there were some fine vocal recitals and one of Smith's few instrumental potpourris (a collection of historical violinists), while TAP offered an excellent series of thematic compilations featuring Met and La Scala singers of the golden age, great twentieth-century

Mozart interpreters, Puccini singers, duets, and famous American singers, as well as miscellaneous potpourris featuring well-known sopranos, tenors, baritones, and contraltos: the latter boasted the only known recording of Florence Wickham--as yet undocumented, retrieved from a "test copy," according to Smith. In 1962, TAP also issued the now infamous "Verdi: Il Trovatore - Di quella pira - 40 Tenors - 80 High C's," a compilation of the aria, probably the first of its kind, that included not only obvious upward transpositions conforming to its title, but also Caruso's famous 1906 version edited into an "unreleased record," that is, transferred at the wrong speed with the resulting penultimate high C edited ludicrously to extend for an immodest fourteen seconds!

What made Smith's private recordings so much more compelling was the bolder *nature* of their content. Relatively few commercial 78s, however rare and desirable, were featured on these LPs, while these were the staple of his and other commercially based collectors' labels of the period. Instead, Smith emphasized noncommercial performances taken from radio and television broadcasts, live performances from the world's great opera houses, private recordings, and anything else that was both rare and worthy. We tend to take the availability of such things for granted today, in light of the fact that major labels and institutions have gradually come to see the financial potential of unlocking their dusty collections of archival materials--in part because of the pioneering efforts of the early pirates. Smith pursued noncommercial recordings with shameless abandon, ignoring copyright restrictions (stated or unstated) with the defiance of a pirate and the zeal of an enthusiast too smitten with the task at hand to even notice, much less bother, with such practical considerations. In later years, as the number of legal threats against him swelled, he was forced to reconsider the breadth of his evasive tactics.

It should be clear from the discography that, much to his credit, Smith was not simply another nostalgic "golden age" chauvinist. He featured countless post war singers on his private labels, sometimes out of choice, sometimes out of necessity, as well as "youngsters" (as he was so fond of referring to them) who were just beginning to make a professional impact.

Though it was alluded to infrequently in his bulletins, Smith's principal aim was to offer collectors unusual, otherwise unavailable material. Because bulletins did not accompany the GAO LPs until October 1958, with the issue of EJS 134 and 135, we were robbed of any formal statement of the series' initial intent, but in retrospect, Smith's objectives were fairly obvious, if at times a bit inconsistent. While there was never a single theme imposed upon the whole of the GAO series, apart from the promise of fine singing by some of the greatest singers of the century, there was a pattern guiding its overall content:

1. Smith's own favorite singers
2. Obscure singers of the past
3. Obscure recordings of well-known singers, past and present
4. Private recordings
5. Metropolitan Opera and Ente Italiano Audizioni Radiofoniche (EIAR)/RAI broadcasts and telecasts
6. Miscellaneous broadcasts and telecasts by major singers, including those taken from regularly scheduled programs
7. In-house concert and operatic recordings
8. Obscure repertory
9. Operatic and opera-related film soundtrack excerpts
10. Compilation performances and forgeries

No priorities are implied here, as Smith generally published what became available to him and what he thought collectors might appreciate hearing. One month might bring two or three Metropolitan Opera broadcasts or a series of potpourris with material drawn from a variety of sources, another, some obscure, otherwise unrecorded operas of European origin.

Smith's favorite singers were obvious at the time to subscribers and should be equally obvious today from the GAO listings: Martinelli, his cherished personal friend (a "second father," he often claimed) was perhaps the best-represented major singer in GAO series. Tibbett, Ponselle, Rethberg, De Luca, Flagstad, Melchior, and Gigli were among the others. Often lending him their own private, unissued, and broadcast recordings, most were probably flattered by his interest and the apparently insatiable appetite of his subscribers.

Antonio Aramburo and Alessandro Moreschi, *Soprano della Cappella Sistina*, were typical examples of the more obscure singers of the past featured in the GAO series. Their records, like many others, remain great rarities even today, and were generally offered by Smith "as is," with little concern for their condition or, in the case of Aramburo, their authenticity. Because he released so many live performances, many celebrated but rarely heard comprimarii were unwittingly featured on the LPs as well, singers active for years at the Met, Covent Garden, La Scala, RAI, and so forth.

Recordings of well-known singers were generally restricted to rare early recordings, tests, and unpublished items. With the advent of Historic Masters and the latest (encouraging) wave of compact discs aimed specifically at the vocal collector, many of these are not nearly so inaccessible today, but most were new to LP when they were issued by Smith, and were often being heard publicly for the first time in decades, or at all.

The private recordings were sometimes studio recordings never intended for circulation or home recordings taken on disc or tape. There were several records made at musical soirées in New York, for example, most in the late 1940s, or in artists' homes. A number of the private records featured throughout the GAO series were actually recorded for, if not by, Smith himself.

The Metropolitan Opera and EIAR/RAI broadcasts were just that, issued either in excerpts or complete as transcribed. Depending on the material available to him at a given time, these were often issued first as excerpts and later as complete performances, with individual arias and ensembles frequently recycled on subsequent releases. During the run of the Golden Age of Opera series, Smith managed, through friends, to gain unofficial access to official NBC line checks, including those of the Met broadcasts: at this point the offerings became more generous and the transfers markedly better, as might be expected. As a result of Smith's uncanny access to EIAR/RAI materials, gleaned from early connections established while he was residing in Rome with his second wife and through trusted, well-maintained friendships, several of these broadcast performances appeared on GAO within months of airing.

The miscellaneous broadcast materials included rarer, less frequently transcribed broadcasts from other houses such as the San Francisco and Chicago Opera companies, shortwave broadcasts from British and European theaters, and radio and television program recitals featuring famous singers. The latter were especially innovative additions to the catalog, considering the frequency with which singers appeared on the air in the 1920s, 1930s, and 1940s, often in regular weekly installments. From a dizzying variety of sources that included official station and network line checks as well as privately made air checks, Smith unearthed hundreds of excerpts from the foremost concert programming of the day, ranging from the "Atwater Kent Hour" shows of the earliest 1930s, to the "Bell Telephone Hour" and "Concerto Martini e Rossi" shows of the 1940s, 1950s, and 1960s. Over the course of several LPs, he sometimes managed to issue the complete musical contents of these broadcasts and telecasts.

In-house recordings, although considerably fewer in number than broadcasts in the GAO series, included operatic performances, live concerts, and in the instance of the Wiener Staatsoper, possible Selenophone (film) transcriptions. As he did with radio programs, Smith issued a remarkable sampling of some of the earliest live performances featuring eminent singers of the pre war era.

Obscure repertory was a Smith specialty that is liable to be taken for granted today. He was rarely at a loss to point out in his bulletins that a current offering had never been recorded or had been so long out of print that he was making it available for the first time in years. Indeed, at a time when Rossini was more or less represented in the LP catalogs only by *Il Barbiere di Siviglia*, *L'Italiana in Algeri*, *La Cenerentola*; Bellini by *Norma*, *I Puritani*, and *La Sonnambula*; and Donizetti by *La Fille du Regiment*, *L'Elisir d'amore*, *Don Pasquale*, *La Favorita*, *Linda di Chamounix*, and *Lucia di Lammermoor*, as well as the usual complement of arias, ensembles, and overtures from less frequently performed works, Smith succeeded in adding to the catalog complete or representative recordings of other obscure operas that many collectors hadn't even heard of, much less actually heard. New works were similarly added for many major composers who were represented on LP at the time by only a handful of operas (Gounod and Massenet) or by no more than a single opera (Leoncavallo, Cilea, and Mascagni), often taken from their initial post war or even twentieth-century revivals. Many of these have lately been "rediscovered" as masterpieces and have subsequently undergone full-blown studio productions in the current zeal to inflate the repertory--in deference to artists and the breadth of the CD catalog. But this was at the time one of Smith's most substantial contributions, and if the performances he released were not always the best (he often complained that some were the "only ones available"), he certainly did more to create an awareness of the void than did any of the major labels, especially in America.

The soundtrack reissues, too, were virtually unique at the time. Having enjoyed the short-lived patronage of Hollywood in the early days of sound film (roughly the eleven years between 1926 and 1937), many major singers left a sizeable legacy of soundtrack performances. Smith was certainly the first to exploit these, unearthing operatic Vitaphone soundtracks and, over the course of two decades, releasing the musical portions of several American and European feature films. Singers like Gigli who continued to appear in films throughout lengthy careers can thus be heard over a twenty-year period in soundtrack excerpts alone.

Another more or less standard feature of the GAO series was the composite performance. These were sometimes deliberate, "creative" efforts boastfully advertised in the bulletins (the manufactured Martinelli-Bonninsegna and Martinelli-Muzio "duets" on EJS 270; the joint Flagstad-Melchior *Siegfried* "duet" on EJS 338, and so on), but frequently they were contrived to overcome deficiencies in the source material or simply to deceive. Most often, portions of commercial recordings or snippets from other live performances were edited into broadcasts to compensate for lost music or bumpy passages. There were also the forgeries--Mapleson and Bettini cylinders that were neither Mapleson nor Bettini cylinders, and other early or rare recordings by singers who have yet to be documented to anyone's satisfaction as having recorded. These will be discussed at some length in the discography.

Smith's LPs, both commercial and private, were generous to a fault in the sheer quantity of their offerings. While many early collector's labels were notorious for their miserly limit of fewer than ten tracks per twelve-inch LP, Smith was more likely to crowd up to a dozen selections per side, especially on the short-lived but cluttered TAP label. However admirable his intentions were, his generosity was not without severe consequences. The kind of *micro*-microgroove cutting that was necessary to achieve such lengthy running times tracked very poorly, especially on the clumsy equipment for which the records were originally intended. It is not unusual, moreover, for even the most sophisticated modern stylus to track between the grooves of these LPs, or to produce a "ghost." Add to this the generally dismal quality of vinyl Smith used, complete with warping and surface bumps, and the careless pitching, and it is easy to understand why his releases still provoke rage, especially as we become more and more accustomed to the improved response and relative quiet of the compact disc.

Throughout the 1960s and 1970s Smith was physically and financially able to devote himself to his private labels. His gloomy accounts of the chronic health problems that plagued him in later life became an endearing motif in his bulletins beginning in the early 1970s, along with constant warnings of his imminent retirement. By the late 1970s, in the midst of the A.N.N.A. series, his predicament was becoming increasingly credible. In fact, not one of the eight A.N.N.A. bulletins published between 1978 and 1981 managed to avoid the subject of his failing health. The fifth bulletin, released in the fall of 1979, announced that A.N.N.A. 1043-1049 would "certainly be the final regular release of A.N.N.A. records and anything that might follow would only be because of an extraordinary discovery and as such would consist of two or three records at the most." But in fact there would be three more bulletins and more than twenty additional LPs. The final bulletin, undated but probably from early 1981, concluded with yet another of his tragic caveats: "If I am fortunate enough to be able to carry on, there will be other releases. I must have grave doubts about this possibility - I live with the Sword of Damocles hanging over my head, so if you do not hear from me again, then God Bless and keep you all."

Having doubtless become accustomed to these dramatic farewells and final best wishes over the preceding decade, few of Smith's subscribers could have suspected what his friends already knew: that the seemingly indestructible Smith legacy was spent. There would be no more releases. Three years later, on 11 July, 1984, Smith died of cancer in Englewood, New Jersey. "God willing," he observed in January 1980, in the sixth A.N.N.A. bulletin, "we will all meet some day in a better world where our mutual love of great music will draw us together forever."

It was only fitting that his last release, A.N.N.A 1072, should have been a potpourri in the grand tradition of so many that preceded it, a collection of operatic excerpts by favorite artists intimately associated with the prodigious if somewhat curious career of Edward Joseph Smith. Among them was Enrico Caruso, Jr.'s "Che gelida manina," privately recorded for Smith back in 1939.

Had our task been merely to report the information stated on the labels and in the monthly EJS bulletins, the published results might have appeared in a matter of months. But most subscribers and collectors have known for years that Smith's labels and bulletins yielded either fragmentary or incorrect information, making them useless, or in the very worst instances, subversive. We found that suspicion, far more than simple vigilance, was the most valuable sentiment cultivated throughout the project--the instinctive denial of Smith's explanations and the abandonment of everything that had been previously assumed to be true by others. Smith was frequently misinformed by those who furnished him with the material, or merely assumed for one reason or another that a performance came from such-and-such a house on such-and-such a date; sometimes, there simply was no information to be found on the original air checks or test pressings that were used; singers' names were at times transcribed from foreign language on-the-air announcements; quite often, especially in the labeling of Metropolitan Opera broadcasts and Toscanini material, any telltale information was deliberately omitted to avoid legal action; and in at least one instance, the name of a singer was changed deliberately to avoid the responsibility of compensating him for its use.

A few examples of GAO labels, shown with their corresponding bulletin entries (as reproduced directly from the actual discs and monthly announcements), should serve to illustrate these points and define with greater clarity the nature and purpose of this book. Compare these to the listings given in the discography:

THE GOLDEN AGE OF OPERA

POTPOURRI (2)

Side 1 — EJS - 142 A — 33 1/3 rpm Microgroove

T. Ruffo: Barbiere di Siviglia—Largo al factotum (1930)
T. Ruffo: Otello: Credo (1930)
N. Melba: Il Pensieroso—Sweet Bird (1904)
L. Melchior: Otello—Dio mi potevi scagliar (1928)
L. Melchior: Otello—Niun mi tema (1928)
F. Chaliapin: Boheme—Vecchia Zimara (1922)
F. Tamagno: Perche—(Fillippi) (1903)

PRIVATE RECORD
NOT FOR SALE

THE GOLDEN AGE OF OPERA

POTPOURRI (2)

Side 2 — EJS - 142 B — 33 1/3 rpm Microgroove

E. Caruso & F. Alda: Carmen—Parle-moi de ma mere (1914)
B. Sayao: Lo Schiavo—Cavatina (1945)
L. Bori & E. Pinza: Mignon—Duet of the Swallows (1936)
A. Aramburo: Otello—Nium mi tema (1902)
G. DeLuca, L. Pons, V. Lazarri: Rigoletto—Quel vecchio maledivami; Si vendetta & Lassu in cielo (1940)
E. Pinza: Xerxes—Ombra mai fu (1944)
B. Gigli & M. Caniglia: Traviata: Brindisi (1938)

PRIVATE RECORD
NOT FOR SALE

Ruffos were taken from unreleased film he made in 1930; Melba was a breakdown in 1904; Melchiors are unpublished tests (1928); Chaliapin, Tamagno & Alda-Caruso are unpublished tests. Sayao was radio broadcast, Bori & Pinza from Met broadcast (1936), Aramburo is only known disc of this Spanish tenor, contemporary and rival of Gayarre. Aramburo was born in 1838 and sang in all the world's major opera houses as a first class spinto until his retirement in 1899. This test record was made in 1902. He died in Montevideo in 1912. The DeLuca, Pons & Lazzari excerpts are from Met broadcast in 1940; the Pinza from a radio broadcast and the Gigli & Caniglia from a Covent Garden appearance in 1938.

EJS 142: "Potpourri (2)." Apart from the fact that many of the dates are given incorrectly on the label, only one of the Melchior Otello items was unpublished, and the Chaliapin had appeared previously as AGSA 11. The Ruffo arias were not taken from an "unreleased film he made in 1930," rather, from two separate films released by M-G-M in 1929 or 1930. The Melba was unpublished owing to an error ("breakdown") toward the end of the aria, and neither the label nor the bulletin mentions that the obbligato is provided by the eminent flutist, Philippe Gaubert. The Gigli-Caniglia duet is not taken from a 1938 Covent Garden appearance (they appeared in Traviata in 1939) and, in fact, still remains a mystery.

THE GOLDEN AGE OF OPERA

LA JUIVE

Act II—Pt. 1

(October 30, 1936)

Side I EJS — 221-A

Microgroove 33⅓ rpm LP

1. Passover Scene: O Dieu de nos peres
2. Dieu che ma voix tremblante
3. Trio: Tu possedes, dit-en
4. Il va venir

With Elisabeth Rethberg, Giovanni Martinelli, Charlotte Boerner, Hans Clemens, Chorus of the San Francisco Opera Association directed by Armando Aginini, San Francisco Symphony Orchestra conducted by Gaetano Merola

PRIVATE RECORD
NOT FOR SALE

THE GOLDEN AGE OF OPERA

LA JUIVE

Act II—Concluded

Act IV—Pt. 2

(October 30, 1936)

1. Duo: Lors qu'a toi je me suis donnee
2. Trio Finale: Et toi que j'accueillis

Side 2 EJS — 221-B

Microgroove 33⅓ rpm LP

Act IV
(March 8, 1927)

3. Ta fille en ce moment
4. Rachel, quand du Seigneur

With Elisabeth Rethberg, Giovanni Martinelli, Hans Clemens, Virgilio Lazzari, San Francisco Symphony Orchestra conducted by Gaetano Merola, Chicago Opera Orchestra conducted by Tullio Serafin

PRIVATE RECORD
NOT FOR SALE

Act II of La Juive, broadcast from the opening of the San Francisco Opera Season, October 30, 1936. Cast includes Elisabeth Rethberg, Giovanni Martinelli, Charlotte Boerner and Hans Clemens under the baton of Gaetano Merola. Also Scene Two of Act IV of La Juive, March 8, 1927 with Martinelli & Virgilio Lazzari, taken from the Chicago Opera Company. (This section some collectors already have if they possess the ASCO double record Martinelli set.) Since many do not, this total of 67 minutes on a single disc includes everything that Martinelli recorded from La Juive Singing is superb - it includes the Passover Scene: Dieu che ma voix tremblante; Il va venir - the big duo and trio including several breathtaking high C's on the part of both Martinelli & Rethberg. Last act is the duet of the Cardinal & Eliazar and concludes with Eleazar's Rachel, quand du Seigneur. Sound is remarkably good considering the age of the record which is one of the most important of all releases since the onset of this series. One record: $3.90.

EJS 221: The side 1 label omits any mention of the fact that this San Francisco performance was supplemented by Martinelli's commercial Victor recordings of the Passover Scene (1928) and an unpublished acoustical "Dieu, que ma moix" (1924). The "Ta fille en ce moment" and "Rachel! quand du Seigneur" on side 2 were taken from two 1927 Vitaphone films with Martinelli and bass Louis D'Angelo, who is given here as "Virgilio Lazzari." (D'Angelo insisted on payment for the use of his name, so Smith simply substituted Lazzari!) As to the attribution of a Chicago Opera performance conducted by Serafin on 8 March, 1927, Martinelli's only Chicago appearances that season were in Ravinia Park (he sang JUIVE there on 26 July); he apparently sang nowhere on 8 March, his closest engagement having been a 17 March studio session for Victor. Nor did Serafin appear in Chicago that season. 8 March, 1927, moreover, would predate the earliest known American operatic broadcast transcriptions, even if such a performance had taken place. The date was apparently chosen at random.

This sort of chaotic documentation was common to both the GAO labels and bulletins for live performances and broadcasts of major works, with casts, conductors, theaters, and even orchestras often hopelessly tangled.

THE GOLDEN AGE OF OPERA

GERALDINE FARRAR

(1935-37)

A

Excerpts of Hansel & Grete'—Prayer
Konigskinder: Cavatina of Fiddler
Walkure: Wotan's Farewell and Wintersturma
Faust: Il est coute

Side I — EJS — 397-A — 33 1/3 rpm LP Microgroove

Damnation of Faust: D'Amour l'ardente flamme
Mefistofele: Lontano, lontano
Traviata: Dite all giovine; A fors e lui, Sempre Libera; Addio, del passato; Di provenza; Liebiamo, Parigi o cara.
I Love Thee (Grieg) and Ode to Music (Schubert).

MARY GARDEN

1. Resurrection (Alfano): Dieu de Grace
2. Dreary Steppe
3. Somewhere a Voice is Calling

PRIVATE RECORD
NOT FOR SALE

THE GOLDEN AGE OF OPERA

LAWRENCE TIBBETT

(1934-37)

Side 2 — EJS — 397-B — 33 1/3 rpm LP Microgroove

1. Rigoletto: Cortigani, vil rassa donata
2. Halleluiah Rhythm
3. Minnelied
4. Carmen: Toreador Song
5. Amor, amor (Pirandelli)
6. Pagliacci: Vesti la giubba
7. Pagliacci: Prologue
8. Road to Mandalay
9. The Glory Road

PRIVATE RECORD
NOT FOR SALE

The third record is somewhat of a potpourri. Side A features Geraldine Farrar in what were her final public appearances after her retirement. The great singer performs fragments of arias from bass through soprano leggiero in recordings dated from 1935-37. Operas represented are: Hansel & Gretel, Konigskinder, Walkure, Faust, Damnation of Faust, Mefistofele and Traviata as well as songs by Grieg and Schubert. Also on the Farrar side are two heretofore unpublished "takes" of Mary Garden- the Dieu de Grace from Alfano's Resurrection and Dreary Steppe of Rachmaninoff. Side B features nine selections by Lawrence Tibbett recorded between 1933 and 1937. These include both the Prologue and Vesti la giubba from Pagliacci, Toreador Song from Carmen, Cortigani from Rigoletto and five songs.

EJS 397: One of the most complicated GAO LPs. It is not mentioned that all but the last two Farrar items were taken from her Metropolitan Opera broadcast Intermission Features of the 1934-1935 season, or that some of those featured here are rehearsal recordings, not live broadcasts. No mention of the sources of the Grieg and Schubert songs is made, and there is no Farrar material included from as late as 1937. "Two heretofore unpublished 'takes' of Mary Garden" are noted in the bulletin, while three are given on the label, but the last is really a 1925 recording of Rosa Ponselle singing "Little Old Garden" by Hewitt! The Tibbett side includes material recorded between 1934 and 1937 according to the label, and 1933 and 1937 according to the bulletin--1928 to circa 1937 is correct. Note also, the incorrect titles and lack of composer credits throughout.

THE LISTING

Format

The format of the listings has been adapted to make all necessary allowances for the various kinds of performances issued: recitals (usually collections of recordings by a single artist), potpourris (collections of recordings by a number of artists), and major works (most often operatic, concert, and broadcast performances).

For the major works, the following descriptions will be used consistently:

1. Complete: These are essentially complete as written, with only minor cuts resulting from changes of reel or transcription disc in the original source.

Single acts of a work, when transferred complete, will be cited as exceptions to the above categories. They will be designated in the heading of an LP ("Act II only"), with an explanatory note added to clarify the circumstances (i.e., when only a single act was broadcast or transcribed, when other acts from the same performance were issued on subsequent LPs, or when no other acts have survived, etc.).

2. Complete as performed: When major deviations from the score are the result of known performance cuts, "complete as performed" will be cited instead.

3. Abridged: Nearly complete, but with significant cuts and noticeable lapses in continuity. An abridged performance, as used here, may still be considered fairly representative of a complete work. A distinction will be made in the endnotes between performance and recording cuts, but either may constitute an "abridged" performance. Recording cuts may be the result of truncation during the original transcribing of a performance, the transfer of an incomplete or damaged source, or the deliberate omission of material for purposes of timing during the production of an LP.

4. Excerpts: a performance with extensive cuts and little or no large-scale continuity. These are no more than an assemblage of highlights of a complete work (the term Smith most often employed) or, in some cases, selections. Excerpts may also include fragments, which will be designated specifically in the listing of individual tracks and discussed, where appropriate, in the endnotes. While Smith often issued excerpts of performances that existed complete, many of the incomplete performances found throughout the GAO series were drawn from broadcasts or concerts that consisted *only* of highlights from a score and so, were presented complete as performed.

5. Adaptation: a special category, more or less unique to broadcast performances. Usually a specially prepared version of a work tailored to fit a specific broadcast schedule, these can be nearly complete or severely cut productions of large-scale works, and very often have added narration or spoken dialogue between musical excerpts to compensate for the loss of score continuity. The extent of the abridgement will be discussed in the endnotes to these issues.

Unless otherwise stated in the endnotes to an individual LP, the citation of these varying states of completeness is based on the recordings themselves, not on the information provided in the accompanying bulletins or on the equally unreliable labels.

Separation bands will usually be noted, but the distribution of selections, when such has been observed or reported, will only be given for the abridged and excerpted operas. The complete operas will bear headings such as "SIDES 1-6 (291 A-F)," followed directly by the musical and discographical information: the division of a complete work over the course of several sides will rarely be noted, as it bears little musical significance.

Indexes

Cumulative indexes follow the discography and include all artists (singers, speakers, accompanists, conductors, instrumental soloists, etc.), works performed, including excerpts, a chronology of live performances from the various houses and concert halls represented, radio and television broadcasts, commercial films, and all LP matrix numbers.

Language of Performance

The language of a performance, given in parentheses, will follow the name of the composer after the works and excerpts performed. The only abbreviations used will be for those languages common to the type of repertory that appeared on Smith's LPs:

(D) Danish	(E) English	(F) French	(G) German
(I) Italian	(N) Neapolitan	(Nw) Norwegian	(P) Portuguese
(R) Russian	(S) Spanish	(Sw) Swedish	

Anything more exotic will likely be exceptional and will appear unabbreviated.

For the sake of uniformity and ease of reference, titles of major works will be given in their original language. An exception will be made in the case of works that are performed almost invariably in translation (Donizetti's *La Favorite* for example is more often performed in Italian as *La Favorita*). Cyrillic titles have been listed in Roman characters in accordance with the most reliable modern citations in an attempt to preserve as much of the original title as possible.

The titles of excerpts will generally be cited in the language in which they are sung, the only exceptions being those where the translation is so unfamiliar as to be irrelevant, for example, the Swedish or Russian text of an Italian or French operatic passage. Discounting these rare exceptions, the translated titles of excerpts will be followed in brackets *without* quotation marks by the excerpt title in its original language. Popular names and "nicknames" will be also be given in brackets, but with quotation marks. As an example:

FAUST, Act IV: Scheinst zu schlafen du im Stübchen [Vous qui faites l'endormie] ["Mephistophélès' Serenade"] (Gounod) (G)

Thus, this aria from *Faust* is sung in German (G), but the original French title of the opera is given rather than the German *Margarethe*, followed by the act from which the aria is drawn, the title of the aria *as sung*, the title (in brackets) in its original language, its familiar "nickname" (quoted in brackets), the composer, and the language designation.

In a few instances, translations could not be found (we searched for an Italian score or libretto of Massenet's *Manon* for four years without success!): here, the excerpts have been given in the original language.

Texts as Sung

Excerpts will be given *as sung*, not as labeled, with as accurate an accounting of starting and ending texts as was possible to supply. Having had to rely on reports in correspondence as well as published discographies when no copy of an EJS LP was available for analysis, it is inevitable that there will be errors. Indeed, even the most reputable published works have been discovered on occasion to be incorrect in this regard. In at least one instance (EJS 366) excerpts from a broadcast performance were listed for a subsequently produced private LP and imposed on the EJS listing with the assumption that the two were identical, and they were not.

Unsung texts, often necessary for ease of identification when an excerpt begins abruptly in mid phrase or in an awkward, unfamiliar place, will precede the text in brackets, designating that it is not actually *heard* in the excerpt(s). For example, *[Che gelida] manina* designates that the first two words of this aria have been omitted for some reason from the transfer, which begins, therefore, at "se la lasci riscaldar"; similarly, *[Che gel]ida manina* would designate that the first word and part of the second have been omitted, and so on.

Another text-related problem has been the libretti consulted: a variety of published libretti have been used by the compilers, some of them from the period of the performances under consideration, others published many years before or after. These often vary wildly, even in their presentation of the original language! Translations, too, have proven a nuisance, as few have been retained over any period of time as "standard." Revisions of, and errors in, libretti have been reconciled with the performances under discussion wherever possible, and in extreme instances will be discussed in an endnote.

Casts

Casts for ensemble performances have been given as comprehensively as possible, using every source available to us, both contemporary and retrospective. These have been supplemented and corrected in every possible instance. As labels are frequently incorrect, every entry has been reviewed carefully for errors.

Playing Speeds

One of the perennial flaws of the EJS issues was indiscriminate pitching, whether in the use of 78.26 rpm as the standard speed for transcribing shellacs from different periods, or in the carelessness with which acetates of live performances were often transferred. We have attempted, therefore, to cite the correct playing speeds of original disc pressings (commercially recorded 78s) and, based upon score pitch or a known transposition, have frequently suggested corrective measures to be taken on the GAO LPs themselves. When acetate discs (the precise speeds of which are generally unknown) were the original source materials used, these corrective measures are based solely on score pitch rather than original playing speeds. When a 78 rpm *re-recording* is known or assumed to have been Smith's immediate source of transfer (for example, IRCC, HRS, or CRS dubbings), some explanation, where appropriate, will be given. Any disputes concerning playing speeds will be discussed in an endnote, along with original keys and transpositions, known or suspected.

The corrective measures prescribed for the LPs are based on careful listening, so that with a variable-speed turntable (essential for the proper reproduction of EJS LPs!) the correct performance pitch may be secured during playback.

Absolute precision in these matters would be considerably more difficult (not to mention impractical) for the live performances, the majority of which were originally recorded on aluminum, laminated metal, or laminated glass acetates ("instantaneous discs"), many of them transcribed off the air ("air checks") or by a prebroadcast station or network line source ("line checks"). A number of EJS LPs were compiled from a collection of official network line checks, in which the pitch often drops slightly between the beginning and the end of a side. Thus, it would be impossible to surmise with any certainty whether the inconsistencies that plague so many of Smith's issues were the fault of the original source material or of its transfer to master tapes: having heard, firsthand, several of the original open-reel tapes furnished to Smith by his collector friends, those which would eventually be used for mastering the LPs, it would be unfair to blame Smith or his engineers entirely for the pitching problems encountered over the course of the GAO, UORC, and A.N.N.A. series.

Moreover, accounting for every pitch irregularity would have required the meticulous scrutinizing of entire operas, though as it turns out, coauthor Calvin Goodwin was willing and able to do just that in countless instances. But normally, only a brief summary will be given in the endnotes, noting passages or complete sides that may have been transferred slightly above or below pitch, with consideration given to any possible transpositions that might have been made during the actual performances. Any deliberate tampering (high Cs manufactured from high B-flats, etc.) will be mentioned in greater detail.

In any case, corrective LP speeds will be given where known.

Dates and Numbering of the LP Issues

The first five Golden Age of Opera issues carried no printed catalog number on their labels, only etched numbers, EJS 100 to EJS 104, in their surrounds. Their function, however, appears to have been the same. Thereafter, catalog numbers, ranging from 105 to 578, appeared on the labels prefixed "EJS."

A discrete "P"-prefix matrix number series (briefly, "CO-P-"), etched into the surround of either side, began to appear irregularly at EJS 374 (*Tosca*) in October 1966. By 1967, the "CO-P-" prefixes had disappeared and the "P-" prefixes were being used exclusively. These numbers will appear in the LP headings beginning at EJS (GAO) 374. A single matrix number was usually assigned to a given *issue*, regardless of the number of discs, and suffixed with a side letter, A-F (thus, CO-P-902A, CO-P-902B, CO-P-902C, etc.). A few larger sets carried sequential matrix *numbers* for each individual disc, rather than a single number appended with the sequential side letters, but this was exceptional.

While these matrix numbers appeared regularly from EJS 374 on, there were exceptions. A few subsequent issues, through the 500 range, still bore GAO catalog numbers only. Earlier issues, as far back as EJS 170, were often remastered and reissued in the 1970s bearing the new "P"-prefix matrix numbers: the earliest documented reissue with the lowest matrix number is matrix P-2426 (EJS 356, originally issued February 1966) from 1971; GAO 170, "Potpourri 5," originally issued January 1960, is the earliest GAO release known to have been reissued (as matrix P-3526 in about June 1974), while the latest GAO reissue, that is, with the *highest* GAO catalog number, is from May-June 1976, matrix P-3925

(EJS 250, originally issued November 1962). These late copies of early issues, pressed during the UORC years of production and sometimes distinguished by their blue print on white or off-white labels (early GAO pressings were invariably printed brown on white), were sometimes sonically superior to their predecessors, and have often been found with pitches improved if not always corrected.

The printed EJS bulletins, which served both to announce and to document the contents of the LPs, carried dates (month only: the year was omitted) designating when the records were ready for shipment, and so will be used as the official source of release dates in the discography. The first EJS bulletin, announcing the release of EJS 134, appeared in October 1958. The release dates of the preceding thirty-four LPs have been dated from correspondence, based upon reports of those subscribers who took care to note the dates of receipt on their copies.

Misnumberings of the EJS LPs were frequent. Some were just careless errors on the label copy--for example, EJS 175 for EJS 275. Sometimes the correct number appeared etched in the wax while the label was simply misprinted, usually carrying the number next to it (EJS 198 and EJS 199, for example, were switched on the labels of those issues). Most often, however, a 1970s checklist of The Golden Age of Opera series was to blame for the many numbering errors that have found their way into print. This checklist, covering the entire series and circulated among subscribers to advertise LPs still available at that time, was incomplete, omitting those LPs no longer available as back stock, and this may have caused the eventual numbering crisis that characterizes it as a whole: it is riddled with numbering errors. These have been corrected in the discography and discussed in the endnotes to those LPs affected. The checklist will be mentioned frequently and referred to throughout the discography simply as the "1970s EJS checklist." An Appendix (pp. 622-623) has been added to the discography as a concordance of these misnumberings.

Special Problems

These will include seemingly undocumentable recordings, forgeries, instances of "artistic editing" and a host of other frustrating complications. In a few instances, we have not been able to substantiate the edition of a score used for a performance when it seems to vary significantly from others. Composite performances, where material has been culled from more than one source and edited together to disguise the fact (a hallmark of the Smith releases), will be analyzed in the endnotes with their respective components identified as precisely as possible. Commercial recordings of major arias and ensembles were frequently inserted into live performances for a variety of reasons, but the reverse has turned up as well (a celebrated example can be found on Smith's earlier commercial label, Allegro, where Martinelli's 1955 studio recording of "A venti'tre ore" from *I Pagliacci*, as issued on Allegro LP 1614, has an inserted high B-natural taken from a 29 February, 1936 Metropolitan Opera broadcast). Such tampering with the recorded facts, when not designed simply to supplement the material available, was apparently contrived as a means of improving what Smith must have considered a less than flawless performance.

Private Correspondence

Smith corresponded regularly with subscribers and close personal friends (often in the margins and on the back of GAO bulletins). A good deal of this correspondence has been made available to us, and will be quoted selectively when found to contain discussion of source material and the like.

TYPES OF RECORDINGS USED

1. **Commercial Recordings**

Wherever possible, commercial recordings have been documented from company ledgers or from acknowledged discographical research. When we have not been able to document a commercial recording with absolute certainty, such will be noted. Only the most reliable secondary sources of documentation have been quoted in the listings: anything taken from questionable sources (especially the information furnished on LP reissues of commercial and private recordings) will carry a question mark and will be discussed in an endnote. We have made every attempt here to exclude the "historical fiction" of the past.

2. **Private Recordings**

Private recordings include noncommercial studio and home recordings, but not unpublished commercial recordings or secretly recorded live performances. As defined here, they were made with no intention of publication, contemporary or retrospective, regardless of whether they were made in a studio or not.

3. **Live Performance Recordings**

Live performances are distinguished as performances played to a live audience. Though there is an unavoidable overlap here with broadcasts (most live performances were transcribed off the air), many were in-house recordings, some professionally made (usually through the public address system), others privately transcribed backstage or via hand-held microphone.

Among these are the celebrated Viennese Selenophone recordings, 7mm nitrate sound-on-film recordings made on modified 35mm (negative) motion picture stock using only the audio portion of the film (the video portion and sprocket holes were sliced off). The negatives could not be played and required positive prints for reproduction. Up to thirty-five minutes of a performance could be recorded without changing reels and, using two machines, there would be no gap between one reel and the next. As with motion picture film, the recordings could be edited and transferred to acetate discs without breaks.

The Selenophone, for all practical purposes, the first commercially marketed "tape" recorder, was developed by Oskar Czeija, head of the Radio Verkehers AG [RAVAG]--Austrian Radio, Vienna. The prototype was developed by 1929 but the process was not exploited until 1937, by which time CBS and NBC were competing for an interest in the device as a means of securing access to European broadcasts (until then, American networks had to rely on shortwave broadcasts for these, though NBC was opposed to using them on a national feed). NBC eventually purchased two of the Selenophone machines from RAVAG and in 1942 transferred the accompanying films to disc. The war put an end to this exchange of broadcasts and probably accounted for the destruction of the other Selenophone films (and negatives) made. Much of the 1937 Salzburg Festival was recorded in this manner, preserving several complete operas conducted by Arturo Toscanini and Bruno Walter. In the mid-1950s, NBC gave one of the machines and the surviving films to Walter Toscanini, the conductor's son, who wanted to transfer the three performances conducted by his father--*Die Meistersinger*, *Falstaff*, and *Die Zauberflöte*--that NBC still held as positive prints. A *Nozze di Figaro* and *Don Giovanni* from the festival, both conducted by Bruno Walter, also survived, but not Toscanini's *Fidelios*, his Verdi *Requiem* and *Te Deum*, or his orchestral broadcasts of 14 and 29 August, 1937, as far as is known. All five of the original nitrate film copies originally purchased by NBC are currently held at the New York Public Library, as is a Selenophone reproducer--the only known functioning example in the world. No original negatives are known to exist. See Donald McCormick's fine, detailed study of the Toscanini Selenophone transcriptions, "The Toscanini Legacy: Part II, the Selenophone," *ARSC Journal*, 22, no. 2 (Fall 1991), pp. 200-206, for a description and analysis of the Selenophone process. See also, Tom Moran's "The Toscanini Legacy," *Opera Monthly* (August 1991), pp. 17-21, and Allan Kozinn's "Racing against Time to Save Sound of Fragile Old Toscanini Recordings," in the *New York Times* (2 January, 1990), pp. B1 and B3. While none of the 1937 Salzburg performances were featured in the GAO series, several others from Vienna were, and excluding the backstage acetates of Herr May, some of these were *perhaps* Selenophone recordings. These have apparently survived as acetate transfers from the original film recordings.

4. **Broadcast Transcriptions**

Radio broadcasts will be given with the call letters and location of the originating station where available, and the network affiliation when appropriate. This is not meant to imply that the originating stations were necessarily the immediate source from which the actual transcriptions were taken: frequently, coast-to-coast network broadcasts were taken off the air in New York City, regardless of where they originated. Several performances were furnished by the artists featured on the LPs (Tibbett, Martinelli, Bonelli, etc.), who had air checks professionally transcribed for their own use by private studios.

Wherever possible, a distinction will be made between these air checks (dubbings of actual AM or FM broadcasts, taken off the air either professionally or by home listeners), line checks (transcriptions made by local stations or networks from transmission lines during a broadcast), and in-house live recordings made at the actual site of a performance.

Off-the-air transcriptions, whether official line checks or home air checks, suffer from a number of pronounced eccentricities, as mentioned earlier: poor tracking, an uneven or off-center cut, distortion, broadcast interference, cross-talk, and inconsistencies of speed, especially between the end of one disc side and the beginning of another. These problems are painfully audible on a number of Smith transfers. Smith's principal source of access to the official NBC Met broadcasts was, at the time, using a turntable without variable speed, which meant that pitches were rarely if ever corrected in the initial phase of transfer (i.e., to open-reel tape)--or elsewhere in the chain of production, it would seem, as so many of the LPs demand constant vigilance. A log of many of the official NBC acetates furnished to Smith also was made available to us, and the relevant information will appear in the listings. This will include the numbers given on the discs as well as the broadcast number(s) assigned to a program.

In the United States, aluminum discs were used through 1935, laminated metal-based acetates taking their place that same year. From about the spring or summer of 1941 through the autumn of 1945, stations and networks (in particular, NBC) began using glass-based acetates, and continued to do so as a concession to conserve metal for the war effort. After the war, metal-based discs were reinstated. Through the 1950s, sixteen-inch transcription discs were the standard, the twelve-inch size being the exception. The inside-start format was discontinued in 1938-1939 in favor of outside-start, though here, too, there are exceptions.

The *New York Times* most often listed regularly scheduled shows under a generic "concert" title in an effort to minimalize unpaid sponsor exposure in its radio logs. Thus, many of the best-known network shows appear there under such bland titles as "Radio Concert," or simply under an artist's name. These shows will be listed under their proper titles in the discography with the sponsor restored. An invaluable source for straightening out these program titles was Harrison B. Summers' *A Thirty-Year History of Programs Carried on National Radio Networks in the United States 1926-1956* (New York: Arno Press/The New York Times, 1971), issued as part of the Arno Press's *History of Broadcasting: Radio to Television* series. Among useful contemporary sources of detailed broadcast listings was the *Radio Guide* (later the *Movie-Radio Guide*), published nationally as a magazine in various cities across America beginning in the 1920s. These, unfortunately, are very scarce in any form, while newspapers are plentiful, so that relatively few issues could be consulted.

Often, substitutions in a broadcast were made. Newspapers relied on "play lists" furnished to them by networks or sponsors. In most cases, these were compiled well in advance of an actual broadcast and rarely reflected any possible changes in musical selections made by the artists. We have had fortunate access to a number of broadcast concert schedules from the 1930s and 1940s, hand annotated by contemporary listeners with a good deal of musical experience. These saviors of the past, bless them, often took it upon themselves to note what was actually sung on a program, allowing us to date and otherwise document performances that would have been lost in anonymity forever. Most substitutions will be discussed in the endnotes, but it should be clear that we have not assumed anything based on either intuition or provenance--least of all program substitutions--simply because something could not be traced. Evidence was our only guide in assigning sources and dates to broadcasts. In some cases, unique (as far as we could tell) performances of unfamiliar repertory have been dated to the only known broadcast on which the artist sang them. Other material, often appearing on different GAO releases, which the artist also sang on a broadcast known to have been preserved, has been provisionally ascribed to that date (hence the notion of provenance), and annotated as such. Where we have information that an artist sang a given selection on a series of dates or different programs, and lacking any evidence that other material from these broadcasts has survived, we have included all known possible broadcast dates and assisting artists.

5. Metropolitan Opera House Broadcasts

The Met broadcasts, heard first over the NBC radio network, began on Christmas Day 1931, with a performance of Humperdinck's *Hänsel und Gretel*, conducted by Vincenzo Bellezza (*I Pagliacci* was also performed on this matinee bill, but was not heard on the air). The earliest Met broadcasts were carried simultaneously over both of the NBC key affiliates in New York City (WEAF and WJZ, NBC Red and Blue, respectively), a practice that continued through the mid-1930s. Eventually, WJZ became the sole originating station.

Beginning on 7 December, 1940 with *Le Nozze di Figaro*, issued in excerpts as EJS 228 in January, 1962, the Met broadcasts were sponsored by Texaco, but prior to this, three other companies had taken a turn as official seasonal sponsors: Lucky Strike cigarettes (1933-1934), Listerine mouthwash (1934-1935), and the Radio Corporation of America (1936-1937). From 1931 to 1934, the matinees were broadcast under the "sustaining" sponsorship of NBC itself.

Contemporary accounts claim that Texaco intervened in response to the on-the-air appeals made during the matinees of the 1939-1940 broadcast season, when a major campaign was launched by the Metropolitan Opera Guild to supplement funding (Giuseppe De Luca's broadcast appeal, made between the second and third acts of the *La Bohème* on 10 February, 1940, is preserved complete on EJS 248, issued in October 1962). Indeed, an estimated 153,000 radio listeners pledged over $325,000 during that season alone. The Texaco broadcasts originated over station WJZ, New York City, and were heard initially over 131 NBC Blue network affiliates throughout the nation. Texaco has continued sponsorship of the broadcasts without interruption to this day, making theirs the longest continuous sponsorship of a program in the history of commercial American broadcasting.

Note that prior to 1942, the National Broadcasting Company (NBC) maintained two separate networks, NBC Red and NBC Blue: WEAF was the key station of the Red network, WJZ the key station of the Blue network (there were also Pacific Coast Red and Blue networks). In 1942, the federal government forced NBC to relinquish one of the two, so that NBC Blue was operated independently as the Blue Network during the 1942-1943 season before evolving into the American Broadcasting Company (ABC) in late 1943.

ABC took over the Met broadcasts from WJZ and the Blue Network in 1943, and was eventually succeeded by CBS in 1958. A joint Texaco-Metropolitan Opera network was contrived in 1960.

The Motion Picture, Broadcasting, and Recorded Sound Division of the Library of Congress (LC) obtained the NBC Radio Collection in 1978, consisting of 175,000 transcription discs (about 80,000 hours): these include some 300 Metropolitan Opera broadcasts from the years 1933 through 1970. A comprehensive index of the pre-1942 matinees and other off-the-air material held by LC was published as *Radio Broadcasts in the Library of Congress 1924-1941: A Catalog of Recordings*, James R. Smart, compiler (Washington, D.C.: Library of Congress, 1982). This index also includes a portion of the Wilfred Pelletier Collection of 575 sixteen-inch transcription discs of Met performances and other miscellaneous broadcasts conducted by Pelletier between 1938 and 1949. Many of the broadcast performances issued on EJS are found in their original form in these two important archival collections. Reference to the Library of Congress tape catalog numbers included in Smart's index (for broadcasts prior to 1 January, 1942) will be made in individual endnotes throughout the discography. Unless otherwise stated, the Metropolitan Opera broadcasts in the LC collection are line checks cited as having been transcribed from station WJZ, New York City.

All New York City Metropolitan Opera broadcasts are Saturday afternoon matinees unless otherwise noted: a lower case "e" in parentheses (e) will be given after the broadcast date to designate the few evening Met performances issued on GAO. This symbol will be used *only* for New York City Met broadcasts; most other radio performances, (excluding regularly scheduled shows of the period) may be assumed to have been evening broadcasts.

All Met broadcasts were heard nationwide over NBC prior to late 1943, and after that, over ABC, and this too may be assumed in the listing. Met tour broadcast citations (Chicago, Cleveland, and Boston, etc.) will carry the day of the performance and the network designation, and should also be assumed to have been afternoon matinees unless otherwise noted.

6. Radio Audizioni Italiana/Radiotelevision Audizioni Italiana (RAI) and Ente Italiano Audizioni Radiofoniche (EIAR) Broadcasts

Prior to the end of the Second World War, Italian Radio bore the name *Ente Italiano Audizioni Radiofoniche* (EIAR); after the war, the name was changed to *Radio Audizioni Italiana* (RAI). With the commencement of commercial television broadcasting in 1954, RAI became *Radiotelevision Audizioni Italiana*, the name it bears to this day.

A distinction will be made wherever possible between recording dates and broadcast dates: by about 1953, most Italian Radio productions were prerecorded for later broadcast. Note that most RAI broadcast dates only indicate the date of *first* public transmission: a performance may or may not have been aired live. Singers' biographies with chronologies and the files of the journal *La Scala* (1950-1960) have been used to ascertain dates of actual recording wherever possible.

Reference will frequently be made to the Gualerzi-Roscioni *50 Anni di Opera lirica all RAI 1931-1980* (see the Selective Bibliography, below) as the "RAI chronicles." It should be noted that this compilation, though of inestimable value, lists only studio performances and dates of the first broadcast (even if prerecorded), not pickups from major houses or studio performances that were recorded but not broadcast. Nor does it include broadcasts of excerpts; only complete works are listed.

7. Film Soundtrack Excerpts

With the exception of the Vitaphone and M-G-M "Metro Movietone Acts" soundtrack excerpts, the many soundtrack items excerpted on EJS were taken from later feature films, primarily the Italian films of Gigli, Schipa and Lauri-Volpi, the Hollywood films of Grace Moore, Lawrence Tibbett, Jan Kiepura, and Nino Martini, and the British films of Tauber. These were an important part of the Smith legacy, giving collectors access, for the first time, to the musical portions of films virtually unseen for decades. In all known instances, optical (sound-on-film) tracks were used as the source--which does much to explain the poor quality of the transfers.

8. Vitaphone Shorts

Edward J. Smith had a large personal collection of Vitaphone operatic shorts, which he used periodically to provide soundtrack performances of important singers. These were poorly transferred from second-, possibly third-generation 16mm sound-on-film copies (the originals were 35mm, sound-on-disc). The rumor has always been that Smith somehow made his way into the Warner Brothers studio and paid some enterprising employee to copy as many of the films as possible from 35mm originals and their corresponding soundtrack discs, at a price of $50.00 per film. This makes for a good story, but is probably not true. I've seen some of the Smith Vitaphone copies, and it is inconceivable that they could possibly have come from anything better than poor 16mm reference or transfer copies--more than likely copies of the 16mm prints distributed in the 1950s for American television. Moreover, having several original

Vitaphone discs in my own collection, the dreadful quality of the dubbings found on Smith's various commercial and private labels suggests that badly scratched, roaring optical soundtracks were his only source: the original discs, when in clean condition, are stunning in their clarity, detail, and sheer volume of sound. Recorded as early as June 1926, they are among the most sophisticated recordings of their day, technically far beyond the commercial studio records of the period.

Excerpts from the Gigli and Martinelli soundtracks appeared on numerous EJS LPs, while EJS 513, a "Film Potpourri," offered a general sampling of excerpts by other singers.

The films were made by Warner Brothers and its subsidiary, the Vitaphone Corporation, beginning in 1926, and were released initially through 1932. The soundtracks were originally recorded using equipment developed by Western Electric through the Bell Laboratories, and were distributed for theatrical use on twelve- and sixteen-inch shellac discs pressed by Victor. In England and Europe, other major labels (HMV, Columbia, Aeolian, etc.) were responsible for the pressings. With one exception, the operatic shorts were one reel in length (approximately four to ten minutes). They were numbered serially and, by 1929 or 1930, appeared under the collective series title, "Vitaphone Varieties." The operatic shorts were shot in New York's Manhattan Opera House (other non operatic Vitaphone shorts were made in the old Vitagraph Studio in Brooklyn, which Warner's had purchased in April 1925). The Austro-Hungarian conductor Herman Heller (1881-?) was in charge of the Vitaphone operatic unit, and was the most frequently credited musical director (indeed, he seems to have conducted the Vitaphone Symphony Orchestra in all of the operatic "Vitaphone Varieties"). For at least one of the shorts, Pasquale Amato's "A Neapolitan Romance" (1928), Heller is credited as the film director as well.

Wherever possible, Vitaphone titles will be given as they appear in the films themselves; otherwise, copyright titles will be cited instead (generally, the major difference between the two is one of punctuation). The "Vitaphone Varieties" serial number will be given, along with the Library of Congress (LC) Copyright Registration Number, the latter preceded by an "MP" prefix, designating "published motion pictures other than photoplays." Production dates for the shorts are sparse, as is other production information generally, but premiere dates will be listed where available, taken from reviews as well as from contemporary Vitaphone release schedules. The original discs often carried dates, but it is not known whether these are recording dates or some sort of "processing" dates. The few disc matrix numbers that have been documented are given in the appropriate endnotes.

Sixty-four Vitaphone shorts featuring singers of operatic importance have been traced.

9. Mapleson Cylinders

The famous Mapleson cylinders of 1901-1903, actual performance recordings taken "live" from the stage of the Metropolitan Opera House, New York City, had a troubled history on EJS (see EJS 267, issued in April 1963), and though they seldom appeared on Smith's LPs, reference will always be made to the subsequently assigned Rodgers and Hammerstein Archives of Recorded Sound "Mapleson Cylinder Project" index numbers. Readers are referred to the following sources:

Hall, David. "The Mapleson Cylinder Project: Repertoire, Performers and Recordings Dates," *Recorded Sound* 83 (January 1983), pp. 21-25.

Hamilton, David, editor and compiler. *The Mapleson Cylinders: Complete Edition 1900-1904*. New York: The Rodgers and Hammerstein Archives of Recorded Sound, New York Public Library, 1985. (A 71-page booklet accompanying the six-LP Mapleson re-recordings, RH 100, which can be reliably consulted for a number of supplementary details, including full texts and sources of the performance extracts).

REISSUES

Subsequent reissues of the material released in the Golden Age of Opera series will be given where known--whether on EJS, UORC, or A.N.N.A. (Smith frequently issued the same performances more than once, boasting that better sources had become available or that better transfers had been miraculously effected)--or on other labels, commercial and private. Many of the less-distinguished private labels simply dubbed the EJS pressings, though fortunately, commercial firms have tended to issue the performances from the best available sources.

Similarly, when Smith issued excerpts from live performances, these were followed frequently (sometimes years later) by the complete performance from which the excerpts were drawn. These will be listed in the endnotes for individual LPs.

Some of the frequently cited private and esoteric collectors' labels active subsequent to the demise of The Golden Age of Opera series in November 1971 include the following, each preceded by the abbreviations that will be used in the endnotes to the GAO listings:

Accanta	Fono Team GmbH, Hamburg/Bellaphon [LPs: Germany] [Issued selectively as BASF in the U.S.]
Accord	Musidisc-Europe [LPs and CDs: France]
AS DISC	Andrea Scarduelli [CDs: Italy]
BJR	Charles Johnson & Santiago Rodriguez [LPs: U.S.A.]
BWS	Bruno Walter Society [LPs: U.S.A.]
CLS	? [LPs: Italy]
Discocorp	Bruno Walter Society [LPs: U.S.A.]
Edizione Lirca	Edizione Lirica (Ed Rosen) [LPs: U.S.A.]
ERR	Historic Operatic Treasures (Ed Rosen) [LPs: U.S.A.]
Estro Armonico	Estro Armonico [LPs: Belgium]
Foyer	Jacques Bertrand [LPs: France]
Frequenz	Salvatore Caruselli [Italy: LPs and CDs]
FWR	Roger W. Frank [LPs: U.S.A.]
GDS	Giuseppe di Stefano [label] (Melodram) [LPs and CDs: Italy]
GFC	GFC (Great Opera Performances Dischi [GOP]) [LPs: Italy]
Glendale	Legend Records [LPs: U.S.A.]
Gioielli della Lirica	Gioielli della Lirica [LPs: Italy]
GOP	Great Opera Performances Dischi (GOP) [LPs and CDs: Italy]
Historic Opera Treasures	*see ERR*
HOPE	Historical Operatic Performances Edition [LPs: U.S.A.]

HRE	Historical Recording Enterprises (Ed Rosen) [LPs: U.S.A.]
HUNT	Hunt Productions (Messaggerie Musicali s.p.a.) [CDs: Italy]
IGI	I Grandi Interpreti (Discocorp) [LPs: U.S.A.]
IGS	? [LPs: U.S.A.]
Italia	Italia [LPs: Italy]
JLT	No Information
Legato Classics	Ed Rosen [CDs: U.S.A.]
Legendary	Legendary Recordings [LPs & CDs: U.S.A.]
Magnificent Editions	Historical Recording Enterprises [LPs: U.S.A.]
MDP	Michael D. Polimeni [LPs: U.S.A.]
Melodram	Ina Del Campo [LPs & CDs: Italy]
MRF	Mauro R. Fuggette (MRF 1-99); Bismark Beane (MRF 100-) [LPs: U.S.A.]
Morgan	Morgan [LPs: ?Germany]
Moviménto Musica	Salvatore Caruselli/WEA Italiana (Warner Communications Co.) [Italy: LPs and CDs]
Music and Arts	Music and Arts Programs of America [CDs: U.S.A.]
Myto	Myto Records S.a.s. (Phonocomp s.p.a./Hunt Productions) [CDs: Italy]
Nuova Era	Nuova Era [CDs: Italy]
OMEGA	Omega [Open-reel tapes only: U.S.A.]
OPA	Operatic Archives (William Seward and John Carreddu Press) [LPs: U.S.A.]
OR	Roger Frank [LPs: U.S.A.]
Parnassus	Parnassus Recordings (Legendary Recordings) [LPs: U.S.A.]
Penzance	Roger W. Frank [LPs: U.S.A.]
Replica	ES Productions/Editoriale Sciascia [LPs: Italy]
Recital Records	Bruno Walter Society [LPs: U.S.A.]
Robin Hood	Robin Hood Records/BJR Enterprises [LPs: U.S.A.]
Rodolphe	Rodolphe/Harmonia Mundi [LPs and CDs: France]
SPA	? [CDs: Italy] (Also issued as budget "Laserlight" CDs in the U.S. Not to be confused with the (1950s) commercial American SPA [Society of Participating Artists, Inc., New York] label
Standing Room Only	Ed Rosen [CDs: U.S.A.]
STR	Stradivarius (Great Opera Performances Dischi [GOP]) [LPs: Italy]
VOCE	VOCE Records [LPs and CDs: U.S.A.]

Some frequently cited, larger-scale commercial labels, a few published by Edward J. Smith, include:

ANNA	A.N.N.A. Record Company (Edward J. Smith) [LPs: U.S.A.]
ASCO	American Stereophonic Corporation (Edward J. Smith) [LPs: U.S.A.]
Club 99	Club 99 (Bernard and Ellen Lebow) [LPs & CDs: U.S.A.]
Harvest	Edward J. Smith [LPs: U.S.] (not to be confused with the American EMI/Capitol subsidiary)
OASI	OASI (William Violi) [LPs & CDs: U.S.A.]
Pearl/Opal	Pavillion Records Ltd. [LPs & CDs: U.K.]

Rococo	Ross, Court & Co. [LPs: Canada]
Symposium	Symposium Records (Eliot B. Levin) [LPs and CDs: U.K.]
TAP:	Top Artist Platters (Edward J. Smith) [LPs: U.S.A.] (issued selectively in the U.K. on both the Rhapsody and Top Rank labels)
TIMA:	Edizioni de Timaclub SIAE (Maurizio Tiberi) [LPs & CDs: Italy]
UORC	Unique Opera Record(s) Corporation/Company (Edward J. Smith) [LPs: U.S.A.]

Often private and institutional collections of tapes and other original source materials will be discussed in endnotes. These include:

StARS (Stanford [University] Archive of Recorded Sound, Palo Alto, CA): tape only unless otherwise specified.
Library of Congress (Washington, DC): tape only unless otherwise specified
Swedish Radio (Sveriges Radio AB, Stockholm): tape only unless otherwise specified
New York Public Library Rodgers & Hammerstein Collection (New York City): various formats
Norwegian Radio (Norsk Rikskringkasting [NRK], Oslo): tape only unless otherwise specified

GENERAL ABBREVIATIONS

Notwithstanding an attempt to be as thorough as possible, general abbreviations have been kept to a minimum, in deference to any inquiries made from outside the collecting community, where the kind of shorthand that has become so widespread among record collectors remains obscure. The following abbreviations, however, will be used throughout the discography:

*	An asterisk, placed before the number of a selection or LP band, designates an endnote
CD	Compact disc (digitally remastered)
CST	Central Standard Time (U.S. time zone: Midwest)
(e)	Evening performance (all others are afternoon matinees): Metropolitan Opera Broadcasts only
EIAR	Ente Italiano Audizioni Radiofoniche (predecessor of RAI)
EP	Extended play, 45 rpm microgroove issues: 7-inch
EST	Eastern Standard Time (U.S. time zone: East coast)
LP	Long-playing 33 1/3 rpm microgroove issues: 7-, 10-, and 12-inch
(m)	Matinee performance (for non-Metropolitan Opera performances only)
Met	Metropolitan Opera House (and Guild), New York City
MST	Mountain Standard Time (U.S. time zone: Western mountain states)
NYC	New York City (all other locations will be given in full)
orch/	Orchestral accompaniment/conductor as noted
orch/?	Orchestral accompaniment/conductor unknown
pf/	Piano accompaniment/pianist as noted
pf/?	Piano accompaniment/pianist unknown
PST	Pacific Standard Time (U.S. time zone: Pacific coast)

RAI Radio[television] Audizioni Italiana (successor of EIAR)
rr Re-recording: *not* pressed from original metal parts
unpub Unpublished (for commercial recordings): these are recordings that were unissued in the form originally intended, usually 78 rpm shellac. Many were eventually pressed and issued on shellac or vinyl, and many subsequently appeared on LP as transfers
( ) Commercial catalog numbers given in parentheses were assigned but not issued
[ ] HMV single-sided catalog numbers given in brackets were assigned to, but issued only as, double-sided discs; these are in fact the "face numbers" of double-sided discs
[ ] Singers whose names appear in brackets among the cast listings for live or broadcast performances are not actually heard on the LP excerpts under discussion: they have been included so that the cast of the original performance can be shown complete

See also language abbreviations listed earlier

All dates will be given *day-month-year*, with the month abbreviated (e.g., 16 Dec 1937) to avoid the familiar European-American conflict of citation.

When specific sides and bands of an LP are referred to in the endnotes, they are given in Roman and Arabic numerals, respectively, for example, II/4 for side 2, band 4; II/4-7 for side 2, bands 4-7 inclusive, and so on.

Orchestras will be distinguished as follows: "orch" designates an unnamed studio orchestra for commercial recording sessions (the Victor or RCA studio orchestra, for example); "studio orch" designates a similarly unnamed orchestra for radio and television studio broadcasts. All other ensembles will be named specifically (e.g., the Orchestra of Radio Italiana [RAI], the Metropolitan Opera House Orchestra, the London Philharmonic Orchestra, etc.). All solo instruments other than piano [pf] will be given in full.

78 RPM LABEL ABBREVIATIONS

AGSA American Gramophone Society/HMV [U.K.], Addison Foster, director: 10-inch shellac pressings from original metal parts
AGSB American Gramophone Society/HMV [U.K.], Addison Foster, director: 12-inch shellac pressings from original metal parts
CRS Collector's Record Shop, New York City, Jack Caidin, director: shellac and vinylite re-recordings unless otherwise noted
G&T Gramophone and Typewriter Ltd. (1900-1908/9)
Gram Gramophone Company, Ltd.: Often referred to as "Dog Concert" (10-inch) and "Dog Monarch" (12-inch) pressings, "Gram" will be used generically for all post Pre-Dog/ pre-HMV Gramophone Company issues, 1909-1914, as well as for Gramophone Company issues of imported recordings (usually American Victors) that remained in print over various label changes

HMA Historic Masters Ltd. [U.K., 1972-]: 10-inch vinyl pressings from original metal parts
HMB Historic Masters Ltd. [U.K., 1972-]: 12-inch vinyl pressings from original metal parts
HMV His Masters Voice/The Gramophone Company, Ltd., 1914-
HRS Historic Record Society, New York City, William Speckin, director: shellac pressings from original metal parts unless otherwise noted
IRCC International Record Collectors' Club, Bridgeport, Connecticut, William Seltsam, director: shellac pressings from original metal parts unless otherwise noted
Pre-Dog Gramophone Company Ltd.: post-G&T, pre-Gramophone issues of the period 1908/9-1910, though the label was retained slightly longer, it would appear, in Russia and Eastern Europe
VA HMV: 10-inch white and gold label "Archive Series," first issued October 1951; shellac discs, a mixture of repressings and electrical transfers
VB HMV: 12-inch white and gold label "Archive Series," first issued October 1951; shellac discs, a mixture of repressings and electrical transfers

Selective Bibliography

CLASSIFIED BIBLIOGRAPHIC SOURCES

The following works will be referred to frequently throughout the notes, sometimes by the author's name, sometimes by the title, but most often by the abbreviations preceding the citations.

Met Annals: Seltsam, William H. *Metropolitan Opera Annals: A Chronicle of Artists and Performers*. New York: H. W. Wilson/Metropolitan Opera Guild, 1947; *First Supplement: 1947-1957*. New York: H. W. Wilson/ Metropolitan Opera Guild, 1957.

RAI Chronology: Gualerzi, Giorgio, and Carlo Marinelli Roscioni. *50 anni di opera lirica alla RAI 1931-1980*. Turin: ERI/Edizioni RAI, 1981.

WERM: Clough, Francis F., and G. J. Cuming. *The World's Encyclopedia of Recorded Music*, and *First Supplement, April, 1950-May-June, 1951*. London: The London Gramophone Corporation & Sidgwick and Jackson Ltd., 1952; *Second Supplement 1951-1952*. London: London Records and Sidgwick and Jackson Ltd., 1953; *Third Supplement 1953-1955*. London: Sidgwick and Jackson Ltd. and the Decca Record Company Ltd., 1957.

Gramophone Shop Encyclopedia: *The Gramophone Shop Encyclopedia of Recorded Music*, R. D. Darrell, compiler. New York: The Gramophone Shop, 1936; 2nd rev. edition, George Clark Leslie, supervising editor. New York: The Gramophone Shop and Simon & Schuster, 1942; 3rd rev. and enl. edition, Robert H. Reid, supervising editor. New York: The Gramophone Shop and Crown, 1949.

MISCELLANEOUS DISCOGRAPHICAL SOURCES

The three editions of Edward Sackville-West and Desmond Shawe-Taylor's *The Record Guide* (London: Collins, 1951-1956) and two *The Record Year* supplements (London: Collins, 1952-1953) were consulted, as were David Hall's *The Record Book* (New York: Smith & Durrell, 1940; supplement, 1941), and *The Record Book: New International Edition* (New York: Durrell, 1948).

Among standard discographical compendia, Roberto Bauer's *Historical Records* (Milano: Martucci, 1937) and *The New Catalogue of Historical Records, 1898-1908/09* (London: Sidgwick & Jackson, 1947); *Vertical Cut Cylinders and Discs* by Victor Girard and Harold M. Barnes (London: British Institute of Recorded Sound, 1964; corrected facsimile reprint, 1971); and the two catalogs of Julian Morton Moses, *The Record Collector's Guide* (New York: Concert Bureau, College of the City of New York, 1936) and *Collectors' Guide to American Recordings, 1895-1925* (New York: American Record Collector's Exchange, 1949; corrected republication, New York: Dover, 1977) were used frequently. Incidental to our research were the many published secondary catalogs of specific record companies (notably, those works devoted to Edison written variously by Dr. Duane D. Deakins, Ronald Dethlefson, Allen Koenigsberg, and Raymond R. Wile), but two, in particular, will be seen throughout the listings to have been indispensable:

Fagan, Ted, and William R. Moran. *The Encyclopedic Discography of Victor Recordings*: (Volume 1) *Pre Matrix Series*, and (Volume 2) *Matrix Series: 1 through 4999*. Westport, CT: Greenwood Press, 1983 and 1986, respectively.

Sears, Richard S. *V-Discs: A History and Discography*. Westport, CT: Greenwood Press, 1980 (*Discographies*, no. 5).

The catalog of the New York Public Library's Library and Museum of the Performing Arts (*Dictionary Catalog of the Rodgers and Hammerstein Archives of Recorded Sound*, 15 vols. [Boston: G. K. Hall, 1981]) was used early on as a source of cross-reference among the various Smith series, GAO, UORC, and A.N.N.A.

GENERAL MUSICAL LEXICONS

The standard lexicons were consulted for reliable and current musicological information: the various editions of *Grove's Dictionary of Music and Musicians*, 1879/89- ; Baker's *Biographical Dictionary of Musicians*, 1900- ; the Thompson *International Cyclopedia of Music and Musicians*, 1938-); and their European counterparts, *Die Musik in Geschichte und Gegenwart*, 1949- ; *La Musica*, 1966- ; and so forth. Older, more obscure works proved most valuable for difficult biographical searches involving less well-known or forgotten performers and works. National bibliographies, most notably the *National Union Catalog Pre-1956 Imprints*, 754 vols. (London: Mansell, 1968-1981), were also used frequently to answer a variety of musicological questions.

The standard sources for information related specifically to opera and operetta include lexicons: Charles Osborne's *The Dictionary of the Opera* (New York: Simon & Schuster, 1983) and Harold Rosenthal and John Warrack's *The Concise Oxford Dictionary of Opera*, 2nd ed. (Oxford and New York: Oxford University Press, 1979), as well as various other opera encyclopedias (David Ewen's *Encyclopedia of the Opera* and *The New Encyclopedia of the Opera* [New York: Hill and Wang, 1955 and 1971, respectively], and so forth). The late Carl Dahlhaus's *Pipers Enzyklopädie des Musiktheaters*, 3 vols. (Munich: Piper, 1986-1991), although not yet complete, was also consulted. Lord Harewood's current revision of *The Definitive Kobbé's Opera Book* (New York: Putnam, 1987) was drafted early on as the authority in such matters as character names and then, throughout the project, into a myriad of other problem-solving roles, as were the many earlier Kobbé editions, 1919- . The opera-plot books of George P. Upton (*The Standard Opera*, various editions, 1885-) often provided information on operas that have since disappeared from the international repertory, just as the various opera books published by the Metropolitan Opera Guild (*The Metropolitan Opera Guide*, 1939- , and *Metropolitan Operagrams*, 1937/8-) proved useful in pinpointing standard cuts in some of the broadcast productions issued in the GAO series.

For the lighter repertory that appeared on GAO, Kurt Gänzl and Andrew Lamb's *Gänzl's Book of the Musical Theatre* (London: Bodley Head, 1988; New York: Schirmer, 1989) and Mark Lubbock's *The Complete Book of Light Opera* (London: Putnam, 1962) were most useful, as were both editions of Gerald Bordman's *American Musical Theater: A Chronicle* (New York and Oxford: Oxford University Press, 1978 and 1992).

In an attempt to document the many singers represented throughout GAO, virtually everything that came our way was pressed into service. In addition to the aforementioned standard biographical lexicons and the three editions of the Kutsch-Riemens *Sängerlexikon* (see the Selective Bibliography below), these included musical Who's Whos, the Pierre Key annuals (*Pierre Key's Music Year Book*, various editions, 1925-), David Ewen's *Living Musicians* series, 1940- , and countless others--in short, anything and everything that was found to list verifiable birth, death, and career dates.

A few of the more obscure but very helpful biographical sources of a more *national* orientation should be cited in full, though the coverage in some is international in overall scope:

Enciclopedia de Musica Brasileira: Erudita, Folklorica, Popolar, 2 vols. São Paulo: Art Editora, 1977.

Gourret, Jean. *Dictionnaire des Cantatrices de L'Opéra de Paris*. Paris: Éditions Albatros, 1987.

------. *Dictionnaire des Chanteurs de L'Opéra de Paris*. Paris: Éditions Albatros, 1982.

Hofsten, Sune. "Sångerbiografier," in "Operan: Röster från Stockholmsoperan under 100 år," Swedish EMI 7C 153 35350/58 [LP] (1977).

The Opera Directory, Ross, Ann, ed. New York: Sterling, 1961.

SONG LITERATURE

Three works were essential for the documentation of the many popular songs that appear throughout the discography. These answered many questions of publication, copyright, and correct authorship:

Fuld, James J. *The Book of World-Famous Music*. New York: Crown, 1966.

Kinkle, Roger D. *The Complete Encyclopedia of Popular Music and Jazz 1900-1950*, 4 vols. New Rochelle, NY: Arlington House, 1974.

Mattfeld, Julius. *Variety Music Cavalcade*. Englewood Cliffs, NJ: Prentice-Hall, 1952; revised ed., 1962; Based upon the author's original "Musical-Historical Cavalcade: 1800-1935," in *Variety Radio Directory 1938-1939* (New York: Variety, 1938), pp. 33-158.

FILM

Sources for film and film soundtrack information included the second and third volumes of the *Catalog of Copyright Entries, Cumulative Series, 1912-1939*, and *1940-1949* (Washington, D.C.: Copyright Office/The Library of Congress, 1951 and 1953); the *American Film Institute Catalog: Feature Films 1921-1930*, Kenneth W. Munden, executive editor (New York and London: Bowker, 1971); and *The Motion Picture Guide*, 12+ vols., by Jay Robert Nash and Stanley Ralph Ross (Chicago: Cinebooks, 1985-).

These, in addition to the various editions of the *Motion Picture Production Encyclopedia* (Hollywood: Hollywood Reporter Press) and other similar industry annuals, provided us with reliable access to much of the filmographic information cited.

SELECTIVE BIBLIOGRAPHY

Given there are many of the specific, often esoteric sources that made our work not only easier but possible, in the final analysis. All but a very few individual articles and discographies from three of the more frequently consulted discographical journals are omitted from the bibliography:

The Record Collector: Ipswich, England; Pontrhydyfen, Port Talbot, Wales; Broomfield, Chelmsford, England, 1946- .

Recorded Sound: *The Journal of the British Institute of Recorded Sound*, 1961-1984, and its predecessor, The British Institute of Recorded Sound *Bulletin*, 1956-1960.

ARSC Journal: *Journal of the Association for Recorded Sound Collections*, 1968- .

Those familiar with the literature of discography will be quick to recognize the use of certain definitive artist and works discographies found in these journals. Discographies will be cited, as appropriate, in the endnotes to individual LPs. In many cases, however, what appeared to be reliable work proved otherwise, so that a great deal of information from published discographies was abandoned and researched anew from primary source materials.

Record liner notes were generally avoided as sources of reliable information. On those very rare occasions when they were consulted and their information was verified, they will be cited directly in the appropriate endnotes.

The works listed below emerged, for a variety of reasons, as among the most important sources available:

Ardoin, John. *The Callas Legacy*. London: Duckworth, 1977; rev. 2nd ed., London: Duckworth 1982/reprint, 1988.

Battaglia, Fernando. *L'arte del canto in Romagna*. Bologna: Bongiovanni Editore, 1979.

Bennett, John (and various coauthors). *Voices of the Past*, 11 vols. Lingfield, Surrey: Oakwood Press, 1956- .

Bishop, Cardell. *San Carlo Opera Company of America*. Santa Monica, CA: The Author, 1980-1981.

Bloomfield, Arthur J. *The San Francisco Opera, 1923-1961*. New York: Appleton-Century-Crofts, 1961.

------. *The San Francisco Opera: 1922-1978*. Sausalito, CA: Comstock Editions, 1978.

Blum, Daniel. *Daniel Blum's Opera World, 1952-* . New York: Putnam, 1955- .

Borgno, Marina. *Franco Corelli: un uomo, una voce*. Parma: Azzali, 1990.

Caamano, Robert. *La Historia del Teatro Colon*, 3 vols. Buenos Aires: Editorial Cinetea, 1969.

Casanova, Carlamaria. *Renata Tebaldi, la voce d'angelo*. Milan: Electa, 1981; Nuova ed., Parma: Azzali, 1987.

Caserta, Gino, and Alessandro Ferrau, eds. *Annuario del Cinema Italiano 1953-1954*. Rome: Cinedizione, 1954.

Cassidy, Claudia. *Lyric Opera of Chicago*. Chicago: Chicago Lyric Opera, 1979.

Cella, Franca. *Leyla Gencer: Romanzo vero di una primadonna*. Venice: CGS, 1986.

Celletti, Rodolfo. *Le Grandi Voci*. Rome: Istituto per la Collaborazione Culturale, 1964.

------. *Il Teatro d'opera in disco 1950-1987*. Milan: Rizzoli, 1988.

Cervetti, Valerio, Claudio Del Monte, and Vincenzo Segreto. *Teatro Regio di Citta di Parma: Cronologia degli Spettacoli Lirici 1929-1979*, 3 vols. and Indici, vol. 4. Parma: STEP, 1979/1982.

Chavez, Edgard de Brito, Jr. *Memorias e Glorias de um Teatro: Sessenta Anos do Teatro Municipal do Rio de Janeiro*. Rio de Janeiro: CEA, 1971.

Christian, Hans, and Harald Hoyer. *Die Wiener Staatsoper 1945-1980*. Wien: (?)Staatsoper, 1981.

Clerico, Cesare. *Giulio Neri - Una vita nella voce*. Turin: Scomegna, 1981.

------. *Tancredi Pasero - Voce verdiana*. Turin: Scomegna, n.d.

Collins, William J. "Beniamino Gigli: Non-Commercial Recordings," *The Record Collector* 35, nos. 8-10 (August-October 1990), pp. 190-240.

------. "Giacomo Lauri-Volpi Live and Private Recordings," *The Record Collector* 34, nos. 11-12 (December 1989), pp. 235-252.

------. "Giovanni Martinelli," *The Record Collector* 25, nos. 7-9 (October 1979), pp. 147-215; 25, nos. 10-12 (February 1980), pp. 221-255 (w. readers' addenda).

Cronstrom, Anne-Marie and Gustave. "Beniamino Gigli," *The Record Collector* 9, nos. 9-10 (February-March 1955), pp. 221-240; 9, nos. 11-12 (April-May 1955), pp. 247-269; 13, nos. 7-8 (September-October 1960), pp. 184-188.

Dahlhaus, Carl. *Pipers Enzyklopädie des Musiktheaters*, 3 vols. Munich: Piper, 1986-1991.

Davis, Ronald. *Opera in Chicago*. New York: Appleton-Century, 1966.

De Oliviera Castro Cequera, Paulo. *Um Secolo de Opera em São Paulo*. São Paulo: (?)publisher, 1954.

Di Cave, Luciano. *Lina Pagliughi*. (?)Rome: Timaclub/Associazione S.ER.M.AR., 1989.

Eaton, Quaintance. *Opera Caravan: Adventures of the Metropolitan Opera on Tour*. New York: Farrar, Straus and Cudahy, 1957/reprint, New York: Da Capo, 1978.

------. *Opera Production: A Handbook*. Minneapolis: University of Minnesota Press, 1961.

------. *Opera Production II: A Handbook*. Minneapolis: University of Minnesota Press, 1974.

La Fenice. Milano: Nuove Edizioni, 1972.

Foschi, Franco. *Omaggio a Beniamino Gigli - Primavera del tenore*. Rome: Bulzoni, 1982.

Frajese, Vittorio. *Dal Costanzi all'Opera*, 4 vols. Rome: Capitolium, 1978.

Frassoni, Edilio. *Due secoli di lirica a Genova*, 2 vols. Genova: C. R. di Genova e Imperia, 1980.

Gatti, Carlo. *Il Teatro alla Scala - Nella Storia e nell'arte (1778-1963)*. Milan: Ricordi, 1964. Appendix: Tintori, Giampiero. *Cronologia completa degli spettacoli e dei concerti*.

Gray, Michael. *Beecham: A Centenary Discography*. New York: Holmes & Meier, 1979.

Griffel, Margaret Ross. *Opera in German: A Dictionary*. Westport, CT: Greenwood Press, 1990.

Hansen, Hans. *Lauritz Melchior: A Discography*. Copenhagen: Nationaldiskoteket, 1972.

------. Melchior discography. In *Tristanissimo: The Authorized Biography of Heroic Tenor Lauritz Melchior*, by Emmons, Shirlee. New York: Schirmer, 1990.

Kelly, Alan. "Chaliapin Discography," *The Record Collector* 20, nos. 8-10 (August 1972), pp. 180-230.

------. *His Master's Voice/La Voce del Padrone: The Italian Catalogue*. Westport, CT: Greenwood Press, 1988 (*Discographies*, no. 30).

-------. *His Master's Voice/La Voix de Son Maitre: The French Catalogue*. Westport, CT: Greenwood Press, 1990 (*Discographies*, no. 37).

Kelly, Alan, and Vladimir Gurvich. Chaliapin discography. In *Chaliapin: A Critical Biography* by Victor Borovsky. New York: Knopf, 1988.

Kolodin, Irving. *The Metropolitan Opera*. New York: Knopf, 1968.

Kutsch, K. J., and Leo Riemens. *A Concise Biographical Dictionary of Singers*, Harry Earl Jones, trans. Philadelphia: Chilton, 1969.

------. *Unvergängliche Stimmen: Klienes Sängerlexikon*. Bern: A. Francke AG Verlag, 1962/1975.

------. *Unvergängliche Stimmen / Sängerlexikon*. Bern and Munich: Francke Verlag, 1982. (Only when appropriate will a distinction be made between these various editions, which will otherwise be referred to in the text uniformly as "Kutsch-Riemens").

Major, Norma. *Joan Sutherland*. London: Macdonald/Queen Anne Press, 1987.

Marinelli, Carlo. *Opere in disco*. Florence: Discanto Edizioni, 1982.

Martinez, Corrado. *40 Anni di attivita artistica del Teatro Massimo di Palermo . . . 1936-1975*. Palermo: Priulla, 1980.

Moore, Edward. *Forty Years of Opera in Chicago*. New York: Horace Liveright, 1930.

Moran, William R., "Edward Joseph Smith . . . An Appreciation and a Project," *The Record Collector* 31, nos. 4-5 (May 1986), pp. 111-114.

------, compiler. *Nellie Melba: A Contemporary View*. Westport, CT: Greenwood Press, 1985 (*Contributions to the Study of Music and Dance*, no. 5).

------. Tibbett discography. In *Lawrence Tibbett: Singing Actor*, edited by Andrew Farkas. Portland, OR: Amadeus Press, 1989, a revision of his earlier Tibbett discography in *The Record Collector* 23, nos. 11-12 (August 1977), pp. 273-286; 24, nos. 1-2 (January 1978), pp. 36-46, the latter with a filmography by Dr. T. R. Bullard.

Moran, William R., and Richard Koprowski. Caruso discography. In *Enrico Caruso: My Father and My Family*, by Enrico Caruso Jr., and Andrew Farkas. Portland, OR: Amadeus Press, 1990.

Neupert, Käte, ed. *Die Besetzung der Bayreuther Festspiele 1876-1960*. Bayreuth: Musica, 1961.

Park, Bill. Ponselle discography. In *Ponselle: A Singer's Life*, by Rosa Ponselle, and James A. Drake. Garden City, NY: Doubleday, 1982.

Parsons, Charles H. *The Mellen Opera Reference Index* (series), 14 vols. Lewiston, NY: Edwin Mellen Press, 1986-1990.
Opera Composers and Their Works, vols. 1-4.
Opera Librettists and Their Works, vols. 5-6.
Opera Premieres: A Geographical Index, vols. 7-8.
Opera Subjects, vol. 9.
Opera Discography, vols. 10-12.
Opera Premieres: An Index of Casts, vols. 13-14.

Peel, Tom, and John Holohan. "Beniamino Gigli Discography," *The Record Collector* 35, nos. 5-7 (May-July 1990), pp. 111-158.

Picchi, Mirto. *Un Trono Vicino al Sol*. Ravenna: Girasole, 1978.

Pinzauti, Leonardo. *Il Maggio Musicale Fiorentino (dalla 1ª alla 30ª edizione)*. Florence: Valecchi, 1967.

Porter, Jack W., and Harald Henrysson. *A Jussi Bjoerling Discography*. Indianapolis: Jussi Bjoerling Memorial Archive, 1982.

Quattrocchi, Vincenzo. *Magda Olivero - Una voce per tre generazioni*. Turin: ?The Author, 1984.

Ricaldone, Marc. Gigli discography. In *The Memoirs of Beniamino Gigli*, by Beniamino Gigli, Darina Silone, trans. London: Cassell, 1957/ reprint, New York: Arno Press/New York Times, 1977.

------. Unpublished 55-page manuscript of the noncommercial Gigli recordings, n.d.

Rosenthal, Harold. *Two Centuries of Opera at Covent Garden*. London: Putnam, 1958.

Sanner, Howard. *Kirsten Flagstad Discography*. Unpublished Master's Thesis, University of Maryland, 1981.

Segond, André. *Renata Tebaldi*. Lyon: Éditions Jacques-Marie Laffont et Associés, 1981.

Shaman, William. *Giuseppe De Luca: A Discography* (Symposium 1038). London: Symposium, 1991.

------. "The Operatic Vitaphone Shorts," *ARSC Journal* 22, no. 1 (Spring 1991), pp. 35-94.

------. "The Vatican G&Ts," in *The Record Collector* 28, nos. 7-8 (December 1983), pp. 146-191; 30, nos. 12-13 (December 1985), pp. 287-293.

Silveri, Paolo. *Paolo Silveri nella vita e nell'arte*. Rome: Bardi, 1983.

Smart, James R., compiler. *Radio Broadcasts in the Library of Congress 1924-1941: A Catalog of Recordings*. Washington, DC: Library of Congress, 1982.

Teatro San Carlo. *Chronache del Teatro S. Carlo 1948-1968*. Naples: Teatro San Carlo, 1968.

Terrace, Vincent. *The Complete Encyclopedia of Television Programs, 1947-1976*, 2 vols. New York: A. S. Barnes, 1976.

Tintori, Giampiero. *Duecento anni di Teatro alla Scala - Cronologia Opere-Baletti-Concerti 1778-1977*. Milano: ?Gutenberg, 1979.

Tognelli, Jole, ed. *Cinquant'anni del Teatro dell'Opera, Roma 1928-1978*. Rome: Bestetti, 1979.

-----. *Cronache del Teatro S. Carlo 1948-1968*. Milano: Ricordi, 1969.

Trezzini, Lambert. *Due secoli di vita musicale - Storia del Teatro Comunale di Bologna*, 2 vols. Bologna: Alfa, 1966.

Wolff, Stéphane. *Un Demi-siècle d'opera-comique*. Paris: Editions André Bonne, 1953.

------. *L'Opéra au Palais Garnier (1875-1962)*. Paris: L'Entr'acte, 1962.

Worth, Paul W., and Jim Cartwright, compilers. *John McCormack: A Comprehensive Discography*. Westport CT: Greenwood Press, 1986 (*Discographies*, no. 21). (Because the works are so similar, Brian Fawcett Johnston's "Count John McCormack / Discography," issued in 1988 as *Talking Machine Review* 74 and 75 (addendum) should be mentioned also as another useful, if controversial, source of McCormack documentation, though its renown seems to have been all but subsumed in the wake of the Worth and Cartwright publication).

Discography of "The Golden Age of Opera" Series

EJS 100: "The Golden Age of Opera" (1 LP)
Issued 1956

SIDE 1 (100 A):

* 1. JEAN DE RESZKE, tenor (Metropolitan Opera House Orchestra/ Philippe Flon): L'AFRICAINE, Act IV: "ô Paradis" (Meyerbeer) (F) [fragments]
Recorded by Lionel Mapleson during a Metropolitan Opera performance, NYC, Friday, 15 Mar 1901 (evening)
a) Sorti de l'onde . . . à nous cet Éden retrouvé!
------ IRCC 183 IRCC L-7004 (LP) R&H 100 (LP)
b) . . . salut! Monde nouveau to end of aria
IRCC 110 IRCC 183 IRCC L-7004 (LP) R&H 100 (LP)

* 2. ADELINA PATTI, soprano (pf/Alfredo Barili): "La Calesera" (Sebastian Yradier) (I)
684½c Craig-y-Nos, Wales, June, 1906 G&T 03085

* 3. FRANCESCO TAMAGNO, tenor (pf/?): HÉRODIADE, Act IV: Adieu donc, vains objects" (Massenet) (F)
3016ft Ospedaletti, February, 1903 G&T 52680

* 4. ERNESTINE SCHUMANN-HEINK, contralto (orch/?Walter B. Rogers): LA CLEMENZA DI TITO, K. 621, Act I: Parto, parto ma tu ben mio (Mozart) (I)
C-8231-3 Camden, 18 Sep 1909 Victor 88196

* 5. EDOUARD DE RESZKE, bass (pf/?Charles Prince): MARTHA, Act III: Chi mi dirà [Lasst mich euch fragen] ["Canzone del Porter"] (Flotow) (I)
1222-1 New York, 1903 Columbia 1222

* 6. CHARLES DALMORES, tenor (orch/?Walter B. Rogers): LE PROPHÈTE, Act III: Roi du ciel (Meyerbeer) (F)
B-4395-3 Camden, 25 Mar 1908 Victor unpub

* 7. MARIANNE BRANDT, contralto (pf/?) LUCREZIA BORGIA, Act II: Trinklied [Il segreto per esser felici] (Donizetti) (G)
Pathé 19261 Vienna, 11 September or 23 November, 1905

* 8. RICCARDO MARTIN, tenor (orch/?Walter B. Rogers): TOSCA, Act III: E lucevan le stelle (Puccini) (I)
B-8658-2 ?Camden, 7 Mar 1910 Victor 87050 Gram 7-52009

* 9. GERALDINE FARRAR, soprano (orch/?Bruno Seidler-Winkler): ROMéO ET JULIETTE, Act I: Je veux vivre dans le rêve ["Waltz Song"] (Gounod) (F)
1315r Berlin, 23 Jun 1906 G&T 33618

* 10. POL PLANÇON, bass (pf/?C.H.H. Booth): LE CAïD, Act I: Enfant chéri . . . Le tambour-major (Thomas) (F)
C-873-1 New York, 23 Dec 1903 Victor 85019 G&T 032019
Victor (15-1034)

SIDE 2 (100 B):

* 1. FERNAND ANSSEAU, tenor (orch/Piero Cappola): TOSCA, Act I: Recondita armonia (Puccini) (I)
Bb-10949-1 London, 15 June, 1927 HMV DA 898 [7-52378]

* 2. LAURITZ MELCHIOR (Metropolitan Opera House Orchestra/Erich Leinsdorf): DIE WALKÜRE, Act I/iii: Ein Schwert verhiess mir der Vater . . . Wärme gewann ich und Tag (Wagner) (G)
Metropolitan Opera broadcast, NYC, 27 Feb 1943

* 3. DAME NELLIE MELBA, soprano (Royal Opera House Orchestra/Vincenzo Bellezza)
Recorded during Melba's Farewell Concert, Covent Garden, London, 8 Jun 1926
a) LA BOHÈME, Act III: Donde lieta usci ["Addio"] (Puccini) (I)
CR-412-1 HMV DB 943 [2-053264] Japanese Victor ND 973
DB 1500
b) "Farewell Speech" (spoken)
CR-421-1 HMV DB 943 [01182] Japanese Victor ND 973

-----

* 4. EDWARD JOHNSON, tenor (orch/Josef Pasternack): FANCIULLA DEL WEST, Act II: Una parola sola . . . Or son sei mesi che mio padre mori (Puccini) (I)
C-23460-2 Camden, 7 Nov 1919 Victor unpub AGSB 63

* 5. LOTTE LEHMANN, soprano (Berlin State Opera Orchestra/Frieder Weissmann): TOSCA, Act II: Nur der Schönheit [Vissi d'arte] (Puccini) (G)
xxB 8321-3 Berlin, 16 Apr 1929 Odeon 0-8736

* 6. FEODOR CHALIAPIN, bass (orch/John Barbirolli): DON GIOVANNI, K. 527, Act I: Catalog Aria (Mozart) (I)
Recorded in Small Queen's Hall, London, 19 June, 1928
a) Part 1: Madamina! Il catalogo è questo . . .
Bb-13832-1A HMV DA 994 [7-52406] Victor 1393
b) Part 2: . . . Nella bionda
Bb-13833-1 HMV DA 994 [7-52407] Victor 1393

* 7. ENRICO CARUSO, "bass" (orch/Walter B. Rogers): LA BOHÈME, Act IV: Vecchia zimarra, senti (Puccini) (I)
B-17198-1 Camden, 23 Feb 1916 Victor "87499" HMV DL 100

NOTES: EJS 100

Labeled only as "The Golden Age of Opera," the surround of this first GAO release bears the matrix number "EJS 100 A & B."

As a general note on playing speeds, all of the commercial shellac recordings included on this LP were transcribed at 78.26 rpm. The original playing speeds and keys for pressings will be given in the notes below.

Side 1 (100 A):

Band 1: The second fragment of "ô Paradis" was originally re-recorded and issued as IRCC 110 (January, 1940), playing in the correct key of G-flat at about 90 rpm. Both fragments were later issued on IRCC 183 (February, 1941), with the speeds adjusted to a more manageable 78.26 rpm. Pitches are correct on EJS 100. Together, these fragments are nos. 1 and 2, respectively, in the Rodgers and Hammerstein Mapleson cylinder index.

Band 2: Reissued as IRCC 17 in April, 1933, and VB 40 in 1951. The key of this performance (and thus, the speed of the G&T and IRCC pressings) is disputed. EMI's complete Patti set (RLS 711 and Electrola C 147-01 500/01 M) pitches it in D-flat at 73.47 rpm, while 76.00, 77.43 and 80.00 rpm have all been suggested to pitch the disc in D major (77.43 seems correct). It has been transcribed here at 78.26 rpm.

Band 3: The original playing speed is 77.64 rpm (F major). Reissued as IRCC 172 in August, 1940. The unpublished version of the aria, matrix 3017ft, was issued as Historic Masters HMA 43, a ten-inch vinyl pressing.

Band 4: The original playing speed is 75.00 rpm (B-flat). Reissued as IRCC 31 in February, 1934, and in the early 1950s as AGSB 21.

Band 5: A new electrically-dubbed master of the "Porter's Song" (W 170728-1) was made in New York on 9 December, 1933 for issue the same month as IRCC 28-B, with De Reszke's original spoken announcement removed. The EJS 100 dubbing carries the announcement, so it may be assumed that an original (single-sided only) copy of Columbia 1222 was used. The original playing speed is 79.00 rpm (D major).

Band 6: The original playing speed is 76.00 rpm (A-flat). Reissued as IRCC 131 in November, 1938.

Band 7: The spoken announcements for Brandt's three Pathés are unclear as to the date of recording, as reflected in the listing above. The original discs have been reported to play at a variety of speeds (stampers vary): the highest estimate reported was 98 rpm for the key of C major. The source used here was undoubtedly the IRCC 3010 re-recording (issued June-July, 1947), pitched correctly at 78.26 rpm. This, and Brandt's PROPHÈTE aria (Pathé 19260) were issued in 1990 on Symposium CD 1085, "The Harold Wayne Collection, Volume 6;" the Schumann "Frühlingsnacht" (Pathé 19259), Brandt's only other recording, appeared on "The Yale Collection, Volume 1," isssued in 1992 as Symposium 1135.

Band 8: The original playing speed is 76.60 rpm (B minor).

Band 9: The original playing speed is 72.00 rpm (F major). Reissued as IRCC 29 in January, 1934.

Band 10. The original playing speed is 78.00 rpm (G major). The Victor "Heritage" issue, 15-1034, was scheduled for issue but was not released.

Side 2 (100 B):

Band 1: The original playing speed is 78.00 rpm (F major).

Band 2: In addition to Melchior's three electrical studio recordings of this excerpt, several broadcasts were examined to determine conclusively the origin of this track. From Metropolitan Opera broadcasts: New York, 17 February, 1940 (Leinsdorf); Boston, 30 March, 1940 (Leinsdorf); New York, 27 February, 1943 (Leinsdorf); New York, 2 December, 1944 (Szell); also, a 22 February, 1941 ***NBC SYMPHONY***

Carnegie Hall broadcast (WJZ, New York City), conducted by Arturo Toscanini, issued commercially on RCA Victor LP LM 2452 (matrix F2 RP 6398-43).

Apart from purely musical similarities (especially instrumental errors), identical audience noises very strongly suggest that the Met broadcast of 27 February, 1943 was the one excerpted here. Note that the EJS 100 dubbing is a half-step HIGH (*Siegmund* enters on C-natural at score pitch).

Traubel's "Hoyotoho!" from this performance appeared on EJS 171 (January, 1960).

Band 3. The original playing speed is 78.26 rpm (D major for the BOHÈME aria). See also EJS 127 (1958).

Band 4: The original playing speed is 76.00 rpm (A minor). AGSB 63 was the only pressing issued.

Band 5: The original playing speed of Lehmann's "Vissi d'arte" is 76.00 rpm (E-flat). Issued in England as Parlophone R 20095 and in the U.S. as Decca 25804.

Band 6: The original playing speed of both sides is 78.26 (D major).

Band 7: Victor "87499" (a bogus single-sided catalog number assigned in 1949) and HMV DL 100 are both ten-inch re-recordings taken from what was thought at the time to be the only extant copy of this unpublished performance, originally owned by Caruso's friend and biographer, Dr. P. Mario Marafioti. The electrically-dubbed master (D9-QB-7758-1A) was prepared in Camden in 1949 and was coupled with a spoken commentary, "Why Caruso Recorded the Coat Song" by Francis Alda and Wally Butterworth, in conjunction with the latter's weekly radio series, ***VOICES THAT LIVE***, on station WJZ, New York City. Victor "87499" was a Red Seal vinyl issue; HMV DL 100 was green-label shellac. The original recording was made at 76.00 rpm (C-sharp minor), but was dubbed at 78.26 rpm for both the Victor and HMV reissues. The EJS 100 dubbing was made at 78.26 rpm, and should be adjusted accordingly.

EJS 101: "The Golden Age of Opera" (3 LPs)
Issued 1956

SIDES 1-6 (101 A-F):

Aïda (Verdi) (I)
Opera in 4 Acts (complete)
Metropolitan Opera House Orchestra and Chorus/Ettore Panizza
Metropolitan Opera broadcast, NYC, 22 Mar 1941

CAST:
Norman Cordon (*The King of Egypt*); Bruna Castagna (*Amneris*); Stella Roman (*Aïda*); Giovanni Martinelli (*Rhadames*); Ezio Pinza (*Ramfis*); Leonard Warren (*Amonasro*); Lodovico Oliviero (*Messenger*); Maxine Stellman (*Priestess*).

NOTES: EJS 101

Rumor has it that the air checks used for this issue came from Stella Roman, who recovered them from a closet! The NBC acetates, which also contained Intermission Features with Milton Cross, Frank Black, Josephine Tuminia, Virgil Thompson, and a number of non-musical dignitaries, have apparently been lost.

EJS 102: "The Golden Age of Opera" (1 LP)
Issued 1956

SIDE 1 (102 A):

TURANDOT (Puccini - completed by Franco Alfano) (I)
Opera in 3 Acts (excerpts)
Royal Opera House Orchestra and Chorus/John Barbirolli
Unpublished live performance recordings, Technical Test Series
TT 2352-1/TT 2352-7, Covent Garden, London, 5 May 1937
[+ EXCEPT AS NOTED]

CAST:
Eva Turner (*Turandot*); Octave Dua (*Emperor Altoum*); Giulio Tomei (*Timur*); Giovanni Martinelli (*Prince Calaf*); Mafalda Favero (*Liù*); Piero Biasini (*Ping*); Angelo Bada (*Pang*); Giuseppe Nessi (*Pong*); [Aristide Baracchi (*Mandarin*)].

* 1. Act I: + a) FAVERO (orch/?Lorenzo Molajoli): Signore, ascolta!
WB 2159 Italian Columbia D 5932 Milan, 1928

b) MARTINELLI: Non piangere, Liù
FAVERO: Noi morrem sulla strada dell'esilio!
TOMEI: Noi morrem!
MARTINELLI: Dell'esilio addolcisci a liu le strade!
. . . chiede colui che non sorride più!
TT 2352-1 unpublished Columbia test

Act II c) TURNER, MARTINELLI, and Chorus: In questa Reggia . . . O Turandot!
TT 2352-2 unpublished Columbia test

d) TURNER, MARTINELLI, and Chorus: Straniero, ascolta!
TT 2352-3 unpublished Columbia test

e) TURNER, DUA, TOMEI, FAVERO, MARTINELLI, and Chorus: Guizza al pari di fiamma
TT 2352-4 unpublished Columbia test

* f) TURNER, DUA, MARTINELLI, and Chorus: Turandot! Turandot! Gloria, gloria, o vincitore . . . O audace! O coraggioso! O forte!
TT 2352-5 unpublished Columbia test

g) MARTINELLI, DUA, and Chorus: . . . il mio nome non sai! . . . to end of Act 2
TT 2352-6 unpublished Columbia test

Act III h) MARTINELLI, BIASINI, BADA, NESSI, and Chorus: Nessun dorma! . . . Di'tu, che vuoi!
TT 2352-7 unpublished Columbia test

SIDE 2 (102 B):

* 1. GIOVANNI MARTINELLI, tenor (Vitaphone Symphony Orchestra/Herman Heller): LA JUIVE, Act IV: J'ai fait peser sur toi mon éternelle haine . . . Rachel! quand du Seigneur (Halévy) (F)
from the soundtrack of the one-reel Warner Brothers-Vitaphone short ***GIOVANNI MARTINELLI, TENOR OF THE METROPOLITAN OPERA COMPANY, SINGING "VA PRONONCER LA MORT" FROM ACT IV OF THE OPERA, "LA JUIVE"*** (1927), New York, circa 1927
Vitaphone Varieties 510
MP 4107; c29 Jun 1927
Premier: Warners' Theater, New York City, 8 Oct 1927

* 2. GIOVANNI MARTINELLI, tenor, and JEANNE GORDON, contralto (Vitaphone Symphony Orchestra/Herman Heller): CARMEN, Act II: Excerpts (Bizet) (F)
a) GORDON: Les tringles des sistres! (first 30 measures and last 28)
b) MARTINELLI: Halte-là . . . Dragons d'Alcala! (beginning at measure 38 of No. 16)
c) GORDON and MARTINELLI: Enfin c'est toi
d) GORDON and MARTINELLI: Je vais dancer . . . Je le veux Carmen . . . La fleur que tu m'avais jetée (complete)
from the soundtrack of the one-reel Warner Brothers-Vitaphone short ***GIOVANNI MARTINELLI, ASSISTED BY JEANNE GORDON IN SELECTIONS FROM CARMEN*** (1927), New York, circa 1927
Vitaphone Varieties 474
MP 3949; c18 Apr 1927
Premiere: Colony Theater, New York City, 12 Apr 1927

* 3. GIOVANNI MARTINELLI, tenor, and GIUSEPPE DE LUCA, baritone (pf/?Emanuel Balaban): "I mulattieri" (Francesco Masini) (I)
Broadcast, ***CARNEGIE POPS CONCERT***, Carnegie Hall, WNYC, NYC, 11 May 1948

* 4. GIOVANNI MARTINELLI, tenor, and GIUSEPPE DE LUCA, baritone (Carnegie Pops Orchestra/Emanuel Balaban): LA FORZA DEL DESTINO, Act III: Solenne in quest'ora (Verdi) (I)
Broadcast, ***CARNEGIE POPS CONCERT***, Carnegie Hall, WNYC, NYC, 11 May 1948

NOTES: EJS 102

Side 1 (102 A):

Band 1: With the exception of Favero's studio recording of "Signore, ascolta," published as Columbia D 5932, these TURANDOT excerpts were recorded live from the stage of Covent Garden by English Columbia (EMI). None were issued, possibly because of the sound quality, which is poor. It has also been suggested that Martinelli's contractural obligation to Victor/HMV prevented their issue.

Virtually identical excerpts were recorded from the 10 May, 1937 performance, cast intact, but with Albanese as *Liù*. Only the first of the three performances of TURANDOT given during this Coronation Season (30 April, with Favero as *Liù*) was *not* recorded, though the first act was broadcast in its entirety. Keith Hardwick, in his "Producer's Note" to the 1988 EMI compact disc issue of these performances, "Puccini: Turandot (Excerpts)," from the "Great Recordings of the Century" series (CDH 7 61074 2), *suggests* that the 5 May performance may have been a *recording* rehearsal: certainly, the lack of applause after Martinelli's 5 May "Nessun dorma" makes this a credible theory considering the outburst we hear after his 10 May rendition.

The original Columbia test pressings were twelve-inch, single-sided shellacs: there were seven masters cut from each of the two recorded performances. In 1958, when the excerpts were first being considered for release on LP (using Dame Eva Turner's original copies), the 10 May set (Technical Test Series TT 2353-1/TT 2353-7) was reported as having survived complete, but the 5 May set (Technical Test Series TT 2352-1/TT 2352-7) was lacking the first act excerpts (TT 2352-1), the end of Act 2 (TT 2352-6), and Martinelli's "Nessun dorma" (TT 2352-7). As Smith certainly had access to these missing discs as early as 1956, his source material must have come from another of the principals, probably his friend, Martinelli. The 10 May excerpts turned up later on EJS 240 (May, 1962) and both sets were coupled on EJS 50X (issued April-May, 1976 amid the UORC bulletins). Smith claimed that EJS 50X was compiled in 1969 at the behest of Martinelli himself, but that the singer died before it could be published. This, too, lends some credibility to the theory that Smith may have secured Martinelli's own copies of the complete excerpts.

The missing Favero "Signore, ascolta!" remains a mystery: it was thought to have preceded Martinelli's "Non piangere, Liù" on TT 2352-1 (her sobbing can be heard throughout the Prince's aria) but considering Smith's access to TT 2352-1, the fact that he was forced to substitute Favero's early commercial recording, EMI's subsequent restoration of the set, and their "official" documentation of the contents of TT 2352-1 in the liner notes, it now seems certain that Favero's "Signore, ascolta!" was recorded on a separate master--if it was recorded at all. Perhaps this master was discarded before pressings were made, owing to some technical flaw. In any event, there seems little hope that the 5 May "Signore, ascolta" still exists.

Note that there are no band separations on the TURANDOT side of EJS 102, and that a bad opening groove and "bump" obstruct the beginning of the "Signore, ascolta!"

Miscellaneous warnings concerning the various Smith TURANDOT issues include mislabelings, possible editing, and the incorrect identification of performances (the second side of EJS 50X, labeled as 10 May, 1937, seems to be a composite of both the 5 and 10 May performances). The dubbing of the 5 May performance on EJS 50X (mislabeled "April 30, 1937") is essentially the same as that on EJS 102, except that a band separation has been added between the Act I excerpts and the "In questa Reggia." EJS 50X also contains Favero's Columbia recording of "Signore, ascolta!," and has the same damaged opening groove found on EJS 102: Smith's engineer in the 1970s has told me that, by 1976, the master tapes for EJS 102 and 240 had been lost, and that 50X was prepared using these earlier LPs as the source.

Individual excerpts from these performances have been included on any number of Martinelli recitals and potpourris, and on a variety of Smith's own commercial labels--ASCO, Celebrity, Allegro Royale, and TAP. The EMI compact disc reconstruction, however, can be acknowledged to supersede all of these in authority as well as in quality.

Band 1f: "Guarda! La mia vittoria . . . Tre enigmi m'hai proposto! . . . Uno soltanto a te ne proporrò" is omitted.

Side 2 (102 B):

Bands 1 and 2: Both of these Vitaphone shorts are given here under their respective copyright titles. A privately-owned print of the CARMEN short carries the date "1926." This short premiered with the May McAvoy programmer, "Matinee Ladies." A contemporary Vitaphone catalog gives the premiere date as 19 April, 1927, but the *New York Times* review (13 April, 1927, p. 29:4) proves otherwise.

In spite of its title, Martinelli omits the first three phrases (16 measures) of this scene in the LA JUIVE excerpt. The film premiered during the run of "The Jazz Singer" at the Warners' Theater in New York City, and reappeared at least once, at the premiere of an obscure May McAvoy-Lionel Barrymore feature, "The Lion and the Mouse."

The CARMEN excerpts were also released by Smith on EJS 470 (May, 1969), Celebrity CTL 1001, Rondo Gold RG 1001 ("La fleur" only), ASCO A-116 (do.), and Celebrity CEL 500 (do.). Similarly, the JUIVE excerpt also appeared on EJS 221 (November, 1961), ASCO A-116, and Celebrity CEL 500.

Bands 3 and 4: This *CARNEGIE POPS CONCERT* was a benefit for American Relief for Italy, Inc. It has been suggested that these duets were recorded by Jack L. Caidin for possible release on his CRS label, but this has not been documented. The piano-accompanied "I mulattieri" was not on the program, and so was probably an unscheduled encore (it seems certain that it was from this broadcast, but reviews do not confirm this). Two other De Luca standards, "Occhi di fata" (Tremacoldo-Denza) and "Voi dormite, Signora" (Pagliari-Tosti), both of which he recorded commercially, were also scheduled, but the next day's reviews do not mention who sang them that evening. These have not appeared on any LP as far as I know, so may not have been transcribed. Also heard during this broadcast were Jean Carlton and Eddy Michaelis in Menotti's THE TELEPHONE.

Both the FORZA duet and the "I mulattieri" can be found on various Smith LPs; in the early 1980s, the former was included on the Pearl LP GEMM 181/2, a Martinelli compilation, where it is listed erroneously as an unpublished excerpt from a "May, 1928" performance. The set was reissued on CD (GEMM 9350 and 9351) in 1988. What appears to be Martinelli's "E lucevan le stelle" from this broadcast appeared later on EJS 270 (May, 1963).

EJS 103/104: "The Golden Age of Opera" (2 LPs)
Issued 1956

SIDES 1-3 (103 A-B and 104 A):

CARMEN (Bizet) (F)
Opera in 4 Acts (excerpts)
Metropolitan Opera House Orchestra and Chorus/Gennaro Pappi
Metropolitan Opera broadcast, Cleveland, NBC, 17 Apr 1937

CAST:
Rosa Ponselle (*Carmen*); René Maison (*Don José*); Hilda Burke (*Micaela*); Julius Huehn (*Escamillo*); Louis D'Angelo (*Zuniga*); Wilfred Engelman (*Morales*); Thelma Votipka (*Frasquita*); Helen Olheim (*Mercédès*); George Cehanovsky (*Dancaire*); Giordano Paltrinieri (*Remendado*).

1. Act I:
   a) PONSELLE and chorus: L'amour est un oiseau rebelle ["Habanera"]
   b) PONSELLE: Près des remparts de Séville ["Seguidilla"]

   Act II:
   c) PONSELLE, VOTIPKA, and OLHEIM: Les tringles des sistres! ["Chanson Bohème"]
   d) HUEHN: Votre toast ["Toreador Song"]
   e) PONSELLE, VOTIPKA, OLHEIM, PALTRINIERI, and CEHANOVSKY: Nous avons en tête une affaire
   f) PONSELLE and MAISON: Halte-là! . . . La fleur que vous m'avais jetée ["Flower Song"]
   g) PONSELLE, MAISON, VOTIPKA, OLHEIM, PALTRINIERI, CEHENOVSKY and D'ANGELO: Holà! Carmen

   Act III:
   h) PONSELLE, VOTIPKA, and OLHEIM: Mêlons! Mêlons! . . . En vain pour éviter ["Card Scene"]

   Act IV:
   i) PONSELLE and HUEHN: Si tu m'aimes, Carmen
   j) PONSELLE, MAISON, and chorus: C'est toi! C'est toi! . . . to end of the opera

SIDE 4 (104 B):

"ROSA PONSELLE, SOPRANO"

* 1. w. studio orch/Andre Kostelanetz: ALCESTE, Act I: Divinités du Styx (Gluck) (I)
Broadcast, ***CHESTERFIELD HOUR***, WABC, NYC, 3 Dec 1934

* 2. w. studio orch/Andre Kostelanetz: DON GIOVANNI, K. 527, Act I: Batti, batti o bel Masetto (Mozart) (I)
Broadcast, ***CHESTERFIELD HOUR***, WABC, NYC, 1 Oct 1934

* 3. w. studio orch/Andre Kostelanetz: FEDRA: O divina Afrodite (Romano Romani) (I)
Broadcast, ***CHESTERFIELD HOUR***, WABC, NYC, 18 Mar 1936

* 4. w. Los Angeles Philharmonic Orch/Erno Rapee: SEMIRAMIDE, Act I: Bel raggio lusinghier (Rossini) (I)
Broadcast, ***GENERAL MOTORS HOUR***, KFI, Hollywood Bowl, Los Angeles, 24 May 1936

* 5. w. Los Angeles Philharmonic Orch/Erno Rapee: LA TRAVIATA, Act III: Addio del passato (Verdi) (I)
Broadcast, ***GENERAL MOTORS HOUR***, KFI, Hollywood Bowl, Los Angeles, 24 May 1936

6. w. studio orch/Andre Kostelanetz: "Ave Maria" (Miguel Sandoval) (I)
Broadcast, ***CHESTERFIELD HOUR***, WABC, NYC, 25 Mar 1936

NOTES: EJS 103/104

The CARMEN excerpts are divided over the first three LP sides without band separations. The same excerpts have appeared on the Metropolitan Opera Guild and Operatic Archives LPs, Met-7 and OPA-10016.

Stephen Fassett (Fassett Recording Studio, 24 Chesnust Street, Boston 8, Mass.") issued private, custom dubbings of the complete CARMEN (as he did with many early recordings), and these may have been the source of this GAO issue.

Side 4 (104 B):

Bands 1-2 and 4-5 were reissued on EJS 191 (October, 1960); bands 1, 2 and 3 later appeared on ANNA 1036 (May-June, 1979).

Band 1: Library of Congress tape: 5063-5 (30-minute broadcast).

Band 2: Library of Congress tape: 5063-1 (30-minute broadcast).

Band 3: Ildebrando Pizzetti (1880-1968) also wrote a three-act setting of d'Annunzio's FEDRA, to the poet's own libretto, that was first produced at La Scala in 1915. Romani's one-act PHEDRA, with a libretto by Lanzoni, premiered in Rome the same year. Ponselle, a friend and pupil of Romani, remained faithful to the work throughout her career, even seeing to its Covent Garden revival in 1931.

Romani was both a noted conductor and accompanist. He recorded as Ponselle's accompanist and as the conductor of the credited "Grande Orchestra" for Columbia in London (74000 matrix series) during the First World War.

Bands 4-5: Though billed as the ***LOS ANGELES PHILHARMONIC*** in the *New York Times*, this concert was among Ponselle's regular ***GENRAL MOTORS HOUR*** broadcasts. Both arias were later reissued on EJS 190 (October, 1960).

EJS 105: "The Golden Age of Opera" (1 LP)
Issued 1956

I PAGLIACCI (Leoncavallo) (I)
Opera in 2 Acts and a Prologue (abridged)
Metropolitan Opera House Orchestra and Chorus/Ferruccio Calusio
Metropolitan Opera broadcast, NYC, 1 Feb 1941

CAST:
Norina Greco (*Nedda*); Giovanni Martinelli (*Canio*); Lawrence Tibbett (*Tonio*); Alessio DePaolis (*Beppe*); Francesco Valentino (*Silvio*).

SIDE 1 (105-A):

1. Prologue: a) TIBBETT: Prologue, "Si può?" (complete)

   Act I: b) CAST and Chorus: Son qua! . . . E parti domattina?

SIDE 2 (105-B):

1. Act I: a) E allor perchè . . . Vesti la giubba . . . to end of the act

   Act II: b) CAST and chorus: Pagliaccio, mio marito ("La Commedia") . . . to end of the opera

NOTES: EJS 105

Lawrence Tibbett had his own Met broadcasts transcribed off-the-air by a New York studio. These he personally loaned to Smith. Portions of this I PAGLIACCI are reported to have been transferred slightly below pitch, in particular, *Nedda's* "Stridono lassù" (the "Ballatella"), and the *Nedda-Silvio* duet, "Decidi il mio destin, Nedda."

Side 1 (105 A):

The orchestral introduction to the Prologue was omitted on EJS 105.

Side 2 (105 B):

The orchestral Intermezzo was omitted from EJS 105, along with the chorus, "Presto affrettiamoci . . ."

EJS 106: "The Golden Age of Opera" (3 LPs)
Issued 1956

SIDES 1-6 (106 A-F):

OTELLO (Verdi) (I)
Opera in 4 Acts (complete)
Metropolitan Opera House Orchestra and Chorus/Ettore Panizza
Metropolitan Opera broadcast, NYC, 24 Feb 1940

CAST:
Giovanni Martinelli (*Otello*); Lawrence Tibbett (*Iago*); Alessio DePaolis (*Cassio*); Giordano Paltrinieri (*Roderigo*); Nicola Moscona (*Lodovico*); George Cehanovsky (*Montano*); Wilfred Engelman (*Herald*); Elisabeth Rethberg (*Desdemona*); Thelma Votipka (*Emilia*).

NOTES: EJS 106

Taken from broadcast transcription discs loaned to Smith by Tibbett. This performance has also appeared on a Metropolitan Opera Guild LP, Met-4.

Library of Congress tape: 5174-11 (complete broadcast).

EJS 107: "The Golden Age of Opera" (3 LPs)
Issued 1956

SIDES 1-5 (107 A-E):

LA TRAVIATA (Verdi) (I)
Opera in 3 Acts (complete)
Metropolitan Opera House Orchestra and Chorus/Ettore Panizza
Metropolitan Opera broadcast, NYC, 5 Jan 1935

CAST:
Rosa Ponselle (*Violetta*); Elda Vettori (*Flora*); Henriette Wakefield (*Annina*); Frederick Jagel (*Alfredo*); Lawrence Tibbett (*Germont*); Angelo Bada (*Gastone*); Alfredo Gandolfi (*Baron Douphol*); Marquis Millo Picco (*Marquis D'Obigny*); Paolo Ananian (*Doctor Grenvil*).

SIDE 6 (107 F):

1. **FIRST INTERMISSION FEATURE:** Milton Cross introduces Geraldine Farrar
   a) GERALDINE FARRAR: Reminisences about LA TRAVIATA in Berlin
   b) GERALDINE FARRAR, soprano: LA TRAVIATA, Act II: Dite alla giovine [fragment] (Verdi) (I)
   c) GERALDINE FARRAR, soprano: LA TRAVIATA, Act II: Di provenza il mar [fragment] (Verdi) (I)
   Metropolitan Opera broadcast, NYC, 5 Jan 1935

2. **SECOND INTERMISSION FEATURE:**
   a) GERALDINE FARRAR: On Ponselle's first LA TRAVIATA (1921) and her own at the Met (28 February 1908)
   b) GERALDINE FARRAR, soprano: LA TRAVIATA, Act I: Ah, fors è lui . . . Sempre libera [fragments] (Verdi) (I)
   Metropolitan Opera broadcast, NYC, 5 Jan 1935

3. **THIRD INTERMISSION FEATURE:**
   a) GERALDINE FARRAR: Analyses LA TRAVIATA . . . talks about singing *Violetta* to Caruso's *Alfredo* and singing for Cosima Wagner early in her career
   b) GERALDINE FARRAR, soprano: LA TRAVIATA, Act III: Addio del passato [fragment] (Verdi) (I)
   c) GERALDINE FARRAR, soprano: LA TRAVIATA, Act I: Tra voi saprò dividere ["Brindisi"] . . . Parigi, o cara [fragments] (Verdi) (I)
   d) GERALDINE FARRAR: Berlin "champaign glass" anecdote
   Metropolitan Opera broadcast, NYC, 5 Jan 1935

NOTES: EJS 107

Taken from broadcast transcription discs loaned to Smith by Tibbett, which included the Farrar Intermission features. The complete performance (without the intermissions) was reissued on Pearl LP GEMM 235/236, and in 1988, as CD GEMM 9317. Smith reissued EJS 107 complete on one of his "special" labels, MOP 2.

Sides 1-5 (107 A-E):

Ponselle's "Ah, fors è lui . . . Sempre libera" was transposed down during the actual performance: the recitative to the cavatina (at "in core ho scolpiti questi accenti") is taken down a half step, and down another half step in the recitative to the cabaletta (at "Che spara or piu?"). Moreover, sagging pitches have been reported between the original transcription discs.

Side 6 (107 F):

For puposes of timing, Farrar's Intermission features for the TRAVIATA were also pre-recorded on 4 January, 1935: these rehearsals or "run-throughs" have survived, and were issued selectively on EJS 397 (May, 1967) and IRCC L-7033 (1968). The excerpts included on EJS 107 were taken *live* off-the-air on 5 January during the actual broadcast. Both the spoken and musical portions of the live Intermission are very similar to their pre-recorded equivalents, at least in content.

See also the endnotes for EJS 397 (I/1a-h).

On 25 November, 1934, the *New York Times* (31:3) carried a feature story entitled "Miss Farrar to Aid Opera Broadcasts," with details of Farrar's appearance the night before on a local WEAF (New York City) broadcast, "The Season's Opera Broadcasts," where she accepted the post of commentator for the Saturday afternoon Met broadcast intermissions being carried nationally over NBC. Introduced as a "raconteuse" by Paul D. Cravath, chairman of the board of the Metropolitan Opera Association, Farrar consented to assume the post beginning with the Christmas broadcast of HÄNSEL UND GRETEL, extending through the entire 1934-1935 broadcast season of fifteen Saturday performances. "It is not going to be my intention to bore you with data or weighty information that you can read for yourself in any encyclopedia of music," she was quoted as saying, "What I should much prefer to do is to make you all aware that opera can be an entertainment as thrilling as the theatre or the movie." Indeed, Farrar's broadcasts tended toward simple demonstrations of leading motifs and other highlights of the score; her singing and playing were delightful, often moving, and surprisingly secure for an aging "raconteuse" who had been retired from the stage for some dozen years.

The 25 December, 1934 broadcast of HÄNSEL UND GRETEL marked another milestone in the annals of the Met Saturday afternoon broadcasts, then celebrating their third anniversary on the air. In an article titled "New Radio Devices to Electrify Christmas Opera / Farrar Rehearses a New Role," the *New York Times* of 16 December, 1934 (X: 19:1) proclaimed that the "nationwide audience is expected to receive the music with greater clarity than ever before," owing to a new radio installation that had been built in the house. New velocity microphones, tubes, and circuits, "evolved through three seasons of opera broadcasting," were credited. Three thousand dollars had been spent to upgrade the facilities: the electricity was changed from direct to alternating current, and special "pockets" were built into the stage to conceal as many microphones as possible. "The control operators' instruments," the article continued, "by which the musical-electricians liven or deaden the various microphones will be located in a box to be known as 'the control room.' Each piece of equipment is in duplicate and two engineers will be assigned to each post in case of emergency and to avoid interruptions in the broadcast." Farrar herself extolled these technical improvements at length during her ROMÉO ET JULIETTE Intermission of 26 January, 1935 (pre-recorded 24 January).

Box 42, which the singer referred to as her "radio nest," was converted into a studio for Farrar's use. There, she held her Intermission Features throughout the season. The broadcast of HÄNSEL UND GRETEL" was reviewed the following day in the *New York Times* (19:4), where it was reported that the second scene was interrupted temporarily by a loud thud, the result of a falling counterweight to one of the drop scenes. Even the orchestra was startled into silence. It was left to the diplomatic skills of announcer Milton Cross to placate the radio audience in the awkward moments that elapsed, though reports that Queena Mario, the *Gretel* that afternoon, had fainted in the wake of the accident were dismissed as untrue. Farrar was not visible during the broadcast, but a number of the 3,000 children present in the audience that day managed to find her backstage after the performance. The *Times*, naturally, was unable to resist the temptation of running a photograph of Farrar enveloped by the smiling faces of her young admirers.

Intermission material from the HÄNSEL UND GRETEL broadcast was pre-recorded on 22 December, 1934. Two of the run-though fragments appeared on EJS 397 and IRCC L-7033.

EJS 108: "The Golden Age of Opera" (3 LPs)
Issued 1956

SIDES 1-6 (108 A-F):

SIMON BOCCANEGRA (Verdi) (I)
Opera in 3 Acts and a Prologue (complete)
Metropolitan Opera House Orchestra and Chorus/Ettore Panizza
Metropolitan Opera broadcast, NYC, 21 Jan 1939

CAST:
Lawrence Tibbett (*Simon Boccanegra*); Elizabeth Rethberg (*Maria Boccanegra*); Ezio Pinza (*Jacopo Fiesco*); Giovanni Martinelli (*Gabriele*); Leonard Warren (*Paolo Albiani*); Louis D'Angelo (*Pietro*); Girodano Paltrinieri (*Captain*); Pearl Besuner (*Maidservant*).

NOTES: EJS 108

Taken from broadcast transcription discs loaned to Smith by Tibbett. A few missing measures are reported between sides of the original transcription discs, the result of the engineer not changing discs quite fast enough. This performance has also appeared on the Metropolitan Opera Guild LP Met-13.

EJS 109: "The Golden Age of Opera" (3 LPs)
Issued 1956

SIDES 1-6 (EJS 109 A-F):

TANNHÄUSER (Wagner) (G)
Opera in 3 Acts (complete)
Metropolitan Opera House Orchestra and Chorus/Artur Bodanzky
Metropolitan Opera broadcast, NYC, 18 Jan 1936

CAST:
Emanuel List (*Hermann*); Lauritz Melchior (*Tannhäuser*); Lawrence Tibbett (*Wolfram*); Hans Clemens (*Walther*); Arnold Gabor (*Biterolf*); Giordano Paltrinieri (*Heinrich*); James Wolfe (*Reinmar*); Kirsten Flagstad (*Elisabeth*); Margaret Halstead (*Venus*); Editha Fleischer (*Shepherd*).

NOTES: EJS 109

Taken from broadcast transcription discs loaned to Smith by Tibbett. Only minor orchestral abridgements have been reported, but it is not known if these were performance, recording, or transfer cuts.

EJS 110: "The Golden Age of Opera" (1 LP)
Issued 1957

"LAWRENCE TIBBETT, BARITONE (1929-1936)"

SIDE 1 (110 A):

* 1. w. studio orch/Wilfred Pelletier: DIE MEISTERSINGER VON NÜRNBERG, Act II: Was duftet doch der Flieder (Wagner) (E)
Broadcast, ***PACKARD HOUR***, WJZ, NYC, 2 Oct 1934

2. w. studio orch/Wilfred Pelletier: MARTHA, Act III: Porter's Song [Lasst mich euch fragen (Flotow) (E)
Broadcast, ***PACKARD HOUR***, WJZ, NYC, 18 Dec 1934

3. w. studio orch/?: LA TRAVIATA, Act II: Di provenza il mar (Verdi) (I)
Broadcast, ***PACKARD HOUR***, 27 Nov 1934; 22 Oct 1935; 17 Dec 1935; or 18 Feb 1936

4. w. studio orch/?Donald Voorhees: SERSE, Act I: Ombra mai fu (Handel) (I)
Broadcast, ***PACKARD HOUR***, WABC, NYC, 19 Nov 1935

5. w. studio orch/?: LES CONTES D'HOFFMANN, Act II: Scintille diamant (Offenbach) (F)
Broadcast, ***PACKARD HOUR***, ?WJZ, NYC, circa 1934

6. w. studio orch/?: ANDREA CHENIER, Act III: Nemico della patria? (Giordano) (I)
Broadcast, ***PACKARD HOUR***, WJZ, NYC, 5 Feb 1935 or 1 Oct 1935

SIDE 2 (110 B):

1. w. studio orch/?Wilfred Pelletier: FALSTAFF, Act II: È sogno, o realtà? (Verdi) (I)
Broadcast, ***PACKARD HOUR***, WJZ, NYC, 19 Feb 1935

2. w. studio orch/?Donald Voorhees: ROMÉO ET JULIETTE, Act I: Mab la riene des mensonges (Gounod) (F)
Broadcast, ***PACKARD HOUR***, WABC, NYC, 10 Mar 1936

3. w. studio orch/?: IL TABARRO: Scorri, fiume eterno! (Puccini) (I)
Broadcast, ***PACKARD HOUR***, 30 October, 1934; 19 Mar 1935; or 12 Nov 1935

4. w. studio orch/?Donald Voorhees: IL TROVATORE, Act II: Il balen del suo sorriso (Verdi) (I)
Broadcast, ***PACKARD HOUR***, WABC, NYC, 25 Feb 1936

5. w. studio orch/?Donald Voorhees: TOSCA, Act II: Già! Mi dicon venal (Puccini) (I)
Broadcast, ***PACKARD HOUR***, WABC, NYC, 25 Feb 1936

6. w. studio orch/?Donald Voorhees: HÉRODIADE, Act II: Vision fugitive (Massenet) (F)
Broadcast, ***PACKARD HOUR***, WABC, NYC, 29 Oct 1935 or 11 Feb 1936

7. w. studio orch/?: FAUST, Act IV: Vous qui faites l'endormie ["Sérénade"] (Gounod) (F)
   Broadcast, ***PACKARD HOUR***, WABC, NYC, ?4 Febr 1936

NOTES: EJS 110

In spite of its subtitle, "1929-1935," this Tibbett recital is drawn exclusively from ***PACKARD HOUR*** broadcasts, 1934-1936.

Tibbett's regular weekly appearances on the ***PACKARD HOUR***--Tuesday evenings over station WJZ, New York City (NBC Blue)--began on 18 September, 1934 and ended, temporarily, on 19 March, 1935. John B. Kennedy was the announcer, and Wilfred Pelletier, long-time Metropolitan Opera conductor, was the director of the credited "Concert Orchestra." On 26 March, 1935, the show was replaced by the dramatic series ***WELCOME VALLEY***.

After a hiatus of nearly six months, during which Tibbett was in Hollywood filming "Metropolitan" for 20th Century-Fox, the ***PACKARD HOUR*** returned on 24 September, 1935 over station WABC, New York City (CBS), occupying the same Tuesday evening slot from 8:30 to 9:00 pm. The "Voorhees Orchestra," under the direction of Donald Voorhees, accompanied the premiere broadcast, which was introduced by Alvan Macauley, president of the Packard Motor Car Company. Voorhees, a pioneering broadcast conductor and erstwhile bandleader on the Edison, Columbia, Pathé, and Hit-of-the-Week labels, probably stayed on as conductor through early 1936, but this is not verified in the radio logs. By 17 March, 1936, Russ Morgan was credited as the conductor.

Where the exact date of a broadcast is uncertain (I/3, 5, and 6; II/3, 6, and 7), so then is the station and the conductor. Pelletier probably conducted all of the WJZ shows through March, 1935, and Voorhees the WABC shows beginning in September of that year.

Side 1 (110 A):

Band 1: The MEISTERSINGER aria is mislabeled "Wahn! wahn" on EJS 110: this misattribution has somehow found its way onto to other LP reissues.

EJS 111: "The Golden Age of Opera" (1 LP)
Issued 1957

"BENIAMINO GIGLI, TENOR (1923-1944)"

SIDE 1 (111 A):

* 1. w. orch/Enrico Sivieri: LO SCHIAVO, Act II: All'istante partir di qui vorrei . . . Quando nascesti tu (Gomes) (I)
   S-093089-1 Rio de Janeiro, 29 Oct 1951 Victor B-5024

* 2. w. orch/Enrico Sivieri: IL GUARANY, Act II: Son giunto in tempo . . . Vanto io pur (Gomes) (I)
   S-093090-1 Rio de Janeiro, 29 Oct 1951 Victor B-5024

* 3. w. Vitaphone Symphony Orchestra/Herman Heller: LA GIOCONDA, Act II: Sia gloria ai canti . . . Cielo e mar! (Ponchielli) (I)
from the soundtrack of the one-reel Warner Brothers-Vitaphone short ***BENIAMINO GIGLI, TENOR OF THE METROPOLITAN OPERA COMPANY SINGING SELECTIONS FROM ACT II OF THE OPERA LA GIOCONDA*** (1927)
New York, circa 1927
Vitaphone Varieties 517
MP 4118; c29 Jun 1927
Premiere: Warners' Theater, NYC, 21 Jun 1927

RIGOLETTO (Verdi) (I)
Opera in 3 Acts (excerpts)
Royal Opera House Orchestra and Chorus/Vittorio Gui
Broadcast, Covent Garden, London, 6 June, 1938

CAST:
Lina Pagliughi (*Gilda*); Olga de Franco (*Maddalena*); [Gladys Palmer (*Giovanna*)]; José Malone (*Countess di Ceprano*); [Dorothy Jennings (*Page*)]; Beniamino Gigli (*Duke of Mantua*); Carlo Tagliabue (*Rigoletto*); Corrado Zambelli (*Sparafucile*); Aristide Baracchi (*Marullo*); [Roderick Lloyd (*Monterone*)]; Octave Dua (*Matteo Borsa*); Frank Sale (*Ceprano*).

* 4. GIGLI, MALONE, TAGLIABUE, BARACCHI, DUA, and SALE: Act I: Questa o quella . . . Partite? crudele! . . . Tutto è festa

* 5 GIGLI, ZAMBELLI, TAGLIABUE, PAGLIUGHI, and DE FRANCO: Act IV: La donna è mobile . . . E non ti basta ancor? (43 measures into the Quartet)

* 6. w. LUCREZIA BORI, soprano (orch/Rosario Bourdon): ROMÉO ET JULIETTE, Act I: Ange adorable (Gounod) (F)
C-27714-1 ?New York, 28 Mar 1923 Victor unpub HMV 2-034033

SIDE 2 (111 B):

* 1. w. TITTA RUFFO, baritone (orch/Rosario Bourdon): LA GIOCONDA, Act I: Enzo Grimaldo, Principe di Santafior (Ponchielli) (I)
CVE-37321-1 Camden, 17 Dec 1926 Victor unpub AGSB 49

* 2. w. TITTA RUFFO, baritone (orch/Rosario Bourdon): LA FORZA DEL DESTINO, Act III: Solenne in quest'ora (Verdi) (I)
CVE-37319-2 Camden, 17 Dec 1926 Victor unpub AGSB 49

* 3. w. TITTA RUFFO, baritone (orch/Rosario Bourdon): LA BOHÈME, Act IV: In un coupè . . . O Mimi, tu piu non torni (Puccini) (I)
CVE-37320-2 Camden, 17 Dec 1926 Victor unpub AGSB 56

MANON (Massenet) (F)
Opera in 5 Acts (excerpts)
Metropolitan Opera House Orchestra and Chorus/Louis Hasselmans;
Deems Taylor, voice-over narration
Metropolitan Opera broadcast, NYC, 5 Mar 1932

CAST:
Grace Moore (*Manon Lescaut*); Aida Doninelli (*Poussette*); Minnie Egener (*Javotte*); Dorothea Flexer (*Rosette*); Beniamino Gigli (*Chevalier Des Grieux*); Giuseppe De Luca (*Lescaut*); Léon Rothier (*Comte Des Grieux*); Angelo Bada (*Guillot de Morfontaine*); [George Cehanovsky (*De Brétigny*)]; [Paolo Ananian (*Innkeeper*)]; [Max Altglas (*Guard*)]; [Arnold Gabor (*Guard*)]; [Paolo Ananian (*Sergeant*)]; [George Cehanovsky (*Archer*)]; [Gina Gola (*Servant*)].

* 4. Act IV: a) Manon! Manon, sphinx étonnant! . . . ah! jamais! A toi [mon amour! A toi mon être!] [35.00 slowing to 32.00 rpm]

Act III: b) MOORE and chorus: [Obéissons quand leur voix appelle . . . Profi]tons bien de la jeunesse . . . Le coeur hèlas! . . . Ah! ah! ["Gavotte"] [32.6 rpm]

Act IV: c) GIGLI, BADA, DE LUCA, and Chorus: [Au jeu!] Au jeu! . . . Permettez-moi de jouer sur parole . . . J'ai perdu [32.6 rpm]

d) GIGLI, BADA, ROTHIER, MOORE, DONINELLI, EGENER, FLEXER, and Chorus: J'y tâcherai! . . . Le guet la conduira [32.6 rpm]

e) GIGLI, BADA, and DE LUCA: [O douleur! L'avenir] nous sépare . . . to end of the act [32.6 rpm]

* 5. w. orchestra/Vito Carnevali: GRISELDA: Per la gloria d'adorarvi (Giovanni Bononcini) (I)

2EA-13688-?	London, 18 Mar 1949	Victor B-5023	HMV (DB 6983)
0EA-14970-1	London, 18 Mar 1949	----	HMV DA 1956

* 6. w. orch/Vito Carnevali: "Tu mancavi a tormentarmi" (Cesti) (I)

2EA-13689-1	London, 18 Mar 1949	Victor B-5023	HMV (DB 6983)

NOTES: EJS 111

Playing speeds for this issue, given below and in the listing (MANON), have been calculated at score pitch.

Side 1 (111 A):

Bands 1 and 2: No take numbers appear in the wax of B-5024. Take numbers and precise date of recording have been taken from the Peel-Holohan Gigli discography (*The Record Collector*, 35/5-8, May-July, 1990, p. 134). Recording speeds for both (78.26 rpm) are correct on EJS 111. Victor 5024 was a Brazilian (only) issue.

Band 3: A print of the GIOCONDA short is reported to bear the date 26 June, 1927. The film premiered alongside the Warner Brothers feature "Old San Francisco," starring Dolores Costello and directed by Alan Crosland.

The recitative only was also issued on Eterna 732 (1959); the entire scene appeared on Scala 861 (1961) and Scala 5001 (circa 1962). Smith later included it on TAP 331 (1961).

Bands 4 and 5: There were three performances of RIGOLETTO during the 1938 Covent Garden season, all with the identical cast, save for a new *Gilda* in the last: 31 May and 6 June with Pagliughi and 10 June with Luella Paikin. Only the 6 June performance was broadcast.

Band 6: The original playing speed is 77.43 rpm, dubbed here at 78.26 rpm. Later issued in the early 1950s as AGSB 58.

Side 2 (111 B):

Bands 1-3: The original recording speed for all three of the Gigli-Ruffo duets is 77.43 rpm, dubbed here at 78.26 rpm.

Band 4: This performance of MANON was the sixteenth Metropolitan Opera broadcast, and is among the earliest from which excerpts survive (only the third and fourth acts were heard on the air). It also preserves one of the few surviving examples of Deems Taylor's controversial voice-over narrations, which were cancelled after the first broadcast season (see also note for EJS 487, issued in November, 1969). It is one of the relatively few Gigli Met broadcasts that has survived (he left after the 1934-1935 season), and one of the very few live performances featuring Grace Moore prior to the outset of her "second" Hollywood career, which began in 1934 with the very successful Columbia feature ***ONE NIGHT OF LOVE***.

The excerpts were originally recorded on a vertical-cut, 8-inch aluminum disc that contained several short segments of miscellaneous items taken off the air. The excerpts heard on EJS 111 are separated by significant (recording) gaps. They represent, essentially, *Des Grieux's* arioso and the trio based on it, the Act III "Gavotte," and the concerted finale.

Note the two fragments from Act III/i: as the Met regularly omitted Act III at the time, Moore, like other sopranos, simply appropriated the "Gavotte" for insertion into Act IV--in place of "Ce bruit de l'or" when the "Coeur-la-Riene scene was cut. The same is true of the abridged 1940 Moore MANON issued as EJS 149 (April, 1959).

Smith reissued the same excerpts from this 1932 performance in much improved sound on ANNA 1033 (May-June, 1979).

Band 5: "Per la gloria d'adorarvi" is taken from the 1722 opera GRISELDA of Giovanni Bononcini (1670-1747), not the 1718 GRISELDA written by his brother, Antonio Maria Bononcini (1677-1726). The family surname is often spelled "Buononcini," but reliable modern sources insist that "Bononcini" is the one observed at present.

In its citation of the LP issue of this recording (ALP 1174), the 1957-1958 HMV catalog credits Parisotti's well-known transcription of the aria that originally appeared in his *Arie Antiche* (Ricordi, 1890), and in Theodore Baker's translated edition, *Anthology of Italian Song of the Seventeenth and Eighteenth Centuries* (Schirmer, 1894).

The ten-inch master, OEA-14970-1, issued on DA 1956, was a transfer from the original twelve-inch master 2EA-13688-?, released as Brazilian Victor B-5023-A. Bennett (*Voices of the Past*, vol. 4, p. 247) lists the DB 6983 coupling of the Bononcini and Cesti items as issued, where the Peel-Holohan *Record Collector* discography, ibid., does not: I have found no catalog citation to substantiate that DB 6983 was ever released. The original playing speed is 78.26 rpm, dubbed correctly on EJS 111.

Band 6: Cesti's "Tu mancavi a tormentarmi" is also found in Parisotti's *Arie Antiche*, and Baker's American edition. The original playing speed is 78.26 rpm, dubbed correctly on EJS 111. Victor 5023 was a Brazilian (only) issue.

EJS 112: "The Golden Age of Opera" (2 LPs)
Issued 1957

SIDES 1-4 (112 A-D):

L'AMORE DEI TRE RE (Italo Montemezzi) (I)
Opera in 3 Acts (complete)
Metropolitan Opera House Orchestra and Chorus/Italo Montemezzi
Metropolitan Opera broadcast, NYC, 15 Feb 1941

CAST:
Ezio Pinza (*Archibaldo*); Richard Bonelli (*Manfredo*); Charles Kullman (*Avito*); Alessio DePaolis (*Flamino*); Nicholas Massue (*Youth*); Grace Moore (*Fiora*); Lucielle Browning (*Maid*); Maxine Stellman (*Young Woman*); Anna Kaskas (*Old Woman*); Reno Mabilli (*Shepherd*).

NOTES: EJS 112

Subsequently issued on the "Magnificent Editions" label. Possible pitch problems have been reported between the three acts, but none specifically.

Library of Congress tape: 12736-64B (complete broadcast).

EJS 113: "The Golden Age of Opera" (3 LPs)
Issued 1957

SIDES 1-6 (113 A-F):

NORMA (Bellini) (I)
Opera in 4 Acts (complete)
Metropolitan Opera House Orchestra and Chorus/Ettore Panizza
Metropolitan Opera broadcast, NYC, 20 Feb 1937

CAST:
Giovanni Martinelli (*Pollione*); Ezio Pinza (*Oroveso*); Gina Cigna (*Norma*); Bruna Castagna (*Adalgisa*); Thelma Votipka (*Clotilde*); Giordano Paltrinieri (*Flavio*).

NOTES: EJS 113

Pressings may vary in pitch: what appear to be the earliest copies of EJS 113 (brown and white label) have been reported as being uniformly in pitch at 33.3 rpm; others seem to be significantly below pitch at this speed. Possibly a new disc master was made at some point from the original tape, played at the incorrect speed.

Library of Congress tape: 15731-89A (complete broadcast).

EJS 114: "The Golden Age of Opera" (1 LP)
Issued 1957

SIDES 1-2 (114 A-B):

LA BOHÈME (Puccini) (I)
Opera in 4 Acts (excerpts: Acts I and III only)
Metropolitan Opera House Orchestra and Chorus/Vincenzo Bellezza
Metropolitan Opera broadcast, NYC, 23 Mar 1935

CAST:
Frederick Jagel (*Rodolfo*); Millo Picco (*Schaunard*); Paolo Ananian (*Benoit*); Elisabeth Rethberg (*Mimi*); [Max Altglass *(Parpignol)*]; Giuseppe De Luca (*Marcello*); Ezio Pinza (*Colline*); [Pompilio Malatesta (*Alcindoro*)]; Nina Morgana (*Musetta*); [Carlo Coscia (*Sergeant*)].

NOTES: EJS 114

Listed in the 1970s "Golden Age of Opera" cumulative checklist as Acts I and II, but this is incorrect. Act I is incomplete and ends with Rethberg's "Mi chiamano Mimi," omitting the "O soave fanciulla." Jagel's "Che gelida manina" is clearly an insert from another source, if not from a different, as yet unidentified performance.

It is especially unfortunate that so little of this broadcast (the last of the 1934-1935 season) appears to have survived, as one of the *Intermission Features* boasted a group of speeches by Met dignitaries, among them outgoing director Gatti-Casazza and his ill-fated successor, Herbert Witherspoon. Irving Kolodin, in *The Metropolitan Opera*, 4th ed. (New York: Kopf, 1966), p. 385, comments that Gatti "spoke a few words of farewell in barely understandable English."

The set plays approximately a quarter-tone low at 33.3 rpm: a playing speed of 33.8-34.00 rpm has been suggested to compensate.

The Rethberg-De Luca "Mimi! Speravo . . . Oh! buon Marcello" from Act III later appeared on ANNA 1039 (May-June, 1979), mislabeled "ANNA 1041" in Smith's fourth ANNA bulletin.

EJS 115: "The Golden Age of Opera" (1 LP)
Issued 1957

SIDES 1-2 (115 A-B):

CAVALLERIA RUSTICANA (Mascagni) (I)
Opera in 1 Act (abridged)
Metropolitan Opera House Orchestra and Chorus/Gennaro Papi
Metropolitan Opera broadcast, Boston, 10 Apr 1937

CAST:
Elisabeth Rethberg (*Santuzza*); Irra Petina (*Lola*); Sydney Rayner (*Turiddu*); Carlo Morelli (*Alfio*); Anna Kaskas (*Lucia*).

NOTES: EJS 115

The abridgement of this performance is orchestral: omitted are the Prelude, the orchestral passages from the end of Rayner's "Siciliana" to the opening chorus of Act I, and the Intermezzo. The entire broadcast does exist, however, and has been published on the Operatic Archives (OPA) label.

Ponselle was scheduled to sing *Santuzza*, but owing to ill health, was replaced at the last minute by Rethberg. The incident and its consequences are discussed at length in Ponselle's autobiography, *Ponselle: A Singer's Life*, co-authored by James Drake (New York: Doubleday, 1982), p. 172.

HÄNSEL UND GRETEL was also performed that afternoon in Boston: highlights of this were issued on EJS 539 in February, 1971. Note that the CAVALLERIA is dated 10 *May*, 1937 on the label of EJS 115.

Excerpts from this performance later appeared on EJS 239 (May, 1962).

EJS 116: "The Golden Age of Opera" (3 LPs)
Issued 1957

SIDES 1-6 (116 A-F):

CARMEN (Bizet) (F)
Opera in 4 Acts (complete)
Metropolitan Opera House Orchestra and Chorus/Louis Hasselmans
Metropolitan Opera broadcast, Boston, 28 Mar 1936

CAST:
Rosa Ponselle (*Carmen*); René Maison (*Don José*); Hilda Burke (*Micaela*); Ezio Pinza (*Escamillo*); Louis D'Angelo (*Zuniga*); George Cehanovsky (*Morales*); Thelma Votipka (*Frasquita*); Helen Olheim (*Mercédès*); Angelo Bada (*Dancaire*); Marek Windheim (*Remendado*).

NOTES: EJS 116

Mislabeled on some copies as EJS 117. Later pressings of the CARMEN, correctly numbered as EJS 116, appeared with a blue-on-white label. The 1970s EJS checklist cites the CARMEN once again as EJS 117.

This performance was issued subsequently by Smith on one of his more obscure private labels, "Great French Operatic Performances of the Century" CAR 1/6 (matrix P-1610), where several inserts were made--most prominently from the second act of the 1 February, 1936 Ponselle-Kullman-Pinza New York performance originally issued as EJS 218 (October, 1961). The 28 March performance subsequently appeared as HRE 253-3.

EJS 117: "The Golden Age of Opera" (4 LPs)
Issued 1957

SIDES 1-8 (117 A-H):

LES HUGUENOTS (Meyerbeer) (I)
Opera in 5 Acts (Acts I - IV only)
Orchestra and Chorus of Radio Italiana [RAI], Milano/Tullio Serafin
RAI broadcast, Milan, ?23 Oct 1955

CAST:
Anna De Cavalieri (*Valentine*); Antonietta Pastori (*Marguerite*); Jolanda Gardino (*Urbain*); Giacomo Lauri-Volpi (*Raoul*); Giuseppe Taddei (*Count Nevers*); Nicola Zaccaria (*Marcel*); Giorgio Tozzi (*Count St.-Bris*); Bianca Furlai (*First Lady/First Young Girl*); Edy Amedeo (*Second Young Girl*); Tommaso Frascati (*Cossé/Bois-Rose*); Dino Formichini (*Tavannes*); Giorgio Tadeo (*Thoré*); Nestore Catalani (*Méru/Maurevert/Second Monk*); Guido Mazzini (*De Retz/An Archer*); Renato Ercolani (*A Servant/A Voice/First Monk*).

NOTES: EJS 117

Mislabeled on some copies as EJS 116. Anna De Cavalieri was the Italian stage name of Anna McKnight.

Act V was not performed, but Acts I-IV are presented here complete as broadcast. Lauri-Volpi's first act "Bianca al par," and his second act duet with Pastori were later issued on the seven-inch Cetra EP 0344. The "Bianca al par" was reissued in 1966 on Cetra SPO 1039 (a 45 rpm single), coupled with Lauri-Volpi's 1955 studio recording of "Spirto gentil" from FAVORITA. *Raoul's* music from this performance was later issued complete on TIMACLUB LP TIMA 17. CLS 17, "Unforgettable Performances," and Gioielli della Lirica GML 64, "Gli Ugonotti," also contain excerpts from the October, 1955 broadcast. The entire performance has also appeared as Replica LP 2401/3.

The date of the original RAI broadcast of UGONOTTI has been difficult to determine: 23 October is a matter of consensus, but 1953, 1954, and 1955 have all been suggested (on 23 October, 1954 a performance of L'ELISIR D'AMORE was broadcast). The RAI chronology gives 1955, as does the Gioielli LP, so 1955 seems the most likely.

A knowledgeable informant has reported that the actual studio recording was made earlier, in the Spring of 1955.

EJS 118: "The Golden Age of Opera" (3 LPs)
Issued 1957

SIDES 1-6 (118 A-F):

LE NOZZE DI FIGARO, K. 492 (Mozart) (I)
Opera in 4 Acts (complete)
Metropolitan Opera House Orchestra and Chorus/Ettore Panizza
Metropolitan Opera broadcast, NYC, 9 Mar 1940

CAST:
John Brownlee (*Almaviva*); Elisabeth Rethberg (*Countess*); Bidú Sayão (*Susanna*); Ezio Pinza (*Figaro*); Jarmila Novotná (*Cherubino*); Irra Petina (*Marcellina*); Alessio DePaolis (*Basilio*); Giordano Paltrinieri (*Don Curzio*); Virgilio Lazzari (*Bartolo*); Louis D'Angelo (*Antonio*); Marita Farell (*Barbarina*); Lucielle Browning (*Peasant Girl*); Maxine Stellman (Peasant Girl).

NOTES: EJS 118

The complete NBC acetates, which include the intermission features, do exist, but having not yet gained access to the official line checks, Smith probably used an alternate off-the-air transcription, possibly one provided by one of the principals.

The performance is presented here virtually complete, with only recitative performance cuts. The four acts are banded over the six LP sides.

Reissued on three CDs by Music and Arts as CD-646.

Library of Congress tape: 5174-3 (complete broadcast).

EJS 119: "The Golden Age of Opera" (3 LPs)
Issued 1957

SIDES 1-6 (119 A-F):

DON GIOVANNI, K. 527 (Mozart) (I)
Opera in 2 Acts (complete)
Metropolitan Opera House Orchestra and Chorus/Bruno Walter
Metropolitan Opera broadcast, NYC, 7 Mar 1942

CAST:
Ezio Pinza (*Don Giovanni*); Rose Bampton (*Donna Anna*); Norman Cordon (*Commandant*); Charles Kullman (*Don Ottavio*); Jarmila Novotná (*Donna Elvira*); Bidú Sayão (*Zerlina*); Alexander Kipnis (*Leporello*); Mack Harrell (*Masetto*).

NOTES: EJS 119

Also issued as Cetra LO-27/3.

EJS 120: "The Golden Age of Opera" (1 LP)
Issued 1957(?)

"EZIO PINZA, BASS"

SIDE 1 (120 A):

1. w. studio orch/Donald Voorhees: AMADIS DE GAULE, Act II: Bois épais (Lully) (F)
   Broadcast, ***BELL TELEPHONE HOUR***, WNBC, NYC, 4 Aug 1947

* 2. w. studio orch/Donald Voorhees: BERENICE, Act II: Si, tra i ceppi (Handel) (I)
   Broadcast, ***BELL TELEPHONE HOUR***, WNBC, NYC, 16 Aug 1948

* 3. w. Detroit Symphony Orchestra/José Iturbi: L'ELISIR D'AMORE, Act I: Udite, o rustici (Donizetti) (I)
   Broadcast, ***FORD SUNDAY EVENING HOUR***, WJR, Detroit, 4 Dec 1938

* 4. w. Metropolitan Opera House Orchestra/Italo Montemezzi: L'AMORE DEI TRE RE, Act I: Italia, Italia! (Montemezzi) (I)
   Metropolitan Opera broadcast, NYC, 15 Feb 1941

* 5. w. Metropolitan Opera House Orchestra/Wilfred Pelletier: LAKMÉ, Act II: Lakmé, ton doux regard se voile (Delibes) (F)
   Metropolitan Opera broadcast, NYC, 6 Jan 1940

6. w. studio orch/Donald Voorhees: LA REINE DE SABA, Act I: Sous les pieds d'une femme (Gounod) (F)
   Broadcast, ***BELL TELEPHONE HOUR***, WNBC NYC, 18 Nov 1946

* 7. w. Metropolitan Opera House Orchestra and Chorus/Giulio Setti: DIE ZAUBERFLÖTE, K. 620, Act II: O Isis und Osiris (Mozart) (G)
   BVE-41299-1 Liederkranz Hall, NYC, 5 Jan 1928 Victor unpub

SIDE 2 (120 B):

* 1. w. BING CROSBY (studio orch/John Scott Trotter):
   a) "Timber Trail" (Hill-Emmerich) (E)
   b) "In the Evening by the Moonlight" (Bland) (E)
   c) "You are my Sunshine" (Davis-Mitchell) (E)
   Broadcast, ***PHILCO MUSIC HALL***, WJZ, NYC, 13 Nov 1946

2. w. PATTI PAGE (studio orch/?Carl Hoff): "When You and I were Young, Maggie" (Johnson-Butterfield) (E)
   Telecast, ***SCOTT MUSIC HALL***, WNBT, NYC, 8 Apr 1953

* 3. w. studio orch and chorus/?: MESSE SOLENNELLE, Op. 12: Panis Angelicus (Frank) (L)
   Telecast(?), source and date unknown, circa 1953

* 4. w. studio orch/?: "Eh Cumpare" (trad.- ?arr.) (I)
   Telecast(?), source and date unknown, circa 1953

* 5. w. studio orch/Donald Voorhees: "Besame mucho" (Velásquez) (S)
   Broadcast, ***BELL TELEPHONE HOUR***, WEAF, NYC, 10 Jul 1944

6. w. studio orch/Donald Voorhees: "In questa tomba oscura," WoO 133 (Carpani-Beethoven) (I)
   Broadcast, ***BELL TELEPHONE HOUR***, WNBC, NYC, 2 Jun 1947

* 7. w. studio orch/Donald Voorhees: "Nebbie" (Negri-Respighi) (I)
   Broadcast, ***BELL TELEPHONE HOUR***, WNBC, NYC, 8 Dec 1947

8. w. studio orch/Donald Voorhees: "The Song of the Flea" [Pesnya Mefistofelya o blokhe] (Goethe-trans. Strugovshehikov-Mussorgsky) (E)
   Broadcast, ***BELL TELEPHONE HOUR***, WNBC, NYC, 4 Aug 1947

9. w. studio orch/Donald Voorhees: "Fiocca di neve" (Cimara) (I)
   Broadcast, ***BELL TELEPHONE HOUR***, WNBC, NYC, 18 Nov 1946

10. w. studio orch/Donald Voorhees: SEVEN SONGS, Op. 47, no. 5: Pilgrim's Song [Blagoslavlyayu vas, lesa] ["Benediction"] (Tolstoy, trans. England-Tchaikowsky) (E)
   Broadcast, ***BELL TELEPHONE HOUR***, WEAF, NYC, 12 Aug 1946

NOTES: EJS 120

Side 1 (120 A):

Band 2: Handel wrote two versions of the aria "Si, tra i ceppi" for BERNICE: Pinza sings the version marked 'Come alla breve,' which begins with two half notes (minims).

Band 3: Also issued in the early 1950s on a 12-inch red vinyl LP, "The Record Collector's Club Peoria, Illinois," no. 2A.

Band 4: The complete 15 February, 1941 L'AMOURE DEI TRE RE was issued on EJS 112 (1957).
Library of Congress tape: 12736-64B (complete broadcast).

Band 5: The 6 January, 1940 LAKMÉ was issued complete as EJS 153 (August, 1959).
Library of Congress tape: 5174-31 (complete broadcast).

Band 7: The original recording speed of this unissued "O Isis und Osiris" (BVE 41299-1) was 77.43 rpm, dubbed at 78.26 rpm on EJS 120.

Side 2 (120 B):

Band 1: Listed as "Timber" on the label of EJS 120. James A. Bland's "In the Evening by the Moonlight" serves here as a transition from "Timber" Trail" to "You are my Sunshine," and is not cited on the label. In the latter, Pinza and Crosby begin to *ad lib*, inserting into the lyrics joking references to the sponsor: "Philco is my Sunshine," ". . . please don't take our sunshine away," etc.

Band 3: The "Panis Angelicus" may be from Pinza's NBC television series, ***BONINO***, a situation comedy than ran from 12 September to 26 December, 1953. At least one song was featured on each show. Donald Voorhees conducted the sessions for ***BONINO***.

Band 4: Julius La Rosa had a major hit recording of "Eh Cumpare" on Cadence 1232 (matrix P-49657-2; E3-CB-4763-1A), issued in August, 1953, as arranged by La Rosa and the conductor of the session, Archie Bleyer. Depending upon the date and origin of this Pinza performance, this may be the version sung here. Like the "Panis Angelicus," this may be from ***BONINO***.

Band 5: "Besame mucho," first published in 1941, was writen by Consuelo Velásquez, with English lyrics by Sunny Skylar. This, according to the original copyright statement and the original 1941 sheet music (Promotora Hispano Americana de Musica, S.A., Mexico - Southern Music Publishing, New York). Later recordings of the song credit the English lyrics to Selig Shaftel. Pinza sings it in Spanish (lyrics by Velásquez). No composer is credited on the label of EJS 120.

Band 7: The *New York Times* listing for this 8 December, 1947 ***BELL TELEPHONE HOUR*** credits Donald Voorhees in one place, and Howard Barlow in another. Voorhees was the regular conductor of the show throughout the 1940s; Barlow was for many years associated with ***THE VOICE OF FIRESTONE***, which followed the ***BELL TELEPHONE HOUR*** on NBC radio. Pinza's daughter, soprano Claudia Pinza, and tenor Glenn Burris were also guests on this particular show.

EJS 121: "The Golden Age of Opera" (2 LPs)
Issued 1958(?)

SIDES 1-3 (121 A-C):

I PAGLIACCI (Leoncavallo) (I)
Opera in 2 Acts and a Prologue (complete)
Metropolitan Opera House Orchestra and Chorus/Gennaro Papi
Metropolitan Opera broadcast, NYC, 29 Feb 1936

CAST:
Queena Mario (*Nedda*); Giovanni Martinelli (*Canio*); Richard Bonelli (*Tonio*); Giordano Paltrinieri (*Beppe*); George Cehanovsky (*Silvio*).

SIDE 4 (121 D):

IL TROVATORE (Verdi) (I)
Opera in 4 Acts (excerpts)
Metropolitan Opera House Orchestra and Chorus/Gennaro Papi
Metropolitan Opera broadcast, NYC, 15 Feb 1936

CAST:
Elisabeth Rethberg (*Leonora*); Kathryn Meisle (*Azuncena*); [Thelma Votipka (*Inez*)]; Giovanni Martinelli (*Manrico*); Richard Bonelli (*Count di Luna*); [Virgilio Lazzari (*Ferrando*)]; [Giordano Paltrinieri (*Ruiz*)]; [Arnold Gabor (*Gypsy*)].

1. MARTINELLI, MEISLE, RETHBERG, AND BONELLI: Act IV/ii complete: Madre, non dormi? . . . to the end of the opera

NOTES: EJS 121

Both the complete I PAGLIACCI and the IL TROVATORE excerpts were taken from broadcast transcription discs originally made for Richard Bonelli in New York.

Side 2 (121 B):

Further excerpts from this 15 February, 1936 performance of IL TROVATORE were featured on EJS 130 (1958).

EJS 122: "The Golden Age of Opera" (3 LPs)
Issued 1958(?)

"GIUSEPPE DE LUCA, BARITONE: TOWN HALL RECITAL"

SIDES 1-3 (122 A-C): Giuseppe De Luca, baritone (pf/Werner Singer)
Golden Jubilee Concert, Town Hall, NYC,
11 Jan 1947

SIDES 4-6 (122 D-F): Giuseppe De Luca, baritone (pf/Gibner King)
Golden Jubilee Concert, Town Hall, NYC,
7 Nov 1947

SIDE 1 (122 A): 11 January, 1947 (part 1)

* 1. L'ORFEO, Act II: Tu sè morta ["Il Pianto d'Orfeo"] (Monteverdi-arr. Respighi) (I)

2. CINQUE CANTI ALL'ANTICA, no. 4: Bella porta di rubini (Respighi) (I)

* 3. [GIULIO SABINO]: Lungi dal caro bene (Giuseppe Sarti) (I)

* 4. L'HONESTA NEGLI AMORI: Già il sole dal Gange (Alessandro Scarlatti) (I)

5. "Beau soir" (Paul Bourget-Claude Debussy) (F)

6. SEPT MÉLODIES: Les Papillons, Op. 2, no. 3 (Gautier-Chausson) (F)

* 7. FORTUNIO, Act II: J'aimais la vieille maison grise ["La Maison grise"] (André Messager) (F)

* 8. "Requiem du coeur" (Viard-Pessard) (F)

SIDE 2 (122 B): 11 January, 1947 (part 2)

* 1. DINORAH (LE PARDON DE PLOëRMEL), Act III: In questo loco, un anno appunto or compie . . . Sei vendicata assai [Ah! mon remords te venge] (Meyerbeer) (I)

2. Remarks by De Luca (E)

3. "La Cennamelle" (Rossellini) (I)

4. "Canta il mare" (Mazzola-Enrico De Leva) (I) * sung twice

5. "'A Vucchella" (d'Annunzio-Tosti) (I)

6. "Voi dormite, Signora" (Pagliara-Tosti) (I)

7. SIETE CANCIONES POPULARES ESPAÑOLAS, no. 4: Dicens que no nos queremos ["Jota"] (Sierra-de Falla) (S)

SIDE 3 (122 C): 11 January, 1947 (part 3)

1. EMIGRANTES: Granadinas (Calleja y Barrera) (S) * sung twice

* 2. "Princesita" (M. F. Palomero-José Padilla) (S)

* 3. LA CANÇIÓN DEL OLVIDO: Marinella (Emilio Serrano y Ruiz) (S)

* 4. "Ninna-nanna" (Theodore Gargiulo) (I) ANNOUNCED BY DE LUCA

* 5. "Mister Jim" (Albert Hay Malotte) (E)

* 6. FALSTAFF, Act II/ii: Quand 'ero paggio (Verdi) (I) ANNOUNCED BY DE LUCA

* 7. "This Little Rose" (William Roy) (E) ANNOUNCED BY DE LUCA

8. "Marietta" (Romilli) (E)

SIDE 4 (122 D): 7 November, 1947 (part 1)

1. "Mi parto" (Bottegari) (I)

* 2. TOLOMEO, Act I: Non lo dirò col labbro (Handel) (I)

* 3. SCHERZI MUSICALE: Maledetto sia l'aspetto (Monteverdi) (I) * sung twice

4. "Con tranquillo riposo i vaghi lumi suoi . . . Sussurrate intorno a Clori Zefiretti" (Pasquini) (I)

* 5. LE NOZZE DI FIGARO K. 492, Act IV: Tutto è disposto . . . Aprite un po'quegl'occhi (Mozart) (I)

* 6. LA DAMNATION DE FAUST, Op. 24, Part II/vi: Pel cielo! Dio! . . . C'era una volta un sire [Vrai dieu! messieurs . . . Une puce gentille] ["Canzone della pulce"] (Berlioz) (I)

7. LA DAMNATION DE FAUST, Op. 24, Part II/vii: Su queste rose [Voici des roses] (Berlioz) (I) (w. 28 measure piano introduction, beginning at the preceding "Andantino")

SIDE 5 (122 E): 7 November, 1947 (part 2)

* 1. LA DAMNATION DE FAUST, Op. 24, Part III/xii: Ed or'! . . . E che fai tu qui all'uscio del damo? [Maintenant, chantons . . . Devant la maison] ["Serenata di Mefistofele"] (Berlioz) (I)

2. FRANCIS ALDA: Remarks / GIUSEPPE DE LUCA: Remarks (E)

3. NUOVE LIRICHE TAGORIANE: Non nascondere il segreto (Alfano) (I)

4. "Serenata, Canti di Strapaese" (Gian Luca Tocchi) (I)

5. "Bergerette" (Giulia Recli) (I)

6. "C'era una volta" (Annibale Bizzelli) (I) * sung twice

SIDE 6 (122 F): 7 November, 1947 (part 3)

1. "Nel giardino" (Francesco Santoliquido) (I)

2. "Dodici!" ["Filastrocca"] (Gian Luca Tocchi) (I)

* 3. LA TRAVIATA, Act II: Mio figlio! Ah quanto soffri . . . Di provenza il mar (Verdi) (I)

* 4. "Ninna-nanna" (Theodore Gargiulo) (I)

* 5. "Dolce Madonna" (Nicola Aloysius Montani) (I)

6. "Marietta" (Romilli) (E)

7. "Serenata Gelata" (Buzzi-Peccia) (I)

NOTES: EJS 122

Though four selections from De Luca's 1947 Town Hall recitals were originally issued by Jack L. Caidin on his CRS label in May, 1948 (items I/4, III/6, IV/5, and IV/6 on EJS 122), Edward J. Smith may have been responsible for the actual recording of the two concerts, possibly in league with Caidin. In his notes to the 1961 ASCO LP A-124, which contains the 7 November, 1947 concert, Smith says as much:

> "At the time of De Luca's Fiftieth Anniversary Concert, this writer [Smith] begged for permission to have the event recorded. De Luca acquiesed (sic) and for the first time in musical history, such a concert was preserved for all time . . . Some of the acetates were worn, but the basic sound is there."

He further noted that the concert(s) were recorded on acetate discs. Beyond the typical extravagance of his claim, it would be foolish to discount altogether Smith's involvement in the project.

Note that De Luca "dedicates" the FALSTAFF "Quand'ero paggio" (III/6), exclaiming with a roguish laugh, ". . . for Mr. Smith." Smith later reissued bands I/1 and 4 from both concerts on his Top Artist Platters (TAP) label. The "Quand'ero paggio" was later included in the first of Caidin's "Famous Records of the Past" (FRP) series in 1955.

Apparently no recordings exist of De Luca's two earlier Town Hall concerts on 11 March and 16 November, 1946.

Speeds are inconsistent over the six sides of EJS 122, but few of the selections require anything more than minor adjustment. All of the operatic items and art songs are sung at score pitch, unless otherwise noted below.

Items marked "ANNOUNCED BY DE LUCA" in the listing are introduced by him. Many others are preceded or followed by comments and audience commotion. Some were sung twice during the recitals, and are so marked.

Side 1 (122 A):

Band 1: Later dubbed on TAP 327.

Band 3: Sung a half step lower than (traditional) score pitch. Sources vary as to the provenance of "Lungi dal caro bene." Some describe it as a song independent of any larger work; others insist that it is an aria, taken variously from GIULIO SABINO (1781) or ARMIDA E RINALDO (1759). Of the two, GIULIO SABINO is cited most often.

The version that De Luca sings here is identical to that recorded by Tebaldi, (London 1571) and Cesare Valletti (RCA LM 2280). Pinza's 1940 commercial recording (Victor 17916-A), an arrangement by Bruno Huhn, is markedly different. Another setting of the text, by Antonio Secchi, was recorded by Florence Easton in 1939 (off-the-air, issued on IRCC 166 in April, 1940), Elisabeth Rethberg in 1941 (off-the-air, issued on EJS 532 in December, 1970), and by Hulda Lashanska in 1923 (Victor 66195 and 964).

Band 4: Sung a half step lower than score pitch. Scarlatti's opera is titled "L'Onesta Negli Amori" on the label of EJS 122. This performance was originally issued as CRS 55 (May, 1948), labeled by Caidin as "November 7, 1947," and later turned up on TAP 315.

Band 7: Sung a half step lower than score pitch.

Band 8: Sung a half step *higher* than score pitch.

Side 2 (122 B):

Band 1: Sung a half step lower than score pitch.

Side 3 (122 C):

Bands 2 and 3: The order of these bands is reversed on the label of EJS 122: they are given in the listing as performed.

Band 4: The composer's name is not given on the various Smith issues of this concert. It does appear, however, on the 16 November, 1946 Town Hall program, when De Luca also sang Gargiulo's "Tarantella." A Schirmer advertisement for the sheet music of the "Ninna-nanna" appeared in the 7 November, 1947 Town Hall program.

Band 5: No composer is given on the label, but "Mister Jim" was in fact written by Albert Malotte--composer of the well-known setting of "The Lord's Prayer" and other popular religious works.

Band 6: Originally issued as CRS 55 (May, 1948) and labeled by Caidin as "November 7, 1947," the "Quand 'ero paggio" was later included on FRP 1. Note De Luca's announcement, ". . . for Mr. Smith."

Band 7: This song was introduced by De Luca at his 16 November, 1946 Town Hall recital. The *New York Times* for 10 November (II/7:1) carried a photograph of the singer, score in hand, with the caption "Giuseppe De Luca Studies a New Song." The composer, William Roy, is noted there as being 16-years old; De Luca's remarks preceding the song confirm this.

Side 4 (122 D):

Band 2: Sung in G major.

Band 3: Sung in E minor.

Band 5: Originally issued (in two parts) as CRS 53 (May, 1948).

Band 6: De Luca sings the recitative but the intervening chorus leading to the aria is omitted. Originally issued (in two parts) as CRS 54 (May, 1948).

Side 5 (122 E):

Band 1: Given as "Serenade of the Gnomes" on the label of EJS 122 and in the original Town Hall program.

Side 6 (122 F):

Band 3: Sung a half step lower than score pitch.

Band 4: See note for Side 3/band 4.

Band 5: De Luca's 15 January, 1907 recording of "Dolce Madonna" (Fonotipia 39938 and Odeon 59076, matrix XPh 2325) credits the song to "G. De Luca," presumably meaning the singer himself, not the 16th-century composer of the same name. His 1946 version in the Decca album "Italian Art Songs" (V-1) (Decca DL 7505, matrix WX-73624, recorded in New York, 13 June, 1946, dubbed as matrix WX-73641) gives it as "Anonymous." Ronald Wise, in his notes for this set, claims that "The lovely and old 'Dolce Madonna' which Mr. De Luca sings in his recitals was 'discovered' by the singer in Italy. He is very jealous of this little musical gem and will not let the penned copy out of his possession for fear that others will copy it and thus 'steal' his prize." Neither EJS 121 nor ASCO A-124 credits the composer.

However, the review of De Luca's 11 March, 1946 Town Hall concert in the *New York Times* (12 March, 1946, 12:2) cites "Montani" as the composer, as does the original program, and mentions that the singer's final set, which included the "Dolce Madonna," was made up primarily of works by "modern Italian" composers. Although Nicola Aloysius Montani (1880-1948) was American by birth (born in Utica, New York), he studied at the Vatican under Dom Lorenzo Perosi, Perpetual Master of the Sistine Chapel, and could--with some justification--be described as an Italian composer.

["EJS 122½"]: "The Golden Age of Opera" (2 LPs)
GRP 1001: "Great Performances of the Past" (2 LPs)
Issued 1957(?)

SIDES 1-4 (EJS 122½ / GRP 1001 A-D):

MISSA SOLEMNIS, Op. 123 (Beethoven) (Greek and Latin)
Mass for Soloists, Chorus and Orchestra in D Major (complete)
New York Philharmonic-Symphony Orchestra and the Schola Cantorum of New York/Arturo Toscanini; Pietro Yon, organ
Broadcast, *NEW YORK PHILHARMONIC*, Carnegie Hall, NYC, WABC, 28 Apr 1935

Elisabeth Rethberg, soprano — Marion Telva, contralto
Giovanni Martinelli, tenor — Ezio Pinza, bass

NOTES: EJS "122½" / GRP 1001

The 1970s checklist of EJS "Golden Age of Opera" releases lists this as EJS 122½, but to date, no copies have been reported actually bearing this number. The set seems to have been issued only on the "Great Performances of the Past" label, number GRP 1001, at about the time EJS 119 was released (1957). Both brown-on-white and later blue-on-white labels have been reported, the former with a title error, "Missa Solennis." The blue-on-white labeled copies are probably improved reissues with a separate P-prefix matrix number.

The performance was dubbed from Marion Telva's acetates, furnished to Smith by Mrs. Richard Bonelli.

EJS 123: "The Golden Age of Opera" (1 LP)
Issued 1958(?)

DER FLIEGENDE HOLLÄNDER (Wagner) (G)
Opera in 3 Acts (Excerpts)
London Philharmonic Orchestra, and Chorus of the Royal Opera House/ Fritz Reiner
Unpublished live performance recordings (HMV):
a) Technical Test Series 6544-1/18 Covent Garden, London, 7 Jun 1937
b) Technical Test Series 6545-1/23 Covent Garden, London, 11 Jun 1937

CAST (7 and 11 June, 1937):
Ludwig Weber (*Daland*); Kirsten Flagstad (*Senta*); Max Lorenz (*Erik*); Mary Jarred (*Mary*); [Ben Williams (*Steersmann*)]; Herbert Janssen (*Holländer*).

SIDE 1 (123 A):

* 1. Act II: FLAGSTAD, JARRED, and Chorus: Traft ihr das Schiff . . . Hilf Himmel! Senta!

2. Act III: WEBER, FLAGSTAD, LORENZ, JANSSEN, and Chorus: Was musst' ich hören! . . . to end of the opera

SIDE 2 (123 B):

* 1. Act II: FLAGSTAD, JANSSEN, AND WEBER: Mein Kind, du siehst mich auf der Schwelle . . . Mögst du, mein Kind . . . to end of the act

NOTES: EJS 123

Note that, for timing purposes, the excerpts are presented here out of sequence.

Three performances of DER FLIEGENDE HOLLÄNDER, all conducted by Fritz Reiner, were given at Covent Garden in June, 1937. The casts for the first two, on 7 and 11 June, were identical, but for the third, on 16 June, Adolph Vogel replaced Ludwig Weber as *Daland* and Torsten Ralf replaced Max Lorenz as *Erik*. The London Philharmonic served as the pit orchestra for the 1936-1938 Covent Garden season.

The first act of 11 June was the only segment broadcast from the three performances. HMV recorded 18 sides from the 7 June performance (Technical Test Series 6544-1/18), 23 sides from 11 June (Technical Test Series 6545-1/23), and three sides from 16 June (Technical Test Series 6546-1/3). Between 10 August and 17 September, 1937, a composite performance taken from the 7 and 11 June recordings was assembled by HMV engineers: none of the three sides taken from 16 June was included.

The original side divisions of the excerpts are not known, but the following transfer information is available:

MATRIX	TRANSFERRED FROM TESTS	DATES OF TRANSFER
2EA 5600-1	6544-1/6545-2	10 Aug 1937
2EA 5601-1	6545-2	10 Aug 1937
2EA 5602-1,2	6545-2,3	10 Aug 1937
2EA 5603-1	6544-4	10 Aug 1937
2EA 5604-1,2	6544-5/6545-5	10 Aug 1937
2EA 5605-1	654?	10 Aug 1937
2EA 5606-1	?	10 Aug 1937
2EA 5607-1	6545-8,9	10 Aug 1937
2EA 5608-1	6545-9,10	10 Aug 1937
2EA 5609-1	6545-10,11	10 Aug 1937
2EA 5609-2	? (possibly 6545-10,11)	17 Sep 1937
2EA 5610-1	6545-12	10 Aug 1937
2EA 5611-1	6545-12,13	10 Aug 1937
2EA 5612-1	6545-13,14	10 Aug 1937
2EA 5613-1	6545-14,15	11 Aug 1937
2EA 5614-1	6545-15/6544-14	11 Aug 1937
2EA 5615-1	6544-14,15	11 Aug 1937
2EA 5616-1	6545-18	11 Aug 1937
2EA 5617-1	6545-22	11 Aug 1937
2EA 5618-1	6545-23	11 Aug 1937

A last matrix number, 2EA 5619-1, transferred from Technical Test Series 6543-1, is cited in the EMI books as "Der Fliegende Holländer," but this is in fact the first side of the 1 June, 1937 Covent Garden GÖTTERDÄMMERUNG, conducted by Furtwängler (Technical Test Series 6543), transferred circa 11-13 August, 1937 to matrices 2EA 5619-1 - 2EA 5646-1. This GÖTTERDÄMMERUNG was issued on EJS 431 (April, 1968). See the endnotes for that issue.

A two-disc compilation of these DER FLIEGENDE HOLLÄNDER performances was issued as EJS 515 in June, 1970, containing two additional excerpts from Act I (Janssen's complete "Die Frist is um," and the Scene, Duet and Chorus, "Weit komm ich her . . . Sogleich die Anker lichten wir" with Janssen, Weber, and Williams) and the Act III Chorus, "Steuermann, lass' die Wacht! . . . So nehmt, der Nachbar hat's verschmäht" with Williams. The speeds and sound quality of this later release were advertised as being noticeably improved, but in fact the speeds were still erratic. Excerpts have also appeared on HRE 234, Recital Records 469, Rococo 1008, and most recently, on a Legato Classics CD (Standing Room Only SRO 808-1); Flagstad's "Traft ihr das Schiff" was included on Orpheum 8404 and Legendary LR 120.

Side 1 (123 A):

Band 1: There are fluctuations in pitch between some of the test sides of *Senta's* Ballad. The opening ("Yo-ho-hoe!") was omitted from EJS 123.

Side 2 (123 B):

Band 1: The original test recordings (as well as the tape from which Smith prepared this issue) contained *Senta's* preceding line, "Treue ihm Ha!," but this was omitted from the EJS 123 transfer.

EJS 124: "The Golden Age of Opera" (1 LP)
Issued 1958

"LAWRENCE TIBBETT, BARITONE"

SIDE 1 (124 A):

* 1. THE EMPEROR JONES, Op. 36 (Eugene O'Neill-Kathleen de Jaffa-Louis Gruenberg) (E)
Opera in 2 Acts, a Prologue and 6 Scenes (adaptation)
w. studio orch/Wilfred Pelletier; JOHN B. KENNEDY, announcer
Broadcast, ***PACKARD HOUR***, WJZ, NYC, 16 Oct 1934

SIDE 2 (124 B):

* 1. w. studio orch and Metropolitan Opera Chorus/Wilfred Pelletier; DEEMS TAYLOR, speaker: THE KING'S HENCHMAN, Act III: Finale (Edna St. Vincent Millay-Deems Taylor) (E)
Broadcast, ***PACKARD HOUR***, WJZ, NYC, 20 Nov 1934

a) Eadgar! Eadgar! King of Britain . . . Kingsmen and Kings behale [pp. 245-249]
b) So. So. Why then, my life . . . and turns away [pp. 257-262] (15 measures, between "ye the ploughman" and "far to the eye," are cut)
c) Nay Maccus, Lay him down . . . to end of the opera [pp. 271-279] (the part of Aelfrida is taken here by the orchestra)

* 2. w. studio orch/?Donald Voorhees: I PAGLIACCI, Act I: Recitar . . . Vesti la giubba (Leoncavallo) (I)
Broadcast, ***PACKARD HOUR***, WABC, NYC, ?21 Jan 1936

* 3. (w. orch and chorus/Alfred Newman): FAUST, Act II/i: Merci de ta Chanson! . . . conduit le bal (Gounod) (F)
from the feature film ***UNDER YOUR SPELL*** (20th Century-Fox, 1936), Hollywood, 1936
LP 6849; c6 November, 1936 (Twentieth Century Fox Film Corp.)
New York Premiere: RKO Palace Theater, NYC, 6 Nov 1936
a) LAWRENCE TIBBET, *bass*; ZARUHI ELMASSION, contralto; and EARL COVERT, baritone, and Chorus: Merci de ta chanson! . . . Dans les airs se brise!
PLCS-97719-1 Victor Special Record
Hollywood, circa August, 1936

b) LAWRENCE TIBBET, *bass*, and Chorus: Buvons! Trinquons! . . . Et qu'on joyeux refrain . . . Un rat plus poltron que brave . . . Le veau d'or . . . conduit le bal"
PCS-97689-1 Victor Special Record
Hollywood, circa August,1936

NOTES: EJS 124:

See also the endnotes for EJS 110 (1957) for details of Tibbett's ***PACKARD HOUR*** appearances. Tibbett created the role of *Brutus Jones* on 7 January, 1933 and *King Eadgar* (THE KING'S HENCHMAN) on 17 February, 1927--both at the Met.

Side 1 (124 A):

Band 1: *John* B. Kennedy (not "Stephen" as given on the label of EJS 124), resident announcer for the ***PACKARD HOUR***, introduces the THE EMPEROR JONES excerpts, a thirty-minute condensation of Gruenberg's 1933 setting of the Eugene O'Neill play. Much of the broadcast is de Jaffa's adaptation of O'Neill (as is much of the opera itself), giving us some idea of Tibbett's extraordinary abilities as a dramatic actor. The dialogue that is intoned, as vaguely designated in Gruenberg's score, is accompanied by orchestra. In addition, Tibbett sings "Standin' in the need of prayer," which he recorded commercially for Victor (CS-81087-2A, recorded on 19 January, 1934 with Pelletier conducting the Metropolitan Opera Orchestra, issued as Victor 7959). An alternate take recorded the same day (CS-81087-1) was issued in 1989 on an RCA Victor-BMG Tibbett CD, 7808-2-RG. Only a fragment of the orchestral Prelude was performed in this broadcast.

The *New York Times* announcement of the broadcast (14 October, 1934, X:11) begins: "Lawrence Tibbett, baritone, will be starred in a radio version of the American opera, 'Emperor Jones,' during this broadcast with Wilfred Pelletier's Orchestra. The opera, based on Eugene O'Neill's play of the same name, tells the story of the Negro Pullman porter . . ."

The actor playing *Smithers* has not been identified. The same broadcast, without Kennedy's spoken introduction, appeared later on a Rococo Tibbett recital (5324).

Side 2 (124 B):

Band 1: THE KING'S HENCHMAN excerpts, narrated by the composer and announced by Tibbett, run approximately fifteen minutes. The quoted pagination is taken from the original 1926 Fischer score.

Tibbett recorded the "Nay, Maccus" commercially on 5 April, 1928 (CVE-43614-1, recorded 5 April, 1928 with Giulio Setti conducting the Metropolitan Opera Orchestra and Chorus, issued as Victor 8103 and 11-8932).

Band 2: Tibbett sings "Vesti la giubba" a whole step lower than score pitch. In addition to the "Vesti la giubba," the 21 January, 1936 broadcast featured Tibbett singing "Oh Dry Those Tears" by Del Riego, Mussorgsky's "Song of the Flea," Guion's "Ma'moiselle Marie," and Wolfe's "Hand Organ Man," accompanied variously by orchestra and by Tibbett's regular accompanist, Stewart Wille.

The performance of *Canio's* aria that later appeared on EJS 397 (May, 1967) is different, and is thought to have been taken from a 25 September, 1934 ***PACKARD HOUR*** broadcast conducted by Wilfed Pelletier. It was sung *without* the recitative, and was taken from a medley billed "Selections from 'Pagliacci'," wherein Tibbett sang excerpts of *Tonio*, *Canio*, and *Silvio* (Tibbett's "Si puo?" from this broadcast was also included on EJS 397).

The "Vesti la giubba" on EJS 124 was later included on the Rococo LP 5324, and in 1979 turned up on a Glendale Tibbett recital (GL 8001) culled largely from broadcast material.

Band 3: Note that Tibbett sings *Méphistophélès* in these FAUST excerpts. The recordings were made for Victor's Hollywood branch sometime between 7 and 21 August, 1936. The original discs have "RCA Victor" labels and backs. The matrix prefix "PLCS" designates a 12-inch ("C") extended-range Western Electric cutter ("S"). "P" designates a pacific coast (Hollywood studios) recording. Both were recorded at 78.26 rpm. "A-67" and "S-25" also appear in the wax of PLCS-97719-1; PCS-97689-1 bears only "S-25." The original discs are given under the titles "Faust Recit. & Des Eeeps" (meaning "Choral des Epéeps" or "Scène des Epées") and "Golden Calf," respectively, along with the film title ***UNDER YOUR SPELL*** (Tibbett's 1936 20th Century Fox swan song), but it is not known if they are soundtrack *masters* used for dubbing the musical sequences or soundtrack transfers. Possibly they were simply made as private records for the artists. They may have been made, according to W.R. Moran, for "local" use by the studio, unlike the many soundtrack masters that have survived from Tibbett's previous Fox feature, ***METROPOLITAN***. Only those Hollywood recordings that were evntually issued (i.e. those in the same matrix block by Benny Goodman, Xavier Cugat, and Eddy Duchin, etc.) were added to Victor's New York files, hence the lack of precise documentation of these Tibbett sides. Six additional Tibbett recordings bearing the title ***UNDER YOUR SPELL*** have also been documented by Mr. Moran as having survived in a private collection: three of these bear Victor "PBS"-prefix matrices, while the others have single-letter (film studio?) matrix numbers only. Tibbett's "Le veau d'or" was featured in the released film, the "Merci de ta chanson!" was not: neither Elmassion or Covert appear listed among the cast of the film. Smith's original explanation for these excerpts was that they were taken from an incomplete studio FAUST which Tibbett had *begun* to record for commercial release! This, according to a long-time Smith associate and charter subscriber to the GAO series.

Arthur Lange was the credited musical director on the film, but it appears that Alfred Newman was the conductor.

The same performance of "Le veau d'or" appeared on Rococo 5324. New transfers of several ***UNDER YOUR SPELL*** numbers will appear in 1993 on the Delos International compact disc DE-5501, a Tibbett recital produced in collaboration with the Stanford Archive of Recorded Sound.

EJS 125: "The Golden Age of Opera" (2 LPs)
Issued 1958

SIDES 1-4 (125 A-D):

GIOVANNA D'ARCO (Verdi) (I)
Opera in 4 Acts (complete)
Orchestra and Chorus of Radio Italiana [RAI], Milano/Alfredo Simonetto
RAI broadcast, Milan, 26 May 1951

CAST:
Renata Tebaldi (*Giovanna d'Arco*); Carlo Bergonzi (*Carlo VII*); Rolando Panerai (*Giacomo*); Antonio Massaria (*Talbot*); Guido Scarinci (*Delil*).

NOTES: EJS 125

The RAI chronology, wherein performances are ordered sequentially, lists this as 26 "Marzo," 1951, but the GIOVANNA D'ARCO falls between performances given on 23 Maggio and 10 Giugno, so "Marzo" may be a misprint. Hence the citation of 26 May, 1951 in the listing above. Both Casanova's and Ségond's Tebaldi biographies confirm the date 26 May, 1951.

EJS 126: "The Golden Age of Opera" (2 LPs)
Issued 1958

SIDES 1-4 (126 A-D):

FIDELIO (Beethoven) (G)
Opera in 2 Acts (Abridged)
Metropolitan Opera House Orchestra and Chorus/Bruno Walter
Metropolitan Opera broadcast, NYC, 22 Feb 1941

CAST:
Herbert Janssen (*Don Fernando*); Julius Huehn (*Don Pizarro*); René Maison (*Florestan*); Kirsten Flagstad (*Leonore*); Alexander Kipnis (*Rocco*); Marita Farell (*Marzelline*); Karl Laufkoetter (*Jaquino*); Emery Darcy (*Prisoner*); John Gurney (*Prisoner*).

NOTES: EJS 126

Neither the "Leonore Overture" nor the "Leonore Overture No. 3" from Act II are included on EJS 126. The dialogue was replaced by recitatives in the original performance which, apart from the orchestral omissions, is given here complete as performed.

This 22 February, 1941 broadcast was subsequently issued on the Bruno Walter Society label (712/713) and on the limited-edition Metropolitan Opera Guild MET 5. The Walter Society issue included a "Leonore Overture No. 3" taken from one of the conductor's many New York Philharmonic broadcasts.

Sides 1 and 2 of EJS 126 are reported to play in pitch at 32.8 rpm.

EJS 127: "The Golden Age of Opera" (1 LP)
Issued 1958

"NELLIE MELBA (1859-1931): FAREWELL PERFORMANCE (June 8, 1926)"

SIDE 1 (127 A):

LA BOHÈME (Puccini) (I)
Opera in 4 Acts (excerpts)
Royal Opera House Orchestra/Vincenzo Bellezza
Recorded during Melba's Farewell Concert, Covent Garden, London, 8 Jun 1926

CAST:
Nellie Melba (*Mimi*); Aurora Rettore (*Musetta*); Browning Mummery (*Rodolfo*); John Brownlee (*Marcello*); Frederick Collier (*Schaunard*); Edouard Cotreuil (*Colline*).

Act III: 1. a) MELBA and BROWNLEE: Entrate . . . C'è Rodolfo?
CR 411-1 HMV unpub
b) MELBA: Donde lieta uscì ["Addio"]
CR 412-1 HMV DB 943 [2-053264] Japanese Victor ND 973
DB 1500
c) MELBA, BROWNLEE, RETTORE, and MUMMERY: Addio, dolce svegliare alla mattina ["Quartet"] . . . to the end of the act (last five orchestral measures omitted)
CR 413-1 HMV unpub

Act IV: 2. a) MELBA, BROWNLEE, RETTORE, MUMMERY, COLLIER, and COTREUIL: Gavotta . . . Minuetto . . . lascia ch'io guardi intor [no]
CR 414-1 HMV unpub
b) MELBA AND MUMMERY: Sono andati? . . . Era buio, e la mantu mi prendevi
CR 415-1 HMV unpub
c) MELBA, MUMMERY, BROWNLEE, RETTORE, COLLIER, and COTREUIL: [Io] Musetta . . . Oh come è bello è morbido . . . to the end of the opera (last two and a half orchestral measures omitted)
CR 416-1 HMV unpub

SIDE 2 (127 B):

1. NELLIE MELBA, soprano, w. Royal Opera House Orchestra/Vincenzo Bellezza [+ EXCEPT AS NOTED]
   Recorded during Melba's Farewell Concert, Covent Garden, London, 8 Jun 1926

   a) OTELLO, Act IV/i: Willow Song (Verdi) (I)
      part 1: Piangea cantando
      CR 417-1 HMV DB 1500 [2-053263] IRCC 2-B
      part 2: Scendean gli augelli
      CR 418-1 HMV unpub
   b) OTELLO, Act IV/ii: Ave Maria piena di grazia (Verdi) (I)
      CR 419-1 HMV unpub

   + c) Lord Stanley of Alderley, Ex-Governer-General of Victoria: "Address" (spoken) (E)
      CR 420-1 HMV unpub

   + d) NELLIE MELBA: "Farewell Speech" (spoken) (E)
      CR 421-1 HMV DB 943 [01182] Japanese Victor ND 973

* 2. NELLIE MELBA, soprano (pf/Landon Ronald): "Distance Tests" [Vocalises on phrases from HAMLET, Act IV: A vos jeux . . . Partagez-vous mes fleurs! ("Mad Scene") (Thomas)]
   4195f Gram unpub HMB 36 London, 11 May 1910

3. NELLIE MELBA, soprano (pf/Landon Ronald): "Pur dicesti, o bocca, bocca bella" (Antonio Lotti) (I)
   4214f Gram unpub London, 19 May 1910

NOTES: EJS 127

The title of the LP is in error--Melba was born 19 May, 1861.

All of the original Covent Garden discs included in this collection were recorded at 78.26 rpm, and dubbed at that speed for EJS 127. The two 1910 Gramophone titles were recorded at 77.43 rpm, and dubbed high at 78.26 rpm. The entire LP was transferred low, necessitating a playing speed of approximately 34.7 rpm to secure correct pitches.

Most of these London recordings have appeared on other labels (EMI, OASI, and Opus among them), and have been published complete on the 1976 EMI set, "Nellie Melba: The London Recordings 1904-1926" (RLS 719).

The Smart catalog lists a twenty-minute excerpt of the live Covent Garden performance as Library of Congress tape 7749-16B, transcribed from BBC 2LO (at the time, the British Broadcasting *Company*), London. The HMV recordings were relays to begin with, but it is not known if this transcription contains any material not recorded by the Gramophone Company (i.e. the Charles Hackett excerpts).

Side 2 (127 B):

Band 2: The recording date of the "Distance Tests"--11 May, 1910--has has been confirmed by the recent BIRS-EMI Historical Masters issue (HMB 36) where it is found hand-written in the wax.

EJS 128: "The Golden Age of Opera" (2 LPs)
Issued 1958

SIDES 1-4 (128 A-D):

LA GIOCONDA (Ponchielli) (I)
Opera in 4 Acts (abridged)
Metropolitan Opera House Orchestra and Chorus/Ettore Panizza
Metropolitan Opera broadcast, NYC, 30 Dec 1939

CAST:
Zinka Milanov (*Gioconda*); Bruna Castagna (*Laura*); Nicola Moscona (*Alvise*); Anna Kaskas (*La Cieca*); Giovanni Martinelli (*Enzo Grimaldo*); Carlo Morelli (*Barnaba*); Wilfred Engelman (*Zuane*); Wilfred Engelman (*Singer*); Giordano Paltrinieri (*Singer*); Giordano Paltrinieri (*Isepo*); Louis D'Angelo (*Monk*); Carlo Coscia (*Steersman*).

NOTES: EJS 128

Presented here is a 115-minute abridgement of the opera. The complete performance was later issued as EJS 225, a "Special Release" in January, 1962 and still later on HOPE LP 201. Speeds for EJS 128 are reported to be quite erratic, ranging from 33.8 to 34.7 rpm.

EJS 129: "The Golden Age of Opera" (1 LP)
Issued 1958

SIDES 1-2 (129 A-B):

TOSCA (Puccini) (I)
Opera in 3 Acts (excerpts: Act I only)
San Francisco Opera House Orchestra and Chorus/Gaetano Merola
San Francisco Opera broadcast, KPO, San Francisco, 15 Oct 1932

CAST:
Claudia Muzio (*Floria Tosca*); Dino Borgioli (*Mario Cavaradossi*); Alfredo Gandolfi (*Scarpia*); Marsden Argall (*Angelotti*); Louis D'Angelo (*Sacristan*); Marek Windheim (*Spoletta*).

NOTES: EJS 129

This performance marked the opening of the San Francisco War Memorial Opera House, and to this day a large bronze plaque, situated just inside the front doors, commemorates the event and its cast. Borgioli's name was, for years, misspelled "Borgiolo" on the marker, but this was eventually corrected.

Much of the broadcast, originally transcribed on 12-inch, vertically-cut aluminum discs, was devoted to the opening ceremonies--a lengthy description of the new opera house, interviews, the arrival of the evening's patrons, and even an account of the street traffic featuring announcer Jennings Peerce. Only the first act of TOSCA was broadcast nationally over NBC Red. The *New York Times* lavished a feature article on the opening of the house the previous Sunday. Apart from the opening preamble, "The Star Spangled Banner," little of this introductory material was included on EJS 129.

EJS 129 is reported to play flat at 33.3 rpm: a speed of approximately 34.7 rpm has been suggested to compensate.

The performance was later issued on the MDP label, and prior to that, on an unnumbered, unlabeled LP that was sold in the Los Angeles and San Francisco areas at about the same time EJS 129 was available. Those responsible for this other private LP may have dubbed it from EJS 129 . . . or vice versa.

EJS 130: "The Golden Age of Opera" (2 LPs)
Issued 1958

Il TROVATORE (Verdi) (I)
Opera in 4 Acts (excerpts)
Metropolitan Opera House Orchestra and Chorus/Gennaro Papi
a) Metropolitan Opera broadcast, NYC, 15 Feb 1936
b) Metropolitan Opera broadcast, NYC, 8 Jan 1938
c) Commercial recordings (see endnotes)

CASTS:	1936 PERFORMANCE	1938 PERFORMANCE
Leonora . . .	[Elisabeth Rethberg] . . .	Zinka Milanov
Azucena . . .	Kathryn Meisle . . .	Bruna Castagna
Inez . . .	[Thelma Votipka] . . .	[Thelma Votipka]
Manrico . . .	Giovanni Martinelli . . .	Giovanni Martinelli
di Luna . . .	Richard Bonelli . . .	Richard Bonelli
Ferrando . . .	[Virgilio Lazzari] . . .	Virgilio Lazzari
Ruiz . . .	[Giordano Paltrinieri] . . .	Giordano Paltrinieri
Gypsy . . .	Arnold Gabor . . .	[Carlo Coscia]

SIDE 1 (130 A):

Act I: 1. LAZZARI, MILANOV, MARTINELLI, and BONELLI: Act I/i complete b) [last few orchestral measures omitted] [circa 34.7 rpm]

*2. a) MILANOV and MARGARET ROGGERO: Ne' tornei . . . Tacea la notte placida . . . Di tale amor (c) [circa 33.8 rpm]

b) MARTINELLI and BONELLI: Deserto sulla terra (b) [beginning 41 measures into No. 5, a few notes to the aria proper) [circa 34.2 rpm]

c) BONELLI, MILANOV, and MARTINELLI: Non m'inganno . . . Infida! Qual voce!" to the end of the scene (b) [repeat of the trio, "Piombi, ah piombi il tuo" to Count di Luna's "Lo condannò," omitted] [circa 34.2 rpm]

SIDE 2 (130 B):

Act II: 1. MEISLE, MARTINELLI, GABOR, and chorus: Act II/i complete (a) [circa 33.7 rpm]

SIDE 3 (130 C):

Act III: 1. LAZZARI, BONELLI, MEISLE, and Chorus: Complete (a) [circa 34.2 rpm]

*2. a) MILANOV and MARTINELLI: Quale d'armi fragor . . . Ah si, ben mio (b) [orchestral introduction to No.18 and the first few lines of Leonora's recitative omitted] [circa 35 rpm]

b) PALTRINIERI, MARTINELLI, MILANOV, and Chorus: Ruiz's entrance, "Manrico?" . . . Di quella pira (b) & (c) [circa 33.3 rpm]

SIDE 4 (130 D):

Act IV: *1. a) MILANOV: Timor di me (b) [first 21 measures omitted] [circa 32.5 rpm]

b) MILANOV: D'amor sull'ali rosee (b) [circa 32.5 rpm]

c) MILANOV, MARTINELLI, and Chorus: Miserere (b) & (c) [circa 33.3 rpm]

2. a) MEISLE and MARTINELLI: Madre, non dormi?. . . Ai nostri monti (a) [circa 34.5 rpm]

b) MILANOV, MARTINELLI, CASTAGNA, and BONELLI: Leonora's entrance, "Son io, Manrico," to end of the opera (b) [circa 35 rpm]

NOTES: EJS 130

Side 1 (130 A):

Band 2: Milanov's "Tacea la note placida" and "Di tale amor" are taken from the complete 1952 IL TROVATORE with Bjoerling (RCA LM 6008; HMV ALP 1112/3 and ALP 1832/3, excerpts on various LPs thereafter), recorded at the RCA studios in New York's Manhattan Center, February-March, 1952, Renato Cellini, conducting. The *Inez* is contralto Margaret Roggero. These inserts are disguised here with bogus surface noise. It has also been suggested that at least a portion of the trio finale to Act I/ii may have been inserted from another Milanov Metropolitan Opera broadcast, possibly one of the four with tenor Kurt Baum.

Martinelli's "Deserto sulla terra" from the 8 January, 1938 Met broadcast appeared on the Pearl CD GEMM 9350 in 1988, still missing the same first notes of the aria. Bonelli's "Il balen" is on the forthcoming Stanford/Delos International Bonelli CDs, DE-5504 and DE-5505.

Side 3 (130 C):

Band 2: Martinelli's "Di quella pira" is a compilation of the aria proper, taken from the 8 January, 1938 Met performance, and the choral "all'armi," dubbed from his commercial Victor recording with soprano Grace Anthony (CVE-41046-2, recorded 17 November, 1927, Giulio Setti conducting the Metropolitan Opera House Orchestra and Chorus, issued as Victor 8109 and HMV DB 1288). An orchestral conclusion from a broadcast performance, with applause, finishes the scene on EJS 130. The aria was transposed a whole step down in both the commercial recording and the Met performance.

Side 4 (130 D):

Band 1: The "Miserere" is also a compilation. Milanov's solos with the Robert Shaw Chorale have been taken from the aforementioned 1952 commercial LP with Bjoerling; Martinelli's solos, and the concluding ensemble, are taken from the Martinelli-Ponselle studio recording (CVE-41637-2, recorded 23 January, 1928, Giulio Setti conducting the Metropolitan Opera House Orchestra and Chorus, issued as Victor 8097 and HMV DB 1199). Ponselle can be heard clearly in the climax. Applause has been added to finish the scene. Note that take CVE-41637-2, not the rarer take -1, was used for the insert.

[ANNA 1030--a two-disc Martinelli recital (with ANNA 1031) issued May-June, 1979--may also contain material from the 8 January, 1938 Met broadcast (the label says "1938"), intermingled with excerpts from the 4 March, 1939 Martinelli-Milanov-Castagna-Bonelli Met performance. A detailed comparison has proven inconclusive so far. EJS 121, issued 1958, contains a lengthy excerpt from Act IV/ii of the 15 February, 1936 Met performance, while UORC 151 (March, 1973) includes the 1936 "Miserere" and fragments from Rethberg's recitative and aria, "D'amor sull'ali."].

EJS 131: "The Golden Age of Opera" (2 LPs)
Issued 1958

SIDES 1-4 (131 A-D):

RIGOLETTO (Verdi) (I)
Opera in 4 Acts (complete)
Metropolitan Opera House Orchestra and Chorus/Gennaro Papi
Metropolitan Opera broadcast, NYC, 11 Mar 1939

CAST:
Jan Kiepura (*Duke of Mantua*); Lawrence Tibbett (*Rigoletto*); Lily Pons (*Gilda*); Virgilio Lazzari (*Sparafucile*); Helen Olheim (*Maddalena*); Thelma Votipka (*Giovanna*); Norman Cordon (*Monterone*); George Cehanovsky (*Marullo*); Giordano Paltrinieri (*Matteo Borsa*); Wilfred Engelman (*Ceprano*); Pearl Besuner (*Countess di Ceprano*); Lucielle Browning (*Page*).

NOTES: EJS 131

Acts 1 and 2 are reported to play in pitch at 33.3 rpm. Act III should be adjusted to 33.00 rpm and Act IV to circa 32.9 rpm. This performance was taken from broadcast transcriptions lent to Smith by Tibbett.

EJS 132: "The Golden Age of Opera" (2 LPs)
Issue 1958

SIDES 1-4 (132 A-D):

ATTILA (Verdi) (I)
Opera in 3 Acts and a Prologue (complete)
Orchestra and Chorus of the Teatro La Fenice, Venezia/Carlo Maria Giulini
RAI broadcast, Venice, 12 Sep 1951

CAST:
Caterina Mancini (*Odabella*); Gino Penno (*Foresto*); Gian Giacomo Guelfi (*Ezio*); Italo Tajo (*Attila*); Aldo Bertocci (*Uldino*); Dario Caselli (*Leone*).

NOTE: EJS 132

The cast, as given above, has been extracted from the RAI chronology. The label of EJS 132 gives Guelfi's forename as "Giacomo," Giulini's middle name as "Mario," and "C. F. Manelli" in the role of Leone.

The February, 1965 bulletin notes that "The worst sound recording we ever released was Verdi's Attila (No. 32). It was virtually sold out before it was discovered how bad was the sound. A good copy of the tape of the opera came into our hands and we re-recorded the work . . . for those who purchased the old set, the cost of the new one will be $3.00 for the two discs - when the old set is returned. For those who did not and who want the work the cost is $6.00."

EJS 133: "The Golden Age of Opera" (2 LPs)
Issued 1958

SIDES 1-4 (133 A-D):

ELISABETTA, REGINA D'INGHILTERRA (Rossini) (I)
Opera in 2 Acts (complete, except for the Overture)
Orchestra and Chorus of Radio Italiana [RAI], Milano/Alfredo Simonetto
RAI broadcast, Milan, 16 Aug 1953

CAST:
Maria Vitale (*Elisabetta*); Lina Pagliughi (*Matilda*); Giuseppe Campora (*Leicester*); Antonio Pirino (*Norfolk*); Ortensia Beggiato (*Enrico*); Mario Carlin (*Guglielmo*).

NOTES: EJS 133

The Overture and Finale of this 1815 opera were taken from Rossini's earlier AURELIANO IN PALMIRA (1813). The Overture, which is omitted from EJS 133, is the one used traditionally for IL BARBIERE DI SIVIGLIA.

Reissued complete on CD as Melodram 27032.

EJS 134: "The Golden Age of Opera" (2 LPs)
Issued October, 1958

SIDES 1-4 (134 A-D):

MERRY MOUNT (Richard L. Stokes-Howard Hanson) (E)
Opera in 4 Acts and 5 Scenes (complete)
Metropolitan Opera House Orchestra and Chorus/Tullio Serafin
Metropolitan Opera broadcast, NYC, 10 Feb 1934

CAST:
Arnold Gabor (*Faint-not-Tinker*); James Wolfe (*Samoset*); Irra Petina (*Desire Annable*); Giordano Paltrinieri (*Jonathan Banks*); Lawrence Tibbett (*Wrestling Bradford*); Gladys Swarthout (*Plentiful Tewke*); Louis D'Angelo (*Praise-God-Tewke*); Alfredo Gandolfi (*Myles Brodrib*); Helen Gleason (*Peregrine Brodrib*); Lillian Clark (*Love Brewster*); Henriette Wakefield (*Bridget Crackston*); Merek Windheim (*Jack Prence*); Göta Ljungberg (*Lady Marigold Sandys*); George Cehanovsky (*Thomas Morton*); Edward Johnson (*Sir Gower Lackland*); Millo Picco (*Jewel Scrooby*); Max Altglass (*Puritan*); Pompilio Malatesta (*Puritan*).

NOTES: EJS 134

EJS 134 was the first "Golden Age of Opera" issue to be announced by a formal bulletin, and so is the first to carry the month of release in these listings.

This performance was the world *stage* premiere of Hanson's opera, which made its concert debut some nine months earlier in Ann Arbor, Michigan on 20 May, 1933. The EJS transfer was taken from aluminum transcription discs made for Tibbett at a New York studio.

All four sides of EJS 134 are reported to play a bit slow at 33.3 rpm.

EJS 135: "The Golden Age of Opera" (3 LPs)
Issued October, 1958

SIDES 1-6 (135 A-F):

LOHENGRIN (Wagner) (G)
Opera in 3 Acts (complete, except for the Act I Prelude)
Metropolitan Opera House Orchestra and Chorus/Erich Leinsdorf
Metropolitan Opera broadcast, NYC, 27 Jan 1940

CAST:
Emanuel List (*King Heinrich*); Lauritz Melchior (*Lohengrin*); Elisabeth Rethberg (*Elsa*); Julius Huehn (*Telramund*); Kerstin Thorborg (*Ortrud*); Leonard Warren (*Herald*).

NOTES: EJS 135

The Prelude to Act I is omitted. The LP is reported to be uniformly in pitch at 33.3 rpm.

Library of Congress tape: 5174-27 (complete broadcast).

EJS 136: "The Golden Age of Opera" (2 LPs)
Issued November, 1958

SIDES 1-4 (136 A-D):

UN BALLO IN MASCHERA (Verdi) (I)
Opera in 4 acts (abridged)
Metropolitan Opera House Orchestra and Chorus/Ettore Panizza
Metropolitan Opera broadcast, NYC, 28 Feb 1942

CAST:
Giovanni Martinelli (*Riccardo*); Richard Bonelli (*Renato*); Stella Roman (*Amelia*); Bruna Castagna (*Ulrica*); Josephine Antoine (*Oscar*); George Cehanovsky (*Sylvan*); Norman Cordon (*Sam*); Nicola Moscona (*Tom*); John Carter (*Judge*); Lodovico Oliviero (*Servant*).

NOTES: EJS 136

Complete as performed except for the Prelude and first few measures of the orchestral introduction to Act II. This performance was taken from transcription discs originally made for Richard Bonelli.

Excerpts from this performance later appeared on the two-disc Martinelli recital, ANNA 1030-1031 (May-June, 1979), taken, it would appear, from a considerably better source. Bonelli's "Alla vita che t'arride" is featured on the forthcoming Stanford-Delos International Bonelli CDs DE-5504 and DE-5505.

EJS 137: "The Golden Age of Opera" (3 LPs)
Issued November, 1958

SIDES 1-6 (EJS 137 A-F):

IL DUCA D'ALBA (Donizetti-reconstructed by Salvi) (I)
Opera in 4 Acts (complete)
Orchestra and Chorus of Radio Italiana [RAI], Roma/Fernando Previtali
RAI broadcast, Rome, 12 Jan 1952

CAST:
Caterina Mancini (*Amelia*); Amedeo Berdini (*Marcello di Bruges*); Gian Giacomo Guelfi (*Duke d'Alba*); Dario Caselli (*Sandoval*); Aldo Bertocci (*Carlo*); Nestore Catalani (*Daniele*); Manfredi Ponz de Leon (*A Publican*).

NOTES: EJS 137

This was at the time the only recorded performance of Matteo Salvi's reconstruction of the Scribe-Donizetti LE DUC D'ALBE, originally written in French (by Donizetti) for the Paris Opéra in 1840, but not produced. Subsequently, a complete 1979 Brussels performance in Italian (with soprano Marina Krilovici and tenor Ottavio Garaventa, de Fabritiis conducting) was issued as MRF 170-5. Donizetti planned the opera in four acts, but completed only the first, part of the second, and passages of the third acts. He also left indications for the vocal line and notes for the orchestration of additional fragments. The incomplete score was recovered from Donizetti's family in Bergamo in 1875 and was to be performed there at the Teatro Riccardi (now the Teatro Donizetti) to celebrate the reburial of the composer and his teacher, Johann Simon Mayr, in the Church of Santa Maria Maggiore, but partisan efforts to avoid violating the composer's reputation saw to it that the venture was eventually abandoned.

Salvi was commissioned to complete the score in 1882 by the publisher Giovanna Lucca (Ricordi had refused to publish the original fragments a year earlier). Salvi's contributions included the Prelude, the orchestration of the passages left incomplete, and *Henri's* fourth Act aria "Angelo casto e bel," which was used to replace the original sketches of "Ange si pur" (aka "Spirto gentil"), the aria that Donizetti himself had subsequently 'borrowed' for the fourth act of LA FAVORITE (1840). Salvi's reconstruction was first produced in Rome at the Teatro Apollo, where it was performed five times between 22 March and 1 April, 1882. Thereafter, it was heard sporadically between 1882 and 1886 in Spain and Italy.

The better known and more frequently-recorded Italian version of the opera, IL DUCA D'ALBA, is Thomas Schipper's reconstruction, first produced in Spoleto at the Teatro Nuovo on 11 June, 1959 as part of Gian Carlo Menotti's "Festival of Two Worlds." Mounted in three acts, it omits most of Salvi's music, but ironically, still manages to contain approximately twenty minutes less of Donizetti's than did the Salvi version.

Smith reissued the same performance, this time taken from "a superb tape," according to his March, 1974 bulletin, on the two-disc UORC 190 (March, 1974).

EJS 138: "The Golden Age of Opera" (2 LPs)
Issued December, 1958

SIDES 1-4 (138 A-D):

LA CENA DELLE BEFFE (Giordano) (I)
Opera in 4 Acts (complete)
Orchestra and Chorus of Radio Italiana [RAI], Milano/Oliviero de Fabritiis
RAI broadcast, Milan, 14 Apr 1956

CAST:
Gigliola Frazzoni (*Ginevra*); Mafalda Micheluzzi (*Lisabetta*); Antonio Annaloro (*Gianetto Malespini*); Anselmo Colzani (*Neri Chiaramantesi*); Liliana Pellegrino (*Laldomine/Cintia*); Pina Leo Tanco (*Fiametta*); Enzo Guagni (*Gabriello Chiaramantesi/Il Trinca*); Franco Calabrese (*Il Tornaquinci*); Aurora Cattelani (*Il Calandra*); Antonio Sacchetti (*Fazio*); Aldo Corelli (*Il Dottore*); Walter Artioli (*Lapo/Un Cantore*).

NOTES: EJS 138

Dated "Milan, 1951" in the December, 1958 EJS bulletin, the correct date, 14 April, 1956, is taken from the RAI chronology.

Reissued in October, 1972 as UORC 124 and later on the Melodram LP MEL-157.

EJS 139: "The Golden Age of Opera" (2 LPs)
Issued December, 1958

SIDES 1-4 (139 A-D):

IL BARBIERE DI SIVIGLIA (Rossini) (I)
Opera in 2 Acts (complete)
Metropolitan Opera House Orchestra and Chorus/Gennaro Papi
Metropolitan Opera broadcast, NYC, 1 Mar 1941

CAST:
Bruno Landi (*Almaviva*); Salvatore Baccaloni (*Dr. Bartolo*); Josephine Tuminia (*Rosina*); John Charles Thomas (*Figaro*); Ezio Pinza (*Don Basilio*); Wilfred Engelman (*Fiorello*); Irra Petina (*Berta*); John Dudley (*Official*).

NOTES: EJS 139

The Overture has been omitted for purposes of timing. Side 1 plays in score pitch at 34.5 rpm. Side 2 plays uniformly at 34.0 rpm (*Rosina's* aria is transposed the customary half-step *up*, *Bailio's* aria the customary half-step *down*). Just after the "La columnia" begins, an overdubbed "canned" laughter, quite distinguishable from the (abundant) laughter of the real audience, is inserted on and off throughout the remainder of the performance. This is often dubbed in at such volume as to overwhelm the music--its source and circumstance are unknown. Baccaloni sings "A un Dottor" for his aria rather than the "Manca un foglio." Sides 3 and 4 both play in score pitch at 34.0 rpm.

As she did in the 19 February, 1941 performance (same cast and conductor), Josephine Tuminia sings Proch's "Theme and Variations" in the lesson scene.

The original NBC acetates (eleven 16-inch sides with Ortha labels, numbered ENG. 183 9-37, broadcast no. 41-46) contain Intermission Features with Milton Cross, Edward Johnson, Edwin MacArthur, Risë Stevens, Walt Disney, and Mrs. Herbert Hoover.

EJS 140: "The Golden Age of Opera" (1 LP)
Issued January, 1959

"LEON ROTHIER (1874-1951) IN OPERA AND SONG (RECORDED 1938-1950)"

SIDE 1 (140 A):

1. w. pf/?Albert Sciaretti: PHILÉMON ET BAUCIS, Act I: Au bruit de lourd marteau (Gounod) (F)
   Broadcast, ***LÉON ROTHIER***, WQXR, NYC, 20 Feb 1938, 10 Apr 1938, 1 Oct 1939, or 14 Apr 1940

* 2. w. pf/?: LES CONTES D'HOFFMANN, Act II: Scintille diamant (Offenbach) (F)
   Broadcast, WQXR, NYC, date unconfirmed

* 3. w. pf/?: LES CONTES D'HOFFMANN, Act I: [Je me nomme] Coppélius (Offenbach) (F)
   Broadcast, WQXR, NYC, date unconfirmed

4. w. pf/?Albert Sciaretti: FAUST, Act IV: Vous qui faites l'éndormie ["Sérénade"] (Gounod) (F)
Broadcast, ***LÉON ROTHIER***, WQXR, NYC, 2 Feb 1941

5. w. pf/?Albert Sciaretti: LA DAMNATION DE FAUST, Op. 24, Part II/vi: Chanson de la puce (Berlioz) (F)
Broadcast, ***LÉON ROTHIER***, WQXR, NYC, 6 Feb 1938

* 6. w. pf/?: OEDIPE à COLONE, Act III/ii : [Mon fils! tu ne l'es plus] . . . tous les droits sont perdus . . . Elle m'a prodigué sa ten dresse et ses soins (Antonio Sacchini) (F)
Broadcast, WQXR, NYC, date unconfirmed

* 7. w. pf/?: MEFISTOFELE, Prologue: Ave Signor! (Boïto) (I)
Broadcast, ***LÉON ROTHIER***, WQXR, NYC, ?2 Feb 1941

8. w. pf/?: LA JUIVE, Act I: Si la rigeur et la vengeance (Halévy) (F)
Broadcast, WQXR, NYC, date unconfirmed

* 9. w. pf/?: IPHIGÉNIE EN AULIDE, Act I: Diane, impitoyable! . . . Brillant auteur de la lumière (Gluck) (F)
Broadcast, WQXR, NYC, date unconfirmed

SIDE 2 (140 B):

* 1. w. pf/?Albert Sciaretti: SARDANAPLE, Act III(?): Nos soldats . . . Le front dans la poussiere (Victorin de Joncières) (F)
Broadcast, ***LÉON ROTHIER***, WQXR, NYC, 22 May 1938, 1 Oct 1939, or 18 May 1941

2. w. pf/?: LA DAMNATION DE FAUST, Op. 24, Part III/xii: Devant la maison ["Sérénade de Méphistophélès"] (Berlioz) (F)
Broadcast, ***LÉON ROTHIER***, WQXR, NYC, 6 Feb 1938

* 3. w. pf/?: LOUISE, Act IV: Louise! Louise! Regarde-moi (Charpentier) (F)
Broadcast, WQXR, NYC, date unconfirmed

* 4. w. pf/?: HAMLET, Act III: O destin de mon frère, hélas! . . . Je t'implore, o mon frère (Thomas) (F)
Broadcast, ***LÉON ROTHIER***, WQXR, NYC, ?17 Mar 1940

* 5. w. COLETTE D'ARVILLE or MARIA SCHACKO, soprano (pf/? or Maurice Abravanel): VÉRONIQUE, Act II: De ci, de là! Ca hin, ca ha! ["Duetto de l'âne"] (Messager) (F)
Broadcast, ***LÉON ROTHIER***, WXQR, NYC, ?11 Dec 1938 (w. *D'ARVILLE*), or WXQR, NYC, 23 Jun 1940 (w. *SCHACKO*)

6. w. pf/? "Plaisir d'amour" (Claris de Florian-G. Martini) (F)
Broadcast, WQXR, NYC, date unconfirmed

* 7. w. pf/?: "Danse macabre" (Cazalis-Saint-Saëns) (F)
Broadcast, WQXR, NYC, date unconfirmed

* 8. w. pf/?: HERCULANUM, Act III: Je crois au Dieu que tout le ciel révère ["Credo"] (Felicien David) (F)
Broadcast, ***LÉON ROTHIER***, WQXR, 31 Mar 1940 or 13 Apr 1941

* 9. w. pf/?: "Le Coeur de ma vie" (Dalcroze) (F)
?Private recording, New York City, April, 1948

NOTES: EJS 140

Rothier's radio show was broadcast locally (and somewhat irregularly) in New York City over station WQXR (Interstate Broadcasting Company) between 1938-1941. His pianist, as noted, was often Albert Sciaretti, and on at least one broadcast (23 June, 1940), Maurice Abravanel.

It has been suggested that if there really is later material included here, as the LP title implies, it may have come from the ***CAROL LONGONE OPERALOGUE***, and that the pianist is perhaps Nicola Rescigno. But it is more likely that everything presented here, except for item II/9, came from Rothier's WQXR broadcasts.

A detailed listing of local New York broadcasts from this period has not yet been found, which explains, if not justifies, why the sources and dates of so many of the selections included here have not been confirmed. The listings in the *New York Times* are incomplete. Alternate dates designate that Rothier is known to have sung the same selection on more than one broadcast, which was very often the case.

EJS 215 (June, 1961), EJS 563 (June, 1971), and UORC 105 (January, 1972) also contain off-the-air Rothier performances, all dated "1938."

Side 1 (140 A):

Band 2: Preceded by a spoken introduction by Rothier.

Band 3: The EJS 140 transfer (and perhaps the original recording) begins abruptly on the word "Coppélius."

Band 6: The label of EJS 140 carries the title OEDIPE ROI, but the facsimile reprint of the Parisian second edition (*Bibliotheca Musica Bononiensis*, Series 4, no. 17. Bologna: Forni Editore Bologna, 1970) cites OEDIPE À COLONE as the original title of this 1786 opera.

The first few measures of Oedipe's recitative, "Mon fils! tu ne l'es plus," are missing from this transfer (and perhaps from the original recording), though they were no doubt performed: the first intelligible line on EJS 140 is "tous les droits sont perdus."

Band 7: The EJS 140 transfer (and perhaps the original recording) is complete through "Tant'è fiaccato," omitting the last line, "di tentarlo al mal."

Band 9: The label of EJS 140 gives "De noirs pressentiments" (sic) from Gluck's IPIGENIE EN TAURIDE (sic). Actually this is not *Thoas'* Act I/ii aria, "De noirs préssentiments mon âme intimidée" from IPHIGÉNIE EN TAURIDE, but *Agamemnon's* aria from the first act of IPHIGÉNIE EN AULIDE, as noted.

An annoying high-pitched whistle can be heard throughout this band.

Side 2 (140 B):

Band 1: As I was unable to find the score of this three-act opera drawn from Byron (debut Théâtre-Lyrique, 8 February, 1867), there remains some question as to the place of this recitative and aria, though the third act aria of *Bélèses*, the high priest, seems likely.

Band 3: This aria is preceded by a spoken introduction by Rothier. The label of EJS 140 gives the aria as "Adieu de la pere" (sic). Jack Caidin issued a different broadcast performance of the "Louise! Louise! Regarde-moi!" on CRS 51-A (May, 1948), dated there as 21 May, 1939.

Band 4: Given on the label of EJS 140 as being from Saint-Saëns' 1883 opera, HENRY VIII.

Band 5: Preceded by a spoken introduction by Rothier in which the singer dissociates Messager's "Duet of the Donkeys" from the Wright-Forrest-Friml-Stothart "Donkey Serenade" from the operetta THE FIREFLY! The performance with Schacko, accompanied by Abravanel from 23 June, 1940 is the only broadcast actually documented, though a possible version with D'Arville on 11 December, 1938, accompanist unknown, has also been reported.

Band 7: Saint-Saëns' vocal setting of the "Danse macabre," with text by Henri Cazalis, was written in 1872 and was first published with orchestral accompaniment in 1873, preceding even the composition of the better-known orchestral version, Op. 40, by a year.

Vladimir Rosing (Parlophone E11247, matrix XE 6395, recorded 1934), Nelson Eddy (Columbia 17309-D, matrix WCO 28059A-17, recorded 1940), Norman Cordon (Victor 2165, matrix BS-063730-1, recorded 1941), and Richard Bonelli (from a 2 February, 1936 ***GENERAL MOTORS HOUR*** broadcast included on EJS 445 in October, 1968) are among the other singers who recorded the song, and even earlier, Lucien Rigaux (Odeon X 60339, matrix XP 3359, recorded circa 1908).

Band 8: Preceded by a spoken introduction by Rothier. Given on the label of EJS 140 as "Credo (David)," *Lilia's* third act aria (no. 15b) is indeed subtitled "Credo" in the original 1860 Paris first edition of the score. Note that the aria is transposed by Rothier, and was originally scored for mezzo-soprano in D major.

Band 9: Smith claimed in private correspondence (January, 1959) that this Dalcroze song was recorded "for me [Smith] personally in April 1948 as a present for a friend for Christmas." The spelling of the title, which was called into question by his correspondent, was, according to Smith, confirmed by Rothier.

EJS 141: "The Golden Age of Opera" (1 LP)
Issued January, 1959

"POTPOURRI (1)"

SIDE 1 (141 A):

* 1. KIRSTEN FLAGSTAD, soprano (Detroit Symphony Orchestra/Ernest Macmillan): DER FREISCHÜTZ, Act II: Leise, leise, fromme Weise (Weber) (G)
Broadcast, ***FORD SUNDAY EVENING HOUR***, WJR, Detroit, 27 Feb 1938

* 2. ROSA PONSELLE, soprano (studio orch/Frank Black): FEDRA: O divini Afrodite (Romano Romani) (I)
Broadcast, ***RCA MAGIC KEY***, WJZ, NYC, 2 May 1937

* 3. BENIAMINO GIGLI, tenor (Rome Opera Orchestra and Chorus/Luigi Ricci):
a) OTELLO, Act I: Esultate! (Verdi) (I)
b) OTELLO, Act III: Dio mi potevi scagliar (Verdi) (I)
From the soundtrack of the feature film ***MAMMA*** (1940)
Cinecittà Studios, Rome, 1-10 Oct 1940.

* 4. GLADYS SWARTHOUT, contralto (studio orch/Al Goodman): ORFEO ED EURIDICE, Act III: Che farò senza Euridice (Gluck) (I)
Broadcast, ***PRUDENTIAL FAMILY HOUR***, WABC, NYC, 11 Apr 1943

* 5. NORINA GRECO, soprano, and JOHN CHARLES THOMAS, baritone (Metropolitan Opera House Orchestra/Paul Breisach): Aïda, Act III: Ciel! mio padre! . . . Coraggio! ei giunge là tutto udrò (Verdi) (I)
Metropolitan Opera broadcast, NYC, 21 Feb 1942

SIDE 2 (141 B):

* 1. MARJORIE LAWRENCE, soprano (studio orch/Donald Voorhees): LA JUIVE, Act II: Il va venir! (Halévy) (F)
Broadcast, ***BELL TELEPHONE HOUR***, WEAF, NYC, 12 Mar 1945

* 2. JAN PEERCE, tenor (NBC Symphony Orchestra/Dr. Frank Black): JUDAS MACABEUS, No. 136: Sound an Alarm (Handel) (E)
Broadcast, ***NBC SYMPHONY ORCHESTRA***, WEAF, NYC, 30 Sep 1945

* 3. ORVILLE HARROLD, tenor (orch/Rosario Bourdon): LAKMÉ, Act I: Fantaisie aux divins mensonges (Delibes) (F)
C-24379-3 New York or Camden, 12 Aug 1920 Victor unpub

* 4. GIUSEPPE CAMPANARI, baritone (orch/?): OTELLO, Act II: Era la notte (Verdi) (I)
Source and date unknown

* 5. VIRGILIO LAZZARI, bass (pf/?): LE MASCHERE, Act I: Quella è una strada e questa è una piazza ["Stutter Song"] (Mascagni) (I)
?Private recording (acetate) ?New York, circa 1948

* 6. ZARA DOLOUKHANOVA, mezzo-soprano (U.S.S.R. Radio Orchestra/ O. Brohn): SEMIRAMIDE, Act I: Ah! quel giorno ognor rammento (Rossini) (I)
[D 2859/5-4] U.S.S.R., 1956 Melodiya D 2858/9 (LP)

* 7. FRANCES ALDA, soprano, and ENRICO CARUSO, tenor (orch/Walter B. Rogers): IL TROVATORE, Act III: Quel suon, quelle preci . . . Ah! che la morte ["Miserere"] (Verdi) (I)
C-8506-1 Camden, 27 Dec 1909 Victor unpub

* 8. GIOVANNI ZENATELLO, tenor (pf/?):
a) OTELLO, Act IV: Niun mi tema (Verdi) (I)
b) [Spoken] Interview (I)
?Broadcast, ?RAI, circa 1948

NOTES: EJS 141

Note that the original playing speeds for items II/3 and 7 given in the notes, below, have been calculated at score pitch. Both were transferred at 78.26 rpm on EJS 141.

Side 1 (141 A):

Band 1: The middle section of the aria, "O wie hell die goldnen Sterne . . . Sende deine Engelscharen," is cut. This performance was later issued on Legendary Records LR 120, along with the only other surviving item from this broadcast--Landon Ronald's "[O Lovely] Night," which was included on EJS 432 (April, 1968). See also the endnote for EJS 432.

Band 2: Library of Congress tape: 15778-63B (complete broadcast).

Band 3: The OTELLO "Niun mi tema" from the ***MAMMA*** soundtrack appeared later on EJS 464 (March, 1969).

Band 4: Listed on the label of EJS 141 as "1944."

Band 5: This duet plays in score pitch at 32.6 rpm.

Side 2 (141 B):

Band 1: The JUIVE aria plays a half-step lower than score pitch at 32.6 rpm (a likely transposition), but sounds much better in score pitch at 33.9 rpm.

Band 2: The label of EJS 141 states "1944," but this is incorrect. Peerce also sang the "Rachel, quand du Seigneur" from Halévy's LA JUIVE on this broadcast.

Band 3: Special vinyl pressings of this unpublished LAKMÉ aria exist. It plays in score pitch at 32.0 rpm: the playing speed of the original recording is 75.00 rpm.

Band 4: A favorite EJS enigma: this Campanari "Era la notte" is definitely NOT an unpublished Victor. Possibly it is an unpublished Columbia from the same 1909 sessions (with orchestral accompaniment) that spawned the two ten-inch NOZZE DI FIGARO titles (4091-1/4092-1), issued as Columbia A740.

William R. Bryant of Portland, Maine, has no record of a Campanari "Era la notte" in his extensive Columbia files, but has reported blanks for the following matrices: 4070, 4075-4076, 4081-4084, 4097, 4099, and 4100-4101.

Band 5: The label of EJS 141 gives the title "Stutter Song," and the date "1948." The performance is thought to have been taken from an acetate made at a private New York party circa that year, possibly at the Ansonia Hotel. It has also been suggested, accordingly, that the pianist may have been Nicola Rescigno, in whose apartment the party took place.

Band 6: Listed incorrectly in Bennett's *Melodiya: A Soviet LP Discography* (Westport, CN: Greenwood Press, 1981), p. 492, as "Bel raggio lusinghier" under the LP catalog numbers D 2858/9 (ten-inch issue, 1956) and D 08057/8 (twelve-inch reissue, 1961). The same performance was reissued again in 1983 on Melodiya M10-42623-24, a Doloukhanova recital. On the latter, both the conductor and the orchestra are credited as in the listing. No 78 rpm issue has been reported. D-2859/5-4 is the matrix number found in the wax of side two of the original LP release, D 2858/9. The recording is described as a broadcast in N. A. Ridley's review of EJS 141 in *The Record Collector*, 12/8&9 (November-December, 1959), p. 201, but it is clearly a studio recording.

The label of EJS 141 gives the singer's surname as "Dulkhanova," the title "In quel giorno" (sic), and the date "1956."

Band 7: This is the unpublished "Miserere," without the Metropolitan Opera House Chorus. Special vinyl pressings of it have circulated for years. The published version, C-8506-3, recorded in New York on 6 January, 1910, and originally issued as Victor 89030 and HMV 2-054007, features the chorus. Plays in score pitch at 32.0 rpm: the playing speed of the original recording is 75.00 rpm. It has been issued on numerous Caruso LPs.

Band 8: No trace of this ?RAI broadcast, made when Zenatello was 72 years old, has been found. The tape from which Smith may have taken it is marked simply "fr. Italian Radio" and "ca. 1948." This tape appears to have been compiled in about 1951, probably from borrowed acetates. The interview (in Italian) was later included on a Club 99 LP, CL 99-25, a Zenatello recital.

The singing is a half-step below score pitch at 33.3 rpm, but sounds fabulous (too fabulous perhaps) in score pitch at 34.6 rpm.

EJS 142: "The Golden Age of Opera" (1 LP)
Issued January, 1959

"POTPOURRI (2)"

SIDE 1 (142 A):

* 1. TITTA RUFFO, baritone (orch/?): IL BARBIERE DI SIVIGLIA, Act I: Largo al factotum (Rossini) (I)
No. 364-6A (a-128) Label No. A-66 (?)New York, (?)28 February, 1929
from the soundtrack of the one-reel (495 ft.) Metro-Goldwyn-Mayer "Metro Movietone Act" short *TITTA RUFFO [SINGS] FIGARO* (1929), ?Hollywood, circa 1929
MP 187; c13 May 1929

* 2. TITTA RUFFO, baritone (orch/?): OTELLO, Act II: Credo in un Dio crudel (Verdi) (I)
Scene 1, 387-7 (a-134) Label No. ? (?)New York, (?)8 March, 1929
from the soundtrack of the one-reel (550 ft.) Metro-Goldwyn-Mayer "Metro Movietone Act" short *TITTA RUFFO SINGING IAGO'S CREDO FROM VERDI'S OPERA OTELLO* (1930), ?Hollywood, circa 1929
MP 1335; c 20 Mar 1930

* 3. NELLIE MELBA, soprano (pf/Landon Ronald; flute/Philippe Gaubert): IL PENSIEROSO, Part I (Milton-Handel) (E)
a) Sweet Bird That Shunn'st the Noie of Folly
b) Error and comment by Melba
(?)13 Great Cumberland Place, London, March, 1904 G&T unpub

* 4. LAURITZ MELCHIOR, tenor (New Symphony Orchestra/John Barbirolli): OTELLO, Act III: Gott! um hast du Gehäuft dieses Elend [Dio! mi potevi!] (Verdi) (G)
CR 2509-1 London, 17 May 1930 HMV D 2037 [32-1480]
Electrola EJ 574

* 5. LAURITZ MELCHIOR, tenor (New Symphony Orchestra/John Barbirolli): OTELLO, Act IV: Jeder Knabe kann mein Schwert mir entreissen [Niun mi tema] (Verdi) (G)
CR 2510-1(?) London, 17 May 1930 HMV unpublished

* 6. FEODOR CHALIAPIN, bass (orch/Rosario Bourdon): LA BOHÈME, Act IV: Vecchia zimarra (Puccini) (I)
B-29247-2 Camden, 3 Jan 1924 Victor unpub HMV (7-52271)
AGSA 11

* 7. "FRANCESCO TAMAGNO" (sic), tenor (pf/?): "Pecche?" ["Perchè?"] (Filippi) (I)
3023 Ospedaletti, 7 Feb 1903 G&T unpub

SIDE 2 (142 B):

* 1. FRANCES ALDA, soprano, and ENRICO CARUSO, tenor (orch/Walter B. Rogers): CARMEN, Act I: Parle-moi de ma mère (Bizet) (F)
C-15483-3 New York, 10 Dec 1914 Victor (89083) unpub

* 2. BIDÚ SAYÃO, soprano (NBC Orchestra/Joseph Stopak): LO SCHIAVO, Act IV/v: O come splendido e bello . . . Come serenamente il mar carezza (Gomes) (I)
Broadcast, ***MUSIC OF THE NEW WORLD***, WEAF, NYC, 29 Apr 1943

* 3. LUCREZIA BORI, soprano; EZIO PINZA, bass (Metropolitan Opera House Orchestra/Louis Hasselmans): MIGNON, Act I: Légère hirondelles (Thomas) (F)
Metropolitan Opera broadcast, NYC, 4 Jan 1936

* 4. JESUS [ANTONIO] ARAMBURO (sic), tenor (pf/?): OTELLO, Act IV: Niun mi tema (Verdi) (I)
Source, format and date unknown

RIGOLETTO (Verdi) (I)
Opera in 3 Acts (Excerpts)
Metropolitan Opera House Orchestra and Chorus/Gennaro Papi
Metropolitan Opera broadcast, WINS, NYC, Tuesday, 12 Mar 1940 (e)

CAST:
[Charles Kullman (*Duke of Mantua*)]; Giuseppe De Luca (*Rigoletto*); Lily Pons (*Gilda*); Virgilio Lazzari (*Sparafucile*); [Anna Kaskas (*Maddalena*)]; [Thelma Votipka (*Giovanna*)]; [Norman Cordon (*Monterone*)]; [George Cehanovsky (*Marullo*)]; [Giordano Paltrinieri (*Borsa*)]; [Wilfred Engelman (*Ceprano*)]; [Maxine Stellman (*Countess di Ceprano*)]; [Edith Herlick (*Page*)].

* 5. a) Act I: DE LUCA and LAZZARI: Quel vecchio maledivami!
b) Act II: PONS and DE LUCA: No, vecchio, t'inganni un vindice avrai . . . Si, vendetta, tremanda vendetta
c) Act III: PONS and DE LUCA: Lassù in cielo, vicino alla madre . . . per voi pregherò / Gilda! mia Gil-[da!] . . . to the end of the opera

* 6. EZIO PINZA, bass (studio orch/Howard Barlow): SERSE, Act I: Frondi tenere . . . Ombra mai fu ["Largo"] (Handel) (I)
Broadcast, ***THE VOICE OF FIRESTONE***, WEAF, NYC, 14 Aug 1944.

* 7. BENIAMINO GIGLI, tenor; MARIA CANIGLIA, soprano (orch/?): LA TRAVIATA, Act I: Libiamo, libiamo (Verdi) (I)
Source and date unknown.

NOTES: EJS 142

Note that the original playing speeds given in the notes below have been calculated at score pitch. All items were transferred at 78.26 rpm for EJS 142.

Side 1 (142 A):

Bands 1 and 2: Only three Ruffo sound film shorts have been documented, all "Metro Movietone Acts" produced by Metro-Goldwyn-Mayer. In addition to the BARBIERE and OTELLO films excerpted here, another, ***TITTA RUFFO AS NELUSKO, THE SLAVE, IN MEYERBEER'S L'AFRICAINE*** (MP 1158), was copyrighted on 10 February, 1930. None of the release dates or premieres could be found. Whether the films were shot in Hollywood or in New York could not be determined with certainty.

The titles given in the listing are those under which the films were copyrighted. The disc numbers appear in the order in which they were transcribed from the original labels (at least three collectors have actually inspected the discs, which were originally found in Sydney, Australia: they are sixteen-inch, lateral-cut, 33.3 rpm, inside-start. One of these informants insists that they were Victor Vitaphone pressings, which is altogether possible). The label of EJS 142 gives the date "1930" for both recordings.

The "Largo al factotum," was performed a half step below score pitch. The label of the original disc cites "495 ft" as the film length, where the Library of Congress Copyright Catalog gives "485 ft."

Band 3: Note that this is the unissued master, (?)13, complete with Melba's comment "No, no . . . oh bother(?) it . . . We'll have to begin it all over again," made just before beginning the cadenza and after a false start. This item later appeared as an "appendix" to the 1976 EMI Melba set, RLS 719. The original playing speed is 75.00 rpm.

Bands 4 and 5: Both given on the label of EJS 142 as recorded in "1928." The original playing speeds for both are 78.26 rpm. Special vinyl pressings of the first take of the "Jeder Knabe kan mein Schwert mir entreissen" (CR 2510-1) have circulated for many years (take three was issued as D 2037 and EJ 574: a detailed comparison of the two surviving takes reveals that the EJS 142 transfer is the unpublished take -1.

Band 6: Given as "1922" on the label of EJS 142. Originally assigned the HMV catalog number 7-52271, but only issued later as AGSA 11. The original playing speed is 76.00 rpm.

Band 7: A great deal of correspondence has been exchanged concerning this notorious recording. I'll attempt to recap its long and curious journey toward documentation.

First, a summary of the discographical facts from W. R. Moran:

> "Some years ago . . . I received shiny new pressings of all the unpublished . . . Tamagno series. Included was the mysterious "Perchè?" which I have before me as I write. All the records in the series, from 3000 to 3022, with the exception of this one record, bear the initials "F.T." in a crude, hand-written circle . . . and all are Francesco Tamagno. While we have no proof that the initials "F.T." in the circle were placed there by the tenor himself, this is certainly a possibility and I would be willing to speculate almost a certainty. This recording of "Perchè?" was first marked (by hand) "3005-" (no "F.T." please note). The "05" part is marked out, and above it is written "23" . . . still no "F.T." Then, to one side, is a factory stamping, in raised letters, meaning it was machine stamped into a metal part at the factory, and not placed there at the time of the actual recording, we find "3023 ft." The fact that number 3023 was at the end of the Tamagno block; the fact that the record in question was first numbered "3005-" and then changed to another number still within the Tamagno group; the fact that the familiar "F.T." in circle is conspicuously missing from the markings made at the recording session, but that the printed "ft" was added by the factory to the group of waxes sent in for processing from the Tamagno session;

> plus the fact that the playing speed of "3023, née 3005" [77.64 rpm] seems to agree with playing speeds determined for 3002 FT through 3008 FT, all permits us to make an "educated guess" that "Perchè?" was recorded during the Tamagno session, and all we have to do is to listen to the recording to know that it is not Tamagno. Those are the facts, and what I consider to be a series of reasonable deductions from them. From this point on, everything is pure speculation, and should be so labeled."

The recording has generated much discussion over the years. Following are some of the highlights, arranged chronologically:

January, 1959: Smith issues the "Perchè?" on EJS 142 as by "Francesco Tamagno." It is dubbed high, making the artist sound at least something like a tenor, if not at all like Tamagno.

In private correspondence to a friend, dated 28 December, 1958, Smith gave the following account:

> I wrote you at length [about] the Tamagno Perchè. I had a friend, Maestro E. G., go to Asti to the home of Carlo Sabajno's son. There he looked up the records (paper records) of the [Tamagno] recording sessions which had Cottone at the piano but Sabajno as supervisor. According to the written notes, Tamagno SANG Perchè--also Celeste Aida, Il vento il cor from Guarany, and Tu che a Dio from Lucia. E.G. 'believes' the other tests are in the home of Sabajno's son, a well to do builder . . . I've been told as well [that] solos by Angelo Masini made in Russia in 1903 and solos by Antonio Cotogni never issued or passed by the baritone [are also there]."

Many subsequent references were made by Smith in correspondence to the Sabajno collection. There is of course no indication in any official source that Cottone served as Tamagno's accompanist for the sessions (I would be astonished to learn that he was ever capable of playing so badly!), or that Sabajno acted as "supervisor." As to the Masini and Cotogni records . . .

April, 1960: John Stratton's article, "3023 ft," appears in the Canadian journal *Record News* (4/8, pp. 297-301). Here, Mr. Stratton contends that the voice is none other than that of the baritone Antonio Cotogni (1831-1918). Comparing it with Cotogni's single, verifiable recording, the duet "I mulattieri" of Francesco Masini, with tenor Francesco Marconi (Pre-Dog 54373, matrix 11180½b, Milan, 1908), Stratton admits that the voice of "Perchè?" sounds "younger" than the voice heard in the Marconi duet, but concludes, "Otherwise however, I must confess it sounds to me the same voice. It may never be possible to establish definitely that the 'Perchè?' actually was sung by Cotogni, but I invite collectors to see if they can establish that it was NOT."

March, 1974: Edward J. Smith reissues the "Perchè?" on UORC 197 ("Potpourri No. 3") as by Cotogni, with no mention that he had previously issued it on EJS 142 as by Tamagno! The bulletin for the UORC release notes that "The Cotogni discs except for the rare I Mulattieri with Francesco Marconi were allegedly non-existent. Test copies belonged to my very good friends Vivian Liff and George Stuart who loaned me tapes for reproduction. The two solos never heard before are the O Casto Fior from Roi de Lahore of Massenet and the song Perchè by Fillipi. Cotogni recorded all three in 1908 when he was 77 years of age."

Of course, UORC 197 presented the "Perchè?" dubbed at a lower, decidedly "baritonal" speed.

Circa December, 1981: The Timaclub of Rome issues this growing catalog of Cotogni records complete on the LP "Le Voci di Roma" (Tima 37)--the "I mulattieri," the "O casto fior," and the "Perchè?" (there as "Pecche'"). Edward J. Smith is credited in the acknowledgements for the LP, incidentally.

July, 1986: When the Timaclub LP was reviewed in *The Record Collector* (31/6-7, July, 1986, pp. 163-166), no mention of any controversy or uncertainty was made. "The album leads off with the three *known* (emphasis mine) recordings by Antonio Cotogni," the author writes, ". . . Only his duet I Mulatieri sung for the most part, frustratingly, in unison with Francesco Marconi, was published commercially. The others circulated for years as mystery test pressings, the ROI DE LAHORE aria often being ascribed to Charles Santley and the Fillipi song, probably recorded around 82 but played at 78, and with a "Tamagno" matrix (R18) being published at least once on private lp as sung by the creator of Otello. The three discs are collected here for the first time on commercial LP."

The question of attribution notwithstanding, the "'Tamagno' matrix (R18)" and the high recording speed/low transfer speed are clearly in error here.

1988: Alan Kelly's note in *His Master's Voice/La Voce Del Padrone: The Italian Catalogue* (Westport, CN: Greenwood Press, 1988, *Discoggraphies*, no. 30), p. [429]:

> "Nothing has been found in any file to suggest that this record was made by another singer than Tamagno. The record is listed in the Register as being by Tamagno."

I interpret Mr. Kelly's note not as an endorsement of Francesco Tamagno as the singer, but as a refutation--based on the facts--of Antonio Cotogni.

Still a final scenario has been suggested, this one, too, as difficult to dispute as it is to prove. The late Robert Zierling of New York City reported a notice, possibly in the *Gazzetta Musicale di Milano*, dated Buenos Aires, 10 August, 1895, establishing that one of Francesco Tamagno's two brothers, Giovanni, is known to have sung Fillipi's "Perchè?" in concert in Buenos Aires around that time. A similar notice, dated Lisbon, 1891, suggests that Francesco Tamagno himself had sung the song at a benefit concert given in the Teatro San Carlo, accompanied on the piano by Marino Mancinelle (indicating, I suppose, that one Tamagno was just as likely to have recorded it as the other).

Obviously lacking here is any evidence that Giovanni Tamagno (or indeed, Antonio Cotogni) was present at *Francesco* Tamagno's Ospedaletti recording sessions in 1903.

I'll add a few of my own conclusions: first, at any speed, the singer of the "Perchè?" sounds nothing like Francesco Tamagno. Second, the Cotogni-Marconi duet offers little in the way of a lucid document of Cotogni's voice, making any comparison with either the "Perchè?" or the "O Casto fior" indecisive at best. Third, until a verifiable recording of Giovanni Tamagno emerges, his candidacy is less than shaky --even certain knowledge that he was present during brother Francesco's recording sessions could establish the attribution of matrix 3023 to him solely on the basis of circumstantial rather than vocal evidence.

Based on the speeds of the "other" Tamagno recordings in this group, the original playing speed of the "Perchè?" should be 77.64 rpm.

Side 2 (142 B):

Band 1: This unpublished duet was originally assigned the catalog number 89083 (later given to the Caruso-De Gogorza "A la luz de la luna," matrix C-21773-2 from 16 April, 1918). 75.00 rpm has been deduced as the original playing speed based on the speed of the other items made at Caruso's 10 December, 1914 session. Three takes were made of the CARMEN duet, all of them marked "destroyed" in the Victor books. The tape from which Smith may have taken the duet notes matrix "C-15483-3;" both Secrist and Bolig, in their respective Caruso discographies, give take 3 as the one assigned catalog number 89083. W.R. Moran's definitive discography in the Enrico Caruso, Jr.-Andrew Farkas *Enrico Caruso: My Father and My Family* (Portland Oregon: Amadeus Press, 1990), p. 632 (note 74) confirms that all transfers came from Alda's own surviving test pressing, "said to be take 3." RCA Victor's complete Caruso issues on LP and CD both observe take 3, as does the recent Pearl CD set.

Band 2: Listed on the label of EJS 142 as "Cavatina" (it is in fact a "Romanza," according to the original piano-vocal score), with the date "1945." This was also issued on IRCC LP L-7020, "Gems from the Repertoire of Bidú Sayão" in 1962, where William Seltsam notes "There are a few imperfections which could not be corrected, for instance, the interference tone in the original recording of the 'Schiavo' aria." This 'whistle' is missing from the EJS 142 dubbing. As Seltsam heralded his as an "authorized edition," he may have secured his copy from Sayão herself. Smith's source is not known, but a "protection" glass-based copy of the original NBC acetates (titled "Inter Amer Univ of the Air / Music of the New World. Salute to the Past" and numbered 21025 and 21026, broadcast no. 43-668) does exist, which labels the SCHIAVO recitative and aria as a "Serenata!"

Band 3: Reported to play flat, necessitating a speed of approximately 34.1 rpm for the score key of D major.

Band 4: Another perennial EJS conversation piece. Smith claimed, in at least one instance, that this recording of ANTONIO ARAMBURO (1838-1905 or 1912), who is listed on the label of EJS 142 with the forename "Jesus," was taken from a "1902 Victor" recorded in Argentina, where the tenor had by then settled. One reliable source claims to have seen the actual disc used for the transfer--an entirely unmarked test pressing. "He had no more reason to say it was Aramburo," I was told by this claimant, "than he did to call it Gayarre or Masini."

Authentic recordings of Aramburo have been documented, however. The singer did make at least eight cylinders in Montevideo in 1901 or 1902 for what appears to have been his own recording company. One of them, a concert cylinder, appeared on the market some years ago, housed in an expensive hand-made wooden box, and was accompanied by a certificate of authenticity signed by the singer himself. An early South American catalog, circa 1902, has been seen carrying several Aramburo titles.

Eight of the cylinders are held at Yale University. Richard Warren, Jr., curator of the Yale collection, informs me that "the cylinders, certificates, and catalog are in [the Yale] collection." He further states that the "Niun mi tema" on EJS 142 does not appear in the catalog carrying the Aramburo titles, but that all of the items owned by Yale *are* found there. Mr. Warren concluded that "the 'Niun mi tema' on EJS 142, in comparison with the Aramburo recordings in

[Yale's] collection, seems to be the voice of a different singer," and that other staff members at the Yale Historical Sound Recordings Collection, who have apparently heard the genuine Aramburo cylinders, "agree on this opinion."

Bands 5 a-c: From a Tuesday evening broadcast over WINS, New York City, sponsored by the New Jersey Milk Fund--specifically, Free Milk Fund for Babies, Inc. The performance was reviewed the next day in the *New York Times* (13 March, p. 28:1) under the title "De Luca Returns to Rigoletto Role." The Free Milk Fund for Babies, Inc. had been founded as a charity in 1926 by Mrs. William Randolph Hearst, hence the broadcast over WINS, a Hearst-owned local station. Between 10 February and 10 March, 1940, numerous accounts of the benefit appeared in the *New York Times*: 10 February, p. 18; 11 February II/3; 25 February, II/2; and 10 March, II/3.

Note that the "Lassù in cielo" is finished by another baritone, Tibbett perhaps (Robert Weede has also been suggested), but this has not been verified: De Luca sings through "Gilda! mia Gil--," at which point the other voice finishes *Gilda's* name and completes the opera. Several Tibbett broadcasts have been examined in an effort to determine the source of the insert, among them, Met, 28 December, 1935 (issued on EJS 213 and EJS 551), Met, 11 March, 1939 (issued on EJS 131), and a 1947 ***STANDARD HOUR*** performance. None of these matches the EJS 142 insert, though they are the most likely sources Smith had at his disposal. The 31 January, 1942 Met broadcast with Weede, issued in excerpts as UORC 117 (May-June, 1972), may also have been the source.

The cut in "Lassù in cielo" (5c) is a performance cut.

The WINS excerpts were later issued on the LP "Giuseppe De Luca In Live Performances 1940-1948" (MDP 015), where we find not only the same baritone insert at the end, but also a Pons insert for *Gilda's* first two phrases of the "Lassù in cielo," which were very dim on the original WINS transcription--as we can hear on EJS 142. The phrases have been replaced on MDP 015 by a fragment taken from a considerably better source, probably a later Pons broadcast. However, they are not from either the 1935 or 1939 Pons-Tibbett Met broadcasts mentioned above.

Band 6: This performance subsequently appeared on EJS 214 (June, 1961).

Band 7: Thought to have been from the 31 May, 1939 Covent Garden relay, but when the latter was first issued complete on EJS 306 in September, 1964, the "Libiamo" turned out to be a different performance. No broadcasts of Gigli and Caniglia were traced containing the excerpt: their other 1939 Covent Garden performances of the opera were not broadcast.

EJS 143: "The Golden Age of Opera" (1 LP)
Issued January, 1959

"SCENES FROM THE FILM DON QUIXOTE (ENGLISH VERSION 1932)" / "SONGS FROM THE FILM DON QUIXOTE (FRENCH VERSION 1932)"

DON QUICHOTTE (DON QUIXOTE) (1933)
Nelson Films, Ltd. - Vandor Films
Presented by DuWorld Pictures, Inc., in association with Valdemar D. Bell
Gaumont-Franco-Film-Aubert Studios, Nice
Director: G. W. Pabst
Collaborator (assistant director) on French-language version: Jean de Limur
Collaborator (assistant director) on English-language version: John Farrow
Director of Production: Constantin Geftman
Scenario: Paul Morand, after the novel by Miguel de Cervantes
Dialogue: Alexandre Arnoux
Camera: Nikolas Farkas and Paul Portier (aka Porter)
Settings (art director): Andrei Andreiev
Costumes: M. Pretzfelder (design); Maison Karinsky (execution)
Editor: Hans Oser
Sound mixing and sychronization: (?) Bell
Assistant sound engineer: H. Rappaport
Western Electric System
Music: Jacques Ibert; additional material: A. S. Dargomizhsky
Conductors: (?) Jacques Ibert and/or (?) Albert Coates
9 Reels, 2260 meters, B&W, approximately 73-83 minutes
LP 5516; cl Jan 1935
Paris Premiere (French version): early April, 1933
London Premiere (English version): 25 May 1933
U.S. Premiere (English version): Cameo Theater, NYC, 22 Dec 1934

CAST:	(French Version)	(English Version)
Don Quixote	. . . Feodor Chaliapin	. . . Feodor Chaliapin
Sancho Panza	. . . Dorville	. . . George Robey
Dulcinée/Dulcinea	. . . Renée Valliers	. . . Renée Valliers
Sancho's Wife	. . . Mady Berry	. . . Emily Fitzroy
The Duchess	. . . Arlette Marchal	. . . Lydia Sherwood
The Niece	. . . Mireille Balin	. . . Sidney Fox
The Priest	. . . Charles Leger	. . . Frank Stanmore
The Gypsy King	. . . ?	. . . Wally Patch
The Duke	. . . ?	. . . Miles Mander
The Captain of Police	. . . C. Martinelli	. . . Oscar Asche
Carrasco	. . . [René] Donnio	. . . [René] Donnio
Servant at Inn	. . . Genica Anet	. . . Genica Anet
1st Innkeeper	. . . Leo Larive	. . . ?
2nd Innkeeper	. . . Pierre Labry	. . . ?

SIDE 1 (143 A):

1. "SCENES FROM THE FILM ***DON QUIXOTE*** (ENGLISH VERSION 1932)" (26:10)

   a) CHALIAPIN, FOX, and DONNIO: Don Quixote Awakes (w. music and dialogue) (E)
   b) "Fanfare" (w. music and dialogue) (E)
   * c) CHALIAPIN: "Bolero: Sierra Nevada" (Dargomizhsky) (w. dialogue: DONNIO and STANMORE) (E)
   d) CHALIAPIN and PATCH: Knighthood Scene and Scene with Dulcinea (w. incidental music from Lully's AMADIS DE GAULE and dialogue) (E)
   * e) CHALIAPIN: "Chanson du départ" ("This Castle New") (Ronsard-Ibert) (E)
   f) CHALIAPIN and ROBEY: The Battle for the Prisoners (w. music and dialogue) (E)
   g) ROBEY: "Knights never eat, Knights never sleep" (?) (E)
   h) CHALIAPIN, ROBEY, MANDER, SHERWOOD, et al: The Duke's Court (w. music and dialogue) (E)

SIDE 2 (143 B):

1. "SCENES FROM THE FILM ***DON QUIXOTE*** (ENGLISH VERSION 1932)" (12:10)

   a) CHALIAPIN: "Chanson du Duc" ("This Song I Sing") (Ronsard-Ibert) (E)
   b) CHALIAPIN, DONNIO, and MANDER: Battle with Carrasco (w. music and dialogue) (E)
   c) CHALIAPIN and ROBEY: Combat with the Windmills (w. music and dialogue) (E)
   d) CHALIAPIN: "Chanson de la morte de Don Quichotte" ("Stop Crying Sancho, my Dear") (Ronsard-Ibert) (E)

* 2. "SONGS FROM THE FILM ***DON QUIXOTE*** (FRENCH VERSION 1932)"

FEODOR CHALIAPIN, bass (orch/Jacques Ibert)
Salle Chopin, Paris, 9 January and 13 March, 1933

a) "Chanson du Duc" (Ronsard-Ibert) (F)
OPG 428-4 13 Mar 1933 HMV DA 1310 [30-10328] HMV VA 25

b) "Chanson du départ" (Ronsard-Ibert) (F)
OPG 429-3 13 Mar 1933 HMV DA 1310 [30-10303] HMV VA 25

c) "Chanson à Dulcinée" (Ronsard-Ibert) (F)
OPG 430-1 9 Jan 1933 HMV DA 1311 [30-10301] HMV VA 26

d) "Chanson de la morte de Don Quichotte" ("Ne pleure pas, Sancho") (Ronsard-Ibert) (F)
OPG 637-1 13 Mar 1933 HMV DA 1311 [30-10475] HMV VA 26

e) FEODOR CHALIAPIN, bass; OLIVE KLINE, soprano (orch/Rosario Bourdon): DON QUICHOTTE, Act V: Finale [Death Scene] (Massenet) (F)
Liederkranz Hall, New York, 7 April, 1927
1) "Oh mon maïtre"
CVE-38334-1 Victor 6693 HMV DB 1096 [2-032114]
6812
2) "Oui! Je fus le chef"
CVE-38335-1 Victor 6693 HMV DB 1096 [2-034042]
6812

NOTES: EJS 143

Most prints of ***DON QUICHOTTE/QUIXOTE*** now in circulation are very badly mutilated, especially those available on videotape: the French-language videos run approximately 64 minutes, while the English-language versions, entitled ***ADVENTURES OF DON QUIXOTE***, consume a mere 53 minutes. This, considering the *original* running time of approximately 83 minutes. There is, however, a subtitled French version available for rental on 16mm that claims to actually run 83 minutes, but it has not been viewed for confirmation.

Both versions were shot between 1932 and 1933 and released in Europe and the U.K. as early as 1933. The film, presumably the English-language version, was not copyrighted in the U.S. until 1 January, 1935 (LP 5516), having premiered in New York City in December, 1934. The Paris premiere was reviewed in the *New York Times* on 23 April, 1933, and in *Variety* on 11 April, so the film must have opened there in about the first week of April. The two versions were shot as *separate* films, and are quite different, each having its own distinctive visual "feel." While the treatment was the same for both, and the screenplays virtually identical, the fact remains that most of the major sequences were re-staged and re-shot.

The English translator(s) of the Ronsard-Ibert songs and the Dargomizhsky "Bolero" ("Sierra Nevada") are not known, nor is the composer of *Sancho's* "Knights never eat, Knights never sleep," sung by George Robey in the English-language version and by Dorville in the French-language version.

Peculiar to the credits of the French-language version are a few technical details (the use of Kodak equipment and the Western Electric recording system, for example) and acknowledgement that Chaliapin sings through the courtesy of "His Master's Voice." The French credits do not identify the actors portraying the *Duke* and the *Gypsy King*, just as the credits of the English-language version omit the names of the two *Inkeepers*, along with any reference to Arnoux's dialogue. "Film Traders Ltd." is given as the distributor of the English version. The transliteration of the Russian names differs slightly between the French and English credits, and the second cameraman is listed as "Portier" and "Porter," respectively. The actress playing the *Servant at the Inn* is identified in both versions as "Genica Anet," but she has been found elsewhere bearing the surname "Athanasiou."

Lee Atwell, in his book, *G. W. Pabst* (Boston: Twayne, 1977), pp. 169-170, further credits Lotte Reiniger with the "Chinese Shadows"--an element of a sequence that has evidently not survived in all prints. Atwell also claims that the well-known Russian character actor (and recorded pianist) Vladimir Sokoloff and a player named "Mafer" are among the French cast members, though their roles are not designated.

The conductor attributions could not be confirmed: neither Ibert (who conducted Chaliapin's commercial HMV recordings of the Ronsard-Ibert songs) nor Coates are listed in the credits. Mention of Coates has not yet been encountered in reliable sources, and is given here only as a *possibility*, however slight.

In spite of the ambiguity of the LP title, the French-language versions of the Ronsard-Ibert songs and the Massenet Finale on side two were taken from Chaliapin's 1933 commercial HMVs, and 1927 commercial Victors, respectively, not from the films. Smith wrote a friend in December, 1958 that his attempts to secure dubbings of the French soundtrack and the unpublished HMVs from the score had failed, hence his use of the relatively common commercial items included on this LP.

Side 1 (143 A):

Band 1 (c and e): From the English-language soundtrack, *not* from the commercial recordings. Note that item c in particular is sung in English, with orchestral accompaniment (Chaliapin recorded the Dargomizhsky "Bolero" in Russian with Piero Coppola at the piano in the Salle Chopin, Paris, 9 January, 1933, matrix OPG 431-1, during the first of the two Ibert-conducted sessions, along with the English versions of the Ronsard-Ibert DON QUICHOTTE songs; the studio "Bolero" remained unpublished until its issue as Historic Masters HMA 46).

Side 2 (143 B):

Band 2: These are commercial, *not* soundtrack recordings. The Ronsard-Ibert and Massenet excerpts were taken from the standard issues, not alternate takes. Olive Kline's *Dulcinée* is heard only in the second part of item 2e (CVE-38335-1). Her name does not appear on the original 1927 Victor labels, but it does on HMV pressings and in HMV catalogs. Chaliapin created Massenet's *Don* in Monte Carlo in 1910, with bass André Gresse as *Sancho*.

The playing speed of the 1933 Ibert titles is 78.26 rpm, reproduced correctly here; the two Massenet sides were recorded at 77. 43 rpm and dubbed at 78.26 rpm on EJS 143.

EJS 144: "The Golden Age of Opera" (1 LP)
Issued January, 1959
"OTELLO JUNE 17, 1926 (COVENT GARDEN) (WITH INCIDENTAL FILL-INS)"

OTELLO (Verdi) (I)
Opera in 4 Acts (Excerpts)
+ Recorded during actual performance, Covent Garden, London, 17 Jun 1926
= Recorded during Melba's Farewell Concert, Covent Garden London, 8 Jun 1926

SIDE 1 (144 A):

Act I: 1. * a) GIOVANNI ZENATELLO, tenor (Orchestra and Chorus of the Teatro La Scala/Carlo Sabajno): Una vela! . . . Esultate! [beginning of the opera to the end of the "Esultate!"]
Ck 1914-2 Milan, 8 Nov 1926 HMV DB 1007 [2-052323]

* b) + GIUSEPPE NOTO, baritone; LUIGI CILLA, tenor; OCTAVE DUA, tenor (Royal Opera House Orchestra and Chorus/ Vincenzo Bellezza): Inaffia l'ugola! ["Brindisi "] . . . bevi, bevi, con me
CR 494-1 HMV (2-054164) unpub

* c) [1] GIOVANNI ZENATELLO, tenor; LINA PASINI-VITALE, soprano (orch/?): Già nella notte densa . . . te ne ramenti
XXPh 4087 Milan, 1910 Fonotipia 74157
[2] GIOVANNI ZENATELLO, tenor; HINA SPANI, soprano (Orchestra of the Teatro La Scala/Carlo Sabajno):
a) Qando narravi
Ck 1918-4 Milan, 3 Dec 1926
HMV DB 1006 [2-054173] Victor 6714
b) Venga la morte
Ck 1919-2 Milan, 9 November, 1926
HMV DB 1006 [2-054174] Victor 6714

Act II: * d) APOLLO GRANFORTE, baritone (Orchestra of the Teatro La Scala/Carlo Sabajno): Vanne: la tua meta gia vedo . . . Credo in un Dio crudel . . . E vecchia fola il Ciel
2M 184-4 Milan, January, 1932
HMV C 2417 [32-2589] Victor [CVS-73211]

* e) + GIOVANNI ZENATELLO, tenor; GIUSEPPE NOTO, baritone (Royal Opera House Orchestra/Vincenzo Bellezza): Mio signore . . . Amore e gelosia vadan dispersi insieme . . . to the end of the chorus
CR 496-1 HMV DB 953 [2-054165] HMV VB 17

* f) + GIOVANNI ZENATELLO, tenor; GIUSEPPE NOTO, baritone (Royal Opera House Orchestra/Vincenzo Bellezza): Non pensateci più . . . Ora e per sempre addio . . . Ardua impresa sarebbe
CR 497-1 HMV DB 953 [2-054166] HMV VB 17

SIDE 2 (144 B):

Act II: 1. * a) APOLLO GRANFORTE, baritone (Orchestra of the Teatro La Scala/Carlo Sabajno): E qual certezza sognate voi se . . . Era la notte . . . in cieco letargo si mutò
2M 240-1 Milan, February, 1932
HMV C 2420 [32-2595] Victor [CVS-73217]
2M 190-7
HMV C 2420 [32-2596] Victor [CVS-73218]

* b) + GIOVANNI ZENATELLO, tenor; GIUSEPPE NOTO, baritone (Royal Opera House Orchestra/Vincenzo Bellezza): [Ah!] mille vite . . . Si, pel ciel . . . to the end of the act
CR 499-1A HMV unpub HMB 17

Act III: * c) + GIOVANNI ZENATELLO, tenor; GIUSEPPE NOTO, baritone (Royal Opera House Orchestra/Vincenzo Bellezza): Dio! mi potevi scagliar . . . Ti nascondi
CR 500-1 HMV unpub HMB 17

* d) + GIOVANNI ZENATELLO, tenor; GIUSEPPE NOTO, baritone; LUIGI CILLA, bass (Royal Opera House Orchestra and Chorus/Vincenzo Bellezza): Tutto è spento . . . Questa è una ragna . . . Evviva il Leon di San Marco!
CR 501-1 HMV DB 955 [2-054167] HMV VB 8

Act IV: * e) = NELLIE MELBA, soprano (Royal Opera House Orchestra/ Vincenzo Bellezza): Salce, Salce ["Willow Song"]
a) Piangea cantando
CR 417-1 HMV DB 1500 [2-053263] IRCC 2
b) Scendean gli augelli
CR 418-1 HMV unpub

* f) = NELLIE MELBA, soprano (Royal Opera House Orchestra/ Vincenzo Bellezza): Ave Maria piena di grazia
CR 419-1 HMV unpub

* g) + GIOVANNI ZENATELLO, tenor; LUIGI CILLA, tenor; EDOUARDO COTREUIL, bass; MICHELE SAMPIERI, tenor (Royal Opera House Orchestra/Vincenzo Bellezza): Niun mi tema . . . to the end of the opera
CR 502-1 HMV DB 955 [2-054168] HMV VB 8

NOTES: EJS 144

In contrast to its title, EJS 144 contains OTELLO excerpts from a variety of different sources, not just the live Zenatello Covent Garden performance. In fact, these "incidental fill-ins" account for more than half of the individual excerpts included.

The Zenatello-Noto-Cilla "live" Covent Garden recordings were gathered subsequently on the EMI Covent Garden set (ALP 3788, in set RLS 742) which also contains the OTELLO excerpts from Melba's farewell. The latter also appear on EMI's 1976 Melba set (RLS 719). In addition, two of the unpublished Zenatello recordings (II/b and c) have been issued by Historic Masters as noted in the listing, pressed from the original parts.

The Granforte solos (I/d and II/a) have been checked against the originals, HMV Album Set 157, C 2413 - C 2428 (32-2582/2612), also issued as Victor Set M-152 (Manual 11363-11378) and AM-152 (Automatic 11379-11394). In at least one instance, the "Era la notte" (2M-240-1 and 2M 190-7), Smith seems to have used the early, echo-ladden Camden LP transfer, CCL 101 (also issued on QALP 10203/5 in Italy, and later on EMI C 153-03885/7--without the echo). Alternate takes on HMV have been found in this set, but none among the solos featured on EJS 144. The Granforte solos were used because, in Smith's estimation, the live Noto recordings were "inferior and badly sung" (correspondence, December, 1958).

Transfer speeds are especially erratic on EJS 144, so rather than speculate as to what went on during its preparation, the speeds of the original discs are given below, where it is assumed that all have been transferred at 78.26 rpm on EJS 144. Listening to this LP with an open score is highly recommended.

Side 1 (144 A):

Item 1a: Only Zenatello is listed on the label of DB 1007. The *Iago*, *Cassio*, and the *Montano* have never been identified. The original playing speed is 76.00 rpm.

Item 1b: The single-sided HMV catalog number (in parentheses) was assigned but not issued. The original playing speed is 78.26 rpm.

Item 1c: The first part of the Zenatello-Spani love duet, "Già nella note densa" to "te ne ramenti," matrix Ck 1917 (9 November, 1926), was unpublished. The first take is marked "destroyed" in the EMI ledgers, the second take as "damaged." To complete the duet, Smith, ever the fox, inserted the first part of the 1910 Zenatello/ Pasini-Vitale Fonotipia performance. It must be said that the patch job was done very nicely: the quality of the recording does little to give away the deception, and it is only the rather striking dissimilarity of the two sopranos, Pasini-Vitale and Spani, that reveals the crime. The original Fonotipia issue, 74157/74158 (matrices XXPh 4087/4088) presented the duet complete on two 12-inch sides from "Già nella note densa" to ". . . ancora un bacio."

Smith made every attempt to secure the unpublished Spani material. The singer confirmed to him that she had indeed recorded the "Già nella note" portion of the duet with Zenatello as well as the "Ave Maria" and "Salce," but had apparently been responsible herself for their rejection--at least the "Ave Maria." The others, he claimed in a January, 1959 letter, had been "destroyed in test pressing stage evidentally" (sic). His only option was to complete the LP using the Pasini-Vitale Fonotipia and the Melba Covent Garden arias.

The playing speed of Fonotipia 74157 is 75.00 rpm; both of the Zenatello-Spani sides play at 76.00 rpm.

Item 1d: Transferred nearly a half step high on EJS 144. CVS-73211 was the domestic matrix number assigned by Victor to this excerpt (side 9 in set M-152): two catalog numbers were assigned sequentially to the double sides of each set format, M and AM (manual and automatic sequence): 11367 and 11383, respectively, for sides 9 and 10. The original playing speed is 77.00 rpm.

Item 1e: The original playing speed is 78.26 rpm.

Item 1f: Zenatello's final "atroce!" preceding Noto's "Non pensateci" on CR 497-1, was omitted here. The original playing speed is 78.26 rpm.

Side 2 (144 B):

Item 1a: Only the last part of 2M 240-1 ("E qual certezza . . . Udite") and the first part of 2M 190-7 ("Era la notte . . . in ceco letargo si mutò") were used here. The beginning of the "Sì pel ciel" duet, "Oh! mostruosa colpa! . . . lo vidi in man di Cassio" that finishes 2M 190-7 is cut. CVS-73217 and CVS-73218 were the matrix numbers assigned by Victor (sides 15 and 16 in sets M-152 and AM-152: catalog numbers 11370 and 11386 correspond to these sides). The original playing speed for both sides is 77.00 rpm, both having been transferred nearly a half step high on EJS 144.

Item 1b: The original playing speed is 78.26 rpm.

Item 1c: The final fifteen orchestral bars at the end of Scene IV which conclude CR 500-1 are omitted here. Transferred slightly below pitch on EJS 144, though the original playing speed is 78.26 rpm.

Item 1d: Transferred on EJS 144 nearly a half step high, though again, the original playing speed is 78.26 rpm.

Items 1e-f: The original playing speed of the three Melba excerpts is 78.26 rpm. See also the note for band 1c above, and the endnotes for EJS 127 (1958).

Item 1g: The original playing speed is 78.26.

EJS 145: "The Golden Age of Opera" (2 LPs)
Issued February, 1959

SIDES 1-3 (145 A-C):

ELEKTRA (R. Strauss) (G)
Opera in 1 Act (abridged "Concert Version")
New York Philharmonic Orchestra/Artur Rodzinski
Broadcast, ***NEW YORK PHILHARMONIC***, WABC, NYC, 21 Mar 1937

CAST:
Rose Pauly (*Elektra*); Charlotte Boerner (*Klytemnestra*); Enid Szantho (*Chrysothemis*); Julius Huehn (*Oreste*); Frederick Jagel (*Aegisthus*); Abrasha Robovsky (*Foster Father of Orestes*); Abrasha Robovsky (*An Old Servant*).

SIDE 4 (145 D):

TANNHÄUSER (Wagner) (G)
Opera in 3 Acts (excerpts)
Metropolitan Opera House Orchestra and Chorus/Erich Leinsdorf
Metropolitan Opera broadcast, NYC, 16 Dec 1939

CAST:
[Emanuel List (*Hermann*)]; Eyvind Laholm (*Tannhäuser*); [Herbert Janssen (*Wolfram*)]; [John Carter (*Walther*)]; [Mack Harrell (*Biterolf*)]; [Giordano Paltrinieri (*Heinrich*)]; [John Gurney (*Reinmar*)]; [Kirsten Flagstad (*Elisabeth*)]; Rose Pauly (*Venus*); [Maxine Stellman (*Shepherd*)].

1. Act I/ii: PAULY and LAHOLM: Geliebter, sag' wo weilt dein Sinn? . . . to end of the Venusburg Scene

NOTES: EJS 145

Sides 1-3 (145 A-C):

Singers responsible for the smaller parts have not been identified. The ELEKTRA is presented complete on EJS 145 as performed in this "concert version," with the following cuts observed:

a) from the end of the opening chords to the beginning of *Elektra's* "Allein! Weh, ganz allein" (pp. 5-20 in the 1908 Fürstner piano-vocal score/reprinted in 1943 by Boosey and Hawkes).

b) from the orchestral "Sehr schnell" immediately preceding *Clytaemnestra's* dialogue, "Lichter! . . . Mehr Lichter!" to *Orest's* "Ich muss hier warten" in the *Elektra-Orest* duet (pp. 115-116).

c) Small cut in the *Maids'* ensemble, "Sie schreit so aus dem Schlaf" (beginning page 210).

The same performance, in improved sound, was reissued in January-February, 1977 as UORC 322.

Side 4 (145 D):

Presented here is the Venusburg scene, without the Overture. Only Pauly and Laholm are heard in this Act I/ii excerpt.

Flagstad's "Dich, teure Halle" from this performance was included on EJS 258 (January, 1963).

Library of Congress tape 5174-7 (complete broadcast).

EJS 146: "The Golden Age of Opera" (2 LPs)
Issued February, 1959

SIDES 1-4 (146 A-D):

OBERTO, CONTE DI SAN BONIFACIO (Verdi) (I)
Opera in 2 Acts (complete)
Orchestra and Chorus of Radio Italiana [RAI], Turin/Alfredo Simonetto
RAI broadcast, Turin, 26 Apr 1951

CAST:
Maria Vitale (*Leonora*); Giuseppe Modesti (*Oberto*); Gino Bonelli (*Riccardo*); Elena Nicolai (*Cuniza*); Lydia Roan (*Imelda*).

NOTES: EJS 146

Reported to play a half-step lower than score pitch at 33.3 rpm. The original February, 1959 bulletin gives the cast as Maria Caniglia, Elena Nicolai, Gianni Poggi, and Tancredi Pasero, with the date 1951; the RAI chronology give the cast as listed above. The Riccardo sounds like Poggi, and no other Bonelli recordings or broadcasts were available to make a detailed comparison (this was apparently his only RAI broadcast). Riccardo's Act I "Son fra voi!" later appeared on EJS 575 (November, 1971), also labeled as by Poggi. Maria Vitale's Act I "Sotto il paterno tetto" was included on EJS 576 (November, 1971).

La Scala subsequently produced OBERTO for the 150th anniversary of Verdi's birth, beginning on 13 February, 1952. The cast included Caniglia, Stignani. Poggi, and Passero (later replaced by Modesti), conducted by Franco Capuana. No other performances of the work were given until a concert performance in London in 1965 (the opera was later revived in Bologne in 1977 and in New York in 1978).

There is little doubt that the performance on EJS 146 is an RAI studio production and not a Scala broadcast--if nothing else, there are no audience noises and no applause. Not having gained access to the RAI archives by 1959, and having heard of the 1952 Scala production, Smith may have unwittingly created the Scala-RAI *composite* cast given in the bulletin.

Parsons' opera discography (the *Mellen Opera Reference Index* series) notes that an Estro Armonico LP (EA-038) was issued as by the RAI cast given in the listing above, but dated 26 *June*, 1951, which may have been Parson's error, Estro Armonico's, or the date of an RAI re-broadcast.

EJS 147: "The Golden Age of Opera" (3 LPs)
Issued March, 1959

SIDES 1-6 (147 A-F):

AÏDA (Verdi) (I)
Opera in 4 Acts (complete)
Metropolitan Opera House Orchestra and Chorus/Ettore Panizza
Metropolitan Opera broadcast, NYC, 6 Feb 1937

CAST:
Norman Cordon (*King of Egypt*); Bruna Castagna (*Amneris*); Gina Cigna (*Aïda*); Giovanni Martinelli (*Radames*); Ezio Pinza (*Ramfis*); Carlo Morelli (*Amonasro*); Giordano Paltrinieri (*Messenger*); Thelma Votipka (*Priestess*).

NOTES: EJS 147:

This Aïda was the Metropolitan Opera debut of soprano Gina Cigna. EJS 147 contains a portion of the Milton Cross commentary following Act III, in which novelist Marcia Davenport bursts into the broadcasting booth to proclaim Cigna's debut the most exciting since Flagstad's (which was only two years earlier, on 2 February, 1935!). Davenport's remark, "It's [Cigna's debut] the biggest news to hit the Italian wing in some time," can be heard on EJS 147.

Library of Congress tape: 15731-87A (complete broadcast).

EJS 148: "The Golden Age of Opera" (1 LP)
Issued March, 1959

BELSHAZZAR (Handel) (E)
Oratorio in 3 Acts (adaptation: Acts II and III only)
Pasadena Civic Orchestra and Festival Chorus/Dr. Richard Lert; William Bergren, assistant conductor
Broadcast, Pasadena Music Festival, Pasadena Civic Auditorium, Pasadena, California, KHJ [Mutual Broadcasting System], Thursday, 23 May 1940
Limited-edition, private 78 rpm pressings, AN-1 through AN-12

CAST:
Charles Kullman (*Belshazzar*); Elizabeth Rethberg (*Nitocris*); [Stan Englund (*Daniel*)]; Joseph (later Brian) Sullivan (*Gobrias*); Douglas Beattie (*Cyrus*); [? (*Arioch*)]; [? (*Messenger*)]; Carla Peterson (*?choir soloist*); Ruth Terry Koechig (*?choir soloist*).

SIDE 1 (148 A):

Act I:
1) KULLMAN: Let Festal joy triumphant reign . . . Each hand the chime melodious raise [internal cuts]
2) RETHBERG and KULLMAN: Recitative: For You, my friends . . . I must prevent thee, son [internal cuts and text changes]
3) RETHBERG and KULLMAN: Recitative: It is the Custom [internal cuts and text changes]
4) CHORUS: Recall, O King [first 8 and last 12 measures]
5) RETHBERG and KULLMAN: They tell you true [first 2 measures] . . . Away! Is then my mother [first 10 measures]
* 6) RETHBERG and KULLMAN: Oh dearer than my life, forbear [internal cuts]

Act II:
* 7) CHORUS: Ye Almighty Gods ("Ye tutelar Gods") [internal cuts and text changes]
8) KULLMAN: Recitative: Where is the God of Judah's boasted pow'r? [internal cuts]
* 9) CHORUS: [Allegro] Sesach!
10) KULLMAN and CHORUS: Oh! Help! Help the King! [text changes]
11) KULLMAN: Call all my wisemen [text changes]
* 12) CHORUS OF WISEMEN (TTB): Alas! too hard a task the King
13) CHORUS: O misery, oh terror! [first 3 measures]
14) RETHBERG: Recitative: Oh king, live forever [internal cuts and text changes]
* 15) ORCHESTRA: "Sinfonia"
16) KULLMAN: Recitative: Art thou Daniel of the Jewish captives? [first 2 measures]
17) KULLMAN: Recitative: . . . I'll read this oracle [internal cuts and text changes]

18) KULLMAN: Recitative: . . . From God the hand was sent . . . The God, whom thou hast dishonored [text changes]
* 19) CHORUS: He Comes

SIDE 2 (148-B):

* 20) CHORUS: See, see from his post Euphrates
21) BEATTIE: You see, my friends, a path to the city [internal cuts and text changes]
* 22) CHORUS: [without text: hummed]

Act III: * 23) ORCHESTRA: "Battle Music"
* 24) RETHBERG: Recitative: All's lost! The fate of Babylon is come! [internal cuts and text changes]
* 25) KULLMAN: Cyrus has conquered Babylon
* 26) RETHBERG and KULLMAN: Recitative and Aria: My Mother, I am dying ["Belshazzar's Death"]
* 27) RETHBERG: I weep and lament
* 28) SULLIVAN: Recitative: To pow'r immortal my first thanks are due [internal cuts]
* 29) PETERSON, KOECHIG, ?SULLIVAN, ?BEATTIE, and CHORUS: Tell it out among the heathen [internal cuts and text changes]
30) BEATTIE: Yes, I will build thy city [internal cuts and text changes]

[Act I]: 31) CHORUS: O glorious Prince [internal cuts and text changes]

NOTES: EJS 148

The edition used for this adaptation was prepared by the conductor, Richard Lert (1885-?). The *Los Angeles Times* mentioned on 19 May, 1940 that "Dr. Lert, recognized authority on Handel's music, has written the orchestration . . . from the original score and has rearranged and dramatized the libretto." Certainly, his version differs significantly from the Chrysander edition of 1864 in content, setting, text, and orchestration. The *Pasadena Star-News* of 25 May, 1940 noted that "neither the verses of the text" or the "soli and choral episodes" were "designated in the customary manner"--Handel's evidently. This live concert performance is at best a sampling of the three-act oratorio: many numbers have been omitted, and those performed are generally shortened, often to less than half their intended length. The recitatives especially have been truncated beyond recognition.

Cyrus was originally scored for contralto, and *Gobrias* for bass, but as is common practice with music of this period, the parts are often reassigned--as was the case in this performance. The parts of *Daniel* (contralto), the *Messenger* (bass), and *Arioch* (tenor) are not heard on EJS 148, and may not have been performed. What part baritone Stan Englund actually sang is unknown, as no baritone soloist appears on EJS 148.

This fifth Pasadena Music Festival, presented by the Festival Association, took place between Monday, 3 June, and Sunday, 9 June, 1940. BELSHAZZAR was proclaimed "the first major performance [of the work] in America." The chorus consisted of 200 voices.

The 78 rpm set that served as the source of this LP was a private issue of six twelve-inch discs. The broadcast, over KHJ, Los Angeles (Mutual Network), was heard locally, as well as on a hookup of some 117 other Mutual affiliates, probably all of them west of the Mississippi. BELSHAZZAR was not broadcast in New York, Minneapolis, or Boston, and only the second and third acts were heard anywhere on the air. Side AN-6 of the original set contains only applause, cast bows, and station identification; similarly, side AN-12 consists of applause, final announcements, and cast identification.

Internal cuts, textual changes, and specific *performance* omissions are noted below against the Chrysander edition, which was still considered definitive at the time.

Side 1 (148 A):

No. 6: The orchestral introduction was omitted.
No. 7: The second "Allegro" section was omitted.
No. 9: The repeat used for this chorus is not designated in the score.
No. 12: The introduction used for this number is not designated in the score
No. 15: Not found in the score: this is not the "Sinfonia" provided by the composer.
No. 19: Not found in the score.

Side 2 (148 B):

No. 20: The "Why, faithless river" section omitted.
No. 22: This humming chorus is not found in the score.
No. 23: This is not the "Martial Symphony" provided by the composer.
No. 24: The "All's lost!" recitative is written for the Messenger, but performed here by Nitocris.
No. 25: Not found in the score.
No. 26: This recitative and aria, titled "Belshazzar's Death" on the original 78s, is not found in the score.
No. 27: Not found in the score.

EJS 149: "The Golden Age of Opera" (2 LPs)
Issued April, 1959

SIDES 1-4 (149 A-D):

MANON (Massenet) (F)
Opera in 4 Acts (abridged)
Metropolitan Opera House Orchestra and Chorus/Wilfred Pelletier
Metropolitan Opera broadcast, NYC, 13 Jan 1940

CAST:
Grace Moore (*Manon*); Annamary Dickie (*Pousette*); Maxine Stellman (*Javotte*); Lucielle Browning (*Rosette*); Richard Crooks (*Des Grieux*); John Brownlee (*Lescaut*); Nicola Moscona (*Count Des Grieux*); Alessio DePaolis (*Guillot*); George Cehanovsky (*De Bretigny*); Louis D'Angelo (*Inkeeper*); Max Altglas (*Guard*); Arnold Gabor (*Guard*); Gina Gola (*Servant*).

NOTES: EJS 149

The abridgement of MANON presented here was apparently the one used frequently by the Met during the 1930s and 1940s, with the work lasting about two hours. Act III, in particular, was all but omitted: Moore's "Gavotte," accordingly, being incorporated into Act IV in place of "Ce bruit de l'or" when the "Coeur-la-Riene" scene was cut. The orchestral Preludes of both the first and second acts were also omitted, but these seem more likely to have been cuts made by Smith for timing purposes when preparing the LP.

The sound quality of EJS 149 is unusually poor, though the constant level problems may suggest faulty source material. The whole performance, moreover, seems to have been transferred high, so that a playing speed of just under 32.0 rpm is required to secure score pitch.

The MANON excerpts on a later Richard Crooks recital (EJS 488, issued November, 1969) appear to be from this performance, in considerably better sound.

Library of Congress tape: 8944-8 (complete broadcast).

EJS 150: "The Golden Age of Opera" (2 LPs)
Issued April, 1959

SIDES 1-4 (150 A-D):

MIGNON (Thomas) (F)
Opera in 3 Acts (abridged)
Metropolitan Opera House Orchestra and Chorus/Wilfred Pelletier
Metropolitan Opera broadcast, NYC, 13 Mar 1937

CAST:
Gladys Swarthout (*Mignon*); Josephine Antoine (*Philine*); Charles Hackett (*Wilhelm Meister*); Ezio Pinza (*Lothario*); Angelo Bada (*Laerte*); Norman Cordon (*Jarno*); Helen Olheim (*Frederic*); Norman Cordon (*Antonio*).

NOTES: EJS 150

The abridgement of this performance is primarily orchestral, but little bits and pieces are cut throughout the score. The principal omissions are the Overture and the beginning of Act III (the introduction and the opening chorus), which then begins with *Lothario's Berçeuse*, "De son coeur j'ai calmé."

Speeds are inconsistent: Acts I and II play at about 32.5 rpm, but Act III is in pitch at closer to 33.00 rpm.

The Library of Congress tape: 15731-96A (complete broadcast).

EJS 151: "The Golden Age of Opera" (2 LPs)
Issued May, 1959

SIDES 1-4 (151 A-D):

LINDA DI CHAMOUNIX (Donizetti) (I)
Opera in 3 Acts (complete)
Orchestra and Chorus of Radio Italiana [RAI], Milano/Alfredo Simonetto
RAI broadcast, Milan, 23 Jul 1953

CAST:
Margherita Carosio (*Linda*); Rina Corsi (*Pierotto*); Gianni Raimondi (*Charles*); Giuseppe Taddei (*Antonio*); Giuseppe Modesti (*Prefect*); Carlo Badioli (*Marquis de Boisfleury*); Maria Teresa Mandalari (*Maddalena*); Guglielmo Fazzini (*Intendant*).

NOTES: EJS 151

This performance subsequently appeared as MRF 115.

EJS 152: "The Golden Age of Opera" (2 LPs)
Issued May, 1959

SIDES 1-4 (152 A-D):

LA FILLE DU REGIMENT (Donizetti) (F)
Opera in 2 Acts (complete)
Metropolitan Opera House Orchestra and Chorus/Gennaro Papi
Metropolitan Opera broadcast, NYC, 28 Dec 1940

CAST:
Lily Pons (*Marie*); Irra Petina (*Marquis*); Salvatore Baccaloni (*Sulpice*); Raoul Jobin (*Tonio*); Louis D'Angelo (*Hortentius*); Wilfred Engelman (*Corporal*); Lodovico Oliviero (*Peasant*); Maria Savage (*Duchesse de Crakentorp*).

NOTES: EJS 152

"La Marseillaise" was interpolated as the Act II Finale in this performance.

First pressings of EJS 152 were found to have defective third and fourth sides (152 C-D). Smith offered replacements of the second disc in the ninth and tenth EJS bulletins (June and August, 1959).

Library of Congress tape: 7749-17A (complete broadcast).

EJS 153: "The Golden Age of Opera" (2 LPs)
Issued August, 1959

SIDES 1-4 (153 A-D):

LAKMÉ (Delibes) (F)
Opera in 3 Acts (complete)
Metropolitan Opera House Orchestra and Chorus/Wilfred Pelletier
Metropolitan Opera broadcast, NYC, 6 Jan 1940

CAST:
Lily Pons (*Lakmé*); Irra Petina (*Mallika*); Annamary Dickie (*Ellen*); Lucielle Browning (*Rose*); Helen Olheim (*Mrs. Benson*); Armand Tokatyan (*Gérald*); Ezio Pinza (*Nilakantha*); George Cehanovsky (*Frederic*); Nicholas (Nicola) Massue (*Hadji*); Lodovico Oliviero (*Fortune Teller*); Lamberto Belleri (*Chinese Merchant*); Wilfred Engelman (*Thief*).

NOTES: EJS 153

Issued slightly out of sequence: the bulletin for June, 1959 carried EJS 155-157, while EJS 153, 154, and 158 were announced in August. There, Smith claimed that the 6 January, 1940 Met broadcast was the earliest complete live performance of LAKMÉ to have survived.

The performance is preserved here complete, evidently as performed, without even orchestral abridgement.

Speeds have been reported to run as high as 33.8 rpm for sides 3 and 4.

The performance later appeared on the Munich-based Discophilia label (DIS/KS-13/15) and on Operatic Archives OPA-1045.

Library of Congress tape: 5174-31 (complete broadcast).

EJS 154: "The Golden Age of Opera" (2 LPs)
Issued August, 1959

SIDES 1-4 (154 A-D):

ROMÉO ET JULIETTE (Gounod) (F)
Opera in 4 Acts (complete)
Metropolitan Opera House Orchestra and Chorus/Emil Cooper
Metropolitan Opera broadcast, NYC, 1 Feb 1947

CAST:
Bidú Sayão (*Juliette*); Mimi Benzell (*Stephano*); Claramae Turner (*Gertrude*); Jussi Bjoerling (*Roméo*); Thomas Hayward (*Tybalt*); Anthony Marlowe (*Benvolio*); John Brownlee (*Mercutio*); George Cehanovsky (*Paris*); Philip Kinsman (*Gregorio*); Kenneth Schon (*Capulet*); Nicola Moscona (*Friar Laurence*); William Hargrave (*Duke of Verona*).

NOTES: EJS 154

This performance is complete as performed, except for the substitution of Sayão's commercial Columbia recording of *Juliette's* "Waltz Song" conducted by Leinsdorf (XCO 31073-1, recorded on 18 August, 1941 and issued as Columbia 17301-D). The plug begins immediately after the orchestral introduction, at "Ah! [je veux vivre]," and continues to the last of the three trills on "Longtemps encor," where the broadcast version is once again restored. The later Toscanini Society issue of the performance (ATS 101-2) also contains this commercial insert. The Met LP reissue used a recently-discovered acetate of Sayão's 1 February, 1947 "Waltz Song." Another unconfirmed report claims that Bjoerling's "Ah! lève-toi soleil" has been inserted on EJS 154 from his commercial recording (2SB 2535-2, recorded in Stockholm, 6 September, 1945, Nils Grevillius, conducting, issued as HMV DB 6249 and Victor 12-0527).

Speeds for EJS 154 are inconsistent: a lenghty and detailed report of this set concluded that all four sides undergo frequent shifts in pitch, many of them abrupt and disorienting. Whether this was a fault of the original transcriptions or something that occurred during their dubbing is not known.

Portions of this broadcast have also appeared on Rococo 5329 (Bjoerling, Vol. 6, "Gounod Recital"), Opera Archives OPA 1008, a Sayão recital, and UORC 350 (September-October, 1977). The commercial "Waltz Song" has appeared on the Odyssey LP Y31151 (1972).

Conductor Emil Cooper (née Kuper, the name under which he recorded with the St. Petersburg Symphony for Polydor) was Russian by birth, a pupil of Nikisch. Before coming to the Met during the 1944 season, he had conducted at the Chicago Civic Opera (1929-1932 and 1939-1943). He was at the Met until 1950, and directed a number of important American and house premieres, including Musorgsky's KHOVANSHCHINA during his last season (a complete performance of the opera under his direction--from the debut season--was issued on UORC 295 in May-June, 1976, excerpts having appeared earlier as EJS 261 in March, 1963).

EJS 155: "The Golden Age of Opera" (2 LPs)
Issued June, 1959

SIDES 1-4 (155 A-D):

I DUE FOSCARI (Verdi) (I)
Opera in 3 Acts (complete)
Orchestra and Chorus of the Teatro La Fenice, Venice/Tullio Serafin
RAI broadcast, Teatro La Fenice, Venice, 27 Dec 1957

CAST:
Leyla Gencer (*Lucrezia Contarini*); Mirto Picchi (*Jacopo Foscari*); Gian Giacomo Guelfi (*Francesco Foscari*); Alessandro Maddalena (*Jacopo Loredano*); Ottorino Begali (*Barbarigo*); Marisa Salimbene (*Pisana*); Augusto Veronese (*An Officer*); Umberto Scaglione (*Servant*).

NOTES: EJS 155

Dated in the June, 1959 bulletin as 31 December, 1957, where the Cella Gencer biography insists that it was the *first* performance of the production on 27 December that was actually broadcast. The Cetra issue of the complete performance (LO-67/2) also cites 31 December, while the Gioielli della Lirica excerpts on GML 76 observe Cella's date.

Gencer's cabaletta and aria, "Tu al cui sguardo," complete with the recitative, are also found on EJS 421, a Gencer recital issued January, 1968. The complete performance was issued recently as Melodram MEL-465.

Speed is low on this set, requiring 34.5 rpm to compensate.

EJS 156: "The Golden Age of Opera" (2 LPs)
Issued June, 1959

SIDES 1-4 (156 A-D):

AROLDO (Verdi) (I)
Opera in 4 Acts (complete)
Orchestra and Chorus of Radio Italiana [RAI], Torino/Arturo Basile
RAI broadcast, Turin, 24 Oct 1951

CAST:
Maria Vitale (*Mina*); Vasco Campagnano (*Aroldo*); Rolando Panerai (*Egberto*); Gianfelice De Manuelli (*Briano*); Miti Truccato Pace (*Elena*); Aldo Bertocci (*Godvino*); Tommaso Soley (*Enrico*).

NOTES: EJS 156

This relatively obscure opera premiered in Rimini on 16 August, 1857. It was a revision of Verdi's own 1850 opera STIFFELIO, with an added fourth act. Both works are based on the same Piave libretto.

This performance also appeared on a ten-LP Cetra set entitled "Maria Vitale," which also included a 5 April, 1952 RAI broadcast of Mercadante's IL GIURAMENTO and the 16 August, 1953 RAI broadcast of ELISABETTA, REGINA D'INGHILTERRA that had appeared earlier as EJS 133 (1958).

Two excerpts from this performance, in better sound, were later included in the STIFFELIO issue, EJS 333 (May, 1965).

EJS 157: "The Golden Age of Opera" (3 LPs)
Issued June, 1959

SIDES 1-6 (157 A-F):

TRISTAN UND ISOLDE (Wagner) (G)
Opera in 3 Acts (abridged)
Metropolitan Opera House Orchestra and Chorus/Artur Bodanzky
Metropolitan Opera broadcast, NYC, 2 Jan 1937

CAST:
Lauritz Melchior (*Tristan*); Kirsten Flagstad (*Isolde*); Ludwig Hofmann (*King Mark*); Julius Huehn (*Kurvenal*); Arnold Gabor (*Melot*); Kerstin Thorborg (*Brangäne*); Hans Clemens (*Shepherd*); James Wolfe (*Steersman*); Karl Laufkoetter (*Sailor's Voice*).

NOTES: EJS 157

Apart from the omission of the Act I Prelude, this performance is presented on EJS 157 complete as performed. A number of performance cuts were made, however, conforming to Bodanzky's standard TRISTAN cuts. These are listed below, using the page-system-measure numbers of the Schirmer piano-vocal score:

Act I: complete except for the Prelude

Act II: 141/4/4: ". . . bot ich dem Tage Trutz!" to 157/4/5: ". . . Doch es rächte" (321 measures)
173/2/4: "Lass den Tag dem Tode weichen!" to 177/5/1: "So stürben wir" (85 measures)
201/4/3: ". . . da Tristan mich verreith?" to 204/4/1: "Diess wundervolle Weib" (48 measures)

Act III: 230/1/1: ". . . noch dir, Isolden, scheint!" to 233/5/3: "Ach, Isolde, süsse holde!" (69 measures)
246/2/4: "Noch ist kein Schiff" to 249/2/1: "Die alte Weise sagt mir's weider" (57 measures)
250/2/3: "vor Sehnsucht nicht zu sterben!" to 253/3/3: "Wie vom Herz zum Hirn" (58 measures)
280/3/1: "uns Beiden vereint erlösche" to 282/3/4: "Tristan! Ha! horch! Er wacht!" (42 measures)

The other Bodanzky cut, 290/2/3: "Todt den Alles! Alles Todt!" to 293/2/3: "Der Wahn häufte die Noth!" observed in the 9 March, 1935 TRISTAN (issued on Smith's "Goldene Aera Richard Wagners" set, GAW 300) was not made in the 1937 broadcast--this 53-measure passage is intact on EJS 157.

Grateful acknowlegment is made to David Hamilton's article, "Tristan in the Thirties: Part I," in the *Musical Newsletter*, 6/4 (Fall, 1976), pp. 22-23. Hamilton estimates that the 733 measures cut represent "something like thirteen percent of the opera," and continues: "Their effect on its proportions is actually more serious, because they are concentrated in only two acts: thus, 22% of Act II, 16% of Act III." (p. 23).

Library of Congress tape: 5174-18 (complete broadcast).

EJS 158: "The Golden Age of Opera" (2 LPs)
Issued August, 1959

SIDES 1-4 (158 A-D):

SALOME (R. Strauss) (G)
Opera in 1 Act (complete)
Metropolitan Opera House Orchestra and Chorus/Fritz Reiner
Metropolitan Opera broadcast, NYC, 12 Mar 1949

CAST:
Frederick Jagel (*Herod*); Kerstin Thorborg (*Herodias*); Ljuba Welitsch (*Salome*); Herbert Janssen (*Jokanaan*); Brian Sullivan (*Narraboth*); Hertha Glaz (*Herodias' Page*); Dezso Ernster (*First Nazarene*); Emery Darcy (*Second Nazarene*).

NOTES: EJS 158

This 1949 performance has been issued on at least three other private LPs: MFR 1, BJR 156-2, and Melodram 039 (later Melodram CD 27042). The 19 January, 1952 Met performance, also with Welitsch, appeared on SJS 701/2, a private label, and on a limited-edition Metropolitan Opera Guild LP (Met 9), coupled with Varnay's 23 February, 1952 ELEKTRA. Portions of Welitsch's 1944 Viennese broadcast, conducted by Lovro von Matačič, have been issued with some frequency on commercial labels, most recently on a Pathé-Marconi EMI Welitsch recital (1012671 M) transferred by Keith Hardwick. Melodram LP 041 contains the commercial HMV version conducted by Beecham, recorded in London 27-29 October, 1947, with Welitsch, Schlüter, Widdop, and Schöffler.

The EJS 158 Finale has been reported by one reputable source as possibly containing patches from the Welisch-Reiner studio recording with the Metropolitan Opera House Orchestra, made in New York, 14 March, 1949, and originally issued in the U.S. as Columbia Set MX-316 (subequently on Columbia LPs ML 2048 [ten-inch] and ML 4795 [twelve-inch], and in 1967 on Odyssey 32 16 077, a Welitsch recital). Details of the commercial Finale, performed without *Herod* and *Herodias*, are as follows:

1. "Ah! Du wolltest mich nicht deiner Mund Küssen lassen"
   XCO-41067-1A 72818-D LX 1241 NY, 14 March, 1949
2. "Öffne doch die Augen"
   XCO-41068-1A 72818-D LX 1241 NY, 14 March, 1949
3. "Oh! Warum hast du mich nicht angesehn, Jochanaan"
   XCO-41069-1A 72819-D LX 1242 NY, 14 March, 1949
4. "Ah! Ich habe ihn geküsst, deinen Mund"
   XCO-41070-1A 72819-D LX 1242 NY, 14 March, 1949

In part three (XCO-41069-1A), the 21-measure *Herod-Herodias* section beginning "Sie ist ein Ungeheuer" is cut to just before rehearsal no. 355; in part four (XCO-41070-1A), *Herod's* "Man töte dieses Weib!" (2 measures) is taken by the orchestra.

Repeated listening and careful analysis has not revealed any "patch" work on EJS 158. I tender the following comparative observations:

1. Sides 1 and 2 of EJS 158 play uniformly in score pitch at 34.5 rpm, while sides 3 and 4 do the same at 31.8 rpm. Some very careful editing would have been required for any insertions, and generally speaking, Smith's patch work is betrayed by careless pitching.

2. The sound throughout the EJS 158 Finale is of uniformly broadcast quality: this is obvious even in spite of the poor surface quality of the LP.

3. There are numerous differences in Welitsch's phrasing throughout the commercial and the live Finales.

4. One measure before rehearsal no. 333, Welitsch's E-sharp ("schön") is flat in the 1949 broadcast, but not on XCO-41068-1A; similarly, five measures before rehearsal no. 337, her A-sharp ("welt war nichts") is flat in the broadcast, but not on XCO-41068-1A.

5. Two measures after rehearsal no. 340, there is a broadcast "beep" (perhaps to announce the hour?) on EJS 158 just before "Warum has du mich" that obviously would have had to have been deliberately dubbed over XCO-41069-1A. Smith rarely went to such lengths to conceal his "creative editing."

6. In the tenth and eleventh measures after rehearsal no. 340, there is a 21-measure cut on EJS 158 between "Augen die Binde eines" and "Ich durste nach deiner Schönheit" (one measure before rehearsal no. 344). Why, if the commercial recording was being used to supplement the broadcast, was this passage not restored by simply patching in that portion from XCO-41069-1A?

7. Two measures after rehearsal no. 360, the A-sharp ("geküsst") is flat in the broadcast, but not on XCO-41070-1A. Moreover, other signs of Welitsch's fatigue are present as we near the end of this live performance.

8. Just before rehearsal no. 351, *Herod* (Jagel) and *Herodias* (Thorborg) are present in the EJS 158 broadcast ("Sie ist ein Ungeheuer"/"Meine Tochter hat recht getan"), and on the last page, Jagel is again heard. The *Herod-Herodias* section is omitted on XCO-41069-1A and the five-measure "Man töte dieses Weib!" is taken only by the orchestra on XCO-41070-1A.

In light of these differences between the 1949 Met Finale and the commercial recording, it would appear that only the smallest portions of the second through fourth sides of the Columbia set could possibly have been used to supplement the broadcast (which subsequent LP reissues show needed no supplementing). With the arena of possible tampering so confined, I am unable to endorse the notion that portions of the commercial Welitsch Finale have been used on the EJS 158 Finale.

It has been suggested that perhaps two editions of EJS 158 might have been prepared, one with inserts, another without. I have reported here from an early pressing of the Smith issue (brown and white label). It is hoped that suspicious collectors will make their own detailed comparisons of the Finale using the various issues of the 1949 and 1952 Met broadcasts, the 1944 Viennese broadcast, and the commercial Columbia issue. Possibly Smith used portions of the November, 1948 Welitsch Finale mounted by Walter Legge and conducted by Karajan, which featured Gertrud Schuster as *Herodias* and Josef Witt as *Herod*. This was not made commercially available by EMI until the late 1970s because of the damaged second side, but the ever-resourceful Mr. Smith may well have had access to some 'underground' source of this recording as early as 1959.

EJS 159: "The Golden Age of Opera" (2 LPs)
Issued September, 1959

SIDES 1-4 (159 A-D):

I CAPULETTI ED I MONTECCHI (Bellini) (I)
Opera in 2 Acts (complete)
Orchestra and Chorus of Radio Italiana [RAI], Roma/Lorin Maazel
RAI broadcast, Rome, 23 Oct 1958

CAST:
Antonietta Pastori (*Giulietta*); Fiorenza Cossotto (*Romeo*); Renato Gavarini (*Tebaldo*); Ivo Vinco (*Lorenzo*); Vittorio Tatozzi (*Capellio*).

NOTES: EJS 159

The label of EJS 159 and the 1970s EJS checklist give 1957 as the date of this performance.

A uniform speed of 32.7 rpm is reported for this issue, which was recorded at an unusually low level.

This performance was later issued as Melodram MEL-003.

EJS 160: "The Golden Age of Opera" (2 LPs)
Issued September, 1959

SIDES 1-4 (160 A-D):

IL PIRATA (Bellini) (I)
Opera in 2 Acts (complete)
Orchestra and Chorus of Radio Italiana [RAI], Torino/Mario Rossi
RAI broadcast, Turin, 9 Feb 1958 (recorded 28 Jun 1957)

CAST:
Anna De Cavalieri (*Imogene*); Mirto Picchi (*Gualtiero*); Walter Monachesi (*Ernesto*); Miti Truccato Pace (*Adele*); Tommaso Spataro (*Itulbo*); [James] Thomas O'Leary (*Goffredo*).

NOTES: EJS 160

Reported to play at a uniform 34.00 rpm. Anna De Cavalieri was the Italian stage name of Anne McKnight.

The *recording* date given above was taken from Mirto Picchi's *Un Trono vicino al sol* (Ravenna: Edizioni del Girasole, 1978).

EJS 161: "The Golden Age of Opera" (1 LP)
Issued October, 1959

SIDES 1-2 (161 A-B):

EMILIA DI LIVERPOOL (Donizetti) (I)
Opera in 2 Acts (abridged and narrated)
Royal Liverpool Philharmonic Orchestra and Chorus/?John Pritchard
?BBC broadcast, Liverpool, 8 Sep 1957

CAST:
Joan Sutherland (*Emilia*); April Cantelo (*Candida*); April Cantelo (*Bettina*); William McAlpine (*Colonel Villars*); Dennis Dowling (*Claudio*); Hervey Alan (*Count Asdrubale*); Bernard Miles (*Narrator*).

NOTES: EJS 161

This abridged and narrated version of EMILIA DI LIVERPOOL is derived from an 1828 revision of the original 1824 score.

The VOCE-30 reissue gives John Pritchard as the conductor on the label and in its advertising, but cites Fritz Spiegl in the liner notes. The performance chronology in Norma Major's *Joan Sutherland* (London: Macdonald/Queen Anne Press, 1987) cites Pritchard as the conductor and the date as 8 September, 1957. As it turns out, the citation of Spiegl on the Voce LP was the result of a misunderstanding: an article on Fritz Spiegl in the 6 September, 1957 (London) *Radio Times* stated that this little-known Donizetti opera "will have its first broadcast performance in the Home Service on Sunday," meaning Sunday the 8th, but this was in fact a reference to the Pritchard performance included here. Speigl's production with the Liverpool Music Group, a concert version of the opera given to mark the 750th anniversary of Liverpool's city charter, had been given nearly three months before on 12 June, 1957, with Doreen Murray as *Emilia*.

McAlpine's character is listed as "Thomas" in Major's Sutherland biography.

Various pitch problems have been reported for EJS 161. The many label misspellings have been corrected in the listing above.

EJS 162: "The Golden Age of Opera" (2 LPs)
Issued October, 1959

SIDES 1-4 (162 A-D):

MARIA DI ROHAN (Donizetti) (I)
Opera in 3 Acts (complete)
Orchestra and Chorus of the Teatro Donizetti, Bergamo/Ettore Gracis
Broadcast, Teatro Donizetti, Bergamo, 30 Oct 1957

CAST:
Roma Sitran (*Maria*); Nicola Tagger (*Riccardo*); Anselmo Colzani (*Enrico*); Nello Romanato (*Armando di Gondi*); Giorgio Giorgetti (*Viscount di Suze*); Vito Susca (*De Fiesque*); Franco Ricciardi (*Aubrey*); Angelo Carli (*A Relative*).

NOTES: EJS 162

Reported to play sharp on all sides: 32.00 rpm has been estimated as the correct playing speed.

In keeping with the original Vienna version of the opera, which premiered on 5 June, 1843, *Armando di Gondi* is sung here by tenor Nello Romanato. Donizetti expanded the role for the Paris version, first heard about six months after the Vienna performance, at which time the role was assumed by contralto Marietta Brambilla (1807-1875). The contralto version seems to have been used for most modern-day performances, including revivals in Naples (1962) and at La Scala (mid 1970s). Flora Rafanelli sang the contralto version at the Teatro La Fenice revival with Scotto and Grilli on 20 March, 1974 (issued as MRF-103).

The 30 October, 1957 performance presented here was later issued on CD as Melodram MEL-151.

EJS 163: "The Golden Age of Opera" (2 LPs)
Issued October, 1959

SIDES 1-4 (163 A-D):

DON QUICHOTTE (DON CHISCIOTTE) (Massenet) (I)
Opera in 5 Acts (complete)
Orchestra and Chorus of Radio Italiana [RAI], Milano/Alfredo Simonetto
RAI broadcast, Milan, 6 Feb 1958

CAST:
Boris Christoff (*Don Quichotte*); Carlo Badioli (*Sancho*); Teresa Berganza (*Dulcinea*); Ornella Rovero (*Pedro*); Pina Malgarini (*Gracia*); Alfredo Nobile (*Rodriguez*); Tommaso Frascati (*Juan*); Carlo Bagno (*Bandit Chief*); Sergio Liviabella (*A Servant*); Tino Berri (*A Servant*); Carlo Castellani (*A Bandit*); Giampaolo Rossi (*A Bandit*); Gianni Bortolotto (*A Bandit*); Pier Luigi Pelitti (*A Bandit*).

NOTES: EJS 163

Complete as performed. The *Four Bandits* at the end of the cast list are speaking parts and are given here as they are found on early labels: their names are not given in the cast listing of the RAI chronology, but appear as above on the Fonit-Cetra issue of the performance (LAR-13). There are, in addition, several spelling errors on the original labels. The title DON QUICHOTTE is given on the records, where the italianate "DON CHISIOTTE" appears on the twelfth EJS bulletin.

The performance has also appeared as Rare Recorded Editions EA-039, and Melodram CD MEL 27027.

EJS 164: "The Golden Age of Opera" (3 LPs)
Issued November, 1959

SIDES 1-6 (164 A-F):

LOUISE (Charpentier) (F)
Opera in 4 Acts (complete)
Metropolitan Opera House Orchestra and Chorus/Sir Thomas Beecham
Metropolitan Opera broadcast, NYC, 20 Feb 1943

CAST:
Grace Moore (*Louise*); Raoul Jobin (*Julien*); Doris Doe (*Mother*); Ezio Pinza (*Father*); Maxine Stellman (*Irma*); Thelma Votipka (*Camille*); Irra Petina (*Gertrude*); Lillian Raymondi (*Apprentice*); Annamary Dickey (*Elise*); Helen Olheim (*Blanche*); Lucielle Browning (*Suzanne*); Maria Savage (*Forewoman*); Mary Van Kirk (*Marguerite*); Anna Kaskas (*Madeleine*); Wilfred Engelman (*Painter*); Lorenzo Alvery (*Philosopher*); Walter Cassel (*Philosopher*); Lodovico Oliviero (*Sculptor*); John Garris (*Poet*); John Dudley (*Student*); George Cehanovsky (*Song Writer*); Maria Savage (*Street Sweeper*); Mona Paulee (*Newspaper Girl*); Lucielle Browning (*Young Rag Picker*); Maxine Stellman (*Milk Woman*); Anna Kaskas (*Coal Picker*); Alessio DePaolis (*Sleep Walker*); Alessio DePaolis (*King of the Fools*); Emery Darcy (*Policeman*); Gerhard Pechner (*Policeman*); John Gurney (*Rag Picker*); Louis D'Angelo (*Junk Man*); Lillian Raymondi (*Street Arab*); John Dudley (*Old Clothes Man*); Tony D'Addozzio (*Bird Food Vendor*); Thelma Votipka (*Artichoke Vendor*); Anna Kaskas (*Watercress Vendor*); Anna Kaskas (*Chair Mendor*); Alessio DePaolis (*Carrot Vendor*); George Cehanovsky (*Rag Vendor*); John Dudley (*Green Peas Vendor*).

NOTES: EJS 164

Complete as broadcast, and in excellent sound. Pitch is reported to be inconsistent over the six sides, however, generally low: 33.8 rpm has been suggested as a base playing speed. Moore transposes her third-act "Depuis le jour" down a half-step.

Later reissued on one of Smith's "special" labels, MOP 1.

EJS 165: "The Golden Age of Opera" (2 LPs)
Issued November, 1959

SIDES 1-4 (165 A-D):

LA BOHÈME (Leoncavallo) (I)
Opera in 4 Acts (complete)
Orchestra and Chorus of the Teatro San Carlo di Napoli/Francesco Molinari-Pradelli
Broadcast, Teatro San Carlo, Naples, 8 Mar 1958

CAST:
Ettore Bastianini (*Rodolfo*); Doro Antonioli (*Marcello*); Rosetta Noli (*Mimi*); Mafalda Masini (*Musette*); Anna di Stasio (*Eufemia*); Walter Monachesi (*Schaunard*); Antonio Sacchetti (*Barbemuche*); Giuseppe Forgione (*Viscount Paolo*); Curzio Flemi (*Colline*); Piero de Palma (*Gaudenzio*); Piero de Palma (*Durand*); Pier Giovanni Filippi (*A Gentleman*); Pier Giovanni Filippi (*A Cad*).

NOTES: EJS 165

Complete as broadcast and, like EJS 164, presented in unusually good sound. Smith's note in the thirteenth EJS bulletin that this is the "Original Edition" of the 1897 Leoncavallo opera is misleading: he adds that "The Bohème is the first edition in which *Marcello* is a tenor and *Rodolfo* is a baritone," which makes it clear that he means only to distinguish Leoncavallo's version from Puccini's. Leoncavallo's was written first, but made its debut more than a year after the Puccini's.

The work was recorded commercially by Cetra in 1963 (LPC-1269). A 1980s revival of the work is reported to have contained nearly twenty minutes of music not contained on either the EJS or Cetra performances, so there were perhaps some "standard" cuts originally associated with the opera. Another commercial release of the opera, on Orfeo CD C-023822, appeared in 1983.

The 1958 live performance presented here was later issued as Melodram MEL-021.

EJS 166: "The Golden Age of Opera" (2 LPs)
Issued December, 1959

SIDES 1-4 (166 A-D):

ANNA BOLENA (Donizetti) (I)
Opera in 2 Acts (abridged)
Orchestra and Chorus of Radio Italiana [RAI], Milano/Gianandrea Gavazzeni
RAI broadcast, Milan, ?17 Jul 1958 (recorded ?11 Jul 1958)

CAST:
Leyla Gencer (*Anna Bolena*); Giulietta Simionato (*Giovanna Seymour*); Plinio Clabassi (*Enrico VIII*); Aldo Bertocci (*Percy*); Anna Maria Rota (*Smeton*); Silvio Maionica (*Lord Rochefort*); Mario Carlin (*Sir Hervey*).

NOTES: EJS 166

Note that the GÖTTERDÄMMERUNG set (EJS 167) was initially assigned the catalog numbers EJS 166 and 167 in error: the ANNA BOLENA is in fact EJS 166 and carries this number in the wax.

There are quite a few recording and broadcast dates given for this performance in various sources. Franca Cella's biography of Gencer, which includes a discography, cites 11 July, 1958 as the date of *recording*, while the label of Gioielli della Lirica GML 29, a Gencer LP recital, gives 17 July, 1958 as the *broadcast* date. Foyer 1015, on the other hand, gives 17 July, *1957* as the broadcast date (only the final scene of the performance is included on this LP), but "1957" is probably a typographical error. The RAI chronology says only that the ANNA BOLENA was broadcast during the 1958-1959 season (the performance itself was somehow omitted from the main body of the text in oversight).

If the performance was indeed recorded on Friday, 11 July, 1958, it is entirely possible that it was first aired on the following Thursday, 17 July, as RAI performances were most often taped for broadcast at a slightly later date during the 1950s. No re-broadcast dates have been reported.

Conductor Gavazzeni prepared the edition of ANNA BOLENA used for the April, 1957 La Scala revival with Callas (where Simionato had assumed the role of *Jane Seymour* and Clabassi the role of *Rochefort*). Presumably this is the version used for the RAI performance, though if so, it was certainly not transferred complete on EJS 166: there are a number of cuts (some of them consisting of whole numbers) made to accomodate the four sides allotted. There are also unintentional transfer cuts: *Anna's* last cavatina, "Al dolce guidami," is heard complete on the Gioielli della Lirica LP, where there is an internal cut on EJS, probably the result of a tape break.

Smith's later Gencer recital, EJS 421 (issued January, 1968), contains a complete ANNA BOLENA Finale beginning several pages before "Al dolce guidami," but this is a 23 November, 1965 RAI concert conducted by Basile. The first-act scene and Finale of the 1958 RAI performance are also found on side six of Robin Hood Records LP RHR 503-C, along with Gencer's live ROBERTO DEVREUX from Naples (issued complete on EJS 307 in October, 1964). There, however, the ANNA BOLENA excerpts are given as 1964!

The complete ?17 July, 1958 broadcast subsequently appeared on Replica RPL 2407/9 and Nuovo Era CD 67130-OM. Excerpts were included on Melodram 081, a two-LP Simionato recital.

The entire performance of ANNA BOLENA is reported to play in pitch at 33.3 rpm on EJS 166.

EJS 167: "The Golden Age of Opera" (2 LPs)
Issued December, 1959

GÖTTERDÄMMERUNG (Wagner) (G)
Opera in 3 Acts and a Prologue (excerpts)
a) Royal Opera House Orchestra and Chorus/Sir Thomas Beecham
Unpublished live performance recordings, Technical Test Series TT 2292-1/TT 2292-16, Covent Garden, London, 14 May 1936
b) Metropolitan Opera House Orchestra and Chorus/Artur Bodanzky
Special Metropolitan Opera broadcast, NYC, WJZ [NBC], 12 May 1939 (evening)
c) New York Philharmonic-Symphony Orchestra and Chorus of the Grand Opera Choral Alliance/Fritz Reiner
Lewisohn Stadium broadcast, WABC, NYC, 22 Jul 1937
d) New York Philharmonic Symphony (sic)/Bruno Walter
Broadcast, ***NEW YORK PHILHARMONIC***, WCBS, NYC, 23 March, 1952

CASTS:	a) 1936 Performance	b) 1939 Performance	c) 1937 Performance
Siegfried ...	Lauritz Melchior	Lauritz Melchior	[Paul Althouse]
Gunther ...	Herbert Janssen	[Julius Huehn]	[Julius Huehn]
Alberich ...	[Eduard Habich]	[Arnold Gabor]	-----
Hagen ...	Emanuel List	[Emanuel List]	[Hudson Carmody]
Brunhilde ...	Frida Leider	Kirsten Flagstad	Florence Easton
Gutrune ...	Maria Nežádal	[Dorothee Manski]	-----
Waltraute ...	Kerstin Thorborg	[Kerstin Thorborg]	Kathryn Meisle
Three Norns ..	[Mary Jarred]	Doris Doe	-----
...	[Constance Willis]	Lucielle Browning	-----
...	[Mae Craven]	Dorothee Manski	-----
Woglinde ...	[Stella Andreva]	[Thelma Votipka]	[Florence Kirk]
Wellgunde ...	[José Malone]	[Irra Petina]	[Irra Petina]
Flosshilde ...	[Margery Booth]	[Doris Doe]	[Edwina Eustis]

SIDES 1-2 (167 A-B):

1. Act I: LEIDER, THORBORG, and MELCHIOR: Altgewohntes Geraüsch . . . jagst du mich hin! (Waltraute Scene) (a)
TT 2292-1 - TT 2292-?

2. Act II: LEIDER, THORBORG, NEŽÁDAL, MELCHIOR, JANSSEN, and LIST: Gegrüsst sei, teurer Held! . . . to the end of the act (a)
TT 2292-? - TT 2292-?

SIDE 3 (167 C):

1. a) Prologue: FLAGSTAD, DOE, BROWNING, and MANSKI: Welch' Licht leuchtet dort? . . . Zur Mutter! Hinab! (Norn Scene) (b)

   b) Act I: FLAGSTAD and MELCHIOR: Zu neuen Taten . . . Heil! Heil! Heil! (b)

SIDE 4 (167 D):

1. Act I: FLORENCE EASTON and KATHRYN MEISLE: Altgewohntes Geräusch raunt meinem Ohr die Ferne . . . Verrath! (Waltraute Scene) (c)

2. Act III: KIRSTEN FLAGSTAD: Starke Scheite (Immolation Scene) (d)

NOTES: EJS 167

This issue was double-numbered EJS 166 and 167 on the original labels, though EJS 166 was later assigned to the ANNA BOLENA: "EJS 166" (A-D) is scratched in the wax of the GÖTTERDÄMMERUNG, however. Speeds are reported to be irregular over all four sides.

Sides 1-2 (167 A-B):

The Beecham performance was recorded by the Gramophone Company "live" from Covent Garden, 14 May, 1936, on Technical Test Series TT 2292-1/TT 2292-16. The excerpts recorded are not specified in Michael H. Gray's *Beecham: A Centenary Discography* (New York: Holmes & Meier, 1979), p. 32. Only Act III of the performance was broadcast, so, as in other instances, Smith *did* have access to the actual HMV test pressings, not broadcast transcriptions.

These same excerpts were later recycled as UORC 234 (January, 1975). The 29th UORC bulletin claims that eighteen minutes were added to the original 90-minute segment presented on EJS 167, pitches were corrected, and the sound quality much improved owing to the "superb sounding copies" used for the UORC reissue. The sound was certainly better, but pitches were by no means correct on UORC 234.

Side 3 (167 C):

The 1939 Met excerpts were taken from a special thirty-five minute broadcast on 12 May, 1939 (7:25-8:00 pm EST) over WJZ, New York City. This included the first and second scenes of GÖTTERDÄMMERUNG with Flagstad, Thorborg, Melchior, and the three *Norns* (the beginning of the opera to measure 749). The performance was given in honor of the Met's World's Fair Spring Season, calling back members of the previous evening's performance of the complete opera (see Seltsam's *Metropolitan Opera Annals*, p. 636). See also the endnote for EJS 489 (December, 1969).

The Lewisohn Stadium broadcast of 22 July, 1937 included the entire Dawn duet and *Siegfried's* Rhine Journey with tenor Paul Althouse, and while these are portions known to have been recorded, neither are included on EJS 166 (the 23:55 segment on EJS 167 ends at *Siegfried's* entrance). Easton's "Zu neuen Taten" from the Prologue of the 1937 performance also appeared on the IRCC LP L-7022, isued in 1963. Extensive excerpts from the performance later appeared on ANNA 1008 (May, 1978), dated as London, 1936.

The Flagstad-Walter excerpt was part of a lengthy broadcast recital which also included Wagner's WESENDONCK LIEDER. The GÖTTERDÄMMERUNG scene was later issued by the Bruno Walter Society on the LP I Grandi Interpreti IGI 328.

EJS 168: "The Golden Age of Opera" (1 LP)
Issued January, 1960

"POTPOURRI (3)"

SIDE 1 (168 A):

UN BALLO IN MASCHERA (Verdi) (I)
Opera in 3 Acts (excerpts)
San Francisco Opera House Orchestra and Chorus/Gennaro Pappi
San Francisco Opera broadcast, KPO [NBC], San Francisco, 23 Oct 1940

CAST:
Elisabeth Rethberg (*Amelia*); [Suzanne Sten (*Ulrica*)]; [Margit Bokor (*Oscar*)]; Jussi Bjoerling (*Riccardo*); Richard Bonelli (*Renato*); [Lorenzo Alvary (*Sam*)]; [Robert Sellon (*Tom*)]; [George Cehanovsky (*Silvano*)]; [Paul Walti (*Judge*)]; [Roy Garden (*Servant*)].

* 1. Act II: RETHBERG, BJOERLING, AND BONELLI:
a) Orchestral introduction to Act II
b) [Ecco l'orido campo] . . . ove s'accoppia . . . Ma dall'arido stelo
c) Teco io sto . . . O qual soave brivido
d) [Ahi mè! s'appressa alcun!] Chi giunge in questo soggiorno della morte? . . . Amico, gelosa t'affido una cura . . . to Renato's "Lo giuro, e sarà"

* 2. ELISABETH RETHBERG, soprano ("Wallenstein Orchestra"/Alfred Wallenstein): PARTENOPE, Act II: Qual farfaletta (Handel) (I)
Broadcast, ***ELISABETH RETHBERG***, WOR, NYC. 1 Aug 1941

* 3. ELISABETH RETHBERG, soprano ("Wallenstein Orchestra"/Alfred Wallenstein): GIULIO CESARE, Act II: V'adoro pupille (Handel) (I)
Broadcast, ***ELISABETH RETHBERG***, WOR, NYC, 1 Aug 1941

SIDE 2 (168 B):

* 1. ELISABETH RETHBERG, soprano ("Wallenstein Orchestra"/Alfred Wallenstein; pf/?): IPHIGÉNIE EN TAURIDE, Act I: Ô race de Pélops, race toujours fatale! . . . Ô toi, qui prolongeas mes jours (Gluck) (F)
Broadcast, ***ELISABETH RETHBERG***, WOR, NYC, 29 Aug 1941

* 2. ELISABETH RETHBERG, soprano ("Wallenstein Orchestra"/Alfred Wallenstein): IDOMENEO, K. 366 Act III/i: Solitudini amiche, aure amorose . . . Zeffiretti lusinghieri (Mozart) (I)
Broadcast, ***ELISABETH RETHBERG***, WOR, NYC, 5 Sep 1941

* 3. RENATA TEBALDI, soprano, and JUSSI BJOERLING, tenor (Metropolitan Opera House Orchestra/Max Rudolf): LA BOHÈME, Act I: Oh! sventata, sventata! La chiave della stanza . . . to the end of the act (Puccini) (I)
Telecast, ***PRODUCERS' SHOWCASE***, NBC-TV, 30 Jan 1956

* 4. ELISABETH RETHBERG, soprano, and EZIO PINZA, bass (San Francisco Opera House Orchestra/Gennaro Papi): LA FORZA DEL DESTINO, Act II: Sull'alba il piede all'eremo (Verdi) (I)
San Francisco Opera House broadcast, San Francisco, KGO [NBC], 28 Oct 1938

NOTES: EJS 168

Side 1 (168 A):

Band 1: Only Act II of the BALLO was heard via national pickup over NBC, a 27-minute broadcast beginning at 9:30 pm (PST).

Bands 2-3: The Rethberg broadcast solos are all from her ten-show summer series which aired over WOR, New York City (Mutual Broadcasting Network) in 1941. The orchestra is credited as the "Wallenstein Orchestra."

Side 2 (168 B):

Bands 1-2: As above, Side I/2-3. The recitative of the IPHIGÉNIE aria is piano accompanied. The IDOMENEO later appeared on EJS 239 (April, 1962).

Band 3: Monday evening, 30 January, 1956 was quite an night to spend in front of the television: present on this ***PRODUCERS' SHOWCASE*** telecast were, in addition to Bjoerling and Tebaldi, Marian Anderson, Zinka Milanov, Jan Peerce, Roberta Peters, Gregor Piatigorsky, Artur Rubenstein, Blanche Thebom, Isaac Stern, Risë Stevens, Leonard Warren, and Mildred Miller. As if that was not enough, Charles Laughton acted as Master of Ceremonies. The joint sponsors were the Ford Motor Company and RCA Victor, and the producer was Sol Hurok. The show was filmed at NBC's Studio 8H, Rockefeller Center Studio in New York City and portions of it were broadcast in color.

The Bjoerling-Tebaldi BOHEME excerpt later appeared on Rococo 1003, Legendary Recordings LR 137, and MDP 026.

Band 4: Only Act II of FORZA was heard over NBC, a 30-minute broadcast beginning at 9:00 pm (PST). The broadcast originated over station KGO, San Francisco.

EJS 169: "The Golden Age of Opera" (1 LP)
Issued January, 1960

"POTPOURRI (4)"

SIDE 1 **(169 A)**:

* 1. BENIAMINO GIGLI, tenor ([?]Rome Opera Orch./Luigi Ricci): DIE WALKÜRE, Act I: Cede il verno ("Winterstürme") (Wagner) (G)
from the soundtrack of the feature film **VERTIGINE/ ADORAZIONE/ *TRAGÖDIE EINER LIEBE*** (1941)
Cinecittà Studios, Rome, August-September, 1941

* 2. EZIO PINZA, bass (studio orch/Donald Voorhees): LE CAïD, Act I: Enfant chéri . . . Le tambour-major (Thomas) (F)
Broadcast, ***BELL TELEPHONE HOUR***, WEAF, NYC, 15 Jan 1945

3. EZIO PINA, bass (studio orch/Donald Voorhees): "L'Heureux vagabond" (Bruneau) (F)
Broadcast, ***BELL TELEPHONE HOUR***, WNBC, NYC, 15 Aug 1949

4. ROSA PONSELLE, soprano (studio orch/Erno Rapee): AïDA, Act I/i: Ritorna vincitor! (Verdi) (I)
Broadcast, ***GENERAL MOTORS HOUR***, Carnegie Hall, NYC, WEAF, 27 Sep 1936

* 5. GIUSEPPE DANISE, baritone (Nicola Rescigno/pf): ANDREA CHENIER, Act III: Nemico della patria? (Giordano) (I)
Private party recording, NYC, 25 Jan 1948

* 6. GIOVANNI MARTINELLI, tenor, and GIUSEPPE DANISE, bass (Nicola Rescigno/pf): LA BOHÈME, Act IV: O Mimi, tu più non torni (Puccini) (I)
Private party recording, NYC, 25 Jan 1948

TANNHÄUSER (Wagner) (G)
Opera in 3 Acts (excerpts: Act III only)
Chicago Opera House Orchestra and Chorus, Edwin McArthur
Chicago Opera broadcast, Chicago, WMAQ [NBC], 27 Nov 1939

CAST:
Paul Althouse (*Tannhäuser*); [Kirsten Flagstad (*Elisabeth*)]; Elen [Carol] Longone (*Venus*); George Czaplicki (*Wolfram*); [Douglas Beattie (*Landgrave*)].

* 7. Act III: LONGONE, ALTHOUSE, and CZAPLICKI: Finale, two measures before Wolfram's "Zu mir! Es ist um dich gethan!" . . . to the end of the opera

SIDE 2 **(169 B)**:

* 1. FREDERICK JAGEL, tenor, and HERVA NELLI, soprano: (studio orch/ Sylvan Levin): MANON LESCAUT, Act II: Tu, tu, amore? . . . O tentatrice (Puccini) (I)
Broadcast, ***MUTUAL'S OPERA CONCERT***, NYC, 26 Aug 1951

* 2. BIDÚ SAYÃO, soprano, and GIUSEPPE DE LUCA, baritone (Metropolitan Opera House Orchestra/Gennaro Pappi): LA BOHÈME, Act III: Mimi! Speravo di trovarvi qui . . . Oh! buon Marcello, aiuto! . . . l'alba s'assopi sopra una panna (Puccini) (I)
Metropolitan Opera broadcast, NYC, 10 Feb 1940

MARTHA (Flotow) (I)
Opera in 4 acts (excerpts)
San Francisco Opera House Orchestra and Chorus, Johann Riedel
San Francisco Opera broadcast, KFRC [NBC], 8 Oct 1944

CAST:
Licia Albanese (*Lady Harriet*); Bruno Landi (*Lionel*); Lorenzo Alvary (*Plunkett*); Salvatore Baccaloni (*Sir Tristan*); [Ronald Goodwin (*Sheriff*)]; Hertha Glaz (*Nancy*); [Georgia Gianopoulos (*Maid*)]; [Kathleen Lawlor (*Maid*)]; [Nevart Levon (*Maid*)]; [Benjamin Martin (*Farmer*)]; [Lelia Gambi (*Farmer's Wife*)]; [Fred Wahlin (*Lackey*)]; [Paul Guenter (*Lackey*)]; [Philip Doan (*Lackey*)]; [Albert Vannucci (*Lackey*)].

* 3. ALBANESE, LANDI, GLAZ, ALVARY, AND BACCALONI: Act III, Finale: Marta, te perdona Iddio (sic) [Ah! che a te perdoni Iddio] [Mag der Himmel euch vergeben] . . . to the end of the act

4. GLADYS SWARTHOUT, contralto (Metropolitan Opera House Orchestra/ Wilfred Pelletier): RISURREZIONE, Act II: Voici l'heure! et lui n'arrive pas! . . . Dieu de grâce ["Giunge il treno ed ei non giunge ancor! . . . Dio pietoso"] (Cesare Hanau-Franco Alfano - P. Ferrier, French translation; after Tolstoy) (F)
Broadcast, ***THE METROPOLITAN OPERA PRESENTS***, WJZ, NYC, 31 Dec 1944

5. MARIAN ANDERSON, mezzo-soprano (studio orch/Donald Voorhees): LE CID, Act III: Pleurez, pleurez mes yeux (Massenet) (F)
Broadcast, ***BELL TELEPHONE HOUR***, WEAF, NYC, 11 Dec 1944

6. MARIAN ANDERSON, mezzo-soprano (studio orch/Donald Voorhees): HÉRODIADE, Act I: Venge-moi d'une suprême offense! . . . Hérode! Hérode! Ne me refusez pas! (Massenet) (F)
Broadcast, ***BELL TELEPHONE HOUR***, WNBC, NYC, 6 Jan 1947

* 7. GIUSEPPE DI STEFANO, tenor (San Francisco Opera Orchestra/ Gaetano Merola): LE CID, Act III: Ô souverain! Ô juge! Ô père! (Massenet) (F)
Broadcast, ***STANDARD HOUR***, KNBC, San Francisco, 15 Oct 1950

NOTES: **EJS 169**

Side 1 (169 A):

Band 1: This same performance was later featured in Gigli's 1946 feature film, ***VOGLIO BENE SOLTANTO A TE***. Apart from Smith's subsequent reissue of it on TAP 331 (1961), it has also appeared on Scala 861 (1961), and Scala 5001 (circa 1962), all three being Gigli recitals. Ricci is definitely the conductor, but it is only suspected that the Rome Opera Orchestra was the accompanying ensemble.

Band 2: This performance was issued as V-Disc 413 (VP 1135) and Navy V-Disc 193 (NVP 1186), matrix D5TC 122, mastered 25 January, 1945.

Bands 5-6: Both of these items were apparently recorded at a private party given at the home of the accompanist, Nicola Rescigno, in New York City.

Band 7: In spite of what the label of EJS 169 claims (Flagstad, Althouse, and Richard Bonelli are listed), Czaplicki is the *Wolfram*, and Flagstad does not appear (by this point in Act III, *Elisabeth* has already made her final exit). Only Act III was broadcast, beginning at 10:25 pm (CST).

Czaplicki made no commercial recordings, but his voice has been preserved in several Chicago Opera broadcasts. An autographed portrait of this artist in the author's collection has his name signed as "Chapliski."

Side 2 (169 B):

Band 1: Smith gives 1955 as the date of the Jagel-Nelli duet.

Band 2: The Sayão-De Luca BOHÈME duet is taken from the complete Met performance of 10 February, 1940 that would later be issued as EJS 248 in October, 1962. This Act III duet turned up in the late 1960s on a private De Luca recital LP, MDP 015. The complete performance on EJS 248 also contains a back-stage interview with De Luca.

Band 3: The label of EJS 169 gives the date 1942 in error.

Band 7: This was a local broadcast only, originating from KNBC, San Francisco.

EJS 170: "The Golden Age of Opera" (1 LP)
Issued January, 1960

"POTPOURRI (5)"

SIDE 1 (170 A):

* 1. EZIO PINZA, bass, and GERTRUD WETTERGREN, contralto (Metropolitan Opera House Orchestra/Maurice de Abravanel): SAMSON ET DALILA, Act II/ii: J'ai gravi la montagne (Saint-Saëns) (F)
Metropolitan Opera broadcast, NYC, 26 Dec 1936

* 2. RICHARD CROOKS, tenor (Metropolitan Opera House Orchestra/Ettore Panizza): LA TRAVIATA, Act II: Lunge da lei . . . De miei bollenti spiriti (Verdi) (I)
Metropolitan Opera broadcast, NYC, 23 Dec 1939

* 3. RICHARD BONELLI, baritone, VIRGILIO LAZZARI, bass, and LODOVICO OLIVIERO, tenor: (Metropolitan Opera House Orchestra/Gennaro Papi): LUCIA DI LAMMERMOOR, Act I: Cruda, funesta smania (Donizetti) (I)
Metropolitan Opera broadcast, NYC, 3 Feb 1940

* 4. LILY PONS, soprano, and RICHARD BONELLI, baritone (Metropolitan Opera House Orchestra/Gennaro Papi): LUCIA DI LAMMERMOOR, Act II: Il pallor funesto . . . Soffriva nel pianto (Donizetti) (I)
Metropolitan Opera broadcast, NYC, 3 Feb 1940

* 5. EZIO PINZA, bass (Metropolitan Opera House Orchestra/Gennaro Papi): LUCIA DI LAMMERMOOR, Act III: Cessi, ah, cessi quel contento . . . Dalle stanze ove Lucia (Donizetti) (I)
Metropolitan Opera broadcast, NYC, 27 Feb 1937

SIDE 2 (170 B):

* 1. GIOVANNI MARTINELLI, tenor, and CESARE FORMICHI, baritone (Royal Opera House Orchestra/Sir Thomas Beecham): OTELLO, Act II: Desdemona rea! . . . Ora e per sempre, addio . . . Non son più vostro alfiere (Verdi) (I)
Broadcast, Covent Garden, London, 19 Apr 1937

* 2. ROSA PONSELLE, soprano (studio orch/Andre Kostelanetz): CAVALLERIA RUSTICANA: Voi lo sapete (Mascagni) (I)
Broadcast, ***CHESTERFIELD HOUR***, WABC, NYC, 11 Mar 1936

3. ROSA PONSELLE, soprano (studio orch/Andre Kostelanetz): "L'Ultima canzone" (Tosti) (I)
Broadcast, ***CHESTERFIELD HOUR***, WABC, NYC, 11 Mar 1936

* 4. MARJORIE LAWRENCE, soprano (?Royal Albert Hall Orchestra/?): SALOME, Finale: Ah! Du wolltest mich nicht deinen Mund küssen lassen . . . to the end of the opera (R. Strauss) (G)
?Concert, ?Royal Albert Hall, London, ?24 Oct 1948

* 5. KIRSTEN FLAGSTAD, soprano (pf/Ernest Lush): "Der Musensohn," D. 764 (Goethe-Schubert) (G)
BBC broadcast, London, 5 Jul 1948

* 6. FRIDA LEIDER, soprano, KERSTIN THORBORG, mezzo-soprano, and KARL KAMANN, baritone (Royal Opera House Orchestra [London Philharmonic] and Chorus/Wilhelm Furtwängler): DIE WALKÜRE, Act II: Hojotoho! . . . des frech frevelnden Paars (Wagner) (G)
Broadcast, Covent Garden, London, 1 Jun 1938

NOTES: EJS 170

Remastered (blue and white label) as matrix P-3526 in early 1974.

Side 1 (170 A):

Band 1: The approximate playing speed is 34.2 rpm. Further excerpts with Pinza, Wettergren, and Maison from this 1936 Met SAMSON were featured subsequently on EJS 186 (July-August, 1960); Wettergren's "Printemps qui commence" on EJS 213 (May, 1961); the "J'ai gravi la montagne" on a PEARL Pinza LP recital (GEMM 162/3), reissued as compact disc GEMM 9304; and extensive excerpts from the complete performance on EJS 516 (June, 1970).
Library of Congress tape: 5174-30 (complete broadcast).

Band 2: The approximate playing speed of this band is 33.8 rpm. About 75 minutes of this TRAVIATA were issued on EJS 540 in February, 1971, while EJS 488, a November, 1969 Crooks recital, also contained a possible short excerpt. See also the Crooks-Jepson duet on EJS 171 (January, 1960).

Bands 3-4: Lazzari and Oliviero appear only momentarily in the "Cruda, funesta." The scene reflects standard cuts made at the Met during this period: the end of *Enrico's* cavatina cuts directly to a single verse of the cabaletta, with the intervening material omitted. The approximate playing speed of Pons' "Il pallor funesto" is 34.5 rpm. Both items appeared in 1992 on the first volume of an IRCC broadcast potpourri (CD 806).
Library of Congress tape: 5174-9 (complete broadcast).

Band 5: See also the Pons-Jagel duet from this performance on EJS 172 (January, 1960) and the more extensive excerpts from the performance issued as EJS 524 (October, 1970). The complete performance was issued as UORC 311 (November-December, 1976).
Library of Congress tape: 15731-93B (complete broadcast).

Side 2 (170 B):

Band 1: This same excerpt appeared later on ANNA 1031, a Giovanni Martinelli recital issued in May-June, 1979. OTELLO was performed that season on 19, 23, and 28 April, 1937 with Formichi as *Iago*; a fourth performance, on 26 June, featured Tibbett in the latter role. 19 April was the opening performance of the Coronation Season.

Bands 2-3: Park's Ponselle discography does not list EJS 170 as a source for these 11 March, 1936 ***CHESTERFIELD HOUR*** excerpts, but they appear to be identical to those on the other Smith issues listed there: EJS 190, UORC 118, ANNA 1036, and ASCO A-125 (CAVALLERIA), EJS 191, and UORC 118 ("L'Ultima canzone"). The latter also appeared on a private MDP LP (MDP 012) in the late 1960s.

Band 4: Date as given on the label of EJS 170, and as reported subsequently in the 1987 Marjorie Lawrence discography featured in *The Record Collector* (32/1-2, January, 1987), pp. 11 and 17. The *London Times* lists no such concert in 1946, 1947, or 1948, so the date and circumstance of this recording remain a mystery. Even *Le Monde* was checked for a possible French performance. Sung in German, it is *not* the commercial recording made in Paris in 1934 (DB 4933/4934), which was sung in French.

This is the complete "concert" version of the SALOME Finale, without *Herod* and *Herodias*. A speed of 33.8 rpm has been suggested, unless Lawrence transposed it down a half-step during the actual performance.

Band 5: Given as "Der Nusensohn" in the bulletin for EJS 170 and on the label. "Der Musensohn" was one of at least seven titles recorded from this Flagstad broadcast, all of which have appeared at one time or another on one of Smith's "private" labels. This particular song was issued again on Legendary Records LP LR 120.

Band 6: This excerpt cuts off in mid-line at *Fricka's* "des frech frevelnden Paars." Only the "Hojotoho!" appears on the later UORC 234 transfer, issued January, 1975, though it is not listed in either the bulletin or on the label of that LP. 33.8 rpm has been suggested as the correct playing speed for the EJS 170 transfer.

Given as 6 January, 1938 on the label, but this is simply an American-for-European date transposition: 1 June is the correct date. The London Philharmonic served as the pit orchestra during the 1938 Grand Opera Season.

EJS 171: "The Golden Age of Opera" (1 LP)
Issued January, 1960

"POTPOURRI (6)"

SIDE 1 (171 A):

* 1. BENIAMINO GIGLI, tenor, and IVA PACETTI, soprano (Royal Opera House Orchestra/Vittorio Gui): TOSCA, Act III: [E lucevan le stelle ed olezzava; La ter] ra, stridea l'uscio . . . Franchigia a Floria Tosca (Puccini) (I)
Broadcast, Covent Garden, London, 2 Jun 1938

2. BENIAMINO GIGLI, tenor, and ARISTIDE BARACCHI, bass (Royal Opera House Orchestra/Vittorio Gui): TOSCA, Act I: Recondita armonia (Puccini) (I)
Broadcast, Covent Garden, London, 15 May 1939

* 3. HELEN TRAUBEL, soprano, and ARTHUR CARRON, tenor (Metropolitan Opera House Orchestra/Wilfred Pelletier): THE MAN WITHOUT A COUNTRY, Act I/i: My dearest, how long it is since we have met (Guiterman-Damrosch/after E.E. Hale) (E)
Metropolitan Opera broadcast, NYC, 22 May 1937

* 4. HELEN TRAUBEL, soprano, and ARTHUR CARRON, tenor (Metropolitan Opera House Orchestra/Wilfred Pelletier): THE MAN WITHOUT A COUNTRY, Act II/ii: My own! My life! My love! (Guiterman-Damrosch/after E.E. Hale) (E)
Metropolitan Opera broadcast, NYC, 22 May 1937

* 5. HELEN TRAUBEL, soprano (Metropolitan Opera House Orchestra/Erik Leinsdorf): DIE WALKÜRE, Act II: Hoyotoho!
?Metropolitan Opera broadcast, NYC, 27 Feb 1943

* 6. MARIO CHAMLEE, tenor (Metropolitan Opera House Orchestra/Wilfred Pelletier): THE BARTERED BRIDE [PRODANÁ NEVĚSTA], Act III: . . . at least you say it so discretely . . . Oh! my adored one! (Smetana) (E)
Metropolitan Opera broadcast, NYC, 8 May 1937

* 7. HELEN JEPSON, soprano, and RICHARD CROOKS, tenor (Metropolitan Opera House Orchestra and Chorus/Ettore Panizza): LA TRAVIATA, Act I: Libiamo, nei lieti calici (Verdi) (I)
?Metropolitan Opera broadcast, NYC, 23 Dec 1939

* 8. MAGGIE TEYTE, soprano (pf/Frederick Stone): CIBOULETTE: "Ce n'était pas la même chose" (Hahn) (F)
BBC broadcast, Wednesday, 26 Nov 1958

SIDE 2 (171 B):

* 1. EZIO PINZA, bass (studio orch/Donald Voorhees): "Nina" ["Tre giorni son che Nina"] (attr. Pergolesi) (I)
Broadcast, ***BELL TELEPHONE HOUR***, WNBC, NYC, 16 Feb 1953

2. EZIO PINZA, bass (studio orch/Donald Voorhees): "Torna a Surriento" (de Curtis-de Curtis) (I)
Broadcast, ***BELL TELEPHONE HOUR***, WNBC, NYC, 11 Jan 1954

* 3. GRACE MOORE, soprano (studio orchestra and chorus/?): NORMA, Act I: Sediziose voci . . . Casta Diva (Bellini) (I)
from the 10-reel Metro-Goldwyn-Mayer feature film *A LADY'S MORALS* (1930), Hollywood, 1929-1930
LP 1680; c27 Oct 1930
New York premiere: Capitol Theater, NYC, 8 Nov 1930

* 4. GRACE MOORE, soprano (studio orchestra and chorus/?): LA FILLE DU REGIMENT, Act I: Chacun le sait ("Rataplan") (Donizetti) (F)
from the 10-reel Metro-Goldwyn-Mayer feature film *A LADY'S MORALS* (1930), Hollywood, 1929-1930
LP 1680; c27 Oct 1930
New York premiere: Capitol Theater, NYC, 8 Nov 1930

* 5. NINO MARTINI, tenor (studio orch/?Nathaniel Shilkret): I PAGLIACCI, Act I: Recitar! . . . Vesti la giubba (Leoncavallo) (I)
from the 8-reel RKO feature film *MUSIC FOR MADAM* (1937), Hollywood, 1937
LP 7450; c1 Oct 1937
New York premiere: Criterion Theater, NYC, Oct 1937

* 6. BENIAMINO GIGLI, tenor (studio orch/?):
a) MIGNON, Act II (Finale): Della morte . . . to the end of the act
b) MARTHA, Act III: Ah! che a te perdoni Iddio . . . Quell' affanno assai mi dice ("Mag der Himmel euch vergeben . . . Todesschmerz hat mich getroffen"] (Flotow) (I)
from the feature film ***NON TI SCORDAR DI ME [VERGISS MEIN NICHT]*** Italia Films GmbH., Berlin, May, 1935
LP 7155 c15 May 1937 (Grand National Films)

DON GIOVANNI (Mozart) (G)
Opera in 2 Acts (excerpts)
Vienna State Opera House Orchestra and Chorus/Josef Krips
Broadcast, Covent Garden, London, 27 Sep 1947

CAST:
[Elisabeth Schwarzkopf (*Donna Elvira*)]; Maria Cebotari (*Donna Anna*); Hilde Güden (*Zerlina*)]; [Erich Kunz (*Leporello*)]; [Paul Schöffler (*Don Giovanni*)]; Richard Tauber (*Don Ottavio*); [Ludwig Weber (*Commandant*)].

* 7. Act I: CEBOTARI and TAUBER: Anima mia, consolati! . . . fa cor! . . . Fuggi, crudele, fuggi! (G)

* 8. EZIO PINZA, bass (Metropolitan Opera House Orchestra and chorus/Bruno Walter): DIE ZAUBERFLÖTE, K. 620, Act II: O Isis and Osiris (Mozart) (E)
?Metropolitan Opera broadcast, NYC, 26 Dec 1942

* 9. EZIO PINZA, bass (Metropolitan Opera House Orchestra and chorus/Bruno Walter): DIE ZAUBERFLÖTE, K. 620, Act II: Within these holy portals ("In diesen heil' gen Hallen") (Mozart) (E)
?Metropolitan Opera broadcast, NYC, 26 Dec 1942

NOTES: EJS 171

Given above are the selections as they appear on the actual record, not as labeled.

Side 1 (171 A):

Band 1: This Gigli-Pacetti duet has been reported as being Gigli and Cigna from Covent Garden, 15 May, 1939, also conducted by Gui, but the 2 June, 1938 performance now appears to be correct.

Bands 3-4: The world premiere of Damrosch's setting of Edward Everett Hale's THE MAN WITHOUT A COUNTRY took place at the Met on Wednesday evening, 12 May, 1937, with Traubel as *Mary Rutledge* and Carron as *Philip Nolan*, making these excerpts "creator" performances. The 22 May, 1937 performance was issued complete as EJS 528 (November, 1970).

Library of Congress tape: 5375-58 (complete broadcast).

Band 5: It is not certain that this "Hoyotoho!" comes from the 27 February broadcast. There is no concert ending, however (the excerpt ends just before *Wotan* sings), so it is presumably taken from a live performance, 27 February, 1943 being the likeliest date. Melchior's "Ein Schwert" from that date was included on EJS 100 (1956).

Band 6: Issued complete as EJS 523 (October, 1970).
Library of Congress tape: 15778-44B (complete broadcast).

Band 7: The date is again uncertain for this duet. It has been checked against the 23 December, 1939 TRAVIATA excerpts issued as EJS 540 in February, 1971: the two "Brindisi" appear to be identical. See also the Crooks "De miei bollenti spiriti" on EJS 170 (January, 1960) and the accompanying note.

Band 8: Teyte's performance of "Ce n'etait-pas la même chose" is preceded by a brief introduction wherein the singer explains that this is a baritone aria from Hahn's 1923 operetta, CIBOULETTE. This broadcast excerpt, along with an interview with the singer from the same program, appeared on the BBC/Caedmon LP "Dame Maggie Teyte, D.B.E." (Arabesque 8069) in 1980, where the date 26 November, 1958 is given; Friday, 28 November has also been reported. Possibly the recording was taped on the 26th for broadcast two days later, or 28 November was a re-broadcast (25 November has also been suggested, but probably in error unless this was a pre-recording date). A Hahn song from the same broadcast later appeared on EJS 478 (September, 1969).

Side 2 (171 B):

Band 1: Pinza's "Nina" is dubbed high--so much so that the singer might be mistaken for a tenor.

Bands 3-4: No musical director seems to have been credited on ***A LADY'S MORALS***, so that the conductor of Moore's operatic scenes is unknown. The film, incidentally, is a highly fictionalized account of the life of Jenny Lind, and was Moore's Hollywood debut.

Band 5: Nathaniel Shilkret is credited as the musical director for ***MUSIC FOR MADAM***, so it can be assumed that he actually conducted Martini's operatic scenes.

Bands 6a-6b: ***NON TI SCORDAR DI ME*** was a 1935 Italian-German production, entitled ***VERGISS MEIN NICHT*** for the German release; an English-language version was shot in Britain in December, 1935 at Worton Hall Studios, Middlesex, by Alexander Korda and issued as ***FORGET ME NOT***. This version was released in 1937 by Grand National Pictures in the U.S. as ***FOREVER YOURS***. The two scenes featured here, from the original Italian-German version, are known to have been shot in Berlin and aboard the ship Bremen in May, 1935. The conductor and orchestra are not credited. The extraordinary musical bridge between the MIGNON and MARTHA excerpts used in the film can be heard on EJS 171: namely, ten seconds of TRISTAN UND ISOLDE! The MIGNON excerpt is preceded on EJS 171 by a few measures of chorus; the end of the scene differs significantly from the printed score.

Band 7: This DON GIOVANNI was Tauber's final stage appearance. The day after, on 28 September, 1947, he appeared on the BBC's ***LIGHT PROGRAMME CONCERT***, and on 4 October he entered the hospital. He died in London on 8 January, 1948. Note that the performance, part of the Wiener Staatsoper's Covent Garden season, was sung in German, but that the translation used has not been determined, hence the listing of the text here in Italian. The same duet was featured later on EJS 452 (December, 1968).

Bands 8-9: It has never been determined with absolute certainty that these excerpts were taken from the 26 December, 1942 Met performance of ZAUBERFLÖTE, but it seems likely that they were. Pinza's only other broadcast of the opera (sung during the War years using Ruth and Thomas P. Martin's celebrated 1941 English translation) was on 1 December, 1945.

Smith first issued this 26 December, 1942 ZAUBERFLÖTE complete on his "Great Mozart Recordings of the Century" label as MJA 5000, a "privately"-announced set of three discs offered in the June, 1964 bulletin to select subscribers on a first-come, first-served basis. There, it was claimed that only twenty-five copies were to be pressed for retstricted sale, with an additional fifteen copies slated for library distribution. Twenty-three copies of MJA 5000 were later offered for general sale in the March, 1973 UORC bulletin, where the set is described as having been produced "some years ago." A formal reissue of the performance on two discs (UORC 210) was announced in June, 1974.

The original network acetates exist but their numbers were not available. They were 16-inch glass discs, complete from the Overture through *Pamina's* second-act "Ach, ich fühl's." Only five minutes of the finale has survived; sides 2 and 3 of the original Act I acetates are missing.

EJS 172: "The Golden Age of Opera" (1 LP)
Issued January, 1960

"POTPOURRI (7)"

SIDE 1 (172 A)

1. RAOUL JOBIN, tenor, and EZIO PINZA, bass (Metropolitan Opera House Orchestra/Louis Fourestier): FAUST, Act I/ii: Mais ce Dieu, que peut-il pour moi? . . . to the end of the scene (Gounod) (F)
   Metropolitan Opera broadcast, NYC, 4 Jan 1947

* 2. GIUSEPPE DE LUCA, baritone (studio orch/Alfredo Antonini): LA FAVORITA, Act III: A tanto amor (Donizetti) (I)
   Broadcast, ***SONG TREASURY***, WOR, Newark, 16 May 1946

3. GIUSEPPE DE LUCA, baritone (studio orch/Alfredo Antonini): "Canta il mare" (Mazzola-de Leva) (I)
   Broadcast, ***SONG TREASURY***, WOR, Newark, 16 May 1946

* 4. LICIA ALBANESE, soprano, and GIUSEPPE DE LUCA, baritone (studio orch/Alfredo Antonini): DON PASQUALE, Act I: Pronta io son . . . Vado, corro (Donizetti) (I)
Broadcast, ***SONG TREASURY***, WOR, Newark, 16 May 1946

* 5. ELISABETH SCHUMANN, soprano (studio orch/?Walter Goehr): 6 ORIGINAL CANZONETTAS, Set II, no. 4, H. XXVIa/34: She Never Told Her Love (Shakespeare-Haydn) (E)
Broadcast, ?***LIGHT PROGRAMME CONCERT***, BBC, London, 23 May 1947

* 6. LILY PONS, soprano, and FREDERICK JAGEL, tenor (Metropolitan Opera House Orchestra/Gennaro Papi): LUCIA DI LAMMERMOOR, Act I: Ah! talor del tuo pensiero . . . Verranno a te sull'aure (Donizetti) (I)
Metropolitan Opera broadcast, NYC, 27 Feb 1937

SIDE 2 (172 B):

* 1. FREDERICK JAGEL, tenor (Metropolitan Opera House Orchestra/Gannaro Papi): LUCIA DI LAMMERMOOR, Act III: Fra poco a me ricovero (Donizetti) (I)
Metropolitan Opera broadcast, NYC, 27 Feb 1937

* 2. BIDÚ SAYÃO, soprano (Metropolitan Opera House Orchestra/Frank St. Leger): SEMIRAMIDE, Act I: Bel raggio lusinghier (Rossini) (I)
Metropolitan Opera broadcast [IL BARBIERE DI SIVIGLIA], Cleveland, NBC, 10 Apr 1943

3. VIRGILIO LAZZARI, bass (Metropolitan Opera House Orchestra and chorus/Cesare Sodero): NORMA, Act I: Ite sul colle, o Druidi (Bellini) (I)
Metropolitan Opera broadcast, NYC, 12 Feb 1944

* 4. JOSEPHINE TUMINIA, soprano (orch/?): DINORAH (LE PARDON DE PLOëRMEL), Act II: Ombra leggiera (Meyerbeer) (I)
?Broadcast, source and date unknown

* 5. GEORGE CEHANOVSKY, baritone (San Francisco Opera Orchestra/Gaetano Merola): ROMÉO ET JULIETTE, Act I: Mab, la reine des mensonges (Gounod) (F)
Broadcast, ***STANDARD HOUR***, KPO, San Francisco, 13 Oct 1946

* 6. CHARLES KULLMAN, tenor (Metropolitan Opera House Orchestra/Cesare Sodero): LA BOHÈME, Act I: Che gelida manina (Puccini) (I)
Metropolitan Opera broadcast, Chicago, ABC, ?29 Apr 1944

7. BIDÚ SAYÃO, soprano, and NINO MARTINI, tenor (Metropolitan Opera House Orchestra/Cesare Sodero): LA BOHÈME, Act I: O soave fanciulla (Puccini) (I)
Metropolitan Opera broadcast, NYC, 4 Mar 1944

NOTES: EJS 172

Side 1 (172 A):

Band 2: The parts of *Fernando* and *Leonora* are omitted here, as is the "Ah! dolce la speme de suo cor seconda" section of the aria.

Band 4: The Albanese-De Luca duet begins at "Pronta io son . . . brava! brava! brava!," cuts to "Collo torto . . . Vado, corro," and concludes with "Serva / Brava" . . . to the end of the scene. Albanese also sang Bizet's "Ouvre ton coeur," Victor Herbert's "Kiss Me Again," and Barroso's "Os quindins de Yaya" on this broadcast.

Band 5: The notes to the live performances in the Juynboll and Seddon Schumann discography in *The Record Collector* (33/3-5, March, 1988), p. 101, claim that "She Never Told Her Love" on EJS 172 was "Probably taken from the ***BBC THIRD PROGRAMME*** broadcast of 31 August, 1947. The accompanist is Frederick Stone," but in fact this selection is accompanied by orchestra. Schumann is known to have performed the song under Walter Goehr's direction on the ***LIGHT PROGRAMME CONCERT*** of 23 May, 1947, hence the provisional attribution given above (her 29 August, 1945 commercial recording, issued on HMV DA 1850, was accompanied on the piano by Gerald Moore).

The song is the fourth of Haydn's 6 ORIGINAL CANZONETTAS, Set II, written in England in 1795. The text is taken from the end of Act II/iv of Shakespeare's TWELFTH NIGHT.

Band 6: The bulletin for EJS 172 says only "1937." Pons and Jagel were featured in more than one LUCIA broadcast. However, the only 1937 radio matinee was on 27 February; the next closest broadcast with these singers was on Saturday, 12 March, 1938, but the latter is not known to exist in any collection (Pons herself didn't have a copy). Extensive excerpts from the 27 February, 1937 performance were later issued as EJS 524 (October, 1970), and the complete performance as UORC 311 (November-December, 1976).

Library of Congress tape: 15731-93B (complete broadcast).

Side 2 (172 B):

Band 1: As above, Side I/6.

Band 2: This was the lesson scene from a Met tour performance of BARBIERE from Cleveland. The aria is performed complete. The entire performance exists in a private collection, from which Smith was furnished this excerpt.

The complete performance was issued as Operatic Archives OPA 1021.

Band 4: This item may have been taken from one of Tuminia's many performances on WOR's ***HOUR OF SONG*** from the early 1940s.

Band 5: This was a local broadcast only, originating from KPO, San Francisco.

Band 6: It has not been determined with absolute certainty that Kullman's "Che gelida manina" came from this Chicago (tour) broadcast over the ABC network. Pinza's "Vecchia zimarra" from the 29 April, 1944 performance appeared later on EJS 186 (July-August, 1960).

EJS 173: "The Golden Age of Opera" (4 LPs)
Issued February, 1960

SIDES 1-8 (173 A-H):

SIEGFRIED (Wagner) (G)
Opera in 3 Acts (complete)
Metropolitan Opera House Orchestra and Chorus/Artur Bodanzky
Metropolitan Opera broadcast, NYC, 30 Jan 1937

CAST:
Lauritz Melchior (*Siegfried*); Karl Laufkoetter (*Mime*); Friedrich Schorr (*Wanderer*); Eduard Habich (*Alberich*); Emanuel List (*Fafner*); Kerstin Thorborg (*Erda*); Kirsten Flagstad (*Brünnhilde*); Stella Andreva (*Forest Bird*).

NOTES: EJS 173

Reissued (blue and white label) as matrix P-3882 and P-3885 in January-February, 1976.

Given as "January 22, 1937" on the label of EJS 173 and in the February, 1960 bulletin. 22 January was an evening performance, however, where 30 January was the matinee.

For some reason Smith announced this LP as "available only in limited quantities . . . on a first come, first served basis."

Late, if not all pressings, are reported to play quite flat, requiring a playing speed of over 35 rpm to secure score pitch.

The final *Siegfried-Brünnhilde* duet later appeared on UORC 159, a collection of Melchior duets issued in May, 1973. There, the pitch is reported to have been corrected, and the sound much improved, owing to Smith's access at that point to the official NBC acetates. A portion of the *Siegfried-Brünnhilde* duet of Act III/iii was used in a Flagstad-Melchior compilation on EJS 338 (September, 1965).

Reissued by the Bruno Walter Society as I Grandi Interpreti IGI 373 (at pitch, ostensibly from the NBC actetates), and more recently on three CDs by Music and Arts as CD-696. The Act III duet appeared on the Metropolitan Opera Guild's MET-100, "Centenial Collection, 1935-1959."

Library of Congress tape: 15731-85A (complete broadcast).

EJS 174: "The Golden Age of Opera" (2 LPs)
Issued March, 1960

SIDES 1-4 (174 A-D):

MARIA STUARDA (Donizetti) (I)
Opera in 3 Acts (complete)
Orchestra and Chorus of the Teatro Donizetti, Bergamo/Oliviero de Fabritiis
RAI broadcast, Teatro Donizetti, Bergamo, 16 Oct 1958

CAST:
Dina Sorresi (*Maria Stuarda*); Renata Heredia-Capnist (*Elisabetta*); Nicola Tagger (*Leicester*); Antonio Zerbini (*Talbot*); Remo Jori (*Cecil*); Laura Zannini (*Anna Kennedy*).

NOTES: EJS 174

This RAI broadcast was a live pickup from the Teatro Donizetti, Bergamo, not a studio performance. Labels and promotional material give soprano Capnist as "Renata Capristi," where Smith's issue of Mascagni's SILVANO on EJS 389 (issued February, 1967) lists the singer more accurately as "Renata Heredia." Dina Sorresi is given as "Soresi" on the labels of EJS 174: she was apparently a chorister with the New York City Opera who had received a grant to study singing in Italy, where she landed the title role for this performance!

Reported to play flat: a range of 34.5-34.7 rpm has been suggested to compensate.

EJS 175: "The Golden Age of Opera" (2 LPs)
Issued March, 1960

SIDES 1-4 (175 A-D):

DINORAH [LE PARDON DE PLOëRMEL] (Meyerbeer) (F)
Opera in 3 Acts (complete)
Orchestra and Chorus of the Théâtre Royale de la Monnaie, Bruxelles/ Maurice Bastin
In-house recording, Théâtre de la Monnaie, Brussels, 29 Mar 1953

CAST:
Giulia Bardi [Sylvia Stahlmann] (*Dinorah*); Gilbert Dubuc (*Höel*); Francis Barthel (*Corentin*); Maurice de Groote (*The Huntsman*); ? (*The Harvester*); ? (*The Goatherders*).

NOTES: EJS 175

This is the earlier Opéra-Comique version of Meyerbeer's 1859 opera, with dialogue. The later version, also prepared by the composer, employed recitative instead.

The bulletin for EJS 175 states that this DINORAH was "Recorded in the theatre (sic) March 29, 1953, during a performance." The tenor singing *Le Faucher* has not been identified, nor have the two *Goatherders*. The sound quality of the performance is markedly substandard. Indeed, even Smith's bulletin says as much, noting that it is " . . . not a good recording, but also it is far from poor. The balance is not always accurate and stage noises at times are annoying."

"Giulia Bardi" was the name under which American soprano Sylvia Stahlman (1929-) sang at the Théâtre de la Monnaie in the early 1950s. She later appeared under her own name in the San Francisco, Chicago, and New York City Opera companies, and from 1961, at the Met, usually in soubrette roles.

Pitch is reported to be correct on all copies at 33.3 rpm.

EJS 176: "The Golden Age of Opera" (2 LPs)
Issued April, 1960

SIDES 1-4 (176 A-D):

DON PASQUALE (Donizetti) (I)
Opera in 3 Acts (complete)
Metropolitan Opera House Orchestra and Chorus/Gennaro Papi
Metropolitan Opera broadcast, NYC, 21 Dec 1940

CAST:
Bidú Sayão (*Norina*); Nino Martini (*Ernesto*); Francesco Valentino (*Doctor Malatesta*); Salvatore Baccaloni (*Don Pasquale*); Alessio DePaolis (*Notary*).

NOTES: EJS 176

Smith gives the opera in four acts, with the two scenes of Act III divided into separate acts. Martini sings his Act I cabaletta, "Mi fa il destin mendico," as well as the "Com'è gentil, down a half step. The *Ernesto-Norena* duet from the final scene, "Tornami a dir," is also transposed down a half-step. Apart from orchestral cuts made for purposes of timing (most of the Act II Prelude and various introductions), the scene for *Don Pasquale* and the servants at the beginning of Act III has been cut on EJS 176. There were several standard Met performance cuts as well.

The April, 1960 bulletin makes note of the excellent sound quality of this release, Smith claiming that "Very probably it [EJS 176] contains the best sound of any of the older broadcasts released to date." The four sides of EJS 176 range from 34.5-34.7 rpm.

EJS 177: "The Golden Age of Opera" (2 LPs)
Issued April, 1960

SIDES 1-4 (177 A-D):

SIMON BOCCANEGRA (Verdi) (I)
Opera in a Prologue and 3 Acts (complete: Acts I-III only)
Metropolitan Opera House Orchestra and Chorus/Ettore Panizza
Metropolitan Opera broadcast, NYC, 16 Feb 1935

CAST:
Lawrence Tibbett (*Simon Boccanegra*); Eisabeth Rethberg (*Maria Boccanegra*); Ezio Pinza (*Jacopo Fiesco*); Giovanni Martinelli (*Gabriele*); Alfredo Gandolfi (*Paolo Albiani*); Louis D'Angelo (*Pietro*); Giordano Paltrinieri (*Captain*); Pearl Besuner (*Maidservant*).

NOTES: EJS 177

The April, 1960 bulletin notes that this performance is complete save for the Prologue which was "defective." Apparently, Tibbett's children were responsible, having spilled molasses on the precious disc! Smith calls the sound quality of this issue "the same type as the Traviata (1935) . . . Recorded on aluminum, it blasts on occasion on high notes and at times is shallow, but the singing is superb." The (5 Jaunary, 1935) TRAVIATA to which Smith referred was issued as EJS 107 in 1956. The Prologue was finally issued in June, 1973 as UORC 161.

Like so many others, the original transcription discs were supplied by Tibbett, who had had them taken off-the-air at a New York studio.

Note that EJS 277, Montemezzi's L'INCANTESIMO (issued September, 1963) was mislabeled EJS 177 on some copies.

EJS 178: "The Golden Age of Opera" (4 LPs)
Issued May, 1960

SIDES 1-8 (178 A-H):

DIE WALKÜRE (Wagner) (G)
Opera in 3 Acts (complete)
Metropolitan Opera House Orchestra and Chorus/Erich Leinsdorf
Metropolitan Opera broadcast, Boston, NBC, 30 Mar 1940

CAST:
Friedrich Schorr (*Wotan*); Kerstin Thorborg (*Fricka*); Marjorie Lawrence (*Brünnhilde*); Lauritz Melchior (*Siegmund*); Lotte Lehmann (*Sieglinde*); Emanuel List (*Hunding*); Dorothee Manski (*Helmwige*); Thelma Votipka (*Gerhilde*); Irene Jessner (*Ortlinde*).

NOTES: EJS 178

Listed in the 1970s EJS checklist as EJS 179: labels and waxes give EJS 178 (see EJS 179, MIGNON). Apart from some minimal performance cuts, the May, 1960 bulletin notes that six minutes are missing from the last act, owing, perhaps, to a fault in the original transcription discs. Like the MIGNON that followed, the WALKÜRE was advertised as being available "in about 60% of the normal quantity."

Reported to play throughout at 34.00 rpm.

EJS 179: "The Golden Age of Opera" (3 LPs)
Issued May, 1960

SIDES 1-6 (179 A-F):

MIGNON (Thomas) (F)
Opera in 3 Acts (complete)
Metropolitan Opera House Orchestra and Chorus/Wilfred Pelletier
Metropolitan Opera broadcast, NYC, 15 May 1937

CAST:
Jennie Tourel (*Mignon*); Josephine Antoine (*Philine*); Armand Tokatyan (*Wilhelm Meister*); Leon Rothier (*Lothario*); Désiré Defrère (*Laerte*); Norman Cordon (*Jarno*); Maria Matyas (*Frederic*); Norman Cordon (*Antonio*).

NOTES: EJS 179

The MIGNON is in fact EJS 179, though the 1970s EJS checklist gives it as EJS 178: the labels and waxes carry the number "EJS 179" (A and B). See also EJS 178, DIE WALKÜRE.

This was Tourel's Metropolitan Opera debut. The May, 1960 bulletin claims that MIGNON was available "only in very limited quantities with about one-third the normal quota of copies." This seems odd considering that it is by no means one of the rarest of the GAO issues. The set was released with a separate flyer proclaiming that the MIGNON was, in addition to Tourel's Met debut, "the only recording of a complete opera starring JENNIE TOUREL." A complete 1944 Met NORMA was issued a month later, however, as EJS 180 (!), and has since appeared on compact disc.

Library of Congress tape: 15778-46A (complete broadcast).

EJS 180: "The Golden Age of Opera" (3 LPs)
Issued June, 1960

SIDES 1-6 (180 A-F):

NORMA (Bellini) (I)
Opera in 2 Acts (complete)
Metropolitan Opera House Orchestra and Chorus/Cesare Sodero
Metropolitan Opera broadcast, NYC, 30 Dec 1944

CAST:
Frederick Jagel (*Pollione*); Norman Cordon (*Orovese*); Zinka Milanov (*Norma*); Jennie Tourel (*Adalgisa*); Thelma Votipka (*Clothilde*); Alessio DePaolis (*Flavio*).

NOTES: EJS 180

The June, 1960 bulletin claims that a full two-thirds of the normal number of pressings had been sent to subscribers prior to publication, and that the NORMA would, therefore, be "an extremely limited edition."

EJS 181: "The Golden Age of Opera" (3 LPs)
Issued June, 1960

SIDES 1-5 (181 A-E):

OTELLO (Verdi) (I)
Opera in 4 Acts (complete)
Metropolitan Opera House Orchestra and Chorus/Ettore Panizza
Metropolitan Opera broadcast, NYC, 12 Feb 1938

CAST:
Giovanni Martinelli (*Otello*); Lawrence Tibbett (*Iago*); Nicholas Massue (*Cassio*); Giordano Paltrinieri (*Roderigo*); Nicola Moscona (*Lodovico*); George Cehanovsky (*Montano*); Wilfred Engelman (*Herald*); Elisabeth Rethberg (*Desdemona*); Thelma Votipka (*Emilia*).

SIDE 6 (181 F):

* 1. ELISABETH RETHBERG, soprano (studio orch/?): LA WALLY, Act I: Ebben, ne andrò lontana (Catalini) (I)
Broadcast, ***ELIZABETH RETHBERG***, WOR, NYC, 22 Aug 1941

* 2. ELISABETH RETHBERG, soprano (NBC Symphony Orchestra/Frank Black): LA FORZA DEL DESTINO, Act IV: Pace, pace, mio Dio (Verdi) (I)
Broadcast, ***THE MAGIC KEY***, WJZ, NYC, 24 Oct 1937

* 3. GIOVANNI MARTINELLI, tenor (pf/Giuseppe Bamboschek): SAMSON ET DALILA, Act III: Vois ma misère, hélas (Saint-Saëns) (F)
TA-33-011 Continental CLP 103 (LP) ?New York, 1950

4. GIOVANNI MARTINELLI (Detroit Symphony Orchestra/Sir Ernest MacMillan): "Agnus Dei" (Bizet) (F)
Broadcast, ***FORD SUNDAY EVENING HOUR***, WJR, Detroit, 6 Mar 1938

* 5. LAWRENCE TIBBETT, baritone (Metropolitan Opera House Orchestra/ Maurice de Abravanel): LES CONTES D'HOFFMANN, Act I: Je me nomme Coppélius (Offenbach) (F)
?Metropolitan Opera broadcast, NYC, ?23 Jan 1937

* 6. LAWRENCE TIBBETT, baritone (dubbed studio orch/Hans Jürgen Walther): DON GIOVANNI, K. 527, Act I: Madamina! Il catalogo è questo (Mozart) (I)
Studio recording, ?New York, circa 1955

NOTES: EJS 181

Sides 1-5 (181 A-E):

The splendid OTELLO offered on EJS 181 was the first Met broadcast of the opera, the 22 December, 1937 evening performance with the same cast having been its first performance in that house since 31 January, 1913, when the principal roles were taken by Slezak, Scotti, and Alda. Martinelli, Tibbett, and Massue would later participate in studio excerpts of OTELLO issued as Victor Set M-620 (HMV Album Series 357), recorded on 3 and 9 May, 1939 in New York, and conducted by Pelletier.

Speeds for this broadcast performance are reported to be inconsistent over the five sides of EJS 181.

Reissued on CD by Music and Arts as CD-645.

Side 6 (181 F):

Band 1: The source and date of the WALLY was taken from the on-the-air announcement which *follows* the aria on the original acetate Smith used for the transfer. The aria is not listed among the official contents of the 22 August, 1941 broadcast, so was undoubtedly a substitution. The original acetate is missing the first two lines of the aria: the source of what has been patched-in to complete it is unknown.

The WALLY and FORZA (I/2) arias were reissued on two subsequent Rethberg recitals: EJS 239 (April, 1962) and Anna 1038 (May-June, 1979).

Band 2: The 24 October, 1937 "Navy Day" broadcast that featured the FORZA aria was indeed a special event, reviewed the next day in the *New York Times* as "a new chapter in radio history." In addition to Rethberg and Black, broadcasting from WJZ's New York City studio with a popular vocal group, the Tune Twisters, the show carried a message from Rear Admiral William D. Leahy, Chief of Naval Operations (appointed Ambassador to France in 1940 by FDR), heard live from Washington D.C., and for the first time ever, a broadcast from a submerged vessel: Submarine R-14, stationed off the coast of New London, Connecticut, in a live relay to a surface craft. Prior to this, only cabled transmissions from a submerged craft had been heard. The *New York Times*, unfortunately, failed to report the full musical contents of the show.

Band 3: This SAMSON aria was originally issued on the LP "Giovanni Martinelli" (subtitled "Metropolitan Opera Memories") issued by the Continental Record Company of New York as CLP 103 (matrixes TA-33-101/011). Giuseppe De Luca's final recordings, made in New York in late January or early February, 1950, were issued as Continental CLP 102 (matrices TA-33-008/009) in the Summer of 1950, so the Martinelli collection must have come out at about the same time or shortly thereafter.

Giuseppe Bamboschek (1890-1969) was a well-known accompanist (at one point for Amato), musical secretary for a time at the Met, and a conductor in that house from 1919 to 1929. Along with Bodanzky, he was one of the first conductors to record with the Metropolitan Opera House Orchestra--for Columbia as early as 1920.

Band 5: It has not been confirmed that this HOFFMANN aria was taken from the 23 January, 1937 Met broadcast. The entire performance was issued on UORC 206 in May, 1974. Bovy's "Elle a fui" appears on EJS 184 (July-August, 1960), and Bada's "Jour et nuit" on EJS 212 (May, 1961).

Library of Congress tape: 15778-97A (complete broadcast).

Band 6: Tibbett's circa 1955 studio "Madamina!" was later issued on a Tibbett recital, Scala/Everest 886. Others among the contemporary LP issues of these late recordings (Hudson, Royale, etc.) contain songs, but no arias.

Conductor Hans Jürgen-Walther has stated to an informant that he conducted the dubbing sessions for the Tibbett "ca. 1955" recordings: it is documented that Walther did the same for the OTELLO, PAGLIACCI, and LUCIA excerpts issued by the Record Corporation of America on labels like Allegro and Allegro Royale, and for recitals of tenor Albert Da Costa and soprano Mary Henderson. My informant, Mr. Ernst A. Lumpe of Soest, Germany, reported that the original recordings were made in New York with a soft harmonium accompaniment to keep pitch, then sent over to Hamburg where Walther, conducting his own "Philharmonia Orchestra of Hamburg," would add the orchestral tracks. Edward J. Smith was of course involved in these releases, along with a New York producer.

EJS 182: "The Golden Age of Opera" (1 LP)
Issued July-August, 1960

"DINO BORGIOLI RECITAL"

SIDE 1 (182 A):

1. w. Ernest Lush/pf: PARIDE ED ELENA, Act I/i: Spiagge amate (Gluck) (I)
   Broadcast, ***THE FRIDAY RECITAL***, BBC, London, 19 Aug 1949

2. w. Ernest Lush/pf: "Presto, presto" (Mazzaferrata) (I)
   Broadcast, ***THE FRIDAY RECITAL***, BBC, London, 19 Aug 1949

3. w. Ernest Lush/pf: "La gondoliera veneziana (Sadero) (I)
   Broadcast, ***THE FRIDAY RECITAL***, BBC, London, 2 Jun 1950

4. w. Ernest Lush/pf: "I pastori" (Pizzetti) (I)
   Broadcast, ***THE FRIDAY RECITAL***, BBC, London, 19 Aug 1949

* 5. w. Ernest Lush/pf: "Invito alla danza" (Respighi) (I)
   Broadcast, ***THE FRIDAY RECITAL***, BBC, London, 19 Aug 1949 or Friday, 2 June, 1950

* 6. w. Ernest Lush/pf: L'ARIANNA: Lasciatemi morire (Monteverdi) (I)
   Broadcast, ***THE FRIDAY RECITAL***, BBC, London, 19 Aug 1949 or Friday, 2 June, 1950

* 7. w. Ernest Lush/pf: "Lunghi, lunghi è amor da me (Fasolo) (I)
   Broadcast, ***THE FRIDAY RECITAL***, BBC, London, 2 Jun 1950

SIDE 2 (182 B):

1. w. Ernest Lush/pf: TRE SONETTI DI PETRARCA, no. 3: Io vidi in terra angelici costumi (Liszt) (I)
   Broadcast, ***THE FRIDAY RECITAL***, BBC, London, 2 Jun 1950

2. w. Frederick Stone/pf: ORONTEA, Act II: Intorno all'idol mio (Cesti) (I)
   Broadcast, ***BBC HOME SERVICE***, BBC, London, 28 Dec 1948

3. w. Frederick Stone/pf: CANZóNI ARGENTINE, no. 3: Canción del carretero (Carlos Lopéz Buchardo) (S)
   Broadcast, ***BBC HOME SERVICE***, BBC, London, 28 Dec 1948

4. w. Ernest Lush/pf: "Luoghi sereni e cari (Donaudy) (I)
   Broadcast, ***THE FRIDAY RECITAL***, BBC, London, 2 Jun 1950

5. w. Ernest Lush/pf: "Ah! mai non cessate" (Donaudy) (I)
   Broadcast, ***THE FRIDAY RECITAL***, BBC, London, 2 Jun 1950

6. w. Ernest Lush/pf: "O luna che fa lume" (Davico) (I)
   Broadcast, ***THE FRIDAY RECITAL***, BBC, London, 2 Jun 1950

NOTES: EJS 182

The July-August, 1960 bulletin claims that this is an English recital from 1944. The numbering of bands is continuous over both labels (1-13), and there are numerous spelling errors throughout, corrected in the listing.

Side 1 (182 A):

Bands 5 and 6: These items were sung on both the 19 August, 1949 and 2 June, 1950 Borgioli broadcasts, so the precise origin of each has not been determined.

Band 7: Borgioli also sang the "Lunghi, lunghi" on ***THE SUNDAY CONCERT*** of 19 June, 1949, but since nothing from this date appeared elsewhere on EJS 182 (or for that matter, on the other EJS Borgioli broadcast recitals that contain BBC material--EJS 223 and EJS 417), it may be assumed that, like the other items featured on EJS 182, the performance was taken from the 2 June, 1950 broadcast.

EJS 183: "The Golden Age of Opera" (1 LP)
Issued July-August, 1960

"KIRSTEN FLAGSTAD, SOPRANO"

SIDE 1 (183 A):

* 1. KIRSTEN FLAGSTAD, soprano; JULIUS HUEHN, baritone; and KARIN BRANZELL, contralto (Metropolitan Opera House Orchestra and Chorus/Abravanel): LOHENGRIN, excerpts (Wagner) (G)
a) Act II/i: complete
b) Act II/ii: through "Hochmut werd'ihr Reu" [Friedrich's "So zieht das Unheil in dies Haus! . . . Ehre soll vergehn" is omitted]
Metropolitan Opera broadcast, NYC, ?27 Mar 1937

SIDE 2 (183 B):

1. KIRSTEN FLAGSTAD, soprano; WINIFRED HEIDT, mezzo-soprano (Detroit Symphony/John Barbirolli): DER FLIEGENDE HOLLÄNDER, Act II: Summ' und brumm' . . . Johohoe! . . . Traft ihr das Schiff (Wagner) (G)
Broadcast, ***FORD SUNDAY EVENING HOUR***, WJR, Detroit, 21 May 1939

* 2. KIRSTEN FLAGSTAD, soprano (pf/?Edwin McArthur): TANNHÄUSER, Act II: Dich, teure Halle (Wagner) (G)
Broadcast, ***KRAFT MUSIC HALL***, KFI, Los Angeles, 25 Aug 1938

* 3. KIRSTEN FLAGSTAD, soprano; MAGGIE TEYTE, soprano (Mermaid Theater Orchestra/Geraint Jones): DIDO AND AENEAS: Act I: Shake the cloud from off your brow . . . to the end of the chorus "The Hero loves as well as you" and the appearance of Aeneas (Purcell) (E)
BBC broadcast, Mermaid Theater, London, 1 Oct 1951

NOTES: EJS 183

Side 1 (183-A):

Band 1: There were two Met LOHENGRINs issued on EJS featuring Flagstad, Huehn, and Branzell--27 March, 1937 under Abravanel, issued complete on UORC 308 (November-December, 1976) and in excerpts on EJS 258 (January, 1963) and 557 (June, 1971); and 19 February, 1938, also under Abravanel, the second act of which was issued as UORC 194 (March, 1974). The EJS 183 excerpts *appear* to have been taken from the 27 March, 1937 performance.

Library of Congress tape: 15778-41A (complete 27 March, 1937 broadcast).

Side 2 (183-B):

Band 2: McArthur has only been tentatively identified as the accompanist on this 25 August, 1938 ***KRAFT*** broadcast, which was not aired nationally.

Band 3: This production marked Teyte's final apearance on the operatic stage. Unlike the 1 October, 1951 performance of DIDO, which has only appeared complete on EJS 546 (March, 1971), portions of the 15 October-28 March, 1952 performances at the Mermaid Theater, London, conducted by Jones, with Schwarzkopf as *Belinda*, were eventually combined and issued commercially as HMV LHMV 1007 (subsequently reissued as World Record Club SH 117), and in the U.S. as Victor LM-2019. The 1 October, 1951 performance was broadcast on BBC Radio III.

EJS 184: "The Golden Age of Opera" (1 LP)
Issued July-August, 1960

"POTPOURRI (8)"

SIDE 1 (184-A)

* 1. a) LUCREZIA BORI, soprano: Speech (unaccompanied) (E)
b) LUCREZIA BORI, soprano (?studio orch/Frank Black): MIGNON, Act I: Connais-tu le pays? (F)
c) LUCREZIA BORI, soprano (?studio orch/Frank Black): EXSULTATE, JUBILATE, K. 165, no. 3: Alleluia (Mozart) (L)
d) LUCREZIA BORI, soprano (?studio orch/Frank Black): RAYMONDA, Op. 57: "La primavera d'oro" [Valse fantasque] (Betti-Glazunov-arr. La Forge) (I)
e) "La Paloma" (Sebastian Yradier) (S)
Broadcast, ***?MAGIC KEY OF RCA***, WJZ, NYC, 25 Dec 1936

2. ELISABETH RETHBERG, soprano (studio orch/Alfred Wallenstein): SELIG IST DER MANN (Cantata), BWV 57: Ich wunschte mir den Tod (J.S. Bach) (G)
Broadcast, ***ELISABETH RETHBERG***, WOR, NYC, 18 Jul 1941

* 3. ROSA PONSELLE, soprano (New York Philharmonic Orch/Erno Rapee): OTELLO, Act IV: Ave Maria (Verdi) (I)
Broadcast, ***GENERAL MOTORS HOUR***, WEAF, NYC, 27 Sep 1936

4. GLADYS SWARTHOUT, contralto (studio orch/Al Goodman): CAVALLERIA RUSTICANA: Voi lo sapete (Mascagni) (I)
Broadcast, ***PRUDENTIAL FAMILY HOUR***, WABC, NYC, 16 Jan 1944

SIDE 2 (184-B):

* 1. a) MARIA JERITZA, soprano: Speech (unaccompanied) (E)
b) MARIA JERITZA, soprano (Vienna Symphony [Orchestra]/?): "I Love You Truly" (Carrie Jacobs Bond) (E)
c) MARIA JERITZA, soprano (Vienna Symphony [Orchestra]/?): PAGANINI, Act II: Liebe, du Himmel auf Erden (Lehar) (G)
Broadcast, ***THE MAGIC KEY OF RCA***, WJZ, NYC, 29 Sep 1935

2. ROSE BAMPTON, soprano (studio orch/Frank Black): IL BARBIERE DI SIVIGLIA, Act I/ii: Una voce poco fà (Rossini) (I)
Broadcast, ***THE MAGIC KEY OF RCA***, WJZ, NYC, 15 Dec 1935

* 3. MARIAN ANDERSON, contralto (studio orch/Frank Black): LA FAVORITA, Act III: O mio Fernando (Donizetti) (I)
Broadcast, ***THE MAGIC KEY OF RCA***, WJZ, NYC, 2 Feb 1936

* 4. a) SUZANNE FISHER, soprano (studio orch/Frank Black): MANON, Act III: Obéissons quand leur voix appelle ["Gavotte"] (Massenet) (F)
b) SUZANNE FISHER, soprano (studio orch/Frank Black): LOUISE, Act III: Depuis le jour (Charpentier) (F)
Broadcast, ***THE MAGIC KEY OF RCA***, WJZ, NYC, 10 Nov 1935

* 5. VINA BOVY, soprano (Metropolitan Opera House Orchestra/Maurice de Abravanel): LES CONTES D'HOFFMANN, Act IV: Elle a fui, la tourterelle (Offenbach) (F)
Metropolitan Opera broadcast, NYC, 23 Jan 1937

NOTES: EJS 184

Side 1 (184-A):

Band 1: This broadcast appeared in the *New York Times* under the title ***CLEVELAND ORCHESTRA; LUCREZIA BORI, SOPRANO***. Rodzinski is given as the conductor. The scheduled bill of fare, however, was given as entirely orchestral, and included the Prelude to Act I of LOHENGRIN, Mussorgsky's "A Night on Bald Mountain," and Mendelssohn's 3rd Symphony. Bori's sequence was perhaps added as a yuletide afterthought, and more than likely originated in NBC's New York studio, probably with Frank Black conducting the NBC Orchestra. Bori's name appears in the daily radio log for 25 December, 1936, but not in the more detailed Sunday, 20 December listing. All of the selections heard here were reissued on EJS 541 (February, 1971).

Band 1d: The "Primavera d'ora" is an arrangement of the "Valse fantasque" from Glazunov's 1896-1897 ballet, RAYMONDA, Op. 57. This vocal arrangement is by Frank La Forge, with an Italian text by Betti. Bori recorded it commercially in Italian as "Love-Tide of Spring" (Victor 6699) in the key of E-flat, titled elsewhere as "Golden Spring."

Band 3: Later issued on EJS 190 (October, 1960) and UORC 118 (May-June, 1972) as an "unpublished Victor," and still later on ANNA 1036 (May-June, 1979).

Side 2 (184-B):

Band 1a-c: This Jeritza broadcast was a complicated affair, having been made up of performances and interviews originating live throughout the world. Jeritza, accompanied by the "Vienna Symphony" according to the *New York Times*, was joined by Walt Disney in Hollywood, "Amos n' Andy" (Correll and Gosden) from station WMAQ, Chicago, and the orchestras of Paul Whiteman, Frank Black, and Walter Damrosch (ensemble unnamed) from New York City. David Sarnoff, president of RCA, broadcast his own message from aboard a ship bound for England. John B. Kennedy--Tibbett's regular announcer on ***THE PACKARD HOUR***--was the master of ceremonies. Mme. Jeritza's conductor was not named. The Lehar is listed only as "Waltz" on the label of EJS 184.

Library of Congress tape: 15994-A (complete broadcast).

Band 3: The July-August, 1960 bulletin lists this as Anderson's American radio debut: it followed closely her American concert debut at New York's Town Hall on 31 December, 1935, and the Carnegie Hall recital that followed on 20 January, 1936.

Band 4: This broadcast was made just prior to Fisher's Met debut as Butterfly on Thursday evening, 26 December, 1935.

Band 5: The complete 23 January, 1937 CONTES with Bovy and Tibbett was issued on UORC 206 (May, 1974). A Tibbett excerpt is featured on EJS 181 (June, 1960), and a Bada excerpt on EJS 212 (May, 1961).
Library of Congress tape: 15778-97A (complete broadcast).

EJS 185: "The Golden Age of Opera" (1 LP)
Issued July-August, 1960

"POTPOURRI (9)"

SIDE 1 (185 A):

* 1. FRANCESCO TAMAGNO, tenor (pf/?): OTELLO, Act IV: Niun mi tema ["Morte d'Otello"] (Verdi) (I)
14FT ?Ospedaletti, 1903 G&T unpub

* 2. FRANCESCO TAMAGNO, tenor (pf/?): HERODIADE, Act IV: Quand nos jours s'éteindront comme une chaste flamme (Massenet) (F)
3022 FT Ospedaletti, February, 1903 G&T unpub

* 3. FRANCESCO TAMAGNO, tenor (pf/?): ANDREA CHENIER, Act I: Un dì, all'azzurro spazio ["Improvviso"] (Giordano) (I)
3005FT Ospedaletti, February, 1903 G&T unpub

* 4. NELLIE MELBA, soprano; JOHN McCORMACK, tenor; G. MARIO SAMMARCO, baritone (New Symphony Orch/Landon Ronald) FAUST, Act V: All'erta! All'erta! o tempo più non è! (Gounod) (I)
4188f London, 11 or 12 May 1910 Gramophone unpub

* 5. NELLIE MELBA, soprano (Gabriel Lapierre/pf): LOUISE, Act III: Depuis le jour (Charpentier) (F)
C-13903-1 Camden, 3 Oct 1913 Victor unpub

* 6. NELLIE MELBA, soprano (New Symphony Orch/Landon Ronald): TOSCA, Act II: Vissi d'arte (Puccini) (I)
4186f London, 11 May 1910 Gramophone unpub

* 7. NELLIE MELBA, soprano (New Symphony Orch/Landon Ronald): DON CÉSAR DE BAZAN, [Entr'Acte]: A Séville, belles Señoras ("Sevillana") (Jules Ruelle-Massenet) (F)
4207f London, 19 May 1910 Gramophone unpub

* 8. MATTIA BATTISTINI, baritone (Carlos Sabajno/pf): "La Partida" (Alvarez) (S)
Ck-1434-2 Milan, 27 Feb 1924 HMV (2-062013) unpub

SIDE 2 (185 B):

* 1. MIGUEL FLETA, tenor (orch/?): ROI D'YS, Act III: Puisqu'on ne peut Fléchir ces jalouses gardiennes . . . Vainement, ma bien aimée ("Aubade") (Lalo) (F)
ON-541-2 Spain, 1931 HMV DA 1208

* 2. JOSE MARDONES, bass (orch/?): IL BARBIERE DI SIVIGLIA, Act I: La calunnia (Rossini) (I)
WKX-131-1 Spain, 1925-1926 (S.A.) Columbia A4060

* 3. JOSE MARDONES, bass (orch/?): LE NOZZE DI FIGARO, K. 492, Act I: Non più andrai (Mozart) (I)
WKX-145-1 Spain, 1925-1926 (S.A.) Columbia A4060

* 4. JOSE MARDONES, bass (orch/?): GLI UGONOTTI, Act I: Con piacer una vecchia mia canzon . . . [Piff! paff!] Finita è pe'frati [Pour les couvents c'est fini] (Meyerbeer) (I)
WK-1368-1 Spain, 1925-1926 Spanish Regal RS2008

* 5. ANNA FITZIU, soprano (orch/?): GOYESCAS, 3rd Cuadro: Porqué entre sombras el ruiseñor ["La Maja y el Ruiseñor"] (Granados) (S)
mtx? ?New York, 1916 Pathé 82001

* 6. GIUSEPPE DE LUCA, baritone (orch/?): ANDREA CHENIER, Act III: Un dì m'era di gioia (Giordano) (I)
XPh 2323 Milan, 15 Jan 1907 Fonotipia unpub

* 7. ADELINA PATTI, soprano: New Year Message to Baron Cederström (unnaccompanied speech) (E)
no mtx no. Craig-y-Nos, Wales, December, 1905 G&T unpub

* 8. ADELINA PATTI, soprano (Landon Ronald/pf): FAUST, Act III: Ah! Je ris de me voir (Gounod) (F)
542f Craig-y-Nos, Wales, December, 1905 G&T unpub

* 9. ADELINA PATTI, soprano (Landon Ronald/pf): "The Banks of Allan Water" (Old Scottish Song-arr. Charles Horn) (E)
555f Craig-y-Nos, Wales, December, 1905 G&T unpub

* 10. ADELINA PATTI, soprano (Landon Ronald/pf): MARTHA, Act II: The Last Rose of Summer [Letzte Rose] (Thomas Moore-Flotow) (E)
546f Craig-y-nos, Wales, December, 1905 G&T unpub
HMB 78

* 11. ADELINA PATTI, soprano (Landon Ronald/pf): CLARI, or THE MAID OF MILAN: Home, Sweet Home (John Howard Payne-Henry R. Bishop) (E)
550f Craig-y-Nos, Wales, December, 1905 G&T unpub

NOTES: EJS 185

Side 1 and bands 6-11 of side 2 are subtitled "Heretofore unpublished acoustics." The Fleta ROY D'YS and the three Mardones titles are electrical, however, and the Fitziu is a commercial Pathé issue, as duly noted in the July-August, 1960 bulletin.

Side 1 (185 A):

Bands 1-3: The original playing speed of these unpublished takes is 77.64 rpm, dubbed here at 78.26 rpm. The OTELLO aria was subsequently issued in the Historic Masters series as HMB 36.

Band 4: The FAUST "Trio" presented here is the unpublished version, 4188f, distinguished by Melba holding her final note with Sammarco and McCormack. The other version, 4190f, in which Melba drops off the final note before her two colleagues, was first issued as IRCC 7 in August, 1932, and subsequently appeared as Irish HMV IRX 1006 and Victor "Heritage" 15-1019. Smith later issued 4188f on ASCO A-110 and Rhapsody 6012, a British label usually taken from his TAP masters. The original playing speed of 4188f is 76.00 rpm, dubbed on EJS 185 at 78.26 rpm.

Bands 5-6: The original playing speeds of these Melba items, both dubbed here at 78.26 rpm, are 76.00 and 77.43 rpm, respectively.

Band 7: This DON CÉSAR "aria" is in fact a vocal arrangement of an "Entr'Acte," with words by Jules Ruelle. The opera was published by Heugel et Cie., copyright 1895.

Melba made three recordings of the piece for the Gramophone Company, none of them issued commercially except on the complete Melba LP set, RLS-719: 4184f (11 May, 1910) is unique in its diminuendos on the long held notes in the internal cadenza; 4206f (19 May, 1910) has a bad vocal glitch on the final note of Melba's rapid, alternating two-note figure before the final cadence; 4207f (19 May, 1910), presented here, has neither the diminuendos or the glitch. A fourth recording was made for Victor on 24 August, 1910 (matrix C-9370-1) and was issued by both Victor and the Gramophone Company on Victor 88252, 88662, and 6216 and HMV DB 711.

The speed of 4207f, dubbed on EJS 185 at 78.26 rpm, is 77.43 rpm.

Band 8: The Battistini "La Partida" was assigned catalog number 2-062013 but was never issued. It was subsequently included on EMI's complete Battistini set, EX 29 0790 3 (issued in the U.S. as Seraphim IG 6153).

Side 2 (185 B):

Band 1: This electrical "Aubade" was issued circa July, 1931. The EMI recording ledgers give no city and no precise date for the actual session.

Bands 2-4: These rare Mardones electricals were not issued in the U.S.: Columbia A4060 is South American, and Regal RS2008 is Spanish. The UGONOTTI was coupled with "La Molinera de Santianes--Canciones asturiana" of Fernandez on the original ten-inch, blue-label Spanish Regal issue.

Band 5: Anna Fitziu (or Fitzhugh) created the role of *Rosario* in the world premiere of GOYESCAS at the Met on 28 January, 1916. Martinelli and De Luca were also in the cast. The aria was issued originally only as 14-inch hill-and-dale Pathé 82001. It was subsequently dubbed as IRCC 3147 in April, 1954 and appeared in the second volume of "The Record of Singing" (EMI RLS 743).

Band 6: De Luca's CHENIER aria is unique in that none of his other Fonotipias from either 1905 or 1907--published or unpublished--was accompanied by orchestra, as this one is.

Bands 7-11: All of the Patti items given here, with the exception of the spoken New Year's greeting to her husband, were originally recorded at 73.47 rpm, and dubbed for EJS 185 at 78.26 rpm. All were later included in EMI's complete Patti set (RLS 711 and German Electrola C 147-01 500/01 M), and more recently on a Pearl CD Patti recital (GEMM 9312). The MARTHA was issued as Historic Masters HMB 78 in 1991.

Band 7: This unaccompanied speech was assigned no matrix number, but is thought to have been recorded during Patti's first session at Craig-y-Nos in December, 1905. It begins, "God bless you, my dear husband, for the New Year, 1906."

Band 9: Given on the label of EJS 185 as "On the Banks."

Band 11: "Home Sweet Home" was adapted by Bishop for his 3-act opera CLARI, or THE MAID OF MILAN (Covent Garden, 3 May, 1823) from his own 3-act musical drama, WHO WANTS A WIFE? (Covent Garden, 16 April, 1816), with a new text by J. H. Paine. The song served as the main theme of CLARI.

EJS 186: "The Golden Age of Opera" (1 LP)
Issued July-August, 1960

"POTPOURRI (10)"

SIDE 1 (186 A):

* 1. EZIO PINA, bass; MAX ALTGLASS, tenor; WILFRED ENGELMAN, bass (Metropolitan Opera House Orchestra and Chorus/Maurice de Abravanel): SAMSON ET DALILA, Act I: Que vois-je? . . . Maudites à jamais (Saint-Saëns) (F)
Metropolitan Opera broadcast, NYC, 26 Dec 1936

* 2. EZIO PINZA, bass; GERTRUDE WETTERGREN, contralto; RENÉ MAISON, tenor (Metropolitan Opera House Orchestra and Chorus/Maurice de Abravanel): SAMSON ET DALILA, Act III: Viens, Dalila . . . to the end of the act (Saint-Saëns) (F)
Metropolitan Opera broadcast, NYC, 26 Dec 1936

* 3. EZIO PINZA, bass (Metropolitan Opera House Orchestra/Cesare Sodero): LA BOHEME, Act IV: Vecchia zimarra senti (Puccini) (I)
Metropolitan Opera broadcast, Chicago, ABC, 29 Apr 1944

* 4. FREDERICK JAGEL, tenor (Metropolitan Opera House Orchestra/Paul Breisach): AÏDA, Act I: Se quel guerrier . . . Celeste Aïda (postlude omitted) (Verdi) (I)
Metropolitan Opera broadcast, NYC, 21 Feb 1942

* 5. MARGARET MATZENAUER, contralto, and MILTON CROSS, announcer (pf/?): AÏDA, Act IV: L'abborita rivale . . . Oh! che mai parlo / Gia! sacerdoti . . . di vita a te sarò (Verdi) (I)
Metropolitan Opera broadcast (Intermission Feature), NYC, 21 Feb 1942

* 6. GIOVANNI MARTINELLI, tenor (Nicolai Rescigno/pf): LA JUIVE, Act IV: Rachel, quand du Seigneur (Halévy) (F)
Private recording (acetate) ?New York City, 25 Jan 1948

Side 2 (186 B):

1. GRACE MOORE, soprano; CHARLES KULLMAN, tenor; GERHARD PECHNER, bass-baritone (Metropolitan Opera House Orchestra/Cesare Sodero): TOSCA, Act I excerpts (Puccini) (I)
a) KULLMAN and PECHNER: Recondita armonia . . . Scherzo coi fanti e lascia stare i santi (Puccini) (I)
b) MOORE and KULLMAN: Mario! Mario! . . . Lo giuro, amore (Va!)
Metropolitan Opera broadcast, NYC, 8 Apr 1944

* 2. JOSEPH SCHMIDT, tenor (orch/?): L'ELISIR D'AMORE, Act II: Una furtiva lagrima (Donizetti) (I)
Broadcast, source and date unknown

* 3. JOSEPH SCHMIDT, tenor (?New York Philharmonic Orch/Erno Rapee): RIGOLETTO, Act IV: La donna è mobile (Verdi) (I)
Broadcast, ***GENERAL MOTORS HOUR***, Carnegie Hall, WEAF, NYC, 7 Mar 1937

* 4. JOSEPH SCHMIDT, tenor (?New York Philharmonic Orch. and chorus/ Erno Rapee): DER ZIGEUNERBARON, Act I: Als flotter Geist (J. Strauss) (G)
Broadcast, ?***GENERAL MOTORS HOUR***, Carnegie Hall, NYC, WJZ, ?11 Apr or ?31 Oct 1937

* 5. VIRGILIO LAZZARI, bass (pf/?): GLI UGONOTTI, Act I: [Piff! Paff!] Finita è pe'frati [Pour les couvents c'est fini] (Meyerbeer) (I)
?Private recording (acetate) New York, circa 1948

6. FREDERICK JAGEL, tenor (Metropolitan Opera House Orchestra/ Wilfred Pelletier): L'AFRICAINE, Act IV: [O paradiso] col divin . . . to the end of the aria
Broadcast, ***THE METROPOLITAN OPERA PRESENTS***, WJZ, NYC, 11 Mar 1945

NOTES: EJS 186

Side 1 (186 A):

Bands 1-2: This trio, along with other extensive excerpts, was reissued on EJS 516 (June, 1970), while the Pinza/Wettergren "J'ai gravi la montagne" from this 1936 Met performance was included earlier on EJS 170 (January, 1960). A Wettergren aria from the performance appeared on EJS 213 (May, 1961).

Library of Congress tape: 5174-30 (complete broadcast).

Band 3: It has not been determined with absolute certainty that the Pinza "Vecchia zimarra" is from the Met Chicago (tour) performance cited. What is probably Kullman's 29 April, 1944 "Che gelida manina" appeared on EJS 172 (January, 1960).

Band 4: The missing postlude was not a performance cut. A Greco-Thomas Act III duet from this performance was featured on EJS 141 (January, 1959).

Band 5: The Matzenauer AÏDA excerpt begins at "L'aborrita," and cuts directly to "Gia! sacerdoti" after "Oh! che mai parlo." The pianist is unknown, but may be Boris Goldovsky.

This intermission feature accompanied the Jagel-Greco AÏDA matinee conducted by Breisach, and is Matzenauer's last known recording as a singer. Milton Cross is heard thanking her and expressing his hope that she will soon be heard in a regular Met performance.

Band 6: Party noises can be heard in the background of the "Rachel."

Side 2 (186 B):

Bands 2-4: The July-August, 1960 EJS bulletin gives all three items as "1937." Schmidt made six appearances on NBC's ***GENERAL MOTORS HOUR*** in 1937. All of them were broadcast from Carnegie Hall with Rapee conducting (Oskar Strauss was also featured as conductor on 10 October). None of the shows is listed as including the ELISIR aria (which Schmidt sang at his Carnegie Hall recital on 26 October, 1937), but it may have been an addition or a substitution. The ZIGEUNERBARON aria may have been performed on either the 11 April or 31 October, 1937 WJZ broadcasts, as excerpts from the opera were prominently featured in both (the 11 April show included a "Treasure Waltz," probably the "Schatz-Walzer," Op. 418, based on themes from ZIGEUNERBARON, which was recorded commercially as a vocal arrangement by Miliza Korjus on Victor 12-0327). The orchestra for all of the Carnegie Hall shows is reported to have been the New York Philharmonic, though it was not credited as such.

Band 5: Lazzari's "Piff! Paff!" was either performed at a private New York City party--probably at the Ansonia Hotel (as the MASCHERE "Stutter Song" on EJS 141 may have been)--in which case the pianist may be Nicola Rescigno, or on a ***CAROL LONGONE OPERALOGUE*** broadcast.

EJS 187 ("The Golden Age of Opera") (1 LP)
Issued September, 1961

PETER IBBETSON (Deems Taylor-Constance Collier/after Du Maurier) (E)
Opera in 3 Acts (Revised Edition) (excerpts)
Metropolitan Opera House Orchestra and Chorus/Tullio Serafin
Metropolitan Opera broadcast, NYC, 17 Mar 1934

CAST:
Edward Johnson (*Peter Ibbetson*); Lawrence Tibbett (*Colonel Ibbetson*); Lucrezia Bori (*Mary*); Gladys Swarthout (*Mrs. Deane*); Ina Bourskaya (*Mrs. Glyn*); Angelo Bada (*Achille*; Léon Rothier (*Major Duquesnois*); Louis D'Angelo (*Chaplain*); Giordano Paltrinieri (*Charlie Plunkett*); Millo Picco (*Guy Mainwaring*); Max Altglass (*Footman*); Phradie Wells (*Diana Vivash*); Grace Divine (*Madge Plunkett*); Philine Falco (*Victorine*); Elda Vettori (*Sister of Charity*); Alfredo Gandolfi (*Manservant*); George Cehanovsky (*Prison Governor*); Alfredo Gandolfi (*Turnkey*).

People of the Dream: George Cehanovsky (*Pasquier de la Marière*); Dorothea Flexer (*Marie Pasquier*); Helen Gleason (*Mme. Seraskier*).

SIDE 1 (187 A):

Act I: a) BOURSKAYA, TIBBETT, PALTRINIERI, and PICCO: Dear friend, what is the poem called? . . . to the end of Colonel Ibbetson's aria, "Si vous croyez que je vais dire" (p. 17-23)

b) SWARTHOUT, GLEASON, CEHANOVSKY, and JOHNSON: Your parents, were they English? . . . She too, I think, is dead (pp. 43-57)

c) ALTGLASS, SWARTHOUT, BORI, BOURSKAYA, WELLS, DIVINE, PALTRINIERI, PICCO, JOHNSON, and TIBBETT: Her Grace, the Duchess of Towers . . . to the end of the act (pp. 66-91)

Act II: a) JOHNSON, ROTHIER and VETTORI: Mon commandant, vous rappelez-vous votre aimi Pasquier? . . . Monsieur. A bientôt (pp. 114-123)

SIDE 2 (187 B):

Act II: JOHNSON and BORI: Do you come often to Paris? . . . to the end of the act (pp. 177-195)

Act III: a) BORI, JOHNSON, and CHORUS: Chantant la savoyarde, dansant la montagnarde En revenant d'Auvergne . . . to the end of the love duet, "Dearest . . . Dearest . . . I have sought you everywhere" (pp. 255-289) (chorus incomplete)

b) BORI, JOHNSON, and CHORUS: I knew that you would come . . . to the end of the opera (pp. 316-329)

NOTES: EJS 187

Taken from Tibbet's aluminum transcriptions. PETER IBBETSON was originally prepared (and numbered) for release in September, 1960, but was witheld for a year and announced in the September, 1961 bulletin. The sound, as the bulletin notes, is poor, ostensibly because Tibbett played the original discs "almost to death." The performance was reissued in February, 1973 as UORC 143.

Heard here is the composer's revision of the original score, which had premiered at the Met on 7 February, 1931 with a similar cast (but with Telva for Swarthout, Windheim for Altglass, Egener for Vettori, and Frigerio, Biondo and Doninelli as the *People of the Dream*).

The pagination given in the listing is taken from the original 1930 version of the score published by Fischer.

34.7 rpm has been suggested for EJS 187 (Act III may require a slightly higher speed), but it would appear that the Act III Finale with Johnson and Bori was performed a half-step below score pitch, possibly as a practical concession to these two veterans.

EJS 188: "The Golden Age of Opera" (3 LPs)
Issued September, 1960

SIDES 1-6 (188 A-F):

FAUST (Gounod) (F)
Opera in 5 Acts (complete)
Metropolitan Opera House Orchestra and Chorus/Wilfred Pelletier
Metropolitan Opera broadcast, Boston, NBC, 6 Apr 1940

CAST:
Richard Crooks (*Faust*); Helen Jepson (*Marguerite*); Ezio Pinza (*Méphistophélès*); Leonard Warren (*Valentin*); Helen Olheim (*Siébel*); Thelma Votipka (*Marthe*); Wilfred Engelman (*Wagner*).

EJS 189: "The Golden Age of Opera" (2 LPs)
Issued September, 1960

SIDES 1-4 (189 A-D):

RIENZI (Wagner) (G)
Opera in 5 Acts (abridged)
?Berlin State Opera House Orchestra and Chorus/?Robert Heger
Broadcast, ?Vienna, circa 1950

CAST:
Gunther Treptow (*Rienzi*); Gerda Scheyrer (*Irene*); Hilde Rössl-Majdan (*Adriano*); Adolf Vogel (*Colonna*); Walter Berry (*Orsini*); Oskar Czerwenka (*Raimondo*); Waldemar Kmentt (*Baroncelli*); Otto Wiener (*Cecchio*); Friedl Riegler (*Friedensbote*).

NOTES: EJS 189

EJS 189 was misnumbered in the wax of all copies as 187 A-D.

This could very possibly be an abridged concert performance of RIENZI, and judging from the cast, is more likely to have come from Vienna than Berlin (as claimed in the September, 1960 bulletin, which cites the Berlin State Opera House Orchestra under Heger). Except for Treptow, the principals--Scheyrer, Rössl-Majdan, and Berry--were all associated at the time with the Vienna State Opera.

The performance, edited with others to make a larger composite, later appeared as Penzance 8, where the portions featured on EJS 189 were attributed by producer Roger Frank to a Vienna broadcast: nothing more could be determined.

In addition to numerous internal cuts, especially in ensembles and orchestral passages, the omissions on EJS 189 can be summarized briefly:

Act I/i:	The ensemble following *Rienzi's* arioso, "Zur Ruhe!." *Raimondo* and *Nobles* omitted at the end of *Rienzi's* aria, "Doch höret ihr der Trompete Ruf."
Act I/ii:	The Trio, "Noch schlägt in seiner Brust."
Act I/iv:	The first verse of chorus, "Befreier, Retter," and the solo parts for *Cecco*, *Adriano*, and *Rienzi* before the final verse.
Act II/i:	The ensemble following the first verse of *Friedensbote's* "Ich sa die Stadt."
Act II/iii:	The reception of the *Ambassadors* through *Adriano's* "Rienzi, sei auf deiner Hut."
Act II/iv:	The Ballet
Act II/v:	The ensemble, "O lasst der Gnade Himmelslicht," through *Rienzi's* "Euch Edlen dieses Volk."
Act III/i:	The orchestral introduction.
Act III/ii:	The battle hymn and ensemble to the entry of the defeated *Nobles*.
Act IV/ii:	The beginning of the *Monks'* chorus, "Vae tibi maledicte."
Act V	Act V/ii-iii: The *Rienzi-Irene* duet and *Adriano-Irene* duet.

The Act II/i Chorus of *Friedensboten* is inserted into the middle of Rienzi's "Des Frieden, des Gesetztes grosse nu."

These cuts are given using the Hollreiser/Dresden State Opera recording (issued in the mid 1970s as HMV SLS 990, Electrola 1C 193-02 776/80 Q, and in the U.S., Angel SELX-3818) as a point of reference. The EMI set (which is not complete) runs a full 200 minutes, where EJS 189 runs just over 100 minutes; the Penzance 8 compilation runs some 230 minutes.

The Act III/ii Finale used for the EJS 189 performance is another mystery, as it is musically quite different from the version used by Hollreiser. Wagner's own 1843 revision was used for the EMI set; the composer's original 1840 version, first performed in Dresden in 1842, was only published as a piano-vocal score; the Felix Mottl-Cosima Wagner-Julius Kniese "revision," probably dating from the 1880s, was published in orchestral score, but was in disrepute even in 1950.

A live performance from the mid 1940s with Max Lorenz was issued some time ago on the Acanta label, but has not been identified conclusively.

The playing speed of the EJS 189 abridgement is about 32.8 rpm.

EJS 190: "The Golden Age of Opera" (1 LP)
Issued October, 1960

"ROSA PONSELLE IN OPERA (1934-37)"

SIDE 1 (190 A):

* 1. w. studio orch/Andre Kostelanetz: ALCESTE, Act I: Divinités du Styx (Gluck) (I)
Broadcast, ***CHESTERFIELD HOUR***, WABC, NYC, 3 Dec 1934

* 2. w. studio orch/Andre Kostelanetz: DON GIOVANNI, K.277, Act I: Batti, batti o bel Masetto (Mozart) (I)
Broadcast, ***CHESTERFIELD HOUR***, WABC, NYC, 1 Oct 1934

* 3. w. Los Angeles Philharmonic Orchestra/Erno Rapee: SEMIRAMIDE, Act I: Bel raggio lusingher (Rossini) (I)
Broadcast, ***GENERAL MOTORS HOUR***, KFI, Hollywood Bowl, Los Angeles, 24 May 1936

4. w. studio orch and chorus/Andre Kostelanetz: CARMEN, Act I: L'amour est un oiseau rebelle ["Habanera"] (Bizet) (F)
Broadcast, ***CHESTERFIELD HOUR***, WABC, NYC, 25 Mar 1936

5. w. studio orch/Andre Kostelanetz: LA VESTALE, Act II: Tu che invoco ["Preghiera"] (Spontini) (I)
Broadcast, ***CHESTERFIELD HOUR***, WABC, NYC, 1 Apr 1936

6. w. studio orch/Erno Rapee: AïDA, Act I: Ritorna vincitor!
Broadcast, ***GENERAL MOTORS HOUR***, WEAF, Carnegie Hall, NYC, 27 Sep 1936

7. w. studio orch/Andre Kostelanetz: CARMEN, Act I: Près des remparts de Séville ["Seguidilla"] (Bizet) (F)
Broadcast, ***CHESTERFIELD HOUR***, WABC, NYC, 26 Feb 1936

SIDE 2 (190 B):

1. a) w. Metropolitan Opera House Orchestra and Chorus/Ettore Panizza: LA TRAVIATA, Act I:
   a) Ah fors è lui (Verdi) (I)
   b) Sempre libera (Verdi) (I)
   Metropolitan Opera broadcast, NYC, 5 Jan 1935

* 2. w. studio orch/Frank Black: FEDRA: O divina Afrodite (Romano Romani) (I)
Broadcast, ***MAGIC KEY OF RCA***, WJZ, NYC, 2 May 1937

3. w. studio orch/Andre Kostelanetz: CARMEN, Act II: Les tringles des sistres! ["Chanson bohème"] (Bizet) (F)
Broadcast, ***CHESTERFIELD HOUR***, WABC, NYC, 4 Mar 1936

* 4. w. studio orch/Erno Rapee: OTELLO, Act IV: Ave Maria (Verdi) (I)
Broadcast, ***GENERAL MOTORS HOUR***, WEAF, Carnegie Hall, NYC, 27 Sep 1936

5. w. studio orch/Andre Kostelanetz: CARMEN, Act III: En vain pour éviter ["Card Scene"] (Bizet) (F)
   Broadcast, ***CHESTERFIELD HOUR***, WABC, NYC, 26 Feb 1936

6. w. studio orch/Andre Kostelanetz: CAVALLERIA RUSTICANA: Voi lo sapete (Mascagni) (I)
   Broadcast, ***CHESTERFIELD HOUR***, WABC, NYC, 11 Mar 1936

* 7. w. Los Angeles Philharmonic Orchestra/Erno Rapee: LA TRAVIATA, Act III: Addio del passato (Verdi) (I)
   Broadcast, ***GENERAL MOTORS HOUR***, KFI, Hollywood Bowl, Los Angeles, 24 May 1936

NOTES: EJS 190

The first of a series of three LPs (EJS 190-192) devoted to Ponselle. Several of the items on EJS 190 appeared in 1956 on EJS 104 (I/1, 2, 3, and II/7); the two TRAVIATA arias on side 2 are from the complete Met broadcast issued the same year as EJS 107 (and subequently reissued on Pearl LP GEMM 235/236 and CD GEMM 9317).

Bands 1, 2, 3, and 6 of side 1, and 2, 4, and 6 of side 2 appeared in May-June, 1979 on ANNA 1036; band 5 of side 1 was included in that same issue on ANNA 1037. UORC 118 (May-June, 1972) contained items II/4 and 6.

Side 1 (190 A):

Bands 1-2: A spoken introduction, probably genuine to this broadcast, precedes the dubbing of this "Batti, batti" on MDP LP 012.
Library of Congress tape: 5063-1 (complete broadcast).

Band 3: Issued earlier on EJS 104 (1956). Though billed as the ***LOS ANGELES PHILHARMONIC*** in the *New York Times*, this concert was among Ponselle's regular ***GENRAL MOTORS HOUR*** broadcasts.

Side 2 (190 B):

Band 2: Library of Congress tape: 15778-63B (complete broadcast).

Band 4: This "Ave Maria" appeared earlier on EJS 184, and was later reissued by Smith on UORC 118, described as an unpublished Victor!

Band 7: See note for I/3. The TRAVIATA was also issued on EJS 104.

EJS 191: "The Golden Age of Opera" (1 LP)
Issued October, 1960

"ROSA PONSELLE IN SONGS BY FRENCH, GERMAN, ITALIAN AND SPANISH COMPOSERS (1925; 1934-37)"

SIDE 1 (EJS 191 A):

* 1. w. studio orch/Erno Rapee: VASCO DA GAMA: "Ouvre ton coeur" (Bizet) (F)
Broadcast, *GENERAL MOTORS HOUR*, WEAF, Carnegie Hall, NYC, 27 Sep 1936

2. w. studio orch/Andre Kostelanetz: "L'ultima canzone" (Tosti) (I)
Broadcast, *CHESTERFIELD HOUR*, WABC, NYC, 11 Mar 1936

3. w. studio orch/Andre Kostelanetz: "Der Erlkönig," D. 328 (Schubert) (G)
Broadcast, *CHESTERFIELD HOUR*, WABC, NYC, 4 Mar 1936

4. w. studio orch/Andre Kostelanetz: "Clavelitos" (Valverde) (I)
Broadcast, *CHESTERFIELD HOUR*, WABC, NYC, 4 Mar 1936

5. w. studio orch/Andre Kostelanetz: "Ave Maria" (Sandoval) (L)
Broadcast, *CHESTERFIELD HOUR*, WABC, NYC, 25 Mar 1936

6. w. pf/?: "Après un rêve," Op. 7, no. 1 (Anon.-trans. Bussine-Fauré) (F)
Private recording, ?Villa Pace, Baltimore, 15 May 1950

7. w. studio orch/Erno Rapee: "Dicitencello vuje" (Falvo) (I)
Broadcast, *GENERAL MOTORS HOUR*, WEAF, Carnegie Hall, NYC, 27 Sep 1936

SIDE 2 (191 B):

1. w. studio orch/Andre Kostelanetz: "El Morenita (Buzzi-Peccia) (S)
Broadcast, *CHESTERFIELD HOUR*, WABC, NYC, 1 Apr 1936

2. w. Los Angeles Philharmonic Orchestra/Erno Rapee: "Marechiare" (Tosti) (I)
Broadcast, *GENERAL MOTORS HOUR*, KFI, Hollywood Bowl, Los Angeles, 24 May 1936

3. w. pf/Igor Chichagov: "Ave Maria" (Luzzi) (L)
Private recording, ?Villa Pace, Baltimore, 7 Dec 1953

4. w. studio orch/Andre Kostelanetz: SIX SONGS, Op. 6, no. 6: None but the Lonely Heart (Tchaikovsky) (E)
Broadcast, *CHESTERFIELD HOUR*, WABC, NYC, 26 Feb 1936

5. w. studio orch/Andre Kostelanetz: "Goodbye" (Whyte-Melville - Tosti) (E)
Broadcast, *CHESTERFIELD HOUR*, WABC, NYC, 1 Apr 1936

6. w. orch/Josef Pasternack: "La Rosita" (Dupont) (S)
BVE-32851-5 Camden, 4 Jun 1925 Victor unpub HMV VA 69

7. w. orch/Josef Pasternack: "La Spagnola" (Di Chiara) (I)
BVE-32873-2 Camden, 5 Jun 1925 Victor unpub HMV VA 69

NOTES: EJS 191

The two private recordings were probably made at Villa Pace, Ponselle's estate in Baltimore, Maryland.

Side 1 (191 A):

Band 1: It would seem that Bizet's venerable "Ouvre ton coeur" originally appeared in the composer's VASCO DA GAMA (1859), a "symphonic ode," but was subsequently published amid other fragments from his obscure and unfinished operatic works in a collection of SEIZE MÉLODIES (1886). This, according to Winton Dean's *Bizet* (London: Dent, 1948), p. 149. Curiously, the second edition of Dean's book, published in 1964, omits any mention of the song by title and supresses the earlier reference to its origin.

Two broadcasts of the song--Lucrezia Bori (1936) and Grace Moore (1940)--appear on EJS 247 (September, 1962), attributed to Bizet's equally obscure IVAN IV (aka IVAN LE TERRIBLE), an unfinished opera composed and revised between 1862 and 1865, but lost until its 1946 concert revival: the work was reconstructed by conductor Henri Busser in 1951 for a belated stage premiere in Bordeaux. The Busser reconstruction was issued in December, 1972 as UORC 135.

EJS 192: "The Golden Age of Opera" (1 LP)
Issued October, 1960

"ROSA PONSELLE IN ENGLISH SONGS (1925; 1934-7)"

SIDE 1 (192 A):

* 1. w. studio orch and chorus/Frank Black: "Carry Me Back to Old Virginny" (Bland) (E)
Broadcast, ***MAGIC KEY OF RCA***, WJZ, NYC, 2 May 1937

2. w. studio orch/Andre Kostelanetz: "The Old Refrain" (Brandl-arr. Kreisler) (E)
Broadcast, ***CHESTERFIELD HOUR***, WABC, NYC, 11 March, 1936

* 3. w. studio orch/Andre Kostelanetz: "The Cuckoo Clock" (Griselle-Young) (E)
Broadcast, ***CHESTERFIELD HOUR***, WABC, NYC, 1 Oct 1934

4. w. studio orch/Andre Kostelanetz: "Night Wind" (Farley) (E)
Broadcast, ***CHESTERFIELD HOUR***, WABC, NYC, 25 Mar 1936

5. w. studio orch/Andre Kostelanetz: "When I Have Sung My Songs" (Ernest Charles) (E)
Broadcast, ***CHESTERFIELD HOUR***, WABC, NYC, 18 Mar 1936

6. w. studio orch/Erno Rapee: "Homing" (Teresa del Riego) (E)
Broadcast, ***GENERAL MOTORS HOUR***, WEAF, Carnegie Hall, NYC, 27 Sep 1936

7. w. studio orch/Andre Kostelanetz: "Comin' Thro' the Rye" (trad.) (E)
   Broadcast, ***CHESTERFIELD HOUR***, WABC, NYC, 11 Mar 1936

* 8. w. studio orch and chorus/Andre Kostelanetz: I Carry You in My Pocket (Magidson-Conrad) (E)
   Broadcast, ***CHESTERFIELD HOUR***, WABC, NYC, 26 Feb 1936

SIDE 2 (192 B):

1. w. studio orch and chorus/Andre Kostelanetz: "Humoresque" (Dvorak) (E)
   Broadcast, ***CHESTERFIELD HOUR***, WABC, NYC, 18 Mar 1936

* 2. w. studio orch/Frank Black: MADEMOISELLE MODISTE, Act: Kiss Me Again (Blossom-Herbert) (E)
   Broadcast, ***MAGIC KEY OF RCA***, WJZ, NYC, 2 May 1937

* 3. w. studio orch/Andre Kostelanetz: "I Love You Truly" (Carrie Jacobs Bond) (E)
   Broadcast, ***CHESTERFIELD HOUR***, WABC, NYC, 1 Oct 1934

4. w. studio orch/Andre Kostelanetz: "Danny Boy" (traditional-Frederick E. Wetherley) (E)
   Broadcast, ***CHESTERFIELD HOUR***, WABC, NYC, 4 Mar 1936

* 5. w. pf/Ponselle: CLARI, or THE MAID OF MILAN: "Home, Sweet Home" (Paine-Bishop) (E)
   Broadcast, ***MAGIC KEY OF RCA***, WJZ, NYC, 2 May 1937

6. w. studio orch/Andre Kostelanetz: "The Cuckoo" (Liza Lehmann) (E)
   Broadcast, ***CHESTERFIELD HOUR***, WABC, NYC, 1 Apr 1936

* 7. w. orch/Josef Pasternack: "The Little Old Garden" ["Sanctuary"] (Hewitt) (E)
   BVE-32850-2 Camden, 1 Jun 1925 Victor unpub HMV VA 67

8. w. orch/Josef Pasternack: "Beloved" (Silberta) (E)
   BVE-32852-5 Camden, 5 Jun 1925 Victor unpub HMV VA 67

NOTES: EJS 192

Side 1 (192 A):

Band 1: Library of Congress tape: 15778-63B (complete broadcast).

Band 3: Library of Congress tape: 5063-1 (complete broadcast).

Band 8: This song is from the score of the 1935 Fox musical, ***HERE'S TO ROMANCE*** which featured, among others, Nino Martini (making his film debut) and Ernestine Schumann Heink. Martini sang the song in the film.

Side 2 (192 B):

Band 2: Library of Congress tape: 15778-63B (complete broadcast).

Band 3: Library of Congress tape: 5063-1 (complete broadcast).

Band 5: See THE note for EJS 185 (II/11) re. CLARI, or THE MAID OF MILAN.
Library of Congress tape: 15778-63B (complete broadcast).

Band 7: Under the title "Somewhere a voice is calling"--as sung by Mary Garden--this performance was accidentally recycled on EJS 397 (May, 1967).

EJS 193: "The Golden Age of Opera" (1 LP)
Issued October, 1960

SIDES 1-2 (193 A-B):

IL TABARRO (Puccini) (I)
Opera in One Act (complete)
Metropolitan Opera House Orchestra and Chorus/Cesare Sodero
Metropolitan Opera broadcast, NYC, 5 Jan 1946

CAST:
Lawrence Tibbett (*Michele*); Frederick Jagel (*Luigi*); Alessio DePaolis (*Tinca*); Virgilio Lazzari (*Talpa*); Licia Albanese (*Giorgetta*); Margaret Harshaw (*Frugola*); Anthony Marlowe (*Song Peddler*); Maxine Stellman and Thomas Hayward (*Lovers*).

EJS 194: "The Golden Age of Opera" (2 LPs)
Issued November, 1960

SIDES 1-4 (194 A-D):

LODOLETTA (Mascagni) (I)
Opera 3 in Acts (complete)
Orchestra and Chorus of Radio Italiana [RAI], Milano/Tullio Serafin
RAI broadcast, Milan, 28 Dec 1957

CAST:
Giuliana [Giulia] Tavolaccini (*Lodoletta*); Giuseppe Campora (*Flammen*); Giulio Fioravanti (*Gianetto*); Elda [Gina] Ercole (*Vannard*); Miti Truccato Pace (*Madwoman*); Amalia Oliva (*Maud*); Antonio Cassinelli (*Antonio*); Antonio Sacchetti (*Franz*); Mario Carlin (*Postman*); Mario Carlin (*A Voice*).

NOTES: EJS 194

The labels of EJS 194 give the date of this performance as 1958.

EJS 195: "The Golden Age of Opera" (2 LPs)
Issued November, 1960

SIDES 1-4 (195 A-D):

IRIS (Mascagni) (I)
Opera in 3 Acts (complete)
Orchestra and Chorus of the Teatro San Carlo di Napoli/Gabriele Santini
Broadcast, Teatro San Carlo, Naples, 6 Feb 1960

CAST:
Clara Petrella (*Iris*); Umberto Borsó (*Osaka*); Ivo Vinco (*Cieco*); Saturno Meletti (*Kyoto*); Aida Stefani (*A Geisha*); Gianni Avolanti (*A Peddler*); Ottavio Taddei (*A Ragpicker*).

EJS 196: "The Golden Age of Opera (1 LP)
Not issued

EJS 196 was prepared as an "Alexander Davidoff" recital, taken, ostensibly, from "live" performances of the mid 1920s. Fortunately, Smith was convinced by Aida Favia-Artsay that this attribution was incorrect, so the LP was never issued in the "Golden Age of Opera" series. Indeed, Davidoff's career supposedly ended in 1924 (*Keutch-Riemans* notes that the onset of deafness rendered him unable to perform from about 1912), after which he remained in Paris as a *regisseur* for the two Russian opera companies in residence there. He recorded for the Gramophone Company in Paris as late as April, 1931, however (a few of these electricals were issued in the plum "E" series), and these records establish without a doubt that the singer in question is *not* Davidoff.

The same material resurfaced in 1981 on ANNA 1068, labeled as live recitals by "Dimitri Smirnoff" from Aeolian Hall and Carnegie Hall, respectively, November, 1926. The Carnegie Hall items further boasted the accompaniment of the Boston Symphony Orchestra under Koussevitsky!

The first side of ANNA 1068 contains the following selections: the SALVATORE ROSA "Star vicna;" Scarlatti's "Se mai senti spirarti sul volto;" Caldara's "Alma del core;" Duparc's "Soupir;" Massenet's "Mon temps s'acheve;" Tosti's "Che fai tu, Luna in ciel;" Purcell's "Rule a Wife and Have a Wife" and "There's not a Swain in the Plain;" the MEISTERSINGER "Prize Song;" Levko's "Sleep, My Beauty" from MAY NIGHT; and Borodin's "Song of the Dark Forest," all with piano accompaniment and all given as Aeolian Hall, New York, November, 1926. Side two includes Prince Sinodal's Romance from DEMON; Tschaikowski's "Don Juan's Serenade;" the ELISIR D'AMORE "Una furtiva lagrima;" three songs by "Roberto Doellnersky;" and Lenki's Air from EUGENE ONEGIN--the Doellnersky songs and the ONEGIN aria are labeled as accompanied by the "Boston Symphony Orchestra: Serge Koussevitsky, Conductor, Carnegie Hall, New York, November, 1926."

The program of Smirnoff's 26 December, 1926 Aeolian Hall concert, accompanied by Prof. C. Shevedov on the piano, was given in the *New York Times* for that day as follows: "Aria" from LA FANCIULLA DEL WEST; Giordano's "Caro mio ben;" "Aria" from WERTHER; the "Serenade" from BARBIERE; the Indian Song from SADKO; Rachmaninoff's "O Cease thy Singing, Maiden Fair" and "Lilacs;" Lenski's Air from ONEGIN; the MANON "Rêve;" Liapunov's "Romance Oriental;" Rubinstein's "Persian Song" (sic); and an "Aria" from THE PEARL FISHERS. His encore was an unnamed song by Tosti. A review of the concert in the *Times* the following day commended the singer for his skillful use of the *voix blanche*, but dismissed his voice as "hard and throaty." This was Smirnoff's only documented New York appearance that year--could there have been others so late in his career?

None of the items featured on A.N.N.A. 1068 correspond to those sung at Smirnoff's Aeolian Hall recital, as given in either contemporary advertisements or reviews. No Boston Symphony concert featuring Smirnoff and Koussevitsky could be found. In fact, no American appearances by Smirnoff prior to the Aeolian Hall date could be documented.

Adding to the mystery is the fact that the recordings are described in the late-1980 ANNA bulletin as live 1926 performances captured on "78 rpm cardboard discs." "For the initial time in America," Smith claimed, "a recording from the stage was undertaken as was the case the same year with Nellie Melba's farewell in London at Covent Garden and Zenatello's Otello at the same house, also in 1926 . . . This is not only a first of one of the great tenors of this century, but also the historic first of recording from the stage in the U.S." Smirnoff's few commercial electricals for Parlophone, HMV, and Columbia make it very unlikely that the tenor featured on ANNA 1068 is him--Smith's tenor has an altogether more dramatic force to his voice. Smith summoned the testimony of long-time Metropolitan Opera baritone George Cehanovsky as "evidence," however: having heard the tenor perform MAY NIGHT in St. Petersburg in 1912, Cehanovsky is noted as endorsing Smirnoff as the singer in question.

ANNA 1068 proved to be one of the most controversial of all of Smith's issues--the identity of the singer remains to be discovered and is still the subject of passionate research by others (see *The Record Collector*, 35/5-7 [May-July, 1990], pp. 179-180). Only recently, a spokesman for one band of American enthusiasts approached co-author Bill Collins at a conference to proclaim that his group had, long ago, placed the mystery tenor, but to date, no information or evidence has been received from them.

The ANNA LP will be analyzed track-by-track in its proper place. It is thought that the unknown composer "Roberto Doellnersky" may prove to be the Rosetta Stone.

EJS 197: "The Golden Age of Opera" (1 LP)
Issued December, 1960

"KIRSTEN FLAGSTAD, SOPRANO / THIRTEEN UNPUBLISHED LIEDER"

SIDE 1 (197 A):

* 1. w. pf/Ernest Lush: SCHWANENGESANG, D. 957: No. 8: Der Atlas (Heine-Schubert) (G)
Broadcast, BBC, London, 5 Jul 1948

* 2. w. pf/Ernest Lush: WINTERREISE, D. 911, No. 15: "Die Krähe" (Müller-Schubert) (G)
Broadcast, BBC, London, 5 Jul 1948

* 3. w. pf/Ernest Lush: "Dem Unendlichen," D. 291 (Klopstock-Schubert) (G)
Broadcast, BBC, London, 5 Jul 1948

* 4. w. pf/Waldemar Alme: ACHT LIEDER, Op. 49, no. 5: Sie wissen's nicht (O. Panizza-R. Strauss) (G)
Broadcast, Norwegian Radio, Oslo, 7 May 1954

* 5. w. pf/Waldemar Alme: DREI LIEDER, Op. 29, no. 3: Nachtgang (Bierbaum-R. Strauss) (G)
Broadcast, Norwegian Radio, Oslo, 7 May 1954

* 6. w. pf/Waldemar Alme: FÜNF LIEDER, Op. 41, no. 4: Wiegenlied (Dehmel-R. Strauss) (G)
Broadcast, Norwegian Radio, Oslo, 7 May 1954

* 7. w. pf/Waldemar Alme: VIER LETZTE LIEDER, AV 150, no. 3: September (Hesse-R. Strauss) (G)
Broadcast, Norwegian Radio, Oslo, 7 May 1954

* 8. w. pf/Waldemar Alme: ACHT LIEDER, Op. 49, no. 1: Waldseligkeit (Dehmel-R. Strauss) (G)
Broadcast, Norwegian Radio, Oslo, 7 May 1954

SIDE 2 (197 B):

* 1. w. pf/Waldemar Alme: "Zur Ruh' zur Ruh'" (Korner-Wolf) (G)
Broadcast, Norwegian Radio, Oslo, 10 May 1954

* 2. w. pf/Waldemar Alme: "Gebet" (Mörike-Wolf) (G)
Broadcast, Norwegian Radio, Oslo, 10 May 1954

* 3. w. pf/Waldemar Alme: "Der Freund" (Eichendorff-Wolf) (G)
Broadcast, Norwegian Radio, Oslo, 10 May 1954

* 4. w. pf/Waldemar Alme: "Gesang Weylas" (Mörike-Wolf) (G)
Broadcast, Norwegian Radio, Oslo, 10 May 1954

* 5. w. pf/Waldemar Alme: "Anakreons Grab" (Goethe-Wolf) (G)
Broadcast, Norwegian Radio, Oslo, 10 May 1954

* 6. w. pf/Waldemar Alme: ITALIENISCHES LIEDERBUCH: "Heb' auf dein blondes Haupt" (Heyse-Wolf) (G)
Broadcast, Norwegian Radio, Oslo, 10 May 1954

* 7. w. pf: Waldemar Alme: "Morgenstimmung" (Reinick-Wolf) (G)
Broadcast, Norwegian Radio, Oslo, 10 May 1954

NOTES: EJS 197

This LP was mislabeled, as EJS 198. Norwegian Radio is properly Norsk Rikskringkasting [NRK].

Side 1 (197 A):

Bands 1-3: This 5 July, 1948 BBC broadcast was live, and was re-broadcast on 7 July over BBC 3. These three items later appeared on ANNA 1016 (September, 1978), while others from the broadcast were issued on EJS 170 (January, 1960) and Legendary Recordings LR 120.

Bands 4-8: The live Norwegian Radio concerts (see also items II/1-9) may have been pre-recorded for later broadcast: tapes of the concerts in a major U.S. archive have only the music, no announcements, and there would have been little point in "sanitizing" live broadcasts in such a manner after they had aired.

Norwegian Radio tape: NRK 3602 and 52369/1.

Side 2 (197 B):

Bands 1-9: Norwegian Radio tape: NRK 3604. In all, Flagstad sang twenty-four songs on this broadcast, all of them preserved on Stanford Archive of Recorded Sound tapes StARS 560000 M3, 560000 M4, and 540900 M3. A few were included on UORC 243 in April, 1975.

Howard Sanner's *Kirsten Flagstad Discography*, p. 104, lists "Lebe wohl" (Mörike-Wolf) and "Über Nacht" (Sturm-Wolf), both from the same broadcast, as among the contents of EJS 198 (given there as EJS 197), but neither is listed on the label and neither appears on the actual discs examined or reported.

EJS 198: "The Golden Age of Opera" (1 LP)
Issued December, 1960

"KIRSTEN FLAGSTAD, SOPRANO"

SIDE 1 (198 A):

* 1. w. orch/?: "Aagots Fjeldsang" (Thrane) (Nw)
NW 347 Oslo, 1914-1915 Odeon 5332A
Odeon 1775

* 2. w. orch/?: "Aa, Ola, Ola min eigen onge" (Folksong) (Nw)
NW 348 Oslo, 1914-1915 Odeon 5332A
Odeon 1775

3. w. orch/?: "Mot Kveld," Op. 42, no. 7 (Jynge - Backer-Grøndahl) (Nw)
BT-172-1 Oslo, 1 Oct 1923 HMV X-1946

4. w. orch/?: PEER GYNT, Op. 23, no. 1: Solveig's Song (Ibsen-Grieg) (Nw)
BT-177-1 Oslo, 2 Oct 1923 HMV X-1940

5. w. orch/?: "Saeterjentens Søndag" (Moe-Bull) (Nw)
BT-178-2 Oslo, 2 Oct 1923 HMV X-1940

* 6. w. pf/Maja Flagstad: "Mainat" (Krag-Sinding) (Nw)
BT-179-1 Oslo, 2 Oct 1923 HMV X-1946

7. w. orch/?: TOLV MELODIER, Op. 33, no. 2: Vaaren (Vinje-Grieg) (Nw)
mtx? Oslo, 1914-1915 Odeon 5348A

8. w. w. orch/?: "Ingalill" (Rosenfeld) (Nw)
mtx? Oslo, 1914-1915 Odeon 5348A

SIDE 2 (198 B):

* 1. w. orch/?: CLARI, or THE MAID OF MILAN: Hjem, Kjaere Hjem [Home, Sweet Home] (Paine-Bishop) (Nw)
mtx? Oslo, 1914-1915 Odeon 5371A

* 2. w. orch/?: "Endun et streif kun av sol" (Backer-Grøndahl) (Nw)
mtx? Oslo, 1914-1915 Odeon 5371A

3. w. pf/Eyvind Alnaes: "Sne" (Rode-Lie) (Nw)
BN-190-1 Oslo, 19 Jan 1929 HMV X-2974 AGSA 35
HMV AL-2265

4. w. pf/Eyvind Alnaes: "Lykken Mellem to Mennesker," Op. 26, no. 1 (Stuckenberg-Alnaes) (Nw)
BN-191-2 Oslo, 19 Jan 1929 HMV X-2974 AGSA 34

5. w. orch/?: "Saeterjentens Søndag" (Moe-Bull) (Nw)
BN-192-2 Oslo, 19 Jan 1929 HMV X-2975 AGSA 34
HMV AL 2265

6. w. orch/?: PEER GYNT, Op. 23, no. 1: Solveig's Song (Ibsen-Grieg) (Nw)
BN-193-1 Oslo, 19 Jan 1929 HMV X-2975 AGSA 35

7. w. orch/?: ROMANCER, Op. 39, no. 4: Millom Roser (Janson-Grieg) (Nw)
BN-194-1 Oslo, 19 Jan 1929 HMV X-3068

8. w. orch/?: ROMANCER, Op. 15, no. 4: Modersorg (Richardt-Grieg) (Nw)
BN-195-1 Oslo, 19 Jan 1929 HMV X-3068

NOTES: EJS 198

This LP, the first listed in the December, 1960 bulletin, was mislabeled "EJS 197" on some labels and in the 1970s EJS checklist.

Offered here is a sampling of Flagstad's earliest recordings, all made in Oslo. Matrix numbers for the acoustical Odeons are given where known: the 5000 catalog series was domestic Norwegian; the 1700 series were European issues. Both the "X"- and "AL"-prefix HMVs are ten-inch Scandanavian issues, the former a plum-label export series (many of which were pressed at Hayes), the latter domestic Norwegian issues. The "BT-prefix HMV matrix numbers are acoustical; those prefixed "BN" are electrical.

Maja Flagstad is identified on the labels as "Fry Maria Flagstad."

These same items later appeared on Harvest 1004 and Legendary recordings LR 120.

Side 1 (198 A):

Bands 1-2: Both of these were re-recorded on IRCC 3040 in October, 1948. See note for EJS 185 (II/11) re. CLARI, or THE MAID OF MILAN.

EJS 199: "The Golden Age of Opera" (1 LP)
Issued December, 1960

"KIRSTEN FLAGSTAD, SOPRANO"

SIDE 1 (199 A):

* 1. w. Oslo Philharmonic Orchestra/Hugo Kramm: SYMPHONIC SUITE FOR SOPRANO, "Mot Blåsno Høgdom (Kielland) (Nw)
Broadcast, Norwegian Radio, Bergen, 27 Sep 1953

SIDE 2 (199 B):

* 1. w. Oslo Philharmonic Orchestra/Hugo Kramm: SOLOKANTATE (*Psalm* 8 and *Esaias* 60, verses 1 to 3-Kvandal) (Nw)
Broadcast, Norwegian Radio, Bergen, 27 Sep 1953

* 2. w. pf/Waldemar Alme: GELLERT LIEDER, Op. 48, nos. 1-6 (Gellert-Beethoven) (G)
a) "Bitten"
b) "Die Liebe des Nächsten"
c) "Vom Tode"
d) "Die Ehre Gottes aus der Natur"
e) "Gottes Macht und Vorsehung"
f) "Busslied"
Broadcast, Norwegian Radio, Oslo, 8 Sep 1954

NOTES: EJS 199

These Norsk Rikskringkasting [NRK] broadcasts have also appeared on Rococo LP 5385 and Harvest LP 1005. Howard Sanner's *Kirsten Flagstad Discography*, p. 108 lists the following Beethoven songs as among the contents of EJS 199, but none of them appears on the labels or on the actual discs examined or reported. All derive from the same 8 September, 1954 Norwegian Radio broadcast that produced the GELLERT LIEDER, and all are accompanied by Waldemar Alme:

1. "Wonne der Wehmuth," Op. 83, no. 1 (Goethe-Beethoven) (G)
2. "Andenken," WoOp. 136 (Matthisson-Beethoven) (G)
3. "Ich liebe dich," WoOp. 123 (Herrosee-Beethoven) (G)
4. "An die Hoffnung," Op. 94 (Tiedge-Beethoven) (G)

Side 1 (199 A):

Band 1: Norwegian Radio tape: NRK 50652/1

Side 2 (199 B):

Band 1: Norwegian Radio tape: NRK 50455/1.

Bands 2a-f: Norwegian Radio tape: NRK 3608.

EJS 200: "The Golden Age of Opera" (1 LP)
Issued December, 1960

"KIRSTEN FLAGSTAD, SOPRANO"

SIDES 1-2 (200 A-B):

DIE WALKÜRE (Wagner) (G)
Opera in 3 Acts (Act I only)
Metropolitan Opera House Orchestra/Artur Bodanzky
Metropolitan Opera broadcast, NYC, 2 Feb 1935

CAST:
Paul Althouse (*Siegmund*); Emanuel List (*Hunding*); [Friedrich Schorr (*Wotan*)]; Kirsten Flagstad (*Sieglinde*); [Gertrude Kappel (*Brünnhilde*]); [Maria Olszewska (*Fricka*); [Dorothee Manski (*Helmwige*); [Phradie Wells (*Gerhilde*)]; [Pearl Besuner (*Ortlinde*)]; [Ina Bourskaya (*Rossweisse*)]; [Philine Falco (*Grimgerde*)]; [Doris Doe (*Waltraute*)]; [Elda Vettori (*Siegrune*)]; [Irra Petina (*Schwertleite*)].

NOTES: EJS 200

Presented here is the complete first act of Flagstad's legendary Met debut. Flagstad's extant Act II fragments later appeared on EJS 444 (October, 1968).

According to the December, 1960 bulletin, the WALKÜRE Act I was copied from Flagstad's own "78 rpm records."

EJS 201: "The Golden Age of Opera" (2 LPs)
Issued January, 1961

SIDES 1-4 (201 A-D):

LORELEY (Catalani) (E)
Opera in 3 Acts (complete)
Orchestra and Chorus of Radio Italiana [RAI], Milano/Alfredo Simonetto
RAI broadcast, Milan, 15 Dec 1954

CAST:
Anna de Cavalieri (*Loreley*); Rina Gigli (*Anna*); Kenneth Neate (*Walter*); Piero Guelfi (*Hermann*); Alfredo Colella (*Rodolfo*).

NOTES: EJS 201

The label of EJS 201 gives the date of this performance as 1960. Pitch is bit high, with 32.5 rpm suggested to compensate.

The third-act duet, "Vieni! Deh vien . . . Deh! ti rammenta," is reported to be an insert from the 1929 Merli-Scacciati commercial Columbia (GQX 10203 and D18066), matrices WBX 489-2 and 490-1, but this has not been confirmed.

Anna De Cavalieri was the Italian stage name of Anne McKnight.

EJS 202: "The Golden Age of Opera" (2 LP)
Issued January, 1961

SIDES 1-4 (202 A-D):

LA WALLY (Catalani) (I)
Opera in 4 Acts (complete)
Orchestra and Chorus of Radio Italiana [RAI], Roma/Arturo Basile
RAI broadcast, Rome, 29 Oct 1960

CAST:
Renata Tebaldi (*Wally*); Giacinto Prandelli (*Giuseppe Hagenbach*); Silvio Maionica (*Stromminger*); Dino Dondi (*Geller*); Jolanda Gardino (*Afra*); Pinuccia Perotti (*Walter*); Dimitri Lopatto (*An Old Soldier*).

NOTES: EJS 202

Subsequently issued as Movimento Musica 03.011, Fonit-Cetra LAR-21 (LP), and Fonit-Cetra CDC-7 (CD). Excerpts were issued as I Gioielli della Lirica LP GML-60 (where the performance is dated 20 October, 1960 in error) and Rodolphe CD RP C 32705.

EJS 203: "The Golden Age of Opera (2 LPs)
Issued February, 1961

SIDES 1-4 (203 A-D):

OTELLO (Rossini) (I)
Opera in 3 Acts (abridged)
Orchestra and Chorus of Radio Italiana [RAI], Roma/Fernando Previtali
RAI broadcast, Rome, 19 Jun 1960

CAST:
Agostino Lazzari (*Otello*); Giuseppe Baratti (*Iago*); Virginia Zeani (*Desdemona*); Herbert Handt (*Rodrigo*); Franco Ventriglia (*Barberigo*); Anna Reynolds (*Emilia*); Alfredo Nobile (*Lucio*); Tommaso Frascati (*The Doge*); [Tommaso Frascati (*A Gondolier*)].

NOTES: EJS 203

Mislabeled on some (early?) copies as EJS 103.

The Overture and the opening of Act III (and thus the role of the *Gondolier*) were omitted from this LP for purposes of timing: Act III begins with *Desdemona's* "Willow Song."

The set is reported to play at pitch at approximately 32.7 rpm.

This same performance was later issued complete as GOP 718, and in stereo, as Replica LP RPL 2419/21, while excerpts have appeared on I Gioielli della Lirica LP GML-47 (dated incorrectly as 18 June, 1960).

EJS 204: "The Golden Age of Opera" (2 LPs)
Issued February, 1961

SIDES 1-4 (204 A-D):

I MASNADIERI (Verdi) (I)
Opera in 4 Acts (complete)
Orchestra and Chorus of Radio Italiana [RAI], Milano/Alfredo Simonetto
RAI broadcast, Milan, 29 Mar 1951

CAST:
Adriana Guerrini (*Amalia*); Ralph Lambert (*Carlo Moor*); Renato Capecchi (*Francesco Moor*); Sesto Bruscantini (*Massimiliano Moor*); Angelo Mercuriali (*Arminio*); Dario Caselli (*Moser*); Guido Scarinci (*Rolla*).

NOTES: EJS 204

Only one cut is made, the Act III chorus, "Le rubi, gli stupri," but this may have been a performance cut.

The February, 1961 bulletin and the disc labels give 1960 as the date of this performance. The RAI chronology gives Rolando Panerai as *Francesco Moor*, while the labels of EJS 204 seem to be correct in their assignment of Capecchi.

From about the middle of Act I to the end of the opera, the pitch sags, requiring a playing speed of 34.3 rpm.

EJS 205: "The Golden Age of Opera" (2 LPs)
Issued March, 1961

SIDES 1-4 (205 A-D):

LO SCHIAVO (Gomes) (I)
Opera in 4 Acts (complete)
Orchestra and Chorus of the Teatro Muncipal, Rio de Janeiro/Santiago Guerra
?In-house performance, Teatro Municipal, Rio de Janeiro, 26 Jun 1959

CAST:
Ida Miccolis (*Ilára*); Lurivel Braga (*Iberé*); Alfredo Colisimo (*Américo*); Luiz Nascimento (*Count Rodrigo*); Antea Claudia (*Contessa di Boissy*); Alvarany Solano (*Goitacá*); Marino Terranova (*Gianfera*); Carlos Dittert (*Leon*).

NOTES: EJS 205

Neither the labels of EJS 205 or the Chavez chronology of the Teatro Municipal give the names of the singers appearing in Act III as the Botocudo, Tapaceá, Tupinambá, Carijó, Caiapó, and Arari chiefs.

The Overture was omitted from EJS 205 for purposes of timing.

This set probably derived from a pre-recorded tape of the performance broadcast in New York City, circa April, 1960, as part of a cultural exchange program.

EJS 206: "The Golden Age of Opera" (3 LPs)
Issued March, 1961

SIDES 1-6 (206 A-F):

LES VÊPRES SICILIENNES (Verdi) (I)
Opera in 5 Acts (complete)
Orchestra and Chorus of Radio Italiana [RAI], Torino/Mario Rossi
RAI broadcast, Turin, 16 Nov 1955 (recorded 30 Sep 1954)

CAST:
Anita Cerquetti (*Elena*); Mario Ortica (*Arrigo*); Carlo Tagliabue (*Guido di Monforte*); Boris Christoff (*Giovanni da Procida*); Miti Truccato Pace (*Ninetta*); Mario Zorgniotti (*Bethune*); Giuliano Ferrein (*Vaudemont*); Tommaso Soley (*Danieli*); Walter Artioli (*Tebaldo*); Cristiano Dalamangas (*Roberto*); Sante Andreoli (*Manfredo*).

NOTES: EJS 206

The label of EJS 206 gives 1954 as the performance date. An Anita Cerquetti performance chronology included in the jacket notes of Timaclub LP Tima 23, a Cerquetti recital, cites 30 September, 1954 as the date of the actual recording, where the RAI chronology gives the broadcast date assigned above: 16 November, 1955. Numerous other spelling and attribution errors on the labels of this set have been corrected in the listing.

EJS 206 plays slightly high, requiring a speed of about 32.8 rpm.

Later issued as MFR 92 and Replica RPL 2433/35.

EJS 207: "The Golden Age of Opera" (1 LP)
Issued April, 1961

IL TROVATORE (Verdi) (I)
Opera in 4 Acts (excerpts)
Metropolitan Opera House Orchestra and Chorus/Ferruccio Calusio
Metropolitan Opera broadcast, NYC, 11 Jan 1941

CAST:
Norina Greco (*Leonora*); Jussi Bjoerling (*Manrico*); Bruna Castagna (*Azucena*); Francesco Valentino (*Count di Luna*); Nicola Moscona (*Ferrando*); Lodovico Oliviero (*Ruiz*); [Maxine Stellman (*Ines*)]; Arthur Kent (*Gypsy*).

SIDE 1 (207 A):

1. Act I: BJOERLING, VALENTINO, and GRECO: Deserto sulla terra to the end of the act

2. Act II: CASTAGNA, BJOERLING, and Chorus: Stride la vampa . . . to the end of the scene

3. Act III: BJOERLING and GRECO: Quale d'armi fragor . . . through Ah si, ben mio

SIDE 2 (207 B):

1. Act III: GRECO, OLIVIERO, and BJOERLING: L'onda dal suoni mistici . . . Di quella pira . . . to the end of the act

2. Act IV: a) GRECO, BJOERLING, and Chorus: Quel suon, quelle preci . . . Ah! che la morte ("Miserere")
   b) BJOERLING, CASTAGNA, GRECO, and VALENTINO: Madre, non dormi! . . . Ai nostri monti . . . to the end of the opera

NOTES: EJS 207

The Act III/ii excerpt beginning with "L'onda de suoni mistici" is listed on the label only as "Di quella pira." Similarly, the Act IV/i-ii excerpts are incorrectly labeled "D'amor sull'ali rosee" to the end of the "Miserere."

The complete 11 January, 1941 performance was subsequently issued as UORC 115 (May-June, 1972), Cetra LO 71, Robin Hood Records RHR 509, HOPE LP 221, and AS CD 1110/1. Excerpts from it have also appeared on a number of Bjoerling recitals: EJS 405 (September, 1967), UORC 350 (September-October, 1977), and Rococo 5304. Greco's "D'amor sull'ali rosee," omitted from EJS 207, later turned up on ANNA 1043, a San Carlo Opera collection issued in the fall of 1979.

EJS 207 plays in pitch at a uniform 34.00 rpm.

EJS 208: "The Golden Age of Opera (1 LP)
Issued April, 1961

DON CARLOS (Verdi) (I)
Opera in 4 Acts (excerpts)
Metropolitan Opera House Orchestra and Chorus/Fritz Stiedry
Metropolitan Opera broadcast, NYC, 11 Nov 1950

CAST:
Jussi Bjoerling (*Don Carlo*); Delia Rigal (*Elisabetta*); Cesare Siepi (*Filippo II*); Fedora Barbieri (*Eboli*); Robert Merrill (*Rodrigo*); Jerome Hines (*The Grand Inquistor*); Lubomir Vichegonov (*Friar*); [Anne Bollinger (*Tebaldo*)]; [Paul Franke (*Count di Lerma*)]; [Emery Darcy (*A Herald*)]; Lucine Amara (*A Heavenly Voice*); [Tilda Morse, dancer (*Countess Aremberg*)].

SIDE 1 (208 A):

Act I: 1. a) BJOERLING, MERRILL, BARBIERI, and RIGAL: Io l'ho perduta to the end of the scene
b) BJOERLING and RIGAL: Io vengo a domandar . . . Signor! Signor!

Act II: 2. BJOERLING, BARBIERI, and MERRILL: Mezzanotte in giardino . . . Qual mai pensier vi trasse qui (Prelude omitted)

SIDE 2 (208 B):

Act II: 1. BJOERLING, BARBIERI, and MERRILL: 'Ed io . . . che tremava al suo aspetto! . . . to the end of the scene

2. BJOERLING, SIEPI, RIGAL, AMARA, and Chorus: Sire! egli è tempo ch'io viva . . . to the end of the act

Act III: 3. MERRILL, BJOERLING, AND SIEPI: Son io, mio Carlo . . . to the end of the Prison Scene

Act IV: 4. BJOERLING, RIGAL, SIEPI, HINES, and VECHEGONOV: È dessa! . . . un detto . . . to the end of the opera

NOTES: EJS 208

Note that this is the four-act version of the opera, not the original five-act version, and that the selections on EJS 208 have been cued accordingly.

The labels of EJS 208 give only act and scene numbers, implying that these appear complete, which they do not.

The complete 11 November, 1950 performance was later issued on three LPs as UORC 121 in September, 1972, and later as Magnificent Editions ME 105-3 and Myto CD MCD 911.35. The opening night performance of the opera (same cast), broadcast over NBC television on 6 November, 1950, has also survived.

The set is reported to play in score pitch at 34.0 rpm, albeit with minor variations throughout.

EJS 209: "The Golden Age of Opera" (1 LP)
Issued April, 1961

RIGOLETTO (Verdi) (I)
Opera in 4 Acts (excerpts)
Metropolitan Opera House Orchestra and Chorus/Cesare Sodero
Metropolitan Opera broadcast, NYC, 29 Dec 1945

CAST:
Leonard Warren (*Rigoletto*); Bidú Sayão (*Gilda*); Jussi Bjoerling (*Duke of Mantua*); Norman Cordon (*Sparafucile*); Martha Lipton (*Maddalena*); Thelma Altman (*Giovanna*); Thelma Altman (*A Page*); William Hargrave (*Monterone*); George Cehanovsky (*Marullo*); Richard Manning (*Matteo Borsa*); John Baker (*Count Ceprano*); Maxine Stellman (*Countess di Ceprano*).

SIDE 1 (209 A):

Act I: 1. Act I complete (Prelude omitted)

Act II: 2. WARREN and SAYÃO: Figlia! . . . Mio padre! . . . è il sol dell'anima

SIDE 2 (209 B):

Act II: 1. BJOERLING, SAYÃO, MANNING, and BAKER: Che m'ami, deh! ripetimi . . . Caro nome

Act III: 2. a) BJOERLING: Ella mi fu rapita . . . Parmi, veder le lagrime
b) BJOERLING, WARREN, and SAYÃO: No, vecchio t'inganni . . . Sì, vendetta

Act IV: 3. a) BJOERLING La donna è mobile
b) BJOERLING, SAYÃO, WARREN, CORDON, and LIPTON: Un dì, se ben . . . Bella figlia dell'amore
c) BJOERLING, WARREN, and SAYÃO: La donna è mobile (reprise) . . . to the end of the opera (with internal cuts)

NOTES: EJS 209

Portions of this performance have also appeared on MDP 026 and 035, as well as on Rococo 5304. It was Reissued complete on two discs in November, 1973 as UORC 176, and subsequently on Melodram 27079, OPA 1019, and Music & Arts CD-636. The recitative to Sayão's "Caro nome" is reported to be inserted from another source on the Music & Arts CD edition, which may also be the case on either of the Smith issues, but this has not been confirmed.

EJS 210: "The Golden Age of Opera" (1 LP)
Issued April, 1961

FAUST (Gounod) (F)
Opera in 5 Acts (excerpts)
Metropolitan Opera House Orchestra and Chorus/Jean Morel
Metropolitan Opera broadcast, NYC, 19 Dec 1959

CAST:
Jussi Bjoerling (*Faust*); Elisabeth Söderström (*Marguerite*); Cesare Siepii (*Méphistophélès*); Robert Merrill (*Valentin*); Mildred Miller (*Siébel*); Thelma Votipka (*Marthe*); Roald Reitan (*Wagner*).

SIDE 1 (210 A):

1. Act I: BJOERLING, SIEPI, and Chorus: Rien! En vain j'interroge [Prologue] . . . Mais ce Dieu . . . to the end of Act I (orchestral Introduction omitted)

2. Act I: MILLER, MERRILL, SIEPI, REITAN, SÖDERSTRÖM, BJOERLING, and [Act II] Chorus: Merci de ta chanson! . . . Ainsi que la brise légère . . .

3. Act III: BJOERLING and SIEPI: Quel trouble inconnu me pénètre? . . . Salut! demeure . . . Alerte, a voilà!

SIDE 2 (210 B):

1. Act III: BJOERLING, SÖDERSTRÖM, SIEPI, and VOTIPKA: Prenez mon bras . . . Il était temps! . . . Il se fait tard!

2. Act IV: BJOERLING, MERRILL, and SIEPI: Que voulez-vous ["Trio du duel"]

5. Act V: BJOERLING, SÖDERSTRÖM, and SIEPI, and Chorus: Arrête! N'as-tu pas promise . . . Ici, docteur, tout m'est soumis / Vains remords . . . Va t'en! . . . Alerte! Alerte! . . . Jugée!

NOTES: EJS 210

The complete 29 December, 1959 performance was subsequently issued on Robin Hood Records RHR 502 and on Myto CD MCD 906.33.

There are a number of minor performance cuts in the Act V excerpts, which come to an abrupt end at *Mephistophélès'* "Jugée!," just as the choral "Apothéose" is beginning.

EJS 211: "The Golden Age of Opera" (2 LPs)
Issued May, 1961

SIDES 1-4 (211 A-D):

LA FORZA DEL DESTINO (Verdi) (I)
Opera in 4 Acts (abridged)
Metropolitan Opera House Orchestra and Chorus/Bruno Walter
Metropolitan Opera broadcast, NYC, 23 Jan 1943

CAST:
Louis D'Angelo (*Marchese*); Stella Roman (*Leonora*); Lawrence Tibbett (*Don Carlos*); Frederick Jagel (*Don Alvaro*); Irra Petina (*Preziosilla*); Ezio Pinza (*Abbot*); Salvatore Baccaloni (*Father Melitone*); Thelma Votipka (*Curra*); Lorenzo Alvary (*Alcade*); Alessio DePaolis (*Trabuco*); John Gurney (*Surgeon*).

NOTES: EJS 211

The Overture and the *Preziosilla* scenes are cut, though Petina's Act II/ii "E solo obliato" may not have been performed. Act III/i in particular is severly abbreviated: with both the Prelude and the opening chorus omitted, it begins at *Don Alvaro's* "La vita è inferno all' infelice . . . Oh, tu che in seno agli angeli" and ends after *Don Carlo's* "Urna fatale del mio destino." All of these cuts appear to have been made by Smith for purposes of timing.

AS Disc reissued the complete performance, presumably from the same broadcast, on CD as AS 409/10, with these cuts restored. In all probability, AS used another transcription source--EJS 211 used the official NBC acetates (the Spanish broadcast NBC acetates had much breakage and were subsequently lost; the acetates used for EJS 211 could not be documented).

Excerpts from another Met broadcast of FORZA--also under Walter's direction--from 27 November, 1943, were issued in rather poor sound as EJS 561 (June, 1971), with Anna Kaskas as *Preziosilla* and Gerhard Pechner as the *Marchese*. EJS 211, by contrast, having been taken from the NBC line-checks, is unusually good, though a speed of 34.5 rpm is needed to secure score pitch.

EJS 212: "The Golden Age of Opera" (1 LP)
Issued May, 1961

"POTPOURRI No. 11"

SIDE 1 (212 A):

* 1. ARMAND TOKATYAN, tenor, JOHN BROWNLEE, baritone, ALESSIO DE PAOLIS, tenor, LICIA ALBANESE, soprano (Metropolitan Opera House Orchestra and Chorus/Gennaro Papi): MADAMA BUTTERFLY, Act I: Quale smania vi prende! Sareste addirittura colto? . . . Amore o grillo . . . Siam giunte. B.F. Pinkerton. Giu . . . Giu (Puccini) (I) [33.9 rpm]
Metropolitan Opera broadcast, NYC, 25 Jan 1941

* 2. ARMAND TOKATYAN, tenor and JOHN BROWNLEE, baritone (Metropolitan Opera House Orchestra and Chorus/Gennaro Papi): MADAMA BUTTERFLY, Act III: Non ve l'avevo detto? . . . Addio, fiorito asil (Puccini) (I) [34.0 rpm]
Metropolitan Opera broadcast, NYC, 25 Jan 1941

* 3. LICIA ALBANESE, soprano and ARMAND TOKATYAN, tenor (Metropolitan Opera House Orchestra and Chorus/Gennaro Papi): MADAMA BUTTERFLY, Act III: Con onor muore . . . to the end of the opera [33.7 rpm]
Metropolitan Opera broadcast, NYC, 25 Jan 1941

* 4. STELLA ROMAN, soprano, and ANNA KASKAS, contralto (Metropolitan Opera House Orchestra/Ferruccio Calusio): CAVALLERIA RUSTICANA: Voi lo sapete . . . Io son dannato (Mascagni) (I) [33.8 rpm]
Metropolitan Opera broadcast, NYC, 1 Feb 1941

* 5. FREDRICK JAGEL, tenor and ANNA KASKAS, contralto (Metropolitan Opera House Orchestra and Chorus/Ferruccio Calusio): CAVALLERIA RUSTICANA: Mamma, quel vino . . . Addio all madre (Mascagni) (I) [32.5 rpm]
Metropolitan Opera broadcast, NYC, 1 Feb 1941

* 6. LEONARD WARREN, baritone (Metropolitan Opera House Orchestra and Chorus/Ettore Panizza): ALCESTE, Act I: Dieu puissant! . . . Perce d'un rayon éclatant (Gluck) (F)
Metropolitan Opera broadcast, NYC, 8 Mar 1941

* 7. ANGELO BADA, tenor (Metropolitan Opera House Orchestra/Maurice de Abravanel): LES CONTES D'HOFFMANN, Act IV: Eh bien quoi! Toujours en colère . . . Jour et nuit (Offenbach) (F) [33.3 rpm]
Metropolitan Opera broadcast, NYC, 23 Jan 1937

SIDE 2 (212 B):

* 1. ROSE BAMPTON, soprano (Metropolitan Opera House Orchestra/Ettore Panizza): ALCESTE, Act I: Divinités du Styx (Gluck) (F) [32.9 rpm]
Metropolitan Opera broadcast, NYC, 8 Mar 1941

* 2. ROBERT WEEDE, baritone (Metropolitan Opera House Orchestra/Ettore Panizza): RIGOLETTO, Act I: Pari siamo (Verdi) (I)
Metropolitan Opera broadcast, NYC, 31 Jan 1942

3. BRUNO LANDI, tenor (Metropolitan Opera House Orchestra/Ettore Panizza): RIGOLETTO, Act II: Ella mi fu . . . Parmi veder lagrime (Verdi) (I) [34.2 rpm]
Metropolitan Opera broadcast, NYC, 31 Jan 1942

* 4. HILDE REGGIANI, soprano and, ROBERT WEEDE, baritone: RIGOLETTO, Act II: (Metropolitan Opera House Orchestra/): Si, vendetta (Verdi) (I) [34.2 rpm]
Metropolitan Opera broadcast, NYC, 31 Jan 1942

5. BRUNO LANDI, tenor (Metropolitan Opera House Orchestra/Ettore Panizza): RIGOLETTO, Act III: La donna è mobile (Verdi) (I) [33.5 rpm]
Metropolitan Opera broadcast, NYC, 31 Jan 1942

6. LILY DJANEL, contralto (Metropolitan Opera House Orchestra and Chorus/Thomas Beecham): CARMEN, Act I: Quand je vous aimerai . . . L'amour est un oiseau rebelle (Bizet) (F) [34.5 rpm]
   Metropolitan Opera broadcast, Chicago, Saturday, 27 Mar 1943

7. NINO MARTINI, tenor (Metropolitan Opera House Orchestra/Frank St. Leger): IL BARBIERE DI SIVIGLIA, Act I: Ecco ridente (Rossini) (I) [34.5 rpm]
   Metropolitan Opera broadcast, Cleveland, NBC, 10 Apr 1943

NOTES: EJS 212

Most of the items on this potpourri were transferred flat: speeds are thus given in the listing for the *consistently-pitched* bands. The Jagel-Kaskas CAVALLERIA excerpt (I/5) and the Bampton ALCESTE aria (II/1) are sharp, and should be reproduced at 32.5 and 32.9 rpm, respectively, while Weede's "Pari siamo" (II/2) is variable.

Side 1 (212 A):

Bands 1-3: The complete 25 January, 1941 BUTTERFLY performance was later issued as EJS 237 (April, 1962).

Bands 4-5: The PAGLIACCI performed after the CAVALLERIA on 1 February, 1941 was issued earlier on EJS 105 (1956).

Band 6: This was the fourth Metropolitan Opera performance of this production of ALCESTE, which made its debut on 24 January, 1941, with Panizza conducting, Warren as the *High Priest*, and Marjorie Lawrence as *Alceste*. Bampton took over the title role after two performances. An abridgement of this 8 March, 1941 broadcast was issued subsequently on the single-disc EJS 545 issue (March, 1971). Speed is variable on the EJS 212 transfer.

Library of Congress tape: 8944-13 (complete broadcast).

Band 7: Bada sings one verse only, a composite of the two in the score. This performance was issued complete on UORC 206 (May, 1974). Tibbett's excerpts have turned up on a number of LPs.

Library of Congress tape: 15778-97A (complete broadcast)

Side 2 (212 B):

Band 1: See the note for Side 1/band 6. Bampton's performance of the ALCESTE aria from the 12 June, 1941 ***TORONOTO PROMENADE CONCERT*** (NBC), Reginald Stweart conducting, has been preserved on the original network acetates (two 16-inch sides, numbered ENG. 183 9-37, broadcast no. 41-257), along with her HÉRODIADE "Il est doux, il est bon."

Band 2: Speed is variable on this transfer.

Band 4: Labeled as Lily Pons and Lawrence Tibbett, but this is from the 31 January, 1942 Met performance represented elsewhere on EJS 212. The "Tutte le feste . . . Sì, vendetta" was included in the first volume of a 1992 IRCC broadcast potpourri (CD 806), taken from private acetates.

EJS 213: "The Golden Age of Opera" (1 LP)
Issued May, 1961

"POTPOURRI No. 12"

SIDE 1 (213 A):

* 1. RICHARD BONELLI, baritone (Detroit Symphony Orchestra/Victor Kolar): IL TROVATORE, Act II: Il balen del suo sorriso (Verdi) (I)
Broadcast, ***FORD SUNDAY EVENING HOUR***, WJR, Detroit, 7 Feb 1937

* 2. LAURITZ MELCHIOR, tenor (M-G-M Studio Orchestra/?Georgie Stoll): MARTHA, Act III: M'appari [Ach, so fromm] (Flotow) (I)
from the soundtrack of the 105-minute Metro-Goldwyn Mayer feature film, ***THIS TIME FOR KEEPS*** (1947), Hollywood, 1946
LP 1271; 3 Oct 1947 (Loew's Inc.)
New York Premiere: Capitol Theater, NYC, 4 Dec 1947

* 3. LAURITZ MELCHIOR, tenor (M-G-M Studio Orchestra/?Georgie Stoll): RIGOLETTO, Act IV: La donna è mobile (Verdi) (I)
from the soundtrack of the 105-minute Metro-Goldwyn Mayer feature film, ***THIS TIME FOR KEEPS*** (1947), Hollywood, 1946
LP 1271; c3 Oct 1947 (Loew's Inc.)
New York Premiere: Capitol Theater, NYC, 4 Dec 1947

4. TOTI DAL MONTE, soprano (orch/?): DON PASQUALE, Act I: Quel guardo il cavaliere . . . So anch'io la vertu magica (Donizetti) (I)
Source and date unknown, circa 1947, probably Italian

* 5. FREDERICK JAGEL, tenor (Metropolitan Opera House Orchestra/ Ettore Panizza): RIGOLETTO, Act IV: La donna è mobile (Verdi) (I)
Metropolitan Opera broadcast, NYC, 28 Dec 1935

* 6. LILY PONS, soprano; HELEN OLHEIM, contralto; FREDERICK JAGEL, tenor; and LAWRENCE TIBBETT, baritone (Metropolitan Opera House Orchestra/Ettore Panizza): RIGOLETTO, Act IV: Bella figlia dell'amore (Verdi) (I)
Metropolitan Opera broadcast, NYC, 28 Dec 1935

* 7. RENÉ MAISON, tenor (Metropolitan Opera House Orchestra/Maurice de Abravanel): SAMSON ET DALILA, Act I: Arrêtez! ô mes frères! (Saint-Saëns) (F)
Metropolitan Opera broadcast, NYC, 26 Dec 1936

* 8. GERTRUDE WETTERGREN, contralto (Metropolitan Opera House Orchestra/Maurice de Abravanel): SAMSON ET DALILA, Act I: Printemps qui commence (Saint-Saëns) (F)
Metropolitan Opera broadcast, NYC, 26 Dec 1936

9. RICHARD BONELLI, baritone (Metropolitan Opera House Orchestra/ Maurice de Abravanel): MANON, Act I: Ne bronchez pas (Massenet) (F)
Metropolitan Opera broadcast, NYC, 13 Feb 1937

10. BIDÚ SAYÃO, soprano: (Metropolitan Opera House Orchestra/ Maurice de Abravanel): MANON, Act I: Voyons, Manon (Massenet) (F)
Metropolitan Opera broadcast, NYC, 13 Feb 1937

SIDE 2 (213 B):

* 1. ELISABETH SCHUMANN, soprano (Wallenstein's Orchestra/Alfred Wallenstein): IL RE PASTORE, K. 208, Act II: L'amerò, sarò costante (Mozart) (I)
Broadcast, ***AMERICA PREFERRED***, WOR, NYC, 28 Feb 1942

* 2. QUEENA MARIO, soprano; IRENE JESSNER, soprano (Metropolitan Opera House Orchestra/Karl Riedel): HÄNSEL UND GRETEL, Act I: Brüderchen, komm tanz mit mir (Humperdinck) (G)
Metropolitan Opera broadcast, NYC, 24 Dec 1937

3. DOROTHEE MANSKI, mezzo-soprano (Metropolitan Opera House Orchestra/Karl Riedel): HÄNSEL UND GRETEL, Act II: Hokus, pokus, Hexenschuss! (Humperdinck) (G)
Metropolitan Opera broadcast, NYC, 24 Dec 1937

* 4. MARIA CANIGLIA, soprano, and GIOVANNI MARTINELLI, tenor (Metropolitan Opera House Orchestra/Ettore Panizza): OTELLO, Act IV: Chi è là? (Verdi) (I)
Metropolitan Opera broadcast, NYC, 3 Dec 1938

* 5. FRIEDRICH SCHORR (Metropolitan Opera House Orchestra/Bodanzky) FIDELIO, Act I: Ha! welch ein Augenblick (Beethoven) (G)
Metropolitan Opera broadcast, NYC, 31 Dec 1938

* 6. ARTHUR CARRON, tenor (Metropolitan Opera House Orchestra and Chorus/Ettore Panizza): AÏDA, Act I: Se quel guerrier io fossi . . . Celeste Aïda (Verdi) (I)
Metropolitan Opera broadcast, NYC, 2 Mar 1940

* 7. STELLA ROMAN (Metropolitan Opera House Orchestra/Panizza): OTELLO, Act IV: Ave Maria (Verdi) (I)
Metropolitan Opera broadcast, NYC, 18 Jan 1941

NOTES: EJS 213

Mislabeled EJS 113, possibly on all copies.

Side 1 (213 A):

Band 1: This performance was later included on EJS 445 (October, 1968).

Bands 2-3: ***THIS TIME FOR KEEPS*** was Melchior's third Hollywood film. Georgie Stoll, M-G-M's musical director and the conductor of Melchior's commercial studio recordings for M-G-M, was credited as the film's musical director, and is presumably the conductor of these soundtrack excerpts.

An arrangement of Cole Porter's "(You are) So Easy to Love," which Melchior sings in the film, was commercially recorded by him in Hollywood for M-G-M on 31 December, 1946 (M-G-M 3003), Stoll conducting, so it is assumed that the actual soundtrack material was probably recorded in late 1946 or early, 1947. Melchior did not record either the "M'appari" or the "La donna è mobile" for M-G-M.

The soundtrack also features a jazzed up "M'appari" with Melchior and Johnnie Johnston.

Band 5-6: Taken from the official NBC acetates: this performance exists nearly complete. Extensive excerpts were issued in April, 1971 as EJS 551 using considerably poorer source material.

Bands 7-8: Both of these SAMSON arias were later reissued on EJS 516 (June, 1970). Other excerpts from the performance had appeared previously on EJS 170 (January, 1960) and 186 (July-August, 1960).

Library of Congress tape: 5174-30 (complete broadcast).

Side 2 (213 B):

Band 1: Given as "1944" on the label of EJS 213.

Band 2: The 24 December, 1937 HÀNSEL UND GRETEL was issued (abridged) as EJS 539 in February, 1971.

Band 4: Library of Congress tape: 7596 (complete broadcast).

Band 5: The complete 31 December, 1938 FIDELIO appeared subsequently on UORC 268 (November-December, 1975), Melodram MEL-307, and Music and Arts CD-619. Excerpts were issued as EJS 231 in February, 1962.

Band 6: Library of Congress tape: 5174-13 (complete broadcast).

Band 7: The complete OTELLO of 18 January, 1941 was later issued as UORC 192 (February, 1974); 70 minutes of highlights were subsequently included on EJS 264 (April, 1963). Pearl reissued the performance complete (labeled 4 December, 1941) in 1988 on LP (GEMM 267-9) and compact disc (GEMM CD 9267).

EJS 214: "The Golden Age of Opera" (1 LP)
Issued June, 1961

"POTPOURRI No. XIII"

SIDE 1 (214 A):

* 1. GRACE MOORE, soprano, and FRANK FOREST, tenor (studio orch/?Isaac Van Grove or Morris W. Stoloff): MADAMA BUTTERFLY, Act I: Vogliatemi bene, un bene piccolino . . . to the end of the act (Puccini) (I)
from the soundtrack of the 9-reel Columbia feature film *I'LL* ***TAKE ROMANCE*** (1937), Hollywood, 1937
LP 7571; c15 Nov 1937
New York Premiere: Radio City Music Hall, NYC, 16 Dec 1937

* 2. JOHN CHARLES THOMAS, baritone (Detroit Symphony Orchestra/Eugene Ormandy): LA FAVORITA, Act II: Ma de malvaggi invan . . . Vien, Leonora (Donizetti) (I)
Broadcast, ***FORD SUNDAY EVENING HOUR***, WJR, Detroit, 10 Mar 1940

* 3. JOHN CHARLES THOMAS, baritone (Detroit Symphony Orchestra/Eugene Ormandy): DON CARLOS, Act III: Son io, mio Carlo . . . Per me giunto è il di supremo (Verdi) (I)
Broadcast, ***FORD SUNDAY EVENING HOUR***, WJR, Detroit, 12 Nov 1939

* 4. JOHN CHARLES THOMAS, baritone (Detroit Symphony Orchestra/Eugene Ormandy): NORFOLK SONGS: Yarmouth Fair (trad.-arr. H. Collins-Warlock) (E)
Broadcast, ***FORD SUNDAY EVENING HOUR***, WJR, Detroit, 12 Nov 1939

* 5. GERALDINE FARRAR, soprano (orch/?Pasternack): MADAMA BUTTERLY, Act II: Un bel di, vedremo (Puccini) (I)
C-5055-4 28 Mar 1917 Victor unpublished

* 6. LAURITZ MELCHIOR, tenor, and MARINA KOSHETZ, soprano (M-G-M studio Orchestra/?Georgie Stoll): AÏDA, Act III: [Pur ti riveggo] ! . . . Tu non m'ami . . . to the end of the duet (with internal cuts) (Verdi) (I)
from the soundtrack of the 97-minute Metro-Goldwyn-Mayer feature film ***LUXURY LINER*** (1948), Hollywood, late 1947
LP 1749; c28 Jul 1948 (Loewe's Inc.)
New York Premiere: Capitol Theater, NYC, 9 Sep 1948

* 7. LEON ROTHIER, bass (pf/?): PELLÉAS ET MÉLISANDE, Act IV/i: Maintenant que le père de Pelléas est sauvé . . . on a tant besoin de beauté aux côtés de la mort [Mélisande's line omitted] (Debussy) (F)
Broadcast, ***LÉON ROTHIER***, WQXR, NYC, 4 Feb 1940

* 8. LINA PAGLIUGHI, soprano, and CARLO TAGLIABUE, baritone (London Philharmonic Orchestra/Vittorio Gui): RIGOLETTO, Act I: No, vecchio t'inganni . . . Sì, vendetta (Verdi) (I)
Broadcast, Covent Garden, London, 31 May 1938

SIDE 2 (214 B):

* 1. GERTRUDE RIBLA, soprano, and DOROTHY STAHL, soprano (orch/Wilfred Pelletier): LA JUIVE, Act IV: [Du Cardinal voici l'ordre] Pourquoi m'arrachez vous à ma sombre demeure? . . . to the end of the scene (one verse of "Dieu tutélaire" only, with abbreviated coda) (Halévy) (F)
Broadcast, ***METROPOLITAN OPERA AUDITIONS OF THE AIR***, WJZ, NYC, 2 May, 1948

* 2. EZIO PINZA, bass (studio orch/Howard Barlow): SERSE, Act I: Frondi tenere . . . Ombra mai fu (Handel) (I)
Broadcast, ***THE VOICE OF FIRESTONE***, WEAF, NYC, 14 Aug 1944

3. LICIA ALBANESE, soprano (studio orch/Alfredo Antonini): LO SCHIAVO, Act: IV: Come serenamente il mar carezza (Gomes) (I)
Broadcast, ***SONG TREASURY***, WOR, Newark, 30 Jan 1947

* 4. LICIA ALBANESE, soprano (San Francisco Symphony Orchestra/Kurt Herbert Adler): CAVALLERIA RUSTICANA: Voi lo sapete (Mascagni) (I)
Broadcast, ?***STANDARD HOUR***, KNBC, San Francisco, 11 Oct 1953

* 5. LILY PONS, soprano (San Francisco Symphony Orchestra/Gaetano Merola): LA TRAVIATA, Act I: Ah! fors'e lui . . . Sempre libera (Verdi) (I)
Broadcast, ***STANDARD HOUR***, KNBC, San Francisco, 28 Oct 1951

6. JOHN McCORMACK, tenor (pf/Gerald Moore): "Nina" ["Tre giorni son che Nina"] (attr. Pergolesi) (I)
OEA-8807-1 London, 19 Jun 1940 HMV IR 1045 AGSA 61

* 7. FEODOR CHALIAPIN, bass (Royal Opera House Orchestra and Chorus/Vincenzo Belezza): MEFISTOFELE, Prologue: Ave Signor! (Boïto) (I)
CR 383-1 Covent Garden, London, 31 May 1926 HMV (DB 940)
CR 384-1 Covent Garden, London, 31 May 1926 HMV (DB 940)

* 8. LÉON ROTHIER, bass, and COLETTE D'ARVILLE, soprano (pf/?): DON GIOVANNI, K. 527, Act I: Là ci darem la mano (Mozart) (I)
Broadcast, ***LÉON ROTHIER***, WQXR, NYC, circa December, 1938

NOTES: EJS 214

Mislabeled as EJS 215 on some copies.
The speeds on this issue are irregular, ranging from 32.00 rpm to 34.5 rpm. Pitching of individual tracks is recommended.

Side 1 (214 A):

Band 1: Given as 1938 on the label of EJS 214 and titled "Bimba non piangere," but the excerpt begins several pages into the scene. Both Van Grove and Stoloff served as music directors on the film, so the actual conductor credit has not be verified.
Score pitch is steady at 33.8 rpm.

Bands 2-4: The Thomas items play in score pitch at 32.00 rpm. Both the DON CARLOS and the FAVORITA arias were later reissued on EJS 531 (December, 1970). The DON CARLOS begins at the beginning of the scene, but the recitative material is abbreviated and *Don Carlos'* lines are omitted.

Band 5: Special pressings exist of this otherwise unpublished performance, originally recorded at 76.60 rpm and transcribed here at 78.26 rpm.

Band 6: Georgie Stoll, M-G-M's musical director and the conductor of Melchior's commercial studio recordings on the M-G-M label, was the music director of this film, and probably the conductor of this soundtrack excerpt.
Melchior recorded a number of selections from the film for the M-G-M label between 23 June and 26 December, 1947, so it may be assumed that the actual soundtrack items featured here were recorded in 1947.
Marina Koshetz, the daughter of Nina Koshetz, had a minor career on the operatic stage and appeared in a few feature films between 1946 and 1967.
Sung a half-step lower than score pitch at 34.4 rpm.

Band 7: See also Side II/8. From Rothier's WQXR radio show (see the endnote for EJS 140): the exact origin of this performance could not be determined. Plays in score pitch at about 34.5 rpm, though a shift in the original transcription discs drops the speed to about 34.2 rpm. Rothier might have transposed the aria down a half-step, which could explain the high playing speed.

Band 8: The London Philharmonic Orchestra served as the pit orchestra during Beecham's 1938 Covent Garden Grand Opera Season.

Plays in score pitch at 32.00 rpm.

This scene was later issued (at correct pitch and with *Monterone's* opening lines restored) on MDP LP 018, "Gigli . . . Live from the Great Opera Houses of the World."

Side 2 (214 B):

Band 1: Given on the label as 1942. Plays at 32.3 rpm.

Band 2: This same performance appeared on EJS 142 (January, 1959). Both 32.7 rpm and 34.0 rpm have been suggested as possible playing speeds, depending upon the key chosen.

Band 4: In spite of reports implying otherwise, no ***SONG TREASURY*** performance by Albanese of the CAVALLERIA aria could be found. Considering the Pons TRAVIATA arias that follow it (II/5), the ***STANDARD HOUR*** "Voi lo sapete" from 10 November, 1953 seems a more likely source.

Band 5: Plays in score pitch at 32.0 rpm.

Band 7: Taken from a live performance. These two sides were assigned the catalog number HMV DB 904, but were never issued on 78. The HMV matrices from this performance were issued on the EMI Covent Garden LP set (RLS 742), where CR 383 and CR 384 are found complete: the EJS 214 dubbing omits the choral introduction from the beginning of CR 383.

Band 8: See note for Side I/7. Transposed down a whole-step, playing here at 34.7 rpm. D'Arville was a member of the Paris Opéra-Comique, and was heard on the ***GENERAL MOTORS HOUR*** several times during the 1935-1936 seasons.

EJS 215: "The Golden Age of Opera" (3 LPs)
Issued June, 1961

SIDES 1-6 (215 A-F):

BORIS GODUNOV (Mussorgsky) (I)
Opera in a Prologue and 4 Acts (complete)
Metropolitan Opera House Orchestra and Chorus/Ettore Panizza
Metropolitan Opera broadcast, NYC, 9 Dec 1939

CAST:
Ezio Pinza (*Boris*); Irra Petina (*Fedor*); Marita Farell (*Xenia*); Anna Kaskas (*Nurse*); Alessio DePaolis (*Shuisky*); George Cehanovsky (*Tchelkaloff*); Nicola Moscona (*Pimenn*); Charles Kullman (*Dimitri*); Kerstin Thorborg (*Marina*); Leonard Warren (*Rangoni*); Norman Cordon (*Varlaam*); Giordano Paltrinieri (*Missail*); Doris Doe (*Innkeeper*); Nicholas Massue (*Simpleton*); John Gurney (*Police Officer*); Wilfred Engelman (*Lovitzky*); Arnold Gabor (*Tcherniakowsky*); Nicholas Massue (*Boyar*).

NOTES: EJS 215

Misnumbered EJS 214 on the 1970s "Golden Age of Opera" checklist.

Taken from official NBC acetates (fourteen 16-inch sides labeled "COPY ORTHACOUSTIC Jun 1 1940," numbered ENG. 183 9-37, broadcast no. 42-38). Performed in Italian and labeled "BORIS GODOUNOFF."

Library of Congress tape: 7749-18 (complete broadcast).

EJS 216: "The Golden Age of Opera" (2 LPs)
Issued September, 1961

SIDES 1-4 (216 A-D)

GIULIETTA E ROMEO (Zandonai) (I)
Opera in 3 Acts (complete)
Orchestra and Chorus of Radio Italiana [RAI], Milano/Angelo Questa
RAI broadcast, Milan, 21 Sep 1955

CAST:
Anna Maria Rovère (*Giulietta*); Angelo Lo Forese (*Romeo*); Renato Capecchi (*Tebaldo*); Ornella Rovero (*Isabella*); Maria Luisa Zeri (*First Maschera*); Maria Luisa Zeri (*First Maidservant*); Maria Luisa Zeri (*First Lady*); Ottavia Torriani (*Second Maschera*); Liliana Pellegrino (*Second Maidservant*); Liliana Pellegrino (*Second Lady*); Dino Formichini (*The Singer*); Salvatore Di Tommaso (*Gregorio*); Antonio Massaria (*Sansone*); Antonio Massaria (*A Crier*); Ugo Novelli (*Bernabo*); Mario Carlin (*Un Montecchio*); Mario Carlin (*A Relative*); Emilio Casolari (*A Servant*).

NOTES: EJS 216

The label of EJS 216 gives 17 May, 1958 as the date of this performance.

This set is reported to play slightly flat, requiring a speed of 33.8 rpm to compensate.

EJS 217: "The Golden Age of Opera" (1 LP)
Issued September, 1961

PELLÉAS ET MÉLISANDE (Debussy) (F)
Opera in 5 Acts (excerpts)
Metropolitan Opera House Orchestra and Chorus/Emil Cooper
Metropolitan Opera broadcast, NYC, 13 Jan 1945

CAST:
Martial Singher (*Pelléas*); Bidú Sayão (*Mélisande*); Margaret Harshaw (*Geneviève*); Lillian Raymondi (*Yniold*); Lawrence Tibbett (*Golaud*); Alexander Kipnis (*Arkel*); Lorenzo Alvary (*Physician*).

SIDE 1 (217 A):

Act I: 1. SAYÃO, TIBBETT, HARSHAW, and KIPNIS: Je ne pourrai plus sortir . . . Voici ce qu'il a écrit à son frère Pelléas . . . Aie soin d'allumer la lampe dès ce soir, Pelléas

Act II: 2. a) SAYÃO and SINGHER: Vous ne savez pas où je vous ai menée? . . . La vérité, la vérité, la vérité
b) TIBBETT: Ah! Ah! tout va bien . . . Il paraît que ce n'est rien

SIDE 2 (217 B):

Act III: 1. a) SAYÃO, SINGHER, and TIBBETT: Mes longs cheveux descendent jusqu'au seuil de la tour! . . . Quels enfants! Quels enfants!
b) SINGHER and TIBBETT: Prenez garde: pour ici . . . Ah! je respire enfin! . . . Tiens, voilà notre mère et Mélisande à une fenêtre de la tour

Act IV: 2. a) KIPNIS: Maintenant que la père de Pelléas est sauvé . . . Comme j'avais pitié de toi ces mois-ci!
b) SAYÃO and SINGHER: Nous sommes venus ici il y a bien longtemps . . . to the end of the act

NOTES: EJS 217

Reissued complete as UORC 187 in January, 1974.

EJS 218: "The Golden Age of Opera" (2 LPs)
Issued October, 1961

SIDES 1-4 (218 A-D):

BEATRICE DI TENDA (Bellini) (I)
Opera in 2 Acts (complete)
Orchestra and Chorus of La Scala, Milano/Antonino Votto
[Live] RAI broadcast, Milan, 10 May 1961

CAST:
Joan Sutherland (*Beatrice*); Giuseppe Campora (*Orombello*); Raina Kabaiwanska (*Agnes de Maino*); Dino Dondi (*Filippo*); Piero De Palma (*Anichino*); Walter Gullino (*Rizzardo del Maino*).

NOTES: EJS 218

Speeds are reported to be erratic on this set: pitching is recommended. The complete performance was later reissued as Cetra DOC-15 and Movimento Musica 03.007.

EJS 219: "The Golden Age of Opera" (1 LP)
Issued October, 1961

CARMEN (Bizet) (F)
Opera in 4 Acts (excerpts)
Metropolitan Opera House Orchestra and Chorus/Louis Hasselmans
Metropolitan Opera broadcast, NYC, 1 Feb 1936

CAST:
Rosa Ponselle (*Carmen*); Charles Kullman (*Don José*); [Susanne Fisher (*Micaela*)]; Thelma Votipka (*Frasquita*); Helen Olheim (*Mercédès*); Ezio Pinza (*Escamillo*); Angelo Bada (*Dancaïre*); Marek Windheim (*Remendado*); Louis D'Angelo (*Zuniga*); [George Cehanovsky (*Morales*)].

SIDE 1 (219 A):

Act I: 1. a) PONSELLE, KULLMAN, and Chorus: Quand je vous aimerai . . . L'amour est un oiseau rebelle . . . Carmen! sur tes pas . . . postlude to Carmen's exit
b) PONSELLE, KULLMAN, and D'ANGELO: Tra la la la la . . . Près des remparts de Séville . . . to the end of the Act

Act II: 2. a) PONSELLE, VOTIPKA, OLHEIM, and D'ANGELO: Les tringles des sistres! . . . Bonsoir, messieurs nos amoureux
b) PINZA, PONSELLE, VOTIPKA, OLHEIM, D'ANGELO, and Chorus: Votre toast, je peux vous le rendre . . . La belle, un mot . . . Eh bien vite, quelles nouvelles

SIDE 2 (219 B):

Act II: 1. PONSELLE, VOTIPKA, OLHEIM, BADA, and WINDHEIM: Nous avons en tête une affaire

2. a) PONSELLE and KULLMAN: Je vais danser en votre honneur . . . Et va t'en, mon garçon, va t'en! retourne à ta caserne!
b) PONSELLE and KULLMAN: Non! tu ne m'aimes pas! . . . Là-bas dans la montagne . . . Non! je ne veux plus t'écouter!

Act III: 3. a) PONSELLE, VOTIPKA, and OLHEIM: Voyons, que j'esssaie à mon tour . . .En vain pour éviter . . . to the end of the scene
Act IV: b) PONSELLE, PINZA, VOTIPKA, OLHEIM, KULLMAN, and Chorus: Si tu m'aimes . . . to the end of the opera

NOTES: EJS 219

Excerpts of this performance were later reissued as part of a two-disc Ponselle recital, ANNA 1037 (May-June, 1979), containing about half of what is included on EJS 219. Smith's 1968 transfer of the 28 March, 1936 Ponselle-Maison-Pinza CARMEN from Boston, issued on "Great French Operatic Performances of the Century, CAR 1/6 (P-1610), seems to use a second-act insert from this 1 February, 1936 performance, beginning after the Gypsy Dance. This insert is not featured--reportedly--on Smith's original issue of the March, 1936 performance on EJS 117 (1957).

Speeds for EJS 219 range from about 34.7 to 35 rpm, with considerable inconsistency over the two sides.

EJS 220: "The Golden Age of Opera" (1 LP)
Issued October, 1961

SIDE 1 (220 A):

TOSCA (Puccini) (I)
Opera in 3 Acts (Act III only)
Orchestra and Chorus of the Chicago Opera/Carlo Peroni
Chicago Opera broadcast, WGN, Chicago, 1 Dec 1941

CAST:
Grace Moore (*Tosca*); Frederick Jagel (*Cavaradossi*); [John Charles Thomas] (*Scarpia*); Giuseppe Cavadore (*Spoletta*); Renato De Cesari (*Jailor*); Margery Mayer (*Shepherd*); ? (*Sciarrone*).

SIDE 2 (220 B):

LA BOHÈME (Puccini) (I)
Opera in 4 Acts (Act III only)
Metropolitan Opera House Orchestra and Chorus/Cesare Sodero
Metropolitan Opera broadcast, NYC, 12 Dec 1942

CAST:
Grace Moore (*Mimi*); Frederick Jagel (*Rodolfo*); [Wilfred Engelmann (*Schaunard*)]; [Salvatore Baccaloni (*Benoit*)]; [Lodovico Oliviero (*Parpignol*)]; Francesco Valentino (*Marcello*); [Ezio Pinza (*Colline*)]; Frances Greer (*Musetta*); [Salvatore Baccaloni (*Alcindoro*)]; John Gurney (*Sergeant*).

NOTES: EJS 220

Side 1 (220 A):

Only the final act of this TOSCA was broadcast over Chicago's Mutual Radio Network affiliate, WGN, also heard over WOR in New York City.

The Moore-Jagel TOSCA was issued complete on UORC 214 (September, 1974) is a 7 February, 1942 Met performance.

Side 2 (220 B):

This BOHÈME third act was taken from the official NBC acetates. The performance has survived complete.

EJS 221: "The Golden Age of Opera" (1 LP)
Issued November, 1961

LA JUIVE (Halévy) (F)
Opera in 5 Acts (excerpts)
San Francisco Opera House Orchestra and Chorus/Gaetano Merola
San Francisco Opera broadcast, KGO [NBC], San Francisco, 30 Oct 1936

CAST:
Giovanni Martinelli (*Eléazar*); Elisabeth Rethberg (*Rachel*); Charlotte Boerner (*Eudoxie*); Hans Clemens (*Léopold*); [Ezio Pinza (*Brogni*)]; [John Howell (*Ruggiero*)]; [John Burr (*Herald*)].

SIDE 1 (221 A)

* 1. Act II: MARTINELLI, RETHBERG, BOERNER, and CLEMENS: Orchestral Entr'Acte . . . O Dieu, Dieu de nos pères . . . to the end of Il va venir! (portion of the orchestral postlude omitted)

SIDE 2 (221 B)

* 1. Act II: MARTINELLI, RETHBERG, BOERNER, and CLEMENS: Lorsqu'à toi je me suis donné . . . to the end of the act (portion of the orchestral postlude omitted, with applause added)

* 2. Act IV: GIOVANNI MARTINELLI, tenor; LOUIS D'ANGELO, bass (Vitaphone Symphony Orchestra/Herman Heller): Ta fille en ce moment
from the soundtrack of the one-reel Warner Brothers-Vitaphone short ***GIOVANNI MARTINELLI, TENOR, ASSISTED BY LOUIS D'ANGELO, BASS, OF THE METROPOLITAN OPERA COMPANY IN A DUET FROM ACT IV OF THE OPERA "LA JUIVE"*** (1927), New York, 1927
Vitaphone Varieties 509
MP 4108; c29 Jun 1927
Premiere: New York City, 12 Jun 1927

* 3. Act IV: GIOVANNI MARTINELLI, tenor (Vitaphone Symphony Orchestra/Herman Heller): J'ai fait peser sur toi mon éternelle haine . . . Rachel! quand du Seigneur
from the soundtrack of the one-reel Warner Brothers-Vitaphone short ***GIOVANNI MARTINELLI, TENOR OF THE METROPOLITAN OPERA COMPANY, SINGING "VA PRONONCER LA MORT" FROM ACT IV OF THE OPERA, "LA JUIVE"*** (1927), New York, 1927
Vitaphone Varieties 510
MP 4107; c29 Jun 1927
Premiere: Warners' Theater, New York City, 8 Oct 1927

NOTES: EJS 221

The contents of this LP was reissued in considerably better sound on Voce LP VOCE-40.

Side 1 (221 A):

Only Act II of this San Francisco performance was broadcast. Smith's source was the official NBC acetates: these contained a long spoken introduction by Marcia Davenport omitted from EJS 221. Davenport *is* heard briefly, however, making comments during the performance.

The original acetates (four 16-inch sides, numbered ENG. 183 9-36, broadcast no. 6-8) have a short side break during the "Si trahison ou perfidité" section of the "Passover Scene," at *Eléazar's* "[ou sur l'im]pie, grand Dieu," which was "repaired" for this LP by inserting the missing line from Martinelli's commercial Victor recording of the scene:

GIOVANNI MARTINELLI (Metropolitan Opera House Orchestra/Giulio Setti): Si trahison ou perfidie ("Passover Scene," Part 2) (F)
CVE-49016-1 24 Dec 1928 Victor 8165 HMV DB 1411

The broadcast is restored at "que tombe ton courroux!"

The "Dieu, que ma voix" heard on this LP was taken from the unpublished second take of Martinelli's acoustical Victor, as sandwiched between edited applause:

GIOVANNI MARTINELLI (orch/Pasternack; harp/Francis J. Lapitino): Dieu, que ma voix (F)
C-31363-2 3 Dec 1924 Victor unpub

This would later be recycled for the Martinelli recital on EJS 470 (May, 1969) along with the unpublished acoustical "Rachel! quand du Seigneur" (C-31364-2) from the same session.

Side 2 (221 B):

Band 2: The November, 1961 bulletin credits *Virgilio Lazzari* as *Cardinal De Brogni* and claims that these Act IV excerpts come from an 8 March, 1927(!) Chicago Opera performance conducted by Tullio Serafin. Louis D'Angelo reportedly wanted Smith to pay him for the use of his name, and so Lazzari's was simply substituted, along with the false performance attribution. This was to be the case with other D'Angelo performances issued throughout the course of the GAO issues.

Band 3: In spite of the film's copyright title (given here), Martinelli omits the first three phrases of *Eléazar's* recitative, which are taken by the orchestra.

This short premiered during the run of Warner Brothers' landmark feature "The Jazz Singer." The soundtrack was included earlier on EJS 102 (1956) and later on ASCO A-116, Smith's Martinelli "Diamond Jubilee" set.

EJS 222: "The Golden Age of Opera" (1 LP)
Issued November, 1961

CARMEN (Bizet) (I)
Opera in 4 Acts (excerpts)
Orchestra and Chorus of the Teatro dell'Opera, Roma/Vincenzo Bellezza
Scalera Film Studio, Rome, June-July, 1949

CAST:
Ebe Stignani (*Carmen*); Beniamino Gigli (*Don José*); Gino Bechi (*Escamillo*); Rina Gigli (*Micaela*); Giulio Tomei (*Zuniga*); Anna Marcangeli (*Frasquita*); Fernanda Cadoni (*Mercédès*); Arturo La Porta (*Dancaïre*); Salvatore De Tommaso (*Remendado*); Guido Mazzini (*Morales*).

SIDE 1 (222 A):

Act I: 1. a) TOMEI and GIGLI: C'est bien là . . . Et vous pouvez juger vous-même
b) STIGNANI and CHORUS: Mais nous ne voyons pas la Carmencita! . . . L'amour est un oiseau rebelle (Habanera)
c) B. GIGLI and R. GIGLI: Quels regards! . . . Parle-moi de ma mère . . . il revoit son village!
d) STIGNANI, B. GIGLI, and TOMEI: Mon officier . . . Tra la la la . . . Ou me conduirez-vous?
e) STIGNANI and B. GIGLI: Près des remparts de Séville (and concluding duet)

SIDE 2 (222 B):

Act II: 1. a) STIGNANI, MARCANGELI, and CADONI: Les tringles des sistres! (1 verse only)
b) BECHI and Chorus: Votre toast! (Toreador Song) (orchestral introduction omitted)
c) B. GIGLI and STIGNANI: Halte-là . . . Enfin c'est toi! (one verse only of José's "Halte-là!)
d) STIGNANI, MARCANGELI, CADONI, B. GIGLI, DE TOMMASO, LA PORTA, TOMEI: Je vais danser . . . Holà! Carmen, holà! . . . to the end of the Act

SIDE 3 (222 C):

Act III: 1. a) STIGNANI and B. GIGLI: Que regardes-tu donc? . . . Qu'importe, après tout le déstin est le maître (Le Dancaïre's opening recitative is omitted)
b) STIGNANI, MARCANGELI, and CADONI: [Mêlons! Mêlons!] . . . En vain pour éviter (opening Frasquita and Mercédès duet omitted)
c) R. GIGLI: C'est des contrebandiers . . . Je dis que rien
d) R. GIGLI and BECHI: Je ne me trompe pas . . . Quelques lignes plus bas
e) B. GIGLI and BECHI: Je suis Escamillo
f) STIGNANI, MARCANGELI, CADONI, B. GIGLI, DE TOMMASO, LA PORTA, BECHI, and Chorus: Holà! Holà! José! . . . to the end of the act

SIDE 4 (222 D):

Act IV: 1. a) BECHI, STIGNANI, MARCANGELI, CADONI, and Chorus: [Les voici, les voici!] . . . Si tu m'aimes, Carmen . . . Place! place! place au seigneur . . . Carmen, un bon conseil (opening chorus, final trio, and orchestral postlude omitted)

b) STIGNANI, B. GIGLI, and Chorus: C'est toi! C'est moi! . . . to the end of the opera

NOTES: EJS 222

This was a soundtrack recording for an unreleased Italian feature film. The November, 1961 bulletin claims that 95% of Gigli's music is represented on this single-disc compilation.

Smith later issued the performance nearly complete as UORC 178 (December, 1973), as did EMI on the LP 3C 153-18255/57. Excerpts have appeared on various private LPs: EJS, the ANNA 1033 Gigli recital (May-June, 1979), Harvest (another Smith label), and Melodram, among others.

The performance is in Italian, but the excerpts have been given here in the original French for ease of reference.

EJS 223: The Golden Age of Opera" (1 LP)
Issued November, 1961

"POTPOURRI NO. 14"

SIDE 1 (223 A)

* 1. TITTA RUFFO, baritone (orch/Rosario Bourdon): "Cubanita" (Huarte-Tito Schipa) (S)
B-31694-1 21 Jan 1925 Victor unpub

* 2. TITO RUFFO, baritone (orch/Rosario Bourdon): PANURGE, Act I: Je suis né . . . Touraine est un pays (Massenet) (F)
BVE-49966-1 18 Feb 1929 Victor unpub

* 3. TITTA RUFFO, baritone (pf/Percy B. Kahn or Gerald Moore) "Mattuttino" (P. Mario Costa) (I)
OB-5462-2 London, 25 Nov 1933 HMV unpub

* 4. TITTA RUFFO, speaker: [Mock] Conversation with Chaliapin (I)
OB-5468-1 London, 24 Nov 1933 HMV unpub

* 5. DINO BORGIOLI (pf/Ernest Lush): "Nina" ["Tre giorni son che Nina"] (attr. Pergolesi) (I)
Broadcast, *BBC HOME SERVICE*, BBC, London, 26 Apr 1948

* 6. DINO BORGIOLI (pf/Ernest Lush): "Non piu d'amore" (Sarconieri) (I)
Broadcast, *BBC HOME SERVICE*, BBC, London, 26 Apr 1948

* 7. DINO BORGIOLI (pf/Ernest Lush): "Donzelle fuggite"(Cavalli) (I)
Broadcast, *BBC HOME SERVICE*, BBC, London, 26 Apr 1948

* 8. LUISA TETRAZZINI, soprano (orch/?Percy Pitt): FAUST, Act II: Aria dei gioielli ["Ah! Je ris"] (I) (Gounod)
Ho 522 London, 20 Jun 1914 HMV unpub

* 9. LUISA TETRAZZINI, soprano (harp and violin/?): "Angel's Serenade" (Braga) (I)
Ho 554c London, 20 Jun 1914 HMV unpub

*10. LUISA TETRAZZINI, soprano (orch/?Percy Pitt): ROSALINDA: Pastorale (Francesco Veracini) (I)
Ho 550c London, 20 Jun 1914 HMV unpub

SIDE 2 (223 B):

* 1. GIUSEPPE DE LUCA, baritone (recitative: pf/?; aria: studio orch/?): DON PASQUALE, Act I: Proprio quella che ci vuole . . . Bella siccome un angelo (Donizetti) (I)
?Broadcast, source and date unknown

* 2. GIUSEPPE DE LUCA, baritone (pf/?): "Mare, mare" (Neapolitan Song-trad.) (Neapolitan)
?Broadcast, source and date unknown

* 3. GLADYS SWARTHOUT, contralto; JAN KIEPURA, tenor (studio orch and and chorus/?): "Processional--Lift Up Thy Voices" (Oscar Hammerstein II-Erich Wolfgang Korngold) (E)
from the 8-reel Paramount feature film, *GIVE US THIS NIGHT* (1936), Hollywood, 1936
LP 6204; c6 Mar 1936 (Paramount Productions, Inc.)
New York Premiere: Paramount Theater, NYC, 3 Apr 1936

* 4. JAN KIEPURA, tenor (with mandolins, ?drums, and chorus/?): IL TROVATORE, Act III: Di quella pira (Verdi) (I)
from the 8-reel Paramount feature film, *GIVE US THIS NIGHT* (1936), Hollywood, 1936
LP 6204; c6 Mar 1936 (Paramount Productions, Inc.)
New York Premiere: Paramount Theater, NYC, 3 Apr 1936

5. GIACOMO LAURI-VOLPI, tenor (RAI Orchestra, Roma/Riccardo Santarelli): WERTHER, Act I: Io non so se son desto ["Je ne sais si je veille"] ["Invocation"] (Massenet) (I)
Broadcast, ***CONCERTO MARTINI E ROSSI***, Rome, 9 Mar 1953

6. GIACOMO LAURI-VOLPI, tenor (RAI Orchestra, Roma/Riccardo\ Santarelli): TOSCA, Act III: E lucevan le stelle (Puccini) (I)
Broadcast, ***CONCERTO MARTINI E ROSSI***, Rome, 9 Mar 1953

7. GIACOMO LAURI-VOLPI, tenor (RAI Orchestra, Roma/Riccardo Santarelli): MANON LESCAUT, Act I: Donna non vidi mai (Puccini) (I)
Broadcast, ***CONCERTO MARTINI E ROSSI***, Rome, 9 Mar 1953

8. GIACOMO LAURI-VOLPI, tenor (RAI Orchestra, Roma/Riccardo Santarelli): IL TROVATORE, Act III/ii: Di quella pira . . . All'armi! (Verdi) (I)
Broadcast, ***CONCERTO MARTINI E ROSSI***, Rome, 9 Mar 1953

* 9. LAURITZ MELCHIOR, baritone (orch/?): IL TROVATORE, Act II: Il balen del suo sorriso (Verdi) (D)
Kpo 414 Copenhagen, January-February, 1913 Odeon A 144375

NOTES: EJS 223

Though the transfers are all surprisingly good, speeds are erratic on this LP and each item should be pitched individually.

Side 1 (223 A):

Band 1: This is *not* the song that the composer, Tito Schipa, recorded for Victor as "A Cuba" in 1924 and again in 1925.
Private vinyl copies of the Ruffo performance exist.

Band 3: Recorded at HMV's Abbey Road studio: both Kahn and Moore were present during the session, but it is not known which of the two accompanied Ruffo.

Band 4: Given on the label of EJS 223 as "Talk: Ruffo and Chaliapin." A second matrix of this mock dialogue was recorded at the same session: OB-5469-1, but this has not appeared on LP as far as I know. Ruffo, of course, speaks both parts.

Bands 5-7: A full LP recital of Borgioli BBC items appeared as EJS 182 in July-August, 1960.

Bands 8-10: All of the unpublished Tetrazzini titles are dated 1910 on the label of EJS 223. 20 June, 1914 is given by Alan Kelly in his *La Voce del Padrone* discography.
The FAUST "Jewel Song" was subsequently reissued on vinyl as Historic Masters HMB 23.

Band 10: This "Pastorale" is from the 1744 operatic setting of ROSALINDA by Francesco Veracini (1690-1768), not RODELINDA of Handel, as implied on the label of EJS 223.

Side 2 (223 B):

Bands 1-2: The source(s) of these two items are still untraced. The label of EJS 223 says only "1948," but neither has been found among De Luca's broadcasts of that year. Nor did a thorough search through the 1946 and 1947 radio logs turn up any possible sources. From their sound, they are obviously broadcasts: the applause after both numbers sounds like that of a large studio audience, as if from a regular studio broadcast. Vocally, both are consistent with other documented De Luca broadcasts of this period.
De Luca's only large-scale performances from this period of late activity were the annual Lewisohn Stadium "Italian Night" concerts on 6 July, 1946 and 12 July, 1947, both accompanied by the New York Philharmonic under Alexander Smallens. Audience attendence at both topped 16,000. Jan Peerce was featured alongside De Luca in both, with a supporting cast of younger singers: Claramae Turner and Marie Rogndahl in 1946, and Rogndahl, Herva Nelli, Charles Danford, and Carlo Tomanelli in 1947. At the first concert De Luca sang only Romilli's "Marietta," "Di provenza" from TRAVIATA, the "Largo al factotum" from BARBIERE, and in duet with Peerce, the "Solenne quest'ora" from FORZA.

A song also credited to him, "Mare chiare"(sic), adds a potential complication. At the 1947 concert he joined Peerce in the "Invano Alvaro!" from FORZA, and participated in a LUCIA Sextette. These concerts were not broadcast, though they may have been recorded.

It is doubtful that either the "Bella siccome" or the "Mare, Mare" are from the CARNEGIE POPS CONCERT of 11 May, 1948 (see EJS 102 and 270), as they are not listed in the radio logs or reviews for that benefit concert and their audience noise and overall "acoustic" is quite dissimilar. Possibly they are from immediately post-War RAI broadcasts: De Luca did appear in a complete RAI LA TRAVIATA on 17 February, 1945 and may well have taken part in others (the only other documented RAI broadcast is a PEARL FISHERS from 4 June, 1936).

In the DON PASQUALE aria, *Don Pasquale's* line in the recitative, "Son tut t'occhi . . . attento a udir vi sto," is taken by the piano. Note that the entire recitative, "Proprio quella che ci vuole . . . Udite," is accompanied only by piano and that the aria, beginning at "Bella siccome un angelo," is with orchestra. The pianist is unknown. It has been suggested that the aria and the recitative may have been taken from different sources, but I do not believe this to be the case: the piano is clearly audible under the orchestra in the aria itself, which suggests that a "patch" has not been made here.

Bands 3 and 4: 3 April, 1936 was the New York preview date of ***GIVE US THIS NIGHT***: the general run of the film began the next day. No music director/conductor for the soundtrack sessions could be found. Unlabeled shellac pressings of other Kiepura excerpts from this film have been reported from private collections.

Bands 5-8: The Lauri-Volpi ***MARTINI E ROSSI*** selections are dated 1961 on the label of EJS 223. Smith reissued a number of these performances on Harvest LP H-1003, and again on ANNA.

Band 9: The Melchior baritone recordings were subsequently issued nearly complete on ASCO 121, and again on UORC 160 (May, 1973). Danacord has issued the same items on both LP and CD in their "Melchior Anthology, Volume 1" (DACO[CD] 311-312).

EJS 224: "The Golden Age of Opera" (4 LPs)
Issued December, 1961

SIDES 1-8 (224 A-H):

DIE MEISTERSINGER VON NÜRNBERG (Wagner) (G)
Opera in 3 Acts (complete)
Metropolitan Opera House Orchestra and Chorus/Erich Leinsdorf
Metropolitan Opera broadcast, NYC, 2 Dec 1939

CAST:
Irene Jessner (*Eva*); Karin Branzell (*Magdalene*); Charles Kullman (*Walther*); Friedrich Schorr (*Hans Sachs*); Walter Olitzki (*Beckmesser*); Emanuel List (*Pogner*); Herbert Janssen (*Kothner*); Max Altglass (*Vogelgesang*); Nicholas Massue (*Zorn*); Lodovico Oliviero (*Moser*); Giordano Paltrinieri (*Eisslinger*); Louis D'Angelo (*Nachtigal*); George Cehanovsky (*Ortel*); James Wolfe (*Foltz*); John Gurney (*Schwartz*); Karl Laufkoetter (*David*); George Cehanovsky (*Night Watchman*).

NOTES: EJS 224

Smith's source for this performance was the official NBC acetates (seventeen 16-inch sides, numbered ENG. 183 9-37, broadcast no. 9-349, and dated "Dec-8-39" in pencil). The same tape of the original acetates was used for the Discocorp 484 reissue.

Library of Congress tape: 5174-18 (complete broadcast).

EJS 225: "The Golden Age of Opera" (3 LPs)
Issued January, 1962 ("Special Release")

SIDES 1-6 (225 A-F)

LA GIOCONDA (Ponchielli) (I)
Opera in 4 Acts (complete)
Metropolitan Opera Orchestra and Chorus/Ettore Panizza
Metropolitan Opera broadcast, NYC, 30 Dec 1939

CAST:
Zinka Milanov (*Gioconda*); Bruna Castagna (*Laura*); Nicola Moscona (*Alvise*); Anna Kaskas (*La Cieca*); Giovanni Martinelli (*Enzo Grimaldo*); Carlo Morelli (*Barnaba*); Wilfred Engelman (*Zuane*); Wilfred Engelman (*Singer*); Giordano Paltrinieri (*Singer*); Giordano Paltrinieri (*Isepo*); Louis D'Angelo (*Monk*); Carlo Coscia (*Steersman*).

NOTES: EJS 225

D'Angelo is listed in both the old and new versions of the *Metropolitan Opera Annals* as the *Monk* and is credited on the label of EJS 225 accordingly, but the call to prayer at the end of Act I sounds nothing like him. However, no last-minute substitution (Wilfred Engelman, perhaps?) could be documented, if indeed there was one.

The original NBC acetates (fourteen 16-inch sides, numbered ENG. 183 9-37, broadcast no. 9-350) have Ortha labels and the pencilled notation "Jan. 5."

A 115 minute abridgement of this performance was issued previously on EJS 128 (1958). Excerpts subsequently appeared on a Martinelli duet recital, UORC 255 (June, 1975) and on HOPE-201. The latter two, like EJS 225, made use of the official NBC acetates of the performance, while EJS 128 was taken from a sub-standard air-check.

The three discs play at score pitch at a uniform 32.3 rpm.

EJS 226: "The Golden Age of Opera" (1 LP)
Issued January, 1962

MISSA SOLEMNIS, Op. 123 (Beethoven) (Greek and Latin) (excerpts)
Cincinnati Symphony and Cincinnati May Festival Chorus/Eugene Goossens
Broadcast, ***CINCINNATI MAY FESTIVAL***, ?WCKY [NBC], Cincinnati, 5 May 1937

Kirsten Flagstad, soprano
Kathryn Meisle, contralto
Frederick Jagel, tenor
Ezio Pinza, bass

SIDE 1 (226 A)

1. FLAGSTAD, MEISLE, JAGEL, PINZA, and Chorus: Kyrie

2. FLAGSTAD, MEISLE, JAGEL, PINZA, and Chorus: Gloria

SIDE 2 (226 B)

1. FLAGSTAD, MEISLE, JAGEL, PINZA, and Chorus: Credo

NOTES: EJS 226

Taken from the official NBC acetates (four 16-inch sides numbered ENG. 183 9-36, broadcast no. 7-30). The original one-hour broadcast cut off in the midst of the "Sanctus" and the "Agnus Dei" was performed after the broadcast had terminated altogether.

EJS 227: "The Golden Age of Opera " (1 LP)
Issued January, 1962

SIDE 1 (227 A):

MANON (Massenet) (F)
Opera in 5 Acts (excerpts)
San Francisco Opera House Orchestra and Chorus/Gaetano Merola
San Francisco Opera Broadcast, KGO [NBC], San Francisco, 13 Oct 1939

CAST:
Bidú Sayão (*Manon*); Tito Schipa (*Des Grieux*); Richard Bonelli (*Lescaut*); [André Ferrier (*Guillot*)]; George Cehanovsky (*De Brétigny*); Margaret Ritter (*Maid*); [Norman Cordon (*Count Des Grieux*)]; [Stanley Noonan (*Guard*)]; [Max Edwards (*Guard*)].

1. SAYÃO, SCHIPA, BONELLI, CEHANOVSKY: Beginning of Act II . . . En fermant les yeux ["Le rêve"]

SIDE 2 (227 B):

CARMEN (Bizet) (F)
Opera in 4 Acts (excerpts)
New York City Center Opera Orchestra and Chorus/Laszlo Halasz
New York City Opera Broadcast, City Center, NYC, WEAF, 26 Feb 1944

CAST:
Jennie Tourel (*Carmen*); Joseph Rogatschewsky (*Don José*); [Mary Martha Briney (*Micaela*)]; [George Czaplicki (*Escamillo*)]; Sidor Belarsky (*Zuniga*); [Hugh Thompson (*Morales*)]; Regina Resnik (*Frasquita*); Rosalind Nadell (*Mercédès*); Emil Renan (*Dancaïre*); Henry Cordy (*Remendado*).

1. RESNIK, NADELL, TOUREL, RENAN, CORDY, ROGATSCHEWSKY, and BELARSKY: Act II: End of the "Votre toast!" ("Toreador Song") . . . to the end of the act.

NOTES: EJS 227

Side 1 (227 A):

Only the second act of this season premiere MANON was broadcast. Smith's source was the official NBC acetates (two 16-inch sides, numbered ENG. 183 9-37, broadcast no. 9-263) which coupled the excerpt with installments of "Pepper Young's Family" and "David Harum." The same excerpt was later issued on MDP 024, a Schipa recital. As the latter was dubbed quite flat, the same may be true of the EJS 227 dubbing.

Side 2 (227 B):

Only Act II of the CARMEN was broadcast over WEAF, a forty-five minute segment beginning at 3:30 pm EST. The performance itself commenced in City Center at 2:15 pm. Tenor Rogatschewsky was substituting for the indisposed Mario Berini.

The January, 1962 bulletin notes clicks in the transfer owing to damage on the original glass acetate. The official NBC Ortha acetates (two 16-inch sides, numbered 31906 and 31907, broadcast no. 44-377) were Smith's source: the first disc of Act II was missing, the second (marked part 3) transcribed here, was broken and repaired.

EJS 228: "The Golden Age of Opera" (1 LP)
Issued January, 1962

LE NOZZE DI FIGARO, K. 492 (Mozart) (I)
Opera in 4 Acts (excerpts)
Metropolitan Opera House Orchestra and Chorus/Ettore Panizza
Metropolitan Opera broadcast, NYC, 7 Dec 1940

CAST:
John Brownlee (*Count Almaviva*); Elisabeth Rethberg (*Countess*); Licia Albanese (*Susanna*); Ezio Pinza (*Figaro*); Jarmila Novotná (*Cherubino*); [Irra Petina (*Marcellina*)]; [Alessio DePaolis (*Don Basilio*)]; [George Rasely (*Don Curzio*)]; Salvatore Baccaloni (*Doctor Bartolo*); [Louis D'Angelo (*Antonio*)]; [Marita Farell (*Barbarina*)]; [Helen Olheim (*Peasant Girl*)]; [Maxine Stellman (*Peasant Girl*)].

SIDE 1 (228 A):

Act I:
1. ALBANESE and PINZA: Cinque, dieci
2. PINZA: Se vuol ballare
3. BACCALONI: La vendetta, si? la vendetta!
4. NOVOTNÁ: Non so più, cosa son, cosa faccio
5. PINZA: Non più andrai

Act II:
6. RETHBERG: Porgi amor qualque ristoro
7. NOVOTNÁ: Voi che sapete

SIDE 2 (228 B)

Act III:
1. ALBANESE and BROWNLEE: Crudel! perche finora
2. BROWNLEE: Hai già vinta la causa!
3. RETHBERG: Dove sono i bei momenti
4. RETHBERG and ALBANESE: Che soave zeffiretto

Act IV:
5. PINZA: Aprite un po' quelgl'occhi
6. ALBANESE: Deh vieni, non tardar

NOTES: EJS 228:

This was the first of Texaco's regularly-sponsored Metropolitan Opera Saturday matinees. Originating from station WJZ in New York City, the performance was broadcast over the NBC Blue network to 131 national affiliates, reaching a potential audience of nearly ten million listeners (the 1939-1940 matinee season was calculated to have attracted some eight million listeners). This special alliance between Texaco and the Met has emerged as kind of American cultural icon, and remains the longest running *continuous* sponsorship in the history of American commercial radio.

The original Ortha label NBC actetates (fourteen 16-inch sides, numbered ENG. 183 9-37, broadcast no. 40-524) also include the Intermission features: "Opera Guild at Home," featuring Lucrezia Bori, Edward Johnson, George W. Sloan, and Mrs. Belmont; an "Opera Question Forum" with Milton Cross, Lawrence Tibbett, Gladys Swarthout, and Olin Downes; and a segment between Acts II and IV, "Our American Way of Life No. 1," with Mrs. Harold Milligan and ex-President Herbert Hoover.

The performance also marked the house debut of Salvatore Baccaloni, who had previously sung *Bartolo* in Philadelphia with the Met four days earlier. It has been reissued complete on LP by the Metropolitan Opera Guild as MET 5.

EJS 229: "The Golden Age of Opera" (1 LP)
Issued January, 1962

DON GIOVANNI, K. 527 (Mozart) (I)
Opera in 2 Acts (excerpts)
Metropolitan Opera House Orchestra and Chorus/Paul Breisach
Metropolitan Opera broadcast, Chicago, NBC, 3 Apr 1943

CAST:
Ezio Pinza (*Don Giovanni*); Zinka Milanov (*Donna Anna*); [Jarmila Novotná (*Donna Elvira*)]; Bidú Sayão (*Zerlina*); Norman Cordon (*The Commandant*); James Melton (*Don Ottavio*); Salvatore Baccaloni (*Leporello*); [Mack Harrell (*Masetto*)].

SIDE 1 (229 A):

Act I: 1. BACCALONI, PINZA, MILANOV, CORDON, and MELTON: Notte e giorno faticar. . . ma qual mai s'offre . . . to the end of the scene
2. BACCALONI: Madamina! Il catalogo
3. SAYÃO and PINZA: La ci darem la mano!
4. MILANOV: Or sai, chi l'onore

SIDE 2 (229 B):

Act I: 1. MELTON: Dalla sua pace la mia dipende
2. PINZA: Finch'han dal vino
3. SAYÃO: Batti, batti
Act II: 4. PINZA: Deh vieni alla finestra
5. SAYÃO: Vedrai, carino
6. MELTON: Il mio tesoro in tanto
7. MILANOV: Non mi dir, bell'idol mio

NOTES: EJS 229

These 3 April 1943 excerpts were taken from aluminum NBC *air-checks*, as all but two of the original network acetates (fifteen 16-inch sides, numbered 12687; 12689-12694, broadcast no. 43-482) were broken: sides 9 and 14 were irreparable; 11 had audible damage, sides 13 and 15 had edge chips missing. The Intermission Features were apparently preserved intact on sides 8 and 9. The final scene was missing on the official network line checks.

Some of the Milanov excerpts were included later on VOCE-118CD.

EJS 230: "The Golden Age of Opera" (2 LPs)
Issued February, 1962

SIDES 1-4 (230 A-D):

UN BALLO IN MASCHERA (Verdi) (I)
Opera in 3 Acts (complete)
Metropolitan Opera House Orchestra and Chorus/Ettore Panizza
Metropolitan Opera broadcast, NYC, 14 Dec 1940

CAST:
Jussi Bjoerling (*Riccardo*); Alexander Sved (*Renato*); Zinka Milanov (*Amelia*); Kerstin Thorborg (*Ulrica*); Stella Andreva (*Oscar*); Arthur Kent (*Sylvan*); Norman Cordon (*Sam*); Nicola Moscona (*Tom*); John Carter (*Judge*); Lodovico Oliviero (*Servant*).

NOTES: EJS 230

The official NBC acetates were used for this issue. These were subsequently lost, so could not be documented. The originals, like contained the lengthy Intermission Features which included among others, Milton Cross, Frank St. Leger, Risë Stevens, and Jarmilla Novotna (on the "Opera Quiz Forum").

The performance was subsequently reissued as Rococo 1003, Historical Operatic Treasures ERR 109-3, Robin Hood Records RHR 516-C, and most recently, as Metropolitan Opera Guild MET 1.

EJS 230 plays nearly a half-step low at 33.3 rpm.

Bjoerling omitted *Riccardo's* third-act aria "Ma se m'è forza perderti" in the actual performance, but does sing the preceding recitative complete.

Library of Congress tape: 7749-53 (complete broadcast).

EJS 231: "The Golden Age of Opera" (1 LP)
Issued February, 1962

FIDELIO, Op. 72 (Beethoven) (G)
Opera in 2 Acts (excerpts)
Metropolitan Opera House Orchestra and Chorus/Artur Bodanzky
Metropolitan Opera broadcast, NYC, 31 Dec 1938

CAST:
Kirsten Flagstad (*Leonora*); René Maison (*Florestan*); Friedrich Schorr (*Don Pizaro*); Marita Farell (*Marzellina*); Emmanuel List (*Rocco*); Karl Laufkoetter (*Jaquino*); Arnold Gabor (*Don Fernando*); Nicholas Massue (*First Prisoner*); Arnold Gabor (*Second Prisoner*).

SIDE 1 (231 A):

1. Act I:
   a) FARELL, FLAGSTAD, LAUFKOETTER, and LIST: Mir ist so wunderbar (Quartet)
   b) SCHORR and Chorus: Ha! welch'ein Augenblich
   c) SCHORR and LIST: Jetzt, Alter, jetzt hat es Eile
   d) FLAGSTAD: Abscheulicher, wo eilst du hin . . . Komm, Hoffnung

SIDE 2 (231 B):

1. Act I: a) FLAGSTAD, LIST, FARELL, LAUFKOETTER, and SCHORR: Nun sprecht, wie ging's? . . . to the end of the act

Act II: b) MAISON, LIST, FLAGSTAD, and SCHORR: Nur hurtig fort . . . to the end of the scene (Finale omitted)

NOTES: EJS 231

The Act I "Goldarie" was not performed. Bodanzky's recitatives were used for the performance in place of the spoken dialogue.

Schorr's first-act aria from this performances also appeared on EJS 213 (May, 1961) and the Act I "Abscheulicher" was issued on a Flagstad recital, EJS 258 (January, 1963). Stanford University has the complete performance on tape (StARS 381231), which subsequently appeared in its entirety as UORC 268 (November-December, 1975) and on CD as Music and Arts as CD-619.

EJS 232: "The Golden Age of Opera" (1 LP)
Issued February, 1962

IL BARBIERE DI SIVIGLIA (Rossini) (I)
Opera in 2 Acts (excerpts)
Metropolitan Opera House Orchestra and Chorus/Gennaro Pappi
Metropolitan Opera broadcast, NYC, 22 Jan 1938

CAST:
Bruno Landi (*Count Almaviva*); Pompilio Malatesta (*Doctor Bartolo*); Lily Pons (*Rosina*); John Charles Thomas (*Figaro*); Ezio Pinza (*Don Basilio*); Wilfred Engelman (*Fiorello*); Irra Petina (*Berta*); Giordano Paltrinieri (*Official*).

SIDE 1 (232 A):

Act I: 1. LANDI: Ecco ridente in cielo
2. THOMAS: Largo al factotum
3. LANDI: Se il mio nome saper ["Serenata"]
4. LANDI and THOMAS: All'idea di quel metallo . . . Numero quindici
5. PONS: Una voce poco fà . . .Io son docile

SIDE 2 (232 B):

Act I: 1. PINZA: La calunnia è un venticello
2. PONS and THOMAS: Dunque io son?
* 3. MALATESTA: Manca un foglio, e già (Romani)
4. PONS: LESSON SCENE:
a) "Villanelle" (Dell'Acqua)
b) DIE ENTFÜHRUNG AUS DEM SERAIL, K. 384, Act I: Ach ich liebte (Mozart) (I)

Act II: 5. MALATESTA, THOMAS, PONS, LANDI, PINZA, PALTRINIERI, and Chorus: Fermi tutti. Eccoli quà . . . to the end of the opera

NOTES: EJS 232

Taken from air-checks belonging to Pons. Issued complete as UORC 129 (November, 1972).

Side 2 (232 B):

Band 3: "Manca un foglio" was written by Pietro Romani, and is frequently interpolated into the first act in place of the aria "A un dottor della mia sorte."

EJS 233: "The Golden Age of Opera" (1 LP)
Issued March, 1962

POTPOURRI 15 ("Tenors")

SIDE 1 (233 A):

ANDREA CHENIER (Giordano) (I)
Opera in 4 Acts (excerpts)
San Francisco Opera House Orchestra and Chorus/Gaetano Merola
San Francisco Opera Broadcast, KGO [NBC], San Francisco, 7 Oct 1938

CAST:
Beniamino Gigli (*Chenier*); Elisabeth Rethberg (*Maddalena*); [Richard Bonelli (*Gérard*)]; Doris Doe (*The Countess*); John Howell (*Fléville*); Lodovico Oliviero (*The Abbot*).

* 1. Act I: HOWELL, RETHBERG, DOE, OLIVIERO, and GIGLI: Commosso, lusingato . . . Un dì, all'azzurro spazio

* 2. BENIAMINO GIGLI, tenor (orch and chorus/?): LA SONNAMBULA, Act I: Prendi, l'anel ti dono (Bellini) (I)
from the soundtrack of the feature film *LACHE BAJAZZO/I PAGLIACCI* (1942), Cinecittà Studios, Rome, May, 1942

* 3. BENIAMINO GIGLI, tenor (orch and chorus/?): I PAGLIACCI, Act I: Recitar . . . Vesti la giubba (Leoncavallo) (I)
from the soundtrack of the feature film *LACHE BAJAZZO/I PAGLIACCI* (1942), Cinecittà Studios, Rome, May, 1942

4. BENIAMINO GIGLI, tenor (Orchestra of Radio Italiana [RAI], Milano/Nino Sanzogno): L'ELISIR D'AMORE, Act II: Una furtiva lagrima (Donizetti) (I)
Broadcast, *CONCERTO MARTINI E ROSSI*, RAI, Teatro Municipale, San Remo, 21 Dec 1953

5. BENIAMINO GIGLI, tenor (Orchestra of Radio Italiana [RAI], Milano/Nino Sanzogno): TOSCA, Act III: E lucevan le stelle (Puccini) (I)
Broadcast, *CONCERTO MARTINI E ROSSI*, RAI, Teatro Municipale, San Remo, 21 Dec 1953

6. BENIAMINO GIGLI, tenor (Orchestra of Radio Italiana [RAI], Milano/Nino Sanzogno): MARTHA, Act III: M'appari [Ach, so fromm] (Flotow) (I)
   Broadcast, *CONCERTO MARTINI E ROSSI*, RAI, Teatro Municipale, San Remo, 21 Dec 1953

SIDE 2 (233 B):

1. GIACOMO LAURI-VOLPI, tenor (Orchestre Maggio Musicale Fiorentino/Carlo Felice Cillario): I LOMBARDI, Act II: La mia letizia infondere (Verdi) (I)
   Broadcast, *CONCERTO MARTINI E ROSSI*, RAI, ?Florence, 11 Feb 1957

* 2. GIACOMO LAURI-VOLPI, tenor (?Luigi Ricci/pf): "Tu sei l'amor mio" (Giacomo Lauri-Volpi) (I)
   Telecast, *ROSSO E NERO*, RAI, circa 1959

* 3.. GIACOMO LAURI-VOLPI, tenor (?Luigi Ricci/pf): FEDORA, Act II: Amor ti vieta (Giordano) (I)
   Telecast, *ROSSO E NERO*, RAI, circa 1959

* 4. GIACOMO LAURI-VOLPI, tenor (pf/?): "Mattinata" (Breschi) (I)
   From the feature film *LA CANZONE DEL SOLE* [*DAS LIED DER SONNE*] (1933), Italia-Film G.m.b.H, Berlin, 1933
   [disc transfer]: Discoteca di Stato-Fono Roma A 102 KR 186 Rome, 1933

* 5. GIACOMO LAURI-VOLPI, tenor (pf/?): "La canzone del sole" (Mascagni) (I)
   From the feature film *LA CANZONE DEL SOLE* [*DAS LIED DER SONNE*] (1933), Italia-Film G.m.b.H, Berlin, 1933
   [disc transfer]: Discoteca di Stato-Fono Roma A 102 KR 186 Rome, 1933

* 6. GIUSEPPE DI STEFANO, tenor, and EBE STIGNANI, contralto (Orchestra of Radio Italiana [RAI], Torino/Oliviero de Fabritiis): LA FAVORITA, Act I: Ah mio bene . . . Fia vero lasciarti (Donizetti) (I)
   Broadcast, *CONCERTO MARTINI E ROSSI*, RAI, Torino, 8 Dec 1952

7. FERRUCCIO TAGLIAVINI, tenor (orch/?): MANON, Act III: Ah, dispar! vision [Je suis seul . . . Ah! fuyez, douce image (Massenet) (I)
   Broadcast, source and date unknown

* 8. FREDERICK JAGEL, tenor (pf/?): SALVATOR ROSA, Act III: Mia piccirella (Gomes) (I)
   Telecast, *PERFORMANCE*, WGBH [NET], Boston, 27 Sep 1960

* 9. FREDERICK JAGEL, tenor (pf/?): LE ROI D'YS, Act III: Vainement, ma bien aimée ["Aubade"] (Lalo) (F)
   Telecast, *PERFORMANCE*, WGBH [NET], Boston, 27 Sep 1960

NOTES: EJS 233

Side 1 (233 A):

Band 1: Only the Act I finale of this performance has survived. Smith's source was the original NBC acetates (six 16-inch sides numbered ENG. 183 9-37). Richard Bonelli's *Gérard* is listed on the label of EJS 233, but does not appear in the Act I segment presented here. The same excerpt was reissued in slightly better sound on the MDP 018 LP "Beniamino Gigli Live . . . From the Great Opera Houses of the World."

Bands 2-3: Both the German- and Italian-language versions of this Gigli feature film were shot in Rome. The SONNAMBULA aria was also included on the afore-mentioned MDP 018 LP, labeled "1939."

Side 2 (233 B):

Bands 2-3: The origin of this telecast has not been determined. Ricci was Lauri-Volpi's regular accompanist throughout the 1950s and so may well be the unnamed pianist here. Lauri-Volpi's 1959 private recording of his own "Tu sei l'amor mio," appeared subsequently on EJS 565 (June, 1971) as "Ah si ben mio, mio solo amor."

Band 4-5: Listed in error as recorded "1953" on the label of EJS 233. The disc transfer cited in the listing, Discoteca di Stato-Roma A 102 KR 186, is a shellac dubbing taken directly from the soundtrack. A Rome broadcast featuring Lauri-Volpi, recorded at the Discoteca di Stato Accademia Filarmonica on 25 November, 1933, was also issued on this label (A 101 KR 171/172), and includes a singing lesson as well as excerpts from BOHÈME, RIGOLETTO, HUGUENOTS, and AFRICAINE. These, and the soundtrack songs featured on EJS 233, later appeared on the LP "Il Favoloso Archivo della Discoteca di Stato." A later Smith-produced Lauri-Volpi recital on Harvest H-1002 contains the "Mattinata" and "La Canzone del sole." Timaclub, too, has reissued much of this non-commercial Lauri-Volpi material.

Band 6: Mr. César Dillon of Buenos Aires has confirmed that this 8 December, 1952 broadcast featured Di Stefano and Stignani, as the label attests. Reports that the soprano was in fact Fedora Barbieri are apparently false.

The same duet subsequently appeared on Fonit Cetra LMR 5024, HRE 302-2, Legendary LR 146-2, Timaclub MPV5, and GDS 1205.

Bands 8-9: This WGBH Jagel recital was issued complete as EJS 533 (December, 1970), along with a 1959 faculty recital at the New England Conservatory in Boston. See the lengthy endnote for that LP.

EJS 234: "The Golden Age of Opera" (1 LP)
Issued March, 1962

SIDES 1-2 (234 A-B)

DIE WALKÜRE (Wagner) (G)
Opera in 3 Acts (excerpts: Act II only)
San Francisco Opera House Orchestra and Chorus/Fritz Reiner
San Francisco Opera Broadcast, KGO [NBC], San Francisco, 13 Nov 1936

CAST:
Kirsten Flagstad (*Brünnhilde*); Friedrich Schorr (*Wotan*); Lauritz Melchior (*Siegmund*); Lotte Lehmann (*Sieglinde*); Kathryn Meisle (*Fricka*); Emanuel List (*Hunding*).

NOTES: EJS 234

Taken from the official NBC acetates. The last measures on the original acetates (at *Wotan's* "Geh' hin, knecht") contain Marcia Davenport's announcements, omitted from EJS 234 by way of an abrupt ending. The network acetates have since been reported as lost. Numerous splices and abrupt changes of speed plague this particular issue, as do sweeping performance cuts: the LP is, accordingly, best approached with score in hand.

Reissued on the Discocorp label as RR-426 and Edizione Lirica as 004-2. The Discocorp issue is pitched poorly, but it does contain some of the Davenport announcements.

EJS 235: "The Golden Age of Opera" (1 LP)
Issued March, 1962

"LILY PONS OPERATIC RECITAL (1935-1941)"

SIDE 1 (235 A)

* 1. w. studio orch/André Kostelanetz: FORTUNIO, Act II: J'aimais la vielle maison grise ["La maison grise"] (Messager) (F)
Broadcast, ***THE CHESTERFIELD HOUR***, WABC, NYC, 1 Jan 1936

* 2. w. studio orch/André Kostelanetz: MIREILLE, Act I: O légère hirondelle (Gounod) (F)
Broadcast, ***THE CHESTERFIELD HOUR***, WABC, NYC, 5 May 1937

* 3. w. studio orch/André Kostelanetz: SADKO, Scene IV: Les diamants chez nous sont innombrables [Ne shchest al masov] ("Song of the Indian Guest") (Rimsky-Korsakov) (F)
Broadcast, ***THE CHESTERFIELD HOUR***, WABC, NYC, ?27 May 1936

4. w. General Motors Symphony Orchestra/Erno Rapee: MIGNON, Act II: Je suis Titania ("Polonaise") (Thomas) (F)
Broadcast, ***GENERAL MOTORS HOUR***, WEAF, Westchester County Theater, White Plains, New York, 6 Dec 1936

* 5. w. studio orch/André Kostelanetz: FORTUNIO, Act III: Si vous croyez ("Chanson de Fortunio") (Messager) (F)
Broadcast, ***THE CHESTERFIELD HOUR***, WABC, NYC, ?27 May 1936

* 6. w. studio orch/André Kostelanetz: LES CONTES D'HOFFMANN, Act II: Les oiseaux dans la charmille (Offenbach) (F)
Broadcast, ***THE CHESTERFIELD HOUR***, WABC, NYC, ?13 May 1936

7. w. studio orch/André Kostelanetz: PEER GYNT, Op. 23/1: Solveig's Song (Grieg) (F)
Broadcast, ***THE CHESTERFIELD HOUR***, WABC, NYC, 13 May 1936

8. w. studio orch/André Kostelanetz: PARYSATIS: La chanson du rossignol (Saint-Saëns) (F)
Broadcast, ***THE CHESTERFIELD HOUR***, WABC, NYC, 26 May 1937

SIDE 2 (235 B):

* 1. w. studio orch/André Kostelanetz: MANON LESCAUT, Act I: C'est l'histoire (Auber) (F)
Broadcast, ***THE CHESTERFIELD HOUR***, WABC, NYC, 16 Jun 1937

2. w. studio orch/Donald Voorhees: LA TRAVIATA, Act I: Ah fors e lui . . . Sempre libera (Verdi) (I)
Broadcast, ***THE BELL TELEPHONE HOUR***, WNBC, NYC, 10 Dec 1951

3. w. Detroit Symphony Orchestra/José Iturbi: DIE ZAUBERFLÖTE, K. 620, Act II: Ah, je le sais [Ach, ich fühl's] (Mozart) (F)
Broadcast, ***FORD SUNDAY EVENING HOUR***, WJR, Detroit, 3 Jan 1937

4. w. Detroit Symphony Orchestra/José Iturbi: EXSULTATE, JUBILATE, K. 165: Alleluja (Mozart) (L)
Broadcast, ***FORD SUNDAY EVENING HOUR***, WJR, Detroit, 3 Jan 1937

5. w. Detroit Symphony Orchestra and male chorus/Eugene Ormandy: LA FILLE DU REGIMENT, Act I: Chacun le sait . . . Il a gangé tant de combats (Donizetti) (F)
Broadcast, ***FORD SUNDAY EVENING HOUR***, WJR, Detroit, 23 Nov 1941

6. w. Detroit Symphony Orchestra/Eugene Ormandy: LA FILLE DU REGIMENT, Act I: Il faut partir, mes bons amis d'armes (Donizetti) (F)
Broadcast, ***FORD SUNDAY EVENING HOUR***, WJR, Detroit, 23 Nov 1941

* 7. w. Detroit Symphony Orchestra/Eugene Ormandy: ROSMONDA D' INGHILTERRA, Act I: ["De surprise . . . Au partir mon coeur renomme"] (sic) (Donizetti) (F)
Broadcast, ***FORD SUNDAY EVENING HOUR***, WJR, Detroit, 23 Nov 1941

* 8. w. General Motors Symphony Orchestra/Erno Rapee: LAKMé, Act II: Où va la jeune Indoue ("Bell Song") (Delibes) (F)
Broadcast, ***GENERAL MOTORS HOUR***, WEAF, Industrial Mutual Association, Flint, Michigan, WFDF, Flint, 12 Apr 1936

9. w. Detroit Symphony Orchestra/José Iturbi: DINORAH [LE PARDON DE PLOëRMEL], Act II: Ombre légère (Meyerbeer) (F)
Broadcast, ***FORD SUNDAY EVENING HOUR***, WJR, Detroit, 3 Jan 1937

NOTES: EJS 235

The air checks used for this issue were submitted to a private collector by Pons herself, and these were passed on to Smith for dubbing. This collector, a well-known Pons authority, was the source of the broadcast dates given in the listing (taken apparently from the discs themselves or perhaps from the singer's own recollections), but these dates do not always agree with the *New York Times* listings: discrepancies will be discussed in the individual endnotes below. Possibly some of the selections (I/2 and I/6) were last-minute substitutions (the two items from the 27 May, 1936 broadcast, I/3 and 5), could not be verified, as the *Times* ran no log for the broadcast).

Several items included here appeared later on various UORC Pons recitals, notably UORC 212 (October, 1974).

The subtitle of the LP, "(1935-1941)," is incorrect, as was so often the case in the GAO series.

Speeds vary slightly from band to band.

Side 1 (235 A):

Band 1: Library of Congress tape: 5063-25 (complete broadcast).

Band 2: Kostelanetz is not listed in the *New York Times* log for the 5 May, 1937 broadcast, but he was undoubtedly the conductor.

Band 3: No program was given for this broadcast in the *New York Times*.

Band 5: No program was given for this broadcast in the *New York Times*.

Band 6: The HOFFMANN aria was not listed in the *New York Times* log for the 13 May, 1936 broadcast.

Side 2 (235 B):

Band 1: Kostelanetz is again not listed in the *New York Times* log, but almost certainly conducted the 16 June, 1937 show.

Band 7: Given as "Mes Amis" from LA FILLE DU REGIMENT on the label of EJS 235.

This aria began its distinguished life in Act I/ii of Donizetti's two-act ROSMONDA D'INGHILTERRA of 1834 as the recitative-aria-cabaletta "Volgon tre lune, ahi! lassa! . . . Perchè non ho del vento . . . Torna, ah! torna, o caro oggetto." The creator of both *Lucia* and *Rosmonda*, Fanny Tacchinardi-Persiani (1812-1867), was probably the first to use the ROSMONDA aria as a substitute for *Lucia's* Act I fountain scene "Regnava nel silenzio" and "Quando rapito in estasi"). Published editions of the substituted aria are many, each with different alterations to the text and music. French scores reveal that by the time LUCIA made its French-language debut at the Théâtre-Italien 12 December, 1837), the adapted ROSMONDA aria ("Perchè non ho del vento") may have already been used, as it would routinely thereafter, to stand in place of the fountain scene or even to supplement the famous "Mad Scene" of Act III, though some sources claim that the ROSMONDA scene was written by Donizetti expressly for this purpose.

Lucette Korsoff recorded the LUCIA DI LAMMERMOOR version on 17 June, 1913 as "Que n'avons-nous des ailes . . . Toi par qui mon coeur rayonne" on French Gramophone 033168, later issued as HMV W217 (matrix 02720½v). More recently, Joan Sutherland recorded the LUCIA version of the aria. Beverly Sills recorded the an abbreviated version of the original ROSMONDA version on her first recital for Westminster (WST-17143), while Lella Cuberli included the complete original ROSMONDA aria on her recital, "Momenti di Belcanto" (Cetra CDC 14). A 1975 Belfast production of ROSMONDA. using the *Opera Rara* edition, appeared complete as UORC 274 (January-February, 1976) and was later reissued in stereo MRF 127-5.

Though Pons was scheduled to sing only excerpts from LA FILLE DU REGIMENT on this 23 November, 1941 broadcast, this aria was probably announced as being from either ROSMONDA or LUCIA. The text she sings here could not be documented as authentic to any version of the aria.

Band 8: Also appearing on this Easter broadcast, and accompanying Pons, was a 1,200-voice choir under the direction of Eduard Ossko.

EJS 236: "The Golden Age of Opera" (1 LP)
Issued March, 1962

AÏDA (Verdi) (I)
Opera in 4 Acts (excerpts)
Metropolitan Opera House Orchestra and Chorus/Wilfred Pelletier
Metropolitan Opera broadcast, NYC, 6 Mar 1943

CAST:
[Lansing Hatfield (*King of Egypt*)]; Bruna Castagna (*Amneris*); Zinka Milanov (); Giovanni Martinelli (*Radames*); Norman Cordon (*Ramfis*); Richard Bonelli (*Amonasro*); [John Dudley] (*Messenger*); Frances Greer (*Priestess*).

SIDE 1 (236 A):

Act I: 1. MARTINELLI: Se quel guerrier io fossi! . . . Celeste Aïda

2. MILANOV: Ritorna vincitor!

Act III: 3. MILANOV, BONELLI, and MARTINELLI: Qui Radames verrà . . . O patria mia . . . Coraggio! ei giunge, la tutto udro

SIDE 2 (236 B):

Act III: 1. MARTINELLI, MILANOV, BONELLI, CASTAGNA, and CORDON: Pur ti riveggo, mia dolce . . . to the end of the act

Act IV: 2. CASTAGNA and MARTINELLI: L'abborrita rivale a me sfuggia . . . through Già i sacerdoti adunansi

Act IV: 3. MILANOV, CASTAGNA, MARTINELLI, GREER and Chorus: La fatal pietra . . . Morir! . . . O terra addio . . . to the end of the opera

NOTES: EJS 236

The bulletin for EJS 236 rightly notes that this AÏDA, from Martinelli's thirtieth consecutive Met season, was his last broadcast in the role of *Radames*. The performance was subsequently reissued complete as EJS 500 (March, 1970) and as Cetra LO-26/3.

EJS 237: "The Golden Age of Opera" (2 LPs)
Issued April, 1962

SIDES 1-4 (237 A-D):

MADAMA BUTTERFLY (Puccini) (I)
Opera in 2 Acts (complete)
Metropolitan Opera House Orchestra and Chorus/Gennaro Pappi
Metropolitan Opera broadcast, NYC, 25 Jan 1941

CAST:
Licia Albanese (*Butterfly*); Lucielle Browning (*Suzuki*); Maxine Stellman (*Kate Pinkerton*); Armand Tokatyan (*B. F. Pinkerton*); John Brownlee (*Sharpless*); Alessio DePaolis (*Goro*); George Cehanovsky (*Yamadori*); John Gurney (*Uncle-Priest*); Wilfred Engelman (*Imperial Commissioner*).

NOTES: EJS 237

The entire performance is reported to play in score pitch at approximately 34.9-35.00 rpm.
Reissued as OPA-1031/32.

EJS 238: "The Golden Age of Opera" (1 LP)
Issued April, 1962

L'ELISIR D'AMORE (Donizetti) (I)
Opera in 2 acts (excerpts)
Metropolitan Opera House Orchestra and Chorus/Giuseppe Antonicelli
Metropolitan Opera broadcast, NYC, 5 Feb 1949

CAST:
Ferruccio Tagliavini (*Nemorino*); Bidú Sayão (*Adina*); Francesco Valentino (*Sgt. Belcore*); Italo Tajo (*Dr. Dulcamara*); Inge Manski (*Gianetta*).

SIDE 1 (238 A):

Act I: 1. a) TAGLIAVINI, MANSKI, SAYÃO, and Chorus: Quanto è bella . . . Della crudele Isotta
b) VALENTINO, SAYÃO, MANSKI, TAGLIAVINI, and Chorus: Come Paride vezzoso . . . a conquistar

SIDE 2 (238 B):

Act I: 1. a) TAGLIAVINI, SAYÃO, and VALENTINO: Caro Elisir! sei mio! . . . Tran, tran, tran . . . to the end of the Trio

Act II: b) TAGLIAVINI and VALENTINO: Venti scudi!
c) SAYÃO and TAJO: Quanto amore!
d) TAGLIAVINI: Una furtiva lagrima
e) SAYÃO: Prendi, prendi, per me sei libero . . . to the end of the opera

NOTES: EJS 238

The Sanguinetti-Williams Tagliavini discography in *The Record Collector*, 29/9-12 (December, 1984), p. 238, claims that this is the 24 December, 1949 Met broadcast, but the 5 February performance is offered as an alternative in the Addendum to the discography that appeared in 30/10-11 (October, 1985), p. 240. 5 February, 1949 appears to be the correct date.

EJS 239: "The Golden Age of Opera" (1 LP)
Issued April, 1962

"ELISABETH RETHBERG OPERATIC RECITAL (1936-1941)"

SIDE 1 (239 A):

1. w. studio orch/Alfred Wallenstein: ALCESTE, Act I: Divinités du Styx (Gluck) (F)
Broadcast, ***ELISABETH RETHBERG***, WOR, NYC, 18 Jul 1941

* 2. w. studio orch/Alfred Wallenstein: L'ENFANT PRODIGUE: L'année en vain chasse l'année! . . . Azaël! Azaël! Pourquoi m'as-tu quitée ["Air de Lia"] (Debussy) (F)
Broadcast, ***ELISABETH RETHBERG***, WOR, NYC, 5 Sep 1941

* 3. w. studio orch/Alfred Wallenstein: IDOMENEO, K. 366, Act III: Solitudini amiche . . . Zeffiretti lusinghieri (Mozart) (I)
Broadcast, ***ELISABETH RETHBERG***, WOR, NYC, 5 Sep 1941

* 4. w. studio orch/Alfred Wallenstein: LA WALLY, Act I: Ebben, ne andrò lontano (Catalani) (I)
Broadcast, ***ELISABETH RETHBERG***, WOR, NYC, 22 Aug 1941

* 5. w. NBC Symphony Orchestra/Alfred Wallenstein: LA FORZA DEL DESTINO, Act IV: Pace, pace, mio Dio (Verdi) (I)
Broadcast, ***MAGIC KEY OF RCA***, WJZ, NYC, 24 Oct 1937

* 6. w. San Francisco Opera House Orchestra/Gennaro Papi: UN BALLO IN MASCHERA, Act II: Sino il rumor de passi miei . . . Ma dall'arido stella divulsa (Verdi) (I)
San Francisco Opera broadcast, KPO [NBC], San Francisco, 23 Oct 1940

SIDE 2 (239 B):

* 1. w. Metropolitan Opera House Orchestra/Ettore Panizza: SIMON BOCCANEGRA, Act I: Come in quest'ora bruna (Verdi) (I)
Metropolitan Opera broadcast, NYC, 21 Jan 1939

* 2. w. Metropolitan Opera House Orchestra/Vincenzo Bellezza: LA BOHÈME, Act I: Si, mi chiamano Mimi (Puccini) (I)
Metropolitan Opera broadcast, NYC, 23 Mar 1935

* 3. w. FREDERICK JAGEL, tenor; Metropolitan Opera House Orchestra/ Vincenzo Bellezza: LA BOHÈME, Act III: Addio senza rancor . . . Donde lieta uscì (Puccini) (I)
Metropolitan Opera broadcast, NYC, 23 Mar 1935

4. w. Metropolitan Opera House Orchestra/Gennaro Papi: CAVALLERIA RUSTICANA: Voi lo sapete (Mascagni) (I)
Metropolitan Opera broadcast, Boston, 10 Apr 1937

* 5. w. Metropolitan Opera House Orchestra/Ettore Panizza: LE NOZZE DI FIGARO, K. 492, Act III: E Susanna non vien! . . . Dove sono (Mozart) (I)
Metropolitan Opera broadcast, NYC, 9 Mar 1940

* 6. w. NBC Symphony Orchestra/Alfred Wallenstein: AÏDA, Act I: Ritorna vincitor! (Verdi) (I)
Broadcast, ***MAGIC KEY OF RCA***, WJZ, NYC, 24 Oct 1937

* 7. w. San Francisco Opera House Orchestra/Gaetano Merola: LA JUIVE, Act II: Il va venir! (Halévy) (F)
San Francisco Opera broadcast, KGO [NBC], San Francisco, 30 Oct 1936

NOTES: EJS 239

EJS 239 was reissued as UORC 1040 (May-June, 1979), part of a two-disc Rethberg set, where the original order selections was retained.

Side 1 (239 A):

Band 2: In addition to the IDOMENEO and L'ENFANT PRODIGUE arias, Rethberg performed Debussy's ARIETTES OUBLIÉES on this 5 September, 1941 broadcast, two of which appeared on EJS 256 (January, 1963). The IDOMENEO had appeared earlier on EJS 168 (January, 1960).

Band 3: Featured earlier on EJS 168 (January, 1960).

Bands 4-5: The WALLY and FORZA arias appeared earlier on EJS 181 (June, 1960). See notes VI/1-2 for that issue.

Band 6: Lengthy excerpts from this BALLO appeared earlier on EJS 168 (January, 1960).

Side 2 (239 B):

Band 1: From the complete 21 January, 1939 BOCCANEGRA issued earlier as EJS 108 (1956).

Bands 2-3: The complete Acts I and III of the BOHÈME appeared earlier as EJS 114 (1957). Only Jagel's final phrase preceding the "Addio" is heard.

Band 4: A slightly-abridged version of this performance (in which Rethberg was substituting for Ponselle) appeared in 1957 as EJS 115: see the endnote for that issue.

Band 5: This NOZZE was issued complete as EJS 118 in 1957.
Library of Congress tape: 5174-3 (complete broadcast).

Band 6: See the endnote for EJS 181 (Side 6/bands 1-2) regarding this 24 October, 1937 "Navy Day" broadcast.

Band 7: Only Act II of this JUIVE was broadcast. What remains of the performance originally appeared on EJS 221 (November, 1961), and was later reissued in considerably better sound as VOCE-40. See the endnote for side 1 of EJS 221.

EJS 240: "The Golden Age of Opera" (1 LP)
Issued May, 1962

TURANDOT (Puccini - completed by Franco Alfano) (I)
Opera in 3 Acts (excerpts)
Royal Opera House Orchestra and Chorus/John Barbirolli
Unpublished live performance recordings, Technical Test Series
TT 2353-1/TT 2353-7, Covent Garden, London, 10 May 1937

CAST:
Eva Turner (*Turandot*); Octave Dua (*Emperor Altoum*); Giulio Tomei (*Timur*); Giovanni Martinelli (*Prince Calaf*); Licia Albanese (*Liù*); Piero Biasini (*Ping*); Angelo Bada (*Pang*); Giuseppe Nessi (*Pong*); [Aristide Baracchi (*Mandarin*)].

Side 1 (240 A):

1. Act I: a) ALBANESE: Signore, ascolta!
TT 2353-1 unpublished Columbia test
b) MARTINELLI: Non piangere, Liù
FAVERO: Noi morrem sulla strada dell'esilio!
TOMEI: Noi morrem!
MARTINELLI: Dell'esilio addolcisci a lui le strade! . . . chiede colui che non sorride più!
TT 2353-1 unpublished Columbia test

2. Act II c) TURNER, MARTINELLI, and Chorus: In questa Reggia . . . O Turandot!
TT 2353-2/2353-3 unpublished Columbia test
d) TURNER, MARTINELLI, and Chorus: Straniero, ascolta!
TT 2353-3 unpublished Columbia test
e) TURNER, DUA, TOMEI, FAVERO, MARTINELLI, and Chorus: Guizza al pari di fiamma
TT 2353-4 unpublished Columbia test
f) TURNER, DUA, MARTINELLI, and Chorus: Turandot! Turandot! Gloria, gloria, o vincitore . . . O audace! O coraggioso! O forte! ["Guarda! La mia vittoria . . . Tre enigmi m'hai proposto! . . . Uno soltanto a te ne proporrò" is omitted]
TT 2353-5 unpublished Columbia test
g) MARTINELLI, DUA, and Chorus: . . . il mio nome non sai! . . . to end of Act 2
TT 2353-6 unpublished Columbia test

3. Act III h) MARTINELLI, BIASINI, BADA, NESSI, and Chorus: Nessun dorma! . . . Di'tu, che vuoi!
TT 2353-7 unpublished Columbia test

SIDE 2 (240 B):

I PAGLIACCI (Leoncavallo) (I)
Opera in 2 Acts (excerpts)
Metropolitan Opera House Orchestra and Chorus/Cesare Sodero
Metropolitan Opera broadcast, NYC, 20 Mar 1943
CAST:
Marita Farell (*Nedda*); Giovanni Martinelli (*Canio*); Leonard Warren (*Tonio*); John Dudley (*Beppe*); Walter Cassel (*Silvio*).

1. Act I: a) WARREN: Si può? (Prologue)
b) MARTINELLI and FARELL: Eh! Eh! vi pare? . . . Un tal gioco, credetemi . . . A ventitrè ore!
c) FARELL: Qual fiamma avea nel guardo . . . Oh! che volo d'augelli (Ballatella)
d) MARTINELLI: Recitar! . . . Vesti la giubba

2. Act II: MARTINELLI, FARELL, WARREN, CASSEL, DUDLEY, and Chorus: Nome di Dio! . . . to the end of the opera

NOTES: EJS 240

Side 1 (240 A):

The same excerpts from the 5 May, 1937 Covent Garden performance of TURANDOT appeared originally on EJS 102 (1956); the complete excerpts from both performances were eventually coupled on a special issue, EJS 50X (April-May, 1976). Excerpts from both turned up elsewhere throughout the run of the GAO, UORC, and ANNA series. EMI released the extant portions from both the 5 and 10 May performances on compact disc CDH 7 61074 2 in 1988.

The Technical Test numbers show the approximate distribution of the excerpts over the seven sides recorded on 10 May.

It has been suggested that Martinelli's high "C" in the "Riddle Scene" ("ti voglio tutto ardente d'amor") has been deliberately extended on this LP through editing.

See the endnote for EJS 102 for a full account of these live performance recordings.

Side 2 (240 B):

The bulletin for EJS 240 gives the date of the PAGLIACCI in error as "March 30, 1943." This was Martinelli's last Met broadcast and his last complete performance of I PAGLIACCI. Farell, in her only Met appearance as *Nedda*, replaced Licia Albanese at the last minute (see *Opera News*, 7/22, 15 March, 1943, pp. 12-13). Also on the bill was a CAVALLERIA RUSTICANA with Milanov and Jagel and the "Dance of the Hours" from Ponchielli's LA GIOCONDA, featuring the Met's resident *Corps de Ballet*. NBC's Spanish broadcast acetates (thirteen 16-inch sides, some inside-start, numbered 11667-11670 for CAVALLERIA and 10750, 311660, 10751, 311661, 10752, 311662, 10753, 311663 for PAGLIACCI, broadcast no. 43-450) have survived, but two sides each of the CAVALLERIA and PAGLIACCI are broken, with sides 1 and 3 missing from the latter.

The complete 20 March, 1943 PAGLIACCI was later issued as EJS 448 (November, 1968): see the note for that issue.

EJS 241: "The Golden Age of Opera" (1 LP)
Issued May, 1962

SIDE 1-2 (241 A-B):

L'AMORE DEI TRE RE (Montemezzi) (I)
Opera in 3 Acts (excerpts)
Metropolitan Opera House Orchestra and Chorus/Giuseppe Antonicelli
Metropolitan Opera broadcast, NYC, 15 Jan 1949

CAST:
Virgilio Lazzari (*Archibaldo*); Robert Weede (*Manfredo*); Charles Kullman (*Avito*); Leslie Chabay (*Flaminio*); [Paul Franke (*Youth*)]; Dorothy Kirsten (*Fiora*); [Thelma Altman (*Ancella*)]; [Paula Lenchner (*Young Woman*)]; [Claramae Turner (*Old Woman*)].

SIDE 1 (241 A):

Act I: 1. LAZZARI, CHABAY, KULLMAN, KIRSTEN, and WEEDE: Act I complete

SIDE II (241 B):

Act II: 1. a) WEEDE and KIRSTEN: Dimmi, Fiora . . . Addio, Fiora!
b) KULLMAN and KIRSTEN: Oh! Fiora! Fiora! . . . Fuggi: ti prego!
c) KULLMAN and KIRSTEN: Addio, Fiora! Ho voluto rivederti . . . Ho sete! Ho sete!
d) LAZZARI, KIRSTEN, and WEEDE: Fiora! Fiora! . . . Vedresti alla sua gola la collana di morte delle mie dite paterne!

Act III: 2. KULLMAN, WEEDE, LAZZARI, and Chorus: [Fiora, Fiora. E' silenzio] . . . anch'ella sarà fredda, irrigidita . . . to the end of the opera

NOTES: EJS 241

Bits and pieces are omitted from Act II (short orchestral passages, the entrance of *Ancella* after *Firoa's* "Fuggi: ti prego!," and the conclusion of the *Fiora-Avito* scene after "Ho sete! Ho sete!") as are the last page and a half of the act--from *Archibaldo's* "Additami la strada con il suono." The Act III finale is complete from the middle of *Avito's* solo scene. These were transfer cuts made for purposes of timing, not performance cuts.

Playing speeds are inconsistent for this LP. The beginning of the opera through *Archibaldo's* aria, plays at 34.4 rpm, albeit with a bit of waver, after which 33.5 rpm is correct through the end of the act; on side 2, "Dimmi, Fiora" plays in score pitch at 34.0 rpm, while the remainder of the second act plays at 33.6 rpm; the Act III finale (II/2) plays at a uniform 32.9 rpm.

EJS 242: "The Golden Age of Opera" (1 LP)
Issued May, 1962

"SINGERS OF THE PAST VOLUME I (1903-1908)"

SIDE 1 (242 A):

* 1. VICTOR MAUREL, baritone (pf/?): IPHIGÉNIE EN TAURIDE, Act I: Le ciel par d'éclatants miracles . . . De noirs préssentiments (Gluck) (F)
1627-F1 Paris, 1903 G&T 2-32809

* 2. LEOPOLDO SIGNORETTI, tenor (pf/?): ERNANI, Act IV: Tutto ora tace . . . Solingo, errante e misero (Verdi) (I)
X-1814 Milan, ?1903 Zonophone X-1814

* 3. FELIA LITVINNE, soprano (?Alfred Cortot/pf): DIE WALKÜRE, Act II/i: Hojotoho! (Wagner) (F)
2274.CS II(f) Paris, 1903 G&T 33163x

4. LEONE CAZAURAN, tenor (Carlo Sabajno/pf): WERTHER, Act III: Ah, non mi ridestar [Pourquoi me réveiller?] (Massenet) (F)
2348L Milan, December, 1904 G&T 52163

* 5. IVAN ERSCHOV [E.B. YERSHOV], tenor (pf/?): LE PROPHÈTE a) Act II: Pour Berthe moi je soupire ["Pastorale"] b) Act V: Versez, versez ["Brindisi"] (Meyerbeer) (R)
95y St. Petersburg, 1903 G&T 022012

* 6. EDYTH WALKER, mezzo-soprano (orch/?Bruno Seidler-Winkler): RIENZI, Act: III Gerechter Gott' . . . In seiner BlÜthe bleicht mein Leben (Wagner) (G)
455s/456s Hamburg, 1908 G&T 043144/043145

* 7. LEOPOLDO SIGNORETTI, tenor (orch/?): LE PROPHÈTE, Act II: Sotto le vaste arcate . . . Sopra Berta [Sous les vastes arceaux . . . Pour Berthe moi je soupire] ["Pastorale"] (Meyerbeer) (I)
1491c Milan, 1908 Pre-Dog 052229

* 8. GUERRINA FABBRI, contralto (pf/Salvatore Cattone): L'ITALIANA IN ALGERI, Act II: Pensa alla patria ["Rondo"] (Rossini) (I)
CON 552-II Milan, October-December, 1903 G&T 053007

SIDE 2 (242 B):

1. TERESA ARKEL, soprano (orch/?): LUCREZIA BORGIA, Prologue: Com'è bello (Donizetti) (I)
503c Milan, 1905 G&T 053062

2. TERESA ARKEL, soprano (orch/?): L'AFRICANA, Act II: In grembo a me [Sur mes genoux, fils du soleil] (Meyerbeer) (I)
501c Milan, 1905 G&T 053060

3. GINO MARTINEZ-PATTI, tenor, and CESARE PREVE, bass (orch/?): L'AFRICANA, Act III: Vengo a voi malgrado l'odio . . . [Je viens à vous malgré la haine] (Meyerbeer) (I)
552c Milan, 1905 G&T 054066

* 4. FRANCESCO NAVARINI, bass, and unknown tenor (orch/?): LUCREZIA BORGIA, Act I: Separarsi all'alba han, per costume . . . Vieni: la mia vendetta (Meyerbeer) (I)
XPh 2397 Milan, 1 Feb 1907 Fonotipia 62026

* 5. LÉON ESCALAÏS, tenor (pf/?): GUILLAUME TELL, Act IV: Asile héréditaire (Rossini) (F)
XPh 489 Milan, ?November, 1905 Fonotipia 39427

* 6. LÉON ESCALAÏS, tenor (pf/?): LE PROPHÈTE, Act III: Roi du ciel et des anges (Meyerbeer) (F)
XPh 495 Milan, ?November, 1905 Fonotipia 39429

* 7. ROSE CARON, soprano (pf/?): SIGURD, Act IV/viii: Sigurd, les Dieux dans leur clémence . . . Des présents de Gunther (Reyer) (F)
XPh 523 Paris, ?20 Dec 1904 Fonotipia 39097
HRS-Odeon 1019

* 8. ROSE CARON, soprano (pf/?): "Prière" (Gounod) (F)
XPh 521 Paris, ?20 Dec 1904 Fonotipia 39096
HRS-Odeon 1019

NOTES: EJS 242

Transfer speeds are high for items 3-6 on the second side.

Side 1 (242 A):

Band 1: Issued along with Maurel's six other G&Ts on the Symposium CD 1101, "The Harold Wayne Collection Volume 9" (1991).

Band 2: Reissued with two other Signoretti Zonofonos on Syposium CD 1065, "The Harold Wayne Collection Volume 1" (1989). The notes for the Symposium issue give the recording date as 1901, but judging from the matrix/catalog number, 1903 seems more likely. In all, Signoretti made five Milanese International Zonophones.

Band 3: From Litvinne's second G&T session. Symposium CD 1101, "The Harold Wayne Colection Volume 9," noted above, both of Litvinne's Paris sessions (December, 1902 and 1903), nearly complete. Cortot's accompaniment for Litvinne's second Paris session is disputed.

Band 5: Not listed on the label of EJS 242. Both the 1903 G&T and Columbia versions can be heard in considerably better sound on the 1983 Melodyia Erschov LP recital, M10 45189 001.

Band 6: Listed as band 5 on the label. Both parts of the RIENZI aria were issued as IRCC 137, announced January, 1939, but this was a dubbing (transfer matrices 2EA 7466-1/7467-1) made in the London in January, 1939.

Band 7: Not listed on the label of EJS 242.

Band 8: Listed as band 6 on the label. Also issued on Symposium CD 1065, "The Harold Wayne Collection Volume 1" (1989), with the speculative recording date October-December, 1903: the EMI ledgers give only the year, 1903.

Side 2 (242 B):

Band 4: Issued in 1992 as Historic Masters HM 83, a vinyl pressing coupled with Navarini's LUCREZIA "Qualunque sia l'effetto" (XPh 2398, originally Fonotipia 62027). The tenor singing *Rustighello's* lines is not named.

Bands 5-6: Recording dates taken from the Bennett-Dennis *Voices of the Past*, vol. 3, *Supplement to "Dischi Fonotipia"* (Lingfield, Surrey: Oakwood Press, 1957).

Bands 7-8: Odeon 1019, sponsored by the Historical Record Society in the 1930s, contains repressings of both of these rare Caron Fonotipias. The recording date given here, 20 December, 1904, is taken from these Odeon labels. The SIGURD title is a creator recording.

EJS 243: "The Golden Age of Opera" (1 LP)
Issued May, 1962

"ROSA PONSELLE IN OPERA & SONG (1934-54)"

SIDE 1 (243 A):

1. w. Ponselle/pf: MANON, Act II: Adieu, notre petite table (Massenet) (F)
   Private coaching session, ?Villa Pace, Baltimore,
   24 Nov 1952

2. w. pf/?: ADRIANA LECOUVREUR, Act I: Io son l'umile (Cilèa) (I)
Private recording ?Villa Pace, Baltimore, 5 Sep 1953

3. w. pf/?: ADRIANA LECOUVREUR, Act IV: Poveri fiori (Cilèa) (I)
Private recording ?Villa Pace, Baltimore, 5 Sep 1953

4. w. pf/?: TRISTAN UND ISOLDE, Act III/iii: Mild und leise ["Liebestod"] (Wagner) (G)
Private recording ?Villa Pace, Baltimore, 6 Sep 1953

5. w. Igor Chichagov/pf: FORTUNIO, Act II: J'aimais la vielle maison grise ["La maison grise"] (Messager) (F)
Private recording RPX 102 ?Villa Pace, Baltimore, 30 Mar 1957

6. w. Ponselle/pf: DIE TOTE STADT, Op. 12, Act I: Glück, das mir verblieb ["Mariettas Lied"] (Korngold) (G)
Private recording RPX 102 ?Villa Pace, Baltimore, 27 Oct 1951

7. w. EZIO PINZA, bass (pf/?): DON GIOVANNI, K. 527, Act I: Là ci darem la mano (Mozart) (I)
Private recording ?Villa Pace, Baltimore, 8 May 1953

8. w. EZIO PINZA, bass, and chorus (pf/?): LA FORZA DEL DESTINO, Act II: La Vergine degli angeli (Verdi) (I)
Private recording ?Villa Pace, Baltimore, 8 May 1953

SIDE 2 (243 B):

1. w. Igor Chichagov/pf: "L'invitation au voyage" (Baudelaire-Duparc) (F)
No no. assigned ?New York, 17 Oct 1954 Victor unpub

2. w. Igor Chichagov/pf: "Ave Maria" (Tosti) (L)
E 4-RC-0722-1 ?New York, 17 Oct 1954 Victor unpub

3. w. Igor Chichagov/pf: AN DIE MUSIK, D. 547: Du holde Kunst (Schober-Schubert) (G)
E 4-RC-0723-1 ?New York, 17 Oct 1954 Victor unpub

* 4. w. studio orch/André Kostelanetz: "A Dream" (C.B. Cory-J.C.Bartlett) (E)
Broadcast, ***CHESTERFIELD HOUR***, WABC, NYC, 26 Nov 1934

* 5. w. studio orch/André Kostelanetz: "What is in the Air Today?" (Eden) (E)
Broadcast, ***CHESTERFIELD HOUR***, WABC, NYC, 26 Nov 1934

6. w. Robert Lawrence/pf: SAMSON ET DALILA, Act II: Amour! viens aider ma faiblesse! (Saint-Saëns) (F)
Private recording RPX 102 ?Villa Pace, Baltimore, 7 Nov 1953

7. w. Robert Lawrence/pf: SAMSON ET DALILA, Act II: Mon coeur s'ouvre à ta voix (Saint-Saëns) (F)
Private recording RPX 102 ?Villa Pace, Baltimore, 7 Nov 1953

* 8. w. studio orch/André Kostelanetz: SAMSON ET DALILA, Act I: Printemps qui commence (Saint-Saëns) (F)
Broadcast, *CHESTERFIELD HOUR*, WABC, NYC, 29 Oct 1934

NOTES: EJS 243

Villa Pace, Ponselle's estate, was located in Baltimore, Maryland.
Many of the selections on EJS 243 were later included in the two-disc Ponselle recital ANNA 1036/1037 (May-June, 1979) as follows: *Side 1*: bands 2 and 3 (ANNA 1036); bands 1, 5, 6, 7, 8 (ANNA 1037); *Side 2*: bands 6 and 8 (ANNA 1037). A few turned up on a private LP issued by the singer, "Rosa Ponselle--By Request" (RPX 102), and subsequently on MDP LPs 012, 029, and 036.

Side 2 (243 B):

Bands 4-5: Library of Congress tape: 5063-5 (complete broadcast).

Band 8: Park's Ponselle discography lists this item as both a private recording of 7 November, 1953, accompanied by Lawrence, and as the 29 October, 1934 Kostelanetz broadcast: it is in fact the broadcast, accompanied by orchestra. The MDP 012 dub contains a spoken introduction by Ponselle.
On EJS 243, the final measures of the "Printemps qui commence" fall at a break in the acetate sides: there is no change of source, only an abrupt change in surface quality.
Library of Congress tape: 5063-3 (complete broadcast).

EJS 244: "The Golden Age of Opera" (2 LPs)
Issued June, 1962

SIDES 1-4 (244 A-D):

KÖNIGSKINDER (Humperdinck) (G)
Opera in 3 Acts (complete)
Orchestra amd Chorus of the Westdeutscher Rundfunk, Köln/Richard Kraus
WDR broadcast, Cologne, ?24 Jul 1953 (recorded November, 1952)

CAST:
Peter Anders (*Der Königssohn*); Käthe Mölker-Siepermann (*Die Gansemagd*); Dietrich Fischer-Dieskau (*Der Spielmann*); Ilse Ihme-Sabich (*Die Hexe*); Fritz Ollendorf (*Der Holzhacker*); Walter Jenkel (*Der Besenbinder*); Karl-Heinz Welbers (*Sein Töchterlein*); Heinrich Nillius (*Der Ratsältester*); Heiner Horn (*Der Wirt*); Hanna Ludwig (*Die Wirtstochter*); Walter Kassek (*Ein Schneider*); Marianne Schröder (*Eine Stallmagd*); Matti Lehtinen (*Ein Torwächter*); Fritz Hallen (*Ein Torwächter*); Maria Plümacher (*Eine Frau*).

NOTES: EJS 244

The bulletin for EJS 244 gives 24 July, 1953 as the *recording* date of this performance. More than likely this was the *broadcast* date (and thus the date it was recorded off-the-air). The recording date given above, November, 1952, was taken from *Zwanzig Jahre WDR 1948-1968*.

The Overture is omitted. No other significant (non-performance) cuts have been reported. Early copies of EJS 244 were pressed out of sequence--in reverse order (Acts III, II, and I) and so, are mislabeled. Late pressings were reassembled in the correct order, and subscribers were invited to return their defective copies. The error was subsequently referred to in the October, 1971 bulletin when this broadcast as reissued as EJS 567. Smith mistakenly implied that the reissue was a different performance.

Note that EJS 344 (October, 1965) is mislabeled "EJS 244."

EJS 245: "The Golden Age of Opera" (2 LPs)
Issued June, 1962

SIDES 1-4 (245 A-D):

HÉRODIADE (Massenet) (F)
Opera in 4 Acts (complete)
?Radio Hilversum Orchestra and Chorus/Albert Wolff
?Radio Hilversum broadcast, Holland, 5 Apr 1957

CAST:
Guy Fouché (*Jean*); Charles Cambon (*Hérod*); Germain Ghislain (*Phanuel*); Andrea Guiot (*Salomé*); Mimi Van Aarden (*Hérodias*); Joseph Burksten (*Vitellius*).

NOTES: EJS 245

A number of misspellings appear on the label of EJS 245: "Planel" for Phanuel, "Gulot" for soprano Guiot, and "Harden" for contralto Mimi van Aarden.

"Radio Hilversum" is presumably the Algemeene Vereniging Radio Omroep [AVRO] or Omroepvereniging [VARA].

EJS 246: "The Golden Age of Opera (3 LPs)
Issued September, 1962

SIDES 1-6 (246 A-F):

LES HUGUENOTS (Meyerbeer) (I)
Opera in 5 Acts (complete)
Teatro all Scala Orchestra and Chorus/Gianandrea Gavazzeni
Broadcast, Teatro all Scala, Milan, 7 Jun 1962

CAST:
Joan Sutherland (*Marguerite de Valois*); Giulietta Simionato (*Valentine*); Fiorenza Cossotto (*Urbain*); Franco Corelli (*Raoul de Nangis*); Nicolai Ghiaurov (*Marcel*); Giorgio Tozzi (*Count St.-Bris*); Wladimiro Ganzarolli (*Count Nevers*); Giuseppe Bertinazzo (*Cossé*); Piero de Palma (*Tavannes*); Alfredo Giacomotti (*Méru*); Antonio Casinelli (*De Retz*); Virgilio Carbonari (*An Archer*); Manuel Spatafora (*Thoré*); Silvio Maionica (*Maurevert*); Walter Gullino (*Bois-Rose*).

NOTES: EJS 246

Of the five HUGUENOTS given during the 1962 La Scala season (28 and 31 May; 2, 7, and 12 June), only the 7 June performance was broadcast.

This HUGUENOTS was issued in Fonit-Cetra's "Document" series (DOC-34) and with numerous pitch problems as MFR 18. More recently, in the late 1980s, Pantheon re-released it on three cassette tapes (XLNC-105, later as C-85082).

EJS 247: "The Golden Age of Opera" (1 LP)
Issued September, 1962

"POTPOURRI No. 16"

SIDE 1 (247 A):

* 1. BENIAMINO GIGLI, tenor (RAI Orchestra, Roma/Nino Antonicelli): LA JUIVE, Act IV: Rachel! quand du Seigneur (Halévy) (F)
Broadcast, ***CONCERTO MARTINI E ROSSI***, Rome, 9 Feb 1953

* 2. RICHARD BONELLI, baritone (orch/Andre Kostelanetz): "La Paloma" (Yradier) (S)
Broadcast, ***CHESTERFIELD HOUR***, WABC, NYC, 20 Apr 1935

* 3. GLADYS SWARTHOUT, contralto; RICHARD BONELLI, baritone (orch/?): DON GIOVANNI, K. 527, Act I: Là ci darem la mano (Mozart) (I)
Broadcast, source and date unknown, circa 1937

* 4. ELISABETH RETHBERG, soprano; EZIO PINZA, bass (NBC Symphony Orchestra/Edwin MacArthur): LE NOZZE DI FIGARO, K. 492, Act III: Crudel, perchè finora (Mozart) (I)
Broadcast, ***NBC SALUTE TO CIVIC MUSIC GROUPS***, WJZ, NYC, 25 Feb 1940

* 5. DUSOLINA GIANNINI, soprano (NBC Symphony Orchestra/Frank Black): AÏDA, Act I: Ritorna vincitor! (Verdi) (I)
Broadcast, ***NBC SALUTE TO CIVIC MUSIC GROUPS***, WJZ, NYC, 25 Feb 1940

* 6. GLADYS SWARTHOUT, contralto; ARMAND TOKATYAN, tenor (NBC Orchestra/Erno Rapee): IL TROVATORE, Act IV/ii: Si, la stanchezza m'opprime . . . Ai nostri monti (Verdi) (I)
Broadcast, ***MAGIC KEY OF RCA***, WJZ, Carnegie Hall, NYC, 30 May 1937

* 7. RAOUL JOBIN, tenor (orch/Wilfred Pelletier): LA GIOCONDA, Act II: Cielo e mar (Ponchielli) (I)
Broadcast, ***[METROPOLITAN] CLEVELAND PRE-OPERA CONCERT***, WHK, Cleveland, 25 Mar 1940

* 8. GLADYS SWARTHOUT, contralto (studio orch/?Robert Armbruster): IL TROVATORE, Act II: Stride la vampa! (Verdi) (I)
Broadcast, ***GLADYS SWARTHOUT PROGRAM***, WEAF, NYC, 31 Mar 1937

SIDE 2 (247 B):

* 1. LUCREZIA BORI, soprano (Detroit Symphony Orchestra/Victor Kolar): VASCO DA GAMA: "Ouvre ton coeur" (Bizet) (F)
Broadcast, ***FORD SUNDAY EVENING HOUR***, WJR, Detroit, 2 Feb 1936

* 2. EBE STIGNANI, contralto; DINO BORGIOLI, tenor; RICHARD BONELLI, baritone (San Francisco Opera House Orchestra/Gaetano Merola): DON CARLOS, Act II: Sei tu, sei tu, bell'adorata . . . Trema per te, falso figliuolo [Rédoutez tout de ma furié] (Verdi) (I)
Broadcast, ***MAGIC KEY OF RCA***, ?KGO [NBC], San Francisco, 30 Oct 1938

* 3. BRUNA CASTAGNA, contralto (Metropolitan Opera House Orchestra/ Frank St. Leger): CARMEN, Act I: Quand je vous aimerai? . . . L'amour est un oiseau rebelle ["Habanera"] (Bizet) (F)
Telecast, ***METROPOLITAN OPERA FUND***, W2XBS [NBC], NYC, 10 Mar 1940

* 4. BRUNA CASTANGNA, contralto (studio orch and male chorus/Robert Armbruster): MIGNON, Act: Connais-tu le pays (Thomas) (F)
Broadcast, ***CHASE AND SANBORN HOUR***, ?KFI, Los Angeles, 1 Aug 1937

* 5. BRUNA CASTANGNA, contralto (studio orch and male chorus/Robert Armbruster): CARMEN, Act II: Les tringles des sistres! ["Chanson Bohème"] (Bizet) (F)
Broadcast, ***CHASE AND SANBORN HOUR***, ?KFI, Los Angeles, 1 Aug 1937

* 6. GRACE MOORE, soprano (orch/Detroit Symphony Orchestra/Franco Ghione): VASO DA GAMA: Ouvre ton coeur (Bizet) (F)
Broadcast, ***FORD SUNDAY EVENING HOUR***, WJR, Detroit, 4 Feb 1940

* 7. MARY GARDEN, soprano; ? Collingwood or Collingworth, announcer: a) Spoken introduction b) (unacc.): HARK! THE MAVIS: "Ca' the yowes to the knowes" ["My bonnie Jeannie"] (Robert Burns) (E)
Broadcast, Chicago, circa 1943

* 8. ROSA PONSELLE, soprano (Igor Chicagov/pf): SKETCHES OF PARIS: In the Luxembourg Gardens (Katherine Lockhart Manning) (E)
No no. assigned ?New York, 19 October, 1954 Victor unpub

NOTES: EJS 247

Side 1 (247 A):

Band 1: The JUIVE aria plays in score pitch at 32.0 rpm.

Bands 2 and 3: These play in C major and at score pitch, respectively, at 34.5 rpm.

Bands 4-5: This concert was given in celebration of the New York Civic Concert Association's tenth anniversary. In addition to Rethberg, Pinza, and Giannini, Kirsten Flagstad appeared singing *Isolde's* "Liebestod," Ania Dorfmann played the second movement of Saint-Saëns' PIANO CONCERTO IN G MINOR, Emanuel Feuermann performed the "Adagio" from Dvorak's CONCERTO FOR CELLO, and Erica Morini played two short works. Edwin McArthur shared the podium with Frank Black. This is the title of the show as given in the *New York Times;* the labels of the original acetates (four 16-inch sides, numbered ENG. 183 9-37, broadcast no. 40-24) give "10th Anniversary of NBC Civic Concert."

Band 5: This plays in score pitch at 32.0 rpm.

Band 6: The "Ai nostri monti" was listed in error as the "Miserere" in the *New York Times* radio log. It plays in score pitch at 34.3 rpm.

Band 7: The original acetates on which this "Pre-Opera Concert" were transcribed (four 16-inch sides, numbered ENG. 183 9-37, broadcast 40-45), are labeled "Cleveland Pre-Opera Concert." The orchestra is unknown: the Met Orchestra was in Baltimore that evening accompanying a BARBIERE. Jobin's assisting artists included Eleanor Steber, Jean Merrill, Annamary Dickey, Arthur Carron, Anna Kaskas, John Carter, and Leonard Warren.

The aria plays in score pitch at 32.8 rpm.

Band 8: The "Stride la vampa" was part of a TROVATORE medley that included the "Anvil Chorus" and "Il balen" (sung by baritone Frank Chapman). Swarthout's rendition is unusually interesting for her realization of all the written trills--expertly performed here.

This was an occasional program heard over the NBC Red network in 1937 on Wednesday evenings, 10:30 pm EST. Armbruster was the resident conductor of the ***CHASE AND SANBORN HOUR***, on which Swarthout also appeared in 1937, but ***GLADYS SWARTHOUT PROGRAM*** was not a ***CHASE AND SANBORN HOUR*** show: the sponsor was National Ice Advertising, Inc.

Swarthout's "Stride la vampa!" plays in score pitch at 34.1 rpm.

Side 2 (247 B):

Band 1: See note for EJS 191 (I/1) regarding Bizet's "Ouvre ton coeur." The label of EJS 247 gives the date as 1935.

Band 2: The label of EJS 247 gives the date as 1935. There are a few minor performance cuts throughout the trio. This excerpt subsequently appeared on OASI 540, an Olivero/Stignani recital, where the entire 30 October, 1938 Stignani San Francisco radio concert is transcribed. This was Stignani's American debut season. The excerpt plays in score pitch at 34.2 rpm.

Library of Congress tape: 15778-86B (complete broadcast).

Band 3: This early telecast was a fund raiser for the Metropolitan Opera Fund, hosted by Edward Johnson, general manager of the Met. The original NBC acetates (four 16-inch sides numbered ENG. 183 9-37, broadcast no. 40-67) feature solos by Jagel, Albanese, and Warren, as well as excerpts from I PAGLIACCI. Castagna's "Habanera" is slightly abridged and without chorus, and plays in score pitch at 34.5 rpm.

Bands 4-5: Both the MIGNON and the CARMEN arias were apparently substitutions on this 1 August, 1937 ***CHASE AND SANBORN HOUR*** broadcast, preserved in its entirety on four 16-inch sides numbered ENG. 183 9-36, broadcast no. 7-223. The show originated from Los Angeles, so it is assumed that KFI (NBC Red) was the source. Castagna sings only one verse of the MIGNON aria, with an extended coda. A humming male chorus chorus accompanies the "Chanson Bohème." 1938 is given as the date for both arias on the label of EJS 247.

Both play in score pitch at 33.1 rpm.

Band 6: See note for EJS 191 (I/1) regarding Bizet's "Ouvre ton coeur." Dated 1938 on the label of EJS 247. A Victor test pressing of Moore singing the song, conducted by Wilfred Pelletier (CS-075263-1, recorded 5 June, 1942) also exists in a private collection, and was made available to Smith; CS-075263-2, also unpublished, has been available for years on "special" vinyl pressings. Neither was used here, however. Moore also sang "Ouvre ton coeur" on a 23 January, 1938 ***FORD SUNDAY EVENING HOUR*** broadcast.

The song plays in score pitch at 34.0 rpm, but Moore may have transposed it down a half step (32.5 rpm).

Library of Congress tape: 9061-3 (complete broadcast).

Band 7: This mysterious item has not yet been fully documented. It begins with Garden's exclamation, "Hello Chicago! This is Mary Garden speaking to you from my charming city of Aberdeen, where I was born." A "Mr. Collingwood" or "Collingworth" is the interviewer who eventually pursuades her to sing ("We don't want you to sing us grand opera, but come on and sing us a little Scottish song").

Unless Garden was deliberately misleading her radio audience ("I am thousands of miles from you tonight," she explains), this brief interview was probably pre-recorded on acetate in Aberdeen for the Chicago broadcast: an international hookup for a live Aberdeen-to-Chicago broadcast during the war was possible but not terribly likely. A reliable source informs me that the interviewer may have been an American Garden enthusiast who actually traveled to Scotland, recorded the interview, possibly in the singer's home, and took it back to the States for the broadcast. Possibly the interview questions were sent to Garden, who recorded her responses on disc. As far as the actual broadcast was concerned, the interviewer may have integrated Garden's pre-recorded responses into a live broadcast--similar to the promotional "open-ended interviews" used by pop radio disc jockeys in the 1960s--or he may have edited both his questions and the singer's answers onto a single disc for air play.

The label of EJS 247 gives the date 1943 and adds that Garden was 71 years old (in fact she would have been either 69 or 70 in 1943), which suggests that the date attributed here is tentative at best. In any event, this 1943 Chicago broadcast has yet to be found.

The title of the song, "one of Robby Burns' loveliest," as Garden describes it, is given as "My Bonnie Jeannie" on the label (actually sung as "My Bonnie Dearier"), but the opening text, as given above, is "Ca' the yowes to the knowes," the first verse of the poem HARK! THE MAVIS. Ralph Vaughan-Williams' setting of the text, similar to that which Garden sings, was recorded in 1928 by the English Singers on Roycroft 160 (Cameo matrix 3008-C).

Band 8: Plays in G major at 32.7 rpm.

EJS 248: "The Golden Age of Opera" (2 LPs)
Issued October, 1962

SIDES 1-4 (248 A-D):

LA BOHÈME (Puccini) (I)
Opera in 4 Acts (complete)
Metropolitan Opera House Orchestra and Chorus/Gennaro Papi
Metropolitan Opera broadcast, NYC, 10 Feb 1940

CAST:
Armand Tokatyan (*Rodolfo*); George Cehanovsky (*Schaunard*); Louis D'Angelo (*Benoit*); Bidú Sayão (*Mimi*); Lodovico Oliviero (*Parpignol*); Giuseppe De Luca (*Marcello*); Ezio Pinza (*Colline*); Louis D'Angelo (*Alcindoro*); Annamary Dickey (*Musetta*); Carlo Coscia (*Sergeant*).

SIDE 2 (248 B):

2. GIUSEPPE DE LUCA, MILTON CROSS, and unnamed interviewer: Intermission Interview with De Luca between Acts II and III

NOTES: EJS 248

This performance, issued complete on EJS 248, was later issued as a private open-reel tape by Omega (Omega No. 18), advertised as having been taken from the offical actetates (NBC acetates of this and several other Met broadcasts did come on the market in 1989, so Omega's claim is probably correct). The De Luca-Sayão "Oh! buon Marcello" from Act III had earlier appeared on EJS 169 (January, 1960). This and the De Luca-Tokatyan "Ah! Mimi, tu più non torni" were later reissued on MDP 015 (where the Act III duet is given on the jacket as "Mimi, io son").

Act I plays at 32.2 rpm until the entrance of Mimi, where there is an interpolation from what appears to be the 3 February, 1945 Met matinee with Sayão and Peerce ("Che viso d'ammalata! . . . A lei. Poco, poco. Cosi? Grazie"), which varies in pitch. Tokatyan's "Che gelida manina" and the end of the love duet were transposed down a half step in the actual performance.

Act II plays at 32.4 rpm.

Act III plays at 32.0 rpm. The last three or four measures of Mimi's "Addio" are patched in from another source--possibly the 3 February, 1945 performance (the singer is definitely Sayão).

Act IV: The introductory chords to this act are followed by a splice, and there is a break a few pages after Mimi's entrance (Schaunard's "Fra mezz'ora [e morata]" through Mimi's "[Ho un po'di tosse!] Ci sono avezza." About a page of music is omitted (odd that nothing was patched in to take its place).

The De Luca interview between Acts II and III was recorded in the singer's dressing room. It is preceded by a lengthy introduction by Milton Cross, given in his familiar Box 44. The actual interviewer is not named in the broadcast. De Luca talks about his return to America, his gratitude at finding his audience so very loyal, and the quality of production at the Met. He closes with a plea of support for the Metropolitan Opera Guild. Another intermission speaker during this broadcast was conductor Walter Damrosch, but his interview does not appear on EJS 248: undoubtedly it was transcribed. This was one of the first in a series of fund-raising Intermission Features that began in the 1939-1940 season, mounted by Henry Souvaine.

EJS 249: "The Golden Age of Opera" (2 LPs)
Issued October, 1962

SIDES 1-4 (249 A-D):

DAS RHEINGOLD (Wagner) (G)
Opera in 1 act (complete)
Metropolitan Opera House Orchestra and Chorus/Artur Bodanzky
Metropolitan Opera broadcast, Boston, 3 Apr 1937

CAST:
Friedrich Schorr (*Wotan*); Julius Huehn (*Donner*); Hans Clemens (*Froh*); René Maison (*Loge*); Eduard Habich (*Alberich*); Karl Laufkoetter (*Mime*); Norman Cordon (*Fasolt*); Emanuel List (*Fafner*); Karin Branzell (*Fricka*); Dorothee Manski (*Freia*); Doris Doe (*Erda*); Stella Andreva (*Woglinde*); Irra Petina (*Wellgunde*); Doris Doe (*Flosshilde*).

NOTES: EJS 249

Library of Congress tape: 15988-1A (complete broadcast).

EJS 250: "The Golden Age of Opera" (2 LPs)
Issued November, 1962

SIDES 1-4 (250 A-D):

FALSTAFF (Verdi) (I)
Opera in 3 acts (complete)
Metropolitan Opera House Orchestra and Chorus/Fritz Reiner
Metropolitan Opera broadcast, NYC, 26 Feb 1949

CAST:
Leonard Warren (*Sir John Falstaff*); Giuseppe Valdengo (*Ford*); Giuseppe Di Stefano (*Fenton*); Leslie Chabay (*Doctor Caius*); Alessio DePaolis (*Bardolph*); Lorenzo Alvary (*Pistol*); Regina Resnik (*Mistress Ford*); Licia Albanese (*Anne*); Cloe Elmo (*Dame Quickly*); Martha Lipton (*Mistress Page*); Ludwig Burgstaller (*Innkeeper*).

NOTES: EJS 250

Late pressings of EJS 250 bear the matrix numbers P-3924/3925, remastered in 1976.

EJS 251: The Golden Age of Opera" (1 LP)
Issued November, 1962

MANON LESCAUT (Puccini) (I)
Opera in 4 acts (excerpts)
Metropolitan Opera House Orchestra and Chorus/Giuseppe Antonicelli
Metropolitan Opera broadcast, NYC, 10 Dec 1949

CAST:
Dorothy Kirsten (*Manon Lescaut*); Jussi Bjoerling (*Des Grieux*); Giuseppe Valdengo (*Lescaut*); Salvatore Baccaloni (*Geronte*); Thomas Hayward (*Edmondo*); Clifford Harvuot (*Sergeant*); [Alessio dePaolis (*Ballet Master*)]; George Cehanovsky (*Innkeeper*); [Jean Madeira (*Musician*)]; Paul Franke (*Lamplighter*); Osie Hawkins (*Captain*).

SIDE 1 (251 A):

Act I: 1. a) BJOERLING, HAYWARD, VALDENGO, BACCALONI, CEHANOVSKY, KIRSTEN, and Chorus: Tra voi belle . . . Cortese damigella . . . Donna non vidi mai
b) KIRSTEN, BJOERLING, and HAYWARD: Vedete? Io son fedel . . . Andiam!

Act II: 2. a) VALDENGO and KIRSTEN: Sei splendida e lucente! . . . È Geronte che fa dei madrigali!
b) KIRSTEN: L'ora, o Tirsi
c) KIRSTEN, BJOERLING, and BACCALONI: Tu amore? . . . Ahimè! Partir dobbiamo!

SIDE 2 (251 B):

Act II: 1. BJOERLING, KIRSTEN, BACCALONI, FRANKE, and HARVUOT: Ah, Manon, mi tradisce . . . to the end of the act

Act III: 2. HARVUOT, BJOERLING, HAWKINS, and Chorus: Presto! In fila! . . . to the end of the act

Act IV: 3. KIRSTEN and BJOERLING: Complete

NOTES: EJS 251

Excerpts from this performance have also appeared on Rococo 5304; the complete broadcast was later issued as UORC 207 (May, 1974).

EJS 252: "The Golden Age of Opera" (1 LP)
Issued November, 1962

"JUSSI BJOERLING OPERA ARIAS AND DUETS (1946-1960)"

SIDE 1 (252 A):

* 1. w. Gothenburg Symphony Orchestra/Nils Grevillius: LOHENGRIN, Act III: I fjärran land [In fernem Land] (Wagner) (Sw)
Broadcast, Gothenburg (Göteborg) Concert Hall, 5 Aug 1960

* 2. w. studio orch/Donald Voorhees: CAVALLERIA RUSTICANA: Mama! Quel vino . . . Addio alla madre (Mascagni) (I) [32.2 rpm]
Broadcast, ***BELL TELEPHONE HOUR***, WNBC, NYC, 4 Apr 1949

* 3. w. studio orch/Donald Voorhees: LA BOHÈME, Act I: Che gelida manina (Puccini) (I) [32.2 rpm]
Broadcast, ***BELL TELEPHONE HOUR***, WNBC, NYC, 7 Nov 1949

* 4. w. Firestone Orchestra/Howard Barlow: I PAGLIACCI: Recitar! . . . Vesti la giubba (Leoncavallo) (I) 32.9 rpm]
Broadcast and Telecast, ***VOICE OF FIRESTONE***, WNBC, NYC, 19 Nov 1951

* 5. w. Firestone Orchestra/Howard Barlow: TURANDOT, Act III: Nessun dorma (Puccini) (I) [32.8 rpm]
Broadcast and Telecast, ***VOICE OF FIRESTONE***, WNBC, NYC, 10 Mar 1952

* 6. w. Gothenburg Symphony Orchestra/Nils Grevillius: EUGEN ONEGIN, Act II: Förbi, förbi [Kuda, kuda] ["Lenski's Air"] (Tchaikowski) (Sw) [33.8 rpm]
Broadcast, Gothenburg (Göteborg) Concert Hall, 5 Aug 1960

* 7. w. studio orch/Donald Voorhees: MANON, Act II: Instant charmant . . . En fermant les yeux (Massenet) (F) [34.3 rpm]
Broadcast, ***BELL TELEPHONE HOUR***, WNBC, NYC, 8 Jan 1951

SIDE 2 (252 B):

1. w. ANNALISA BJOERLING, soprano (San Francisco Opera Orchestra/ Gaetano Merola): ROMÉO ET JULIETTE, Act IV: Va! je t'ai pardonné . . . Nuit d'Hymenée (Gounod) (F) [31.8 rpm]
Broadcast, ***STANDARD HOUR***, KNBC, San Francisco, 23 Oct 1949

* 2. w. ANNALISA BJOERLING (Firestone Orchestra/Howard Barlow): LA BOHÈME, Act I: O soave fanciulla (Puccini) (I) [31.5 rpm]
Broadcast and Telecast, ***VOICE OF FIRESTONE***, WNBC, NYC, 6 Mar 1950

3. w. ANNALISA BJOERLING (Ray Noble and His Orchestra): ROMÉO ET JULIETTE, Act I: Ange adorable (Gounod) (F) [32.4 rpm]
Broadcast, ***EDGAR BERGEN AND CHARLIE McCARTHY SHOW***, CBS, Hollywood, 11 Nov 1951

* 4. w. ANNALISA BJOERLING (Ray Noble and His Orchestra): MAYTIME: Will You Remember (Sweetheart)? (Wood-Young-Romberg) (E)
Broadcast, ***EDGAR BERGEN AND CHARLIE McCARTHY SHOW***, CBS, Hollywood, 2 Dec 1951

* 5. w. DOROTHY KIRSTEN, soprano (Metropolitan Opera House Orchestra/Fausto Cleva): FAUST, Act III: Il se fait tard . . . O nuit d'amour . . . Tête folle! (Gounod) (F) [31.9 rpm]
Metropolitan Opera broadcast, NYC, 23 Dec 1950

* 6. w. Detroit Symphony Orchestra/Eugene Ormandy: MANON, Act III: Ah, fuyez, douce image (Massenet) (F)
Broadcast, ***FORD SUNDAY EVENING HOUR***, WJR, Detroit, 13 Jan 1946

NOTES: EJS 252

Labels have been reported as reversed on at least some copies of EJS 252. Much of this material has appeared elsewhere on various private collectors' labels: Legendary, MDP, and HRE, as well as on the other Smith issues cited below.

Note that the tenor's wife, Annalisa Bjoerling, a noted soprano in her own right, came out of retirement to perform--with some success--with her husband.

Speeds for the individual bands of the LP are given in the listing above or in the corresponding endnotes below.

Side 1 (252 A):

Band 1: This broadcast was apparently Bjoerling's final public appearance (he died 9 September, 1960). Tranferred high, requiring a speed below 30.0 rpm.

Band 2: This broadcast was originally transcribed on a 16-inch, 33.3 rpm U.S. Government disc entitled "Voice of America, Program No. 115" (matrix D-45632, master no. DS-1066), which also contains a 15 March, 1948 ***BELL TELEPHONE HOUR*** Bjoerling broadcast.

The other two selections sung by Bjoerling on this 4 April broadcast later surfaced on Legendary LR 138 and HRE 214-2.

Band 3: The other two items sung by Bjoerling on this broadcast were later include on EJS 365 (May, 1966).

Band 4: Another selection from this broadcast later appeared on EJS 279 (October, 1963) and still later on Legendary LR 138.

Band 5: Other selections from this broadcast later appeared on EJS 279 (October, 1979), ANNA 1017 (September, 1978), and Legendary LR 138, among others.

Band 6: See the note for item I/1.

Band 7: Other Bjoerling items from this broadcast, along with portions of a 23 October, 1950 ***BELL TELEPHONE HOUR*** show, were originally transcribed on a 16-inch, 33.3 rpm U.S. Government disc entitled "Voice of America, Concert Hall Program No. 70" (master no. DS-2451). Portions of the 8 January broadcast appeared on EJS 337 (June, 1965), EJS 366 (May, 1966), and numerous private labels.

Side 2 (252 B):

Band 2: Bjoerling's "Salut! demeure" from this broadcast appeared later on UORC 350 (September-October, 1977).

Band 4: The speed of this band could not be verified owing to the possibility of transposition.

Band 5: The complete 23 December, 1950 FAUST performance was later issued as UORC 110 (April, 1972).

Band 6: The speed of this item varies but eventually settles at 33.0 rpm.

EJS 253: "The Golden Age of Opera" (2 LPs)
Issued December, 1962

SIDES 1-4 (253 A-D):

LA DONNA DEL LAGO (Rossini) (I)
Opera in 2 acts (complete)
Orchestra and Chorus of the Maggio Musicale Fiorentino/Tullio Serafin
?Broadcast, Maggio Musicale Fiorentino, Teatro Comunale, Florence, 9 May 1958

CAST:
Rosanna Carteri (*Elena*); Cesare Valletti (*Giacomo V*); Eddy Ruhl (*Rodrigo di Dhu*); Irene Compañez (*Malcolm Graeme*); Paolo Washington (*Douglas d'Angus*); Carmen Piccini (*Albina*).

NOTES: EJS 253

Rossini's early LA DONNA DEL LAGO, based on Walter Scott's LADY OF THE LAKE, dates from 1819. Whether this performance was an in-house recording or a broadcast has not been determined. Transcribed on EJS 253 complete as performed, with substantial performance cuts reported.

EJS 254: "The Golden Age of Opera" (2 LPs)
Issued December, 1962

SIDES 1-4 (254 A-D):

NERONE (Boïto) (I)
Opera in 4 Acts (complete)
Orchestra and Chorus of the Teatro San Carlo di Napoli/Franco Capuana
?Broadcast, Teatro San Carlo, Naples, 30 Nov 1957

CAST:
Mirto Picchi (*Nerone*); Mario Petri (*Simon Mago*); Gian Giacomo Guelfi (*Fanuel*); Anna Di Cavalieri (*Asteria*); Adriana Lazzarini (*Rubria*); Ferruccio Mazzoli (*Tigellino*); Piero De Palma (*Gobrias*); Piero De Palma (*First Passer-by*); Plinio Clabassi (*Dositeo*); Anna Di Stasio (*Perside*); Valeria Escalar (*Cerinto*); Nino Fanelli (*Il Tempiere*); Augusto Frati (*Second Passer-by*); Gennaro Chiocca (*Slave*); Gianni Bianchi (*Terpnos*).

NOTES: EJS 254

The date of this performance is given in error as 10 November, 1957 in the December, 1962 bulletin. Whether this was an in-house recording or a broadcast has not been determined. Anna De Cavalieri was the Italian stage name of Anne McKnight.

There is a (non-performance) cut in the middle of Act III, made by Smith for purposes of timing--from *Asteria's* "Vengo da dove [non s'esce mai vivi]" to *Fanuel's* "[ti pregai tanto] l'alto abbandon del lagrimato error!"--but this NERONE is otherwise given complete as originally performed. It was reissued on four LPs as Cetra LO-56.

Playing speeds for EJS 254 are unusually complicated:
Side 1: Act I (beginning): 33.6 gradually rising to 34.0 rpm
Side 2: Act I (conclusion) and Act II (beginning): 34.0 rpm
Side 3: Act II (conclusion): 34.0 rpm rpm
Act III (beginning): to the afore-mentioned cut: 34.0
Act III (conclusion): 33.6 rpm
Act IV (beginning): 33.5 rpm
Side 4: Act IV (conclusion): 33.5 rpm

EJS 255: "The Golden Age of Opera" (1 LP)
Issued January, 1963

"ELISABETH RETHBERG RECITAL (1928-41)"

SIDE 1 (255 A):

1. w. studio orch/Alfred Wallenstein: Ah, perfido!, Op. 65 (Metastasio-Beethoven) (I)
Broadcast, ***ELISABETH RETHBERG***, WOR, NYC, 11 Jul 1941

2. w. studio orch/Alfred Wallenstein: SELIG IST DER MANN, BWV 57, no. 3: Ich wünschte mir den Tod (J.S. Bach) (G)
Broadcast, ***ELISABETH RETHBERG***, WOR, NYC, 18 Jul 1941

3. w. Detroit Symphony Orchestra/Fritz Reiner: FIDELIO, Op. 72, Act I: Abscheulicher! Wo eilst du hin? . . . Komm, Hoffnung (Beethoven) (G)
Broadcast, ***FORD SUNDAY EVENING HOUR***, WJR, Detroit, 30 Jan 1938

SIDE 2 (255 B):

* 1. w. studio orch/Alfred Wallenstein: IRISH SONGS: O Might I But My Patrick Love (Beethoven) (E)
Broadcast, ***ELISABETH RETHBERG***, WOR, NYC, 25 Jul 1941

2. w. studio orch/Alfred Wallenstein: DIE SCHÖNE MÜLLERIN, D. 795, no. 2: Wohin? (Müller-Schubert) (G)
Broadcast, ***ELISABETH RETHBERG***, WOR, NYC, 11 Jul 1941

3. w. studio orch/Alfred Wallenstein: WINTEREISSE, D. 911, no. 5: Der Lindenbaum" (Müller-Schubert) (G)
Broadcast, ***ELISABETH RETHBERG***, WOR, NYC, 11 Jul 1941

4. w. studio orch/Alfred Wallenstein: "Der Erlkönig," D. 328 (Goethe-Schubert) (G)
Broadcast, ***ELISABETH RETHBERG***, WOR, NYC, 11 Jul 1941

* 5. w. studio orch/Alfred Wallenstein: "Gretchen im Zwinger"/ "Gretchens Bitte" [Ach, neige], D. 564 (Goethe-Schubert) (G)
Broadcast, ***ELISABETH RETHBERG***, WOR, NYC, 11 Sep 1941

6. w. studio orch/Alfred Wallenstein: MYRTHEN, Op. 25, no. 1: Widmung (Rückert-Schumann) (G)
Broadcast, ***ELISABETH RETHBERG***, WOR, NYC, 11 Jul 1941

7. w. studio orch/Alfred Wallenstein: LIEDER UND GESÄNGE II, Op. 51, no. 2: Volksliedchen (Rückert-Schumann) (G)
   Broadcast, ***ELISABETH RETHBERG***, WOR, NYC, 11 Jul 1941

8. w. studio orch/Alfred Wallenstein: LIEDER UND GESÄNGE II, Op. 51, no. 3: Ich wandre nicht (Rückert-Schumann) (G)
   Broadcast, ***ELISABETH RETHBERG***, WOR, NYC, 11 Jul 1941

NOTES: EJS 255

EJS 255 contains, among other selections, all of the music Rethberg performed on her 11 July, 1941 WOR broadcast. The studio orchestra was credited in the *New York Times* as "Wallenstein's Orchestra" for this Rethberg summer series.

A number of these selections were later included on ANNA 1038-1039 (May-June, 1979), a two-disc Rethberg recital.

Side 2 (255 B):

Band 1: Credited in the *New York Times* as from Beethoven's "Three Scotch Songs."

Band 5: Based on the subtitle of the LP ("1928-41") and the comparatively youthful sound of the soprano's voice--which may simply be the result of poor pitching--it has been suggested that this, like the two songs featured on EJS 256, is an unpublished Brunswick recording, but it is more likely that this performance of "Gretchens Bitte" was the one featured on Rethberg's final WOR broadcast on 11 September, 1941.

EJS 256: "The Golden Age of Opera" (1 LP)
Issued January, 1963

"ELISABETH RETHBERG RECITAL (1928-41)"

SIDE 1 (256 A):

1. w. studio orch/Alfred Wallenstein: MöRIKELIEDER, No. 25: Schlafendes Jesuskind (Mörike-Wolf) (G)
   Broadcast, ***ELISABETH RETHBERG***, WOR, NYC, 8 Aug 1941

2. w. studio orch/Alfred Wallenstein: MöRIKELIEDER, No. 16: Elfenlied (Mörike-Wolf) (G)
   Broadcast, ***ELISABETH RETHBERG***, WOR, NYC, 8 Aug 1941

3. w. studio orch/Alfred Wallenstein: MöRIKELIEDER, No. 6: Er ist's" (Mörike-Wolf) (G)
   Broadcast, ***ELISABETH RETHBERG***, WOR, NYC, 8 Aug 1941

* 4. w. pf/?: GESÄNGE, Op. 17, no. 2: Ständchen, (Osterwald-Robert Franz) (G)
   Broadcast, ***ELISABETH RETHBERG***, WOR, NYC, 29 Aug 1941

5. w. studio orch/Alfred Wallenstein: GESÄNGE, Op. 17. no. 6: Im Herbst (Müller-Robert Franz) (G)
Broadcast, ***ELISABETH RETHBERG***, WOR, NYC, 29 Aug 1941

* 6. w. studio orch/Alfred Wallenstein: LIEDER UND GESÄNGE [LIEDER UND GESÄNGE AUS DER JUGENDZEIT], no. 1: Frühlingsmorgen (R. Leander-Mahler) (G)
Broadcast, ***ELISABETH RETHBERG***, WOR, NYC, 22 Aug 1941

7. w. studio orch/Alfred Wallenstein: DAS KNABEN WUNDERHORN, no. 4: Rheinlegendchen (Mahler) (G)
Broadcast, ***ELISABETH RETHBERG***, WOR, NYC, 22 Aug 1941

8. w. studio orch/Alfred Wallenstein: ARIETTES OUBLIÉES, no. 1: C'est l'extase (Verlaine-Debussy) (F)
Broadcast, ***ELISABETH RETHBERG***, WOR, NYC, 5 Sep 1941

9. w. studio orch/Alfred Wallenstein: ARIETTES OUBLIÉES, no. 2: Il pleure dans mon coeur (Verlaine-Debussy) (F)
Broadcast, ***ELISABETH RETHBERG***, WOR, NYC, 5 Sep 1941

10. w. studio orch/Alfred Wallenstein: "Marienlied" (Novalis-Joseph Marx) (G)
Broadcast, ***ELISABETH RETHBERG***, WOR, NYC, 18 Jul 1941

11. w. studio orch/Alfred Wallenstein: "Venezianisches Wiegenlied" (Anon.-Joseph Marx) (G)
Broadcast, ***ELISABETH RETHBERG***, WOR, NYC, 18 Jul 1941

12. w. studio orch/Alfred Wallenstein: "Und Gestern hat mir Rosen gebracht" (Singer-Joseph Marx) (G)
Broadcast, ***ELISABETH RETHBERG***, WOR, NYC, 18 Jul 1941

13. w. studio orch/Alfred Wallenstein: "Hat dich die Liebe berührt" (Heyse-Joseph Marx) (G)
Broadcast, ***ELISABETH RETHBERG***, WOR, NYC, 18 Jul 1941

SIDE 2 (256 B):

1. w. pf/?: SECHS LIEDER, Op. 17, no. 2: Ständchen (Schack-R. Strauss) (G)
Source and date unknown

2. w. studio orch/Alfred Wallenstein: VIER LIEDER, Op. 27, no. 4: Morgen (Mackay-R. Strauss) (G)
Broadcast, ***ELISABETH RETHBERG***, WOR, NYC, 25 Jul 1941

* 3. w. NBC Orchestra/Alfred Wallenstein: VIER LIEDER, Op. 27, no. 4: Morgen (Mackay-R. Strauss) (G)
Broadcast, ***MAGIC KEY OF RCA***, WJZ, NYC, 24 Oct 1937

* 4. w. studio orch/Alfred Wallenstein: WESENDONCK-LIEDER, no. 2: Stehe still (Mathilde Wesendonk-Wagner) (G)
Broadcast, ***ELISABETH RETHBERG***, WOR, NYC, 29 Aug 1941

5. w. studio orch/Alfred Wallenstein: WESENDONCK-LIEDER, no. 4: Schmerzen (Wagner) (G)
Broadcast, ***ELISABETH RETHBERG***, WOR, NYC, 29 Aug 1941

6. w. pf/?: MYRTHEN, Op. 25, no. 3: Der Nussbaum (Mosen-Schumann) (G)
   Source and date unknown
7. w. pf/?: "Es steht ein Baum in jenen Tal" (Wilhelm Taubert) (G)
   Source and date unknown

* 8. (w. studio orch/?Frank Black): "It was a Dream" [Ich hatte einst ein schönes Vaterland] (Eduard Lassen)
   matrix unknown   Chicago, 1928-1929   Brunswick 15147

* 9. (w. studio orch/?Frank Black): "A Moonlight Song," Op. 42, no. 2 (Mills-Cadman)
   matrix unknown   Chicago, 1928-1929   Brunswick 15147

NOTES: EJS 256

The studio orchestra was credited as "Wallenstein's Orchestra" for Rethberg's 1941 summer series.

A number of these selections were later included on ANNA 1038-1039 (May-June, 1979), a two-disc Rethberg recital.

Side 1 (256 A):

Band 6: "Frühlingsmorgen" is not among the set of three Mahler songs credited in the *New York Times* radio log for this broadcast, but the source of the performance seems certain, as cited above. The other works performed on this 22 August, 1941 broadcast were included on EJS 532 in December, 1970.

Side 2 (256 B):

Band 3: This particular broadcast is discussed at some length in the notes for EJS 181 (VI/1-2).

Band 4: Only Wagner's "Schmerzen" and "Traume" from the WESENDONCK-LIEDER are listed in the *New York Times* radio log, but the 29 August, 1941 broadcast is almost undoubtedly the source of the "Stehe still," which may have been a substitution.

Bands 8-9: Rumored to be unpublished Brunswick studio recordings, these two songs were in fact issued as ten-inch Brunswick 15147, matrices unknown (matrix numbers rarely appear on post-1923 Brunswick pressings). Hence the subtitle of this LP, ("1928-41"). J. B. Richards' early discography of Rethberg in *The Record Collector* identified the coupling initially as Brunswick 15147 (3/4, April, 1948, p. 53), but then, omitting any mention of either song in a later Rethberg article (8/1, January, 1953, p. 10), assigned 15147 for Rethberg's ten-inch version of the Gardenia-Densmore "A Spring Fancy," coupled in the U. S. and Australia with Grace Moore's "Pour toi," and in the U.K. with Rethberg's "By a Lonely Forest Pathway." These couplings were in fact issued as Brunswick 15146. There are reports, however, that British Brunswick pressings were often recoupled with catalog number errors, so Richards may have been correct in implying that "A Spring Fancy" was *also* issued as 15147 in the U.K. Rethberg Brunswicks 15146-15148 are listed in American catalogs of issues "up to Jan. 1, 1930," but they do not appear the 1928 edition or in the 1928-1929 Australian catalog.

The composer of "It was a Dream" is given on Brunswick labels as "Lassen" (Eduard Lassen, 1830-1904). The song is in fact Lassen's ""Er war ein Traum," with the opening text, "Ich hatte einst ein schönes Vaterland." The title is translated in Schirmer music catalogs as "Ah! tis a Dream!" and in Krehbeil's anthology, *Famous Songs* (Cincinnati: John Church, 1902) as "It was a Dream." Lassen's song is not not be confused with the popular 1875 song "It was a Dream" by Robert E. Francillon and Frederick H. Cowen.

At the time of these recordings, Frank Black was Brunswick's musical director, so it is assumed that he conducted the session(s).

EJS 257: "The Golden Age of Opera" (1 LP)
Issued January, 1963

SIDES 1-2 (257 A-B):

PARSIFAL (Wagner) (G)
Opera in 3 Acts (Act II only)
Royal Philharmonic Orchestra and Royal Opera House Chorus/Karl Rankl
Broadcast, Covent Garden, London, 22 Jun 1951

CAST:
Franz Lechleitner (*Parsifal*); Kirsten Flagstad (*Kundry*); Otakar Kraus (*Klingsor*); Audrey Bowman (*Flowermaiden*) Patricia Howard (*Flowermaiden*); Adele Leigh (*Flowermaiden*); ?Blanche Turner (*Flowermaiden*); Barbara Howitt (*Flowermaiden*); ?Monica Sinclair (*Flowermaiden*); [Sigurd Bjoerling (*Amfortas*)]; [Ludwig Weber (*Gurnemanz*)]; [Michael Langdon (*Titurel*)]; [Thorstein Hannesson (*Knight of the Grail*)]; [Rhydderich Davies (*Knight of the Grail*)]; [Adele Leigh (*Esquire*)]; [Monica Sinclair (*Esquire*)]; [William McAlpine (*Esquire*)]; [John Cameron (*Esquire*)].

NOTES: EJS 257

The *Flowermaidens* are not credited on the label. The original cast list gives only five *Flowermaidens*, but Sinclair, having sung one of the Knappen in Act I, may have been the likeliest sixth in the second-act ensemble. Bjoerling and Weber, neither of whom appear in Act II, are listed in error on the label.

The last two bars of the act are omitted on EJS 257. The performance was reissued in 1989 as Legato Classics CD LCD-144-1, where the end of the act is completed with another, unidentified performance.

EJS 258: "The Golden Age of Opera" (1 LP)
Issued January, 1963

"KIRSTEN FLAGSTAD MEMORIAL (1937-1949)"

SIDE 1 (258 A):

* 1. w. RENÉ MAISON, tenor (Metropolitan Opera House Orchestra and Chorus/Maurice de Abravanel): LOHENGRIN, Act III: End of the Bridal Chorus . . . Das süsse Lied verhallt . . . to the death of Telramund (Wagner) (G)
Metropolitan Opera broadcast, NYC, 27 Mar 1937

* 2. w. MARGARETHE KLOSE, contralto (London Philharmonic Orchestra and Royal Opera House Chorus/Sir Thomas Beecham): TRISTAN UND ISOLDE, Act I: Liess' er das Steuer jetz zur Stund' . . . O Süsse! Traute! (Wagner) (G)
Unpublished live performance recordings (HMV):
Technical Tests Series 6547-?, Covent Garden, London, 18 Jun 1937

* 3. w. Metropolitan Opera House Orchestra/Erich Leinsdorf: TANNHÄUSER, Act II: Dich, teure Halle! (Wagner) (G)
Metropolitan Opera broadcast, NYC, 16 Dec 1939

SIDE 2 (258 B):

* 1. w. Metropolitan Opera House Orchestra/Artur Bodanzky: FIDELIO, Op. 72, Act I: Abscheulicher! Wo eilst du hin? . . . Komm, Hoffnung (Beethoven) (G)
Metropolitan Opera broadcast, NYC, 31 Dec 1938

2. w. LAURITZ MELCHIOR, tenor; GERTRUDE WETTERGREN, contralto, and JULIUS HUEHN, baritone (Metropolitan Opera House Orchestra/Artur Bodanzky): TRISTAN UND ISOLDE, Act II: O sink hernieder . . . Rette dich, Tristan (Wagner) (G)
Metropolitan Opera broadcast, NYC, 29 Jan 1938

* 3. w. San Francisco Opera House Orchestra/Gaetano Merola: DER FLIEGENDE HOLLÄNDER, Act II: Trafft ihr das Schiff ("Senta's Ballad") (Wagner) (G)
Broadcast, ***STANDARD HOUR***, San Francisco War Memorial Opera House, KPO, San Francisco, 9 Oct 1949

NOTES: EJS 258

Side 1 (258 A):

Band 1: Extensive excerpts of this performance later appeared on EJS 557 (June, 1971) and UORC 308 (November-December, 1976).
Library of Congress tape: 15778-41A (complete broadcast).

Band 2: The complete 18 June, 1937 TRISTAN was recorded by HMV on Technical Test Series 6547 according to Sanner's Flagstad discography (p. 155, no. 96). Michael Gray's Beecham discography claims that only Act III was recorded, on Test Series TT 6548-39/65 (p. 38), while Sanner assigns TT 6548 to the 22 June, 1937 TRISTAN (p. 155, no. 97)

--a performance not listed as having been recorded at all by Gray. In any event, none of these TRISTAN recordings were issued commercially (only brief passages from live 1936 and 1937 Covent Garden productions of GÖTTERDÄMMERUNG and MEISTERSINGER were released on shellac). The Act I of 18 June later appeared as UORC 302 (September, 1976), while excerpts appeared on Recital Records RR 5382. Discocorp, in their Melchior Anthology, issued both the 18 and 22 June second acts as RR-223. Melodram CD 37029 may, similarly, be a compilation of the two performances. ANNA 1050 and 1051 (circa January, 1980) presented a rather more troublesome composite of both which, along with subsequent LP and CDs releases, will be discussed at length in the note for EJS 465 (April, 1969).

Band 3: Library of Congress tape: 5174-7 (complete broadcast).

Side 2 (258 B):

Band 1: The complete performance exists as Stanford Archive of Recorded Sound tape StARS 381231 MI-2 and was later issued as UORC 268 (November-December, 1975).

Band 3: Given as 9 November, 1949 on the label of EJS 258. Set Svanholm appeared with Flagstad on this broadcast, excerpts of which were later issued on LP as VOCE-98.

EJS 259: "The Golden Age of Opera" (3 LPs)
Issued February, 1963

SIDES 1-6 (259 A-F):

SEMIRAMIDE (Rossini) (I)
Opera in 2 Acts (complete)
Orchestra and Chorus of the Teatro alla Scala, Milano/Gabriele Santini
Broadcast or in-house recording, Teatro alla Scala, Milan, 19 Dec 1962

CAST:
Joan Sutherland (*Semiramide*); Giulietta Simionato (*Arsace*); Wladimiro Ganzarolli (*Assur*); Gianni Raimondi (*Idreno*); Ferruccio Mazzoli (*Oroë*); Giuseppe Bertinazzo (*Mitrano*); Antonio Zerbini (*L'Ombra di Nino*); Manuela Bianchi Parro (*Azema*).

NOTES: EJS 259

In spite of the claim made in the February, 1963 EJS bulletin, no evidence has been found verifying that any of the seven Scala SEMIRAMIDE performances from the 1962-1962 season were broadcast, so it may be that EJS 259 was compiled from an in-house recording.

Complete as performed in four (rather than the original two) acts: Act II begins with Sutherland's "Bel raggio;" Act III begins at the start of the original Act II (the *Semiramide-Assur* duet); Act IV begins at *Assur's* "Mad Scene."

Speeds are irregular: Act I plays in score pitch at 34.0 rpm, Act II at 34.2 rpm, and Act III and IV at 34.7 rpm and higher.

The performance was later issued as Fonit-Cetra DOC-40.

EJS 260: "The Golden Age of Opera" (1 LP)
Issued February, 1963

SIDES 1-2 (A-B):

I PAGLIACCI (Leoncavallo) (I)
Opera in 2 Acts (complete)
Metropolitan Opera House Orchestra and chorus/Vincenzo Bellezza
Metropolitan Opera broadcast, NYC, 10 Mar 1934

CAST:
Queena Mario (*Nedda*); Giovanni Martinelli (*Canio*); Lawrence Tibbett (*Tonio*); Alfio Tedesco (*Beppe*); George Cehanovsky (*Silvio*).

NOTES: EJS 260

The February, 1963 bulletin notes that this performance is the earliest surviving *complete* broadcast performance from the Met and that it was the first broadcast of I PAGLIACCI from that house. However, the 10 February, 1934 MERRY MOUNT (issued as EJS 134 in October, 1958) obviously pre-dates the PAGLIACCI by a month. Moreover, the 13 January, 1910 PAGLIACCI from the Met with Caruso, Amato, and Bella Alten, a broadcast mounted by Lee De Forest and heard only as far away as New Jersey, was obviously the first airing of the opera.

This PAGLIACCI is also one of the relatively few surviving recordings of soprano Queena Mario, who appears to have made no commercial recordings; the voice of Alfio Tedesco, too, apart from an ERNANI "O sommo Carlo" with Giuseppe De Luca and Grace Anthony, recorded in New York City 5 April, 1928 (matrix CVE-43615-2, issued on Victor 8174), survives in only a handful of broadcast transcriptions.

This performance was later reissued on the private ERR 126 LP. The SALOME performed on the same 10 March, 1934 broadcast was issued as EJS 506 (April, 1970), with only minor cuts.

EJS 261: "The Golden Age of Opera" (1 LP)
Issued March, 1963

SIDES 1-2 (261 A-B):

KHOVANSHCHINA [KHOVANCHINA] (Mussorgsky) (E)
Opera in 5 Acts (excerpts)
Metropolitan Opera House Orchestra and Chorus/Emil Cooper
Metropolitan Opera broadcast, NYC, 25 Feb 1950

CAST:
Risë Stevens (*Marfa*); Polyna Stoska (*Susanna*); Anne Bollinger (*Emma*); Charles Kullman (*Prince Vassili Golitsin*); Jerome Hines (*Dossifé*); Lawrence Tibbett (*Prince Ivan Khovansky*); Brian Sullivan (*Andrei Khovansky*); Robert Weede (*Shaklovity*); Leslie Chabay (*The Scrivener*); Osie Hawkins (*Varsonoviev*); Clifford Harvuot (*Kuska*); Emery Darcy (*Streltsy*); Denis Harbour (*Streltsy*); Philip Kinsman (*Streltsy*).

NOTES: EJS 261

Misnumbered as EJS 262 on the 1970s "Golden Age of Opera" checklist, but given correctly as EJS 261 on discs and labels.

The complete performance was issued as UORC 295 in May-June, 1976.

Mussorgsky's KHOVANSHCHINA was left unfinished, and was completed and orchestrated by Rimski-Korsakov. Its first performance was given in St. Petersburg on 21 February, 1886. The first Met performance of the work (in English) was on 16 February, 1950, with the same cast and conductor heard in this 25 February broadcast.

Prince Ivan was Tibbett's last *new* role at the Met in his final season there, though this broadcast was not his final performance: in addition to a 28 February TOSCA (a gala testimonial for Edward Johnson), he sang four performances of KHOVANSCHINA, the last, his final stage appearance at the Met, on 24 March, 1950.

EJS 262: "The Golden Age of Opera" (1 LP)
Issued March, 1963

"POTPOURRI NO. 17"

SIDE 1 (262 A):

* 1. BENIAMINO GIGLI, tenor (Orchestra of Radio Italiana [RAI], Milano/Alfredo Simonetto): L'AFRICANA, Act IV: O Paradiso [ô Paradis!] (Meyerbeer) (I)
Broadcast, ***CONCERTO MARTINI E ROSSI***, RAI, Teatro Muncipale, San Remo, 27 Dec 1954

* 2. BENIAMINO GIGLI, tenor (Orchestra of Radio Italiana [RAI], Milano/Alfredo Simonetto): WERTHER, Act III: Ah, non mi ridestar [Pourquoi me réveiller?] (Massenet) (I)
Broadcast, ***CONCERTO MARTINI E ROSSI***, RAI, Teatro Muncipale, San Remo, 27 Dec 1954

* 3. BENIAMINO GIGLI, tenor (Orchestra of Radio Italiana [RAI], Milano/Alfredo Simonetto): L'ARLESIANA, Act II: È la solita storia del pastor ["Lamento di Federico"] (Cilèa) (I)
Broadcast, ***CONCERTO MARTINI E ROSSI***, RAI, Teatro Muncipale, San Remo, 27 Dec 1954

* 4. BENIAMINO GIGLI, tenor (Orchestra of Radio Italiana [RAI], Milano/Alfredo Simonetto): ANDREA CHENIER, Act I: Un dì, all'azzurro spazio ["Improvviso"] (Giordano) (I)
Broadcast, ***CONCERTO MARTINI E ROSSI***, RAI, Teatro Muncipale, San Remo, 27 Dec 1954

* 5. GRACE MOORE, soprano (Columbia Studio Orchestra/Pietro Cimini): LA TRAVIATA, Act I: Follie! Follie! . . . Sempre libera (Verdi) (I)
from the 9-reel Columbia feature film, ***ONE NIGHT OF LOVE*** (1934), Hollywood, 1933-1934
LP 4862; c30 Jul 1934
New York premiere: Radio City Music Hall, 6 Sep 1934

* 6. GRACE MOORE, soprano (Columbia Studio Orchestra and chorus/Pietro Cimini): "Ciribiribin" (Carlo Tiochet-A. Pestalozza) (I)
from the 9-reel Columbia feature film, ***ONE NIGHT OF LOVE*** (1934), Hollywood, 1933-1934
LP 4862; c30 Jul 1934
New York premiere: Radio City Music Hall, 6 Sep 1934

* 7. GRACE MOORE, soprano (Columbia Studio Orchestra/Pietro Cimini, and pf/?): MARTHA II: Die Letzte Rose ('Tis the Last Rose of Summer)(Moore-Flotow) (E)
from the 9-reel Columbia feature film, ***ONE NIGHT OF LOVE*** (1934), Hollywood, 1933-1934
LP 4862; c30 Jul 1934
New York premiere: Radio City Music Hall, 6 Sep 1934

* 8. GRACE MOORE, soprano (Columbia Studio Orchestra/Pietro Cimini): CARMEN, Act I: La voila! . . . L'amour est un oiseau rebelle ["Habanera"] (Bizet) (F)
from the 9-reel Columbia feature film, ***ONE NIGHT OF LOVE*** (1934), Hollywood, 1933-1934
LP 4862; c30 Jul 1934
New York premiere: Radio City Music Hall, 6 Sep 1934

* 9. GRACE MOORE, soprano, and unidentified baritone (Columbia Studio Orchestra and chorus/Pietro Cimini): MADAMA BUTTERFLY, Act I: Ah! quanto cielo . . . Ancora un passo un via (Puccini) (I)
from the 9-reel Columbia feature film, ***ONE NIGHT OF LOVE*** (1934), Hollywood, 1933-1934
LP 4862; c30 Jul 1934
New York premiere: Radio City Music Hall, 6 Sep 1934

*10. GRACE MOORE, soprano (Columbia Studio Orchestra/Pietro Cimini): MADAMA BUTTERFLY, Act II: Piangi? Perchè? . . . Un bel dì, vedremo (Puccini) (I)
from the 9-reel Columbia feature film, ***ONE NIGHT OF LOVE*** (1934), Hollywood, 1933-1934
LP 4862; c30 Jul 1934
New York premiere: Radio City Music Hall, 6 Sep 1934

SIDE 2 (262 B):

1. FEODOR CHALIAPIN, bass (pf/?): "On the Hills of Georgia" [Na kholmakh Gruzii], Op. 3, no. 4 (Rimsky-Korsakov) (R)
5303ae St. Petersburg, 12 Jan 1914 HMV unpub

* 2. FEODOR CHALIAPIN, bass (pf/?): "The Prisoner" [Plennik], Op. 78, no. 6 (Polonsky-Rubinstein) (R)
5301ae St. Petersburg, 12 Jan 1914 HMV unpub HM 91

3. FEODOR CHALIAPIN, bass (pf/?): "When Yesterday We Met" [Vchera my vstrechilis], Op. 26, no. 13 (Polonsky-Rachmaninoff) (R)
5304ae St. Petersburg, 12 Jan 1914 HMV unpub

ROMÉO ET JULIETTE (Gounod) (F)
Opera in [4] Acts (excerpts)
Metropolitan Opera House Orchestra and Chorus/Louis Hasselmans
Metropolitan Opera broadcast, NYC, 26 Jan 1935

CAST:
[Eide Norena (*Juliette*)]; Charles Hackett (*Roméo*); Gladys Swarthout (*Stephano*); [Henriette Wakefield (*Gertrude*)]; Angelo Bada (*Tybalt*); Max Altglass (*Benvolio*); Giuseppe De Luca (*Mercutio*); [Millo Picco (*Paris*)]; Paolo Ananian (*Gregorio*); Louis D'Angelo (*Capulet*); [Léon Rothier (*Friar Laurence*)]; Arthur Anderson (*Duke of Verona*).

4. DE LUCA, HACKETT, SWARTHOUT, D'ANGELO, ANANIAN, ALTGLASS, BADA, ANDERSON, and Chorus: Act III: [De]puis hier je cherche en vain mon maître! . . . et du prince et du ciel!

* 5. GLADYS SWARTHOUT, contralto (studio orch/?): LA FAVORITA, Act III: Fia dunque vero, o ciel? . . . O mio Fernando (Donizetti) (I)
Broadcast, source and date unknown, circa 1935

* 6. JAN PEERCE, tenor (studio orch/George Sebastian): IL TROVATORE, Act III: Di quella pira (Verdi) (I)
Broadcast, ***GREAT MOMENTS IN MUSIC***, WABC, NYC, 24 Jan 1945

* 7. JAN PEERCE, tenor (studio orch/George Sebastian): IL BARBIERE DI SIVIGLIA, Act I: Ecco ridente in cielo (Rossini) (I)
Broadcast, ***GREAT MOMENTS IN MUSIC***, WABC, NYC, 13 Jun 1945

* 8. JAN PEERCE, tenor (studio orch/?): ANDREA CHENIER, Act I: Un dì, all'azzurro spazio ["Improvviso"] (Giordano) (I)
?Broadcast, source and date unknown

* 9. JAN PEERCE, tenor, and ANNE ROSELLE, soprano (studio orch/?): ANDREA CHENIER, Act IV: Vicino a te s'acqueta (Giordano) (I)
?Broadcast, source and date unknown

NOTES: EJS 262

Misnumbered as EJS 263 on the 1970s "Golden Age of Opera" checklist, but given correctly as EJS 262 on discs and labels.

Side 1 (262 A):

Bands 1-4: These Gigli ***MARTINI E ROSSI*** items have appeared on a number of private LPs and CDs. This broadcast was shared with soprano Maria Callas, though she performed no duets with Gigli. Callas' ARMIDA aria was included on EJS 360 (March, 1964), though all four of her 27 December, 1954 arias have been gathered on a number of other private LPs.

Bands 5-10: Louis Silvers is credited as the composer of the incidental music for the Columbia film ***ONE NIGHT OF LOVE*** along with Gus Kahn and Victor Scherzinger, the film's director. Dr. Pietro Cimini is credited as the music director, and so is probably the conductor of these excerpts. Silvers, however, was a well-known studio music director in his own right (at Warner Brothers in the 1920s and 1930s), making Cimini's attribution as conductor provisional.

Moore's studio recordings of songs from the film, made in New York on 4 October, 1934 with the Metropolitan Opera House Chorus and a studio orchestra conducted by Wilfred Pelletier, included only the Pestalozza "Ciribiribin" and the title song, issued on Brunswick 6994 (matrices B-16101-A/16102-A). She recorded the BUTTERFLY "Un bel dì" on Decca 29000 in Los Angeles on 27 November, 1935 (matrix DLA-284-C), as credited to the film ***LOVE ME FOREVER***.

All but the MARTHA "Last Rose" were issued on Parnassus LP PAR 1010, a Moore recital, to which the film's title song was also added.

Band 7: Begins with piano, but eventually the orchestra fades in.

Band 9: Tenor Paul Ellis, identified only as "*Pinkerton*" in the film credits, is heard in this scene, but prior to the excerpt presented here. The *Sharpless*, who is heard on EJS 262, could not be identified.

Side 2 (262 B):

Band 2: Also known by the title "The Captive." Reissued in 1992 as a vinyl pressing, Historic Masters HM 91, coupled with the unpublished Slonov "A Word of Farewell" (5300ae) from the same session.

Band 4: The label of EJS 262 notes that eight minutes of Act III are included. This portion of Act III/ii is presented in five sections with significant recording cuts. The performance was reissued complete as UORC 175 (November, 1973) with this scene intact as performed.

Band 5: Swarthout's FAVORITA aria is not listed on the label of EJS 262, nor have the date and broadcast source been determined: she sang the aria often on the radio making the identification of this version difficult.

Bands 6-7: Carried over WABC-AM and -FM, New York City.

Band 8-9: Labels date the two CHENIER titles as "1944," but this could not be verified.

EJS 263: "The Golden Age of Opera" (2 LPs)
Issued March, 1963

SIDES 1-4 (263 A-D):

DIE TOTE STADT (Paul Schott-Erich Wolfgang Korngold) (G)
Opera in 3 Acts (complete)
Orchestra and Chorus of the Bayrischer Staatsoper, Munich/Fritz Lehmann
Broadcast or in-house recording, Bayrischer Staatsoper, Munich, circa summer, 1954

CAST:
Maud Cunitz (*Marietta/Apparition of Marietta*); Karl Friedrich (*Paul*); Benno Kusche (*Frank*); Hans Braun (*Pierrot/Fritz*); Lilian Benningsen (*Brigitta*); ? (*Juliette*); ? (*Lucienne*); ? (*Victorin*); ? (*Gaston*); ? (*Graf Albert*).

NOTES: EJS 263

Misnumbered as EJS 261 on the 1970s "Golden Age of Opera" checklist, but given correctly as EJS 263 on discs and labels.

The complete cast of this obscure performance could not be documented. It is not known, moreover, whether this was taken from a broadcast or an in-house recording.

A speed of about 32.8 rpm has been suggested to maintain score pitch.

EJS 264: "The Golden Age of Opera" (1 LP)
Issued April, 1963

OTELLO (Verdi) (I)
Opera in 4 Acts (excerpts)
Metropolitan Opera House Orchestra and Chorus/Ettore Panizza
Metropolitan Opera broadcast, NYC, 18 Jan 1941

CAST:
Giovanni Martinelli (*Otello*); Lawrence Tibbett (*Iago*); [Alessio DePaolis (*Cassio*)]; [John Dudley (*Roderigo*)]; [Nicola Moscona (*Lodovico*)]; [George Cehanovsky (*Montano*)]; [Wilfred Engelman (*Herald*)]; Stella Roman (*Desdemona*); [Thelma Votipka (*Emilia*)].

SIDE 1 (264 A):

Act I: 1. a) MARTINELLI and Chorus: Esultate! . . . Evviva Otello! Evviva! evviva! evviva!
b) MARTINELLI and ROMAN: Già nella notte densa . . . to the end of the act

Act II: 2. a) TIBBETT: Vanne; la tua meta già vedo . . . Credo in un Dio crudel . . . è vecchia fola il Ciel!
b) TIBBETT, MARTINELLI, and Chorus: Dove guardi splendono raggi . . . Ora e per sempre addio . . . Oh! monstruosa colpa! [ending "Sangue! Sangue!"]

SIDE 2 (264 B):

Act II: 1. MARTINELLI and TIBBETT: Si pel ciel . . . to the end of the act

Act III: 2. MARTINELLI and ROMAN: Il fazzoletto voglio . . . Dio! mi potevi scagliar . . . Cielo! Oh, gioia

Act IV: 3. ROMAN: Piangea cantando nell'erma landa . . . Ave Maria

4. MARTINELLI: Niun mi tema . . . to the end of the opera

NOTES: EJS 264

This splendid OTELLO, issued complete as UORC 192 in February, 1974, was reissued as Robin Hood RHR 508 (3 LPs). Pearl reissued it again, first as LP GEMM 267-9, and in 1988, as GEMM CD 9267 (labeled as in "Stereo"!). Both EJS 264 and UORC 192 presented the performance in excellent sound, obviously taken from line checks (Smith had access to "official" NBC acetates by this time), and it is possible, judging from the slow-moving surface noise, that Pearl may have availed themselves of the UORC reissue when preparing their own.

Whether intentionally or not, the performance date assigned to the Pearl issues was 4 December, 1941 (a Thursday evening performance with the same cast and conductor that was neither broadcast or recorded as far as is known).

EJS 265: "The Golden Age of Opera" (1 LP)
Issued April, 1963

SIDES 1-2 (265 A-B):

FAUST (Gounod) (F)
Opera in 5 Acts (excerpts)
Metropolitan Opera House Orchestra and Chorus/Sir Thomas Beecham
Metropolitan Opera broadcast, NYC, 30 Jan 1943

CAST:
Raoul Jobin (*Faust*); Ezio Pinza (*Méphistophélès*); John Charles Thomas (*Valentin*); Wilfred Engelman (*Wagner*); Licia Albanese (*Marguerite*); Lucielle Browning (*Siébel*); [Thelma Votipka (*Marthe*)].

SIDE 1 (265 A):

Act I: 1. JOBIN and PINZA: Mais ce Dieu, que peut-il pour moi? . . . À moi les plaisirs . . . to the end of the act

Act II: 2. a) THOMAS, ENGELMAN, BROWNING, and Chorus: O sainte médaille . . . Avant de quitter ces lieux
b) THOMAS, PINZA, and Chorus: Un rat plus poltron que brave . . . Le veau d'or

Act III: 3. JOBIN: Quel trouble inconnu me pénètre . . . Salut! demeure

4. ALBANESE: Je voudrais bien savoir . . . Il était un Roi de Thulé . . . Les grands seigneurs . . . Ah! Je ris de me voir ["Jewel Song"]

SIDE 2 (265 B):

Act III: * 1. PINZA, ALBANESE, and JOBIN: Il était temps! . . . Ô nuit étends sur eux ton ombre . . . Laisse-moi . . . Ô nuit d'amour . . . Ne brisez pas le coeur de Marguerite / Divine pureté! . . . to the end of the act

Act IV: * 2. a) PINZA, JOBIN, and THOMAS: Qu'attendez-vous encore? . . . Vous qui faites l'endormie ["Sérénade"] . . . Que voulez-vous messieurs . . . verser le sang du frère que j'outrage!
b) THOMAS, ALBANESE, BROWNING, and Chorus: Merci! merci! . . . Écoute-moi bien, Marguerite ["Death of Valentin"] . . . to the end of the act

Act V: 3. JOBIN, ALBANESE, and PINZA: Marguerite! Marguerite! Ah! c'est la voix du bien-aimé . . . Alerte! alerte! . . . to the end of the Trio

NOTES: EJS 265

Labeled as "Act I / Act II, Part One" on side 1 and "Act II, Concluded / Acts III, IV & V" on side 2. The listing above shows the correct division of the excerpts.

EJS 265 was transferred a half-step below score pitch at 33.3 rpm (the Act II excerpt, I/2, slightly lower). Jobin's "Salut! demeure" (and the preceding recitative) were transposed down a half step in the actual performance.

This performance was later issued complete as Magnificent Editions ME 104-3 and as AS CD 1104/5. Two Thomas excerpts from the performance were included on EJS 531 (December, 1970).

Side 2 (265 B):

Band 1: The duet is nearly complete: "Tu veux . . . Tu me brises le coeur!" was cut in the actual performance, resuming at "partez Hélas! j'ai peur."

Band 2b: The "Death of Valentin" is complete, but the last choral and orchestral measures of Act IV were omitted from EJS 265.

EJS 266: "The Golden Age of Opera" (1 LP)
Issued April, 1963

CARMEN (Bizet) (F)
Opera in 4 Acts (excerpts: Act II only)
San Francisco Opera House Orchestra and Chorus/Gaetano Merola
San Francisco Opera broadcast, KPO [NBC], San Francisco, 2 Nov 1940

CAST:
Marjorie Lawrence (*Carmen*); Raoul Jobin (*Don José*); Ezio Pinza (*Escamillo*); [Verna Osborne (*Micaela*)]; Lorenzo Alvary (*Zuniga*); George Cehanovsky (*Dancaïre*); Alessio DePaolis (*Remendado*); Thelma Votipka (*Frasquita*); Alice Avakian (*Mercédès*).

SIDES 1-2 (266 A-B)

1. LAWRENCE, JOBIN, PINZA, ALVARY, CEHANOVSKY, DE PAOLIS, VOTIPKA, AVAKIAN, and Chorus: Act II (complete)

NOTES: EJS 266

Only Act II was broadcast. The first few notes of the Prelude are missing, ostensibly because they were obscured by the announcement preceding the music. The NBC line-checks were the source of this issue. Network acetetates of the third act of a 25 April, 1940 St. Louis Grand Opera CARMEN with Lawrence and Kiepura also survive.

EJS 267: "The Golden Age of Opera" (1 LP)
Issued April, 1963

SIDE 1 (267 A): "PURPORTED MAPLESON CYLINDERS (1888-1904)"

This first side of EJS 267, "Purported Mapleson Cylinders (1888-1904)," is perhaps Smith's most notorious issue. Beyond all of the "creative" editing, the clandestine inserts within live performances, and the litany of miscellaneous errors that will always be summoned against him, these Mapleson fakes are probably his least forgivable prank or, as has often been suggested by those who knew him best, his most naive undertaking. Only the legendary FAUST "Salve dimora" labeled as sung by "Jean De Reszke (OR SOME OTHER TENOR)" on EJS 452 (December, 1968)--in reality a 1904 Milanese Columbia sung by tenor Angelo Santini--seems as outrageous in retrospect.

The April, 1963 bulletin describes EJS 267 as a "highly controversial disc," containing "what purports to be fourteen excerpts from Mapleson cylinders not yet published . . . We accepted the tape copy of the Mapleson cylinders and felt they should be published immediately." Philip R. Miller and Dr. A. F. R. Lawrence are mentioned as two "prominent and well-known collector-musicians" who pronounced them outright forgeries. Smith then offers his own indictment of the cylinders:

> " . . . in no instance at the end of solos is there any applause as would be certain to have occurred; that many solos allegedly from performances have concert endings which are clipped short of the final notes so concluding chords are not heard; that the orchestras are invariably of acoustic quality rather than the fuller sound of performance cylinders published before - that no record of these cylinders has ever existed in the Mapleson file; that some of the singers seem to be personalities we all know and that those we don't know are always more clear than singers who should be identifiable. Lastly, the surface noise and blasts seem to be mechanically produced by modern methods of juggling volume controls. This evidence is damning and would seem to condemn the discs (sic) beyond redemption, yet the specter of doubt does remain and because of the importance of the cylinders should they be authentic, we are publishing them somewhat reluctantly but with this warning: that they may be - and probably are faked."

If these observations were not enough to create suspicion, the subtitle of the LP, "(1888-1904)," should have been, as none of the artists said to be included were singing at the Met as early as 1888: the two earliest, Eames and De Reszke, both made their Met debuts in 1891. And of course no known vocal Mapleson have been authenticated as having been made at the Met after January-February, 1904 (or as early as 1888, though the latter may be a misplaced reference to side 2).

Smith himself was not responsible for engineering these forgeries, but his motives for issuing them will always be debated. It doesn't seem likely that he was driven either by the thought of potential profit or a sense of satire; possibly he was simply taken in himself, intoxicated--as anyone might be--by the splendid possibility of so many hitherto-unknown Mapleson cylinders being discovered and published for the first time in 1963. In an April, 1963 letter he boasted of having tapes of "Caruso's debut on Mapleson cylinders with bits of the La donna è mobile & the Quartet--all faked--but done so expertly as to *defy detection*" (emphasis mine). That he was aware OF THIS from the outset makes him ultimately responsible for them.

In discussing the proper way to document this issue with those closest to the project, it was decided to list the contents as given on the label and to make no attempt to solve the riddles of identification, though in fact, the sources of most were quickly discovered. Most were taken from scarce commercial recordings of the artists named (Eames and Reiss, for example), while others (De Reszke, Ternina, etc.) were pure folly from unrelated sources. The dubbings are appalling, as they were perhaps meant to be--a coupling of fake surface noise (effected by placing a stylus in the locked running groove of a shellac disc, hence the pronounced periodicity of the scratch, rumble, and clicks), Mapleson-like breaks in the continuity, and deliberately obscure transfers, so that no real discographical service is rendered in identifying the sources. Indeed, would it be necessary in a Schumann-Heink or Witherspoon discography to devote more than a footnote to the fact that a disfigured fragment of their 30 July, 1907 Victor recording of "Weiche, Wotan" (matrix C-4732-1, issued as Victor 88092 and G&T 043090) appears on EJS 267, labeled as a "Schumann-Heink & Van Rooy" Mapleson cylinder? And wouldn't Van Rooy be better served by a simple and unequivocal assurance that he simply had nothing whatsoever to do with this "live" RHEINGOLD fragment?

Following are the contents of the side as given on the label of EJS 267, corrected and annotated to show full titles and names:

1. IL TROVATORE: Miserere: [Lillian] Nordica & [Emilio] De Marchi
IL TROVATORE: Di quella pira: [Georg] Anthes
IL TROVATORE: Abbietta zingara: [Marcel] Journet
MEFISTOFELE: Ave Signor: [Pol] Plançon

2. SIEGFRIED: Forging Song: J.[ean] De Reszke
ROMÉO ET JULIETTE: Valse: [Emma] Eames
TRISTAN UND ISOLDE: Liebestod: [Milka] Ternina
DER FLIEGENDE HOLLÄNDER: Ballad: [Johanna] Gadski

3. LA BOHÈME: Che gelida manina: [Albert] Saléza
FAUST: Jewel Song: [Lillian] Nordica
SIEGFRIED: Zwangvolle: [Albert] Reiss

4. TOSCA: Act I (sic): [Milka] Ternina & [Giuseppe] Cremonini
TANNHÄUSER: Dich teure: [Milka] Ternina
DAS RHEINGOLD: Weiche: [Ernestine] Schumann-Heink & [Anton] Van Rooy

None of the above are authentic, and only a handful of the singers cited on the label appear on the disc from any source.

SIDE 2 (267 B): "GREAT PERSONALITIES"

Band 1:

* a) FREDERICK ARTHUR STANLEY, BARON OF PRESTON (1841-1908): Speech at the Toronto Industrial Exhibition: "[Mr. President] and Gentlemen . . . We bid you a very hearty welcome" (E)
Toronto, 11 Sep 1888 Unnumbered [Edison] cylinder

* b) ALFRED LORD TENNYSON (1809-1892): THE CHARGE OF THE LIGHT BRIGADE, II: "Theirs not to make reply . . . Noble six hundred!" (Tennyson) (E)
?Farringford, Isle of Wight, 15 May 1890 Unnumbered [Edison] cylinder

* c) SARAH BERNHARDT (1844-1923): La Prière pour nos enemies (Louis Payen) (F)
mtx unknown New York, ?January, 1918 Aeolian Vocalion B22035

* d) COUNT LEV TOLSTOY (1828-1910): "Thoughts from the book FOR EVERY DAY" ["Qu'est-ce que la religion"] (Tolstoy) (F)
6877r Vásnaya Polyána, ?16/29 Oct or ?18/31 Oct 1909
Gramophone 31329 Symposium 1029

Band 2:

* a) SIR ARTHUR SULLIVAN (1842-1900): Speech of praise addressed to Thomas Edison: "Dear Mr. Edison . . . For myself, I can only say . . . Arthur Sullivan" (E)
Little Menlo, London, 5 Oct 1888 Unnumbered [Edison] cylinder

* b) ROBERT BROWNING (1812-1889): HOW THEY BROUGHT THE GOOD NEWS FROM GHENT TO AIX: "I sprang to the stirrup, and Joris, and he; I galloped, Dirck galloped, we galloped all three" (Browning) (E)
Little Menlo, London, 1888 or 1889 Unnumbered [Edison] cylinder

* c) EDWIN BOOTH (1833-1893): OTHELLO, I/iii: [after "Most potent, grave, and reverend signiors]: "She wished she had not heard it . . . And I loved her that she did pity them (Shakespeare) (E)
New York, ?March, 1890 Unnumbered ?private cylinder

* d) OSCAR WILDE (1854-1900): THE BALLAD OF READING GAOL, VI: "In Reading Gaol by Reading town . . . By all let this be heard" (Wilde) (E)
Source and date unknown

Band 3:

* a) TOMMASO SALVINI (1829-1916): SAUL, II/i: David? Io l'odio . . . ch'io già vaneggio!" ["Il sogno di Saul"] (Vittorio Alfieri) (I)
X-1559 Milan, ?20 Apr 1903 Disco Zonofono X-1559

* b) SIR HENRY IRVING (1838-1905): RICHARD III, I/i: Now is the winter of our discontent . . . He capers nimbly in a lady's chamber (Shakespeare) (E)
?Surrey, 9 May 1898 Unnumbered [private] cylinder

* c) GIANNI VIAFORA (?-?), GIACOMO PUCCINI (1858-1924), ELVIRA PUCCINI (1861-1934), and possibly GINA CIAPARELLI-VIAFORA (1881-1936): Staged address (I)
M-1420-1 New York, ?24 Feb 1907 Unnumbered B&S Columbia

* d) WILLIAM SIDNEY PORTER [O. HENRY] (1862-1910): "This is William Sydney Porter speaking, [eh] better known to you, no doubt, as O. Henry . . . Goodbye, folks!" (E)
U.S., circa 1910 ?Private Edison cylinder

Band 4:

* a) WILLIAM EWART GLADSTONE (1809-1898): Speech: A Message of Thanks to Thomas A. Edison: "As to the future consequences . . . wonder upon wonders are opening before us" (?excerpt only) (E)
?Little Menlo, London, date unknown Unnumbered [Edison] cylinder

* b) P.[HINEAS] T.[HOMAS] BARNUM (1810-1891): "I wish to give my parting thanks to the British public . . . P. T. Barnum" (E)
London, 17 Feb 1890 Unnumbered Edison cylinder

* c) KENNETH LANDFREY (?-?): Speech and demonstration of the bugle sounded at Waterloo and by him at Balaclava on 25 October, 1854: "I am trumpeter Landfrey" . . . bugle solo (E)
Edison House, North Cumberland Avenue, London, 2 Aug 1890
Unnumbered [Edison] cylinder

* d) FLORENCE NIGHTINGALE (1820-1910): "God bless my dear old comrades of Balaclava . . . Florence Nightingale" (E)
"Florence Nightingale's House," London, 30 Jul 1890
Unnumbered [Edison] cylinder

Band 5:

* a) RUDYARD KIPLING (1865-1936): [Speech to Canadian Authors]: "We know that when all the men who do things have done them . . . it is only words--nothing but words--that live to show the present how men worked and thought in the past" (E)
?Broadcast, Royal Society of St. George, BBC, London, 6 May 1935

* b) KAISER WILHELM [Friedrich Wilhelm Viktor Albert, Wilhelm II] (1859-1941): Address on "Die deutschen Volk" (G)
Source and date unknown

* c) DAME ELLEN TERRY (1847-1928): THE MERCHANT OF VENICE, IV/i: "The Quality of mercy is not strain'd . . . And that same prayer doth teach us all to render the deeds of mercy" (Shakespeare) (E)
B-9988-3 New York, 28 Feb 1911 Victor 64194 HMV 2-3535

* d) SIR HERBERT BEERBOHM TREE (1853-1917): TRILBY, Act I: Ach! Wunderschön! . . . And you shall see nothing, hear nothing, think nothing but Svengali, Svengali, Svengali! ["Svengali Mesmerizes Trilby"] (Du Maurier-Paul M. Potter) (E)
3751e London, early March, 1906 G&T 1313 HMV E162

Band 6:

* a) NIKOLAI LENIN (1870-1924): Speech (excerpt only) (R)
[N56-48] Moscow, 1919 USSR 56-48 (in set 5289-50)

* b) JOSEPH STALIN (1879-1953): Speech (excerpt) (R)
Broadcast, Red Square, Moscow, 7 Nov 1941

* c) MAHATMA GANDHI (1869-1948): from HIS SPIRITUAL MESSAGE: "There is an indefinable, mysterious power that pervades everything . . . and yet, defies all proof" (Gandhi) (E)
WA-12082-1 London, 17 October, 1931 Columbia LB-67; 17523-D

* d) ALBERT EINSTEIN (1879-1955): "We should strive not to use violence in fighting for our cause, but by non-participation in anything you believe is evil." (E)
?Broadcast or telecast, date unknown

NOTES: EJS 267

Side 2 (267 B):

Many of these important spoken-word items have appeared elsewhere, often in better sound and complete, but a detailed analysis of the items included on EJS 267 was nonetheless warranted. Note that the same selections were reissued more or less intact as the second side of UORC 323 in January-February, 1977 (the Browning cylinder was further truncated there), this time coupled with genuine Bettini, Edison, Pathé, and Mapleson cylinders.

A majority of these personality items appeared on at least three earlier LPs that may well have been among Smith's sources for EJS 267 and UORC 323. The first, issued in 1951, was "Hark! The Years" (Capitol Records S-282, reissued in 1965 as T-2334), which contains the same excerpts of Lenin, Gandhi, Einstein, Landfrey, and Florence Nightingale. The second was the two-volume set "History Speaks," originally issued on the Gotham label in the 1950s (matrices 933 A-B and 934 A-B) and reissued by the Voices of the Past Recording Society of New York: this contained the excerpts of Browning, Landfrey, Stanley, Nightingale, Barnum, Sullivan, O. Henry, and Terry on Volume I, and Tennyson, Tolstoy, Kipling, and Gladstone on Volume II, albeit with the constant interruption of narrator James Harbur. The third was "The Voices of the 20th Century" (Coral CRL 57308), also from the mid 1950s, written and produced by Bud Greenspan and narrated by Henry Fonda: included were Landfrey, Nightingale, a Booth excerpt, Barnum, Kipling, Einstein, and Gandhi. The Capitol LP was compiled under the auspices of G. Robert Vincent, while the Gotham set, engineered by Walter L. Welch, co-author of the monumental *From Tin Foil to Stereo* (Indianapolis: Sams, 1959/1976), was issued out of the Edison Foundation Re-recording Laboratory at Syracuse University. Rococo 4002, "Authors and Actors" (1972), includes better dubbings of the O. Henry, Kipling, Irving, Terry, Booth, Beerbohm-Tree, Bernhardt, and Salvini items, while Argo SW 510, "Great Actors of the Past" (1977), compiled by actor Richard Bebb, contains fine dubbings of the Terry, Beerbohm-Tree, Booth, Irving, and Salvini recordings. These LPs and others will be cited frequently below and are highly recommended for comparison.

Band 1:

Item a) Complete here as recorded. Note that this is a recording of **Frederick Arthur Stanley, Baron of Preston** (of Stanley Cup fame) and not, as is so often stated, explorer Sir Henry Morton Stanley (1841-1904). The label of EJS 267 cites "Lord Stanley," correctly designating Frederick Arthur Stanley, who was created Baron of Preston in 1886 and was, at the time of this recording, the Governor General of Canada--hence his presence at the 1888 Toronto Industrial Exhibition.

Until recently this cylinder was thought to be the oldest extant sound recording, but in fact a number of cylinders, some assumed to have been recorded as early as mid 1888, have since been unearthed at the Edison Site in West Orange, New Jersey.

Item b): The Tennyson cylinders are documented in "The Tennyson Phonograph Records," written for the *BIRS Bulletin* (no. 3, Winter, 1956, pp. 2-8) by the poet's great-grandson, Sir Charles Tennyson.

There, a provisional date and place of recording (15 May, 1890 at Farringford, Tennyson's residence) is established for at least some of the recitations by means of a family diary entry for that date, though it could not be determined whether this was written by the poet's wife or by his eldest son, Hallam. A similar entry describing Tennyson's adventures with the Edison cylinder machine sent to him by Col. Gouraud, also entered on 15 May 1890, was found in the diary of Tennyson's daughter.

Two groups of Tennyson recitations are documented in Sir Charles' article: twenty-three *original* "soft wax" and twelve "hard black wax" cylinders. Four of the "soft wax" recordings contain portions of "The Charge of the Light Brigade," but the extent of each fragment is not specified. Of these, Sir Charles assesses the sound quality of one as "very good," another as "good in parts," and the remaining two as "unintelligible." The "hard black wax" cylinders, described as having been "pressed from a set of copper matrices," were prepared in about 1921, according to Sir Charles, molded directly from what was probably another group of (lost) soft-wax cylinders, date unknown (indeed, considering that the twenty-three *original* "soft wax" cylinders with a provisional recording date of May, 1890 remained in playable condition as late as 1956, it hardly seems possible that molds could have been taken from them without doing irreparable damage).

HMV dubbed a "Light Brigade" fragment in the Transfer Room at Hayes in late 1934 (matrix 0EA-275-1), but the source of this copy is unclear: Sir Charles speculates that the HMV disc matrix was probably made from the same group of "hard black wax" cylinders that included a "Light Brigade" fragment dubbed by the BBC (BBC Library No. 22133), but says nothing about whether BBC Library No. 22133 and the HMV transfers actually contain the same reading (another BBC transfer--Recorded Programmes Permanent Library No. 18941--is listed explicitly as having been taken from 0EA-275-1). He does suggest, however, that BBC No. 22133 and HMV 0EA-275-1 were taken from a different group of *original* Tennyson recordings, that is, not from the twenty-three "soft wax" cylinders thought to have been recorded at Farringford on or about 15 May, 1890.

0EA-275-1, which includes stanzas 2-5 of "Light Brigade," was probably the source used for the EJS issues and other LPs, for whatever its origin, it would have been the most accessible form of the recording and thus the most likely to have been copied. Judging from Sir Charles' description of the 0EA-275-1 dubbing, the EJS 267 transfer is apparently complete as recorded or retrieved.

A splendid MAUDE fragment (Part I: XXII/xi) from Sir Charles' inventory of the "soft wax" group has also appeared on LP, notably on a BBC potpourri of Tennyson works read by others issued in 1972 as CMS/BBC 639.

Unless the rumored cylinder by Cardinal Henry Edward Manning (b. 15 July, 1808) ever turns up, Tennyson (b. 6 August, 1809) appears to have been--by birthdate, not his age at the time--the oldest person whose voice has survived on record, followed in close succession by William Ewart Gladstone (b. 29 December, 1809), Pope Leo XIII [née Vincenzo Gioacchino Pecci] (b. 2 March, 1810), Phineas T. Barnum (b. 5 July, 1810), and poet Robert Browning (b. 7 May, 1812).

Item c): Incomplete on EJS 267. Reissued complete and in considerably better sound on ANNA 1044 (Fall, 1979), a Bernhardt/Coquelin collection compiled for Smith by Richard Bebb. Three original copies of this vertically-cut Vocalion disc have been examined by a reliable source who reports that none bore visible matrix numbers.

Item d): Complete as recorded. Symposium Records has reissued the complete Tolstoy Gramophone recordings as pressings on three twelve-inch vinyl discs, the last being single-sided:

French version:	6877r	Gram 31329	Symposium 1029A (10-inch)
English version:	6878r	Gram 1412	Symposium 1029B (10-inch)
Russian version:	6879r	Gram 21407	Symposium 1030A (10-inch)
German version:	6880r	Gram 2-41114	Symposium 1030B (10-inch)
Russian version:	411s	Gram 021000	Symposium 1056 (12-inch)

The date given on these reissues is 18/31 October, 1909 (slashed to designate Julian versus Roman dates), but Tolstoy's diaries, edited and translated by R. F. Christian (TOLSTOY'S DIARIES, 2 vols, Cambridge: Cambridge University Press/New York: Scribner's Sons, 1985, Volume II: 1895-1910) contain the following entry:

> [...] 16 October [1909] [S. T.] Semyonov came, and he persuaded me [Tolstoy] that I couldn't refuse the phonograph recording that I had promised. It was very unpleasant for me. I had to agree.
>
> . . . In the evening six people came [to Vásnaya Polyána] with the gramophone and phonograph. It was very depressing. I couldn't refuse and I had to prepare something as best I could. [...]" (pp. 635-636).

No previous or subsequent references to the recordings appear in this edition of the diaries. What Tolstoy meant by the six people coming "with the gramophone and phonograph" is unclear, but Christian does provide a note stating that he "was regretting his promise to record his voice for the Society of Workers of the Periodical Press and Literature (sic), but was persuaded to keep it" (no. 211, p. 729). The connection between the Russian branch of the Gramophone Company and what appears to have been the sponsor of the Tolstoy recordings, the "Society of Workers of the Periodical Press and Literature" is alluded to in a MOLVA article reprinted in the notes accompanying the Symposium reissue:

> "Yesterday Messrs I. A. Bieloussoff and I. I. Mitropolsky, members of the Society of Literature and the Periodical Press (sic), Mr. A. G. Micheles (sic), manager of the Gramophone Company Limited, the engineer Max Hampe and the photographer N. S. Nikolsky (of Otto Renard's), returned from an interesting visit to Yassnaia Poliana (sic), in connection with the recording of the voice of Count Leo Tolstoy on gramophone discs . . . the records will be published by the Gramophone Company, with the consent of Count Tolstoy, for the profit of the Society of Literature and the Periodical Press."

I found no reference outside of the diaries to Tolstoy's friend, S. T. Semyonov, a peasant writer, or his role in persuading Tolstoy to make the recordings.

For the listing, I have given the date in Tolstoy's diary entry, 16 October, 1909 (Julian), as well as the dates given in the Symposium notes (18/31 October, 1909). Alan Kelly (*His Master's Voice/La Voix de son Maître*, Westport, CT: Greenwood Press, 1990), p. 65, gives 31 October, 1909. It should be mentioned, however, that Tolstoy's diaries are not an entirely reliable source of dates and other details. He often reveals himself to have been confused about when events actually occurred and was rarely able to distinguish one day of the week from the next in retrospect. Indeed, phrases in the vein of "yesterday or the day before, I cannot remember" are quite common throughout.

As to the work being read, the MOLVA article mentions that "Having expressed some thoughts about the use of the gramophone for schools, Tolstoy made with his own hand some notes in his *Thoughts for Every Day*, which he advised Mr. Micheles (sic) to make use of for recording purposes." Neither the recorded excerpts read by Tolstoy or these *Thoughts for Every Day* could be found among his *oeuvre*, though "notes in his Thoughts for Every Day" may simply imply spontaneous observations scribbled into a diary.

Band 2:

Item a) Complete as recorded. The authenticity of this Sullivan recording has been disputed for years. The announcement begins "Little Menlo, October the 5th, 1888. Now listen to the voice of Sir Arthur Sullivan," at which point Sullivan enters, closing his address by expressing his fear that "so much hideous (and) bad music may be put on record forever." Sullivan's speech, without the opening announcement, has been transferred well on Pearl's 1984 two-LP set "The Art of the Savoyard Volume II" (GEMM 282/3).

Item b) Incomplete. The original announcement by Col. Gouraud ("My dear Edison! My dear Edison! . . . Robert Browning. Now listen to his voice") that precedes Browning's brief recitation has been omitted from EJS 263, but has turned up on other LPs. The poet recites two lines of "How they brought the good news from Ghent to Aix" (substituting "saddle" for "stirrip" and "with Joris" for "and Joris") and stumbles through the next three ("Behind shut the postern . . . the lights sank to rest") before stopping to tell his audience, "I'm terribly sorry, but I can't remember *me* own poem . . . [undecipherable] . . . Robert Browning." At this point on the original cylinder, those present join in a rousing finale ("Bravo! Bravo! Bravo! Hip Hip Hurrah! Hip Hip! Hurrah! Hip Hip! Hurrah! Bravo" . . . [applause]) that has been omitted here.

Item c): Incomplete. Recently included complete (begining at "Most potent, grave, and reverend signiors") on the 1990 Pearl CD "The Great Shakespearians" (GEMM CD 9465), where it has been transferred from another LP--probably Argo's "Great Actors of the Past," which included the complete recording. A Booth HAMLET "To be, or not to be," presumably from the same date, has also been reported, but no reissue information has been confirmed.

Item d): Source and date unknown. This "Oscar Wilde" cylinder has always been disputed, if only because it so strongly conforms to certain misguided expectations engendered by Wilde's alleged homosexuality. Moreover, the "clicky" surface noise that we hear on the EJS 267 dubbing sounds quite unconvincing. The excerpt as presented here may be complete (I've not heard another dubbing), though the last four lines of verse VI are for some reason omitted. The announcement, presumably by Wilde, is "The Ballad of Reading Gaol, Verse Six."

Richard Ellmann's superb Wilde biography, *Oscar Wilde* (New York: Knopf, 1988), gives several contemporary accounts of Wilde's speaking voice and manner of speaking. Author Max Beerbohm described it as "a mezzo voice, uttering itself in leisurely fashion, with every variety of tone" (p. 38), while actress Lillie Langtry found it "one of the most alluring voices that I have ever listened to, round and soft, and full of variety and expression" (p. 111). Helen Potter, an American who later impersonated Wilde in public performance, recalled that his voice was "clear, easy, not forced." (p. 164). Poet Walt Whitman disparaged his "English society drawl," but defended his enunciation as "better than I ever heard in a young Englishman or Irishman before" (p. 170) and actor Sir Seymour Hicks further testified that there was no trace of an Irish accent in his delivery (p. 38). Whether any of these descriptions conform to what we hear in the cylinder is a matter of opinion. For those interested in pursuing this further, Ellmann's biography (pp. 629-630) also reproduces an analysis of Wilde's speaking voice taken from Helen Potter's book *Impersonations* (New York: Edgar S. Werner, 1891). Potter used Wilde's study "Lecture on Art" as a vehicle for this analysis, carefully transcribing accents and pauses in precise phonetic notation.

Band 3:

Item a): SAUL, one of Vittorio Alfieri's (1749-1803) best-known dramas, was completed in 1782, and bears a dedication date of October, 1784. The performance is announced as "Il sogno di Saul," apparently by Salvini himself, and is given here complete as recorded.

Apart from some apparent recordings for Bettini, Salvini left only three commercial discs, all issued on the light-blue Disco Zonofono label. The date assigned in the listing is derived from the seven Caruso sides that immediately preceded Salvini's. All but X-1547, X-1562, and X-1565 are accounted for immediately before and after the three Salvini discs, as follows, so it is unlikely that there were other Salvini Zonophones:

X-1540: A. GARULLI
X-1541: E. BENDAZZI-GARULLI
X-1542 to 1546: A. GARULLI
X-1547: ?
X-1548 to X-1549: A. GARULLI
X-1550 to X-1556: CARUSO [19 April, 1903]
X-1557: SALVINI: OTHELLO, (?) IV/iii
X-1558: SALVINI: HAMLET, III/i: "Essere o non essere"
X-1559: SALVINI: SAUL, II/i: "Il sogno di Saul"
X-1560: SIGNORINA FRANCESCATTI ("Bambina di anni 8"): "Variazioni de Prock"
X-1561: DE NEGRI
X-1562: ?
X-1563 to X-1564: DE NEGRI . . . etc.
X-1565: ?
X-1566: DE NEGRI

Item b): Incomplete. The original recording goes as far as "Why, I, in this weak piping time of peace." This, and an excerpt from Act IV/ii of Tennyson's BECKET, occupy a private cylinder apparently made during one of Irving's visits to Sir Henry Morton Stanley and Lady Stanley at their home in Surrey. The BECKET excerpt closes with the announcement "Henry Irving, 9 May 1898." See Richard Bebb's articles "The Actor Then and Now" in *Recorded Sound*, 47 (July, 1972), pp. 85-93, and 48 (October, 1972), pp. 115-124; and "The Voice of Henry Irving: An Investigation," in *Recorded Sound*, 68 (October, 1977), pp. 727-32. Mr. Bebb has long contemplated the authenticity of the Irving recordings, his vivid analyses based on their provenance and style, specifically, Irving's pronunciation of the English language, the quality of his voice and its production, and the alleged "strangeness" of his vowel sounds--all issues that figured prominently in contemporary assessments of him. What emerges, especially in Bebb's BBC presentation, "The Voice of Henry Irving: An Investigation" (Radio 3, 23 October 1975, revised broadcast 18 June, 1977), is a model for the effective analysis of historical spoken word performances. Bebb concluded that at least four (probably five) of the known Irving cylinders, including the RICHARD III excerpt, appear to be genuine. Along with an excerpt from HENRY VIII, the RICHARD III appears--with the dated announcement intact--on the ARGO "Great Actors of the Past," compiled by Mr. Bebb.

Item c) Complete as recorded. Announced as recorded by the "Columbia Phonograph Company, New York" by Puccini's friend, Gianni Viafora, who appears to occupy the lion's share of the disc. Maestro Puccini's is the second voice heard (he closes by exclaiming "America forever!"), followed by Elvira Puccini's. Cries of "evviva!" punctuate throughout.

Viafora was a well-known illustrator and caricaturist (a collection of his drawings entitled *Caricature* was published in 1919 by Brentano's in New York). I've been told, but cannot substantiate, that he held some position with Columbia at the time: indeed he appears to announce himself in the recording as a representative of the Company.

Smith received this item from a well-known British collector who claimed that it was a "Message from the composer and his wife on the occasion of their leaving the U.S.A. Feb. 21 1907 / Columbia Silver and Black Label. No Number" (sic). The letter that accompanied the original 5-inch open-reel tape used for the LP reads: "Dear Eddie,---Here it is at last! . . . The first part is spoken by Gianni Diapora (sic), then Puccini, then Elvira. Isn't it marvelous that he uses the words from BUTTERFLY!" (meaning only "America forever!" from the Act I *Sharpless-Pinkerton* duet). The tape, however, is *not* a dubbing of the original disc: on both transfers included, the sound of a stylus being placed on a slow-moving vinyl record and the second "layer" of surface noise are unmistakable. Nor is the black and silver Columbia original numberless--Smith's supplier may have never seen the original disc. Christopher Sullivan of Norwich was able to contact the BBC in 1987 to see if they knew of an original pressing of the recording. Through the kindness of Mr. Derek Lewis, BBC's archivist, Mr. Sullivan discovered that a copy was indeed held by the BBC--a standard black and silver "test" or "promotional" label without artist or title, bearing only the matrix number "M-1420-1." This number, according to Columbia researcher William R. Bryant of Portland, Maine, falls between xylophonist Thomas Mills' "Dixie Blossoms" (M-1419) on Columbia 3628, and Will F. Denny's rendition of Dave Reed's "My Word! What a Lot of It" (M-1421) on Columbia 3638, both issued in June, 1907. The occasion of Puccini's 1906-1907 visit to America was a six-week, four-opera tribute sponsored by the Metropolitan Opera to accompany the American premieres of MANON LESCAUT on 18 January, and MADAMA BUTTERFLY on 11 February, 1907. The recording itself sounds suspiciously similar to Columbia's other staged "descriptive" spoken-word specialties from this period, but its authenticity seems never to have been questioned.

Item d): Complete as recorded. Also disputed, date and source unknown. Porter talks briefly about his "secret" of writing the sort of "drawn-from-life" fiction that, along with his surprise endings, have immortalized him. The speaker's southern drawl is pronounced (he was born in Greensboro, North Carolina) and his manner is as relaxed and natural as can be imagined. Indeed, if this ca. 1910 cylinder is authentic, it may be the most extraordinarily unaffected, relaxed address ever given on a pre-World War I recording, which is among the reasons its authenticity has so often been questioned. But then, considering the many other more inviting possibilities, why would anyone go to such lengths to fake an O. Henry cylinder? Then again, I'm told that a recently-denounced Walt Whitman cylinder came from the same batch that included the Wilde and O'Henry recordings.

The same recording also appeared on the Gotham LP as well as on Rococo 4002, where it is identified by Canadian historian J. B. McPherson as having been transcribed from an original Edison cylinder.

Band 4:

Item a) Incomplete. The EJS 267 dubbing lasts only seconds: "As to the future consequences, it is impossible to anticipate them. All I see is that wonder upon wonders are opening before us." Some have speculated that Gladstone was referring here to Edison's Phonograph. Smith's source was probably the second volume of the Gotham set, where the same brief recording appears in considerably better sound.

Another Gladstone recording, well transfered on Argo's 1970 LP set "The Wonder of the Age: Mr. Edison's New Talking Phonograph" (ZPR 122/3) was dubbed from a 1936 U.K. Decca transfer, matrix OC-249-1. It begins "The request that you have done me the honor to make, to receive the record of my voice" and ends with Gladstone giving his name. The two sentences heard on EJS 267 and the Gotham LP are nowhere to be found in the Argo transfer. However, the authenticity of the cylinder dubbed on Argo, given as recorded in London on 22 November, 1888 and sent to the U.S., has been disputed with the claim that Gladstone, reluctant to record himself, sent a representative to do so in his place. Whether or not the Gladstone message on EJS and Gotham is authentic (it is certainly a different recording of a different voice than the one on the Argo LP) has not been determined as far as I know, nor has the date of the recording.

In the U.S., one of the Gladstone recordings was issued in about 1940 as National Vocarium TNV-125 (matrix CS-046635-1).

Item b) Complete as recorded. While it is generally documented as having been recorded in the U.S., the circa 1941 National Vocarium TNV-133 dubbing (matrix CS-047312-1), containing introductory remarks by renowned educator William Lyon Phelps, gives the place and date of recording as London, 17 February, 1890, at a banquet in Barnum's honor given by Sir Henry Irving. Certainly, Barnum's remarks sound as if his departure from England was imminent, not behind him.

Item c) Complete as recorded. To date, no one has been able to identify Trumpeter Landfrey or to verify that a) such a person ever existed, b) he was a trumpeter at Balaclava if he did, or that c) this recording is authentic as announced. In a letter to *The Historic Record* (25, October, 1992, p. 7), Joe Pengelly of Plymouth claimed that there is evidence that "Landfrey . . . would travel round the pubs offering to blow his bugle for the price of a pint," and contends that the bugler may be buried in Brighton. No evidence of either claim is provided, however. The cylinder begins with Landfrey speaking: "I am trumpeter Landfrey, one of the surviving trumpeters of the charge of the Light Brigade at Balaclava . . ." He then describes the bugle that we are about to hear as the one used at at Waterloo (reportedly by J. Edwards, Field Trumpeter to Lord Edward Somerset, Commander of the Household Troops, to sound the charge of the 1st Life Guards) and, by him, at Balaclava. A woman's voice, possibly the same which announces the Florence Nightingale cylinder (4d), then announces: "Recorded at Edison House, North Cumberland Avenue, London, August 2nd, 1890," at which point Landfrey gives forth a ferocious (and exceptionally well-recorded) charge on the bugle.

Issued on shellac in about 1939 as National Vocarium RV-22 (matrix CS-043155-1), with a spoken introduction by Robert L. ("Believe it or Not") Ripley.

Item d) Incomplete. The *original* Florence Nightingale cylinder begins with a female voice announcing: "At Florence Nightingale's house, London, July the 30th, 1890." Nightingale then enters: "When I am no longer even a memory, just a name, I hope my voice may perpetuate the great work of my life. God bless my dear old comrades of Balaclava, and bring them safe to shore. Florence Nightingale." This is severely truncated on EJS 267. See also the note for Landfrey (4c) above. A third cylinder featuring other survivors of Balaclava is also rumored to have been made in an appeal for funds.

A transfer matrix of this cylinder was made (by Decca?) in 1934, numbered TEBN-7, and may have been the version prepared for the British Empire Cancer Campaign, later announced for sale in the U.S. by IRCC in September, 1936. It was also issued on shellac in the U.S. in 1939 as red-label National Vocarium CS-041359-1 (dubbed September, 1939: BS-041358 and BS-041360 are dated 27 August and 27 September, 1939, respectively). A copy at Yale University (white label, typed), distributed by IRCC and obviously a later dubbing, bears the matrix number LCS-047309-1, and the catalog number TNV-130.

Band 5:

Item a) Incomplete. The Kipling has been only provisionally identified. It seems almost certain to be electrical, and may have come from a 6 May, 1935 Royal Society of St. George BBC broadcast that is known to have survived (the Library of Congress has a 6-minute shortwave transcription of it, catalogued as tape 6312-38). The liner notes for Rococo 4002, where a lengthier excerpt from the same speech is included, say only that it is "a transcription from a late broadcast." The dubbing on the Gotham LP is identical to that on EJS 267 and may well have been Smith's immediate source.

Item b) Probably incomplete, but no other dubbing of it has turned up for comparison. It is suggested by Bescoby-Chambers (ibid, p. 120), that this may be a private recording made after the First World War when the Kaiser was in exile in Holland. I have not been able to identify it beyond that. The only other Wilhelm II recording I've encountered appeared in a German Ariola LP set (71 096 KW) entitled "Deutschlands Weg in die Diktatur Originalaufnahmen aus Jahren von 1914 bis 1939: Der Erste Weltkrieg, 1914-1918." A transcription of the 4 August, 1914 speech given there (which seems to have been recorded two days later) does not match the excerpt heard on EJS 267.

Item c) Dubbed complete on EJS 267. *Portia's* final lines of the "Mercy Speech" ("I have spoke thus much . . . Must needs give sentence 'gainst the merchant there") were omitted from the original recording. HMV 2-3535 was a single-sided (only) HMV "Catalog No. 2" issue.

Item d): Complete as recorded. TRILBY, based on the 1894 novel by George Louis Palmella Busson Du Maurier and dramatized in four acts by Paul Meredith Potter (1853-1921), a journalist-turned-dramatic critic-turned playwright, was apparently never published, and was performed from a prompt script. The latter, which carries two short scenes in the first and second acts interpolated by Tree himself (as sanctioned by Du Maurier) and written in his own hand, is said to be all that has survived. Two German translations of the Potter adaptation by Emanuel Lederen *were* published, however, the first in Berlin, publisher unknown, the other by Reclam/Universal-Bibliothek in Leipzig (1897). The only modern English-language publication of Potter's dramatization appears in *The Golden Age of Melodrama: Twelve 19th Century Melodramas*, abridged and introduced by Michael Kilgarriff (London: Wolfe, 1974), which credits Samuel French Ltd. for the use of the afore-mentioned prompt script.

Tree first saw the play in Philadelphia while on tour in the U.S. and secured the British rights directly from Potter--over the strong objections of his half-brother, Max Beerbohm, who thought it "utter nonsense." Tree's inaugural production went up on 7 September, 1895 at the Theater Royal, Manchester, before its formal opening on 30 October at the Haymarket Theater, London, where it ran for more than six months. Though ill-received by critics, it enjoyed great success. William Archer's often-quoted review in *The Theatrical "World" of 1895* accused Tree of doing with *Svengali* "what comes easiest to him, luxuriating in obvious and violent gestures and grimaces, expending no more thought on the matter than is involved in the adroit use of his personal advantages" (p. 333). But there seems to have been little doubt that this was, in many respects, the actor's greatest public triumph. Indeed, the profits from TRILBY enabled him to hasten the completion of Her Majesty's Theater, London, where he would remain until 1917 as manager and leading player. Tree himself was quoted as having dismissed the entire TRILBY phenomenon as "hogwash."

Twenty-year-old Dorothea Baird (1875-1933) created a sensation as *Trilby*. She retired from the stage in 1913 after seventeen years as a member of Sir Henry Irving's company.

The actress heard on this record has never been identified and is not named on the original G&T, Gramophone, or subsequent red-and black-label HMV "Catalogue No. 2" issues. Tree's notoriety for tampering at will with the author's original text is nowhere in evidence in this remarkable excerpt, which follows the prompt script nearly word-for-word.

Band 6:

Item a) Incomplete. Louis Fischer, in his *The Life of Lenin* (New York: Harper & Row, 1964), pp. 511-512, notes that Lenin "inscribed eight records in 1919. All eleven (sic) original plates found a safe repository in the Education Commissariat." Fischer further claims that the records were made in the "gramophone-inscribing-studio in Moscow." The records included speeches on a proposed new tax system, the nature of "concessions," and cooperatives. Several of these 1919 sides were eventually dubbed on a group of six vinyl 78s, with Lenin on six sides and Stalin on the remaining five (the last being blank), issued on the USSR label in the late 1940s or early 1950s as red-label vinylite set 5289-50. The Lenin matrices are N-56-48, N-59-48, N-110-48, N-111-48, N-130-48, and N-163-48. The EJS 267 excerpt consists of the first part of side one, USSR 56-48 (matrix N56-48), with an added voice-over announcement in English and orchestral background music not found on the original recording. The announcer begins, "A speech of Lenin's on the Red Army has been safeguarded for posterity. Listen to the voice of Lenin." Lenin is then heard in the background, "translated" throughout. The original source of this *edited* version with the voice-over is not known, but it is most likely a fragment taken from a broadcast or newsreel made years after Lenin's death. In the brief portion of the speech presented on EJS 267, Lenin lashes out against the capitalists of England, America, and France, whom he felt were waging ideological and economic war against Russia.

This same fragment *with* voice-over turned up earlier on a 7-inch 33.3 rpm "Voices of the Past" disc (X-501) entitled "Stalin and Lenin," issued by Rare Records of New York City in the 1950s (matrix 7HLP 70), but begins abruptly with the announcer's "Listen to the voice of Lenin," so could not have been the source used for EJS 267. Smith does not date the Lenin excerpt; the Rare Records transfer claims incorrectly that it is the "only known recording of Lenin, 1921." Both the USSR 78s and Fischer's biography give the date 1919.

A commercial Pathé issue of Lenin's voice is also rumored.

Item b) The EJS 267 Stalin excerpt is without introduction or narration, but closes with the applause of a large crowd. The "Voices of the Past" LP X-501 mentioned above (Lenin) also contains the same excerpt, but with an added introduction ("You are listening to one of the rare recorded speeches of Marshal Stalin") and a translation in English by journalist Edward R. Murrow. In fact, the "Voices of the Past" issue "borrowed" the Stalin excerpt from the first volume of the Columbia Murrow LP "I Can Hear it Now, 1933-1945" (Columbia 4095), originally issued in 1949. The EJS 267 excerpt, while from the same speech, lacks Murrow's voice-over, so was obviously taken from a different source. Again, Smith makes no attempt to assign a date, where the "Voices of the Past" LP gives 1944. The Columbia LP correctly cites this as Stalin's famous 7 November, 1941 speech given to mark the 24th anniversary of the October Revolution. In his *A History of the USSR From Lenin To Khrushchev*, translated from the French by Patrick O'Brian (New York: David McKay, 1962/1964), p. 376, Louis Aragon gives an especially vivid description of the scene:

> "On the 7th [of November, 1941] the review took place in Red Square, which wore the face of deep winter; the soldiers were in their cold-weather clothing; tanks and infantry furrowed the snow. Budyenny, vice-commissar for defence, opened the parade. On leaving the square, the troops marched straight to their battle-positions."

Stalin's 7 November speech was reprinted in PRAVDA (XV, pp. 32-35) the next day. Note that the five Stalin recordings in the USSR set 5289-50 are all *1945* recordings.

Item c) Gandhi's "His Spiritual Message" was issued in two parts on Columbia LB-67 in the U.K. and on 17523-D in the U.S. The recording was made during his last tour of Britain. The second part, recorded at the same session, is matrix WA-12083-1. The excerpt on EJS 267 comprises the first three sentences of part one, probably taken from the Coral LP "The Voices of the 20th Century."

Item d) The Einstein excerpt has been severely truncated and decontextualized through deliberate editing, and was probably appropriated from the earlier Coral LP. There, as on EJS 267, we hear only: "We should strive not to use violence in fighting for our cause, but by non-participation in anything you believe is evil." What

Einstein actually said was: "I believe that Gandhi's views were the most enlightened of all the political men of our time. We should strive to do things in his spirit, not to use violence in fighting for our cause, but by non-participation in anything you believe is evil." The entire quote may be heard on the Capitol LP "Hark, the Years!" and on a ten-inch Heritage LP "Conquest by Love / The Voice and Teachings of Mahatma Gandhi" (HG-0050) issued in 1953, where it is buried in the second band of side 2.

The source and date of the quote are unknown. There are many similar printed and spoken endorsements of Gandhi by Einstein, who held the Indian leader in high esteem throughout his life. As Gandhi is referred to in the past tense in this particular statement, it was obviously spoken after 30 January, 1948 and was probably taken from a broadcast or perhaps a telecast. G. Robert Vincent is credited as the source compiler of "Hark! the Years" on which the Einstein fragment first appeared, but the catalogue of the Vincent Voice Library at Michigan State University (*Dictionary Catalog of the G. Robert Vincent Voice Library at Michigan State University, East Lansing, Michigan*, Leonard E. Cluley and Pamela N. Engelbrecht, eds. (Boston: G. K. Hall, 1975), pp. 143-144, gives no appropriate sources dating from the late 1940s or early 1950s.

EJS 268: "The Golden Age of Opera" (2 LPs)
Issued May, 1963

SIDES 1-4 (268 A-D):

DIE ÄGYPTISCHE HELENA (R. Strauss) (G)
Opera 2 in acts (complete)
Orchestra and Chorus of the Bayrischer Staatsoper/Joseph Keilberth
?Broadcast, Bayrischer Staatsoper, Munich, 10 Aug 1956

CAST:
Leonie Rysanek (*Helena*); Bernd Aldenhoff (*Menelas*); Annalies Kupper (*Aithra*); Hermann Uhde (*Altair*); Richard Holm (*Da-Ud*); Ira Malaniuk (*Die alles-wissende Muschel*); Lilian Benningsen (*First Dienerin der Aithra*); Antonie [Antonia] Fahberg (*Second Dienerin der Aithra*); Lotte Schädle (*First Elf*); Doris Pilling (*Second Elf*); Gertrud Friederich (*Third Elf*); Gertrud Vollath (*Fourth Elf*).

NOTES: EJS 268

This performance was part of the 1956 Münchner Festpielwochen. Smith later reissued it under the title "Helen of Egypt" on one of his private "foreign" labels, the **Richard Strauss** series, SP 1, which also came to include performances of INTERMEZZO, FEUERSNOT, and DIE LIEBE DER DANAË, all of which had previously been issued in the "Golden Age of Opera" series. Smith claimed that these later issue were done at the behest of a "Strauss Society," and that the names of the operas were deliberately translated into English to avoid legal complications.

This may be an in-house recording (as rumored) not a broadcast.

The SP 1 issue is reported to play slow at 33.3 rpm, which may also be the case with EJS 268.

EJS 269: "The Golden Age of Opera" (1 LP)
Issued May, 1963

SIDES 1-2 (269 A-B):

LA JOLIE FILLE DE PERTH (Bizet) (E)
Opera 4 in acts (acts 1 and 2 only)
Royal Philharmonic Orchestra and BBC Chorus/Sir Thomas Beecham
BBC broadcast, London, 5 Oct 1956

CAST:
Mattiwilda Dobbs (*Catherine Glover*); Alexander Young (*Henry Smith*); Kevin Miller (*Duke of Rothsay*); David Ward (*Ralph*); Anna Pollak [Pollack] (*Mab*); Owen Brannigan (*Simon Glover*).

NOTES: EJS 269

All four acts of this performance were broadcast. The label of EJS 269 states that the opera is presented complete, but only the first two acts were included. Acts 3 and 4 were eventually made available on EJS 438 in June, 1968, where Smith stated that "Not having a score to consult, we thought the opera was complete on a single disc [EJS 269]. Now it seems we released acts one and two and acts three and four are now available on a single record [EJS 438]."

This disc, and EJS 438, were reissued together in the January, 1972 UORC bulletin.

EJS 270: "The Golden Age of Opera" (1 LP)
Issued May, 1963

"GIOVANNI MARTINELLI GOLDEN ANNIVERSARY"

SIDE 1 (EJS 270 A)

* 1. "CLAUDIA MUZIO, soprano, and GIOVANNI MARTINELLI, tenor" (orchs/Wilfred Pelletier and Lorenzo Molajoli): OTELLO, Act I: Già nella notte . . . Ed io vedea . . . to the end of the act (Verdi) (I)
[A combination of two commercial recordings of the Act I/iii duet: MUZIO and FRANCESCO MERLI, conducted by Molajoli on Columbia BQX 2510 (matrices BX 1369-1 and 1370-1), recorded in Milan in 1933, and the MARTINELLI-HELEN JEPSON on Victor 15801/15802 (matrices CS-036875-1 and CS-036876-1), recorded in ?New York, 9 March, 1939 and issued as Victor set M-620. Merli's and Jepson's parts have simply been spliced out, with Muzio's and Martinelli's combined to create this composite.]

* 2. "CELESTINA BONINSEGNA, soprano, and GIOVANNI MARTINELLI, tenor" (pf/Carlo Sabajno; Metropolitan Opera House Orchestra and Chorus/Giulio Setti): IL TROVATORE, Act III: Quel suon, quelle preci . . . Ah! che la morte ["Miserere"] (Verdi) (I)
[As above, a bogus mating of Martinelli and Boninsegna, taken from the electrical MARTINELLI-PONSELLE version, Victor 8097 (matrix CVE-41637-2), recorded in New York on 23 January, 1928, and the BONINSEGNA-GIOVANNI VALLS acoustical, G&T 54056 (matrix 2179L), recorded (with piano by Sabajno) in Milan in 1904.]

* 3. w. GIORDANO PALTRINIERI, tenor (Metropolitan Opera House Orchestra and Chorus/Ettore Panizza): NORMA, Act I: Meco all'altar (Bellini) (I)
Metropolitan Opera broadcast, NYC, 20 Feb 1937

* 4. (w. orchestra and chorus of La Scala Opera of Philadelphia/ Giuseppe Bamboschek): OTELLO, Act I: Esultate (Verdi) (I)
In-house recording, La Scala Opera, Philadelphia, 16 Apr 1948

* 5. (w. pf/Giuseppe Bamboscheck--recitative; Nicola Rescigno--aria): LA FANCIULLA DEL WEST, Act III: Vi ringrazio, Sonora . . . Ch'ella mi creda (Puccini) (I)
Recitative: from the LP "Giovanni Martinelli"
TA-33-010 Continental CLP 103 New York, early 1950
Aria: private recording New York, January, 1948

6. (w. Carole Longone/pf): SAMSON ET DALILA, Op. 47, Act I: Arrêtez! ô mes frères! (Saint-Saëns) (F)
Private recording, ***CAROL LONGONE OPERALOGUE***, New York, circa March, 1950

7. w. CLARAMAE TURNER, contralto (Carole Longone/pf): SAMSON ET DALILA, Op. 47, Act II: En ces lieux (Saint-Saëns) (F)
Private recording, ***CAROL LONGONE OPERALOGUE***, New York, circa March, 1950

8. w. CLARAMAE TURNER, contralto, and LLOYD HARRIS, baritone (Carole Longone/pf): SAMSON ET DALILA, Op. 47, Act I: Je viens célébrer la victoire (Saint-Saëns) (F)
Private recording, ***CAROL LONGONE OPERALOGUE***, New York, circa March, 1950

SIDE 2 (EJS 270 B):

* 1. (w. orch/?): TOSCA, Act III: E lucevan le stelle (Puccini) (I)
Broadcast, circa 1948

* 2. (w. studio orch/Donald Voorhees): LA JUIVE, Act IV: Rachel, quand du Seigneur (Halévy) (F)
Broadcast, ***PACKARD HOUR***, WJZ, NYC, 15 Jan 1935

* 3. (w. studio orch/Donald Voorhees): "By the Bend in the River" (Bernhard Haig-Clara Edwards) (E)
Broadcast, ***PACKARD HOUR***, WJZ, NYC, 15 Jan 1935

* 4. w. QUEENA MARIO, soprano (studio orch/Donald Voorhees): MADAMA BUTTERFLY, Act I: Give me your lovely hands [Dammi ch'io baci] (Puccini) (E)
Broadcast, ***PACKARD HOUR***, WJZ, NYC, 15 Jan 1935

I PAGLIACCI (Leoncavallo) (I)
Opera in 2 Acts (excerpts)
Chicago Opera Orchestra and Chorus/Maurice Abravanel
Chicago Opera broadcast, Chicago, 11 Nov 1940

CAST:
Helen Jepson (*Nedda*); John Charles Thomas (*Tonio*); Giovanni Martinelli (*Canio*); George Czaplicki (*Silvio*); Jose Mojica (*Beppe*).

5. Act II: JEPSON, THOMAS, MARTINELLI, CZAPLICKI, MOJICA and Chorus: A stanotte. E per sempre . . . No, Pagliaccio non son! . . . to the end of the opera

6. (w. Metropolitan Opera House Orchestra/Ettore Panizza) SIMON BOCCANEGRA, Act II: O inferno . . . Sento avvampar nell'anima (Verdi) (I)
   Metropolitan Opera broadcast, NYC, 16 Feb 1935

7. w. GIUSEPPE DANISE, baritone (pf/Pietro Cimara): OTELLO, Act II: Oh! mostruoso colpa! . . . Si, pel ciel marmoreo giuro! (Verdi) (I)
   Private recording, Ansonia Hotel, NYC, 1948

NOTES: EJS 270

Side 1 (270 A):

Bands 1-2: Smith had this to say in the May, 1963 bulletin: "Since Martinelli sang with, but never recorded with either [Muzio or Boninsegna], we wish to pay tribute to the magnificent tape dubbing and transferring done by the indefatigable Dr. A.F.R. Lawrence, who painstakingly removed the partners of the ladies from other recordings, and substituted Martinelli. Both duets are superb - and we challange collectors to fault the tape from the standpoint of musicality or sound."

The late Dr. Lawrence, to be sure, was Smith's first, and arguably most ingenious creator of performances that never were . . .

Band 3: Library of Congress tape: 15731-89A (complete broadcast).

Band 4: Martinelli was associated with the Philadelphia La Scala Opera in the 1940s and 1950s, possibly because of his old friend and accompanist Giuseppe Bamboschek. He was also on the 1948 roster of the San Carlo Opera, which was on tour in New York in April, 1948, but Cardell Bishop's *San Carlo Opera Company of America*, 2nd ed., 1936-1955 (Santa Monica, California: the author, 1981) lists no performances by him that season. Extensive excerpts from this OTELLO appeared later on EJS 409 (October, 1967).

Band 5: The recitative of this scene was taken from Martinelli's 1950 Continental LP recital, a commercial studio recording; the aria proper is from a private recording, made two years earlier.

Side 2 (270 B):

Bands 1: Reported to be from the ***CARNEGIE POPS CONCERT*** of 11 May, 1948, broadcast over WNYC, New York City, a benefit for American Relief for Italy, Inc. Radio logs list no "E lucevan le stelle," however--only Tosti's "Voi dormite, Signora," Denza's "Occhi di fata" (two De Luca perennials, both presumably sung by him), the FORZA "Solenne quest'ora," and "other works by . . . Donaudy." These, in addition to orchestral selections by the Carnegie [Hall] Pops Orchestra, conducted by Emmanuel Balaban, and Menotti's THE TELEPHONE with Jean Carlton and Eddy Michaelis (given in the *New York Times* as "Michaels"). The Martinelli-De Luca duets from this broadcast concert were previously issued on EJS 102 (1956); the FORZA duet later appeared on ANNA 1030 (May-June, 1979), and the other, Masini's "I mulattieri," on UORC 375 (December, 1977). Thereafter, both appeared on other commercial LPs. See also the note for EJS 102 (II/3-4).

Bands 2-4: Martinelli and Mario were substituting on this broadcast for Lawrence Tibbett, the ***PACKARD HOUR***'s regular featured artist, who was singing in Hartford, Connecticut on 15 January, 1935.

Band 5: This PAGLIACCI was broadcast in its entirety, but to date, has not appeared complete on LP.
See the note on Czaplicki for EJS 169 (I/7).

EJS 271: "The Golden Age of Opera" (1 LP)
Issued June, 1963

SIDES 1-2 (271 A-B):

IL GIOVEDÌ GRASSO (Donizetti) (I)
Opera in 1 act (complete)
Orchestra of Radio Svizzera-Italiana [CORSI]/Edwin Loehrer
Broadcast, CORSI, ?Montecenere, Mar 1962

CAST:
Bruna Rizzoli (*Nina*); Maria Minetto (*Camilla*); Irene Bassi (*Stefania*); Juan Oncina (*Ernesto*); Nestore Catalani (*Sigismondo*); James Loomis (*The Colonel*); Rodolfo Malacarne (*Teodoro*); Teodoro Rovetta (*Cola*).

NOTES: EJS 271

There are numerous label errors on EJS 271: the parts of *Camilla* and *Stefania* are given as "Carmela" and "Stefanina," respectively; *Ernesto* and *Oncina* are omitted from the cast listing; and the "Radio Suisse and Chorus" are given instead of the correct Radio Svizzera-Italiana. In fact, there is no chorus part for IL GIOVEDÌ GRASSO. The June, 1963 bulletin claims that the performance was "Broadcast from Switzerland in Italian . . ." This was probably a CORSI broadcast (Società Cooperative per la Radiotelevisione nella Svizzera Italiana, or "Radio Svizzera-Italiana:" Montecenere is the location of the transmitter.

EJS 272: "The Golden Age of Opera (1 LP)
Issued June, 1963

SIDES 1-2 (272 A-B):

I PURITANI (Bellini) (I)
Opera in 3 acts (excerpts)
Orchestra and Chorus of Radio Italiana [RAI], Roma/Fernando Previtali
RAI broadcast, Rome, Saturday, 5 Jan 1952

CAST:
Lina Pagliughi (*Elvira*); Mario Filippeschi (*Arturo*); Rolando Panerai (*Riccardo*); Sesto Bruscantini (*Giorgio*); Lucia Quinto (*Queen Enrichetta*); Enzo Mori (*Sir Benno Robertson*).

NOTES: EJS 272

Reported to have been recorded on 4 January for broadcast the next day, Pagliughi herself claimed that the recording was made on 1 January, 1952.

Highlights in this 67-minute condensation include only major arias and ensembles: from Act 1, Filippeschi's "A te o cara" and Panerai's "Ah! per sempre" and "Bel sogno beato;" from Act 2, Pagliughi's "Qui la voce," Bruscantini's "Cinta di rose," and the *Riccardo-Giorgio* duet, "Suoni la tromba;" from Act 3, Filippeschi's "Vieni, vieni fra queste braccia," and "Credeasi misera." The performance was issued complete as UORC 102 (January, 1971).

EJS 273: "The Golden Age of Opera (1 LP)
Issued June, 1963

DAS LIEBESVERBOT (Wagner) (G)
Opera in 2 acts (excerpts)
Orchestra of the Radio Beromünster, Bern, and Chorus of Radio Bern/ Meinhard von Zallinger
Broadcast, Radio Beromünster, Bern, 1963

CAST:
Edith Lang (*Isabella*); Vera Schlosser (*Mariana*); Ingeborg Fanger (*Dorella*); Ralph Telasko (*Friederich*); Lorenz Fehenberger (*Claudio*); Leonhard Packl (*Luzio*); Wolfram Martz (*Angelo*); Andreas Camillo Agrelli (*Brighella*); Franz Lindauer (*Danieli*); Jakob Soltermann (*Pontio Pilato*).

SIDE 1 (273 A):

Act I:
1. Overture
2. PACKL, MARTZ, FANGER, SOLTERMANN, AGRELLI, and LINDAUER: Opening Scene to the entrance of Claudio
3. SCHLOSSER and LANG: Salve Regina . . . Göttlicher Frieden, himmlische Ruh'
4. PACKL and LANG: Es ist ein Mann
5. TELASKO and LANG: Wohlan so rede . . . Kennst du das Lied

SIDE 2 (273 B):

Act I: 1. TELASKO and LANG: Kennst du das Lied (conclusion) . . . to the beginning of the ensemble "Was ist geschehn"

Act II: 2. FEHENBERGER and LANG: Wo Isabella bleibt (with introduction)
3. TELASKO: So spät und noch kein Brief (with introduction and recitative)
4. LANG and SCHOLSSER: Verweile hier . . . Welch wunderbar Erwarten
5. PACKL and Chorus: Ihr junges Volk ["Karnavalslied"]

NOTE: EJS 273

The June, 1963 bulletin implies that this is a 1963 English broadcast, meaning perhaps that the air-checks used were from the BBC. The exact date of the performance could not be determined.

The second-act *Isabella-Mariana* scene ("Verweile hier . . . Welch wunderbar Erwarten") and the "Karnavalslied" are presented here in reverse order, but whether this was done in the actual performance or by Smith (and then, deliberately or not) could not be confirmed.

EJS 274: "The Golden Age of Opera" (1 LP)
Issued June, 1963

DIE FEEN (Wagner) (G)
Opera in 3 acts (excerpts)
BBC Northern Orchestra and Singers/Leo Wurmser
BBC broadcast, London, Wednesday, 22 May 1963

CAST:
Elisabeth Fretwell (*Ada*); Elisabeth Fretwell (*Lora*); Ronald Dowd (*Arindal*); Otakar Kraus (*Gernot*); Otakar Kraus (*Morald*); Otakar Kraus (*Groma*); Otakar Kraus (*The Fairy King*).

SIDE 1 (274 A):

Act I: 1. Overture
2. Chorus: Schwinget euch auf
3. DOWD: Da hörten plötzlich Donner wir erschallen . . . Wo find ich dich

Act II: 4. Chorus: Weh! uns! Weh!
5. FRETWELL and Chorus: Was drängt euch so . . .O musst die Hoffnung schwinden

Act I: 6. KRAUS: War einst'ne böse Hexe wohl

SIDE 2 (274 B):

Act II: 1. FRETWELL: Weh' mir, so nah' die fürchterliche Stunde

Act III: 2. DOWD, FRETWELL, and KRAUS: Hallo! Hallo!
3. DOWD and FRETWELL: Oh ihr, des Busens Hochgefühl
4. KRAUS, FRETWELL, DOWD, and Chorus: Du Sterblicher drangst ein in unser Reich . . . to the end of the opera

NOTES: EJS 274

Note that the excerpts are presented out of score order, as listed above.

EJS 275: "The Golden Age of Opera" (2 LPs)
Issued September, 1963

SIDES 1-4 (275 A-D):

GUGLIELMO RATCLIFF (Mascagni) (I)
Opera in 4 acts (complete)
Orchestra and Chorus of Radio Italiana [RAI], Roma/Armando La Rosa Parodi
RAI broadcast, Rome, 30 Jul 1963

CAST:
Pier Miranda Ferraro (*Guglielmo Ratcliff*); Renata Mattioli (*Maria*); Giovanni Ciminelli (*Count di Douglas*); Ferruccio Mazzoli (*MacGregor*); Vito Tatone (*Lesley*); Miti Truccato Pace (*Margherita*); Saturno Meletti (*Tom*); Giovanni Amodeo (*Robin*); Giovanni Amodeo (*John*); Eva Jakabfy (*Willie*); Augusto Pedroni (*Dick*); Andrea Mineo (*Bell*); Arrone Ceroni (*Taddie*); Arrone Ceroni (*A Servant*).

NOTES: EJS 275

Mislabeled on some copies as EJS 175.
This issue is apparently complete as performed, but with extensive cuts in the original score.
Reissued on LP (in stereo) as MFR 57-S, where the performance date is given as August, 1963, and on CD as Nuova Era 2336/7.

EJS 276: The Golden Age of Opera" (1 LP)
Issued September, 1963

SIDES 1-2 (276 A-B):

LA BETULIA LIBERATA, K. 118 (Metastasio-Mozart) (I)
Sacred Oratorio (1771) (complete as performed)
Orchestra and Chorus of Radio Italiana [RAI], Torino/Mario Rossi
RAI broadcast, Turin, 30 May 1952

CAST:
Elisabeth Schwarzkopf (*Amital*); Boris Christoff (*Achior*); Cesare Valletti (*Ozia*); Miriam Pirazzini (*Giudetta*); Luisa Vincenti (*Cabri*); Luigia [?Luisa] Vincenti (*Carmi*).

NOTES: EJS 276

Reportedly misnumbered on some copies as EJS 176.

Complete as performed and broadcast. Score items no. 1 and 11 were omitted in the actual performance, and the recitatives were truncated.

Vincenti is given as "Luisa" on EJS 276, but this is probably Luigia Vincenti, a soprano active at RAI in the early 1950s.

EJS 277: "The Golden Age of Opera" (1 LP)
Issued September, 1963

SIDES 1-2 (277 A-B):

L'INCANTESIMO (Montemezzi) (I)
Opera in 1 act (complete)
NBC Symphony Orchestra/Italo Montemezzi
NBC Symphony Orchestra broadcast, WEAF [NBC], NYC, 9 Oct 1943

CAST:
Alexander Sved (*Folco*); Mario Berini (*Rinaldo*); Vivian Della Chiesa (*Griselda*); Virgilio Lazzari (*Salamone*).

NOTES: EJS 277

Misnumbered on some copies as EJS 177.

This is the world premiere of Montemezzi's last opera. It was subsequently staged in Verona in 1952, but apparently has yet to be published in score. There is, however, a libretto, published by Ricordi.

EJS 278: "The Golden Age of Opera" (1 LP)
Issued October, 1962

SIDES 1-2 (278 A-B):

L'OCCASIONE FA IL LADRO (Rossini) (I)
Opera in 1 act (complete)
Orchestra and Chorus of the Radio Svizzera-Italiana/Edwin Loehrer
Broadcast, Radio Svizzera-Italiana [CORSI], place and date unknown

CAST:
Jolanda Meneguzzer (*Berenice*); Juan Oncina (*Count Alberto*); Nestore Catalani (*Don Parmenione*); Maria Minetto (*Ernestina*); Fernando Corena (*Martino*); Adriano Ferrario (*Don Eusebio*).

NOTE: EJS 278

Label errors include the mispelling of *Don Parmenione*, *Ernestina*, and *Don Eusebio* as "*Don Sarmenione*," "*Ernestine*," and "*Don Ernesto*," respectively.

EJS 279: "The Golden Age of Opera" 1 LP)
Issued October, 1963

"JUSSI BJOERLING IN OPERA AND SONG (1939-1954)"

SIDE 1 (279 A):

* 1. (w. studio orch/Donald Voorhees): AÏDA, Act I: Se quel guerrier io fossi . . . Celeste Aïda (Verdi) (I)
Broadcast, ***BELL TELEPHONE HOUR***, WNBC, Carnegie Hall, NYC, 12 Mar 1951

* 2. (w. studio orch/Donald Voorhees): I PAGLIACCI, Act I: Recitar . . . Vesti la giubba (Leoncavallo) (I)
Broadcast, ***BELL TELEPHONE HOUR***, WNBC, Carnegie Hall, NYC, 12 Mar 1951

* 3. (w. Orchestra of the Algemeene Vereniging Radio Omroep [AVRO], Hilversum Frieder Weissmann): MESSA DA REQUIEM: Ingemisco tamquam reus (Verdi) (L)
AVRO broacast, Hilversum, Holland, 8 Jun 1939

* 4. (w. Orchestra of the Algemeene Vereniging Radio Omroep [AVRO], Hilversum/Frieder Weissmann): FAUST, Act III: Salut! demeure chaste et pure (Gounod) (F)
AVRO broacast, Hilversum, Holland, 8 Jun 1939

* 5. (w. Orchestra of the Algemeene Vereniging Radio Omroep [AVRO], Hilversum/Frieder Weissmann): LA BOHÈME, Act I: Che gelida manina (Puccini) (I)
AVRO broacast, Hilversum, Holland, 8 Jun 1939

* 6. (w. Orchestra of the Harmonien Music Society [Bergen Symphony Orchestra]/Carl Garaguly): SERSE, Act I: Frondi tenere . . . Ombra mai fu (Handel) (I)
Bergen Music Festival, Concert Palace, Bergen, Norway, 9 Jun 1954
Pre-recorded broadcast, ***WORLD MUSIC FESTIVAL***, WCBS, New York City, 18 Jul 1954

* 7. (w. Orchestra of the Harmonien Music Society [Bergen Symphony Orchestra]/Carl Garaguly): "Pietà Signor" (Niedermeyer/attr. Stradella) (I)
Bergen Music Festival, Concert Palace, Bergen, Norway, 9 Jun 1954
Pre-recorded broadcast, ***WORLD MUSIC FESTIVAL***, WCBS, New York City, 18 Jul 1954

SIDE 2 (279 B):

* 1. (w. studio orch/Donald Voorhees): "Sylvia" (Scollard-Speaks) (E)
Broadcast ***BELL TELEPHONE HOUR***, WNBC, Rockefeller Center, NYC, 10 Mar 1952

* 2. (w. studio orch/Donald Voorhees): "L'alba separa dalla luce l'ombra" (Tosti) (I)
Broadcast ***BELL TELEPHONE HOUR***, WNBC, Rockefeller Center, NYC, 10 Mar 1952

* 3. (w. studio orch/Donald Voorhees): THE PRINCESS PAT: Neapolitan Love Song (Blossom-Herbert) (E)
Broadcast ***BELL TELEPHONE HOUR***, WNBC, Rockefeller Center, NYC, 10 Mar 1952

4. (w. studio orch/Donald Voorhees): "The Rose of Tralee" (Glover) (E)
Broadcast ***BELL TELEPHONE HOUR***, WNBC, Carnegie Hall, NYC, 12 Mar 1951

* 5. (w. pf/James W. Quillian): "Tristans död" (Rangström) (Sw)
Broadcast, ***SWEDEN IN MUSIC***, WNYC, Carnegie Hall, NYC, 11 Apr 1949

* 6. (w. pf/James W. Quillian): "I drömmen du ar mig nära" (Sjögren) (Sw)
Broadcast, ***SWEDEN IN MUSIC***, WNYC, Carnegie Hall, NYC, 11 Apr 1949

* 7. (w. pf/James W. Quillian): "Jungfrun under lind" (Peterson-Berger) (Sw)
Broadcast, ***SWEDEN IN MUSIC***, WNYC, Carnegie Hall, NYC, 11 Apr 1949

* 8. (w. studio orch and Chorus/Howard Barlow): MESSE SOLENELLE À SAINTE CÉCILE: Sanctus (Gounod) (L)
Broadcast, ***VOICE OF FIRESTONE***, WEAF, Rockefeller Center, NYC, 15 Apr 1946

* 9. (w. studio orch and Chorus/Howard Barlow): "We gather together" [Wilt heden nu treden] (trad.-arr. Kremser) (E)
Broadcast and telecast, ***VOICE OF FIRESTONE***, WNBC, Rockefeller Center, NYC, 19 Nov 1951

NOTES: EJS 279

Side 1 (279 A):

Bands 1-2: The PAGLIACCI and AÏDA arias were later issued on HRE 214-2. The "Celeste Aïda" also appeared on UORC 350 (September-October, 1977), Legendary LR 137-2, and Glendale GL 8006.

Bands 3-5: The "Ingemisco" subsequently appeared on MDP 026, as did the "Salut! Demeure," which also turned up on HRE 214-2 and 376-2, and as an insert in the live Wiener Staatsoper performance of 1937 presented on EJS 337 (June, 1965). The three 8 June, 1939 items included on EJS 279, along with Bjoerling's other three numbers from this AVRO broadcast, later appeared on ANNA 1005 (May, 1978) and ERR 121-1.

Bands 6-7: The ***WORLD MUSIC FESTIVAL***, heard over CBS on 18 July, 1954, had been pre-recorded in Bergen on 9 June, 1954. The Oslo Philharmonic was also featured, playing an arrangement of a Bach Toccata, along with pianist Ivar Johnsen who, accompanied by the Bergen Symphony, performed Grieg's Piano Concerto in A Minor. In addition to the Handel and Niedermeyer, Bjoerling sang songs of Grieg and Sibelius as well as the "Ingemisco" from the Verdi REQUIEM. Both the "Ombra mai fu" and the "Pieta Signor" later appeared on ANNA 1017 (September, 1978) and MDP 035, which contains all but one of the vocal selections from the broadcast.

Side 2 (279 B):

Bands 1-3: "Sylvia" was later issued on HRE 214-2 and Legendary LR 138. The Tosti song also appeared on the Legendary recital, as well as on Rococo 5341, which also included the PRINCESS PAT excerpt.

Bands 5-7: This ***SWEDEN IN MUSIC*** broadcast was given on behalf of the Swedish Seamen's Welfare Fund. Contralto Karin Branzell and baritone Joel Berglund were also featured, along with conductors Fritz Busch and Max Rudolf. The broadcast was heard on WNYC-AM and -FM, New York City.

Band 5: Labeled "Tristan's Death" by McMillan on EJS 279. Later issued on the MDP Bjoerling recital, MDP 026.

Bands 6-7: Both songs also appeared on MDP 026.

Band 8: Later issued on Rococo 5329.

Band 9: Labeled "Prayer of Thanksgiving" as arranged by Kremser on EJS 279. Later issued on Legendary LR 138.

EJS 280: "The Golden Age of Opera" (2 LPs)
Issued October, 1963

SIDES 1-4 (280 A-D):

LA PIETRA DEL PARAGONE (Rossini) (I)
Opera in 2 acts (complete as performed)
Orchestra and Chorus of the Piccola Scala, Milano/Nino Sanzogno
La Piccola Scala (?)broadcast, Milan, 6 Jun 1959

CAST:
Fiorenza Cossotto (*Clarice*); Ivo Vincó (*Count Asdrubale*); Alvinio Misciano (*Gioconda*); Giulio Fioravanti (*Pacuvio*); Renato Capecchi (*Macrobio*); Eugenia Ratti (*Donna Fulvia*); Silvana Zanolli (*The Baroness*); Franco Calabrese (*The Majordomo*).

NOTES: EJS 280

Complete as performed, but with extensive score cuts. The overture to LA PIETRA DEL PARAGONE (1812), heard in this performance, was recycled by the composer a year later for TANCREDI

The performance was later issued as Fonit-Cetra DOC-4.

EJS 281: "The Golden Age of Opera" (3 LPs)
Issued November, 1963

SIDES 1-5 (281 A-E):

OTELLO (Verdi) (I)
Opera in 4 Acts (complete)
Metropolitan Opera House Orchestra and Chorus/Ettore Panizza
Metropolitan Opera broadcast, NYC, 3 Dec 1938

CAST:
Giovanni Martinelli (*Otello*); Lawrence Tibbett (*Iago*); Alessio DePaolis (*Cassio*); John Dudley (*Roderigo*); Nicola Moscona (*Lodovico*); George Cehanovsky (*Montano*); Wilfred Engelman (*Herald*); Maria Caniglia (*Desdemona*); Thelma Votipka (*Emilia*).

SIDE 6 (281 F):

AïDA (Verdi) (I)
Opera in 4 acts (excerpts)
Chicago Opera House Orchestra and Chorus/Paul Breisach
Chicago Opera broadcast, WGN, Chicago, 9 Dec 1940

CAST:
Rose Bampton (*Aïda*); Giovanni Martinelli (*Radames*); Elza [Elsa] Zebranska (*Amneris*); Carlo Morelli (*Amonasro*); [Virgilio Lazzari] (*Ramfis*); [Giuseppe Cavadore (*Messenger*)]; [Virginia Wallace (*Priestess*)].

* 1. Act III: MARTINELLI, BAMPTON, and CZAPLICKI: Aïda! . . . Tu non m'ami--Va! . . . Sì: fuggiam da questa mura . . . to the end of the act

2. Act IV: ZEBRANSKA and MARTINELLI: Già i sacerdoti adunansi . . . Temo sol la tua pietà (through the postlude of the duet before Amneris' "Ohime! morir mi sento")

3. Act IV: MARTINELLI, BAMPTON, and ZEBRANSKA: Scene ii complete

NOTES: EJS 281

Sides 1-5 (281 A-E):

Library of Congress tape: 7596 (complete broadcast).

Side 6 (281 F):

Band 1: Only Acts III and IV were broadcast. *Ramfis'* two lines, "Guardie, olà!" and "Li inseguite!," were omitted, hence Lazzari's absence from the preserved excerpts.
Library of Congress tape: 8944-46A (excerpts).

EJS 282: "The Golden Age of Opera (1 LP)
Issued November, 1963

"RENATA TEBALDI / LICIA ALBANESE"

SIDE 1 (282 A):

* 1. RENATA TEBALDI, soprano (San Francisco Opera Orchestra/Gaetano Merola): ADRIANA LECOUVREUR, Act I: Troppo, signori . . . Io son l'umile ancella (Cilèa) (I)
Broadcast, *STANDARD HOUR*, KFI, Los Angeles, 12 Nov 1950

* 2. RENATA TEBALDI, soprano, and ROBERT WEEDE, baritone (San Francisco Opera Orchestra/Gaetano Merola): LA TRAVIATA, Act II: [Pura siccome un angelo] . . . l'amato e amante giovine . . . Dite alla giovine (Verdi) (I)
Broadcast, *STANDARD HOUR*, KFI, Los Angeles, 12 Nov 1950

* 3. RENATA TEBALDI, soprano, and GIUSEPPE DI STEFANO (San Francisco Opera Orchestra/Gaetano Merola): MADAMA BUTTERFLY, Act I: [Bimba dagli occhi] . . . Somiglio la Dea della luna . . . (Puccini) (I)
Broadcast, *STANDARD HOUR*, KNBC, San Francisco, 16 Oct 1950

4. RENATA TEBALDI, soprano (Orchestra of Radio Italiana, Turno/Carlo Maria Giulini): LE NOZZE DI FIGARO, Act II: Porgi amor (Mozart) (I)
Broadcast, *CONCERTO MARTINI E ROSSI*, RAI Torino, Turin, 26 Nov 1951

SIDE 2 (282 B):

1. RENATA TEBALDI, soprano (Orchestra of Radio Italiana, Turino/ Carlo Maria Giulini): LOUISE, Act III: Depuis le jour (Charpentier) (I)
Broadcast, *CONCERTO MARTINI E ROSSI*, RAI Torino, Turin, 26 Nov 1951

2. RENATA TEBALDI, soprano (studio orch/Donald Voorhees): STABAT MATER, No. 8: Inflammatus (Rossini) (L)
Broadcast, *BELL TELEPHONE HOUR*, WNBC, NYC, 19 Nov 1956

3. RENATA TEBALDI, soprano (studio orch/Donald Voorhees): "Cantares" (Turina) (S)
Broadcast, *BELL TELEPHONE HOUR*, WNBC, NYC, 19 Nov 1956

* 4. LICIA ALBANESE, soprano, and SET SVANHOLM, tenor (San Francisco Opera Orchestra/Gaetano Merola): OTELLO, Act I: Già nella notte densa (Verdi) (I)
Broadcast, *STANDARD HOUR*, KPO, San Francisco, 26 Oct 1947

* 5. LICIA ALBANESE, soprano; SET SVANHOLM, tenor; LEONARD WARREN, baritone; and CLARAMAE TURNER, mezzo-soprano (San Francisco Opera Orchestra/Gaetano Merola): OTELLO, Act II: D'un uom che geme (Verdi) (I)
Broadcast, *STANDARD HOUR*, KPO, San Francisco, 26 Oct 1947

* 6. LICIA ALBANESE, soprano, and SET SVANHOLM, tenor (San Francisco Opera Orchestra/Gaetano Merola): OTELLO, Act III: [Dio ti giocondi] . . . dell'alma mia sovrano (Verdi) (I)
Broadcast, ***STANDARD HOUR***, KPO, San Francisco, 26 Oct 1947

NOTES: EJS 282

Several items begin very abruptly a few bars after the excerpts commenced in performance, presumably the fault of the air-checks used for the dubbings. Smith notes in the November, 1963 that, for the OTELLO excerpts, while none are complete, they nonetheless "contain 90% of the music."

Side 1 (282 A):

Bands 1-3: These ***STANDARD HOUR*** excerpts were later issued on VOCE-86.

Side 2 (282 B):

Bands 4-7: Lawrence Tibbett and Thelma Votika, not Leonard Warren and Claramae Turner, are credited as the *Iago* and *Emilia* on the label of EJS 282 and in the accompanying bulletin. This confuses the 7 October, 1947 cast of the San Francisco Opera production (Albanese, Svanholm, Tibbett, Chabay as *Roderigo*, and Votipka as *Emilia*) with the 26 October, 1947 ***STANDARD HOUR*** excerpts actually presented here. However, Turner's first appearance as *Emilia* in the San Francisco Opera production of OTELLO was on 16 October, 1948, with Albanese, Svanholm, Warren, and Chabay. It would appear that the 1948 season was a more likely time for this particular cast to undertake the ***STANDARD HOUR*** adaptation presented here, but the date 26 October, 1947 has been confirmed.

The same excerpts, along with others from this performance, later appeared--with the cast correctly identified--on EJS 321 (February, 1965).

EJS 283: "The Golden Age of Opera" (2 LPs)
Issued December, 1963

SIDES 1-4 (283 A-D):

EURYANTHE (Weber-arr. Kurt Honolka) (G)
Opera in 3 acts (arrangement: complete as performed)
Orchestra and Chorus of the Westdeutschen Rundfunk and Chorus of Kölnischer Rundfunk [WDR], Köln/Joseph Keilberth
WDR broadcast, Cologne, December, 1958

CAST:
Dorothea Siebert (*Euranthe*); Marianne Schech (*Eglantine* [*Claudia*]); Josef Traxel (*Adolar* [*Gerard*]); Gustav Neidlinger (*Lysiart*); Walter Kreppel (*King Ludwig VI*); André Peysang (*A Messenger*).

NOTES: EJS 283

Kreppel's surname is given as "Kreppl" on the label of EJS 283 and the date of the performance is listed as 1960.

Honolka's arrangement of EURYANTHE is sweeping in its changes: the text is markedly dissimilar to the original Helmina von Chezy libretto (especially after the first act), and there are a great many cuts made in the music. Apparently Honolka's version was not published and exists, I am told, "only as a mimeograph copy for companies interested in performing it."

Among the changes are the character names *Eglantine* and *Adolar*, which became "*Claudia*" and "*Gerard,*" respectively--though in fact, the new names are never used in the text.

The recording date was taken from *Zwanzig Jahre Musik im Westdeutscher Rundfunk* 1948-1964 (Köln: Westdeutschen Rundfunk, 1968).

EJS 284: "The Golden Age of Opera" (2 LPs)
Issued December, 1963

SIDES 1-4 (284 A-D):

GERUSALEMME (JÉRUSALEM) (Verdi) (I)
Opera in 4 acts (complete as performed)
Orchestra and Chorus of the Teatro La Fenice, Venezia/Gianandrea Gavazzeni
?Broadcast, Teatro La Fenice, Venice, 24 Sep 1963

CAST:
Giacomo Aragall (*Gaston*); Emilio Savoldi (*The Count of Toulouse*); Gian Giacomo Guelfi (*Roger*); Leyla Gencer (*Hélène*); Mirella Fiorentini (*Isaure*); Antonio Zerbini (*Ademaro*); Franco Ghitti (*Raymond*); Alessandro Maddalena (*The Emir of Ramla*); Alessandro Maddalena (*A Soldier*); Ottorino Begali (*An Officer*); Virgilio Carbonari (*A Herald*).

NOTES: EJS 284

GERUSALEMME was originally produced in 1843 as I LOMBARDI ALLA PRIMA CROCIATA, the libretto by Temistocle Solera. As such, it is generally acknowledged to have been the first Verdi opera performed in America (Palmo's Opera House, New York, 3 March, 1847). The opera was revised for the Paris Opera in 1847 as JÉRUSALEM, with substantial changes to the music and a new French libretto by Royer and Vaëz. A second revision--with the story altered, much of the music rewritten, and the text translated back into Italian--was scheduled to premiere at La Scala in 1848, but the production was never mounted. This Teatro La Fenice performance was apparently the world premiere of this last version of the opera, performed more than a century after Verdi's final efforts to revise the score and libretto. The December, 1963 bulletin notes that "JÉRUSALEM now contains about 30% of the original LOMBARDI; 35% of the Paris production and 35% of the 'new' production for La Scala - in other words - a virtually new Verdi opera." One of the cuts in this performing version is the "Polonaise," one of the score's better-known show pieces, recorded by Blanche Arral on 18 March, 1909 and issued as Victor 74146 (later as Victor Heritage 15-1016).

This 1963 performance has had a distinguished career on LP, beginning with EJS 284. Subsequently it appeared on MRF 89 (2 discs), JLT 0010 (3 discs, advertised as stereophonic), and Hope 249. The Morgan 6403 issue on 3 LPs bears the date 19 November, *1964*, but Cella's Gencer chronology lists no performances between the final 24 September, 1963 GERUSALEMME and a DON CARLOS in Rome in December.

EJS 284 seems to play accurately at a speed of approximately 34.2 rpm. The use of possibly more than one source of the performance has also been suggested, owing to the abrupt changes in speed and sound quality.

EJS 285: "The Golden Age of Opera" (1 LP)
Issued December, 1963

"KIRSTEN FLAGSTAD TRIBUTE"

SIDE 1 (285 A):

1. (w. Havana Symphony/Clemens Krauss): DER FLIEGENDE HOLLÄNDER, Act II: Trafft ihr das Schiff [Senta's Ballad] (Wagner) (G)
   In-house concert recording, Havana, Sunday, 24 Oct 1948

2. (w. Havana Symphony/Clemens Krauss): WESENDOCK LIEDER, no. 1: Der Engel (Wesendock-Wagner) (G)
   In-house concert recording, Havana, Sunday, 24 Oct 1948

3. (w. Havana Symphony/Clemens Krauss): WESENDOCK LIEDER, no. 2: Stehe Still (Wesendock-Wagner) (G)
   In-house concert recording, Havana, Sunday, 24 Oct 1948

4. (w. Havana Symphony/Clemens Krauss): WESENDOCK LIEDER, no. 3: Im Treibhaus (Wesendock-Wagner) (G)
   In-house concert recording, Havana, Sunday, 24 Oct 1948

5. (w. Havana Symphony/Clemens Krauss): WESENDOCK LIEDER, no. 4: Schmerzen (Wesendock-Wagner) (G)
   In-house concert recording, Havana, Sunday, 24 Oct 1948

6. (w. Havana Symphony/Clemens Krauss): WESENDOCK LIEDER, no. 5: Träume (Wesendock-Wagner) (G)
   In-house concert recording, Havana, Sunday, 24 Oct 1948

SIDE 2 (285 B):

1. (w. Havana Symphony/Clemens Krauss): "Ah! Perfido," Op. 65 (Metastasio-Beethoven) (G)
   In-house concert recording, Havana, Sunday, 24 Oct 1948

2. w. SET SVANHOLM, tenor (San Francisco Opera Orchestra/Gaetano Merola): TRISTAN UND ISOLDE, Act II: O sink'hernieder (Wagner) (G)
   Broadcast, ***STANDARD HOUR***, KNBC, San Francisco, 9 Oct 1949

3. (San Francisco Opera Orchestra/Gaetano Merola): TRISTAN UND ISOLDE, Act III: Mild und leise [Liebestod] (Wagner) (G)
Broadcast, ***STANDARD HOUR***, KNBC, San Francisco, 9 Oct 1949

NOTES: EJS 285

The Havana concert presented on the first side was apparently not broadcast, but was preserved as an in-house recording. The two ***STANDARD HOUR*** excerpts on side 2 were reissued from the original KNBC acetates on VOCE-98.

EJS 286: "The Golden Age of Opera (2 LPs)
Issued January, 1964

SIDES 1-4 (286 A-D):

L'AFRICAINE (Meyerbeer) (I)
Opera in 5 acts (complete as performed)
Orchestra and Chorus of the Teatro San Carlo di Napoli/Franco Capuana
In-house recording, Teatro San Carlo, Naples, Wednesday, 18 Dec 1963

CAST:
Nicola Nikoloff (*Vasco da Gama*); Antonietta Stella (*Selika*); Aldo Protti (*Nelusko*); Margherita Rinaldi (*Inès*); Ivo Vinco (*Don Pedro*); Enrico Campi (*Don Diego*); Paride Venturi (*Don Alvaro*); Plinio Clabassi (*Grand Inquisitor*); Plinio Clabassi (*Grand Brahmin*); Armanda Bonato (*Anna*); Vittorio Pandano (*A Priest*); Guido Malfatti (*A Sailor*).

NOTES: EJS 286

Copies of EJS 286 have been reported bearing reversed labels--side 1 for 2 and side 3 for 4--but the waxes are correctly marked.

This slightly more than two-hour version of L'AFRICAINE seems to conform to the versions used when the opera was still a part of the standard repertory, with the same standard cuts more or less. Recent revivals have restored the work to a three-hour running time. The San Carlo ballet was apparently on strike in December, 1963, which--if true--may explain some of the extensive cuts to Act IV in this production.

Speeds over the four sides range from 33. 5 rpm (Acts II-V) to 33.8 rpm (Act I). The performance was reissued complete as Melodram MEL 459.

EJS 287: "The Golden Age of Opera" (1 LP)
Issued January, 1964

SIDES 1-2 (287 A-B):

LE PORTRAIT DE MANON (Massenet) (F)
Opera in 1 act (complete)
Orchestra of Radio Italiana [RAI], Milano/Mario Rossi
RAI broadcast, Milan, 14 Dec 1950

CAST:
Carla Schlean (*Aurore*); Tamara Del Remo (*Jean*); Renato Capecchi (*Des Grieux*); Tommaso Spataro (*Tiberge*).

NOTES: EJS 287

LE PORTRAIT DE MANON is Massenet's own 1894 sequel to MANON, sung here by an Italian company in French, with the original French dialogue intact. The label of EJS 287 and the January, 1964 bulletin give "Mario Fighera" as the conductor.

EJS 288: "The Golden Age of Opera" (1 LP)
Issued January, 1964

SIDE 1 (288 A):

"AIDA / ACT II: SCENE TWO / ACT IV: SCENE ONE"

AÏDA (Verdi) (I)
Opera in 4 acts (excerpts)
London Philharmonic Orchestra and Royal Opera House Chorus/Vincenzo Bellezza
Broadcast, Covent Garden, London, 15 May 1936

CAST:
Elisabeth Rethberg (*Aïda*); Giacomo Lauri-Volpi (*Radames*); Gertrude Wettergren (*Amneris*); John Brownlee (*Amonasro*); Ezio Pinza (*Ramfis*); Eduard Habich (*The King of Egypt*); [Octave Dua (*A Messenger*)]; [Josephine Wray (*Priestess*)].

* 1. a) Act II/ii: HABICH, LAURI-VOLPI, PINZA, RETHBERG, WETTERGREN, BROWNLEE, and Chorus: End of the ballet . . . Gloria all'Egitto, ad Iside . . . to the end of the scene

b) Act IV/i: WETTERGREN and LAURI-VOLPI: L'aborrita rivale a me sfuggia . . . Già i sacerdoti adunansi . . . Oh! ch'io non vegga quelle bianche larve!

SIDE 2 (288 B):

"TENOR RECITAL"

1. BENIAMINO GIGLI, tenor (Orchestra of the RAI, Roma/Nino Antonicelli): LES PÊCHEURS DE PERLES, Act I: Mi par d'udir ancora (Bizet) (I)
   Broadcast, *CONCERTO MARTINI E ROSSI*, Rome, RAI, 9 Feb 1953

2. BENIAMINO GIGLI, tenor (Orchestra of the RAI, Roma/Nino Antonicelli): LODOLETTA, Act III: Se Franz dicesse il vero . . . Ah! ritrovarla (Mascagni) (I)
   Broadcast, ***CONCERTO MARTINI E ROSSI***, RAI, Rome, 9 Feb 1953

3. BENIAMINO GIGLI, tenor (Orchestra of the RAI, Roma/Nino Antonicelli): FEDORA, Act II: Amor ti vieta (Giordano) (I)
   Broadcast, ***CONCERTO MARTINI E ROSSI***, RAI, Rome, 9 Feb 1953

* 4. GIOVANNI MARTINELLI, tenor (pf/Giuseppe Bamboschek): TOSCA, Act III: E lucevan le stelle (Puccini) (I)
   Broadcast, ***BIRTHDAY BALL FOR THE PRESIDENT***, WABC, Ritz Carlton Hotel, NYC, 25 Jan 1937

* 5. GIOVANNI MARTINELLI, tenor (pf/Giuseppe Bamboschek): "Mattinata" (Leoncavallo) (I)
   Broadcast, ***BIRTHDAY BALL FOR THE PRESIDENT***, WABC, Ritz Carlton Hotel, NYC, 25 Jan 1937

6. LAURITZ MELCHIOR, tenor (Band of the Tivoli Boys Guard, Kobenhavn/?): DER VAR ENGANG: Midsommervise (Lange-Müller) (D or Sw)
   Live concert recording, Tivoli Gardens, Copenhagen, June, 1963

7. LAURITZ MELCHIOR, tenor (Band of the Tivoli Boys Guard, Kobenhavn/?): "Flaget" (Rygard) (D or Sw)
   Live concert recording, Tivoli Gardens, Copenhagen, June, 1963

8. LAURITZ MELCHIOR, tenor (Band of the Tivoli Boys Guard, Kobenhavn/?): HJERTETS MELODIER, Op. 5, no. 3: "Jeg elsker dig" (Grieg) (Sw)
   Live concert recording, Tivoli Gardens, Copenhagen, June, 1963

9. FERRUCCIO TAGLIAVINI, tenor (San Francisco Opera Orchestra/ Gaetano Merola): LE CID, Act III: O souverain! O juge! O père!
   Broadcast, ***STANDARD HOUR***, KNBC, San Francisco, 16 Oct 1949

10. TITO SCHIPA, tenor (studio orch/?): "Nina" ["Tre giorni son che Nina"] (Pergolesi) (I)
   from the soundtrack of the feature film ***TRE UOMINI IN FRAK*** (1933) Caesar Film, Roma, 1932

NOTES: EJS 288

Side 1 (288 A):

It has been reported that the Act II/ii AÏDA excerpt, through Amonasro's "Ma tu, o Re," features Lubja Welitsch as *Aïda*, probably taken from her 11 March, 1950 Met broadcast (subsequently issued complete as Melodram MEL 011 and in excerpts as Penzance 20), at which point the 1936 Covent Garden performance begins, as cited above. In addition to Welitsch, the Met cast would feature Lorenzo Alvary (*King of Egypt*), Ramon Vinay (*Radames*), Margaret Harshaw (*Amneris*), and Robert Merrill (*Amonasro*), conducted by Emil Cooper.

Side 2 (288 B):

Bands 4 and 5: Billed in the *New York Times* as the "January 30th Birthday Ball for the President," and described as "President Roosevelt Outlines Purpose of Birthday Ball," this program presented FDR, broadcasting direct from the White House, Martinelli, from the Ritz Carlton Hotel in New York City, Dr. Charles Mayo of the Mayo Clinic, Rochester, Minnesota (addressing, ostensibly, the new "March of Dimes" program for polio victims, innaugurated by FDR in 1938), Henry L. Doherty and Carl Byoir, chairman and general director, respectively, of the Democratic National Committee, and the Paulist Choir under the direction of the renowned Rev. William J. Finn. Two CBS affiliates, WABC (NYC), WJR (Detroit), and the independent WOR (Bemberger Broadcasting System), New York City and Newark, broadcast the show simultaneously from 10:30-11:00 pm.

EJS 289: "The Golden Age of Opera" (1 LP)
Issued February, 1964

MADAMA BUTTERFLY (Puccini) (E)
Opera in 3 acts (adaptation)
Studio Orchestra and Chorus/Wilfred Pelletier
Broadcast, ***STANDARD BRANDS HOUR***, WEAF, NYC, 16 Dec 1934

CAST:
Elisabeth Rethberg (*Butterfly*); Joseph Bentonelli (*B.H. Pinkerton*); Douglas Stanbury (*Sharpless*); Norman Cordon (*Bonzo*); Erwin Munch (*Goro*); Clemence Gifford (*Suzuki*); Deems Taylor (*Narrator*).

SIDE 1 (289 A):

1. Act I:
   a) BENTONELLI and STANBURY: Affonda l'ancora all ventura . . . America forever!
   b) MUNCH, RETHBERG, and Chorus: Ecco! Son giunte . . . Ancora un passo . . . Siam giunte
   c) CORDON, RETHBERG, MUNCH, and BENTONELLI: Cio-Cio San! . . . Hou! Cio-Cio San!
   d) GIFFORD: E Izaghi ed Izanami Sarundasico . . . e Kami
   e) RETHBERG and BENTONELLI: Vogliatemi bene, un bene piccolino . . . to the end of the act

   [Chase and Sanborn commercial exerpt]

   Act II:
   f) GIFFORD: E Izaghi ed Izanami . . . mai piu, mai più
   g) RETHBERG: Ah, la fede ti manca . . . through Un bel dì

SIDE 2 (289 B):

1. Act II:
   a) RETHBERG and GIFFORD: Trionfa il mio amor! . . . Corolle di verbene, petali d'ogni ["Flower Duet"]

   Act III:
   b) BENTONELLI: Addio, fiorito asil . . . Ah! son vil!
   c) RETHBERG: Tu? tu? tu? piccolo Iddio! . . . to the end of the opera

NOTES: EJS 289

The contents of this performance have been given in the original language for ease of reference.

The ***STANDARD BRANDS HOUR***, sponsored by Chase and Sanborn, inaugurated this series of radio adaptations of operas in English during the 1934 season, all conducted by Pelletier, with most featuring a major Metropolitan Opera artist "surrounded," as Smith puts it in the February, 1964 bulletin, "by a group of American youngsters from the Chicago and San Francisco seasons" (sic). Toward the end of the series, the "youngsters" were displaced altogether by members of the established old guard. In all, there appear to have been fourteen of these broadcasts between between 2 December, 1934 and 17 March, 1935, as opposed to the "39" shows claimed in the February bulletin: the first was a RIGOLETTO with John Charles Thomas, Josephine Antoine, Roderick Cross, Ruth Gordon, and Bentonelli, and the last a TROVATORE with Martinelli, Bampton, Hilde Burke, and Robert Weede. EJS 290 features the Bori-Bentonelli MANON adaptation, and EJS 291 the Stückgold-Bentonelli-Weede CARMEN. Deems Taylor, whose voice-over narrations had been banished two years earlier from the Saturday afternoon Met broadcasts on NBC, was back providing a còntinuous narration for these one-hour adaptations. Uncredited actors are heard portraying the characters in dialogue between the major arias and ensembles.

Shortly after the series concluded, WJZ of New York City inaugurated its own series of hour-long operatic adaptations (in the original languages, however) under the title ***MUSIC HALL OF THE AIR***, conducted by Erno Rapee and featuring a number of notable singers.

Smith claimed that, along with the material used for the Bentonelli recital, EJS 292, the three surviving broadcasts presented on EJS 289-291 were taken from Bentonelli's own personal copies.

A portion of a Chase and Sanborn coffee commercial can be heard on side one of the BUTTERFLY between the first and second acts.

EJS 290: "The Golden Age of Opera" (1 LP)
Issued February, 1964

MANON (Massenet) (E)
Opera in 5 Acts (adaptation)
Studio Orchestra and Chorus/Wilfred Pelletier
Broadcast, ***STANDARD BRANDS HOUR***, WEAF, NYC, 27 Jan 1935

CAST:
Lucrezia Bori (*Manon*); Joseph Bentonelli (*Des Grieux*); ?Douglas Stanbury (*Count Des Grieux*); Deems Taylor (*Narrator*).

SIDE 1 (290 A):

1. Act I: a) Prelude (cut/w. Taylor's narration)
b) BORI: Combien ces femmes . . . Voyons, Manon
c) BORI and BENTONELLI: Non! Non! Votre liberté . . . Nous vivrons à Paris!

Act II: d) BORI: Allons! Il le faut! . . . Adieu, notre petite table
e) BENTONELLI: En fermant les yeux

Act III: f) Chorus: Quelle éloquence!

SIDE 2 (290 B):

1. Act III: a) BENTONELLI: Ah! fuyez, douce image
b) BORI and BENTONELLI: Ah, rends moi ton amour! . . . N'es-ce plus ma main que cette main presse?

Act IV: c) BORI: Obéissons, quand leur voix appelle ["Gavotte"]
d) BORI, BENTONELLI and Count Des Grieux: Oui, je viens t'arracher à la honte!

Act V: e) BORI and BENTONELLI: Seul amour de mon âme!

NOTES: EJS 290

As with the EJS 289 BUTTERFLY, the contents of this MANON have been given in the original language for ease of reference.

Note that the *Count Des Grieux* was not listed in the *New York Times* radio log, and could not be identified conclusively: Stanbury, who sang in other broadcasts in the series, constitutes what we feel is an educated guess.

See also the endnote for EJS 189 regarding this ***STANDARD BRANDS HOUR*** series of broadcasts.

Bori, forgetting the terms of the ocassion, begins the Act III duet (II/1b) in French before switching back immediately to English!

EJS 291: "The Golden Age of Opera" (1 LP)
Issued February, 1964

"CARMEN (HIGHLIGHTS)"

CARMEN (Bizet) (E)
Opera in 4 Acts (adaptation)
Studio Orchestra and Chorus/Wilfred Pelletier
Broadcast, ***STANDARD BRANDS HOUR***, WEAF, NYC, 3 Mar 1935

CAST:
Grete Stückgold (*Carmen*); Joseph Bentonelli (*Don José*); Robert Weede (*Escamillo*); Helen Marshall (*Michaela*); ? (*Frasquita*); ? (*Mercédès*); Deems Taylor (*narrator*).

SIDE 1 (291 A):

1. Act I: a) STüCKGOLD: L'amour est un oiseau rebelle ["Habanera"]
b) STüCKGOLD: Tralalalalala, coupe-moi, brûle-moi
c) STüCKGOLD and BENTONELLI: Près des remparts de Séville ["Seguidilla"]

Act II: d) STüCKGOLD and Frasquita and Mercédès: Les tringles des sistres! ["Chanson Bohème"]
e) WEEDE: Votre toast ["Toreador Song"]
f) BENTONELLI: Halte-là! Qui va là?
g) BENTONELLI: La fleur que tu m'avais jetée

SIDE 2 (291 B):

1. Act II: a) STüCKGOLD and BENTONELLI: [Holà! Carmen, holà!] . . . Tonnerre! . . . to the end of the act [portion]

Act III: b) STüCKGOLD: En vain pour éviter ["Card Scene"]
c) MARSHALL: Je dis que rien ["Micaela's Air"]
d) WEEDE: Toreador en garde! . . . to the end of the act

Act IV: e) WEEDE and STüCKGOLD: Si tu m'aimes, Carmen
f) BENTONELLI and STüCKGOLD: Tu ne m'aimes donc plus?

NOTES: EJS 291

As with the EJS 289 BUTTERFLY and 290 MANON, the contents of this CARMEN have been given in the original language for ease of reference.

Note that the *Frasquita* and *Mercédès*, featured in the "Chanson Bohème," were not identified in the *New York Times* radio log, so could not be identified.

See also the note for EJS 189 regarding this ***STANDARD BRANDS HOUR*** series of broadcasts.

EJS 292: "The Golden Age of Opera" (1 LP)
Issued February, 1964

"JOSEPH BENTONELLI RECITAL (1929-1960)"

SIDE 1 (292 A):

* 1. (w. Los Angeles Philharmonic Orchestra/Otto Klemperer): LA BOHÈME, Act I: Che gelida manina (Puccini) (I)
Broadcast, ***GENERAL MOTORS PROMENADE CONCERT***, KECA [NBC], Hollywood Bowl, Los Angeles, 6 Jun 1937

* 2. w. LUCREZIA BORI, soprano (Los Angeles Philharmonic Orchestra/ Otto Klemperer): LA BOHÈME, Act I: O soave fanciulla (Puccini) (I)
Broadcast, ***GENERAL MOTORS PROMENADE CONCERT***, KECA [NBC], Hollywood Bowl, Los Angeles, 6 Jun 1937

* 3. (w. Los Angeles Philharmonic Orchestra/Otto Klemperer): FAUST, Act III: Salut! demeure (Gounod) (F)
Broadcast, ***GENERAL MOTORS PROMENADE CONCERT***, KECA [NBC], Hollywood Bowl, Los Angeles, 6 Jun 1937

* 4. (w. studio orch/Donald Voorhees): RIGOLETTO, Act III: La donna è mobile (Verdi) (I)
Broadcast, ***PACKARD HOUR***, WABC, NYC, 7 Jan 1936

5. (w. studio orch/?): Ay-ay-ay (Friere) (S)
?Broadcast, source and date unknown, circa 1935

6. (w. studio orch/?): CAVALLERIA RUSTICANA: O Lola ch'ai di latti ["Siciliana"] (Mascagni) (I)
?Broadcast, source and date unknown, circa 1937

7. (w. studio orch/?): IL BARBIERE DI SIVIGLIA, Act I: Ecco ridente (Rossini) (I)
?Broadcast, source and date unknown

8. (w. studio orch/?): WERTHER, Act I: Perchè tremar? . . . O natura [Pourquoi? . . . O nature] (Massenet) (I)
?Broadcast, source and date unknown

9. (w. studio orch/?): MARTHA, Act III: M'appari [Ach, so fromm] (Flotow) (I)
?Broadcast, source and date unknown

SIDE 2 (292 B):

1. (w. harpsichord/?): "Non più fra sassi" (Porpora) (I)
Source and date unknown, circa 1955

2. (w. harpsichord/?): "Contemplar almen chi s'ama (Porpora) (I)
Source and date unknown, circa 1955

3. (w. pf/?): L'ENFANT PRODIGUE: Ces airs joyeux (Debussy) (F)
Source and late unknown, circa 1955

4. (w. pf/?): TAVERN SONGS OF THE RENAISSANCE
a) Quoi que cupidon nous flatte (F)
b) Camarades, sans nous à battre (F)
c) Quoi! Toujours des chansons à boire (F)
d) Entendez-vous le carillon verre (F)
Source and date unknown, circa 1960

5. (w. harpsichord): LES INDES GALANTES, Act ?: Invocation et Hymne au Soleil (Rameau) (F)
Source and date unknown, circa 1960

* 6. w. GRACE MOORE, soprano (studio orch/?): MAYTIME: Will You Remember? (Wood-Young-Romberg) (E)
Broadcast, ***VICK OPEN HOUSE***, KFI, [NBC] Hollywood, 2 Mar 1936

7. w. GRACE MOORE, soprano (studio orch/?): THE BLUE PARADISE: Auf wiederseh'n (Reynolds-Romberg) (E)
Broadcast, source unknown, circa 1936

* 8. w. NADINE CONNER, soprano (studio orch/?): "Song of Songs" (M. Vaucaire-C. Lucas-Moya) (E)
?Broadcast, source and date unknown, circa 1937

NOTES: EJS 292

It is noted in the February, 1964 bulletin that the material presented in this recital was given to Smith by Bentonelli himself, but documentation beyond that is sparse. Bentonelli (née Joseph Horace *Benton*, according to his autobiography, and *Benter*, according to Kutsch-Riemans) appeared on the radio often in the 1930s: one concert in particular, a 19 January, 1935 solo recital on the ***CHESTERFIELD HOUR***, may well have been recorded, coming between Ponselle's last appearance as a regular on the show (23 December, 1934) and Bori's first (21 January, 1935). The three intervening programs, 31 December, 1934 to 16 January, 1935, were given in the radio logs of the *New York Times* only as "The Kostelanetz Orchestra."

Side 1 (292 A):

Bands 1-3: The BOHÈME items were from a "Concert Presentation" of the opera featured as part of this broadcast, which aired over WJZ (NBC Blue) in New York City, and probably originated over the Los Angeles Blue Network affiliate, KECA, not KFI.

Band 4: No other off-the-air Bentonelli "La donna è mobile" could be found, but it seems very likely that this ***PACKARD HOUR*** broadcast, a half-hour version of RIGOLETTO, was the source. Performed were the "Pari siamo," "Caro nome," "Cortigiani," "Piangi, fanciulla," "La donna è mobile," the third-act Quartet, and the "Lassù in cileo." The *Gilda* was probably Josephine Antoine, the Maddalena, Myrtle Leonard. The "Cortigiani" from this broadcast may be the one dubbed on EJS 397. Two Tibbett-Bentonelli-Antoine-Leonard RIGOLETTO Quartets from 1935-1936 (otherwise unidentified) also exist in a private collection.

Side 2 (292 B):

Band 6: Introduced by Grace Moore on the air. Josef Pasternack's Orchestra was the featured ensemble for the CBS ***VICK OPEN HOUSE*** broadcasts beginning in 1937, but Moore's conductor on these early NBC shows could not be documented.

Band 8: Labeled "Songs of Songs."

EJS 293: "The Golden Age of Opera" (2 LPs)
Issued March, 1964

SIDES 1-4 (293 A-D):

LA GAZZA LADRA (Rossini) (I)
Opera in 2 acts (complete)
Orchestra and Chorus of the Wexford Festival/John Pritchard
Wexford Festival, Wexford, October, 1959

CAST:
Trevor Anthony (*Fabrizio Vingradito*); Elisabeth Bainbridge (*Lucia*); Nicola Monti (*Gianetto*); Mariella Adani (*Ninetta*); Paolo Pedani (*Fernando Villabella*); Giorgio Tadeo (*Gottardo*); Janet Baker (*Pippo*); Griffith Lewis (*Isacco*); Julian Moyle (*Antonio*); Dennis Wicks (*Giorgio*).

NOTES: EJS 293

The Wexford Festival has been an annual event since 1951.
There were large performance cuts made in this particular performance, the first revival of LA GAZZA LADRA in the twentieth century. A complete performance of the work appeared in March, 1974 as UORC 193 and still later on Italia ITL-70056.
Sides three and four of this set have been reported defective on virtually all copies, with heavy pressing bumps.

EJS 294: "The Golden Age of Opera" (1 LP)
Issued March, 1964

SIDES 1-2 (294 A-B):

ADINA, or IL CALIFFO DI BAGDAD (Rossini) (I)
Opera in 1 act (complete)
Orchestra dell' Angelicum di Milano/Bruno Rigacci
?RAI Broadcast, Milan, 30 Sep 1963

CAST:
Mariella Adani (*Adina*); Mario Spina (*Selimo*); Giorgio Tadeo (*The Calibe*); Florindo Andreolli (*Ali*); Paolo Pedani (*Mustafà*).

NOTES: EJS 294

The April, 1964 bulletin noted that by "some incredible circumstance as yet unexplained, some of the discs of Rossini's Adina-Il Califfo di Bagdad . . . had a first side a major fifth in pitch above normal (sic). The work has been re-cut and repressed." Subscribers were invited to ask for copies of the new pressings and were advised to keep or destroy the old ones.
The performance was reissued (in pitch) as VOCE-32.

EJS 295: "The Golden Age of Opera (1 L)
Issued March, 1964

"POTPOURRI NO. 18"

SIDE 1 (295 A):

1. LILLIAN NORDICA, soprano (pf/?): SALVATORE ROSA, Act I: Mia piccerella (Gomes) (I)
30681-1 New York, 16 February, 1911 Columbia unpub

* 2. JOHN McCORMACK, tenor (pf/Edwin Schneider): "Love's Roses" (Frances Ring-Martin Broones) (E)
Broadcast, ***NBC SPECIAL TRIBUTE TO THOMAS MEIGHAN***, WEAF, NYC, 20 Aug 1935

* 3. JOHN McCORMACK, tenor (pf/Edwin Schneider): "Believe me if all those endearing young charms" (Moore-trad. Irish/arr. Schneider) (E)
Broadcast, ***NBC SPECIAL TRIBUTE TO THOMAS MEIGHAN***, WEAF, NYC, 20 Aug 1935

* 4. MATTIA BATTISTINI, baritone (pf/?): "Caro mio ben" (Giordani) (I)
301 Milan, 1920 Fonotecnica C 3003 / C 5008

5. GIUSEPPE DI STEFANO, tenor (Orchestra and Chorus of Radio Italiana [RAI]/?): LA SPOSA VENDUTA [PRODANÁ NEVESTA/THE BARTERED BRIDE], Act II: Puo alcun pensare [Jak mozna verít/Es muss gelingen!] (Smetena) (I)
Broadcast, ?*CONCERTO MARTINI E ROSSI*, date unknown

* 6. LAURITZ MELCHIOR, tenor (pf/?): AÏDA, Act I: Se quel guerrier io fossi . . . Celeste Aïda (Verdi) (I)
Private recording, 1962

7. LAWRENCE TIBBETT, baritone (pf/?): LES CONTES D'HOFFMANN, Act III: Scintille diamant (Offenbach) (F)
Private recording, circa 1936

* 8. LAWRENCE TIBBETT, baritone (pf/?): "Noël (A Catholic tale I have to Tell)" (?)
Private recording, circa 1936

9. RICHARD BONELLI, baritone (pf/?): DIE WALKÜRE, Act I: Winterstürme (Wagner) (G)
Private recording, circa 1959

10. RICHARD BONELLI, baritone (pf/?): MONNA VANNA, Act ?: C'est-ne pas un vieillard (Fevier) (F)
Private recording, circa 1959

SIDE 2 (295 B):

* 1. LUCREZIA BORI, soprano (Los Angeles Philharmonic Orchestra/Otto Klemperer): "English Lavender" ["Who'll buy my lavender?] (Edward German) (E)
Broadcast, *GENERAL MOTORS PROMENADE CONCERT*, KECA, Hollywood Bowl, Los Angeles, 6 Jun 1937

2. EZIO PINZA, bass (Studio orch/Frank Black): LE NOZZE DI FIAGRO, K. 492, Act I: Non più andrai (Mozart) (I)
Broadcast, *MAGIC KEY OF RCA*, WJZ, NYC, 30 Jan 1938

* 3. EBE STIGNANI, contralto (orch/?): ERCOLE SU'L TERMODONTE (Vivaldi) (I)
a) Onde chiare che sussurrate; b) Da due venti
?RAI broadcast, circa 1957

* 4. BORIS CHRISTOFF, bass (Orchestra of the RAI/?): HENRY VIII, Act I: Qui donc commande, quand il aime (Saint-Saens) (F)
Broadcast, ?*CONCERTO MARTINI E ROSSI*, RAI, circa 1956

* 5. JARMILA NOVOTNÁ, soprano (orch/?): LA BOHÈME, Act I: Si, mi chiamano Mimi (Puccini) (I)
Source and date unknown, circa 1944 or 1948

* 6. RICHARD TAUBER, tenor (Studio orch/George Melachrino): OLD CHELSEA: My heart and I (Richard Tauber) (E)
BBC broadcast, London, 20 Jan 1946

7. RICHARD TAUBER, tenor (pf/Percy B. Kahn): SCHWANENGESANG, D. 957, no. 4: Leise flehen ["Ständchen"] (Rellstab-Schubert) (G)
   BBC broadcast, London, 20 Jan 1946

8. RICHARD TAUBER, tenor (pf/Percy B. Kahn): "Laughing and weeping" [Lachen und weinen], D. 777 (Rellstab-Schubert) (E)
   BBC broadcast, London, 20 Jan 1946

9. RICHARD TAUBER, tenor (Studio orch/George Melachrino): BLOSSOM TIME: Love comes at blossom time (Donnelly-Berté-Romberg) (E)
   BBC broadcast, London, 20 Jan 1946

10. RICHARD TAUBER, tenor (Studio orch/George Melachrino): DAS LAND DES LÄCHELNS, Act II: You are my heart's delight [Dein ist mein ganzes Herz] (Lehár) (E)
   BBC broadcast, London, 20 Jan 1946

NOTES: EJS 295

Side 1 (295 A):

Bands 2-3: This broadcast originated from the studios of station WEAF (NBC-Red) in New York City and from the BBC, London. In New York, it was broadcast between 7:15 and 7:45 pm on 20 August; in London, of course, it was already 21 August, which may explain the confusion about its documentation in the various McCormack discographies. McCormack was joined in New York by actress Charlotte Greenwood; in London, former New York City mayor James J. "Jimmy" Walker was heard immediately after the tenor, offering his greetings, along with actors Sir Seymour Hicks and Joseph Coyne, actress Bessie Love, and the Debroy Somers Band. The tribute had been arranged by NBC vice president John F. Royal.

The original NBC acetates, four in all, are numbered PLT 181 1M 5-35 (broadcast no. 5-24).

Irish actor Thomas Meighan (b. 1879) was ill at the time with pneumonia at his home in Great Neck, Long Island. His was a long and distinguished career that came to include a number of feature films as late as the mid 1930s. He died in Great Neck on 8 July, 1936, less than a year after the tribute broadcast.

The broadcast was announced in the *New York Times* on 20 August, 1935 (p. 23: 8), and reviewed under the title "J. J. Walker Heard Here in Broadcast" on 21 August (p. 17: 1).

Band 4: Issued also by Fonografia Nazionale, Milano, and the Société Suisse des Disques Phonographiques, Zurich. Included on the set, "Mattia Battistini: King of Baritones" (EMI EX29 0790 3 and Seraphim 1G-6153 in the U.S.) in 1986.

Band 6: Not the German-language version found on EJS 322 (March, 1965). This version is otherwise undocumented.

Band 8: Also included on UORC 197 (March, 1974), where the "Noël" is given as Tibbett's "own version of a Christmas Noel, sung at a party." The lyrics begin "May all my enemies go to hell . . . Noël, Noël, Noël."

Side 2 (295 B):

Band 1: Joseph Bentonelli was also featured in this broadcast: his selections appeared earlier on EJS 292 (February, 1964). Station KECA was the local NBC Blue affiliate in Los Angeles. Other items from this 6 June, 1937 broadcast appeared on EJS 425 (February, 1968), including "English Lavender," and later, on the Bori recital, EJS 541 (February, 1971).

Band 3: This single Stignani band actually contains two separate arias from Vivaldi's opera ERCOLE SU'L TERMODONTE, as given.

Band 4: Labeled as "Tant le pape est ostile," a corruption of the recitative, "Donc le pape est hostile." The recitative, however, does not appear on the EJS 295 transfer.

Band 5: Given on the label of EJS 295 as 1944, but reported to be 1948, source unknown. It could not be a 1944 Met broadcast, as Sayão was the featured *Mimi* in both of the BOHÈME radio matinees aired in 1944 and 1945.

Band 6: Tauber's operetta, OLD CHELSEA, made its debut at the Prince's Theater, London, on 17 February, 1943. See also the endnote for EJS 511 (May, 1970).

EJS 296: "The Golden Age of Opera" (2 LPs)
Issued April, 1964

SIDES 1-3 (296 A-C):

LE CONVENIENZE ED INCONVENIENZE TEATRALI (Donizetti) (I)
Opera 2 in acts (complete)
Orchestra and Chorus dell'Angelicum di Milano/Bruno Rigacci
?RAI broadcast, Milano, 20 Sep 1963

CAST:
Renato Capecchi (*Mamm'Agata*); Mariella Adani (*Corilla*); Giorgio Tadeo (*Procolo*); Alberta P. Gonzales (*Luigia*); Paolo Montarsolo (*Biscroma Strappaviscere*); Stefania Malagù (*Dorotea*); Herbert Handt (*Guglielmo*); Paolo Pedani (*Impresario*); Dino Mantovani (*Prospero*).

SIDE 4 (296 D):

PIGMALIONE (Donizetti) (I)
Opera in 1 act (complete)
Orchestra of the Teatro Donizetti, Bergamo/Armando Gatto
Broadcast, Teatro Donizetti, Bergamo, 3 Dec 1963

CAST:
Doro Antonioli (*Pigmalione*); Orianna Santunioni Finzi (*Galatea*).

NOTES: EJS 296

The CONVENIENZE ED INCONVENIENZE TEATRALI was later issued as VOCE-5, and the PIGMALIONE as Melodram MEL-029 and VOCE-15.

PIGMALIONE, a one-act *scena drammatica*, was Donizetti's first opera, written in Bologna in 1816, but not produced until 13 October, 1960 (Teatro Donizetti, Bergamo). The manuscript is held in the Biblioteque Nationale, Paris.

EJS 297: "The Golden Age of Opera (2 LPs)
Issued April, 1964

SIDES 1-4 (297 A-D):

L'INGANNO FELICE (Rossini) (I)
Opera 1 in act (complete)
Orchestra Antonio Scarlatti di Napoli/Carlo Franci
RAI broadcast, Naples, 17 Dec 1963

CAST:
Emilia Cundari (*Isabella*); Fernando Jacopucci (*Bertrando*); Paolo Montarsolo (*Batone*); Giorgio Tadeo (*Tarabotto*); Sergio Pezzetti (*Ormondo*).

NOTES: EJS 297

This performance was later reissued on LP as VOCE-4 and on CD (in stereo) as AS 1001.

EJS 298: The Golden Age of Opera" (2 LPs)
Issued May, 1964

SIDES 1-4 (298 A-D):

LEONORA (sic) [**FIDELIO**] (Beethoven) (G)
Opera in acts (complete)
?Bayerischer Rundfunk Orchestra and Chorus/Hans Altmann
Broadcast, Bayerischer Rundfunk, Munich, circa 1951

CAST:
Paula Baumann (*Leonora*); Julius Patzak (*Florestan*); Lore Wissmann (*Marzelline*); Richard Holm (*Jaquino*); Georg Weiter (*Rocco*); Georg Hann (*Don Fernando*); Richard Misske (*Don Pizzaro*); Walter Praetorius (*First Prisoner*); Gustav Bley (*Second Prisoner*).

NOTES: EJS 298

This is the original 1805 version of Beethoven's FIDELIO. The May, 1964 bulletin suggests that the music differs some 30-40% from the better-known revison.

EJS 299: "The Golden Age of Opera (1 LP)
Issued May, 1964

SIDES 1-2 (299 A-B):

CRISPINO E LA COMARE (Federico and Luigi Ricci) (I)
Opera in 4 acts (excerpts)
Orchestra and Chorus of Radio Italiana [RAI], Milano/Alfredo Simonetto
RAI broadcast, Milan, circa 1950

CAST:
Franco Calabrese (*Crispino Tacchetto*); Graziella Sciutti (*Annetta*); Lydia Roan (*La Comare*); Giovanni Gazzera (*The Count del Fiore*); Pier Luigi Latinucci (*Don Fabrizio*); Giorgio Giorgetti (*Don Mirabolano*); Pasquale Lombardi (*Don Asdrubale di Caparotta*); [? (*Lisetta*)]; [? (*Bortolo*)].

NOTES: EJS 299

Presumably presented complete here as perfomed and broadcast. The parts of *Lisetta* and *Bortola* do not appear in the recorded excerpts, and are not identified on the labels of EJS 299.

Act I/i ends after the "Crispino misero . . . Paga! Paga!" ensemble. Act I/ii is complete. Act II is given from the opening to the end of "Io non sono più l'Anetta." Act III/i and ii are nearly complete, with only the opening chorus omitted, beginning at *Don Fabrizio's* "Vediam se in farmacia. Scene iii goes only as far as the famous "Doctors' Trio," which is also omitted. Act IV is complete with a few internal cuts in Scene ii.

The date of this performance is provisional, based on the fact that 1950 was the centenary of the Ricci's opera, that tenor Gazzera sang for RAI only in the 1949-1950 season, and that Roan and Lombardi were active at RAI only in the 1948-1952 seasons (though Lombardi had sung earlier for EIAR in 1934 and 1935). The May, 1964 bulletin, however, claims that the work "dates from this [?1964] year," which may mean a re-broadcast.

EJS 300: "The Golden Age of Opera" (1 LP)
Issued May, 1964

SIDES 1-2 (300 A-B):

ARIADNE AUF NAXOS (R. Strauss) (G)
Opera in 1 act and a Prologue (complete, but with Prelude omitted)
Orchestra of the Reichssender, Stuttgart/Clemens Krauss
Broadcast, Reichssender [Reichs-Rundfunk], Berlin or Stuttgart, 6 Nov 1935

CAST:
Viorica Ursuleac (*Ariadne*); Helge Roswaenge (*Bacchus*); Erna Berger (*Zerbinetta*); Miliza Korjus (*Najade*); Gertrud Rünger (*Dryade*); Ilonka Holndonner (*Echo*); Karl Hammes (*Harlekin*); Benno Arnold (*Scaramuccio*); Eugen Fuchs (*Truffaldin*); Erich Zimmermann (*Brighella*).

NOTES: EJS 300

This Radio Berlin performance was reissued as BASF KFB-21806 and Acanta 21.806.

EJS 301: "The Golden Age of Opera" (1 LP)
Issued June, 1964

SIDES 1-2 (301 A-B):

LE NOZZE DI FIGARO, K. 492 (Mozart) (I)
Opera in 4 acts (Act II only)
San Francisco Opera House Orchestra and Chorus/Erich Leinsdorf
San Francisco Opera broadcast, KPO [NBC], San Francisco, 12 Oct 1940

CAST:
Ezio Pinza (*Figaro*); Bidú Sayão (*Susanna*); Elisabeth Rethberg (*The Countess*) John Brownlee (*Count Almaviva*); Risë Stevens (*Cherubino*); Gerhard Pechner (*Doctor Bartolo*); Irra Petina (*Marcellina*); Alessio De Paolis (*Don Basilio*); Mari Monte (*Barbarina*); George Cehanovsky (*Antonio*); [Robert Ballagh (*Don Curzio*)].

NOTES: EJS 301

This was the opening-night performance of the 1940 San Francisco season. The original NBC acetates from which this issue was drawn (three 16-inch sides with Orthacoustic labels, numbered ENG. 183 9-37, broadcast no. 40-345) end abruptly in the midst of the Act II Finale: the completion of the performance on EJS 301 is taken from another, as yet untraced (?Metropolitan Opera) broadcast.

EJS 302: "The Golden Age of Opera" (1 LP)
Issued June, 1964

SIDE 1 (302 A):

IL BARBIERE DI SIVIGLIA (Rossini) (I)
Opera in 2 acts (excerpts)
Orchestra and Chorus of the Palacio de las Bellas Artes, Mexico City/ Renato Cellini
Broadcast, Palacio de las Bellas Artes, Mexico City, XEN, 7 Jul 1949

CAST:
Giulietta Simionato (*Rosina*); Giuseppe Di Stefano (*Count Almaviva*); Enzo Mascherini (*Figaro*); [Cesare Siepi (*Don Basilio*)]; [Gerhard Pechner (*Doctor Bartolo*)]; [Concha de los Santos (*Berta*)]; Francisco Tortolero (*Fiorello*).

1. Act I:
   a) DI STEFANO: Ecco ridente
   b) MASCHERINI: Largo al factotum

   c) DI STEFANO and MASCHERINI: All'idea di quel metallo . . . Numero quindici
   d) SIMIONATO: Una voce poco fà
   e) SIMIONATO and MASCHERINI: Dunque io son?

   Act III: f) MASCHERINI, SIMIONATO, and DI STEFANO: Ah qual colpo . . . Alla scala del balcone

SIDE 2 (302 B):

MIGNON (Thomas) (I)
Opera in 3 acts (excerpts)
Orchestra and Chorus of the Palacio de las Bellas Artes, Mexico City/ Umberto Mugnai
Broadcast, Palacio de las Bellas Artes, XEN, Mexico City, 28 Jun 1949

CAST:
Giulietta Simionato (*Mignon*); Luz Verdad Guajardo (*Philine*); Giuseppe di Stefano (*Wilhelm*); Cesare Siepi (*Lothario*); Gilberto Cerda (*Laërte*); Ignacio Ruffino (*Jarno*); Graciela Milera (*Fredéric*).

Act I:
1. GUAJARDO, SIMIONATO, DI STEFANO, SIEPI, CERDA, and RUFFINO: Quel est, je veux le savoir
2. DI STEFANO, SIEPI, and GUAJARDO: Eh quoi! mon cher Laërte . . . Que de grâce
3. SIMIONATO: Demain, dis-tu? . . . Connais-tu le pays
4. SIMIONATO and SIEPI: Légères hirondelles

Act II:
5. SIMIONATO: Je connais un pauvre enfant ["Styrienne"]
6. MILERA: Me voici dans son boudoir
7. DI STEFANO: Adieu, Mignon! courage!
8. SIMIONATO: Elle est aimée!
9. SIEPI and SIMIONATO: As-tu souffert? as-tu pleuré?
10. GUAJARDO: Oui, pour ce soir je suis reine des fées . . . Je suis Titania ["Polonaise"]

NOTES: EJS 302

Side 1 (302 A):

Issued more recently on a Giuseppe De Stefano (label) CD, GDS 105.

Side 2 (302 B):

Sung in Italian: the excerpts are listed above in the original French for ease of reference.

The act two Rondo-Gavotte of *Frédéric*, "In veder l'amata stanza" [Me voici dans son boudoir] is interpolated into the *Frédéric-Wilhem* duet, "C'est moi! j'ai tout brisé," that follows *Mignon's* "Styrienne." This was apparently first performed by Zélia Trebelli-Bettini (1834-1892) in the 1870 Drury Lane production with Christine Nilsson.

The 1949 series of summer Palacio de las Bellas Artes performances with Di Stefano and Simionato, from which the BARBIERE and MIGNON were drawn, continued on EJS 303 with the WERTHER excerpts and on EJS 319 (February, 1965), a complete LA FAVORITA.

The MIGNON is reported to have appeared on an early HRE LP, catalog number unknown. Excerpts were reissued (1992) on "Golden Age of Opera" CD 128/129 (not the Smith GAO series, of course), coupled with excerpts from the 22 June, 1948 Palacio de las Bellas Artes RIGOLETTO, originally issued as EJS 559 in June, 1971.

EJS 303: "The Golden Age of Opera" (1 LP)
Issued June, 1964

WERTHER (Massenet) (I)
Opera in 4 acts (excerpts)
Orchestra and Chorus of the Palacio de las Bellas Artes, Mexico City/ Renato Cellini
Broadcast, Palacio de las Bellas Artes, Mexico City, XEN, 3 Jul 1949

CAST:
Giuseppe Di Stefano (*Werther*); Giulietta Simionato (*Charlotte*); Fausto Del Prado (*Albert*); Eugenia Rocca Bruna (*Sophie*); Ignacio Ruffino (*Le Bailli*); [Gilberto Cerda (*Johann*)]; [Francesco Tortolero (*Schmidt*)].

SIDE 1 (303 A):

Act I: 1. a) DI STEFANO: Alors, c'est bien ici . . . O Nature pleine de grâce
b) DI STEFANO, RUFFINO, SIMIONATO, ROCCA BRUNA, and DEL PRADO: O spectacle idéal d'amour et d'innocence
c) SIMIONATO, DI STEFANO, and RUFFINO: Il faut nous séparer . . . to the end of the act

Act II: 2. a) DI STEFANO: Un autre est son époux! . . . tout mon être en pleure!
b) DEL PRADO and DI STEFANO: Je vous sais un coeur loyal et fort . . . Et ce sera ma part de bonheur sur la terre
d) ROCCA BRUNA, DI STEFANO, DEL PRADO, and SIMIONATO: Du gai soleil . . . to the end of the act

SIDE 2 (303 B):

Act III: 1. a) SIMIONATO: Werther! Werther! . . . et tu frémiras!
b) SIMIONATO, ROCCA BRUNA, and DI STEFANO: Va! laisse couler mes larmes . . . Pourquoi me réveiller?

Act IV: 2. a) SIMIONATO, DI STEFANO, ROCCA BRUNA, and Chorus: Complete (from the end of the Entr'acte)

NOTES: EJS 303

As with the MIGNON on EJS 302, the WERTHER is sung here in Italian: the excerpts are listed above in the original French for ease of reference. The complete performance was issued in April, 1971 as EJS 547 and later, on Cetra LO-30/3.

EJS 304: "The Golden Age of Opera" (2 LPs)
Issued June, 1964

GRISÉLIDIS (Massenet) (F)
Opera in 3 acts (abridged)
Orchestra and Chorus of the Office de Radiodiffusion Télévision Française [ORTF], Paris/Robert Allpress
ORTF broadcast, Paris, 1963

CAST:
Géneviève Moizan (*Griséldis*); Fréda Betti (*Fiamina*); Lina Dachary (*Bertrade*); Xavier Depraz [Depras] (*The Devil*); Claude Genty (*The Marquis*); André Malabrera (*Alain*); Georges Jollis (*The Priest*); Lucien Lovano (*Gondebaud*).

SIDE 1 (304 A) - SIDE 2 (304 B):

Prologue - Act II (part 1)

SIDE 3 (304 C):

1. Act II (part 2)
2. Act III

LA NAVARRAISE (Massenet) (F)
Opera in 2 acts (complete)
Orchestra and Chorus of the Office de Radiodiffusion Télévision Française [ORTF], Paris/Jean-Claude Hartemann
ORTF broadcast, Paris, November, 1963

CAST:
Géneviève Moizan (*Anita*); Alain Vanzo (*Araquil*); Jacques Mars (*Garrido*); Lucien Lovano (*Remigio*); Joseph Peyron (*Ramon*); Marcel Vigneron (*Bustamente*).

3. Act I (part 1)

SIDE 4 (304 D):

1. Conclusion

NOTES: EJS 304

Sides 1-3 (GRISÉLIDIS):

It has been suggested that the *Priest*, "G. Jollis," may in fact be Gabriel Jullia, who sang at the Opéra-Comique for decades beginning in 1931. However, Jullia's only documented performances of GRISÉLIDIS in that house had him in the role of *Gondebaud*. Conductor Allpress has been cited elsewhere as "Alpress," as labeled on EJS 304.

Massenet's 1901 opera was originally mounted in three acts and a Prologue, as given here, though some contemporary sources cite *two* acts and a prologue. It is presented on EJS 304 complete as performed, with a number of minor performance cuts (a few bars of the Act I Prelude for example), and the following recording cuts in Act II, all seemingly made by Smith--possibly for purposes of timing, but more than likely because of a damaged source tape:

a) nearly the first two pages of the *Devil's* opening aria (the truncation of the Act II Prelude leading into the opening scene seems to have been a *performance* cut).

b) In II/iii, from after *Grisélidis'* scene ending "Ainsi soit-il," to the duet of the *Devil* and *Fiamina*, "Quand nous vimes le marquis;" after *Grisélidis'* "Il partit au printemps" (just before the offstage women's chorus, "Je vous salue, Marie"), *Grisélidis'* line, "Protégez le père et l'enfant" is also missing.

c) From after *Grisélidis'* "J'obérai! Voici l'anneau" to the *Devil's* "Des bois obscures," omitting the end of II/iv and all of II/v.

Act III begins abruptly with the *Grisélidis-Marquis* duet at "Avant de vous parler, suis-je votre epouse?," but this may be a cut in the original source tape.

The entire set is sharp at 33.3 rpm: the Prologue plays in score pitch at about 31.5 rpm; Act I plays correctly at about 31.8 rpm, and Act II at 32.00 rpm: all rise slightly throughout their duration.

Note that GRISÉLIDIS occupies all of sides 1 and 2 and the first two bands of side 3; LA NAVARRAISE begins at band three of side 3 and concludes (unbanded) on side 4.

EJS 305: "The Golden Age of Opera" (2 LPs)
Issued September, 1964

SIDES 1-4 (305 A-D):

IL CORSARO (Verdi) (I)
Opera in 3 acts (complete)
Orchestra and Chorus of the Vacanze Musicali and the Istituzione Universitaria dei Concerti di Roma/ Victor Wollny
In-house or private recording, ?Rome, 29 Aug 1963

CAST:
Aldo Bottion (*Corrado*); Maria Battinelli (*Medora*); Virginia De Notaristefani (*Gulnara*); Silvano Carroli (*Seid*); Vito Brunetti (*Giovanni*); Giorgio Grimaldi (*Selimo*); Mario Guggia (*A Eunuch*); Vincenzo Taddeo (*A Slave*).

NOTES: EJS 305

The September, 1964 bulletin describes IL CORSARO as one of two hitherto [1964] unrecorded Verdi operas (the other is not mentioned!). The bulletin further states that the performance originated in Rome and boasts a "good cast of young Italians."

Smith claimed privately that he arranged the performance himself and that it was recorded professionally. It was probably not broadcast, and may not have even been a public performance, as there is no applause.

EJS 306: "The Golden Age of Opera" (2 LPs)
Issued September, 1964

SIDES 1-4 (306 A-D):

LA TRAVIATA (Verdi) (I)
Opera in 3 acts (complete)
London Philharmonic Orchestra and Royal Opera House Chorus/Pietro Cimara
Broadcast, Covent Garden, London, 31 May 1939

CAST:
Maria Caniglia (*Violetta*); Beniamino Gigli (*Alfredo*); Mario Basiola (*Germont*); Maria Huder (*Flora*); Aristide Baracchi (*Baron Douphol*); Norman Walker (*Grenvil*); Adelio Zagonara (*Gastone*); Booth Hitchin (*Marquis d'Obigny*); Gladys Palmer (*Annina*); Octave Dua (*Giuseppe*).

NOTES: EJS 306

According to the September, 1964 bulletin, *Germont's* second-act aria, "Di provenza il mar," was omitted from the performance "for some reason--we cannot find out why," as Smith put it. Possibly it was simply not transcribed, but it seems unlikely that it would not have been sung. As *Basiola* appears not to have recorded it commercially, Giuseppe De Luca's commercial electrical version, recorded in New York (probably in Liederkranz Hall), was plugged in instead, as noted in the EJS bulletin:

GIUSEPPE DE LUCA, baritone (Metropolitan Opera House Orchetra/Giulio Setti): Di provenza il mar
CVE-51151-2   10 Apr 1929   Victor 7086 HMV DB 1340 [42-614]

EJS 307: "The Golden Age of Opera" (2 LPs)
Issued October, 1964

SIDE 1-4 (307 A-D):

ROBERTO DEVEREUX ossia IL CONTE D'ESSEX (Donizetti) (I)
Opera in 3 acts (complete)
Orchestra and Chorus of the Teatro San Carlo di Napoli/Mario Rossi
Broadcast, Teatro San Carlo, Naples, 2 May 1964

CAST:
Leyla Gencer (*Elisabetta*); Ruggiero Bondino (*Roberto Devereux*); Piero Cappucilli (*Duke of Nottingham*); Anna Maria Rota (*Sara*); Gabriele De Julis (*Lord Cecil*); Silvano Pagliuca (*Sir Gualtiero Raleigh*); Bruno Grella (*A Page*); Bruno Grella (*Nottingham's Servant*).

NOTES: EJS 307

Noted in the October, 1964 bulletin as the first recording of this 1837 Donizetti opera.

The entire performance requires a playing speed of about 31.5 rpm. Correctly pitched and in better sound, it was subsequently reissued as Robin Hood Records RHR 503-C, and more recently, as Hunt CD 545 and Foyer FO-1042.

EJS 308: "The Golden Age of Opera" (1 LP)
Issued October, 1964

LA FANCIULLA DEL WEST (Puccini) (I)
Opera in 3 acts (abridged)
Orchestra and Chorus of the Teatro dell'Opera, Roma/Oliviero de Fabritiis
In-house wire recording, Teatro dell'Opera, Rome, 24 Jan 1952

CAST:
Giacomo Lauri-Volpi (*Dick Johnson*); Maria Caniglia (*Minnie*); Raffaele De Falchi (*Jack Rance*); Saturno Meletti (*Sonora*); Alfredo Colella (*Ashby*); Adelio Zagonara (*Nick*); Nino Mazziotti (*Trin*); Virgilio Stocco (*Bello*); Paolo Caroli (*Harry*); Mino Russo (*Joe*); Giuseppe Forgione (*Happy*); Gino Conti (*José Castro*); Fernando Delle Fornaci (*Pony Express Rider*).

SIDE 1 (308 A):

1. Act I: CANIGLIA and assembled cast: Che cos' è stato? [Minnie's entrance] . . . to the end of the act

SIDE 2 (308 B):

1. Act II: LAURI-VOLPI, CANIGLIA, and assembled cast: Hello! [Johnson's entrance] . . . to the end of the act

2. Act III: LAURI-VOLPI, DE FALCHI, CANIGLIA, MELETTI, and Chorus: Ch'ella mi creda . . . to the end of the opera

NOTES: EJS 308

The original performance *recording* was abridged. The October, 1964 bulletin claims that it was "originally taken on wire and then transferred to tape," and that "the orchestra sound is poor - but the singing is tremendous." The last two points cannot be disputed.

EJS 309: The Golden Age of Opera" (1 LP)
Issued November, 1964

MANON LESCAUT (Puccini) (I)
Opera in 4 acts (excerpts)
Orchestra and Chorus of Radio Italiana [RAI], Milano/Alfredo Simonetto
RAI broadcast, Milan, 24 or 29 Dec 1950

CAST:
Adriana Guerrini (*Manon Lescaut*); Beniamino Gigli (*Chevalier Des Grieux*); Mario Borriello (*Lescaut*); Mario Zorgnotti (*A Sergeant*); Renato Pasquali (*Captain*); [Pasquale Lombardi (*Geronte de Ravoir*)]; [Gino Del Signore (*Edmondo*)]; [Mario Zorgnotti (*An Innkeeper*)]; [Jole Farolfi (*A Singer*)]; [Ercole Pirelli (*Dancing Master*)]; [Ercole Pirelli (*A Lamplighter*)].

SIDE 1 (309 A):

1. Act I: a) Prelude
b) GIGLI: Tra voi belle
c) GIGLI, GUERRINI, and BORRIELLO: Cortese damigella . . . Donna non vidi mai
d) GUERRINI, GIGLI, and BORRIELLO: Vedete? Io son fedele . . . Che dite?! Il vero!

2. Act II: a) BORRIELLO and GUERRINI: Sei splendida e lucente! . . . In quelle trine morbide
b) GUERRINI and GIGLI: Tu, tu, amore, tu! . . . Dolcissimo soffrir!

SIDE 2 (309 B):

1. Act II: c) GIGLI and GUERRINI: Senti, di qui partiamo . . . Sarò fedele e buona, lo giuro, lo giuro!

1. Act III: a) Intermezzo
b) ZORGNOTTI, GIGLI, DE PASQUALI, and Chorus: Presto! In fila! . . . No! pazzo son! Guardate . . . to the end of the act

2. Act IV: GUERRINI and GIGLI: Sola, perduta, abbandonata! . . . to the end of the opera

NOTES: EJS 309

Note that this LP was issued out of sequence in November, 1964, where EJS 310, also part of Smith's celebration of the fiftieth anniversary of Gigli's operatic debut, appeared the previous month. The November bulletin incorrectly dates the MANON LESCAUT as 19 June, 1952. EJS 329 (April, 1965) and ANNA 1033 (May-June, 1979) included the Gigli-Guerrini Act IV "Tutto su me ti posa" (to the beginning of "Sola, perduta") that is missing from EJS 309, but on both LPs it is listed as sung by Gigli and Caniglia.

The MANON LESCAUT was performed complete and broadcast complete in Italy, but the tape made available to non-commercial American radio stations by RAI-USA contained only the material that appears on EJS 309, which probably used the official American broadcast tape as its source. The date of the original performance was 24 December: it is not known whether the 29 December MANON LESCAUT was another performance or simply an Italian rebroadcast.

Zorgnotti is given the surname "Zotti" on the label of EJS 309, and Renato De Pasquali the name "Nino Pasquale."

Speeds are reported to begin at 33.8 rpm, shifting to about 34.00 at Guerrini's "In quelle trine;" Act IV requires a speed of 34.2 rpm.

EJS 310: "The Golden Age of Opera" (1 LP)
Issued October, 1964

"BENIAMINO GIGLI / 50th ANNIVERSARY RECORD"

SIDE 1 (310 A):

1. w. Orquesta Sinfonica do Radio Gazeta, Sao Paulo/Armando Belardi: WERTHER, Act III: Ah, non mi ridestar [Pourquoi me réveiller?] (Massenet) (I)
   Broadcast, Orquesta Sinfonico do Radio Gazeta, Auditorium do Radio Gazeta, Sao Paulo, 7 Oct 1951

2. w. Orquesta Sinfonica do Radio Gazeta, Sao Paulo/Armando Belardi: RIGOLETTO, Act IV: La donna è mobile (Verdi) (I)
   Broadcast, Orquesta Sinfonico do Radio Gazeta, Auditorium do Radio Gazeta, Sao Paulo, 7 Oct 1951

3. w. Orquesta Sinfonica do Radio Gazeta, Sao Paulo/Armando Belardi: "Quanno a ffemmena vo'" (De Crescenzo) (N)
   Broadcast, Orquesta Sinfonico do Radio Gazeta, Auditorium do Radio Gazeta, Sao Paulo, 7 Oct 1951

4. w. JOAQUIN VILLA, baritone (Orquesta Sinfonica do Radio Gazeta, Sao Paulo/Armando Belardi): LA FORZA DEL DESTINO, Act IV: Fratello--Riconoscimi . . . Le minaccie i fieri accenti
   Broadcast, Orquesta Sinfonico do Radio Gazeta, Auditorium do Radio Gazeta, Sao Paulo, 7 Oct 1951

* 5 w. La Scala Orchestra/Pietro Mascagni: CAVALLERIA RUSTICANA: O Lola ch'ai di latti ["Siciliana"] (Mascagni) (I)
   ?2BA 3811-3 HMV DB 3960 Milan, April, 1940

6. w. RAI Orchestra/Nino Sanzogno: L'ELISIR D'AMORE: Una furtiva lagrima (Donizetti) (I)
   Broadcast, ***CONCERTO MARTINI E ROSSI***, RAI, Teatro Municipale, San Remo, 21 Dec 1953

SIDE 2 (310 B):

1. w. RAI Orchestra/Nino Sanzogno: ANDREA CHENIER, Act I: Un dì, all'azzurro spazio ["Improvviso"] (Giordano) (I)
   Broadcast, ***CONCERTO MARTINI E ROSSI***, RAI, Teatro Municipale, San Remo, 21 Dec 1953

2. w. string orch/Rainaldo Zamboni; organ/Herbert Dawson: ELLENS DRITTER GESANG, D.839, no. 6: Ave Maria [Ave Maria! Jungfrau mild!] (Schubert) (L)
   2EA 10684-1 London, 26 Nov 1947 HMV DB 6619 Victor 12-0400

3. w. RAI Orchestra/Nino Antonicelli: LES PÊCHEURS DE PERLES, Act I: Mi par d'udir ancora [Je crois entendre encore] (Bizet (I)
   Broadcast, ***CONCERTO MARTINI E ROSSI***, RAI, Rome, 9 Feb 1953

4. w. RAI Orchestra/Nino Antonicelli: LODOLETTA, Act III: Se Franz dicesse il vero . . . Ah! ritrovarla (Mascagni) (I)
   Broadcast, ***CONCERTO MARTINI E ROSSI***, RAI, Rome, 9 Feb 1953

5. w. RAI Orchestra/Nino Antonicelli: FEDORA, Act II: Amor ti vieta (Giordano) (I)
   Broadcast, ***CONCERTO MARTINI E ROSSI***, RAI, Rome, 9 Feb 1953

* 6. w. RAI Orchestra/Armando La Rosa Parodi: TURANDOT, Act III: Nessun dorma (Puccini) (I)
   Broadcast, ***CONCERTO MARTINI E ROSSI***, RAI, Torino, 22 Jan 1951

NOTES: EJS 310

Side 1 (310 A):

Band 5: A bogus applause track concludes this commercial recording (from the 1940 complete CAVALLERIA on HMV, conducted by the composer), ostensibly to disguise its commercial origin.

Because the original April, 1940 Milanese matrix was broken in transit from Italy, Gigli remade the "Siciliana" in London on 26 November, 1947 (matrix 2EA 10685-1) for the post-War British and American 78 issues of the set. Which version is used on EJS 310 could not be determined.

Side 2 (310 B):

Band 6: Gigli sings an encore of the "Nessun dorma."

EJS 311: "The Golden Age of Opera" (2 LPs)
Issued November, 1964

SIDES 1-4 (311 A-D):

LA CAMPANNA SOMMERSA (Respighi) (I)
Opera in 4 acts (complete)
Orchestra and Chorus of Radio Italiana [RAI], Milano/Franco Capuana
RAI broadcast, Milan, 11 Jul 1956

CAST:
Margherita Carosio (*Rautendelein*); Umberto Borsó (*Enrico*); Rina Malatrasi (*Magda*); Lucia Danieli (*The Witch*); Rolando Panerai (*The Undine*); Plinio Clabassi (*The Curate*); Tommaso Frascati (*The Satyr*); Angel[ic]a Vercelli (*Elf*); Marisa Pintus (*Elf*); Bruna Ronchini (*Elf*); Graziella Cattaneo (*Child*); Graziana Gasperoni (*Child*); Pier Luigi Latinucci (*The Maestro*); Angelo Mercuriali (*The Barber*).

EJS 312: "The Golden Age of Opera" (2 LPs)
Issued November, 1964

SIDES 1-3 (312 A-C):

CECILIA (Refice) (I)
Azione sacra in 3 Episodes (complete)
Orchestra and Chorus of Radio Italiana [RAI], Milano/Oliviero De Fabritiis
RAI broadcast, Milan, 2 Nov 1955

CAST:
Maria Pedrini (*Cecilia*); Alvinio Misciano (*Valeriano*); Armando Dadò (*Tiburzio*); Saturno Meletti (*Amachio*); Plinio Clabassi (*Bishop Urbano*); Maria Fornaro (*The Angel*); Palmira Vitali Marini (*Blind Woman*); Valiano Natali (*A Freed Slave*); Bruno Bassi (*A Slave*).

SIDE 4 (312 D):

2. a) CLAUDIA MUZIO, soprano (orch and chorus/Licinio Refice):
CECILIA, Act I: L'annuncio (Refice) (I)
CBX 1335-2/1336-2 Milan, ?19 Apr 1934 — Columbia BQX 2500; Columbia LCX 19; Columbia 9089-M; 9148-M

b) CLAUDIA MUZIO, soprano (orch and chorus/Licinio Refice):
CECILIA, Act III: La morte di Cecilia (Refice) (I)
CBX 1366-1/1367-1 Milan, ?6-7 Jun 1935 — Columbia BQX 2503; Columbia LCX 24; Columbia 9149-M

NOTES: EJS 312

Dated 1954 on the label of EJS 312. Maria Fornaro is not credited. The 1970s EJS checklist gives the ambiguous citation "Pedrini & Muzio: 78 rpm discs (2) - RAI - 1954," meaning only that Muzio's two commercial Columbia recordings from Refice's 1934 *Azione sacra* (text by E. Mucci), the composer conducting, have been added to side four of this 1955 RAI performance. Muzio also recorded Refice's "Ombra di nube" (CBX 1365-1) and "Ave Maria" (CBX 1368-1) during the June, 1935 session. She created the role of *Cecilia* at Rome's Teatro Reale on 15 February, 1934.

The BQX and LCX prefixes are Italian and English, respectively; the M-suffix is American. The American issues appeared in Set X-112. The Milan dates are taken from the Angel Muzio LP, COLC 101, which contains some of the preceding and following matrices (but neither of the Refice arias): CBX 1337 is dated 19 April, 1934; CBX 1359-1364 are dated 5-6 June, 1935, and CBX 1375 is dated 11 June, 1935.

EJS 312 plays nearly a semi-tone low at 33.3 rpm. The 1955 broadcast was later issued on the two-disc Melodram LP, MEL 167.

EJS 313: "The Golden Age of Opera" (1 LP)
Issued December, 1964

GUNTRAM (R. Strauss) (G)
Opera in 3 acts (excerpts)
BBC Scottish Orchestra/Norman Del Mar
BBC broadcast, ?London, 24 May 1964

CAST:
Robert Thomas (*Guntram*); Marie Collier (*Freihild*).

SIDE 1 (313 A):

Act I: 1. Prelude

Act II: 2. THOMAS: Prelude . . . Ich schaue ein glanzvoll prunkendes Fest

SIDE 2 (313 B):

Act II: 1. COLLIER: Fass'ich sie bang
2. COLLIER and THOMAS: Heil dir, Geliebter

NOTES: EJS 313

The roughly 50 minutes of excerpts featured here were thought at the time to be all that remained of Strauss' 1894 version of GUNTRAM and this is noted in Smith's December, 1964 bulletin, which further insists that the name of the opera is "Guthram."

EJS 314: "The Golden Age of Opera" (3 LPs)
Issued December, 1964

SIDES 1-6 (314 A-F):

DIE LIEBE DER DANAE (R. Strauss) (G)
Opera in 3 acts (complete)
Wiener Philharmoniker and Chorus of the Wiener Staatsoper/Clemens Krauss
Broadcast, Salzburg Festival, Salzburg, 14 Aug 1952

CAST:
Annelies Kupper (*Danae*); Paul Schöffler (*Jupiter*); Josef Traxel (*Merkur*); Josef Gostic (*Midas*); Laszlo Szemere (*Pollux*); Anny Felbermayr (*Xanthe*); Dorothea Siebert (*Semele*); Ester [Esther] Rethy (*Europa*); Georgine von Milinkovič (*Alkmene*); Sieglinde Wagner (*Leda*); August Jaresch (*First King*); Erich Majkut (*Second King*); Harald Pröglhöf (*Third King*); Franz Bierbach (*Fourth King*).

NOTES: EJS 314

Strauss' 1943 DIE LIEBE DER DANAE, the composer's last opera, was set to premiere at the 1944 Salzburg Festival with Ursuleac, Taubmann, and Hotter, Krauss conducting, but this was cancelled after the 16 August dress rehearsal (it had originally been scheduled to open the festival on 5 August). The Salzburg Festival had been given partial exemption from the 20 July, 1944 "Total War" edict, but at the last moment all public performances were cancelled, the only exception being a Bruckner Eighth Symphony conducted by Furtwängler on 14 August of that year.

Consequently, this 14 August, 1952 performance was the world *public* premiere of the opera. Conductor Clemens Krauss was the sole participant of the original 1944 production to take part.

The February, 1965 bulletin notes that "After publication, it was discovered that side three of Liebe der Danae was a major fifth (sic) too high. This has been re-run and those who received defective copies may have a new one by writing." The second edition, on the other hand, plays *low* at 33.3 rpm!

Later issued by Smith in his "Richard Strauss" series as SP 4, under the title DANAE'S LOVE, with the speeds uncorrected. The Bruno Walter Society reissued the performance on three LPs as part of their Recital Records Series, RR 464, and Melodram issued it as MEL-111.

EJS 315: "The Golden Age of Opera" (2 LPs)
Issued January, 1965

SIDES 1-4 (315 A-D):

BENVENUTO CELLINI (Berlioz) (F)
Opera in 2 acts (complete)
Orchestra of the Suisse Romande and Chorus of the Grand Theatre, Génève/Louis de Froment
?Broadcast, Radio Suisse, Geneva, circa November, 1964

CAST:
Nicolai Gedda (*Benvenuto Cellini*); Andrée Esposito (*Teresa*); Jacques Doucet (*Fieramosca*); Michel Hamel (*Ascanio*); Nicolai Ghiuselev (*Clement VII*); André Vessières (*Balducci*); Pierre Voillier (*Francesco*); Georgio [Georg] Pappas (*Bernadino*); Hugues Cuénod (*Inn Keeper*); Olof de Wyzanowsky (*An Officer*).

NOTES: EJS 315

The January, 1965 bulletin claims that this performance, "not in regular release," was given the previous November in Geneva and that "only 25 copies are available of this work, the balance having been subscribed to in advance in Europe." Whether or not this was really true has not been determined. In any event, the exact date of the broadcast could not be found.

EJS 316: "The Golden Age of Opera" (2 LPs)
Issued February, 1965

SIDES 1-4 (316 A-D):

LA FIGLIA DEL REGGIMENTO [LA FILLE DU RÉGIMENT] (Donizetti) (I)
Opera in 2 Acts (complete)
Orchestra and Chorus of Radio Italiana [RAI], Milano/Franco Mannino
RAI telecast, Milan, 11 Dec 1960

CAST:
Anna Moffo (*Marie*); Giuseppe Campora (*Tonio*); Giulio Fioravanti (*Sergeant Sulpice*); Jolanda Gardino (*The Marquise*); Antonio Cassinelli (*Hortensius*); Teodoro Rovetta (*A Corporal*); Tommaso Frascati (*A Peasant*).

NOTES: EJS 316

Issued out of sequence in February, 1965 (EJS 317 and 318 had appeared the previous month). Smith noted in the February bulletin that "we turned out copies of the Figlia del Regimento (sic) with Anna Moffo and Giuseppe Campora for the soprano. What was intended only as a private release turned out to be so magnificent a performance vocally and sound wise, that we requested permission to issue it as no really good Figlia is currently available. Miss Moffo granted this permission and 48 sets are available on a first come first served basis." One wonders if this request was tendered also to RAI, especially in light of the fact that the February, 1965 bulletin says nothing of the performance's origin and the 1970s EJS checklist lists it as "(1959 - Scala)."

The performance was subsequently reissued as Melodram MEL 27018.

EJS 317: "The Golden Age of Opera" (2 LPs)
Issued January, 1965

SIDES 1-4 (317 A-D):

PARISINA D'ESTE (Donizetti) (I)
Opera in 3 acts (complete)
Orchestra and Chorus of the Teatro Comunale di Bologna/Bruno Rigacci
?Broadcast, Teatro dei Rinnovati, Siena, 17 Sep 1964

CAST:
Marcella Pobbe (*Parisina*); Renato Cioni (*Ugo*); Giulio Fioravanti (*Azzo*); Franco Ventriglia (*Ernesto*); Margherita Pogliano (*Imelda*).

NOTES: EJS 317

Generally known simply as PARISINA, the title that appears in all historical references to, and scores of, the work, Smith has for some reason assigned the title PARISINA D'ESTE to EJS 317. The performance may have been part of the Settimana Chigiana festival held annually at the Accademia Chigiana in September.

The version of the opera performed here is a revision by conductor Rigacci, who was moved, apparently, to replace what he considered weak parts of the score with other Donizetti fragments--among them, passages from the composer's CATERINA CORNARO (1842).

The February, 1965 bulletin notes that "at least a third of the copies of Parisina D'Este had sides one and two with stripped grooves which result in a horrible grounding (sic) sound for 5-10 seconds in those spots when played. [These are] . . . replaceable upon notification."

The performance was subsequently reissued as Melodram MEL-171.

EJS 318: "The Golden Age of Opera" (2 LPs)
Issued January, 1965

GÖTTERDÄMMERUNG (Wagner) (G)
Opera in 3 acts and a Prologue (excerpts)
Orchestra and Chorus of the Teatro alla Scala, Milan/Wilhelm Furtwängler
Broadcast, La Scala, RAI, Milan, ?2 Apr 1950

CAST:
Kirsten Flagstad (*Brünnhilde*); Max Lorenz (*Siegfried*); Ludwig Weber (*Hagen*); Josef Herrmann (*Gunther*); Hilde Konetzni (*Gutrune*); Elisabeth Höngen (*Waltraute*)]; [Alois Pernerstorfer (*Alberich*)]; [Margret Weth-Falke (*First Norn*)]; [Margaret Kenney (*Second Norn*)]; [Hilde Konetzni (*Third Norn*)]; [Magda Gabory (*Woglinde*)]; [Margarita Kenny (*Wellgunde*)]; [Sieglinde Wagner (*Flosshilde*)].

SIDE 1 (318 A):

1. FLAGSTAD and LORENZ: Prologue: Zu neuen Taten

SIDE 2 (318 B):

2 HERRMANN, LORENZ, FLAGSTAD, WEBER, KONETZNI, and Chorus: Act II: Gegrüsst sei, teurer Held! . . . to the end of the act

SIDE 3-4 (318 C-D):

GÖTTERDÄMMERUNG (Wagner) (G)
Opera in 3 acts and a Prologue (Act III only)
Orchestra and Chorus of Radio Italiana [RAI], Roma/Wilhelm Furtwängler
RAI broadcast, Rome, 31 May 1952

CAST:
Kirsten Flagstad (*Brünnhilde*); Ludwig Suthaus (*Siegfried*); Josef Greindl (*Hagen*); Josef Herrmann (*Gunther*); Hilde Konetzni (*Gutrune*); Julia Moor (*Woglinde*); Ruth Michaelis (*Flosshilde*); Elisabeth Lindermeier (*Wellgunde*).

NOTES: EJS 318

The January, 1965 bulletin lists these performances as "two La Scala broadcasts of February, 1950 and May, 1952."

The 1950 production of GÖTTERDÄMMERUNG was performed on 2, 4, and 6 April, 1950. The Bruno Walter Society's Recital Records issue, authorized by Frau Elisabeth Furtwängler, carries 2 April as the broadcast date. This well-known performance has been issued in its entirety on a number of LPs (notably by Discocorp, Fonit-Cetra, Everest, and in the complete La Scala Furtwängler RING cycle issued as an 11-disc Murray Hill set) and has recently been reissued on CD by both Murray Hill and HUNT, the latter as CDWFE 351d. The GÖTTERDÄMMERUNG was also issued complete on four discs as EJS 538 in February, 1971. See also the endnote for EJS 538.

Only Act III was performed on the 31 May, 1952 radio concert, which was subsequently reissued in 1982 as Fonit Cetra LP FE-20.

EJS 319: "The Golden Age of Opera" (2 LPs)
Issued February, 1965

SIDES 1-4 (319 A-D):

LA FAVORITA (Donizetti) (I)
Opera in 4 acts (complete)
Orchestra and Chorus of the Palacio de las Bellas Artes, Mexico City/ Renato Cellini
Broadcast, Palacio de las Bellas Artes, XEN and XENN-FM, Mexico City, 12 Jul 1950

CAST:
Giuseppe Di Stefano (*Fernando*); Giulietta Simionato (*Leonora*); Enzo Mascherini (*Alfonso*); Cesare Siepi (*Baldassare*); Rosa Rodriguez (*Inez*); Francesco Tortolero (*Don Gasparo*).

NOTES: EJS 319

Excerpts from three of these 1949 summer Palacio de las Bellas Artes performances, all featuring Di Stefano and Simionato, appeared earlier on EJS 302 and 303, issued June, 1964.

Only the first page of the Overture is given before yielding to the Act I Prelude. De Stefano sings an encore of the second strophe of the Act IV "Spirto gentil."

Speeds are reported to be erratic over the course of the four sides: side 1 begins at 34.7 rpm, eventually slowing to 33.8 at Fernando's entrance; thereafter, the prevailing speed of Acts I and II is 34.7 rpm. Most of the second disc plays at score pitch at 34.00 rpm, but Act IV climbs gradually to about 34.7 rpm.

Subsequently reissued on LP as Cetra LO 2/3 and on CD as Standing Room Only SRO 816.

EJS 320: "The Golden Age of Opera" (1 LP)
Issued February, 1965

SIBERIA (Giordano) (I)
Opera in 3 acts (Acts II and III complete)
Orchestra Sinfonica e Coro di Milano/Piero Argento
?RAI broadcast or studio recording, circa 1951

CAST:
Adriana Guerrini (*Stephana*); Aldo Bertocci (*Vassili*); Luigi Borgonovo (*Gleby*); Renata Broilo (*The Girl*); Mario Pinazzi (*The Sergeant*); Mario Pinazzi (*The Cossack*); Nino Pasquali (*The Captain*); Nino Pasquali (*The Governor*); Pier Luigi Latinucci (*The Invalid*); Giuliano Ferrein (*The Inspector*).

NOTES: EJS 320

Though the cast of this SIBERIA includes a number of RAI regulars, it is not listed in the RAI chronology because it was not a complete performance. Moreover, only those cast members who appear in the second and third acts are given on the label of EJS 320 (omitted are the first-act characters *Nikona*, *Alexis*, *Ivan*, *Miskinsky*, and *Walinoff*), implying that perhaps no more than the second and third acts were performed or recorded. It may be that Smith had mounted this as a studio recording for one of the many small commercial labels for which he furnished "imported" operatic performances in the 1950s, the SIBERIA perhaps having gone unissued in that form.

Act II is given complete on side 1, along with the Prelude and Chorus ("Dalle nuvole à il ciel") of Act III; side 2 completes Act III with what appear to be a few minor *performance* cuts in the chorus parts.

Rosciani's Guerrini chronology/discography in Georgio Feliciotti's *Adriana Guerrini: Una voce che ritorna* (Bologne: Bongiovanni, 1980) does not mention this performance among the soprano's RAI broadcasts, so this may well be an unissued studio recording.

EJS 321: The Golden Age of Opera" (1 LP)
Issued February, 1965

SIDE 1 (321 A):

OTELLO (Verdi) (I)
Opera in 4 acts (excerpts)
San Francisco Opera Orchestra/Gaetano Merola
Broadcast, ***STANDARD HOUR***, KPO, San Francisco, 26 Oct 1947

CAST:
Set Svanholm (*Otello*); Licia Albanese (*Desdemona*); Leonard Warren (*Iago*); Leslie Chabay (*Cassio*); Claramae Turner (*Emilia*).

* 1. Act I: a) SVANHOLM and ALBANESE: Già nella notte densa

Act II: b) ALBANESE, SVANHOLM, WARREN, and TURNER: D'un uom che geme . . . Dammi la dolce e lietà parola del perdon
c) SVANHOLM and WARREN: Ah! mille vite gli donasse Iddio! . . . Sì, pel ciel

Act III: d) ALBANESE and SVANHOLM: [Dio ti giocondi] . . . dell'alma mia sovrano . . . Ma riparlar vi debbo di Cassio
e) WARREN, CHABAY, and SVANHOLM: [L'attendi], e intanto, giacchè non si stanca mai . . . to the end of the scene

Act IV: a) SVANHOLM: Niun mi tema

SIDE 2 (321 B):

LA GIOCONDA (Ponchielli) (I)
Opera in 4 acts (excerpts)
San Francisco Opera Orchestra/Gaetano Merola
Broadcast, ***STANDARD HOUR***, KPO, San Francisco, 19 Oct 1947

CAST:
Kurt Baum (*Enzo Grimaldo*); Stella Roman (*Gioconda*); Leonard Warren (*Barnaba*); Blanche Thebom (*Laura*); Margaret Harshaw (*La Cieca*).

1. Act I: a) HARSHAW: Voce di donna [solo part only]
b) BAUM and WARREN: Enzo Grimaldo, Principe di Santafior . . . O grido di quest'anima

Act II: c) BAUM: Cielo e mar!
d) THEBOM and BAUM: [Enzo adorato!] Ma il tempo vola . . . Deh! non tremar! . . . Laggiù nelle nebbie remote
e) THEBOM: Ho il cuor gonfio di lagrime . . . Stella del marinar
f) THEBOM and ROMAN: Chi sei? . . . L'amo come il fulgor del creato!

Act IV: g) ROMAN: Suicidio!
h) ROMAN, BAUM, and THEBOM: Ecco la barca . . . Addio, Gioconda, addio! [internal cuts]
i) WARREN and ROMAN: Così, mantieni il patto? . . . to the end of the opera

NOTES: EJS 321

Apparently in an effort to create some sort of continuity between the sections performed, both the OTELLO and GIOCONDA excerpts suffer from clipped introductions and postludes throughout, the result of disc changes: these were taken from air checks, not from line checks, the official ***STANDARD HOUR*** acetates having not yet become available to Smith.

Side 1 (321 A):

The Act I love duet, the Act II quartet, and the Act III "Dio ti giocondi" had appeared previously on EJS 282 (November, 1963). Also performed on this broadcast, but not included on EJS 321, were the Act I "Inaffia l'ugola," Warren's Act II "Credo," and Albanese's Act IV "Willow Song" and "Ave Maria" (all but the "Credo" with internal cuts in the actual performance). The same "Si, pel ciel" was reissued on a 1992 IRCC broadcast potpourri (CD 807) where it is dated 1948.

See also the endnote for EJS 282 (II/4-7) relating to this 26 October, 1947 ***STANDARD HOUR*** OTELLO.

Side 2 (321 B):

The Prelude and Warren's Act I "O monumento" were also broadcast, but were not included on EJS 321. The same cast of principals appeared in the San Francisco Opera production of GIOCONDA on 30 September, 1947.

The label of EJS 321 mistakenly gives Thebom as *La Cieca* and Harshaw as *Laura*. The transfer is reported as slightly high, 33.00 rpm being the recommended playing speed.

EJS 322: "The Golden Age of Opera" (1 LP)
Issued March, 1965

"LAURITZ MELCHIOR / 75th BIRTHDAY ANNIVERSARY"

SIDE 1 (322 A):

* 1. a) w. orch/?: DIE WALKÜRE, Act I: Winterstürme (Wagner) (G)
7742-2 Berlin, 1924 Parlophone 1011
P 1903
E 10352 (U.K.)

b) w. FRIDA LEIDER, soprano (orch/?Leo Blech): DIE WALKÜRE, Act I: Du bist der Lenz (Wagner) (G)
1485½as Berlin, November-December, 1923 Polydor 72934
[B 25033]

c) w. FRIDA LEIDER, soprano (orch/?Leo Blech): DIE WALKÜRE, Act I: Wie dir die Stirn . . . O süsseste Wonne (Wagner) (G)
1486as Berlin, November-December, 1923 Polydor 72934
[B 25034]

d) w. orch/?Leo Blech: DIE WALKÜRE, Act I: Siegmund heiss'ich (Wagner) (G)
1489as Berlin, November-December, 1923 Polydor 72867
[B 22183]

* 2. w. orch/?: IL TROVATORE, Act II: Il balen (Verdi) (D)
Kpo 414 Copenhagen, March, 1913 Odeon A 144275

3. w. HOLGER HANSEN, bass (orch/?): GLUNTARNE: Slottsklockan (Wennerberg) (D)
742-½ar Copenhagen, circa 1920-1921 Nordisk Polyphon 84316

4. w. HOLGER HANSEN, bass (orch/?): GLUNTARNE: En solnedgång i Eklundshofskogen (Wennerberg) (D)
314as Copenhagen, circa 1920-1921 Nordisk Polyphon 84031

* 5. w. KIRSTEN FLAGSTAD, soprano; KARIN BRANZELL, mezzo-soprano; and LAWRENCE TIBBETT, baritone (NBC Symphony Orchestra/Eugene Goossens): "Suomis sång" ["Synnoves sång"] (Johan Ludvig Runeberg-Fredrik Pacius) (Finnish)
Broadcast, ***BENEFIT CONCERT FOR FINLAND***, Carnegie Hall, WJZ, NYC, 27 Dec 1939

SIDE 2 (322 B):

* 1. w. pf/?: SCHWANENGESANG, D. 957, No. 8: Der Atlas (Heine-Schubert) (G)
New York, ?1963

* 2. w. pf/?: SCHWANENGESANG, D. 957, No. 13: Der Doppelgänger (Schubert) (G)
New York, ?May, 1961

* 3. w. pf/?: VIER LIEDER, Op. 27, No. 3: Heimliche Aufforderung (J. H. Mackay-R. Strauss) (G)
New York, ?May, 1961

* 4. w. pf/?: ACHT LIEDER AUS LETZTE BLÄTTER, Op. 10, No. 1: Zueignung (H. von Gilm-R. Strauss) (G)
New York, ?May, 1961

* 5. w. pf/?: "Torna a Surriento (De Curtis) (I)
New York, ?May, 1961

* 6. w. pf/?: "The Lord's Prayer" (Malotte) (E)
New York, ?May, 1961

* 7. w. pf/?: "I Believe" (Sammy Cahn-Jule Styne) (E)
New York, ?May, 1961

* 8. w. pf/?: AÏDA, Act I: Holde Aïda [Celeste Aïda] (Verdi) (G)
Hamburg, 5 April, 1960, or New York, circa 1963

* 9. w. pf/?: LE PROPHÈTE, Act III: Roi du ciel (Meyerbeer) (G)
?Hamburg, 5 April, 1960

10. w. American Symphony Orchestra/Leopold Stokowski: HJERTETS MELODIER, Op. 5, no. 3: Ich liebe dich [Jeg elsker dig] (Grieg) (G)
In-house recording, Woodruff Hall, Adelphi College, Long Island, New York, 18 Apr 1963

NOTES: EJS 322

This Melchior LP, like the Gigli recital issued the same month, commemorated the fact that both tenors were born on the same day, 20 March, 1890. Smith later reissued the majority of the early Melchior acousticals on the UORC "Memorial Albums" of May and June, 1973: UORC 160, Volume II (the baritone recordings), and UORC 165, Volume IV (the tenor recordings). Danacord has reissued the complete Melchior acousticals on the first two volumes of their "Melchior Anthology," DACO[CD] 311-312 and 313-314, currently available on compact disc.

Side 1 (322 A):

Band 1: No conductor is given on the labels for the majority of Melchior's 1924 Berlin Parlophones, though Paul Breisach and Frieder Weissmann are named on the Melchior-Bettendorf TANNHÄUSER and LOHENGRIN duets, which are some 100 matrix numbers later than the "Winterstürme."

Band 2: Melchior sings here, of course, as a baritone. The "Il balen" is from his second recording session, the first having been for Odeon in Copenhagen in January-February, 1913. The other selections on EJS 322 are all early tenor recordings.

Band 5: This benefit concert, broadcast live from Carnegie Hall over NBC, 9:00-10:45pm (EST), was billed variously as a "Program of Scandinavian Music" and "Finnish Relief Fund Benefit Concert," and included three Norwegian, three Danish, three American, and three Sibelius songs. Also performed were two Sibelius tone poems, "Finlandia," Op. 26, and the slightly less well-known "En Saga," Opus 9 of 1892. The first edition of Hansen's Melchior discography, p. 27, claims that it was "recorded off-the-air by Melotone Studios . . . and distributed privately by Mr. Melchior." Smith's source was a Melotone disc given to a private collector by Melchior himself.

The concert was sponsored by the Finnish Relief Fund, of which ex-President Herbert Hoover was the chairman, and mounted for the benifit of the Lotta Svaard Finnish Women's Organization. Mrs. Lawrence Tibbett was chairman of the Ticket Committee. Guests included the Finnish Minister to the U.S., the Finnish Consul General, and a long list of important political patrons. The *New York Times* reported the concert ("Concert Tonight to Help Finland," 27 December, 1939, p. 5) and noted that Goossens had been "released" from the Cincinnati Symphony Orchestra to conduct the NBC Symphony Orchestra. The "Suomis sång" is the Finnish National Anthem, with a text by Runeberg (1804-1877). Both Pacius (1809-1891) and "Kjerulf" have been cited as the composer, the latter's setting as arranged by Frank Black. This performance will be featured on a forthcoming Delos International Tibbett CD (DE-5501) produced in collaboration with the Stanford University Archive of Recorded Sound.

Side 2 (322 B):

Bands 1-9: Hansen, q.v. notes that "According to Dr. A. F. Lawrence and Mr. W. R. Moran," these items "were all recorded in New York, and not as previously supposed Hamburg." An undated, piano-accompanied OTELLO "Esultate," possibly from this period, was later provided with a dubbed orchestral accompaniment (Smith was involved in this practice earlier as a producer of commercial LPs in the 1950s) and appeared with other unpublished Melchior items on ASCO LP A-121. These 1960-1963 items are all *studio* recordings.

Current information, however, not yet published but reported by a reliable source, claims that the "Holde Aïda" and perhaps the PROPHÈTE aria (bands 8 and 9) were in fact recorded privately in Hamburg on 5 April, 1960.

EJS 323: "The Golden Age of Opera" (1 LP)
Issued March, 1965

SIDES 1 and 2 (323 A-B):

GLI ZINGARI (Leoncavallo) (I)
Opera 1 in act (complete)
Dutch Radio Orchestra/Fulvio Vernizzi
Broadcast, Dutch Radio [sic], November, 1963

CAST:
Edy Amedeo (*Fleana*); Aldo Bertocci (*Radu*); Vinicio Cocchieri (*Tamar*); Jan Derksen (*Old Man*).

NOTES: EJS 323

Amedeo's forename is given as Editta on the label of EJS 323: possibly this is genuine, though "Edy" appears to be the name under which she most often performed.

This short Leoncavallo opera was first produced at London's Hippodrome in September, 1912. The Dutch network responsible for this broadcast could not be determined from the available description.

EJS 324: "The Golden Age of Opera (1 LP)
Issued March, 1965

PÉNÉLOPE (Fauré) (F)
Opera in 3 acts (excerpts)
Orchestra and Chorus of the Office de Radiodiffusion Télévision Française [ORTF], Paris/Désiré-Émile Inghelbrecht
ORTF broadcast, Théâtre des Champs-Elysées, Paris, recorded 24 May 1956

CAST:
Régine Crespin (*Pénélope*); Raoul Jobin (*Ulysse*); Christiane Gayraud (*Euryclée*); Robert Massard (*Eurymacque*); Bernard Demigny (*Ctesippe*); Joseph Peyron (*Antinoüs*); Françoise Ogéas (*Melanthe*); Nicole Robin (*Eurynome*); Nicole Robin (*Phylo*); Michel Hamel (*Léodès*); Michel Hamel (*The Shepherd*); Genevieve Macaux (*Alkandre*); Madeleine Gagnard (*Cléone*); André Vessières (*Eumée*).

SIDE 1 (324 A):

1. Act I: a) Prelude and Choeur des servantes fileuses
   b) CRESPIN, JOBIN, GAYRAUD, DEMIGNY, PEYRON, OGÉAS, ROBIN, MASSARD: Vous n'avez fait qu'éveiller dans mon sein . . . to the end of Scene viii

SIDE 2 (324 B):

1. Act II: a) CRESPIN, JOBIN, and GAYRAUD: Mais toi-même tu pleures pourquoi? . . . through Pénélope's exit

   Act III: b) Assembled Cast: Il a tendu . . . to the end of the opera

NOTES: EJS 324

The actual broadcast date is not known. This performance was subsequently issued complete on CD as Rodolphe RPC 32447/8.

EJS 325: "The Golden Age of Opera" (1 LP)
Issued March, 1965

IL TROVATORE (Verdi) (I)
Opera in 4 acts (excerpts)

<u>*SOURCES*</u>

a) Orchestra and Chorus of the Teatro Colón, Buenos Aires/Ettore Panizza
Broadcast, Teatro Colón, Buenos Aires, 7 Jul 1948
CAST:
Beniamino Gigli (*Manrico*); Maria Caniglia (*Leonora*); Fedora Barbieri (*Azucena*); Carlos Guichandut (*Count di Luna*); [Luisa Perlotti (*Ines*)].

b) "Mexico City" source and date unknown
CAST:
? (*Manrico*); Leonora Maria Caniglia (*Leonora*); Fedora Barbieri (*Azucena*); Paolo Silveri (*Count di Luna*).

c) Source and date unknown
CAST:
? (*Manrico*); ? (*Leonora*); Fedora Barbieri (*Azucena*); Paolo Silveri (*Count di Luna*).

d) Rome Opera House Orchestra and Chorus/Tullio Serafin
From the soundtrack of the feature film ***[LA VITA DI] GIUSEPPE VERDI*** (1938), Cinecittà Studios, Rome, 1938
CAST:
Beniamino Gigli (*Manrico*); Apollo Granforte (*Count di Luna*).

e) Orchestra of Radio Italiana [RAI], Torino/?
Broadcast, ***CONCERTO MARTINI E ROSSI***, RAI, Turin, 26 Jan 1953
CAST:
Maria Caniglia (*Leonora*); Paolo Silveri (*Count di Luna*).

f) Sources and casts unknown

SIDE 1 (325 A):

1. Act I:
   a) Prelude (b)
   b) CANIGLIA: Tacea la notte (a)
   c) CANIGLIA and ?: Quanto narrasti di turbamento . . . Detto, che intendere l'almo non sà (b)
   d) CANIGLIA: Di tale amor (without Ines) (a)
   e) Unknown soprano & SILVERI: Tacea la notte . . . A noi supremo; E tal momento (c)
   f) GIGLI and GRANFORTE: Il trovator! io fremo . . . Deserto sulla terra (d)
   g) SILVERI: Non m'inganno! Ella scende! (b)

h) CANIGLIA, GIGLI, and GUICHANDUT: E, dissenato! Vieni . . . Conte! (a)
i) SILVERI: Al mio disegno vittima . . . to the beginning of the trio (b)
j) CANIGLIA, GIGLI, and GUICHANDUT: Unison part of the trio . . . to the end of the act (a)

2. Act II: a) BARBIERI: Stride la vampa (c)

SIDE 2 (325 B):

1. Act III: a) GIGLI: Ah! si, ben mio (a)

b) GIGLI (orch/?): Di quella pira
OBA-4190-3 Milan, 30 November, 1940
HMV DA 5398 Victor 10-1475

Act IV: c) CANIGLIA: D'amor sull'ali rosee (a)
d) Unknown Chorus: Miserere d'un'alma già vicina (opening) (f)
e) CANIGLIA and GIGLI: [Miserere] Sull'orrida torre . . . to the end of the Miserere (a)
f) SILVERI and CANIGLIA: Udiste . . . Mira d'acerbe lagrima . . . Colui vivrà (e)
g) GUICHANDUT and CANIGLIA: Vivra! Contende il giubilo (a)

Act IV: h) BARBIERI / +GIGLI and CLOE ELMO (orch/?): Turba feroce . . . Ai nostri monti (c)
+2BA 3650-2 HMV DB 5385 Victor 12-0767
Milan, 23 January, 1940

i) CANIGLIA, GIGLI, and GUICHANDUT: Prima che d'altri vivere . . . Manrico! (a)
j) Unknown singers: Madre! Oh Madre, Addio! . . . Ov'è mio figlio? (f)
k) A morte ei corre! . . . to the end of the opera (f)

NOTES: EJS 325

Co-author William Collins has called this "the most diabolical disc ever to issue from the often obfuscatory studio of Eddie Smith." His analysis, summarized here, was originally published in his own "Beniamino Gigli: Non-Commercial Recordings," in *The Record Collector*, 35/8-10 (August-September, 1990), note 109, pp. 216-217. The March, 1965 EJS bulletin notes only that "Since no Di quella pira existed from this performance, poetic license was taken and a commercial version (virtually unknown) was used." In fact, a great deal of "poetic license" was taken when this tangled and confusing compilation was patched together.

In the above listing, six sources are detailed: (a) the Buenos Aires live performance quoted in the EJS bulletin, which did *not* feature Silveri as *Count di Luna*; (b) an undocumented live performance featuring Barbieri and Silveri, which Smith explained privately was from "Mexico City" (nothing could be found from the Palacio de las Bellas Artes and no such performance is mentioned by Silveri in his autobiography); (c) another unknown source that obviously featured

Barbieri and Silveri; (d) a Gigli-Granforte soundtrack excerpt from the Italian feature film, ***GIUSEPPE VERDI*** (aka ***LA VITA DI GIUSEPPE VERDI***); (e) a ***CONCERTO MARTINI E ROSSI*** broadcast, and (f) a generic designation for sources (and thus, casts) which we were unable to identify at all. The sources from which each excerpt are designated by the appropriate letter after the texts. Side II/b and h are taken from commercial Gigli recordings, the latter apparently combining an unknown live Barbieri performance with Gigli's part taken from his HMV duet with Cloe. Side II/d uses the chorus opening from an electrical recording of the "Miserere" which has not been identified. Thus, the documentation of the contents of this LP remains tentative.

Smith reissued the same "Ah! si, ben mio" as well as the same portion of the "Miserere" on ANNA 1032 (May-June, 1979). Caniglia's "D'amor sul'ali rosee," the "Miserere," and the "Mira d'acerbe . . . Vivrà!" used here later appeared on the LP "Maria Caniglia . . . Live" (MDP 014), while Gigli's "Deserto sulla terra" (through the end of the scene) and "Mal reggendo" turned up on "Beniamino Gigli . . . Live" (MDP-018).

Though transpositions have been reported as probable in some of the excerpts featured on EJS 325, it may be that several of the excerpts were simply pitched incorrectly, as they were on the later MDP issues.

EJS 326: "The Golden Age of Opera" (2 LPs)
Issued April, 1965

SIDES 1-4 (326 A-D):

SAPHO (Massenet) (F)
Opera in 5 acts (abridged)
Orchestra and Chorus of the Office de Radiodiffusion Télévision Française [ORTF], Paris/Pierre-Michel LeConte
ORTF broadcast, ?Paris, circa 1961

CAST:
Géneviève Moizan (*Fanny Legrand*); Jean Mollien (*Jean Gaussin*); Robert Massard (*Caoudal*); Lucien Lovano (*Césaire*); Joseph Peyron (*La Bordiere*); Christine Jacquin (*Iréne*); Solange Michel (*Divonne*).

NOTES: EJS 326

The label of side 4 notes "Act III (PART CUT)," meaning that everything is missing up to *Caoudal's* entrance. The opera appears to have been broadcast complete, so this was probably a simple, if not especially praiseworthy space-saving measure.

A number of labeling errors might also be mentioned: character names ("*Cesar*," "*La Borderie*," "*Yvonne*" for *Divonne*), and the conductor's surname, given as "Le Comte."

EJS 327: "The Golden Age of Opera" (1 LP)
Issued April, 1965

DIE WALKÜRE (Wagner) (G)
Opera in 3 acts (excerpts)
Orchestra and Chorus of the Teatro alla Scala, Milano/Wilhelm Furtwängler
Broadcast, La Scala, Milan, RAI (Rome and Turin), ?9 Mar 1950

CAST:
Kirsten Flagstad (*Brünnhilde*); Gunther Treptow (*Siegmund*); Hilde Konetzni (*Sieglinde*); Ferdinand Frantz (*Wotan*); Ludwig Weber (*Hunding*); [Elisabeth Höngen (*Fricka*)]; Ilona Steingruber (*Helmwige*); Walburga Wegner (*Gerhilde*); Karen Marie Cerkall (*Ortlinde*); Dagmar Schmedes (*Waltraute*); Margaret Kenney (*Siegrune*); Margret Weth-Falke (*Rossweise*); Sieglinde Wagner (*Grimgerde*); Polly Batic (*Schwertleite*).

SIDE 1 (327 A):

1. Act II: a) FRANTZ and FLAGSTAD: Nun zäume dein Ross . . . Hojotoho!
   b) FLAGSTAD, TREPTOW, KONETZNI, WEBER, and FRANTZ: Siegmund! Sieh'auf mich . . . to the end of the act

SIDE 2 (327 B):

1. Act III: a) FLAGSTAD and FRANTZ: Tönend erklang mir . . . Leb' wohl, du kühnes . . . to the end of the opera

NOTES: EJS 327

This production was performed on 9, 13, and 16 March, 1950, and it is not known which was actually broadcast in its entirety. It was issued complete from a different source on the three-disc EJS 534 in January, 1971, and many times after on a variety of commercial labels, among them, Fonit Cetra CFE 101-(18). See also the endnote for EJS 534.

EJS 328: "The Golden Age of Opera" (1 LP)
Issued April, 1965

"ELISABETH SCHUMANN"

SIDE 1 (328 A):

1. ELISABETH SCHUMANN, soprano (pf/Ernest Lush): Lecture-Recital
   a) "Das Veilchen," K. 476 (Goethe-Mozart) (G)
   b) "Lachen und weinen," D. 777 (Rückert-Schubert) (G)
   c) SECHS LIEDER, no. 6: Mausfallensprüchlein (Mörike-Wolf) (G)
   d) "Vergebliches Ständchen," Op. 84, no. 4 (Zuccalmaglio-Brahms) (G)

   BBC Studios, London, 13 October, 1950 for broadcast, ***BBC THIRD PROGRAMME***, BBC, London, 22 Feb 1951

SIDE 2 (328 B):

1. ELISABETH SCHUMANN, soprano (pf/Ernest Lush): Lecture-Recital
   a) VIER LIEDER, Morgen, Op. 27, no. 4 (Mackay-R. Strauss) (G)
   b) "Die Forelle," D. 550 (Schubart-Schubert) (G)
   c) SPANISCHES LIEDERBUCH, Weltiche Lieder, No. 2: In dem Schatten meiner Locken (Anon.-Wolf) (G)
   BBC Studios, London, 16 November, 1951 for broadcast, ***BBC THIRD PROGRAMME***, BBC, London, 31 Jan 1952

NOTES: EJS 328

Schumann was 65 and 66 years old, respectively, when these lecture-recitals were given. She died in New York on 23 April, 1952. The original tapes of both have been retained in the BBC Archives.

EJS 329: "The Golden Age of Opera" (1 LP)
Issued April, 1965

"BENIAMINO GIGLI"

SIDE 1 (329 A):

* 1. w. BBC Opera Orchestra/Stanford Robinson: LA RONDINE, Act III: Se vuoi seguirmi . . . Dimmi che vuoi (Puccini) (I)
BBC broadcast, London, 25 Apr 1952

* 2. w. BBC Opera Orchestra/Stanford Robinson: "Bella, bellina" (Giulia Recli) (I)
BBC broadcast, London, 25 Apr 1952

* 3. w. BBC Opera Orchestra/Stanford Robinson: FEDORA, Act II: Amor ti vieta (Giordano) (I)
BBC broadcast, London, 25 Apr 1952

* 4. w. BBC Opera Orchestra/Stanford Robinson: "Ideale" (Errico-Tosti) (I)
BBC broadcast, London, 25 Apr 1952

* 5. w. Orchestra of the Teatro alla Scala/Franco Ghione: ANDREA CHENIER, Act IV: Come un bel dì di maggio (Giordano) (I)
Broadcast, La Scala, Milan, 28 Feb 1937

* 6. a) w. ROSETTA PAMPANINI, soprano (Orchestra of the Teatro alla Scala/Franco Ghione): ANDREA CHENIER, Act IV: Tu sei la mèta dell'esistenza mia! . . . La nostra morte . . . Infinito! Amore! (Giordano) (I)
Broadcast, La Scala, Milan, 28 Feb 1937

b) w. MARIA CANIGLIA (La Scala Orchestra/Oliviero de Fabritiis): ANDREA CHENIER, Act IV: È la morte! . . . to the end of the opera (Giordano) (I)
2BA 4812-? Milan, November, 1941
HMV DB 5435 Victor 12-0605

* 7. w. Orchestra of the Teatro alla Scala/Gino Marinuzzi: MANON, Act III: Io son sola . . . Ah, dispar, vision [Je suis seul . . . Ah, fuyez, douce image] (Massenet) (I)
Broadcast, La Scala, Milan, 10 Mar 1937

8. w. MAFALDA FAVERO, soprano (Orchestra of the Teatro alla Scala/ Gino Marinuzzi): MANON, Act III: No, fu sogno lusinghiero [Ce rêve insensé . . . Ecouté-moi! Rapelle-toi!] ["St. Suplice" Scene] (Massenet) (I)
Broadcast, La Scala, Milan, 10 Mar 1937

* 9. w. ADRIANA GUERRINI, soprano (Orchestra of Radio Italiana, Milano/Alfredo Simonetto): MANON LESCAUT, Act IV: Tutta su me ti posa . . . lieta novella poi vieni a recar! (Puccini) (I)
RAI broadcast, Milano, 24 or 29 Dec 1950

SIDE 2 (329 B):

1. w. Ente Italiano Audizioni Radiofoniche [EIAR] Symphony, Roma and the Cappella Sistina/Lorenzo Perosi: NATALITA'[NATALITIA]: Finale (Breviary-Lorenzo Perosi) (I)
EIAR broadcast, Vatican, 25 Dec 1937

IL GIUDIZIO UNIVERSALE (G. Salvadori-P. Miscatelli-Lorenzo Perosi) (L and I)
Oratorio (excerpts)
Ente Italiano Audizioni Radiofoniche [EIAR] Symphony, Roma and the Cappella Sistina/Don Lorenzo Perosi
EIAR broadcast, Vatican, 25 Dec 1937

CAST:
Beniamino Gigli (*Cristo*); Licia Albanese (*L'angelo di pace*); Gianna Pederzini (*Lo spirito della giustizia*).

2. b) GIGLI, ALBANESE, PEDERZINI, and CAPPELLA SISTINA: Le Beatitudine
c) GIGLI and CAPPELLA SISTINA: Le Benedizione
d) ALBANESE and CAPELLA SISTINA: L'Inno della pace
e) PEDERZINI and CAPPELLA SISTINA: L'Inno della Giustizia

NOTES: EJS 329

Side 1 (329 A):

Bands 1-4: The completion of Gigli's 25 April, 1952 BBC concert was issued in June, 1965 on EJS 336.

Bands 5-6: Taken from a complete performance. The original broadcast acetates break off at "Infinito! Amore!," so the final pages of the score were patched in from the 1941 complete CHENIER issued commercially by HMV and Victor. A later MDP Gigli recital (MDP-018), which also included the RONDINE and MANON excerpts presented on EJS 329, featured the same CHENIER duet, but places the broadcast in Rome.

Band 7: Because the broadcast acetate was incomplete, the recitative, up to the line "Sacro, che dona la fe?," and the last words, "dispar, vision, vision," were taken from Gigli's commercial HMV recording of the aria, DB 6346 (matrix 2EA 11511-2), recorded in Milan on 13 December, 1946.

Band 9: The label of EJS 329 says only "Duo Finale with Maria Caniglia." This MANON LESCAUT was broadcast complete by RAI on 24 December, 1950 and rebroadcast on 29 December. It is possible, however, that the 29 December broadcast was a *different* performance, not simply a rebroadcast. Smith's tape came from the RAI-USA tape which contained only an abridgement of the opera. Taken together, numerous Smith issues (EJS 309, EJS 329, EJS 563, UORC 336, and ANNA 1033) eventually completed the entire American abridgement of Act IV as broadcast. See also the endnote for EJS 309 (November, 1964).

Side 2 (329 B):

Smith's source of this Vatican broadcast was the official NBC actetates made from the original shortwave broadcast entitled "Christmas Day at the Vatican," carried over WEAF, New York City (NBC Red). For the American broadcast it was announced only as NATALITA'. The original EIAR broadcast also included Gigli in a selection from Perosi's 1899 oratorio IL NATALE DEL REDENTOR and additional music from IL GIUDIZIO UNIVERSALE (1904). Perosi (1872-1956) was the Perpetual Master of the Sistine Chapel from 1898 until his death. This broadcast was the world premiere of his oratorio NATALITA'. A 1950 performance of IL GIUDIZIO UNIVERSALE, also featuring Gigli, was issued in November, 1965 as EJS 345.

Library of Congress tape: 15778-65B (1 hour and 6 minute ?American shortwave broadcast).

EJS 330: "The Golden Age of Opera" (2 LPs)
Issued May, 1965

SIDE 1-4 (330 A-D):

IL FURIOSO ALL'ISOLA DI SAN DOMINGO (Donizetti) (I)
Opera in 3 acts (complete)
Orchestra and Chorus of the Accademia Musicale Chigiana/Franco Capuana
?Broadcast, Settimana Chigiana, Siena, 14 Sep 1958

CAST:
Gabriella Tucci (*Eleonora*); Giulia [Giuliana] Tavolaccini (*Marcella*); Ugo Savarese (*Cardenio*); Nicola Filacuridi (*Fernando*); Alfredo Mariotti (*Kaidamá*); Silvio Maionica (*Bartolomeo*).

NOTES: EJS 330

The character *Kaidamá* is given as "*Kaidana*" on the label of EJS 330. The performance was part of the Settimana Chigiana, held annually at the Accademia Musicale Chigiana in September.

Subsequently reissued as Cetra LO 80/2 and Melodram MEL-156.

EJS 331: "The Golden Age of Opera" (1 LP)
Issued May, 1965

SIDE 1 (331 A):

IL MATRIMONIO SEGRETO (Cimarosa) (I)
Opera in 2 acts (excerpts)
Orchestra and Chorus of the Teatro alla Scala, Milano/Mario Rossi
Broadcast, La Scala, 22 Mar 1949

CAST:
Tito Schipa (*Paolino*); Boris Christoff (*Count Robinson*); Alda Noni (*Carolina*); Hilde Güden (*Elisetta*); Fedora Barbieri (*Fidalma*); Sesto Bruscantini (*Geronimo*).

* 1. Act I: a) BARBIERI: E'vero che in casa io sono
b) NONI, GüDEN, and BARBIERI: Signora sorellina
c) SCHIPA and NONI: Cara non dubitar ["Cara! cara!"]
d) SCHIPA and NONI: Io ti lascio, perchè uniti
e) CHRISTOFF, BARBIERI, GüDEN, and NONI: Senza tante cerimonie

* 2. w. pf/?: LA RONDINE, Act III: Dimmi che vuoi (Puccini) (I)
Source unknown, 2 Sep 1964

* 3. w. pf/?: LA RONDINE, Act III: No! non lasciarmi solo! (Puccini) (I)
Source unknown, 2 Sep 1964

* 4. w. pf/?: "Inno a Diana" (Puccini) (I)
Source unknown, 2 Sep 1964

SIDE 2 (331 B):

* 1. TITO SCHIPA, tenor (pf/?): IRIS, Act I: Apri la tua finestra (Mascagni) (I)
Source unknown, 2 Sep 1964

* 2. TITO SCHIPA, tenor (w. pf): FEDORA, Act II: Amor ti vieta (Giordano) (I)
Source unknown, 2 Sep 1964

* 3. TITO SCHIPA, tenor (w. pf/?): IL POMPEO, Act : O cessate di piagarmi (Scarlatti) (I)
Source unknown, 2 Sep 1964

* 4. TITO SCHIPA, tenor (w. pf/?): PARIDE ED ELENA, Act I: O del mio dolce ardor (Gluck) (I)
Source unknown, 2 Sep 1964

5. TITO SCHIPA, tenor (w. pf/?): "Luna piangente" (?Caslar) (I)
from the soundtrack of the feature film, ***TRE UOMINI IN FRAK*** (1933), Caesar Film, Roma, 1932

6. TITO SCHIPA, tenor (w. orch/?): "Ti voglio bene" (Caslar) (I)
from the soundtrack of the feature film, ***TRE UOMINI IN FRAK*** (1933), Caesar Film, Roma, 1932

7. TITO SCHIPA, tenor (w. orch/?): "Io son un immenso tenore" (Caslar) (I)
   from the soundtrack of the feature film, ***TRE UOMINI IN FRAK*** (1933), Cesar Film, Roma, 1932

8. TITO SCHIPA, tenor (w. salon orch/?): "Melancolia de mi alma" (Caslar) (S)
   from the soundtrack of the feature film, ***TRE UOMINI IN FRAK*** (1933), Caesar Film, Roma, 1932

9. TITO SCHIPA, tenor (w. orch/?): "Quando nei tuoi occhi trema il pianto" (Caslar) (I)
   from the soundtrack of the feature film, ***TRE UOMINI IN FRAK*** (1933), Caesar Film, Roma, 1932

*10. TITO SCHIPA, tenor (w. orch/?): "Nina" ["Tre giorni son che Nina"] (Pergolesi) (I)
   from the soundtrack of the feature film, ***TRE UOMINI IN FRAK*** (1933), Caesar Film, Roma, 1932

11. TITO SCHIPA, tenor (w. orch/?): "Marechiare" (Tosti) (I)
   from the soundtrack of the feature film, ***TRE UOMINI IN FRAK*** (1933), Caesar Film, Roma, 1932

NOTES: EJS 331:

Side 1 (331 A):

Band 1: These excerpts from Act I of IL MATRIMONIO SEGRETO are not given in score order on EJS 331 which, using the letters given in the listing, would actually be: c, d, b, a, and e.

Further excerpts from Act I ("Si, corraggio mi faccio" to the end of the act) were issued in June, 1966 on EJS 371.

Bands 2-4: Smith gives the date 2 September, 1964 for these recordings (as well as for Side II/bands 1-4), but their source has not been verified. According to Renzo D'Andrea's *Tito Schipa nella vita, nell' arte, nel suo tempo* (n.p.: Schena, 1981), Schipa was in Lecce during the winter of 1963-1964 and arrived back in New York on 4 February, 1964. He took up residence at 70/71 Groton Street in Forest Hills, Long Island, the same New York suburb into which Eddie Smith would move in November, 1964 (68/34 Fleet Street), as announced in the EJS bulletin of that month. Schipa remained in Long Island through December, 1964 at which point he went to Italy for Christmas, returning to the United States sometime in late December, 1964 or early January, 1965 to meet his final illness (he died in New York on 16 December, 1965). It is entirely possible, given his friendship with Smith and the latter's residence in September, 1964 (84/25 Elmhurst Avenue, Elmhurst, Long Island), that these 2 September, 1964 recordings were mounted by Smith somehere in the New York area.

Schipa's age at the time is given as 77 in the May, 1965 bulletin, but the tenor's date of birth has always been disputed.

Bands 2-3: Schipa created the role of *Ruggero* in Puccini's LA RONDINE in Monte Carlo, 27 March, 1917, which makes these creator recordings. It has been suggested that the excerpts were made at Smith's suggestion precisely because of that, just as Martinelli was persuaded to record the "Ah, guardarmi e taci" from Giordano's MADAME SANS-GENE in 1957 for release on Smith's "Last of the Titans" Martinelli compilation on Rondo Gold RG 1001.

Band 4: Puccini's obscure "Inno a Diana" dates from 1899.

Side 2 (331 B):

Bands 1-4: See the note for Side I/2-4.

Band 10: This soundtrack "Nina" appeared earlier on EJS 288 (January, 1964).

EJS 332: "The Golden Age of Opera (1 LP)
Issued May, 1965

DER FREISCHÜTZ (Weber) (G)
Opera in 3 acts (excerpts)
Orchestra and Chorus of the Wiener Staatsoper/Joseph Krips
Backstage recording, Wiener Staatsoper, Vienna, ?10 May 1933
Orchestra and Chorus of the Salzburg Festival/Hans Knappertsbusch
?Broadcast, Salzburg Festival, Salzburg, 3 Aug 1939

CASTS:	1933 PERFORMANCE	1939 PERFORMANCE
Max	Franz Völker	Franz Völker
Caspar	---	Michael Bohnen
Agathe	Elisabeth Rethberg	[Tiana Lemnitz]
Kuno	Karl Ettl	Carl Bissutti
Samiel	---	Volker Soetber

SIDE 1 (332 A):

Act I:
1. VÖLKER, BOHNEN, and BISSUTTI, and Chorus: O diese Sonne (1939)
2. VÖLKER: Nein, langer trag'ich . . . Durch die Wälder, durch die Auen (1933)
3. BOHNEN and VÖLKER: Hier im erd'schen Jammertal [w. spoken dialogue] (1939)
4. BOHNEN: Schweig! Schweig! (1939)

Act II:
5. RETHBERG: Wie nahte mir . . . Leise, leise, fromme Weise (1933)
6. BOHNEN, VÖLKER, and SOETBER: Samiel! Samiel! Eins! . . . to the end of the "Wolf's Glen Scene" (1939)
7. RETHBERG: Und ob die Wolke [first verse only] (1933)

SIDE 2 (332 B):

DER ROSENKAVALIER (R. Strauss) (G)
Opera in 3 acts (excerpts)
Orchestra and Chorus of the Wiener Staatsoper/Hans Knappertsbusch
In-house recording, Wiener Staatsoper, Vienna, 22 April, 1936
Orchestra and Chorus of the Wiener Staatsoper/Hans Knappertsbusch
In-house recording, Wiener Staatsoper, Vienna, 13 June, 1937

CASTS:	22 APRIL, 1936	13 JUNE, 1937
Marschallin	. . . Lotte Lehmann	. . . Hilde Konetzni
Octavian	. . . Eva Hadrabová	. . . Margit Bokor
Sophie	. . . Elisabeth Schumann	. . . Elisabeth Schumann
Baron Ochs	. . . Fritz Sternek	. . . Fritz Krenn
Faninal	. . . Viktor Madin	. . . Hermann Wiedemann
Marianne	. . . Aenne Michalski	. . . Aenne Michalski
Valzacchi	. . . William Wernigk	. . . Hermann Gallos
Annina	. . . Bella Paalen	. . . Bella Paalen
Majordomo of Faninal	. . . (Ralph) Telasko	. . . William Wernigk
Majordomo of Marschallin	. . . --- Tomek	. . . ?
Police Commissioner	. . . Karl Ettl	. . . Viktor Madin
Wirt	. . . Georg Maikl	. . . ?Georg Maikl
Italian Singer	. . . [Koloman von Pataky]	. . . [Emmerich Godin]
Notary	. . . [Alfred Muzzarelli]	. . . [Alfred Muzzarelli]
Modistin	. . . [-- Nemeth]	. . . [Rosa Braun]
Animal Trainer	. . . [Anton Arnold]	. . . [Anton Arnold]
Orphans	. . . [?Maria Mathias]	. . . [Maria Mathias]
	. . . [Molly Jonas]	. . . [Molly Jonas]
	. . . [?Rosa Brunnbauer]	. . . [Rosa Brunnbauer]

Act I:
1. BOKOR: Prelude . . . Wie du warst! wie du bist! (1937)
2. KONETZNI: Und Nachmittag werd'ich Ihm . . . Jetzt sei Er gut und folg' Er mir (1937)
3. Orchestra: Postlude . . . to the end of the act (1936)

Act II:
4. MADIN, MICHALSKI, and TELASKO: Ein ernster Tag, ein grosser Tag! . . . Den edlen und gestrengen Herrn von Lerchenau! (1936)
5. SCHUMANN and MICHALSKI: [Demütigen] und recht bedenken . . . Sie reissen den Schlag auf! (1937)
* 6. BOKOR and SCHUMANN: Mir is die Ehre widerfahren . . . den will ich nie vergessen bis an meinen Tod (1936 and 1937)

Act III:
7. KRENN, PAALEN, GALLOS, MADIN, SCHUMANN, BOKOR, and KONETZNI [and Cast]: Leupold, wir gehn! . . . Geh' Er und mach' Er seinem Hof (1937)
8. KONETZNI, BOKOR, and SCHUMANN: Hab mir's gelobt . . . In gottes Namen! (1937)
9. BOKOR, SCHUMANN, KONETZNI, and WIEDEMANN: War ein Haus wo . . . beieinand' für alle Zeit und Ewigkeit! [orchestral conclusion omitted] (1937)

NOTES: EJS 332

Side 1 (332 A):

The label of EJS 332 and the bulletin for May, 1965 claim that the FREISCHÜTZ is taken from a single performance with Rethberg, Völker, and Bohnen, conducted by "Boehme." Actually, the Rethberg Wiener Staatsoper performance from this date was conducted by Krips, and did not feature Bohnen. Those excerpts featuring Bohnen are from the 1939 Salzburg Festival, conducted by Knappertsbusch. EJS 332 features all but about 15-30 seconds of the surviving material from the 1933 performance, recorded backstage at the Staatsoper. The surviving excerpts from the 1939 performance also contain Lemnitz's two arias, but these, remarkably, were never issued on a Smith LP, despite his access to them.

The date of the 1933 performance is disputed: both 10 April and 10 May, 1933 are claimed as accurate.

Speed is reported at about 33.1 rpm for all bands but 1 and 6, which require 33.8 rpm.

Side 2 (332 B):

The label of EJS 332 reads "With Lotte Lehmann, Jarmila Novotna, Fritz Wiedemann, Orchestra of the Staatsoper, Vienna, conducted by Richard Strauss (1936)." The May, 1965 bulletin reiterates this. In fact, this is a composite of two Staatsoper performances given on 22 April, 1936 and 13 June, 1937, both conducted by Knappertsbusch. Lehmann was in the 1936 cast, but nothing of her is to be heard in the EJS 332 composite. HERMANN (not Fritz!) Wiedemann appeared only in the 1937 production. The 1936 *Octavian* is disputed: some sources name Jarmila Novotná, but the Vienna *Neue freie Presse*, from which the above 1936 listing is taken, gives Eva Hadrabová. In any case, neither are heard here. The 1936 *Modistin* is *not* soprano *Maria* Nemeth; the 1936 *Majordomo of Marschallin*, retrieved only as "Tomek," may be Zivojin *Tomič*.

The excerpts derive from two sets of acetates recorded backstage at the Staatsoper: approximately 17 minutes has survived from the 1936 performance and about 27 minutes from 1937. EJS 332 uses all that is available from 1937 (except for small cuts made so that the excerpts close at cadences), but only two excerpts and a bridge passage from 1936 (see also the endnote for II/6).

Speed is reported slightly flat throughout the ROSENKAVALIER.

Band 6: This excerpt appears to be a composite of passages from both the 1936 and 1937 performances, i.e. two 3 ½-minute acetates from 1937, and a bridge from 1936, as follows:

a) BOKOR and SCHUMANN: Mir is die Ehre widerfahren . . . wie Rosen vom hochheiligen Para[dies] (1937)
b) SCHUMANN: [Para]dies. Ist Ihm nicht auch? (1936)
c) BOKOR and SCHUMANN: Ist wie ein Gruss vom Himmel . . . Jetzt aber kommt mein Herr Zukünftiger (1937)

EJS 333: "The Golden Age of Opera" (1 LP)
Issued May, 1965

SIDE 1 (333 A):

STIFFELIO (Verdi) (I)
Opera in 3 acts (excerpts)
pf/? and organ/?
?Broadcast, Centro Sperimentale, Venice, 1965

CAST:
Aldo Bottion (*Stiffelio*); Virginia De Notaristefani (*Lina*); Silvano Carroli (*Stankar*); Silvano Carroli (*Jorg*).

1. Act I:
   a) CARROLI: O santo libro (w. pf)
   b) CARROLI, BOTTION, and DE NOTARISTEFANI: Soli noi siamo . . . Vidi dovunque gemere . . . Ah! v'appare in fronte scritto (w. pf)

   Act II:
   c) VASCO CAMPAGNANO, tenor; MARIA VITALE, soprano; ROLANDO PANERAI, baritone; and ALDO BERTOCCI, tenor (Orchestra of Radio Italiana [RAI], Torino/Arturo Basile: Ah! Era vero . . . Un accento proferite . . . non negarmi, per pieta!
   RAI broadcast, Turin, 24 Oct 1951

   Act III:
   d) MARIA VITALE, soprano; VASCO CAMPAGNANO, tenor; ROLANDO PANERAI, baritone; and GIANFELICE DE MANUELLI, bass (Orchestra of Radio Italiana [RAI], Torino/Arturo Basile: Egli un patto proponeva
   RAI broadcast, Turin, 24 Oct 1951
   e) CARROLI and DE NOTARISTEFANI: Non puniscimi Signore (w. organ)
   f) CARROLI, BOTTION, DE NOTARISTEFANI: Stiffelio! Eccomi! (w. pf)

SIDE 2 (333 B):

ALZIRA (Verdi) (I)
Opera in 2 acts and a Prologue (excerpts)
pf/?; Student Orchestra of the Centro Sperimentale, Venezia/?
?Broadcast, Centro Sperimentale, Venice, 1965

CAST:
Virginia De Notaristefani (*Alzira*); Aldo Bottion (*Zamoro*); Silvano Carroli (*Gusmano*); Silvano Carroli (*Alvaro*).

1. Prologue
   a) Overture (orchestra)
   b) DE NOTARISTEFANI, BOTTION, and CARROLI: Sorgete! Prigioniero! . . . Un Inca, eccesso orribile! (w. pf)

   Act I:
   c) DE NOTARISTEFANI: Da Gusman, su fragil barco (w. pf)
   d) DE NOTARISTEFANI, BOTTION, and CARROLI: Nella polve, genuflesso (w. pf)

   Act II:
   e) DE NOTARISTEFANI, BOTTION, and CARROLI: Scegli! Il pianto, l'angoscia (w. pf)

GLORIA (Cilèa) (I)
Opera in 3 acts (excerpts)
?Orchestra of the Radio Italiana [RAI]/?
?RAI broadcast, date unknown

CAST:
Agostino Lazzari (*Lionetto Ricci*); Gabriella Tucci (*Gloria*).

2. Act II: a) Intermezzo (orchestra)
b) LAZZARI: Pur dolente son io
c) TUCCI: O mia cuna fiorita

NOTES: EJS 333

Side 1 (333 A):

Verdi's unsuccessful STIFFELIO, with its text by Piave after the 1849 play LE PASTEUR OU L'ÉVANGILE ET LE FOYER by Émile Souvestre and Eugène Bourgeois, was first produced at the Teatro Grande, Triste, on 16 November, 1850. The libretto was later revised as the four-act AROLDO, which premiered in Rimini on 16 August, 1857.

The orchestrally-accompanied inserts were taken from the 1951 RAI broadcast of AROLDO issued in June, 1959 as EJS 156.

In 1965, only the piano-vocal score of STIFFELIO was available, the orchestral score having been withdrawn by the composer when the opera was revised, which explains the accompaniment of the excerpts from the Centro Sperimentale production. "Non puniscimi Signore" was originally scored with organ accompaniment in STIFFELIO, so that its conversion from the piano accompaniment back to organ was easily accomplished for this performance.

In addition to the conductor of this student production, if there was one, neither the pianist or organist could be identified. Soprano De Notaristefani was an RAI regular in the early 1960s.

A 1968 performance of STIFFELIO was issued complete in March, 1969 as EJS 461.

Side 2 (333 B):

Band 1: The orchestral score to Verdi's 1845 ALZIRA does exist in spite of its failure and the composer's disdain for it, so it is not known why only the Overture was played by the orchestra in this performance. More ambitious revivals of the work have been heard since 1967. Both the "Sorgete!" (item b) and "Da Gusman" (item c) are given without their cabalettas.

Band 2: This performance of Cilèa's last produced opera, the obscure GLORIA, text by Colautti, was not taken from a complete RAI broadcast, hence its absence from the RAI chronology. An RAI ***CONCERTO MARTINI E ROSSI*** broadcast has also been suggested as a possible source, but the origin of the performance remains obscure. The work made its debut under Toscanini's direction at La Scala on 15 April, 1907, with Amato, Zenatello, and Kruszelnicka heading the cast. A complete 1969 RAI performance later appeared as EJS 477 (September, 1969). Tenor Mirto Picchi's "Pur dolente son io" appeared on EJS 360 (Potpourri 19) in March, 1966, and was later included on a Timaclub Picchi recital.

Band 2: This performance of Cilèa's last produced opera, the obscure GLORIA, text by Colautti, was not taken from a complete RAI broadcast, hence its absence from the RAI chronology. An RAI ***CONCERTO MARTINI E ROSSI*** broadcast has also been suggested as a possible source, but the origin of the performance remains obscure. The work made its debut under Toscanini's direction at La Scala on 15 April, 1907, with Amato, Zenatello, and Kruszelnicka heading the cast. A complete 1969 RAI performance later appeared as EJS 477 (September, 1969). Tenor Mirto Picchi's "Pur dolente son io" appeared on EJS 360 (Potpourri 19) in March, 1966, and was later included on a Timaclub Picchi recital.

EJS 334: "The Golden Age of Opera" (1 LP)
Issued May, 1965

"MARIA JERITZA"

SIDE 1 (334 A):

SALOME (R. Strauss) (G)
Opera in 1 act (excerpts)
Wiener Philharmoniker/Leopold Reichberger [Hugo Reichenberger]
?Broadcast, Wiener Staatsoper, Vienna, 29 Apr 1933

CAST:
Maria Jeritza (*Salome*); Emil Schipper (*Jochanaan*); Georg Maikl (*Narraboth*).

* 1. JERITZA, MAIKL, and SCHIPPER: Jochanaan, ich bin verliebt . . . Entweihe nicht den Temple des Herrn, meines Gottes / Ich kann es nicht ertragen . . . Knie nieder am ufer des Sees, ruf ihn an

* 2. JERITZA: Ah! Du wolltest mich deinen Mund küssen lassen, Jochanaan . . . die ihren Geifer gegen mich spie

CAVALLERIA RUSTICANA (Mascagni) (G)
Opera in 1 Act (excerpts)
Wiener Philharmoniker/Leopold Reichberger [Hugo Riechenberger]
?Broadcast, Wiener Staatsoper, Vienna, 26 Sep 1933

CAST:
Maria Jeritza (*Santuzza*); Helge Roswaenge (*Turiddu*); Emil Schipper (*Alfio*).

3. JERITZA and ROSWAENGE: L'hai voluto, e ben to sta! . . . No, no, Turiddu

4. JERITZA and SCHIPPER: Il ver . . . Infami loro

5. w. FRANZ VöLKER, tenor (Wiener Philharmoniker/Clemens Krauss): DIE WALKÜRE, Act II: deinem Drohen trotz'ich mit ihm! . . . Auf der Walstatt seh'ich dich wieder! (end of the "Todesverkundigung")
?Broadcast, Wiener Philharmoniker, Vienna, 11 Jun 1933

SIDE 2 (334 B):

DON CARLOS (Verdi) (G)
Opera in 5 acts (excerpts)
Orchestra and Chorus of the Wiener Staatsoper/Bruno Walter
In-house recording, Wiener Staatsoper, Vienna, 16 Dec 1936
In-house recording, Wiener Staatsoper, Vienna, 6 Jan 1937

CASTS:	16 DECEMBER, 1936	6 JANUARY, 1937
Elisabeth . . .	Hilde Konetzni . . .	Hilde Konetzni
Princess of Eboli . . .	Elena Nikolaidi . . .	Elena Nikolaidi
Don Carlos . . .	Franz Völker . . .	Norbert Ardelli
Rodrigo . . .	Frederick Ginrod . . .	Frederick Ginrod
Philip II . . .	Alexander Kipnis . . .	Alexander Kipnis
Grand Inquisitor . . .	Alfred Jerger . . .	Alfred Jerger
Friar . . .	Herbert Alsen . . .	Carl Bissutti

Act IV: *1. a) KIPNIS: Dormirò sol, nel manto mio regal . . . giornata è giunta [a sera] (1936)
b) ?KIPNIS: a sera . . . la vôlta nera
c) KIPNIS (Berlin State Opera Orchestra/Clemens Schmalstich): Là nell'avello dell'Escurial . . . Amor per me non ha! (G)
BLR-6208-2 Berlin, 1 Apr 1930
Electrola EW 88 (30-3629) HMV E 610 (30-3629)
HMV V 208 (30-3629)

* 2. JERGER and KIPNIS: Ovunque avra vigor . . . Sta ben! . . . Ed io, l'inquisitor . . . Perchè mi trovo io qui? (1936)

3. KONETZNI and NIKOLAIDI: Io son straniera in questo sol! . . . Fra l'esiglio ed il vel sceglier potrete! (1936)

* 4. NIKOLAIDI: Versar, versar, sol posso pianto . . . Lo salverò (1936)

5. VÖLKER, KIPNIS, and JERGER: Tu più figlio non h'ai! . . . to the end of the scene (1936)

Act V: * 6. VÖLKER and KONETZNI: Vago sogno m'arrise! . . . che fugge in terra ognor! (1936)

* 7. BISSUTTI and JERGER, and Chorus: Il duolo della terra . . . [Act I] Monk's Chorus . . . to the end of the opera (1937)

NOTES: EJS 334

Side 1 (334 A):

Bands 1-2: Labeled on EJS 334 as conducted by Richard Strauss, but this was disproven quite some time ago (see Peter Morse's Strauss discography in the *ARSC Journal*, 9/1, 1977, p. 57).

Side 2 (334 B):

Note that the DON CARLOS excerpts, sung in German, are given here in the more familiar Italian.

This is another of the very complicated Smith issues. EJS 334 is labeled as "Elisabeth Reining (sic), Elena Nicolaidi, Franz Völker, Alexander Kipnis, Alfred Jerger, and Alexander Sved. Orchestra and Chorus of the Vienna Staatsoper conducted by Bruno Walter (February 16, 1936)." The May, 1965 bulletin gives the same information. *Maria* Reining sang in neither of the performances excerpted on EJS 334, and Sved, who was announced as the *Rodrigo* for the 16 December, 1936 performance, was replaced by Frederick Ginrod, heard here.

There was no performance at the Staatsoper on 16 February, 1936. The production was first mounted on 16 December of that year, so this dating was probably the result of a smudge on the original acetate labels. (16/2/36 for 16/12/36). Three performances of DON CARLOS have survived in excerpts from this season: 16 December, 1936, 6 January, 1937, and 7 December, 1937, all recorded on acetates by a certain "Herr May," or so legend insists.

Two private catalogs--one from Good Sound Associates, the other from a private New York collection--have issued materials from what was determined to be three of that season's performances of DON CARLOS--"February 16, 1936" (sic), which is really 16 December, 1936; "January 5, 1937," which was in fact 6 January, 1937 (as there was no performance of the work on 5 January); and 7 December, 1937.

The private collection lists a combined 22 minutes/15 seconds from the December, 1936 and January, 1937 performances with "Reining or H. Konetzni" as Elisabeth (Reining appeared as *Elisabeth* only on 7 December, 1937, making either the date or the attribution incorrect), as well as a 7-minute excerpt of *Philip's* Act IV aria and scene with the *Grand Inquisitor*.

Good Sound Associates listed three excerpts: a 10-minute scene with Konetzni, Nikolaidi, Völker, Alsen, and Kipnis dated 2/16/36 (sic) and two scenes with Reining and Todor Mazaroff, one 15-minutes in duration dated 1/5/37 (sic), the other 20-minutes long and dated 12/7/37. The conductor for all three exerpts is given as Walter.

The cast of the 7 December, 1937 performance--conducted by Wolfgang Martin, not Walter--is given below for comparison with those of 16 December, 1936 and 6 January, 1937:

Maria Reining (*Elisabeth*); Elena Nikolaidi (*Princess of Eboli*); Todor Mazaroff (*Don Carlos*); Piero Pierotic (*Don Rodrigo*); Herbert Alsen (*Philip II*); Alfred Jerger (*Grand Inquistor*); Carl Bissutti (*Friar*).

Co-author Bill Collins researched this issue with great care, and furnishes his own analysis:

"I obtained a tape of the 16 December, 1936, 6 January and 7 December, 1937 performances as sold by still another "private" outlet, Mr. Tape, the contents of which are as follows:

No. 1: Presumably 16 December, 1936, this is identical to the first six bands of EJS 334, with some minor cosmetic differences, and one major difference--as in no. 2 below.

No. 2: Presumably 6 January, 1937, a repeat of the music on band 6 of EJS 334 (the Act V duet between *Carlos* and *Elisabeth*) with a different tenor and an acetate break not found in no. 1, plus the music in band 7 of EJS 334.

No. 3: Presumably 7 December, 1937. The *Carlos-Rodrigo* duet from Act I, the *Carlos-Elisabeth* duet from Act II, and the *Carlos-Princess Eboli-Rodrigo* "Garden" duet and trio from Act III, none of which is on EJS 334.

"The problem of dating the EJS 334 excerpts involves the discrepancies between the two private listings for 16 December, 1936 and 6 January, 1937 (given incorrectly there as 5 January). If Good Sound Associates is correct, only the first three or four bands of EJS 334 are from the 16 December performance, with Völker's contribution being a few lines from the [Prison Scene] finale. However, Good Sound Associates is demonstrably wrong in its listing of Reining and Mazaroff as the singers in the duet--unless the duet is from 7 December, 1937 and is out of musical order. Unfortunately, I am aware of no commercial recordings by Ardelli (none are listed in any of the Kutsch-Riemens editions) with which to match the second version of the Act V duet. The voice does sound *a bit* like Mazaroff, I must admit. But if that is so, then is it Ardelli on EJS 344?

"My own solution is necessarily subjective: if we take the timings given on the tape from the private New York collection, then those two selections add up to the total of all the music from 16 December and 6 January, counting both versions of the duet. If Mr. Tape's order is correct, then Herr May recorded only the second version of the duet and the fragment of the 6 January finale, and only the second excerpt appears on EJS 344 from that date. It would be odd if Herr May had neglected to record Völker but *did* record Ardelli--rather like omitting Domingo but catching Carlo Bini at a later performance! So, in the band-by-band breakdown of EJS 334, I would assign bands 1-6 to 16 December, 1936 and band 7 to 6 January, 1937.

"As a postscript, The Teletheater LP of the Wiener Staatsoper 1936 (Teletheater 76.23589) issued the Act V duet found on EJS 334 as being from the 16 December, 1936 performance with Völker and Konetzni, which would seem to confirm my speculations, at least for that excerpt."

Band 1: There is an audible cut at *Philip's* "a sera" running through "la vôlta nera," but the source of the patch is unknown. It may or may not be Kipnis, but appears not to have been taken from his 1930 Berlin HMV (sung in German as "Könnte doch die Krone"), as the end of the aria, beginning at "Là nell'avello dell'Escurial," certainly has. HMV V 208 was the Scandanavian issue.

Band 2: There is an acetate break between *Philip's* "Sta ben!" and the *Grand Inquistor's* "Ed io, l'inquisitor." The excerpt ends after the chords preceding "Perchè mi trovo qui?"

Band 4: There are gaps in the acetate immediately preceding and following *Princess Eboli's* "Un dì mi resta," and these are patched in from some unknown (probably commercial) source.

Band 6: *Elisabeth's* "marziale" passage is omitted, an established custom.

Band 7: After the *Grand Inquistor's* "È la voce di Carlos!," the *Monks* reprise their Act I chorus. The original acetates end with an upward orchestral *tutti* cut from EJS 334. This ending, including the reappearance of the *Monk's* chorus, follows no published score and appears to be in keeping with the long-standing tradition of ending DON CARLOS with a custom-made finish.

EJS 335: "The Golden Age of Opera" (2 LPs)
Issued June, 1965

SIDES 1-4 (335 A-D):

LA GAZZETTA (Rossini-revised Ugo Rapolo)
Opera in 2 acts (complete)
Orchestra of the Antonio Scarlatti di Napoli and the Coro del Teatro San Carlo, Napoli/Franco Carracciolo
?Broadcast, Teatro di Corte, Palazzo Reale, Naples, 27 Sep 1960

CAST:
Gianna Galli (*Doralice*); Angelica Tuccari (*Lisetta*); Bianca Maria Casoni (*Madama La Rosa*); Agostino Lazzari (*Alberto*); Mario Borriello (*Filippo*); Italo Tajo (*Don Pomponio Storione*); Carlo Cava (*Traversen*); Leonardo Monreale (*Anselmo*).

NOTES: EJS 335

Subsequently reissued on Fonit-Cetra LAR-17 and VOCE-12.

EJS 336: "The Golden Age of Opera" (1 LP)
Issued June, 1965

SIDE 1 (336 A):

AÏDA (Verdi) (I and G)
Opera in 4 acts (excerpts)
Wiener Philharmoniker Orchestra and Chorus of the Wiener Staatsoper/Karl Alwin
In-house recording, Wiener Staatsoper, Vienna, 23 May 1937

CAST:
Beniamino Gigli (*Radames*); Maria Nemeth (*Aïda*); Rosette Anday (*Amneris*); Alexander Sved (*Amonasro*); Alexander Kipnis (*Ramfis*); Nikolaus [Nicola] Zec (*The King of Egypt*).

1. Act I:
   * a) GIGLI: [Se quel] guerrier io fossi . . . Celeste Aïda
   - b) GIGLI: D'un sogno avventuroso . . . a tal onor prescelto
   - c) GIGLI, NEMETH, ANDAY, KIPNIS, and ZEC: Iside venerata . . . Guerra, guerra e morte allo stranier

   Act II:
   - d) GIGLI, KIPNIS, and ZEC: O Re, pei sacri numi . . . fra noi resti col padre Aïda

   Act III:
   - e) GIGLI and NEMETH: Pur ti riveggo . . . Fuggire! Fuggire!
   * f) GIGLI and NEMETH: Sovra una terra estrania . . . la si schiude un ciel d'amore
   - g) GIGLI and NEMETH: Vieni meco, insiem fuggiamo . . . a noi duce fia l'amor
   - h) GIGLI, NEMETH, ANDAY, SVED, and KIPNIS: No, tu non sei colpevole . . . to the end of the act

Act IV: i) GIGLI and ANDAY: Di me discolpe i giudici . . . Morire!
j) GIGLI and ANDAY: Per essa anch'io la patria . . . Ed ella? sparve ne piu novella s'ebbe
k) GIGLI and NEMETH and Chorus: La fatal pietra . . . troppo sei bella
l) GIGLI, NEMETH, ANDAY, and Chorus: O terra addio! . . . to the end of the opera

SIDE 2 (336 B):

* 1. w. BBC Opera Orchestra/Stanford Robinson: "Caro mio Ben" (Giordani) (I)
BBC broadcast, London, 25 Apr 1952

* 2. w. BBC Opera Orchestra/Stanford Robinson: "Plaisir d'amour" (Claris de Florian-G. Martini) (F)
BBC broadcast, London, 25 Apr 1952

* 3. w. BBC Opera Orchestra/Stanford Robinson: MARTHA, Act III: M'appari [Ach, so fromm] (Flotow) (I)
BBC broadcast, London, 25 Apr 1952

* 4. w. BBC Opera Orchestra/Stanford Robinson: L'AFRICAINE, Act IV: Mi batte il cor . . . O Paradiso! [Pays merveilleux . . . Ô Paradis!] (Meyerbeer) (I)
BBC broadcast, London, 25 Apr 1952

* 5. w. BBC Opera Orchestra/Stanford Robinson: I PAGLIACCI, Act I: Recitar . . . Vesti la giubba (Leoncavallo) (I)
BBC broadcast, London, 25 Apr 1952

* 6. w. Philharmonia Orchestra/Stanford Robinson: "Core 'ngrato" (Cardillo) (I)
BBC Studios, London, 31 Oct 1952 for BBC broadcast, 25 Dec 1952

* 7. w. Philharmonia Orchestra/Stanford Robinson: L'ELISIR D'AMORE: Una furtiva lagrima (Donizetti) (I)
BBC Studios, London, 31 Oct 1952 for BBC broadcast, 25 Dec 1952

* 8. w. Philharmonia Orchestra/Stanford Robinson: LES PÊCHEURS DE PERLES, Act I: Mi par d'udir ancora [Je crois entendre encore] (Bizet) (I)
BBC Studios, London, 31 Oct 1952 for BBC broadcast, 25 Dec 1952

* 9. w. Max Salpeter, violin; Philharmonia Orchestra/Stanford Robinson: WTC I, Prelude 1: "Ave Maria" (J. S. Bach-arr. Gounod) (L)
BBC Studios, London, 31 Oct 1952 for BBC broadcast, 25 Dec 1952

*10. GIGLI: Speech (E)

NOTES: EJS 336

Side 1 (336 A):

Note that Gigli sang *Radames* in Italian, while the rest of the cast sang in German. For easier recourse to the score, the original Italian text is given in the listing.

Excerpts e, f, g, h, k, and l later appeared on MDP 018.

Band 1a: Three measures are cut at the end of the "Celeste Aïda," presumably a break in the original transcription.

Band 1f: Speed is slightly low on this excerpt. On the MDP 018 Gigli recital, *Aïda's* cabaletta is completed using excerpts from a different live performance featuring Nemeth.

Side 2 (336 B):

Bands 1-5: The remainder of this 25 April, 1952 BBC broadcast was issued on EJS 329 (April, 1965). Thereafter, excerpts were featured elswhere on EJS, MDP, Glendale, and EMI.

Bands 6-10: The remainder of this 31 October, 1952 broadcast recording session appeared on EJS 357 (February, 1966). There is no applause at the end of the songs and arias because the show was pre-recorded for a Christmas Night broadcast, but applause has been spliced in on EJS 336 after the concluding speech.

Band 10: Gigli's speech is preceded by an unknown announcer.

EJS 337: "The Golden Age of Opera" (1 LP)
Issued June, 1965

FAUST (Gounod) (Sw-G)
Opera 5 in acts (excerpts)
Wiener Philharmoniker Orchestra and Chorus of the Wiener Staatsoper/ Josef Krips
In-house recording, Wiener Staatsoper, Vienna, 7 Mar 1937

CAST:
Jussi Bjoerling (*Faust*); Alexander Kipnis (*Méphistophélès*); Ester [Esther] Rethy (*Marguerite*); Alexander Sved (*Valentin*); Dora Komarek (*Siebel*); [Bella Paalen (*Marthe*)]; [Georg Monthy (*Wagner*)].

SIDE 1 (337 A):

* 1. Act I:
- a) BJOERLING: Eh bien! Puisque la mort . . . Salut! Ô mon dernier matin! . . . Vains échos
- b) BJOERLING and KIPNIS: Mais ce Dieu . . . Maudites soyez-vous
- c) BJOERLING and KIPNIS: À moi les plaisirs . . . Je puis contenter ton caprice
- d) BJOERLING and KIPNIS: Et maintenant, maître . . . to the end of the act

Act II: e) SVED: Avant de quitter ces lieux
f) KIPNIS, [Je ferai mon mieux] pour n'ennuyer personne . . . Le veau d'or
g) BJOERLING, KIPNIS, RETHY, and KOMAREK: Ne permettez-vous pas . . . through the finale

Act III: h) BJOERLING (Orchestra of the Algemeene Vereniging Radio Omroep [AVRO], Hilversum/Frieder Weissmann): Salut! demeure (F)
AVRO broadcast, Hilversum, Norway, 8 Jun 1939

i) BJOERLING and RETHY: Il se fait tard . . .Quelle soit pour ton coeur l'oracle du ciel même
j) BJOERLING and RETHY: Eternelle! . . . dans nos deux âmes
k) BJOERLING, KIPNIS, and RETHY, Marguerite! . . . to the end of the act

Act IV: l) BJOERLING, KIPNIS and RETHY: Quittons ces lieux! . . . Anges purs, anges radieux . . . to the end of the opera

"JUSSI BJOERLING RECITAL"

SIDE 2 (337 B):

* 1. w. Wiener Philharmoniker Orchestra/Victor de Sabata: AÏDA, Act I: Se quel guerrier io fossi . . . Celeste Aïda (Verdi) (Sw-G)
In-house recording, Wiener Staatsoper, Vienna, 7 Jun 1936

* 2. w. Wiener Philharmoniker Orchestra/Karl Alwin: I PAGLIACCI, Act I: Recitar! . . . Vesti la giubba (Leoncavallo) (Sw)
In-house recording, Wiener Staatsoper, Vienna, 12 Mar 1937

* 3. w. MARGIT BOKOR, soprano (Wiener Philharmoniker Orchestra/Karl Alwin): I PAGLIACCI, Act II: Non Pagliacco non son . . . é il nome del tuo ganzo (Leoncavallo) (Sw-G)
In-house recording, Wiener Staatsoper, Vienna, 12 Mar 1937

* 4. w. Orchestra of the Algemeene Vereniging Radio Omroep [AVRO], Hilversum/Frieder Weissmann: L'AFRICAINE, Act IV: Mi batte il cor . . . O Paradiso! [Pays merveilleux . . . Ô Paradis] (Meyerbeer) (I)
AVRO broadcast, Hilversum, Holland, 8 Jun 1939

* 5. w. Orchestra of the Algemeene Vereniging Radio Omroep [AVRO] Hilversum/Frieder Weissmann: MANON, Act II: En fermant les yeux (Massenet) (F)
AVRO broadcast, Hilversum, Holland, 8 Jun 1939

* 6. w. Orchestra of the Algemeene Vereniging Radio Omroep [AVRO] Hilversum/Frieder Weissmann: CARMEN, Act II: La fleur que tu m'avais jetée (Bizet) (F)
AVRO broadcast, Hilversum, Holland, 8 Jun 1939

* 7. w. studio orch/Donald Voorhees: MANON LESCAUT, Act II: Donna non vidi mai (Puccini) (I)
Broadcast, ***BELL TELEPHONE HOUR***, WNBC, NYC, 8 Jan 1951

* 8. w. studio orch/Donald Voorhees: ANDREA CHENIER, Act IV: Come un bel dì maggio (Giordano) (I)
Broadcast, ***BELL TELEPHONE HOUR***, WNBC, NYC, 23 Oct 1950

* 9. w. orch/Nils Grevillius: RIGOLETTO, Act III: La donna è mobile (Verdi) (I)
2SB 441-2 Concert Hall, Small Auditorium, Stockholm, 4 Dec 1936
HMV DB 1548 Victor 4372
HMV IR 420 Victor JE 100
Victor HL 54

*10. w. orch/Nils Grevillius: CAVALLERIA RUSTICANA: O Lola, bort till dig [O Lola, ch'ai di latti] ["Siciliana"] (Mascagni) (Sw)
OPA 236-1 [?Concert Hall], Stockholm, 3 Mar 1934 HMV X-4265

NOTES: EJS 337

The many dating errors on the labels of this issue appear to be the result of confusing European and American dating styles when the label copy was compiled. Most excerpts have been given in the listing in their original language.

Side 1 (337 A):

Band 1a-1: The FAUST excerpts, recorded backstage during a complete performance, are dated 5 May, 1937 on the label of EJS 337.

Note that Bjoerling sang *Faust* in Swedish, while the rest of the cast sang in German. Bjoerling's "Salut, demeure," taken from the 8 June, 1939 AVRO broadcast conducted by Weissmann (see side II/4-6), is sung in French and had appeared earlier on EJS 279 (October, 1963). All of the FAUST excerpts included here were later recycled on HRE 214-2 and HRE 376-2, both of which used the 1939 "Salut, demeure" insert.

Item 1g falls just short of the conclusion of the Act II Finale.

Side 2 (337 B):

Band 1: Dated 6 July, 1936 on the label of EJS 337. This "Celeste Aïda" was taken from a complete performance sung in Swedish by Bjoerling and in German by the remainder of the cast, with Maria Nemeth in the title role. Other excerpts from the performance appeared on EJS 405 (September, 1967), HRE 376-2, and MDP 026.

Bands 2-3: Dated 3 December, 1937 on the label of EJS 337. From a complete performance of I PAGLIACCI. Note that Bokor sang *Nedda* in German, while Bjoerling sang *Canio* in Swedish. These two excerpts are apparently all that survive from the performance: both were later issued on HRE 376-2, while Bjoerling's "Vesti la giubba" also appeared on MDP 026.

Bands 4-6: Three other selections from this 8 June, 1939 concert, including the "Salut! demeure" inserted into the 7 March, 1937 Wiener Staatsoper FAUST on side 1, appeared earlier on EJS 279 (October, 1963). The complete 8 June, 1939 broadcast (six items by Bjoerling) was later included on ANNA 1005 (May, 1978) and ERR 121-1.

Bands 7-8: Two other Bjoerling items from this broadcast, along with the MANON LESCAUT, later appeared on EJS 367 (May, 1966), while the MANON "Rêve" and MANON LESCAUT arias were included on HRE 214-2 (the MANON has appeared on many other private labels).

Both the MANON LESCAUT and the CHENIER arias appeared originally on a 16-inch 33.3 rpm transcription disc labelled "Voice of America, Concert Hall Program No. 70" (master DS-2451) issued by the U.S. Government. See also the endnote for EJS 367 (I/4-6).

Band 9: HMV IR 420 is an Irish issue; Victor JE 100 and HL 54 are Japanese. The Porter-Henrysson Bjoerling discography explains that the company ledgers give the recording date as 4 December, 1936, but that the Small Auditorium was used for recording only on 1 and 3 December (p. 31n).

Band 10: The original label of X-4265 reads "Siciliana ur 'Pa Sicilien." This performance has appeared on a number of commercial Bjoerling LPs.

EJS 338: "The Golden Age of Opera" (1 LP)
Issued September, 1965

"KIRSTEN FLAGSTAD 70th BIRTHDAY DISC"

SIDE 1 (338 A):

1. w. Detroit Symphony Orchestra/Frederick Stock: STABAT MATER: Inflammatus (Rossini) (L)
   Broadcast, ***FORD SUNDAY EVENING HOUR***, WJR, Detroit, 21 Apr 1935

* 2. w. pf/Waldemar Alme: "Rain Has Fallen" (Joyce-Barber) (E)
   Broadcast, Norwegian Radio, Oslo, ?9 Sep 1954

* 3. w. pf/Waldemar Alme: "Music I Heard With You" (Aiken-Richard Hageman) (E)
   Broadcast, Norwegian Radio, Oslo, ?9 Sep 1954

* 4. w. pf/Waldemar Alme: GITANJALI: The Sleep that Flits on Baby's Eyes (Tagore-John Alden Carpenter)
   Broadcast, Norwegian Radio, Oslo, ?9 Sep 1954

* 5. w. pf/Waldemar Alme: "With the Tide" (O'Brien-Winter Watts) (E)
   Broadcast, Norwegian Radio, Oslo, ?9 Sep 1954

* 6. w. pf/Waldemar Alme: "The White Peace" (Macleod-Bax) (E)
   Broadcast, Norwegian Radio, Oslo, ?9 Sep 1954

* 7. w. pf/Waldemar Alme: "Cradle Song" (Colm-Bax) (E)
   Broadcast, Norwegian Radio, Oslo, ?9 Sep 1954

* 8. w. pf/Waldemar Alme: "Speak, Music" (Benson-Elgar) (R)
   Broadcast, Norwegian Radio, Oslo, ?9 Sep 1954

* 9. w. pf/Waldemar Alme: "The Little Road to Bethlehem" (Rose-Michael Head) (E)
Broadcast, Norwegian Radio, Oslo, ?9 Sep 1954

* 10. w. pf/Waldemar Alme: "Love's Philosophy" (Shelley-Delius) (E)
Broadcast, Norwegian Radio, Oslo, ?9 Sep 1954

* 11. w. pf/Waldemar Alme: "Love Went A-Riding" (Coleridge-Bridge) (E)
Broadcast, Norwegian Radio, Oslo, ?9 Sep 1954

SIDE 2 (338 B):

* 1. w. orch/?Wilfred Pelletier or ?Boris Morros: DIE WALKÜRE, Act II: Hoyotoho! (Wagner) (G)
from the soundtrack of the 10-reel feature film, ***THE BIG BROADCAST OF 1938*** (1938), Hollywood, circa Spring, 1937
LP 7843 c18 Feb 1938 (Parmamount Pictures, Inc.)
New York Premiere: Paramount Theater, NYC, 9 Mar 1938

* 2. a) w. LAURITZ MELCHIOR, tenor (Metropolitan Opera House Orchestra/Artur Bodanzky): SIEGFRIED, Act III/iii: Heil dir, Sonne! . . . birg' meinen Muth mir nicht mehr! (Wagner) (G)
Metropolitan Opera broadcast, NYC, 30 Jan 1937

b) w. LAURITZ MELCHIOR tenor: SIEGFRIED, Act III/iii: [. . . Dort seh'ich Grane . . . mir in die Brust] (Wagner) (G)
Flagstad portion: Philharmonia Orchestra/George Sebastian
2EA 15697-2 London, 12-13 Jun 51 HMV BLP 1035 (LP)
Victor LHMV 1024 (LP)
Melchior portion: w. London Symphony/Robert Heger
2B 2898-2 London, 29 May 1932 HMV DB 1711

c) w. LAURITZ MELCHIOR, tenor ((Metropolitan Opera House Orchestra/Artur Bodanzky): SIEGFRIED, Act III/iii: [brach nun die Lohe . . . to the end of the opera (Wagner) (G)
Metropolitan Opera broadcast, NYC, 30 Jan 1937

NOTES: EJS 338

Mislabeled and misnumbered in the wax as EJS 238. This error has found its way into Sanner's Flagstad discography (item 91, p. 42, and item 934, p. 149), and in both editions of Hansen's Melchior discography (item 042, p. 30).

Side 1 (338 A):

Band 1: Dated March, 1935 on the label of EJS 338.

Bands 2-11: These ten English songs from 9 September, 1954 are listed by Sanner (items 577-586, p. 109), but they are not given there as having appeared on EJS 338. They are dated on the label of EJS 338 as 14 March, 1955, with accompanist Alme given as "Almo." That they were actually broadcast over Norsk Rikskringkasting [NRK] on 9 September, 1954 is disputed, though this is the broadcast date given by Sanner.

Norwegian Radio tape: NRK 3609. Stanford Archive of Recorded Sound tape: StARS 560000 MI/M2; New York Public Library tape: F-VIII/F-IX.

Side 2 (338 B):

Band 1: From the soundtrack of ***THE BIG BROADCAST OF 1938***, Flagstad's only Hollywood (or commercial) film appearance. In full *Brünnhilde* regalia and playing herself, she is introduced by the ship's "master of ceremonies," Bob Hope, and sings only the WALKÜRE aria. Tenor Tito Guizar and bandleader Shep Fields also appear in cameos. Sanner (note 91, p. 152) gives Pelletier as Flagstad's conductor, but this could not be confirmed elsewhere: Boris Morros was the film's credited musical director.

Like the "Inflammatus" on side 1, this performance subsequently appeared on Legendary Records LR 120.

Band 2: A compilation, taken from the 30 January, 1937 Met performance with Melchior (issued complete as EJS 173 in February, 1960) and the two separate commercial recordings given in the listing. From approximately "Dort seh'ich Grane" through "mir in die Brust," an insert is made from the commercial recordings: the Melchior portion taken from his 1932 London HMV set with soprano Florence Easton, conducted by Heger, and the Flagstad portion taken from her 1951 London HMV set with tenor Set Svanholm, conducted by Sebastian. Considering that the basis of this scene is the Met broadcast, which does exist complete, the reason the compilation was made remains vague. Smith is known to have had access to the official NBC acetates at this point, so that the missing portion of the Act III/iii *Siegfried-Brünnhilde* duet was available to him.

It has been suggested that in fact, the compilation was released as a "favor" to Danish collector Knut Hegermann-Lindencrone. The "compilation" aspect is noted in the September, 1965 EJS bulletin, but without source details. According to Smith, it was "painstakingly put together magnificently by Knut Hegermann-Lindencrone, the famed Danish collector and great personal friend of both artists [Flagstad and Melchior]. Both Madame Flagstad while alive, and Melchior, heard the tape and were much impressed with it and requested copies. Mr. Lindencrone agreed to make his tape available for release for which we think all collectors who acquire this disc will be most grateful."

Library of Congress tape: 15731-85A (complete 1937 Met broadcast).

EJS 339: "The Golden Age of Opera" (2 LPs)
Issued September, 1965

SIDES 1-4 (339 A-D):

ZELMIRA (Rossini) (I)
Opera in 2 acts (complete)
Orchestra and Chorus of the Teatro San Carlo di Napoli/Carlo Franci
Broadcast, Teatro San Carlo, Naples, 10 Apr 1965

CAST:
Virginia Zeani (*Zelmira*); Nicola Tagger (*Ilo*); Gastone Limarilli (*Antenore*); Paolo Washington (*Polidoro*); Anna Maria Rota (*Emma*); Guido Mazzini (*Leucippo*); Giuseppe Moretti (*Eacide*); Enrico Campi (*High Priest*).

NOTES: EJS 339

Mislabeled and misnumbered in the wax as EJS 239.
Subsequently reissued as MRF 93, Melodram MEL-164, and GFC 043/4.

EJS 340: "The Golden Age of Opera" (2 LPs)
Issued September, 1965

SIDES 1-4 (340 A-D):

IL GUARANY (Gomes) (I)
Opera 4 in acts (complete)
Orchestra and Chorus of the Teatro Municipal, Rio de Janeiro/
Francesco Molinari-Pradelli
Broadcast, Teatro Municipal, Rio de Janeiro, 21 Aug 1964

CAST:
Joao Gibin (*Percy*); Gianna D'Angelo (*Cecilia*); Piero Cappucilli (*Gonzales*); Massimiliano Malaspina (*Il Cacico*); Nicola Zaccaria (*Don Antonio*); Victor Prochet (*Don Alvaro*); Luiz Nascimento (*Alonso*); Nino Crimi (*Ruy Bento*); Alvary Solano (*Pedro*).

NOTES: EJS 340

Mislabeled and misnumbered in the wax as EJS 240.

EJS 341: "The Golden Age of Opera" (1 LP)
Issued October, 1965

LUCIA DI LAMMERMOOR (Donizetti) (I)
Opera in 3 acts (excerpts)
a) Orchestra and Chorus of the Palacio de la Bellas Artes, Mexico City/Renato Cellini
Broadcast, Palacio de la Bellas Artes, XEOY [Radio Mexico], Mexico City, 13 Aug 1946 and/or 24 Aug 1946
b) Orchestra and Chorus of the Metropolitan Opera House/Pietro Cimara or Fausto Cleva
Metropolitan Opera broadcast, NYC, 17 Jan 1948 (Cimara), 1 Jan 1949 (Cimara), or 29 Dec 1951 (Cleva)

CASTS:	Mexico City, 1946	Metropolitan Opera, 1948-1950
Lucia	. . . Lily Pons	. . . Lily Pons
Edgar	. . . Ferruccio Tagliavini	. . . Ferruccio Tagliavini
Sir Henry	. . . Ivan Petrov	. . . [various]
Raymond	. . . Roberto Silva	. . . [various]
Arthur	. . José Arraita/Joaquin Alverez	. . [various]
Alice	. . . Concha de los Santos	. . . Thelma Votipka
Norman	. . . [?Carlos Sagarminaga]	. . . [various]

SIDE 1 (341 A):

Act I: * 1. ?PETROV: Cruda, funesta smania [33.3 rpm]
Private [?broadcast] recording, source and date unknown

* 2. a) PONS: Regnava nel silenzio . . . poi ratta dileguò [32.3 rpm] (b)
b) PONS and DE LOS SANTOS: e l'onda pria si limpida . . . al mio penar [32.9 rpm] (a)
c) PONS and VOTIPKA: Quando rapito in estasi . . . to the end of the act [32.3 rpm] (b)

3. a) VOTIPKA, PONS, and TAGLIAVINI: Egli s'avanza . . . Sulla tomba . . . Cedi, cedi a me [32.3 rpm] (b)
b) DE LOS SANTOS, PONS, and TAGLIAVINI: si, potrei compirlo ancor, ancor! . . . Io di te memoria viva sempre, o cara, serberò [32.9 rpm] (a)
c) PONS and TAGLIAVINI: Verrano a te . . . to the end of the scene [32.3 rpm] (b)

Act II: 4. PETROV and PONS: Appressati, Lucia . . . to the end of the scene [32.9 rpm] (a)

SIDE 2 (341 B):

Act II: 1. TAGLIAVINI, PETROV, SILVA, ARRAITA or ALVAREZ, DE LOS SANTOS, and PONS: Chi mi frena ["Sextette"] . . . to the end of the scene [32.8 rpm] (a)

Act III: 2. PONS: Il dolce suono . . . to the end of the ["Mad"] scene [32.7 rpm] (a)

3. TAGLIAVINI, SILVA, and Chorus: Tombe degli'avi miei . . . to the end of the opera [32.7 rpm] (a)

NOTES: EJS 341

Mislabeled and misnumbered in the wax as EJS 241. Both the October, 1965 bulletin and the label claim that the performance comes from Mexico City, June, 1947.

All that is certain about this issue is that at least four different sources were used: a private recording, almost certainly Petrov, singing the Act I "Cruda, funesta;" two Mexican broadcasts from the 1946 featuring Pons, Tagliavini, and Petrov, both aired over XEOY, Mexico City, and one of three Pons-Tagliavini-Votipka Met broadcasts of 1948-1951.

The Sanguinetti-Williams Tagliavini discography in *The Record Collector*, 29/9-12 (December, 1984), cites no 13 August, 1946 LUCIA broadcast, and claims that EJS 341 comes from a 22 June, 1947 Mexican broadcast (p. 238), though earlier, in the broadcast chronology, this date is given as *20* June, 1947. In fact, Tagliavini's only Mexico City appearances were made during the 1946 season; the only June broadcasts during the 1947 season were CHENIER (10 June), FORZA (17 June), and RIGOLETTO (24 June), and while other operas were broadcast that season (BALLO, SAMSON, ROMÉO, WALKÜRE, MANON, FAUST, and SIEGFRIED), none are known to circulate as transcriptions. LUCIA, moreover, was not in the

1947 Palacio de la Bellas Artes season repertory, so the Sanguinetti-Williams dates are clearly in error. Of the 1946 broadcasts (FAUST, BOHÈME, DON GIOVANNI, BUTTERFLY, TRAVIATA, AÏDA, CARMEN, TOSCA, and two LUCIAs), several have survived, including the Kirsten TRAVIATA, a Winifred Heidt-Ramon Vinay CARMEN, and the Roman-Tagliavini TOSCA excerpts issued as EJS 374 (October, 1966). Which of the two LUCIAs was used for EJS 341 (24 August, with Alvarez replacing Arraita as Arthur, was a season's-end performance) has not been determined with any certainty.

Pons, Tagliavini, and Votipka appeared together in three Met LUCIA broadcasts: on 17 January, 1948 and 1 January, 1949, both conducted by Cimara, and on 29 December, 1951, conducted by Cleva. None of these was issued complete by Smith (the 1949 broadcast was later released as Melodram CD 27513), so it is not known to which he might have had even partial access in 1965.

Because of the erratic pitching, owing in part to the different sources used, playing speeds are given in brackets after each excerpt.

Side 1 (341 A):

Band 1: The "Cruda, funesta smania" seems to be Petrov, and has been tentatively attributed to a private recording (source unknown, but most likely from a broadcast). The orchestra that accompanies him is a most undistinguished ensemble. There are no other singers present, nor is there a chorus; applause erupts at the end of the aria and only the cavatina is sung--all tell-tale signs of a broadcast performance.

Band 2a: Sung a half-step *higher* than score pitch, a routine transposition for Pons.

Side 2 (341 B):

Band 2: Sung a half-step higher than score pitch, also a common Pons transposition. There are several minor performance cuts. One report claims that Pons' "Mad Scene," too, cuts back and forth between the Met and Mexico City performances, but this may confuse the frequent tape cuts or acetate breaks with actual changes of source.

Band 3: Sung a half-step lower than score pitch. The orchestral introduction is omitted.

EJS 342: "The Golden Age of Opera" (1 LP)
Issued October, 1965

SIDES 1-2 (342 A-B):

GÖTTERDÄMMERUNG (Wagner) (G)
Opera 3 in acts (excerpts)
London Philharmonic Orchestra and Royal Opera House Chorus/Wilhelm Furtwängler
Broadcast, Covent Garden, London, 7 Jun 1938

CAST:
Frida Leider (*Brünnhilde*); Lauritz Melchior (*Siegfried*); Wilhelm Schirp (*Hagen*); Herbert Janssen (*Gunther*); Anny Von Stosch (*Gutrune*); [Kerstin Thorborg (*Waltraute*)]; [Adolf Vogel (*Alberich*)]; [Mary Jarred (*First Norn*)]; [Constance Willis (*Second Norn*)]; [Mae Craven (*Third Norn*)]; [Stella Andreva (*Woglinde*)]; [Betty Thompson (*Wellgunde*)]; [Freda Townson (*Flosshilde*)].

1. Act II: JANSSEN, MELCHIOR, LEIDER, SCHIRP, STOSCH, and Chorus: Heil! Heil dir, Gunther . . . to the end of the act

NOTES: EJS 342

This performance was from Leider's final season at Covent Garden.

Mislabeled and misnumbered in the wax as EJS 242. Dated on the label as 6 July, 1938. Only Act II was broadcast, on BBC Regional. Smith later reissued excerpts from this performance on UORC 234 (January, 1975).

EJS 343: "The Golden Age of Opera" (1 LP)
Issued October, 1965

"GIOACOMO LAURI-VOLPI"

SIDE 1 (343 A):

1. w. orch/Ino Savini: TOSCA, Act I: Recondita armonia (Puccini) (I)
In-house recording, Piazza della Republica, L'Ariccia, 24 Jul 1965

2. w. orch/Ino Savini: LUISA MILLER, Act II: Ah! fede negar potessi . . . Quando le sere (Verdi) (I)
In-house recording, Piazza della Republica, L'Ariccia, 24 Jul 1965

* 3. w. GUIDO GUARNERA, baritone (orch/Ino Savini): LES PÊCHEURS DE PERLES, Act I: Del tempio al limitar [Au fond du temple] (Bizet) (I)
In-house recording, Piazza della Republica, L'Ariccia, 24 Jul 1965

4. w. orch.Ino Savini: RIGOLETTO, Act III: La donna è mobile (Verdi) (I)
In-house recording, Piazza della Republica, L'Ariccia, 24 Jul 1965

5. w. orch/Ino Savini: TURANDOT, Act III: Nessun dorma (Puccini) (I)
In-house recording, Piazza della Republica, L'Ariccia, 24 Jul 1965

* 6. w. organ/Ino Savini: SERSE, Act I: Ombra mai fu ["Largo"] (Handel) (I)
In-house recording, Chiesa dell'Assunzione, L'Ariccia, 25 Jul 1965

7. w. organ/Ino Savini: "Panis Angelicus" (Franck) (L)
In-house recording, Chiesa dell'Assunzione, L'Ariccia, 25 Jul 1965

8. w. organ/Ino Savini: "Salve Regina" (Mercadante) (L)
In-house recording, Chiesa dell'Assunzione, L'Ariccia, 25 Jul 1965

SIDE 2 (343 B):

1. w. pf/?Lauri-Volpi: RIGOLETTO, Act I: Questa o quella (first verse only) (Verdi) (I)
Private recording, Lauri-Volpi's home, Rome, 25 May 1964

2. w. pf/?Lauri-Volpi: "'A Vucchella" (Tosti) (I)
Private recording, Lauri-Volpi's home, Rome, 25 May 1964

3. w. pf/?Lauri-Volpi: AÏDA, Act I: Celeste Aïda (Verdi) (I)
Private recording, Lauri-Volpi's home, Rome, 25 May 1964

* 4. w pf/?Lauri-Volpi: LA FANCIULLA DEL WEST, Act I: Se volete che strana cosa! . . . Quello che tacete . . . Cio che avremmo (Puccini) (I)
Private recording, Lauri-Volpi's home, Rome, 25 May 1964

5. w. pf/?Lauri-Volpi: LOHENGRIN, Act I: Merce, merce, cigno [Nun sei bedankt, mein lieber Schwan] (Wagner) (I)
Private recording, Lauri-Volpi's home, Rome, 25 May 1964

6. w. pf/?Lauri-Volpi: I PURITANI, Act I: A te, o cara (Bellini) (I)
Private recording, Lauri-Volpi's home, Rome, 25 May 1964

7. w. pf/?Lauri-Volpi: WTC I, Prelude 1: "Ave Maria" (Bach-arr. Gounod) (L)
Private recording, Lauri-Volpi's home, Rome, 25 May 1964

NOTES: EJS 343

Mislabeled and misnumbered in the wax as EJS 243.

The 24 July, 1965 concert in the Piazza della Republica was Lauri-Volpi's 50th Anniversary Concert and was announced as his public farewell.

Side 1 (343 A):

Bands 3 and 6: Later issued on Timaclub LP TIMA 4.

Side 2 (343 B):

Giancarlo Bongiovanni, who has published other home recordings of Lauri-Volpi on his own Bongiovanni label, reported that the tenor provided his own piano accompaniments on these 25 May, 1964 recordings and that this was his customary practice. By all accounts Lauri-Volpi was a skilled pianist. Thus, the claim made on the label of EJS 343 and in the October, 1965 bulletin is probably correct.

Band 4: Lauri-Volpi begins at the point where *Johnson* and *Minnie* are alone, proceeds through *Johnson's* arioso, and with minor cuts, continues to the end of the act, singing most of *Minnie's* lines as well. EJS 370 (June, 1966) contains a 1963 private recording of the same passage beginning at "Cio che avremmo," later issued on Bongiovanni LP GB 1025.

EJS 344: "The Golden Age of Opera" (2 LPs)
Issued October, 1965

SIDES 1-4 (344 A-D):

INTERMEZZO (R. Strauss) (G)
Opera in 2 acts (complete)
Bayrischer Staatsoper Orchestra and Chorus/Joseph Keilberth
Broadcast, Münchner Festpiel, Munich, 27 Apr 1963

CAST:
Hermann Prey (*Robert Storch*); Hanny Steffek (*Christine*); Ferry Gruber (*Baron Lummer*); Anny Felbermayr (*Anna*); Alfred Poell (*A Notary*); Judith Hellwig (*The Notary's Wife*); Waldemar Kmentt (*Kapellmeister Stroh*); Oskar Czerwenka (*Kommerzienrat*); Alois Pernersdorfer (*Counsel: Zustizrat*); Ludwig Welter (*Kammersänger*); Peter Rille (*The Young Franzl*); Helene Volpenka (*Cook*); Irene Woloch (*Resi*).

NOTES: EJS 344

Mislabeled and misnumbered in the wax as EJS 244.
Later issued under the title INTERLUDE as SP 2, part of the obscure "Richard Strauss" series released as one of Smith's "special labels." Smith claimed that the English title of the later release was used to avoid copyright complications.
The bulletin for EJS 344 boasts that this was the "initial recording of the opera." The broadcast date given above is taken from the Melodram reissue (MEL-113) and is thought to be correct.

EJS 345: "The Golden Age of Opera" (1 LP)
Issued November, 1965

SIDES 1-2 (345 A-B):

IL GIUDIZIO UNIVERSALE (G. Salvadori-P. Miscatelli-Lorenzo Perosi) (L and I)
Oratorio (complete)
Orchestra and Chorus of the Accademia di Santa Cecilia, Roma/Don Lorenzo Perosi
Live recording, Pontifical Gregorian University, Vatican City, 4 May 1950

CAST:
Beniamino Gigli (*Cristo*); Marcella Pobbe (*L'Angelo della Pace*); Gianna Pederzini (*Lo Spirito della Giustizia*).

NOTES: EJS 345

Mislabeled and misnumbered in the wax as EJS 245.

Excerpts from a 1937 Vatican broadcast of Perosi's 1904 oratorio IL GIUDIZIO UNIVERSALE, featuring Gigli, Albanese, and Pederzini, were issued on EJS 329 (April, 1965). A portion of this 1950 performance ("Decedite a me maledicti") was issued on Italian RCA ML 40003-10.

The November, 1965 bulletin claims that the performance was "the world premiere, conducted by the then 78 year old composer in 1950," but this is obviously not the case in light of the 1937 broadcast (the actual premiere date could not be found). Perosi, moreover, was in fact 77 at the time of the 1950 performance, this being some eight months short of his 78th birthday (born 20 December, 1872).

EJS 346: "The Golden Age of Opera" (1 LP)
Issued November, 1965

SIDES 1-2 (346 A-B):

CAVALLERIA RUSTICANA (Mascagni) (Sw and I)
Opera in 1 act (complete)
Orchestra and Chorus of the Royal Opera, Stockholm/Kurt Bendix
Broadcast, Royal Opera House, Stockholm, Swedish Radio, 8 Dec 1954

CAST:
Jussi Bjoerling (*Turiddu*); Aase Nordmo-Lövberg (*Santuzza*); Georg Swedenbrant (*Alfio*); Bette Bjoerling (*Lola*); Margit Sehlmark (*Mamma Lucia*).

NOTES: EJS 346

Mislabeled and misnumbered in the wax as EJS 246.

Performed in Swedish, except for Bjoerling's *Turiddu*, which is sung in Italian. The performance is complete as performed, lacking only the Act II "Intermezzo," which was omitted from EJS 346 for purposes of timing. 8 December, 1954 was the recording date: the first broadcast of the performance was on 30 August, 1955.

Swedish Radio tape: 55/1039:1.

EJS 347: "The Golden Age of Opera" (1 LP)
Issued November, 1965

SIDE 1 (347 A):

AÏDA (Verdi) (Sw)
Opera in 4 acts (excerpts)
Orchestra and Chorus of the Royal Opera, Stockholm/Leo Blech
Broadcast, Royal Opera House, Swedish Radio, Stockholm, 5 Jan 1939

CAST:
Set Svanholm (*Radames*); Inez Kohler (*Aïda*); Gertrude Wettergren (*Amneris*); Leon Bjoerker (*Ramfis*); Folke Jonsson (*The King of Egypt*); Georg Sedenbrandt (*Messenger*).

1. Act I/i: complete

SIDE 2 (347 B):

DIE MEISTERSINGER VON NÜRNBERG (Wagner) (Sw)
Opera in 3 acts (excerpts)
Orchestra and Chorus of the Royal Opera, Stockholm/Nils Grevillius
Broadcast, Royal Opera House, Swedish Radio, Stockholm, 13 Sep 1939

CAST:
Set Svanholm (*Walther*); Joel Berglund (*Hans Sachs*); Joseph Herou (*Beckmesser*); Conny Molin (*Kothner*); Leon Bjoerker (*Pogner*); Olle Strandberg (*Vogelgesang*); Oskar Ralf (*Zorn*); Folke Cembraeus (*Eisslinger*); Gösta Kjellertz (*Moser*); Sven Herdenberg (*Nachtigale*); Gösta Lindberg (*Ortel*); Sven D'Ailly (*Schwarz*); Sigurd Bjoerling (*Foltz*).

1. Act I: ASSEMBLED CAST: Am stillen Herd . . . to the end of the act

FANAL (Kurt Atterberg) (Sw)
Opera in 3 acts (excerpts)
Orchestra and Chorus of the Royal Opera, Stockholm/Nils Grevillius
Broadcast, Royal Opera House, Swedish Radio, Stockholm, 29 Jan 1934

CAST:
Jussi Bjoerling (*Martin Skarp*); Helga Görlin (*Rosamund*); Gösta Bäckelin (*Vassal*); Joel Berglund (*Jost*); Leon Bjoerker (*Duke*).

* 2. Act III: ASSEMBLED CAST: Finale, Nu, bröder, ändas våra strider . . . to the end of the opera

NOTES: EJS 347

Side 2 (347 B):

Band 2: Atterburg's FANAL made it debut at the Royal Opera, Stockolm, on 27 January, 1934, probably with a cast identical or nearly identical to the 29 January, 1934 performance given here. The opera was performed complete on 29 January, but only Act III was broadcast. This appears to be the earliest surviving live performance of Jussi Bjoerling.

The Act III Finale was later issued on the 1977 Swedish EMI set, "Operan: Röster från Stockholms-operan under 100 år" (7C 153 35350/58).
Swedish Radio tape: L-B 306:1-2.

EJS 348: "The Golden Age of Opera" (2 LPs)
Issued November, 1965

SIDES 1-4 (348 A-D):

L'EQUIVOCO STRAVAGANTE (Rossini) (I)
Opera in 2 acts (complete)
Orchestra dell'Accademia Musicale Chigiana, and Coro dei Cantori Pisane/Alberto Zedda
?Broadcast, Teatro dei Rinnuovati, Siena, 7 Sep 1965

CAST:
Margherita Rinaldi (*Ernestina*); Pietro Bottazzo (*Ermanno*); Carlo Badioli (*Gamberotto*); Paolo Pedani (*Buralicchio*); Elena Barcis (*Rosalia*); Florindo Andreolli (*Frontino*); ? (*Angela*).

NOTES: EJS 348:

This performance was probably part of the Settimana Chigiana festival, held annually at the Accademia Chigiana in September.

EJS 349: "The Golden Age of Opera" (1 LP)
Issued December, 1965

LE NOZZE DI FIGARO, K. 492 (Mozart) (Sw)
Opera in 4 acts (excerpts)
Orchestra and Chorus of the Royal Opera, Stockholm/Herbert Sandberg
Broadcast, Royal Opera House, Swedish Radio, Stockholm, 9 May 1937

CAST:
Joel Berglund (*Figaro*); John Forsell (*Count Almaviva*); Helga Görlin (*Susanna*); Britta Hertzberg (*The Countess*); Elsa Ekendahl (*Cherubino*); Gota Allard (*Marcellina*); Olle Strandberg (*Don Basilio*); Emile Stiebel (*Doctor Bartolo*); Folke Jonsson (*Antonio*).

SIDE 1 (349 A):

Act I:
a) BERGLUND and GÖRLIN: Cinque, dieci . . . Guarda un po'mio caro Figaro
b) FORSELL, GÖRLIN, EKENDAHL, and STRANDBERG: Ah, son perduto . . . Cosa sento! . . . to the end of the trio.
c) BERGLUND: Non più andrai

Act II:
d) EKENDAHL: Voi che sapete
e) HERTZBERG, FORSELL, EKENDAHL, and GÖRLIN,: Chi picchia alla mia porta? . . . Susanna, starà qui finchè torniamo
f) FORSELL, HERTZBERG, and GÖRLIN: Tutto è come il lasciai . . . Apprender potrà

g) FORSELL, GÖRLIN, BERGLUND, ALLARD, HERTZBERG, and STIEBEL, and JONSSON: Son venuti a sconcertarmi . . . to the end of the act

SIDE 2 (349 B):

Act III: a) FORSELL and GÖRLIN: Che imbarazzo e mai questo . . . Crudel! perchè finora . . . Vedro, mentr'io sospiro
b) HERTZBERG: E Susanna non vien! . . . Dove sono i bei momenti?

Act IV: c) BERGLUND: Aprite un po'quegl'occhi
d) EKENDAHL, HERTZBERG, GÖRLIN, BERGLUND, FORSELL, and STRANDBERG: Pian, pianin le andró più presso . . . to the end of the opera

NOTES: EJS 349

Though sung in Swedish [FIGAROS BROLLOP], the excerpts are given here in the original Italian for ease of reference.

John Forsell, age 68 at the time and Director of Stockholm's Royal Opera, was the teacher of Joel Berglund, Set Svanholm, and Jussi Bjoerling, among others, and was himself a prolific recorder during the acoustical period. This broadcast is especially interesting as he made no commercial electrical recordings.

EJS 350: "The Golden Age of Opera" (1 LP)
Issued December, 1965

SIDES 1-2 (350 A-B):

CAVALLERIA RUSTICANA (Mascagni) (I)
Opera in 1 act (complete)
Orchestra and Chorus of the Teatro San Carlo di Napoli/Franco Patané
Broadcast, Treatro San Carlo, Naples, ?8 Jan 1952

CAST:
Beniamino Gigli (*Turiddu*); Adelina Campi (*Santuzza*); Piero Guelfi (*Alfio*); Amalia Pini (*Lola*); Irene Acampora (*Mamma Lucia*).

NOTES: EJS 350

Complete, but with orchestral abridgements made for purposes of timing. The PAGLIACCI on EJS 351 was performed on the same evening. Gigli was just three months shy of his 62nd birthday.

The date of the CAVALLERIA and PAGLIACCI performances is disputed: 5, 8, and 12 January, 1952 have all been reported, 8 January most reliably.

Excerpts from this CAVALLERIA later appeared on the Italian HMV set "Beniamino Gigli: Edizione Completa" (153-54010/17).

EJS 351: "The Golden Age of Opera" (1 LP)
Issued December, 1965

SIDES 1-2 (351 A-B):

I PAGLIACCI (Leoncavallo) (I)
Opera in 2 acts (complete)
Orchestra and Chorus of the Teatro San Carlo di Napoli/Franco Patané
Broadcast, Teatro San Carlo, Naples, ?8 Jan 1952

CAST:
Beniamino Gigli (*Canio*); Pina Malgarini (*Nedda*); Giuseppe Gentile (*Tonio*); Saturno Meletti (*Silvio*); Piero De Palma (*Beppe*).

NOTES: EJS 351

See the endnote for EJS 350 regarding the broadcast date. The "Vesti la giubba" and "Vo'il nome" also appeared on EMI's Gigli "Edizione Completa" set (153-54010/17).

EJS 352: "The Golden Age of Opera" (2 LPs)
Issued December, 1965

SIDES 1-4 (352 A-D)

FEUERSNOT (R. Strauss) (G)
Opera in 1 act (complete)
?Orchestra and Chorus of the Wiener Staatsoper/Ernst Märzendorfer
?Broadcast, ?Wiener Staatsoper, Vienna, 1964

CAST:
Gerhard Stolze (*Schweiker von Gundelfingen*); Alfons Herwig (*Ortolf Sentlinger*); Marcella Pobbe (*Diemut*); ? (*Elspeth*); ? (*Wigelis*); ? (*Margret*); Hans Friederich (*Kunrad*); Otakar Schöfer (*Jörg Pöschel*); Hans Braun (*Hämerlein*); Franz Fuchs (*Kofel*); Alois Pernersdorfer (*Kunz Gilgenstock*); Erich Majkut (*Ortlieb Tulbeck*); Sonia Draksler [Drachsler] (*Ursula*); ? (*Roger Aspeck*); ? (*Walpurg*).

NOTES: EJS 352

Later issued under the title FIRE FAMINE as SP 3 in Smith's obscure special-label "Richard Strauss" series. The English title was used there, according to Smith, to avoid copyright entanglements.

The bulletin for EJS 352 claimed that this was the first commercial recording of the work--just as the bulletin for EJS 344 had for the INTERMEZZO.

By 1964, the Vienna Staatsoper had yet to perform FEUERSNOT in the post-War era. Possibly this was a concert performance done at the Staatsoper or elsewhere in Vienna, or perhaps a radio performance by some other opera company. The orchestra may be the Vienna Philharmonic, or simply another ensemble using the name "Wiener Staatsoper Orchester" for the occasion. One unconfirmed theory places this as a concert performance given as part of the Wiener Festwochen.

Schöfer's surname is given as "Schoffer" on the label of EJS 352.

EJS 353: "The Golden Age of Opera" (2 LPs)
Issued January, 1966

SIDES 1-4 (353 A-D):

LE SIÈGE DE CORINTHE [L'ASSEDIO DI CORINTO] (Rossini) (I)
Opera in 3 acts (complete as performed)
Orchestra and Chorus of the Teatro San Carlo di Napoli/Gabriele Santini
In-house recording, Teatro San Carlo, Naples, 2 Jan 1952

CAST:
Renata Tebaldi (*Pamira*); Mario Petri (*Maometto II*); Mirto Picchi (*Cleomene*); Miriam Pirazzini (*Neocle*); Augusto Romani (*Omar*); Anna Maria Borrelli (*Ismene*); Raffaele Arié (*Jero*); Piero De Palma (*Adraste*).

NOTES: EJS 353

Complete as performed, save for the Overture, but missing nearly 25% of Rossini's original 1826 score. LE SIÈGE DE CORINTHE, given here under its Italian title, was a revision of Rossini's own three-act opera, MAOMETTO II (1820). Thomas Schipper's restoration of LE SIÈGE DE CORINTHE, produced at La Scala in 1969 and at the Met in April, 1975, was longer than the version performed here and incorporated material from the original MAOMETTO II.

This 1952 San Carlo performance was a semi-offical in-house recording. Borrelli's surname is given as "Boriello" on the label of EJS 353.

The performance was reissued as HRE 298.

EJS 354: "The Golden Age of Opera" (2 LPs)
Issued January, 1966

SIDES 1-4 (354 A-D):

L'ELISIR D'AMORE (Donizetti)
Opera in 2 acts (complete)
Orchestra and Chorus of the Teatro San Carlo di Napoli/Gianandrea Gavazzeni
In-house recording, Teatro San Carlo, Naples, 17 Jan 1953

CAST:
Beniamino Gigli (*Nemorino*); Rina Gigli (*Adina*); Giuseppe Taddei (*Belcore*); Italo Tajo (*Doctor Dulcamara*); Anna Maria Borrelli (*Gianetta*).

NOTES: EJS 354

As with EJS 353, this was a semi-offical in-house recording. "The performance was not broadcast," the January, 1966 bulletin points out, "but taken on theatre (sic) equipment." Minor dips in pitch are also noted in the bulletin.

Reissued as MDP 008, but excerpts have appeared on EMI and on the two-disc Gigli compilation, ANNA 1032-1033 (May-June, 1979).

EJS 355: "The Golden Age of Opera" (2 LPs)
Issued February, 1966

SIDES 1-4 (355 A-D):

L'AMICO FRITZ (Mascagni) (I)
Opera in 3 acts (complete)
Orchestra and Chorus of the Teatro San Carlo di Napoli/Gianandrea Gavazzeni
In-house recording, Teatro San Carlo, Naples, 7 Feb 1951

CAST:
Beniamino Gigli (*Fritz*); Rina Gigli (*Suzel*); Afro Poli (*David*); Miriam Pirazzini (*Beppe*); Iginio Ricco (*Federico*); Luciano Della Pergola (*Hanezo*); Irene Acampora (*Caterina*).

NOTES: EJS 355

Another semi-official in-house recording. As they were for EJS 354, minor dips in pitch were reported in the accompanying bulletin for EJS 355.

The performance was reissued as MDP-002.

EJS 356: "The Golden Age of Opera" (2 LPs)
Issued February, 1966

SIDES 1-4 (356 A-D):

ZAZÀ (Leoncavallo) (I)
Opera in 4 acts (complete)
Orchestra and Chorus of the Teatro San Carlo di Napoli/Franco Ghione
In-house recording, Teatro San Carlo, Naples, 2 Jan 1950

CAST:
Mafalda Favero (*Zazà*); Giacinto Prandelli (*Milio Dufresne*); Carlo Tagliabue (*Cascart*); Agnese Dubbini (*Anaide*); M. Valeria Zazo (*Natalia*); Lydia Malisci (*Floriana*); Rosa Morelli (*Signora Dufresne*); Gerardo Gaudioso (*Bussy*); Carlo Badioli (*Courtois*); Gianni Avolanti (*Augusto*); Luciano Della Pergola (*Marco*); Sonia Lo Giudice (*Toto*).

NOTES: EJS 356

Problems in sound--orchestral "wows" and pronounced surface noise --are noted in the February, 1966 bulletin, which also claimed that this was, at the time, the only available recording of the complete ZAZÀ: this appears to have been true, at least in the U.S.

Late repressings bear the 1971 matrix number P-2426.

EJS 357: "The Golden Age of Opera" (1 LP)
Issued February, 1966

"BENIAMINO GIGLI IN OPERA AND SONG (1934-55)"

SIDE 1 (357 A):

ROMÉO ET JULIETTE (Gounod) (I)
Opera in 5 acts (excerpts)
Orchestra and Chorus of the Teatro alla Scala/Gabriele Santini
Broadcast, La Scala, Milan, 5 Apr 1934

CAST:
Beniamino Gigli (*Roméo*); Mafalda Favero (*Juliette*); Aristide Baracchi (*Gregorio*).

* 1. Act II: Abridged

* 2. w. MAGDA OLIVERO (Orchestra of the Teatro Reale dell'Opera, Roma/Mario Rossi): ADRIANA LECOUVREUR, Act I: La dolcissima effigie (Cilèa) (I)
Broadcast, Teatro Reale dell'Opera, Rome, 20 Mar 1940

3. w. the Orchestra and Chorus of the Teatro Reale dell'Opera/ Oliviero de Fabritiis: IL TROVATORE, Act III: Di quella pira (Verdi) (I)
Broadcast, Teatro Reale Dell'Opera, Rome, 9 Dec 1939

* 4. w. PIA TASSINARI, soprano (Orchestra and Chorus of the Teatro Reale dell'Opera/Vincenzo Bellezza): MANON, Act II: O dolce incanto . . . Chiudo gli occhi [Instant charmant . . . En fermant les yeux] (Massenet) (I)
Broadcast, Teatro Reale Dell'Opera, Rome, 8 Apr 1938

* 5. w. LUDWIG WEBER, bass (Orchestra and Chorus of the Bayrischer Staatstheater, München/Giuseppe Becce): MANON LESCAUT, Act III: Ah! Non v'avvicinate . . . No, pazzo son! (Puccini) (I)
from the soundtrack of the feature film, ***DU BIST MEIN GLÜCK*** [***TU SEI LA VITA MIA***] (1936), Tobis Klangfilm, Munich, June-July, 1936

SIDE 2 (357 B):

1. w. CARLO MORELLI, baritone (Orchestra of the Teatro alla Scala/ Gabriele Santini): LA FORZA DEL DESTINO, Act IV: Invano Alvaro! . . . Le minaccie i fieri accenti (Verdi) (I)
Broadcast, La Scala, Milan, 31 Mar 1934

2. w. Orchestra and Chorus of the Bayrischer Staatstheater, München/ Giuseppe Becce: AÏDA, Act I: Celeste Aïda (Verdi) (I)
from the soundtrack of the feature film, ***DU BIST MEIN GLÜCK*** [***TU SEI LA VITA MIA***] (1936), Tobis Klangfilm, Munich, June-July, 1936

* 3. w. Philharmonia Orchestra/Stanford Robinson: "Marechiare" (Tosti) (I)
BBC Studios, London, 31 Oct 1952 for BBC broadcast, 25 Dec 1952

* 4. w. Philharmonia Orchestra/Stanford Robinson: "Che 'sso turanto a fa" (Di Veroli) (I)
BBC Studios, London, 31 Oct 1952 for BBC broadcast, 25 Dec 1952

* 5. w. Philharmonia Orchestra/Stanford Robinson: "Maria, Mari" (Di Capua) (I)
BBC Studios, London, 31 Oct 1952 for BBC broadcast, 25 Dec 1952

6. w. BBC Theater Orchestra/Stanford Robinson: L'ELISIR D'AMORE, Act II: Una furtiva lagrima (Donizetti) (I)
BBC broadcast, London, 24 Mar 1955

7. w. BBC Theater Orchestra/Stanford Robinson: "Torna e Surriento" (De Curtis) (I)
BBC broadcast, London, 24 Mar 1955

8. w. BBC Theater Orchestra/Stanford Robinson: TOSCA, Act III: E lucevan le stelle (Puccini) (I)
BBC broadcast, London, 24 Mar 1955

9. w. pf/Dino Fedri: "Ritorna ancor!" (Di Veroli) (I)
BBC broadcast, London, 24 Mar 1955

10. w. pf/?: MARTHA, Act III: M'appari [Ach, so fromm] (Flotow) (G)
from the soundtrack of the feature film, *UNA VOCE NEL TUO CUORE* (1949), Cinecittà Studios, Rome, July, 1949

NOTES: EJS 357

Many of the excerpts on this LP have been reissued a number of times--by EMI, MDP, the Timaclub, and Legato Classics. Some also appeared later on the Gigli set, ANNA 1032-1033 (May-June, 1979).

Side 1 (357 A):

Band 1: There are several cuts in this ROMÉO Act II, some of them recording cuts, others performance cuts. There is a break, possibly in the original transcription, near the end of the chorus of *Retainers*, while the subsequent encounter between *Gertrude* and *Gregorio* is omitted altogether, along with the exit of the chorus and the scene between *Juliette* and the *Nurse*--the recording begins again at *Roméo's* "O nuit divine" in Scene v.

ANNA 1032 and 1033, a Gigli recital issued in May-June, 1979, also included much of this material broken over two sides.

The EJS 357 excerpt plays in score pitch at 32.5 rpm.

Band 2: Given as 1939 on the label of EJS 357. Plays in pitch at 32.5 rpm.

Band 4: This same excerpt is dated 13 April, 1944 on MDP 018. Gigli *did* sing MANON in Rome on that date, but 8 April, 1938 is in fact the correct date of this Teatro Reale performance with Tassanari.

Band 5: Ludwig Weber is not credited on the label of EJS 357. The "Donna non vidi mai" from this soundtrack later appeared on EJS 464 (March, 1969).

Side 2 (357 B):

Band 3-5: The completion of this 25 December, 1952 Gigli broadcast was issued on EJS 336 (June, 1965).

EJS 358: "The Golden Age of Opera" (2 LPs)
Issued March, 1966

SIDES 1-2 (358 A-B):

LA BOHÈME (Puccini) (I)
Opera in 4 acts (complete)
Orchestra and Chorus of the Teatro San Carlo di Napoli/Tullio Serafin
In-house recording, Teatro San Carlo, Naples, 10 Jan 1951

CAST:
Renata Tebaldi (*Mimi*); Giacomo Lauri-Volpi (*Rodolfo*); Tito Gobbi (*Marcello*); Elda Ribetti (*Musetta*); Saturno Meletti (*Schaunard*); Giulio Neri (*Colline*); Carlo Badioli (*Benoit*); Carlo Badioli (*Alcindoro*); Gianni Avolanti (*Parpignol*); Silvio Santarelli (*Sergeant*).

EJS 359: "The Golden Age of Opera" (1 LP)
Issued March, 1966

SIDES 1-2 (359 A-B):

MESSA DA REQUIEM ["MANZONI REQUIEM"] (Verdi) (L)
Requiem Mass for Orchestra, Chorus and Soloists (excerpts)
Orchestra and Chorus of the Ente Italiano Audizioni Radiofoniche [EIAR], Roma; Chamber Orchestra of Rome; Choruses of Firenza and Verona/Victor De Sabata; Constantino Constantini, chorus master
Broadcast, Basilica di Santa Maria degli Angeli, Rome, 14 Dec 1940

Maria Caniglia	Beniamino Gigli
Ebe Stignani	Tancredi Pasero

NOTES: EJS 359

Only the "Dies Irae," "Sanctus," and "Libera Me" are included on EJS 359.

Cetra made disc matrices of this performance for archival reasons (as they did for most EIAR broadcasts), numbers NN230-NN244. The Timaclub reissue of the same movements (Tima 69/70) claimed that EJS 359 was transferred from long-playing actetate copies of inferior quality produced for EIAR at the same time (intended for short-term reference only). Where this information came from, or whether it is true, is not known.

Reissued on a Hunt CD, "Capolavori" (2-CDLSMH-34046), coupled with a 1951 La Scala MANZONI REQUIEM conducted by De Sabata.

EJS 360: "The Golden Age of Opera" (1 LP)
Issued March, 1966

"POTPOURRI 19"

SIDE 1 (360 A):

* 1. a) AMEDEO BERDINI (orch/?): ISABEAU, Act II: O popolo di vil . . . E passerà la viva creatura (Mascagni) (I)
Broadcast, ?*CONCERTO MARTINI E ROSSI*, RAI, date unknown

b) RENATO CIONI, tenor, and ANNA MARIA ROTA, soprano (Orchestra of Radio Italiana [RAI]/?): LUISA MILLER, Act I: Duchezza . . . Dall'aule raggianti di vano splendor (Verdi) (I)
Broadcast, *CONCERTO MARTINI E ROSSI*, RAI, date unknown

* 2. MARIA CALLAS, soprano (Orchestra of Radio Italiana [RAI], Milano/ Alfredo Simonetto): ARMIDA, Act II: D'amore al dolce impero (Rossini) (I)
Broadcast, *CONCERTO MARTINI E ROSSI*, RAI, Teatro Municipale, San Remo, 27 Dec 1954

* 3. MIRTO PICCHI, tenor (Orchestra of Radio Italiana [RAI], Milano/ Carlo Felice Cillario): GLORIA, Act II: L'assedio or non e più! . . . Pur dolente son io (Cilèa) (I)
Broadcast, *CONCERTO MARTINI E ROSSI*, RAI, Milan, 2 Dec 1957

4. BORIS CHRISTOFF, bass (Orchestra of Radio Italiana [RAI]/?): IPHIGENIE EN AULIDE, Act II: Ah! Qual debolezza . . . O tu, la cosa mia più cara [Ah! Quelle faiblesse . . . O toi, l'objet le plus aimable] (Gluck) (I)
Broadcast, *CONCERTO MARTINI E ROSSI*, RAI, date unknown

5. FLORIANA CAVALLI, bass (Orchestra of Radio Italiana [RAI]/?): DEJANICE, Act III: Una cetra, perchè? Colà, nell'oasi ["Canzone Egiziaca"] (Catalani) (I)
Broadcast, *CONCERTO MARTINI E ROSSI*, RAI, date unknown

SIDE 2 (360 B):

1. CESARE VALLETTI, tenor, and PLINIO CLABASSI, baritone (pf/?): LES SOIRÉES MUSICALES, no. 12: "Li marinai" (Pepoli-Rossini) (I
Broadcast, *CONCERTO MARTINI E ROSSI*, RAI, date unknown

2. MARGHERITA CAROSIO, soprano (Orchestra of Radio Italiana [RAI]/?): IL RE, Act I: Colombello, sposarti (Giordano) (I)
Broadcast, *CONCERTO MARTINI E ROSSI*, RAI, ?Milan, 3 Dec 1956

* 3. MARGHERITA CAROSIO, soprano (orch/Pietro Mascagni): NERONE, Act II: Perche dovrei tremare . . . Canto notte e di (Mascagni) (I)
Filmed live performance, La Scala, Milan, January-February, 1935 or April, 1937

* 4. TERESA BERGANZA, mezzo-soprano (Orchestra A. Scarlatti di Napoli/ Bruno Bartoletti): [I CASTI AMORI D'] ORONTEA, Act II: Intorno all'idol mio (Cesti-rev. Vito Frazzi) (I)
Live performance, house unknown, Naples, date uncertain

5. GIULIETTA SIMIONATO, contralto (Orchestra of Radio Italiana [RAI], Milano/Nino Sanzogno): TRANCREDI, Act I: O patria . . . Di tanti palpiti (Rossini) (I)
   Broadcast, ***CONCERTO MARTINI E ROSSI***, RAI, Milan, 29 Apr 1959

6. FEDORI BARBIERI, soprano (Orchestra of the Maggio Musicale Fiorentino/Carlo Felice Cillario): DON SEBASTIANO, Act I: Ov'e in cielo . . . Terra adorata (Donizetti) (I)
   Broadcast, ***CONCERTO MARTINI E ROSSI***, RAI, ?Florence, 11 Feb 1957

7. MARIA CANIGLIA, soprano (Orchestra of Radio Italiana [RAI]/?): NERONE, Act I: A notte cupa (Boïto) (I)
   Broadcast, ***CONCERTO MARTINI E ROSSI***, RAI, Turin, 26 Jan 1953

NOTES: EJS 360

The March, 1966 bulletin claimed that the *raison d'être* of this "most unusual" potpourri was the inclusion of "a dozen selections which have *almost* never been put on disc--either in the acoustic, electric or LP days" (emphasis mine). The vast majority of items, as can be seen in the listing, come from ***CONCERTO MARTINI E ROSSI*** broadcasts, many of them as yet undocumented.

Side 1 (360 A):

Band 1: The ISABEAU aria, which shares band one with the LUISA MILLER duet, is not listed on the label of EJS 360; the tenor singing it has not been identified, nor has the broadcast source. It is not Del Monaco's 1952 ***CONCERTO MARTINI E ROSSI*** performance, featured on UORC 151 (March, 1973), though the provenance would certainly have seemed appropriate. Amedeo Berdini has been suggested as the tenor heard here.

In contrast to the LP title, Bernardo De Muro recorded the aria in Milan on 7 March, 1912, as a matter of fact, as issued on Gramophone 052340, HMV DB 557, and Victor 74372 (matrix 02348v).

Band 2: The complete 27 December, 1954 Callas RAI broadcast has appeared on a variety of labels (BJR, ERR, Opera Viva, Morgan, etc.), as have excerpts from it, including the ARMIDA. She shared the program with Beniamino Gigli, whose four arias (they performed no duets) first appeared complete on EJS 262 (March, 1963) and subsequently on a number of other private LPs and CDs.

Band 3: Picchi's "Pur dolente son io" later appeared on a Timaclub Picchi recital (Tima 62). Other excerpts from GLORIA were featured on EJS 333 (May, 1965); a complete 1969 performance was issued as EJS 477 (September, 1969).

Side 2 (360 B):

Band 3: This is a creator record: Carosio sang the role of the *Slave* in the Epilogue of the world premiere of Mascagni's NERONE on 16 January, 1935 at La Scala. It has been reported that Mascagni's NERONE so displeased Mussolini that the opera was only printed privately, never published.

Filmed at one of fifteen Scala performances of the opera: there were ten given between January and February, 1935 and five in April, 1937, all conducted by the composer and featuring Pertile in the title role. Productions of the opera were also mounted in Livorno, Genova, Naples, and Bologna between the Scala premiere and the end of the Second World War.

A second excerpt from the same film, "Addio, Nerone," also sung by Carosio, appeared on EJS 483 (October, 1969), and has turned up on a commercial videotape entitled "La Scala" (currently in circulation) which boasts a brief glimpse of Pertile. A longer excerpt, possibly containing both of Carosio's solos, is also available on another videotape edition in limited circulation from a New York company. Both Carosio excerpts were later issued on MFR 81.

Band 4: From a complete performance of the Frazzi revision, which runs half the length of the original Cesti score.

EJS 361: "The Golden Age of Opera" (2 LPs)
Issued April, 1966

SIDES 1-4 (361 A-D):

LE JONGLEUR DE NOTRE DAME (Massenet) (F)
Opera in 3 acts (complete)
Orchestra and Chorus of Radio Nederland/Albert Wolff
Broadcast, Radio Nederland, ?Hilversum, Holland, date unknown

CAST:
Jean Villars (*Jean*); Leon Combe (*Boniface*); A. Percik (*The Prior*); Henk Darel (*The Musician Monk*); Jo Sixtra (*The Sculptor Monk*); Simon van der Hask (*The Poet Monk*); Jean Bergsen (*The Painter Monk*); Leonie Smits (*Angel*); Katherine Hasel (*Angel*).

NOTES: EJS 361

This *may* have been an international broadcast over Radio Netherlands International (properly, Radio Nederland Wereldomroep, Hilversum) or a VARA or AVRO broadcast.

EJS 362: "The Golden Age of Opera" (1 LP)
Issued April, 1966

SIDE 1-2 (362 A-B):

VIOLANTA, Op. 8 (Korngold) (G)
Opera in 1 act (complete)
Orchestra of Radio Verkehers AG [RAVAG], Austria/-- Kassowitz
Radio RAVAG broadcast, Austria, circa 1949

CAST:
Ilona Steingruber (*Violanta*); Willi Friederich (*Simone Trovari*); Erich Majkut (*Alfonso*); ? (*Giovanni Bracca*); Rotilda Busch or Ursula Boesch (*Bice*); ? (*Barbara*); ?Leopold Winklehofer (*Matteo*); ? (*Soldiers*); ? (*Maidservants*).

NOTES: EJS 362

Radio RAVAG was the predecessor of the Austrian Broadcasting Corporation (ORF). It is listed as "Radio Ravak" on the labels of EJS 262 and in the accompanying bulletin.

Except for the two principals, the cast assign-ment is tentative, as labels give only the artists' names, many of them misspelled. Winklehofer is given, but which role he sang is especially vague.

DER RING DES POLYKRATES (see EJS 363) and VIOLANTA (given on labels and in the April, 1966 bulletin as *LA* VIOLANTA) were Korngold's first and second operas, respectively, both produced initially at the Munich Opera on 28 March, 1916.

The suggested playing speed for EJS 362 is 32.3 rpm.

EJS 363: "The Golden Age of Opera" (1 LP)
Issued April, 1966

SIDES 1-2 (363 A-B):

DER RING DES POLYKRATES, Op. 7 (Korngold) (G)
Opera in 1 act (complete)
Orchestra of Radio Verkehers AG [RAVAG], Austria/Hans Swarowsky
Radio RAVAG broadcast, Austria, circa 1949

CAST:
Walter Berry (*Florian*); Waldemar Kmentt (*Wilhelm Arndt*); ?Ursula Boesch (*Lieschen*); Erich Majkut (*Peter Vogel*).

NOTES: EJS 363

See the note for EJS 362. The Wiener Staatsoper is given as the source on the labels of EJS 363 and in the April, 1966 bulletin. Conductor Swarowsky's surname is given as "Berowsky." Boesch is given as *Lieschen* in a private catalog.

EJS 364: "The Golden Age of Opera" (1 LP)
Issued April, 1966

"RICHARD TAUBER ARIAS AND SONGS"

SIDE 1 (364 A):

* 1. w. Algemeene Verniging Radio Omroep [AVRO], Hilversum Orchestra/ Nico Treep: DER FREISCHÜTZ, Act I: Nein, länger trag'ich die Qualen . . . Durch die Wälder, durch die Auen (Weber) (G)
AVRO broadcast, Hilversum, Holland, 18 Jul 1939

* 2. w. Algemeene Verniging Radio Omroep [AVRO], Hilversum Orchestra/ Nico Treep: LOHENGRIN, Act III: In fernem Land (Wagner) (G)
AVRO broadcast, Hilversum, Holland, 18 Jul 1939

3. w. pf/?: SECHS LIEDER, Op. 48, no. 6: Ein Traum [En drom] (Bodenstedt-Grieg) (G)
   Source and date unknown

* 4. w. orch/?: DAS LAND DES LÄCHELNS, Act II: You are my heart's delight [Dein is mein ganzes Herz!] (Lehár) (E)
   Source and date unknown

* 5. w. Detroit Symphony/Wilfred Pelletier: FRASQUITA, Act II: Schatz, ich bitt'dich . . . Hab' ein blaues Himmelbett (Lehár) (G)
   Broadcast, ***FORD SUNDAY EVENING HOUR***, WJR, Detroit, 29 Jan 1939

6. w. Detroit Symphony and Chorus/Franco Ghione: LES CONTES D'HOFFMANN, Act I: Es war einmal am Hofe Eisenach [Il était une fois à la cour d' Eisenach!] ["Légende de Kleinzach"] (Offenbach) (G)
   Broadcast, ***FORD SUNDAY EVENING HOUR***, WJR, Detroit, 26 Mar 1939

7. w. pf/?: "Die Princessen" (Bjørnson-Grieg) (G)
   Source and date unknown

SIDE 2 (364 B):

1. w. pf/?: ROMANZEN UND BALLADEN II, Op. 49, no. 1: Die beiden Grenadieren (Schumann) (G)
   Source and date unknown

2. w. orch and chorus/?: DER ZIGEUNERBARON, Act I: Als flotter Geist (J. Strauss) (G)
   Source and date unknown

3. w. orch/?: DER EVANGELIMANN, Act II: Selig sind, die Verfolgung leiden (Kienzel) (G)
   Source and date unknown

4. w. pf/?: VIER LIEDER, Op. 27, no. 3: Heimliche Aufforderung (Mackay-R. Strauss) (G)
   Source and date unknown

* 5. w. Detroit Symphony and chorus/Franco Ghione: DER SINGENDE TRAUM: You Mean the World to Me [Du bist die Welt für mich] (Richard Tauber) (E)
   Broadcast, ***FORD SUNDAY EVENING HOUR***, WJR, Detroit, 26 Mar 1939

* 6. w. pf/?: LAND WITHOUT MUSIC: Heaven in a Song (Oscar Straus) (E)
   from the feature film ***LAND WITHOUT MUSIC [FORBIDDEN MUSIC]*** (1936)
   Capitol Films/General Film Distributors, London, 1936 (U.K.) World Pictures, 1938 (U.S.)

NOTES: EJS 364

The April, 1966 bulletin contains a minimal amount of information on this recital, calling it "a solo record of off-the-air material of Richard Tauber between 1939 and 1946." This would appear to be more accurate, judging from those items actually documented, than the description given in James Dennis' Tauber discography in *The Record Collector* (18/10, October, 1969), p. 238, which dates all of the contents as "circa 1937." Such is clearly not the case. Possibly this was the result of likening EJS 364 to the later Tauber recital on EJS 440 (September, 1968), which was indeed made up entirely of 1937 ***GENERAL MOTORS HOUR [CONCERT]*** broadcast excerpts.

Side 1 (364 A):

Bands 1-2: The proper playing speed of the FREISCHÜTZ is 32.8 rpm, where the LOHENGRIN is in score pitch at 32.4 rpm. A CARMEN "Flower Song" from this broadcast was later included on EJS 452 (December, 1968).

Band 4: Only the last refrain is included here. This is not the 20 January, 1946 BBC performance included on EJS 295 (March, 1964). The proper playing speed of the aria is 33.7 rpm.

Band 5: Library of Congress tape: 8944-50 (complete broadcast).

Side 2 (364 B):

Bands 5-6: Described in the April, 1966 bulletin as "a pair of popular English ballads"! LAND WITHOUT MUSIC (1936), released in the U.S. in 1938 as FORBIDDEN MUSIC, was a political satire in the form of an original operetta. Tauber's co-stars were Diana Napier and Jimmy Durante. The film was directed by Walter Forde. World Pictures, the U.S. distributor of the film, was also responsible for the release of Jean Renoir's 1938 Academy Award nominee, "Grand Illusion."

EJS 365: "The Golden Age of Opera" (3 LPs)
Issued May, 1966

SIDES 1-4 (365 A-F):

DIE SCHWEIGSAME FRAU (R. Strauss) (G)
Opera in 3 acts (complete)
Wiener Philharmoniker and Chorus of the Wiener Staatsoper/Karl Böhm
Broadcast, Salzburg Festival, Salzburg, 8 Aug 1959

CAST:
Hans Hotter (*Sir Morosus*); Georgine von Milinkovič (*Housekeeper*); Hermann Prey (*Barber*); Hilde Güden (*Aminta*); Fritz Wunderlich (*Henry Morosus*); Pierette Alarie (*Isotta*); Hetty Plümacher (*Carlotta*); Joseph Knapp (*Morbio*); Karl Dönch (*Vanuzzi*); Alois Pernersdorfer (*Farfallo*).

NOTES: EJS 365

This performance is complete except for standard performance cuts. It has appeared more recently on the two-disc Melodram LP, MEL 27071 and on OD LP 1000/1/2 as "The Silent Wife."

EJS 366: The Golden Age of Opera" (1 LP)
Issued May, 1966

IL TROVATORE (Verdi) (I)
Opera in 4 acts (excerpts)
London Philharmonic Orchestra and the Royal Opera House Chorus/ Vittorio Gui
Broadcast, Covent Garden, London, 12 May 1939

CAST:
Jussi Bjoerling (*Manrico*); Gina Cigna (*Leonora*); Mario Basiola (*Count di Luna*); Gertrude Wettergren (*Azucena*); Corrado Zambelli (*Ferrando*); Maria Huder (*Ines*); Octave Dua (*Ruiz*); Giuseppe Zammit (*A Messenger*); [Leslie Horsman] (*An Old Gypsy*).

SIDE 1 (366 A):

Act I: 1. HUDER, CIGNA, BASIOLA, BJOERLING, and Chorus: Ne'tornei. V'apparvo . . . Tacea la notte placida . . . to the end of the act

Act II: 2. BJOERLING and WETTERGREN: Soli or siamo . . . Mal reggendo . . . to the end of the scene
3. CIGNA, HUDER, BASIOLA, ZAMBELLI, DUA, BJOERLING, and Chorus: E deggio e posso crederlo? . . . to the end of the act

SIDE 2 (366 B):

Act III: * 1. CIGNA, BJOERLING, DUA, and Chorus: Quale d'armi fragor . . . Ah! sì, ben mio . . . Di quella pira . . . to the end of the act

Act IV: * 2. DUA, CIGNA, and BJOERLING: D'amor sull'ali rosee . . . Quel suon . . . scordarmi! di te . . . Come albeggi, la scure al figlio . . . Mira! di acerbe lagrime . . . to the end of the scene
3. BJOERLING, CIGNA, WETTERGREN, and BASIOLA: Che! Non m'inganno! . . . to the end of the opera

NOTES: EJS 366

The Porter and Henrysson Bjoerling discography (p. 72) claims that this performance, which appears to exist only in the excerpts presented here, was not recorded either by the Royal Opera House or by the BBC, but that it does appear to have been broadcast. They note that it was "possibly recorded on film," which may mean a backstage recording, a motion picture, or something similar: the BBC was also using motion picture film for recording at about this time--a technique similar to that of the Selenophone (see the INTRODUCTION for more information on the Selenophone).

Similar excerpts, with what appears to be an added Act I/ii fragment from a Stella Roman Met broadcast, later appeared on MDP 004--as on EJS 366, transferred at inconsistent pitch. Note that Porter and Henrysson's Bjoerling discography used the MDP issue to document the texts *as sung*, not EJS 366, and that this has been corrected in the listing accordingly.

Side 2 (366 B):

Band 1: "L'onda de suoni mistici . . . Gioje di casto amor!" is cut.

Band 2: The *Monks'* opening "Miserere" is cut, as is "Tu vedrai che amore . . . Udiste." The scene commences again at "Come albeggi," as noted, and proceeds through "Mira! di acerbe . . . Vivrà! Contende il giubilo" to the end of the scene.

EJS 367: "The Golden Age of Opera" (1 LP)
Issued May, 1966

"JUSSI BJOERLING IN OPERA AND SONG (Volume 2)"

SIDE 1 (367 A):

* 1. w. Harmonien Music Society Orchestra [Bergen Symphony Orchestra]/Carl Garaguly: SEX DIGTE, Op. 25, no. 2: En Svane (Ibsen-Grieg) (N)
Bergen Music Festival, Concert Palace, Bergen, Norway, 9 Jun 1954
Pre-recorded broadcast, ***WORLD MUSIC FESTIVAL***, CBS, 18 Jul 1954

* 2. w. Harmonien Music Society Orchestra [Bergen Symphony Orchestra]/Carl Garaguly: HJERTETS MELODIER, Op. 5, no. 3: Jeg elsker dig" (Anderson-Grieg) (N)
Bergen Music Festival, Concert Palace, Bergen, Norway, 9 Jun 1954
Pre-recorded broadcast, ***WORLD MUSIC FESTIVAL***, CBS, 18 Jul 1954

* 3. w. studio orch/Donald Voorhees: ACHT LIEDER AUS LETZTE BLÄTTER, Op. 10, no. 1: Zueignung (Gilm-R. Strauss) (G)
Broadcast, ***BELL TELEPHONE HOUR***, WNBC, NYC, 23 Oct 1950

* 4. w. studio orch/Donald Voorhees: Op. 21, no. 5: "Lilacs" ["Siren'"] (Beketova-Rachmaninoff) (E)
Broadcast, ***BELL TELEPHONE HOUR***, WNBC, NYC, 15 Mar 1948

* 5. w. studio orch/Donald Voorhees: "Clorinda" (Morgan) (E)
Broadcast, ***BELL TELEPHONE HOUR***, WNBC, NYC, 15 Mar 1948

* 6. w. studio orch/Donald Voorhees: "Mattinata" (Leoncavallo) (I)
Broadcast, ***BELL TELEPHONE HOUR***, WNBC, NYC, 15 Mar 1948

* 7. w. studio orch/Donald Voorhees: "Jeannie With the Light Brown Hair" (Stephen Collins Foster) (E)
Broadcast, ***BELL TELEPHONE HOUR***, WNBC, NYC, 7 Nov 1949

* 8. w. studio orch/Donald Voorhees: SECHS LIEDER, Op. 17, no. 2: Ständchen (Schack-R. Strauss) (G)
Broadcast, ***BELL TELEPHONE HOUR***, WNBC, NYC, 7 Nov 1949

* 9. w. studio orch/Donald Voorhees: "Jungfrun under Lind" (Peterson-Berger) (Sw)
Broadcast, ***BELL TELEPHONE HOUR***, WNBC, NYC, 8 Jan 1951

* 10. w. studio orch/Donald Voorhees: "For You Alone" (P.J. O'Reilly-Henry E. Geehl) (E)
Broadcast, ***BELL TELEPHONE HOUR***, WNBC, NYC, 8 Jan 1951

* 11. w. Metropolitan Opera House Orchestra/Fausto Cleva: RIGOLETTO, Act III: La donna è mobile (Verdi) (I)
Telecast, ***ED SULLIVAN SHOW***, CBS-TV, NYC, 17 Feb 1957

* 12. w. HILDE GÜDEN, soprano, and THELMA VOTIPKA, mezzo-soprano (Metropolitan Opera House Orchestra/Fausto Cleva): RIGOLETTO, Act I: Signor nè principe . . . È il sol dell'anima (Verdi) (I)
Telecast, ***ED SULLIVAN SHOW***, CBS-TV, NYC, 17 Feb 1957

SIDE 2 (367 B):

* 1. w. San Francisco Symphony Orchestra/Gaetano Merola: LA GIOCONDA, Act II: Cielo e mar! (Ponchielli) (I)
Broadcast, ***STANDARD HOUR***, KNBC, San Francisco, 30 Sep 1951

* 2. w. San Francisco Symphony Orchestra/Gaetano Merola: TOSCA, Act III: E lucevan le stelle (Puccini) (I)
Broadcast, ***STANDARD HOUR***, KNBC, San Francisco, 30 Sep 1951

* 3. w. studio orch/Donald Voorhees: SADKO, Scene IV: My Heathen Guests [Ne shchest almasov] (Rimsky-Korsakov) (E)
Broadcast, ***BELL TELEPHONE HOUR***, WNBC, NYC, 15 Nov 1948

* 4. w. studio orch/Donald Voorhees: L'AFRICAINE, Act IV: Mi batte il cor . . . O Paradiso! [Pays merveilleux . . . Ô Paradis] (Meyerbeer) (I)
Broadcast, ***BELL TELEPHONE HOUR***, WNBC, NYC, 23 Oct 1950

* 5. w. studio orch/Donald Voorhees: ANDREA CHENIER, Act IV: Come un bel dì di maggio (Giordano) (I)
Broadcast, ***BELL TELEPHONE HOUR***, WNBC, NYC, 23 October, 1950

* 6. w. studio orch/Donald Voorhees: MANON LESCAUT, Act I: Donna non vidi mai (Puccini) (I)
Broadcast, ***BELL TELEPHONE HOUR***, WNBC, NYC, 8 Jan 1951

* 7. w. ELEANOR STEBER, soprano (studio orch/Howard Barlow): IL TROVATORE, Act IV: Quel suon . . . Ah, che la morte ognora ["Miserere"] (Verdi) (I)
Broadcast, ***VOICE OF FIRESTONE***, WEAF, NYC, 21 Jan 1946

* 8. w. ELEANOR STEBER, soprano (studio orch/Howard Barlow): MAYTIME: Will You Remember (Sweetheart)? (Wood-Young-Romberg) (E)
Broadcast, ***VOICE OF FIRESTONE***, WEAF, NYC, 21 Jan 1946

NOTES: EJS 367

Side 1 (367 A):

Bands 1-2: See also the endnote for EJS 279 (October, 1963). Other items from this concert appeared on UORC 350 (September-October, 1977) and ANNA 1017 (September, 1978). MDP 035 contains the entire broadcast.

Band 3: Apart from the CHENIER and AFRICAINE items featured here, a Rachmaninoff song from this broadcast was issued on HRE 214-2.

Bands 4-6: All three of these songs were originally coupled on V-Disc 863-A. "Clorinda" also appeared on a 16-inch 33.3 rpm transcription disc labelled "Voice of America, Concert Hall Program No. 70" (master DS-2451) issued by the U.S. Government. The MANON aria from this broadcast later appeared on UORC 350. See also the endnote for EJS 337 (II/7-8).

Bands 7-8: The BOHÈME aria from this broadcast appeared earlier on EJS 252 (November, 1962) and later on HRE 214-2.

Bands 9-10: Both the "Jungfrun under Lind" and the MANON LESCAUT aria (II/6) were also included on "Voice of America, Concert Hall Program No. 70" (see the endnote for I/4-6).

This 8 January, 1951 broadcast is complete on EJS 367 except for the MANON "Rêve," issued earlier on EJS 252 (November, 1962) and later on UORC 350.

Bands 11-12: These two RIGOLETTO excerpts comprise Bjoerling's entire contribution to the 17 February, 1957 ***ED SULLIVAN*** show.

Side 2 (367 B):

Bands 1-2: The original transcription disc for this ***STANDARD HOUR*** broadcast is in the Stanford University Archive of Recorded Sound. The two Sayão duets from the broadcast later appeared on UORC 350; UORC 340 (May-June, 1977) also includes the Tosti "L'alba separa."

Duets from this 30 September, 1951 broadcast were later issued on VOCE-119 CD.

Band 3: Swedish Radio tape: L-B+ 23534

Bands 4-5: See the endnote for I/3. The CHENIER aria was issued earlier on EJS 337 (June, 1965); both arias later appeared on HRE 214-2.

Band 6: See the endnote for I/9-10. The MANON LESCAUT aria appeared on EJS 337 and later on HRE 214-2.

Bands 7-8: Later issued on Legendary LR 141, a Steber broadcast recital.

EJS 368: "The Golden Age of Opera" (2 LPs)
Issued June, 1966

SIDES 1-4 (368 A-D):

LUCREZIA BORGIA (Donizetti) (I)
Opera in 2 acts and a Prologue (complete)
Orchestra and Chorus of the Teatro San Carlo di Napoli/Carlo Franci
Broadcast, Teatro San Carlo, Naples, 31 Jan 1966

CAST:
Leyla Gencer (*Lucrezia Borgia*); Giacomo Aragall (*Gennaro*); Mario Petri (*Don Alfonso di Ferrara*); Anna Maria Rota (*Maffio Orsini*); Giuseppe Moretti (*Jeppo Liverotti*); Alfredo Colella (*Don Apostolo Gazella*); Salvatore Catania (*Ascanio Petrucci*); Mario Guggia (*Oloferno Vitellozzo*); Augusto Frati (*Gubetta*); Franco Ricciardi (*Rustighello*); Emilio Savoldi (*Astolfo*).

NOTES: EJS 368

This LUCREZIA BORGIA is presented here complete as performed. Conductor Franci's forename is given as "Paulo" on the label of EJS 368. Cella's Gencer biography notes that this is the second performance of the production, and that the first, on 29 January, 1966, was *not* broadcast because bass Mario Petri was ill.

The same complete performance was reissued as Hunt CD 544, dated *29* January, 1966.

Sides 1 and 2 play at a uniform 34.4 rpm; the first band of side 3 plays at 33.8 rpm, the second band at 34.0 rpm, as does side 4.

EJS 369: "The Golden Age of Opera" (2 LPs)
Issued June, 1966

SIDES 1-4 (369 A-D):

FERNAND[O] CORTEZ (Spontini) (I)
Opera in 3 acts (complete)
Orchestra and Chorus of the Teatro San Carlo di Napoli/Gabriele Santini
Broadcast, Teatro San Carlo, Naples, 15 Dec 1951

CAST:
Gino Penno (*Fernand Cortez*); Renata Tebaldi (*Amazily*); Piero De Palma (*Alvaro*); Aldo Protti (*Telasco*); Italo Tajo (*Montezuma*); Antonio Cassinelli (*Priest*); Afro Poli (*Morales*); Augusto Romani (*A Prisoner*); Gerardo Gaudioso (*Another Prisoner*); Gianni Avolanti (*A Sailor*); Luigi Paolillo (*A Mexican Officer*).

NOTES: EJS 369

Excerpts from this performance later appeared on Giuseppe di Stefano GDS 4002, a Tebaldi recital.

EJS 370: "The Golden Age of Opera" (1 LP)
Issued June, 1966

"GIACOMO LAURI-VOLPI RECITAL"

SIDE 1 (370 A):

RIGOLETTO (Verdi)
Opera in 4 acts (excerpts)
Orchestra and Chorus of Radio Italiana [RAI], Roma/Fernando Previtali
RAI broadcast, Rome, 14 Jun 1947

CAST:
Lina Pagliughi (*Gilda*); Giacomo Lauri-Volpi (*Duke of Mantua*); Tito Gobbi (*Rigoletto*); Fernanda Cadoni (*Maddalena*); Carlo Platania (*Monterone*); Lydia Melisci (*Giovanna*); ? (*A Page*); [Bruno Sbalchiero (*Sparafucile*)]; [Lydia Melisci (*Countess Ceprano*)]; M. Mancini (*Ceprano*); [M. Mancini (*An Usher*)]; [Mario Silvani (*Marullo*)]; Salvatore di Tommaso (*Borsa*).

Act I:
1. GOBBI and PAGLIUGHI: Figlia! Mio Padre! . . . Deh non parlare al misero
2. LAURI-VOLPI and PAGLIUGHI: Ah! inseparabile . . . È il sol dell'anima . . . Addio, speranza ed anima

Act II:
* 3. LAURI-VOLPI: Parmi veder le lagrime . . . Scorrendo uniti remoto via
4. [Page], MANCINI, DI TOMMASO, GOBBI, and Chorus: Al suo sposo parlar vuol . . . Cortigiani, vil razza dannata
5. PLATANIA, GOBBI, and PAGLIUGHI: Nè fulmine o un ferro . . . Sì, vendetta

Act III:
* 6. LAURI-VOLPI (Orchestra of the Ente Italiano Audizioni Radiofoniche [EIAR], Milano/Giuseppe Morelli): "La donna è mobile (Verdi) (I)
Broadcast, ***CONCERTO PER LE FORZE ARMATI***, EIAR, Milan, 11 Nov 1941
7. LAURI-VOLPI, CADONI, GOBBI, and PAGLIUGHI: Ogni saggezza chiudesi . . . Bella figlia dell'amore

SIDE 2 (370 B):

* 1. w. Orchestra of the Ente Italiano Audizioni Radiofoniche [EIAR], Milano/Giuseppe Morelli: TURANDOT, Act III: Nessun dorma (Puccini) (I)
Broadcast, ***CONCERTO PER LE FORZE ARMATI***, EIAR, Milan, 11 Nov 1941

* 2. w. Orchestra of the Ente Italiano Audizioni Radiofoniche [EIAR], Milano/Giuseppe Morelli: "Andalucia" (Granados) (S)
Broadcast, ***CONCERTO PER LE FORZE ARMATI***, EIAR, Milan, 11 Nov 1941

* 3. w. Orchestra Magio Musicale Fiorentino/Carlo Felice Cillario: TOSCA, Act I: Recondita armonia (Puccini) (I)
Broadcast, ***CONCERTO MARTINI E ROSSI***, RAI, 11 Feb 1957

* 4. w. Orchestra Magio Musicale Fiorentino/Carlo Felice Cillario: LA FANCIULLA DEL WEST, Act III: Ch'ella mi creda (Puccini) (I)
Broadcast, ***CONCERTO MARTINI E ROSSI***, RAI, 11 Feb 1957

5. w. pf/Lauri-Volpi: LA FAVORITA, Act I: Una vergine un angiol di Dio (Donizetti) (I)
Private recording, 1963

6. w. pf/Lauri-Volpi: LA FANCIULLA DEL WEST, Act II: Ma non vi avrei rubato . . . Or son sei mesi (Puccini) (I)
Private recording, 1963

* 7. w. pf/Lauri-Volpi: LA FANCIULLA DEL WEST, Act I: Quello che tacete . . . Cio che avremmo . . . Come ha detto? . . . Un viso d'angelo! (Puccini) (I)
Private recording, 1963

* 8. w. pf/Lauri-Volpi: I PURITANI, Act I: A te o cara (Bellini) (I)
Private recording, 1963

* 9. LINA PAGHLIUGHI, soprano (Orchestra of Radio Italiana [RAI], Milano/Carlo Maria Giulini): LORD INFERNO: Milord, le vostre parole (Ghedini) (I)
RAI broadcast, Milan, 22 Oct 1952

NOTES: EJS 370

Side 1 (370 A):

This 14 June, 1947 RIGOLETTO was broadcast complete, but to date has only been issued as excerpts. Reissued by Smith on ANNA 1040 (May-June, 1979) and later, as Melodram CD 15508. The *Page* was not identified in the original RAI broadcast.

Band 3: The ANNA 1040 dubbing also contains the recitative "Ella mi fu rapita," omitted from EJS 370.

Band 6: Also issued on ANNA 1040 and Timaclub TIMA 4, a Lauri-Volpi recital. There is no indication on the label of EJS 370 that this was taken from a source other than the complete 14 June, 1947 performance.

Side 2 (370 B):

Bands 1-2: Later issued on Timaclub TIMA 4. Dated 1942 on the label of EJS 370.

Bands 3-4: Dated 1961 on the label of EJS 370. These items have been reissued on a number of labels (Timaclub, Replica, and Fonit-Cetra); the TOSCA later appeared on ANNA 1041 (May-June, 1979).

Band 7: Lauri-Volpi sings both *Johnson* and *Minnie* in this patchwork of Act I passages. Reissued on Bongiovanni LP GB 1025. See also the endnote for EJS 343 (II/4).

Band 8: Reissued on ANNA 1040.

Band 9: This 22 October, 1952 performance was the world premiere of Ghedini's one-act "radio opera," LORD INFERNO, written for the RAI. The aria included is a soprano solo by Pagliughi, who created the role of *Jenny*. Also featured in the broadcast were Cloe Elmo (*Gambogi*), Agostino Lazzari (*Narrator*), Renato Capecchi (*Lord*), Giovanni Fabbri (*Aeneas*), and Mario Carlin (*Garble*).

The work was later revised as L'IPOCRITA FELICE (1956).

EJS 371: "The Golden Age of Opera" (1 LP)
Issued June, 1966

IL MATRIMONIO SEGRETO (Cimarosa) (I)
Opera in 2 acts (excerpts)
Orchestra and Chorus of the Teatro alla Scala, Milano/Mario Rossi
?Broadcast, La Scala, Milan, 22 Mar 1949

CAST:
Tito Schipa (*Paolino*); Boris Christoff (*Count Robinson*); Alda Noni (*Carolina*); Hilde Güden (*Elisetta*); Fedora Barbieri (*Fidalma*); Sesto Bruscantini (*Geronimo*).

SIDE 1 (371 A):

1. Act I: Si, coraggio mi faccio . . .

SIDE 2 (371 B):

1. Act I: . . . to the end of the act

* 2. TITO SCHIPA, tenor (Orchestra of the Teatro alla Scala, Milano/ Franco Ghione): WERTHER, Act I: Io non so se son desto . . . O natura [Je ne sais si je veille . . . O nature] (Massenet) (I)
Broadcast, La Scala, Milan, EIAR, 27 April, 1934
\+ OBA-5023-2 HMV DA 5420 Milan, March-April, 1942

3. TITO SCHIPA, tenor (Orchestra of the Teatro alla Scala, Milano/ Franco Ghione): WERTHER, Act I: Ah! perche quando ardate [Ah! pourvu que je vois . . . C'est que l'image] (Massenet) (I)
Broadcast, La Scala, Milan, EIAR, 27 Apr 1934

4. TITO SCHIPA, tenor and GIANNA PEDERZINI, contralto (Orchestra of the Teatro alla Scala, Milano/Franco Ghione): WERTHER, Act III: Ah non mi ridestar [Pourquoi me réveiller?] (Massenet) (I)
Broadcast, La Scala, Milan, EIAR, 27 Apr 1934

5. TITO SCHIPA, tenor and GIANNA PEDERZINI, contralto (Orchestra of the Teatro alla Scala, Milano/Franco Ghione): WERTHER, Act IV: No! Io muoio . . . to the end of the opera [Non, Charlotte, je meurs . . . to the end of the opera] (Massenet) (I)
Broadcast, La Scala, Milan, EIAR, 27 Apr 1934

NOTES: EJS 371

The WERTHER excerpts, along with a few scenes from this IL MATRIMONIO SEGRETO, later appeared on MDP 024, a Schipa recital.

Side 1 (371 A):

The label of EJS 371 says that the IL MATRIMONIO excerpts are from Act II, but what is given is Act I/x--from "Si, corraggio mi faccio" to the end of the act, which concludes on the first band of side 2. It is complete as performed except for minor lapses in the continuity resulting from actetate breaks. EJS 331 (May, 1965) contained other excerpts from the same performance of Act I, the total of the two LPs being some 90 percent of the act as broadcast.

SIDE 2 (371 B):

The WERTHER scenes presented here were subsequently included on the Timaclub LP TIMA 41, with Pederzini's Act III letter aria added. UORC 221, a Schipa recital issued in October, 1974, included the Act I duet, the "Ah non mi ridester," and the death scene, but attributed these to Schipa and Coe Glade--San Francisco Opera, 22 November, 1935, conducted by Merola (Schipa sang Werther in Italian, the rest of the cast sang in the original French).

Band 2: David Hamilton, in his article "Discoveries," (*ARSC Journal*, 18/1-3, 1986, pp. 249-250) notes that the "O natura" from the broadcast is completed on EJS 371 with Schipa's 1942 commercial HMV recording of the aria inserted at the wrong pitch.

EJS 372: "The Golden Age of Opera" (2 LPs)
Issued September, 1966

SIDES 1-4 (372 A-D):

GIULIO CESARE (Handel) (I)
Opera in 3 acts (complete)
Orchestra and Chorus of the Teatro San Carlo di Napoli/Herbert Albert
?In-house recording, Teatro Grande, Pompeii, 6 Jul 1950

CAST:
Cesare Siepi (*Giulio Cesare*); Renata Tebaldi (*Cleopatra*); Gino Sinimberghi (*Sesto Pompeo*); Elena Nicolai (*Cornelia*); Antonio Cassinelli (*Tolomeo*); Fernando Piccinni (*Achille*); Gerardo Gaudioso (*Curio*); Gerardo Gaudioso (*Nireno*).

NOTES: EJS 372

The source of this performance is unclear. It sounds more like an in-house recording than a broadcast, and so was, perhaps, another of the semi-offical San Carlo backstage transcriptions featured among the 1966 GAO offerings.

This GIULIO CESARE was later issued as HRE 378.

EJS 373: "The Golden Age of Opera" (2 LPs)
Issued September, 1966

SIDES 1-4 (373 A-D):

LE DONNE CURIOSE (Wolf-Ferrari) (I)
Opera in 3 acts (complete)
Orchestra and Chorus of Radio Italiana [RAI], Milano/Alfredo Simonetto
RAI broadcast, Milan, 30 Aug 1958

CAST:
Mafalda Micheluzzi (*Rosaura*); Eugenia Ratti (*Colombina*); Ester Orel (*Eleanora*); Gabriella Carturan (*Beatrice*); Carlo Franzini (*Florindo*); Carlo Badioli (*Arlecchino*); Paolo Pedani (*Lelio*); Renato Capecchi (*Pantalone*); Silvio Maionica (*Ottavio*); Angelo Mercuriali (*Leandro*); Florindo Andreolli (*Asdrubale*); Walter Artioli (*Almoro*); Renato Berti (*Alvise*); Bruno Cioni (*Lunardo*); Arrigo Cattelani (*Momolo*); Vittorio Tatozzi (*Menego*).

EJS 374: "The Golden Age of Opera" (1 LP)
Issued October, 1966
MATRIX CO-P-902

TOSCA (Puccini) (I)
Opera in 3 acts (abridged)
a) Orchestra and Chorus of the Palacio de las Bellas Artes, Mexico City/Walter Herbert
Broadcast, Palacio de las Bellas Artes, Mexico City, XEOY, 6 Aug 1946
b) Orchestra and Chorus of the Metropolitan Opera House/Giuseppe Antonicelli
Metropolitan Opera broadcast, NYC, 21 Jan 1950

CASTS:		Mexico City, 1946		Metropolitan Opera, 1950
Tosca	. . .	Stella Roman	. . .	Stella Roman
Cavaradossi	. . .	Ferruccio Tagliavini	. . .	Ferrucico Tagliavini
Scarpia	. . .	Alexander Sved	. . .	Alexander Sved
Angelotti	. . .	Gilberto Cerda	. . .	[Lorenzo Alvary]
Sacristan	. . .	Francisco Alonso	. . .	Gerhard Pechner
Sciarrone	. . .	Francisco Alonso	. . .	Clifford Harvuot]
Spoletta	. . .	Carlos Sagarminaga	. . .	Alessio DePaolis
A Shepherd	. . .	[Oralia Dominguez]	. . .	[Thelma Altman]
A Jailor	. . .	[Manuel Carreno]	. . .	[Lawrence Davidson]

SIDE 1 (374 A):

Act I: 1. a) TAGLIAVINI, ALONSO, CERDA, and ROMAN: Recondita armonia . . . La vita mi costasse, vi salverò! (a)
b) SVED, ROMAN, ALONSO, SAGARMINAGA, and Chorus: Tosca? Che non mi veda . . . to the end of the act (a)

SIDE 2 (374 B):

Act II: 1. a) SVED, ROMAN, ALONSO, and TAGLIAVINI: Ed ora fra noi parliamo da buoni amici . . . Salvatelo! Io? Voi! (a)

b) ROMAN and SVED: Quanto? Quanto? Il prezzo! . . . Vissi d'arte (a)

Act III: 2. a) TAGLIAVINNI: E lucevan le stelle (a)
b) TAGLIAVINI and ROMAN: Ah! Franchigia . . . venne all'orrendo amplesso (a)
* c) ROMAN and TAGLIAVINI: Io quella lama gli piantai nel cor . . . Gli occhi ti chiuderò con mille baci e mille ti dirò nomi d'amor (b)
* d) ROMAN, ?PECHNER, DE PAOLIS, and Chorus: Com'è lunga l'attesa! . . . to the end of the opera (b)

NOTES: EJS 374

Original 1966 pressings of EJS 374 were the first to bear separate matrix numbers etched into the wax: prior to this, the GAO numbers served as both the catalog and matrix number. See the note on matrix numbers in the INTRODUCTION TO THE DISCOGRAPHY.

Side 2 (374 B):

The conclusion of the third act--specifically, items c and d--were almost certainly taken from a different source than the quoted 1946 Mexico City performance, though such is not noted in the October, 1966 EJS bulletin or on the labels of EJS 374. Roman's declining vocal resources appear evident: probably the 21 January, 1950 Met broadcast conducted by Antonicelli was used here, featuring Roman's *Tosca*, Tagliavini's *Cavaradossi*, Sved's *Scarpia*, and Alessio DePaolis' *Spoletta*. DePaolis, in particular, can be heard clearly in the finale of the EJS 374 performance.

EJS 375: "The Golden Age of Opera" (2 LPs)
Issued October, 1966
MATRIX CO-P-906

SIDES 1-4 (375 A-D):

RISURREZIONE (Alfano) (I)
Opera in 4 acts (complete)
Orchestra and Chorus of Radio Italiana [RAI], Milano/Oliviero de Fabritiis
RAI broadcast, Milan, 1 Mar 1952

CAST:
Carla Gavazzi (*Katiusha*); Nicola Filacuridi (*Dimitri*); Gino Orlandini (*Simonson*); Jole Jacchia (*Sofia*); Jole Jacchia (*La Korablewa*); Lydia Pratis (*Matrena*); Lydia Pratis (*La Gobba*); Maria Teresa Mandalari (*Anna*); Jole Farolfi (*Vera*); Jole Farolfi (*Fenitchka*); Angela Moretti (*La Rossa*); Carla Macelloni (*Fedia*); Eraldo Coda (*Kritzloff*); Eraldo Coda (*Head of the Guards*); Giulio Biellesi (*A Station Clerk*); Fernando Valentini (*A Watchman*); Fernando Valentini (*An Official*); Aldo Roggi (*First Peasant*); Fernando Valentini (*Second Peasant*); Aldo Roggi (*A Cossack*).

EJS 376: "The Golden Age of Opera" (2 LPs)
Issued October, 1966
MATRIX CO-P-913

SIDES 1-4 (376 A-D):

I CAVALIERI DI EKEBÙ (Zandonai) (I)
Opera in 4 acts (complete)
Orchestra and Chorus of Radio Italiana [RAI], Milano/Alfredo Simonetto
Recorded 31 Mar 1957 for first RAI broadcast, Milan, 16 Jan 1958

CAST:
Rina Malatrasi (*Anna*); Mirto Picchi (*Gösta Berling*); Fedora Barbieri (*Commandant*); Giampiero Malaspina (*Cristiano*); Nicola Zaccaria (*Sintram*); Maria Amadini (*L'ostessa*); Nicoletta Panni (*A Young Woman*); Mario Carlin (*Liecrona*); Bruno Cioni (*Samzelius*); Arrigo Cattelani (*A Cavalier*).

NOTES: EJS 376

Issued here as performed, with Act III/i and the part of Anna's mother omitted--a standard cut, apparently, in Italy. This RAI performance was reissued subsequently as MRF 167. The October, 1966 bulletin notes that "The recording itself is magnificent in sound and could easily have been presented in stereo" . . . whatever that means.

Some copies of EJS 376 are misnumbered 375 on all four labels.

Fonit-Cetra issued a complete I CAVALIERI (LMA 3020) on 3-LPs with Gianandrea Gavazzeni conducting the RAI Orchestra. The only other representative vocal recordings from the opera date from the Swedish premiere (Royal Opera, Stockholm, September-October, 1928): a set of collected excerpts on Odeon featuring soprano Britta Hertzberg, mezzo-soprano Irma Bjoerk, contralto Kirsten Thorborg, tenor Ejnar Beyron, and baritone Einar Larsson. Hertzberg and Beyron were also featured on a Scandanavian HMV issue of vocal selections (HMV Z 185).

EJS 377: "The Golden Age of Opera" (2 LPs)
Issued November, 1966
MATRIX CO-P-960

SIDES 1-4 (377 A-D):

LA PRISE DE TROIE (Berlioz) (F)
Opera in 3 acts (complete)
Royal Philharmonic Orchestra and BBC Theater Chorus/Sir Thomas Beecham
Broadcast relay, ***THIRD PROGRAMME***, BBC, ?London, 3 Jun 1947

CAST:
Marisa Ferrer (*Cassandre*); Jean Giraudeau (*Enée*); Charles Cambon (*Chorebe*); Irene Joachim (*Ascagne*); Colin Cunningham (*Helenus*); Yvonne Cork (*Hecube*); Charles-Paul (*Panthée*); Ernest Frank (*The Ghost of Hector*); Scott Joynt (*Priam*); Dennis Dowling (*A Trojan Soldier*); Dennis Dowling (*A Greek Captain*).

NOTES: EJS 377

LA PRISE DE TROIE is a three-act version of Acts 1 and 2 of LES TROYENS, as revised by Berlioz in 1863 to secure a performance. It's companion, the five-act LES TROYENS À CARTHAGE (see EJS 378), consisted of Acts 3-5 of the complete opera. LES TROYENS, in the form in which it was originally conceived, made its belated debut under Felix Mottl in Karlsruhe on 6 and 7 December, 1890.

David Cairn's essay, "The Operas of Berlioz," in *Opera on Record 2*, edited by Alan Blyth (New York: Beauford, 1983), pp. 158-163, notes that both of the BBC productions are riddled with small performance cuts, possibly the result of the version used: at the time, the only score available was from Choudens, a Paris publisher.

There seems to be some question as to when the performances were actually broadcast: they were certainly mounted and recorded successively on 3 and 4 June, 1947, but may not have been broadcast until later that week.

EJS 378: "The Golden Age of Opera" (3 LPs)
Issued November, 1966
MATRIX: CO-P-965

SIDES 1-6 (378 A-F):

LES TROYENS À CARTHAGE (Berlioz) (F)
Opera in 5 acts and a Prologue (complete)
Royal Philharmonic Orchestra and BBC Theater Chorus/Sir Thomas Beecham
Broadcast relay, ***THIRD PROGRAMME***, BBC, ?London, 4 Jun 1947

CAST:
Marisa Ferrer (*Didon*); Jean Giraudeau (*Enée*); Yvonne Cork (*Anna*); Yvonne Cork (*The Ghost of Cassandre*); Frans [Franz] Vroons (*Iopas*); Maria Braneze (*Ascagne*); Charles-Paul (*Panthée*); Charles Cambon (*Narbal*); Charles Cambon (*The Ghost of Chorebe*); Colin Cunningham (*Hylas*); Ernest Frank (*First Soldier*); Scott Joynt (*Second Soldier*); Scott Joynt (*The Ghost of Priam*); Stearn Scott (*Mercure*).

NOTES: EJS 378

See the endnote for EJS 377.

EJS 379: "The Golden Age of Opera" (1 LP)
Issued December, 1966
MATRIX: CO-P-1007

FEDORA (Giordano) (I)
Opera in 3 acts (abridged)
Orchestra and Chorus of the Teatro Municpal, Rio de Janeiro/Nino Sanzogno
Broadcast, Teatro Municipal, Rio de Janeiro, 20 Aug 1951

CAST:
Beniamino Gigli (*Loris*); Elena Nicolai (*Fedora*); Diva Pieranti (*Olga*); Paulo Fortes (*De Siriex*); Giuseppe Modesti (*Cirillo*); Antonio Lembo (*Grech*); Heraldo De Marco (*Rouvel*); Carmen Pimentel (*A Savoyard*); Enrico Silvieri, piano (*Lazinski*); Ernesto De Marco (*Boroff*); [Carmen Pimentel (*Dimitri*)]; [Heraldo De Marco (*Desiré*)]; [Geraldo Chagas (*Michele*)].

SIDE 1 (379 A):

1. Act I:
   a) NICOLAI: O grandi occhi lucenti
   b) MODESTI: Egli mi disse "Andiamo al Tiro!" . . . O nostro padre!

   Act II:
   a) NICOLAI, GIGLI, FORTES, E. DE MARCO, PIERANTI, H. DE MARCO, and Chorus: Oh! Il Signor De Siriex . . . Risponda!
   b) FORTES: La donna russa
   * c) GIGLI (w. BBC Opera Orchestra/Stanford Robinson): Amor ti vieta
     BBC broadcast, London, 25 April, 1952
   d) PIERANTI, NICOLAI, and GIGLI: Principessa, se aveste . . . Infame! Più non mi sfuggi!
   e) NICOLAI, GIGLI, and SIVIERI (pf): Loris Ipanoff, oggi lo Zar . . . to the end of the act

SIDE 2 (379 B):

1. Act III: Complete (opening chorus omitted)

NOTES: EJS 379

This performance later appeared on the American Edizione Lirica label (EL 002); excerpts from the Act II Finale have been issued on ANNA 1032 (May-June, 1979), MDP 018, and EMI 153-54010/17, the Gigli "Edizione Completa."

The "Amor ti vieta" derives from Gigli's 25 April, 1952 BBC concert, other portions of which were included on EJS 329 (April, 1965), EJS 336 (June, 1965), and ANNA 1032. The Edizione Lirica LP uses the same "Amor ti vieta," but gives the date as 12 August, 1951.

EJS 380: "The Golden Age of Opera" (2 LPs)
Issued December, 1966
MATRIX: CO-P-1004

LA FORZA DEL DESTINO (Verdi) (I)
Opera in 4 acts (excerpts)
Orchestra and Chorus of the Teatro Municipal, Rio de Janeiro/Antonio Votto
Broadcast, Teatro Municipal, Rio de Janeiro, 16 Aug 1951

CAST:
Beniamino Gigli (*Don Alvaro*); Elisabetta Barbato (*Leonora*); Enzo Mascherini (*Don Carlo*); Giulio Neri (*Padre Guardiano*); Guilherme Damiano (*Fra Melitone*); Giuseppe Modesti (*Marquis de Calatrava*); Carmen Pimentel (*Curra*); ?Antonio Lembo (*A Surgeon*); [Anna Maria Canali (*Preziosilla*)]; [Nino Crimi (*Trabucco*)]; [?Antonio Lembo (*Alcalde*)].

SIDE 1 (380 A):

1. Act I: a) Overture
b) BARBATO, PIMENTEL, GIGLI, and MODESTI: Me pellegrina ed orfana . . . to the end of the act
c) GIGLI: Dressing room interview beteen acts

SIDE 2 (380 B):

1. Act II: BARBATO and NERI, and Chorus: Sono giunta! grazie, a Dio! . . . Madre, Madre, pietosa Vergine . . . La vergine degli angeli . . . to the end of the scene

SIDE 3 (380 C):

1. Act III: GIGLI, MASCHERINI, LEMBO, and Chorus: O tu che in seno . . . Urna fatale del mio destino . . . to the end of the scene

SIDE 4 (380 D):

1. Act IV: NERI, MASCHERINI, DAMIANO, GIGLI, BARBATO, and Chorus: Giunge qualcun! Aprite! . . . to the end of the opera

NOTES: EJS 380

The Finale of this performance later appeared on ANNA 1033 (May-June, 1979). Other excerpts have turned up on HRE 259 and on EMI 153-54010/17, the Gigli "Edizione Completa."

EJS 381: "The Golden Age of Opera" (2 LPs)
Issued December, 1966
MATRIX P-1014

SIDES 1-4 (381 A-D):

MARINO FALIERO (Donizetti) (I)
Opera in 3 acts (complete)
Orchestra and Chorus of the Teatro Donizetti, Bergamo/Adolfo Camozzo
?Broadcast, Teatro Donizetti, Bergamo, 12 Oct 1966

CAST:
Agostino Ferrin (*Marino Faliero*); Margherita Roberti (*Elena*); Angelo Mori (*Fernando*); Lina Rossi (*Irene*); Carlo Meliciani (*Israele Bertucci*); Virgilio Carbonari (*Steno*); Gianfranco Manganotti (*Leoni*); Gianfranco Manganotti (*A Gondolier*); Emilio Savoldi (*Pietro*); Ottorino Begali (*Guido*); Ottorino Begali (*Vincenzo*).

NOTES: EJS 381

Carbonari's foremane is given as "Virginio" on the label of EJS 381. The premiere date of the work given in the December, 1966 bulletin, 30 May, 1830, is incorrect: the work made its debut at the Théâtre-Italien, Paris, on 12 March, 1835.

The performance was later issued as Melodram MEL-27030.

EJS 382: "The Golden Age of Opera" (1 LP)
Issued January, 1967
MATRIX: CO-P-1042

"BENIAMINO GIGLI / RECITAL / RIO DE JANIERO, 1951"

SIDE 1 (1-13) - SIDE 2 (1-2):
Beniamino Gigli, tenor; pf/Enrico Sivieri
In-house recording, Teatro Jão Caetano, Rio de Janeiro, 23 Oct 1951

SIDE 2 (3-12):
Beniamino Gigli, tenor; pf/Enrico Sivieri
In-house recording, Teatro Jão Caetano, Rio de Janeiro, 25 Oct 1951

SIDE 1 (382 A):

<u>23 October, 1951</u> **(part 1)**

1. MANON LESCAUT. Act I: Tra voi, belle (Puccini) (I)

2. "Quanno il diavol naque" (Donaudy) (I)

3. "Vaghissima sembianza" (Donaudy) (I)

4. "O del mio amato ben" (Donaudy) (I)

5. "Bella bellina: (Giulia Recli) (I)

6. "Mimosa" (Froes) (P)

7. "Vidalita" (Williams) (S)

8. LUISA MILLER, Act II: Ah! fede negar potessi . . . Quando le sere al placido (Verdi) (I)

9. I PAGLIACCI, Act I: Recitar . . . Vesti la giubba (Leoncavallo) (I)

10. RIGOLETTO, Act III: La donna è mobile (Verdi) (I)

11. L'AFRICAINE, Act IV: Mi batte il cor . . . O Paradiso [Pays merveilleux . . . Ô Paradis] (Meyerbeer) (I)

12. "Rondine al nido" (De Crescenzo) (I)

13. "LA FANCIULLA DEL WEST, Act III: Ch'ella mi creda (Puccini) (I)

SIDE 2 (382 B):

<u>25 October, 1951</u> (part 1)

1. TOSCA, Act III: E lucevan le stelle (Puccini) (I)

<u>23 October, 1951</u> (part 2)

* 2. "Mattinata" (Leoncavallo) (I)

<u>25 October, 1951</u> (part 2)

3. L'ELISIR D'AMORE, Act II: Una furtiva lagrima (Donizetti) (I)

4. WTC I, Prelude 1: "Ave Maria" (J. S. Bach-arr. Gounod) (L)

5. LES PÊCHEURS DE PERLES, Act I: Mi par d'udir ancora [Je crois entendre encore] (Bizet) (F)

6. "Core 'ngrato" (Cardillo) (N)

7. WERTHER, Act III: Ah, non mi ridestar [Pourquoi me réveiller?] (Massenet) (F)

8. "Ideale" (Errico-Tosti) (I)

9. "Musica proibita" (Gastaldon) (I)

10. "Povera Pulcinella" (Buzzi-Peccia) (I)

11. "Ah! L'ammore che 'ffa fa'" (De Curtis) (N)

12. "Torna a Surriento" (De Curtis) (N)

NOTES: EJS 382

The 23 October concert is presented here complete as performed. Note that the TOSCA aria was the last item performed on 25 October and the Leoncavallo "Mattinata" the last performed on 23 October, and that the two have been placed out of order on EJS 382.

The last six items of the 25 October concert were later included on EJS 403 (June, 1967) and EJS 464 (March, 1969). The entire concert was later issued on HRE-213.

EJS 383: "The Golden Age of Opera" (2 LPs)
Issued January, 1967
MATRIX: P-1039

SIDES 1-4 (383 A-D):

MACBETH (Verdi) (I)
Opera in 4 acts (complete)
Scottish Orchestra and the Glyndebourne Festival Chorus/Berthold Goldschmidt
?Broadcast, Edinburgh Festival, Edinburgh, 27 Aug 1947

CAST:
Margherita Grandi (*Lady Macbeth*); Francesco Valentino (*Macbeth*); Italo Tajo (*Banquo*); Walter Midgley (*Macduff*); Andrew McKinley (*Malcolm*); Vera Terry (*Lady's Attendant*); André Orkin (*An Assassin*); André Orkin (*A Physician*).

NOTES: EJS 383

Taken from the first Edinburgh Festival, a production of the Glyndebourne Opera Company sponsored by the Glyndebourne Society.

EJS 384: "The Golden Age of Opera" (1 LP)
Issued January, 1967
MATRIX CO-P-1040

SIDE 1 (384 A):

LA BOHÈME (Puccini) (Sw)
Opera in 4 acts (Act I only)
Orchestra and Chorus of the Royal Opera House, Stockholm/Nils Grevillius
Broadcast, Royal Opera House, Stockholm, 21 Mar 1940

CAST
Jussi Bjoerling (*Rodolfo*); Hjördis Schymberg (*Mimi*); Sven Herdenberg (*Marcello*); Karl Richter (*Schaunard*); Leon Bjoerker (*Colline*); Folke Cembraeus (*Benoit*).

1. Act I (complete)

SIDE 2 (384 B):

LE CANZONE DEI RICORDI (R. Paliara-Giuseppe Martucci) (I)
Poemetto Lirico (complete)
NBC Symphony Orchestra/Arturo Toscanini
Broadcast, ***NBC SYMPHONY ORCHESTRA***, WJZ, NYC, 29 Mar 1941

Bruna Castagna, mezzo-soprano

NOTES: EJS 384

Side 1 (384 A):

The BOHÈME is dated incorrectly as 25 May, 1940 on the label of EJS 384. The first act was recorded by the Swedish Broadcasting Corporation, but may not have actually been broadcast until 17 July, 1977, according to the Porter-Henrysson Bjoerling discography.

The complete Act I presented here has also appeared as HRE 281-2.

Swedish Radio tape: L-B 4141

Side 2 (384 B):

The CANZONE DEI RICORDI is given on the label of EJS 384 and in the January, 1967 bulletin as a *1939* performance from the Teatro Colon Orchestra, conducted by Ettore Panizza. This was done undoubtedly to avoid the same threats of legal action leveled by the Toscanini estate when Smith issued the 1935 New York Philharmonic MISSA SOLEMNIS on EJS 122½/Great Performances of the Past GRP 1001 in 1957. The work was originally published with piano accompaniment (1888) and later revised for orchestra (1900).

This 29 March, 1941 broadcast also featured Wagner's "Eine Faust-ouvertüre," Schumann's Second Symphony, and Tommasini's "Carnival of Venice."

EJS 385: "The Golden Age of Opera" (1 LP)
Issued January, 1967
MATRIX P-1041

LES DEUX JOURNÉES (Cherubini) (F)
Opera in 3 acts (excerpts)
Royal Philharmonic Orchestra and BBC Theater Orchestra/Sir Thomas Beecham
Broadcast, ?*THIRD PROGRAMME*, BBC, London, 2 or 19 Dec 1947

CAST:
Janine Micheau (*Constance*); Charles-Paul (*Mikeli*); Pierre Giannotti (*Count Armand*); Fabian Smith (*Commandant*).

SIDE 1 (385 A):

Act I: * 1. CHARLES-PAUL: Guide mes pas, o providence
* 2. MICHEAU and GIANNOTTI: Me séparer de mon epoux tu m'appartiens, et je défie

Act III: * 3. MICHEAU, GIANNOTTI, and SMITH: Approchons-nous bien doucement
* 4. CHARLES-PAUL and Chorus: Livrons-nous tous à la gaîté

SIDE 2 (385 B):

* 1. ?BBC THEATER CHORUS (Royal Philharmonic Orchestra/Sir Thomas Beecham): THAMOS, KÖNIG IN AEGYPTEN, K. 345, Act I, No. 1: Schon weichet dir, Sonne! (Mozart) (G)
BBC broadcast, London, 5 Jul 1948

* 2. ROYAL PHILHARMONIC ORCHESTRA/SIR THOMAS BEECHAM: THAMOS, KÖNIG IN AEGYPTEN, K. 345, Act II-III: Interlude [No. 3, Andante] (Mozart)
BBC broadcast, London, 5 Jul 1948

* 3. ROGER RICO, bass (Royal Philharmonic Orchestra and ?BBC Theater Chorus/Sir Thomas Beecham): THAMOS, KÖNIG IN AEGYPTEN, K. 345, Act V, No. 7b: Ihr Kinder des Staubes (Mozart) (G)
BBC broadcast, London, 5 Jul 1948

4. DOROTHY BOND, soprano (Royal Philharmonic Orchestra/Sir Thomas Beecham): LA CLEMENZA DI TITO, K. 621, Act II: S'altro che lagrime (Mozart) (I)
BBC broadcast, London, 27 Jun 1948

5. ROSANNA GIANCOLA, contralto; MARGARET RITCHIE, soprano; and TREVOR ANTHONY, bass (Royal Philharmonic Orchestra/Sir Thomas Beecham): LA CLEMENZA DI TITO, K. 621, Act I: Se al volto (Mozart) (I)
BBC broadcast, London, 27 Jun 1948

NOTES: EJS 385

Side 1 (385 A):

There were two BBC broadcasts of LES DEUX JOURNÉES--on 2 and 19 December, 1947. EJS 285 credits the 2 December performance, while the VOCE-73 reissue gives 19 December: both appear to be identical despite the varying quality of their transfers. The EJS 385 performance was subsequently issued complete on the two-disc UORC 174 (November, 1973). Reference to the "Bax Orchestra" as the accompanying ensemble--whatever that may have been--has also been made in print.

Side 2 (385 B):

Bands 1-3: THAMOS has since been given a *new* Köchel number, 336a.

EJS 386: "The Golden Age of Opera" (1 LP)
Issued February, 1967
MATRIX: CO-P-1071

SIDES 1-2 (386 A-B):

BOCCACCIO (Von Suppé) (E)
Operetta in 3 acts (excerpts)
Pro Arte Orchestra/Leo Wurmser
?BBC broadcast, ?London, date unknown

CAST:
Peter Leeming (*Pietro*); Geoffrey Chard (*Boccaccio*); John Mitchinson (*Scalza*); Michael Maurel (*?Ausrufer*); Dennis Dowling (*?Leonetto*); Patricia Kern (*Peronella*); Shirley Minty (*?Beatrice*); Elizabeth Harwood (*?*); Ann Robson (*?Isabella*); Patricia Reakes (*?Fiametta*); John Noble (*Checco*).

NOTES: EJS 386

This appears to be a BBC studio broadcast performance, with narration replacing the original dialogue.

The label of EJS 386 lists the singers but not their corresponding roles. The assignment of the roles in the listing above is, therefore, provisional: there are too few basses, but it seems unlikely that tenor Mitchinson or baritone Maurel double in some of the minor roles; conversely, there are too *many* women given for the available roles!

Chard's surname is given on the label and in the February, 1967 bulletin as "Charo."

EJS 387: "The Golden Age of Opera" (1 LP)
Issued February, 1967
MATRIX P-1072

SIDES 1-2 (387 A-B):

LES BRIGANDS (Offenbach) (G)
Operetta in 3 acts (abridged)
Orchestra and Chorus of the Norddeutschen Rundfunk, Hamburg/Fred Walker
Broadcast, Norddeutschen Rundfunk [NDR], Hamburg, 1961

CAST:
Helge Roswaenge (*Falsacappa*); Gertrud Freedmann (*Fiorella*); Peter Minich (*Fragoletto*); Wolfgang Volz (*Pietro*); Erland Erlandson (*Antonio*); Richard Munch (*Gloria-Cassis*); Kurt Marschner (*Campotasso*); Richard Capellman (*The Duke of Mantou*); ? (*The Captain*); Harold Enns (*Carmagnola*); Fritz Gollnitz (*Pippo*); Rudiger Pobl (*Adolphe*); Erna Maria Duske [Duschke] (*The Princess*); ? (*Zerlina*); ? (*Fiametta*); ? (*The Duchess*); ? (*The Marquis*); ? (*Bianca*); ? (*Cicinella*); Jürgen Förster (*Brigand*); Caspar Bröcheler (*Brigand*); Mathieu Ahlersmeyer (*Brigand*).

NOTES: EJS 387

Reported to be misnumbered as EJS 388 on at least some copies.

Entitled DIE BANDITEN, EJS 387 contains all of the vocal music actually broadcast, but omits the Overture and most of the (German) dialogue, which consumed nearly a half hour of this roughly 90-minute performance. Only the dialogue spoken over the music is retained. Act II, as performed here, deviates from the French score, which may be indicative of some vaguely "standard" German version of the opera in use at the time. This may explain the omission of some of the missing characters as well.

EJS 388: "The Golden Age of Opera" (1 LP)
Issued February, 1967
MATRIX P-1073

SIDES 1-2 (388 A-B):

LE MÉDECIN MALGRÉ LUI (Gounod) (F)
Opera in 3 acts (complete)
Orchestra and Chorus of the Radio Italiana [RAI], Roma/Nino Sanzogno
RAI broadcast, Rome, 25 Mar 1962

CAST:
Scipio Colombo (*Sganarelle*); Luisella Ciaffi Ricagno (*Martine*); Paolo Montarsolo (*Valére*); Antonio Pietrini (*Lucas*); Eric Tappy (*Léandre*); Miti Truccato Pace (*Jacqueline*); Andrée Aubéry Luc[c]hini (*Lucinde*); Italo Tajo (*Geronte*); [Roberto Bertea (*Recitante*)].

NOTES: EJS 388

Reported to be misnumbered as EJS 387 on at least some copies.

This obscure work is based on Molière's 1666 play of the same title (THE DOCTOR IN SPITE OF HIMSELF), with a libretto by Gounod, Jules Barbier and Michel Carré. First produced at the Paris Théâtre-Lyrique on 15 January, 1858, it was Gounod's only attempt at comic opera. Note that this RAI performance is sung in the original French.

The score itself, something of a cross between opéra-comique and incidental music, consists of fourteen musical numbers separated by long stretches of Molière's original dialogue. The dialogue appears to have been replaced by narration for this performance (*vis* Bertea's *Recitante*), and omitted altogether from EJS 388. The music is presented here complete, but the "Choeur des fagottiers" (No. 5) has been placed between the Overture and the first vocal number--obviously a performance alteration.

The label of EJS 388 is riddled with errors, making chaos of both the singers' names and the parts they play. Tappy, who was apparently billed as *Erico* Tappy for the original broadcast, is listed on the label as "*Leondre*," playing the *role* of "Eric Tappy!" The above listing has been corrected.

The MÉDECIN excerpted on MRF 157 is a different performance taken from French Radio.

EJS 388 is slightly below pitch at 33.3 rpm.

EJS 389: "The Golden Age of Opera" (1 LP)
Issued February, 1967
MATRIX CO-P-1078

SIDES 1-2 (389 A-B):

SILVANO (Mascagni) (I)
Opera in 2 acts (complete)
Orchestra of Radio Italiana [RAI], Milano/Pietro Argento
RAI broadcast, Milan, 6 Oct 1954

CAST:
Renata Heredia-Capnist (*Matilde*); Vittoria Palombini (*Rosa*); Aldo Bertocci (*Silvano*); Filippo [Philip] Maero (*Renzo*).

NOTES: EJS 389

This performance of Mascagni's fifth opera (1895) was made available in considerably better sound as MRF 81. The EJS 390 transfer is among the most appalling of the series.

EJS 390: "The Golden Age of Opera" (1 LP)
Issued February, 1967
MATRIX: CO-P-1079

SIDE 1 (390 A):

FIDELIO, Op. 72 (Beethoven) (G and E)
Opera in 3 acts (excerpts)
Orchestra of the Royal Opera House/Karl Rankl
Broadcast, Covent Garden, London, 21 May 1951

CAST:
Kirsten Flagstad (*Leonora*); Howell Glynne (*Rocco*); Elisabeth Schwarzkopf (*Marzelline*); Dennis Stevenson (*Jaquino*); [Tom Williams (*Don Pizarro*)].

* 1. a) SCHWARTZKOPF, FLAGSTAD, GLYNNE, and STEVENSON: Act I: Mir ist so wunderbar
b) FLAGSTAD: Abscheulicher! wo eilst du hin?

* 2. KIRSTEN FLAGSTAD, soprano (pf/Waldemar Alme): ROMANCER OG SANGE, Op. 18, no. 4: Efteraarsstormen (Richardt-Grieg) (Nw)
Broadcast, Norwegian Radio, Oslo, 29 May 1954

* 3. KIRSTEN FLAGSTAD, soprano (pf/Waldemar Alme): ROMANCER (AELDRE OG NYERE), Op. 39, no. 5: I liden høit der oppe (Lie-Grieg) (Nw)
Broadcast, Norwegian Radio, Oslo, 29 May 1954

* 4. KIRSTEN FLAGSTAD, soprano (pf/Waldemar Alme): FEM DIGTE, Op. 70, no. 3: Lys Natt (Benzon-Grieg) (Nw)
Broadcast, Norwegian Radio, Oslo, 29 May 1954

* 5. KIRSTEN FLAGSTAD, soprano (pf/Waldemar Alme): FEM DIGTE, Op. 26, no. 1: Et Håb (Paulsen-Grieg) (W)
Broadcast, Norwegian Radio, Oslo, 29 May 1954

* 6. KIRSTEN FLAGSTAD, soprano (pf/Waldemar Alme): SEX DIGTE, Op. 25, no. 5: Borte (Ibsen-Grieg) (Nw)
Broadcast, Norwegian Radio, Oslo, 29 May 1954

* 7. KIRSTEN FLAGSTAD, soprano (pf/Waldemar Alme): FEM DIGTE, Op. 69, no. 1: Der gynger en båt på bølge (Benzon-Grieg) (Nw)
Broadcast, Norwegian Radio, Oslo, 29 May 1954

* 8. KIRSTEN FLAGSTAD, soprano (pf/Waldemar Alme): HJERTETS MELODIER, Op. 5, no. 3: Jeg elsker dig (Andersen-Grieg) (Nw)
Broadcast, Norwegian Radio, Oslo, 29 May 1954

* 9. KIRSTEN FLAGSTAD, soprano (pf/Waldemar Alme): DIGTE, Op. 60, no. 5: Og jeg vil ha' meg en hjertenskjaer (Krag-Grieg) (Nw)
Broadcast, Norwegian Radio, Oslo, 29 May 1954

SIDE 2 (390 B):

SIEGFRIED (Wagner) (G)
Opera in 3 acts (excerpts)
Orchestra of the Teatro alla Scala, Milan/Wilhelm Furtängler
Broadcast, La Scala, Milan, 22 Mar 1950
CAST:
Set Svanholm (*Siegfried*); Kirsten Flagstad (*Brünnhilde*); [Josef Herrmann (*Wanderer*)]; [Elisabeth Höngen (*Erda*)]; [Alois Pernerstorfer (*Alberich*)]; [Emil Markwort (*Mime*)]; [Ludwig Weber (*Fafner*)]; [Julia Moor (*Forest Bird*)].

* 1. SVANHOLM and FLAGSTAD, soprano: Act III: Heil dir, Sonne! Heil dir, Licht! . . . to the end of the opera

NOTES: EJS 390

Side 1 (390 A):

Band 1: Act I of this 22 March, 1950 FIDELIO was broadcast complete, but no further excerpts are known to survive. The two numbers sung here are connected by the English dialogue used in the performance--the music was sung in the original German. The quartet is preceded and followed by dialogue, then cuts to the "Abscheulicher," which is complete, cutting short only the final chord.

The correct speed for these excerpts is 31.8 rpm.

Bands 2-9: Sanner's Flagstad discography lists this 29 May, 1954 broadcast concert (pp. 105-106, items 547-554), but does not assign EJS 390 as a published source. The songs are dated 1954 in the February, 1967 bulletin, and incorrectly as 23 June, 1954 on the label of EJS 390. It is not clear whether the recital was pre-recorded for broadcast over Norsk Rikskringkasting [NRK].

The bulletin notes also that among the eight Grieg songs are "a couple she never did commercially," but this is true only of no. 6, "Borte."

Norwegian Radio tape: NRK 3606; Stanford University Archive of Recorded Sound tape: StARS 560000 M5; New York Public Library tape: F-XI.

Side 2 (390 B):

Band 1: The complete 22 March, 1950 La Scala SIEGFRIED was issued on the four-disc UORC 123 (October, 1972) as well as on the Murray Hill Furtwängler RING cycle (940477), Everest 475/3, and Recital Records RR 420 (Bruno Walter Society). Fonit-Cetra has issued excerpts from the performance on compact disc CDC-16.

A speed of approximately 31.8 rpm places this duet at score pitch.

EJS 391: "The Golden Age of Opera" (1 LP)
Issued March, 1967
MATRIX P-1139

SIDES 1-2 (391 A-B):

IL BACIO (Zandonai) (I)
Opera in 2 acts (complete)
Orchestra and Chorus of Radio Italiana [RAI], Milano/Francesco Molinari-Pradelli
RAI broadcast, Milan, 10 Mar 1954

CAST:
Rosetta Noli (*Vestilia*); Lina Pagliughi (*Mirta*); Angelo Lo Forese (*Marzio*); Rossana Papagni (*A Girl*); Giuseppina Salvi (*The Matron*); Anna Maria Rota (*The Novice*); Walter Artioli (*Narcisino*); Walter Artioli (*Nicodeme*); Angelo Mercuriali (*A Foolish Relative*); Virgilio Carbonari (*Narcisone*); Lido Maffeo (*An Irascible Relative*); Franco Valenti (*The Father Guardian*); Giulio Fioravanti (*A Pilgrim Friar*); Plinio Clabassi (*An Older Priest*); Cristiano Dalamangas (*Another Relative*).

NOTES: EJS 391

This broadcast was the world premiere of the two acts of IL BACIO completed by the composer. The work was written between 1940 and 1944 to a libretto by Rossato and Mucci, after G. Keller. The March, 1967 EJS bulletin incorrectly dates the performance as 1953.

Reported to be be slightly sharp at 33.3 rpm.

EJS 392: "The Golden Age of Opera" (2 LPs)
Issued March, 1967
MATRIX: P-1137 / P-1138

SIDES 1-4 (392 A-D):

IL CAMPIELLO (Wolf-Ferrari) (I)
Opera in 3 acts (complete)
Orchestra and Chorus of Radio Italiana [RAI], Milano/Ettore Gracis
RAI broadcast, 3 Sep 1963

CAST:
Elena Rizzieri (*Gasparina*); Silvana Zanolli (*Lucieta*); Jolanda Meneguzzer (*'Gnese*); Laura Zannini (*Orsola*); Giuseppe Savio (*Zorzeto*); Mario Borriello (*Astolfi*); Silvio Maionica (*Anzoleto*); Agostino Ferrin (*Fabrizio*); Mario Guggia (*Dona Canete*); Angelo Mercuriali (*Dona Pasqua*).

EJS 393: "The Golden Age of Opera" (2 LPs)
Issued March, 1967
MATRIX: P-1140 / P-1142

SIDES 1-4 (393 A-B):

ALI BABA (Cherubini-revised Vito Frazzi) (I)
Opera in 4 acts and a Prologue (complete)
Orcehstra and Chrous of the Teatro alla Scala, Milano/Nino Sanzogna
Broadcast, La Scala, Milan, 15 Jun 1963

CAST:
Teresa Stich-Randall (*Delia*); Orianna Santunione Finzi (*Morgiane*); Alfredo Kraus (*Nadir*); Wladimiro Ganzarolli (*Ali Baba*); Paolo Montarsolo (*Aboul Hassan*); Lorenzo Testi (*Ours-Kan*); Agostino Ferrin (*Thamar*); Piero De Palma (*Calaf*); Virgilio Carbonari (*Phaor*).

NOTES: EJS 393

As noted in the March, 1967 bulletin, much of the music for ALI BABA was taken from Chrubini's earlier works--the opera FANISKA (1806) and the unsuccessful ballet, ACHILLE À SCYROS (1804), to which a new overture was added. ALI BABA was Cherubini's last opera, produced at the Paris Opéra 22 July, 1833.

This performance was later issued as MRF C-05 and Melodram 170.

EJS 394: "The Golden Age of Opera" (2 LPs)
Issued April, 1967
MATRIX P-1176

SIDES 1-4 (394 A-D):

MADAME SANS-GÊNE (Giordano) (I)
Opera in 3 acts (complete)
Orchestra and Chorus of Radio Italiana [RAI], Milano/Arturo Basile
RAI broadcast, Milan, 10 Aug 1957

CAST:
Magda Laszló (*Caterina*); Danilo Vega (*Lefèbvre*); Carlo Tagliabue (*Napoleone*); Danilo Cestari (*Count Niepergg*); Danilo Cestari (*Vinaigre*); Carlo Perucci (*Fouché*); Irene Callaway (*Toniotta*); Irene Callaway (*Queen Carolina*); Maria Montereala (*Giulia*); Maria Montereala (*Princess Elisa*); Renato Berti (*Despreaux*); Maria Luisa Malacchi (*La Rossa*); Maria Luisa Malacchi (*Signora di Bülow*); Maria Luisa Malacchi (*A Voice*); Enzo Viaro (*Gelsomino*); Enzo Viaro (*De Brigode*); Enzo Viaro (*Roustan*); Aurora Cattelani (*Leroy*).

EJS 395: "The Golden Age of Opera (3 LPs)
Issued April, 1967
MATRIX EJS 395 A-F

SIDES 1-6 (395 A-F):

HERCULES [ERACLE] (Handel) (I)
Oratorio (complete)
Orchestra and Chorus of the Teatro alla Scala, Milano/Lovro von Matačič
Broadcast, La Scala, Milan, 29 Dec 1958

CAST:
Elisabeth Schwarzkopf (*Jole*); Fedora Barbieri (*Dejanira*); Franco Corelli (*Illo*); Ettore Bastianini (*Lica*); Jerome Hines (*Eracle*); Agostino Ferrin (*A High Priest*); Vittorio Tatozzi (*A Weaver*); Adriana Macchiaioli (*Erastia*).

EJS 396: The Golden Age of Opera" (2 LP)
Issued May, 1967
MATRIX P-1267

SIDES 1-4 (396 A-D):

ALZIRA (Verdi) (I)
Opera in 2 acts and a Prologue (complete)
Orchestra and Chorus of the Teatro dell'Opera, Roma/Franco Capuana
Broadcast, Teatro dell'Opera, Rome, RAI, 12 Feb or 16 Mar 1967

CAST:
Virginia Zeani (*Alzira*); Gianfranco Cecchele (*Zamoro*); Cornell McNeil (*Gusmano*); Carlo Cava (*Alvaro*); Saverio Forzano (*Ovando*); Mario Rinaudo (*Ataliba*); Bianca Bortoluzzi (*Zulma*); Sergio Tedesco (*Otumbo*).

NOTES: EJS 396

ALZIRA (1845), based on Voltaire's ALZIRE, OU LES AMÉRICAINES (1730), libretto by S. Cammarano, was one of Verdi's few genuine failures. This broadcast was taken from the first production of its modern revival.

This performance is dated 12 February, 1967 in Roger Beaumont's excellent Zeani discography in *The Record Collector*, 36/1 (March, 1991), p. 51. The conflict between the two dates has not been resolved.

The performance has been reissued on MRF-8, Melodram CD 27013, Verona CD 27042/43, and GFC 036/7.

EJS 397: "The Golden Age of Opera" (1 LP)
Issued May, 1967
MATRIX: P-1270

SIDE 1 (397 A):

"GERALDINE FARRAR (1935-37) / MARY GARDEN"

1. a) w. pf/Geraldine Farrar: HÄNSEL UND GRETEL, Act II: When I lay me down to sleep [Abends, will ich schlafen geh'n] (Humperdinck) (E)
   Recorded Metropolitan Opera House, NYC, 22 December, 1934
   [Rehearsal for Metropolitan Opera broadcast, ***INTERMISSION FEATURE***, 25 Dec 1934]

* b) w. pf/Geraldine Farrar: KÖNIGSKINDER, Act III: O Where are you gone, dear children? [Wohin bist du gegangen] (Humperdinck) (E)
   Recorded Metropolitan Opera House, NYC, 22 Dec 1934
   [Rehearsal for Metropolitan Opera broadcast, ***INTERMISSION FEATURE***, 25 Dec 1934]

* c) w. pf/Geraldine Farrar: DIE WALKÜRE, Act III: Farewell thou fairest, best belov'd child [Leb' wohl] ["Wotan's Farewell"] (Wagner) (E)
   Recorded Metropolitan Opera House, NYC, 26 Jan 1935
   [Rehearsal for Metropolitan Opera broadcast, ***INTERMISSION FEATURE***, 2 Feb 1935]

* d) w. pf/Geraldine Farrar: DIE WALKÜRE, Act I: Medley: Winter storms have waked to a magic moon [Winterstürme] . . . You are the spring [Du bist der Lenz] (Wagner) (G)
   Recorded Metropolitan Opera House, NYC, 26 Jan 1935
   [Rehearsal for Metropolitan Opera broadcast, ***INTERMISSION FEATURE***, 2 Feb 1935]

* e) w. pf/Geraldine Farrar: ROMÉO ET JULIETTE, Act II: Qui m'écoute . . . je t'aime! (Gounod) (F)
   Recorded Metropolitan Opera House, NYC, 24 Jan 1935
   [Rehearsal for Metropolitan Opera broadcast, ***INTERMISSION FEATURE***, 26 Jan 1935]

* f) w. pf/Geraldine Farrar: LA DAMNATION DE FAUST, Part IV: D'amour l'ardente flamme [fragment] (Berlioz) (F)
   Recorded Metropolitan Opera House, NYC, 15 Mar 1935
   [Rehearsal for Metropolitan Opera broadcast, ***INTERMISSION FEATURE***, probably 16 Mar 1935]

* g) w. pf/Geraldine Farrar: MEFISTOFELE, Act III: Lontano, lontano [fragment] (Boïto) (I)
   Recorded Metropolitan Opera House, NYC, 15 Mar 1935
   [Rehearsal for Metropolitan Opera broadcast, ***INTERMISSION FEATURE***, probably 16 Mar 1935]

* h) w. pf/Geraldine Farrar: LA TRAVIATA, fragments:
1. Act II: Dite alla giovine . . . ah sventura
2. Act II: Di provenza
3. Act I: Ah, fors è lui
4. Act I: Sempre libera . . . sempre lieta ne'ritrovi
5. Act III: Addio del passato . . . gia sono pallenti
6. Act I: Tra voi saprò dividere ["Brindisi"]
7. Act III: Parigi, o cara . . . la mia salute rifiorira

Recorded Metropolitan Opera House, NYC, 4 Jan 1935
[Rehearsal for Metropolitan Opera broadcast, ***INTERMISSION FEATURE***, 5 Jan 1935]

* i) w. pf/Geraldine Farrar: HJERTETS MELODIER, Op. 5, no. 3: I Love Thee [Jeg elsker dig] (Anderson-Grieg) (E)
Source and date unknown

* j) w. pf/?Geraldine Farrar or Frank Black: AN DIE MUSIK, D. 547: Thou gracious art [Du holde Kunst] (Schober-Schubert) (E)
Electrical Transcription, ***AMERICAN RADIATOR HOUR*** [Auditon], MS-88878-1 / MS 88879-1 New York, circa March, 1935

"MARY GARDEN"

* 2. w. orch/Rosario Bourdon: RISURREZIONE, Act II: Voici l'heure! . . . Dieu de grâce [Giunge il treno . . . Dio pietoso] (Alfano) (F)
?CVE-36735-5 Camden, 3 Nov 1926 Victor unpub

* 3. w. pf/Jean Dansereau: "The Dreary Steppe," Op. 5, no. 1 ["Over the Stepp"] (Gretchaninov) (E)
?BVE-36733-5/-8 Camden, 24 Dec 1926, or 22 Nov 1927
Victor unpub

* 4. ROSA PONSELLE, soprano (w. orch/Josef Pasternack): "Little Old Garden" ["Sanctuary"] (Hewitt)
BVE-32850-2 Camden, 1 Jun 1925 Victor unpublished HMV VA 67

SIDE 2 (397 B):

"LAWRENCE TIBBETT (1934-37)"

* 1. w. orch/Alexander Smallens: RIGOLETTO, Act II: Cortigiani, vil razza dannata (Verdi) (I)
CS-02173-2 New York or Camden, 19 October, 1936
Victor (14182) unpub

* 2. w. orch/Alexander Smallens: "Hallelujah Rhythm" (Jacques Wolfe) (E)
CS-02175-1 or -1A New York or Camden, 19 October, 1936
Victor unpub

3. w. orch/Wilfred Pelletier: "Minnelied" (Brahms) (E)
Broadcast, ***PACKARD HOUR***, WJZ, NYC, 27 Nov 1934

* 4. w. orch/Wilfred Pelletier or Donald Voorhees: CARMEN, Act II: Votre toast ["Toreador Song"] (Bizet) (F)
Broadcast, ***PACKARD HOUR***, WJZ, NYC, 18 Sep 1934 or 14 Jan 1936

* 5. w. orch/?: "Amor, amor" (Pirandelli) (I)
Broadcast, ?*PACKARD HOUR*, circa 1937

* 6. w. orch/Wilfred Pelletier: I PAGLIACCI, Act I: Vesti la giubba (Leoncavallo) (I)
Broadcast, ***PACKARD HOUR***, WJZ, NYC, ?25 Sep 1934

* 7. w. orch/Wilfred Pelletier: I PAGLIACCI, Act I: Si pùo? [Prologue] (Leoncavallo) (I)
Broadcast, ***PACKARD HOUR***, WJZ, NYC, 25 Sep 1934

8. w. pf/Stewart Wille: "On the Road to Mandalay" (Kipling-Speaks) (E)
CVE-45190-1 New York or Camden, 29 May 1928 Victor unpub

* 9. w. pf/?Stewart Wille: "De Glory Road" (Clement Wood-Jacques Wolfe) (E)
from the soundtrack of the feature film, ***METROPOLITAN***
(20th Century-Fox, 1935)
Hollywood, April-August, 1935
LP 6065 c8 Nov 1935 (Twntieth Century-Fox Film Corp.)
New York premiere: Radio City Music Hall, NYC, 17 Oct 1935

NOTES: EJS 397

Side 1 (397 A):

The Farrar Intermission features were recorded in Box 42 of the Metropolitan Opera House. Though heard *live* on-the-air, those featured here are rehearsals, pre-recorded for purposes of timing a few days prior to their intended broadcasts. All were recorded on 12-inch aluminum discs at 78 rpm, inside start. They are not numbered, but all are designated as broadcast no. 5-9 and all but 1a and 1b have plain NBC labels (the latter two have no labels). See the note for EJS 107 (1956) for details of these programs. With the exception of two fragments from "The Four Marguerites" (16 March, 1935) and the complete TRAVIATA Intermission (5 January, 1935), only the pre-recorded *rehearsal* versions, the "run-throughs," appear to have survived. All of the Intermission items featured on EJS 397 subsequently appeared in lengthier form on the IRCC LP L-7033 (1968), except the pre-recorded TRAVIATA "Di provenza" and the "Marguerites" of Berlioz and Boïto (the live versions of the latter two were included subsequently on IRCC L-7033). The title of EJS 397 is incorrect: all of this material dates from 1933-1935.

At 33.3 rpm, pitches are slightly flat for the Farrar excerpts.

Note that in all cases the excerpts performed here are *fragments*, usually no more than the first few phrases of the arias and ensembles.

The spoken introductions (by Farrar) for the two Wagner items (1c-d) and the TRAVIATA "Ah fors è lui" have been omitted from EJS 397, though they are contained on the original acetates.

Band 1a-b: Originally recorded on five twelve-inch aluminum sides. Farrar created the role of the *Goose Girl* in KÖNIGSKINDER at the Met on 28 December, 1910. Gruber's "Silent Night," which has not yet appeared on LP, was also performed on the broadcast (Farrar's pre-recorded version exists). John L. Johnston, president of Listerine, that season's sponsor of the Met broadcasts, also appeared during the intermission.

Farrar's piano introduction to the HÄNSEL UND GRETEL and postlude to the KÖNIGSKINDER are omitted from EJS 397, as are her lengthy opening remarks for both.

Bands 1c-d: Farrar's piano postlude to "*Wotan's* Farewell" is retained here, where it was shortened on IRCC L-7033. Her lengthy spoken introductions to the Wagner excerpts, however, have been omitted from EJS 397. The original twelve-inch aluminum discs (four sides) carry the label date "26 Jan 35."

Bands 1e: Labeled as "FAUST: Il est coute" on EJS 397. The original aluminum acetates of this performance (three twelve-inch sides), pre-recorded two days before the actual broadcast and dated "1/24/35" on the labels, also contain a spoken excerpt by Farrar from the Act II/ii balcony scene of Shakespeare's ROMEO and JULIET ("O gentle Romeo, If thou dost love, pronounce it faithfully . . . Which the dark night hath so discovered"), offered in contrast to Gounod's realization of the same scene. Bisecting the Gounod is a noisy acetate break between "je t'aime," where the EJS 397 transfer ends, and "N'accuse pas mon coeur . . . A trahi le mistère," the point at which the second acetate ends This concluding section can be heard on IRCC L-3033. "Et je te crois! . . . Comme tu peux te fier à moi-même!" was consumed altogether by the change of discs, while *Roméo's* five lines were omitted by the singer.

The 26 January, 1935 ROMÉO broadcast is preserved in its entirety as UORC 175 (November, 1973), but without the Farrar Intermission excerpts: the live versions of these two short extracts are not known to have been transcribed. Farrar's description of the new electrical equipment installed for the 1934-1935 broadcast season, to which she devoted a good deal of time during this Intermission, has yet to appear on LP.

Band 1f-g: The live broadcast versions of the Berlioz and Boïto excerpts were originally issued by IRCC as "The Four Marguerites," first on the 12-inch 78 rpm IRCC 144 (May, 1939) and later on the ten-inch LP IRCC L-7001 (August, 1954) and twelve-inch IRCC L-7033, "Memories of Geraldine Farrar" (1968). The first and second Marguerites, missing from EJS 397 but included on the IRCC issues, were Schubert's ("Gretchen am Spinnrade," introduced by Farrar as "Margarethe am Spinnrade") and Gounod's. The two excerpts appearing on EJS 397 were pre-recorded a day earlier on a single twelve-inch aluminum side: in the broadcast version, Farrar translates "D'amour l'ardente flamme" as "Love is the Ardent Flame," whereas "The Flame of Ardent Love" was offered in the pre-recorded version; the broadcast version, moreover, begins with a five-note arpeggio in the piano introduction, while the run-through begins with a different four-note arpeggio. The Boïto varies more in the spoken introductions, wherein Farrar omits her original reference to "*Faust's* awakening under his [*Mefistofele's*] influence" from the broadcast version. The MEFISTOFELE introduction is severely cut, however, on the EJS 397 transfer.

"The Four Marguerites" was broadcast during the intermission of the 16 March, 1935 AÏDA. The original acetates for both lack the introductions by Milton Cross that might have explained Farrar's unexpected choice of material. The IRCC bulletin no. 83 for May, 1939 notes that all of the fragments were "recorded electrically from the Metropolitan Opera House . . . [and] issued by special permission of Miss Farrar and the National Broadcasting Company," so that the possibility that these recordings were used (or re-used) for a more appropriate broadcast seems slight.

Band 1h: Pre-recorded a day before the 5 January, 1935 Met broadcast of the Ponselle TRAVIATA, as issued complete as EJS 107 (1956) and on one of Smith's "special" labels, MOP 2, a two-disc reissue of EJS 107. The Farrar intermission excerpts featured on these LPs were in fact recorded *live* from the actual broadcast: the pre-recorded versions are noticeably different in both the musical performances and Farrar's commentaries. In addition to her singing and her analysis of the opera, this intermission (as pre-recorded and broadcast live) contains anecdotes about hearing Ponselle's *Violetta* for the first time in 1921, singing the role to Caruso's *Alfredo* in 1908 (she claims 1907), and her own early performances of the opera, notably in Berlin. IRCC L-7033 contains the pre-recorded versions, but without the "Di provenza" and much of the running commentary.

In an especially interesting introduction to the "Addio del passato," Farrar recalls performing the aria for Cosima Wagner during her early years in Berlin, impressing the matron of Bayreuth in spite of the fact that she was unable to perform a Wagner excerpt at the gathering!

Band 1i: Announced by Farrar, "'I Love Thee,' by Edvard Grieg." This item is *not* from American Radiator audition of 1933 (see 1j below).

Band 1j: This Schubert song, announced and sung in English, was taken from two undated RCA Victor electrical transcriptions labeled "American Radiator Company Audition (Geraldine Farrar)," matrices MS-88878-1 and MS-88879-1. These were apparently studio-recorded auditions for "Geraldine Farrar's Sunday Evenings at Home," to be sponsored by American Radiator, and featured soprano Louise Bernhardt, baritone George Reynolds, and conductor Frank Black, who may have accompanied Farrar's "Ode to Music." Bernhardt sang "Last Night the Nightingale Woke Me" and the DON GIOVANNI "Là ci darem la mano" with Reynolds; Reynolds sang Del Riego's "O, Dry those Tears."

Farrar was slated to introduce two "young American singers" on each broadcast, then accompany herself in a song at about midpoint. Louise Bernhardt was featured on this program and is introduced on the original discs as having made her Chicago Opera debut "last year under Mr. Witherspoon." Witherspoon only managed the 1931-1932 Chicago season, and it would appear from Ronald Davis' *Opera in Chicago* (New York: Appleton-Century, 1966) that Bernhardt's first performance there was 2 January, 1932, suggesting a 1933 recording date. Bernhardt's New York Town Hall debut took place on Sunday, 27 October, 1935, which has lead some to suspect that this radio audition may date from as late as November, 1935. The matrix numbers, however, tell still another story: CS-88807-1 was recorded on 1 March, 1935 and BS-88843-1 on 6 March, 1935, and while a block of numbers may well have been held back out of sequence for these NBC "MS"-prefix transcriptions, March, 1935 seems the likeliest recording date for these Farrar items.

American Radiator sponsored a half-hour show beginning in the 1934-1935 season, officially titled the ***AMERICAN RADIATOR HOUR***, but also known as the ***FIRESIDE RECITAL***, for which this Farrar audition may have been a prototype. The show's regular conductor was Frank Black and the featured artists were bass-baritone Sigurd Nilsson and tenor Hardesty Johnson (Nilsson was a regular from 1935 to 1937). These shows ran on Sunday evenings for 15-minutes over station WEAF, New York City. No evidence has been found documenting any actual Farrar broadcasts from 1933, which suggests, obviously that Farrar's was an audition (what would be called a "pilot" today), for a show that either failed to sell, or which Farrar evidentally decided against pursuing.

"Ode to Music," without the spoken introduction heard on EJS 397, was issued on IRCC L-7033 in 1968 (from Farrar's own copy of the transcriptions), labeled circa 1931.

Bands 2-3: Unpublished takes. These differ significantly from the published versions of the RISURREZIONE aria on Victor 6623 (CVE-36735-6, recorded in Camden, 3 November, 1926) and the Gretchaninov song on Victor 1539 (BVE-36733-11, recorded in New York, 5 November, 1929): the beginning phrases of *Caterina's* recitative and the last phrase of the aria make the unpublished and published takes easy to distinguish; similarly, Garden's phrasing of the first measures of the Gretchaninov song is entirely different in the take used on EJS 397.

Determining the actual take numbers used here is more difficult: presumably, only takes marked "hold" in the Victor books *should* have survived, but exceptions to this logical assumption have been documented elsewhere.

The disposition of the RISURREZIONE aria is as follows, where "d" is "destroy," "h" is "hold," and "m" is "master." Take -5, which will appear on "The Mary Garden Edition," a Romophone CD currently in preparation, was probably the one used on EJS 397:

CVE-36735-1, 2, 3	26 Oct 1926	d, d, d		
-4, 5, 6	3 Nov 1926	d, h, m	Victor 6623	AGSB 44

The Gretchaninov takes are more complicated. More than likely, tests of either take -5 or take -8 survived:

BVE-36733-1	25 Oct 1926	d		
-2, 3	26 Oct 1926	d, d		
-4	9 Dec 1926	d		
-5, 6, 7	24 Dec 1926	h, d, d		
-8, 9	22 Nov 1927	h, d		
-10, 11	5 Nov 1929	d, m	Victor 1539	HMV VA 18

An alternate, unpublished take of Garden's electrical LOUISE "Depuis le jour" (probably matrix CVE-40736-1, recorded in New York, 23 November, 1927), accompanied by pianist Jean Dansereau, was issued on the LP "Unforgettable Voices in Unforgotten Performances from the French Operatic Repertoire" (Victrola VIC 1394 and Italian RCA LM 20115) in 1969, and will appear, along with ten other unpublished Garden Victors, on the afore-mentioned CD, "The Mary Garden Edition," produced by Ward Marston for the Romophone label. The unpublished Gretchaninov take(s), however, was not slated for inclusion on that CD.

Band 4: Labeled as Mary Garden's "Somewhere a Voice is Calling" on EJS 397 (meaning the unpublished take, BVE-40735-4, recorded in New York, 5 November, 1929, Dansereau accompanying). This is in fact Ponselle's "Little Old Garden," unpublished except as HMV "Archive" series VA 67, and which had already appeared on EJS 192 (October, 1960). This is take -2: both BVE-32850-1 and -3 were marked "d" in the Victor books.

The unpublished fourth take of Garden's "Somewhere a Voice is Calling" has circulated for years on special vinyl pressings, and was eventually included on EJS 452, "Potpourri 22" (December, 1968), where the title and singer are at least identified correctly. Subsequently, the unpublished first take from 22 November, 1927 appeared on the Voce LP "Great Singers" (VOCE-88); both takes 1 and 4 will apear on the forthcoming Romophone CD.

Side 2 (397 B):

Many of these Tibbett performances have appeared on LP, just as many of the unpublished Victors have circulated privately as special vinyl pressings.

Band 1: This "Cortigiani" has more recently appeared on OASI 5861 and Met 404.

Band 2: It is not known which of the unpublished takes of the "Hallelujah Rhythm" survived, though CS-02175-1 and 1A contain the same performance recorded on different lathes.

Band 4: The 18 September, 1934 show, conducted by Pelletier, was Tibbett's first regularly-scheduled ***PACKARD HOUR*** appearance. The 1936 broadcast was conducted by Voorhees. The performance plays in score pitch at 34.5 rpm. See the endnote for EJS 110 (1957) for details of Tibbett's ***PACKARD HOUR*** appearances.

Band 5: "Pirandelli" is given as the composer in the standard Tibbett discographies, but this may be the work of violinist and composer Pier Adolfo *Tirindelli* (1858-1937), who was active as a teacher at the Cincinnati Conservatory from 1920.

Bands 6-7: The "Vesti la Guibba" is sung a half-step below score pitch, and without the recitative--though in fact there is no evidence that the recitative was *not* performed, and was simply omitted from either the original transcription or from this LP dubbing. Another broadcast version of the aria from 21 January, 1936, sung *with* the recitative, appeared earlier on EJS 124 (1958): see the endnote for EJS 124 (II/2). The 24 September, 1934 broadcast contained a medley billed "Selections from Pagliacci," in which Tibbett sang excerpts of *Tonio*, *Canio* and *Silvio*--the likeliest source of the two PAGLIACCI arias featured on EJS 397 (almost certainly the source of the "Prologue").
Both PAGLIACCI excerpts play in their correct pitches at 34.2 rpm.

Band 8: Unlike the 10 October, 1935 Victor recording of "On the Road to Mandalay" (CS-95371-1, issued as Victor 11877, 11-8862 and HMV DB 3036), this version begins with an introduction taken from the chorus of the song.

Band 9: An acetate of this performance, taken from the original recording, not the soundtrack, is announced "13 hundred, F-93" by a male voice, while a disc of alternate endings is reported to be numbered 1378-25. The complete acetate performance is identical to the one featured on EJS 397, and has turned up on a number of other LPs (OASI 586, Glendale GL 8001, etc.). It is definitely the version featured on the actual soundtrack of ***METROPOLITAN***. "De Glory Road" was coprighted in 1928, and carries a dedication to Paul Robeson, who never chose to record it.

EJS 398: "The Golden Age of Opera" (1 LP)
Issued May, 1967
MATRIX P-1268

"VICTORIA DE LOS ANGELES"

SIDE 1 (398 A):

* 1. a) w. pf/Pablo Casals: Op. 107, no. 3: Das Mädchen spricht (Gruppe-Brahms) (G)
Source and date unknown
b) w. pf/Pablo Casals: Op. 43, no. 2: Die Mainacht (Hölty-Brahms) (G)
Source and date unknown
c) w. pf/Pablo Casals: Op. Op. 71, no. 3: Geheimnis (Candidus-Brahms) (G)
Source and date unknown
d) w. pf/Pablo Casals: Op. 49, no. 4: "Wiegenlied" (Scherer-Brahms) (G)
Source and date unknown
e) w. pf/Pablo Casals: Op. 84, no. 4: Vergebliches Ständchen (trad.-Brahms) (G)
Source and date unknown

IL COMBATTIMENTO DI TANCREDI E CLORINDA (Monteverdi) (I)
Dramatic cantata (complete)
Orchestra of the Teatro São Carlos, Lisbon/Napoleone Annovazzi
?Broadcast, Teatro São Carlo, Lisbon, 10 Nov 1944

CAST:
Victoria de Los Angeles (*Narrator*); Maria Del Pilar Farcada (*Clorinda*); Raimundo Torres (*Tancredi*).

* 2. Complete

SIDE 2 (398 B):

* 1. * a) w. guitar/Victoria De Los Angeles: Spanish Song (sic)
Private party, Lisbon, 12 Nov 1944
* b) w. guitar/Victoria De Los Angeles: Spanish Song (sic)
Private party, Lisbon, 12 Nov 1944
* c) w. guitar/Victoria De Los Angeles: Spanish Song (sic)
Private party, Lisbon, 12 Nov 1944
* d) w. pf/?: Op. 49, no. 4: "Wiegenlied" (Scherer-Brahms) (G)
Private party, Lisbon, 12 Nov 1944
* e) w. male voices: "Spanish Song" (sic)
Private party, Lisbon, 12 Nov 1944
* f) w. guitar/Victoria De Los Angeles: Spanish Song (sic)
Private party, Lisbon, 12 Nov 1944
g) w. RAIMUNDO TORRES, baritone (pf/?): LA SERVA PADRONE, No. 4: Lo conosco a quegli occhietti (Pergolesi) (I)
Private party, Lisbon, 12 Nov 1944
h) w. RAIMUNDO TORRES, baritone (pf/?): LA SERVA PADRONE, No. 7: Per te ho io nel core (Pergolesi) (I)
Private party, Lisbon, 12 Nov 1944

* 2. w. ?Bayreuth Festival Orchestra/?Wolfgang Sawallisch: TANNHÄUSER, Act II: Dich, teure Halle! (Wagner) (G)
Broadcast, Bayreuth Festival, Bayreuth, 23 Jul 1961 or 26 Jul 1962

NOTES: EJS 398

Side 1 (398 A):

Band 1: The source and date of these Brahms songs, accompanied by Casals, has not been determined. Prades (France) and Puerto Rico have been suggested as the location of the recording(s) or broadcast(s).

Band 2: This 10 November, 1944 Lisbon performance of Monteverdi's IL COMBATTIMENTO DI TANCREDI E CLORINDA is given in the May, 1967 bulletin as De Los Angeles' debut, but in fact, accounts of this important occasion vary. By some, she made her debut three years earlier in 1941 while a student at the Barcelona Conservatory in Monteverdi's ORFEO, and her professional stage debut in the same year at the Teatro Victoria in Barcelona as *Mimi*. An obscure De Los Angeles biography claims that she first sang professionally in Lisbon in 1942. Other sources claim that her recital debut was made in Barcelona in *May*, 1944 and her operatic debut at the Teatro Liceo, Barcelona, in January, 1945 as the *Countess* in NOZZE. The 1992 edition of *Baker's Biographical Dictionary of Musicians*, p. 42, claims that her operatic debut was at the Barcelona Teatro *Lirico* (sic) in 1946!

The COMBATTIMENTO may have been a back-stage recording, not a broadcast.

Side 2 (398 B):

Band 1: According to the May, 1967 bulletin and other credible reports, the eight items sung here were recorded at a private party in Lisbon two days after De Los Angeles' debut.

The identity of the "Spanish Songs" has not been determined.

Band 1d: Introduced by an unidentified American. Henry Pleasants, who was serving in the American G-2 intelligence unit at the time, wrote about the European musical scene for a number of publications while stationed there during the Second World War, has been suggested as the announcer. But when asked about this recently at his home in London, Mr. Pleasants denied his presence at the party.

Band 1e: Sung by several male voices, with De Los Angeles providing the obbligato.

Band 2: De Los Angeles never sang *Elisabeth* at the Met or for RAI, so this "Dich, teure Halle!" probably came from one of several Bayreuth Festival performances, where she sang the role in 1961 and 1962. A July 1961 performance, with Dietrich Fischer-Dieskau, Grace Bumbry, and Wolfgang Windgassen, conducted by Wolfgang Sawallisch and broadcast on 23 July, 1961, has appeared on several private LPs (Melodram, HRE, etc.), so is the likeliest choice. However, the first performance of the following season, on 26 July, 1962, may also have been broadcast, after which De Los Angeles was replaced by Anja Silja.

EJS 399: "The Golden Age of Opera" (1 LP)
Issued May, 1967
MATRIX: P-1269

SIDE 1 (399 A):

LOHENGRIN (Wagner) (G)
Opera in acts (excerpts)
Orchestra and Chorus of the Bayreuth Festival/Wilhelm Furtwängler
Broadcast, Bayreuth Festival, Bayreuth, 19 Jul 1936

CAST:
Franz Völker (*Lohengrin*); Maria Müller (*Elsa*); Margarete Klose (*Ortrud*); Josef Von Manowarda (*King Heinrich*); [Jaroslav Prohaska] (*Telramund*); [Herbert Janssen (*The King's Herald*)].

* 1. a) Radio announcement (in German)

Act III: b) CAST and Chorus: Prelude . . . Das süsse Lied verhallt . . . Atme ich Wonnen, die nur Gott verleiht!
c) MANOWARDA and Chorus: [Horn passage] . . . Heil König Heinrich! . . . Die Mannen sind's des Telramund
d) VÖLKER and Chorus: In fernem Land . . . Hör ich so seine höchste
e) VÖLKER, KLOSE, and MÜLLER: Mein lieber Schwan . . . to the end of the opera

SIDE 2 (399 B):

* 1. MAX LORENZ, tenor; ANNI KONETZNI, soprano; and MARGARETE KLOSE, contralto (Wiener Philharmoniker/Wilhelm Furtwängler): TRISTAN UND ISOLDE, Act II: [Nie wieder erwarchens wahnlos hold bewusster] Wunsch . . . Einsam wachend in der Nacht ["Brangänes Wachtlied"] (Wagner) (G)
Broadcast, Wiener Staatsoper, Vienna, 25 Dec 1941

2. KIRSTEN FLAGSTAD, soprano (Royal Philharmonic Orchestra/Sir Thomas Beecham): TRISTAN UND ISOLDE, Act III: Mild und liese ["Liebestod"] (Wagner) (G)
Broadcast, ***ROYAL PHILHARMONIC CONCERT***, BBC, London, 21 Dec 1952

DER FLIEGENDE HOLLÄNDER (Wagner)
Opera in 3 acts (excerpts)
Wiener Philharmoniker and Chorus of the Wiener Staatsoper/Leopold Reichwein
Broadcast, Wiener Staatsoper, Vienna, 29 Mar 1942

CAST:
Hans Hotter (*Holländer*); Hilde Konetzni (*Senta*).

3. Act I: a) HOTTER and Chorus: Die Frist ist um . . . Ew'ge Vernichtung, nimm mich auf
b) HOTTER: Durch Sturm und bösen Wind verschlagen . . . so sollst du sicher deines Verteils sein

Act II: c) HOTTER and KONETZNI: Wie aus der Ferne längst vergang'ner Zeiten . . . lass es die Kraft der Treue sein!

NOTES: EJS 399

Side 1 (399 A):

Issued subsequently on Fonit-Cetra FE 25 and Acanta FK 40.23520.

A number of 1936 LOHENGRIN excerpts conducted by Heinz Tietjen, the Artistic Director of Bayreuth from 1931-1944, have appeared on LP (American Telefunken TH 97003 and TH 97008), but these are commercial recordings, originally issued on Telefunken 78s and its subsidiary label, *Bayreuth*. The cast of these is identical, however, to that of the 19 July, 1936 Furtwängler performance given here.

Preiser also issued a 1942 performance of LOHENGRIN with virtually the same cast, Ludwig Hofmann replacing Manowarda.

Side 2 (399 B):

Band 1: Dated *1942* on the label of EJS 399 and in the May, 1967 bulletin.

Band 2: Flagstad also sang the Wagner WESENDONCK LIEDER on this broadcast recital, accompanied by the Royal Philharmonic under Beecham.

EJS 400: "The Golden Age of Opera" (2 LPs)
Issued June, 1967
MATRIX: P-1300

SIDES 1-4 (400 A-D):

EDGAR (Puccini) (I)
Opera in 4 acts (complete)
Fulham Municipal Orchestra, and Chorus of the Hammersmith Opera Company/Joseph Vandernoot
In-house recording, Hammersmith Opera, Fulham, England, 6 Apr 1967

CAST:
Edward Byles (*Edgar*); Angela Rubini (*Fidelia*); Doreen Doyle (*Tigrana*); Michael Rippon (*Frank*); Graham Nicholls (*Gualtiero*).

NOTES: EJS 400

The June, 1967 bulletin notes that Puccini's second opera, EDGAR, first performed at La Scala on 21 April, 1889, was until EJS 400, "utterly unrepresented locally by even a single commercial disc on 78 or long playing records." Evidently, "locally" meant the U.S., for as matter of fact, the Scala Orchestra recorded the third act Intermezzo in the early 1930s, issued on HMV S 10368.

EJS 401: "The Golden Age of Opera" (1 LP)
Issued June, 1967
MATRIX P-1302

SIDES 1-2 (401 A-B):

MESE MARIANO (Giordano) (I)
Opera in 1 act (complete)
Orchestra and Chorus of the Teatro San Carlo di Napoli/Franco Carracciolo
Broadcast, Teatro San Carlo, Naples, 4 Feb 1967

CAST:
Clara Petrella (*Carmela*); Ada Finelli (*The Countess*); Giampiero Malaspina (*The Rector*); Rosa Laghezza (*Mother Superior*); Mafalda Micheluzzi (*Sister Pazienza*); Vittoria Magnaghi (*Sister Celeste*); Maja Sunara (*Sister Cristiana*); Pia Ferrara (*Sister Agnese*); Lia Palumbo (*Sister Maria*); Luciana Lattes (*A Child*); Rosella Colosimo (*A Child*).

EJS 402: The Golden Age of Opera" (1 LP)
Issued June, 1967
MATRIX P-1301

IL TROVATORE (Verdi) (I)
Opera in 4 acts (excerpts)
Orchestra and Chorus of the Royal Opera, Stockholm/Herbert Sandberg
Broadcast, Royal Opera, Stockholm, 6 Mar 1960

CAST:
Hjördis Schymberg (*Leonora*); Jussi Bjoerling (*Manrico*); Hugo Hasslo (*Count di Luna*); Kerstin Meyer (*Azucena*); [Ingeborg Kjellgren (*Inez*)]; Olle Sivall (*Ruiz*); Sture Ingebretsen (*A Messenger*); [Erik Saeden (*Ferrando*)]; Bertil Alstergard (*A Gypsy*).

SIDE 1 (402 A):

Act I: 1. BJOERLING, HASSLO, SCHYMBERG, INGEBRETSEN: Deserto sulla terra . . . to the end of the act

Act II: 1. MEYER, BJOERLING, ALSTERGARD, and Chorus: Mesta è la tua canzon! . . . Mal reggendo . . . Un momento può involarmi

SIDE 2 (402 B):

Act III: 1. BJOERLING, SCHYMBERG, and SIVALL and Chorus: Alto è il periglio! . . . Ah! si, ben mio . . . Di quella pira

Act IV: 2. a) SCHYMBERG, BJOERLING, and Chorus: Miserere . . . Quel suon
b) BJOERLING, MEYER, SCHYMBERG, and HASSLO: Madre? Non dormi? . . . through the end of the opera

NOTES: EJS 402

Though broadcast in its entirety, this TROVATORE has never been issued complete on LP. The "Alto è il periglio! . . . Ah si, ben mio" later appeared on HRE 215-1.

Swedish Radio tape: MK 60/142 (complete broadcast).

EJS 403: "The Golden Age of Opera" (1 LP)
Issued June, 1967
MATRIX P-1303

"BENIAMINO GIGLI IN OPERA"

SIDE 1 (403 A):

* 1. w. MARION TALLEY, soprano (Vitaphone Symphony Orchestra/Herman Heller): LUCIA DI LAMMERMOOR, Act I: Lucia perdona . . . sulla tomba . . . Verranno a te sull'aure (Donizetti) (I)
from the soundtrack of the one-reel Warner Brothers-Vitaphone short ***MARION TALLEY, SOPRANO, AND BENIAMINO GIGLI, TENOR, OF THE METROPOLITAN OPERA COMPANY SINGING VERRANNO A TE SULL'AURA (BORNE ON THE SIGHING BREEZE) FROM ACT 1 OF THE OPERA LUCIA DI LAMMERMOOR*** (1927), New York, 1926-1927
Vitaphone Varieties 499
MP 3973; c30 Apr 1927
Premiere: New York City, 28 May 1927

* 2. a) w. CORRADO ZAMBELLI, bass, and CARLO TAGLIABUE, baritone (London Philharmonic Orchestra and the Royal Opera House Chorus/Vittorio Gui): RIGOLETTO, Act III: La donna è mobile (Verdi) (I)
Broadcast, Covent Garden, London, 6 Jun 1938

b) w. MARION TALLEY, soprano; JEANNE GORDON, contralto; and GIUSEPPE DE LUCA, baritone (Vitaphone Symphony Orchestra/ Herman Heller): RIGOLETTO, Act III: Un dì, se ben rammentomi . . . Bella figlia del'amore (Verdi) (I)
from the sountrack of the one-reel Warner Brothers-Vitaphone short ***QUARTETTE FROM RIGOLETTO; MARION TALLEY, GIUSEPPE DE LUCA, BENIAMINO GIGLI, AND JEANNE GORDON, SINGING THE QUARTETTE NUMBER FROM THE 3rd ACT OF VERDI'S OPERA, RIGOLETTO*** (1927), New York, 1926-1927
Vitaphone Varieties 415
MP 3923; c4 Apr 1927
Premiere: Selwyn Theater, New York City, 3 Feb 1927

* 3. w. GIUSEPPE DE LUCA, baritone (Vitaphone Symphony Orchestra/ Herman Heller): LES PÊCHEURS DE PERLES, Act I: Sei tu che dinnanzi mi sta . . . Del tempio al limitar [C'est toi! toi qu' enfin je revois . . . Au fond du temple] (Bizet) (I)
from the soundtrack of the one-reel Warner Brothers-Vitaphone short ***BENIAMINO GIGLI AND GIUSEPPE DE LUCA IN DUET FROM ACT I OF "THE PEARL FISHERS" (PESCATORI DI PERLE) . . . BIZET*** (1928), New York, ?6 Apr 1927
Vitaphone Varieties 518
MP 4826; c15 Mar 1928
Premiere: Warners' Theater, New York City, 14 Mar 1928

SIDE 2 (403 B):

* 1. a) w. ELISABETTA BARBATO, soprano (Orchestra of the Teatro Municipal, Rio de Janeiro/Rainaldo Zamboni): TOSCA, Act I: Perchè chiuso? . . . non la sospiri . . . Ma falle gli occhi neri! (Puccini) (I)
Broadcast, Teatro Municipal, Rio de Janeiro, 3 Sep 1947

b) ELISABETTA BARBATO, soprano (Orchestra of the Teatro Municipal, Rio de Janeiro/Rainaldo Zamboni): TOSCA, Act II: Vissi d'arte (Puccini) (I)
Broadcast, Teatro Municipal, Rio de Janeiro, 3 Sep 1947

c) w. Orchestra of Radio Italiana [RAI], Milano/Nino Sanzogno: TOSCA, Act III: E lucevan le stelle (Puccini) (I)
Broadcast, ***CONCERTO MARTINI E ROSSI***, Teatro Municipale, San Remo, 21 Dec 1953

d) w. ELISABETTA BARBATO, soprano, and ALESSIO DEPAOLIS, tenor (Orchestra of the Teatro Municipal, Rio de Janeiro/Rainaldo Zamboni): TOSCA, Act III: Amaro sol per te m'era il morire . . . to the end of the opera (Puccini) (I)
Broadcast, Teatro Municipal, Rio de Janeiro, 3 Sep 1947

* 2. w. pf/Enrico Sivieri: I PAGLIACCI, Act I: Recitar . . . Vesti la giubba (Leoncavallo) (I)
In-house recording, Teatro Jão Caetano, Rio de Janeiro, 25 Oct 1951

* 3. w. pf/Enrico Sivieri: LO SCHIAVO, Act II: All'istante partir . . . Quando nascesti (Gomes) (I)
In-house recording, Teatro Jão Caetano, Rio de Janeiro, 25 Oct 1951

* 4. w. pf/Enrico Sivieri: LA BOHÈME, Act I: Che gelida manina (Puccini) (I)
In-house recording, Teatro Jão Caetano, Rio de Janeiro, 25 Oct 1951

NOTES: EJS 403

Band 1: Given in the listing under the film's copyright title. The excerpt begins at "Lucia perdona," lacks the first solo portions of the "Verranno a te," and skips to the duet a few pages further on. The "Si, si, allor" is also omitted, and the duet concludes at "Rammentati." There is clearly a cut just before the concerted "Verranno a te," evidence perhaps that Smith's source was lacking the solo section omitted. The film itself seems not to have survived intact: Smith had access only to the soundtrack, and because the film has not been seen, it is impossible to determine whether the cuts in the duet were actual performance cuts.

Claims that Ferruccio Tagliavini has been plugged into the EJS 403 transfer (taken from one of the five surviving Pons-Tagliavini LUCIA broadcasts) are disputed. To my ear, there are no such inserts.

The short premiered alongside the Warner Brothers part-talking feature "The Glorious Betsy" which, in addition to Dolores Costello, featured baritone Pasquale Amato as Napoleon (a là MADAME SANS-GÈNE), though regrettably, not in any of the sound sequences. Bass Andrés [Perelló] de Segurola also appeared, singing the "Marseillaise" to great critical acclaim.

The LUCIA duet was later issued on two Pearl Gigli compilations, GEMM 202-6 and GEMM 9367.

Band 2: a) The Covent Garden "La donna è mobile" and the Vitaphone Quartet are joined together for musical continuity. The four excerpts from Acts I-III of the Covent Garden performance have appeared on numerous LPs.

b) Given in the listing under the film's copyright title. The short premiered alongside the Warner Brothers feature "When a Man Loves," with John Barrymore.

This soundtrack was later issued on the Pearl Gigli set, GEMM 202-6.

Band 3: The original Vitaphone disc bears the date 6 April, 1927, probably the recording date, though the short was copyrighted and released in 1928. As in their commercial Victor recording of the duet (CVE-41071-2, recorded 28 November, 1927 and issued as Victor 8084 and HMV DB 1150), Gigli and De Luca sing through "Elle fuit!" (quoting the original French text), but begin pages earlier at "C'est toi!"

Gigli sued the Vitaphone Corporation for witholding his contracted salary on this film. The case was eventually settled out of court, the singer receiving "about $10,000" in compensation. Apparently Warner Brothers was dissatisfied with the photography, which Gigli's attorneys, Freudenberg and Mattuck of New York City, argued was not their client's fault. What role, if any, De Luca might have played in this squabble is not known. See "Gigli Settles Suit on Film Appearance" in the *New York Times* (2 February, 1928), p. 17.

The short premiered alongside the Warner Brothers feature "Tenderloin," with Dolores Costello.

Contrary to my own report in "The Operatic Vitaphone Shorts" (*ARSC Journal*, 22/1, Spring, 1991, pp. 62 and 85), this soundtrack did *not* appear on Eterna LP 732 and VEB-Eterna 8-20-757: included there was the acoustical Gigli-Pacini version (matrix 1055aj, recorded 5 December, 1919) issued as HMV 2-054109 and DB 269.

SIDE 2 (403 B):

Band 1: These appear to be the only excerpts to have survived from this 3 September, 1947 TOSCA.

1c: The "E lucevan le stelle" is credited implicitly as part of the Rio performance in the June, 1967 bulletin and on the label of EJS 403, but it was taken from the ***MARTINI E ROSSI*** broadcast cited in the listing. The other three arias performed by Gigli on the broadcast appeared on EJS 233 (March, 1962), EJS 310 (October, 1964), and a number of other private LPs.

Bands 2-4: This 25 October, 1951 concert was eventually completed over the course of EJS 382 (January, 1967), EJS 464 (March, 1969), EJS 403, and UORC 184 (January, 1974). A portion of the concert later appeared on HRE 213.

EJS 404: "The Golden Age of Opera" (2 LP)
Issued September, 1967
MATRIX P-1385

SIDES 1-4 (404 A-D):

SAFFO (Pacini) (I)
Opera in 3 acts (complete)
Orchestra and Chorus of the Teatro San Carlo di Napoli/Franco Capuana
Broadcast, Teatro San Carlo, Naples, 1, 5, or 9 Apr 1967

CAST:
Leyla Gencer (*Saffo*); Tito Del Bianco (*Faone*); Louis Quilico (*Alcandro*); Franca Mattiucci (*Climene*); Vittoria Magnaghi (*Dirce*); Mario Guggia (*Ippia*); Maurizio Piacente (*Lisimaco*).

NOTES: EJS 404

Cella's Gencer biography gives the date as 1 April, 1967. The MRF (MRF-10) and Hunt (HN 541) reissues give the date as 7 April. EJS 404 says only 1967. Cella reports that four performances were scheduled, but because of a strike, only two were actually given. *The Chronache del Teatro di San Carlo 1948-1968* (Milan: Ricordi, 1969) claims that *three* performances, on 1, 5, and 9 April, were given, though it is not mentioned there which was broadcast.

The EJS 404 transfer plays at score pitch at 34.00 rpm.

EJS 405: "The Golden Age of Opera" (1 LP)
Issued September, 1967
MATRIX P-1382

"JUSSI BJOERLING IN OPERA (1936-1948)"

SIDE 1 (405 A):

1. w. studio orch/Erno Rapee: LA BOHÈME, Act I: Che gelida manina (Puccini) (I)
   Broadcast, ***GENERAL MOTORS HOUR***, Carnegie Hall, WJZ, NYC, 28 Nov 1937

2. w. studio orch/Erno Rapee: RIGOLETTO, Act III: La donna è mobile (Verdi) (I)
   Broadcast, ***GENERAL MOTORS HOUR***, WJZ, Carnegie Hall, NYC, 28 Nov 1937

3. w. studio orch/Erno Rapee: AÏDA, Act I: Se quel guerrier io fossi . . . Celeste Aïda (Verdi) (I)
   Broadcast, ***GENERAL MOTORS HOUR***, WJZ, Carnegie Hall, NYC, 28 Nov 1937

4. w. studio orch/Erno Rapee: "Land, du valsignade" (Althén) (Sw)
   Broadcast, ***GENERAL MOTORS HOUR***, WJZ, Carnegie Hall, NYC, 28 Nov 1937

* 5. w. MARIA JERITZA, soprano (studio orch/Erno Rapee): CAVALLERIA RUSTICANA: Jag är ej slav, förgäves du grater [Bada, Santuzza, schiavo non sono] (Mascagni) (Sw and I)
Broadcast, ***GENERAL MOTORS HOUR***, WJZ, Carnegie Hall, NYC, 28 Nov 1937

6. w. Wiener Philharmoniker/Victor DeSabata: AÏDA, Act I: Vore je utkarad . . . Ljuva Aïda [Se quel guerrier io fossi . . . Celeste Aïda] (Verdi) (Sw)
In-house recording, Wiener Staatsoper, Vienna, 7 Jun 1936

* 7. a) w. MARIA NEMETH, soprano (w. Wiener Philharmoniker/Victor DeSabata: AÏDA, Act III: Pur ti riveggo . . . Fuggir! Fuggire! (Verdi) (Sw and G)
In-house recording, Wiener Staatsoper, Vienna, 7 Jun 1936
b) w. MARIA NEMETH, soprano (w. Wiener Philharmoniker/Victor DeSabata: AÏDA, Act III: Va, va t'attende all'ara Amneris . . A noi duce fia l'amor (Verdi) (Sw and G)
In-house recording, Wiener Staatsoper, Vienna, 7 Jun 1936
c) w. ALEXANDER SVED, baritone, and MARIA NEMETH, soprano (w. Wiener Philharmoniker/Victor DeSabata: AÏDA, Act III: No! tu non sei colpevole . . . Là del tuo cor, del tuo (Verdi) (Sw and G)
In-house recording, Wiener Staatsoper, Vienna, 7 Jun 1936

SIDE 2 (405 B):

* 1. w. BIDÚ SAYÃO, soprano; GEORGE CEHANOVSKY, baritone; NICOLA MOSCONA, bass; and FRANK VALENTINO, baritone; and (Metropolitan Opera House Orchestra/Giuseppe Antonicelli): LA BOHÈME, Act I: Non sono in vena . . . to the end of the act (Puccini) (I)
Metropolitan Opera broadcast, NYC, 25 Dec 1948

* 2. w. Metropolitan Opera House Orchestra and Chorus/Ferruccio Calusio: IL TROVATORE, Act III: Ah! si, ben mio . . .Di quella pira (Verdi) (I)
Metropolitan Opera broadcast, NYC, 11 Jan 1941

* 3. w. AUDREY SCHUCH, soprano (New Orleans Opera Orchestra/Walter Herbert): UN BALLO IN MASCHERA, Act III: Forse la soglia attinse . . . Si, rivederti, Amelia (Verdi) (I)
In-house recording, New Orleans Opera House, 20 Apr 1950

NOTES: EJS 405

The subtitle of this LP, "(1936-48)," is incorrect.

Side 1 (405 A):

Bands 1-5: Announcer Milton Cross noted on the air that this was Bjoerling's American debut as a tenor (he had toured the U.S. as a boy soprano in the earliest 1920s and recorded for Columbia as part of the Bjoerling Trio with his brothers, Olle and Gösta), as does the September, 1967 EJS bulletin and the *New York Times* for 28 November. EJS 405 includes all of the surviving Bjoerling items, but most have appeared selectively on other EJS LPs and on the MDP and Historical Opera Treasures labels. The Althén song was not listed in the *New York Times* radio log, but it *was* performed on the show. Jeritza's solos from the broadcast were issued on EJS 418 (December, 1967).

Band 5: Bjoerling sang *Turridu's* part in Swedish, while Jeritza sang *Santuzza* in Italian.

Bands 6-7: Dated 1936 in the September, 1967 bulletin. Bjoerling sang *Radames* in Swedish, while the other roles were sung in German. These were most likely back-stage Selenophone recordings.

These excerpts were reissued on HRE 376-2.

Side 2 (405 B):

Band 1: The September, 1967 bulletin gives this as a San Francisco performance. The complete Christmas, 1948 BOHÈME was issued on the two-disc UORC 180 (December, 1973) and later on Robin Hood RHR 515-B.

Band 2: Dated 1946 on the label of EJS 405 and placed as "San Francisco" in the September, 1967 bulletin. The recitative between the aria and the cabaletta has been omitted here. Thus, neither *Ruiz* (Lodovico Oliviero) or *Leonora* (Norina Greco) are heard.

The complete performance was issued on two LPs as UORC 115 (May-June, 1972), HOPE 221, Cetra LO 71, and Robin Hood RHR 509-B. Excerpts have been recycled on several private labels, as well as on Rococo 5304, a Bjoerling recital.

Band 3: This performance was privately recorded in its entirety, but to date has not been issued complete in any form. Scattered excerpts from Acts I-III later appeared on EJS 468 (May, 1969).

Bjoerling frequently omitted *Ricardo's* third-act aria, as in this performance, but he does interpolate a stunning high "C" on the penultimate syllable of the concluding "d'amor."

EJS 406: "The Golden Age of Opera" (1 LP)
Issued September, 1967
MATRIX P-1384

LA TRAVIATA (Verdi) (Sw)
Opera in 4 acts (excerpts)
Orchestra and Chorus of the Royal Opera, Stockholm/Herbert Sandberg
Broadcast, Royal Opera, Stockholm, 29 Aug 1939

CAST:
Hjördis Schymberg (*Violetta*); Jussi Bjoerling (*Alfredo*); Conny Molin (*Germont*); Georg Svensson (*Baron Douphol*); Göta Allard (*Flora*); Olle Strandberg (*Gastone*); Folke Jonsson (*Marquis d'Obigny*); Gösta Lindberg (*Doctor Grenvil*); Margit Sehlmark (*Annina*); [Ryno Wallin (*Giuseppe*)]; [Bertil Alstergard (*A Messenger*)].

SIDE 1 (406 A):

Act I: 1. BJOERLING, SCHYMBERG, CAST, and Chorus: Sla i och drick ur! [Libiamo, libiamo]

2. SCHYMBERG, BJOERLING and STRANDBERG: Er bild förbi mig har svätat [Un di felice]

3. SCHYMBERG and BJOERLING: En darskap, ja darskap [Follie! Follie! . . . Sempre libera]

Act II: 4. BJOERLING: Ack, här hos henne jag . . . Brännande blodets känela [Lunge da lei . . . De'miei bollenti spiriti

* 5. BJOERLING, SCHYMERG, MOLIN, CAST, and Chorus: Ack tarar lindrar ju . . . Ah, Alfredo, jag dig äskar . . . Min stolther, min glädje [Che fai? Nulla. Scrivevi . . . Ritorna di tuo padre orgoglio e vanto . . . to the orchestral postlude of "Di provenza"]

SIDE 2 (406 B):

Act III: 1. SCHYMBERG, BJOERLING, CAST, and Chorus: Jag honom bett mig följa [Invitato a qui seguirmi] . . . to the end of the act

Act IV: 2. SCHYMBERG, BJOERLING, and CAST: En glädje? Ack säg mig! [Signora. Che t'accadde? . . . Alfredo? Amato Alfredo! . . . Parigi, o cara . . .to the the end of the opera

NOTES: EJS 406

This performance was recorded in its entirety by Swedish Radio. Act II was first broadcast on 17 September, 1939, Acts III and IV on 10 November, 1939, and the entire performance--belatedly--on 15-17 April, 1975. The label of EJS 406 says only "1941."

Issued complete as UORC 269 (November-December, 1975) and on a Swedish Radio LP, RMLP 1272/73. HRE 281-2 included the "Brindisi" and "Un di felice."

EJS 406 plays at a uniform 32.2 rpm.

Swedish Radio tape: L-B+ 4014 (complete performance).

Side I (406 A):

Band 5: This transfer ends after the orchestral introduction to "Di provenza:" the aria itself is omitted, and picks up at the orchestra postlude. "Amami, Alfredo" is follwed by an orchestral restatement and a coda that could not be identified in the score.

EJS 407: "The Golden Age of Opera" (1 LP)
Issued September, 1967
MATRIX P-1383

LA REGINETTA DELLE ROSE (Leoncavallo) (I)
Opera in 3 acts (excerpts)
Orchestra and Chorus of Radio Italiana [RAI], Torino/Cesare Gallino
RAI broadcast, Turin, 23 Feb 1951

CAST:
Lina Pagliughi (*Lillian*); Ornella d'Arrigo (*Anita de Rios Negros*); Lina Avogadro (*Mikalis*); Emilio Renzi (*Principe Max*); Giuseppe Diani (*Don Pedro*); Luigi Latinucci (*Sparados*); Giuliano Ferrein (*Kradomos*).

SIDE 1 (407 A):

1. Act I: a) No. 1: ORCHESTRA: Quadriglia [Musica sulla scena]
b) No. 4: PAGLIUGHI and RENZI: Duettino del baciamino
c) No. 6: PAGLIUGHI: Valzer delle rose
d) No. 9: RENZI and PAGLIUGHI: Romanza-Duetto-Finale

Act II: e) No. 4: D'ARRIGO and DIANI: Duettino del telefono
f) No. 6: PAGLIUGHI and RENZI: Valse-Duetto
g) No. 8: CAST: Settimana della congiura

Act III: h) No. 3: PAGLIUGHI and DIANI: Duettino all'addio
i) No. 5: RENZI: Serenata degli avi
j) No. 8: RENZI, D'ARRIGO, DIANI, and PAGLIUGHI: Finale

SIDE 2 (407 B):

L'ITALIANA IN LONDRA (Cimarosa-rev. Guido Confalonieri) (I)
Opera in 2 acts (complete)
Orchestra of Radio Italiana [RAI], Milano/Ennio Gerelli
RAI broadcast, Milan, 4 Jul 1954

CAST:
Ilva Ligabue (*Donna Livia*); Luisa Villa (*Fanny*); Rodolfo Malacarne (*Milord*); Paolo Montarsolo (*Polidoro*).

NOTES: EJS 407

Side 1 (407 A):

This performance was broadcast as part of RAI Torino's operetta series. The original dialogue from this 1912 Leoncavallo "light opera" was performed but was removed from EJS 407, presumably for purposes of timing. The September, 1967 bulletin claims that although the dialogue has been cut, "the music is intact." This is not the case, however. Pagliughi was also featured in a 12 February, 1949 RAI broadcast of the work with tenor Cesare Valetti, the Act I Finale of which appeared later on EJS 452 (December, 1968).

Side 2 (407 B):

The title of the opera is given as "L'ITALIANA IN ALGERI" in both the September, 1967 bulletin and on the label of EJS 407. Moreover, conductor Gerelli's surname is given as "Girelli," Montarsolo's as "Montarsoni," Ligabue's forename as "Iva," and the date of the performance as *1953*.

Confalonieri's "revision" of Cimarosa's lengthy 1779 Neapolitan opera buffa amounted to a different plot, the removal of some of the characters, and a substantially different text. The September, 1967 bulletin correctly notes that the revision is presented complete at 31 minutes, where Cimarosa's original score runs over two hours.

EJS 408: "The Golden Age of Opera" (2 LPs)
Issued October, 1967
MATRIX P-1404

SIDES 1-4 (408 A-D):

MONTE IVNOR (Rocca) (I)
Opera in 3 acts (complete)
Orchestra and Chorus of Radio Italiana [RAI], Torino/Armando LaRosa Parodi
Recorded 16 Mar 1957 for RAI broadcast, Turin, 17 Oct 1957

CAST:
Leyla Gencer (*Edali*); Miriam Pirazzini (*Naike*); Renato Gavarini (*Imar*); Anselmo Colzani (*Wladimiro Kirlatos*); Nestore Catalani (*Tepurlov*); Jorge [Giorgio] Algorta (*Gregor Miroj*); Leonardo Monreale (*Captain of the Gendarmes*); Leonardo Monreale (*Maravaid*); Jole de Maria (*Kuttarin*); Augusto Pedroni (*Danilo*); Salvatore Di Tommaso (*Droboj*); Walter Brunelli (*Ivanaj*); Walter Brunelli (*A Worker*).

NOTES: EJS 408

Lodovico Rocca, composer of the better-known DYBBUK (La Scala, 24 March, 1934), based MONTE IVNOR (Teatro Reale, Rome, 23 December, 1939) on Franz Werfel's 1933 novel, *Vierzig Tage des Musa Dagh*, using a libretto by Cesare Meano.

EJS 409: "The Golden Age of Opera" (1 LP)
Issued October, 1967
MATRIX P-1401

OTELLO (Verdi) (I)
Opera in 4 acts (excerpts)
Orchestra and Chorus of the La Scala Opera, Philadelphia/Giuseppe Bamboschek
La Scala Opera, Philadelphia, 16 Apr 1948

CAST:
Giovanni Martinelli (*Otello*); Cesare Bardelli (*Iago*); June Haas-Kelly (*Desdemona*); John Carmen Rossi (*Cassio*); [Lloyd Harris (*Lodovico*)]; [John Lawler (*Montano*)]; [Mildred Ippolito (*Emilia*)]; [Cesare Curzi (*Roderigo*)]; [? (*A Herald*)].

SIDE 1 (409 A):

Act I:
1. MARTINELLI and Chorus: Esultate! . . . Evviva!
2. MARTINELLI and HAAS-KELLY: Gia nella notte . . . to the end of the act

Act II:
3. BARDELLI and MARTINELLI: E un' idra fosca . . . Un tal proposto spezza di mie labbra il suggello
4. BARDELLI and MARTINELLI: Non pensateci più . . . Ora e per sempre addio
5. BARDELLI and MARTINELLI: [Era la notte] E allora il sogno in cieco letargo si mutò . . . Sì, pel ciel . . . to the end of the act

Act III: * 6. a) HAAS-KELLY, MARTINELLI, and BARDELLI: Dio ti giocondi o sposo . . . Dio! mi potevi . . . Cassio è là!
b) MARTINELLI: Là! Cielo! gioia! Orror!
Metropolitan Opera broadcast, NYC, date unknown

Act IV: 7. MARTINELLI, ROSSI, and Chorus: Niun mi tema . . . to the end of the opera

SIDE 2 (409 B):

"ARMAND TOKATYAN (1944-48)"

1. w. orch/?: L'ARLESIANA, Act II: È la solita storia ["Lamento di Federico"] (Cilèa) (I)
   Source and date unknown

2. w. orch/?: EUGEN ONEGIN, Act II: Kuda, kuda ["Lenski's Air"] (Tchaikowski) (R)
   Source and date unknown

3. w. IRMA GONZALES, soprano (orch/?): CARMEN, Act I: Votre mère avec moi . . . Parle-moi de ma mère (Bizet) (F)
   Source and date unknown

4. w. orch/?: TURANDOT, Act I: Non piangere, Liù (Puccini) (I)
   Source and date unknown

5. w. orch/? TOSCA, Act III: E lucevan le stelle (Puccini) (I)
Source and date unknown

6. w. orch/?: TURANDOT, Act III: Nessun dorma (Puccini) (I)
Source and date unknown

7. w. ESPERANZA VASQUEZ (orch/?): TOSCA, Act I: Perchè chiuso?
Source and date unknown

8. w. orch/?: "When Shadows Fall" (Manning) (E)
Source and date unknown

9. w. orch/?: "Nostalgia" (Tota Nacho) (S)
Source and date unknown

NOTES: EJS 409

Side 1 (409 A):

This OTELLO, the last of Martinelli's career, exists complete, but has not yet been issued in its entirety. The tenor was 62 at the time. The "Là! Cielo! gioia! Orror!" that concludes "Dio ti giocondi" was patched in from an unknown live (Martinelli) performance to finish the scene--taken probably from one of several surviving Met broadcasts.

Side 2 (409 B):

The October, 1967 bulletin says only that the Tokatyan side is "culled from appearances in Mexico City in 1944 and 1948," but the concerts themselves have not been documented.

EJS 410: "The Golden Age of Opera" (1 LP)
Issued October, 1967
MATRIX P-1405

SIDES 1-2 (410 A):

DIE WALKÜRE (Wagner) (G)
Opera in 3 acts (Act I only)
Danish Radio Symphony Orchestra/Thomas Jensen
Broadcast, Danmarks Radio, Copenhagen, 31 Mar 1960

CAST:
Lauritz Melchior (*Siegmund*); Dorothy Larsen (*Sieglinde*); Mogens Wedel (*Hunding*).

NOTES: EJS 410

This WALKÜRE was apparently Melchior's last appearance (albeit on the concert platform) in a complete act of a Wagner opera. The tenor was 70 at the time. According to Shirlee Emmons, in her book *Tristanissimo: The Authorized Biography of Heroic Tenor Lauritz Melchior* (New York: Schirmer, 1990):

> "Because he had conceived the idea for the concert, Knud Hegermann-Lindencrone was allowed to install his stereo equipment in a little study just beside the concert hall." Here, with Kleinchen [Melchior's wife] at his side, Hergermann-Lindencrone made a stereo recording, parallel to the broadcast mono version, that became the only stereo recording of Lauritz Melchior" (pp. 308-309).

EJS 410 used the monaural broadcast as its source. An orchestral fanfare is heard at the end: this may have preceded an on-stage tribute to Melchior on his 70th birthday, which he had celebrated eleven days earlier.

Hunding is given on the label as "*Hunting*" Reissued on both LP and CD by Danacord.

Speed is sharp throughout the first two scenes, requiring a speed of about 31.00 rpm; Scene 3 is correct at 33.00 rpm; the finale is in score pitch at 33.3 rpm.

Hergermann-Lindencrone's stereophonic recording of the scene was used for the transfer on Danacord's "Melchior Anthology, Vol. 4" (DACOCD 319-321), issued in 1987.

EJS 411: "The Golden Age of Opera" (1 LP)
Issued October, 1967
MATRIX P-14010 (sic)

SIDES 1-2 (411 A-B):

L'HÔTELLERIE PORTUGAISE (Cherubini) (I)
Opera in 1 act (complete)
Orchestra and Chorus of Radio Italiana [RAI], Milano/Enrico Piazza
RAI broadcast, Milan, 1 January, 1953

CAST:
Ilva Ligabue (*Donna Gabriella*); Luigina Villa (*Ines*); Franco Taino (*Don Carlos*); Giovanni Fabbri (*Pedrillo*); Paolo Pedani (*Don Roselbo*); Otello Borgonovo (*Inigo*); Paolo Montarsolo (*Rodrigue*).

NOTES: EJS 411

Issued under the Italian title L'OSTERIA PORTOGHESE, but misspelled "L' Ostebia Portugais" in the October, 1967 bulletin. The odd LP matrix number was probably the result of a machining error and may be *P-1410*.

EJS 412: "The Golden Age of Opera" (2 LPs)
Issued November, 1967
MATRIX P-1447

SIDES 1-4 (412 A-D):

PIA DE'TOLOMEI (Donizetti) (I)
Opera in 2 acts (complete)
Orchestra and Chorus of the Teatro Comunale, Bologna/Bruno Rigacci
Broadcast, Settimana Chigiana, Siena, 3 Sep 1967

CAST:
Jolanda Meneguzzer (*Pia*); Walter Alberti (*Nello della Pietra*); Florindo Andreolli (*Rodrigo de Tolomei*); Aldo Bottion (*Ghino degli Armieri*); Franco Ventriglia (*Piero*); Franco Ventriglia (*Lamberto*); Barbara Testa (*Bice*); Paride Venturi (*Ubaldo*).

NOTES: EJS 412

This performance, apparently the first twentieth-century revival of Donizetti's obscure 1837 opera, was a production of the Accademia Chigiana, Siena. See the review in *High Fidelity/Musical America*, 17 (November, 1967), p. M-31.

Listed in error in the November, 1967 bulletin as "EJS 413." The discs are marked and the labels printed as EJS 412, which also concurs with the 1970s EJS checklist.

Reissued as Melodram CD 37017, along with a 1962 Teatro San Carlo MARIA DI ROHAN with Zeani, only portions of which Smith ever issued himself. UORC 109 (February, 1972) includes Bottion's "Non può dirti la parola" from this complete PIA DE'TOLOMEI.

EJS 413: "The Golden Age of Opera" (2 LPs)
Issued November, 1967
MATRIX P-1448

SIDES 1-4 (413 A-B):

OBERON (Weber) (I)
Opera in 3 acts (complete)
Orchestra and Chorus of Radio Italiana [RAI], Milano/Vittorio Gui
RAI broadcast, Milan, 24 Oct 1957

CAST:
Anita Cerquetti (*Rezia*); Miriam Pirazzini (*Fatima*); Fernanda Cadoni (*Puck*); Mirto Picchi (*Oberon*); Petre Munteanu (*Huon*); Piero De Palma (*Scerasmino*); ? ["Degli Abbati" (*Narrator*)].

NOTES: EJS 413

Similar to EJS 412, this LP is listed in error in the November, 1967 bulletin as "EJS 414." The discs and labels both carry the catalog number EJS 413, as does the 1970s EJS checklist.

The listing given above is taken from the RAI chronology: the labels of EJS 413 are incomprehensibly sloppy in their citation of the singers' and characters' names. The November, 1967 bulletin, moreover, dates the performance as *1958*. The narrator, omitted from this LP, may have been Valerio Degli Abbati.

Huon's Act I aria, "Von Jugend auf in dem Kampfgefild" (No. 5) was almost certainly transposed by Munteanu down a half-step. The first few measures of the Act II Quartet, "Über die blauen Wogen," were omitted from EJS 413, probably the result of a careless error.

Speeds are erratic over all four sides. The entire opera is slow at 33.3 rpm: side 1 begins at 34.5 rpm before eventually winding down to about 34.2 rpm. The other sides are similarly unpredictable, requiring varying speeds of from 34.00 to 34.5 rpm. Constant pitching is advised.

EJS 414: "The Golden Age of Opera" (1 LP)
Issued November, 1967
MATRIX P-1449

"BENIAMINO GIGLI IN OPERA (1938-47)"

AÏDA (Verdi) (I)
Opera in 4 acts (excerpts)
Orchestra and Chorus of the Teatro Municipal, Rio de Janeiro/Oliviero de Fabritiis or Nino Stinco
Broadcast, Teatro Municipal, Rio de Janeiro, 20 or 30 Aug 1947
[+ except as noted]

CAST:
Elisabetta Barbato (*Aïda*); Beniamino Gigli (*Radames*); Ebe Stignani (*Amneris*); Raffaele De Falchi (*Amonasro*); Giulio Neri (*Ramfis*); [Americo Basso (*King of Egypt*)]; [Nino Crimi (*A Messenger*)]; ? (*High Priestess*).

SIDE 1 (414 A):

* 1. Act I: +a) w. Münchener Philharmoniker/Giuseppe Becce: Celeste Aïda from the soundtrack of the feature film ***DU BIST MEIN GLÜCK*** [***TU SEI LA VITA MIA***] (1936), Tobis, Munich, June-July, 1936

b) STIGNANI, GIGLI, and BARBATO: Qual insolita gioia . . . Vieni, o diletta, appressati . . . nè s'agita più grave cura in te?

Act III: c) GIGLI, BARBATO, DE FALCHI, STIGNANI and NERI: Pur ti riveggo . . . to the end of the act

Act IV: d) STIGNANI, GIGLI, NERI, and Chorus: Scene i (complete)

SIDE 2 (414 B):

* 1. Act IV: a) GIGLI and BARBATO: La fatal pietra . . . O terra addio . . . A noi si schiude il ciel, e l'alme erranti
+b) w. MARIA CEBOTARI, soprano, and MARIA HUDER, soprano (Rome Opera Orchestra and Chorus/Tullio Serafin): Volano al raggio dell'eterno di . . . to the end of the opera
from the soundtrack of the feature film ***GIUSEPPE VERDI*** (1938), Cinecittà, Rome, July, 1938

* 2. w. MARIA CANIGLIA, soprano (Orchestra of the Teatro Colon, Buenos Aires/Ettore Panizza): ADRIANA LECOUVREUR, Act II: Taci! Lasciami dir . . . No! no che giova? . . . nell' ombra languirò (Cilèa) (I)
Broadcast, Teatro Colón, Buenos Aires, 14 May 1948

* 3. w. MARIA CANIGLIA, soprano (Orchestra of the Teatro Colon, Buenos Aires/Ettore Panizza): ADRIANA LECOUVREUR, Act IV: Serbato a un trono egli è . . . No, la mia fronte . . . No, più nobile . . . Deh, vien sul cor (Cilèa) (I)
Broadcast, Teatro Colón, Buenos Aires, 14 May 1948

* 4. w. Detroit Symphony Orchestra/Eugene Ormandy: L'ELISIR D'AMORE, Act II: Una furtiva lagrima (Donizetti) (I)
Broadcast, ***FORD SUNDAY EVENING HOUR***, WJR, Detroit, 2 Oct 1938

* 5. w. Detroit Symphony Orchestra/Eugene Ormandy: RIGOLETTO, Act I: Questa o quella (Verdi) (I)
Broadcast, ***FORD SUNDAY EVENING HOUR***, WJR, Detroit, 2 Oct 1938

* 6. w. Detroit Symphony Orchestra/Eugene Ormandy: MARTHA, Act III: M'appari [Ach, so fromm] (Flowtow) (I)
Broadcast, ***FORD SUNDAY EVENING HOUR***, WJR, Detroit, 2 Oct 1938

* 7. w. Detroit Symphony Orchestra/Eugene Ormandy: PAGLIACCI, Act I: Recitar! . . . Vesti la giubba (Leoncavallo) (I)
Broadcast, ***FORD SUNDAY EVENING HOUR***, WJR, Detroit, 2 Oct 1938

* 8. w. orch/Herbert Meyer: "La canzone del clown" (Zandonai) (I)
from the soundtrack of the feature film ***CASA LONTANA*** [***DER SINGENDE TOR***] (1939), Cinecittà, Rome, June-July, 1939

NOTES: EJS 414

Side 1 (414 A):

Band 1: Co-author William Collins' report in his Gigli non-commercial discography in *The Record Collector* 35/8-10 (August-October, 1990), p. 200, that these excerpts were taken from the 30 August, 1947 performance may not be correct. There were three performances that season--on 20, 24, and 30, August, 1947. Fabritiis conducted the 20 and 24 August performances, while Nino Stinco conducted on 30 August. On good authority, it may well have been the initial "gala" performance of 20 August that is presented here. Note that there is no indication in the November, 1967 bulletin or on the label of EJS 414 that the "Celeste Aïda" was taken from the ***DU BIST MEIN GLÜCK*** soundtrack.

Side 2 (414 B):

Band 1: In the continuation of the Rio de Janeiro AÏDA, the orchestral introduction to "La fatal pietra" is omitted; the original acetate breaks off during the final reprise of "O terra addio," hence the Cebotari-Huder soundtrack insert of the final phrases, not mentioned either on the label or in the accompanying bulletin.

Bands 2-3: The label of EJS 414 dates this performance as Rome, 1940, but this perhaps confuses the Gigli-Olivero performance of the opera given that year at the Teatro Reale dell'Opera in Rome. Two additional excerpts from the 1948 Teatro Colón performance, featuring Fedora Barbieri (not heard here) as *La Principessa*, were later issued on MDP 014. The excerpts given here were later recycled on Smith's two-LP Gigli set, ANNA 1032-1033 (May-June, 1979). A Gigli-Caniglia IL TROVATORE (see EJS 325) conducted by Panizza also survives in excerpts, as do excerpts from an unpublished MANON LESCAUT, both from the 1948 Rio de Janeiro season.

Bands 4-7: The November, 1967 bulletin notes that this ***FORD SUNDAY EVENING HOUR*** marked Gigli's first performance in America after six seasons abroad (he left the Met after the 1931-1932 season).

Band 8: Listed as "Cavaliere, son qua" from LA CENA DELLE BEFFE on the label of EJS 414 and as a film fragment from the Giordano opera in the November, 1967 bulletin. In fact, the Giordano aria was not performed in ***CASA LONTANA***.

EJS 415: "The Golden Age of Opera" (2 LPs)
Issued December, 1967
MATRIX P-1472

SIDES 1-4 (415 A-D):

EURYANTHE (Weber) (G)
Opera in 3 acts (abridged)
BBC Orchestra and Chorus/Fritz Stiedry
BBC broadcast, London, 30 Sep or 1 Oct 1955

CAST:
Joan Sutherland (*Euryanthe*); Marianne Schech (*Eglantine*); Frans [Franz] Vroons (*Adolar*); Otakar Kraus (*Lysiart*); Kurt Böhme (*King Ludwig VI*); ? (*Bertha*); ? (*Rudolph*).

NOTES: EJS 415

Presented here complete as performed, but with significant performance cuts. Norma Major's Sutherland biography notes that there were two performances of EURYANTHE broadcast on the dates given in the listing: it is not known which was presented here.

EJS 416: "The Golden Age of Opera" (1 LP)
Issued December, 1967
MATRIX P-1473

SIDES 1-2 (416 A-B):

PIEDIGROTTA (Ricci-rev. Renzo Parodi) (I)
Opera in 3 acts (complete)
Orchestra A. Scarlatti di Napoli and Coro di Napoli/Nino Sanzogno
RAI broadcast, Naples, 14 Oct 1967

CAST:
Dora Gatta (*Rita*); Rita Talarico (*Marta*); Giovanna Fioroni (*Crezia*); Edda Vincenzi (*Stella*); Giuseppina Arista (*Lena*); Franco Bonisolli (*Achille*); Alberto Rinaldi (*Renzo*); Domenico Trimarchi (*Don Polifemo*); Ugo Savarese (*Don Deucalione*); Paolo Montarsolo (*Manicotto*); Florindo Andreolli (*Cardillo*); Angelo Degli Innocenti (*A Coffee Merchant*); Aronne Ceroni (*A Brandy Merchant*); Aronne Ceroni (*A Voice*).

NOTES: EJS 416

Presented complete as performed, but without the considerable amount of dialogue (in Neapolitan dialect) found in the score. Ricci's 1852 opera was originally titled LA FESTA DI PIEDIGROTTA. Parodi's revision of it compresses Ricci's four acts into three, retaining the essence of the first two acts, but omitting a good deal in the third act and the Finale. The revised third act omits verses for *Renzo* and *Deucalione* through the love song, "Lo guorno che vedette de Catarina," leaving intact only the verses sung by *Achille* and *Don Polifemo*. Ricci's original Finale--a lengthy octet, a Rondo for *Rita*, and a martial finale for military band--was replaced by Parodi with a reprise of the Tarantella which opens Act III.

This performance was reissued with dialogue intact as VOCE-66.

EJS 417: "The Golden Age of Opera" (1 LP)
Issued December, 1967
MATRIX P-1474

SIDE 1 (417 A):

"DINO BORGIOLI"

* 1. w. pf/?: FALSTAFF, Act III: Dal labbro il canto estasiato vola (Verdi) (I)
?BBC broadcast, London, ?17 Jan 1941

2. w. pf/Ernest Lush: IL MATRIMONIO SEGRETO, Act III: Pria che spunti in ciel (Cimarosa) (I)
Broadcast, ***BBC HOME SERVICE***, BBC, London, 19 Jun 1949

3. w. pf/Ernest Lush: "E canta il grillo" (Billi) (I)
Broadcast, ***BBC HOME SERVICE***, BBC, London, 19 Jun 1949

4. w. pf/?: L'ELISIR D'AMORE, Act II: Una furtiva lagrima (Donizetti) (I)
   Source and date unknown

5. w. pf/Josephine Lee: "O bellissimi capelli" (Falconieri) (I)
   Broadcast, ***THE SUNDAY CONCERT***, BBC Home Service, London, 22 Aug 1948

6. w. pf/Frederick Stone: "Clair de lune" (Szulc) (F)
   BBC broadcast, London, 28 Dec 1948

7. w. pf/Josephine Lee: "Fior di campo" (Broghi) (I)
   Broadcast, ***THE SUNDAY CONCERT***, BBC Home Service, London, 22 Aug 1948

8. w. pf/Josephine Lee: "Tarantella Napolitana" (Sadero) (I)
   Broadcast, ***THE SUNDAY CONCERT***, BBC Home Service, London, 22 Aug 1948

* 9. w. pf/?: "A tornata a Surriento" [sic] (?)
   Source and date unknown

* 10. w. pf/?: "Mama" (?) (I)
   Source and date unknown

11. w. pf/Josephine Lee: "O luna che fa lume" (Davico) (I)
   Broadcast, ***THE SUNDAY CONCERT***, BBC Home Service, London, 22 Aug 1948

* 12. w. pf/?: "Nuttata 'e sentimento" (Capolongo) (N)
   Source and date unknown

13. w. pf/Josephine Lee: "Lungi, lungi è amor da me" (G. B. Fasolo) (I)
   Broadcast, ***THE SUNDAY CONCERT***, BBC Home Service, London, 22 Aug 1948

SIDE 2 (417 B):

"FERRUCCIO TAGLIAVINI"

1. w. pf/?: RIGOLETTO, Act II: Parmi veder le lagrime (Verdi) (I)
   ?Broadcast, Radio Mexico, ?Mexico City, circa 1946

2. w. pf/?: LA BOHÈME, Act I: Che gelida manina (Puccini) (I)
   ?Broadcast, Radio Mexico, ?Mexico City, circa 1946

3. w. pf/?: CAVALLERIA RUSTICANA: O Lola ch'ai di latti ["Siciliana"] (Mascagni) (I)
   ?Broadcast, Radio Mexico, ?Mexico City, circa 1946

4. w. pf/?: MARTHA, Act III: M'appari [Ach, so fromm] (Flotow) (I)
   ?Broadcast, Radio Mexico, ?Mexico City, circa 1946

5. w. pf/?: L'ELISIR D'AMORE, Act II: Una furtiva lagrima (Donizetti) (I)
   ?Broadcast, Radio Mexico, ?Mexico City, circa 1946

* 6. w. pf/?: "Ay di mí" (Alberto Mendez Canvin-Teofilo Vargas) (S)
?Broadcast, Radio Mexico, ?Mexico City, circa 1946

* 7. w. pf/?: "Agonía" [Yarabí] (Alberto Mendez Canvin-Teofilo Vargas) (S)
?Broadcast, Radio Mexico, ?Mexico City, circa 1946

* 8. w. pf/?: "Nostalgia de amores" [Pasacalle] (Alberto Mendez Canvin-Teofilo Vargas) (S)
?Broadcast, Radio Mexico, ?Mexico City, circa 1946

NOTES: EJS 417

EJS 182 (July-August, 1960) and EJS 223 (November, 1961) also presented recital material from Borgioli's BBC radio appearances, the bulk of which seem to have come from 26 April, 22 August, and 28 December, 1948; 19 June and 19 August, 1949; and 2 June, 1950. It has been reported that the wartime broadcasts came at a time when BBC staffing did not allow for the proper documentation of transmissions, which may account for those for which the source and date are unknown.

Together, EJS 182, EJS 223, and EJS 417 include most of the material from these documented broadcasts, an exception being the Guarini-Caccini "Amarilli, mia bella" from 28 December, 1948.

Side 1 (417 A):

Band 1: 17 January, 1941 has been reported as the broadcast date of the FALSTAFF aria, and is given as such on the label of EJS 417, but this could not be confirmed in the *Radio Times* of London, which lists no Borgioli broadcast on that date. Only the first act of the Salzburg FALSTAFF with Borgioli (20 August, 1936) was broadcast shortwave.

Bands 9 and 10: These are not the familiar "Torna a surriento" of De Curtis or the "Mama" of Bixio. The composers are unknown.

Band 12: The recital-hall echo on the "Nuttata 'e sentimento" suggests either a live performance or a home recording.

Side 2 (417 B):

Given as Mexico City, 1940 in the December, 1967 bulletin, but in fact, Tagliavini did not appear in Mexico City until 1946 (see EJS 341 from October, 1965 and EJS 374 from October, 1966). However, the Spanish songs suggest that a Latin American origin is likely. The sound of this material is clean and forward, further suggesting a pre-recorded broadcast, and the time gaps between the selections easily allow for on-the-air announcements. A Radio Mexico broadcast of 1946 has been offered as a logical compromise.

The bulletin for this LP further states that "incidentally, these are the earliest recordings we have found of the tenor," which may be true if *we have found* is emphasized. There may be an extant Mozart REQUIEM from 1939 featuring Tagliavini, issued on Heliodor 8805, though this was dated 5 December, 1941 in Luigi Bellingardi's De Sabata discography in Teodoro Celli's *L'arte de Victor De Sabata* (Torino: ERI, 1978), and depending upon the true provenance of the present recital, a number of commercial Cetras recorded as early as 1940.

Band 6: Given as "Ay di me" on the label of EJS 417 with "Pascolle" attached. "Pasacalle," which belongs with band 8, is a rhythm of the High Mountains, or Andes, and is Bolivian/Peruvian in origin.

Band 7: Given as "El agonia" on the label of EJS 417. "Yarabí" (spelled "Yaravi" on the label) is also an Andes rhythm of Bolivian/Peruvian origin.

Band 8: Given the title "Canvin" on the label of EJS 417--in reality, the lyricist's surname! This is the "pasacalle" noted above.

EJS 418: "The Golden Age of Opera" (1 LP)
Issued December, 1967
MATRIX P-1475

"POTPOURRI No. 20"

SIDE 1 (418 A):

* 1. a) JOSEF SCHMIDT, tenor (orch/Erno Rapee): LA BOHÈME, Act I: Che gelida manina (Puccini) (I)
Broadcast, ***GENERAL MOTORS HOUR***, WJZ, Carnegie Hall, NYC, 7 Nov 1937

b) GRACE MOORE, soprano (orch/Erno Rapee): LA BOHÈME, Act I: Si, mi chiamano Mimi (Puccini) (I)
Broadcast, ***GENERAL MOTORS HOUR***, WJZ, Carnegie Hall, NYC, 7 Nov 1937

c) GRACE MOORE, soprano, and JOSEF SCHMIDT, tenor (orch/Erno Rapee): LA BOHÈME, Act I: O soave fanciulla (Puccini) (I)
Broadcast, ***GENERAL MOTORS HOUR***, WJZ, Carnegie Hall, NYC, 7 Nov 1937

* 2. a) JOSEF SCHMIDT, tenor (orch/Erno Rapee): TOSCA, Act I: Recondita armonia (Puccini) (I)
Broadcast, ***GENERAL MOTORS HOUR***, WJZ, Carnegie Hall, NYC, 7 Nov 1937

* b) GRACE MOORE, soprano (orch/Erno Rapee); TOSCA, Act II: Vissi d'arte (Puccini) (I)
Broadcast, ***GENERAL MOTORS HOUR***, WJZ, Carnegie Hall, NYC, 7 Nov 1937

* c) JOSEF SCHMIDT, tenor (orch/Erno Rapee): TOSCA, Act III: [E lucevan le stelle . . . ed olez]zava la terra (Puccini) (I)
Broadcast, ***GENERAL MOTORS HOUR***, WJZ, Carnegie Hall, NYC, 7 Nov 1937

* d) ROBERT WEEDE, baritone (orch and chorus/Erno Rapee): TOSCA, Act I: Tre sbirri . . . Te Deum (Puccini) (L and I)
Broadcast, ***GENERAL MOTORS HOUR***, WJZ, Carnegie Hall, NYC, 7 Nov 1937

* 3. a) GRACE MOORE, soprano (orch/Erno Rapee): MADAMA BUTTERFLY, Act II: Piangi? perchè? . . . Un bel dì, vedremo (Puccini) (I)
Broadcast, ***GENERAL MOTORS HOUR***, WJZ, Carnegie Hall, NYC, 7 Nov 1937

* b) GRACE MOORE, soprano, and JOSEF SCHMIDT, tenor (orch/Erno Rapee): MADAMA BUTTERFLY, Act I: Vogliatemi bene . . . to the end of the act (Puccini) (I)
Broadcast, ***GENERAL MOTORS HOUR***, WJZ, Carnegie Hall, NYC, 7 Nov 1937

SIDE 2 (418 B):

* 1. MARIA JERITZA, soprano (orch/Erno Rapee): DER ZIGEUNERPRIMAS, Act II: O komm mit mir ich tanz mit dir ins Himmelreich hin ein (Kálmán) (G)
Broadcast, ?***GENERAL MOTORS HOUR***, WJZ, Carnegie Hall, NYC, 3 Oct 1937

* 2. MARIA JERITZA, soprano, and DONALD DICKSON, baritone (orch/Erno Rapee): DON GIOVANNI, K. 527, Act I: Reich mir die Hand, mein Leben [Là ci darem la mano] (Mozart) (G)
Broadcast, ***GENERAL MOTORS HOUR***, WJZ, Carnegie Hall, NYC, 3 Oct 1937

* 3. MARIA JERITZA, soprano, and JOSEF SCHMIDT, tenor (orch/Erno Rapee): FAUST, Act III: Ô nuit d'amour! ciel radieux (Gounod) (F)
Broadcast, ***GENERAL MOTORS HOUR***, WJZ, Carnegie Hall, NYC, 3 Oct 1937

* 4. GRACE MOORE, soprano (orch/Erno Rapee): LOUISE, Act III: Depuis le jour (Charpentier) (F)
Broadcast, ***GENERAL MOTORS HOUR***, WJZ, Carnegie Hall, NYC, 24 Oct 1937

* 5. GRACE MOORE, soprano (orch and chorus/Erno Rapee): MANON, Act III: Obéissons quand leur voix appelle ["Gavotte"] (Gounod) (F)
Broadcast, ***GENERAL MOTORS HOUR***, WJZ, Carnegie Hall, NYC, 24 Oct 1937

* 6. GRACE MOORE, soprano (orch/Erno Rapee): "English Lavender" ["Who'll Buy My Lavender?"] (Edward German) (E)
Broadcast, ***GENERAL MOTORS HOUR***, WJZ, Carnegie Hall, NYC, 24 Oct 1937

* 7. GRACE MOORE, soprano (St. Louis Symphony Orchestra/Vladimir Golschmann): I PAGLIACCI, Act I: Stridono lassù ["Ballatella"] (Leoncavallo) (I)
Broadcast, ***GENERAL MOTORS HOUR***, KWK, Municipal Auditorium, St. Louis, 21 Nov 1937

* 8. MARIA JERITZA, soprano (orch/Erno Rapee): JEANNE D'ARC, Act I: Adieu, forêts [Prostitye vi, kholmi] (Tchaikowsky) (F)
Broadcast, ***GENERAL MOTORS HOUR***, WJZ, NYC, 28 Nov 1937

* 9. MARIA JERITZA, soprano (orch/Erno Rapee): "Carry Me Back to Old Virginny" (Bland) (E)
Broadcast, ?***GENERAL MOTORS HOUR***, WJZ, NYC, 28 Nov 1937

NOTES: EJS 418

Most of these ***GENERAL MOTORS HOUR*** excerpts are introduced by Milton Cross. The FAUST duet is preceded by audience laughter, the result, it has been suggested, of the audience's possible reaction to a five-foot *Faust* and a nearly six-foot *Marguerite*.

Some of the Schmidt material (I/1a-c, 2a and c, and 3b) appeared subsequently on MDP-019, "The Legendary Tenor Joseph Schmidt," while a few of Moore's solos (I/3a and II/4-7) found there way onto MDP-027, "Grace Moore . . . Live!" Melodram compact disc CDM 18035 also featured several excerpts from this 7 November, 1937 Carnegie Hall broadcast as well as some of the other Moore solos included on EJS 418.

Side 1 (418 A):

Bands 1-3: An all-Puccini concert. The "O soave fanciulla" was a substitution not listed in the *New York Times* radio logs.

Band 2b: The last "perchè me ne rimuneri così?" appears to be spliced in from another source--possibly the 9 February, 1946 Met broadcast issued in excerpts on EJS 456 (January, 1969).

Band 2c: A break in the original source (perhaps a bad groove skip) consumes the first line of the aria after the orchestral introduction.

Band 2d: *Spoletta's* solo lines are omitted.

Band 3b: The end of the duet, from Moore's final "O quanti occhi fisi," appears to have been taken from the soundtrack of ***I'LL TAKE ROMANCE*** (Columbia, 1937). The excerpt cuts off abruptly after her final note, omitting the postlude. The entire BUTTERFLY excerpt from this feature film, with tenor Frank Forest, appeared earlier on EJS 214 (June, 1961): see that issue (I/1) for details on the film.

Side 2 (418 B):

Bands 1-3: The 3 October, 1937 broadcast of the ***GENERAL MOTORS HOUR*** was billed as the season premiere of a "permanent concert group" to include (in addition to Jeritza, Schmidt, and Dickson) Grace Moore, Helen Jepson, Erna Sack, Jussi Bjoerling, and Richard Tauber. Moore and Jepson would broadcast from Hollywood, Sack and Bjoerling from Stockholm, and Tauber from Derby, England. The accompanying orchestra is noted at 70 pieces. The "invited guests" at this premiere gathering numbered 3,000.

Jeritza's ZIGEUNERPRIMAS aria is the only Jeritza item not listed among the contents of the show (Stolz's "Im prater" is), so may have been a substitution: provenance seems clearly to dictate its origin.

Bands 4-6: This 24 October broadcast also featured Richard Tauber and the 70 piece "General Motors Orchestra." The tenor performed the PAGLIACCI "Vesti la giubba," a Grieg song, an aria from Lehár's FRASQUITA, and with Moore, the Act IV love duet from ROMÉO ET JULIETTE and TROVATORE "Miserere," so evidently, he, too, was on hand at

Carnegie Hall (it was noted on 3 October that he would be heard direct from Derby). Tauber's portion of the broadcast was issued complete on EJS 440 (September, 1968).

Band 7: Moore and Tauber were broadcasting with the St. Louis Symphony on 21 November, probably from the studios of KWK, the local NBC Blue affiliate. He was heard doing "M'appari" from MARTHA, the Johann Strauss-Korngold "Song of Love," and the Grieg "Vaaren." Together they performed the Schubert "Ständchen." The latter three appeared on EJS 440 (September, 1968).

Bands 8-9: Fritz Kreisler's "Liebesleid," not "Carry Me Back to Old Virginny," is shown as having been sung by Jeritza on this 28 November broadcast. The Bland song could not be found elsewhere among her broadcasts, though Jeritza often sang similar fare on the radio. It is assumed that this was a substitution and that the origin of the performance given in the listing is correct.

Jussi Bjoerling, billed as "Tenor of the Royal Opera at Stockholm," made his American radio debut on this broadcast, singing three solos and the "Tu qui Santuzza" from CAVALLERIA RUSTICANA with Jeritza. These excerpts appeared earlier on EJS 405 (September, 1967).

EJS 419: "The Golden Age of Opera" (3 LPs)
Issued January, 1968
MATRIX P-1500

SIDES 1-6 (419 A-F):

DON GIOVANNI, K. 527 (Mozart) (I)
Opera in 2 acts (complete)
Wiener Philharmoniker Orchestra and Chorus of the Wiener Staatsoper/ Wilhelm Furtwängler
Broadcast, Salzburg Festival, Festspielhaus, Salzburg, July-August, 1950

CAST:
Tito Gobbi (*Don Giovanni*); Ljuba Welitsch (*Donna Anna*); Elisabeth Schwarzkopf (*Donna Elvira*); Anton Dermota (*Don Ottavio*); Erich Kunz (*Leporello*); Irmgard Seefried (*Zerlina*); Alfred Poell (*Masetto*); Josef Greindl (*The Commandant*).

NOTES: EJS 419

The Salzburg performance from which this transfer was taken has not been identified precisely. The first performance that season was on 27 July, 1950, followed on 31 July, 4, 18, and 29 August. There appears to be general agreement that the 27 July performance, subsequently issued as Melodram MEL 713, is *not* the same performance. The Hunt Furtwängler discography in Jaeger's *Furtwängler: Analyse Dokument Protokoll* (Zurich: Atlantis Musikbuch, 1986), p. 195, gives August, 1950, with the claim that the EJS 419 performance is the same one found on Olympus 9109, Discocorp RR 407, and Turnabout THS 65154-6. Poell is not identified on the label of EJS 419.

The set plays noticeably flat at 33.3 rpm.

EJS 420: "The Golden Age of Opera" (1 LP)
Issued January, 1968
MATRIX P-1502

LA VALSE DE PARIS
A Lux Films Release
Director: Marcel Achord
Screenplay: Marcel Achord
Photographer: Christian Matras
Sets: Bakst and André Clavel
Costumes: Christian Dior
Paris Premiere: ?
New York Premiere (as "Paris Waltz"): Paris Theater, NYC, 22 Aug 1950

CAST:
Pierre Fresnay (*Offenbach*); Yvonne Printemps (*Hortense Schneider*); Jacques Charon (*Berthelier*); Alexandre Astruc (*Achard*); Jacques Castelot (*The Duke of Morny*); Claude Sainval (*The Prince*); Pierre Dux (*Russian General*); Lucien Nat (*Napolean III*); Robert Manuel (*Dupuis*); André Roussin (*Henri Meilhac*); Noëlle Norman (*Marie Prideau*); Denise Provençe (*Brigitte*); Raymonde Allain (*Empress Eugenie*); Renné Senac [sic] (*Mother of Hortense*).

SIDE 1 (420 A):

* 1. a) PRINTEMPS (pf/?): LE CHANSON DE FORTUNIO: Si vous croyez (Offenbach) (F)
b) PRINTEMPS and Chorus (orch/?): LA VIE PARISENNE, Act II: Je suis veuve d'un colonel (Offenbach) (F)
c) PRINTEMPS and unidentified tenor and baritone (orch/?): LA VIE PARISIENNE, Act II, Finale: Volontiers je fais longue pause (Offenbach) (F)
d) PRINTEMPS (pf/?): ORPHÉE AUX ENFERS: Waltz (vocal exercises) (Offenbach) (F)

* 2. PRINTEMPS and unidentified baritone (orch/?): LA PERICHOLE, Act II: Mon Dieu, que les hommes sont bêtes (Offenbach) (F)

3. PRINTEMPS and Chorus (orch/?): MADAME FAVART, Act I: Ma mère aux vignes m'en voyait ["Ronde des Vignes"] (Offenbach) (F)

4. PRINTEMPS (orch/?): LA PERICHOLE, Act I: O mon cher amant, je te jure ["La lettre"] (Offenbach) (F)

SIDE 2 (420 B):

* 1. a) PRINTEMPS (orch/?): ORPHÉE AUX ENFERS: Waltz (vocalise) (Offenbach-arr.) (F)
b) PRINTEMPS (orch/?): LA BELLE HÉLÈNE, Act II: Oui! c'est un rêve (Offenbach-arr.) (F)

* 2. PRINTEMPS and FRESNAY (orch/?): MADAME L'ARCHIDUC, Act ?: Pas ça (Offenbach) (F)

* 3. PRINTEMPS and Chorus (pf/?): LA GRANDE-DUCHESSE DE GÉROLSTEIN, Act I: Ah! que j'aime les militaires (Offenbach) (F)

4. PRINTEMPS (orch/?): LA GRANDE-DUCHESSE DE GÉROLSTEIN, Act II: Dites-lui qu'on l'a remarqué (Offenbach) (F)

* 5. a) FRESNAY and two unidentified male actors: DIALOGUE
b) PRINTEMPS (orch/?): LA VIE PARISIENNE: fragments (Offenbach) (F)
c) PRINTEMPS (orch/?): LA GRANDE-DUCHESSE DE GÉROLSTEIN: fragments (Offenbach) (F)

* 6. FRESNAY and unidentifed male actor: DIALOGUE
b) PRINTEMPS (orch/?): LA BELLE HÉLÈNE, Act II: Dis-moi, Vénus ["Invocation à Vénus"] (Offenbach-arr.) (F)
c) PRINTEMPS and Chorus (orch/?): LA BELLE HÉLÈNE, Act II: Oui! c'est un rêve (Offenbach-arr.) (F)

NOTES: EJS 420

I have not seen the film ***LA VALSE DE PARIS***, and have thus been unable to contextualize the excerpts included on this LP. In the U.S., the film was publicized as "The stories of Offenbach to be taken lightly, and with a great deal of laughter."

Pierre Fresnay was the husband of Yvonne Printemps (they married in 1934). Alexandre Astruc (1923-), an actor here, eventually emerged as a successful screenwriter and director in the late 1940s. Writer and director Marcel Achard (1899-1974) and cinematographer Christian Matras (1903-1977) were both eminent figures in the French cinema.

Side 1 (420 A):

Band 1d: This is a vocal "exercise" sung to the waltz theme.

Band 2: This appears to be some sort of rehearsal scene.

Side 2 (420 B):

Band 1: This is a vocalise sung to the waltz theme. Both 1a and 1b have been re-orchestrated in a syrupy 1930s style.

Band 2: The original text to "Pas ça" has been altered here.

Band 3: Printemps sings only fragments of the "Ah! que j'aime les militaires," followed by the refrain with chorus. Like I/2 above, this appears to be some sort of rehearsal scene.

Band 5: Labeled "Potpourri: Story of Tristan & Isolde." This is a dialogue between Offenbach (Fresnay) and two unidentified characters, but without any reference to *Tristan*! Printemps is heard in the distance from time to time in fragmentary excerpts from LA VIE PARISIENNE and LA GRANDE-DUCHESSE DE GÉROLSTEIN.

Band 6: The dialogue between Offenbach (Fresnay) and an unidentified character contains some passing reference to *Tristan*. Printemps is heard in fragments from LA BELLE HÉLÈNE: the reprise of "Oui! c'est un rêve" at the close of the film has been re-orchestrated in a style vaguely reminiscent of Mantovani.

EJS 421: "The Golden Age of Opera" (1 LP)
Issued January, 1968
MATRIX P-1501

"LEYLA GENCER"

SIDE 1 (421 A):

1. w. Orchestra of Radio Italiana [RAI], Milano/Arturo Basile: ROBERTO DEVEREUX, Act III: Vivi, ingrato a lei d'accanto (Donizetti) (I) [34.00 rpm]
   RAI broadcast, Milan, 23 Nov 1965

* 2. w. Orchestra of Radio Italiana [RAI], Milano/Arturo Basile: ANNA BOLENA, Act II: Piangete voi . . . Al dolce guidami . . . Coppia iniqua (Donizetti) (I) [34.00 rpm]
   RAI broadcast, Milan, 23 Nov 1965

* 3. w. MAFALDA MASINI, mezzo-soprano (Orchestra and Chorus of the Maggio Musicale Fiorentino/Francesco Molinari-Pradelli): MARIA STUARDA, Act II: Oh nube che lieve per l'aria . . . Nella pace nel mesto riposo (Donizetti) (I) [32.3 rpm]
   Broadcast, Maggio Musicale Fiorentino, Teatro Comunale, Florence, 2 May 1967

* 4. w. FRANCO RICCIARDI, tenor, MARIO PETRI baritone, and AUGUSTO FRATI, bass-baritone (Orchestra of the Teatro San Carlo di Napoli/ Carlo Franci): LUCREZIA BORGIA, Prologue: Tranquillo ei posa . . . Com'è bello (Donizetti) (I) [32.8 rpm]
   Broadcast, Teatro San Carlo di Napoli, Naples, 31 Jan 1966

5. w. Orchestra of the Teatro Massimo, Palermo/Vittorio Gui: MACBETH, Act II: La luce langue (Verdi) (I) [32.6 rpm]
   Broadcast, Teatro Massimo, Palermo, 14 Jan 1960

SIDE 2 (421 B):

* 1. w. GIORGIO GIORGETTI, baritone, and O. CAROSSI, mezzo-soprano (Orchestra and Chorus of the Maggio Musicale Fiorentino/Vittorio Gui): LA BATTAGLIA DI LEGNANO, Act I: Voi lo dicesti . . . Quante volte come un dono . . . A frenarti, o cor, nel petto (Verdi) (I) [32.4 rpm]
   Broadcast, Maggio Musicale Fiorentino, Teatro della Pergola, Florence, 10 May 1959

2. w. Orchestra of the Teatro dell'Opera, Roma/Gianandrea Gavazzeni: LES VÊPRES SICILIENNES, Act V: Mercè, dilette amiche [Merci, jeunes amies] ["Bolero"] (Verdi) (I) [32.00 rpm]
   Broadcast, Teatro dell'Opera, Rome, 5 Dec 1964

3. w. Wiener Philharmoniker/Gianandrea Gavazzeni: SIMON BOCCANEGRA, Act I: Com'e in quest'ora bruna (Verdi) (I) [32.00 rpm]
   Broadcast, Salzburg Festival, Felsenreitschule, Salzburg, 9 Aug 1961

* 4. w. MARISA SALIMBENI, soprano (Orchestra and Chorus of the Teatro La Fenice/Tullio Serafin): I DUE FOSCARI, Act I: No! Mi lasciate! . . . Tu al cui sguardo . . . O patrizii, tremate (Verdi) (I) [33.3 rpm]
Broadcast, Teatro La Fenice, Venice, 26 Dec 1957

5. w. Orchestra of Radio Italiana [RAI], Milano/Arturo Basile: NABUCCO, Act II: Ben io t'invenni . . . Anch'io dischiuso un giorno (Verdi) (I) [33.3 rpm]
RAI Broadcast, Milan, 23 Nov 1965

* 6. w. GIACOMO ARAGALL, tenor (Orchestra of the Teatro La Fenice/ Gianandrea Gavazzeni): GERUSALEMME, Act II: D'un padre, ohime! l'immagine . . . Fuggiamo! Sol morte [Une pensée amène] (Verdi) (I)
Broadcast, Teatro La Fenice, Venice, 24 Sep 1963

NOTES: EJS 421

Side 1 (421 A):

Band 1: 10 May, 1959 was the *prima* of the production of BATTAGLIA, and is the performance noted as having been broadcast in the Cella Gencer biography. *14* May has also been suggested, but there is no evidence that this second performance was actually broadcast, that the 10 May performance was rebroadcast on that date, or that a second performance has ever circulated. The complete 10 May performance was subsequently reisssued by Replica.

Band 2: The chorus and other soloists were omitted in the *Scena Finale* of this concert version of ANNA BOLENA.

Band 3: 2 May, 1967 was the first performance of this production, and the one known to have been broadcast. The GFC 001/3 LP issue of the performance gives this date, where the Nuova Era CD edition, culled from the archives of the Maggio Musicale, contains a different performance, and is dated only as "1967." EJS 421 appears to be identical to the GFC issue, and has been independently documented as having been taken from the 2 May, 1967 broadcast.

Band 4: Reported to be from the 5 June, 1967 Rome performance, but this has been compared to the complete 1966 Naples performance issued as EJS 368 in June, 1966, and more recently on a Hunt CD: the two Prologue excerpts are identical.

Side 2 (421 B):

Band 4: The complete FOSCARI was earlier issued as EJS 155 (June, 1959). See the endnote for that LP regarding the date of the performance.

Band 6: This was originally the Act III love duet in I LOMBARDI, the predecessor of GERUSALEME. The speed is unknown, but the recitative begins in G, the first part of the duet in E, and the second part in A.

EJS 422: "The Golden Age of Opera" (1 LP)
Issued February, 1968
MATRIX P-1536

ERNANI (Verdi) (I)
Opera in 4 acts (excerpts)
Orchestra and Chorus of the Maggio Musicale Fiorentino/Dimitri Mitropoulos
Broadcast, Maggio Musicale Fiorentino, Teatro Comunale, Florence, 14 Jun 1957

CAST:
Mario Del Monaco (*Ernani*); Anita Cerquetti (*Elvira*); Ettore Bastianini (*Carlo V*); Boris Christoff (*Silva*); Athos Cesarini (*Riccardo*); Lucianna Boni (*Giovanna*); Aborian Neagu (*Jago*).

SIDE 1 (422 A):

1. Act I: a) DEL MONACO and Chorus: Scene i: Mercè, diletti amici . . . Come rugiada al cespite . . . O tu che l'alma adora
b) CERQUETTI, BASTIANINI, BONI, DEL MONACO, CHRISTOFF, CESARINI, NEAGU and Chorus: Scene ii: complete

SIDE 2 (422 B):

1. Act II: a) DEL MONACO, CERQUETTI, and CHRISTOFF: Oro, quant'oro ogn'avido . . . Ah, morir potessi adesso!
b) BASTIANINI, CHRISTOFF, CERQUETTI, CESARINI, BONI, DEL MONACO, and Chorus: Lo vedremo, veglio audace . . . to the end of the scene

Act III: c) BASTIANINI: O de' verd'anni miei
d) BASTIANINI, DEL MONACO, CERQUETTI, and Chorus: La volontà del ciel sarà mia . . . O sommo Carlo

Act IV: e) DEL MONACO, CERQUETTI, and CHRISTOFF: Cessaro i suoni . . . to the end of the opera

NOTES: EJS 422

This performance was issued complete on Fonit-Cetra DOC-36, Melodram MEL-27016, and CLS AMDRL 32 814. Excerpts appeared subsequently on I Gioielli della Lirica GML 33.

EJS 423: "The Golden Age of Opera" (1 LP)
Issued February, 1968
MATRIX P-1537

NABUCCO [NABUCODNOSOR] (Verdi) (I)
Opera in 4 acts (excerpts)
Orchestra and Chorus of the Omroepvereniging [VARA]/Fulvio Vernizzi
Broadcast, VARA, Hilversum, Holland, 13 Apr 1961

CAST:
Dino Dondi (*Nabucco*); Anita Cerquetti (*Abigaille*); Ugo Trama (*Zaccaria*); Ugo Trama (*High Priest*); Giampaolo Corradi (*Ismaele*); Giampaolo Corradi (*Abdallo*); Giovanna Fioroni (*Fenena*); Gerry De Groot (*Anna*).

SIDE 1 (423 A):

1. Act I: a) CERQUETTI, CORRADI, and FIORONI: Guerrieri, è preso il tempio . . . Io t'amava!

   Act II: * b) CERQUETTI, TRAMA, CORRADI, DONDI, FIORONI, DE GROOT, and Chorus: Lo vedeste? Fulminando . . . Tremin gl'insani . . . O vinti, il capo a terra! . . . to the end of the act

   c) CERQUETTI, and TRAMA: Ben io t'invenni . . . Anch'io dischiuso un giorno . . . Salgo gia dal trono aurato

SIDE 2 (423 B):

1. Act II: a) CORRADI and Chorus: Che si vuol? Chi mai ci chiama?

   b) DE GROOT, CORRADI, FIORONI, DONDI, CERQUETTI, and TRAMA: Deh, fratelli, perdonate . . . S'appressan gl'istanti . . . Chi mi toglie il regio scettro

   Act III: c) TRAMA, CORRADI, DONDI, and CERQUETTI: Eccelsa donna, che d'Assiria . . . Donna, chi sei? . . . Oh, di qual'onta aggravasi . . . Deh, perdona, deh, perdona

   Act IV: d) ASSEMBLED CAST and Chorus: O dischiuso è il firmamento . . . to the end of the opera

NOTES: EJS 423

Side 1 (423 A):

Band 1b: For some unknown reason, this excerpt reaches the conclusion of the ensemble, to *Nabucco's* "O vinti, il capo a terra," then repeats the section beginning "Viva Nabucco!" before proceeding to the end of the act. It is doubtful that this ocurred in the actual performance.

The Cerquetti chronology included in Timaclub LP Tima 23 gives no date for this performance, where the I Gioielli della Lyrica LP GML 78 gives 24 April, 1960.

EJS 424: "The Golden Age of Opera" (1 LP)
Issued February, 1968
MATRIX P-1538

TANNHÄUSER (Wagner) (G and I)
Opera in 3 acts (excerpts)
Orchestra and Chorus of the Teatro San Carlo di Napoli/Karl Böhm
Broadcast, Teatro San Carlo, Naples, 12 Mar 1950

CAST:
Hans Beirer (*Tannhäuser*); Renata Tebaldi (*Elisabeth*); Carlo Tagliabue (*Wolfram*); Boris Christoff (*Landgraf*); [Livia Pery (*Venus*)]; [Petre Munteanu (*Walther*)]; [Augusto Romani (*Biterolf*)]; [Gianni Avolanti (*Heinrich*)]; [Igino Ricco (*Reinmar*)]; [Gilda Martini Rossi (*A Young Shepherd*)].

SIDE 1 (424 A):

Act I:
1. TEBALDI, BEIRER, and TAGLIABUE: Dich, teure Halle . . . Gepriesen sei die Stunde! . . . Heinrich!
2. CHRISTOFF: Gar veil und schön
3. TAGLIABUE: Blick'ich umher

SIDE 2 (424 B):

Act I:
1. CHRISTOFF, TEBALDI, TAGLIABUE, BEIRER, and Chorus: Ha! Der Verruchter! . . . Himmels Mittlerin verkannt!

Act III:
2. TEBALDI: Allmächt'ge Jungfrau
3. TAGLIABUE: Wie Todesahnung . . . O du mein holder Abenstern
4. TAGLIABUE and BEIRER: Doch sprich! Du pilgertest nach Rom? . . . Inbrust im Herzen ["Rome Narrative"] . . . im Venusberg drangen wir ein!

NOTES: EJS 424

Note that Beirer sang the title role in German while the rest of the cast sang in Italian. The original German text is given in the listing for ease of reference.

The *Chronache del Teatro S. Carlo 1948-1968* (Milan: Ricordi, 1969) lists Max Lorenz as the *Tannhäuser* on 12 March, 1950, as does the reissue of the complete performance on HRE 201-3. Lorenz was indeed scheduled to sing the title role, but was forced to cancel because of ill health. Co-author Collins has a letter from Hans Beirer confirming this, as well as photographs of the placard outside the theater, and of Beirer and Tebaldi on stage.

The performance was later issued complete as HRE 201-3. Excerpts appeared on the Standing Room Only CD SRO 834-1, "Tebaldi Sings "Wagner," coupled with excerpts from her 1954 Naples LOHENGRIN.

EJS 424 plays a bit sharp at 33.3 rpm.

EJS 425: "The Golden Age of Opera" (1 LP)
Issued February, 1968
MATRIX P-1535

"POTPOURRI NO. 21"

SIDE 1 (425 A):

* 1. LOTTE LEHMANN, soprano (NBC Orchestra/Frank Black): TOSCA, Act II: Vissi d'arte (Puccini) (I)
Broadcast, ***THE MAGIC KEY OF RCA***, WJZ, NYC, 3 Apr 1938

* 2. LOTTE LEHMANN, soprano (NBC Orchestra/Frank Black): ACHT LIEDER AUS LETZTE BLÄTTER, Op. 10, no. 1: Zueignung (von Gilm-R. Strauss) (G)
Broadcast, ***THE MAGIC KEY OF RCA***, WJZ, NYC, 3 Apr 1938

* 3. LOTTE LEHMANN, soprano (pf/Erno Balogh): Das Mädchen spricht, Op. 107, no. 3 (Gruppe-Brahms)
Broadcast, ***THE MAGIC KEY OF RCA***, WJZ, NYC, 3 Apr 1938

* 4. LOTTE LEHMANN, soprano (pf/Erno Balogh): Wiegenlied, Op. 49, no. 4 (Scherer-Brahms) (G)
Broadcast, ***THE MAGIC KEY OF RCA***, WJZ, NYC, 3 Apr 1938

* 5. LUCREZIA BORI, soprano (Los Angeles Philharmonic Orchestra/Otto Klemperer): LA BOHÈME, Act I: Si, mi chiamano Mimi (Puccini) (I)
Broadcast, ***GENERAL MOTORS HOUR***, KECA [NBC], Hollywood Bowl, Los Angeles, 6 Jun 1937

* 6. LUCREZIA BORI, soprano (Los Angeles Philharmonic Orchestra/Otto Klemperer): "English Lavender" ["Who'll Buy My Lavender?"] (Edward German) (E)
Broadcast, ***GENERAL MOTORS HOUR***, KECA [NBC], Hollywood Bowl, Los Angeles, 6 Jun 1937

* 7. LUCREZIA BORI, soprano (Los Angeles Philharmonic Orchestra/Otto Klemperer): "Clavelitos" (Valverde) (S)
Broadcast, ?***GENERAL MOTORS HOUR***, ?KECA [NBC], Hollywood Bowl, Los Angeles, 6 Jun 1937

8. ROSE PAULY, soprano (Detroit Symphony Orchestra/Fritz Reiner): ACHT LIEDER AUS LETZTE BLÄTTER, Op. 10, no. 8: Allerseelen (von Gilm-R. Strauss) (G)
Broadcast, ***FORD SUNDAY EVENING HOUR***, WJR, Detroit, 20 Feb 1938

* 9. MARIA JERITZA, soprano (Carnegie Hall Promenade Orchestra/Erno Rapee): CAVALLERIA RUSTICANA: Voi lo sapete (Mascagni) (I)
Broadcast, ***GENERAL MOTORS HOUR***, WJZ, Carnegie Hall, NYC, 23 May 1937

10. LAURITZ MELCHIOR, tenor (Detroit Symphony Orchestra/José Iturbi): DIE MEISTERSINGER VON NÜRNBERG, Act III: Morgenlich leuchtend ["Prize Song"] (Wagner) (G)
Broadcast, ***FORD SUNDAY EVENING HOUR***, WJR, Detroit, 17 Oct 1937

SIDE 2 (425 B):

* 1. GALLIANO MASINI, tenor (Detroit Symphony Orchestra/Eugene Ormandy): TOSCA, Act I: Recondita armonia (Puccini) (I)
Broadcast, ***FORD SUNDAY EVENING HOUR***, WJR, Detroit, 12 Dec 1937

* 2. GALLIANO MASINI, tenor (Detroit Symphony Orchestra/Eugene Ormandy): RIGOLETTO, Act I: Questa o quella (Verdi) (I)
Broadcast, ***FORD SUNDAY EVENING HOUR***, WJR, Detroit, 12 Dec 1937

* 3. GALLIANO MASINI, tenor (Detroit Symphony Orchestra/Eugene Ormandy): TOSCA, Act III: E lucevan le stelle (Puccini) (I)
Broadcast, ***FORD SUNDAY EVENING HOUR***, WJR, Detroit, 12 Dec 1937

* 4. GALLIANO MASINI, tenor (Detroit Symphony Orchestra/Eugene Ormandy): AÏDA, Act I: Se quel guerrier io fossi . . . Celeste Aïda (Verdi) (I)
Broadcast, ***FORD SUNDAY EVENING HOUR***, WJR, Detroit, 12 Dec 1937

* 5. ELISABETH RETHBERG, soprano (Detroit Symphony Orchestra/Fritz Reiner): FIDELIO, Op. 72, Act I: Abscheulicher! Wo eilst du hin? . . . Komm, Hoffnung (Beethoven) (G)
Broadcast, ***FORD SUNDAY EVENING HOUR***, WJR, Detroit, 30 Jan 1938

6. ELISABETH RETHBERG, soprano (Detroit Symphony Orchestra/Fritz Reiner): VIER LIEDER, Op. 27, no. 4: Morgen (Mackay-R. Strauss) (G)
Broadcast, ***FORD SUNDAY EVENING HOUR***, WJR, Detroit, 30 Jan 1938

7. ELISABETH RETHBERG, soprano (Detroit Symphony Orchestra/Fritz Reiner): "Spring Fancy" (Densmore) (E)
Broadcast, ***FORD SUNDAY EVENING HOUR***, WJR, Detroit, 30 Jan 1938

* 8. ERNA SACK, soprano (orch/?): "Frühlingsstimmen-Walzer," Op. 410 (Richard Genée-J. Strauss) (G)
Broadcast, ***THE MAGIC KEY OF RCA***, WJZ, NYC, 22 Mar 1936

* 9. ERNA SACK, soprano (orch/?): "La Foletta" (Marchesi) (I)
Broadcast, ***THE MAGIC KEY OF RCA***, WJZ, NYC, 22 Marc 1936

NOTES: EJS 425

Side 1 (425 A):

Band 1-4: The Lehmann broadcast was an "Army Day Salute," with pickups, according to the *New York Times*, "from stratasphere and bombing planes and from United States Army Bases." General Malin Craig of the Joint Chiefs of Staff also spoke on the program. The Lehmann titles are announced by Milton Cross.

Bands 2 and 3 later appeared on the Bruno Walter Society LP "In Memoriam / Lotte Lehmann" (BWS 729).

Bands 5-7: This 6 June, 1937 Hollywood Bowl broadcast, which included an abridged "concert presentation" of LA BOHÈME, also featured tenor Joseph Bentonelli: two of his solos from the broadcast and the duets with Bori were included on EJS 292 (February, 1964). Bori's

"English Lavender" was included earlier on EJS 295 (March, 1964). The concert was broadcast over WJZ (NBC Blue) in New York City, so probably originated over the Los Angeles Blue Network affiliate, KECA, not KFI.

The "Clavelitos" was not listed on the program in the *New York Times*, and may have been a last minute substitution. On the other hand, Bori *did* sing the song often on the radio (on the ***CHESTERFIELD HOUR*** of 6 March, 1935, for example), so Smith may have had access to another broadcast source.

Band 9: Jeritza's co-star on this broadcast was tenor Lanny Ross.

Side 2 (425 B):

Bands 1-5: Billed as Masini's American radio debut.

Band 5: This performance appeared earlier on EJS 255 (January, 1963).

Bands 8-9: Frank Black conducted the orchestra on this broadcast for Sack's co-star, tenor Lanny Ross, but Sack herself was heard live from Dresden, orchestra and conductor unknown.

EJS 426: "The Golden Age of Opera" (1 LP)
Issued February, 1968
MATRIX P-1558

"STELLA ROMAN"

SIDE 1 (426 A):

1. a) w. Metropolitan Opera House Orchestra and Chorus/Fausto Cleva): NORMA, Act I: Casta diva . . . Ah! bello a me ritorna (Bellini) (I)
   XCO 34725- New York, 14 May 1945 Columbia unpublished
   XCO 34726- New York, 14 May 1945 Columbia unpublished

   * b) JENNIE TOUREL, soprano (w. Metropolitan Opera House Orchestra/ Fausto Cleva): NORMA, Act I: Sospirar non vista . . . Deh! Proteggimi, o Dio! (Bellini) (I)
   XCO 34727- New York, 14 May 1945 Columbia unpublished

   c) w. JENNIE TOUREL, soprano (w. Metropolitan Opera House Orchestra/Fausto Cleva): NORMA, Act I: E come e quando nacque tal fiamma in te? . . . Dolce qual arpa armonica . . . Ah! si fa core (Bellini) (I)
   XCO 34728- New York, 14 May 1945 Columbia unpublished
   XCO 34880- New York, 4 Jun 1945 Columbia unpublished

   d) w. JENNIE TOUREL, soprano (w. Metropolitan Opera House Orchestra/Fausto Cleva): NORMA, Act II: Odi! Purgar quest' aura . . . Mira o Norma! (Bellini) (I)
   XCO-34881- New York, 4 Jun 1945 Columbia unpublished
   XCO-34882- New York, 4 Jun 1945 Columbia unpublished
   XCO-34883- New York, 4 Jun 1945 Columbia unpublished

SIDE 2 (426 B):

* 1. w. Los Angeles Philharmonic Orchestra/Artur Rodzinski: DIE TOTE STADT, Act I: Glück, das mir verblieb ["Mariettas Lied"] (Korngold) (G)
Broadcast, ***LOS ANGELES PHILHARMONIC***, Hollywood Bowl, Los Angeles, 18 Jul 1950

* 2. w. Los Angeles Philharmonic Orchestra/Artur Rodzinski: ANDREA CHENIER, Act III: La mamma morta (Giordano) (I)
Broadcast, ***LOS ANGELES PHILHARMONIC***, Hollywood Bowl, Los Angeles, 18 Jul 1950

* 3. w. Los Angeles Philharmonic Orchestra/Artur Rodzinski: MANON LESCAUT, Act II: In quelle trine morbide (Puccini) (I)
Broadcast, ***LOS ANGELES PHILHARMONIC***, Hollywood Bowl, Los Angeles, 18 Jul 1950

* 4. w. orch/Howard Barlow; TOSCA, Act II: Vissi d'arte (Puccini) (I)
Broadcast, ***THE VOICE OF FIRESTONE***, WEAF, Rockefeller Center, New York City, 22 Apr 1946

5. w. Metropolitan Opera House Orchesta/Cesare Sodero: LA BOHÈME, Act I: Si, mi chiamano Mimi (Puccini) (I)
Metropolitan Opera broadcast, NYC, 2 Mar 1946

6. w. Metropolitan Opera House Orchesta/Cesare Sodero: LA BOHÈME, Act III: Donde lieta usci ["Addio"] (Puccini) (I)
Metropolitan Opera broadcast, NYC, 2 Mar 1946

NOTES: EJS 426

The second side of this LP (EJS 426 B) has no matrix number in the wax.

Side 1 (426 A):

Band 1a-d: Except for matrix XCO 34727, which appeared on the Odyssey LP Y2 32880, a 1974 Tourel tribute recital, EJS 426 has been the only issue of these NORMA performances. The take numbers used here could not be documented. Legato Classics compact disc LCD 139-1, "Legends of Opera," included the NORMA excerpts, all incorrectly dated as 1948.

The "Sospirar non vista . . . Deh! Proteggimi" (I/1b) features only Tourel.

Side 2 (426 B):

Bands 1-3: Taken, ostensibly, from Armed Forces Radio Service transcriptions of this 1950 Hollywood Bowl performance, but the actual discs could not be documented. IRCC CD 806, the first volume of "A 1940s Radio Hour," included the CHENIER and MANON LESCAUT arias, incorrectly dated as 1946.

Band 4: Roman's co-star on this 22 April, 1946 broadcast was baritone Igor Gorin.

EJS 427: "The Golden Age of Opera" (2 LPs)
ISSUED March, 1968
MATRIX P-1565

SIDES 1-4 (427 A-D):

LA DAME BLANCHE (Boïeldieu) (F)
Opéra-comique in 3 acts (complete)
Orchestra and Chorus/Jean Fournet
Broadcast, ?Amsterdam, 28 Nov 1964

CAST:
Nicolai Gedda (*Georges Brown*); Erna Spoorenberg (*Anne*); Frans [Franz] Vroons (*Dickson*); Mimi Van Aarden (*Jennie*); Sophia Van Sante (*Marguerite*); Guus Hoekman (*Gaveston*); Henk Driessen (*MacIreton*).

NOTES: EJS 427

Though the origin of this broadcast could not be determined, it has been suggested that the accompanying ensemble was the Concertgebouw Orchestra.

Subsequently issued on HRE and on the two-disc Melodram CD 27053. Both the EJS and Melodram issues are filled with cast misspellings, and there remains some doubt as to whether Van Aarden and Van Sante are reversed in their role assignment (both *Jennie* and *Marguerite* were scored originally for soprano: Van Aarden was a contralto, Van Sante a mezzo).

With the exception of *Anna's* third act recitative and aria, which were omitted from EJS 427 altogether, there are only a few very minor cuts made in the score. These were probably all performance cuts and not done by Smith for timing purposes, as he had plenty of room to squeeze them in.

Splices are apparent throught the performance. Speeds generally run betweem 33.4 and 33.5 rpm, with occasional flights upward to 33.8 rpm.

EJS 428: "The Golden Age of Opera" (2 LPs)
Issued March, 1968
MATRIX P-1571

SIDES 1-4 (428 A-D):

ALESSANDRO STRADELLA (Flotow) (G)
Opera in 3 acts (complete)
Orchestra and Chorus of the Landestheater, Linz/Siegfried Meik
?Broadcast, Landestheater, Linz, date unknown

CAST:
Waldemar Kmennt (*Stradella*); Hanny Steffek (*Leonore*); Ludwig Cinika (*Bassi*); Paul Conrad (*Malvolio*); Franz Glawatsch (*Barbarino*).

EJS 429: "The Golden Age of Opera" (1 LP)
Issued March, 1968
MATRIX P-1570

L'OCA DEL CAIRO, K. 422 (Mozart) (G)
Opera in 2 acts (complete)
München Kammerorchester and Chorus/Günther Weissenborn
Sommerliche Musiktage Hitzacker, Kurhaus, Waldfrieden,
28 or 29 Jul 1966

CAST:
Paul Medina (*Don Pippo*); Charlotte Lehemann (*Celidora*); Georg Selden (*Biondello*); Kurt Westi (*Calandrino*); Gertraut Stoklasse (*Lavinia*); Ilse Hollweg (*Auretta*); Ernst Gerold Schramm (*Chichibio*); [?Marlies Pommerien (*?Donna Pantea*)].

SIDE 1 (429 A):

* 1. Orchestra: unidentified Overture
* 2. Chorus: unidentified chorus
* 3. No. 1: HOLLWEG and SCHRAMM: Cosi si fa
* 4. No. 2: HOLLWEG: Se fosse qui nasconso
* 5. No. 3: SCHRAMM: Ogni momento
* 6. No. 4: HOLLWEG and SCHRAMM: Ho un pensiero nel cervello

SIDE 2 (429 B):

* 1. No. 5: MEDIAN, HOLLWEG, and SCHRAMM: O pazzo, o pazzo . . . Siano pronte alle gran nozze
* 2. No. 6: LEHEMANN, HELDEN, STOCKLASSA, and WESTI: S'oggi, oh Dei
* 3. No. 7: ASSEMBLED CAST and Chorus: Su, via putti, presto, presto!

NOTES: EJS 429

The listing and the notes below have been cued to the original critical edition, *W. A. Mozart Sämtliche Werke* [*Mozart's Werke*] (Leipzig: Breitkopf & Härtel, 1877-1910), volume 24, no. 37. L'OCA DEL CAIRO has also been published in the *Neue Ausgabe Sätliche Werke* (Salzburg: International Mozart Foundation, 1956-) as volume 2:5, no. 13, published in 1960.

Mozart left L'OCA DEL CAIRO (THE GOOSE OF CAIRO) incomplete after scoring six numbers of Act I, and a duet that is not included in the original Abbe Giambattista Varesco libretto (I/6 above).

Conceived in two acts, the opera was composed in 1783. Mozart evidently abandoned it as his interest and trust in the quality of the libretto began to diminish. The surviving fragments were first published by Johann Anton André in 1855, and because Mozart left a detailed description of the construction of the second act (in letters of December, 1783), several attempts--in several languages--to finish the work were subsequently made, beginning with a French version by T.C. Constantin and V. Wilder (Fantaisies-Parisiennes, Paris, 6 June, 1867), which added a Rondo-Quartet, "Ah, che ridere!," the Overture from Mozart's own two-act LO SPOSO DELUSO, K. 430, and the finale from Francesco Bianchi's 1783 two-act opera LA VILLANELLA RAPITA (this finale was originally a Mozart composition interpolated into the Bianchi score). Concert performances of the original L'OCA DEL CAIRO fragments go back even further, to Frankfurt, 1860. See Alfred Lowenberg's *Annals of Opera 1597-1940*, 2nd revised and corrected ed. (New York: Rowman and Littlefield, 1970), coumns 992-993, for a detailed summary of the opera's performance history. Edward Dent, in his book *Mozart's Operas: A Critical Study*, 2nd ed. (London: Oxford University Press, 1947), dismissed these various editions of the opera as "foolish attempts . . . to add another opera of Mozart to the repertory by patching these and other fragments together on the basis of a new libretto" (pp. 101-102). Indeed, as late as 1952, Hans Erismann based his three-act DON PEDROS HEIMKEHR (London: Kalmus) on these and other Mozart fragments.

Hans Redlich's Italian adaptation of the work (Sadler's Wells, 30 May, 1940) seems the likeliest to have been used for the performance heard on EJS 429, but his used only the music from L'OCA DEL CAIRO, with no borrowings from other Mozart compositions, leaving the Overture and opening chorus unexplained.

The German translation used for the performance could not be traced: the original Italian text taken from the Breitkopf and Härtel complete works has been given instead.

The spelling of cast names is unusually chaotic on the label of EJS 429: the *Celidora* is NOT "Lotte *Lehmann*," but Charlotte *Lehemann* (listed by Kutsch-Riemens as "*Lehmann*"). The labels and the March, 1968 bulletin give the performance date as 1966, where a private catalog with access to Smith's original source materials gives 1959. Professor Carlo Marinelli of Rome furnished us the date of the performance, its provenance, and what appear to be the correct cast names. Prof. Marinelli also mentioned that contralto Marlies Pommerien, not heard in the present excerpts, sang in the performance, but without a character assigned--he has suggested *Donna Pantea*.

The bulletin describes L'OCA DEL CAIRO as a "hithertofore unknown work by Mozart," and further misleads by saying that "The opera is listed as K. 422 in the compilation of Mozart works, but it did not receive a hearing until it was given by the Munich chamber orchestra." In addition to the early public performances cited by Lowenberg, Luigi Arditi mounted an important production of the Constantin-Wilder version at Drury Lane on 12 May, 1870, with an Italian libretto by G. Zaffira and recitatives added by Giovanni Bottesini.

Side 1 (429 A):

Bands 1 and 2: The overture and chorus could not be identified; their source is unknown.

Band 3: No. 1 in the original score. Partially scored by Mozart for strings, with winds (heard in this performance) to be added.

Band 4: No. 2 in the original score. Partially scored by Mozart for strings through measure 5, with winds to be added; realized from there using the completed string part. No. 2 of the appendix to the *Mozart's Werke* is a vocal line for an alternate aria for *Biondello*, "Che parli, che dica," not performed here. An alternate sketch of "Se fosse qui nascoso" also appears as No. 3 in the appendix.

Band 5: No. 3 in the original score. The first eleven measures were partially scored by Mozart for oboe, horn, trombone, and strings. The text does not appear in Varesco's libretto. The *Mozart's Werke* edition has a slightly different version of the aria as No. 1 of the appendix.

Band 6: No. 4 in the original score. The first seven measures of the duet (and sporadic measures throughout) were partially scored by Mozart for oboe, bassoon, horn and strings.

Side 2 (429 B):

Band 1: No. 5 in the original score.

Band 2: No. 6 in the original score. Only the first dozen measures were partially scored by Mozart--for strings, oboe, and horn. Alternate inserts for the quartet appear as No. 4 in the appendix to the *Mozart's Werke*.

Band 3: No. 7 in the original score. The first twenty measures were sketched by Mozart for strings, oboe, and horn. The Finale begins as a quartet and eventually comes to entangle the entire cast. A "Coda del primo Finale" appears as No. 5 of the appendix to the *Mozart's Werke*.

EJS 430: "The Golden Age of Opera" (2 LPs)
Issued April, 1968
MATRIX P-1584

ISABEAU (Mascagni) (I)
Opera in 3 acts (complete)
Orchestra Sinfonica di San Remo/Tullio Serafin
?Broadcast, Teatro dell'Opera de Casino, San Remo, late January, 1962

CAST:
Marcella Pobbe (*Isabeau*); Pier Miranda Ferraro (*Folco*); Piero Francia (*Il Cavaliere Faidit*); Renata Davinci (*Ermyntrude*); Rinaldo Rola (*King Raimondo*); Orazio Gualtieri (*Cornelius*); Licia Galvano (*Giglietta*); Anna Lia Bazzani (*Ermyngarde*); ? (*A Herald*); ? (*An Old Man*); ? (*Two Voices*).

NOTES: EJS 430

The orchestra is not identified on the label of EJS 430 or in the April, 1968 bulletin.

This live performance was part of the second International Festival of Melodramma, which produced only two works that season--Mascagni's ISABEAU (1911) and his penultimate opera, IL PICCOLO MARAT (1921). *Opera News* (26/19, 24 March, 1962), p. 7, gives no precise date for the ISABEAU, only late January.

The same cast was later featured in a group of studio-recorded excerpts issued commercially on Cetra LPC 55034, which acknowledged the production of the opera mounted in San Remo. Note that the Cetra excerpts were not taken from an RAI broadcast, but may have been an RAI *recording* originally intended for broadcast. Such was the case with Catalini's DEJANICE, issued on EJS 472 (June, 1969), and Donizetti's MARINO FALIERO, issued on the Historical Recording Enterprises label.

There have apparently been no reissues of the complete live performance featured here: though it also featured both Pobbe and Ferraro, the ISABEAU issued as MRF 97-S was taken from the 1972 Naples revival conducted by Ugo Rapalo.

Playing speeds for EJS 430 range from 33.8 to 34.00 rpm, except for the first few minutes of Act III which require a speed of 33.5 rpm.

EJS 431: "The Golden Age of Opera" (2 LPs)
Issued April, 1968
MATRIX P-1590

GÖTTERDÄMMERUNG (Wagner) (G)
Opera in 3 acts (excerpts)
London Philharmonic Orchestra and Chorus of the Royal Opera House/
Wilhelm Furtwängler
Unpublished live performance recordings (HMV):
Technical Test Series 6543 1/28, Covent Garden, London, 1 Jun 1937

CAST:
Kirsten Flagstad (*Brünnhilde*); Lauritz Melchior (*Siegfried*); Ludwig Weber (*Hagen*); Herbert Janssen (*Gunther*); Maria Nežádal (*Gutrune*); Kerstin Thorborg (*Waltraute*); [Eugen Fuchs (*Alberich*)]; [Mary Jarred (*Norn*)]; [Constance Willis (*Norn*)]; [Mae Craven (*Norn*)]; [Stella Andreva (*Woglinde*)]; [José Malone (*Wellgunde*)]; [Linda Seymour (*Flosshilde*)].

SIDE 1 (431 A):

* 1. Prologue: FLAGSTAD and MELCHIOR: Orchestral bridge from Norn scene . . . Zu neuen Taten . . . to the end of the Prologue
?2EA 5621-1/5622-1 Unpublished HMV tests

2. Act I: FLAGSTAD, THORBORG, and MELCHIOR: Altgewohntes Geräusch . . . [ ]
?2EA 5623-1/5629-1 Unpublished HMV tests

SIDE 2 (431 B):

1. Act I: FLAGSTAD, THORBORG, and MELCHIOR: [Altgewohntes Geräusch] . . . to the end of the act
?2EA 5623-1/5629-1 Unpublished HMV tests

2. Act II: JANSSEN, MELCHIOR, FLAGSTAD, WEBER, and Chorus: Heil! Heil dir, Gunther! . . . Wo bärgest du den Ring, den du von mir erbeutet?
?2EA 5630-?/5645-1 Unpublished HMV tests

SIDE 3 (431 C):

1. Act II: FLAGSTAD, MELCHIOR, WEBER, NEŽÁDAL, JANSSEN, and Chorus: Ha! Dieser war es, der mir den Ring entriss . . . to the end of the act
?2EA 5630-?/5645-1 Unpublished HMV tests

SIDE 4 (431 D):

3. Act III: WEBER, FLAGSTAD, and NEŽÁDAL: Her den Ring! . . . Schweigt eures Jammers! . . . to the end of the opera
?2EA 5630-?/5645-1 Unpublished HMV tests

NOTES: EJS 431

HMV recorded 28 sides from the 1 June, 1937 GÖTTERDÄMMERUNG (Technical Test Series 6543-1/[28]): these were transfered by HMV engineers between circa 11 and 13 August, 1937, as noted in detail below:

MATRIX	TRANSFERRED FROM TESTS	DATE OF TRANSFER
2EA 5619-1	[?]	[?]
2EA 5620-1	[?]	[?]
2EA 5621-1	[?]	[?]
2EA 5622-1	[?]	[?]
2EA 5623-1	6543-5	11 Aug 1937
2EA 5624-1	6543-6	11 Aug 1937
2EA 5625-1	6543-6, 7	11 Aug 1937
2EA 5626-1	6543-7, 8	11 Aug 1937
2EA 5627-1	6543-8, 9	11 Aug 1937
2EA 5628-1	6543-9, 10	11 Aug 1937
2EA 5629-1	6543-10, 11	11 Aug 1937
2EA 5630-1, 2	6543-11, 12	11 Aug 1937
2EA 5631-1	6543-12, 13	12 Aug 1937
2EA 5632-1	6543-14, 15	12 Aug 1937
2EA 5633-1	6543-15	12 Aug 1937
2EA 5634-1	6543-16	12 Aug 1937
2EA 5635-1	6543-17	12 Aug 1937
2EA 5636-1	6543-17, 18	12 Aug 1937
2EA 5637-1	6543-18, 19	12 Aug 1937
2EA 5638-1	6543-19, 20	12 Aug 1937
2EA 5639-1	6543-20, 21	12 Aug 1937
2EA 5640-1	6543-21-23 (sic)	13 Aug 1937
2EA 5641-1	6543-23 (sic)	13 Aug 1937
2EA 5642-1	6543-23, 24	13 Aug 1937
2EA 5643-1	6543-25	13 Aug 1937
2EA 5644-1	6543-26	13 Aug 1937
2EA 5645-1	6543-26, 27	13 Aug 1937
2EA 5646-1	6543-Finale	[?]

The division of the excerpts over the transfer 2EA-prefix matrices is approximate, with ackowledgement to Sanner's Flagstad discography (Sanner ackowledges Danish collector Knud Hegermann-Lindencrone for details of this approximate division, based ostensibly on test pressings inspected by the latter). Note that the Prologue excerpt includes the beginning of the orchestral Rhine Journey and that the complete Act I/iii is divided over the last band of side 1 and the first of side 2.

2EA 5619-1 is marked DER FLIEGENDE HOLLÄNDER, but is part of the GÖTTERDÄMMERUNG group of matrices. The 7 and 11 June, 1937 HOLLÄNDER, issued as EJS 123 (1958), was Technical Test Series 6544-6545 (transfer matrices 2EA 5600-5618). See also the endnote for EJS 123.

Only Act III of this complete GÖTTERDÄMMERUNG was broadcast.

Transferred high on EJS 431, requiring a range of roughly 32.7-32.8 rpm over the course of the four sides.

The performance was subsequently reissued on the Bruno Walter Society's Recital Records label, RR 429.

Stanford Archive of Recorded Sound tape: StARS 560000 M14.

EJS 432: "The Golden Age of Opera" (1 LP)
Issued April, 1968
MATRIX P-1588

"KIRSTEN FLAGSTAD (1937-50)"

SIDE 1 (432 A):

* 1. w. Philharmonia Orchestra/Wilhelm Furtwängler: VIER LETZTE LIEDER, A.V. 150, nos. 1-4:
a) No. 3: Beim Schlafengehen (Hesse-R. Strauss)
b) No. 2: September (Hesse-R. Strauss)
c) No. 1: Frühling (Hesse-R. Strauss)
d) No. 4: Im Abendrot (Eichendorff-R. Strauss)
Broadcast, Albert Hall, London, 22 May 1950

* 2 a) w. New York Philharmonic Orchestra/Erno Rapee: WESENDONCK LIEDER, no. 5: Träume (Wesendonck-Wagner) (G)
Broadcast, ***GENERAL MOTORS HOUR***, WEAF, NYC, 28 Mar 1937

b) w. pf/Edwin McArthur: "Die Forelle," D. 550 (Schubart-Schubert) (G)
Broadcast, ***GENERAL MOTORS HOUR***, WEAF, NYC, 28 Mar 1937

* 3. a) w. Detroit Symphony Orchestra/José Iturbi: DIE WALKÜRE, Act I: Du bist der Lenz (Wagner) (G)
Broadcast, ***FORD SUNDAY EVENING HOUR***, WJR, Detroit, 3 Oct 1937

b) w. pf/José Iturbi: "Still wie die Nacht," Op. 326, no. 27 (Dole-Böhm) (G)
Broadcast, ***FORD SUNDAY EVENING HOUR***, WJR, Detroit, 3 Oct 1937

SIDE 2 (432 B):

* 1. w. Philadelphia Orchestra/Eugene Ormandy: GÖTTERDÄMMERUNG, Act III: "Immolation Scene" (Wagner) (G)
Philadelphia, 17 Oct 1937 Victor unpublished
a) Starke Scheite schichtet mir dort . . . trog keiner wie er!
CS-013069-?
b) Wisst ihr, wie das ward? . . . Ruhe! Ruhe, du Gott!
CS-013070-?
c) Mein erbe nun . . . ?
CS-013071-1
d) "Finale" (sic) . . . to the end of the opera
CS 013072-1

* 2. a) w. pf/José Iturbi: "Love Went A-Riding" (Coleridge-Bridge) (E)
Broadcast, ***FORD SUNDAY EVENING HOUR***, WJR, Detroit, 3 Oct 1937
b) w. Detroit Symphony Orchestra and Chorus/José Iturbi: "The Old Folks at Home" ["Swanee River"] (Stephen C. Foster) (E)
Broadcast, ***FORD SUNDAY EVENING HOUR***, WJR, Detroit, 3 Oct 1937

* 3. a) Speech by FLAGSTAD (E)
b) w. orch and chimes/?: "Stille Nacht, heilige Nacht" (Gruber) (G)
Broadcast, [***CHRISTMAS EVE SPECIAL***], WEAF and WJZ [NBC], 24 Dec 1937

* 4. w. Detroit Symphony Orchestra/Sir Ernest MacMillan: SUMMERTIME: Night ["O Lovely Night"] (Teschemacher-Landon Ronald) (E)
Broadcast, ***FORD SUNDAY EVENING HOUR***, WJR, Detroit, 27 Feb 1938

* 5. FLAGSTAD Interview
a) "On Singing Wagner" (E)
b) unaccompanied: DIE WALKÜRE: Act I: fragment ["Todesverkündigung" Scene] (Wagner) (G)
BBC broadcast, London, 28 Jun 1950

NOTES: EJS 432

Side 1 (432 A):

Band 1: This was the world premiere of Strauss's VIER LETZTE LIEDER, written in 1948. Flagstad sang the four songs out of their customary order, as listed above. The concert was broadcast over BBC 3.

Sanner, in his Flagstad discography (notes 292-95, p. 161), claims that Smith used a tape supplied by collector Richard Bebb (a close friend of Smith's and a frequent source of material for his LPs) that was dubbed from acetates presumably taken off-the-air by the late British collector Thomas N. H. Godfrey. A rumor that Godfrey's transcriptions were taken from the dress rehearsal, not the actual performance, seems unlikely considering how difficult such a task might have proven at the time. Sanner also mentions a rumor that EMI may have recorded either the concert or the dress rehearsal, but he concludes that "this can be neither authoritatively confirmed or denied." The songs were later issued on Turnabout THS 65116 and Cetra LO 501.

Band 2: In addition to these titles, Flagstad also performed Landon Ronald's "O Lovely Night" on this 28 March, 1937 broadcast, but no known complete copy has survived. Her 27 February, 1938 performance of the song appears as II/4 of EJS 432.

The "Träume" and "Forelle" subsequently appeared on Legendary Records LR 120.

Band 3a-b: Like items II/2a-b, these were subsequently issued on Legendary LR 120. Together, the four items constitute Flagstad's entire performance on this 3 October, 1937 broadcast.

Side 2 (432 B):

Band 1: The full listing of takes, all recorded on 17 October, 1937, and including the "A" suffix duplicates recorded simulataneously, follows, with asterisks designating those takes known to exist either as tests or "special pressings" in private collections. The actual division of the last two parts of the scene is not known:

CS-013069-1* (marked "inferior")
-1A
-2* (marked "superior)
-2A
-3*
-3A
CS-013071-1*
-1A

CS-013070-1*
-1A
-2*
-2A
CS-013072-1* (marked only "Finale")

The Flagstad recital on Victrola VIC 1517 and its German equivalent (26.41399AG) used takes CS-013069-3, CS-013070-2, CS-013071-1, and CS-013072-1 according to Sanner (notes 114-17, p. 155). It has not been possible to ascertain which takes of parts 1 and 2 were used for EJS 432.

Exactly where the final part (matrix CS-013072-1) begins is unknown: it is only marked as the "Finale" of the scene.

Band 2a-b: See the endnote for band I/3a-b.

Band 3: From an NBC Christmas Eve broadcast special. Flagstad's speech mentions the recently-deceased Ernestine Schumann Heink and the contralto's traditional Christmas Eve rendering of "Stille Nacht." The question of whether this is Flagstad's 1937 or 1938 broadcast (she appeared in Christmas Eve shows for both years) has not been resolved, but 1937 is generally regarded as correct.

The same performance and speech were subsequently issued on Legendary LR 120 and 136.

Stanford University Archive of Recorded Sound tape: 560218 MI.

Band 4: Many commercial recordings of this well-known Ronald song were labeled using the title "O Lovely Night." Subsequently issued on Legendary LR 120. Flagstad's FREISCHÜTZ "Leise, leise" from this broadcast appeared earlier on EJS 141 (January, 1959). A Grieg "Tak for tit rad," Op. 21, no. 4, and a Bull "Solitude on the Mountains," both performed on the broadcast, are not known to have been transcribed.

Band 5: This interview was reprinted in *Opera News*, 15/15 (29 January, 1951). Flagstad sings the WALKÜRE passages unaccompanied and at score pitch, in response to the question of how she usually warms up. The interviewer has not been identified. Carried over BBC 3, the interview may have been transcribed here complete as broadcast, but this is unclear.

EJS 433: "The Golden Age of Opera" (2 LPs)
Issued May, 1968
MATRIX P-1611

SIDES 1-4 (433 A-D):

DIE FEEN (Wagner) (G)
Opera in 3 acts (complete as performed)
Orchestra and Chorus of the Internationalen Jugend-Festpieltreffen, Bayreuth/John Bell
Broadcast, Bayreuth Festpielhaus, Bayreuth, Aug 1967

CAST:
Hanna Rumowska [Rumowska-Machnikowska] (*Ada*); Marie-Therese Martin (*Farzana*); Roswitha Korff (*Zemira*); Jill Gomez (*Lora*); Barbara Kendall (*Drolla*); Hans-Reiner Schwarzbeck (*Fairy King*); Miroslav Frydlewicz (*Arindal*); Christopher Davies (*Morald*); Jiri Berdych (*Gernot*); Kenneth Ridgeway (*Gunther*); Lionel Fawcett (*Harold*); Walter Eschenbacher (*A Messenger*); Joseph Becker (*Voice of Groma*).

NOTES: EJS 433

Presented here complete as performed, omitting nearly an hour of the original score.

EJS 434: "The Golden Age of Opera" (2 LPs)
Issued May, 1968
MATRIX P-1612

SIDES 1-3 (434 A-C):

L'AMORE MEDICO (Wolf-Ferrari) (I)
Opera in 2 acts (complete)
Orchestra and Chorus of Radio Italiana, Milano/Arturo Basile
RAI broadcast, Milan, 12 Mar 1969

CAST:
Jolanda Meneguzzer (*Lucinda*); Emilia Ravaglia (*Lisetta*); Agostino Lazzari (*Clitandro*); Giuseppe Valdengo (*Arnolfo*); Domenico Trimarchi (*Doctor Desfonandres*); Paolo Pedani (*Doctor Macroton*); Florindo Andreoli (*Doctor Bahis*); Elio Castellano (*Doctor Tomes*); Elio Castellano (*A Notary*).

SIDE 4 (434 D):

MANON LESCAUT (Puccini) (I)
Opera in acts (Act III only)
Orchestra and Chorus of Teatro alla Scala, Milan/Arturo Toscanini
Broadcast, La Scala, Milan, 11 May 1946

CAST:
Mafalda Favero (*Manon Lescaut*); Giovanni Malipiero (*Chevalier Des Grieux*); Mariano Stabile (*Lescaut*); Carlo Forti (*Captain*); Giuseppe Nessi (*A Lamplighter*).

1. FAVERO, MALIPIERO, STABILE, FORTI, and NESSI: Act III (complete)

2. TANCREDI PASERO, bass; GIOVANNI MALIPIERO, tenor; RENATA TEBALDI, soprano; and JOLANDA GARDINO, mezzo-soprano (Orchestra and Chorus of Teatro alla Scala, Milan/Arturo Toscanini): MOSÈ IN EGITTO, Act III: Dal tuo stellato soglio (Rossini) (I)
   Broadcast, La Scala, Milan, 11 May 1946

NOTES: EJS 434

Side four was taken from the 11 May, 1946 re-opening of La Scala. Smith was by this time having problems with the Toscanini estate, compelling him to omit the Maestro's name from labels and bulletins.

L'AMORE MEDICO is in pitch at 33.3 rpm, where the MANON LESCAUT and presumably, the MOSÈ on side 2 require a speed of about 34.6 rpm.

The Scala excerpts have reappeared on various LPs, most recently on the three-CD Legato Classics set, "Toscanini at La Scala" (Standing Room Only SRO 802-3).

EJS 435: "The Golden Age of Opera" (1 LP)
Issued May, 1968
MATRIX P-1615

SIDES 1-2 (435 A-B):

DJAMILEH (Bizet) (F)
Opera in 1 act (complete)
Orchestra and Chorus of the Office de Radiodiffusion Télévision Française [ORTF]/?Robert Allpress
ORTF broadcast, circa 1950s

CAST:
?Andrea Guiot (*Djamileh*); ?Guy Fouché (*Haroun*); ?Claude Genty (*Splendiano*).

NOTES: EJS 435

The label lists five singers for this three-character opera. The others mentioned, Géneviève Moizan (labeled "Geraldine") and Louise Darclay, seem the least likely of the five to have participated. Allpress is labeled "Alpress." The date of the performance could not be verified.

EJS 436: "The Golden Age of Opera" (3 LPs)
Issued June, 1968
MATRIX P-1638 / P-1639 / P-1640

SIDES 1-6 (436 A-F):

ROBERT LE DIABLE (Meyerbeer) (I)
Opera in 5 acts (complete as performed)
Orchestra and Chorus of the Maggio Musicale Fiorentino/Nino Sanzogno
Broadcast, Maggio Musicale Fiorentino, Teatro Comunale, Florence, 7 May 1968

CAST:
Giorgio Merighi (*Roberto*); Boris Christoff (*Bertram*); Renata Scotto (*Isabelle*); Stefania Malagù (*Alice*); Gianfranco Manganotti (*Raimbaud*); Giovanni Antonini (*Albert*); Marisa Sansoni (A Lady-in-Waiting); Ottavio Taddei (*Herald*); Dino Formichini (*Master of Ceremonies*); Graziano Del Vivo (*A Monk*); Enzo Guagni (*First Knight*); Valiano Natali (*Second Knight*); Augusto Frati (*Third Knight*); Mario Frosini (*Fourth Knight*); Roberto Ferraro (*First Gambler*); Giuliano Ferrarini (*Second Gambler*); Giorgio Giorgetti (*Third Gambler*); Guerrando Rigiri (*Fourth Gambler*).

NOTES: EJS 436

ROBERT is presented here complete as performed, at about 158 minutes, with internal cuts and the virtual omission of the character of *Alice*. Repeats of the ensembles are also cut. All told, nearly an hour of the original score has been omitted. The June, 1968 bulletin claims that "Needless to say this is a first performance of the work, complete on three discs," and that "The sound is brilliant - virtually stereophonic" (sic), a favorite Smith superlative.

Reissued as MRF-20 and Melodram 37024. The 1985 Paris Opera production issued on Legendary is billed as a "complete" performance (at 206 minutes), but it, too, has internal cuts.

EJS 437: "The Golden Age of Opera" (1 LP)
Issued June, 1968
MATRIX P-1645

SIDES 1-2 (437 A-B):

COLOMBO (Gomes) (I)
"Poema Vocale-Sinfonico"in 4 acts (complete)
Orchestra Sinfonica do São Paulo/Armando Belardi
Broadcast, ?Teatro Municipal, São Paulo, December, 1963

CAST:
Constanzo Mascitti (*Colombo*); Paulo Adonis (*The Friar*); Lucia Quinto Morsella (*Isabella*); Sergio Albertini (*King Fernando*); Mariangela Rea (*Donna Mercede*); Joao Calil (*Don Ramiro*); Paulo Scavoro (*Don Diego*).

NOTES: EJS 437

COLOMBO was written for the Columbus Festival of 1892, in celebration of the 400th anniversary of Columbus' voyage and was first performed in Milan on 12 October, 1892. The other major operatic work written to commemorate the discovery of America, Alberto Franchetti's CRISTOFORO COLOMBO, made its debut six days earlier at the Carlo Felice in Genoa. There were two versions of the Gomes COLOMBO, variously referred to as a "scenic cantata" and an "oratorio:" it is the shorter of the two which is performed here complete.

The "Opera Municipal[e]" noted in the June, 1968 EJS bulletin is assumed to mean the Teatro Municipal, as noted above.

EJS: 438: "The Golden Age of Opera" (1 LP)
Issued June, 1968
MATRIX P-1644

SIDES 1-2 (438 C-D [sic]):

LA JOLIE FILLE DE PERTH (Bizet) (E)
Opera 4 in acts (acts 3 and 4 only)
Royal Philharmonic Orchestra and BBC Chorus/Sir Thomas Beecham
BBC broadcast, London, 5 Oct 1956

CAST:
Mattiwilda Dobbs (*Catherine Glover*); Alexander Young (*Henry Smith*); Kevin Miller (*Duke of Rothsay*); David Ward (*Ralph*); Anna Pollak [Pollack] (*Mab*); Owen Brannigan (*Simon Glover*).

NOTES: EJS 438

This issue was made to complete EJS 269 (May, 1963), which included only the first two acts of LA JOLIE FILLE DE PERTH. All four acts of this performance were broadcast. In the June, 1968 bulletin Smith stated that "Not having a score to consult, we thought the opera was complete on a single disc [EJS 269]. Now it seems we released acts one and two and acts three and four are now available on a single record [EJS 438]."

This single disc is labeled EJS 438-C and -D, with matrix suffixes to match (P-1664-C and -D, respectively). Both EJS 269 and EJS 438 were reissued in the January, 1972 UORC bulletin.

EJS 439: "The Golden Age of Opera" (3 LPs)
Issued September, 1968
MATRIX P-1691 / P-1692 / P-1693

SIDES 1-6 (439 A-F):

LA JUIVE (Halévy) (F)
Opera in 5 acts (complete as performed)
Orchestra and Chorus of the Koniglijke Oper, Ghent/Robert Ledent
In-house recording, Koninglijke Oper, Ghent, 1964

CAST:
Tony Poncet (*Eléazar*); Gery Brunin (*Rachel*); Tadeusz Wierzbicki (*Cardinal Brogni*); Stany Bert (*Léopold*); Lia Rottier (*Eudoxie*); Aurelio Burzi (*Ruggiero*); Jef Van Den Berghen (*Albert*).

NOTES: EJS 439

The September, 1968 bulletin notes that this performance "was not broadcast - so this is a house recording." No further information has emerged to contradict this.

The complete performance was reissued on LP as Melodram MEL 169.

EJS 440: "The Golden Age of Opera" (1 LP)
Issued September, 1968
MATRIX P-1696

"RICHARD TAUBER IN OPERA AND SONG (Volume 2)"

SIDE 1 (440 A):

* 1. w. orch/Erno Rapee: I PAGLIACCI, Act I: On with the Motley [Recitar . . . Vesti la giubba] (Leoncavallo) (E)
Broadcast, ***GENERAL MOTORS HOUR***, Carnegie Hall, WJZ, NYC, 24 Oct 1937

* 2. w. orch/Erno Rapee: SECHS LIEDER, Op. 48, no. 6: Ein Traum [En drøm] (von Bodenstedt-Grieg) (G)
Broadcast, ***GENERAL MOTORS HOUR***, Carnegie Hall, WJZ, NYC, 24 Oct 1937

* 3. w. orch/Erno Rapee: FRASQUITA, Act II: Schatz, ich bitt' dich . . . Hab'ein blaues Himmelbett (Lehár) (G)
Broadcast, ***GENERAL MOTORS HOUR***, Carnegie Hall, WJZ, NYC, 24 Oct 1937

* 4. w. GRACE MOORE, soprano (orch/Erno Rapee): ROMéO ET JULIETTE, Act IV: Roméo! qu'as-tu donc? . . . Non, ce n'est pas le jour (Gounod) (F)
Broadcast, ***GENERAL MOTORS HOUR***, Carnegie Hall, WJZ, NYC, 24 Oct 1937

5. w. orch/Erno Rapee: O lieb, so lang [Liebestraum, Op. 60, no. 3] (Freiligrath-Liszt) (G)
Broadcast, ***GENERAL MOTORS HOUR***, Carnegie Hall, WJZ, NYC, 14 Nov 1937

* 6. w. orch and Chorus/Erno Rapee: ZIGEUNERLIEBE, Act III: Hör ich Cymbalklänge ["Marishka"] (Lehár) (G)
Broadcast, ***GENERAL MOTORS HOUR***, Carnegie Hall, WJZ, NYC, 14 Nov 1937

SIDE 2 (440 B):

* 1. a) w. orch/Erno Rapee: GRÄFIN MARITZA, Act I: Grüss mir mein Wien (Kálmán) (G)
Broadcast, ***GENERAL MOTORS HOUR***, Carnegie Hall, WJZ, NYC, 14 Nov 1937
b) w. ERNA SACK, soprano (orch and chorus/Erno Rapee): DIE LUSTIGE WITWE, Act II: Come to the Pavilion With Me [Sieh dort den kleinen Pavillon] (Lehár) (E)
Broadcast, ***GENERAL MOTORS HOUR***, Carnegie Hall, WJZ, NYC, 14 Nov 1937

* 2. w. St. Louis Symphony Orchestra/Vladimir Golschmann: TOLV MELODIER, Op. 33, no. 2: Letzter Frühling [Vaaren] (Vinje-Grieg) (G)
Broadcast, ***GENERAL MOTORS HOUR***, KWK, Municipal Auditorium, St. Louis, 21 Nov 1937

* 3. w. St. Louis Symphony Orchestra/Vladimir Golschmann: DAS LIED DER LIEBE: Dort rauscht und plauscht der Wienerwald ["Geschichten aus dem Wienerwald"] (J. Strauss-arr E.W. Korngold) (G)
Broadcast, ***GENERAL MOTORS HOUR***, KWK, Municipal Auditorium, St. Louis, 21 Nov 1937

* 4. w. GRACE MOORE, soprano (w. St. Louis Symphony Orchestra/Vladimir Golschmann): SCHWANENGESANG, D. 957, no. 4: Leise flehen ["Ständchen"] (Rellstab-Schubert) (E)
Broadcast, ***GENERAL MOTORS HOUR***, KWK, Municipal Auditorium, St. Louis, 21 Nov 1937

* 5. w. orch/Erno Rapee: MIGNON, Act II: Adieu, Mignon! (Thomas) (F)
Broadcast, ***GENERAL MOTORS HOUR***, Carnegie Hall, WJZ, NYC, 12 Dec 1937

* 6. w. orch/Erno Rapee: LES ERINNYES: Invocation ["Élégie"] (Gallet-Massenet) (F)
Broadcast, ***GENERAL MOTORS HOUR***, Carnegie Hall, WJZ, NYC, 12 Dec 1937

* 7. w. orch/Erno Rapee: CARMEN, Act II: La fleur que tu m'avais jetée ["Flower Song"] (Bizet) (F)
Broadcast, ***GENERAL MOTORS HOUR***, Carnegie Hall, WJZ, NYC, 12 Dec 1937

NOTES: EJS 440

The subtitle of the LP title ("Volume 2") probably refers to the earlier Tauber recital on EJS 364 (April, 1966), though the two do not share the same title. Most of the selections are introduced by the show's regular host, Milton Cross. See the endnote for EJS 418 (December, 1967) (II/1-3) for details about this series of ***GENERAL MOTORS HOUR*** broadcasts.

Grace Moore's solos from the 24 October, 1937 broadcast appeared earlier on EJS 418 (II/4-6), as did her PAGLIACCI "Ballatella" from 21 November (II/7): see the related endnotes for those LPs.

The 14 November broadcast (I/5-6 and II/1a-b), billed as "Hungarian-Italian Night," featured, in addition to Tauber's performances, Erna Sack singing "Una voce poco fà" from BARBIERE and "Funiculì, funiculà," violinist Michel Piastro playing Sarasate's "Ziegeunerweisen," and orchestral selections of Kodály and Wolf-Ferrari. Tauber's numbers are presented on EJS 440 complete.

Side 1 (440 A):

Band 1: Plays at score pitch at 33.8 rpm.

Band 2: Given in the *New York Times* radio log as Grieg's "Ich liebe dich" [Jag elsker dag] from HJERTETS MELODIER, Op. 5, no. 4.
Plays in score pitch at 33.8 rpm.

Band 3: Announced by Milton Cross as "My Little Nest of Heavenly Blue." Plays in score pitch at 33.1 rpm.

Band 4: Plays in score pitch at 33.1 rpm.

Band 6: Announced during the broadcast as "Marishka," the title also given on the label of EJS 440 and in the *New York Times* radio listing. Where this "familiar name" may have come from is unknown. The song is sung by the character *Ilona*, betrothed to *Kajetán*: but as it turns out, the creator of *Kajetán* in the 8 January, 1910 Vienna premiere was Hubert *Marischka*--a coincidence, no doubt. The correct playing speed could not be determined, owing to probable transposition.

Side 2 (440 B):

Band 1a-b: The first few phrases of the GRÄFIN MARITZA aria are missing from the EJS 440 transcription, though Milton Cross' introduction was somehow left intact. The LUSTIGE WITWE duet is performed by Sack and Tauber as a medley, using an orchestral segue. The Lehár is perhaps best known in this Adrian Ross translation, "Love in My Heart," and is arranged here as a full duet to give Sack a bit more to do.

The correct playing speed of this band is 32.3 rpm.

Band 2: The probable playing speed for the Grieg is 33.0 rpm.

Band 3: "Dort rauscht" is Korngold's arrangement of Strauss's "G'schichten aus dem Wienerwald" ("Tales of the Vienna Woods"), Op. 325. It is given under the title "Song of Love" in the *New York Times* radio listing and on the label of EJS 440, a reference to Korngold's 1931 DAS LIED DER LIEBE, a three-act operetta based on themes of Johann Strauss, text by Ludwig Herzer. The playing speed of this item could not be determined, owing to possible transposition.

Band 4: Plays in score pitch at 33.0 rpm.

Bands 5-7: This 12 December broadcast of French music also featured bass Alexander Kipnis and soprano Marta Krásová, the latter singing the "Mon coeur" from SAMSON ET DELILA and Debussy's "Beau Soir." Kipnis sang *Méphistophéles'* "Sérénade" from FAUST and Flégier's "Le Cor."

Band 5: Plays in score pitch at 33.8 rpm.

Band 6: The famous "Élégie" was adapted by Massenet from the "Invocation" of his incidental music to Leconte de Lisle's 1873 drama, LES ERINNYES.

The correct playing speed could not be determined.

Band 7: Plays in score pitch at 33.5 rpm. While this "Flower Song" was almost undoubtedly taken from the 12 December broadcast, it was not listed among the contents of the show in the *New York Times* radio log, and was probably a substitution.

EJS 441: "The Golden Age of Opera" (1 LP)
Issued September, 1968
MATRIX P-1697

LES PÊCHEURS DE PERLES (Bizet) (I)
Opera in 3 acts (excerpts)
Orchestra and Chorus of Teatro San Carlo di Napoli/Gabriele Santini
Broadcast, Teatro San Carlo, Naples, 30 January, 2 or 6 Feb 1954

CAST:
Ferruccio Tagliavini (*Nadir*); Giuseppe Taddei (*Zurga*); Margherita Carosio (*Leila*); Vito De Taranto (*Nourabad*).

SIDE 1 (441 A):

Act I 1. TAGLIAVINI, TADDEI, and Chorus: Ma vien talun? . . . Della giungla e della selva [Mais qui vient là? . . . Des savanes et des forêts]

2. TADDEI, TAGLIAVINI, and Chorus: Sei tu che dinnanzi . . . Del tempio al limitar [C'est toi! qu'enfin je revois! . . . Au fond du temple]

3. TAGLIAVINI: A quella voce . . . Mi par d'udir ancora [A cette voix . . . Je crois entendre encore]

4. CAROSIO, DE TARANTO, and Chorus: Brahma, gran Dio! [O Dieu Brahma!] . . . to the end of the act

Act II: 5. CAROSIO: Siccome un dì [Comme autrefois dans la nuit sombre]

SIDE 2 (441 B):

Act II: 1. TAGLIAVINI and CAROSIO: Della mia vita . . . Non hai compreso [De mon amie . . . Ton coeur n'a pas compris le mien!]

Act III: 2. TADDEI: Il nembo si calmò [L'orage s'est calmé]

3. TADDEI and CAROSIO: Chi vegg'io . . . Qual m'assal mio terror [Qu'ai-je vu? . . . Ce mot seul a ranimé ma haine et ma fureur!]

4. DE TARANTO, TADDEI, CAROSIO, TAGLIAVINI, and Chorus: Tetre divinità [Sombres divinités] . . . to the end of the opera

NOTES: EJS 441

It is not known which of the three performances of PÊCHEURS given during the 1954 San Carlo season was actually broadcast andtrans-cribed.

EJS 442: "The Golden Age of Opera" (2 LPs)
Issued October, 1968
MATRIX P-1717 / P-1718

SIDES 1-4 (442 A-D):

HAMLET (Thomas) (F)
Opera in 5 acts (complete)
Orchestra and Chorus of the Koninglijke Oper, Ghent/André Cuyckens
Broadcast, Koninglijke Oper, Ghent, 1968

CAST:
Gilbert Dubuc (*Hamlet*); Georgette Cooleman (*Ophélie*); Christian Portanier (*Claudius*); Lucienne Delvaux (*Gertrude*); Stany Bert (*Laërte*); ? (*Marcellus*); ? (*Horatio*); ? (*The Ghost*); ? (*Polonius*); ? (*First Gravedigger*); ? (*Second Gravedigger*).

NOTES: EJS 442

The October, 1968 bulletin notes that EJS 442 was the first complete performance of Thomas' HAMLET on LP. This is probably true: the first complete *commercial* recording of the opera appears to have been London's digital release featuring Dame Joan Sutherland. It has been rumored that this "Ghent" performance was in fact a student production from the Manhattan School of Music, under the possible direction of its then-president, baritone John Brownlee, but Dubuc is quite recognizably the *Hamlet* here.

Most copies were issued with one or more sides pressed off-center.

EJS 443: "The Golden Age of Opera" (1 LP)
Issued October, 1968
MATRIX P-1712

SIDES 1-2 (443 A-B):

LA BOULANGÈRE A DES ÉCUS (Offenbach) (F)
Opéra-bouffe in 3 acts (abridged)
Orchestra and Chorus of the Office de Radiodiffusion Télévision Française [ORTF], Paris/Jean-Paul Kreder
ORTF broadcast, ?Paris, date unknown

CAST:
Lina Dachary (*Margot*): Claudine Collart (*Toinon*); Denise Dupleix (*Mme. de Parabère*); Jeannette Levasseur (*Mme. de Sabran*); Aimé Doniat (*Bernadille*); Lucien Huberty (*The Commissioner*); Raymond Amade (*Ravanne*); Gaston Rey (*Coquebert*); Jacques Pruvost (*Delicat*); Gérard Friedmann (*Flaméche*); René Lenoty (*The Swiss Captain*); Yves Kervyn (*The Thief*); Pierre Saugeay (*A Financier*); Michel Martin (*The Little Thief*).

NOTES: EJS 443

The performance date has not been documented. The original French dialogue (or narration) from the actual broadcast was omitted from EJS 443, probably for purposes of timing. Musical cuts have also been reported. Conductor Kreder's surname is given as "Creder" on the labels of EJS 443.

EJS 444: "The Golden Age of Opera" (1 LP)
Issued October, 1968
MATRIX P-1713

"THE GOLDEN AGE OF WAGNER"

SIDE 1 (444 A):

* 1. ELSA ALSEN, mezzo-soprano (Philharmonic-Symphony of New York/Arturo Toscanini): TRISTAN UND ISOLDE (Wagner) (G)
a) ORCHESTRA: Prelude (last few measures) [32.8 rpm]
b) ALSEN: Act III: Mild und leise . . . Wie sie schwellen [Liebestod] [32.8 rpm]
Broadcast, ***NEW YORK PHILHARMONIC SYMPHONY ORCHESTRA*** (sic), Metropolitan Opera House, WABC, NYC, 27 Nov 1932

* 2. PAUL ALTHOUSE, tenor, and ELSA ALSEN, mezzo-soprano (Philharmonic-Symphony of New York/Arturo Toscanini): DIE WALKÜRE (Wagner) (G)
Act I: a) Ein Schwert verhiess' mir der Vater . . . Glimmt nur noch lichtlose Gluth! [32.8 rpm]
b) [Ein Waffe lass' mich dir] weisen . . . Der Männer sippe . . . Lacht in den Saal! [32.8 rpm]
Broadcast, ***NEW YORK PHILHARMONIC SYMPHONY ORCHESTRA*** (sic), Metropolitan Opera House, WABC, NYC, 27 Nov 1932
c) PAUL ALTHOUSE, tenor (Metropolitan Opera House Orchestra/Artur Bodanzky): DIE WALKÜRE, Act I: Winterstürme (Wagner) (G) [32.8 rpm]
Metropolitan Opera broadcast, NYC, 2 Feb 1935

DIE WALKÜRE (Wagner) (G)
Opera 3 in acts (excerpts)
Metropolitan Opera House Orchestra/Artur Bodanzky
Metropolitan Opera broadcast, NYC, 2 Feb 1935

CAST:
Kirsten Flagstad (*Sieglinde*); Paul Althouse (*Siegmund*); Emanuel List (*Hunding*).

* 3. Act II: a) FLAGSTAD and ALTHOUSE: Hinweg! Hinweg! flieh die Entweihte! . . . Was je Schande dir schuf das büsst nun des Frevlers [Blut!] [32.0 rpm]
b) FLAGSTAD and ALTHOUSE: Horch! die Hörner, hörst du den Ruf? . . . Schwester! Geliebte! . . . orchestral introduction to Scene iv (first 15 measures) [32.0 rpm]
c) FLAGSTAD, ALTHOUSE, and LIST: Kehrte der Vater nun heim . . . Wehalt! Wehalt! Steh' mir zum Streit, sollen dich Hunde nicht halten! [32.0 rpm]

SIDE 2 (444 B):

DIE MEISTERSINGER VON NÜRNBERG (Wagner) (G)
Opera in 3 acts (excerpts)
London Philharmonic Orchestra and Chorus of the Royal Opera House/Sir Thomas Beecham
Published live performance recordings (Columbia)
Technical Test Series TT 2294/1-37, Covent Garden, London, 20 May 1936

CAST:
Torsten Ralf (*Walther*); Tiana Lemnitz (*Eva*); Rudolph Bockelmann (*Hans Sachs*); Ludwig Weber (*Pogner*); [Heddle Nash] (*David*); [Margery Booth (*Magdalena*)]; [Herbert Janssen (*Kothner*)]; [Karl August Neumann (*Beckmesser*)].

* 1. Act I: a) LEMINITZ, and Chorus: Overture (final measures) . . . Da zu dir der Heiland kam . . . Dort am Fluss Jordan [31.8 rpm]
CAX 7910-1 Dubbed: 2 January, 1937 Columbia LX 645

Act III: b) Chorus: Wach auf, es nahet gen den Tag . . . Heil Nürnbergs theurem Sachs! [31.8 rpm]
CAX 7913-1 Dubbed: 2 January, 1937 Columbia LX 645

c) RALF, BOCKELMANN, WEBER, LEMNITZ, and Chorus: Morgenlich leuchtend . . . Vorüber nun all' Herz-beschwer [31.8 rpm]
CAX 7914-1 Dubbed: 4 January, 1937 Columbia LX 646
CAX 7915-1 Dubbed: 4 January, 1937 Columbia LX 646

* 2. a) HANS HOTTER, baritone, and WILLIAM WERNIGK, tenor (Wiener Philharmoniker/Hans Knappertsbusch): SIEGFRIED, Act I: wer wird aus den starken Stücken . . . Nothung das Schwert . . . was schwebt dort und webt (Wagner) (G) [33.3 rpm]
Broadcast, Wiener Staatsoper, Vienna, 10 Dec 1943

b) MAX LORENZ, tenor; ELISABETH SCHUMANN, soprano; and WILLIAM WERNIGK,tenor (Wiener Philharmoniker/Hans Knappertsbusch): SIEGFRIED, Act II: Was ihr mir nützet, weiss ich nicht . . . Er sinnt, und erwägt der Beute Werth (Wagner) (G) [32.5 rpm]
Broadcast, Wiener Staatsoper, Vienna, 16 Jun 1937

c) MAX LORENZ, tenor, and ELISABETH SCHUMANN, soprano (Wiener Philharmoniker/Hans Knappertsbusch): SIEGFRIED, Act II: [nun] sing'! Ich lausche dem Gesang . . . Wie find' ich zum Felsen den Weg'? (Wagner) (G) [32.5 rpm]
Broadcast, Wiener Staatsoper, Vienna, 16 Jun 1937

* 3. LOTTE LEHMANN, soprano; HANS HERMANN NISSEN, baritone; and PAUL ALTHOUSE, tenor (Chicago Opera House Orchestra/Egon Pollak): TANNHÄUSER, Act II: Orchestral introduction (last few bars) . . . Dich, teure Halle! . . . O Fürstin! Gott! [Steht auf! Lasset mich!] (Wagner) (G) [32.7 - variable]
Broadcast, Chicago [Civic] Opera, ?WLS, Chicago, 1 Nov 1930

NOTES: EJS 444

Another of the more complicated Smith issues. Label misspellings like "*Mox* Lorenz" have been corrected in the listing, along with the many inaccuracies of attribution.

Side 1 (444 A):

Bands 1-2: Given on the label of EJS 444 as "New York Philharmonic, Nov. 27, 1932," with no conductor named, probably to avoid further legal entanglements with the ever-vigilant Toscanini estate. This was Toscanini's final broadcast of the 1932 season (he left for Italy shortly therafter) and also included Beethoven's Third Symphony. The original aluminum discs from which the EJS transfer was made have been identified conclusively from announced excerpts--also on the discs--of soprano Luella Melius in a performance of LAKMÉ, given over station WOR, New York City, at 10:00 pm the same day.

There is of course no mention in the October, 1968 bulletin or on the label that the WALKÜRE scene had been extended by inserting Althouse's "Winterstürme" (2c) from the 2 February, 1935 Met performance. See also the endnote I/3, below.

Band 3: This WALKÜRE was Flagstad's Met debut. All that survives of Act II is presented here, while the complete Act I had appeared earlier as EJS 200 (December, 1960). The correct date--2 February, 1935--is given on the label of EJS 444.

Side 2 (444 B):

The label for EJS 444 states that, on this side, "Conductors include Artur Bodanzky, Sir Thomas Beecham, Ernst Kraus, and Giorgio Polacco." Knappertsbusch was probably confused initially with conductor *Clemens* Krauss (1893-1954), who did conduct a number of performances at the Staatsoper in the 1930s, many of which were featured on various EJS LPs (see, for example, the 1933 GÖTTERDÄMMERUNG on EJS 460 from February, 1969); but exactly how the German tenor *Ernst Kraus* (1863-1941) made his way into all of this is anybody's guess. Giorgio Polacco (1873-1960), resident conductor of the Chicago Civic Opera between 1922 and 1930, is given as the conductor of the 1930 TANNHÄUSER excerpt on band 3, when in fact Egon Pollak (1879-1933) directed the performance.

Band 1: The MEISTERSINGER excerpts featured here were all commercially released, as dubbed from the original Technical Tests onto 12-inch "CAX"-prefix matrices on 2 and 4 January, 1937. British Columbia recorded a number of Technical Tests from the 1936 Covent Garden season, including four of Beecham's Wagner performances: GÖTTERDÄMMERUNG (14 May), tests TT 2292/1-16; MEISTERSINGER (20 May), tests TT 2294/1-37; RHEINGOLD (21 May), tests TT 2295/1-?; and another GÖTTERDÄMMERUNG (29 May), tests TT 2296/1-7. The first GÖTTERDÄMMERUNG and the RHEINGOLD were experimental, where four commercial discs were released from the second GÖTTERDÄMMERUNG (Columbia LX 636/637, issued as Set X-83 in the U.S.) and from the MEISTERSINGER excerpted on EJS 444 (Columbia LX 645/646, issued as Set X-87 in the U.S.).

The label of EJS 444 describes the MEISTERSINGER excerpts as the "Finale of opera with: Tina Lemnitz, Margery Booth; Torsten Ralf; Heddle Nash; Rudolph Bockelmann; Karl August Neumann; Herbert Janssen; Ludwig Weber. April 27, 1936," but only Lemnitz, Ralf, Bockelmann, and Weber are heard in the segments that have survived (Lemnitz, Booth, Neumann, and Weber were making their respective London debuts in these roles). The date Smith assigns was the date of the first MEISTERSINGER of the season, not the one actually recorded by Columbia. Lemnitz can be heard clearly above the chorus in the opening "Da zu dir der Heiland kam."

The 14 May GÖTTERDÄMMERUNG material appeared earlier on EJS 167 (December, 1959) and again on the two-LP UORC 234 (January, 1975). Weber's "*Hagen's* Watch" from the 29 May GÖTTERDÄMMERUNG (CAX 7909-1: LX 637) and the four 20 May MEISTERSINGER matrices included on EJS 444 were later featured in considerably better sound on EMI's 1979 LP set "Royal Opera House Covent Garden / Historic Recordings of Actual Performances" (RLS 742).

Band 2: The label of EJS 444 reads: "Forest Bird Scene with Mox Lorenz (sic), Elisabeth Schumann and Hans Hotter. June 16, 1937," with the Wiener Staatsoper properly identified. According to Henry Hall of Sydney, Australia, Hotter himself denied his participation in these 1937 excerpts arguing that he had not sung at the Wiener Staatsoper prior to 1942; the first excerpt seems to include Hotter, however, as taken from the 1943 performance cited in the listing. The Hotter excerpts are dated precisely in a collection of Viennese materials which surfaced in mid 1960s, with timings conforming to what is heard on EJS 444.

The conductor is listed on the label of EJS 444 as "Ernst Kraus," (see note, above) but both performances excerpted here were in fact conducted by Knappertsbusch.

Band 3: There are three breaks in this excerpt, probably acetate breaks from copies taken of the original aluminum disc(s). This has long been assumed to be the oldest surviving excerpt from a live American operatic broadcast. Indeed, Smith refers to it in the October, 1968 bulletin as a "virtually pre-foetal [sic] radio performance" (the paradox not withstanding, "pre-foetal" was a favorite Smith expression, and was used more than once in the run of EJS bulletins to emphasize age). The performance hails from Lehmann's first season in Chicago (she had made her debut as *Sieglinde* only four days earlier on 28 October, 1930). There was a second TANNHÄUSER given on 13 November, 1930, but it was not broadcast--only Act II of the 1 November performance was heard on-the-air, in a one-hour network hookup.

Egon Pollak, who conducted in Chicago between 1929 and 1932, directed this performance, not Giorgio Polacco, as stated on the label.

Note that the playing speed of this excerpt is an unsteady 32.7 rpm, possibly the fault of the original transcription discs.

EJS 445: "The Golden Age of Opera" (1 LP)
Issued October, 1968
MATRIX P-1719

"RICHARD BONELLI / Baritone (1938-55)"

SIDE 1 (445 A):

1. w. Detroit Symphony Orchestra/Fritz Reiner: FAUST, Act II: Avant de quitter ces lieux (Gounod) (F)
   Broadcast, ***FORD SUNDAY EVENING HOUR***, WJR, Detroit, 25 Dec 1938

2. w. orch/Erno Rapee: IL BARBIERE DI SIVIGLIA, Act I: Largo al factotum (Rossini) (I)
   Broadcast, ***GENERAL MOTORS HOUR***, WEAF, NYC, 2 Feb 1936

* 3. w. Detroit Symphony Orchestra/Victor Kolar: IL TROVATORE, Act II: Il balen del suo sorriso (Verdi) (I)
   Broadcast, ***FORD SUNDAY EVENING HOUR***, WJR, Detroit, 7 Feb 1937

4. w. orch/Andre Kostelanetz: TANNHÄUSER, Act III: Wie Todesahnung . . . O du mein holder Abenstern (Wagner) (G)
   Broadcast, ***CHESTERFIELD HOUR***, WABC, NYC, 2 Mar 1935

* 5. w. orch and Chorus/?Victor Kolar: "Swing Low, Sweet Chariot" (Negro Spiritual-H.T. Burleigh-arr.?) (E)
   Broadcast, ***FORD SUNDAY EVENING HOUR***, WJR, Detroit, 1937

* 6. w. orch/Erno Rapee: "Danse macabre" (Cazalis-Saint-Saëns) (F)
   Broadcast, ***GENERAL MOTORS HOUR***, WEAF, NYC, 2 Feb 1936

7. w. orch/Erno Rapee: "Captain Stratton's Fancy" (John Masefield-Deems Taylor) (E)
   Broadcast, ***GENERAL MOTORS HOUR***, WEAF, NYC, 2 Feb 1936

SIDE 2 (445 B):

* 1. w. orch/Hans Jürgen-Walter: FEDORA, Act II: La donna russa (Giordano) (I)
   Private recording, circa 1955

2. w. orch/Andre Kostelanetz: LE ROI DE LAHORE, Act IV: Auxtroupes du Saltin . . . Promesse de mon avenir O Sitâ (Gounod) (F)
   Broadcast, ***CHESTERFIELD HOUR***, WABC, NYC, 23 Feb 1935

* 3. w. ?Detroit Symphony Orchestra/Victor Kolar: SERSE, Act I: Ombra mai fu ["Largo"] (Handel) (I)
   Broadcast, ?***FORD SUNDAY EVENING HOUR***, WJR, Detroit, ?23 Dec 1934

4. w. orch/Erno Rapee: DIE TOTE STADT, Act II: Mein sehnen, mein Wähnen? ["Pierrotlied" or "Pierrot's Dance"] (Korngold) (G)
   Broadcast, ***GENERAL MOTORS HOUR***, WEAF, NYC, 2 Feb 1936

* 5. w. orch/Hans Jürgen-Walther: ZAZÀ, Act IV: Zazà, piccola zingara (Leoncavallo) (I)
   Private recording, circa 1955

6. w. Detroit Symphony Orchestra/Victor Kolar: HÉRODIADE, Act II: Ce breuvage pourrait me donner un tel rêve . . . Vision fugitive (Massenet) (F)
   Broadcast, ?***FORD SUNDAY EVENING HOUR***, WJR, Detroit, 16 Mar 35

7. w. orch/Kostelanetz: HAMLET, Act II: O vin, discaccia la tristezza [O vin, dissipe ma tristesse] ["Brindisi"] (Thomas) (I)
   Broadcast, ***CHESTERFIELD HOUR***, WABC, NYC, 16 Feb 35

* 8. w. orch/Andre Kostelanetz: "On the Road to Mandalay" (Kipling-Speaks) (E)
   Broadcast, ***CHESTERFIELD HOUR***, WABC, NYC, 2 Mar 1935

NOTES: EJS 445

Bonelli has been an especially difficult artist to document, owing to his long and active career as a radio singer, primarily in the mid 1930s. Like Tibbett, he often sang familiar selections time and again, thus making some titles impossible to pin down--even given the often-binding logic of provenance.

Bonelli's *regular* appearances on the ***CHESTERFIELD HOUR*** during the 1934-1935 season began on 2 February, 1935 and ended on 30 March, though he was featured irregularly throughout 1935. Soprano Greta Stückgold had been the featured artist through 28 December, 1934, and Lucrezia Bori followed Bonelli on 6 April, 1935. Between Stückgold and Bonelli was a single appearance by soprano Mary Eastman on 5 January and three by the Koselanetz Orchestra with chorus between 12 and 26 January.

Items II/2 and 7 were not scheduled, according to the *New York Times* radio logs, but have been documented from the original acetates furnished to Smith.

The October, 1968 bulletin concludes that Bonelli, along with Tibbett and Thomas, was one of the three "greatest American baritones of the initial half of the 20th Century." Smith, and one of his subscribers, a well-known American collector and major contributor to the GAO series, knew the popular baritone well, and were always anxious to see his unpublished performances issued, as Bonelli made so few commercial recordings (acousticals and a few electricals for Brunswick, and a handful of Columbias recorded in New York and Los Angeles in 1940). Bonelli himself was an eager supporter of Smith's activities, and often made copies of his own performances available for transfer.

A number of the broadcast selections included here (I/1 and 4; II/2, 4, 6-8) will be included on Delos International compact discs DE-5504 and DE-5505, to be published in collaboration with the Stanford University Archive of Recorded Sound in 1993.

Side 1 (445 A):

Band 3: This "Il balen" was issued earlier on EJS 213 (May, 1961).

Band 5: The date has not been confirmed. Bonelli announces the selection on the original acetate, but was been cut from EJS 445. The arranger is unknown and the conductor is dependent upon the date of the broadcast (it may have been Alexander Smallens, for example).

Band 6: See the endnote on Saint-Saën's vocal setting of "Danse macabre" for EJS 140 (January, 1959), II/7. This Bonelli version is an arrangement, with a spoken introduction by Milton Cross.

Side 2 (445 B):

Band 1: This, and the ZAZÀ (II/5) was a late private recording made in New York with a dim piano accompaniment, to which an orchestral backing was later dubbed in Europe. Conductor Hans Jürgen-Walther disclosed to an informant that he dubbed many such recordings with his own "Philharmonia Orchestra of Hamburg" for release on the Record Company of America labels, with which Smith was affiliated. It is known that the Bonelli-Martinelli I PAGLIACCI material on Allegro Royale 1614 was done in this manner. See the endnote for EJS 181 (June, 1960), II/6. The FEDORA aria was also featured on Allegro Royale 1639.

Band 3: Bonelli sang the "Largo" and the "Vision fugitive" (II/6) on this broadcast, but this has not been *proven* to be the source of this particular transfer (it would be the earliest excerpt from the ***FORD SUNDAY EVENING HOUR*** included on any EJS LP). He undoubtedly sang both arias on numerous other broadcasts.

Band 8: The original acetate of this performance has a spoken introduction by Bonelli.

EJS 446: "The Golden Age of Opera" (2 LPs)
Issued November, 1968
MATRIX P-1736 / P-1737

SIDES 1-4 (446 A-D):

TANCREDI (Rossini) (I)
Opera in 2 acts (complete as performed)
Orchestra and Chorus of Radio Italiana [RAI], Milano/Mario Rossi
RAI broadcast, Milan, 28 June, 1968 [recorded Auditorium Pedrotti, Pesaro, 27 Jun 1968]

CAST:
Anna Reynolds (*Tancredi*); Rita Talarico (*Amenaide*); Giampaolo Corradi (*Argerio*); Luigi Roni (*Orbazzano*); Anna Di Stasio (*Isaura*); Aronne Ceroni (*Ruggiero*); Gabriele De Julis (*Soloist*); Walter Artioli (*Soloist*); Enzo Viaro (*Soloist*).

NOTES: EJS 446

Complete as performed at about 95 minutes: the November, 1968 bulletin claims that "the opera is presented in its entirety," but the original score runs about 175 minutes. The Act II duet, originally for *Tancredi* and *Argerio*, is sung here by *Tancredi* and *Amenaide*, with the text slightly altered to acommodate the modified dramatic context. Similarly, *Ruggiero*, usually sung by a woman, is sung by Aronne Ceroni. Many of the *secco* recitatives have been retained in this performance--more of them, in fact, than in other, later revivals of the work.

The bulletin also bemoans that "the youngsters who sing . . . here do so cleanly and accurately but are not gifted with the fantastic bravura of the singers of Rossini's time . . . with a Sutherland, a Horne, a Bergonza [sic]--the opera would be more like what Rossini had in mind."

The correct playing speed of the performance is approximately 34.2 rpm.

EJS 447: "The Golden Age of Opera" (1 LP)
Issued November, 1968
MATRIX P-1738

"EVA TURNER, DINO BORGIOLI: PUCCINI RECITAL"

SIDE 1 (447 A):

1. GEORGE HANCOCK, baritone, JOHN TORNEY, tenor, DINO BORGIOLI, tenor, and EVA TURNER, soprano (Augmented BBC Theater Orchestra/Stanford Robinson): MADAMA BUTTERFLY, Act I: Ed è bella la sposa? . . . Amore o grillo . . . Ancora un passo . . . Siam giunte. B. F. Pinkerton. Giù! (Puccini) (I)
   Broadcast, ***BBC REGIONAL PROGRAMME***, London, 8 Nov 1938

2. EVA TURNER, soprano (Augmented BBC Theater Orchestra/Stanford Robinson): MADAMA BUTTERFLY, Act II: Un bel dì vedremo (Puccini) (I)
   Broadcast, ***BBC REGIONAL PROGRAMME***, London, 8 Nov 1938

3. DINO BORGIOLI, tenor (Augmented BBC Theater Orchestra/Stanford Robinson): LA BOHÈME, Act I: Che gelida manina (Puccini) (I)
   Broadcast, ***BBC REGIONAL PROGRAMME***, London, 8 Nov 1938

4. DINO BORGIOLI, tenor, and EVA TURNER, soprano (Augmented BBC Theater Orchestra/Stanford Robinson): LA BOHÈME, Act I: O soave fanciulla (Puccini) (I)
   Broadcast, ***BBC REGIONAL PROGRAMME***, London, 8 Nov 1938

5. DINO BORGIOLI, tenor (Augmented BBC Theater Orchestra/Stanford Robinson): TOSCA, Act III: E lucevan le stelle (Puccini) (I)
   Broadcast, ***BBC REGIONAL PROGRAMME***, London, 8 Nov 1938

SIDE 2 (447 B):

1. a) BOYS' CHOIR (Augmented BBC Theater Orchestra/Stanford Robinson): TURANDOT, Act II: Dal deserto al mar . . . Tutto splenderà! (Puccini) (I)
   Broadcast, ***BBC REGIONAL PROGRAMME***, London, 8 Nov 1938

   b) EVA TURNER, soprano, and DINO BORGIOLI, tenor (Augmented BBC Theater Orchestra and Chorus/Stanford Robinson): TURANDOT, Act II: In questa reggia . . . Al principe straniero offri la prova ardita, O Turandot! (Puccini) (I)
   Broadcast, ***BBC REGIONAL PROGRAMME***, London, 8 Nov 1938

2. DINO BORGIOLI, tenor, and JOHN TORNEY, tenor (Augmented BBC Theater Orchestra and Chorus/Stanford Robinson): TURANDOT, Act II: Tre enigmi m'hai proposto! . . . to the end of act (Puccini) (I)
   Broadcast, ***BBC REGIONAL PROGRAMME***, London, 8 Nov 1938

3. JOHN TORNEY, tenor, and DINO BORGIOLI, tenor (Augmented BBC Theater Orchestra/Stanford Robinson): MANON LESCAUT, Act I: A noi t'unisce amico . . . Tra voi, belle . . . Dillo a me! (Puccini) (I)
   Broadcast, ***BBC REGIONAL PROGRAMME***, London, 8 Nov 1938

4. JOHN TORNEY, tenor, and DINO BORGIOLI, tenor (Augmented BBC Theater Orchestra and Chorus/Stanford Robinson): MANON LESCAUT, Act I: Ma bravo! . . . Viaggiatori eleganti, galanti! (Puccini) (I)
   Broadcast, ***BBC REGIONAL PROGRAMME***, London, 8 Nov 1938

* 5. DINO BORGIOLI, tenor (pf/?):
   a) Interview with Borgioli (I)
   a) "O luna che fa lume (Davico) (I)
   b) "I pastori" (Pizetti) (I)
   Broadcast, ***RADIOCORRIERE DELLA LIBERTÀ***, BBC London, ?1 Nov 1943

NOTES: EJS 447

The Turner-Borgioli material, broadcast over BBC on 8 November, 1937, is thought to have actually been pre-recorded in March, 1936. Soprano Nora Gruhn (or Grühn) was also listed as one of the soloists for the broadcast, so other selections must have been performed which were not included on EJS 447.

Side 2 (447 B):

Band 1: The "In questa Reggia" is preceded in the broadcast by a boys' choir singing the "Dal deserto al mar" from Act I.

Band 5: This Borgioli interview was a BBC broadcast to fascist Italy. Because of the lack of personnel during the War, the BBC's "Programme as Broadcast" schedules were suspended, rendering inaccessible the means of documenting precisely many of the performances that have survived as transcriptions. The Borgioli interview suggests that Italy was still firmly under the arm of fascist rule, and is thus thought to date from about the time of the singer's first BBC Overseas Service broadcast on 1 November, 1943. Had the interview been any later, Borgioli might have offered listeners a slightly different message.

The pianist is unknown.

EJS 448: "The Golden Age of Opera" (1 LP)
Issued November, 1968
MATRIX P-1739

SIDES 1-2 (448 A-B):

I PAGLIACCI (Leoncavallo) (I)
Opera in 2 acts (complete)
Metropolitan Opera House Orchestra and Chorus/Cesare Sodero)
Metropolitan Opera broadcast, NYC, 20 Mar 1943

CAST:
Giovanni Martinelli (*Canio*); Marita Farell (*Nedda*); Leonard Warren (*Tonio*); John Dudley (*Beppe*); Walter Cassel (*Silvio*).

NOTES: EJS 448

Accompanied on this matinee bill by a CAVALLERIA RUSTICANA with Milanov and Jagel, and the GIOCONDA "Dance of the Hours" performed by the Met's *Corps de Ballet*. Excerpts from this PAGLIACCI, Martinelli's last perfomance of the work at the Met and his last Met broadcast, had appeared earlier on EJS 240 (May, 1962). Licia Albanese had originally been scheduled as the *Nedda*, according to *Opera News*, 7/22 (15 March, 1943), pp. 12-13. This was Farell's first and last *Nedda* at the Met. See the endnote for EJS 240 regarding the original NBC acetates.

This LP requires constant monitoring of the pitch, as the playing speeds are inconsistent.

EJS 449: "The Golden Age of Opera" (1 LP)
Issued November, 1968
MATRIX P-1740

SIDES 1-2 (449 A-B):

GENEVIÈVE DE BRABANT (Offenbach) (F)
Opéra-bouffe in 3 acts (complete)
Orchestra and Chorus of the Office de Radiodiffusion Télévision Française [ORTF], Paris/Jean-Paul Kreder
ORTF broadcast, ?Paris, date unknown

CAST:
Lina Dachary (*Geneviève*); Huguette Hennetier (*Brigitte*); Gabrielle Ristori (*Isoline*); Germaine Parrat (*Christine*); Emmanuele Jarot (*Bradamante*); Raymond Amade (*Drogan*); Joseph Peyron (*Sifroy*); Jean-Christophe Benoit (*Charles Martel*); Gaston Rey (*Golo*); René Terrason (*Grabuge*); Michel Fauchey (*Vanderprout*); Aimé Doniat (*Pitou*); René Lenoty (*Narcisse*); Pierre Roy (*Péterpip*).

NOTES: EJS 449

This performance is complete *musically*, lacking only the original dialogue. This is not the later ORTF performance of GENEVIÈVE DE BRABANT issued in stereo (though labeled as mono) on Bourg compact disc BGC 10.11.

EJS 450: "The Golden Age of Opera" (2 LPs)
Issued December, 1968
MATRIX P-1757 / P-1758

DIE WALKÜRE (Wagner) (G)
Opera in 3 acts (Act III only)
London Philharmonic Orchestra and Chorus of the Royal Opera House/ Wilhelm Furtwängler
Unpublished live performance recordings (HMV), Covent Garden, London, 26 May 1937

CAST:
Kirsten Flagstad (*Brünnhilde*); [Lauritz Melchior (*Siegmund*)]; Rudolph Bockelmann (*Wotan*); Maria Müller (*Sieglinde*); [Kerstin Thorborg (*Fricka*)]; [Ludwig Weber (*Hunding*)]; Mae Craven (*Gerhilde*); Thelma Bardsley (*Ortlinde*); Linda Seymour (*Waltraute*); Gladys Ripley (*Schwertleite*); Elsa Stenning (*Helmwige*); Edith Coates (*Siegrune*); Gwladys Garside (*Grimgerde*); Evelyn Arden (*Rossweise*).

SIDES 1-3 (450 A-C):

1. CAST: Act III complete
 2EA 5237-1 to 2EA 5252-1 HMV unpublished

SIDE 4 (450 D):

* 1. a) NANNY LARSEN-TODSEN, soprano, and EMIL [ERIK] ENDERLEIN, tenor (Orchestra of the Berlin Staatsoper/Leo Blech): GÖTTERDÄMM-ERUNG, Prologue: Zu neuen Taten . . . Brünnhilde brennt dann ewig heilig dir in der Brust! (Wagner) (G)
 CLR-3967-1/1A Berlin Staatsoper, Berlin, 19 Mar 1928
 HMV unpub

b) NANNY LARSEN-TODSEN, soprano, and EMIL [ERIK] ENDERLEIN, tenor (Orchestra of the Berlin Staatsoper/Leo Blech): GÖTTERDÄMM-ERUNG, Prologue: Lass' ich Liebste, dich hier in der Lohe heiliger Hut . . . to the end of the Prologue (Wagner) (G)
 CLR-3968-1/1A Berlin Staatsoper, Berlin, 19 Mar 1928
 HMV unpub

* 2. EMIL [ERIK] ENDERLEIN, tenor, and NANNY LARSEN-TODSEN, soprano (Orchestra and Männerchor of the Berlin Staatsoper/Leo Blech): GÖTTERDÄMMERUNG, Act II: Helle Wehr, Heilige Waffe! . . . thu' es der Glückliche gleich! (Wagner) (G)
 CLR-3969-1A/2/3 Berlin Staatsoper, Berlin, 19 Mar 1928
 HMV unpub

* 3. a) NANNY LARSEN-TODSEN, soprano, and IVAR ANDRESEN, bass (Orchestra of the Berlin Staatsoper/Leo Blech): GÖTTERDÄMM-ERUNG, Act II: Welches Unhold's List . . . wie doch der Recke mir wich'? (Wagner) (G)
 CLR-3975-1/1A Berlin Staatsoper, Berlin, 21 Mar 1928
 HMV unpub

b) NANNY LARSEN-TODSEN, soprano, IVAR ANDRESEN, bass, and HERBERT JANSSEN, baritone (Orchestra of the Berlin Staatsoper/Leo Blech): GÖTTERDÄMMERUNG, Act II: O Undank . . . Verrieth er mich? (Wagner) (G)
CLR-3976-1/1A/2 Berlin Staatsoper, Berlin, 21 Mar 1928
HMV unpub

c) NANNY LARSEN-TODSEN, soprano, IVAR ANDRESEN, bass, and HERBERT JANSSEN, baritone (Orchestra of the Berlin Staatsoper/Leo Blech): GÖTTERDÄMMERUNG, Act II: Dich verriet er . . . to the end of the act (Wagner) (G)
CLR-3977-1/1A/2/2A Berlin Staatsoper, Berlin, 21 Mar 1928
HMV unpub

NOTES: EJS 450

Sides 1-3 (450 A-C):

The WALKÜRE Act II recordings were apparently not technical tests. HMV matrices 2EA 5253 and 2EA 4800 may also have contained portions of the performance, but this has not been confirmed. The latter was documented from Flagstad's own collection and was simply marked "Die Walküre." None of these live recordings was issued commercially by the Gramophone Company.

Pitch is inconsistent over the course of the three WALKüRE sides, and ranges from about 33.7 to 34.3 rpm.

The entire third act was reissued subsequently on the Bruno Walter Society's Recital Records label as RR 417 and on Acanta 40.23520 FK. The "Nicht straf ich dich erst" appeared on Sonor 98-256901/08 and Acanta 40.23502 FK, and Bockelmann's "Abschied" on BASF [Acanta] HB 22863-0.

Stanford University Archive of Recorded Sound tape: 560000 M13

Side 4 (450 D):

Bands 1-3: The December, 1969 bulletin does not claim these GÖTTERDÄMMERUNG excerpts to be live performance recordings (as has been suggested), but does list bass Ludwig Weber among the participants, which is incorrect. These are landline recordings made at the Staatsoper by D. E. Larter and G. W. George, and relayed to a Berlin studio for transcripition (hence the "CLR" matrix prefix). Takes are given in the listing as they are found in the company recording ledgers: it is not known which takes survived for inclusion here. Matrices CLR 3970-3974, if they were used, are not given in the ledgers for this performance. A note on the recording sheets for the sessions says "All poor balance, records lack life and brightness." Tenor Enderlein is given in the ledgers as Emil Enderlien, the name under which he recorded for Pathé and Polydor.

These excerpts play in score pitch at 34.2 rpm.

Band 3: The last three excerpts, from "Welches Unhold's List" to the end of the opera (CLR 3975-3977), appeared subsequently on the Preiser "Lebindige Vergangenheit" Larsen-Todsen recital, LV 174, but the takes used are not given in the jacket listing.

EJS 451: "The Golden Age of Opera" (1 LP)
Issued December, 1968
MATRIX P-1759

"DIE WALKÜRE ACT I AND II"

SIDE 1 (451 A):

* 1. ALEXANDER KIPNIS, bass, and LAURITZ MELCHIOR, tenor (Metropolitan Opera House Orchestra/Erich Leinsdorf): DIE WALKÜRE, Act I: Heilig ist mein Herd . . . Sieh', wie sie gierig dich frägt! (Wagner) (G)
Metropolitan Opera broadcast, NYC, 6 Dec 1941

* 2. MARIA MÜLLER, soprano, and FRANZ VÖLKER, tenor (Wiener Philharmoniker/Wilhelm Furtwängler): DIE WALKÜRE, Act I: Labung beit' ich dem lechzenden Gaumen . . . Schmecktest du [mir ihn zu?] (Wagner) (G)
In-house recording, Wiener Staatsoper, Vienna, 13 or 17 Feb 1936

3. SET SVANHOLM, tenor (Wiener Philharmoniker/Hans Knappertsbusch): DIE WALKÜRE, Act I: Ein Schwert verhiess' mir der Vater . . . Ist es der Blick der blühenden Frau (Wagner) (G)
In-house recording, Wiener Staatsoper, Vienna, 15 Jun 1941

* 4. MAX LORENZ, tenor, and HILDE KONETZNI, soprano ((Wiener Philharmoniker/Hans Knappertsbusch): DIE WALKÜRE, Act I: Nächtiges Dunkel deckte mein Aug' . . . Der Männer Alle (Wagner) (G)
In-house recordings, Wiener Staatsoper, Vienna, 1 Dec 1943

SIDE 2 (451 B):

* 1. HILDE KONETZNI, soprano, and MAX LORENZ, tenor (Wiener Philharmoniker/Hans Knappertsbusch): DIE WALKÜRE, Act I: So kühn sie sich müh' ten . . . to the end of the act (Wagner) (G)
In-house recording, Wiener Staatsoper, Vienna, 1 Dec 1943

* 2. FRIEDERICH SCHORR, baritone, and KERSTIN THORBORG, contralto (Metropolitan Opera House Orchestra/Erich Leinsdorf): DIE WALKÜRE, Act II: Der alte Sturm! Die alte Müh' . . . to the end of the scene (Wagner) (G)
Metropolitan Opera broadcast, NYC, 6 Dec 1941

NOTES: EJS 451

Side 1 (451 A):

Band 1: In addition to the Schorr-Thorborg duet on side 2 (see note, below) of EJS 451, other portions of this broadcast appeared on EJS 543 (March, 1971). Given as a Chicago performance in the December, 1968 bulletin.

Band 2: It is not known whether this excerpt was taken from the 13 or the 17 February, 1936 Vienna performance.

Band 4: This selection begins on I/4, and concludes on II/1. Various reports have been examined as to just how much of this 1 December, 1943 performance exists. Like the DON CARLOS on EJS 334 (May, 1965), it was recorded on acetates by a certain Herr May. One private collection claims nearly 25 minutes of the performance, about comparable to what is given here on I/4 and II/1. The first five minutes appears to be genuine, or at least consistent in sound quality. At *Sieglinde's* "Eine Waffe las mich dir weisen," however, the transcription becomes cleaner, more professional sounding. It has been suggested that Reichsrundfunk tapes--possibly of Konetzni and Lorenz, but not necessarily--have been inserted here without notice.

See also the endnote for the DON CARLOS on side 2 of EJS 334 for a more detailed discussion of Herr May's Vienna Staatsoper recordings.

Side 2 (451 B):

Band 1: See the note for I/4 above.

Band 2: Taken from the official NBC acetates. This excerpt is undated on the label of EJS 451. There are four extant Thorborg-Schorr WALKÜRE broadcasts from the Met: the first two, 16 January and 18 December, 1937, contain acetate breaks which omit music heard on the present excerpt; the third, 30 March, 1940 was compared and found to be musically dissimilar, indicating that the 6 December, 1941 broadcast, the fourth, was used here. Like I/1 above, this is given as Chicago, with no conductor named. Extended excerpts from the 6 December, 1941 WALKÜRE later appeared on EJS 543 (March, 1971).

EJS 452: "The Golden Age of Opera" (1 LP)
Issued December, 1968
MATRIX P-1762

"POTPOURRI 22"

SIDE 1 (452 A):

* 1. ANGELO SANTINI, tenor (pf/?): FAUST, Act III: Salve dimora [Salut! Demeure] (Gounod) (I)
10384-1 Milan, 1904 B&S Columbia 10384 Columbia A580

* 2. FEODOR CHALIAPIN, bass, and JOSEPH HISLOP, tenor (Orchestra of the Royal Opera House/Eugene Goossens): FAUST, Act I: Eh, bien! Que t'en semble? . . . to the end of the act (Gounod) (F)
CR 2101-1 Live performance, Covent Garden, London, 22 Jun 1928
HMV unpublished 1928

* 3. MARIA CEBOTARI, soprano, and RICHARD TAUBER, tenor (Wiener Philharmoniker/Josef Krips): DON GIOVANNI, K. 527, Act I: Anima mia, consolati! fa cor! . . . Fuggi, crudele, fuggi . . . Lascia, o cara (Mozart) (G)
Broadcast, Covent Garden, London, 27 Sep 1947

* 4. RICHARD TAUBER, tenor (Wiener Philharmoniker/Josef Krips): DON GIOVANNI, K. 527, Act I: [Dalla sua pace] quel ch'a lei piace (Mozart) (G)
Broadcast, Covent Garden, London, 27 Sep 1947

* 5. RICHARD TAUBER, tenor (Wiener Philharmoniker/Josef Krips): DON GIOVANNI, K. 527, Act II: Il mio tesoro . . . che sol di stragi e morte (Mozart) (G)
Broadcast, Covent Garden, London, 27 Sep 1947

* 6. RICHARD TAUBER, tenor (Orchestra of the Algemeene Vereniging Radio Omroep [AVRO]/Nico Treep): CARMEN, Act II: La fleur que tu m'avais jetée ["Flower Song"] (Bizet) (F)
AVRO broadcast, Hilversum, Holland, 18 Jul 1939

* 7. UGO TRAMA, bass (Orchestra of the Radio Italiana [RAI]/?): ATTILA, Act I: Uldino, Uldino . . . Mentre gonfiarsi l'anima . . . Oltre quel limite (Verdi) (I)
Broadcast, ?***CONCERT MARTINI E ROSSI***, circa 1964

SIDE 2 (452 B):

* 1. CESARE VALLETTI, tenor, and LINA PAGLIUGHI, soprano (Orchestra of Radio Italiana [RAI], Torino/?Cesare Gallino): LA REGINETTA DELLE ROSE, Act I: [Lontano, lontano, Lilian] E tutta trionfa di sole (Leoncavallo) (I)
RAI broadcast, Turin, 26 Feb 1949

* 2. MATTIA BATTISTINI, baritone (pf/?): "Ideale" (Errico-Tosti) (I)
301 Milan, circa 1920 Fonotecnica C 3002 C 5002

3. GIUSEPPE DI STEFANO, tenor (Orchestra of Radio Italiana [RAI]/?): DER VOGELHÄNDLER, Act II: Qui vent'anni pien d'amor [Wie mein Ahnl zwanzig Jahr] (Zeller) (I)
Broadcast, ?***CONCERT MARTINI E ROSSI***, date unknown

* 4. GIULETTA SIMIONATO, contralto (pf/?): Te voglio bene assaje ["Tte vojo bene assaje"] (attr. Donizetti) (I)
Source and date unknown

* 5. RICHARD CROOKS, tenor (orch/Alfred Wallenstein): IRIS, Act I: Apri la tua finestra (Mascagni) (I)
Broadcast, ***VOICE OF FIRESTONE***, WEAF, NYC, 29 Dec 1941

* 6. RICHARD CROOKS, tenor (orch/Alfred Wallenstein): "Land of Hope and Glory" ["Pomp and Circumstance"] (Benson-Elgar) (E)
Broadcast, ***VOICE OF FIRESTONE***, WEAF, NYC, 11 Nov 1940

* 7. MARY GARDEN, soprano (pf/Jean Dansereau): "Somewhere a Voice is Calling" (Newton-Tate) (I)
BVE-40735-4 Victor unpublished, New York, 5 Nov 1929

* 8. JOHANNES BRAHMS, pianist: "Hungarian Dance No. 1 in G Minor" [fragment] (Brahms)
Edison cylinder Vienna, ?2 Dec 1889

* 9. ROSA PONSELLE, soprano (orch/Josef Pasternack): SCHWANENGESANG, D. 957, no. 4: Leise flehen ["Ständchen"] (Rellstab-Schubert) (E)
Broadcast, ***ATWATER KENT [RADIO] HOUR***, WEAF, NYC, 7 Dec 1930

*10. ROSA PONSELLE, soprano (orch/Josef Pasternack): CARMEN, Act I: L'amour est un oiseau rebelle . . . et si je t'aime ["Habanera"] (Bizet) (F)
Broadcast, ***ATWATER KENT [RADIO] HOUR***, WEAF, NYC, 7 Dec 1930

*11. GERALDINE FARRAR, soprano (orch/Nathaniel Shilkret): CARMEN, Act I: [L'amour est un oiseau rebelle] Et si je t'aime ["Habanera" fragment] (Bizet) (F)
Broadcast, ***PACKARD HOUR***, WJZ, NYC, 29 Jun 1931

*12. a) GERALDINE FARRAR, soprano (orch/Nathaniel Shilkret): CARMEN, Act I: Près des remparts de Séville . . . Près des reparts de Séville (Bizet) (F)
Broadcast, ***PACKARD HOUR***, WJZ, NYC, 29 Jun 1931

b) GERALDINE FARRAR, soprano (orch/Walter B. Rogers): CARMEN, Act I: Chez mon ami Lillas Pastia . . . to the end of the aria ["Seguidilla"] (Bizet) (F)
C-15477-1 New York, 9 Dec 1914 Victor 88511 HMV 2-033049
6108 DB 244

*13. ERNESTINE SCHUMANN-HEINK, contralto (orch/Rosario Bourdon): DAS RHEINGOLD: [Weiche, Wotan!] . . . Wie alles war, weisss ich . . . dir rat ich, meide den Ring! (Wagner) (G)
?CVE-55615-2 New York or Camden, 17 Jul 1929
Victor 7107 AGSB 1

*14. Two unidentified sopranos and unidentified mezzo-soprano (orch/?): DAS RHEINGOLD: Rheingold! Rheingold! Rheines Gold! (Wagner) (G)
Broadcast, source and date unconfirmed

NOTES: EJS 452

Side 1 (452 A):

Band 1: One of the best-known of the EJS forgeries, labeled "Jean De Reszke: (OR SOME OTHER TENOR): Faust: Salve dimora (1896)," and preceded by a spoken announcement, "Salve dimora, [sung by] Jean De Reszke. Bettini Record." Only one verse of the aria is sung--in Italian, with piano accompaniment, and at score pitch (A-flat).

The surface noise consists of a detached, hollow swish, the periodicity of which is obviously the result of a stylus being placed in the run-off groove of a disc. The noise is constant, without the clicks and knocks--the transient noise--one normally expects from a recording of this vintage. Then, too, the piano lacks that characteristically "watery" sound that, except for French G&Ts of the period 1902-1903, is virtually unique to Bettini's cylinders. Bettini himself is generally acknowledged to be the announcer on all of the surviving *authentic* cylinders. The slightly accented voice we hear introducing the "De Reszke" performance barks out his words very deliberately, and in English, unlike Bettini himself, who announced in the language of the performance, and then, at an almost incomprehensible speed. The real giveaway, however, is the close of the announcement, "Bettini Record," which as W.R. Moran has pointed out, is an anomaly among Bettini cylinders, the only one encountered with an announcement that mentions the make of the record (see W.R. Moran. "The Legacy of Gianni Bettini," in *The Record Collector*, 16/7-8 (September, 1965), p. 169). Neither of the two Bettini discs known to have survived (Romeo Berti on 1239 and Polaire [née Emile Marie Bouchard, 1877-1939] on 1223) are announced.

This recording circulated privately a few years before Smith released it on EJS 451. These private pressings apparently bore the legend "Faust / Salve dimora / Jean De Reszke, tenor / Bettini Cylinder / 1892-1898." Moran presented a fascinating analysis of this private issue in a lecture entitled "The Archivists' Responsibility," given at an Association for Recorded Sound Collections (ARSC) conference held at UCLA on 22 November, 1968. This was recorded and has circulated on cassette. There, Moran examines not only the various physical aspects of the forgery, but also many of the ethical issues it raises.

The December, 1968 bulletin is one of Smith's longest, devoting most of the discussion to the "De Reszke" performance. "The story of the finding of this disc (sic) is most interesting," it begins: "It was brought to a school teacher in New York by a 14 year old boy who said that his grandfather had quite a few cylinder discs (sic) in his barn and asked the teacher, whom he knew to be a collector, if he would be interested in hearing them. The teacher provided a tape recorder and the boy taped a group of Edison 1905 cylinders and the disputed De Reszke. The teacher, then quite excited asked for the original, but the boy claimed he had broken this disc (sic) along with several others in getting them off the machine on which he had played them but not until he had taped them." Finding the *cylinder discs* in grandfather's barn was a bit corny even for Smith--in fact, one collector told me privately that Smith had originally told him that the cylinder was found in an attic! That a 14-year-old would be placidly entrusted with the task of taping fragile cylinders by any knowledgeable collector, breaking record after record on the mandrel (though not before a tape of each had been secured for posterity) seems almost quaint when we consider that this is nothing more than an excuse for making the "De Reszke" cylinder inaccessible to physical scrutiny. But at this point, the bulletin takes a more interesting turn. Testimonials from Richard Bonelli, Maggie Teyte, Bidu Sayao, and Giuseppe [Joseph] Bentonelli--all De Reszke pupils for whom Smith played the "Salve dimora"--are offered, though significantly, none of them is quoted. "All agreed unanimously that it probably was Jean De Reszke," Smith wrote, "and Bentonelli, who had studied *Faust* with him, showed me his score with De Reszke's markings for legato and proper phrasing all of which conformed to the record." Richard Bonelli later recanted his endorsement saying that he really couldn't be so certain after nearly a half century, and that any good tenor of the *French* school of that time might be passed off successfully as De Reszke. As it turned out, the artist was an Italian of no identifiable pedigree.

Smith reported only two "violent objections" to the issue of the "Salve dimora," tendered by Desmond Shawe-Taylor and William Moran, neither of whom believed it was real. Among Moran's immediate concerns was the more than two-minute length of the recording, to which Smith replied in correspondence (September, 1968): ". . . did you see [the] article in *Hobbies* (September) which discloses that Edison had a four minute cylinder on the market in the early 1890's--and advertised it--in England in 1891 (page 92)--this would take away 50% of the objections throw[n] in the way of the alleged Jean De Reszke--I've got to follow this up--." Ultimately, ignoring the pleas of Moran and Shawe-Taylor, Smith went ahead with the issue, stating that "the 10% chance that this may be legitimate makes it worthwhile to publish it." But he did take Moran's suggestion, tendered in personal correspondence in the Summer of 1968, of challenging collectors to examine obscure renditions of the aria among their own holdings in the hope that the identity of the singer might be established conclusively. The sweepstakes winner was *Hobbies* regular, Aida Favia-Artsay who, in the January, 1969 bulletin, is credited with solving the mystery, and identifying the Santini performance on Columbia 10384. "So, unfortunately," Smith concluded in the January bulletin, "another possibility of finding a De Reszke disc has gone down the drain."

There is no doubt that the recording is 10384-1 by the obscure Angelo Santini. As if Favia-Artsay's word were not enough, I have synchronized the EJS 452 dubbing with my own single- and double-sided copies of the Santini disc, both of which are take -1. Santini sings the aria at score pitch. Columbia A580, incidentally, is coupled with Gina [Viafora] Ciaparelli's "Musetta's Waltz," matrix 3178-2.

As with the faked Mapleson cylinders on EJS 267 (April, 1963), the culpability for this forgery is difficult to establish: Smith was either a dupe, a willing participant, or was directly responsible. The same must hold true for the "Schumann-Heink" RHEINGOLD solo on the second side of this LP.

Band 2: Act I was recorded complete from the stage of Covent Garden. The final duet consisted of the last three parts: CR 2099-1, 2100-1, and 2101-1, the last of which is featured here. Only two of the 22 June, 1928 excerpts were published on 78, Hislop's "Salut! Demeure" and the Chaliapin-Hislop "Nous nous retrouverons," issued DB 1189. All twelve were subsquently released by EMI on the 1979 live Covent Garden set, RLS 742.

Bands 3-5: Taken from Tauber's final *stage* appearance, but contrary to the label of EJS 452, this was not the "last performance of [his] life:" in fact, he sang the next day, 28 September, 1947, on the BBC ***LIGHT PROGRAMME CONCERT***. He was hospitalized on 4 October and died of of cancer on 8 January, 1948.

This DON GIOVANNI was part of the Wiener Staatsoper's season at Covent Garden and was sung in German.

The "Dalla sua pace" begins at "quel ch'a lei piace." The "Il mio tesoro" fades at "che sol di stragi e morte" and is described as "truncated" on the label of EJS 452. The same Tauber-Cebotari duet appeared on EJS 171 (January, 1960). See that entry (II/7) for the entire cast listing.

Band 6: Given as Holland, June, 1939 on the label of EJS 452, with [Massimo] Freccia as the conductor. Two other arias from this 18 July, 1939 broadcast had appeared earlier on EJS 364 (April, 1966).

Band 7: Dated 1964 on the label of EJS 452. *Uldino's* lines are cut.

Side 2 (452 B):

Band 1: Dated 1950 on the label of EJS 452. Extensive highlights of Pagliughi's 1951 RAI performance of this three-act opera were issued earlier on EJS 407 (September, 1967). Presented here is a portion of the 1949 Act I finale, which cuts off before the entrance of the chorus. The work was not broadcast complete.

Gallino is known to have conducted the 1951 RAI production of LA REGINETTA DELLE ROSE, but it could not been verified that he was the conductor of this 1949 performanace.

Band 2: Battistini's rare Fonotecnica sides can be found in excellent sound on the 1986 EMI set, "Mattia Battistini: King of Baritones" (EMI EX 29 0790 3 and Seraphim IG-6153). EJS 452 cites "Societe Phonographique" as the original 78 label.

Band 4: This "Canzone Napoletana" is attributed to Donizetti. Given on the label of EJS 452 as "Tte vojo bene assaje" and sung in Italian.

Bands 5-6: Both are dated 1940 on the label of EJS 452. Crooks most likely transposed the IRIS down the familiar half-step, at which pitch it plays at 33.3 rpm. The Elgar is identified in the *New York Times* radio log as "Pomp and Circumstance" ("Land of Hope and Glory" was the 1902 vocal version, with lyrics by Arthur C. Benson).

Band 7: Private vinyl pressings of this unpublished Garden performance have been in circulation for years, verifying that take 4 was definitely used here. The Voce "Great Singers" LP (VOCE-88) transferred the unpublished take 1 from 22 November, 1927 in considerably better sound. In take 1, Garden's last two notes are the same (B-natural); in take 4, she ends on the tonic (B-natural to the E-natural above).

See also the endnote for EJS 397 (May, 1967), II/4.

Band 8: The Brahms cylinder, announced by the composer himself, has most recently appeared in a digital restoration effected at the Phonogrammarchiv der Österreichischen Akademie der Wissenschaften, and released in 1983 on their 7-inch EP, "Johannes Brahms und sein Freundeskreis" (PHA EP 5). The sound is a bit peculiar there, but astonishingly clear. A much less distinguished dubbing appeared in 1977 on the LP "Landmarks of Recorded Pianism, Volume 1," issued by the International Piano Archives and Desmar as IPA 117.

Previously, the provenance of the recording has been given as Brahms' home in Vienna, Summer, 1889. The Vienna Phonogrammarchiv claims, from the announcement, that it was made on 2 December, 1889 in the home of Dr. Fellinger (recorded, undoubtedly, by Edison's indefatigable European agent, Col. Gouraud. The liner notes for PHA EP 5 transcribe Brahm's announcement as: "Dezember 1889, im Haus von Dr. Fellinger, bei (by?) Herrn Dr. Brahms, Johannes Brahms!" (sic). Bescoby-Chambers' *The Archives of Sound* (Lingfield, Surry: Oakwood Press, 1964), p. 126, mentions Brahms' friend *Maria* Fellinger in this connection. The IPA LP transcribes Brahms' announcement as: "Grüsse an Herrn Doktor Edison. I am Dr. Brahms . . . Johannes Brahms."

Bands 9-10: Only fragments of these very early Ponselle broadcast selections are presented here. The "Ständchen," sung in English, is incomplete; the CARMEN begins at the second verse and ends prematurely at "et si je t'aime." Both are incorrectly dated *8* December, 1930 on the label of EJS 452.

Though this particular broadcast was conducted by Josef Pasternack, Victor's veteran musical director, the ***ATWATER KENT [RADIO] HOUR*** was at the time under the musical direction of Donald Voorhees, who would later go on to conduct the ***BELL TELEPHONE HOUR*** for decades. Ponselle shared this 7 December, 1930 broadcast with violinist Michael Rosenker.

Bands 11-12: This broadcast was Farrar's radio debut, "her only professional appearance to survive on discs before her official retirement in 1932," as the December bulletin puts it, which should be taken to mean outside of studio recordings. The show, originating from WJZ, New York City, aired on Monday evenings at 10:00 pm. Only the end of the "Habanera" (from the last line) is preserved on EJS 452. The "Seguidilla" is fragmentary and is completed with Farrar's 9 December, 1914 Victor recording of the aria (matrix C-15477-1, issued as Victor 88511/6108 and HMV 2-033049/DB 244). There is also an internal announcement referring to Farrar. The December bulletin attributes the truncation of these fragments to the fact that in 1930, home recording devices were limited to one minute of recording time--a plausible theory, albeit one which could not be verified.

Bands 13-14: This infamous Schumann-Heink broadcast, if authentic, would be the earliest surviving Met broadcast fragment. It is "alleged to be Feb. 26, 1932: Bodanzky," according to the label of EJS 452, though neither the city nor the house is mentioned there. "The actual origin of the performance," the December bulletin claims, "remains shrouded in mystery."

Schumann-Heink's commercial electrical version of "Weiche, Wotan" can be made to synchronize effortlessly with the last pages of the "live" performance found on EJS 452. The beginning of the EJS transfer, on the other hand, is filled with tiny cuts and other irregularities of speed (even outside of the fact that it was transferred nearly a minor third too low) and so cannot be synchronized as easily. But in fact, the two appear to be identical, down to the most minor performances nuances. That the commercial version may have been used by Smith would also explain the rather extreme dissimilarity of sound between *Erda's* solo and the *Rhinemaiden* finale that follows, which sounds definitely to have been taken from a very early live broadcast.

The *Rhinemaidens* for the two possible broadcast finales, both conducted by Bodanzky (26 February, 1932 with Schumann-Heink, and 27 January, 1933 with Olszewska) were as follows:

		26 February, 1932	27 January, 1933
Woglinde	. . .	Editha Fleisher	Editha Fleisher
Wellgunde	. . .	Phradie Wells	Rose Bampton
Flosshilde	. . .	Marie von Essen	Doris Doe

The problem with the 26 February, 1932 *attribution*, a Friday afternoon matinee which began at 2:30 pm EST, is the 26 February, *broadcast*, carried over WJZ, New York City (NBC Blue) from 3:00-4:00 pm EST: there is simply no possibility that *Erde's* warning could have actually been heard on-the-air between those times. A regularly-scheduled program featuring Harry Kogen's Orchestra followed at 4:00 pm, so it is extremely doubtful that the Met broadcast would have exceeded its allotted one-hour slot that day.

The 27 January, 1933 matinee broadcast, with Olszewska as *Erda*, has also been suggested as a possible source, but Schumann-Heink is unmistakable here. The Olszewska broadcast may be the source, however, for the ending fragment which follows Schumann-Heink's solo. It, too, was a Friday matinee that began at 2:30 pm EST, heard over WEAF, New York City (NBC Red) from 3:15-5:00 pm, so the conclusion of the opera *would* have been heard on-the-air and may well have been transcribed.

Another possibility, however remote, is that *Erda's* solo was performed on another, as yet undocumented network radio show by Schumann-Heink (her 1935 show, for example, sponsored by Hoover Vacuum cleaners), with the RHINEGOLD finale inserted from another (broadcast) source. A recitative and aria from Mendelssohn's ST. PAUL, "And he journeyed . . . But the Lord is Mindful of His Own," was recorded on a Western Electric disc during one of Schumann-Heink's vaudeville appearance at New York's Roxy Theater on 11 January, 1931 (matrix BTL 1318), but no extant RHEINGOLD excerpts are known to have been performed there (the Mendelssohn has survived, however, suggesting that the sources of such extraordinary non-commercial materials appear to be quite inexhaustible!). Nor were any RHEINGOLD excerpts performed on Schumann-Heink's 1934 show, sponsored by Gerber.

Note that both of the fragments play in score pitch at 34.7 rpm.

EJS 453: "The Golden Age of Opera" (1 LP)
Issued December, 1968)
MATRIX P-1760

SIDE 1 (453 A):

JULIE (Spontini) (I)
Opera in 1 act (complete)
?Orchestra of Teatro dei Rinnovati, Siena/Bruno Rigacci
Broadcast, Teatro dei Rinnovati, Siena, 5 Sep 1968

CAST:
Valeria Mariconda (*Julie*); Ugo Trama (*Mondor*); Giancarlo Montanaro (*Verseuil*); Amilcare Blaffard (*Valcour*).

SIDE 2 (EJS 453 B):

IL COMBATTIMENTO DI TANCREDI E CLORINDA (Monteverdi) (I)
Dramatic cantata (complete)
Orchestra of Teatro San Carlo di Napoli/Nino Sanzogno
?In-house recording, Teatro San Carlo, Naples, 12 Apr 1952

CAST:
Giuletta Simionato (*Testo*); Cesare Valetti (*Tancredi*); Ornella Rovero (*Clorinda*).

NOTES: EJS 453

Side 1 (453 A):

The music is complete as performed, but the dialogue has been omitted from EJS 543. The autumn festival in Siena usually employed the Orchestra of the Teatro Comunale, Firenze, but it could not be determined if that was the case here.

This performance of JULIE was later issued on a two-disc Voce LP (VOCE-51), coupled with an RAI performance of Spontini's MILTON.

EJS 454: "The Golden Age of Opera" (2 LPs)
Issued January, 1969
MATRIX P-1776 / P-1777

SIDES 1-4 (454 A-D):

LA STRANIERA (Bellini) (I)
Opera in 2 acts (complete)
Orchestra and Chorus of Teatro Massimo, Palermo/Nino Sanzogno
In-house recording, Teatro Massimo, Palermo, 10 Dec 1968

CAST:
Renata Scotto (*Alaide*); Renato Cioni (*Arturo*); Enrico Campi (*Lord Montolino*); Elena Zilio (*Isoletta*); Domenico Trimarchi (*Baron Valdeburgo*); Maurizio Mazzieri (*Priore degli Spedalieri*); Glauco Scarlini (*Osburgo*).

NOTES: EJS 454

LA STRANIERA originally appeared as a two-act opera, but it is presented here in four acts--possibly the way in which it was given in Palermo. There are a number of performance cuts and rearrangements: *Isoletta's* prominent second-act scene, for example, is shaved of its cabaletta, with the cavatina injected into the beginning of the Act I. The original eighth scene of Bellini's two-act setting (II/2) is also cut, and begins in the middle of the chorus, "Qui non visti."

Labeling errors ("Scarinci" for Scarlini, etc.), have been corrected in the listing above.

Speeds are erratic: the entire first side seems steady at 33.3 rpm; side 2 plays at 33.0 rpm with the exception of the second band, which requires a speed of 32.0 rpm to secure score pitch.

This performance was subsquently reissued on the two-LP MRF 30 and on a two-CD Melodram issue, MEL-27039.

EJS 455: "The Golden Age of Opera" (1 LP)
Issued January, 1969
MATRIX P-1778

SIDE 1 (455 A): "ROSSINI"

1. CARMEN GONZALES, contralto (?Orchestra of Radio Italiana [RAI]/ ?Nino Bonavolonta): DEMETRIO E POLIBIO, Act I: Pien di contento in seno (Rossini) (I)
   ?RAI broadcast, place and date unknown

2. CARMEN GONZALES, soprano, and FRANCINE GIRONES, soprano (?Orchestra of Radio Italiana [RAI]/?Nino Bonavolonta): DEMETRIO E POLIBIO, Act I: Questo cor ti giura amore (Rossini) (I)
   ?RAI broadcast, place and date unknown

3. CARLO GAIFA, tenor (?Orchestra of Radio Italiana [RAI]/?Nino Bonavolonta): CIRO IN BABILONIA, Act ?: Avrai tu pur vendetta (Rossini) (I)
   ?RAI broadcast, place and date unknown

4. FRANCINE GIRONES, soprano (?Orchestra of Radio Italiana [RAI]/ ?Nino Bonavolonta): CIRO IN BABILONIA, Act ?: Deh, per me non v'affliggete (Rossini) (I)
   ?RAI broadcast, place and date unknown

5. CARLO GAIFA, tenor, and FRANCINE GIRONES, soprano (?Orchestra of Radio Italiana [RAI]/?Nino Bonavolonta): CIRO IN BABILONIA, Act ?: È questa o principessa, il pensier mio . . . T'arrendi, t'arrendi (Rossini) (I)
   ?RAI broadcast, place and date unknown

SIDE 2 (455 B): "ROSSINI-ZANDONAI"

1. FRANCINE GIRONES, soprano, CARLO GAIFA, tenor, and CARMEN GONZALES, contralto (?Orchestra of Radio Italiana [RAI]/?Nino Bonavolonta): CIRO IN BABILONIA, Act ?: Oh, qual dolci . . . Fiero nell'anima (Rossini) (I)
   ?RAI broadcast, place and date unknown

2. ?ORCHESTRA OF RADIO ITALIANA [RAI]/?NINO BONAVOLONTA: LA FARSA AMOROSA: Overture (Zandonai)
   ?RAI broadcast, place unknown, circa 1968-1969

3. ALBERTO RINALDI, baritone (?Orchestra of Radio Italiana [RAI]/ ?Nino Bonavolonta): LA FARSA AMOROSA, Act ?: Quante donne, quante spose (Zandonai) (I)
   ?RAI broadcast, place unknown, circa 1968-1969

4. NICOLETTA PANNI, soprano (?Orchestra of Radio Italiana [RAI]/ ?Nino Bonavolonta): LA FARSA AMOROSA, Act ?: Passo i miei di tranquilla (Zandonai) (I)
   ?RAI broadcast, place unknown, circa 1968-1969

5. MIRELLA PARUTTO, mezzo-soprano (?Orchestra of Radio Italiana [RAI]/?Nino Bonavolonta): LA FARSA AMOROSA, Act ?: Stanotte aparecchio il lettucio nel bosco (Zandonai) (I)
   ?RAI broadcast, place unknown, circa 1968-1969

6. NICOLETTA PANNI, soprano (?Orchestra of Radio Italiana [RAI]/ ?Nino Bonavolonta): IL GRILLO DEL FOCOLARE, Act I: Si, è l'anima canora (Zandonai) (I)
   ?RAI broadcast, place unknown, circa 1968-1969

7. ALBERTO RINALDI, baritone (?Orchestra of Radio Italiana [RAI]/ ?Nino Bonavolonta): IL GRILLO DEL FOCOLARE, Act III: Canto ancor, picciol grillo (Zandonai) (I)
   ?RAI broadcast, place unknown, circa 1968-1969

NOTES: EJS 455

Many labeling errors have been corrected in the listing above, but the acts from which these obscure arias were taken could not be determined. Provenance, and in the case of the Zandonai items, dates, are only approximate and could not be verified.

EJS 456: "The Golden Age of Opera" (1 LP)
Issued January, 1969
MATRIX P-1780

SIDE 1 (456 A): "GRACE MOORE"

LOUISE (1938)
Société Parisienne de Production des Films
Distributed in the U.S. by European Film Distributors
A Mayer and Burstyn Release
Director: Abel Gance
Screenplay: Steve Passeur (from Charpentier's 4-act opera)
English-language titles: Deems Taylor
Photography: Kurt Coutant
Musical director: Louis Beydts
Supervision: Gustave Charpentier
Conductor: Eugène Bigot
Filmed: Paris, September, 1938
72-85 minutes B&W
Paris Premiere: ?1938
London Premiere: 1939
New York Premiere: Little Carnegie Theater, NYC, 2 Feb 1940
CAST:
Grace Moore (*Louise*); Georges Thill (*Julien*); André Pernet (*The Father*); Suzanne Despres [speaking] (*The Mother*); Ginette Leclerc (*Lucienne*); Pauline Carton (*Forelady*); Rivers Cadet (*The Singer*); Jacqueline Prevot (*Seamstress*); Le Vigan (*Gaston*); Jacqueline Gaulter (*Alphonsine*); Beauchamp (*Philosopher*); Peres (*Sculptor*); ?Arthur Endrèze (*The Ragman*).

1. Act I: a) THILL, and MOORE: O coeur ami! . . . Et mon coeur chantait les matines d'amour!
   b) PERNET and DESPRES: Le bonheur, vois-tu [Despres *speaks* the Mother's lines]

   Act II: *c) UNIDENTIFIED SINGERS: Les cris de Paris
   *d) MOORE: Une voix mystérieuse
   e) THILL and Chorus: Dans la cité lointaine
   f) ?ENDRÈZE: Un père cherche sa fille
   Act III: *g) MOORE: Depuis le jour

2. GRACE MOORE, soprano (Concertgebouw Orchestra/Willem Mengelberg): MADAMA BUTTERFLY, Act II: Un bel di, vedremo (Puccini) (I)
   Broadcast, Amsterdam, Jun 1936

3. GRACE MOORE, soprano (Concertgebouw Orchestra/Willem Mengelberg): "Ciribiribin" (Carlo Tiochet-A. Pestalozza) (I)
   Broadcast, Amsterdam, Jun 1936

SIDE 2 (456 B): "CONCHITA SUPERVIA & GRACE MOORE"

EVENSONG (1934)
Gaumont-British Pictures
Distributed by Fox
Producer: Michael Balcon
Director: Victor Saville
Scenario and dialogue: Edward Knoblock
Adaptation: Dorothy Farnum
Based on the play by Knoblock and the novel by Beverley Nicholls
Photography: Mutz Greenbaum
Editor: Otto Ludwig
Musical Director: Mischa Spoliansky
Songs: Mischa Spoliansky
Lyrics: Edward Knoblock
9 reels; 83 minutes; B&W
LP 5184 c17 Sep 1934 (Gaumont British Picture Corp., Ltd.)
London Premiere: ?
New York Premiere: Roxy Theater, NYC, 16 Nov 1934

CAST:
Evelyn Laye (*Mme. Irela [Maggie]*); Fritz Kortner (*Kober*); Alice Delysia (*Madam Valmond*); Carl Esmond (*Archduke Theodore*); Emlyn Williams (*George Murray*); Muriel Aked (*Tremlowe*); Patrick O'Moore (*Bob McNeil*); Dennis Val Norton (*Sovino*); Arthur Sinclair (*Pa McNeil*); Conchita Supervia (*Baba L'Étoile*); Browning Mummery (*Tenor Soloist*).

1. a) SUPERVIA (orch/Levy): LA BOHÈME, Act II: Quando m'en vo' ["Musetta's Waltz"] (Puccini) (I) [Dialogue over by Laye and Williams]
   b) LAYE and SUPERVIA: Dialogue (argument scene)
   c) SUPERVIA (pf/?): LAS HIJAS DEL ZEBEDEO: Al pensar en el dueño (José Estremera-Chapí) (S) [Dialogue over by Laye and Williams]
   d) SUPERVIA (guitar/?): "Los ojos negros" (trad.-Barta) (S)
   e) SUPERVIA (guitar/?): Unidentified song (S) [Dialogue over by Laye and Williams]
   f) SUPERVIA (pf/?): LA CENERENTOLA, Act II: Non più mesta (Rossini) (I) [A few bars of the final rondo only]
   g) LAYE (orch/Levy): LA BOHÈME, Act I: [Si, mi chiamano Mimi] Il primo bacio dell'aprile . . . Ahime, non hanno odore (Puccini) (I) [Fades into ending titles music by Spoliansky]

* 2. LAWRENCE TIBBETT, baritone (Metropolitan Opera House Orchestra/ Cesare Sodero): TOSCA, Act II: Ha più forte sapore la conquista vïolenta . . . Io vo' gustar quanto più posso dell'opra divina! (Puccini) (I)
Metropolitan Opera broadcast, NYC, 9 Feb 1946

* 3. GRACE MOORE, soprano, and LAWRENCE TIBBETT, baritone (Metropolitan Opera House Orchestra/Cesare Sodero): TOSCA, Act II: Salvatelo! Io? Voi! . . . Vissi d'arte (Puccini) (I)
Metropolitan Opera broadcast, NYC, 9 Feb 1946

* 4. LAWRENCE TIBBETT, baritone, and GRACE MOORE, soprano (Metropolitan Opera House Orchestra/Cesare Sodero): TOSCA, Act II: E qual via scegliete? . . . to the end of the act (Puccini) (I)
Metropolitan Opera broadcast, NYC, 9 Feb 1946

NOTES: EJS 456

Side 1 (456 A):

Band 1: Abel Gance's poorly-received filmization of Charpentier's ***LOUISE*** (dated 1939 in the January bulletin) contains only about 35 minutes of the original score, which has been arranged throughout, making more substantial solos from parts originally scored for more than one voice. Apart from a few orchestral and choral passages, EJS 456 omits from the original soundtrack the Act III *Louise-Julien* duet "Jolie! Tu regrettes d'être venue!" the "Choeur d'Apotéose," an additional solo for *Louise* that is not in the original opera, the *Father's* "Reste, Repose-toi" from Act IV, and the film's finale, which begins with an off-stage chorus and a scene with Moore, Pernet, and Despres beginning "Paris m'appelle." Moore's added solo and the music that finishes the "Choeur d'Apothéose" were either written by Charpentier, who is credited as the supervisor of the film, or by the film's musical director, Louis Beydts. One informed source insists that the *Ragman's* solo just before Moore's "Depuis le jour" is sung by baritone Arthur Endrèze, but he could not be found in any cast listing.

How the film was received in Paris is difficult to say. English critics were not impressed, and the New York City premiere at the Little Carnegie on 57th Street was entirely undistinguished. Today the film is considered a low point in the otherwise brilliant career of director Gance. Pitches are correct at 33.3 rpm.

Band 1a: There are internal cuts made in this duet.
Band 1c: *Julien's* "Ah! chanson de Paris!" is not included in this excerpt.
Band 1d: This is *Irma's* solo in the original score.
Band 1g: Moore sings the "Depuis le jour" at score pitch. There is a tape break in the middle of the aria.

Band 3: Moore announces her encore, "Ciribiribin," and the audience erupts in laughter--presumably an indication of their delight.

Side 2 (456 B):

Band 1: Note that most of Supervia's vocals are overlayed with dialogue. Tenor Browning Mummery, though he did appear in the film, seems not to appear in any of the excerpts presented on EJS 456. The January bulletin claims that "the whole sound track, talking and singing of this scene, is presented" (sic). Alec Guinness, at the beginning of his long and distinguished career, is reported in one source as having had a small role in the film. Evelyn Laye was a fine popular singer in her own right, and made many commercial recordings in England. She would later be featured in a broadcast excerpt with John McCormack on ANNA 1026 (January, 1979).

Supervia's "Los ojos negros" and "Musetta's Waltz" were subsequently included on a 1992 Pearl CD, "The Unknown Supervia" (GEMM CD 9969).

The playing speed of the *EVENSONG* selections is 33.0 rpm.

Bands 2-4: Given as "Cincinnati 1945" on the label of EJS 456 and reissued as such on the second volume of a 1992 IRCC broadcast potpourri (CD 807). Jan Peerce was the *Cavaradossi*. The "Gia mi struggea" section of the "Salvatelo! . . . Vissi d'arte" is missing about four measures, this being an acetate or tape break, not a performance cut. Similarly, the "E qual via scegliete?" has a break of a few measures.

The three TOSCA excerpts are erratic, hovering around an approximate speed of 32.7 rpm.

EJS 457: "The Golden Age of Opera" (1 LP)
Issued January, 1969
MATRIX P-1781

"MARIO LANZA"

SIDE 1 (457 A):

* 1. (w. Los Angeles Philharmonic Orchestra/Eugene Ormandy): L'ELISIR D'AMORE, Act II: Una furtiva lagrima (Donizetti) (I)
AFRS broadcast, Hollywood Bowl, Los Angeles, 28 Aug 1947

* 2. (w. Los Angeles Philharmonic Orchestra/Eugene Ormandy): ANDREA CHENIER, Act I: Un dì, all'azzurro spazio ["Improvviso"] (Giordano) (I)
AFRS broadcast, Hollywood Bowl, Los Angeles, 28 Aug 1947

* 3. (w. Los Angeles Philharmonic Orchestra/Eugene Ormandy): TOSCA, Act III: E lucevan le stelle (Puccini) (I)
AFRS broadcast, Hollywood Bowl, Los Angeles, 28 Aug 1947

* 4. w. FRANCES YEEND, soprano (Los Angeles Philharmonic Orchestra/ Eugene Ormandy): LA TRAVIATA, Act IV: Parigi, o cara (Verdi) (I)
AFRS broadcast, Hollywood Bowl, Los Angeles, 28 Aug 1947

* 5. w. FRANCES YEEND, soprano (Los Angeles Philharmonic Orchestra/ Eugene Ormandy): MADAMA BUTTERFLY, Act I: Vogliatemi bene (Puccini) (I)
AFRS broadcast, Hollywood Bowl, Los Angeles, 28 Aug 1947

* 6. w. FRANCES YEEND, soprano (Los Angeles Philharmonic Orchestra/ Eugene Ormandy): LA BOHÈME, Act I: O soave fanciulla (Puccini) (I)
AFRS broadcast, Hollywood Bowl, Los Angeles, 28 Aug 1947

SIDE 2 (457 B):

* 1. (w. M-G-M Orchestra/Miklos Rosza): "Agnus Dei" (Bizet) (L)
AFRS broadcast, *METRO-GOLDWYN-MAYER CONCERT*, Hollywood Bowl, Los Angeles, 24 or 28 Jul 1948
no matrix assigned V-Disc unpublished

* 2. (w. M-G-M Orchestra/Miklos Rosza): TURANDOT, Act III: Nessun dorma (Puccini) (I)
AFRS broadcast, *METRO-GOLDWYN-MAYER CONCERT*, Hollywood Bowl, Los Angeles, 24 or 28 Jul 1948
no matrix assigned ?V-Disc unpublished

* 3. w. KATHRYN GRAYSON, soprano (M-G-M Orchestra/Miklos Rosza): LA BOHÈME, Act I: O soave fanciulla (Puccini) (I)
AFRS broadcast, ***METRO-GOLDWYN-MAYER CONCERT***, Hollywood Bowl, Los Angeles, 24 or 28 Jul 1948
no matrix assigned V-Disc unpublished

* 4. w. KATHRYN GRAYSON, soprano (M-G-M Orchestra/Miklos Rosza): EILEEN: Thine alone (Blossom-Herbert) (E)
AFRS broadcast, ***METRO-GOLDWYN-MAYER CONCERT***, Hollywood Bowl, Los Angeles, 24 or 28 Jul 1948
no matrix assigned ?V-Disc unpublished

5. (w. studio orch/Ray Noble): I PAGLIACCI, Act I: Vesti la giubba (Leoncavallo) (I)
Broadcast, ***EDGAR BERGEN AND CHARLIE McCARTHY SHOW***, NBC, Dallas, 15 Feb 1948

* 6. (w. pf/Paul Baron): "Santa Lucia" (T. Cottrau) (I)
Telecast, ***CHRISTOPHER PROGRAM***, Rome. early October, 1957

* 7. (w. pf/Paul Baron): "Because You're Mine" (Sammy Cahn-Nicholas Brodsky) (E)
Telecast, ***CHRISTOPHER PROGRAM***, Rome. early October, 1957

* 8. (w. pf/Paul Baron): ELLENS DRITTER GESANG, D. 839: Ave Maria (Schubert) (L)
Telecast, ***CHRISTOPHER PROGRAM***, Rome. early October, 1957

9. (w. orch and chorus/?Giacomo Spadoni): THE VAGABOND KING, Act I: Some Day (Friml) (E)
Telecast, ***SHOWER OF STARS***, CBS, Hollywood, 28 Oct 1954

NOTES: EJS 457

The January, 1969 bulletin claims that advanced requests for this recital resulted in only 27 copies being left for general consumption.

Side 1 (457 A):

Bands 1-6: This live concert from the Hollywood Bowl was broadcast over the Armed Forces Radio Service. It was not carried nationally as far as could be determined. It is dated 28 August, 1947 on the label of EJS 457 and in an AFRS summary sheet, but a photograph of Lanza standing outside of the Hollywood Bowl on the day of the concert has been reported, with the date *27* August clearly visible. However, the *Los Angeles Times* listing shows that this Thursday evening program was in fact *28* August, 1947.

This concert was originally transcribed on War and Navy Departments Armed Forces Radio Service discs ("the Voice of Information and Education"). The Lanza discs are labeled "Hollywood Bowl Series / Eugene Ormandy, Conductor / Mario Lanza, Tenor Soloist / Frances Yeend, Soprano Soloist," with a "Property of United States Government" notice at the bottom. The 28 August, 1947 selections are from the Hollywood Bowl Series H-38-57 (1947 Series, Volume IX), Program No. 57, a four-disc set in seven parts, matrices U-98403, U-98405, U-98408, U-98412, U-98414, U-98417, and U-19421. The AFRS ledgers from which these recordings have been documented did not include a breakdown of the individual numbers performed (as they did for the John Charles Thomas AFRS concert material on EJS 531 and 564), so individual matrices could not be assigned in the listing above.

The TOSCA aria is announced by Lanza.

Side 2 (457 B):

Bands 1-4: A concert from the Hollywood Bowl, recorded live by V-Disc, though none of the Lanza titles was apprently issued. A page from the V-Disc logs has been reported verifying the date Wednesday, 28 July, (the concert is dated Tuesday, 27 July, 1948 on the label of EJS 457), but Sears' afore-mentioned V-Disc discography, pp. 613-615, gives most of the Lanza titles in the listing above and states that "A ***METRO-GOLDWYN MAYER CONCERT*** was held in the Hollywood Bowl, Hollywood California, in the summer of 1948," with the precise date of Saturday, *24* July given further on. This seems to preclude the likelihood that two such concerts were given that summer. Sears also gives the orchestra personnel (p. 614). Other performers appearing at the concert included Lionel Barrymore (as narrator) and Andre Previn (as pianist). Only two sides were issued from the concert, both orchestral, on V-Disc 888. Of the Lanza and Lanza-Grayson material, Sears lists only the "Agnus Dei," Grayson's "Sempre libera" from TRAVIATA, the BOHÈME duet, and "Aria No. 2," featuring Lanza and the orchestra, which one might assume to be the "Nessun dorma."

The Los Angeles Philharmonic Orchestra's contract for the Hollywood Bowl summer season stipulated a Tuesday-Thursday-Saturday schedule; 24 July was a Saturday, making 28 July, the following Wednesday, a more likely date for the M-G-M Studio Orchestra to have made an appearance, so the date of the concert has yet to be resolved.

Because the available AFRS ledgers for the 1947-1948 Hollywood Bowl series do not give titles for the Lanza material, only dates and matrices, it could not be determined whether the 24/28 July, 1948 concert was part of the four-disc, seven part AFRS Hollywood Bowl Series H-38-57, documented above for the 28 August, 1947.

The M-G-M studio Orchestra of the late 1940s and 1950s was one of the busiest and best studio ensembles, releasing several remarkable commercial LPs on the M-G-M label, most important among them being their readings of the modern repertory, all of which are highly sought by collectors.

The "Nessun dorma" and the EILEEN duet are announced by Lanza.

Bands 6-8: Little is known of this ***CHRISTOPHER PROGRAM*** except that it may have been filmed in Rome in early October, 1957, may not have been telecast in America, and was probably connected in some way to the Catholic Christophers Society, founded in New York City in 1945 by James Keller, M.M. In *The New Catholic Encyclopedia* (18 vols., New York: McGraw-Hill, 1967), vol. 3, p. 664, Keller himself wrote of the group's concern with "the great spheres of influence"--namely, government, education, and media: hence the Christophers' prolific activities in publishing, radio, and television.

Other 33 1/3 rpm transcriptions from the ***CHRISTOPHER PROGRAM*** have been reported, undocumented except for a "program" number and the names of the performers on the labels. If the show *was* broadcast in the U.S., it was probably seen in syndication.

"Because You're Mine" was the title song of Lanza's 1952 M-G-M feature film.

Band 9: This live ***SHOWER OF STARS*** episode was telecast in color and featured in addition to Lanza, Edgar Bergen and Charlie McCarthy, dancer Sheree North, and Gene Nelson. As noted in the listing, Spadoni, a former M-G-M studio conductor, was probably at the podium.

Lanza's "Some Day" has also been reported as a 1951 Chrysler broadcast conducted by Ray Sinatra, but this could not be confirmed.

EJS 458: "The Golden Age of Opera" (2 LPs)
Issued February, 1969
MATRIX P-1791 / P-1792

SIDES 1-4 (458 A-D):

GENOVEVA (Schumann) (I)
Opera in 4 acts (complete)
Orchestra and Chorus of Radio Italiana [RAI], Torino/Vittorio Gui
RAI broadcast, Turin, 14 May 1961

CAST:
Consuelo Rubio (*Genoveva*); Fedora Barbieri (*Margaretha*); Nicola Filacuridi (*Golo*); Mario Borriello (*Siegfried*); Franco Calabrese (*Hidulfus*); Giorgio Tadeo (*Drago*); Renzo Gonzales (*Balthasar*); Lido Freschi (*Caspar*).

NOTES: EJS 458

Schumann's only opera, the rarely-performed GENOVEVA, was written to a text by Robert Reinick (altered by the composer), based on both Johann Ludwig Tieck's 1799 tragedy, *Das Leben und Tod der heiligen Genoveva* and Christian Friedrich Hebbel's 1843 version of the story, *Genoveva*. The opera was first produced in Leipzig on 25 June, 1850. Note that it was performed here in translation.

The performance was later reissued as Melodram MEL 031.

EJS 459: "The Golden Age of Opera" (2 LPs)
Issued February, 1969
MATRIX P-1793 / P-1794

SIDES 1-4 (459 A-D):

LE ASTUZIE FEMMINILI (Cimarosa-rev. Barbara Giuranna) (I)
Opera in 2 acts (complete)
Orchestra of A. Scarlatti di Napoli/Mario Rossi
Broadcast, Teatro di Corte, Palazzo Reale, Naples, 25 Sep 1959

CAST:
Graziella Sciutti (*Bellina*); Sesto Bruscantini (*Don Giampaolo*); Franco Calabrese (*Don Romualdo*); Luigi Alva (*Filandro*); Renata Mattioli (*Ersilia*); Anna Maria Rota (*Leonora*).

NOTES: EJS 459

This was a live broadcast over RAI. Described in the February, 1969 bulletin as an "epic of female shrewdness," it was recommended to Smith, he says, by bass Salvatore Baccaloni, who considered the 1794 opera one of the finest comic opera he himself had sung during his long career.

The performance was later issued on LP as VOCE-42.

EJS 460: "The Golden Age of Opera" (1 LP)
Issued February, 1969
MATRIX P-1795

SIDE 1 (460 A):

GÖTTERDÄMMERUNG (Wagner) (G)
Opera in 3 acts (excerpts)
Wiener Philharmoniker/Clemens Krauss
In-house recording, Wiener Staatsoper, Vienna, 15 Jun 1933

CAST:
Gertrude Kappel (*Brünnhilde*); Gertrude Rünger (*Waltraute*); Wanda Achsel (*Gutrune*); Gertrude Rünger (*First Norn*); Bella Paalen (*Second Norn*); Enid Szantho (*Third Norn*); Josef Von Manowarda (*Hagen*); [Josef Kalenberg (*Siegfried*)]; [Emil Schipper (*Gunther*)]; [Hermann Wiedemann (*Alberich*)]; [Luise Helletsgruber (*Woglinde*)]; [Eva Hadrabová (*Wellgunde*)]; [Enid Szantho (*Flosshilde*)].

1. Prologue: a) RÜNGER, PAALEN, and SZANTHO: Welche licht leuchtet dort? . . . schling' ich das Seil, und singe
b) RÜNGER, PAALEN, and SZANTHO: weisst du, wie das wird? . . . zu Hauf geschichtete Scheite

Act I: c) KAPPEL and RÜNGER: Mehr als Walhalls Wonne . . . zu mir nie steure mehr her!

Act III: d) VON MANWARDA, KAPPEL, and ACHSEL: Des Alben Erbe . . . Starke Scheite . . . to the end of the opera

SIDE 2 (460 B):

PARSIFAL (Wagner) (G)
Opera in 3 acts (excerpts)
Wiener Philharmoniker and Chorus of the Wiener Staatsoper/Felix Weingartner
In-house recording, Wiener Staatsoper, Vienna, 11 Apr 1936

CAST:
Alexander Kipnis (*Gurnemanz*); Kerstin Thorborg (*Kundry*); [Alfred Jerger (*Amfortas*)]; [Gunnar Graarud (*Parsifal*)]; [Nicola (Nikolaus) Zec (*Titurel*)]; [Hermann Wiedemann (*Klingsor*)].

* 1. a) Prelude (37 measures: 8-43)

Act I: b) KIPNIS and Chorus: Nun achte wohl . . . Zum letzten Liebesmahle gerüs[tet Tag für Tag]
c) Boys' Choir: Nehmet hin mein Blut, Nehmet hin meinen Leib . . . auf dass ihr mein' gedenkt (with preceding 12 measures and bridge to Titurel's "Oh! Heilige Wonne!")
d) KIPNIS: Was stehst du noch da? . . . Weisst du, was du sah'st? (with preceding 19 measures)

Act II: d) THORBORG: Den Waffen fern . . . wann sie suchend dann dich ereilt
e) THORBORG: Pein und Lachen . . . in dir entsündigt sein und erlöst!

Act III: f) Chorus: Beginning of the Transformation Scene . . . er birgt die heilige Kraft, der Gott

PARSIFAL (Wagner) (G)
Opera in 3 acts (excerpts)
Wiener Philharmoniker/Clemens Krauss
In-house recording, Wiener Staatsoper, Vienna, 13 Apr 1933

CAST:
Richard Mayr (*Gurnemanz*); [Gertrud Rünger (*Kundry*)]; [Emil Schipper (*Amfortas*)]; [Gunnar Graarud (*Parsifal*)]; [Nicola (Nikolaus) Zec (*Titurel*)]; [Hermann Wiedemann (*Klingsor*)].

* 2. Act I: a) MAYR: Das is ein And'res . . . Ich stürm' herbei von dannen Klingsor
b) MAYR: Du tatest das? . . . siehst du den Blick?
Act III: c) MAYR: Von dorther kam das Stöhnen . . . heiligsten Morgen heut' (6 measures)

NOTES: EJS 460

These three sets of fragments are in-house recordings. The originals, like most transcribed backstage at the Staatsoper in the 1930s, are reported to be in a private Viennese collection. Few of the fragments are properly separated by breaks which, coupled with the appalling sound, leads to frustrating listening (Smith, in the February bulletin, warns that to "those interested in good sound and forward reproduction of that sound, my advice is to stay away and not buy this disc"). The 11 April, 1936 PARSIFAL excerpts are noted as having been recorded on non-professional "home" equipment.

Side 1 (460 A):

The label of EJS 460 gives Heger as the conductor of the GÖTTERDÄMMERUNG excerpts. In fact, for the 1933 season, Heger conducted RHEINGOLD on 10 June and SIEGFRIED on 13 June; the 11 June WALKÜRE and the 15 June GÖTTERDÄMMERUNG presented here were conducted by Krauss. The *Waltraute*, Gertrude Rünger (1899-1965), is mistaken in the bulletin for coloratura soprano Gertrude *Runge* (1880-1948), "who was well past 50," Smith explains, "and who had been recording as early as 1901." Runge's career was a relatively minor one, centered in Weimar and Mannheim, but she had a vast repertory and recorded extensively.

The same GÖTTERDÄMMERUNG excerpts appeared later on UORC 347 (September-October, 1977).

Side 2 (460 B):

Weingartner is given as the conductor of both PARSIFAL performances, but in fact, he did not conduct the opera in Vienna during the 1933 season: two performances were conducted by Krauss and two by Robert Heger, both with Richard Mayr as *Gurnemanz*. Another excerpt from this 1933 performance subsequently appeared on the Teletheater label, helping to confirm 13 April as the correct date of the fragments on EJS 460. The discography in Christopher Dyment's Weingartner book, *Felix Weingartner: Recollections and Recordings* (Rickmansworth: Triad Press, 1976), correctly asserts that Weingartner did not conduct PARSIFAL in Vienna in 1933, but goes on to say "nor did Richard Mayr take part in it" (p. 85). The original Staatsoper playbill for 13 April, 1933, however, contradicts this: Mayr, who is described there as an honorary member of the company ("Ehrenmitglied") was the *Gurnemanz* and Krauss was the conductor, unless a substitution occurred at the last minute.

EJS 461: "The Golden Age of Opera" (2 LPs)
Issued March, 1969
MATRIX: P-1801 / P-1802 / P-1803

SIDES 1-4 (461 A-D):

STIFFELIO (Verdi) (I)
Opera in 3 acts (complete)
Orchestra and Chorus of Teatro Regio di Parma/Peter Maag
Broadcast, Teatro Regio, Parma, 29 Dec 1968

CAST:
Gastone Limarilli (*Stiffelio*); Angeles Gulin (*Lina*); Walter Alberti (*Stankar*); Beniamino Prior (*Raffaele*); Antonio Zerbini (*Jorg*); Lidia Gastaldi (*Dorotea*); Mario Carlin (*Federico*).

NOTES: EJS 461

Sides 1 and 2 are matrices P-1801-A/B, respectively, side 3 is P-1802-C, and side 4 is P-1803-D. The ROSENKAVALIER that follows on EJS 462 was assigned matrices P-1803-A/B.

Gulin is given as "Angeles Dominguez" in the March, 1969 bulletin, and as "Angeles Gulin Dominguez" in Nuova Era CD edition of this performance on 2284/5. See note on STIFFELIO for EJS 333 (May, 1965).

EJS 462: "The Golden Age of Opera" (1 LP)
Issued March, 1969
MATRIX P-1803

SIDES 1-2 (462 A-B):

DER ROSENKAVALIER (R. Strauss) (G)
Opera in 3 acts (Act III only)
San Francisco Opera House Orchestra and Chorus/George Sebastian
San Francisco Opera broadcast, 18 Oct 1945

CAST:
Lotte Lehmann (*Marschallin*); Risë Stevens (*Octavian*); Nadine Conner (*Sophie*); Lorenzo Alvary (*Baron Ochs*); Walter Olitzki (*Faninal*); Hertha Glaz (*Annina*); Alessio DePaolis (*Valzacchi*); Mack Harrell (*Police Commissioner*); John Garris (*Wirt*).

NOTES: EJS 462

Matrix P-1803-D was used for the fourth side of the STIFFELIO (EJS 461).

Act III of the ROSENKAVALIER, presented here complete as performed, was the only act broadcast. Lehmann can be heard to change the line at the beginning of the trio so as to omit the high B-flat.

This LP, along with EJS 463, was advertised as being available in extremely limited quantity (21 copies) owing to the fact that contributors, as well as eleven subscribers "who purchase everything every month regardless of what is issued," were said to have consumed 27 of the 48 copies pressed. It is further claimed that these two performances were produced originally only for libraries and universities.

The entire LP plays in score pitch at 32.8 rpm.

EJS 463: "The Golden Age of Opera" (1 LP)
Issued March, 1969
MATRIX P-1804

SALOME (R. Strauss)
Opera 1 in act (excerpts)
Orchestra of the Wiener Staatsoper/Richard Strauss
In-house recordings, Wiener Staatsoper, Vienna
15 Feb 1942 and 6 May 1942

CASTS		15 February, 1942	6 May, 1943
Salome	. . .	Else Schulz	Else Schulz
Herodias	. . .	Melanie Bugarinovič	Melanie Bugarinovič
Jokanaan	. . .	Paul Schöffler	Hans Hotter
Herod	. . .	Josef Witt	Joachim Sattler
Narraboth	. . .	Anton Dermota	Anton Dermota
Page	. . .	?	?
First Soldier	. . .	?	?
Second Soldier	. . .	?	?
First Nazarene	. . .	?	?
Second Nazarene	. . .	?	?
First Jew	. . .	?	?
Second Jew	. . .	?	?
Third Jew	. . .	?	?
Fourth Jew	. . .	?	?
Fifth Jew	. . .	?	?

SIDE 1 (463 A):

1. DERMOTA, Page, First and Second Soldiers, and SCHOFFLER: Füsse weisse Tauben sind . . . die Ohren der Tauben geöffnet. Heiss ihn schweigen! (1942)

2. SCHÖFFLER, SCHULZ, and DERMOTA: Wo ist er, dessen Sündenbecher jetzt voll ist? . . . Wo ist sie, die sich den jüngen Männern der Egypter gegeben hat (with 42 measures of the orchestral passage leading into Scene iii, beginning 3 measures before no. 62) (1942)

3. DERMOTA, SCHULZ, and SCHÖFFLER: [Prinzessin, ich flehe, geh'hin] ein . . . Jokanaan! Ich bin verliebt in deinen Leib . . . Entweihe nicht den Tempel des Herrn, meines Gottes! (1942)

4. HOTTER and SCHULZ: [Niemals], Tochter Babylons, Tochter Sodoms, Niemals! . . . Du bist verflucht (with 7 measures of the orchestral postlude to the scene) (1943)

* 5. a) First, Second, Third, Fourth, and Fifth Jews, First Nazarene, WITT, SCHÖFFLER, 2nd Nazarene, BUGARINOVIČ, and SCHULZ: [Das kann nicht sein, seit den] Tagen des Propheten Elias sind mehr als dreihundert Jahre vergangen . . . Erkommt ein Tag, da wird die Sonne finster werden (1942)

b) HOTTER, BUGARINOVIČ, SATTLER, and SCHULZ: wie ein schwarzes Tuch . . . über der Terrasse schwebte? Warum kann ich nicht sehn diesen Vogel? (1943)

* 6. WITT or SATTLER and SCHULZ: Ah! Herrlich! Wundervoll . . . Was ist es? das du haben möchtest, Salome? (beginning in the middle of Salome's Dance, 8 measures after letter R) (?)

* 7. SCHULZ: Ja, ich will ihn jetzt küssen deinen Mund, Jokanaan . . . Dein Lieb war eine Elfenbeinsäule auf silbernen Füssen (?)

* 8. SCHULZ: Nichts in der Welt war so schwarz wie dein Haar . . . Deine Stimme war ein Weirauchgefäss und wenn [ich dich ansah] (?)

SIDE 2 (463 B):

* 1. SCHULZ and SATTLER or WITT: [Warum hast du mich nicht angesehn, Jok]anaan? Du legtest über deine Augen . . . Sie ist ein Ungeheuer, deine Tochter (?)

ELEKTRA (R. Strauss) (G)
Opera in 1 act (excerpts)
Metropolitan Opera House Orchestra/Artur Bodanzky
Metropolitan Opera broadcast, 3 Dec 1932

CAST:
Gertrude Kappel (*Elektra*); Göta Ljungberg (*Chrysothemis*); Karin Branzell (*Klytemnestra*); [Rudolf Laubenthal (*Aegisthus*)]; [Freidrich Schorr (*Orestes*)]; [Siegfried Tappolet (*Foster Father of Orestes*)]; [Grace Divine (*Confidant*)]; [Pearl Besuner (*Trainbearer*)]; [Marek Windheim (*Young Servant*)]; [Arnold Gabor (*Old Servant*)]; [Dorothee Manski (*Overseer*)]; [Doris Doe (*Serving Woman*)]; [Ina Bourskaya (*Serving Woman*)]; [Philine Falco (*Serving Woman*)]; [Helen Gleason (*Serving Woman*)]; [Margaret Halstead (*Serving Woman*)].

* 2. KAPPEL, LJUNGBERG, and BRANZELL: Lebens Leben aus ihnen sturzen ["Elektra's Monologue] . . . further fragments

* 3. JULIUS PATZAK, tenor (?Bavarian State Opera Orchestra/R. Strauss): SECHS LIEDER, Op. 17, no. 2: Ständchen (Schack-R. Strauss/orch. Felix Mottl) (G)
Broadcast, Munich or Vienna, 15 Sep 1944

* 4. JULIUS PATZAK, tenor (?Bavarian State Opera Orchestra/R. Strauss): FÜNF LIEDER, Op. 32, no. 1: Ich trage meine Minne (Henckell-R. Strauss/orch. Robert Heger) (G)
Broadcast, Munich or Vienna, 15 Sep 1944

* 5. JULIUS PATZAK, tenor (Bavarian State Opera House Orchestra/ R. Strauss): VIER LIEDER, Op. 27, no. 4: Morgen (Mackay-R. Strauss/orch. R. Strauss) (G)
Broadcast, Munich or Vienna, 15 Sep 1944

* 6. JULIUS PATZAK, tenor (Bavarian State Opera House Orchestra/ R. Strauss): VIER LIEDER, Op. 27, no. 3: Heimliche Aufforderung (Mackay-R. Strauss/orch. Robert Heger) (G)
Broadcast, Munich or Vienna, 15 Sep 1944

NOTES: EJS 463

See the endnote for EJS 462 on the limited availability of this LP. The March, 1969 bulletin claims that a 1945 *Marschallin's* Monologue by Lotte Lehmann is included on the LP, but this is in error.

The bulletin also acknowledged at length the passing of Giovanni Martinelli on 2 February, 1969, and announced the issue of the three-disc "Giovanni Martinelli: In Memoria" set on Celebrity Records CEL 500, the proceeds of which went entirely to the tenor's estate.

Side 1 (463 A):

The label of EJS 463 gives 15 February, 1942 for all of the SALOME excerpts, when in fact they were taken from two different Wiener Staatsoper performances--15 February and 6 May, 1942--both conducted by the composer. There were evidently nine private acetate sides made from these two performances. See Peter Morse's Strauss discography in the *ARSC Journal*, 9/1, (1977), pp.41-42, for a detailed account, as summarized here and in the listing above.

The *Herodias* for both performances, Bugarinovič, seems to have been known initially under the name Milada Bugarinovič, but is generally referred to with the forename Melanie (or Mela), as she came to be known when recording for Decca in the mid 1950s.

The EJS 463 excerpts correspond to the following original acetate sides, with the performance date given where known:

EJS 463 BANDS	ACETATE NUMBERS AND DATES	EJS 463 BANDS	ACETATE NUMBERS AND DATES
1	1 (February)	6	7 (?)
2	2 (February)	7	8 (?)
3	3 (February)	8	9 (?)
4	4 (May)	9	9 (?)
5	5 (February) & 6 (May)		

Band 5: There is a cut from 15 February to 6 May mid-measure on *Jokanaan's* line "Erkommt ein Tag, da wird die Sonne finster *werdem / wie* ein schwarzes Tuch." The first part (5a), taken from acetate 5, is with Schöffler; the second (5b), taken from acetate 6, features Hotter.

Bands 6-8: It has not been determined from which of the two performances these excerpts were drawn.

Band 8: Only eighteen measures of the Finale are presented here, beginning at *Salome's* "Nichts in der Welt war so schwarz wie dein Haar" (5 measures after no. 335) and ending "Deine Stimme war ein Weirauch-gefäss, und wenn" (3 measures after no. 338). There is a 22-measure gap ("ich dich ansah . . . Warum hast du mich nicht angesehn, Jok[anaan?]"), at which point side 2 band 1 picks up at "[Jok]anaan? Du legtest über deine Augen" (6 measures after no. 340).

Side 2 (463 B):

Band 1: It has not been determined from which of the two performances this excerpt was drawn. See also the note for I/8, above.

Band 2: This was the Met premiere of Strauss' ELEKTRA. The American debut of the 1909 opera was given at New York's Manhattan Opera House on 1 February, 1910, performed in French.

Three excerpts, amounting to some eight minutes, are presented here, beginning with a portion of *Elektra's* monologue (Kappel) as noted. This is followed by a brief passage for *Chrysothemis* (Ljungberg) and a lengthier passage for *Elektra*, *Chrysothemis*, and *Klytemnestra* (Branzell).

All three excerpts have been transferred low and require pitching.

Bands 3-6: 15 September, 1944 was the *broadcast* (not performance), date of these songs: through his correspondence, it has been established that Strauss was at his home in Garmisch on 13-15 September, 1944. The songs were probably recorded the same month, however, though exactly where remains a mystery. Patzak was a resident singer at the Bavarian State Opera in 1944, which prompted Peter Morse (ibid, p. 49) to suggest Munich rather than Vienna as the probable site of recording. Patzak himself confirmed that he had indeed broadcast the songs to the composer's accompaniment in 1944.

These four performances appeared on Rococo 5348 credited to the Bavarian Radio Orchestra conducted by Strauss, and all but the "Morgen" on BASF LP 10.22055-9 (where the "Ich trage meine Minne" is given as the Vienna State Opera Orchestra conducted by Clemens Krauss and the others as the Barvarian State Opera Orchestra conducted by Strauss). Another BASF issue of "Ich trage meine Minne" (22.21807-4) credits the Berlin German Opera House Orchestra, conducted by Artur Rother. Two other Patzak items supposedly conducted by the composer--a different "Morgen" and a "Freundliche Vision," Op. 48, no. 1--are disputed by Morse, despite their inclusion on a BASF LP (10.22055-9) as Strauss-conducted performances. On that LP the two are given as the Bavarian State Opera House Orchestra/Strauss and the Weiner Staatsoper Orchestra/Krauss, respectively. See Morse, pp. 48-49, for a detailed analysis of these Patzak recordings and their various long-playing incarnations.

Discounting possible transpositions, both 32.5 or 33.8 rpm yield plausible pitches.

Band 3: Patzak was apparently fond of these orchestrated versions and in fact, recorded several for Polydor with the Berlin State Opera House Orchestra under Julius Prüwer in the earliest 1930s--among them, the "Ständchen," coupled with "Cäcilie" on Polydor B43396/5 (matrixes 2646½ BH and 2645 BH, respectively).

Band 5: This is the first recording of Strauss' orchestration of "Morgen."

EJS 464: "The Golden Age of Opera" (1 LP)
Issued March, 1969
MATRIX P-1805

"BENIAMINO GIGLI (1927-1955)"

SIDE 1 (464 A):

* 1. w. pf/?Vito Carnevali: "Mírame así" (Eduardo Sánchez de Fuentes) (S)
* 2. w. pf/?Vito Carnevali: "Bergère Légère: (Weckerlin) (F)
* 3. w. pf/?Vito Carnevali: "Come Love, With Me" (Falbo-Carnevali) (E)
* 4. w. pf/?Vito Carnevali: "O Sole mio" (Capurro-di Capua) (I)
from the soundtrack of the one-reel Warner Brothers-Vitaphone short, **BENIAMINO GIGLI OF THE METROPOLITAN OPERA COMPANY IN "A *PROGRAM OF CONCERT FAVORITES" a: "BERGÈRE LÉGÈRE" b: "MIRIAME ASSI" c: "COME LOVE, WITH ME" d: "O SOLE MIO"*** (sic) (1927), New York, circa 1927
Vitaphone Varieties 498
MP 3978; c6 May 1927
Premiere: Colony Theater, New York City, circa July, 1927

* 2. w. MILLO PICCO, baritone, MINNIE EGENER, contralto, and Chorus of the Metropolitan Opera House (Vitaphone Symphony Orchestra/Herman Heller): CAVALLERIA RUSTICANA: Intanto, amici, qua . . . Viva il vino spumeggiante . . . A voi tutti salute . . . Addio alla madre . . . to the end of the opera (Mascagni) (I)
from the soundtrack of the one-reel Warner Brothers-Vitaphone short, ***BENIAMINO GIGLI IN CAVALLERIA RUSTICANA SUPPORTED BY MILLO PICCO, MINNIE EGENER, AND CHORUS OF METROPOLITAN OPERA CO. ACCOMPANIMENT BY VITAPHONE SYMPHONY ORCHESTRA, HERMAN HELLER CONDUCTING*** (1927), New York, circa 1927
Vitaphone Varieties 414
MP 3915; c4 Apr 1927
Premiere: Colony Theater, New York City, 5 Apr 1927

* 6. (w. Orchestra of the Bayrischer Staatstheater/Giuseppe Becce): MANON LESCAUT, Act I: Donna non vidi mai (Puccini) (I)
from the soundtrack of the feature film ***DU BIST MEIN GLÜCK [TU SEI LA VITA MIA]*** (1936), Tobis, Munich, June-July, 1936

* 7. (w. orch/Luigi Ricci): OTELLO, Act IV: [Niun mi tema] Ho un arma ancor (Verdi) (I)
from the soundtrack of the feature film ***MAMMA*** (1940), Cinecittà, Rome 1-10 Oct 1940

8. w. ERNA BERGER, soprano (Berlin State Opera Orchestra/Alois Melichar): LA TRAVIATA, Act II: Mi chiamaste? Che bramate? . . . Va! Va! (Verdi) (I)
from the soundtrack of the feature film ***AVE MARIA*** (1936), Tobis, Berlin, May, 1936

SIDE 2 (464 B):

1. (w. Philharmonia Orchestra/Stanford Robinson): "Omaggio a Bellini" (Chopin-arr. Glynski) (I)
2EA-14231-1 London, 4 Oct 1949 HMV unpub

* 2. (w. Philharmonia Orchestra/Stanford Robinson): "Inno alla Patria" (Chopin-?arr. Glynski) (I)
2EA-14233-1 London, 4 Oct 1949 HMV unpub

* 3. w. RINA GIGLI, soprano (Orchestra of the Ente Italiano Audizioni Radiofoniche [EIAR], Roma/Giuseppe Morelli: AÏDA, Act IV/ii: La fatal pietra . . . O terra addio (Verdi) (I)
Broadcast, ***CONCERTO PER LE FORZE ARMATI***, EIAR, Rome, 27 Dec 1942

* 4. (w. pf/Luigi Ricci): "Rondine al Nido" (De Crescenzo) (I)
Broadcast, ***CONCERTO PER LE FORZE ARMATI***, EIAR, Rome, 27 Dec 1942

* 5. (w. London Symphony Orchestra/Dino Fedri): "Ritorna ancor!" (De Veroli) (I)
OEA-18271-? London, 23 Mar 1955 HMV unpub

* 6. (w. London Symphony Orchestra/Dino Fedri): "Luntano, luntano" (Volonnino) (I)
OEA-18269-? London, 23 Mar 1955 HMV unpub

7. (Berlin State Opera Orchestra/Alois Melichar): HÄNSEL UND GRETEL, Act II: Nel bosco c'e un ometto [Ein Männlein steht im Wald] (Humperdinck) (I)
from the soundtrack of the feature film ***AVE MARIA*** (1936), Tobis, Berlin, May, 1936

* 8. (w. pf/Enrico Sivieri): "Se vuoi goder la vita" (Bixio) (I)
In-house recording, Teatro Jão Caetano, Rio de Janeiro, 25 Oct 1951

* 9. (w. pf/Enrico Sivieri): "Maria, Marì" (Di Capua) (I)
In-house recording, Teatro Jão Caetano, Rio de Janeiro, 25 Oct 1951

NOTES: EJS 464

Several of the items found on EJS 464 have appeared more recently in better sound on Legato Classics CD LCD-106-1, billed a recital of "live" Gigli recordings (many of which are not "live" at all).

Side 1 (464 A):

Bands 1-4: The order of the songs as given in the original film title does not correspond to the actual order in which they were sung: EJS 464 presents them in their correct performance order, as given above. Titles and composers, which have been misspelled on, or omitted from, the label of EJS 464 (and misspelled in the title card of the film itself) have been corrected in the listing. Carnevali's accompaniment is noted in a 1950s Associated Artists Productions catalog, *Programs of Quality from the Quality Studio, Warner Brothers* (New York: n.d.), published circa 1957. Beyond that, this could not be verified (Carnevali did *not* accompany Gigli's 9 April, 1925 Victor recording of "Come Love, With Me," BVE-32148-2, issued on Victor 1096 and HMV DA 732).

26 June, 1927 is the release date given in a contemporary Vitaphone release schedule for this Gigli short, but no reviews mention its having yet been added to the bill. This was the last day the

Warner Brothers feature "The Missing Link" played at the Colony Theater in New York City. On 27 June, "The First Auto" with Barney Oldfield premiered there, and reviews show that the Gigli short had still not taken its place on the program. The short was probably added in early July, 1927.

Contrary to my own report in "The Operatic Vitaphone Shorts" (*ARSC Journal*, 22/1, Spring, 1991, p. 63), the "Mírame así" (spelled "assi" on the film's title card), is not a traditional tune, but rather, the work of Cuban composer Eduardo Sánchez de Fuentes (1874-1944).

Band 5: The CAVALLERIA short begins with the "Brindisi," omitting the choral introduction and the concluding duet with *Turiddu* and *Lola*. The Finale is complete without *Lola*. Egener is *Mamma Lucia* and Picco is *Alfio*. A contemporary Vitaphone release schedule claims that the short premiered at the third Vitaphone show (Selwyn Theater, New York City, 3 February, 1927) alongside the John Barrymore feature "When a Man Loves," but reviews contradict this. The CAVALLERIA actually made its bow during the run of "The Fourth Commandment" at the Colony Theater on 5 April of that year, replacing at the last minute a Schumann-Heink Vitaphone short (Vitaphone Varieties No. 379, copyright 1927) that, according to *Variety* (86/12, 6 April, 1927, p. 26), was held up in final production.

The CAVALLERIA short was shown complete in the U.S. on the Public Broadcasting System in 1986 and has circulated widely on video.

Band 6: Gigli's "Ah! Non v'avvicinate" from the soundtrack of ***DU BIST MEIN*** appeared earlier on EJS 357 (February, 1966).

Band 7: Two other OTELLO arias from the soundtrack of ***MAMMA*** appeared earlier on EJS 141 (January, 1959).

Side 2 (464 B):

Band 2: This little-known Chopin arrangement could not be documented.

Bands 3-4: The complete 27 December, 1942 broadcast was later issued on ANNA 1027 (January, 1979). Note that for the AÏDA duet, *Amneris* was omitted. The AÏDA is dated 20 October, 1939 on the label of EJS 464, but this has been disproven by Gigli scholar Marc Ricaldone, who noted that the Bixio "Mama" from this EIAR broadcast had not yet been written! However, co-author William Collins' citation of this being an Act II/ii excerpt in his non-commercial Gigli discography in *The Record Collector*, 35/8-10 (August-September, 1990), p. 86, was a typographical error.

Bands 5-6: Both of these songs are from Gigli's last studio sessions, London, 22-23 March, 1955, from which nothing was issued commercially.

Band 8-9: The other items from this 25 October, 1951 recital were included on EJS 382 (January, 1967) and EJS 403 (June, 1967).

EJS 465: "The Golden Age of Opera" (4 LPs)
Issued April, 1969
MATRIX P-1819 / P-1820 / P-1821 / P-1822

SIDES 1-8 (465 A-H):

TRISTAN UND ISOLDE (Wagner) (G)
Opera in 3 acts (complete)
London Philharmonic Orchestra and Chorus of the Royal Opera House/Fritz Reiner
Unpublished live performance recordings (HMV):
Pt. 1: 2EA 3357-1/2EA 3358-1
Pt. 2: 2EA 3296 - 2EA 3345 (all first takes)
Covent Garden, London, 11 Jun 1936

CAST:
Kirsten Flagstad (*Isolde*); Lauritz Melchior (*Tristan*); Sabine Kalter (*Brangäne*); Herbert Janssen (*Kurvenal*); Emanuel List (*King Mark*); Frank Sale (*Melot*); Leslie Horsman (*Steersman*); Roy Devereux (*A Young Sailor*); Octave Dua (*A Shepherd*).

NOTES: EJS 465

Of the four TRISTANs conducted by Reiner at Covent Garden in 1936 (18 and 22 May, 2 and 11 June), only the 11 June performance appears to have been recorded by HMV. Two blocks of matrices have been documented, pressings of which exist in private collections. It was once though that the *end* of the score had been taken from either the 18 or 22 May, 1936 Reiner performances (2EA 3296-2EA 3345) and that the *beginning* of the score had been taken from either the 22 May or even more likely, the 2 June performance (2EA 3357-2EA 3358), but David Hamilton's review of the 1992 EMI CD reissue of this historic Flagstad-Melchior collaboration ("Recordings," in *Opera Quarterly*, 9/3, Spring, 1993, pp. 162-167) notes that Philip Hart, author of a forthcoming Reiner biography, has established through correspondence that only the 11 June performance was transcribed.

Act I of 18 May, Act II of 22 May was broadcast over BBC National, Act III of 2 June over BBC Regional. While producer Walter Legge has stated in print that these BBC transmissions may have been the actual source of the various LP transfers (see his "Piracy on the High C's," *About the House*, 4/2, Spring, 1973, pp. 48ff), David Hamilton, in his earlier article "Tristan in the Thirties: Part II" (*Musical Newsletter*, 6/4, Fall, 1976), p. 17, n. 56, logically suggests that these LPs sound more like in-house recordings than line- or air-checks. The April, 1969 EJS bulletin is vague as to the source, saying only that "The recording is so forward, so devoid of 78 scratch and so live that one could almost consider making a pseudo stereo (sic) recording of it. Without any question, it is the most brilliant sounding recording to have survived from the 1930s, and is the equal in sound to any commercial recording made up to the advent of tape." Fortunately, Smith resisted the temptation of making a "pseudo stereo" transfer of it for EJS 465.

The 18 May, 1936 performance marked Flagstad's London debut. Rosenthal mentions in his history of Covent Garden that anticipation was high and that "an all-night queue formed outside the gallery on 17 May" (p. 508). Flagstad was suffering from a bad cold as well as an injury sustained during her attendance at the 14 May GÖTTERDÄMMERUNG with Leider, but her *Isolde* was nonetheless a complete success.

The 11 June, performance presented here was subsequently reissued on the Bruno Walter Society's Recital Records (RR 471) and more recently (1992) on VAI Audio VAIA-1004-3, a 3-CD set taken from a set of extant test pressings. The 1992 EMI reissue on CD CHS7-64037-2 consists of Act I and the second part of Act III conducted by Reiner, coupled with the Act II and beginning of Act III from the 18 and 22 June, 1937 Covent Garden performances conducted by Beecham (Technical Test series TT 6547 and 6548), with Flagstad, Melchior, Margarete Klose and Karin Branzell (*Brangäne*), Herbert Janssen and Paul Schöffler (*Kurvenal*), Sven Nilsson (*King Mark*), Booth Hitchin (*Melot*), Parry Jones (*Sailor*), Octave Dua (*Shepherd*), and Leslie Horsman (*Steersman*), respectively. The individual sides of Beecham's 22 June Technical Test series have been documented as TT 6548-39/56, but those of the 18 June performance (TT 6547) have not.

Excerpts from the 18 June 1937 Beecham performance appeared on EJS 258 (January, 1963) and Recital Records RR 5382; subsequently, Act I was issued as UORC 302 (September, 1976) and portions of the first and second acts on Discocorp RR 223. Act II of the 22 June, 1937 performance was excerpted on ANNA 1051 (circa January, 1980) while sections of Acts I and II and and the complete Act III were issued as Discocorp RR 223. ANNA 1050, and possibly Melodram 37029, featured a composite of the two Beecham performances.

Hamilton's 1993 *Opera Quarterly* article, cited above, is highly recommended to anyone with even a passing interest in understanding the complicated history of these Covent Garden TRISTANs.

EJS 465 requires constant monitoring of pitch, though the variations in speed tend to be minor: a range of 33.0-33.7 rpm is suggested.

See also the endnote accompanying EJS 258.

EJS 466: "The Golden Age of Opera" (1 LP)
Issued April, 1969
MATRIX P-1823

"BLANCHE ARRAL"

SIDE 1 (466 A):

1. a) w. pf/?Corinne Wilson: INDIGO UND DIE VIERZIG RÄUBER: Ja, so singt man in der Stadt, wo ich geboren ["Waltz"] (J. Strauss) (G)
   b) w. pf/?Corinne Wilson: MIGNON, Act I: Connais-tu le pays? (Thomas) (F)
   c) ORCHESTRA: Unidentified work
   d) w. pf/?Corinne Wilson: "La Véritable Manola" (Bourgeois) (F)
   Broadcast, ***BLANCHE ARRAL***, WOR, New York City, ?1 Jun 1935
   Pre-recorded at ?WOR, New York City, ?6 Apr 1935

2. a) w. pf/?Corinne Wilson: "Pourquoi ne pas m'aimer?" (?Berger) (F)
b) w. pf/?Corinne Wilson: "Parle-moi d'amour" (fragments) (Lenoir) (F)
c) w. pf/?Corinne Wilson: "Valse Bleue" (Margis) (F)
d) w. pf/?Corinne Wilson: "Wake Up" (Phillips) (E)
Broadcast, ***BLANCHE ARRAL***, WOR, New York City, ?18 May 1935
Pre-recorded at ?WOR, New York City, ?6 Apr 1935

SIDE 2 (466 B):

1. * a) w. pf/?Corinne Wilson: "Le Chanson de Margot" (?Lecocq) (F)
b) w. pf/?Corinne Wilson: DER BETTELSTUDENT: Czardas (Millöcker) (G)
c) w. pf/?Corinne Wilson: "El bolero grande" (Vasseur) (F)
Broadcast, ***BLANCHE ARRAL***, WOR, New York City, ?15 Jun 1935
Pre-recorded at ?WOR, New York City, ?20 Apr 1935

2. a) w. pf/?Corinne Wilson: "Regina coeli" (Amurel) (L)
* b) w. pf/?Corinne Wilson: LE TIMBRE D'ARGENT, Act ?: Air du Troubadour (Saint-Saëns) (F)
* c) w. pf/?Corinne Wilson: L'AMOUR MOUILLÉ: Valse des oiseaux (Varney) (F)
Broadcast, ***BLANCHE ARRAL***, WOR, New York City, ?22 Jun 1935
Pre-recorded at ?WOR, New York City, ?20 Apr 1935

NOTES: EJS 466

Because of the order imposed here by Smith, EJS 466 is *thought* to contain the second, third, fourth, and fifth broadcasts of soprano Blanche Arral's short-lived 15-minute show, a pre-recorded program syndicated by the Bamberger Broadcasting System and heard over WOR, New York City at 3:00 pm on four Saturday afternoons in May and June, 1935. The first broadcast presented here is actually announced as the second show, and because three more follow, it has been assumed that the first show was omitted and that there were at least five broadcasts in the series. I could find evidence of only four shows, however, the first on 18 May, followed by three more on 1, 15, and 22 June, 1935, so I suspect that Smith has included all of the broadcasts and simply dubbed them out of order. The dates given above, except for I/1, are therefore tentative: the dates are correct, but their actual assignment to each of the shows could only be speculated. The shows have been given under single headings to clarify their contents.

Smith gives only two dates for the shows presented here: 6 April, 1935 for the first two, and 20 April, 1935 for the second two. These were probably dates retrieved from the original broadcast discs, remembering that the show was pre-recorded for syndication and thus, distributed in recorded form. Certainly, there were no Arral broadcasts before 18 May, so that these April dates could not correspond to off-the-air transcriptions or line-checks. This implies--if Smith's dates are accepted as accurate--that the shows were all recorded the previous month in two studio sessions. On all but the second show (I/1) the pianist is identified as Corinne Wilson (or perhaps "Williston"--it is difficult to tell from the spoken announcements, and she was not listed in the *New York Times* radio logs), so it is assumed that she was the accompanist for all of them: if indeed the two shows on side 1 were both pre-recorded on the same day, this would seem logical.

Note that Arral made commercial recordings of many of the titles heard here--for Bettini, Edison, and Victor. She appears not to have made any commercial electrical recordings, which makes these broadcasts especially valuable, despite her advanced age--she was about six months shy of 71 at the time. WOR replaced the Arral programs with "Rambles in Erin" on 29 June, and this, in turn, with weekly recitals by soprano Isabelle Guarnieri.

The format was more or less standard for each broadcast: the announcer, "Mr Mack" (or "Monsieur Mack," as she refers to him), introduces the singer as "Madame Blanche Arral, the prima donna of five continents." Arral sings "Mme Arral's March" (otherwise unidentified) to the accompaniment of a studio orchestra, reminisces about her career with the sycophantic prodding of Mr. Mack, sings a few songs to piano accompaniment, and responds to letters sent in by listeners. The shows closed with a second rendition of Arral's march.

From the few solos possible to pitch from a score, this LP seems to require a speed of about 34.4 rpm.

Side 2 (466 B):

Band 1 a-c: This may be the "Couplets de Margot" from LA CIGALE ET LA FOURMI of Lecocq that Arral recorded years before for Bettini under her real name, Mme. Clara Lardinois. Arral recorded both the "Czardas" and "El bolero grande" for Victor in 1909 (64098 and 64107, respectively).

Band 2b: This is not the usual "Le bonheur est chose légère" from Saint-Saëns LE TIMBRE D'ARGENT.

Band 2c: The cadenza performed here is announced as Arral's own. Late Victor labels of Arral's famous studio recording of this aria (matrix B-6912-1, recorded 19 March, 1909 and issued as Victor 64099) credit her as the composer, though all Victor catalogs credit Varney.

EJS 467: The Golden Age of Opera" (2 LPs)
Issued May, 1969
MATRIX P-1844 / P-1845

SIDES 1-4 (467 A-D):

AGNES VON HOHENSTAUFEN (Spontini) (I)
Opera in 3 acts (complete)
Orchestra and Chours of the Maggio Musicale Fiorentino/Vittorio Gui
Andrea Morosini, chorus master
Broadcast, Maggio Musicale Fiorentino, Teatro Comunale, Florence, 9 May 1954

CAST:
Lucille Udovick (*Agnese*); Dorothy Dow (*Irmengarde*); Franco Corelli (*Enrico di Braunschwig*); Francesco Albanese (*Filippo di Hohen-staufen*); Enzo Mascherini (*Duke of Borgogna*); Anselmo Colzani (*Enrico il Leone*); Gian Giacomo Guelfi (*The Emperor Enrico IV*); Arnold van Mill (*The Archbishop of Magonza*); Giorgio [Jorge] Algorta (*A Squire*); Valiano Natali (*Teobaldo*); Valerio Meucci (*The Herald*); Lido Pettini (*First Judge*); Raniero Rossi (*Second Judge*).

NOTES: EJS 467

Spontini's last opera, AGNES VON HOHENSTAUFEN, performed here in Italian as AGNESE DI HOHENSTAUFEN, was set to a libretto by Ernst Raupach and was first produced in Berlin 12 June, 1829 (the first act premiered in Berlin on 28 May, 1827). This particular production was the first of the twentieth century, though the premiere is given in Rosenthal and Warrack's *The Concise Oxford Dictionary of Opera*, 2nd corrected ed. (Oxford: Oxford University Press, 1980/1985), p. 4 as 14 May, 1954, with Tebaldi, under the direction of Tullio Serafin. In fact, Tebaldi was singing at La Scala in Tchaikowski's ONEGIN on 10 May, 1954, so this claim doesn't seem likely. EJS 467 gives only 1954, while the Melodram CD issue of the same performance (MEL 27055) gives 9 May, 1954. The performances was also reissued as Cetra LO-25/3.

Apparently the opera was of vast length, even in its original form. This performance, though perhaps not complete, runs slightly over two hours. More recent revivals, it is said, have added even more music.

EJS 468: "The Golden Age of Opera (1 LP)
Issued May, 1969
MATRIX P-1846

UN BALLO IN MASCHERA (Verdi)
Opera in 3 acts (excerpts)
Orchestra and Chorus of the New Orleans Opera/Walter Herbert
In-house recording, New Orleans Opera, New Orleans, 20 Apr 1950

CAST:
Jussi Bjoerling (*Riccardo*); Suzy Morris (*Amelia*); Marko Rothmüller (*Renato*); Martha Larrimore (*Ulrica*); Audrey Schuch (*Oscar*); Norman Treigle (*Sam*); Jack Dabdoub (*Tom*); [Henri Feux] (*Silvano*); [George Berger (*Judge*)]; [George Berger (*Amelia's Servant*)].

SIDE 1 (468 A):

Act I:
1. SCHUCH, BJOERLING, TREIGLE, DABDOUB, and Chorus: S'avanza il conte . . . La rivedrà nell'estasi
2. SCHUCH and BJOERLING: Volta la terrea. Fronte alle stelle . . . to the end of the scene
3. BJOERLING and CHORUS: Or tu Sibilla . . . Di' tu se fedele
4. BJOERLING and LARRIMORE: È scherzo od è follia

Act II:
5. BJOERLING and MORRIS: Teco io sto! Gran Dio! . . . O qual soave brivido

SIDE 2 (468 B):

Act II:
1. MORRIS, BJOERLING, ROTHMÜLLER: Ahimè! Taci. S'appressa alcun . . . Per salvarti da lor . . . Fuggi, fuggi per l'orrida via

Act III: 2. BJOERLING, MORRIS, and ROTHMÜLLER: A tal colpa è nulla il pianto . . . Morrò! ma prima in grazia

3. BJOERLING and SCHUCH: Forse la soglia attinse . . . Vo' rivederti, Amelia

4. SCHUCH: Saper vorreste

5. MORRIS, BJOERLING, ROTHMÜLLER, SCHUCH, and Chorus: Ah! Perchè qui? fuggite! . . . to the end of the opera

NOTES: EJS 468

The Act III duet with Bjoerling and Audrey Schuch was included earlier on EJS 405 (September, 1967). The performance was privately recorded, but to date has not appeared complete on LP. See also the endnote for EJS 405 (II/3).

The same excerpts appeared more recently on Legato Classics CD LCD 154-1.

EJS 469: "The Golden Age of Opera" (1 LP)
Issued May, 1969
MATRIX P-1847

"THREE TENORS"

SIDE 1 (469 A):

* 1. GIACOMO LAURI-VOLPI, tenor (Orchestra of Radio Italiana [RAI], Milano/Oliviero de Fabritiis): OTELLO, Act III: Dio, mi potevi (Verdi) (I)
Broadcast, ***CONCERTO MARTINI E ROSSI***, Milan, 10 Jan 1955

* 2. GIACOMO LAURI-VOLPI, tenor (Orchestra of Radio Italiana [RAI], Milano/Oliviero de Fabritiis): TURANDOT, Act III: Nessun dorma (Puccini) (I)
Broadcast, ***CONCERTO MARTINI E ROSSI***, Milan, 10 Jan 1955

* 3. GIACOMO LAURI-VOLPI, tenor (Orchestra of Radio Italiana [RAI], Milano/Oliviero de Fabritiis): IL TROVATORE, Act III: Di quella pira (Verdi) (I)
Broadcast, ***CONCERTO MARTINI E ROSSI***, Milan, 10 Jan 1955

* 4. GIACOMO LAURI-VOLPI, tenor (Orchestra of Radio Italiana [RAI], Milano/Alfredo Simonetto): L'AFRICAINE, Act IV: Mi batte il cor . . . O paradiso! [Pays merveilleux . . . Ô paradis] (Meyerbeer) (I)
Broadcast, ***CONCERTO MARTINI E ROSSI***, Milan, 11 Jan 1954

* 5. a) GIACOMO LAURI-VOLPI, tenor (Orchestra of Radio Italiana [RAI], Milano/Alfredo Simonetto): LUISA MILLER, Act II: Ah! fede negar potessi . . . Quando le sere (Verdi) (I)
Broadcast, ***CONCERTO MARTINI E ROSSI***, Milan, 11 Jan 1954
b) GIACOMO LAURI-VOLPI, tenor (Orchestra of Radio Italiana [RAI], Milano/Mario Rossi): LUISA MILLER, Act II: L'ara o l'avello apprestami (Verdi) (I)
RAI broadcast, Rome, 13 Feb 1951

* 6. TITO SCHIPA, tenor (pf/?): "Torna a Surriento (de Curtis-de Curtis) (I)
?Broadcast, Moscow, circa October, 1957

* 7. TITO SCHIPA, tenor (pf/?): "O' ciucciarello" (Oliviero) (I)
?Broadcast, Moscow, circa October, 1957

* 8. TITO SCHIPA, tenor (pf/?): "Granada" (Lara) (S)
?Broadcast, Moscow, circa October, 1957

* 9. TITO SCHIPA, tenor (pf/?): "Chi se nne scorda cchiu" (Barthelemy) (I)
?Broadcast, Moscow, circa October, 1957

*10. TITO SCHIPA, tenor (pf/?): "Marechiare" (Tosti) (I)
?Broadcast, Moscow, circa October, 1957

SIDE 2 (469 B):

* 1. TITO SCHIPA, tenor (pf/?Franz Beeldsnijder): IL PIRRO E DEMETRIO, Act ?: Rugiadose, odorose, violette graziose (A. Scarlatti) (I)
Broadcast, Holland, 3 Nov 1959

* 2. TITO SCHIPA, tenor (pf/?Franz Beeldsnijder): "Desesperdamente" (Ruiz Lopez) (S)
Broadcast, Holland, 3 Nov 1959

I PAGLIACCI (Leoncavallo) (I)
Opera in 2 acts
Orchestra and Chorus/?
from the soundtrack of the feature film ***LACHE BAJAZZO*** [***I PAGLIACCI***] (1942), Tobis, Berlin, May, 1942

CAST:
Beniamino Gigli (*Canio*); Adriana Perris (*Nedda*); Leone Paci (*Tonio*); Mario Borriello (*Silvio*); Adelio Zagonara (*Beppe*).

* 3. Act II: Vo' il nome . . . No, Pagliaccio non son! . . . to the end of the opera (Leoncavallo) (I)

* 4. BENIAMINO GIGLI, tenor (Orchestra of Ente Italiano Audizioni Radiofoniche [EIAR], Torino/Umberto Berrettoni): MEFISTOFELE, Epilogue: Giunto sul passo estremo (Boïto) (I)
Broadcast, ?***CONCERTO MARTINI E ROSSI***, Turin, 10 Mar 1941

* 5. BENIAMINO GIGLI, tenor (Orchestra of the Teatro alla Scala, Gabriele Santini): LA FORZA DEL DESTINO, Act III: O tu che in seno agli angeli (Verdi) (I)
Broadcast, La Scala, Milan, 31 Mar 1934

* 6. BENIAMINO GIGLI, tenor (pf/?): "La camiciola della vita" (trad.) (Marche dialect)
Private recording, Milan, 20 Mar 1934

* 7. BENIAMINO GIGLI, tenor (pf/Luigi Ricci): "Mamma" (Bixio) (I)
Broadcast, ***CONCERTO PER LE FORZE ARMATI***, Rome, 27 Dec 1942

8. BENIAMINO GIGLI, tenor (orch/?): LA FAVORITA, Act IV: Spirto gentil (Donizetti) (I)
   from the soundtrack of the feature film *TAXI DI NOTTE [BAMBINO]* (1950), Cinecittà, Rome, June, 1950

* 9. BENIAMINO GIGLI, tenor (pf/Eric Robinson; small orch and chorus/Eric Robinson): "Adeste fidelis" (trad.) (L)
   Private recording, Via Serchio, Recanati, 12 Dec 1955 for broadcast, ***MUSIC FOR YOU***, BBC, London, 25 Dec 1955

* 10. BENIAMINO GIGLI, tenor (pf/Eric Robinson; small orch/Eric Robinson): "Wiegenlied," Op. 49, no. 4 (Brahms) (G)
   Private recording, Via Serchio, Recanati, 12 Dec 1955 for broadcast, ***MUSIC FOR YOU***, BBC, London, 25 Dec 1955

NOTES: EJS 469

Side 1 (469 A):

Bands 1-5: These items have appeared on several LPs, among them Timaclub TIMA 25. ANNA 1041 (May-June, 1979) reissued all but the LUISA MILLER and TROVATORE arias.

Band 5: The cabaletta, "L'ara o l'avello apprestami," was added from a complete recording of the 13 February, 1951 RAI, Roma broadcast conducted by Mario Rossi, a performance issued as Cetra 3221 and reissued as Cetra-Soria 1221 (with possible additions from another RAI performance) and Cetra LPO 2022. To this, bogus applause was added on EJS 469.

Bands 6-10: Schipa's 1957 Russian tour found him concertizing in Moscow, Leningrad, and Riga, but it is thought that these five recordings, reissued in 1992 on Pearl CD GEMM 9988, were from a Moscow broadcast. The accompanist is unknown. One source claims that the 1957 recordings were made for, and released by, Melodiya.

Side 2 (469 B):

Bands 1 and 2: A Schipa recital on EKR CD-10 gives cites Franz Beeldsnijder as Schipa's pianist for the 31 October, 1959 concert in Volendam, Holland: it is likely, therefore, that Beeldsnijder also accompanied the 3 November, 1959 Dutch broadcast excerpted here.

Band 3: Other excerpts from ***LACHE BAJAZZO*** were included on EJS 233 (March, 1962).

Band 4: It is not certain that this is from a ***MARTINI E ROSSI*** broadcast.

Band 5: Only excerpts appear to have survived from this complete Scala performance. The Act IV "Invano Alvaro!" of Gigli and Carlo Morelli was issued earlier on EJS 357 (February, 1966).

Band 6: In addition to the song, sung in the Marche dialect, Gigli talks to his daughter, Rina. This has been reissued on Pearl's multi-disc Gigli set, GEMM 202-6.

Band 7: The entire 27 December broadcast was later issued on ANNA 1027 (January, 1979).

Bands 9-10: These are Gigli's last available recordings as a singer: his final commercial sessions, from which no titles were published, were made in London in March, 1955. The two Christmas items were recorded at the tenor's villa, Via Serchio, on 12 December, 1955, with Eric Robinson accompanying at the piano. Robinson then conducted accompaniments to them with a small orchestra (and a chorus for the "Adeste fidelis") at the BBC Studios, London, for the 25 December, 1955 broadcast.

EJS 470: "The Golden Age of Opera" (1 LP)
Issued May, 1969
MATRIX P-1848

"GIOVANNI MARTINELLI / RECITAL TWO"

SIDE 1 (470 A):

* 1. w. LIVIA MARRACCI, soprano (Vitaphone Symphony Orchestra/Herman Heller): MARTHA (Flotow) (I)
a) VITAPHONE SYMPHONY ORCHESTRA/ HERMAN HELLER: Overture ("Maestoso" section)
b) MARTINELLI: Act III: [Qui sola, vergin rosa] . . . Sul cespite tremante . . . Ove son io? lo sento! . . . M'appari [Ach, so fromm]
c) MARTINELLI and MARRACCI: Act IV: Per te pietà giammai! . . . to the end of the duet
d) MARTINELLI and MARRACCI: Act IV: Suona l'ora del godere, l'istante del piacer . . . to the end of the finale
from the soundtrack of the one-reel Warner Brothers-Vitaphone short ***GIOVANNI MARTINELLI SINGING M'APPARI FROM MARTHA BY VON FLOTOW ASSISTED BY LIVIA MARRACCI*** (1929), New York, circa 1929
Vitaphone Varieties 932
MP 971; c21 Dec 1929
Premiere: unknown

* 2. w. JEANNE GORDON, contralto (Vitaphone Symphony Orchestra/Herman Heller): CARMEN, Act II (excerpts) (Bizet) (F)
a) GORDON: Les tringles des sistres! (first 30 measures and last 28)
b) MARTINELLI: Halte-là . . . Dragons d'Alcala! (beginning at measure 38 of no. 16)
c) GORDON and MARTINELLI: Enfin c'est toi
d) GORDON and MARTINELLI: Je vais danser . . . Je le veux Carmen . . . La fleur que tu m'avais jetée
from the soundtrack of the one-reel Warner Brothers Vitaphone short ***GIOVANNI MARTINELLI, ASSISTED BY JEANNE GORDON IN SELECTIONS FROM CARMEN*** (1927), New York, circa 1927
Vitaphone Varieties 474
MP 3949; c18Apr 1927
Premiere: Colony Theater, New York City, 12 Apr 1927

* 3. (w. orch/Joseph Pasternack): LA JUIVE, Act IV: Rachel, quand du Seigneur (Halévy) (F)
C-31363-2 Camden, 3 Dec 1924 Victor unpub

* 4. (w. orch/Joseph Pasternack): LA JUIVE, Act II: Dieu, que ma voix tremblante (Halévy) (F)
C-31364-2 Camden, 3 Dec 1924 Victor unpub

SIDE 2 (470 B):

1. (w. pf/Joseph Furgiuele): "Plaisir d'amour" (Claris de Florian-G. Martini) (F)
Private recording, New York, 1958-1960

2. (w. pf/Joseph Furgiuele): LA MOLINARA: Nel cor più non mi sento (Paisiello) (I)
Private recording, New York, 1958-1960

* 3. (w. Chicago Opera House Orchestra/Kurt Herbert Adler): MARTHA, Act III: M'appari [Ach, so fromm] (Flotow) (I)
Broadcast, Grant Park, Chicago, 21 Aug 1941

4. w. OLGA TREVISAN, soprano (pf/Nicola Rescigno): LA BOHÈME, Act I: O soave fanciulla (Puccini) (I)
Private party recording, New York City, Jan 1948

5. (w. pf/Joseph Furgiuele): LA BOHÈME, Act III: Mimì è una civetta! (Puccini) (I)
Private recording, New York, 25 Apr 1963

* 6. (w. pf/Joseph Furgiuele): LA FANCIULLA DEL WEST, Act II: Or son sei mesi (Puccini) (I)
Private studio recording, New York, 17 Apr 1962

NOTES: EJS 470

Side 1 (470 A):

Band 1: Dated 1927 on the label of EJS 470. Note that in the film, Martinelli is joined on camera by Marracci as he sings "Sul cespite tremante" (preceded by the orchestra playing "The Last Rose of Summer"). *Martha's* strophe is cut from the Act IV duet (1c) and the chorus is omitted from the finale (1d). The selections are presented on EJS 470 as a continuous medley, as they are in the actual film.

33.8 rpm appears to be the correct speed, with "M'appari" a half-step below score pitch, the "Per te pietà giammai" at score pitch, and the Act IV finale a half-step *above* score pitch.

No details of the life or career of Livia Marracci (given as "Lydia" on EJS 470) could be found: parts 1c and 1d of this Vitaphone short were reissued on UORC 255 (June, 1975) with her surname spelled "Meracci."

Band 2: Given here is the copyright title. The short premiered alongside the May McAvoy feature "Matinee Ladies." A contemporary Vitaphone release schedule gives the premiere date as 19 April, 1927, but reviews prove otherwise. An original disc is reported bearing the date 1926. 33.5 rpm is the correct pitch of this band.

The Martinelli-Bourskay AÏDA short (Vitaphone Varities 1024, copyright 1930) is often attributed to Jeanne Gordon, but the CARMEN was in fact the latter's only Vitaphone appearance with Martinelli. See also the endnote accompanying EJS 102 (1956), which also includes the CARMEN short.

Bands 3 and 4: Neither of Martinelli's acoustical JUIVE recordings was issued commercially. Take 6 of the "Rachel" and take 5 of the "Dieu, que ma voix," both recorded electrically on 22 June, 1925, were issued as Victor 6545 and HMV DB 865. The unpublished (electrical) take 5 of the "Rachel" has circulated in private pressings.

Both of the JUIVE arias play in score pitch at 33.5 rpm.

Side 2 (470 B):

Band 2: Depending on the key chosen, both 32.6 or 34.00 rpm yield stable pitchs.

Band 3: This "M'appari" is from a Grant Park broadcast recital. The liner notes for Celebrity CEL 500, Smith's "Giovanni Martinelli: In Memoria" tribute, claim that it was from Soldiers' Field, Chicago, a reference to a 16 August, 1941 broadcast performance conducted by Henry Weber. Martinelli did *not* sing the MARTHA aria that day, however.

34.5 rpm is required to secure the score key of F, barring a possible downward transposition.

Band 4: 34.1 rpm yields score pitch: as he does not attempt the high C (one of the party guests *does* in the background, along with soprano Trevisan!) Martinelli may not have bothered transposing it.

Band 5: At 32.5 rpm the "Mimi è una civetta!" is sung a whole-step below score pitch; at 33.8 rpm, it is sung a half-step below.

Band 6: The FANCIULLA aria has a spoken introduction by Lady Mayer, as well as an acknowledgement of the ovation by Martinelli, at which point we hear the start of the aria as recorded in playback. It is sung a half-step below score pitch at 32.9 rpm. See the endnote for EJS 475 (June, 1969) regarding the Mayer Lectures.

Reissued in 1978 at the correct speed (33.3 rpm) and in better sound on the Italian RCA LP "Giovanni Martinelli: Incisioni 1914-1962" (VL 42434), part of the *L'eta d'oro del Belcanto* series, where it is introduced by Martinelli himself. The original version of this LP, "La voce e l'arte di Giovanni Martinelli" (Italian RCA LM-20142), issued in the mid 1960s, did not contain the FANCIULLA recording.

The singer claims that he recorded the "Or son sei mesi" in a New York studio, possibly at RCA, fifty years *to the day* he made his first recordings in London for Edison. He confirms the date given in the listing, 17 April, 1962. Actually, his first recording for Edison, a test, was probably made on 21 May, 1912, and the rest the following September. The label of EJS 470 claims that the "Or son sei mesi" was recorded in London, hence the original introduction on EJS 470 by Lady Mayer (the May, 1969 bulletin obliquely mentions "a scene from Martinelli's London appearances in 1962"). The recording is monaural on both EJS 470 and on VL-42434, and scarcely of contemporary studio quality, but the performance itself is simply splendid. Martinelli's voice, it would seem, had changed little over the course of fifty years, and unlike so many elderly singers making last recordings in the twilight of their lives, his singing is still firm and unmistakable.

EJS 471: "The Golden Age of Opera" (2 LPs)
Issued June, 1969
MATRIX P-1865 / P-1866

SIDES 1-4 (471 A-D):

LA VEDOVA SCALTRA (Wolf-Ferrari) (I)
Opera in 3 acts (complete)
Orchestra and Chorus of Radio Italiana [RAI], Milano/Nino Sanzogno
RAI telecast, Milan, 16 Jul 1955

CAST:
Alda Noni (*Rosaura*); Agostino Lazzari (*Count of Bosco Nero*); Amilcare Blaffard (*M. Le Bleau*); Carlo Badioli (*Don Alvaro of Castiglia*); Antonio Cassinelli (*Milord Runebif*); Dora Gatta (*Marionette*); Renato Capecchi (*Arlecchino*); Giorgio Onesti (*Birif*); Florindo Andreolli (*Foletto*); Arrigo Cattelani (*Don Alvaro's Servant*).

NOTES: EJS 471

There are noticeable gaps in the continuity of this telecast, but it is not known whether these are performance, recording, or transfer cuts.

The performance was reissued as MRF 182.

EJS 472: "The Golden Age of Opera" (1 LP)
Issued June, 1969
MATRIX P-1861

DEJANICE (Catalani) (I)
Opera in 4 acts (excerpts)
?Orchestra of Radio Italiana [RAI]/Danilo Belardinelli
?RAI broadcast, place and date unknown

CAST:
Giovanna Di Rocco (*Dejanice*); Alba Bertoli (*Argelia*); Pier Miranda Ferraro (*Admeto*); Carmine Matranga (*Dardano*); Lorenzo Gaetani (*Labdaco*).

SIDE 1 (472 A):

1. ORCHESTRA: Prelude

Act I:
2. BERTOLI: Amore! Adolescente ancora
3. FERRARO: Solo! O ciel!
4. DI ROCCO, MATRANGA, and FERRARO: Nata di regi

Act II:
5. GAETANI: Melctar! Melctar!
6. FERRARO: Orea vita corsaro
7. DI ROCCO and BERTOLI: Deh! nella tua s'afflesi

SIDE 2 (472 B):

Act III:
1. FERRARO and METRANGA: Il re corsaro in questa seglia
2. ORCHESTRA: Dance of the Heterae
3. DI ROCCO: Cola, nell'oasi

ACT IV: 4. ORCHESTRA: Prelude
5. BERTOLI and FERRARO: Mesciam nel mesto calice

NOTES: EJS 472

This DEJANICE is probably from an RAI broadcast of excerpts, complete as aired: the RAI chronology does not list incomplete performances, which explains its omission there.

EJS 473: "The Golden Age of Opera" (1 LP)
Issued June, 1969
MATRIX P-1862

I PURITANI (Bellini) (I)
Opera in 3 acts (excerpts)
Orchestra of the American Opera Society/Richard Bonynge
In-house recording, Carnegie Hall, New York City 16 or 24 Apr 1963 or Philadelphia, 18 Apr 1963

CAST:
Joan Sutherland (*Elvira*); Nicolai Gedda (*Arturo*); Ernest Blanc (*Sir Riccardo Forth*); Justino Diaz (*Sir George Walton*); Betty Allen (*Queen Enrichetta*); Raymond Michalski (*Lord Walton*); ? (*Sir Benno Robertson*).

SIDE 1 (473 A):

1. Act I: a) BLANC and [BRUNO]: Or dove fuggo io mai? . . . Ah, per sempre . . . Bel sogno beato [33.3 - 33.5 rpm]
b) GEDDA, SUTHERLAND, DIAZ, MICHALSKI, and Chorus: A te, o cara [33.8 rpm]
c) SUTHERLAND, GEDDA, ALLEN, DIAZ, and Chorus: Son vergin vezzosa [33.8 rpm]
d) SUTHERLAND, [BRUNO], BLANC, DIAZ, and Chorus: Dolente morrà! Arturo! tu ritorni, t'appressa ancor . . . Oh vieni al tempio (last portion of the Act I Finale omitted) [33.9 - 34.5 rpm]
Act II: e) DIAZ and Chorus: Cinta di fiori [34.5 rpm]

SIDE 2 (473 B):

1. Act II: a) SUTHERLAND, BLANC, DIAZ, and Chorus: O rendetemi la speme . . . Qui la voce . . . Vien, diletto [34.5 rpm]
b) BLANC and DIAZ: Il rival salvar tu dei . . . Suoni la tromba [34.0 rpm]

Act III: c) SUTHERLAND and GEDDA: Vieni fra queste braccia [34.2 rpm]
d) GEDDA, SUTHERLAND, BLANC, DIAZ, and Chorus: Credeasi misera [34.2 rpm]
e) SUTHERLAND, GEDDA, BLANC, DIAZ, and Chorus: Suon d'araldi! Un messaggio . . . to the end of the opera [34.2 rpm]

NOTES: EJS 473

This was a concert performance, significantly abridged. The part of *Benno Robertson*, not found in any cast listing, was all but omitted and seems not to have been sung by a tenor, as originally scored. It is possible that Michalski, the only low-voiced cast member not heard at some point in duet with *Benno*, sang what was left of the role.

The American Opera Society mounted three performances, as noted in the listing, and it has never been established which of these was recorded (none of the three was broadcast). Smith, in the June, 1969 bulletin, says only that "the sound . . . is not good, since it was a house performance (sic) and not a broadcast." The complete performance issued on the two-disc MFR 39 is supposed to have been taken from the 18 April Philadelphia performance, but this has not been compared to EJS 473: Smith may have had access to a tape of one of the New York performances. Another semi-private tape issue of PURITANI is cataloged as Philadelphia, 18 April, 1963.

The 16 April Carnegie Hall performance marked the New York debut of conductor Bonynge.

Note that some of the often-transposed arias, *Arturo's* "A te, o cara" and "Credeasi misera," and the Act III *Elvira-Arturo* duet are sung in score pitch, even given the graduating speeds encountered over the two sides. The conclusion of Act III includes the 'Malibran' cabaletta finale, "Ah, sento, o mio bel angelo."

EJS 474: "The Golden Age of Opera" (1 LP)
Issued June, 1969
MATRIX P-1863

ZEMIRE ET AZOR (Grétry) (F)
Opera in 4 acts (excerpts)
Orchestra of the Office de Radiodiffusion Télévision Française [ORTF], Paris/Tony Aubin
ORTF broadcast, date unknown

CAST:
Claudine Collart (*Zémire*); Lise Arseguet (*Fatme*); Janine Capderou (*Lisbe*); Robert Andreozzi (*Azor*); Claude Genty (*Sander*); Joseph Peyron (*Ali*).

SIDE 1 (474 A):

Act I:
1. GENTY: No. 2: Le malheur me rend intrepide
2. PEYRON: No. 3: Les ésprits dont on nous fait peur
3. ANDREOZZI: No. 6: Ne va pas me tromper

Act II:
4. COLLART, ARSEGUET, and CAPDEROU: No. 7: Veillons mes soeurs
5. COLLART: No. 8: Rose cherie
6. COLLART and PEYRON: No. 10 bis: Je veux le voir

SIDE 2 (474 B):

Act III: 1. ANDREOZZI: No. 11: Ah! Quel tourment
2. COLLART: No. 14: La fauvette
3. ANDREOZZI: No. 13: Du moment qu'on aime
4. GENTY, ARSEGUET, and CAPDEROU: No. 15: Ah! Laissez-moi la pleurir a

Act IV: 5. PEYRON: No. 16: J'en suis encore tremblant
6. COLLART, GENTY, ARSEGUET, and CAPDEROU: No. 17: Ah! Je tremble

NOTES: EJS 474

The two final arias and ensemble finale to Act IV were probably performed, being of great dramatic importance to the opera, but were omitted here, possibly for purposes of timing or because Smith's source tape was incomplete. If the performance was narrated (and it probably was), this, too, has been cut.

Note that two of the third-act excerpts are given on EJS 474 out of score order: whether this was a performance rearrangement or a production oversight is not known.

Janinine Capderou is given as "Capdereau" on the label of EJS 474, but as "Capderou" on an MRF set of Dukas' ARIANE ET BARBE-BLEU.

EJS 475: "The Golden Age of Opera" (1 LP)
Issued June, 1969
MATRIX P-1864

"VERDI / BY GIOVANNI MARTINELLI"

SIDES 1-2 (475 A-B)

GIOVANNI MARTINELLI, speaker: A talk on the interpretation of Verdi's operas (E)
Private recording, The Mayer Lectures, 1962, Second Series, for the British Institute of Recorded Sound, Royal Institute of Great Britain, London, 23 May 1962

NOTES: EJS 475

The Mayer lectures were founded in 1961 by Sir Richard and Lady Mayer. The label of EJS 475 reads: "A discourse on the interpretation of the operas of Giuseppe Verdi by Giovanni Martinelli, as presented in England, the United States and Italy by the tenor, 1962-1968." The June, 1969 bulletin clarifies this by explaining that much of the same lecture material was given by Martinelli in the U.S., the U.K. and Italy "in at least 20 major cities and Universities" between 1962 and 1968, but that the speeches given under the auspices of the BIRS were the ones recorded and issued here. Martinelli had been invited to speak on the occasion of the 50th anniversary of his Covent Garden debut. "At the request of Martinelli," the bulletin continues, "all proceeds from the sale of this disc after costs of production are to be turned over to the Britsh Institute of Recorded Sound. To this end, copies will not be limited to the normal 100"--a figure, incidentally, that seemed to change over the course of the GAO series as the need arose.

The recordings used by Martinelli as illustrations in his 23 May, 1962 lecture have been omitted from EJS 475.

See also the endnote for EJS 470 (May, 1969) regarding Lady Mayer.

The 24 May, 1962 BIRS Mayer Lecture by Martinelli on the *verismo* school was issued as EJS 481 (October, 1969). A RIGOLETTO "Ella mi fu rapita" from a 1964 London teaching session later appeared on EJS 512 (May, 1970).

At least three of Martinelli's American lectures, one given for the San Francisco Opera Guild on 7 February, 1967, and one each from Seattle, Washington, Portland, and Oregon, around the same time, *may* have been preserved by Smith, who accompanied Martinelli on the tour. In a March, 1967 letter to a subscriber, Smith noted that "I [Smith] recorded all three of Martinelli's performances and filmed *it* as well" (sic). Smith was referring to either the three Seattle performances of TURANDOT (March, 1967), or to the lectures, it is not clear, though the TURANDOTs seem likelier (a segment from one of the 1967 TURANDOTs has circulated on videotape). Exactly which of the "performances" he means to designate here as "it" could not be determined, nor could the present location of the film(s) themselves--whatever they might have been.

EJS 476: "The Golden Age of Opera" (2 LPs)
Issued September, 1969
MATRIX P-1881 / P-1882

SIDES 1-4 (476 A-D):

BELISARIO (Donizetti)
Opera 3 in acts (complete)
Orchestra and Chorus of Teatro la Fenice, Venezia/Gianandrea Gavazzeni
Broadcast, Teatro la Fenice, Venice, 9 May 1969

CAST:
Leyla Gencer (*Antonina*); Giuseppe Taddei (*Belisario*); Mirna Pecile (*Irene*); Umberto Grilli (*Alamiro*); Nicola Zaccaria (*Giustiniano*); Rina Pallini (*Eudora*); Bruno Sebastian (*Eutropio*); Giovanni Antonini (*Eusebio*); Augusto Veronese (*Ottario*); Alberto Carusi (*A Centurion*).

NOTES: EJS 476

Reissued in stereo on MRF 37-S (LP) and on CD by Melodram (MEL 27051) and Verona (27048/9). Hunt CD 586 contains a later production of the opera with Gencer and Renato Bruson, but also includes as an appendix, excerpts from the 1969 production--dated *14* and *17* May, 1969.

EJS 477: "The Golden Age of Opera" (2 LPs)
Issued September, 1969
MATRIX P-1929 / P-1930

SIDES 1-3 (477 A-C):

GLORIA (Cilèa) (I)
Opera in 3 acts (complete)
Orchestra and Chorus of Radio Italiana [RAI], Torino/Fernando Previtali
RAI broadcast, Turin, 8 Jul 1969

CAST:
Margherita Roberti (*Gloria*); Flaviano Labò (*Lionetto*); Lorenzo Testi (*Bardo*); Ferruccio Mazzoli (*Aquilante*); Anna Maria Rota (*La Senese*); Enrico Campi (*The Bishop*).

SIDE 4 (477 D):

IL BARBIERE DI SIVIGLIA (Rossini) (I)
Opera in 2 acts (excerpts)
Orchestra of the Chicago Opera House/Emil Cooper
Broadcast, Chicago Opera, WGN, Chicago, 8 Dec 1941

CAST:
Josephine Antoine (*Rosina*); Nino Martini (*Count Almavia*); Richard Bonelli (*Figaro*); Vittorio Trevisan (*Doctor Bartolo*); Virgilio Lazzari (*Don Basilio*); Tina Paggi (*Berta*).

* 1. Act II: a) ANTOINE: Lesson Scene: LA PERLE DU BRÉSIL: Charmant oiseau ["Couplets du Mysoli"] (David) (F)
b) ANTOINE, TREVISAN, BONELLI, MARTINI, LAZZARI, amd PAGGI: Bella voce! bravissima! . . . Il vechietto cerca moglie . . . mi convien così crepar!
c) ANTOINE, MARTINI, and BONELLI: A quel tuo vil Conte Almaviva . . . Zitti, Zitti

NOTES: EJS 477

Side 1 (477 B):

This performance of GLORIA, coupled with excerpts from a Paris Radio performance of Leoncavallo's LA BOHÈME, was reissued as MRF 189.

Side 2 (477 B):

This BARBIERE was broadcast locally over Chicago station WGN from 10:00 pm CST (through the conclusion of the performance) and nationally over the Mutual network between 10:00-11:15 pm CST.

Antoine's "Charmant oiseau" is given complete (both verses), beginning abruptly in the first vocal phrase. The scene continues uninterrupted with minor cuts through *Berta's* "Il vechietto." "Dunque voi Don Alonzo . . . ma per pietà! is cut, and the score picks up at the trio "A quel tuo vil Conte Almaviva," again, with minor cuts. The side ends at the completion of the "Zitti, Zitti."

EJS 478: "The Golden Age of Opera" (1 LP)
Issued September, 1969
MATRIX P-1928

"MAGGIE TEYTE"

SIDE 1 (478 A):

* 1. (w. pf/Frederick Stone): DIDO AND AENEAS, Act III: Thy hand, Belinda . . . When I am laid in earth (Purcell) (E)
Broadcast, *GENERAL OVERSEAS SERVICE*, BBC, London, 2 Jun 1950

* 2. (w. pf/Frederick Stone): "If music be the food of love" (Shakespeare-Purcell) (E)
Broadcast, *GENERAL OVERSEAS SERVICE*, BBC, London, 2 Jun 1950

* 3. (w. pf/Frederick Stone): "Gentil gallant de France (Cedric Wallis) (F)
Broadcast, *GENERAL OVERSEAS SERVICE*, BBC, London, 2 Jun 1950

* 4. (w. pf/Frederick Stone): "Vielle chanson de chasse" (trad.-arr. Manning) (F)
Broadcast, *GENERAL OVERSEAS SERVICE*, BBC, London, 2 Jun 1950

* 5. (w. pf/Frederick Stone): "Heures d'été" (Baton) (F)
Broadcast, *GENERAL OVERSEAS SERVICE*, BBC, London, 2 Jun 1950

* 6. (w. pf/Frederick Stone): "Dein blaues Auge," Op. 59, no. 8 (Groth-Brahms) (G)
Broadcast, *GENERAL OVERSEAS SERVICE*, BBC, London, 2 Jun 1950

* 7. (w. pf/Frederick Stone): "Kennst du das Land?" ["Mignon"] (Goethe-Wolf) (G)
Broadcast, *GENERAL OVERSEAS SERVICE*, BBC, London, 2 Jun 1950

* 8. (w. pf/Frederick Stone): "Psyché" (Corneille-Paladilhe) (F)
Broadcast, *GENERAL OVERSEAS SERVICE*, BBC, London, 2 Jun 1950

* 9. (w. pf/Frederick Stone): "Si mes vers avaient des ailes" (Hugo-Hahn) (F)
Broadcast, *GENERAL OVERSEAS SERVICE*, BBC, London, 2 Jun 1950

SIDE 2 (478 B):

* 1. (w. pf/Rita Mackay): "The Fields are full" (Armstrong) (E)
BBC broadcast, London, 15 Aug 1937

* 2. (w. pf/?): "En sourdine" (Verlaine-Hahn) (F)
BBC broadcast, London, 26 Nov 1958

* 3. w. JOHN McCORMACK, tenor (pf/Gerald Moore): "Still is the Night" Op. 112, no. 1 (Goetze) (E)
2EA 9652-1 Abbey Road, London, 25 Nov 1941 HMV unpub

4. (w. studio orch/Donald Voorhees): LE NOZZE DI FIGARO, K. 492, Act II: Voi che sapete (Mozart) (I)
Broadcast, *BELL TELEPHONE HOUR*, WEAF, NYC, 20 Aug 1945

5. (w. studio orch/Donald Voorhees): MANON, Act II: Adieu, notre petite table (Massenet) (F)
   Broadcast, ***BELL TELEPHONE HOUR***, WEAF, NYC, 26 Aug 1946

6. (w. studio orch/Donald Voorhees): LA BOHÈME, Act I: Si, mi chiamano Mimi (Puccini) (I)
   Broadcast, ***BELL TELEPHONE HOUR***, WEAF, NYC, 25 Feb 1946

7. (w. studio orch/Donald Voorhees): LA BOHÈME, Act III: Donde lieta usci ["Addio"] (Puccini) (I)
   Broadcast, ***BELL TELEPHONE HOUR***, WNBC, NYC, 4 Nov 1946

8. (w. studio orch/Donald Voorhees): JEANNE D'ARC, Act I: Adieu, forêts [Prostitye vi, kholmi] (Tchaikowski) (F)
   Broadcast, ***BELL TELEPHONE HOUR***, WNBC, NYC, 30 Jun 1947

* 9. (w. pf/Gerald Moore): CIBOULETTE: Ce n'était pas la même chose (Hahn) (F)
   OEA-11017-2 London, 20 May 1946 HMV unpub HMB 76

NOTES: EJS 478

Side 1 (478 A):

Bands 1-9: This complete broadcast was reissued in 1980 on the Arabesque Teyte recital 8069, a BBC/Caedmon co-production.

Side 2 (478 B):

Band 1: Other early BBC items accompanied by Mackay (dated *only* 1937) have been issued by Decca and London.

Band 2: Another excerpt from this 26 November, 1958 Teyte BBC broadcast appeared earlier on EJS 171 (January, 1960). This is the broadcast date given on Arabesque 8069, though 25 and 28 November have also been reported. 25 November seems clearly to be in error, unless it was a pre-recording date, while 28 November *may* be a re-broadcast. Interviews with the singer (excerpts of which are included on the Arabesque LP) punctuated her musical numbers.

Band 3: The McCormack duet was dubbed on 24 December, 1947 to transfer matrices 2EA 9652-1T1, 1T2, and 1T3. It has appeared on two Teyte recital LPs, Rococo 5319 and "L'Exquise Maggie Teyte" (EMI RLS 716), as well as Arabesque 8124, a McCormack recital.

Note that this is not Böhm's "Still wie die Nacht," Op. 326, no. 27. There is disagreement, however, as to the actual composer of the song. Worth and Cartwright (*John McCormack: A Comprehensive Discography*. Westport, CT: Greenwood Press, 1986, *Discographies*, No. 21), p. 88, cite Alma Goetz and an English translation by Mrs. J. P. Morgan; Brian Fawcett Johnston's *Count John McCormack: Discography*, issued as *Talking Machine Review*, 74 (Summer, 1988), p. 44, gives *Carl* Götze as the composer and Elizabeth M. Lockwood as the lyricist. The famous Bori-Tibbett version (Victor 3043/1747 and HMV DA912, matrix BVE-28854-3, recorded 1 June, 1927) is titled "Calm as the Night," with Carl Goetz credited as the composer.

Band 9: The first commercial release of this unpublished 1946 operetta aria, recorded at the Abbey Road studio, London, was on EMI's Teyte collection, RLS 7033. It was subsequently issued as Historic Masters HMB 76, a vinyl 78 pressing.

EJS 479: "The Golden Age of Opera" (1 LP)
Issued October, 1969
MATRIX P-1946

SIDE 1 (479 A):

GERMANIA (Franchetti) (I)
Opera in a Prologue, two scenes, and epilogue (excerpts)
Orchestra and Chorus of Radio Italiana [RAI]/?Pietro Argento
?RAI broadcast, place and date unknown

CAST:
Aldo Bertocci (*Frederick Loewe*); Nelly Pucci (*Ricke*); Attilio D'Orazi (*Karl Worms*).

* 1. Scene iv: a) ORCHESTRA and Chorus: Intermezzo sinfonico

Scene i: b) BERTOCCI: Son come molti un profugo
c) D'ORAZI: Ferito, prigionier
d) PUCCI: All'ardente desio
Epilogue: e) BERTOCCI and PUCCI: O tu che mi soccorri

SIDE 2 (479 B):

GIOVANNI GALLURESE (Montemezzi) (I)
Opera in 3 acts (excerpts)
Orchestra and Chorus of Radio Italiana [RAI]/?
?RAI broadcast, place and date unknown

CAST:
Gianni Poggi (*Giovanni Gallurese*); Floriana Cavalli (*Maria*); Enzo Pasquiero (*The Voice of a Child*).

* 1. Act I: a) PASQUIERO and POGGI: Orchestral introduction . . O picciochedola . . . O, con che calma eterna
b) CAVALLI: Sorge Aurora, la vergine fragrante

Act III: c) POGGI and CAVALLI: O l'amore o la morte

* 2. GIUSEPPE GISMONDO, tenor (?Orchestra of Radio Italiana [RAI]/?): DON JUAN DE MANARA, Act ?: Signor si! Ancor t'offesi (Alfano) (I)
?RAI Broadcast, place and date unknown

* 3. FLORIANA CAVALLI, soprano (?Orchestra of Radio Italiana [RAI]/?): IL DOTTORE ANTONIO, Act III: Nave, nave, nera (Alfano) (I)
?RAI Broadcast, place and date unknown

* 4. GIUSEPPE GISMONDO, tenor (?Orchestra of Radio Italiana [RAI]/?): CYRANO DI BERGERAC, Act I: Io getto con grazia il capello ["Je jette avec grâce mon feutre"] (Alfano) (I)
?RAI Broadcast, place and date unknown

NOTES: EJS 479

Side 1 (479 A):

Smith *may* have chosen these excerpts with the vocal collector in mind, omitting *Loewe's* two well-known arias in deference to the fact that so many important tenors had recorded them, beginning with Enrico Caruso, the creator of the role. The fact remains, however, that MRF 176-S coupled the identical excerpts with a complete ZAZà, implying that either nothing more was recorded or has survived of this GERMANIA or that MRF simply stole their material from EJS 479. *Ricke's* aria from the first scene, "All'ardente desio" (labeled "Tu non sei buono") was also recorded by it creator, Amelia Pinto (1878-1946) on G&T 53239 (matrix 1775b) in Milan on 11 April, 1902, one month to the day after the work's premiere at La Scala. The creator of *Worms*, G. Mario Sammarco, recorded "Ferito, prigionier" on G&T 52371 (matrix 1705b) in March, 1902 and again in 1903 on G&T 052027 (matrix CON 692). He also recorded *Worms'* farewell from Scene ii, "Ascolta! Io morirò!" in 1909, issued on Fonotipia 92335 (matrix XPh 3467). Another aria, *Worms'* "Tu m'eri innanzi" from the Prologue, was recorded by both Pasquale Amato and Domenico Viglione Borghese for Fonotipia. Giovanni Bardi made what may be the only recording of the Scene ii "Vide un tiranno" of *Stapps*, issued Pathé 86360/10076/5005 in Milan in the teens.

Dating this probable RAI broadcast has proven impossible. It is not listed in the RAI chronology, as it was undoubtedly an incomplete performance. It can be placed easily between 1959 and 1969, however: Bertocci was active with RAI between 1948 and 1975, conductor Argento between 1950 and 1973, Pucci between 1958 and 1970, and D'Orazi between 1959 and 1977. EJS 479 was released in October, 1969, the possible overlap being 1959-1969.

Side 2 (479 B):

Band 1: GIOVANNI GALLURESE (1905) was Montemezzi's first produced opera. This performance, too, has proven difficult to date. Poggi sang complete operas for RAI from 1952-1954, and Cavalli's activity peaked between 1959 and 1960 (she returned briefly in 1967-1968). 1960 has been suggested tentatively, at a point when the operatic careers of both overlapped.

The baritone's few lines in the Act III duet (1c) were omitted from the performance.

Bands 2-4: These performances probably came from RAI's Alfano concerts of the late 1950s and early 1960s (CYRANO was broadcast complete during the 1961-1962 season, but with Agostino Lazzari in the title role). ***CONCERTO MARTINI E ROSSI*** has also been suggested as a probable source. Gismondo (given as "Gismondi" on the label of EJS 479) and Cavalli were at their peak of activity at RAI in 1959 and 1960, though both were still singing in the late 1960s.

EJS 480: "The Golden Age of Opera" (1 LP)
Issued October, 1969
MATRIX P-1947

SIDE 1 (480 A): "ROSSINI / ROMANZI / PART TWO"

1. NICOLETTA PANNI, soprano, and ELENA ZILIO, contralto (pf/Giorgio Favaretto): ALBUM ITALIANO, no. 6: Le gi[t]tane (Torre-Rossini) (I)
   RAI broadcast, date unknown

2. ELENA ZILIO, contralto (pf/Giorgio Favaretto): ALBUM ITALIANO, no. 7: Ave Maria (Rossini) (L)
   RAI broadcast, date unknown

3. LAJOS KOZMA, tenor (pf/Giorgio Favaretto): ALBUM ITALIANO, no. 11: Il fanciullo smarrito (Castellani-Rossini) (I)
   RAI broadcast, date unknown

4. NICOLETTA PANNI, soprano (pf/Giorgio Favaretto): MORCEAUX RÉSERVÉS, no.11: Mi lagnerò tacendo ["Ariette à l'Ancienne"] (J.-J.Rousseau-Rossini) (I)
   RAI broadcast, date unknown

5. NICOLETTA PANNI, soprano (pf/Giorgio Favaretto): MISCELLANÉE DE MUSIQUE VOCALE, No. 1: Ariette villageoise (J.-J. Rousseau-Rossini) (I)
   RAI broadcast, date unknown

6. LAJOS KOZMA, tenor (pf/Giorgio Favaretto): MORCEAUX RÉSERVÉS, no. 2: L'esule ["L'Éxile"] (Torre-Rossini) (I)
   RAI broadcast, date unknown

7. NICOLETTA PANNI, soprano (pf/Giorgio Favaretto): ALBUM FRANÇAISE, No. 9: "Élégie" ["Adieux à la vie"] (?E. Pacini-Rossini) (I)
   RAI broadcast, date unknown

SIDE 2 (480 B): "SONGS OF DONIZETTI, VERDI, RICCI"

1. GIUSEPPE DI STEFANO (pf/R. Furlan): "La conocchia" ["Quann'a lo bello mio vojo parlare"] (Donizetti) (I)
   ?RAI broadcast, date unknown

* 2. ANGELICA TUCCARI, soprano (pf/R. Furlan): Lu trademiento ["Aje, tradetore, tu m'haje lassata"] (Donizetti) (I)
   ?RAI broadcast, date unknown

3. ANGELICA TUCCARI, soprano (pf/R. Furlan): "Tengo 'no 'nnamurato" (Donizetti) (I)
   ?RAI broadcast, date unknown

4. ANGELICA TUCCARI, soprano (pf/R. Furlan): Amor Marinaro ["Me vojo fà na casa"] (Donizetti) (I)
   ?RAI broadcast, date unknown

5. GIUSEPPE DI STEFANO (pf/R. Furlan): "Le Crépuscule" ["L'aube naît et la porte est close"] (Hugo-Donizetti) (I)
   ?RAI broadcast, date unknown

6. ROSANNA CARTERI, soprano (pf/R. Furlan): "Canzone dell'ape" (Donizetti) (I)
   ?RAI broadcast, date unknown

7. LAJOS KOZMA, tenor (pf/R. Furlan): SEI ROMANZE, no. 3: Ad una stella (A. Maffei-Verdi) (I)
   ?RAI broadcast, date unknown

8. LAJOS KOZMA, tenor (pf/R. Furlan): "Brindisi" (A. Maffei-Verdi) (I)
   ?RAI broadcast, date unknown

9. ANGELICA TUCCARI, soprano (pf/R. Furlan): "L'amor e una pietanza" (Luigi Ricci) (I)
   ?RAI broadcast, date unknown

10. ANGELICA TUCCARI, soprano (pf/R. Furlan): "Disame di si" (Luigi Ricci) (I)
    ?RAI broadcast, date unknown

11. ANGELICA TUCCARI, soprano (pf/R. Furlan): C'EST POUR VOUS, no. 1: 'sta bene all'erta" (Federico Ricci) (I)
    ?RAI broadcast, date unknown

12. ANGELICA TUCCARI, soprano (pf/R. Furlan): C'EST POUR VOUS, no. 5: Dolente istoria (Federico Ricci) (I)
    ?RAI broadcast, date unknown

NOTES: EJS 480

The title of this LP is especially odd insofar as there was no "Part One" of Rossini "Romanzi" issued on "The Golden Age of Opera" label, and because the plural of "romanza" is "romanze."

The Rossini songs on side 1 are known to be from RAI broadcasts, while those of Donizetti, Verdi, and Ricci are only suspected to be. No dates for any of the performances have been confirmed.

Soprano Nicoletta Panni (1933-) is described in the October, 1969 bulletin as the "granddaughter" of baritone Giuseppe De Luca, while Kolodin, in *The Metropolitan Opera* (New York: Knopf, 1968), p. 699, insists she was his "grand-niece." Neither claim has been confirmed: De Luca had only one child, a daughter, Wally (born 1903) about whom nothing is known. The second edition of the Kutsch-Riemens (1982), pp. 528-529 mentions nothing of Panni's lineage. It is noted there that her only (sic) recordings were issued on EJS, ("Arien von Mercandante"), a reference, ostensibly, to EJS 558 (June, 1971). The Rossini songs on EJS 480 are not mentioned at all, nor the other recordings she made for a variety of commercial Italian (LP) labels.

Side 1 (480 A):

All of these Rossini songs are taken from the thirteen-volume PÉCHÉS DE VIEILLESSE (1857-1868): the upper-case collection titles given in the listing are the titles of the individual volumes.

Side 2 (480 B):

Band 2: Labeled "Sei traditore" on EJS 480.

EJS 481: "The Golden Age of Opera"
Issued October, 1969
MATRIX P-1948

"GIOVANNI MARTINELLI DISCUSSES THE VERISMO SCHOOL"

SIDES 1-2 (481 A-B):

1. GIOVANNI MARTINELLI, speaker: "My Association with the Composers of the *Verismo* School" (E)
   Private recording, The Mayer Lectures, 1962, Second Series, for the British Institute of Recorded Sound, Royal Institute of Great Britain, London, 24 May 1962

NOTES: EJS 481

Martinelli's 23 May, 1962 Mayer Lecture appeared as EJS 475 (June, 1969). In this second talk, the tenor discusses the *verismo* phenomenon, the beginnings of his own career, and his relationship with a number of important *verismo* composers--Puccini, Leoncavallo, Mascagni, Giordano, Boïto, etc. All proceeds from the sale of the LP were again donated to the British Institute of Recorded Sound, according to the October, 1969 bulletin.

Though this was not the case on EJS 475, the recorded examples used by Martinelli as illustrations for this second lecture *were* included on EJS 481, as follows:

Side 1 (481 A):

1. GIANNI VIAFORA, GIACOMO PUCCINI, ELVIRA PUCCINI, and possibly GINA CIAPARELLI-VIAFORA, speakers: Staged address
   M-1420-1 New York, ?24 Feb 1907 Unnumbered B&S Columbia
   [Given here as Puccini talking about his NY visit. This recording is described in detail in the endnotes for EJS 267 (April, 1963), II/3c].

2. GIOVANNI MARTINELLI, tenor, and EVA TURNER, soprano (Orchestra and Chorus of the Royal Opera House /John Barbirolli): TURANDOT, Act II: O Principi, che a lunghe carovane . . . offri la prova ardita, O Turandot! ["Riddle Scene"] (Puccini) (I)
   TT-2352-5 (part) Covent Garden, London, 5 or 10 May 1937
   HMV unpub
   [Virtually identical scenes were recorded on two sets of technical tests from the 1937 Coronation Season TURANDOTs at Covent Garden (series 2352-1/7 and TT 2353-1/7). Both sets of excerpts were issued complete in 1988 by EMI on CD (CDH 7 61074 2). The 5 May appeared earlier on EJS 102 (1956) and were later coupled with the 10 May excerpts on EJS 50X (April-May, 1976). See the detailed endnote for these performances for EJS 102].

3. FEODOR CHALIAPIN, bass (Orchestra of the Royal Opera House/Vincenzo Bellezza): MEFISTOFELE, Act I: Son lo spirito che nega (Boïto (I)
   CR-388-1 Covent Garden, London, 31 May 1926
   HMV DB 942 Victor 15-1042
   [A live relay performance recording from Covent Garden. The Victor pressing was issued as part of their red-vinylite "Heritage" series in 1949. Only four of the nine sides recorded from this performance were issued on shellac: four of the nine (three published, one unpublished) appeared on the EMI Covent Garden set, RLS 742].

Side 2 (481 B):

4. LUCREZIA BORI, soprano (orch/?Josef Pasternack): IRIS, Act II: Un di (ero piccina) al tempio (Mascagni) (I)
   C-15824-2 New York or Camden, 23 May 1915
   Victor 88524 HMV 2-053120
   DB 152
   [One of Bori's rarer acoustical operatic Victors, one of only four that were not doubled in 1924].

5. FRANCESCO TAMAGNO, tenor (pf/?): SAMSON ET DALILA, Act I: Figli miei, v'arrestate [Arrêtez! ô mes frères!] (Saint-Saëns) (I)
   3019 ft G&T 52681 Victor 95008 Ospedaletti, Feb 1902
   [The published version, reissued as HMV DR 101 and VA 62. The unpublished version, matrix 3018 ft, was issued as Historic Masters HM 85 in 1992, a vinyl 78 pressing coupled with Battistini's 1902 DEMON aria (G&T 52670)].

6. MIGUEL FLETA, tenor (orch/Sabajno): GIULIETTA E ROMEO, Act III: Giulietta, son io (Zandonai) (I)
   CE-393-1 Milan, 17 Apr 1922 HMV 2-052210 Victor 74775
   DB 524 6391

EJS 482: "The Golden Age of Opera" (1 LP)
Issued October, 1969
MATRIX EJS 482 A & B

"GLADYS SWARTHOUT"

SIDE 1 (482 A):

1. (w. studio orch/Al Goodman): JEANNE D'ARC, Act I: Adieu, forêt [Prostitye vi, kholmi] (Tchaikowsky) (F)
   Broadcast, ***PRUDENTIAL FAMILY HOUR***, WABC, NYC, 30 Jan 1944

* 2. (w. studio orch/Al Goodman): PIQUE DAME, Act I: My Tender Playmate [Podruggy mili] ["Pauline's Song"] (Tchaikowsky) (E)
   Broadcast, ***PRUDENTIAL FAMILY HOUR***, WABC, NYC, 6 Feb 1944

3. (w. studio orch/Al Goodman): HERODIADE, Act I: Celui dont la parole . . . Il est doux, il est bon (Massenet) (F)
   Broadcast, ***PRUDENTIAL FAMILY HOUR***, WABC, NYC, 13 Dec 1942

4. (w. studio orch/Al Goodman): LE NOZZE DI FIGARO, K. 492, Act I: Non so più cosa son, cosa faccio (Mozart) (I)
   Broadcast, ***PRUDENTIAL FAMILY HOUR***, WABC, NYC, 9 Jan 1944

5. (w. studio orch/Howard Barlow): LE NOZZE DI FIGARO, K. 492, Act II: Voi che sapete (Mozart) (I)
   Broadcast, ***VOICE OF FIRESTONE***, WEAF, NYC, 4 Dec 1944

6. (w. Detroit Symphony Orchestra/Eugene Ormandy): IL BARBIERE DI SIVIGLIA, Act I: Una voce poco fà (Rossini) (I)
   Broadcast, ***FORD SUNDAY EVENING HOUR***, WJR, Detroit, 28 Nov 1937

* 7. (w. studio orch/Al Goodman): LE PROPHÈTE, Act II: Ah! mon fils (Meyerbeer) (F)
   Broadcast, ***PRUDENTIAL FAMILY HOUR***, WABC, NYC, 22 Mar 1942

* 8. w. HELEN JEPSON, soprano (Detroit Symphony Orchestra/Fritz Reiner): LAKMÉ, Act I: Viens, Mallika . . . Dôme épais (Delibes) (F)
   Broadcast, ***FORD SUNDAY EVENING HOUR***, WJR, Detroit, 13 Apr 1941

SIDE 2 (482 B):

1. (w. studio orch/Erno Rapee): LA GIOCONDA, Act I: Voce di donna (Ponchielli) (I)
   Broadcast, ***GENERAL MOTORS HOUR***, WEAF, NYC, 19 Jan 1936

2. (w. Cleveland Orchestra/Artur Rodzinski): ORFEO ED EURIDICE, Act III: Che farò senza Euridice (Gluck) (I)
   Broadcast, ***MAGIC KEY OF RCA***, WEAF, NYC, 22 Nov 1936

* 3. (w. Detroit Symphony Orchestra/Franco Ghione): NADESHDA, Act : What means Ivan? . . . Oh! My heart is weary (Goring-Thomas) (E)
   Broadcast, ***FORD SUNDAY EVENING HOUR***, WJR, Detroit, 16 Apr 1939

4. (w. Detroit Symphony Orchestra/Eugene Ormandy): RINALDO, Act II: Armida dispietata! . . . Lascia ch'io pianga (Handel) (I)
   Broadcast, ***FORD SUNDAY EVENING HOUR***, WJR, Detroit, 16 May 1937

5. (w. orch/?William Daly): LA FAVORITA, Act III: O mio Fernando (Donizetti) (I)
   Broadcast, ***FIRESTONE CONCERT***, WEAF, NYC, 1934

6. w. FRANK CHAPMAN, baritone (studio orch/?William Daly): DON GIOVANNI, K. 527: Act I: Là ci darem la mano (Mozart) (I)
   Broadcast, ***FIRESTONE CONCERT***, WEAF, NYC, date?

7. w. FRANK CHAPMAN, baritone (studio orch/?William Daly): LA FAVORITA, Act II: Leonora! Leonora! deh! taci! In questo suolo . . . Ah! l'alto ardor! . . . to the end of the duet (Donizetti) (I)
   Broadcast, ***FIRESTONE CONCERT***, WEAF, NYC, 22 Oct 1934

8. w. FRANK CHAPMAN, baritone (studio orch/?William Daly): MAYTIME: Will You Remember (Sweetheart)? (Wood-Young-Romberg) (E)
   Broadcast, ***FIRESTONE CONCERT***, WEAF, NYC, 1934

NOTES: EJS 482

The October, 1969 bulletin claims that contralto Gladys Swarthout heard all of the selections contained on this informal memorial issue some two years before her death on 7 July, 1969, and had requested that Smith publish them.

Side 1 (482 A):

Band 2: As with other Swarthout broadcasts of this period, the 6 February, 1944 show was heard over both WABC-AM and WABC-FM. Clean air-checks may well have been transcribed from FM, and these could easily be confused with line-checks, so striking was the difference at the time between commercial AM and FM transmission.

Band 7: Swarthout also sang the PROPHÈTE aria on the 23 January, 1944 ***PRUDENTIAL*** broadcast and many times before that, so 22 March, 1942 is by no means certain here.

Band 8: The LAKMÉ duet was a substitution for the originally-scheduled BUTTERFLY "Flower Duet."

Side 2 (482 B):

Band 3: Labeled "Madsche: My Heart is Weary" and given as 1934. The NADESHDA aria was sung by Swarthout on 16 April, 1939, but nothing else from the broadcast (Rachmaninov's "The Floods of Spring," Pittaluga's "Romance de Solita," etc.) appeared on EJS, making provenance a problem in assigning this date with any certainty.

Possiby the label is correct and the aria is from 1934, in which case it would probably be from the ***FIRESTONE CONCERT***, accompanied by William Daly's orchestra. See the endnote below for items II/5-8. The contents of these earliest Swarthout shows were rarely documented in the *New York Times* radio logs, or for that matter, in such national radio publications as *Radio Guide*, making the precise identification of some of this material virtually impossible.

Bands 5-8: As mentioned above, William Daly conducted the early Swarthout ***FIRESTONE CONCERT*** broadcasts, hence the provisional attribution here. Though the dates of bands II/5, 6, and 8 could not be determined, they are undoubtedly from this weekly program which, at the time, also featured baritone Lawrence Tibbett. During the 1937-1938 season, the show's title was changed permanently to ***THE VOICE OF FIRESTONE***.

EJS 483: "The Golden Age of Opera" (1 LP)
Issued October, 1969
MATRIX P-1950

SIDE 1 (483 A):

CAVALLERIA RUSTICANA (Mascagni) (I)
Opera in 1 act (excerpts)
Orchestra and Chorus of the Opera Italiano d'Olanda/Pietro Mascagni
Broadcast, Dutch Radio, The Hague, 7 Nov 1938

CAST:
Lina Bruna Rasa (*Santuzza*); Antonio Melandri (*Turiddu*); Maria Meloni (*Lola*); ?Rina Galli Toscani (*Mamma Lucia*); [Afro Poli (*Alfio*)].

* 1. a) BRUNA RASA: Voi lo sapete
b) BRUNA RASA, MELANDRI, and MELONI: Tu qui, Santuzza? . . . Fior di giaggiolo . . . No, no, Turiddu
c) BRUNA RASA, MELANDRI, and TOSCANI: Mamma, quel vino e generoso . . . to the end of the opera

* 2. MARGHERITA CAROSIO, soprano (orch/Pietro Mascagni): NERONE, Act III: O mio Nerone, io muoio . . . Addio, Nerone (Mascagni) (I)
Filmed live performance, La Scala, Milan, January-February, 1935 or April, 1937

SIDE 2 (483 B):

LES PÊCHEURS DE PERLES (Bizet) (I)
Opera in 3 acts (excerpts)
Orchestra/Edmondo de Vecchi
Broadcast, The Hague, Netherlands, 17 Mar 1940

CAST:
Luigi Fort (*Nadir*); Scipio Colombo (*Zurga*); Diana Miceli (*Leila*).

1. Act I: a) COLOMBO and FORT: Sei tu che dinnanzi . . . Del tempio al limitar [C'est toi! qu'enfin je revois! . . . Au fond du temple]
b) FORT: A quella voce . . . Mi par d'udir ancora [A cette voix . . . Je crois entendre encore]
c) MICELI and FORT: Brahma gran Dio . . . Nei di (?) ciel [O Dieu Brahma! . . . Dans le ciel sans voiles]

NOTES: EJS 483

Side 1 (483 A):

Band 1: This CAVALLERIA is reportedly a production of the Opera Italiana d'Olanda (Italian Opera [Company] of Holland) according to a recent reissue on Bongiovanni compact disc GB-1050-2, which is also the source of Toscani's participation as *Mamma Lucia*.

Band 2: See the lengthy note on this NERONE film for EJS 360 (March, 1966), II/3, on which Carosio's "Canto notte e di" appeared. Carosio created the role of the *Slave* in the 16 January, 1935 La Scala production of the opera. There were seven Scala performances between January and February of that year, and five in April, 1937, all conducted by the composer and featuring Pertile in the title role. It is not known which of these were filmed and recorded.

EJS 484: "The Golden Age of Opera" (4 LPs)
Issued October, 1969
MATRIX ?P-1956 / P-1957 / P-1958 / P-1959

SIDES 1-8 (484 A-H):

PARSIFAL (Wagner) (G)
Opera in 3 acts (complete)
Metropolitan Opera House Orchestra and Chorus/Artur Bodanzky (Acts I III) and Erich Leinsdorf (Act II)
Metropolitan Opera broadcast, NYC, Friday, 15 Apr 1938 (matinee)

CAST:
Lauritz Melchior (*Parsifal*); Kirsten Flagstad (*Kundry*); Friedrich Schorr (*Amfortas*); Norman Cordon (*Titurel*); Emanuel List (*Gurnemanz*); Arnold Gabor (*Klingsor*); Doris Doe (*A Voice*); George Cehanovsky (*First Knight*); Louis D'Angelo (*Second Knight*); Natalie Bodanya (*Esquire*); Helen Olheim (*Esquire*); Giordano Paltrinieri (*Esquire*); Karl Laufkoetter (*Esquire*); Susanne Fisher (*Flower Maiden*); Irra Petina (*Flower Maiden*); Helen Olheim (*Flower Maiden*); Hilda Burke (*Flower Maiden*); Thelma Votipka (*Flower Maiden*); Doris Doe (*Flower Maiden*).

NOTES: EJS 484

This PARSIFAL was a special Good Friday broadcast matinee. Bodanzky suffered a heart seizure in the midst of Act I, but returned to conduct Act III. Leinsdorf, age twenty-six at the time, had only made his Metropolitan Opera debut a few months earlier when he conducted DIE WALKüRE on 21 January, 1938.

The October, 1969 bulletin notes that "the man who recorded the opera was a superb musician and he chose his [acetate] breaks most carefully." The opera is stated to be at least 95% complete, missing only "10 seconds every seven minutes," the result of changing the original transcription discs.

It is also stated, and rightly, that this is the only *complete* Melchior-Flagstad PARSIFAL to have survived (for that matter, the only complete PARSIFAL recorded by either singer). The only commercially-issued recordings from the opera featuring the two together were the seven sides of the "Herzeleide" scene made for Victor on 23 and 24 November, 1940, a U.S. release only.

Only 19 copies of EJS 484 were advertised in the bulletin as being available for general sale, the other 29 having been sold out in advance of publication. A speed range of 34.5 - 34.7 rpm has been prescribed for the first and third sides.

EJS 485: "The Golden Age of Opera" (1 LP)
Issued November, 1969
MATRIX P-1968

SIDE 1 (485 A):

AïDA (Verdi) (I)
Opera in 4 acts (excerpts)
Orchestra and Chorus of the Teatro Reale dell'Opera, Roma/Oliviero de Fabritiis
Shortwave broadcast, Terme di Caracalla, Rome, 5 Aug 1939

CAST:
Iva Pacetti (*Aïda*); Beniamino Gigli (*Radames*); Ebe Stignani (*Amneris*); Andrea Mongelli (*Ramfis*); Ernesto Dominici (*The King of Egypt*); Nino Mazzetti (*A Messenger*); Pina Tassi (*High Priestess*); [Benvenuto Franci (*Amonasro*)].

* 1. Act I: GIGLI, STIGNANI, PACETTI, DOMINICI, MAZZETTI, MONGELLI, and Chorus: [Celeste Aïda] . . . tu sei regina, tu di mia vita sei lo splendor . . . to the end of the act

SIDE 2 (485 B):

AïDA (Verdi) (I)
Opera in 4 acts (excerpts)
Metropolitan Opera House Orchestra and Chorus/Ettore Panizza
Metropolitan Opera broadcast, NYC, 4 Feb 1939

CAST:
Zinka Milanov (*Aïda*); Beniamino Gigli (*Radames*); Bruna Castagna (*Amneris*); [Ezio Pinza (*Ramfis*)]; [Norman Cordon (*The King of Egypt*)]; [Giordano Paltrinieri (*A Messenger*)]; [Thelma Votipka (*High Priestess*)]; Carlo Tagliabue (*Amonasro*).

* 1. a) Act III: GIGLI, MILANOV, TAGLIABUE, and CASTAGNA: Pur ti riveggo . . . to the end of the act

b) Act IV: MILANOV, GIGLI, CASTAGNA, and Chorus: Nelle tue braccia desiai morire . . . to the end of the opera

NOTES: EJS 485

Side 1 (485 A):

The excerpts from this Teatro dell'Opera performance were taken from the original NBC acetates of the American shortwave broadcast (three 16-inch sides, numbered ENG. 183 9-37, broadcast no. 9-160). The recitative and first lines of Gigli's "Celeste Aïda" are spliced in from another, untraced source.

Side 2 (485 B):

Ramfis' two lines at the close of Act III (1a) are not sung here by Pinza, a practice that was apparently not unheard of at the time (examples from Chicago Opera performances have also survived). Thus, Pinza is not heard on EJS 485.

The same excerpts appeared later on MRF 43.

EJS 486: "The Golden Age of Opera" (2 LPs)
Issued November, 1969
MATRIX P-1978 / P-1979

SIDES 1-4 (486 A-D):

CONCHITA (Zandonai) (I)
Opera in 4 acts (complete)
Orchestra and Chorus of Radio Italiana [RAI], Torino/Mario Rossi
RAI broadcast, Turin, 16 Sep 1969

CAST:
Antonietta Stella (*Conchita*); Aldo Bottion (*Mateo*); Anna Maria Rota (*Mother of Conchita*); Giovanna Di Rocco (*Dolores*); Lorenza Canepa (*Estella*); Emma De Santis (*A Lady*); Rosina Cavicchioli (*Rufina*); Angela Rocco (*A Mother*); Rosetta Arena (*Enrichetta*); Rosetta Arena (*A Caretaker*); Ennio Buoso (*A Fruit Vendor*); Ennio Buoso (*A Guide*); Renato Ercolani (*A Bystander*); Fernando Valentini (*A Bystander*); Enzo Viaro (*A Bystander*); Amilcare Blaffard (*First Englishman*); Andrea Mineo (*Second Englishman*); Andrea Mineo (*A Banderillero*); Carlo Gaifa (*A Voice*); Gianni Socci (*The Inspector*); Saturno Meletti (*Garcia*); Guido Pasella (*Tonio*).

NOTES: EJS 486

The cast, as labeled, has been corrected in the listing above.

Reissued complete on two LPs as MRF 178, where it is dated 1976--possibly the date of a re-broadcast.

The entire set seems to play uniformly in pitch at about 34.3 rpm.

EJS 487: "The Golden Age of Opera" (3 LPs)
Issued November, 1969
MATRIX: P-1980 / P-1981 / P-1982

SIDES 1-5 (487 A-E):

PELLÉAS ET MÉLISANDE (Debussy) (F)
Opera in 5 acts (complete)
Metropolitan Opera House Orchestra and Chorus/Louis Hasselmans
Milton Cross, voice-over narration
Metropolitan Opera Broadcast, Boston, 7 Apr 1934

CAST:
Edward Johnson (*Pelléas*); Lucrezia Bori (*Mélisande*); Ezio Pinza (*Golaud*); Léon Rothier (*Arkel*); Ina Bourskaya (*Geneviève*); Ellen Dalossy (*Little Yniold*); Louis D'Angelo (*A Physician*).

SIDE 6 (487 F):

DER FLIEGENDE HOLLÄNDER (Wagner) (G)
Opera in 3 acts (excerpts)
Philharmonic-Symphony Orchestra of New York/Bruno Walter
Broadcast, ***NEW YORK PHILHARMONIC SYMPHONY ORCHESTRA*** (sic), WABC, Carnegie Hall, NYC, 23 Dec 1934

CAST:
Friedrich Schorr (*Holländer*); Dorothee Manski (*Senta*); Emanuel List (*Daland*).

* 1. Act I: SCHORR: Die Frist is um

* 2. Act II: MANSKI, LIST, and SCHORR: Ach, möchtest du, bleicher Seemann sie finden! . . . to the end of the act

NOTES: EJS 487

Side 1 (487 A):

The PELLÉAS is presented here in unusually poor sound, even considering the date. The November, 1969 bulletin compares it to "Berliner discs on LP and at its worst (less than 10%) - like Mapleson cylinders." The use of a single hanging microphone obviously didn't help matters much, as the singers constantly fade in and out as they walked about the stage, adding dim vocals to the roaring surface noise (see the endnote to EJS 107 (1956) for details of the new sound system installed at the Met in 1934 for broadcast purposes). There are numerous minor cuts of a few measures between each change of transcription disc ("10 seconds . . . every seven minutes," according to the November, 1969 bulletin), but the performance is otherwise complete, except for the first two and a half pages of Act IV.

In personal correspondence (February, 1970), Smith noted that "I had been tracking down an old music professor for years--finally last June I got him in a small Pennsylvania town--just before I was to visit him--he had a heart attack . . . then his physician, also an opera lover, let me visit and I managed to take away the Wagnerian discs I am now publishing [e.g. the three TRISTANs, released as EJS 499 and 502 in March, 1970]--he had an RCA Victor Home recorder . . . he played each [finished transcription] from 80-100 times--nothing but noise left--finally my engineer designed a needle which played the side walls of the grooves and that is what we have gotten and what I am releasing." It is not certain, but seems likely, that the PELLÉAS was part of this batch of early Met broadcasts. David Hamilton (see note for EJS 499) claimed that the transcriptions were the work of a *dentist*!

The bulletin also notes that this was the first live operatic Bori performance discovered complete (the 1934 PETER IBBETSON, excerpts of which appeared in September, 1961 as EJS 187, would not be offered complete until the issue of UORC 143 in February, 1973) and the first complete Johnson performance in a language other than English: in fact, Johnson's only other complete performance transcriptions, both from the Met and both from 1934, are the MERRY MOUNT issued on EJS 134 (October, 1958) and the PETER IBBETSON.

The label of EJS 487 gives [Paolo] Ananian as the *Physician*, but this is in error.

The earliest Met broadcasts offered listeners a voice-over commentary by Deems Taylor, a practice which was quickly modified and eventually banished (see the note for EJS 111, II/4). Milton Cross can be heard here, however, beginning in Act II and continuing intermittently thereafter describing the scene--though fortunately, only during the interludes that punctuate the singing.

The set plays in fairly constant score pitch at 34.3 rpm.

Side 6 (487 F):

This two-hour ***PHILHARMONIC*** concert also featured the Overture to DER FLIEGENDE HOLLÄNDER, the "Ride of the Valkyries," and Schorr's "*Wotan's* Farewell." The Schorr WALKÜRE transcription was so badly warped that it could not be used (the beginning of this warpage can be heard toward the end of the HOLLÄNDER excerpts included here).

The correct playing speeds are 34.7 rpm for the Act I monologue and 34.00 rpm for the second-act ensemble. Applause is heard at the end of both excerpts.

Manksi omits the cadenza at the end of the first part of the Act II duet, while the Finale has sustained the usual performance abridgement.

EJS 488: The Golden Age of Opera" (1 LP)
Issued November, 1969
MATRIX: P-1991

"RICHARD CROOKS (1938-1943)"

SIDE 1 (488 A):

* 1. w. studio orch/Alfred Wallenstein or Howard Barlow: WERTHER, Act III: Pourquoi me réveiller? (Massenet) (F)
Broadcast, ***VOICE OF FIRESTONE***, WEAF, NYC, 23 Jan 1939 or 16 Oct 1944

* 2. w. studio orch/Alfred Wallenstein: SERSE, Act I: "Holy Thou Art" [Ombra mai fu] (Handel) (E)
Broadcast, ***VOICE OF FIRESTONE***, WEAF, NYC, 19 Apr 1943

* 3. w. studio orch/Alfred Wallenstein or Howard Barlow: SADKO, Scene IV: Les diamants chez nous sont innombrables [Ne shchest almasov] (Rimsky-Korsakov) (F)
Broadcast, ***VOICE OF FIRESTONE***, WEAF, NYC

4. w. Detroit Symphony Orchestra/José Iturbi: LOHENGRIN, Act III: Mein lieber Schwan (Wagner) (G)
Broadcat, ***FORD SUNDAY EVENING HOUR***, WJR, Detroit, 16 Oct 1938

* 5. w. Detroit Symphony Orchestra/Fritz Reiner or Victor Kolar, or studio orch/Alfred Wallenstein or Howard Barlow: L'ELISIR D'AMORE, Act II: Una furtiva lagrima (Donizetti) (I)
Broadcast, ***FORD SUNDAY EVENING HOUR***, WJR, Detroit, or ***VOICE OF FIRESTONE***, WEAF, NYC

6. w. studio orch/?: DIE WALKÜRE, Act I: Winterstürme (Wagner) (G)
   Broadcast, source and date unknown

* 7. w. HELEN JEPSON, soprano (Metropolitan Opera House Orchestra/Ettore Panizza): LA TRAVIATA, Act I: Un dì felice, eterea (Verdi) (I)
   Metropolitan Opera broadcast, NYC, 23 Dec 1939 or Cleveland, 13 Apr 1940

* 8. w. Metropolitan Opera House Orchestra/Ettore Panizza: LA TRAVIATA, Act II: Lunge da lei . . . De' miei bollenti spiriti (Verdi) (I)
   Metropolitan Opera broadcast, NYC, 23 Dec 1939 or Cleveland, 13 Apr 1940

SIDE 2 (488 B):

1. w. HELEN JEPSON, soprano (Metropolitan Opera House Orchestra and Chorus/Ettore Panizza: LA TRAVIATA, Act II: Invitato a qui seguirmi (Verdi) (I)
   Metropolitan Opera broadcast, NYC, 23 Dec 1939 or Cleveland, 13 Apr 1940

2. w. HELEN JEPSON, soprano (Metropolitan Opera House Orchestra/Ettore Panizza): LA TRAVIATA, Act III: O mia Violetta . . . Parigi, o cara (Verdi) (I)
   Metropolitan Opera broadcast, NYC, 23 Dec 1939 or Cleveland, 13 Apr 1940

* 3. w. EZIO PINZA (Metropolitan Opera House Orchestra/Wilfred Pelletier): FAUST, Act I: Mais ce Dieu (Gounod) (F)
   Metropolitan Opera broadcast, NYC, 16 Mar 1940 or Boston, 6 Apr 1940

* 4. w. Metropolitan Opera House Orchestra/Wilfred Pelletier: FAUST, Act III: Salut! demeure (Gounod) (F)
   Metropolitan Opera broadcast, NYC, 16 Mar 1940, or Boston, 6 Apr 1940

* 5. w. GRACE MOORE, soprano (Metropolitan Opera House Orchestra/Wilfred Pelletier): MANON, Act II: Instant charmant . . . En fermant les yeux (Massenet) (F)
   Metropolitan Opera broadcast, NYC, 13 Jan 1940

* 6. w. Metropolitan Opera House Orchestra and Chorus/Wilfred Pelletier: MANON, Act III: Je suis seul . . . Ah! fuyez, douce image (Massenet) (F)
   Metropolitan Opera broadcast, NYC, 13 Jan 1940

NOTES: EJS 488

The November, 1969 bulletin notes that Crooks was, at the time, "desperately ill in California" and that "this record is being issued in the hope that it will give him and his admirers some idea of the art of the tenor in his prime in the late 1930's and early 1940's." Crooks died in California on 29 September, 1972.

The TRAVIATA excerpts from 23 December, 1939 have appeared on various Smith LPs, e.g. EJS 170 and 171 from January, 1960, and EJS 540 from February, 1971, which presented extensive excerpts.

Side 1 (488 A):

Band 1: The 1939 broadcast was conducted by Wallenstein and the 1944 broadcast by Barlow. The latter was heard over both WEAF-AM and -FM.

Band 2: The translation sung here, "Holy Thou Art," has nothing to do with the original Italian text of the aria, though it was billed as Handel's "Largo."

Band 3: Crooks sang the SADKO aria on at least three ***FIRESTONE*** shows: 12 January, 1942 conducted by Wallenstein, and on 20 March and 23 October, 1944 conducted by Barlow.

Band 5: Crooks sang the "Una furtiva lagrima" frequently: on the ***FORD SUNDAY EVENING HOUR*** (23 January, 1938 conducted by Reiner, and 24 March, 1940 conducted by Kolar) and on ***THE VOICE OF FIRESTONE*** (9 May, 1938, 26 December, 1938, 1 December, 1941, and 23 March, 1942 conducted by Wallenstein; and 18 October, 1943 and 1 May, 1944 conducted by Barlow). The 1 May, 1944 performance was issued as V-Disc 327 and Navy V-Disc 107 (Victor master D4TC 150).

Side 2 (488 B):

Bands 3-4: The complete 6 April, 1940 Boston performance was issued as EJS 188 (September, 1960). The complete 16 March, 1940 performance was issued as UORC 275 (January-February, 1976). The original acetates of the 16 March performance (eight 16-inch discs with Ortha labels, numbered ENG. 183 9-37, broadcast no. 40-67) included Intermission Features with Milton Cross, Helen Jepson, and John Erskine (former president of Julliard) from Hollywood, as well as Herbert H. Lehmann, the governor of New York.

Library of Congress tape: 8944-11 (complete 16 March, 1940 New York City broadcast).

Bands 5-6: Library of Congress tape: 8944-8 (complete broadcast).

EJS 489: "The Golden Age of Opera" (4 LPs)
Issued December, 1969
MATRIX: P-2008 / P-2009 / P-2010 / P-2011

SIDES 1-7 (489 A-G):

GÖTTERDÄMMERUNG (Wagner) (G)
Opera in 3 acts (complete)
Metropolitan Opera House Orchestra and Chorus/Artur Bodanzky
Metropolitan Opera broadcast, NYC, 11 Jan 1936 (matinee) and 12 May 1939 (evening)

CAST:
Lauritz Melchior (*Siegfried*); Marjorie Lawrence (*Brünnhilde*); Friedrich Schorr (*Gunther*); Ludwig Hofmann (*Hagen*); Eduard Habich (*Alberich*); Dorothee Manski (*Gutrune*); Kathryn Meisle (*Waltraute*); Editha Fleischer (*Woglinde*); Irra Petina (*Wellgunde*); Doris Doe (*Flosshilde*); Doris Doe (*First Norn*); Irra Petina (*Second Norn*); Dorothee Manski (*Third Norn*); [Max Altglass (*Vassal*)]; [Arnold Gabor (*Vassal*)].

SIDE 8 (489 H):

DER FLIEGENDE HOLLÄNDER (Wagner) (G)
Opera in 3 acts (excerpts)
Orchestra and Chorus of the Bayreuth Festival, Bayreuth/Karl Elmendorff
Broadcast, Bayreuth Festpielhaus, Bayreuth, WJZ, NYC, 4 Aug 1939 (matinee)

CAST:
Maria Müller (*Senta*); Rudolf Bockelmann (*Holländer*); Ludwig Hofmann (*Daland*); [Franz Völker (*Erik*)]; [Ria Focke (*Mary*)]; [Erich Zimmermann (*Steersman*)].

* 1. Act II: a) HOFMANN, MÜLLER, and BOCKELMANN: Mein Kind, du siehst mich auf der Schwelle . . . to the end of the act

Act III: b) Chorus: Beginning of the act . . . Steht euch nach frischem wein der Sinn?

NOTES: EJS 489

Side 1 (489 A):

A portion of the Prologue, the *Siegfried-Brünnhilde*, "Zu neuen Taten" (beginning at "Durch deine Tugend allein soll so ich *Taten noch* wirken?"), is markedly superior to the rest of this very noisy and increasingly warped transcription, and has been inserted from the half-hour GÖTTERDÄMMERUNG excerpt broadcast with Melchior and Flagstad over station WJZ, New York City on the evening of 12 May, 1939. This presentation in honor of the Met's World's Fair Spring Season Fair was originally issued complete on EJS 167 in December, 1959. Melchior's only other surviving broadcasts of the opera's Prologue are the 1 June, 1937 Covent Garden performance (issued in April, 1968 as EJS 431), and a 22 February, 1941 ***NBC SYMPHONY*** program over WJZ, NYC. The Covent Garden performance also featured the *Brünnhilde* of Flagstad, where the

NBC SYMPHONY broadcast, conducted by Toscanini, featured Helen Traubel. The latter performance exists, but was never issued by Smith.

The vocal insert was compared to both Flagstad performances and matches the 1939 World's Fair broadcast: note that Flagstad sings a high A instead of the written high C at the end of the duet. Bodanzky's distinctive conducting of the scene, moreover, is reported to be obvious to some. Two instrumental inserts--part of *Siegfried's* Rhine Journey in the Prologue and the "Funeral March" from Act III (to *Gutrune's* "War das sein Horn?")--could not be so easily identified: they were not featured in the brief 12 May, 1939 broadcast, obviously, and Bodanzky appears not to have recorded either commercially, so that virtually any studio recording(s) might have been substituted, if not another, cleaner broadcast performance.

The Prologue and the first two acts play best at 33.5 rpm, with the exception of the final trio of Act II which requires 34.5 rpm. Act III plays at a uniform 33.5 rpm.

Side 2 (489 B):

These HOLLÄNDER excerpts were taken from a half-hour afternoon broadcast carried via shortwave over station WJZ [NBC], New York City. The label of EJS 489 gives Margarethe Klose as *Mary* (in spite of the fact that the Act II excerpt begins after *Mary's* exit) and Victor de Sabata as the conductor, a misattribution that came directly from the actual NBC announcement heard on this transfer. Further, the announcer mentions Völker, though he was not heard on the broadcast, and omits any mention of Bockelmann.

The New York Times radio log published on the Sunday before the broadcast, carried the following item: "Dusolina Giannini, Margarethe Klose, Maria Müller and Franz Völker *have been assigned principal roles* in Wagner's opera, 'The Flying Dutchman,' portions of which will be broadcast. Victor de Sabata is the conductor" (emphasis mine). In fact, there were five performances of HOLLÄNDER that season at Bayreuth, with Müller as *Senta*, Hofmann as *Daland*, Völker as *Erik*, Focke as *Mary*, Zimmermann as the *Steersman*, and Bockelmann sharing the title role with Jaroslav Prohaska. All were conducted by Karl Elmendorff according to *Die Besetzung der Bayreuther Festpiele 1876-1960*. De Sabata's and Klose's 1939 Bayreuth season was limited to TRISTAN UND ISOLDE, and Giannini never sang at Bayreuth. Possibly this description was the result of an inaccurate pre-broadcast press release, hence the ambiguity of the principal roles having been "assigned."

The *New York Times* gives the time of broadcast as 1:30-2:00 pm EST, making this an evening performance and a broadcast matinee. The original NBC acetates (two 16-inch discs, two sides, numbered ENG. 183 9-37, broadcast 9-160), are titled "Beyrouth [sic] Musical Festival," and couple the HOLLÄNDER excerpts with two installments of a soap opera. Transmission in Act II becomes very poor on the original acetates after "Versank' ich jetzt."

The excerpts play in score pitch at 33.8 rpm.

EJS 490: "The Golden Age of Opera" (2 LPs)
Issued December, 1969
MATRIX P-2001 / P-2002

SIDES 1-4 (490 A-D):

LE MASCHERE (Mascagni) (I)
Opera in 3 acts and a Prologue (complete)
Orchestra and Chorus of the Teatro Verdi, Trieste/Bruno Bartoletti
Broadcast, Teatro Verdi, Trieste, 11 Nov 1961

CAST:
Antonio Cassinelli (*Pantalone de'Bisognosi*); Cesy Broggini (*Rosaura*); Ferrando Ferrari (*Florindo*); Michele Cazzato (*Doctor Graziano*); Elena Rizzieri (*Colombina*); Amedeo Berdini (*Brighella*); Giampiero Malaspina (*Captain Spavento*); Sergio Tedesco or Mario Ferrara (*Arlecchino Batocchio*); Afro Poli (*Tartaglia*); Carlo Piccinato [speaker] (*Giocadio*).

NOTES: EJS 490

Mascagni first revised his unsuccessful 1901 *commedia dell'arte* opera for a 1916 Turin production, removing large portions of the original score. Subsequent revisions resulted in the version performed here.

The character *Rosaura* is given as "*Rolanda*" on the label of EJS 490. Carlo Piccinato, who speaks the part of *Giocadio*, was an eminent stage director at the San Francisco Opera from the 1940s through the 1960s, primarily in attendance of the Italian and French repertory.

The correct playing speed of both EJS discs is 34.5 rpm.

The complete performance was reissued on the two-LP set MRF 44.

EJS 491: "The Golden Age of Opera" (1 LP)
Issued December, 1969
MATRIX: P-2004

SIDES 1-2 (491 A-B):

EDIPO RE (Leoncavallo) (G)
Opera in 1 act (complete)
Orchestra of Radio Beromünster, Bern, and Bern Radio Chorus/Nello Santi
Radio Beromünster broadcast, Bern, date unknown

CAST:
Ernst Gutstein (*Edipo*); Edith Lang (*Jocasta*); Libero De Luca (*Creonte*); Manfred Rohrl (*A Corinthian*); Peter Lagger (*Tiresia*); Wolfram Merty (*A Shepherd*); Peter Suter (*A Watchman*).

NOTES: EJS 491

Manfred Rohrl is given as "Fred Rohri" on the label of EJS 491. This was Leoncavallo's final opera, produced posthumously at the Chicago Opera on 31 December, 1920 with Titto Ruffo in the title role (the company mounted only three performances of the work in Chicago and one at the Manhattan Opera House in New York City on 21 February, 1921). The January, 1970 bulletin notes with regret that the only performance available at the time was this one in German: up to that time, it had been produced in Italy only as a 13 October, 1939 EIAR broadcast from Turin, though it was subsequently mounted by RAI, Roma for broadcast on 21 December, 1972.

The opera was later staged at the Teatro San Carlo, Naples, on 23 May, 1970, a performance preserved on MRF-139.

EJS 492: "The Golden Age of Opera" (3 LPs)
Issued January, 1970
MATRIX: P-2024 / P-2026 / P-2027

SIDES 1-6 (492 A-F):

DER MEISTERSINGER VON NÜRNBERG (Wagner) (G)
Opera in 3 acts (complete)
Metropolitan Opera House Orchestra and Chorus/Artur Bodanzky
Metropolitan Opera broadcast, NYC, 22 Feb 1936

CAST:
Friedrich Schorr (*Hans Sachs*); Elisabeth Rethberg (*Eva*); René Maison (*Walther*); Karin Branzell (*Magdalene*); Hans Clemens (*David*); Eduard Habich (*Beckmesser*); Emanuel List (*Pogner*); Julius Huehn (*Kothner*); Marek Windheim (*Vogelgesang*); Louis D'Angelo (*Nachtigal*); Arnold Gabor (*Ortel*); Angelo Bada (*Zorn*); Max Altglass (*Moser*); Giordano Paltrinieri (*Eisslinger*); James Wolfe (*Foltz*); Dudley Marwick (*Schwartz*); Arnold Gabor (*Watchman*).

NOTES: EJS 492

Note that matrix number P-2025, used for the MARINA on EJS 493, is missing from the sequence of individual MEISTERSINGER discs.

There are several minor orchestral cuts, made here for timing, the most important of which is the Prelude to Act II. The sound is very poor, arguably as bad as anything issued by Smith. Indeed, whole sections are inaudible beneath the noise. The January, 1970 bulletin mentions only that it is "heavy with rumble" and further, that "one must listen through it as tho a waterfall were between the listener and the music" (sic). "Those interested in sound" are warned to "stay away!" The performance has since appeared in better sound on a four-CD set, Music and Arts 652.

Speeds are erratic over the course of the six sides, which range from 32.00 to nearly 34.00 rpm.

EJS 493: "The Golden Age of Opera" (1 LP)
Issued January, 1970
MATRIX P-2025

SIDES 1-2 (493 A-B):

MARINA (Camprodón y Lafont-Carrión-Arrieta y Correra) (S)
Opera/*Zarzuela* in 3 acts (complete as recorded)
Coros y Orquesta Sinfonico Columbia, Barcelona/M. Daniel Montorio
Trumpet Soloist: Álvaro Mont. (sic)
Studio Recording, Columbia, Barcelona, circa October, 1929 (12 discs)
Spanish Issue: Regal RS 6504-RS 6515; Columbia ZG 1100-ZG 1111
Italian Issue: Columbia GQX 10000-GQX 10011
Argentinian Issue: Columbia 264780-264791
U.S. Issue: 67769-D - 67780-D (Opera Set OP 11: manual)
70903-D - 70914-D (Opera Set OP 11: automatic)

CAST:
Mercedes Capsir (*Marina*); Hipólito Lázaro (*Jorge*); José Mardones (*Pascual*); Marcos Redondo (*Roque*).

Act I:
1. ORCHESTRA: Prelude to Act I
WKX 180-2 (13071)
2. CAPSIR and Chorus: Brilla el mar
WKX 159-2 (13047)
3. CAPSIR and Chorus: Brilla el mar
WKX 175-2 (13066)
4. CAPSIR: Pensar en él
WKX 173-2 (13064)
5. CAPSIR: Ya sus ojos
WKX 174-1 (13065)
6. CAPSIR and MARDONES: Yo tosco y rudo trabajador
WKX 169-1 (13059)
7. LÁZARO, MARDONES, and Chorus: Costa la de Levante
WKX 170-1 (13060)
8. CAPSIR, LÁZARO, and Chorus: Al ver en la immensa Ilanura del Mar ["Salide de Jorge"]
WKX 171-1 (13061)
9. CAPSIR, LÁZARO, MARDONES, and REDONDO: Seca tus lágrimas ["Cuarteto"]
WKX 160-2 (13048)
10. CAPSIR, LÁZARO, MARDONES, and REDONDO: Serena tu rostro ["Cuarteto"]
WKX 161-1 (13049)
11. LÁZARO and REDONDO: Feliz morada
WKX 167-1 (13056)

Act II:
12. Chorus: Marinero, Marinero ["Barcarola"]
WKX 178-3 (13069)
13. CAPSIR, MARDONES, and Chorus: La novia, no parece
WKX 176-2 (13067)
14. CAPSIR, LÁZARO, MARDONES, REDONDO, and Chorus: Act II Finale
WKX 162-2 (13050)

Act III: 15. MONT. (sic), trumpet, and Orchestra: Prelude to Act III
WKX 179-1 (13070)
16. LÁZARO and Chorus: A beber, a beber
WKX 157-1 (13045)
17. LÁZARO, REDONDO, and Chorus: Pero no importa
WKX 158-2 (13046)
18. CAPSIR, LÁZARO, and REDONDO: No sabes tú que yo tenia
WKX 165-1 (13054)
19. CAPSIR, LÁZARO, and REDONDO: En las alas del deseo
W294155-1 [WKX 166-?]
20. REDONDO: Seguidillas
WKX 163-1 (13051)
21. REDONDO and Chorus: Dichoso aquél que tiene
WKX 164-2 (13052)
22. CAPSIR and LÁZARO: Marina yo parto muy lejos de aquí
WKX 172-2 (13062)
23. CAPSIR: Rondó Final
WKX 168-3 (13057)
24. MARDONES and Chorus: Niña de los ojos negros
WKX 177-2 (13068)

NOTES: EJS 493

EJS 493 was Smith's first attempt at reissuing a complete, previously-published studio recording on LP. The side-for-side excerpts have been given in the listing as they appear on the original (American) Columbia labels, but these are not reliable, and should not be taken as precise indications of the actual side breaks.

MARINA was written originally as a two-act *zarzuela*, libretto by Francisco Camprodón y Lafont (1816-1870), later modified by M. Ramos Carrión for the work's transformation into a 3-act "grand opera." Pascual Juan Emilio Arrietta y Correra (1823-1894), the composer, is usually referred to on record labels simply as "Arrieta." As a *zarzuela*, MARINA made its debut in Madrid at the Teatro del Circo on 21 September, 1855 and was first heard as a grand opera at the Teatro del Real on 16 March, 1871. It remained very popular in Spanish speaking countries and was also performed in Italy, but only two productions could be traced to the U.S.: a modest premiere at the Spanish-American Amsterdam Opera House in New York City on 20 December, 1916 and a staged performance with piano in San Francisco in 1974.

Lázaro and Capsir both sang MARINA frequently, the former more or less regularly in Spain from 1929 to 1935. Subsequent performances in Barcelona (1944) and Havana (1950) have also been traced to him.

The Columbia set appears to have been issued in only four countries, on twelve twelve-inch discs in 1929 and 1930. In the U.S., it first appeared as single discs and was only later repackaged as a two-volume album in Columbia's Opera Set series. An abridged six-disc performance of the work, recorded in South America, was issued there as Victor set VM-S5 in the early 1930s. Tenor Miguel Fleta recorded prominent excerpts from it (some with tenor José Palet), most often in ensemble, while Marcos Redondo, featured on the Columbia set, recorded the "Seguidillas" for Spanish Odeon 0-184234; a whole series of late acoustical solos and ensembles were recorded by Palet for HMV in both Italy and Spain.

The conductor of the 1929 complete performance is given as "Monterio" on American Columbia albums, where "Montorio" is cited elsewhere, including an early advertisement in the 1931 Gramophone Shop *Encyclopedia of the World's Best Recorded Music* (second edition), p. 340. The trumpet soloist is given simply as "Álvaro Mont." on American labels.

The only irregularity in the set is side 19, part two of the *Marina-Jorge-Roque* trio, "En las alas del deseo." The original matrix number of this side was WKX 166, take unknown, but all American copies bear the number 294155-1, with the Western Electric "W" prefix. From the sound, this appears to be an electrical dubbing of the original, not a retake, probably made to correct level problems--indeed, Capsir's passages at the end are very forward and may not have passed the wear test on pressings taken from the original master. When or where this dubbing was made is unknown. It can only be assumed that it was of more or less contemporary Spanish origin. This practice was not at all uncommon for Columbia, though such transfers were often effected by their domestic affiliates. In the Kerstin Thorborg/Charles Kullman DAS LIED VON DER ERDE, for example, conducted by Bruno Walter and recorded live at the Vienna Musikvereinsaal on 24 May, 1936, the original matrix of the first part of Thorborg's "Von Schönheit" (CHAX 130-1) was used for the English Mahler Society issues of the set and possibly on European pressings as well, while all American copies used a domestic dubbing of this side (XCO-23381-1 on Columbia 11056-D), probably to correct some technical flaw in the original recording. It remains to be seen if the Spanish, Argentinian, or Italian issues used the original matrix for side 19 of the MARINA.

EJS 494: "The Golden Age of Opera" (1 LP)
Issued January, 1970
MATRIX P-2052

SIDE 1 (494 A) - SIDE 2 (494 B):

LE CHÂTEAU À TOTO (Offenbach) (F)
Operetta in 3 acts (complete)
Orchestra and Chorus of the Office de Radiodiffusion Télévision Française [ORTF], Paris/Marcel Couraud
ORTF broadcast, Paris, date unknown

CAST:
Raymond Amade (*Toto*); Dominique Tirmont (*Crecy-Crecy*); Jacques Pruvost (*Pitou*); Aimé Doniat (*Massepain*); Monique Stiot (*Catherine*); Lina Dachary (*Jeanne*); Linda Felder (*The Viscountess*).

SIDE 2 (494):

L'ÎSLE DE TULIPATAN (Offenbach) (F)
Operetta in 1 act (complete)
Orchestra and Chorus of the Office de Radiodiffusion Télévision Française [ORTF], Paris/Marcel Cariven
ORTF broadcast, Paris, 3 Mar 1958
CAST:
Dominique Tirmont (*Cacatois XXII*); Jacques Pruvost (*Romboidal*); Lina Dachary (*Alexis*); Denise Benoit (*Theodorine*); Joseph Peyron (*Hermosa*).

NOTES: EJS 494

The dialogue has been removed from both of these performances for timing purposes. Note that LE CHÂTEAU À TOTO occupies all of side 1 and the first band of side 2, with L'ÎSLE DE TULIPATAN given complete as the second band of side 2.

The date of LE CHÂTEAU À TOTO remains a mystery. Conductor Marcel Couraud is mistakenly given as the conductor of L'ÎSLE DE TULIPATAN on the label of EJS 494. René Lenoty and a singer with the surname Dassy are assigned a place in the cast of L'ÎSLE DE TULIPATAN in at least one source, but their roles and their participation could not be documented elsewhere. Possibly this was a second broadcast using most, but not all, of the cast presented in the listing above.

EJS 495: "The Golden Age of Opera" (1 LP)
Issued January, 1970
MATRIX P-2033

SIDES 1-2 (495 A-B):

LE ROI L'A DIT (Delibes) (F)
Opera in 3 acts (abridged)
Orchestra and Chorus of the Office de Radiodiffusion Télévision Française [ORTF], Paris/Tony Aubin
ORTF broadcast, Paris, date unknown

CAST:
Bernard Demigny (*Marquis de Moncontour*); Janine Capderou (*Marquise de Moncontour*); Monique Stiot (*Philomele*); ? (*Chimene*); Claudine Collart (*Javotte*); ? (*Mathilde*); ? (*Angelique*); Joseph Peyron (*Benoit*); ? (*Miton*); ? (*Pacome*); Lucien Huberty (*Baron de Merlussac*); ? (*Gautru*); ? (*Marquis de Flarembel*); ? (*Marquis de la Bluette*).

NOTES: EJS 495

This performance is presented nearly complete, the Overture and Entr'Acts having been omitted, along with numbers 15 and 16 of Act III and all of the spkoen dialogue. A few internal cuts in other numbers have been made throughout the score. It is not known whether these were performance cuts or timing cuts, but it seems unlikely that the Overture and the original dialogue were not performed.

Several label misspellings have been corrected in the listing above.

The playing speed for the LP appears to be about 32.6 rpm.

SPECIAL RELEASE
Edison Foundation STE 100
Issued January, 1970
MATRIX STE 100 A & B

"GIOVANNI MARTINELLI / TENOR / (1885-1969)"

SIDE 1:

1. RICHARD BEBB, speaker: Introduction

* 2. w. orch/?: TOSCA, Act I: Recondita armonia (Puccini) (I)
1215-S1 London, July, 1912 Edison 82018
82036

* 3. w. orch/?: TOSCA, Act III: E lucevan le stelle (Puccini) (I)
1216-S1, S2 London, July, 1912 Edison 82505
82036

* 4. w. orch/?: LA BOHÈME, Act I: Che gelida manina (Puccini) (I)
1229-S1, S2 London, July, 1912 Edison 82515

* 5. w. orch/?: MANON LESCAUT, Act I: Donna non vidi mai (Puccini) (I)
1232-S1, S2 London, July, 1912 Edison 82507

* 6. w. orch/?: RIGOLETTO, Act III: La donna è mobile (Verdi) (I)
1231-S3 London, July, 1912 Edison 82515

* 7. w. orch/?: LA GIOCONDA, Act II: Cielo e mar! (Ponchielli) (I)
1230-S1, S2 London, July, 1912 Edison 83002

SIDE 2:

* 1. w. orch/?: AÏDA, Act I: Celeste Aïda (Verdi) (I)
19047-A West Orange, 13 Feb 1929 Edison 82351 (vertical)
N738-B West Orange, 13 Feb 1929 Edison 47003 (lateral)

* 2. w. orch/?: MARTHA, Act III: M'appari [Ach, so fromm] (Flotow) (I)
19050-A West Orange, 14 Feb 1929 Edison 82351 (vertical)
N741-A West Orange, 14 Feb 1929 Edison 47003 (lateral)

* 3. w. orch/?: I PAGLIACCI, Act I: Recitar! . . . Vesti la giubba (Leoncavallo) (I)
19051-A, B West Orange, 14 Feb 1929 Edison unpub (vertical)
N742-A West Orange, 14 Feb 1929 Edison unpub (lateral)

* 4. w. orch/?: LA GIOCONDA, Act II: Cielo e mar! (Ponchielli) (I)
19068-A, B West Orange, 2 Mar 1929 Edison unpub (vertical)
N759-B West Orange, 2 Mar 1929 Edison unpub (lateral)

* 5. w. pf/Joseph Furgiuele: FRANCESCA DA RIMINI, Act III: Perchè volete voi (Zandonai) (I)
Private recording, New York City, 23 November, 1968

NOTES: STE 100

The last issue advertised in the January, 1970 bulletin was this special LP prepared under the auspices of the Thomas Alva Edison Foundation, numbered STE 100. This is one of the few "special" issues to actually receive extensive bulletin advertising during the run of the "The Golden Age of Opera" series.

The LP contained the first and last recordings of Martinelli's career: the six issued Edison Diamond Discs he recorded in London in 1912, four of the 1929 Edison electricals, only two of which had been issued on shellac, and the "Perchè volete voi" from Zandonai's FRANCESCA DA RIMINI, recorded especially for the Edison Foundation on 23 November, 1968. The latter, subsequently issued on UORC 105 (January, 1972), was Martinelli's final record, made less than three months before his death in New York on 2 February, 1969 (he was the first to sing *Paolo* at both Covent Garden and the Met, in 1914 and 1916, respectively). An opening address, originally scheduled to be given (and recorded) by Martinelli himself, is spoken on his behalf by actor Richard Bebb, the tenor's long-time friend and an associate of Edward J. Smith. The LP was a joint venture of the Thomas Alva Edison Re-Recording Laboratory at Syracuse University, New York, and the Edison National Historical Site, West Orange, New Jersey, though Smith, too, was instrumental in its production. This disc could be purchased directly from Smith with the other "Golden Age of Opera" LPs offered that month, but all profits went to the Edison Foundation. A special decorative flyer was issued with the January, 1970 bulletin alongside a publication price list for other LPs and open-reel tapes available from the Edison Foundation.

Fortunately this LP, which is very rare in its original form, was reissued complete in 1975 as Mark 56 722, and repackaged a year later as part of the oddly-titled Murray-Hill set "First Recorded Opera" M60084 (M-50712), issued in the U.S. by Outlet Book and Publisher's Central Bureau.

Side 1:

There is some doubt as to the date of Martinelli's first recordings, made for Edison in London: July, 1912 has been largely accepted as accurate. The preceding matrices, 1202-1208, were recorded in New York between 19 August and 3 September of that year; the block that followed, from 1233, began in New York on 4 September, 1912. More than likely, the London block of matrices, 1209-1232, was simply allotted, and recorded out of sequence.

Bands 1-3: The takes used here could not be determined.

Band 1: Bebb reads Martinelli's prepared address, beginning: "These words were approved by Maestro Martinelli shortly before his death. As an old friend and admirer, I've been asked to read them for him."

Band 2: Martinelli's first published recording. A cylinder voice trial, consisting of phrases from the IL TROVATORE "Di quella pira" and the "Cujus animam" from Rossini's STABAT MATER, preceded them on 21 May, 1912. Edison 82018 was coupled with Charles Hackett's 1912 New York recording of "Then You'll Remember Me" from THE BOHEMIAN GIRL (matrix 1258).

Band 3: My own copy of Edison 82055, coupled with the Venetian Instrumental Quartet, bears the etched matrix number 1216-*18* in mirror image.

Band 4: Take S2 seems to have been the only one passed: original copies of the the disc bear the etched matrix number 1229-2.

Band 5: Edison 82507 was coupled with Reed Miller's "Siciliana" from CAVALLERIA RUSTICANA (matrix 2007).

Band 6: My own copy of Edison 82515 bears the etched matrix number 1231-*10*.

Band 7: Edison 83002 was coupled with Carmen Melis' "Dir che ci sono al mondo" from ZAZÀ (matrix D124), recorded in New York on 31 January or 3 February, 1910: both Melis takes S3 and S4 were used for this coupling, and were the earliest Diamond Disc masters actually issued.

Side 2:

Martinelli's rare 1929 Edison electricals were approved for issue both as paper-label Diamond Discs and as black-label lateral pressings (Edison "thins"). Multiple takes of bands 1 and 2 may have been issued.

Bands 1-2: Later issued on OASI 596, a Martinelli recital.

Band 3: The vertical and lateral takes A and the vertical take B were approved but not issued. It is not known which survived for use here.

Band 4: The lateral take B and vertical takes A and B were approved, but none of these was issued. Take A is known to have been used for this transfer of the "Cielo e mar," however.

Band 5: At 33.3 rpm the aria is sung a whole-step below score pitch, a likely transposition considering the date and circumstances of the recording.

EJS 496: "The Golden Age of Opera" (3 LPs)
Issued February, 1970
MATRIX: P-2063 / P-2064 / P-2065

SIDES 1-6 (496 A-F):

DER ROSENKAVALIER (R. Strauss) (G)
Opera in 3 acts (complete)
Metropolitan Operea House Orchestra and Chorus/Artur Bodanzky
Metropolitan Opera broadcast, 5 Feb 1938

CAST:
Kerstin Thorborg (*Octavian*); Lotte Lehmann (*Marschallin*); Emanuel List (*Baron Ochs*); Suzanne Fisher (*Sophie*); Friedrich Schorr (*Faninal*); Doris Doe (*Annina*); Angelo Bada (*Valzacchi*); Nicholas Massue (*Italian Singer*); Dorothee Manski (*Marianne*); [Madeleine Leweck (*Negro Boy*)]; Hans Clemens (*Marshcallin's Major-Domo*); Natalie Bodanya (*Orphan*); Lucielle Browning (*Orphan*); Anna Kaskas (*Orphan*); Thelma Votipka (*Milliner*); Max Altglass (*Animal Vendor*); [Sergei Temoff (dancer) (*Hairdresser*)]; Arnold Gabor (*Notary*); Ludwig Burgstaller (*Leopold*); Karl Laufkoetter (*Faninal's Major-Domo*); Karl Laufkoetter (*Innkeeper*); Norman Cordon (*Police Commissioner*).

NOTES: EJS 496

Complete as performed, save for the loss of few measures at each change of actetate. Speeds vary throughout the entire performance (not radically) and most everything seems to be a bit sharp at 33.3 rpm. A range of 32.7 (most of Act III) to perhaps 33.0 rpm seems appropriate.

EJS 497: "The Golden Age of Opera" (2 LPs)
Issued February, 1970
MATRIX: P-2070 / P-2071

SIDES 1-4 (497 A-D):

ADRIANA LECOUVREUR (Cilèa) (I)
Opera in 4 acts (complete)
Orchestra and Chorus of the Teatro San Carlo di Napoli/Mario Rossi
Broadcast, Teatro San Carlo, Naples 28 Nov 1959

CAST:
Magda Olivero (*Adriana Lecouvreur*); Franco Corelli (*Maurizio*); Giulietta Simionato (*The Princess de Bouillon*); Ettore Bastianini (*Michonnet*); Antonio Cassinelli (*Prince de Bouillon*); Mariano Caruso (*Abbe di Chazeuil*); Rosanna Zerbini (*Mlle. Jouvenot*); Anna di Stasio (*Mlle. Dangeville*); Augusto Frati (*Quinault*); Renato Ercolani (*Poisson*); ? (*Major-Domo*).

NOTES: EJS 497

This very well-known performance has been issued countless times since the appearance of EJS 497, usually in considerably better sound: on LP as MRF 47, Melodram MEL 043, Cetra Documents DOC 19, Replica 2454/56, HOPE 246, and Morgan MOR 5901; and on CD, as Melodram 27009.

EJS 498: "The Golden Age of Opera" (1 LP)
Issued February, 1970
MATRIX P-2072

SIDE 1 (498 A) - SIDE 2 (498 B):

JEAN DE PARIS (Boieldieu) (F)
Opera in 2 acts (complete)
L'Ensemble Madrigal and the Orchestra of of the Office de Radiodiffusion Télévision Française [ORTF], Paris/Jean-Paul Kreder
ORTF broadcast, Paris, date unknown

CAST:
Joseph Peyron (*Jean*); Denise Boursin (*The Princess*); Monique Stiot (*Lorenza*); Henri Gui (*The Seneschal*); Gérard Friedmann (*Olivier*); Aimé Doniat (*Pedrigo*).

SIDE 2 (498 B):

LE SERPENT À PLUMES (Delibes) (F)
Opera in 1 act (excerpts)
Orchestra and Chorus of the Office de Radiodiffusion Télévision Française [ORTF], Paris/M. Martignoni
ORTF broadcast, Paris, date unknown

CAST:
Florence Raynal (*Mme. Croquesac*); Monique Stiot (*Mariette*); Gaston Rey (*M. Croquesac*); Philippe Andrey (*Beau Mignon*); Joseph Peyron (*Isidore*); René Lenoty (*The Savant*).

NOTES: EJS 498

The dialogue has been omitted from both performances for purposes of timing. The Boieldieu occupies all of side 1 and the first band of side 2, with the Delibes excerpts as band 2 of the second side. The extent to which the LE SERPENT A PLUMES has been excerpted here (or abridged) could not be determined.

EJS 499: "The Golden Age of Opera" (2 LPs)
Issued March, 1970
MATRIX: P-2090 / P-2091

SIDE 1 (499 A):

TRISTAN UND ISOLDE (Wagner) (G)
Opera in 3 acts (excerpts)
Metropolitan Opera House Orchestra and Chorus/Artur Bodanzky
Metropolitan Opera broadcast, NYC, 3 Mar 1933

CAST:
Lauritz Melchior (*Tristan*); Frida Leider (*Isolde*); Maria Olszewska (*Brangäne*); Friedrich Schorr (*Kurvenal*); James Wolfe (*Steersman*); [Ludwig Hofmann (*King Mark*)]; [Arnold Gabor (*Melot*)]; [Hans Clemens (*A Shepherd*)]; [Hans Clemens (*A Young Sailor*)].

* 1. Act I: a) WOLFE, LEIDER, OLSZEWSKA, SCHORR, and MELCHIOR: Wehe'! Ach wehe, mein Kind! . . . Was wohl erwiedertest du?
b) LEIDER and OLSZEWSKA: Fluch dir, Verruchter! . . . Wie magst du dich betören, nicht hell zu sehn noch hören!
c) OLSZEWSKA, LEIDER, SCHORR, MELCHIOR, and Chorus: Kennst du der Mutter Künste nicht? . . . Ehrfurcht hielt mich in acht

2. Act II: a) LEIDER: Dem Freund zu lieb erfand diese List . . . nun willst du den Treuen schelten?
b) LEIDER and OLSZEWKA: Besser als du sorgt er für mich . . . die sie webt aus Lust [und Leid]

SIDE 2 (499 B):

TRISTAN UND ISOLDE (Wagner) (G)
Opera in 3 acts (excerpts)
Metropolitan Opera House Orchestra and Chorus/Artur Bodanzky
Metropolitan Opera broadcast, NYC, 11 Mar 1933

CAST:
Lauritz Melchior (*Tristan*); Frida Leider (*Isolde*); Maria Olszewska (*Brangäne*); Gustav Schützendorf (*Kurvenal*); James Wolfe (*Steersman*); Ludwig Hofmann (*King Mark*); Arnold Gabor (*Melot*); Hans Clemens (*A Shepherd*); Hans Clemens (*A Young Sailor*).

* 1. Act I: a) Orchestra: Prelude (one-minute fragment *in progress*)
b) LEIDER and OLSZEWSKA: Nimmermehr! Nicht heut' nicht Morgen! . . . zerschlag' es [dies trotzige Schiff]
c) WOLFE, LEIDER, OLSZEWSKA, SCHÜTZENDORF, and MELCHIOR: Wehe'! Ach wehe, mein Kind! . . . Was wohl erwiedertest du?
d) LEIDER and OLSZEWSKA: Fluch dir, Verruchter! . . . Welch eitles Zürnen?
e) LEIDER, OLSZEWSKA, SCHÜTZENDORF, MELCHIOR, and Chorus: Der Mutter Rat gemahnt mich recht . . . Herr Tristan trete nah (with orchestral passage preceding Tristan's "Begehrt, Herrin, was Ihr wünscht")

SIDE 3 (499 C):

1. Act II: a) MELCHIOR and LEIDER: Soll der Tag noch Tristan wecken? . . . O süsse Nacht . . . erhabne Liebesnacht!
b) MELCHIOR and GABOR: Der öde Tag zum Letzten mal . . . Das sollst du, Herr, mit sagen ob [ich ihn recht verklagt] (with orchestral passage preceding Tristan's first lines)
c) HOFMANN: Die kein Himmel erlöst, warum mir diese Hölle? Die klein Elend sühnt, warum mir diese Schmach?
d) MELCHIOR: aus Eifer verreit mich der Freund . . . to the end of act

* 2. Act III: MELCHIOR and SCHÜTZENDORF: [Ich] war wo ich von je gewesen . . . was je sich Minne gewinnt!

SIDE 4 (499 D):

1. Act III: MELCHIOR, SCHÜTZENDORF, LEIDER, WOLFE, CLEMENS, OLSZEWSKA, GABOR, and HOFMANN: Und Kurwenal, wie? Du sähst sie nicht? . . . Mild und leise . . . to the end of the opera

NOTE: EJS 499

In addition to its detailed analysis of these rare 1933 performances, David Hamilton's article, "Tristan in the Thirties: Part I and Part II" (*Musical Quarterly*, 6/4, Fall, 1976, pp. 19-24; 7/2, Spring, 1977, pp. 6-19) also summarizes the standard score cuts used at the Met (and by Bodanzky) through 1935 (Part I, p. 22): these are given in the endnotes for EJS 157 (June, 1959). Hamilton also notes that, in addition to the acetate breaks necessitated by his single recording machine, the *dentist* who recorded these early broadcasts off-the-air had to stop whenever he had a patient! (Part I, pp. 21-22). But comparing these to the 1934 TRISTAN excerpts issued on EJS 502, it has also been suggested that a TRISTAN buff, in pursuit of favorite passages which he or she especially preferred, was at work here, eager to record these parts of the score from any and all sources--unlike many early off-the-air enthusiasts, many of whom tended simply to record excerpts not available on commercial recordings. Smith's account of the source of these transcriptions is a bit different still (see the endnote for EJS 487 from November, 1969). The March, 1970 EJS bulletin, again using that favorite Smith expression, notes that the broadcasts "date from the *foetal* days of recording," by which he meant off-the-air recording presumably. The surface noise on both of these 1933 TRISTANs is overwhelming.

The entire LP seems to have been transferred about a half-step below score pitch.

Side 1 (499 A):

Band 1c: An acetate break omits the *Isolde-Kurvenal* section, "für ungebüsste Schuld die böt' . . . nun harrt, wie er mich hört!"

Side 2 (499 B):

Band 1c: An acetate break omits two sections of this scene: "Sollich ihn bitten, dich zu grüssen? . . . Befehlen liess' dem Eigenholde" and "[getreulich dein' ich ihr] der Frauen höchster Ehr' . . . liess ich das [Steuer]."

Side 3 (499 C):

Band 2: An acetate break omits ". . . mein mit leidest du . . . Dies furchtbare Sehnen."

EJS 500: "The Golden Age of Opera" (2 LPs)
Issued March, 1970
MATRIX: P-2098 / P-2099

SIDES 1-4 (500 A-B):

AÏDA (Verdi) (I)
Opera in 4 acts (complete)
Metropolitan Opera House Orchestra and Chorus/Wilfred Pelletier
Metropolitan Opera broadcast, NYC, 6 Mar 1943

CAST:
Lansing Hatfield (*The King of Egypt*); Bruna Castagna (*Amneris*); Zinka Milanov (*Aïda*); Giovanni Martinelli (*Radames*); Norman Cordon (*Ramfis*); Richard Bonelli (*Amonasro*); John Dudley (*A Messenger*); Frances Greer (*Priestess*).

NOTES: EJS 500

The March, 1970 bulletin notes that "The recordings used for the dubbing came from Rio de Janeiro and were in superb condition." Taken from original NBC actetates, the end of the performance includes a bit of the curtain calls narrated by the *Spanish* announcer used by NBC to preside over line checks destined for eventual re-braodcast in South America, which explains the Rio connection.

This performance was excerpted on EJS 326 (March, 1962) and later appeared complete as Cetra LO 26.

Speeds are irregular, requiring a range of speeds of about 33.3 rpm to 34.5 rpm.

EJS 501: "The Golden Age of Opera" (2 LPs)
Issued March, 1970
MATRIX: P-2092 / P-2097

SIDES 1-4 (501 A-D):

DIE WALKÜRE (Wagner) (G)
Opera in 3 acts (excerpts)
Metropolitan Opera House Orchestra and Chorus/Artur Bodanzky
Metropolitan Opera broadcast, NYC, 3 Feb 1934

CAST:
Paul Althouse (*Siegmund*); Gertrude Kappel (*Sieglinde*); Frida Leider (*Brünnhilde*); Ludwig Hofmann (*Wotan*); Karin Branzell (*Fricka*); Emanuel List (*Hunding*); Dorothee Manski (*Helmwige*); Phradie Wells (*Gerhilde*); Margaret Halstead (*Ortlinde*); Ina Bourskaya (*Rossweise*); Philine Falco (*Grimgerde*); Doris Doe (*Waltraute*); Elda Vettori (*Siegrune*); Irra Petina (*Schwertleite*).

SIDE 1 (501 A):

Act I: 1. a) ALTHOUSE, KAPPEL, and LIST: Begining of the opera . . . mein Wort hörtest du hüte dich wohl!
* b) ALTHOUSE (Metropolitan Opera House Orchestra/Artur Bodanzky): Ein Schwert verhiess mir der Vater
Metropolitan Opera broadcast, NYC, 2 Feb 35

Act II: * 2. LEIDER (Royal Opera House Orchestra/Wilhelm Furtwängler): Hojotoho!
Broadcast, Covent Garden, London, 1 June, 1938

SIDE 2 (501 B):

Act II: 1. LEIDER and HOFMANN: Schlimm, fürcht' ich . . . den Freien erlang' ich mir nicht!

SIDE 3 (501 C):

Act II: 1. a) LEIDER: So sah ich Siegvater nie . . . through the first measures of the orchestral passage between Scenes ii and iii.
b) LEIDER and ALTHOUSE: Orchestral introduction to the *Todesverkundigung*, Scene iv . . . Zu Walvater, der dich gewählt, führ' ich dich: Nach Walhall [folgst du mir]

Act III: 1. a) LEIDER, HALSTEAD, DOE, VETTORI, BOURSKAYA, MANSKI, PETTINA, FALCO, and KAPPEL: Schützt mich und helft in höchster Not! . . . Siegfried erfreu' sich des Sieg's!
b) KAPPEL, HOFMANN, HALSTEAD, DOE, VETTORI, BOURSKAYA, MANSKI, PETTINA, FALCO, and LEIDER: Dir, Treuen dank' ich heiligen Trost! . . . Wo ist Brünnhild'? Wo die Verbrecherin?
c) HALSTEAD, DOE, VETTORI, BOURSKAYA, MANSKI, PETTINA, FALCO, LEIDER, and HOFMANN,: Weh! Weh! Schwester! O schwester! . . . War es so schmählich . . . zähme die Wuth, und deute mir hell die dunk[le Schuld]

SIDE 4 (501 D):

Act III: 1. LEIDER and HOFMANN: [War ist so schmählich . . . zu verstossen] dein trautestes Kind! . . . Leb' wohl, du kühnes . . . to the end of the opera

NOTES: EJS 501

Playing speeds hover around 32.6 - 32.7 rpm until the line "Der augen leuchtendes Paar" in *Wotan's* Farewell on side 4, where it ascends suddenly to 33.1 rpm, rising gradually to 33.3 rpm and remaining variable through the end of the opera.

Note the matrix gap (P-2092 and P-2097) for this set.

Side 1 (501 A):

Band 1b: Althouse's "Ein Schwert," taken from the 2 February, 1935 Met broadcast, had appeared earlier on EJS 444 (October, 1968) along with the surviving portions of Act II from the same performance. The complete Act I of 2 February, 1935 was issued as EJS 200 (December, 1960). Conducted by Bodansky, this was Flagstad's Met debut.

Band 2: Leider's "Hoyotoho!" was taken from the 1 June, 1938 Covent Garden performance, originally issued on EJS 170 (January, 1960), where it included *Wotan's* and *Fricka's* lines before and after the solo.

EJS 502: "Golden Age of Opera" (1 LP)
Issued March, 1970
MATRIX P-2100

TRISTAN UND ISOLDE (Wagner) (G)
Opera in 3 acts (excerpts)
Metropolitan Opera House Orchestra and Chorus/Artur Bodanzky
Metropolitan Opera broadcast, NYC, 6 Jan 1934

CAST:
Lauritz Melchior (*Tristan*); Gertrude Kappel (*Isolde*); Doris Doe (*Brangäne*); Friedrich Schorr (*Kurvenal*); James Wolfe (*Steersman*); [Ludwig Hofmann (*King Mark*)]; [Arnold Gabor (*Melot*)]; [Hans Clemens (*A Shepherd*)]; [Hans Clemens (*A Young Sailor*)].

SIDE 1 (502 A):

1. Act I: a) WOLFE, KAPPEL, and DOE: Weh'! Ach wehe, mein Kind! . . . Furcht der Herrin ich, Isolde
b) KAPPEL and DOE: Fluch dir, Verruchter! . . . Wie magst du dich betören, nicht hell zu seh'n noch hören!
* c) KAPPEL, DOE, SCHORR, and MELCHIOR: Kennst du der Mutter Künste nicht? . . . gegen sein eigen Gemahl?

SIDE 2 (502 B):

1. Act II: KAPPEL, DOE, and MELCHIOR: [Dem Freund] zu Lieb erfand diese List . . . An meiner Brust!
2. Act III: * a) MELCHIOR and SCHORR: [doch, was ich sah,] das kann ich dir nicht sagen . . . was je Minne sich gewinnt!
   b) DOE and KAPPEL: Hörst du uns nicht? . . . Mild und leise . . .to the end of the opera

NOTES: EJS 502

The label of EJS 502 identifies all of the principals, but Hofmann, Gabor, and Clemens are not heard in these excerpts, as shown in the cast listing above.

Side 1 (502 A):

Band 1c: This excerpt begins in Scene iii. An acetate break omits *Isolde's* "Nun leb' wohl, Brangäne! . . . Grüss' mir die Welt, grüsse mir Vater und Mutter!" and *Brangäne's* "Was ist's? Was sinnst du?"

Side 2 (502 B):

Band 2a: An acetate break omits *Tristan's* ["nur was ich leide,] das kannst du nicht leiden!"

EJS 503: **"The Golden Age of Opera" (2 LPs)**
Issued March, 1970
MATRIX P-2504 / P-2505

SIDES 1-4 (503 A-D):

I LOMBARDI [ALLA PRIMA CROCIATA] (Verdi) (I)
Opera in 4 acts (complete)
Orchestra and Chorus of the Teatro dell'Opera, Roma/Gianandrea Gavazzeni
Broadcast, Teatro dell'Opera, Rome, 20 Nov 1969

CAST:
Renata Scotto (*Giselda*); Luciano Pavarotti (*Oronte*); Ruggero Raimondi (*Pagano*); Umberto Grilli (*Arvino*); Anna Di Stasio (*Viclinda*); Mario Rinaudo (*Pirro*); Fernando Jacopucci (*Prior of Milan*); Alfredo Colella (*Acciano*); Sofia Mezzetti (*Sofia*).

NOTES: EJS 503

The broadcast date given above has been taken from Scotto's autobiography: December, 1969 has also been reported, but could not be verified.

This performance has been reissued on LP (MRF 48 and Robin Hood RHR 519-C) and more recently on CD (Verona 27081/2 and Legato Classics LCD 148-2).

A more or less uniform playing speed of 32.4 rpm has been suggested for EJS 503.

EJS 504: "The Golden Age of Opera" (2 LPs)
Issued April, 1970
MATRIX P-2118 / P-2119

LOHENGRIN (Wagner) (G)
Opera in 3 acts (excerpts)
Metropolitan Opera House Orchestra and Chorus/Artur Bodanzky
Metropolitan Opera broadcast, NYC, 24 Mar 1934

CAST:
Lauritz Melchior (*Lohengrin*); [Ludwig Hofmann (*King Henry*)]; Elisabeth Rethberg (*Elsa*); [Gustav Schützendorf (*Telramund*)]; Maria Olszewska (*Ortrud*); [George Cehanovsky (*Herald*)].

SIDES 1-3 (504 A-C):

Act I: a) RETHBERG: Einsam in trüben Tagen [Elsa's Dream"]
b) MELCHIOR: Nun sei bedankt, mein lieber Schwan

Act II: c) RETHBERG: Euch Lüften, die mein Klagen
d) RETHBERG and OLSZEWSKA: Du Ärmste kannst wohl nie ermessen

Act III: e) RETHBERG and MELCHIOR: Das süsse Lied verhallt . . . Einsam, wenn Niemand wacht nie sei der Welt er zu Gehör gebracht!
f) MELCHIOR: Atmest du nicht mit mir die süssen Düfte
g) MELCHIOR: In fernem Land . . . Mein lieber Schwan

TANNHÄUSER (Wagner) (G)
Opera in 3 acts (excerpts)
Metropolitan Opera House Orchestra and Chorus/Artur Bodanzky
Metropolitan Opera broadcast, NYC, 12 Jan 1935

CAST:
Lauritz Melchior (*Tannhäuser*); [Ludwig Hofmann (*Hermann*)]; Richard Bonelli (*Wolfram*); Hans Clemens (*Walther*); Arnold Gabor (*Biterolf*); [Giordano Paltrinieri (*Heinrich*)]; James Wolfe (*Reinmar*); Maria Müller (*Elisabeth*); Dorothee Manski (*Venus*); Lillian Clark (*Shepherd*).

SIDE 4 (504 D):

1. Act II: BONELLI, MELCHIOR, CLEMENS, GABOR, MÜLLER, and Chorus: Blick'ich umher . . . In seinen Sünden fahr'er hin! (before Elisabeth's "Zurück von ihm!")

2. Act III: a) BONELLI: Wohl wusst' ich hier . . . O! würd'ihr Lind'rung nur ertheilt!
b) MÜLLER: [Allmächt'ge Jungfrau] . . . rufe ich! Lass mich im Staub . . . nur anzufleh'n für seine Schuld!
c) BONELLI: Wie Todesahnung . . . O du mein holder Abenstern (orchestral postlude to scene omitted)
d) MELCHIOR, BONELLI, MANSKI, CLEMENS, CLARK, GABOR, WOLFE, and Chorus: Hör'an, Wolfram! Hör'an! . . . Inbrunst im Herzen ["Rome Narrative"] . . . to the end of the opera

NOTES: EJS 504

The April, 1970 bulletin notes that the TANNHÄUSER excerpts were transcribed during a severe thunder storm, accounting by implication for the unusually poor sound. Roughly thirteen minutes of Act II are included and twenty-four of Act III, all that was "available for saving," according to Smith. The original air checks were probably recorded at 33 1/3 rpm, hence the poor sound. There are short gaps in the continuity throughout, corresponding to the original side breaks. The Act III excerpts end just short of the opera's finale, in the midst of the concluding chorus.

Bonelli's "Blich'ich umher" is included in the forthcoming Delos International/Stanford Arvive of Recorded Sound Bonelli CDs, DE-5504 and DE-5505.

EJS 505: "The Golden Age of Opera" (2 LPs)
Issued April, 1970
MATRIX P-2120 / P-2121

SIDES 1-4 (505 A-D):

FOSCA (Gomes) (I)
Opera in 4 acts (complete)
Orchestra and Chorus of the Teatro Municipal, São Paulo/Armando Belardi
Broadcast, Teatro Municipal, São Paulo, 14 Sep 1966

CAST:
Ida Miccolis (*Fosca*); Sergio Albertini (*Paolo*); Costanzo Mascitti (*Cambro*); Agnes Ayres (*Delia*); Mario Rinaudo (*Gajolo*); Roman Carillo (*Michele Giotto*); José Perotta (*The Doge of Venice*).

NOTES: EJS 505

This performance is in approximate score pitch at 33.3 rpm. Later reissued on three LPs as VOCE-81.

EJS 506: "The Golden Age of Opera" (1 LP)
Issued April, 1970
MATRIX P-2122

SIDES 1-2 (506 A-B):

SALOME (R. Strauss) (G)
Opera in 1 act (abridged)
Metropolitan Opera House Orchestra and Chorus/Artur Bodanzky
Metropolitan Opera Broadcast, NYC, 10 Mar 1934

CAST:
Max Lorenz (*Herod*); Dorothee Manski (*Herodias*); Göta Ljungberg (*Salome*); Friedrich Schorr (*Jokanaan*); Hans Clemens (*Narraboth*); Doris Doe (*Page*); Emanuel List (*Nazarene*); Hans Clemens (*Nazarene*); Marek Windheim (*A Jew*); Giordano Paltrinieri (*A Jew*); Angelo Bada (*A Jew*); Max Altglass (*A Jew*); James Wolfe (*A Jew*); Louis D'Angelo (*A Soldier*); Arnold Gabor (*A Soldier*); Alfredo Gandolfi (*Cappadocian*); Helen Gleason (*A Slave*).

NOTES: EJS 506

This broadcast came from the Met's revival season of Strauss' SALOME, the premiere of the production having been mounted on 13 January, 1934. The original Met premiere (the first American performance of the opera) was conducted by Alfred Hertz on 22 January, 1907 and featured Olive Fremstad, Marion Weed, Karel Burrian, and Anton Van Rooy, and though a critical triumph, it proved a "moral" fiasco, resulting in the banishment of the work from that house for more than a quarter of a century.

The 10 March, 1934 performance is transcribed here nearly complete, save for acetate breaks and the deliberate omission of the "Dance of the Seven Veils" for purposes of timing. There is only one notable performance cut, in the scene where *Salome* and *Herod* dispute the substitution of *Jokanaan's* head.

Side 1 plays in pitch at 34.4 rpm, while side 2, beginning at *Herod's* "Es ist vorüber. Horch! Hört Ihr es nicht?" (no. 69 in the full score), plays at 33.3 rpm.

Considering its date, the recording is remarkably good. The PAGLIACCI performed on the same Saturday afternoon bill was issued as EJS 260 in February, 1963.

EJS 507: "The Golden Age of Opera" (1 LP)
Issued April, 1970
MATRIX P-2123

SIDE 1 (507 A) - SIDE 2 (507 B):

LA FALCE (Catalani) (I)
Opera in 1 act (complete)
Orchestra of the Radio Italiana [RAI], Milano/Ferruccio Scaglia
RAI broadcast, Milan, 7 Feb 1970

CAST:
Antonietta Cannarile (*Zohra*); Luigi Infantino (*Seid*).

SIDE 2 (507 B):

2. ?Orchestra of the Radio Italiana [RAI]/Edoardo Brizio: IL REGGENTE: Overture (Mercadante)
   ?RAI broadcast, place and date unknown

3. MARIA LUISA BARDUCCI, soprano (?Orchestra of the Radio Italiana [RAI]/Edoardo Brizio): IL REGGENTE, Act I: Si, d'amor, d'amore insano" (Mercadante) (I)
   ?RAI broadcast, place and date unknown

4. GIOVANNI CIMINELLI, baritone (Orchestra of the Radio Italiana [RAI]/ Edoardo Brizio): IL REGGENTE, Act III: Muoia! Su questa fronte . . . Nuova ferita (Mercadante) (I)
   ?RAI broadcast, place and date unknown

NOTES: EJS 507

The labels of EJS 507 give Cannarile as "Cannarile Berdini" and Barducci as "Mana" Luisa Barducci. LA FALCE occupies all of side 1 and the first band of side 2; the IL REGGENTE excerpts are found as the second, third, and fourth bands of side 2.

LA FALCE, libretto by Boïto, was Catalani's first opera (1875). A complete IL REGGENTE from a 1970 Siena performance appeared in December of that year as EJS 528.

EJS 508: "The Golden Age of Opera" (1 LP)
Issued May, 1970
MATRIX P-2140

SIDES 1-2 (508 A-B):

TOSCA (Puccini) (G)
Opera in 3 acts (excerpts)
Source and date unknown

CAST:
?Carla Martinis (*Tosca*); ?Rudolf Schock (*Cavaradossi*); ?Joseph Metternich (*Scarpia*).

NOTES: EJS 508

Labeled as Ljuba Welitsch (*Tosca*), Helge Roswaenge (*Cavaradossi*), and Joseph Metternich (*Scarpia*), conducted by Rudolph Moralt, Berlin Staatsoper, 1946, but neither Welitsch or Roswaenge are present. Metternich, on the other hand, may have been the *Scarpia* here. The May, 1970 bulletin goes so far as to rave about Roswaenge's upper register which, it is said, "rings like a bell"! See William J. Collins, "Rosvaenge on LP," *The Record Collector*, 25/5&6 (August, 1979), p. 133. The other singers featured (*Spoletta*, *Sciarrone*, and the *Sacristan*) are not given on the label of EJS 508 and could not be determined.

EJS 509: "The Golden Age of Opera" (1 LP)
Issued May, 1970
MATRIX P-2141

LA BOHÈME (Puccini) (I)
Opera in 4 acts (excerpts)
Metropolitan Opera House Orchestra and Chorus/Gennaro Pappi
Metropolitan Opera broadcast, NYC, 13 Jan 1938

CAST:
Bruno Landi (*Rodolfo*); Grace Moore (*Mimi*); Carlo Tagliabue (*Marcello*); Muriel Dickson (*Musetta*); George Cehanovsky (*Schaunard*); Ezio Pinza (*Colline*); [Louis D'Angelo (*Benoit*)]; [Louis D'Angelo (*Alcindoro*)]; [Max Altglass (*Parpignol*)]; [Carlo Coscia (*Sergeant*)].

SIDE 1 (509 A):

Act I: 1. a) Orchestral introduction to the opera to the entrance of Marcello
* b) LANDI, MOORE, CEHANOVSKY, PINZA, and TAGLIABUE: Non sono in vena . . . Che gelida manina . . . Si, Mi chiamano Mimi . . . to the end of the act

Act II: 2. a) LANDI, PINZA, TAGLIABUE, and CEHANOVSKY: Due posti . . . Io non dò che un accessit!
b) DICKSON, TAGLIABUE, D'ANGELO, and MOORE: Quando m'en vo soletta per la via . . . Quella gente che dirà?

Act III: * 3. TAGLIABUE, MOORE, and LANDI: Mimi? Speravo di trovarvi qui . . . Addio! Che vai?

SIDE 2 (509 B):

Act III: 1. MOORE, LANDI, TAGLIABUE, and DICKSON: Donde lieta usci . . . to the end of the act

Act IV: * 2. a) TAGLIABUE and LANDI: In un coupé . . . O Mimi, tu più non torni
b) TAGLIABUE, DICKSON, LANDI, CEHANOVSKY, MOORE, and PINZA: Musetta! . . . C'è Mimi che mi segue e che sta male . . . Vecchia zimarra, senti . . . to the end of the opera

NOTES: EJS 509

Side 1 (509 A):

Band 1b: Another, unidentified source featuring Moore's *Mimi* was used for the passage "[il primo bacio dell' aprile è] mio! . . . Germoglia in un vaso una rosa" in the "Si, Mi chiamano Mimi," from the sound of it, probably a studio recording.

Landi sings "Che gelida manina" down the customary half step. Similarly, *Mimi's* "V'aspettan gli amici" is preceded by a half-step modulation downward, observed through the end of the act.

Band 3: There is a six-measure break from the *Marcello-Mimi* "[Che far dunque? O mia] *vita*!" to *Mimi's* last "Ahimè, morir!." This break also consumes the orchestral passage leading up to *Rodolfo's* "Che? Mimi! Tu qui?"

Side 2 (509 B):

Band 2: The original performance acetates end just before the last line of the *Rodolfo-Marcello* duet: this, and the orchestral postlude, have been inserted from another, unidentified source on EJS 509.

EJS 510: "The Golden Age of Opera" (1 LP)
Issued May, 1970
MATRIX P-2142

SIDES 1 (510 A):

RITA [ou LE MARI BATTU] (Donizetti) (F)
Opera in 1 act (complete)
Orchestra of the Office de Radiodiffusion Télévision [ORTF], Paris/Pierre-Michel LeConte
Recorded at the ORTF Studios, Paris, 12 Dec 1968 for ORTF broadcast, date unknown

CAST:
Odile Pietti (*Rita*); Bernard Demigny (*Gasparo*); Joseph Peyron (*Beppe*).

SIDE 2 (510 B):

UNE ÉDUCATION MANQUÉE (Chabrier) (F)
Operetta in 1 act (?complete)
Orchestra of Radio Svizzera-Italiana/Edwin Loehrer
Broadcast, Radio Svizzera-Italiana, place and date unknown

CAST:
Jean-Christophe Benoit (*Maître Pausanias*); Annalies Gamper (*Gontran de Boismassif*): Monique Linval (*Hélène de la Cerisale*).

NOTES: EJS 510

The dialogue and narration for the Chabrier operetta were omitted from EJS 510. A different performance of UNE ÉDUCATION MANQUÉE later appeared on MRF-187.

EJS 511: "The Golden Age of Opera" (1 LP)
Issued May, 1970
MATRIX P-2143

SIDES 1-2 (511 A-B):

OLD CHELSEA (Richard Tauber and Bernard Gruhn) (E)
Operetta (excerpts)
?BBC Studio Orchestra/Serge Krisch
Broadcast, BBC, London, 7 May 1943

CAST:
Richard Tauber (*Jacob Bray*); Carole Lynne (*Mary Fenton*); Nancy Browne (*Nancy Gibbs*); Betty Percheron (*Christine*); Charles Hawtrey (*Peter Crawley*); Marie O'Neill (*Mistress Murphy*); Francis Robert (*Lord Randeleigh*); Warde Morgan (*Sir Percy Chudleigh*); Elisabeth Aveling (*Lady Walgrave*); C. Jarvis Walker (*Sir Roger Woodville*); Ester Moncrieff (*Countess Stafford*); Edward Stirling (*Narrator*).

NOTES: EJS 511

Tauber's operetta made its debut in Birmingham in September, 1942 and enjoyed a lengthy run at the Prince's Theater, London, beginning on 17 February, 1943. In all, there were some 700 performances of the work. Tauber, Lynne, Brown, and Hawtrey were among the original cast members. This BBC adaptation is thought to be incomplete, but without a score, it is difficult to tell. Note that a majority of the cast members are actors, not singers, and so will be listed in the INDEX OF ARTISTS simply as "vocalists" in deference to the present circumstances.

EJS 512: "The Golden Age of Opera" (1 LP)
Issued May, 1970
MATRIX EJS 512 A & B

"GIOVANNI MARTINELLI RECITAL NO. 3"

SIDE 1 (512 A):

IL TROVATORE (Verdi) (I)
Opera in 4 acts (excerpts)
Metropolitan Opera House Orchestra and Chorus/Gennaro Pappi
Metropolitan Opera broadcast, NYC, 4 Mar 1939

CAST:
Zinka Milanov (*Leonora*); Giovanni Martinelli (*Manrico*); Bruna Castagna (*Azucena*); Richard Bonelli (*Count di Luna*).

Act I: * 1. MARTINELLI, MILANOV, and BONELLI: Anima mia . . . to the end of the scene

Act II: * 2. MARTINELLI and CASTAGNA: Mal reggendo . . . selvaggio ed eremo . . . to the end of the scene

Act III: * 3. MARTINELLI and Chorus: Ah! sì, ben mio . . . Di quella pira

Act IV: * 4. MARTINELLI, MILANOV, and CASTAGNA: Parlar non vuoi

* 5. w. JOSEPHINE ANTOINE, soprano (Metropolitan Opera House Orchestra and Chorus/Ettore Panizza): UN BALLO IN MASCHERA, Act I: La rivedrà nell' estasi (Verdi) (I)
Metropolitan Opera broadcast, NYC, 28 February, 1942

* 6. w. JOSEPHINE ANTOINE, soprano (Metropolitan Opera House Orchestra and Chorus/Ettore Panizza): UN BALLO IN MASCHERA, Act I: Di tu se fedele (Verdi) (I)
Metropolitan Opera broadcast, NYC, 28 February, 1942

* 7. w. JOSEPHINE ANTOINE, soprano (Metropolitan Opera House Orchestra and Chorus/Ettore Panizza): UN BALLO IN MASCHERA, Act III: Forse la soglia attinse . . . Ma se m'è forza perderti (Verdi) (I)
Metropolitan Opera broadcast, NYC, 28 February, 1942

* 8. w. Metropolitan Opera House Orchestra and Chorus/Ettore Panizza: NORMA, Act I: Meco all'altar di Venere (Bellini) (I)
Metropolitan Opera broadcast, NYC, 20 February, 1937

SIDE 2 (512 B):

* 1. w. ELISABETH RETHBERG, soprano (Metropolitan Opera House Orchestra/Ettore Panizza): SIMON BOCCANEGRA, Act I: Vieni a mirar la cerula (Verdi) (I)
Metropolitan Opera broadcast, NYC, 16 February, 1935

* 2. w. EZIO PINA, bass (Metropolitan Opera House Orchestra/Ettore Panizza): SIMON BOCCANEGRA, Act I: Propizio ei giunge . . . Vieni a me, ti benedico (Verdi) (I)
Metropolitan Opera broadcast, NYC, 16 February, 1935

* 3. w. Vitaphone Symphony Orchestra/Herman Heller: I PAGLIACCI, Act I: Recitar! . . . Vesti la giubba (Leoncavallo) (I)
from the soundtrack of the one-reel Warner Brothers-Vitaphone short ***GIOVANNI MARTINELLI, TENOR OF THE N.Y. METROPOLITAN OPERA COMPANY IN "VESTI LA GIUBBA" FROM THE OPERA "I PAGLIACCI" BY LEONCAVALLO*** (1926), New York, ?21 June, 1926
Vitaphone Varieties 198
MP 3836; c12 Mar 1927
Premiere: Warners' Theater, NYC, 6 Aug 1926

* 4. w. Vitaphone Symphony Orchestra/Herman Heller: "Torna a Surriento" (G. Paghara-De Curtis) (I)
from the soundtrack of the one-reel Warner Brothers-Vitaphone short ***GIOVANNI MARTINELLI SINGING "COME BACK TO SORRENTO" [AND] "NINA"*** (1931), Hollywood, circa 1930-1931
Vitaphone Varieties 1213
MP ?2312; ?c5 Feb 1931

* 5. w. Vitaphone Symphony Orchestra/Herman Heller: "Nina" (Tanara-de Leva) (I)
from the soundtrack of the one-reel Warner Brothers-Vitaphone short ***GIOVANNI MARTINELLI SINGING "COME BACK TO SORRENTO" [AND] "NINA"*** (1931), Hollywood, circa 1930-1931
Vitaphone Varieties 1213
MP ?2312; ?c5 Feb 1931

* 6. w. pf/?: "Santa Lucia" (Cottrau) (I)
from the soundtrack of a one-reel Paramount newsreel ["Say it With Song"], Children's Aid Society benefit, New York, circa 1934.
Paramount [Sound] News
Copyright Registration information unknown

* 7. w. pf/Boris Goldovsky: LA GIOCONDA, Act III: Già ti veggo (Ponchielli) (I)
Metropolitan Opera broadcast, ***INTERMISSION FEATURE***, NYC, 2 Apr 1955

8. w. pf/Joseph Furgiuele: LUISA MILLER, Act II: Quando le sere al placido (Verdi) (I)
Private recording, 1958

9. w. pf/? and unidentified pupil: RIGOLETTO, Act II: Ella mi fu rapita (Verdi) (I)
   Private recording, teaching session, London, 1964

* 10. w. pf/Joseph Furgiuele: AÏDA, Act I: Il sacro suolo (Verdi) (I)
   Private recording, New York, circa winter, 1968

* 11. unaccompanied: OTELLO, Act IV: Niun mi tema, s'anco armato mi vede (Verdi) (I)
   Private recording, lecture, May, 1968

NOTES: EJS 512

Side 1 (512 A):

Bands 1-4: The "Di quella pira" from this TROVATORE was later recycled on UORC 197 (March, 1974), but the entire performance is not known to have survived. Acetate breaks omit *Leonora* (Milanov) and *Ruiz* (Giordano Paltrinieri) from the "Ah! si, ben mio" (I/3).

Bands 5-7: The complete 28 February, 1942 BALLO (missing only a few orchestral passages) was issued as EJS 136 in November, 1958. The "Non sai tu" from Act I surfaced later on UORC 255 (June, 1975), as did several excerpts on ANNA 1031 (May-June, 1979).

Band 8: The 20 February, 1937 NORMA was issued complete as EJS 113 in 1957. The "Meco all'altar" and "In mia man" have appeared on various Smith issues.
Library of Congress tape: 15731-89A (complete broadcast).

Side 2 (512 B):

Bands 1-2: This SIMON BOCCANEGRA was issued complete without the Prologue as EJS 177 in April, 1960; the Prologue was issued separately on UORC 161 (June, 1973). Excerpts have appeared on various Smith issues. See also the endnote for EJS 177.

Band 3: From the first Vitaphone show, accompanying the debut of the John Barrymore feature, "Don Juan." The short proved so successful that it was subsequently recycled throughout the late 1920s and early 1930s. The original program for the 6 August show is said to credit the accompaniment to the New York Philharmonic conducted by Henry Hadley, but this seems unlikely: the New York Philharmonic has been documented only as having been featured in their own shorts, not in an accompanying role for other artists--if for no other reason that the prohibitive expense: 80 of the regular 107 players were used, at a cost to the studio of $900.00 an hour. In any event, this claim could not be substantiated.

The original PAGLIACCI disc bears the recording date 21 June, 1926 in the wax; a "Matrix" number 300107; "M 200," the meaning of which is unknown; "Rec. #33," probably designating the playing speed; the fader (e.g. volume control) setting "V +9;" and the singer's name.

Band 4-5: This short also featured the Albertieri Dancers in Rossini's "La Danza." The film was not copyrighted under the title given in the listing: this may be the short copyrighted as *MARTINELLI No. 2*, MP 2312 on 5 February, 1931. It is certainly a post-1930 release, as it carries the "Brunswick Radios Used Exclusively" logo on the title card (Warner's assumed control of Brunswick in April, 1930). The premiere date is not known.

Band 6: This has been reported variously as a sequence from a circa 1934 *Paramount [Sound] News* newsreel, depicting a fund-raiser for New York's Children's Aid Society, and a 1934 Children's Aid Society broadcast (see William J. Collins' Martinelli discography in *The Record Collector*, 25/7-9, October, 1979, p. 195). No appearances by Martinelli corresponding to such a benefit could be traced between 1928 and 1941 but the newsreel, bearing the *sequence* title "Say it With Song" and the dateline New York, is in circulation on video. No copyright information for the newreel itself could be found. In the original film Martinelli is seen on stage in long shot surrounded by children; this brief sequence is announced by Gregory Abbott and the song itself is first sung by the children. Only one verse of "Santa Lucia" is sung, ending in a medium closeup shot of Martinelli.

Band 7: This Met *Intermission Feature* was heard during the broadcast of the Zinka Milanov-Kurt Baum-Leonard Warren GIOCONDA of 2 April, 1955.

Band 10: Smith claimed that he made every attempt to assemble a recording of the *Messenger's* scene with Martinelli (in the role in which he made his unofficial debut in 1908) with Del Monaco as *Radames*, Simionato as *Amneris*, Siepi as the *King*, and Tebaldi in the title role. Exclusive recording contracts, he further claimed, prevented him from doing so. A version with full orchestra and chorus was also contemplated, but this piano-accompanied version was the final result. It is one of Martinelli's last recordings (he died on 2 February, 1969). In correspondence of April, 1968, Smith mentions that Martinelli "has now finished his recording" of the AÏDA scene, along with a FANCIULLA "Una parola sola" not issued on GAO, and a RONDINE aria later issued on EJS 566 in June, 1971.

Band 11: Only the opening lines (as given) of *Otello's* death are sung. Labeled "Last public singing, May, 1968" on EJS 512. Taken from a lecture, this is *not* Martinelli's last recording, however: that distinction seems to belong to the FRANCESCA DA RIMINI "Perchè volete voi" first issued in January, 1970 on STE 100 (see the endnote for that issue between GAO 495 and 496), recorded in New York City on 23 November, 1968.

EJS 513: The Golden Age of Opera" (1 LP)
Issued May, 1970
MATRIX EJS 513 A & B

"FILM POTPOURRI"

SIDE 1 (513 A):

* 1. ERNESTINE SCHUMANN-HEINK, contralto (pf/Josefin H. Vollmer; Vitaphone Symphony Orchestra/Herman Heller): Der Erlkönig," D. 328 (Goethe-Schubert) (G)
from the soundtrack of the one-reel Warner Brothers Vitaphone short ***MME. ERNESTINE SCHUMANN-HEINK a) DER ERLKÖNIG (GERMAN) b) TREES c) PIRATE DREAMS /JOSEFIN H. VOLLMER--AT THE PIANO*** (1927), New York, circa 1927
Vitaphone Varieties 568
MP 4163; c18 Jul 1927
Premiere: Warners' Theater, NYC, 15 Aug 1927

* 2. ERNESTINE SCHUMANN-HEINK, contralto (pf/Josefin H. Vollmer): "Trees" (Joyce Kilmer-Oscar Rasbach) (E)
from the soundtrack of the one-reel Warner Brothers Vitaphone short ***MME. ERNESTINE SCHUMANN-HEINK a) DER ERLKÖNIG (GERMAN) b) TREES c) PIRATE DREAMS /JOSEFIN H. VOLLMER--AT THE PIANO*** (1927), New York, circa 1927
Vitaphone Varieties 568
MP 4163; c18 Jul 1927
Premiere: Warners' Theater, NYC, 15 Aug 1927

* 3. MARIA CEBOTARI, soprano, and EZIO PINZA, bass (Wiener Philharmoniker/Karl Böhm): DON GIOVANNI, K. 527, Act I: [Là ci darem la mano] Vorrei e non vorrei (Mozart) (I)
from the soundtrack of a European film documentary, title unknown, Salzburg Festival (rehearsal), July, 1938

* 4. NINO MARTINI, tenor (orch/?): L'ELISIR D'AMORE, Act II: Una furtiva lagrima (Donizetti) (I)
Source and date unknown

5. BENIAMINO GIGLI, tenor and speaker; MARIELLA GUIDOTTA, interviewer (unaccompanied):
a) Interview on how to sing a Neapolitan Song (I)
b) "O sole mio" (fragments) (Capurro-di Capua) (I)
c) Unidentified folk song in the style of a street urchin (I)
Broadcast, ***FESTA DI PIEDIGROTTA***, RAI, Naples, 14 Sep 1952

* 6. CHARLES HACKETT, tenor (pf/?): DON GIOVANNI, K. 527, Act II: Il mio tesoro (Mozart) (I)
from the soundtrack of the one-reel Warner Brothers Vitaphone short ***CHARLES HACKETT SINGING "IL MIO TESORO INTANTO" [and] "O PARADISO"*** (1929), New York, circa 1929
Vitaphone Varieties 916
MP 881; c25 Nov 1929
Premiere: unknown, circa 1929

* 7. CHARLES HACKETT, tenor (pf/?): L'AFRICAINE, Act IV: Mi batte il cor . . . O Paradiso! [Pays merveilleux . . . Ô Paradis] (Meyerbeer) (I)
from the soundtrack of the one-reel Warner Brothers Vitaphone short ***CHARLES HACKETT SINGING "IL MIO TESORO INTANTO" [and] "O PARADISO"*** (1929), New York, circa 1929
Vitaphone Varieties 916
MP 881; c25 Nov 1929
Premiere: unknown, circa 1929

* 8. CHARLES HACKETT, tenor, and ROSA LOW, soprano (Vitaphone Symphony Orchestra/Herman Heller): ROMÉO ET JULIETTE, Act V: C'est là! Salut! tombeau! . . . to the end of the opera (Gounod) (F)
from the soundtrack of the one-reel Warner Brothers Vitaphone short ***CHARLES HACKETT AND ROSA LOW / ROMÉO ET JULIETTE TOMB SCENE*** (?1930), New York, circa 1930
Vitaphone Varieties 1143
MP ?; copyright date unknown
Premiere: unknown, circa 1930

* 9. JOHN CHARLES THOMAS, baritone (pf/?) "Danny Deever," Op. 2, no. 7 (Kipling-Damrosch) (E)
from the soundtrack of the one-reel Warner Brothers Vitaphone short ***JOHN CHARLES THOMAS, OUTSTANDING AMERICAN BARITONE, SINGING A: "DANNY DEEVER" B: "IN THE GLOAMING"*** (1927), New York, 1927
Vitaphone Varieties 493
MP 3964; c19 Apr 1927
Premiere: New York City, 23 Apr 1927

SIDE 2 (513 B):

* 1. GIUSEPPE DE LUCA, baritone (Vitaphone Symphony Orchestra/Herman Heller): IL BARBIERE DI SIVIGLIA, Act I: Largo al factotum (Rossini) (I)
from the soundtrack of the one-reel Warner Brothers Vitaphone short ***GIUSEPPE DE LUCA, OF THE METROPOLITAN OPERA COMPANY, AS FIGARO, SINGING "LARGO AL FACTOTUM" FROM "THE BARBER OF SEVILLE"*** (1927), New York, circa 1927
Vitaphone Varieties 488
MP 3979; c6 May 1927
Premiere: ?Colony Theater, NYC, 14 May 1927

* 2. FRANCES ALDA, soprano (pf/?): MARTHA, Act II: The Last Rose of Summer [Letzte Rose] (Flotow) (E)
from the soundtrack of the one-reel Warner Brothers Vitaphone short ***MME. FRANCES ALDA SINGING THE LAST ROSE OF SUMMER AND BIRTH OF MORN*** (?1929), New York, circa 1929
Vitaphone Varieties 805
MP 588; c30 Aug 1929
Premiere: unknown, circa 1929

* 3. FRANCES ALDA, soprano (pf/?): "Birth of Morn" (Paul Lawrence Dunbar-Franco Leone) (E)
from the soundtrack of the one-reel Warner Brothers Vitaphone short ***MME. FRANCES ALDA SINGING THE LAST ROSE OF SUMMER AND BIRTH OF MORN*** (?1929), New York, circa 1929
Vitaphone Varieties 805
MP 588; c30 Aug 1929
Premiere: unknown, circa 1929

* 4. FRANCES ALDA, soprano (pf/Frank La Forge; organ/Dr. Clarence Dickinson): OTELLO, Act IV: Ave Maria piena di grazia (Verdi) (I)
from the soundtrack of the one-reel Warner Brothers Vitaphone short ***MME. ALDA SINGING "AVE MARIA" BY VERDI*** (?1930), New York, circa 1930
Vitaphone Varieties 943
MP 1188; c17 Feb 1930
Premiere: unknown, circa 1930

* 5. ROSA RAISA, soprano (pf/?): "Plaisir d'amour" (Claris de Florian-G. Martini) (F)
from the soundtrack of the one-reel Warner Brothers Vitaphone short ***MME. RAISA OFFERS "PLAISIR D'AMOUR" (JOYS OF LOVE) - PADRE G. MARTINI / "LA PALOMA" - S. YRADIER*** (1928), New York, circa 1928
Vitaphone Varieties 2546
MP 5052; c2 Jun 1928
Premiere: New York City, 8 Jul 1928

* 6. ROSA RAISA, soprano (pf/?): "La Paloma" (Sebastian Yradier) (S)
from the soundtrack of the one-reel Warner Brothers Vitaphone short ***MME. RAISA OFFERS "PLAISIR D'AMOUR" (JOYS OF LOVE) - PADRE G. MARTINI / "LA PALOMA" - S. YRADIER*** (1928), New York, circa 1928
Vitaphone Varieties 2546
MP 5052; c2 Jun 1928
Premiere: New York City, 8 Jul 1928

* 7. ROSA RAISA, soprano, and GIACOMO RIMINI, baritone (Vitaphone Symphony Orchestra/Herman Heller): IL TROVATORE, Act IV: Udiste? Come albeggi . . . Mira, di acerbe lagrime . . . Vivrà! Contende il giubilo (Verdi) (I)
from the soundtrack of the one-reel Warner Brothers Vitaphone short ***ROSA RAISA, SOPRANO, AND GIACOMO RIMINI, BARITONE, OF THE CHICAGO OPERA COMPANY IN SELECTION FROM ACT IV OF "IL TROVATORE"*** (1927), New York, circa 1927
Vitaphone Varieties 524
MP 4120; c29 Jun 1927
Premiere: New York City, 6 Jun 1927

NOTES: EJS 513

Despite the title given to this LP, the Martini ELISIR aria (I/4) has not been verified as a soundtrack excerpt. The majority of the selections were taken from Vitaphone shorts, but it should be made clear that these dubbings were made from noisy optical prints, not from the original 12- and 16-inch soundtrack discs. Accordingly, a few of the items presented are virtually unlistenable. See the **INTRODUCTION** for a brief summary of the Warner Brothers-Vitaphone short subjects.

Side 1 (513 A):

Bands 1-2: The third selection sung in this 1927 short was "Pirate Dreams" (Louise A. Garnet-Charles Huerter), issued by Smith on EJS 563 in June, 1971. Schumann-Heink recorded all three songs electrically for Victor. The introduction to "Erlkönig" is played first by the orchestra, then repeated by Vollmer, who accompanies thereafter. "Trees" is accompanied by piano only.

This short premiered during the run of the Warner Brothers feature "Old San Francisco."

Band 3: This rehearsal begins at the second part of the duet. Taken from a German or Austrian film documentary on the 1938 Salzburg Festival, this sequence has turned up on videoptape, so could at least be verified as a soundtrack excerpt.

Band 4: This "Una furtiva lagrima" could not be found among the songs and arias performed in Martini's feature films: "Paramount on Parade" (Paramount, 1929); "Here's to Romance" (Fox, 1935), "The Gay Desperado" (Pickford-Lasky-United Artists, 1936), "Music for Madam (RKO, 1937), and "One Night With You" (Two Cities-Universal, 1948). However, for some of these films, only contemporary reviews and published decriptions could be consulted. By 1970, Smith had demonstrated access only to "Music for Madam" (see EJS 171) and gives the date of the "Una furtiva lagrima" as 1937 in the May bulletin, but the only operatic aria Martini sang in that film was the "Vesti la giubba."

Bands 6-7: This short begins with the pianist playing the introduction to the aria. Hackett walks onto the set, puts down his hat and coat, and begins singing--as if late in arriving!

Band 8: This film was apparently not submitted for copyright. The "Brunswick Radios Used Exclusively" notice in the credits suggests a post-April, 1930 release (Warner Brothers assumed control of Brunswick in April, 1930).

Rosa Low's surname appears as "Bow" on EJS 513. She claimed to be a protégée of baritone Victor Maurel and made her professional debut at Aeolian Hall, New York City, in 1924. Thereafter she was a featured member of the Washington and Philadelphia Civic Opera Companies and the San Carlo Opera.

Band 9: This Thomas short most likely made its debut at the New York City and Brooklyn Strand Theaters alongside the Warner Brothers feature "The Better 'Ole" (the program advertised an accompanying "Vitaphone Concert"). Less likely, but possible, is that it was added to the bill of the John Barrymore feature "When a Man Loves" at the Colony Theater.

Side 2 (513 B):

Band 1: The premiere date is taken from a contemporary Vitaphone schedule but could not be verified beyond that. The short seems to have premiered during the run of the Warner Brothers feature "The Missing Link."

Bands 2-3: Given here is the title under which this short was copyrighted. "Birth of Morn," from the poem "Dawn," one of Dunbar's *Lyrics of Lowly Life* from 1896, is titled "An Angel Robed" on EJS 513--the first words of the text.

Band 4: Pianist La Forge and organist Dickinson (both frequent studio accompanists for Victor) are cited in a mid 1950s Associated Artists Productions distribution catalog, *Programs of Quality from the Quality Studio, Warner Brothers* (New York: aap, Inc., circa 1957), but not in the film's credits. The original Vitaphone release schedule suggests that the short was best suited for Easter, Lent, Christmas, and New Years, and that ". . . Mme. Alda's name has tremendous box-office value. Her recent retirement from opera to devote her talents to radio broadcasting has gained world-wide publicity." Cast in a convent setting rather than *Desdemona's* bed chamber (hence the omission of OTELLO from the title), Alda appears attired in a habit, surrounded by strolling nuns!

Bands 5-6: Raisa's male accompanist is seen throughout the short, but has not been identified and is not credited on the title card. The short made its New York City premiere either at the Warner's Theater alongside "The Lion and the Mouse," or at the Mark Strand with "The Lights of New York," Warner's first all-talking feature.

Band 7: This short probably made its debut at the Colony Theater in New York City alongside the "The Missing Link," which was advertised as having an additional "Vitaphone Concert" on the bill. It was eventually recycled to accompany "The Terror" at the Warners' Theater on 16 August, 1928.

EJS 514: "The Golden Age of Opera" (2 LPs)
Issued June, 1970
MATRIX P-2162 / P-2163

SIDES 1-4 (514 A-D):

LES ABENCÉRAGES or L'ÉTENDARD DE GRENADE (Cherubini) (I)
Opera in 3 acts (complete)
Orchestra and Chorus of the Maggio Musicale Fiorentino/Carlo Maria Giulini
Broadcast, Maggio Musicale Fiorentino, Teatro Comunale, Florence, May, 1957

CAST:
Anita Cerquetti (*Noraima*); Louis Roney (*Almansor*); Alvinio Misciano (*Consalvo*); Mario Petri (*Alemar*); Paolo Washington (*Alamir*); Aborian [Aurelian] Neagu (*Alderren*); Valiano Natali (*Kaled*); Lydia Forcelli (*Ezilora*); Augusto Frati (*Octair*); Carla Caravita (*Maid*); Maria Bertolini (*Maid*); Lorenzo Testi (*?*).

NOTES: EJS 514

Cherubini's 1813 opera is given here in Italian as GLI ABENCERRAGI. This performance, from the first modern revival of the work, was subsequently reissued complete as Cetra LO 66 (dated incorrectly as 1956) and MRF 52. The Cerquetti chronology included in Timaclub recital Tima 23 mentions that the first of three performances of the ABENCERRAGI was given on 9 May, 1957. Neagu is labeled "Magu;" Lydia Forcelli could not be verified, but she is given as Lydia "Toncelli" on the MRF 52 release.

The EJS 514 transfer is slightly flat at 33.3 rpm.

EJS 515: "The Golden Age of Opera" (2 LPs)
Issued June, 1970
MATRIX ?P-2171 / P-2172

DER FLIEGENDE HOLLÄNDER (Wagner) (G)
Opera in 3 acts (excerpts)
London Philharmonic Orchestra, and Chorus of the Royal Opera House/ Fritz Reiner
Unpublished live performance recordings (HMV):
a) Technical Test Series 6544-1/18, Covent Garden, London, 7 Jun 1937
b) Technical Test Series 6545-1/23, Covent Garden, London, 11 Jun 1937

CAST (7 and 11 June, 1937):
Ludwig Weber (*Daland*); Kirsten Flagstad (*Senta*); Max Lorenz (*Erik*); Mary Jarred (*Mary*); Ben Williams (*Steersman*); Herbert Janssen (*Holländer*).

SIDE 1 (515 A):

Act I: 1. JANSSEN and Chorus: Die Frist is um . . . Ew'ge Vernichtung, nimm mich auf!

2. JANSSEN, WEBER, WILLIAMS, and Chorus: Weit komm' ich her . . . Sogleich die Anker lichten wir

SIDE 2 (515 B):

Act II: * 1. FLAGSTAD, JARRED, and Chorus: Introduction . . . Summ' und brumm' . . Traft ihr das Schiff . . . Hilf Himmel! Senta!

SIDE 3 (515 C):

Act III: * 1. WEBER, FLAGSTAD, and JANSSEN: Mein Kind, du siehst mich auf der Schwelle . . . Mögst du, mein Kind . . . to the end of the act

SIDE 4 (515 D):

Act III: 1. WILLIAMS and Chorus: Steuermann, lass' die Wacht! . . . So nehmt, der Nachbar hat's verschmäht!

2. LORENZ, FLAGSTAD, JANSSEN, JARRED, WEBER, and Chorus: Was musst' ich hören? Gott! . . . to the end of the opera

NOTES: EJS 515

Three performances of DER FLIEGENDE HOLLÄNDER, all conducted by Fritz Reiner, were given at Covent Garden in June, 1937. The casts for the first two (7 and 11 June) were identical, but for the third, on 16 June, Adolph Vogel replaced Ludwig Weber as *Daland*, and Torsten Ralf replaced Max Lorenz as *Erik*. The London Philharmonic served as the pit orchestra during for 1936-1938 Covent Garden season.

HMV recorded 18 sides from the 7 June performance (Technical Test Series 6544-1/18), 23 sides from 11 June (Technical Test Series 6545-1/23), and three sides from 16 June (Technical Test Series 6546-1/3). Between 10 August and 17 September, 1937, a composite performance taken from the 7 and 11 June recordings was assembled by HMV engineers: none of the three sides taken from 16 June was included. The first act of 11 June was the only segment broadcast from the three performances.

Excerpts from this performance were first issued on the single-disc EJS 123 (circa 1958). The original HMV side divisions of the excerpts are not known, but matrix information is available: see the lengthy endnote for EJS 123 for a full accounting of the original HMV technical tests and transfer matrices. Smith notes in the June, 1970 bulletin that the sound and pitch problems of the original issue, EJS 123, have been corrected here, but while the sound is noticeably better, pitch varies over the course of the four sides, which range in speed from 33.3-34.7 rpm. Excerpts have also appeared on HRE 234, Recital Records RR 469, Rococo 1008 and most recently, on a Legato Classics CD, Standing Room Only SRO 808-1. Legendary LR 120 and Orpheum 8404 included only Flastad's "Traft ihr das Schiff."

A last matrix number, 2EA 5619-1, transferred from Technical Test Series 6543-1, is cited in the EMI books as "Der Fliegende Holländer," but this is in fact the first side of the 1 June, 1937 Covent Garden GÖTTERDÄMMERUNG, conducted by Furtwängler (Technical Test Series 6543), transferred circa 11-13 August, 1937 to matrices 2EA 5619-1 - 2EA 5646-1. This GÖTTERDÄMMERUNG was issued on EJS 431 (April, 1968). See also the endnote for EJS 431.

Side 2 (515 B):

Band 1: There are fluctuations in pitch between some of the test sides of the *Senta's* Ballad.

Side 3 (515 C):

Band 1: The original test recordings (as well as the tapes from which Smith prepared his issues) contained *Senta's* preceding line, "Treue ihm Ha!," but this was omitted from both EJS 123 and EJS 515.

EJS 516: The Golden Age of Opera" (1 LP)
Issued June, 1970
MATRIX P-2164

SAMSON ET DALILA (Saint-Saëns) (F)
Opera in 3 acts (excerpts)
Metropolitan Opera House Orchestra and Chorus/Maurice De Abravanel
Metropolitan Opera broadcast, NYC, 26 Dec 1936

CAST:
René Maison (*Samson*); Gertrude Wettergren (*Dalila*); Ezio Pinza (*High Priest*); Emanuel List (*Old Hebrew*); [John Gurney (*Abimelech*)]; [Angelo Bada (*Philistine Messenger*)]; Max Altglass (*Philistine*); Wilfred Engelman (*Philistine*).

SIDE 1 (516 A):

1. Act I: a) MAISON: Arrêtez! ô mes frères!
b) PINZA, ALTGLASS, and ENGELMAN: Que vois-je? . . . Maudites à jamais
c) WETTERGREN, MAISON, and LIST: Je viens célébrer la victoire . . . Printemps qui commence
2. Act II: WETTERGREN and PINZA: Prelude . . . Amour! viens aider ma faiblesse! . . . Mort au chef des hebreux!

SIDE 2 (516 B):

1. Act II: MAISON and WETTERGREN: En ces lieux . . . Mon coeur s'ouvre à ta voix . . . to the end of the act

* 2. Act III: MAISON, PINZA, WETTERGREN, and Chorus: Vois ma misère, hélas! . . . to the end of the opera

NOTES: EJS 516

Several of the excerpts included here appeared variously on EJS 170 (January, 1960), EJS 186 (July-August, 1960), and EJS 213 (May, 1961).

The Act III Chorus, "L'aube qui blanchit" and the orchestral "Bacchanale" were omitted from EJS 516.

Library of Congress tape: 5174-30 (complete broadcast).

EJS 517: "The Golden Age of Opera" (1 LP)
Issued June, 1970
MATRIX P-2165

SIDES 1-2 (517 A-B):

DICHTER UND BAUER [POET AND PEASANT] (Von Suppé) (G)
Opera in 3 acts (excerpts)
?"Volkner" Orchestra and Chorus of Radio Linz/Dr. Leopold Mayer
Source and date unknown

CAST:
Friedrich Nidetzky (*Stanislov*); Rudolph Christ (*Peter*); Antonie [Antonia] Fahberg (*Vervina*); Kurt Toema (*Verbios*); Liselotte Schmidt (*Putzie*); Kurt Schossman (*Zivonimir*); Gertrude Burgstaller (*Marie Teresa*); Hasso Dagner (*Niklaus*); Ernst Zeller (*Ignaz*); Adolf Schmitt-Rahner (*Corporal*).

NOTES: EJS 517

Label misspellings include "Mayr" for conductor Mayer, "Lisa-Lotte" for Schmidt, "Ernest" for Zeller, and "Frederick" for Nidetzky. Other names (Toema, Schossman, Dagner, and Schmitt-Rahner) could not be confirmed: names were often transcribed by Smith direct from radio announcements, which may explain many of these and other frequent misspellings. Nor could the "Volkner" Orchestra could not be confirmed--Linz has no "Volkstheater." "Radio Linz" may be Radio Verkehers AG [RAVAG] or Österreichischer Rundfunk [ORF].

The June bulletin mentions that there was no dialogue, and because the score of POET AND PEASANT is extremely rare, it could not be determined whether the music is complete here or whether the dialogue was simply omitted from the original performance.

EJS 518: "The Golden Age of Opera" (1 LP)
Issued June, 1970
MATRIX P-2166

"FOUR GREAT TENORS"

SIDE 1 (518 A):

* 1. LUCIANO PAVAROTTI, tenor, GABRIELLA TUCCI, soprano, ALDO PROTTI, baritone, and RUGGERO RAIMONDI, bass (Orchestra and Chorus of the Teatro Massimo Bellini, Catania/Argeo Quadri): I PURITANI, Act I: A te, o cara (Bellini) (I)
Broadcast, Teatro Massimo Bellini, Catania, Sicily, 22 Mar 1968

* 2. LUCIANO PAVAROTTI, tenor, and MIRELLA FRENI, soprano (Orchestra and Chorus of Radio Italiana [RAI], Roma/Riccardo Muti): I PURITANI, Act III: Vieni, vieni fra queste braccia (Bellini) (I)
RAI broadcast, Rome, ?7 Oct 69/recorded 8 Jul 1968

* 3. LUCIANO PAVAROTTI, tenor, MIRELLA FRENI, soprano, SESTO BRUSCANTINI, bass, and BONALDO GIAIOTTI, bass (Orchestra and Chorus of Radio Italiana [RAI], Roma/Riccardo Muti): I PURITANI, Act III: Credeasi misera (Bellini) (I)
RAI broadcast, Rome, ?7 Oct 69/recorded 8 Jul 1968

* 4. LUCIANO PAVAROTTI, tenor (Orchestra and Chorus of Radio Italiana [RAI], Roma/Carlo Maria Giulini): STABAT MATER, No. 2: Cujus animam (Rossini) (L)
RAI broadcast, Rome, recorded 22 Dec 1967

* 5. LUCIANO PAVAROTTI, tenor, RENATA SCOTTO, soprano, FERNANDO JACOPUCCI, tenor, GIOVANNI CIAVOLA, bass, and BIANCA BORTOLUZZI, mezzo-soprano (Orchestra of the Teatro dell'Opera, Roma/Carlo Maria Giulini): RIGOLETTO, Act I: Che m'ami! Deh! ripetimi . . . Addio. Addio speranza ed anima (Verdi) (I)
Broadcast, Teatro dell'Opera, Rome, 19 Nov 1966

* 6. FRANCO CORELLI, tenor (Orchestra of the Teatro alla Scala/Antonio Votto): LA VESTALE, Act III: L'alma mia s'abandona al suo furore . . . Ah no! s'io vivo ancora (Spontini) (I)
Broadcast, Teatro alla Scala, Rome, 7 Dec 1954

* 7. FRANCO CORELLI, tenor (Orchestra of the Teatro alla Scala/ Gianandrea Gavazzeni): LA BATTAGLIA DI LEGNANO, Act I: O magnanima e prima . . . La pia materna mano (Verdi) (I)
Broadcast, Teatro alla Scala, Rome, 7 Dec 1961

* 8. FRANCO CORELLI, tenor (orch/?): LE CID, Act III: Ô souverain, ô juge, ô père (Massenet) (F)
Source and date unknown

SIDE 2 (518 B):

* 1. ALFREDO KRAUS, tenor (Orchestra of RAI/?): GUILLAUME TELL, Act IV: O muto asil del pianto [Asile héréditaire] (Rossini) (I)
Source and date unknown

* 2. ALFREDO KRAUS, tenor (Orchestra of RAI/?): GUILLAUME TELL, Act I: Il piccol'legno ascendi (Rossini) (I)
Source and date unknown

* 3. ALFREDO KRAUS, tenor (orch/?): RIGOLETTO, Act II: Possente amor mi chiama (Verdi) (I)
Source and date unknown

* 4. ALFREDO KRAUS, tenor, and UNKNOWN SINGERS (orch/?): LUCIA DI LAMMERMOOR, Act II: Sconsigliato! in queste porte chi ti guida? . . . Esci! fuggi! (Donizetti) (I)
Source and date unknown

* 5. NICOLAI GEDDA, tenor (orch/?): CASTOR ET POLLUX, Act I: Eclatez fières trompettes (Rameau) (F)
Source and date unknown

* 6. NICOLAI GEDDA, tenor (Royal Opera House Orchestra/John Pritchard): BENVENUTO CELLINI, Act III: Seul pour lutter . . . Sur les monts les plus sauvages (Berlioz) (F)
Broadcast, Covent Garden, London, 1966

* 7. NICOLAI GEDDA, tenor (orch/?): LES PÊCHEURES DE PERLES, Act I: Je crois entendre encore (Bizet) (F)
Source and date unknown

NOTES: EJS 518

Many of the selections on this LP, unless otherwise unspecified in the notes below, seem to play in pitch at a uniform 33.7 rpm.

Side 1 (518 A):

Band 1: Extensive excerpts from this March, 1968 PURITANI were issued as Melodram CD MEL 15001.

Bands 2-3: This July, 1968 PURITANI was issued complete on Nuova Era CD 2342/44. A 7 October, 1969 performance with this cast is also given in the RAI chronicles, but 8 July, 1968 is thought to be the correct *recording* date. The duet, transposed down the traditional half-step, rises in pitch at *Elvira's* entrance. Verona CD 27029/31 contains the entire performance, but dated July, 1969.

Band 4: The other soloists featured in this STABAT MATER included contralto Shirley Verrett, bass Nicola Zaccaria, and soprano Teresa Zylis-Gara. The broadcast date could not be determined, only the recording date. The performance was subsequently issued complete as Verona CD 27060/1.

Band 5: The *Borsa*, *Ceprano*, and *Giovanna* are given on a Laserlight Pavarotti CD reissue of this excerpt (15104), the SPA "Gala" equivalent (GL 302), and on a private tape of the complete performance.

Band 6: From the complete performance of LA VESTALE with Maria Callas and Ebe Stignani, later issued as UORC 217 (September, 1974). It has also appeared on the ERR, Cetra, Estro Armonica and Raritas labels. The EJS 518 transfer is in pitch at 33.3 rpm.

Band 7: Plays in score pitch at 34.2 rpm.

Band 8: Corelli never sang the role of *Rodrigue* on the stage, so it is assumed that this was taken from a concert performance. The aria was probably transposed down a half-step (Corelli was notorious for doing so in concert), playing here at a speed of 33.8 rpm.

Side 2 (518 B):

Bands 1-2: These TELL arias are both in pitch at 33.3 rpm and sound as if they were taken from Kraus' commercial Spanish recordings.

Bands 3: This aria sounds as if it was recorded with a hand-held microphone from the audience. Only one verse is given here, in pitch at 33.1 rpm.

Band 4: In pitch at 34.5 rpm. The source, and thus, the other singers present, have not been identified.

Band 5: This aria is the Act I "1er Air pour les [deux] Athlètes," sung here as a solo.

Band 6: Transferred (or performed?) a half-step below score pirch.

Band 7: The recitative is not sung here. At 34.2 rpm, the aria is transposed down a whole step into the key of G minor, the customary transposition being A-flat minor. In any event, a downward transposition seems unlikely for Gedda. The recording is crude, as if taken with a hand-held microphone.

EJS 519: "The Golden Age of Opera" (2 LPs)
Announced June, 1970
MATRIX P-2192

SIDES 1-4 (519 A-D):

ARMIDA (Rossini) (I)
Opera in 3 acts (complete)
Orchestra and Chorus of the Teatro la Fenice, Venezia/Carlo Franci
Broadcast, Teatro la Fenice, Venice, 3 Apr or 16 Jun 1970

CAST:
Cristina Deutekom (*Armida*); Pietro Bottazzo (*Rinaldo*); Edoardo Gimenez (*Gernando*); Eduardo Gimenez (*Ubaldo*); Ottavio Garaventa (*Goffredo*); Ottavio Garaventa (*Carlo*); Bernardino Trotta (*Eustazio*); Giovanni Antonini (*Astarotte*); Alessandro Maddalena (*Idraote*).

NOTES: EJS 519

Announced in the June, 1970 bulletin, but not issued or made available until the following September, Smith claimed that this Italian broadcast was scheduled for 16 June, 1970 and that he hoped to have the discs ready by 23 June! The orders, he promised, would be processed in two days, as he was scheduled to fly to London on 25 June. Possibly the broadcast was pre-recorded on 3 April, another date reported for this performance, or 16 June was a scheduled *re-broadcast*. EJS 519 was also listed in the September bulletin.

EJS 520: "The Golden Age of Opera" (3 LPs)
Issued September, 1970
MATRIX P-2209 / P-2210 / P-2211

SIDES 1-6 (520 A-F):

MITRIDATE, RÈ DI PONTO, K. 87 (Mozart) (I)
Opera in 3 acts (complete as performed)
Orchestra of the Mozarteum, Salzburg/Leopold Hager
Broadcast, Mozarteum, Salzburg, 1970

CAST:
Stanley Kolk (*Mitridate*); Meredith Zara (*Aspasia*); Edith Gabry (*Silfare*); Brigitte Fassbänder (*Farnace*); Ileana Cotrubas (*Ismene*); Peter Baillie (*Marzio*); Reingard Didusch (*Arbate*).

NOTES: EJS 520

This obscure work, Mozart's second opera, and his first *opera seria*, was produced in Milan in December, 1770 when he was 14 years old. The parts of *Sifare* and *Farnace* were originally intended for male soprano and alto, respectively. The extent of the cuts in this performance (which is presented here complete as broadcast, presumably), is unknown.

EJS 521: "The Golden Age of Opera" (3 LPs)
Issued September, 1970
MATRIX P-2217 / P-2218 / P-2219

SIDES 1-6 (521 A-F):

PALESTRINA (Pfitner) (G)
Opera in 3 acts (complete)
Wiener Philharmoniker and Chorus of the Wiener Staatsoper/Robert Heger
Broadcast, Wiener Staatsoper, 16 Dec 1965

CAST:
Fritz Wunderlich (*Giovanni Pierluigi da Palestrina*); Christa Ludwig (*Silla*); Sena Jurinac (*Ighino*); Gottlob Frick (*Pope Pius IV*); Walter Berry (*Giovanni Morone*); Gerhard Stolze (*Bernardo Novagerio*); Walter Kreppel (*Cardinal Christoph Madruscht*); Otto Wiener (*Carlo Borromeo*); Ludwig Welter (*The Cardinal of Lorraine*); Peter Klein (*Abdisu*); Harald Pröglhöf (*Anton Brus von Müglitz*); Robert Kerns (*Count Luna*); Gerhard Unger (*The Bishop of Budoja*); Erich Majkut (*Theophilus of Imola*); Alois Pernerstorfer (*Avosmediano*); Hans Braun (*Bishop Ercole Severolus*); Fritz [Friederich] Sperlbauer (*Dandini von Grossetto*); Kurt Equiluz (*The Bishop of Fiesole*); Ljubomir Pantscheff (*The Bishop of Feltre*) Hans Christian (*A Spanish Bishop*); Dagmar Hermann (*A Young Physician*); Herbert Lackner (*Chapel Singer*); Siegfried Rudolf Frese (*Chapel Singer*); Kurt Equiluz (*Chapel Singer*); Karl Terkal (*Chapel Singer*); Ljubomir Pantscheff (*Chapel Singer*); Hilde Rössl-Majdan (*The Apparition of Lucretia*); Gerhard Unger (*Apparition*); Herbert Lackner (*Apparition*); Karl Terkal (*Apparition*); Ljubomir Pantscheff (*Apparition*); Kurt Equiluz (*Apparition*); Tugomir Franc (*Apparition*); Robert Kerns (*Apparition*); Frederick Guthrie (*Apparition*); Harald Pröglhöf (*Apparition*); Mimi Coertse (*Angelic Voice*); Lucia Popp (*Angelic Voice*); Gundula Janowitz (*Angelic Voice*).

NOTES: EJS 521

The "*Chapel Singers*" listed above are in fact "*Chapel Singers of Santa Maria Maggiore*;" similarly, the "*Apparitions*" are "*Apparitions of Nine Dead Composers*."

Following Act I, unbanded and uncredited, is the "Song of the Woodbird" ("Tauben von Gurre!") from Part I of Schoenberg's GURRELIEDER, sung by Janet Baker, source unknown. This was apparently on the tape from which Smith took the PALESTRINA, and perhaps not knowing the opera well, he assumed that it was part of Pfitzner's 1917 work.

The PALESTRINA was reissued on three CDs as Myto MCD 92259.

The September, 1970 bulletin contains a slightly premature farewell, wherein Smith announces the "final year of permanent releases on the Golden Age of Opera." Actually, there would be eleven more bulletins and more than fifty LPs to follow, but the series did indeed end in November, 1971.

EJS 522: "The Golden Age of Opera" (3 LPs)
Issued October, 1970
MATRIX P-2250 / P-2251 / P-2252

SIDES 1-6 (522 A-F):

LE PROPHÈTE (Meyerbeer) (F)
Opera in 5 acts (complete)
Orchestra and Chorus of Radio Italiana [RAI], Torino/Henry Lewis
RAI broadcast, Turin, 8 Sep 1970 (recorded 10 Jul 1970)

CAST:
Margherita Rinaldi (*Berthe*); Marilyn Horne (*Fides*); Nicolai Gedda (*Jean*); Fritz Peter (*Jonas*); Boris Carmeli (*Mathisen*); Robert Amis El Hage (*Zacharie*); Alfredo Giacomotti (*Count Oberthal*).

Other Soloists: Maria Del Fante; Emma De Santis; Giovanna Di Rocco; Osvaldo Alemanno; Pio Bonfanti; Salvatore Catania; Aronne Ceroni; Mario Chiappi; Sergio Gaspari; Ivo Ingram; Paolo Mazzotta; Antonio Pirino; ?*Fernando* Valentini.

NOTES: EJS 522

No program could be found to place character names with the many singers listed merely as "soloists." These are undoubtedly the *peasants, soldiers, merchants, children, anabaptists, prisoners*, etc., called for in the various acts.

The RAI chronicles give the last singer, Valentini, as baritone *Francesco Valentino* (aka Frank Valentino, 1907-1991), a well-known Met baritone whose only EIAR/RAI performances appear to have been in 1937. Smith muddied the waters further by listing *Fernando Valentino*. Almost undoubtedly it is tenor Fernando Valentini, active at RAI between 1946 and 1972, and featured elsewhere among the GAO issues.

This transfer plays in score pitch at 34.00 rpm. The performance has been reissued several times: as MRF 65, BJRS-121 (apparently its first *true* stereo issue), Foyer 2CF-2035, Myto CD MCD 903.18, and Rodolphe CD RPV 32687/9.

EJS 523: "The Golden Age of Opera" (2 LPs)
Issued October, 1970
MATRIX P-2253 / P-2254

SIDES 1-4 (523 A-D):

THE BARTERED BRIDE [PRODANÁ NEVĚSTA] (Smetana) (E)
Opera in 3 acts (complete)
Metropolitan Opera House Orchestra and Chorus/Wilfred Pelletier
Metropolitan Opera broadcast, NYC, 8 May 1937

CAST:
Wilfred Engelman (*Krušina/Kruschina*); Lucielle Browning (*Kathinka/ Ludmilla*); Hilda Burke (*Mařenka/Marie*); John Gurney (*Micha*); Anna Kaskas (*Agnes/Hata*); George Rasely (*Wenzel/Vašhek*); Mario Chamlee (*Hans/Janík*); Louis D'Angelo (*Kecal*/Kezal); Norman Cordon (*Springer/ Ringmaster*); Natalie Bodanya (*Esmeralda*); Ludwig Burgstaller (*Muff/ Murru*).

NOTES: EJS 523

Given here complete as performed, with only minor cuts owing to acetate breaks. This is evidently the only complete operatic performance of American tenor Mario Chamlee (née Archer Chamlee) that has survived. Chamlee's third-act aria, "Oh! my adored one," had been issued previously on EJS 171 (January, 1960).

Library of Congress tape: 15778-44B (complete broadcast).

EJS 524: "The Golden Age of Opera" (1 LP)
Issued October, 1970
MATRIX P-2255

LUCIA DI LAMMERMOOR (Donizetti) (I)
Opera in 3 acts (excerpts)
Metropolitan Opera House Orchestra and Chorus/Gennaro Papi
Metropolitan Opera broadcast, NYC, 27 Feb 1937

CAST:
Lily Pons (*Lucia*); Frederick Jagel (*Edgar*); John Brownlee (*Sir Henry Ashton*); Ezio Pinza (*Raymond*); Nicholas Massue (*Arthur*); Thelma Votipka (*Alice*); Angelo Bada (*Norman*).

SIDE 1 (524 A):

Act I: 1. BROWNLEE, PINZA, BADA, and Chorus: Cruda, funesta smania . . . Fuggir non piò, non piò!

2. PONS, VOTIPKA, and JAGEL: Regnava nel silenzio . . . Quando rapito . . . Verranno a te . . . to the end of the act

Act II: 3. BROWNLEE and PONS: Appressati, Lucia . . . Soffriva nel pianto

SIDE 2 (524 B):

Act II: 1. PONS and BROWNLEE: Che fia? Suonar di giubilo . . . Se tradirmi tu potrai

2. JAGEL, BROWLEE, PONS, PINZA, MASSUE, VOTIPKA, and Chorus: Chi mi frena ["Sextet"] . . . to the end of the act

Act III: 3. PINZA, PONS, and Chorus: Dalle stanze, ove Lucia . . . Il dolce suono ["Mad Scene"] . . . a me ti dona un Dio

4. JAGEL, PINZA, and Chorus: Tu che a Dio spiegasti . . . to the end of the opera

NOTES: EJS 524

The "Cruda, funesta" plays in score pitch at 33.3 rpm, but a range of 33.8-34.00 rpm is necessary for the remainder of the excerpts.

Pons makes her usual upward transpositions of the first-act "Regnava nel silenzio . . . Quando rapito" and the third-act "Mad Scene."

Excerpts from this performance appeared earlier on EJS 170 and EJS 172, both from January, 1960.

Library of Congress tape: 15731-93B (complete broadcast).

EJS 525: "The Golden Age of Opera" (2 LPs)
Issued November, 1970
MATRIX EJS 525 A & B / P-2293

SIDES 1-4 (525 A-D):

HANS HEILING (Marschner) (G)
Opera in 3 acts and a Prelude (complete)
Orchestra and Chorus of Westdeutscher Rundfunk [WDR], Köln/Joseph Keilberth
Broadcast, WDR, Cologne, 1967

CAST:
Hermann Prey (*Hans Heiling*); Leonore Kirschstein [Kirchstein] (*Anna*); Liane Synek (*King of Earth Spirits*); Karl Josef Hering (*Konrad*); Hetty Plümacher (*Gertrude*); Hans Franzen (*Stephan*); Harald Meister (*Niklas*).

NOTES: EJS 525

This performance was reissued complete as MRF 70. Kirschstein's surname has been found in some sources as "Kirchstein."

EJS 526: "The Golden Age of Opera" (2 LPs)
Issued November, 1970
MATRIX P-2290 / P-2291

SIDES 1-4 (526 A-D):

L'ASSASSINIO NELLA CATTEDRALE (Pizzetti) (I)
Opera in 2 parts (complete)
Orchestra and Chorus of Radio Italiana [RAI], Torino/Ildebrando Pizzetti
RAI broadcast, Turin, 5 Dec 1958

CAST:
Nicola Rossi-Lemeni (*Thomas Beckett*); Aldo Bertocci (*A Herald*); Virginia Zeani (*First Corifee*); Anna Maria Rota (*Second Corifee*); Mario Ortica (*First Priest*); Mario Borriello (*Second Priest*); Adolfo Cormanni (*Third Priest*); Rinaldo Pelizzoni (*First Tempter*); Paolo Montarsolo (*Second Tempter*); Silvio Maionica (*Third Tempter*); Marco Stefanoni (*Fourth Tempter*); Rinaldo Pelizzoni (*First Knight*); Paolo Montarsolo (*Second Knight*); Silvio Maionica (*Third Knight*); Marco Stefanoni (*Fourth Knight*).

NOTES: EJS 526

Rossi-Lemeni, Bertocci, Ortica, Cormanni, Pelizzoni, and Stefanoni were creators of their respective roles at the 1 March, 1958 La Scala premiere of the opera, conducted by Gianandrea Gavazzeni. Pizzetti's setting of T.S. Eliot's 1935 dramatic poem "Murder in the Cathedral" was based on a translation by Alberto Castelli. Leyla Gencer and Gabriella Carturan created the roles sung here by Zeani and Rota. There was also a concert perfomance of the opera prior to this broadcast, conducted by László Halasz at Carnegie Hall on 17 September, 1958, with Rossi-Lemeni as *Becket*. This RAI broadcast, noted ambiguously in a postcript to the *December*, 1970 GAO bulletin as "the world premiere broadcast under [Pizzetti's] baton," was reissued as Legendary LR 143-2, while the Scala world premiere has appeared as HOPE 242.

The matrix numbers for this LP run P-2290-A through P-2291-B, C, and D for each of the four sides.

EJS 527: "The Golden Age of Opera" (2 LPs)
Issued November, 1970
MATRIX P-2286 / P-2287

THE MAN WITHOUT A COUNTRY (Arthur Guiterman-Walter Damrosch) (E)
Opera in 2 acts (complete)
Metropolitan Opera House Orchestra and Chorus/Wilfred Pelletier
Metropolitan Opera broadcast, 22 May 1937

CAST:
Arthur Carron (*Philip Nolan*); Helen Traubel (*Mary Rutledge*); George Rasely (*Blennerhassett*); Joseph Royer (*Aaron Burr*); John Gurney (*Colonel Morgan*); Nicholas Massue (*Parke*); Lodovico Oliviero (*Fairfax*); Wilfred Engelman (*Lieutenant Pinckney*); George Cehanovsky (*Lieutenant Reeve*); Donald Dickson (*Negro Boatman*); Daniel Harris (*Officer*); Donald Dickson (*Officer*); Nicholas Massue (*Officer*); Nicholas Massue (*Midshipman*); Donald Dickson (*Midshipman*); Daniel Harris (*Midshipman*); John Gurney (*Midshipman*); George Rasely (*Midshipman*); Joseph Royer (*Boatswain*); George Rasely (*Admiral*); Thelma Votipka (*American Girl*); Maxine Stellman (*American Girl*); Lucielle Browning (*American Girl*); Maria Matyas (*American Girl*); Jarna Paull (*American Girl*).

Speaking Roles: Norman Cordon (*Captain Morris*); Donald Dickson (*Midshipman Denton*); John Gurney (*Midshipman Ahern*); Robert Nicholson (*Surgeon*); Robert Nicholson (*Captain Sedley*); Louis D'Angelo (*Sergeant O'Neill*); Ludwig Burgstaller (*Private Schwartz*); Robert Nicholson (*Officer*); Lodovico Oliviero (*Officer*); Louis D'Angelo (*Commodore Decatur*).

NOTES: EJS 527

The November bulletin gives Damrosch as the conductor of this performance, noting that "it was broadcast no fewer than four times in 1937, mostly with the same people in the cast and always with Damrosch conducting." Actually, there were only four *performances* of the work that season, only one of which was broadcast. The world premiere on the evening of 12 May was indeed conducted by the composer, the others, including this broadcast, by Pelletier. The Met's final production of the work, also conducted by Pelletier, was on 17 February, 1937.

The 22 May cast featured here is identical to that of the world premiere.

An excerpt from this broadcast appeared earlier on EJS 171 (January, 1960).

Library of Congress tape: 5375-58 (complete broadcast).

EJS 528: "The Golden Age of Opera" (2 LPs)
Issued December, 1970
MATRIX P-2327 / P-2328

SIDES 1-4 (528 A-D):

IL REGGENTE (Mercadante) (I)
Opera in 3 acts (complete)
Orchestra dell'Angelicum, Milano, and Chorus of the Maggio Musicale Fiorentino/Bruno Martinotti
Broadcast, Teatro dei Rinnovati, Siena, 2 Sep 1970

CAST:
Giorgio Merighi (*The Count of Murray*); Licinio Montefusco (*The Duke of Hamilton*); Maria Chiara (*Amelia*); Dino Formichini (*Lord Howe*); Vittorio Bruni (*Lord Kilkardy*); Elena Zilio (*Oscar*); Linda Vajna (*Meg*); Dino Formichini (*Scoto*); José Sanchez Cordova (*A Servant*).

NOTES: EJS 528

This performance was subsequently reissued as Myto CD MCD 905.28.

EJS 529: "The Golden Age of Opera" (1 LP)
Issued December, 1970
MATRIX P-2318

"BENIAMINO GIGLI / BRITISH RECITALS (1949)"

SIDE 1 (529 A):

1. w. pf/Ivor Newton: LA TRAVIATA, Act II: Lunge da lei . . . De'miei bollenti spiriti (Verdi) (I)
   BBC broadcast, The Dome, Brighton, England, 13 Oct 1949

2. w. pf/Ivor Newton: DON GIOVANNI, K. 527, Act I: Dalla sua pace (Mozart) (I)
   BBC broadcast, The Dome, Brighton, England, 13 Oct 1949

3. w. pf/Ivor Newton: "Caro mio ben" (Giordani) (I)
   BBC broadcast, The Dome, Brighton, England, 13 Oct 1949

4. w. pf/Ivor Newton: "O del mio amato ben" (Donaudy) (I)
   BBC broadcast, The Dome, Brighton, England, 13 Oct 1949

5. w. pf/Ivor Newton: LA FAVORITA, Act IV: Favorita del re . . . Spirto gentil (Donizetti) (I)
   BBC broadcast, The Dome, Brighton, England, 13 Oct 1949

6. w. pf/Ivor Newton: "La Casarella" (De Veroli) (I)
   BBC broadcast, The Dome, Brighton, England, 13 Oct 1949

SIDE 2 (529 B):

1. w. pf/Vito Carnevali: "Plaisir d'amour" (Claris de Florian-G. Martini) (I)
   BBC broadcast, City Hall, Sheffield, England, 30 Mar 1949

2. w. pf/Vito Carnevali: LE ROI D'YS, Act III: Puisqu'on était . . . Vainement, ma bien aimée ["Aubade"] (Lalo) (F)
   BBC broadcast, City Hall, Sheffield, England, 30 Mar 1949

3. w. pf/Vito Carnevali: CARMEN, Act II: Il fior che avevi a me tu dato [La fleur que tu m'avais jetée] ["Flower Song"] (Bizet) (I)
   BBC broadcast, City Hall, Sheffield, England, 30 Mar 1949

4. w. pf/Vito Carnevali: "Core 'ngrato" (Cardillo) (N)
   BBC broadcast, City Hall, Sheffield, England, 30 Mar 1949

5. w. pf/Vito Carnevali: LO SCHIAVO, Act II: All'istante partir . . . Quando nascesti tu (Gomes) (I)
   BBC broadcast, City Hall, Sheffield, England, 30 Mar 1949

6. w. pf/Vito Carnevali: RIGOLETTO, Act III: La donna è mobile (Verdi) (I)
   BBC broadcast, City Hall, Sheffield, England, 30 Mar 1949

NOTES: EJS 529

The Brighton and Sheffield concerts are both presented here complete as performed and broadcast. Glendale LP GL 8005 contained all but the TRAVIATA aria and "Caro mio ben" from Brighton, and all but the "Core 'ngrato" from Sheffield, as well as two selections from Gigli's 31 October, 1952 BBC concert (issued on EJS 336 and 357).

EJS 530: "The Golden Age of Opera" (1 LP)
Issued December, 1970
MATRIX P-2319

CAVALLERIA RUSTICANA (Mascagni) (I)
Opera in 1 act (excerpts)
Metropolitan Opera House Orchestra and Chorus/Nino Verchi
In-house recording, Metropolitan Opera House, NYC, 16 Nov 1959 (evening)

CAST:
Jussi Bjoerling (*Turiddu*); Giulietta Simionato (*Santuzza*); Walter Cassel (*Alfio*); Rosalind Elias (*Lola*); Thelma Votipka (*Mamma Lucia*).

SIDE 1 (530 A):

1. BJOERLING: O Lola, ch'ai di latti ["Siciliana"]

2. BJOERLING and SIMIONATO: Tu qui, Santuzza? . . . mia è troppo forte l'angoscia mia

3. BJOERLING, ELIAS, CASSEL, VOTIPKA, SIMIONATO, and Chorus: Comare Lola, ve ne andate via . . . Viva il vino spumeggiante . . . Mamma, quel vino è generoso . . . to the end of the opera

SIDE 2 (530 B):

1. JUSSI BJOERLING, tenor (orch/Nils Grevillius): ANDREA CHENIER, Act IV: Come un bel dì, di maggio (Giordano) (I)
   OSB 2397-2 HMV DA 1836 Victor 10-1323 Concert Hall, Small Auditorium, Stockholm, 27 Mar 1944

* 2. JUSSI BJOERLING, tenor (Swedish Radio Symphony Orchestra/Tor Mann): MANON, Act III: Je suis seul . . . Ah! fuyez, douce image (Massenet) (F)
   Broadcast, Swedish Radio, Concert Hall, Large Auditorium, Stockholm, 28 Sep 1945

* 3. JUSSI BJOERLING, tenor ((Swedish Radio Symphony Orchestra/Tor Mann): LES PÊCHEURS DE PERLES, Act I: Je crois entendre encore (Bizet) (F)
   Broadcast, Swedish Radio, Concert Hall, Large Auditorium, Stockholm, 28 Sep 1945

* 4. JUSSI BJOERLING, tenor (Swedish Radio Symphony Orchestra/Tor Mann): L'ELISIR D'AMORE, Act II: Una furtiva lagrima (Donizetti) (I)
   Broadcast, Swedish Radio, Concert Hall, Large Auditorium, Stockholm, 28 Sep 1945

* 5. JUSSI BJOERLING, tenor ((Swedish Radio Symphony Orchestra/Tor Mann): L'ARLESIANA, Act II: È la solita storia ["Lamento di Federico"] (Cilèa) (I)
   Broadcast, Swedish Radio, Concert Hall, Large Auditorium, Stockholm, 28 Sep 1945

* 6. JUSSI BJOERLING, tenor (Stockholm Radio Orchestra/Sixten Ehrling): "En ballad om Lameks söner" (Rangström) (Sw)
   Broadcast, Swedish Radio, Concert Hall, ?Large Auditorium, Stockholm, 31 Jan 1942

* 7. JUSSI BJOERLING, tenor (Stockholm Radio Orchestra/Sixten Ehrling): "En ballad om Narren och Döden" (Rangström) (Sw)
   Broadcast, Swedish Radio, Concert Hall, ?Large Auditorium, Stockholm, 31 Jan 1942

* 8. JUSSI BJOERLING, tenor (Stockholm Radio Orchestra/Sixten Ehrling): "En ballad om god sömn" (Rangström) (Sw)
   Broadcast, Swedish Radio, Concert Hall, ?Large Auditorium, Stockholm, 31 Jan 1942

NOTES: EJS 530

The CAVALLERIA was taken from a private, in-house recording of this Monday evening performance. The complete performance was issued AS HRE 301-2.

Side 2 (530 B):

Bands 2-5: This Sveriges Radio AB broadcast is presented here complete except for the Massenet "Élégie," which was subsequently issued on ANNA 1045 (Fall, 1979). Portions of the broadcast were reissued on MDP 026 and 035 and Swedish Radio SRLP 1354/55.
Swedish Radio tape: L-B+ 6451.

Bands 6-8: This was the world premiere of these three songs by Swedish composer Ture Rangström (1884-1947). All three were reissued on the Swedish Radio LP SRL 1354/55. The "O Paradiso!" and "Cielo e mar," sung by Bjoerling in the first half of the broadcast, have apparently not survived.
Swedish Radio tape: L-B 2665.

EJS 531: "The Golden Age of Opera" (1 LP)
Issued December, 1970
MATRIX P-2320

"JOHN CHARLES THOMAS"

SIDE 1 (531 A):

* 1. w. Detroit Symphony Orchestra/Eugene Ormandy: LA FAVORITA, Act II: Ma de malvag'invan . . . Vien Leonora (Donizetti) (I)
Broadcast, ***FORD SUNDAY EVENING HOUR***, WJR, Detroit, 10 Mar 1940

* 2. w. Detroit Symphony Orchestra/Eugene Ormandy: DON CARLOS, Act III: Son io, mio Carlo . . . . Per me giunto è il di supremo (Verdi) (I)
Broadcast, ***FORD SUNDAY EVENING HOUR***, WJR, Detroit, 12 Nov 1939

* 3. w. VINA BOVY, soprano (Metropolitan Opera House Orchestra/Ettore Panizza): LA TRAVIATA, Act II: Pura siccome un angelo (Verdi) (I)
Metropolitan Opera broadcast, NYC, 11 Dec 1937

* 4. w. Los Angeles Philharmonic Orchestra/Eugene Ormandy: LA TRAVIATA, Act II: Di provenza il mar (Verdi) (I)
D-28195x AFRS H-38-61 [Record II/part 2] AFRS broadcast, Hollywood Bowl, Los Angeles, 13 Jul 1948

* 5. w. Los Angeles Philharmonic Orchestra/Eugene Ormandy: HÉRODIADE, Act I: Salomé! Salomé! (Massenet) (F)
D-28195x AFRS H-38-61 [Record II/part 2] AFR broadcast, Hollywood Bowl, Los Angeles, 13 Jul 1948

SIDE 2 (531 B):

* 1. w. Metropolitan Opera House Orchestra/Sir Thomas Beecham: FAUST, Act II: Avant de quitter ces lieux (Gounod) (F)
Metropolitan Opera broadcast, NYC, 30 Jan 1943

* 2. w. Metropolitan Opera House Orchestra/Sir Thomas Beecham: FAUST, Act IV: Écoutez-moi bien, Marguerite ["Death of Valentine"] (Gounod) (F)
Metropolitan Opera broadcast, NYC, 30 Jan 1943

* 3. w. MARIO CHAMLEE, tenor (orch/?Frank Black): LA FORZA DEL DESTINO, Act III: Solenne in quest'ora (Verdi) (I)
X15640 Brunswick unpublished Chicago, April-May, 1925

* 4. w. orch/Victor Young: ANDREA CHENIER, Act III: Nemico della patria? (Giordano) (I)
Broadcast, ?***JOHN CHARLES THOMAS PROGRAM***, WEAF, NYC, circa January, 1944

* 5. w. orch and chorus/Victor Young: CARMEN, Act II: Votre toast ["Toreador Song"] (Bizet) (F)
Broadcast, ?***JOHN CHARLES THOMAS PROGRAM***, WEAF, NYC, circa 1943-1945

* 6. w. ROSA PONSELLE, soprano (pf/?): "The Old Folks at Home" ["Swannee River"] (Stephen C. Foster) (E)
Live recording, "Eisenhower for President" Rally, 5th Regiment Armory, Baltimore, Maryland, 25 Sep 1952

NOTES: EJS 531

Side 1 (531 A):

Bands 1-2: Both the FAVORITA and DON CARLOS arias appeared earlier on EJS 214 (June, 1961). Two songs from this 12 November, 1939 broadcast were later included on EJS 564 (June, 1971).

Band 3: Extensive excerpts from this TRAVIATA appeared on one of Smith's "special labels," Voix Illustres Belges 601, and the entire performance was issued as UORC 285 (May-June, 1976).

Bands 4-5: The body of this concert consisted of songs, all of which were subsequently included on EJS 564 (June, 1971). See the extensive endnote for that LP.

These AFRS items were originally transcribed on private Army-Navy Air Force Armed Forces Radio Service discs ("The Voice of Information and Education"). The Thomas discs examined are labeled "Personal Presentation Copy / Dr. Karl Wecker / Hollywood Bowl 1948," Wecker apparently being the individual for whom these copies were pressed (the Wecker copies are held at Stanford University but were not necessarily the ones used to compile EJS 531). The bottom of the label carries a private-use notice dated 12 July, 1947. The selections included here are from the Hollywood Bowl Series H-38-61, Program No. 61, a five-disc set in nine parts, matrices D-28194/D-28202 (parts D-28195 and D-28197 are suffixed "x").

Bands 1-2: Extensive excerpts from this performance were originally issued as EJS 265 (April, 1943). Magnificent Editions ME 104-3 contains the entire performance, as does AS compact disc 1104/5.

Band 3: Frank Black was, at the time, Brunswick's musical director, and so was presumably the conductor of this session.

Thomas and Chamlee, under the respective pseudonyms "Enrico Martini" and "Mario Rodolfi," recorded this FORZA duet in 1916, issued as vertical-cut Lyric 7016-A, with Chamlee's "Flower Song" from CARMEN on the other side: the latter is matrix 6163-1, but the FORZA matrix is not visible on the original disc. There is another extant Brunswick test of them singing the duet, matrix X15591. Chamlee eventually recorded the duet with Richard Bonelli, as issued on Brunswick.

Bands 4-5: Labeled as 1945 on EJS 531. This may be the "Nemico della patria?" slated for, but not issued on, V-Disc, which was thought to be from one of Thomas' Westinghouse broadcasts. It does *not* date from a "ca. January, 1944" Westinghouse broadcast, however, as suggested by Sears (p. 869).

The ***JOHN CHARLES THOMAS PROGRAM*** (aka ***THE WESTINGHOUSE PROGRAM WITH JOHN CHARLES THOMAS***) sponsored by Westinghouse, was heard on Sunday afternoons from 2:30-3:00 pm EST over NBC during the 1943-1946 broadcast seasons. Victor Young was the conductor of his own studio orchestra, augmented by the Ken Darby Singers.

Band 6: Announced by Thomas with remarks by Ponselle. Thomas refers to the pianist as "Sir," without identifying him further. This live recording comes from an "Eisenhower for President" Rally held in the 5th Regiment Armory in Baltimore and was originally issued on a rare 10-inch LP, "Rosa's Christmas Gift" (GR 101), produced and distributed privately by Ponselle (100 copies). The duet later appeared on OASI 527.

Ponselle's autobiography, pp. 222, gives a detailed acount of the rally and the repertory performed. An acetate of the performance, with Ponselle's "The Star Spangled Banner," exists in a private collection.

EJS 532: "The Golden Age of Opera" (1 LP)
Issued December, 1970
MATRIX P-2321

"SOPRANO POTPOURRI (No. 23)"

SIDE 1 (532 A):

* 1. ROSA PONSELLE, soprano (pf/Romano Romani): LA FORZA DEL DESTINO, Act IV: Pace, pace, mio Dio (Verdi) (I)
matrix unknown New York, 3 Apr 1918 Columbia test

* 2. ROSA PONSELLE, soprano (orch and chorus/André Kostelanetz): CAVALLERIA RUSTICANA: "Ave Maria" [Intermezzo] (Mascagni) (L)
Broadcast, ***CHESTERFIELD HOUR***, WJZ, NYC, 8 Oct 1934

* 3. ROSA PONSELLE, soprano (orch/André Kostelanetz): THE CHOCOLATE SOLDIER, Act I: My Hero (Oscar Straus) (E)
Broadcast, ***CHESTERFIELD HOUR***, WJZ, NYC, 8 Oct 1934

* 4. ROSA PONSELLE, soprano (orch/André Kostelanetz): "La golondrina" (trad.-arr. ?Serradell) (S)
Broadcast, ***CHESTERFIELD HOUR***, WJZ, NYC, 15 Oct 1934

5. ROSA PONSELLE, soprano (pf/?Romano Romani): "Could I?" ["Vorrei"] (Tosti) (E)
Private recording, ?Villa Pace [Maryland], 1 Oct 1949

* 6. ELISABETH RETHBERG, soprano (orch/Alfred Wallenstein): GIULIO SABINO: Lungi dal caro bene (G. Sarti) (I)
Broadcast, ***ELISABETH RETHBERG***, WOR, NYC, 22 Aug 1941

* 7. ELISABETH RETHBERG, soprano (orch/Alfred Wallenstein; harp/?): "Amarilli, mia bella" (A. Guarini-Caccini) (I)
Broadcast, ***ELISABETH RETHBERG***, WOR, NYC, 22 Aug 1941

* 8. ELISABETH RETHBERG, soprano (orch/Alfred Wallenstein): LIEDER UND GESÄNGE [AUS DER JUGENDZEIT], No. 3: Hans und Grethe (Mahler) (G)
Broadcast, ***ELISABETH RETHBERG***, WOR, NYC, 22 Aug 1941

9. ELISABETH RETHBERG, soprano (pf/Alfred Wallenstein): "Liebst du um Schönheit" (Rückert-Mahler) (G)
Broadcast, ***ELISABETH RETHBERG***, WOR, NYC, 22 Aug 1941

* 10. ELISABETH RETHBERG, soprano (orch/Alfred Wallenstein): "Have You But Seen a Whyte Lilie Grow?" (sic) (Old English) (E)
Broadcast, ***ELISABETH RETHBERG***, WOR, NYC, 22 Aug 1941

* 11. ELISABETH RETHBERG, soprano (orch/Alfred Wallenstein): AYRES, Book I: Come againe sweet love doth now envite (Dowland) (E)
Broadcast, ***ELISABETH RETHBERG***, WOR, NYC, 22 Aug 1941

SIDE 2 (532 B):

* 1. ?LILLIAN NORDICA, soprano (pf/?): DIE WALKÜRE, Act II: Hoyotoho! (Wagner) (G)
M-95 New York, Late 1906 or early 1907 Columbia unpub

* 2. LILLIAN NORDICA, soprano (pf/?): SALVATOR ROSA, Act III: Mia piccirella (Gomes) (I)
30681-1 New York, 16 Feb 1911 Columbia unpub

* 3. FRANCES ALDA, soprano (orch/Rosario Bourdon; harp/Francis J. Lapitino): MARTHA, Act II: The Last Rose of Summer [Letzte Rose] (Flotow) (E)
B-29491-5 ?Camden, 4 Apr 1924 Victor unpub

* 4. FRANCES ALDA, soprano (orch/Rosario Bourdon): L'AMICO FRITZ, Act III: Non mi resta che il pianto (Mascagni) (I)
B-28101-2 or -3 ?Camden, 7 Jun 1923 Victor unpub

5. ELISABETH SCHUMANN, soprano (pf/John Wills): SECHS GEDICHTE, Op. 36, no. 4: An den Sonnenschein (Reinick-Schumann) (G)
Broadcast, BBC, London, 14 Oct 1945

6. ELISABETH SCHUMANN, soprano (pf/John Wills): "Therese," Op. 86, no. 1 (Keller-Brahms) (G)
Broadcast, BBC, London, 14 Oct 1945

7. ELISABETH SCHUMANN, soprano (pf/John Wills): "Ich atmet' einer Linden Duft," WoP, no. 4 (Rückert-Mahler) (G)
Broadcast, BBC, London, 14 Oct 1945

* 8. NELLIE MELBA, soprano (pf/Landon Ronald):
a) FOUR SONGS OF THE HILL: Away on a Hill (Landon Ronald) (E)
b) A CYCLE OF LIFE, No. 2: Down in the Forest ("Spring") (Harold Simpson-Landon Ronald) (E)
Cc148-1 Hayes, Middlesex, 12 May 1921 HMV unpub

* 9. ADELINA PATTI, soprano (pf/Alfredo Barili): "Within a Mile o' Edinboro' Town" (James Hook) (E)
678c Craig-y-nos, Wales, June, 1906 G&T (03080) unpub

* 10. JARMILA NOVOTNA, soprano (Orchestra and Chorus of the Wiener Staatsoper/Franz Lehár): GIUDITTA, Scene iv: Meine Lippen sie küssen so heiss' (Lehár) (G)
Broadcast, Wiener Staatsoper, Vienna, 20 Jan 1934

* 11. JARMILA NOVOTNA, soprano (orch/André Kostelanetz): DIE LUSTIGE WITWE, Act II: Es lebt eine Vilja ["Viljalied"] (Lehár) (E)
Broadcast, ***COCA-COLA SHOW***, WABC, NYC, 13 Feb 1944

* 12. JARMILA NOVOTNA, soprano (orch/?): FAUST, Act III: Ah! je ris ["Jewel Song"] (Gounod) (F)
Broadcast, source unknown, circa 1943

NOTES: EJS 532

The label of EJS 532 numbers the selections by artist--thus, Ponselle, 1-5, Rethberg, 1-5, etc. (actually, Rethberg is misnumbered 1, 2, 4, 5, 6). Abrupt beginnings and endings are found throughout this particular LP.

Side 1 (532 A):

Band 1: This was Ponselle's first recording, subsequently reissued on ANNA 1037 (May-June, 1979) and OASI 621. The label of EJS 532 gives the date *February*, 1918. The January, 1971 GAO bulletin carried a fascinating postcript: "Rosa Ponselle telephoned to say that the Pace mio Dio from Forza released last month on Potpourri 23 did not date from February 1918 as was indicated on the test record but from April or May 1918. 'I had never heard of Pace Mio Dio in February, let alone sung the aria,' said Madame Ponselle." That the incorrect date appeared on the actual "test record," or that Smith had access to the disc itself could not be confirmed.

The correct playing speed of the EJS 532 transfer is 33.8 rpm.

Bands 2-3: The correct playing speed for both bands is 33.8 rpm. The "Ave Maria" is the well-traveled arrangement of the CAVALLERIA "Intermezzo" recorded by many other singers. This Ponselle performance was reissued on MDP-029.

Library of Congress tape: 5063-1 (complete broadcast).

Band 4: Library of Congress tape: 5063-2 (complete broadcast).

Bands 6-11: Rethberg's portion of this 22 August, 1941 broadcast is presented here complete, except for the "Glück, das mir verblieb" from Korngold's DIE TOTE STADT and two other Mahler songs issued earlier on EJS 256 (January, 1963).

Band 6: Variously attributed to Sarti's GIULIO SABINO (1781) and ARMIDA E RINALDO (1759), but more often to the former. The correct playing speed is 32.5 rpm.

Band 7: The *New York Times* notes that "Amarilli" is here scored for lute and orchestra, but the performance is accompanied by solo harp and orchestra. The correct playing speed is 32.8 rpm.

Band 9: This song, no. 7 of a Mahler collection titled SIEBEN LIEDER AUS LETZTER ZEIT by its publisher, is not listed on the label of EJS 532.

Bands 10-11: The correct playing speed for both is 32.8 rpm.

SIDE 2 (532 B):

Bands 1-2: Nordica's unpublished WALKÜRE (matrix 30659-1, recorded in New York on 3 February, 1911) was first issued as a re-recording in May, 1937 on single-sided IRCC 95. Taken from a test pressing found in a Los Angeles junk shop, the recording was dubbed by Columbia on 16 April, 1937 as transfer matrix XP-20986-1. In a veiled reference to the original IRCC issue, the label of EJS 532 claims that the "Hoyotoho" included here is an "unpublished, different take of 30659," but only 30659-1 has been documented as a *genuine* Nordica recording.

For this LP, Smith used a Columbia test pressing bearing the matrix number M-95 (late 1906 or early 1907) and "Olive Fremstad" witten on the label in white ink. There are no other known 1906-1907 Nordica matrices in the area of M-95, nor are there *any* Fremstad recordings from that period: the latter is known to have recorded for Columbia only between 1911 and 1915 (her own issued "Hoyotoho" on Columbia A 1451 was tenb-inch, recorded on 28 October, 1913, matrix 39073-1). W.R. Moran, who has published definitive discographies of both Nordica and Fremstad, has reported that neither he, William Seltsam, or Mrs. Mary Watkins Cushing, Fremstad's biographer (*The Raibow Bridge*, New York: Putnam, 1954/R: New York: Arno Press, 1977) believed the M-95 "Hoyotoho" to be Fremstad, though Moran and Seltsam agreed that it could *possibly* be Nordica--in fact, Seltsam refused to release it on the IRCC label because of the uncertainty, but this, characteristically, did not stop Smith from issuing it without reservation or explanation. In any event, it is NOT the same "Hoyotoho" issued on IRCC 95, and the identity of the singer remains provisional.

Both versions of the WALKÜRE (30659-1 and M-95) and the SALVATORE ROSA aria appeared later on a Sunday Opera Records Nordica recital, SYO 6 (Acoustographic AG-4267, a "complete" Nordica set, did not include the M-95 version of the "Hoyotoho!").

Band 3: Vinyl "special pressings" of the MARTHA aria have been in circulation for years. Smith reported this as matrix B-29491-2 to one prominent collector, but the performance has been identified conclusively as take -5. It was dubbed a half-step low on EJS 532 at about 71.0 rpm: the correct speed of the original recording is 76.0 rpm.

Band 4: The L'AMICO FRITZ aria plays a half-step below score pitch at 33.3 rpm, but it is unlikely that Alda transposed it: like the MARTHA aria, it was probably reproduced at 71.0 rpm rather than a more likely 75-77 rpm. Takes -2 and -3 of B-28101 are marked "hold" in the Victor ledgers, but there are no pressings--"special" or otherwise--to compare to the performance on EJS 532. It is not known to which Smith managed to secure access.

Band 8: Subsequently issued on the 1976 EMI "Nellie Melba: The London Recordings 1904-1926" (RLS 719). The original playing speed is 76.60 rpm, transcribed high on EJS 532 at 78.26 rpm.

Band 9: Subsequently reissued on EMI's complete Patti issues (RLS 711 and Electrola C 147-01 500/01 M), where it was transferred at 72.00 rpm: 76.60 rpm has also been suggested as the proper speed. The catalog number 03080 was assigned, but the recording was not issued. The title of this song varies from source to source: it is labeled "Within a Mile o' Edinboro' Town" on EJS 532 and "Within a mile <u>of</u> Edinboro town" on the original label of the published version, G&T 03064 (matrix 557f), while "'<u>Twas</u> within a mile o' Edinboro' Town" and "'Twas within a mile" have also found their way into print.

Band 10: Heralded in the December, 1970 as a "January 12, 1934 broadcast of a song from Giuditta in the world premiere presentation of that opera." This excerpt is indeed from the premiere, but in fact, the opera made its debut at the Wiener Staatsoper on 2<u>0</u> January, 1934 with Novotna in the title role, Tauber as *Octavio*, Margit Bokor as *Anita*, and Lehár on the podium. WEAF (NBC), New York City, broadcast fifty-five minutes of the premiere direct from Vienna (1:00-1:55 pm EST) before yielding the air to that week's Metropolitan Opera matinee. It is not known how much of the GIUDITTA, outside of this fragment, still exists.

The original chorus part is featured in this live performance, as well as the instrumental interlude between verses, complete with dancing and castanets. This, in fascinating contrast to Novotna's famous commercial recording of "Meine Lippen" (matrix Ve 2011-1) made during her Vienna Odeon session of 11 January, 1934 with Richard Tauber, Lehár conducting.

Even at 34.00 rpm the aria is sung in D major, a whole step below score pitch, so it seems likely that the proper speed of this band is about 36.00 rpm. Both the recording and the transfer are surprisingly good, given the vintage and the source.

Band 11-12: The correct playing speed of both is 34.0 rpm. The ***COCA-COLA SHOW*** (aka ***THE PAUSE THAT REFRESHES***) was broadcast on both WABC-AM and -FM and also featured violinist (and erstwhile Victor artist) E. Robert Schmitz.

EJS 533: "The Golden Age of Opera" (1 LP)
Issued December, 1970
MATRIX: P-2322

"FREDERICK JAGEL"

SIDE 1 (533-A):

1. w. pf/?: EURIDICE, Scene 5: Gioite al canto mio ["Invocation"] (Peri) (I)
   Telecast, ***PERFORMANCE***, WGBH [NET], Boston, 27 Sep 1960

2. w. pf/?: LUISA MILLER, Act II: Quando le sere al placido (Verdi) (I)
   Telecast, ***PERFORMANCE***, WGBH [NET], Boston, 27 Sep 1960

3. w. pf/?: SALVATORE ROSA, Act I: Mia piccirella (Gomes) (I)
   Telecast, ***PERFORMANCE***, WGBH [NET], Boston, 27 Sep 1960

4. w. pf/?: LE ROI D'YS, Act III: Vainement ma bien aimée ["Aubade"] (Lalo) (F)
   Telecast, ***PERFORMANCE***, WGBH [NET], Boston, 27 Sep 1960

5. w. pf/?: MANON LESCAUT, Act I: Donna non vidi mai (Puccini) (I)
   Telecast, ***PERFORMANCE***, WGBH [NET], Boston, 27 Sep 1960

6. w. pf/?: ANDREA CHENIER, Act I: Un dì, all'azzurro spazio ["Improvviso"] (Giordano) (I)
   Telecast, ***PERFORMANCE***, WGBH [NET], Boston, 27 Sep 1960

7. w. pf/?: DIE MEISTERSINGER VON NÜRNBERG, Act III: Morgenlich leuchtend ["Preislied"] (Wagner) (G)
   Telecast, ***PERFORMANCE***, WGBH [NET], Boston, 27 Sep 1960

SIDE 2 (533 B):

1. w. pf/Felix Wolfes: CANTATA NO. 17, WER DANKT OPFERT, DER PREISET MICH, BWV 17: Einer aber unter ihnen . . . Welch Übermaass der Güte schenkst du mir! (J. S. Bach) (G)
   In-house recording, Jordan Hall, New England Conservatory, Boston, 11 January, 1959

2. w. pf/Felix Wolfes: ROMANCES, Op. 33, no. 1: Keinen hat es noch gereut (Tieck-Brahms) (G)
   In-house recording, Jordan Hall, New England Conservatory, Boston, 11 January, 1959

3. w. pf/Felix Wolfes: ROMANCES, Op. 33, no. 3: Sind es Schmerzen, sind es Freuden (Tieck-Brahms) (G)
   In-house recording, Jordan Hall, New England Conservatory, Boston, 11 January, 1959

4. w. pf/Felix Wolfes: ROMANCES, Op. 33, no. 9: Ruhe, Süssliebchen (Tieck-Brahms) (G)
   In-house recording, Jordan Hall, New England Conservatory, Boston, 11 January, 1959

5. w. pf/Felix Wolfes: ROMANCES, Op. 33, no. 14: Wie froh und frisch (Tieck-Brahms) (G)
   In-house recording, Jordan Hall, New England Conservatory, Boston, 11 January, 1959

6. w. pf/Felix Wolfes: VIER LIEDER, Op. 27, no. 3: Heimliche Aufforderung (J. H. Mackay-R. Strauss) (G)
   In-house recording, Jordan Hall, New England Conservatory, Boston, 11 January, 1959

7. w. pf/Felix Wolfes: DREI LIEDER, Op. 29, no. 1: Traum durch die Dämmerung (Bierbaum-Strauss) (G)
   In-house recording, Jordan Hall, New England Conservatory, Boston, 11 January, 1959

8. w. pf/Felix Wolfes: VIER LIEDER, Op. 27, no. 2: Cäcilie (Hart-R. Strauss) (G)
   In-house recording, Jordan Hall, New England Conservatory, Boston, 11 January, 1959

9. w. pf/Felix Wolfes: FÜNF LIEDER, Op. 48, no. 1: Freundliche Vision (Bierbaum-R. Strauss) (G)
   In-house recording, Jordan Hall, New England Conservatory, Boston, 11 January, 1959

NOTES: EJS 533

This ***PERFORMANCE*** recital, heard in simulcast over WGBH-Radio and Television, Boston, was recorded when Jagel was just short of 63 and is given here complete as aired (WGBH was a key affiliate of the National Educational Network [NET]--now the Public Broadcasting System [PBS]). Jagel's accompanist is not known, but was in all probability Felix Wolfes, who accompanied all of Marjorie Lawrence's American Victor recordings, 1939-1940. All of the selections are announced by an unknown announcer and sung in the original score keys. The SALVATORE ROSA and ROI D'YS arias appeared earlier on EJS 233 (March, 1962).

Station WGBH sustained a fire in 1963 which destroyed its archives, making any further details unlikely to turn up.

The New England Conservatory of Music concert was a free afternoon faculty recital and was not broadcast (both Jagel and Wolfes were members of the Conservatory's voice faculty, the former from 1949-1970). In addition to the items presented here, Jagel sang arias of Puccini and a Cimara song. Chausson's 1893 "Poème de l'amour et de la mer" was performed by the Conservatory Orchestra, with Jagel as the featured soloist. The Strauss "Freundliche Vision" was one of four encores and is announced on EJS 533 by Jagel.

EJS 534: "The Golden Age of Opera" (3 LPs)
Issued January, 1971
MATRIX P-2352 / P-2353 / P-2354

SIDES 1-6 (534 A-F):

DIE WALKÜRE (Wagner) (G)
Opera in 3 acts (abridged)
Orchestra of the Teatro alla Scala/Wilhelm Furtwängler
Broadcast, Teatro alla Scala, Milan, ?9 Mar 1950

CAST:
Gunther Treptow (*Siegmund*); Hilde Konetzni (*Sieglinde*); Ferdinand Frantz (*Wotan*); Kirsten Flagstad (*Brünnhilde*); Ludwig Weber (*Hunding*); Elisabeth Höngen (*Fricka*); Ilona Steingruber (*Helmwige*); Walburga Wegner (*Gerhilde*); Karen Marie Cerkall (*Ortlinde*); Dagmar Schmedes (*Waltraute*); Margaret Kenney (*Siegrune*); Margret Weth-Falke (*Rossweisse*); Sieglinde Wagner (*Grimgerde*); Polly Batic (*Schwertleite*).

NOTES: EJS 534

WALKÜRE was performed complete on 9, 13, and 16 March, 1950 and broadcast in its entirety, though which of the three performances was heard on the air remains unresolved. Three recordings of the complete La Scala Ring Cycle are said to exist at RAI, Roma (acetates) and Torino (tape transfers).

The EJS 534 issue, unlike its many commercial successors, omits *Wotan's* "Der der Liebe fluchte . . . trügent verraten wer mir traut" from Act II/ii, along with *Brünnhilde's* intervening "Doch der Wälsung Siegmund? Wirkt er nicht selbst?." Both were restored on the Fonit-Cetra CFE-101-(18) release of the complete Furtwängler Ring Cycle and on numerous other LPs and CDs issued subsequently on the Everest, Murray Hill, and Robin Hood labels.

EJS 327 (April, 1965) contained excerpts from Acts II and III of the same performance, though taken, ostensibly, from a different source.

EJS 535: "The Golden Age of Opera" (1 LP)
Issued January, 1971
MATRIX P-2357

SIDES 1-2 (535 A-B):

LUCREZIA (Respighi-complete by Elsa Olivieri-Sangiacomo Respighi) (I)
Opera in 1 act and 3 scenes (complete)
Orchestra and Chorus of Radio Italiana [RAI], Milano/Oliviero de Fabritiis
RAI broadcast, Milan, 12 Sep 1958

CAST:
Anna De Cavalieri (*Lucrezia*); Miti Truccato Pace (*The Voice*); Walter Brunelli (*Collatino*); Renato Gavarini (*Bruno*); Mario Sereni (*Tarquinio*); Franca Marghinotti (*Servia*); Dedy Montano (*Venilia*); Giovanni Ciavola (*Tito*); Giovanni Ciavola (*Valerio*); Valerio Meucci (*Arunte*); Fernando Corena (*Spurio Lucrezio*).

NOTES: EJS 535

Respighi's last opera, completed by his wife and written to a libretto by Guastalla, made its debut at La Scala on 24 February, 1937, with Gino Marinuzzi conducting. Maria Caniglia (for Maria Carbone), Pablo Civil, and Ebe Stignani were among the principals of the original production.

Anna De Cavalieri was the Italian stage name of Anne McKnight.

EJS 536: "The Golden Age of Opera" (1 LP)
Issued January, 1971
MATRIX P-2358

ARIADNE AUF NAXOS (R. Strauss) (G)
Opera in 1 act and a Prologue (excerpts)
Royal Philharmonic Orchestra/Sir Thomas Beecham
Unpublished studio recording (HMV), London, 13-15 Oct 1947

CAST:
Maria Cebotari (*Ariadne*); Karl Friedrich (*Bacchus*); Gwladys Garside (*Dryade*); Edith Furmedge (*Echo*); Margaret Field-Hyde (*Najade*); Margaret Field-Hyde (*Zerbinetta*).

SIDE 1 (536 A):

* 1. CEBOTARI, FRIEDRICH, GARSIDE, FURMEDGE, and FIELD-WHITE: Ein schönes Wunder . . . to the end of the opera

Side 2 (536 B):

* 1. LOTTE LEHMANN, soprano (pf/Paul Ulanowsky): SIX [6] ORIGINAL CANZONETTAS, Set II, no. 4, H. XXXVIa/34: She never told her love (Shakespeare-Haydn) (E)
Broadcast, ?, 8 January, 1949

* 2. LOTTE LEHMANN, soprano (pf/Paul Ulanowsky): MYRTHEN, Op. 25, no. 1: Widmung ["Du meine Seele, du mein Herz"] (Rückert-Schumann) (G)
Broadcast, ?, 8 January, 1949

* 3. LOTTE LEHMANN, soprano (pf/Paul Ulanowsky): "Londonderry Air" (trad.) (E)
Broadcast, ?, 8 January, 1949

* 4. LOTTE LEHMANN, soprano (pf/Paul Ulanowsky): Drink to me only with thine eyes (Ben Jonson-trad.) (E)
Broadcast, ?, 8 January, 1949

* 5. LOTTE LEHMANN, soprano (pf/Paul Ulanowsky): SCHWANENGESANG, D. 957, no. 4: Leise flehen ["Ständchen"] (Rellstab-Schubert) (G)
Broadcast, ?, 8 January, 1949

* 6. LOTTE LEHMANN, soprano (pf/Paul Ulanowsky): Op. 34, no. 2: Auf Flügeln des Gesanges (Heine-Mendelssohn) (G)
Broadcast, ?, 8 January, 1949

* 7. LOTTE LEHMANN, soprano (Seattle Symphony Orchestra/Carl Bricker): "Die junge Nonne," D. 828 (Craigher-de Jachelutta - Schubert) (G)
Broadcast, ***SEATTLE FIRST ANNIVERSARY VJ DAY FESTIVAL***, University of Washington Stadium, KIRO, Seattle, 11 August, 1946

* 8. LOTTE LEHMANN, soprano (Seattle Symphony Orchestra/Carl Bricker): "Der Jüngling an der Quelle," D. 300 (Salis-Seewis - Schubert) (G)
Broadcast, ***SEATTLE FIRST ANNIVERSARY VJ DAY FESTIVAL***, University of Washington Stadium, KIRO, Seattle, 11 August, 1946

* 9. LOTTE LEHMANN, soprano (Seattle Symphony Orchestra/Carl Bricker): "Der Erlkönig," D. 328 (Goethe-Schubert) (G)
Broadcast, ***SEATTLE FIRST ANNIVERSARY VJ DAY FESTIVAL***, University of Washington Stadium, KIRO, Seattle, 11 August, 1946

*10. LOTTE LEHMANN, soprano (Seattle Symphony Orchestra/Carl Bricker): WESENDONCK-LIEDER, no. 5: "Träume" (Wesendonck-Wagner) (G)
Broadcast, ***SEATTLE FIRST ANNIVERSARY VJ DAY FESTIVAL***, University of Washington Stadium, KIRO, Seattle, 11 August, 1946

NOTES: EJS 536

Side 1 (536 A):

It is said that Beecham would not pass this commercially-recorded ARIADNE Finale because of his dissatisfaction with tenor Karl Friedrich. The assignment of the three *nymphs* has been taken from the British RCA LP of the performance (RL 42821). The Beecham Society also issued it as WSA 510 (in set WSA 509/12).

Though the precise division of the scene over the six sides is unknown, the following matrix information for the ARIADNE is available, given in what appears to be the proper *musical* order. Those takes underlined were the ones approved for publication:

2EA 12421-1, 2	14 Oct 47	2EA 12423-1, 2	14 Oct 47
-3	15 Oct 47	2EA 12424-1, 2	14 Oct 47
2EA 12419-1, 2	13 Oct 47	2EA 12420-1, 2	13 Oct 47
2EA 12422-1, 2, 3	14 Oct 47	-3, 4	13 Oct 47

Side 2 (536 B):

Bands 1-6: The source of the first six Lehmann items is disputed. All but the Haydn appeared on an undocumented 8 January, 1949 broadcast hosted by Lionel Barrymore. "She never told her love" may have been a last-minute addition to the program. This broadcast appears without any further identification or explanation in Gary Hickling's Lehmann discography in Beaumont Glass' *Lotte Lehmann: A Life in Opera & Song* (Santa Barbara, California: Capra Press, 1982), pp. 317-318, notes 452 and 463. Lehmann gave recitals in New York in 1949 (though she was already a permanent resident of Santa Barbara) and so, could have been there in January, but no New York broadcast could be found on this date. In all probability, this was a local or perhaps regional west-coast radio appearance.

EJS 536 claims that all of these Lehmann recordings were made "between 1944 and 1946."

Bands 7-10: This was a local three-hour broadcast over station KIRO, Seattle (Queen City Broadcasting Company) in celebration of VJ Day. It was heard from 2:00-5:00 pm PST and consisted of Lehmann's four songs, orchestral selections, local choirs, and political speeches. The original acetates are preserved in the archives of station KIRO.

EJS 537: "The Golden Age of Opera" (1 LP)
Issued January, 1971
MATRIX P-2359

SIDES 1-2 (537 A-B):

FIERRABRAS, D. 796 (Schubert) (G)
Opera in 3 acts (abridged)
Orchestra and Chorus of the Staatsoper, Bern/Hans Müller-Kray
Studio recording, Office Suisse de Radiodiffusion et Télévision [SSR], Radio Bern, and Süddeutscher Rundfunk, Stuttgart, 1-16 Apr 1959
Broadcast, SSR, Bern, Switzerland, 1959

CAST:
Otto von Rohr (*King Karl*); Sieglinde Kahmann (*Emma*); Raymond Wolansky (*Roland*); Hans Ulrich Mielsch (*Ogier*); Fritz Wunderlich (*Eginhard*); Rudo Timper (*Fierrabras*); Hetty Plümacher (*Florinda*); Melanie Geissler (*Maragond*); Manfred Rohrl (*Brutamonte*).

NOTES: EJS 537

Included on EJS 537 are Acts I and II, through number 15. Smith probably received an incomplete tape of the complete performance, part of a special Schubert cycle mounted as a joint production by Radio Bern [SSR] and Süddeutscher Rundfunk, Stuttgart in 1959: it was not a *public* Staatsoper performance. The recording was made between 1 and 16 April, 1959, but the exact broadcast date could not be determined. No. 3 of the first act was omitted entirely in the actual performance, where nos. 4 and 6 sustained large internal cuts.

The complete performance was subsequently issued on CD as Myto MCD 890.01.

EJS 538: "The Golden Age of Opera" (4 LPs)
Issued February, 1971
MATRIX P-2366 / P-2367 / P-2368 / P-2369

SIDES 1-8 (538 A-H):

GÖTTERDÄMMERUNG (Wagner) (G)
Opera in acts (complete)
Orchestra and Chorus of the Teatro alla Scala/Wilhelm Furtwängler
Broadcast, Teatro alla Scala, Milan, ?2 Apr 1950

CAST:
Max Lorenz (*Siegfried*); Kirsten Flagstad (*Brünnhilde*); Ludwig Weber (*Hagen*); Josef Herrmann (*Gunther*); Hilde Konetzni (*Gutrune*); Alois Pernerstorfer (*Alberich*); Elisabeth Höngen (*Waltraute*); Margret Weth-Falke (*First Norn*); Margaret Kenney (*Second Norn*); Hilde Konetzni (*Third Norn*); Magda Gabory (*Woglinde*); Margherita Kenney (*Wellgunde*); Sieglinde Wagner (*Flosshilde*).

NOTES: EJS 538

This production of GÖTTERDÄMMERUNG was performed on 2, 4, and 6 April, 1950. The Bruno Walter Society's Recital Records issue, authorized by Frau Elisabeth Furtwängler, gives 2 April as the broadcast date. As with the abridged WALKÜRE on EJS 534, three recordings of the complete La Scala Ring Cycle are said to exist at RAI, Roma (acetates) and Torino (tape transfers), but which of these was used for EJS 538 is not certain: it is identical, however, to the performance issued by the Bruno Walter Society.

The complete GÖTTERDÄMMERUNG was also included on the Fonit-Cetra CFE 101-(18) release of the complete Furtwängler Ring Cycle and on numerous other sets issued subsequently on Everest, Murray Hill, Discocorp, Robin Hood, and Hunt. Excerpts appeared earlier on EJS 318 (January, 1965).

EJS 539: "The Golden Age of Opera" (1 LP)
Issued February, 1971
MATRIX P-2370

SIDES 1-2 (539 A-B):

HÄNSEL UND GRETEL (Humperdinck) (G)
Opera in 3 acts (abridged)
Metropolitan Opera House Orchestra and Chorus/Karl Riedel
Metropolitan Opera broadcast, Boston, 10 Apr 1937

CAST:
Irene Jessner (*Hänsel*); Queena Mario (*Gretel*); Dorothee Manski (*Witch*); Doris Doe (*Gertrude*); Arnold Gabor (*Peter*); Lucielle Browning (*Sandman*); Stella Andreva (*Dewman*).

NOTES: EJS 539

Only minor cuts were made on EJS 539 (the accompanying bulletin boasted that "90% of the most important music of the work" was included): the three Preludes are omitted, along with the Act II/iii Pantomime and the *Dewman's* opening solo in Act III.

Speeds range from 33.3 rpm (Act I), 33.7 rpm raising to 34.3 rpm just before the *Sandman's* solo (Act II), and 33.7 rpm (Act III).

The CAVALLERIA RUSTICANA performed the same afternoon in Boston was issued as EJS 115 (1957).

EJS 540: "The Golden Age of Opera" (1 LP)
Issued February, 1971
MATRIX P-2364

LA TRAVIATA (Verdi) (I)
Opera in 3 acts (excerpts)
Metropolitan Opera House Orchestra and Chorus/Ettore Panizza
Metropolitan Opera broadcast, NYC, 23 Dec 1939

CAST:
Helen Jepson (*Violetta*); Richard Crooks (*Alfredo*); Lawrence Tibbett (*Germont*); Thelma Votipka (*Flora*); Lucielle Browning (*Annina*); Alessio DePaolis (*Gastone*); Wilfred Engelman (*Baron Douphol*); George Cehanovsky (*Marquis d'Obigny*); Louis D'Angelo (*Doctor Grenvil*).

SIDE 1 (540 A):

Act I:
1. CROOKS, JEPSON, and Chorus: Libiamo! ["Brindisi"]
* 2. JEPSON and CROOKS: Oh, Qual pallor! . . . Un dì felice
3. JEPSON and CROOKS: È strano! . . . Ah, fors' è lui . . . Sempre libera . . . to the end of the act

Act II:
* 4. CROOKS: Lunge da lei per me non v'ha diletto! . . . De miei bollenti spiriti
5. TIBBETT, and JEPSON: Madamigella Valery? . . . Pura siccome un angelo . . . Dite alla giovine

SIDE 2 (540 B):

Act II:
1. JEPSON and TIBBETT: Imponete! . . . Felice siate. Addio!
2. TIBBETT and CROOKS: Di provenza il mar . . . Che dici? Ah ferma!
3. JEPSON, CROOKS, TIBBETT, DEPAOLIS, VOTIPKA, ENGELMAN, and Chorus: Invitato a qui seguirmi . . . to the end of the act

Act III:
4. JEPSON: "Teneste la promessa" . . . Addio del passato
5. BROWNING, JEPSON, CROOKS, TIBBETT, and D'ANGELO: Signora! Che t'accade? . . . to the end of the opera

NOTES: EJS 540

This performance plays at a more or less uniform 33.7 rpm, except for occasional, very slight variances in either direction.

The Act I "Un dì felice" scene is slightly abridged, but the off-stage dance music preceding "Oh qual pallor!" is left intact. Similarly, the orchestral introduction preceding Crooks' Act II recitative and aria *is* included.

Excerpts from this performance appeared on both EJS 170 and 171 in January, 1960 and on EJS 488 in November, 1969.

EJS 541: "The Golden Age of Opera" (1 LP)
Issued February, 1971
MATRIX P-2371

"LUCREZIA BORI RECITAL"

SIDE 1 (541 A):

* 1. w. ?studio orch/Frank Black): EXSULTATE, JUBILATE, K. 165, no. 3: Alleluia (Mozart) (L) [33.3 rpm]
Broadcast, ?***MAGIC KEY OF RCA***, WJZ, NYC, 25 Dec 1936

* 2. w. studio orch/André Kostelanetz or Frank Black): RAYMONDA, Op. 57: La primavera d'oro [Valse fantasque] (Betti-Glazunov-arr. La Forge) (I) [32.2 or 33.6 rpm]
Broadcast ***CHESTERFIELD HOUR***, WABC, NYC, 3 Nov 1937 or ***MAGIC KEY OF RCA***, WJZ, NYC, 25 Dec 1936

* 3. w. Detroit Symphony Orchestra/Victor Kolar: VASCO DA GAMA: Ouvre ton coeur (Bizet) (F) [33.6 rpm]
Broadcast, ***FORD SUNDAY EVENING HOUR***, WJR, Detroit, 2 Feb 1936

* 4. w. studio orch/Eugene Goossens or Frank Black: MIGNON, Act I: Connais-tu le pays (Thomas) (F) [33.8 rpm]
Broadcast ***OPERA GUILD BROADCAST***, WJZ, NYC, 30 Dec 1934 or ***MAGIC KEY OF RCA***, WJZ, NYC, 25 Dec 1936

* 5. w. studio orch/André Kostelanetz: LOUISE, Act III: Depuis le jour (Charpentier) (F) [34.8 rpm]
Broadcast ***CHESTERFIELD HOUR***, WABC, NYC, ?6 Mar 1935

* 6. w. Los Angeles Philharmonic Orchestra/Otto Klemperer: LA BOHÈME, Act I: Si, mi chiamano Mimi (Puccini) (I) [34.2 rpm]
Broadcast, ***GENERAL MOTORS PROMENADE CONCERT***, KECA, Hollywood Bowl, Los Angeles, 6 Jun 1937

* 7. w. JOSEPH BENTONELLI, tenor (Los Angeles Philharmonic Orchestra/ Otto Klemperer): LA BOHÈME, Act I: O soave fanciulla (Puccini) (I) [33.5 rpm]
Broadcast, ***GENERAL MOTORS PROMENADE CONCERT***, KECA, Hollywood Bowl, Los Angeles, 6 Jun 1937

8. w. studio orch/Eugene Goossens: L'ENFANT PRODIGUE: L'année en vain chasse l'année! . . . Azaël! Azaël! Pourquoi m'as-tu quitée? ["Air de Lia"] (Debussy) (F)
   Broadcast ***OPERA GUILD BROADCAST***, WJZ, NYC, 30 Dec 1934

* 9. w. ?studio orch/Frank Black: "La Paloma" (Sebastian Yradier) (S)
   Broadcast, ?***MAGIC KEY OF RCA***, WJZ, NYC, 25 Dec 1936

SIDE 2 (**541 B**):

1. I PAGLIACCI, Act I: Qual fiamma ["Ballatella"] (Leoncavallo) (I) [33.3 rpm]
   Broadcast, source and date unconfirmed

2. LA FIGLIA DEL REGGIMENTO (Donizetti) (I) [34.3 rpm]
   a) Act I: Convien partir [Il faut partir]
   b) Act I: Lo dice ognun [Chacun le sait]
   Broadcast, source and date unconfirmed

* 3. w. Los Angeles Philharmonic Orchestra/Otto Klemperer: MANON, Act III: Obéissons quand leur voix appelle ["Gavotte"] (Massenet) (F) [34.2 rpm]
   Broadcast, ***GENERAL MOTORS PROMENADE CONCERT***, KECA, Hollywood Bowl, Los Angeles, 6 Jun 1937

* 4. a) "Cantares" (Joaquin Turina) (S)
   Broadcast, source and date unconfirmed
   b) w. studio orch/Eugene Goossens: SIETE CANÇIONES POPULARES ESPAÑOLAS, no. 4: Jota (De Falla) (S)
   Broadcast ***OPERA GUILD BROADCAST***, WJZ, NYC, 30 Dec 1934 or ***FORD SUNDAY EVENING HOUR***, WJR, Detroit, 2 Feb 1936
   c) CANÇIÓN DEL OLVIDO: Marinella (Emilio Serrano y Ruiz) (S)
   Broadcast, source and date unconfirmed
   d) w. pf/?: 20 CANTOS DE ESPAÑA, no. 20: "Polo" (Joaquin Nin y Castellano) (S)
   Broadcast ***OPERA GUILD BROADCAST***, WJZ, NYC, 30 Dec 1934
   e) w.pf/?: "Clavelitos" (Estic-Valverde) (S)
   Broadcast ***CHESTERFIELD HOUR***, WABC, NYC, 6 Mar 1935

* 5. a) w. pf/?: FOUR SONGS, Op. 2, no 2: The Rose has charmed the nightingale [Plenivshis'rozoy, solovey] (A. Kol'tsov - Rimsky-Korsakov) (E)
   Broadcast, source and date unconfirmed
   b) w. pf/?: SIX SONGS, Op. 38, no. 3: At the Ball [Sred schumnovo bala] (Tolstoy-Tchaikowsky) (E)
   Broadcast, source and date unconfirmed
   c) w. pf/?: "My Native Land," Op. 1, no. 4 (Tolstoy-Grechaninov) (E)
   Broadcast, source and date unconfirmed

6. w. orch/?: "Long, Long Ago" (T.H. Bayly) (E)
   Broadcast, source and date unconfirmed

NOTES: EJS 541

The label of EJS 541 gives 1934-1937 as the inclusive dates of these excerpts, which is probably not far from the truth. The peak of Bori's broadcasting activities came in the period of late 1934-1937: her early appearances on the ***OPERA GUILD BROADCAST***, sponsored by Chase and Sanborn, conducted by Goossens (who is listed in the *New York Times* as "conductor of," not *conducting*, the Cincinnati Symphony: this New York-based program surely used a studio orchestra, not the Cincinnati Symphony) and announced by Deems Taylor; the ***STANDARD BRANDS HOUR*** series of opera adaptations in English (see EJS 289-291 from February, 1964); a three-month stint on the ***CHESTERFIELD HOUR*** (21 January, 1935-15 April, 1935), replacing Rosa Ponselle; and her 1936-1937 appearances on the ***FORD SUNDAY EVENING HOUR***, ***MAGIC KEY OF RCA***, and ***GENERAL MOTORS [HOUR] PROMENADE CONCERTS***. Making these excerpts especially difficult to identify is the fact that, like Tibbett, Rothier, and Bonelli, Bori sang many of her most popular selections on several broadcasts, sometimes only a week apart, making provenance the only reasonable guide (i.e. when other selections from a given broadcast appeared on other EJS LPs, one assumes that Smith had access to that particular program, easing the choice of source--this being the case for the LOUISE "Depuis le jour" and the ***OPERA GUILD/MAGIC KEY*** discrepancies in the listing). Moreover, the first five ***CHESTERFIELD*** broadcasts (21 January-18 February, 1935) were not given detailed descriptions in the *New York Times* radio logs, rendering the repertory for those shows unidentifiable.

See also the endnote for EJS 292 (February, 1964) regarding the Ponselle-Kostelanetz-Bori "transition" on the ***CHESTERFIELD HOUR***.

Speeds vary on EJS 541 and are given in the listing where known.

Side 1 (541 A):

Band 1: Originally issued on EJS 184 (July-August, 1960).

Band 2: "La primavera d'oro" is Frank Laforge's arrangement of the "Valse fantasque" from Glazunov's 1896-1897 ballet, RAYMONDA, Op. 57. The key in which Bori sang this is unknown, but her commercial recording of the song, entitled "Love-Tide of Spring" on Victor 6699, with its Italian text by Betti, was sung in E-flat, hence the two possible playing speeds prescribed above. The ***MAGIC KEY*** performance was issued on EJS 184, though the source and date are based there only on provenance.

Band 3: This "Ouvre ton coeur" appeared earlier on EJS 247 (September, 1962). See also the endnote for EJS 191 (October, 1960) regarding the source of this well-known song.

Band 4: Originally issued on EJS 184 (July-August, 1960).

Band 5: Bori performed the LOUISE aria on 24 February as well as on 6 March, 1935, but considering that the "Clavelitos" from 6 March appears on this LP (II/4e), and that nothing has yet emerged from the 24 February show, the second broadcast is a reasonably safe guess.

Bands 6-7: This joint concert of Bori and Joseph Bentonelli included a "Concert Presentation" of BOHÈME, from which these two items were taken. Two of Bentonelli's solos were included on EJS 292 (February, 1964), along with the "O soave fanciulla" given here; Bori's "Who'll buy my lavender?" appeared on both EJS 295 (March, 1964) and EJS 425 (February, 1968). The broadcast was heard over WJZ, New York City, so probably originated over the Los Angeles Blue Network affiliate, WECA, not KFI.

Band 9: Originally issued on EJS 184 (July-August, 1960).

Side 2 (541 B):

Band 3: The MANON "Gavotte" recently appeared on IRCC CD 803, dated 21 January, 1935--one of the Bori ***CHESTERFIELD*** shows that has remained undocumented owing to a lack of radio log information. It has also been documented as having been performed on the 6 June, 1937 broadcast, however. See also the note for I/6-7.

Band 4d: Though identified as the "Polo," no. 7 of Manuel De Falla's SIETE CANÇIONES POPULARES ESPAÑOLAS, this is in fact the "Polo" of Nin y Castellano, the text of which is quite different. The pianist is unknown: only a "seventy-piece orchestra" is listed in the *New York Times* for this broadcast.

Band 4e: The pianist is unknown: only "concert orchestra and chorus" are listed in the *New York Times* for this broadcast.

Band 5a: Also known under the more accurate transliteration, "Enslaved by the rose, the nightingale."

EJS 542: "The Golden Age of Opera" (2 LPs)
Issued March, 1971
MATRIX P-2397 / P-2398

SIDES 1-4 (542 A-D):

OLYMPIA [OLYMPIE] (Spontini) (I)
Opera in 3 acts (complete)
Orchestra and Chorus of the Teatro alla Scala/Gianandrea Gavazzeni
Broadcast, Teatro alla Scala, Milan, 1 Jun 1966

CAST:
Pilar Lorengar (*Olympie*); Fiorenza Cossotto (*Statire*); Franco Tagliavini (*Cassandre*); Gian Giacomo Guelfi (*Antigone*); Nicola Zaccaria (*The Hiérophant*); Silvio Maionica (*Hermas*); Elvira Rizzotti (*Priestess*); Sophia Mezzetti (*Priestess*); Aurora Cattelani (*Priestess*).

NOTES: EJS 542

This performance was reissued on LP as Melodram MEL-029 and on CD as Giuseppe di Stefano GDS 21021.

EJS 543: "The Golden Age of Opera" (1 LP)
Issued March, 1971
MATRIX P-2399

DIE WALKÜRE (Wagner) (G)
Opera in 3 acts (excerpts)
Metropolitan Opera House Orchestra and Chorus/Erich Leinsdorf
Metropolitan Opera broadcast, NYC, 6 Dec 1941

CAST:
Lauritz Melchior (*Siegmund*); Helen Traubel (*Brünnhilde*); Astrid Varnay (*Sieglinde*); Friedrich Schorr (*Wotan*); [Alexander Kipnis (*Hunding*)]; [Kerstin Thorborg (*Fricka*)]; [Maria Van Delden (*Helmwige*)]; [Thelma Votipka (*Gerhilde*)]; [Maxine Stellman (*Ortlinde*)]; [Lucielle Browning (*Rossweisse*)]; [Mary Van Kirk (*Grimgerde*)]; [Doris Doe (*Waltraute*)]; [Helen Olheim (*Siegrune*)]; [Anna Kaskas (*Schwertleite*)].

SIDE 1 (543 A):

Act I: 1. MELCHIOR and VARNAY: Ein Schwert verheiss mir der Vater . . . to the end of the act
Act II: 2. SCHORR and TRAUBEL: Nun zäume dein Ross, Reisige Maid! . . . Hoyotoho!

SIDE 2 (543 B):

Act II: 1. TRAUBEL and MELCHIOR: Siegmund! Sieh' auf mich! . . . Auf der Walstatt grüss' ich dich wieder!

Act III: 2. SCHORR and TRAUBEL: In festen Schlaf verschliess' ich dich . . . to the end of the opera

NOTES: EJS 543

This was Traubel's first Met *Brünnhilde* and Varnay's stage debut (she was substituting for Lotte Lehmann, and sang *Sieglinde* without rehearsal). Excerpts from the first and second acts of this broadcast appeared earlier on EJS 451 (December, 1968).

Speeds range from 33.8 slowing to 33.3 rpm for the Act I excerpt, 34.0 rpm for Act II/i, and 33.3 for the entire second side of the LP.

EJS 544: "The Golden Age of Opera" (1 LP)
Issued March, 1971
MATRIX P-2402

TANNHÄUSER (Wagner) (G)
Opera in 3 acts (excerpts)
Metropolitan Opera House Orchestra and Chorus/George Szell
Metropolitan Opera broadcast, NYC, 19 Dec 1942

CAST:
Helen Traubel (*Elisabeth*); Kerstin Thorborg (*Venus*); Lauritz Melchior (*Tannhäuser*); Herbert Janssen (*Wolfram*); Alexander Kipnis (*Hermann*); John Garris (*Walther*); Emery Darcy (*Heinrich*); Osie Hawkins (*Biterolf*); John Gurney (*Reinmar*); [Maxine Stellman (*Shepherd*)].

SIDE 1 (544 A):

Act II: 1. TRAUBEL, JANSSEN, MELCHIOR, and KIPNIS: Dich, teure Halle . . . da sie Gehört, dass du des Festes Füstin seist

* 2. MELCHIOR, TRAUBEL, JANSSEN, KIPNIS, GARRIS, DARCY, HAWKINS, GURNEY, and Chorus: Dir, Göttin der Liebe, soll mein Lied ertönen . . . to the end of the act

SIDE 2 (544 B):

Act III: 1. TRAUBEL, JANSSEN, MELCHIOR, THORBORG, and CHORUS: Almächt'ge Jungfrau . . . to the end of the opera

NOTES: EJS 544

Side changes on the original acetates cause slight pitch variations throughout, but the first Act II excerpt, in particular, begins fast (about 34.7 rpm) before gradually slowing to 34.0 rpm. A score is useful here. The speed of *Elisabeth's* opening solo in Act III is rather variable, but beginning at *Wolfram's* "O du mein holder Abendstern," side 2 plays at a consistent 34.0 rpm.

The complete performance was subsequently issued as Music and Arts CD-664 and AS compact disc CD 1101/3.

Side 1 (544 A):

Band 2: Ensemble cuts were made in the actual performance.

EJS 545: "The Golden Age of Opera" (1 LP)
Issued March, 1971
MATRIX P-2403

ALCESTE (Gluck) (F)
Opera in 3 acts (excerpts)
Metropolitan Opera House Orchestra and Chorus/Ettore Panizza
Metropolitan Opera broadcast, NYC, 8 Mar 1941

CAST:
René Maison (*Admetus*); Rose Bampton (*Alceste*); Leonard Warren (*High Priest*); Arthur Kent (*The Voice of Apollo*); [George Cehanovsky (*Herald*]; [Alessio DePaolis (*Evander*)]; [Marita Farell (*A Woman*)]; [Maxine Stellman (*Leader of the People*)]; [Helen Olheim (*Leader of the People*)]; [Wilfred Engelman (*Leader of the People*)].

SIDE 1 (545 A):

Act I: 1. BAMPTON and Chorus: Grands dieux! du destin qui m'accable (with internal and chorus cuts)

2. WARREN and Chorus: Dieu puissant! . . . Suspendez vos sacrés mystères (with internal chorus cuts; chorus *reprise* omitted)

3. BAMPTON and WARREN: Où suis-je? . . . Non! ce n'est point un sacrifice! . . . Arbitres du sort des humains . . . Tes destins sont remplis . . . Déjà la mort s'apprête . . . Divinités du Styx! (with internal cuts)

Act II: 4. a) MAISON, BAMPTON, and Chorus: O moments délicieux! . . . Bannis la crainte et les alarmes . . . Ciel! Tu pleures? . . . Toi! ciel! Alceste! (with internal cuts)
b) MAISON, BAMPTON, and Chorus: Barbare! Non, sans toi je ne puis vivre . . . tu n'en doutes pas (Chorus omitted)

SIDE 2 (545 B):

Act II: 1. MAISON, BAMPTON, and Chorus: Et pour sauver mes jours . . . Grand dieux! pour mon époux j'implore vos secours . . . C'est à moi seule à remplir votre oracle
2. BAMPTON: Dérobez-moi vos pleurs . . . Ah! malgré moi mon faible coeur partage ["O ciel! quel supplice" section truncated]

Act III: 3. BAMPTON: Grand Dieux, soutenez mon courage! . . . Ah, divinités implacables! [Chorus, "Malheureuse!," omitted]
4. a) BAMPTON, MAISON, and Chorus: Ciel! Admète! . . . Alceste, au nom des dieux . . . Alceste! Alceste!
b) BAMPTON, MAISON, and Chorus: Alceste! Alceste! Adieu cher époux. Arrêtez!
c) KENT: Poursuis o digne ils du souverain des cieux!
Act II: d) ORCHESTRA: *Divertissement*, No 2: Contredanse
Act III: e) MAISON and BAMPTON: Ô mes amis! Ô mes enfents! . . . Nos malheurs sont finis
f) ORCHESTRA (flute/Nicola Laucella): *Divertissements*
No. 1: Entrée de la danse
No. 2: Marche
No. 3: Solo de flûte
No. 6: Chaconne
Act II: g) CHORUS: Vivez, aimez des jours dignes d'envie

NOTES: EJS 545

The internal cuts and Act II interpolations in the last act are *performance* alterations. Note that the Act II "Barbare! Non, sans toi je ne puis vivre" at the end of the first side continues without break on side 2.

The acetates of bands 1 and 4f contain abrupt, disorienting drops in pitch, especially the orchestral "Chaconne," which slides downward in stages.

The "Solo de flûte" was probably played by Nicola (aka Nicholas) Laucella (1882-1952), a member of the Met Orchestra from 1918 to 1943 and before that, the New York Philharmonic (1906-1918). Laucella made several recordings--acoustical solos and duets, and with the Longo Trio, ensembles on Pathé and Emerson. He provided the obbligato for Giuseppe De Luca's I GIOIELLI DELLA MADONNA "Serenata" in 1930, issued as Victor 3066 and HMV DA 1169.

Arias of Bampton and Warren appeared earlier on EJS 212 (May, 1961): see the endnote for that issue regarding this production of ALCESTE.

Library of Congress tape: 8944-13 (complete broadcast).

EJS 546: "The Golden Age of Opera" (1 LP)
Issued March, 1971
MATRIX P-2404

SIDES 1-2 (546 A-B):

DIDO AND AENEAS (Purcell) (E)
Opera in 3 acts and a Prologue (complete)
Mermaid Theater Orchestra/Geraint Jones; 'cello continuo/Ambrose Gaumblett
Broadcast, Mermaid Theater, London, 1 Oct 1951

CAST:
Kirsten Flagstad (*Dido*); Thomas Hemsley (*Aeneas*); Maggie Teyte (*Belinda*); Edith Coates (*Sorceress*); Arda Mandikian (*First Witch*); Ilsa Steinora (*Second Witch*); Eilidh McNab (*First Lady*); Ann Dowdall (*Second Lady*); Murray Dickie (*Spirit*); Powell Lloyd (*Sailor*).

NOTES: EJS 546

This performance was heard over BBC 3. Dated incorrectly as September, 1951 on the label of EJS 546. The opening scene of this performance with Flagstad and Teyte appeared earlier on EJS 183 (July-August, 1960).

This production of DIDO marked Teyte's final stage appearance.

EJS 547: The Golden Age of Opera" (2 LPs)
Issued April, 1971
MATRIX P-2439 / P-2440

SIDES 1-4 (547 A-B):

WERTHER (Massenet) (I)
Opera in 4 acts (complete)
Orchestra and Chorus of the Palacio de las Bellas Artes, Mexico City/Renato Cellini
Broadcast, Palacio de las Bellas Artes, Mexico City, ?XEN and XENN-FM, 3 Jul 1949

CAST:
Giuseppe Di Stefano (*Werther*); Giulietta Simionato (*Charlotte*); Fausto Del Prado (*Albert*); Eugenia Rocca Bruna (*Sophie*); Ignacio Ruffino (*Le Bailli*); Gilberto Cerda (*Johann*); Francesco Tortolero (*Schmidt*); ? (*Käthchen*); ? (*Brühlmann*).

NOTES: EJS 547

Excerpts from this performance appeared earlier on EJS 303 (June, 1964) and Cetra LO-30. Excerpts from other 1949 Palacio de las Bellas Artes performances were featured over the course of several "Golden Age of Opera" LPs: 302-303 and 319 (June, 1964-February, 1965).

EJS 548: "The Golden Age of Opera" (2 LPs)
Issued April, 1971
MATRIX P-2437 / P-2438

DIE MEISTERSINGER VON NÜRNBERG (Wagner) (G)
Opera in 3 acts (excerpts)
Orchestra and Chorus of the Berlin Staatsoper/Leo Blech
Live recording (HMV), Theater Unter den Linden, Berlin, 22 May 1928

CAST:
Friedrich Schorr (*Hans Sachs*); Robert Hutt (*Walther*); Elfriede Marherr-Wagner (*Eva*); Emanuel List (*Pogner*); Leo Schützendorf (*Beckmesser*); Carl Jöken (*David*); [Lydia Kindermann (*Magdalene*)].

SIDES 1-3 (548 A-C):

Act I: 1. JÖKEN, HUTT, and Chorus: [Wer alles das merkt, weiss und kennt,] wird doch immer noch nicht Meister genennt . . . Dorthin! Hierher!
CLR 4165-1A/4166-1 HMV EJ 277
2. LIST: [Nun hört, und versteht mich recht!] Das schöne Fest . . . Eva, mein einzig Kind, zur Eh'!
CLR 4168-1/4169-1A HMV EJ 278

Act II: 3. JÖKEN and Chorus: Heil!, Heil zur Eh' dem jungen Mann! . . . Juchhei! Juchhei! Johannistag! ["Chorus of Apprentices"]
CLR 4072-1T1 HMV EJ 279
4. JÖKEN, SCHORR, LIST, and MARHERR-WAGNER: Hab ich heut' Singstund? . . . Hör' wohl ein Meister deinen Wahl
CLR 4171-1A HMV 279
5. SCHORR, SCHÜTZENDORF, HUTT, MARHERR-WAGNER, and Chorus: Jerum! Jerum! . . . to the beginning of the riot scene
CLR 4174-1/4175-1A HMV 280
CLR 4176-1/4177-1AT1 HMV 281
CLR 4178-1 HMV 282

Act III: 6. JÖKEN and SCHORR: End of Act III Prelude . . . Gleich! Meister! . . . Kann mir gar nicht mehr denken wie der Knieriemen thut!
CLR 4180-1A HMV EJ 282
CLR 4182-1 HMV EJ 283
7. SCHORR, MARHERR-WAGNER, and HUTT: Grüss Gott, mein Ev'chen . . . Nehmt eu'ren Stand!
CLR 4185-1 HMV EJ 283
CLR 4186-1A/4187-1 HMV EJ 284
8. HUTT and Chorus: Sankt Crispin, lobet ihn! ["Cobbler's Chorus"] . . . Dance of the Apprentices
CLR 4189-1 HMV EJ 285
9. JÖKEN and Chorus: Entrance of the Mastersingers . . . Wach auf! Wolken geht
CLR 4190-1A HMV EJ 285
10. SCHORR and Chorus: Verachtet mir die Meister nicht . . . to the end of the opera
CLR 4194-1A/4195-1 HMV EJ 286

SIEGFRIED (Wagner) (G)
Opera in 3 acts (excerpts)
Metropolitan Opera House Orchestra and Chorus/Fritz Stiedry
Metropolitan Opera broadcast, NYC, 10 Feb 1951

CAST:
Set Svanholm (*Siegfried*); Helen Traubel (*Brünnhilde*); [Peter Klein (*Mime*)]; [Ferdinand Frantz (The *Wanderer*)]; [Gerhard Pechner (*Alberich*)]; [Deszö Ernster (*Fafner*)]; [Karin Branzell (*Erda*)]; [Erna Berger (*Forest Bird*)].

SIDE 4 (548 D):

1. Act III: TRAUBEL and SVANHOLM: Heil dir, Sonne! . . . to the end of the opera

NOTES: EJS 548

Side 1 (548 A):

This live MEISTERSINGER consisted of 31 matrices (CLR 4165-CLR 4195), only twenty of which were actually issued (Electrola EJ 277-EJ 286). The performance itself, if not the recording of it, was mounted to mark the 115th anniversary of the composer's birthday. See A. F. R. Lawrence's thorough analysis of these recordings, "Die Meistersinger - 1928," in the *British Institute of Recorded Sound Bulletin*, 8 (Spring, 1958), pp. 2-5. Lawrence claims that the unissued masters (all first takes or alternates recorded simultaneously on a second cutter, suffixed -1A) were destroyed: certainly, Smith had access here only to the published sides.

The original division of the Electrola set, as taken from labels and from the recording ledgers, is given below, including all of the unpublished masters. All were recorded at the same 22 May, 1928 performance. Note that the first three excerpts from Act II were numbered out of sequence and that the listing for EJS 548, above, reflects the actual starting and ending texts recorded. Matrix CLR 4172-1T1 was defective, and was issued on EJ 279 as a dubbing, numbered CL 4<u>0</u>72-1T1. *Some* late pressings of EJ 281 used the transfer matrix CLR-4177-1AT1, but the original, CLR 4177-1A, is also known to have been used on EJS 281.

Act I:

Hilf Gott! Will ich denn Schuster sein?
CLR 4165-1A EJ 277
Trotz grossem Fleiss und Emsigkeit
CLR 4166-1 EJ 277
Ja, ja, dem Merker!
CLR 4167-1 unpublished
Das schöne Fest
CLR 4168-1 EJ 278
In deutschen Landen
CLR 4169-1A EJ 278
Ein jedes Meistergesanges Bar
CLR 4170-1 unpublished

Act II:

Hab' ich heut' Singstund?
CLR 4171-1A EJ 279
Johannistag! Johanistag!
CLR 4172-1 unpublished (*defective*)
CL 4<u>0</u>72-1T1 EJ 279 (*dubbing*)
Was giebt's? Treff' ich dich wieder am Schlag?
CLR 4173-1 unpublished (*defective*)
Jerum! Jerum! (part 1)
CLR 4174-1 EJ 280
Jerum! Jerum! (part 2)
CLR 4175-1A EJ 280
Schweigt doch! Weckt ihr die
CLR 4176-1, EJ 281
Wlch' toller Spuck!
CLR 4177-1A EJ 281
CLR 4177-1AT1 EJ 281
Sachs! Seht, ihr bringt mich um
CLR 4178-1 EJ 282
Was ist das für Zanken und Streit!
CLR 4179-1 unpublished

Act III:

Prelude (first part only)
CLR 4180-1 unpublished
Gleich, Meister! Hier!
CLR 4181-1A EJ 282
Blumen und Bänder seh'ich dort?
CLR 4182-1 EJ 283
Wahn! Wahn!
CLR 4183-1 unpublished
Doch eines Abend's spät
CLR 4184-1 unpublished
Grüss Gott, mein Ev'chen!
CLR 4185-1 EJ 283
Weilten die Sterne
CLR 4186-1A EJ 284
Was ohne deine Liebe
CLR 4187-1 EJ 284
Selig, wie die Sonne ["Quintet"]
CLR 4188-1 unpublished
Sankt Krispin, lobet ihn!
CLR 4189-1 EJ 285
Entrance of the Meistersingers
CLR 4190-1A EJ 285
Morgen ich leuchte
CLR 4191-1 unpublished
Morgenlich leuchtend im rosigen Schein
CLR 4192-1 unpublished
Abendich dämmernd umschloss mich die Nacht
CLR 4193-1 unpublished
Verachtet mir die Meister nicht
CLR 4194-1A EJ 286
Ehrt eure deutschen Meist
CLR 4195-1 EJ 286

The complete excerpts were reissued on LP by Discocorp as *I Grandi Interpreti* IGA 298 and later on Pearl CD GEMM 9340.

Side 2 (548 B):

This Act III SIEGFRIED excerpt is taken from one of the Saturday-afternoon Ring Cycle performances of the 1950-1951 Met season. The RHEINGOLD from this cycle was issued as UORC 276 (January-February, 1976).

EJS 549: "The Golden Age of Opera" (1 LP)
Issued April, 1971
MATRIX P-2435

SIDES 1-2 (549 A-B):

IL RITORNO [DIE HEIMKEHR AUS DER FREMDE] (Mendelssohn) (I)
Opera in 1 act (complete)
Orchestra and Chorus of Radio Italiana [RAI], Milano/Alfredo Simonetto
RAI broadcast, Milan, 21 Feb 1954

CAST:
Ester Orel (*Lisbeth*); Rina Corsi (*Ursula*); Hugues Cuénod (*Hermann*); Silvio Maionica (*Kauz*); Giuseppe Ciabattini (*The Burgermeister*); Igino Bonazzi (*Martin*).

EJS 550: "The Golden Age of Opera" (1 LP)
Issued April, 1971
MATRIX P-2441

BORIS GODUNOV (Mussorgsky) (R and I)
Opera in 4 acts (excerpts)
Metropolitan Opera House Orchestra and Chorus/George Szell
Metropolitan Opera broadcast, 13 Feb 1943

CAST:
Alexander Kipnis (*Boris*); Irra Petina (*Feodor*); René Maison (*Dimitri*); Kerstin Thorborg (*Marina*); [Marita Farell (*Xenia*)]; [Anna Kaskas (*Nurse*)]; [Alessio DePaolis (*Schouisky*)]; [George Cehanovsky (*Tchelkaloff*)]; [Nicola Moscona (*Pimenn*)]; [Leonard Warren (*Rangoni*)]; [Norman Cordon (*Varlaam*)]; [John Dudley (*Missail*)]; [Doris Doe (*Innkeeper*)]; [John Garris (*Simpleton*)]; [John Gurney (*Police Officer*)]; [Osie Hawkins (*Sergeant*)]; [Lansing Hatfield (*Lovitzky*)]; [Lorenzo Alvary (*Tcherniakowsky*)]; [Emery Darcy (*Boyar*)]; [Maxine Stellman (*Peasant*)]; [Helen Olheim (*Peasant*)]; [Lodovico Oliviero (*Peasant*)]; [Wilfred Engelman (*Peasant*)].

SIDE 1 (550 A):

Act I: 1. KIPNIS and Chorus: My heart is sad . . . to the end of the scene

Act II: 2. PETINA and KIPNIS: And you, my son, so busy? . . . Mine is the highest power

3. KIPNIS: Ah! for some air! I am suffocating here! . . . to the end of the act

Act III: * 4. MAISON and THORBORG:

a) Stasera, presso alla fonte . . . Ah, mia divina! (to the beginning of the "Polonaise")

b) Dimitri, Zarevic, Dimitri . . . E lei, Marina! Tu, mia regina! . . . to the end of the scene

5. KIPNIS, PETINA, and Chorus: Farewell, my son, I am dying . . . to the end of the opera

SIEGFRIED (Wagner) (G)
Opera in 3 acts (excerpts)
Metropolitan Opera House Orchestra and Chorus/Artur Bodanzky
Metropolitan Opera broadcast, NYC, 10 Dec 1938

CAST:
Carl Hartmann (*Siegfried*); Kirsten Flagstad (*Brünnhilde*); [Erich Witte (*Mime*)]; [Friedrich Schorr (*The Wanderer*)]; [Adolf Vogel (*Alberich*)]; [Norman Cordon (*Fafner*)]; [Anna Kaskas (*Erda*)]; [Natalie Bodanya (*Forest Bird*)].

SIDE 2 (550 B):

Act III: 1. FLAGSTAD and HARTMANN: Heil dir, Sonne! . . . to the end of the opera

NOTES: EJS 550

Side 1 (550 A):

Note that while Kipnis sings *Boris* in Russian, the rest of the cast sang in Italian, hence the listing of the contents above in English (for Russian) and Italian. The other *Boris* at the Met that season was Pinza: see EJS 561 (June, 1971).

The Act III/ii excerpt omits *Rangoni*, and thus, his dialogue with *Dimitri* after "Voce divina!" (the excerpt cuts off before the Polonaise).

This side plays in score pitch at 33.3 rpm.

Side 2 (550 B):

Other excerpts from the second and third acts of this SIEGFRIED (without Flagstad) are said to exist.

Most of the acetate sides used to compile this SIEGFRIED excerpt seem to stabilize at 34.0 rpm, except in the middle of "Ewig war ich," where there is a shift to 34.7 rpm. A violent splice at *Siegfried's* re-entry, finds the speed descending to 33.3 rpm through the finale.

EJS 551: "The Golden Age of Opera" (1 LP)
Issued April, 1971
MATRIX P-2436

RIGOLETTO (Verdi) (I)
Opera in 3 acts (excerpts)
Metropolitan Opera House Orchestra and Chorus/Ettore Panizza
Metropolitan Opera broadcast, NYC, 28 Dec 1935

CAST:
Lawrence Tibbett (*Rigoletto*); Lily Pons (*Gilda*); Frederick Jagel (*The Duke of Mantua*); Virgilio Lazzari (*Sparafucile*); Helen Olheim (*Maddalena*); Alfredo Gandolfi (*Monterone*); Hubert Raidich (*Count di Ceprano*); Giordano Paltrinieri (*Borsa*); George Cehanovsky (*Marullo*); Charlotte Symons (*Countess di Ceprano*); Thelma Votipka (*Giovanna*); Paolina Tomisani (*A Page*); ? (*Usher*).

SIDE 1 (551 A):

Act I: * 1. JAGEL, PALTRINIERI, CEHANOVSKY, TIBBETT, RAIDICH, GANDOLFI, and Chorus:
a) Beginning of the opera . . . Questa o quella
b) Gran nuova gran nuova! . . . Un'ora fatale fu questa per te

* 2. TIBBETT, LAZZARI, PONS, JAGEL, and VOTIPKA:
a) Quel vecchio maledivami! . . . Pari siamo
b) Giovanna, ho dei rimorsi . . . E il sol dell'anima

Act II: 3. JAGEL: Ella mi fu rapita! . . . Parmi, veder le lagrime

SIDE 2 (551 B):

Act II: * 1. CEHANOVSKY, RAIDICH, TOMISANI, TIBBETT, PONS, PALTRINIERI, [Usher], and Chorus:
a) [Povero Rigoletto] . . . Buon giorno, Rigoletto . . . Non lasciamo d'osservar
b) Compiuto pur quanto a fare mi resta . . . to the end of the act

Act III: 2. PONS, TIBBETT, LAZZARI, OLHEIM, JAGEL, and Chorus:
a) E l'ami? Sempre . . . La donna è mobile . . . Bella figlia dell'amore
b) Della vendetta alfin giunge l'istante! . . . Lassù in cielo . . . to the end of the opera

NOTES: EJS 551

This was Tibbett's first Met *Rigoletto*, and Votipka's first *Giovanna* (previously she had taken the role of *Countess di Ceprano*). Ostensibly, Smith had access to Tibbett's acetates of this performance, thought to be the only known copy, but missing two sides from the conclusion of Act II. The Act III quartet appeared earlier on EJS 213 (May, 1961).

34.0 rpm is the correct playing speed for bands 1 and 2 of the first side, while 33.6 rpm is required for the third band; side 2 is in pitch 33.6 rpm except for the final scene between *Gilda* and *Rigoletto*, which requires 34.3 rpm. The cuts noted below were almost undoubtedly made by Smith for purposes of timing.

Side 1 (551 A):

Band 1: The Prelude to the opera and the scene with the *Duke* and the *Count* and *Countess di Ceprano* are omitted.

Band 2: The "Veglia, o donna" is omitted.

Side 2 (551 B):

Band 1: *Gilda's* "Tutte le feste" is omitted. The *Usher* is not identified in either edition of the Metropolitan Opera annals, but is heard in this excerpt.

EJS 552: "The Golden Age of Opera" (2 LPs)
Issued May, 1971
MATRIX P-2468 / P-2469

SIDES 1-2 (552 A-B):

LA FANCIULLA DEL WEST (Puccini) (I)
Opera in 3 acts (complete)
Orchestra and Chorus of the Teatro dell'Opera, Roma/Vincenzo Bellezza
Broadcast, Teatro dell'Opera, Rome, 30 Mar 1957

CAST:
Giacomo Lauri-Volpi (*Dick Johnson*); Magda Olivero (*Minnie*); Gian Giacomo Guelfi (*Jack Rance*); Giulio Tomei (*Ashby*); Arturo La Porta (*Sonora*); Adelio Zagonara (*Nick*); Alfredo Colella (*Jake Wallace*); Salvatore di Tommaso (*Trin*); Virgilio Ascorro (*Sid*); Giuseppe Forgione (*Bello*); Paolo Carroli (*Harry*); Enzo Titta (*Larkins*); Corinna Vozza (*Wowkle*); Pietro Paserotti (*Billy*); Gino Conti (*José Castro*); Marco Rogani (*Pony Express*).

NOTES: EJS 552

Lauri-Volpi's two major arias from this performance later appeared on ANNA 1040 (May-June, 1979).

EJS 553: "The Golden Age of Opera" (3 LPs)
Issued May, 1971
MATRIX P-2470 / P-2471 / P-2472

SIDES 1-5 (553 A-E):

UN BALLO IN MASCHERA (Verdi) (I)
Opera in 3 acts (complete)
Royal Philharmonic Orchestra and Glyndebourne Festival Chorus/ Vittorio Gui
Broadcast, Edinburgh Festival, Edinburgh, September, 1949

CAST:
Mirto Picchi (*Riccardo*); Ljuba Welitsch (*Amelia*); Paolo Silveri (*Renato*); Alda Noni (*Oscar*); Jean Watson (*Ulrica*); Ian Wallace (*Sam*); Hervey Alan (*Tom*); Francis Loring (*Silvano*); George Israel (*Judge*); ? (*Servant*).

SIDE 6 (553 F):

OLYMPIA [OLYMPIE] (Spontini) (I)
Opera in 3 acts (excerpts)
Orchestra and Chorus of the Maggio Musicale Fiorentino/Tullio Serafin
Broadcast, Maggio Musicale Fiorentino, Florence, 14 May 1950

CAST:
Renata Tebaldi (*Olympie*); Giorgio Kokolios-Bardi (*Cassandre*); Mario Petri (*Antigone*); Elena Nicolai (*Statire*); Giacomo Vaghi (*Le Hiérophant*); ? (*Hermas*).

* 1. Act III: TEBALDI, KOKOLIOS-BARDI, PETRI, NICOLAI, VAGHI, [Hermas], and Chorus: Ô saintes lois de la nature . . . to the end of the act

2. LJUBA WELITSCH, soprano (BBC Theater Orchestra/James Robertson): LE NOZZE DI FIGARO, K. 492, Act II: Ihr, die ihr Triebe [Voi che sapete] (Mozart) (G)
Broadcast, BBC, London, 26 Sep 1948

3. LJUBA WELITSCH, soprano (BBC Theater Orchestra/James Robertson): TOSCA, Act II: Nur die Schönheit [Vissi d'arte] (Puccini) (G)
Broadcast, BBC, London, 26 Sep 1948

4. LJUBA WELITSCH, soprano (BBC Theater Orchestra/James Robertson): PRODANÁ NEVĚSTA [THE BARTERED BRIDE], Act III: Endlich allein . . . Wie Fremde und Todt [Och, jaký to žal] (Smetena) (G)
Broadcast, BBC, London, 26 Sep 1948

NOTES: EJS 553

The BALLO was taken from the third Edinburgh Festival, a production of the Glyndebourne Opera Company sponsored by the Glyndebourne Society, and was subsequently reissued as Melodram MEL-019.

The May, 1971 bulletin quotes at length a justification of "*why* another Ballo in Maschera," authored by the Earl of Harewood which appeared originally in the May, 1971 issue of *Opera*. This portion of the essay was subsequently republished in (now) Lord Harewood's article on BALLO in *Opera on Record*, Alan Blyth, ed. (London: Hutchinson & Co., 1979, and New York: Harper and Row, 1982), p. 260.

The OLYMPIE Act III/i is apparently the only surviving excerpt from this festival performance, which is known to have been broadcast in its entirety.

EJS 554: "The Golden Age of Opera" (3 LPs)
Issued May, 1971
MATRIX P-2473 / P-2474 / P-2475

SIDES 1-6 (554 A-F):

LE DUE ILLUSTRI RIVALI (Mercadante) (I)
Opera in 3 acts (complete)
Orchestra and Chorus of the Teatro la Fenice, Venezia/Ettore Gracis
Broadcast, Teatro la Fenice, Venice, 9 Dec 1970

CAST:
Claudia Parada (*Bianca*); Vasso Papantoniu (*Elvira*); Georgio Pappas (*Gusmano*); Amedeo Zambon (*Alvaro*); Antonio Liviero (*Armando di Foix*); Alessandro Maddalena (*Inigo*); Maurizio Mazzieri (*Enellina*).

SIDE 6 (554-F):

2. FRANCINE GIRONES, soprano, and GIOVANNA FIORONI, mezzo-soprano (Orchestra of A. Scarlatti di Napoli/Massimo Pradella): ADELAIDE E COMINGO, Act ?: Dove son? (Giovanni Pacini) (I)
   Broadcast, ?, 1970

3. GIORGIO GRIMALDI, tenor (Orchestra of Radio Italiana [RAI], Milano/Luciano Rosada): LA SPOSA FEDELE, Act ?: Si, venite (Giovanni Pacini) (I)
   RAI broadcast, date unknown

4. CARLO MICALUCCI, baritone (?Orchestra of Radio Italiana [RAI]/?): GLI ARABI NELLE GALLIE, Act ?: Piangerò più (Giovanni Pacini) (I)
   ?RAI broadcast, date unknown

NOTES: EJS 554

This performance of DUE ILLUSTRI RIVALI was reissued as MRF 88.

EJS 555: "The Golden Age of Opera" (3 LPs)
Issued June, 1971
MATRIX P-2542 / P-2543 / P-2544

SIDES 1-6 (555 A-F):

L'AFRICAINE (Meyerbeer) (I)
Opera in 5 acts (complete)
Orchestra and Chorus of the Teatro Comunale, Firenze/Riccardo Muti
In-house recording, Maggio Musicale Fiorentino, Teatro Comunale, Florence, 30 Apr 1970

CAST:
Veriano Luchetti (*Vasco da Gama*); Jessye Norman (*Selika*); Gian Giacomo Guelfi (*Nelusko*); Mietta Sighele (*Ines*); Agostino Ferrin (*Don Pedro*); Gianfranco Casarini (*Don Diego*); Dino Formichini (*Don Alvaro*); Giuliana Matteini (*Anna*); Graziano Dal Vivo (*Grand Inquisitor*); Mario Rinaudo (*Grand Brahmin*); Ottavio Taddei (*Usher*); Ottavio Taddei (*Priest*); Valiano Natali (*First Sailor*); Mario Frosini (*Second Sailor*).

NOTES: EJS 555

The AFRICAINE was subsequently reissued as MRF 85.

The June, 1971 bulletin brought still another dramatic but premature farewell from Smith: "All good things must end," he begins, "and so, my friends, after 17 years, the Golden Age of Opera's regular series of releases will cease to be with this June issue." The statistics which followed ("a total of 566 releases of 725 LP discs . . . not including eighteen other discs which were special releases") were slightly less that accurate, but certainly close enough to impress upon us the enormity of Smith's undertaking, not to mention the extent of his contribution--yet to be matched in its quality of offerings. There would be a gap in GAO at this point: where a September bulletin usually followed, the next group of LPs (EJS 567-571) would not come until October, the penultimate GAO issue, followed by a last offering of seven discs in November, 1971.

EJS 556: "The Golden Age of Opera" (2 LPs)
Issued June, 1971
MATRIX P-2552 / P-2553

TRISTAN UND ISOLDE (Wagner) (G)
Opera in 3 acts (excerpts)
Metropolitan Opera House Orchestra and Chorus/Erich Leinsdorf
Metropolitan Opera broadcast, NYC, 6 Feb 1943

CAST:
Lauritz Melchior (*Tristan*); Helen Traubel (*Isolde*); Alexander Kipnis (*King Mark*); Julius Huehn (*Kurvenal*); Emery Darcy (*Melot*); Kerstin Thorborg (*Brangäne*); Karl Laufkoetter (*Shepherd*); John Gurney (*Steersman*); John Garris (*Sailor's Voice*).

SIDE 1 (556 A):

Act I: 1. TRAUBEL, THORBORG, GARRIS, HUEHN, MELCHIOR, and chorus: Wer wagt mich zu höhnen? . . . Weh' mir! Nahe das Land! (to the end of Scene iii)

SIDE 2 (556 B):

Act I: 1. MELCHIOR, TRAUBEL, THORBORG, HUEHN, and Chorus: Begehrt, Herrin . . . to the end of the act

SIDE 3 (556 C):

Act II: 1. MELCHIOR, TRAUBEL, THORBORG, DARCY, and KIPNIS: Isolde! Geliebte! Tristan! Geliebte! . . . O sink' hernieder, Nacht der Liebe! . . . to the end of the act

SIDE 4 (556 D):

Act III: 1. HUEHN, MELCHIOR, TRAUBEL, GURNEY, THORBORG, DARCY, and KIPNIS: Bist du nun todt? . . . Mild und leise . . . to the end of the opera

EJS 557: The Golden Age of Opera" (1 LP)
Issued June, 1971
MATRIX P-2554

LOHENGRIN (Wagner) (G)
Opera in 3 acts (excerpts)
Metropolitan Opera House Orchestra and Chorus/Maurice de Abravanel
Metropolitan Opera broadcast, NYC, 27 Mar 1937

CAST:
René Maison (*Lohengrin*); Kirsten Flagstad (*Elsa*); Karin Branzell (*Ortrud*); Julius Huehn (*Telramund*); Ludwig Hofmann (*King Heinrich*); Arnold Gabor (*Herald*).

SIDE 1 (557 A):

Act I: 1. **HOFMANN** and Chorus: Hört! Grafen, Edle, Freie von Brabant! . . . Jetzt rede das der Drangsal Grund ich weiss

2. **FLAGSTAD, HOFMANN, HUEHN,** and Chorus: Mein armer Bruder . . . So ist es Zeit, dass nun der Ruf ergeh (to one bar before "Wer hier im Gotteskampf")

3. **MELCHIOR, HOFMANN, FLAGSTAD,** and Chorus: Ein Wunder! ein Wunder ist gekommen . . . Schau' ich den herren wonniglichen Mann (one bar before "Nun hört! Euch Volk")

4. **MELCHIOR, HUEHN, HOFMANN, FLAGSTAD,** and **BRANZELL**: Nun hört mich, und achtet wohl . . . to the end of the act

SIDE 2 (557 B):

Act II: 1. **FLAGSTAD** and **BRANZELL**: Euch lüften, die mein Klagen . . . In liebe!

2. **BRANZELL** and **FLAGSTAD**: Entweihte Götter! . . . durch Ihren Hochmuth werd' ihr Reu'

Act III: 3. **MAISON** and **FLAGSTAD**: Das süsse Lied verhallt . . . Rette dich! Dein Schwert! Dein Schwert!

4. **MAISON, HOFMANN, FLAGSTAD,** and Chorus: In fernem Land . . . Welch' harte Noth thust du uns an!

NOTES: EJS 557:

Excerpts from this performance were featured earlier on EJS 183 (July-August, 1960) and EJS 258 (January, 1963).

Library of Congress tape: 15778-41A (complete broadcast).

EJS 558: "The Golden Age of Opera" (1 LP)
Issued June, 1971
MATRIX P-2536

SIDE 1 (558 A):

DON GIOVANNI, K. 527 (Mozart) (I)
Opera in 2 acts (excerpts)
Orchestra and Chorus of the St. Louis Opera/Laszlo Halasz
Broadcast, St. Louis Opera, KMOX [CBS], St. Louis, 16 Apr 1941

CAST:
Ezio Pinza (*Don Giovanni*); Tito Schipa (*Don Ottavio*); Anne Roselle (*Donna Anna*); Vivian Della Chiesa (*Donna Elvira*); Margit Bokor (*Zerlina*); Lorenzo Alvary (*Leporello*); Carlos Alexander (*Masetto*); [Nicola Moscona (*The Commandant*)].

SIDE 2 (558 B): "MERCADANTE"

1. NICOLETTA PANNI, soprano (orch/?): ELISA E CLAUDIO, Act ?: Miei cari figli . . . Giusto ciel (Mercadante) (I)
   ?Broadcast, source and date unknown

* 2. MAGDA OLIVERO, soprano (Orchestra of Radio Italiana [RAI], Milano/Rino Maione): PELAGIO, Act ?: Ah, più ferve la pugna . . . Un infelice non infelice (Mercadante) (I)
   RAI broadcast, Milano, 25 Nov 1970 (recorded 10 Sep 1970)

* 3. ETTORE BASTIANINI, baritone (pf/Luciano Bettarini; 'cello/Massimo Amfiteatroff): "Il sogno" (Mercadante) (I)
   RAI broadcast, city unknown, circa May-June, 1957

4. MAGDA OLIVERO, soprano (Orchestra of Radio Italiana [RAI], Milano/Rino Maione): LE SETTE ULTIME PAROLE DI NOSTRO SIGNORE: Di mille colpe (Mercadante) (I)
   RAI broadcast, Milano, 25 Nov 1970 (recorded 10 Sep 1970)

NOTES: **EJS 558**

The DON GIOVANNI is presented here complete as it was broadcast nationally (45 minutes) over CBS. The final measures of Schipa's "Il mio tesoro" are heard behind a CBS announcement giving the cast of the production and promoting upcoming network broadcasts.

Side 2 (558 B):

Band 1: See the endnote for EJS 480 (October, 1969) regarding Panni.

Band 2: Labeled "Bianca's aria" on EJS 558. The date of this recording and broadcast is taken from Vincenzo Quattrocchi's *Magda Olivero: Una voce per tre generazioni* (Torino: ?The Author, 1984).

Band 3: Given on the label of EJS 558 as "Il bacio," accompanied by piano and string quartet. Marina Boagno and Gilberto Starone's *Ettore Bastianini: Una voce di Bronzo e di Vellutto* (Parma: Azzali Editori, 1991) give the title as "Il sogno," as well as the correct details of accompaniment and the approximate date. Three other songs were recorded by Bastianini with piano and cello for the same broadcast:

"Non posso credetervi" (Bossi), "Ovunque tu" (van Westerhout), and "Eterna memoria" (Ponchielli). RAI presumably broadcast all four, but when, and on what program, could not be determined.

Band 4: Labeled "Dalle sette parole di nostra Signore" on EJS 588, probably transcribed literally from the Italian announcement given on the broadcast by someone unfamiliar with the actual title of this Mercadante "Sacred Drama." See also the endnote for II/2.

EJS 559: "The Golden Age of Opera" (1 LP)
Issued June, 1971
MATRIX P-2539

RIGOLETTO (Verdi) (I)
Opera in 3 acts (excerpts)
Orchestra and Chorus of the Palacio de las Bellas Artes, Mexico City/Renato Cellini
Broadcast, Palacio de las Bellas Artes, XEX, Mexico City, 22 Jun 1948

CAST:
Giuseppe Valdengo (*Rigoletto*); Nadine Conner (*Gilda*); Giuseppe Di Stefano (*The Duke of Mantua*); Ignacio Rufino (*Sparafucile*); Oralia Dominguez (*Maddalena*); [Rafael Lerdo de Tejada (*Monterone*)]; Luz Farfan (*Giovanna*); Francesco Alonso (*Count di Ceprano*); [?] (*Countess di Ceprano*); ?Carlos Sagarminaga (*Borsa*); ? (*Marullo*); ? (*A Page*); [? (*An Usher*)].

SIDE 1 (559 A):

Act I: * 1. DI STEFANO and ?SAGARMINAGA: Orchestral Introduction to the opera . . . Questa o quella

2. VALDENGO, RUFINO, CONNER, FARFAN, and DI STEFANO: Quel vecchio maledivami! . . . Caro nome

SIDE 2 (559 B):

Act II: 1. DI STEFANO: Ella mi fu rapita! . . . Parmi veder le lagrime

2. [Marullo], VALDENGO, ALONSO, [Page], and ?SAGARMINAGA: Povero Rigoletto . . . Cortigiani, vil razza dannata

3. VALDENGO and CONNER: Compiuto pur quanto . . . Sì, vendetta . . . to the end of the act

Act III: 4. DI STEFANO, VALDENGO, DOMINGUEZ, and CONNER: La donna è mobile . . . Un dì, se ben rammentomi . . . Bella figlia dell'amore ["Quartet"]

5. VALDENGO, RUFINO, and CONNER: Della vendetta alfin giunge l'istante! . . . Lassù in cielo . . . to the end of the opera

NOTES: EJS 559

The orchestral Introduction to the opera is included here, but the Prelude has been omitted.

Sagarminaga sang *Matteo Borsa* frequently in Mexico City, before and after the the 1948 season (comprimarii seem not to have changed very much in Mexico City at the time), hence the speculation in the listing that he took the role in this broadcast.

Other broadcasts from the Palacio de las Belles Artes were issued on EJS 302-303,and 319 (June, 1964-February, 1965), as was a complete WERTHER on EJS 547 (April, 1971).

Excerpts from this RIGOLETTO were reissued in 1992 on the post-Smith "Golden Age of Opera" label (CD 128/192), coupled with excerpts from the 28 June, 1949 Palacio de las Bellas Artes MIGNON that had originally appeared on EJS 302 in June, 1964.

EJS 560: "The Golden Age of Opera" (1 LP)
Issued June, 1971
MATRIX P-2538

MANON (Massenet) (I)
Opera in 4 acts (excerpts)
Orchestra and Chorus of the Palacio de las Bellas Artes, Mexico City/Renato Cellini
Broadcast, Palacio de las Bellas Artes, XEX, Mexico City, 6 Jul 1948

CAST:
Irma Gonzales (*Manon*); Giuseppe Di Stefano (*Des Grieux*); Giuseppe Valdengo (*Lescaut*); [Robert Silva (*Count des Grieux*)]; [Carlos Sagarminaga (*Guillot*)]; Gilberto Cerda (*De Bretigny*); [Anamaria Feuss (*Pousette*)] [Concha de los Santos (*Javotte*)]; [Gilda Cossio (*Rosette*)].

SIDE 1 (560 A):

Act I: 1. a) Prelude (first 29 measures)
b) GONZALES and VALDENGO: Je suis encore tout étourdie . . . J'en suis à mon premier voyage!
c) VALDENGO, GONZALES, and DI STEFANO: Ne bronchez pas . . . Voyons, Manon . . . Ah! partons!

Act II: 2. a) DI STEFANO, GONZALES, VALDENGO, and CERDA: Manon! Avez-vous peur que mon visage . . . On l'appelle Manon . . . Enfin, les amoureux . . . ah! partez!
b) GONZALES: Allons! Il le faut! . . . Adieu, notre petite table . . . Adieu!

SIDE 2 (560 B):

Act II: 1. GONZALES and DI STEFANO: C'est lui! Que ma pâleur ne me trahisse . . . Instant charmant . . . En fermant les yeux

Act III: 2. a) DI STEFANO: Je suis seul! . . . Ah! fuyez, douce image
b) GONZALES, DI STEFANO, and Chorus: Ces murs silencieux . . . N'est-ce plus ma main que cette main presse? . . . to the end of the act

Act V: 3. a) DI STEFANO and VALDENGO: Begining of the act . . . Va t'en!
b) DI STEFANO, VALDENGO, and GONZALES: Capitaine, ô gué . . . Ah! Des Grieux! . . . to the end of the opera

NOTES: EJS 560

The omissions in the scenes presented here appear to have been performance cuts. The broadcast microphone must have been placed very near the prompter's box, as his constant patter is heard throughout.

The set plays about a half-step low at 33.3 rpm.

EJS 561: "The Golden Age of Opera" (1 LP)
Issued June, 1971
MATRIX P-2540

LA FORZA DEL DESTINO (Verdi) (I)
Opera in 4 acts (excerpts)
Metropolitan Opera House Orchestra and Chorus/Bruno Walter
Metropolitan Opera broadcast, NYC, 27 Nov 1943

CAST:
Stella Roman (*Leonora*); Frederick Jagel (*Don Alvaro*); Lawrence Tibbett (*Don Carlo*); Ezio Pinza (*Abbott*); [Anna Kaskas (*Preziosilla*)]; [Lorenzo Alvary (*Alcade*)]; [John Gurney (*A Surgeon*)]; [Alessio DePaolis (*Trabuco*)]; [Salvatore Baccaloni (*Brother Melitone*)]; [Frederick Lechner (*Marquis de Calatrava*)]; [Thelma Votipka (*Curra*)].

SIDE 1 (561 A):

Act I: 1. ROMAN: Me pellegrina ed orfana

Act II: 2. TIBBETT: Son Pereda, son ricco d'onore
3. ROMAN and Chorus: Son giunta, grazie, o Dio! . . . Madre pietosa Vergine

Act III: 4. JAGEL: La vita e inferno all'infelice invano . . . O, tu che in seno agli angeli
5. TIBBETT: Urna fatale . . . Ah! egli e salvo!

Act IV: 6. JAGEL and TIBBETT: Le minaccie, i fieri accenti
7. ROMAN: Pace, pace, mio Dio

SIDE 2 (561 B):

Act IV: 1. ROMAN, TIBBETT, JAGEL, and PINZA: Finale

BORIS GODUNOV (Mussorgsky) (I)
Opera in 4 acts (excerpts)
Metropolitan Opera House Orchestra and Chorus/George Szell
Metropolitan Opera broadcast, 4 Dec 1943

CAST:
Ezio Pinza (*Boris*); Thelma Altman (*Feodor*); Armand Tokatyan (*Dimitri*); Kerstin Thorborg (*Marina*); Leonard Warren (*Rangoni*); [Marita Farell (*Zenia*)]; [Anna Kaskas (*Nurse*)]; [Alessio DePaolis (*Schouisky*)]; [Mack Harrell (*Tchelkaloff*)]; [Nicola Moscona (*Pimenn*)]; [Salvatore Baccaloni (*Varlaam*)]; [John Dudley (*Missail*)]; [Doris Doe (*Innkeeper*)]; [John Garris (*Simpleton*)]; [John Gurney (*Police Officer*)]; [Osie Hawkins (*Sergeant*)]; [Gerhard Pechner (*Lovitzky*)]; [Lorenzo Alvary (*Tcherniakowsky*)]; [Emery Darcy (*Boyar*)]; ?[Maxine Stellman (*Peasant*)]; ?[Helen Olheim (*Peasant*)]; ?[Lodovico Oliviero (*Peasant*)]; ?[Wilfred Engelman (*Peasant*)].

Act III: 2. TOKATYAN and THORBORG: Stasera, presso alla fonte . . . Ah, mia divina! ["Fountain Duet"]
3. PINZA, ALTMAN, and Chorus: Addio mio figlio . . . to the end of the opera

NOTES: EJS 561

An abridgement of another FORZA from this season with the same principals (23 January, 1943) had been issued as EJS 211 in May, 1961. Taken from the official NBC acetates, the latter was produced in excellent sound.

Speed problems plague the 27 November, 1943 FORZA, requiring a base speed of about 34.0 rpm, ascending to 34.2 rpm in places. There is a change of source toward the end of Jagel's "O tu che in seno," probably to the January performance. It lasts only a few bars before switching back to the rougher surfaces of the November air-checks.

The other *Boris* that season, singing in Russian, was Kipnis. See EJS 550 (April, 1971). Note that Pinza, like the rest of the cast, sings here in Italian.

EJS 562: "The Golden Age of Opera" (1 LP)
Issued June, 1971
MATRIX P-2537

AÏDA (Verdi) (I)
Opera in 4 acts (excerpts)
Metropolitan Opera House Orchestra and Chorus/Paul Breisach
Metropolitan Opera broadcast, NYC, 21 Feb 1942

CAST:
Norina Greco (*Aïda*); Frederick Jagel (*Radames*); Bruna Castagna (*Amneris*); John Charles Thomas (*Amonasro*); Lansing Hatfield (*The King of Egypt*); Nicola Moscona (*Ramfis*); John Dudley (*A Messenger*); Thelma Votipka (*High Priestess*).

SIDE 1 (562 A):

Act I: 1. MOSCONA and JAGEL: Si, corre voce che l'Etiope ardisca . . . Celeste Aïda

2. GRECO, CASTAGNA, JAGEL, HATFIELD, DUDLEY, and MOSCONA: Ohimè! di guerra fremere . . . Su del Nilo al sacro lido

3. MOSCONA and JAGEL, and Chorus: Il sacro brando dal Dio temprato . . . Nume, custode e vindice . . . to the end of the act

Act II: 4. THOMAS, GRECO, CASTAGNA, JAGEL, HATFIELD, and Chorus: Suo padre anch'io pugnai . . . Ma tu, o re tu signore possente

5. JAGEL, HATFIELD, CASTAGNA, MOSCONA, GRECO, and Chorus: Per lo splendor della tua corona . . . to the end of the act

SIDE 2 (562 B):

Act III: 1. GRECO: Del Nilo i cupi vortici . . . O patria mia

Act IV: 2. CASTAGNA, JAGEL, and Chorus: Io, di sua morte origine! . . . Disperato, tremendo è il mio dolore!
3. GRECO, JAGEL, CASTAGNA, and Chorus: Immenso, immenso, Ftha del mondo . . . O terra, addio! . . . to the end of the opera

NOTES: EJS 562

The original acetates of the second-act finale (I/5) end abruptly in the midst of the final choral passage: a different, as yet unidentified performance has been inserted on EJS 562 to complete the scene.

Excerpts from this performance were issued earlier on EJS 141 (January, 1959) and EJS 186 (July-August, 1960). Greco's "O patria mia" was issued from a different source on IRCC CD 806 in 1992, a 1940s broadcast potpourri.

EJS 563: "The Golden Age of Opera"
Issued June, 1971
MATRIX P-2551

"SIXTY-TWO AND OVER"

SIDE 1 (563 A):

* 1. LUCIEN FUGÈRÈ, baritone (orch/Elie Cohen): DIE ZAUBERFLÖTE, K. 620, Act II: La vie est un voyage [Ein Mädchen oder Weibchen] (Mozart) (F)
WL 1481 Paris, 1928 Columbia D 13092

* 2. ADELINA PATTI, soprano (pf/Alfredo Barili): "La Calesera" (Sebastian Yradier) (S)
684½c Craig-y-Nos, Wales, June, 1906 G&T 03085 IRCC 17

* 3. GIUSEPPE DE LUCA, baritone (pf/?): LA DAMA DI PICCHE, Act III: Se all'egual di vaghi augelli [Yesli v milyye devetsi] ["Tomsky's Song"] (Tchaikowski) (I)
TA-33-009 New York, late January or early February, 1950
Continental CLP 102/CLP-1003

* 4. CHARLES SANTLEY, baritone (pf/?Landon Ronald): LE NOZZE DI FIGARO, K. 492, Act I: Ehi, capitano . . . Non più andrai (Mozart) (I)
WCG 187-R London, 10 June, 1903 G&T 052000

* 5. LEO SLEZAK, tenor (pf/?): MYRTHEN, Op. 25, no. 3: Der Nussbaum (Mosen-Schumann) (G)
1091½bmI ?Berlin, early 1928 Polydor 19924 [B62238]

* 6. MATTIA BATTISTINI, baritone (orch/Carlo Sabajno): PARIDE ED ELENA, Act I: O del mio dolce ardor (Gluck) (I)
CK 1428-2 Milan, 25 February, 1925 HMV 2-052256

* 7. BLANCHE MARCHESI, soprano (pf/Agnes Bedford): "Amuri, amuri" ["Sicilian Cart Driver's Song"] (trad.-arr. Sadero)
TTP 854-1 London, 1936 HMV JH 9 IRCC 89

* 8. GUSTAV WALTER, tenor (pf/?): SCHWANENGESANG, D. 957, no. 12: Am Meer (Heine-Schubert)
332i Vienna, 1904 G&T 042097

* 9. FEODOR CHALIAPIN, bass (pf/G. Godinsky): "Song of the Volga Boatman" [Ei ukhnyem!] (trad.-arr. Chaliapin/Koenemann) (R)
8113-4 Tokyo, 6 February, 1936 Victor 14901

10. LÉON ROTHIER, bass (pf/?): LA JUIVE, Act III: Vous qui du Dieu vivant (Halévy) (F)
Broadcast, ***LÉON ROTHIER***, WQXR, NYC, date unknown

* 11. MARCEL JOURNET, bass (orch/Henri Büsser): FAUST, Act II: Le veau d'or (Gounod) (F)
CG 882-2 Paris, September, 1930 HMV C 2126 [52-700]
AF 421 [52-700]

* 12. VICTOR CAPOUL, tenor (pf/?): JOCELYN, Act II: Cachés dans cet asile . . . Oh! ne t'éveille pas ["Berceuse"] (Godard) (F)
XPh 564-4 Paris, early 1905 Fonotipia (39089)

* 13. NELLIE MELBA, soprano (pf/Harold Craxton): "Swing Low, Sweet Chariot" (trad.-arr. Burleigh) (E)
Cc 9553-1A Small Queens Hall, London, 17 Dec 1926
HMV DB 989 [03894] Victor 6733

* 14. GEORGE HENSCHEL, baritone (pf/George Henschel): SECHS GEDICHTE, Op. 90, no. 1: Lied eines Schmiedes (Lenau-Schumann) (G)
WA 8086-1 London, 12 Nov 1928 Columbia D 1658; 4129-M

SIDE 2 (563 B):

* 1. ERNESTINE SCHUMANN-HEINK (pf/Josefin H. Vollmer): "Pirate Dreams" (Louise A. Garnett-Charles Huerter) (E)
from the soundtrack of the one-reel Warner Brothers Vitaphone short ***MME. ERNESTINE SCHUMANN-HEINK a) DER ERLKÖNIG (GERMAN) b) TREES c) PIRATE DREAMS / JOSEFIN H. VOLLMER--AT THE PIANO*** (1927), New York, circa 1927
Vitaphone Varieties 568
MP 4163; c18 Jul 1927
Premiere: Warners' Theater, NYC, 15 Aug 1927

* 2. LILY PONS, soprano (Fort Worth Opera Orchestra/Karl Krueger): LUCIA DI LAMMERMOOR, Act I: Quando rapita in estasi (Donizetti) (I)
In-house recording, Fort Worth Opera House, 30 Nov 1962

* 3. BENIAMINO GIGLI, tenor, and LESANDRO SARGENTI, bass (Orchestra of the Teatro Municipal, Rio de Janeiro/Antonio Votto: MANON LESCAUT, Act III: Ah! Guai a chi . . . No, Pazzo son! Guardate! (Puccini) (I)
Broadcast, Teatro Municipal, Rio de Janeiro, 31 Aug 1951

* 4. RICHARD BONELLI, baritone (orch/?Hans Jürgen-Walther): Faust, Act II: Avant de quitter ces lieux (Gounod) (F)
Private recording, 1955

5. LAURITZ MELCHIOR, tenor (pf/?): OTELLO, Act II: Tu, indietro, fuggi . . . Ora e per sempre addio (Verdi) (I)
Private recording, circa 1962

* 6. ?HIPOLITO LÁZARO, tenor (organ/?): "Plegaria a la Virgen" (V. Balaquer-F. M. Alvarez) (S)
In-house recording or broadcast, unknown live performance, circa 1964

* 7. TITO SCHIPA, tenor (pf/Albert Carlo Amato): MARTHA, Act III: M'appari [Ach, so fromm] (Flotow) (I)
In-house recording, Town Hall, NYC, 3 Oct 1962

* 8. GIOVANNI MARTINELLI, tenor (pf/Joseph Furgiuele): GIANNI SCHICCHI: Firenze è come un albero fiorito (Puccini) (I)
Private recording, ?New York, 1965

* 9. DOUBROVSKY, bass, and Chorus (unaccompanied): "Song of the Flea" [Pesnya Mefistofelya o blokhe] (Goethe-trans. Strugovshchikov-arr. Mussorgsky) (R)
?Live performance recording, source and date unknown

* 10. FREDERICK JAGEL, tenor (pf/?): NORFOLK SONGS: Yarmouth Fair (H. Collins-Warlock) (E)
Source and date unknown

* 11. KIRSTEN FLAGSTAD, soprano (Danish Radio Orchestra/Johann Hye-Knudsen): ALCESTE, Act I: Divinités du Styx (Gluck) (D)
Broadcast, Danmarks Radio, Copenhagen, 14 Apr 1957

* 12. GIACOMO LAURI-VOLPI, tenor (pf/?Lauri-Volpi): TOSCA, Act III: E lucevan le stelle (Puccini) (I)
Private recording, ?Lauri-Volpi's home, Rome, circa 1955

NOTES: EJS 563

Smith refered to this collection in the June 1971 bulletin as a "Social Security record," containing as it does recorded performances of veteran singers over the age of 62.

Side 1 (563 A):

Band 1: Fugère's Columbia recordings were reissued complete on Symposium CD 1125 in 1992.

Band 2: Reissued as IRCC 17 in April, 1933. Smith first issued the "Calesera" on EJS 100 (1956). See the endnote for that issue (I/2) regarding the playing speed and subsequent LP issues.

Band 3: De Luca's Continental LP, recorded just months before his death on 26 August, 1950, was originally entitled "The Art of Bel Canto / Songs of the Great Masters," but was eventually reissued with a new front cover sticker bearing the subtitle "Memorial Album" to mark the singer's passing. The matrix numbers are TA-33-008-1 and TA-33-009 for sides 1 and 2, respectively. Both "CLP-102" and "CLP-1003" appear as catalog numbers. This studio session, his last, was recorded in a single day according to Smith's liner notes for ASCO-124 (De Luca's 7 November, 1947 Town Hall recital) and is thought to have been produced either by Smith himself or by Jack Caidin of the Collectors Record Shop. Indeed, as with other selections from the LP, the DAMA DI PICCHE aria later turned up on commercial LPs issued both by Smith (TAP 304) and Caidin (Famous Records of the Past FRP 8).

Pianist and erstwhile Met conductor Giuseppe Bamboschek is credited as Martinelli's accompanist for the latter's 1950 Continental sessions (CLP-103: matrices TA-33-010/011), and so may have accompanied De Luca's: no accompanist is named on the De Luca LP, however.

Band 4: Landon Ronald may have been Santley's accompanist on 10 June, 1903 (he has been more or less established as the accompanist for the 8 June session), but this will always be disputed. This famous NOZZE recording has also appeared on Rococo 1, Rococo 5204, Cantelina 6242, the first volume of "The Record of Singing" (RLS 5204) and its predecessor, and in 1991, on "The Harold Wayne Collection Volume 7" (Symposium CD 1093).

Band 5: Slezak's pianist is not named on the original Polydor label.

Band 6: The complete Battistini was issued by EMI in the Set "Mattia Battistini: King of Baritones" (EMI EX 29 0790 3 in the U.K. and Seraphim IG 6153 in the U.S.).

Band 7: Marchesi's 1936 and 1937 electricals received limited distribution in the (private) buff-label HMV JH (10-inch) and JG (12-inch) series. The IRCC issues were announced in February, 1937.

Band 8: Walter was the oldest German singer (by birthdate) to record. The "Am Meer," perhaps his best-known recording, has been issued time and again on LP and now, on compact disc.

Band 9: This was Chaliapin's last recording, issued only as Victor 14901.

Band 11: This "Veau d'or" is from the complete 1930 FAUST with Journet, Vezzani, and Berthon, issued as HMV Album 115 (C 7420-C 7439) and Victor Set M-105. The recording dates from approximately September, 1930: no ledger information (weekly returns) could be secured. AF 421 was the Spanish issue.

Band 12: The Capoul solo, his only recording, was assigned catalog number 39089, but was not issued commercially--that number was eventually given to Ackté's LOHENGRIN "Elsa's Dream" (XPh 4-2). Rose Caron's Paris matrices XPh 521 and 523 have been dated 20 December, 1904, so it is reasonable to assume that Capoul's XPh 564, in spite of the high take number, is from early 1905.

Band 13: This was Melba's last recording. It has appeared in better sound on several subsequent issues, including EMI's 1976 Melba set (RLS 719).

Band 14: Columbia D 1658 and 4129-M were British and American issues, respectively. The second take of WA 8086, also recorded 12 November, 1928, was unissued.

SIDE 2 (563 B):

Band 1: The other songs featured in this film short were issued on EJS 513 (May, 1970). The short premiered during the run of the Warner Brothers feature "Old San Francisco." Schumann-Heink recorded all three songs electrically for Victor.

Band 2: This "Quando rapita" was taken from Pons' operatic farewell performance. The *Edgardo* was Placido Domingo. A photograph from the performance was reproduced in the booklet that accompanied the 1976 LP "Lily Pons, Coloratura Assoluta" (Columbia 34294).

Band 3: This Teatro Municipal performance was identified subsequent to co-author William Collins' research for his non-commercial Gigli discography in *The Record Collector* 35/8-10 (August-September, 1990).

Band 4: These late Bonelli recordings were probably made in New York, circa 1955. The original harmonium accompaniment was replaced by orchestra in Hamburg by conductor Hans Jürgen-Walther. A "Zazá, piccola zingara" from the same period appeared on EJS 445 (October, 1968). See the lengthy endnote for that LP regarding these sessions.

Band 6: Whether or not this is really Lázaro has remained a matter of speculation. Late Cuban performances (1950) have been traced to him, but at approximately age 77--assuming that Smith's date is correct--his would be the best-preserved voice on record. Indeed, his singing seems to have improved significantly since the wayward, often outrageous days of his prime. The scooping and expansiveness we hear in this song are certainly reminiscent of Lázaro, but the splendid tone and unhampered breathing seem unlikely for a septuagenarian. The more realistic key of A (B-flat at the highest) is much more becoming than the higher pitch chosen for this transfer.

W. R. Moran discovered that the song, given simply as "Church Song" on the label of EJS 563, is the same "Plegaria a la Virgen" sung by Supervia on Odeon 195085 (matrix SO 6051, recorded 6 March, 1930) and earlier, by Emilio Sagi-Barba on Spanish Gramofono, as issued in the U.S. on Victor 61212 and 45286.

Band 7: This 3 October, 1962 recital was Schipa's first New York City concert appearance since 1947. See Harold Schonberg's review of the program in the *New York Times* (4 October, 1962), p. 43:1. Notable among the attending dignitaries were Franco Corelli, Licia Albanese, Rose Bampton, Carmela Ponselle, conductor Fausto Cleva, and "assorted masestri, soprani, tenori and bassi." The concert was advertised in the *Times* as standing room only and the hall was indeed packed to the aisles.

Band 8: This same private recording was included on the Martinelli Puccini recital (EJS 566) also issued in June, 1971.

Band 9: "Doubrovsky" is mentioned in the bulletin as "a bass, born in 1874 in Russia and still singing, after a 77 year career. A recording made in performance in 1970 is included." Who "Doubrovsky" was (or perhaps *is*?) remains a mystery, as do the circumstances of this recording. The band is mislabeled as number ten on the label of EJS 563. The arrangement of this well-known song seems to drift a bit in the middle.

Band 10: Jagel's "Yarmouth Fair" ends abruptly on a dissonant chord, signifying either an error on the part of the accompanist or a cut-off of the source. This may be from one of Jagel's late WGBH, Boston, telecasts: see the endnotes for EJS 233 (March, 1962) and 533 (December, 1970).

Band 11: This performance of the Paris version of ALCESTE sung in Danish (translation by Thygessen) was broadcast complete. Legendary Records LR 120 also contains the "Divinitiés du Styx."

Danish Radio tape: DR 4379/1957; Stanford Archive of Recorded Sound tape: StARS 570414 MI-2.

Band 12: Probably recorded at Lauri-Volpi's home in Rome, with the singer accompanying himself at the piano (as he often did). See the endnote for EJS 343 (October, 1965) regarding Lauri-Volpi's private recordings. There is "knocking" throughout the entire track.

EJS 564: "The Golden Age of Opera" (1 LP)
Issued June, 1971
MATRIX P-2541

SIDE 1 (564 A):

"JOHN CHARLES THOMAS SONGS"

* 1. w. Detroit Symphony Orchestra/Eugene Ormandy: "When I think upon the maidens" (Philip Ashbrooke-Michael Head) (E)
Broadcast, ***FORD SUNDAY EVENING HOUR***, WJR, Detroit, 12 Nov 1939

* 2. w. Detroit Symphony Orchestra/Eugene Ormandy: NORFOLK SONGS: Yarmouth Fair (H. Collins-Peter Warlock) (E)
Broadcast, ***FORD SUNDAY EVENING HOUR***, WJR, Detroit, 12 Nov 1939

3. w. Los Angeles Philharmonic Orchestra/Eugene Ormandy): "Roll, Jordan, Roll" (trad.-arr. Hall Johnson)
D-28198 AFRS broadcast, Hollywood Bowl, Los Angeles, 13 Jul 1948 AFRS H-38-61 [Record III/pt. 5]

4. w. Los Angeles Philharmonic Orchestra/Eugene Ormandy): "Shallow Brown" (trad.-arr. Percy Grainger) (E)
D-28198 AFRS broadcast, Hollywood Bowl, Los Angeles, 13 Jul 1948 AFRS H-38-61 [Record III/pt. 5]

5. w. Los Angeles Philharmonic Orchestra/Eugene Ormandy): "Charity" (Emily Dickinson-Richard Hageman) (E)
D-28199 AFRS broadcast, Hollywood Bowl, Los Angeles, 13 Jul 1948 AFRS H-38-61 [Record IV/pt. 6]

6. w. Los Angeles Philharmonic Orchestra/Eugene Ormandy): "Mah Lindy Lou" (Lily Strickland) (E)
D-28199 AFRS broadcast, Hollywood Bowl, Los Angeles, 13 Jul 1948 AFRS H-38-61 [Record IV/pt. 6]

7. w. Los Angeles Philharmonic Orchestra/Eugene Ormandy): "Ye Banks and Braes o' Bonnie Doon" (Robert Burns--trad.) (E)
D-28199 AFRS broadcast, Hollywood Bowl, Los Angeles, 13 Jul 1948 AFRS H-38-61 [Record IV/pt. 6]

8. w. Los Angeles Philharmonic Orchestra/Eugene Ormandy): "Blow me eyes!" ["Sea Chanty"] (Wallace Irwin-Albert H. Malotte) (E)
D-28199 AFRS broadcast, Hollywood Bowl, Los Angeles, 13 Jul 1948 AFRS H-38-61 [Record IV/pt. 6]

9. w. Los Angeles Philharmonic Orchestra/Eugene Ormandy): "Every time I feel the spirit" (trad.-arr. Hall Johnson) (E)
D-28199 AFRS broadcast, Hollywood Bowl, Los Angeles, 13 Jul 1948 AFRS H-38-61 [Record IV/pt. 6]

10. w. Los Angeles Philharmonic Orchestra/Eugene Ormandy): "Drink to me only with thine eyes" (Ben Jonson-trad.) (E)
D-28198 AFRS broadcast, Hollywood Bowl, Los Angeles, 13 Jul 1948 AFRS H-38-61 [Record III/pt. 5]

SIDE 2 (564 B):

"ALESSANDRO MORESCHI, CASTRATO"

* 1. ALESSANDRO MORESCHI, soprano (pf/?): PETITE MESSE SOLENNELE: Crucifixus (Rossini) (L) [A-flat major]
1755b Rome 3-5 Apr 1902 G&T 54764 Victor 5064
91039

* 2. ALESSANDRO MORESCHI, soprano (pf/?): [DIES IRAE]: "Pie Jesu" (Ignace Leybach) (L) [G minor]
2183h Rome, April, 1904 G&T 54774 Victor 61115
Gram C3711 52042
HMV P 328

3. ALESSANDRO MORESCHI, soprano (pf/?; organ/?): "Hostias et preces (Eugenio Terziani) (L) [F major]
2184h Rome, April, 1904 G&T 54775 Victor 61118
Gram C3711 52043
HMV P 328

4. ALESSANDRO MORESCHI, soprano, and the CAPELLA SISTINA (organ/?): "Et incarnatus est et Crucifixus (Luigi Pratesi) (L) [first note is B-flat]
1762b Rome, 3-5 Apr 1902 G&T 54770

5. ALESSANDRO MORESSCHI, soprano, and the CAPELLA SISTINA/ Alessandro Moreschi (pf/?; organ/?): "Oremus pro Pontifice" (Emilio Calzanera) (L) [A-flat major/ends G-flat major]
284i Rome, April, 1904 G&T 054757 Victor 71015
Gram M3738 6334
HMV D 830

* 6. ALESSANDRO MORESCHI, soprano, CESARE BOEZI, tenor, SIG. DADÒ, bass, and Chorus of Boys/Alessandro Moreschi (pf/?; organ?): MESSA DI SAN BONAVENTURA: "Laudamus te" (Gaetano Capocci) (L) [F major]
2199h Rome, April, 1904 G&T 54780 Victor 61116
Gram C3715 893
HMV P330

* 7. ALESSANDRO MORESCHI, soprano (pf/?; violin/?): WTC, I, Prelude I: Ave Maria (J.S. Bach-arr. Gounod) (L) [G major]
2187h Rome, April, 1904 G&T 54777
52045
Gram C3729

8. ALESSANDRO MORESCHI, soprano (pf/?): "Ideale" (Errico-Tosti) (I) [A major]
4374a Rome, 3-5 Apr 1902 G&T 54758

* 9. EMANUELE BUCALO, baritone (pf/Carlo Sabajno): CAVALLERIA RUSTICANA: O Lola ch'ai di latti ["Siciliana"] (Mascagni) (I)
2297L Milan, Nov-Dec 1904 G&T 52157 Zonophone X-99272

* 10. FERRUCCIO CORRADETTI, baritone, and ELISA PETRI, mezzo-soprano (orch/?): I DUE GATTI: Duetto comico imitativo ["Comic Duet of Two Cats"] (Berthold) (I)
XPh 2529 Milan, circa April, 1907 Fonotipia 62003

NOTES: EJS 564

Side 1 (564 A):

Bands 1-2: "Yarmouth Fair" was not scheduled for Thomas's 12 November, 1939 *FORD* broadcast, but the source is almost certain. It, along with the DON CARLOS aria from this broadcast, appeared earlier on EJS 214 (June, 1961). The DON CARLOS aria also appeared on EJS 531 (December, 1970).

Bands 3-10: These AFRS items were originally transcribed on private Army-Navy-Air Force Armed Forces Radio Service discs. The Thomas Discs examined are labeled "Personal Presentation Copy / Dr. Karl Wecker / Hollywood Bowl 1948," Wecker apparently being the individual for whom these copies were pressed (Wecker's copies are held at Stanford University, but were not necessarily the ones used to compile EJS 564). The bottom of the label carries a private-use notice dated 12 July, 1947. The selections included here are from the Hollywood Bowl Series H-38-61, Program No. 61, a five-disc set in nine parts, matrices D-28194/D-28202 (parts D-28195 and D-28197 are suffixed "x").

The TRAVIATA and HÉRODIADE arias that began the broadcast were included earlier on EJS 531 (December, 1970). Note the label misspellings of many of the songs on EJS 564: "Lindy Lou," "Ye banks and braes," and "I will pray" for "Every time I feel the spirit" (the last words of the chorus of this song). A *Los Angeles Times* review mentions that Thomas sang half a dozen encores: only "Roll, Jordan, Roll," "Shallow Brown," and "Drink to me only with thine eyes" are listed on the actual program, so the others included were probably from among these encores. The AFRS ledgers list "Blow me eyes!" as "Sea Chanty," with the handwritten annotations "When I was young - Blow me light - Blow me eyes She did;" "Ye Banks and Braes o' Bonnie Doon" is given there as "My Bonnie Doon."

Also included in series H-30-61 were the Overture to DIE MEISTERSINGER, the "Nocturne and Scherzo" from Mendelssohn's A MIDSUMMER NIGHT'S DREAM, a "Biographical Sketch of Eugene Ormandy," spoken presumably, and Franck's Symphony in D Minor.

Side 2 (564 B):

For a full accounting of the 1902-1904 Vatican G&Ts, see this author's "The Vatican G&Ts," in *The Record Collector*, 28/7-8 (December, 1983), pp. 146-191 and 30/12-13 (December, 1985), pp. 287-293.

The 1902 Moreschi G&Ts were recorded at speeds ranging from 75.0-77.0 rpm, where the 1904 recordings require 73.47 rpm for the 10-inch discs and 75.00 rpm for the 12-inch. The transfers on EJS 564 are high. The proper keys of performance have been given for each of the eight solos.

All of the Moreschi solos and ensembles were issued in 1984 on the Pearl LP "Alessandro Moreschi: The Last Castrato - Complete Vatican Recordings" (OPAL 823), reissued as OPAL CD 9823. Several other labels have issued a handful of the Moreschi solos, including ASCO, a Smith label, Belcanto, Rubini, and Timaclub. The Bach-Gounod "Ave Maria" was included on the first volume of "The Record of Singing" (RLS 724 and its successor, RLS 7705), and the "Hostias et preces" on the 1977 German EMI issue "75 Jahre - Die Stimme Seines Herrn."

The accompanying "Choir of Boys" ("Coro di raggazi" on the original labels and "voci bianchi" in many of the original scores) is presumably the treble section of the Capella Sistina. Similarly, "Chorus of Roman Singers" (II/5) appears on several early labels, but this, too, was probably meant to designate a part of the same choir. Moreschi himself is described on G&T labels as "Soprano della Capella Sistina:" while he was a *castrato*, it has been claimed in print that he was in fact a congenital eunuch.

Band 2: Though subtitled "Dies Irae," the part of the Requiem Mass from which the "Pie Jesu" is taken, this setting was not part of a larger work as far as could be ascertained.

Band 6: Tenor Cesare Boezi was the brother of the eminent Italian composer-conductor Ernesto Boezi (1856-1946), but the identity of Sig. Dadò remains a mystery. Later accounts of a Vatican Trio and Quartet that toured the U.S. and recorded for Lyrophone in New York mention a bass *Marianno* Dadò, while the better-known *Augusto* Dadò recorded in the first decade of the century for G&T and Odeon.

Band 7: This very peculiar transfer of the Bach-Gounod "Ave Maria" has never been explained. Unlike the original (as heard on "The Record of Singing" and the Pearl Moreschi recital) it sounds as if it was transfered by microphone using an acoustical phonograph. There is a severe banging in the piano arpeggios, virtually no surface noise, and a remote, floating sound to Moreschi's solo quite unlike anything retrievable from the proper electrical reproduction of the original disc. But it *is* the Moreschi version, matrix 2187h.

Bands 9-10: The June, 1971 bulletin claims that these were both "taken from early Fonotipia records," which is not the case. The Bucalo CAVALLERIA is notable as being "sung in the cat key!" Sabajno's accompaniment is credited on the original black G&T label. Nothing about the DUE GATTI could be traced, nor its stated composer, Berthold.

EJS 565: "The Golden Age of Opera" (1 LP)
Issued June, 1971
MATRIX P-2550

"GIACOMO LAURI-VOLPI / RECITAL 1955-59"

SIDE 1 (565 A):

IL TROVATORE (Verdi) (I)
Opera in 4 acts (excerpts)
Orchestra of Radio Omroepvereniging [VARA]/Arturo Basile
Broadcast, Radio VARA, Hilversum, Holland, 16 Oct 1954

CAST:
Giacomo Lauri-Volpi (*Manrico*); Gigliola Frazzoni (*Leonora*); Rolando Panerai (*Count di Luna*); Franca Marghinotti (*Azucena*); ? (*Ruiz*); ?Georgio [Jorge] Algorta (*Ferrando*); [? (*Ines*)].

Act I: 1. LAURI-VOLPI and PANERAI: Deserto sulla terra
2. PANERAI, FRAZZONI, and LAURI-VOLPI: Di geloso amor sprezzato

Act II: 3. MARGHINOTTI, LAURI-VOLPI, and [Ruiz]: [Cure non spesi] a risanar le tante ferite . . . Mal reggendo
4. LAURI-VOLPI and MARGHINOTTI: Un momento può involarmi . . . Tu la spremi del mio cor!

Act IV: 5. LAURI-VOLPI, FRAZZONI, and MARGHINOTTI: Parlar non vuoi? . . . to the end of the trio

LA FAVORITA (Donizetti) (I)
Opera in 4 acts (excerpts)
Orchestra of Radio Omroepvereniging [VARA]/Arturo Basile
Broadcast, Radio VARA, Hilversum, Holland, 6 Oct 1954

CAST:
Giacomo Lauri-Volpi (*Fernando*); Franca Marghinotti (*Leonora*); Giorgio [Jorge] Algorta (*Baldassare*); ?Rolando Panerai (*Alfonso*); [? (*Ines*)]; [? (*Don Gasparo*)].

Act I: 6. LAURI-VOLPI and ALGORTA: Una vergine, un angel di Dio

Act IV: 7. LAURI-VOLPI: Spirto gentil

* 8. LAURI-VOLPI and MARGHINOTTI: Vieni, ah! vien, io m'abbandono alla gioia

9. GIACOMO LAURI-VOLPI, tenor (pf/?Lauri-Volpi): GUGLIELMO TELL, Act IV: O muto asil . . . Corriam, corriam [Asile héréditaire . . . Amis, amis] (Rossini) (I)
Private recording, ?Lauri-Volpi's home, Rome, circa 1959

10. GIACOMO LAURI-VOLPI, tenor (pf/?Lauri-Volpi): POLIUTO, Act II: Che vuoi . . . Sfolgorò divino raggio (Donizetti) (I)
Private recording, ?Lauri-Volpi's home, Rome, circa 1959

SIDE 2 (565 B):

* 1. GIACOMO LAURI-VOLPI, tenor (pf/:Lauri-Volpi): I PURITANI, Act III: Son già lontani . . . Corre a valle, corre a monte (Bellini) (I)
Private recording, ?Lauri-Volpi's home, Rome, circa 1959

* 2. GIACOMO LAURI-VOLPI, tenor (pf/:Lauri-Volpi): I PURITANI, Act III: Vieni fra queste braccia (Bellini) (I)
Private recording, ?Lauri-Volpi's home, Rome, circa 1959

* 3. ?ANTONIO PIRINO, tenor (pf/:Lauri-Volpi): I PURITANI, Act III: Credeasi misera (Bellini) (I)
Private recording, ?Lauri-Volpi's home, Rome, circa 1959

4. GIACOMO LAURI-VOLPI, tenor (pf/:Lauri-Volpi): WERTHER, Act III: Ah, non mi ridestar [Traduire . . . Pourquoi me réveiller?] (Massenet) (I)
Private recording, ?Lauri-Volpi's home, Rome, circa 1959

* 5. GIACOMO LAURI-VOLPI, tenor (pf/:Lauri-Volpi): MANON, Act I: [Pardonnez-moi! Je ne sais] (Massenet) (I)
Private recording, ?Lauri-Volpi's home, Rome, circa 1959

* 6. GIACOMO LAURI-VOLPI, tenor (pf/:Lauri-Volpi): MANON, Act III: Chiudo gli occhi [Mais le bonheur est passager . . . Instant charmant . . . En fermant les yeux] ["Le Rêve"] (Massenet) (I)
Private recording, ?Lauri-Volpi's home, Rome, circa 1959

7. GIACOMO LAURI-VOLPI, tenor (pf/:Lauri-Volpi): FAUST, Act III: Qual turbamento in cor mi sento . . . Salve dimora [Quel trouble inconnu me pénètre! . . . Salut! demeure] (Gounod) (I)
Private recording, ?Lauri-Volpi's home, Rome, circa 1959

8. GIACOMO LAURI-VOLPI, tenor (pf/:Lauri-Volpi): CARMEN, Act II: Il fior che avevi a me tu dato [La fleur que tu m'avais jetée] (Bizet) (I)
Private recording, ?Lauri-Volpi's home, Rome, circa 1959

* 9. GIACOMO LAURI-VOLPI, tenor (pf/:Lauri-Volpi): "Tu sei l'amor mio" (Lauri-Volpi) (I)
Private recording, ?Lauri-Volpi's home, Rome, circa 1959

10. GIACOMO LAURI-VOLPI, tenor (Orchestra of Radio Omroepvereniging [VARA]/Arturo Basile/Arturo Basile): I LOMBARDI, Act II: La mia letizia infondere (Verdi) (I)
Broadcast, AVRO, Hilversum, Holland, 10 Oct 1954

11. GIACOMO LAURI-VOLPI, tenor (Orchestra of Radio Omroepvereniging [VARA]/Arturo Basile/Arturo Basile): TOSCA, Act III: E lucevan le stelle (Puccini) (I)
Broadcast, AVRO, Hilversum, Holland, 10 Oct 1954

NOTES: EJS 565

At least some pressings of this LP have the label for EJS 563 pressed onto both sides of the disc, with the EJS 565 label pasted over. See EJS 343 (October, 1965) for a note on Lauri-Volpi's private recordings.

Side 1 (565 A):

The TROVATORE was broadcast complete. Only *Manrico's* verse of the "Mal reggendo" (I/3) is included on EJS 565. The label claims that these are "excerpts of [Lauri-Volpi's] final performance of opera (. . . 1959 at age 67) with Mancini and Mascherini (Teatro dell'Opera, Roma)." In fact, the cast of Lauri-Volpi's final TROVATORE on 7 February, 1959 included Lucia Danieli, Ugo Savarese, and Enzo Mascherini, and is not documented as having survived. Silvio Serbandini's Lauri-Volpi discography in the reprint of the tenor's autobiographical *A Viso Aperto* (Bologna: Edizioni Bongiovanni, 1983) insists that the excerpts presented on EJS 565 are from the 1954 VARA broadcast given in the listing. Indeed, the excerpts are identical to those credited as 1954 on the Timaclub LP Tima 17, and the mezzo-soprano appears to be Marghinotti on both the TROVATORE and the well-documented FAVORITA.

Side 2 (565 B):

Bands 1-3: Lauri-Volpi adds comments between the three PURITANI excerpts. The label of EJS 565 credits the "F above high C" of the "Credeasi misera" (II/3) to Lauri-Volpi, but the voice is obviously not his. Serbandini's afore-mentioned discography names tenor Antonio Pirino as the voice responsible. Giancarlo Bongiovanni, in correspondence with co-author William Collins, has confirmed this.

Band 5: Lauri-Volpi sings only one line of *Manon's* music, "Il mio nome Manon:" the piano play the rest.

Band 6: Lauri-Volpi apparently sings *Manon's* single line during the recitative.

Band 9: Labeled "Ah si ben mio, mio sol amor" on EJS 565. Lauri Volpi's 1959 ***CONCERTO MARTINI E ROSSI*** performance of the song appeared on EJS 233 (March, 1962).

EJS: 566: "The Golden Age of Opera" (1 LP)
Issued June, 1971
MATRIX P-2549

"GIOVANNI MARTINELLI AND GIACOMO PUCCINI"

SIDE 1 (566 A):

* 1. w. orch/?Walter B. Rogers: LA BOHÈME, Act I: Che gelida manina (Puccini) (I)
C-14236-1 24 Dec 1913 Victor 74381 HMV 2-052085
6192 DB 335

2. w. orch/?Walter B. Rogers: TOSCA, Act I: Recondita armonia (Puccini) (I)
B-14276-1 8 Jan 1914 Victor 64420 HMV 7-52060
731 DA 285

* 3. w. orch/?Walter B. Rogers: TOSCA, Act III: E lucevan le stelle (Puccini) (I)
BVE-14277-5 10 Mar 1926 Victor 1208 HMV DA 842

4. w. orch/?Walter B. Rogers: MANON LESCAUT, Act I: Donna non vidi mai (Puccini) (I)
B-14341-1 16 Jan 1914 Victor 64410 HMV 7-52056
738 DA 331

* 5. w. pf/Giuseppe Bamboschek: MANON LESCAUT, Act II: Ah! Manon, mi tradisce (Puccini) (I)
TA-33-010 New York, 1950 Continental CLP 103

* 6. w. pf/Giuseppe Bamboschek: MANON LESCAUT, Act III: No, pazzo son. Guardate! (Puccini) (I)
TA-33-010 New York, 1950 Continental CLP 103

* 7. w. pf/Giuseppe Bamboschek: LA FANCIULLA DEL WEST, Act III: Vi ringrazio, Sonora . . . Ch'ella mi creda (Puccini) (I)
TA-33-010 New York, 1950 Continental CLP 103

* 8. w. pf/Joseph Furgiuele: LA FANCIULLA DEL WEST, Act II: Una parola sola . . . Or son sei mesi (Puccini) (I)
Private studio recording, New York, 17 Apr 1962

9. w. FRANCES ALDA, soprano (orch/Josef Pasternack): LA BOHÈME, Act I: O soave fanciulla (Puccini) (I)
C-22245-2 Camden, 20 Apr 1918 Victor 88598 HMV 2-054091
89132 DK 100
8002

* 10. w. pf/Joseph Furgiuele: LA BOHÈME, Act III: Mimi è una civetta (Puccini) (I)
Private recording, New York, 25 Apr 1963

* 11. w. GIUSEPPE DANISE, baritone (pf/Nicola Rescigno): LA BOHÈME, Act IV: O Mimi, tu più non torni (Puccini) (I)
Private recording, Ansonia Hotel, New York City, 25 Jan 1948

SIDE 2 (566 B):

* 1. w. Royal Philharmonic Orchestra/John Barbirolli: TURANDOT, Act I: Non piangere, Liù (Puccini) (I)
TT-2352-1 Unpublished Columbia Technical Test
Covent Garden, London, 5 May 1937

* 2. w. Royal Philharmonic Orchestra/John Barbirolli: TURANDOT, Act III: Nessun dorma (Puccini) (I)
TT 2352-7 Unpublished Columbia Technical Test
Covent Garden, London, 5 May 1937

3. w. FRANCES ALDA, soprano (orch/Josef Pasternack): MADAMA BUTTERFLY, Act I: Dicon ch'oltre mare . . .O quanti occhi fisi (Puccini) (I)
C-22246-1 Camden, 20 Sep 1918 Victor 89163 HMV 2-054123
8002 DK 100

* 4. w. pf/Giuseppe : MADAMA BUTTERFLY, Act II: Addio, fiorito asil (Puccini) (I)
TA-33-011 New York, 1950 Continental CLP 103

* 5. w. pf/Joseph Furgiuele: GIANNI SCHICCI, Act : Firenze è come un albero fiorito (Puccini) (I)
Private recording, ?New York, 1965

* 6. a) w. Seattle Opera Orchestra/Giuseppe Patanè: TURANDOT, Act II: Un giuramento atroce mi costringe (Puccini) (I)
In-house recording, Seattle Opera House, Seattle, 21 Jan 1967
b) Calaf's responses (inserted)
Private recording, New York, March, 1967

* 7. w. pf/Joseph Furgiuele: IL TABARRO: Hai ben ragione (Puccini) (I)
Private recording, ?New York, 1966

* 8. w. pf/Joseph Furgiuele: EDGAR, Act III: Bella signora (Puccini) (I)
Private recording, ?New York, 1967

* 9. w. pf/Joseph Furgiuele: LA RONDINE, Act I: Chi il bel sogno di Doretta (Puccini) (I)
Private recording, New York, circa winter, 1968

NOTES: EJS 566

The dates for the private recordings accompanied by Furgiuele were taken from an annotated list compiled by Smith himself and submitted to co-author William Collins for the latter's Martinelli discography in *The Record Collector*, 25/7-9 (October, 1979) and 25/10-12 (February, 1980).

Side 1 (566 A):

Band 1: From Martinelli's first Victor session, this was his first recording for that company.

Band 3: Transferred here at 78.26 rpm, the original playing speed of this early electrical commercial issue is 75.00 rpm.

Band 5-7: Taken from Martinelli's 1950 Continental LP, recorded in New York--probably in a single session as De Luca's (CLP 102) apparently was. Bamboschek is identified as Martinelli's accompanist on the label of CLP 103. See the endnote for EJS 563 (June, 1971), I/3.

Band 8: Released earlier on EJS 470 (May, 1969): see the endnote for that issue regarding this private studio session and subsequent releases of the FANCIULLA aria.

Band 10: This appeared earlier on EJS 470.

Band 11: The Danise duet appeared earlier on EJS 169 (January, 1960). This, and a Danise ANDREA CHENIER solo, were apparently recorded at a private party given at the home of accompanist Nicola Rescigno. Smith reported to co-author William Collins, when the latter was compiling his Martinelli discography, that the accompanist was Pietro Cimara, but this is unlikely.

Side 2 (566 B):

Bands 1-2: Taken from the live Covent Garden performance of 5 May, 1937--one of two recorded by Columbia as Technical Tests from the famous Coronation Season TURANDOTs featuring Martinelli and Eva Turner. The complete 5 May excerpts were reissued earlier on EJS 102 (1956). EJS 240 (May, 1962) included the 10 May performance (Technical Tests 2353-1/7), while EJS 50X (April-May, 1976) was a composite of both performances.

It has been suggested, because of the lack of applause in the 5 May set, that this was a *recording* rehearsal. See the lengthy endnote for EJS 102 regarding these TURANDOT technical tests.

Band 4: See note for I/5-7 above.

Band 5: Issued earlier on EJS 563.

Band 6: The 1967 Seattle TURANDOT was Martinelli's last stage appearance, in which he sang the *Emperor Altoum* in three performances. He recorded *Calaf's* responses two months later, and they were simply inserted into the *Emperor's* brief scene. See the endnote for EJS 475 (June, 1969).

Bands 7-9: Also released by Smith on the Martinelli compilation, "Giovanni Martinelli: In Memoria" (Celebrity CEL 500). Smith mentioned in correspondence from April, 1969 that the RONDINE aria, as well as the AÏDA Messenger scene (issued on EJS 512 in May, 1970) and a FANCIULLA "Una parola sola" (*not* the one issued on EJS 470 and 566), was "now finished."

EJS 567: "The Golden Age of Opera" (2 LPs)
Issued October, 1971
MATRIX P-2698 / P-2699

SIDES 1-4 (567 A-D):

KÖNIGSKINDER (Humperdinck) (G)
Opera in 3 Acts (complete)
Orchestra and Chorus of Westdeutscher Rundfunk [WDR], Köln/Richard Krauss
Recorded for WDR broadcast, Cologne, November, 1952/Broadcast ?24 July 1953

CAST:
Peter Anders (*A King's Son*); Käthe Mölker-Siepermann (*A Goose-girl*); Dietrich Fischer-Dieskau (*A Fiddler*); Ilse Ihme-Sabich (*A Witch*); Fritz Ollendorf (*A Woodcutter*); Walter Jenkel (*A Broom maker*); Karl-Heinz Welbers [boy soprano] (*A Child*); Heinrich Nillius (*Senior Councillor*); Heiner Horn (*Innkeeper*); Hanna Ludwig (*Innkeeper's Daughter*); Walter Kassek (*A Tailor*); Marianne Schröder (*A Stable Maid*); Matti Lehtinen (*A Gate Keeper*); Fritz Hallen (*A Gate Keeper*); Maria Plümacher (*A Woman*).

NOTES: EJS 567

Previously issued, from another source, on EJS 244 (June, 1962). The October, 1971 bulletin claims that "a much finer *version* of [KÖNIGSKINDER] has come to light" (emphasis mine), implying a different performance, but in fact, both are identical. The bulletin for that issue gave 24 July, 1953 as the recording date. More than likely this was the broadcast date (and thus the date it was recorded off-the-air). The recording date given above, November, 1952, was taken from *Zwanzig Jahre WDR 1948-1968*.

All significant (non-performance) cuts made on the EJS 244 issue have been restored on EJS 567. Early copies of EJS 244 were pressed out of sequence--in reverse order (Acts III, II, and I), where later pressings were reassembled in the correct order: subscribers were invited to return their defective copies. The correct order was also restored on EJS 567.

In the October, 1971 bulletin Smith claimed that "The Golden Age of Opera" would continue at least through November so that the material "which [has] not been made available and which probably never will be made available commercially" could be published. "Since the initial release in this series took place in November, 1944 (sic!)," he added, "it will enable the series to be rounded out to an exact 17 years," and that "I am still permitted to proceed with such publication since no law as yet prohibiting it has passed." This was undoubtedly a reference to what would eventually become the Copyright Revision Act of 1976. Already in the works by 1971, it contained, among other things, many sweeping reforms of the mechanical copyright provisions of 1909. But considering that UORC and ANNA would extend through 1980, the passage of the new copyright law ultimately did little to inhibit Smith's activities--fortunately.

EJS 568: "The Golden Age of Opera" (2 LPs)
October, 1971
MATRIX P-2707 / P-2708

SIDES 1-4 (568 A-D):

LA MUETTE DE PORTICI (Auber) (F)
Opera in 5 acts (complete)
Orchestra and Chorus of the Office de Radiodiffusion Télévision [ORTF], Paris/Jean Doussard
Broadcast, ORTF, Paris, 11 Jun 1971

CAST:
Monique De Pondeau (*Elvire*); Pierre Lanni (*Masaniello*); André Malabrera (*Alphonse*); Yves Bisson (*Pietro*); Bernard Demigny (*Borella*); ? (*Lorenzo*).

NOTES: EJS 568

There are many internal cuts, including the last 30 pages of Act I, vast portions of Act II, the chorus "Au marché qui vient" and "Tarantella" of Act III, and the first few measures of Act IV. It is not known whether these were performance or transcription omissions, or simply cuts made by Smith for purposes of timing. The Act I Ballet sounds as if it has been spliced in, but no other probable source could be determined.

The four sides of the set are unbanded and unidentified by act. The exact breakdown by side is as follows:

Side 1:	Act I	(part 1)	Side 3:	Act III	(part 2)
Side 2:	Act I	(part 2)		Act IV	(part 1)
	Act II	(with cuts)	Side 4:	Act IV	(part 2)
	Act III	(part 1)		Act V	(complete)

Speeds vary over the course of the four sides. Up to the first part of the Ballet, side 1 plays at 33.3 rpm, after which score pitch is secure at 34.0 rpm. Side 2 begins at 33.7 rpm (the end of the Ballet), slowing to 32.6 rpm for Act II, rising gradually to 32.8 rpm at the recitative before "Amour sacré de la patrie," and still higher to 33.3 rpm by the end of the side. Side 3 plays correctly at 33.3 rpm and side 4 at 32.5 rpm.

EJS 569: "The Golden Age of Opera" (2 LPs)
Issued October, 1971
MATRIX P-2709 / P-2710

SIDES 1-4 (569 A-B):

ELISA E CLAUDIO (Mercadante) (I)
Opera in 2 acts (complete)
Orchestra and Chorus of the Teatro San Carlo di Napoli/Ugo Rapalo
Broadcast, Teatro San Carlo, Naples, 31 Jan 1971

CAST:
Virginia Zeani (*Elisa*); Agostino Lazzari (*Claudio*); Giovanna Fioroni (*Carlotta*); Ugo Trama (*Count Arnoldo*); Domenico Trimarchi (*Marchese Tricufazio*); Maria Luisa Carboni (*Silvio*); Ennio Buoso (*Celso*); Guido Malfatti (*Luca*).

NOTES: EJS 569

This performance was subsequently issued complete on two LPs as MRF-94. The spoken dialogue was included on both the EJS and MRF issues.

EJS 570: "The Golden Age of Opera" (1 LP)
Issued October, 1971
MATRIX P-2711

SIDES 1-2 (570 A-B):

ELENA DA FELTRE (Mercadante) (I)
Opera in 3 acts (Adaptation)
Orchestra A. Scarlatti di Napoli and the Chorus of Radio Italiana [RAI]/Armando Gatto
RAI broadcast, Naples, 16 Dec 1970

CAST:
Orianna Santunione Finzi (*Elena*); Licia Falcone (*Imberga*); Angelo Mori (*Ubaldo*); Vito Tatone (*Boemondo*); Guido Guarnera (*Guido*); Ettore Geri (*Gualtiero*).

SIDE 1 (570 A):

1. GUARNERA and MORI: Diletto amica--Elena! . . . Io gelo!
2. FINZI: Del tremendo Eccelin . . . Ah! si del tenero
3. MORI and FINZI: Il mio sangue i giorni miei
4. FINZI, GUARNERA, MORI, FALCONE, and TATONE, and Chorus: Ah! dura terra e non ti schiudi ancora

SIDE 2 (570 B):

5. FINZI: Madre, che in ciel!
6. GUARNERA and FINZI: Ardon gia le sacrefaci
7. FINZI, MORI, and GERI, and Chorus: Tace la squilla . . . Chi giunge, Ubaldo

NOTES: EJS 570

ELENA DA FELTRE is presented here complete as broadcast, as a 70-minute adaptation. The performance was reissued on CD as VOCE-121.

EJS 571: "The Golden Age of Opera" (1 LP)
Issued October, 1971
MATRIX P-2712

SIDES 1-2 (571 A-B):

ZANETTO (Mascagni) (I)
Opera in 1 act (complete)
Orchestra and Chorus of Radio Italiana [RAI], Milano/Tito Petralia
RAI broadcast, 18 Apr 1970 (recorded 26 Jun 1969)

CAST:
Giuseppina Arista (*Zanetto*); Pina Malgarini (*Silvia*).

NOTES: EJS 571

Reissued as a free "bonus" LP by MRF (MRF-18), coupling this performance with a May-June, 1955 La Scala broadcast of the opera that featured Rosanna Carteri as *Silvia* and Giulietta Simionato as *Zanetto* (Antonino Votto, conducting), along with other Mascagni material.

EJS 572: "The Golden Age of Opera" (3 LPs)
Issued November, 1971
MATRIX P-2734 / P-2735 / P-2736

SIDES 1-6 (572 A-F):

DIE ZAUBERFLÖTE, K. 620 (Mozart) (G)
Opera in 2 acts (complete)
Wiener Philharmoniker and Chorus of the Wiener Staatsoper/Wilhelm Furtwängler
Broadcast, Salzburg Festival, Salzburg, 27 Jul 1949

CAST:
Joseph Greindl (*Sarastro*); Walther Ludwig (*Tamino*); Irmgard Seefried (*Pamina*); Wilma Lipp (*Queen of the Night*); Karl Schmitt-Walter (*Papageno*); Peter Klein (*Monostatos*); Edith Oravez (*Papagena*); Paul Schöffler (*The Speaker*); Hermann Gallos (*First Priest*); Karl Dönch (*Second Priest*); Gertrud Grob-Prandl (*First Lady*); Sieglinde Wagner (*Second Lady*); Elisabeth Höngen (*Third Lady*); Elisabeth Rütgers (*First Youth*); Ruthilde Boesch (*Second Lady*); Polly Batic (*Third Youth*); Ernst Häfliger (*First Warrior*): Hermann Uhde (*First Warrior*).

NOTES: EJS 572

The November, 1971 bulletin, the last in the "Golden Age of Opera" Series, claimed that this Salzburg Festival recording was taken "from 78 rpm discs," hence the quality of the sound. No disc source could be documented, however, only mention of an archival copy--format unknown--at the Rundfunk im Amerikanischen Sektor Berlins [RIAS], Berlin.

This 1949 ZUBERFLÖTE was subsequently issued as Cetra LO-9/3 and Foyer FO-1028.

Note that several of these last GAO issues were released out of matrix sequence.

EJS 573: "The Golden Age of Opera" (2 LPs)
Issued November, 1971
MATRIX P-2740 / P-2741

SIDES 1-4 (573 A-D):

PÉNÉLOPE (Fauré) (F)
Opera in 3 acts (complete)
Orchestra and Chorus of the Office de Radiodiffusion Télévision [ORTF]/Désiré-Émile Inghelbrecht
Broadcast, ORTF, Paris, date unknown

CAST:
Micheline Grancher (*Pénélope*); Gerard Serkoyan (*Ulysse*); Christine Gayraud (*Euryclée*); Françoise Ogeas (*Melantho*); Marguerite Papuet (*Alkandre*); Michel Hamel (*Eumée*); Michel Roux (*Antinous*); Gérard Friedmann (*Eurymaque*); ? (*Phylo*); ? (*Cléone*); ? (*Ctesippe*); ? (*Léodès*).

NOTES: EJS 573

The full cast of this performance could not be documented.

EJS 574: "The Golden Age of Opera" (1 LP)
Issued November, 1971
MATRIX P-2737

DIE ENTFÜHRUNG AUS DEM SERAIL, K. 384 (Mozart) (G)
Opera in 3 acts (excerpts)
Orchestra and Chorus of Norddeutschen Rundfunk [NDR], Hamburg/Hans Schmidt-Isserstedt
Broadcast, NDR, Hamburg, 1946

CAST:
Erna Berger (*Konstanze*); Martina Wulf (*Blonde*); Walther Ludwig (*Belmonte*); Alfred Pfeifle (*Pedrillo*); Theo Hermann (*Osmin*).

SIDE 1 (574 A):

Act I: 1. a) HERMANN and LUDWIG: Wer ein Liebchen hatt gefunden
b) BERGER: Ach, ich liebte

Act II: c) WULFF: Durch Zärtlichkeit
d) BERGER: Martern aller Arten
e) LUDWIG: Wenn der Freude Tränen

SIDE 2 (574 B):

Act III: 1. a) LUDWIG and BERGER: Welch' ein Geschich
b) LUDWIG, BERGER, WULFF, PFEIFLE, and HERMANN: Nie werd'ich deine Huld . . . to the end of the opera

AÏDA (Verdi) (G)
Opera in 4 acts (excerpts)
Wiener Philharmoniker and Chorus of the Wiener Staatsoper/Bruno Walter
In-house recording, Weiner Staatsoper, Vienna, 26 Sep 1937

CAST:
Maria Nemeth (*Aïda*); Todor Mazaroff (*Radames*); Kerstin Thorborg (*Amneris*); Alexander Sved (*Amonasro*); Herbert Alsen (*Ramfis*); Carl Bissutti (*The King of Egypt*).

Act I: 2. a) MAZAROFF: Celeste Aïda

Act II: b) SVED, NEMETH, ALSEN, MAZAROFF, THORBORG, BISSUTTI, and Chorus: Ma tu, [O] Re . . . E rafferma dei Prenci il poter

Act III: c) MAZAROFF, NEMETH, SVED, THORBORG, and ALSEN: Nel fiero anelito . . . to the end of the act

Act IV: d) THORBORG and MAZAROFF: Già i sacerdoti adunansi
e) NEMETH, MAZZAROFF, and THORBORG: O terra addio . . . to the end of the opera

NOTES: EJS 574

The AÏDA, sung here in German, was taken backstage on disc; it was not broadcast. Acetate breaks account for minor omissions, especially in the Act III "Nel fiero anelito" (II/2c).

EJS 575: "The Golden Age of Opera" (1 LP)
Issued November, 1971
MATRIX P-2742

"TENOR SOLOS (GIUSEPPE VERDI)"

SIDE 1 (575 A):

* 1. ?GINO BONELLI, tenor (Orchestra of Radio Italiana [RAI], Torino/ Alfredo Simonetto): OBERTO, CONTE DI SAN BONIFACIO, Act I: Son fra voi! Gia sorto è il giorno (Verdi) (I)
RAI broadcast, Turin, 26 Apr 1951

2. CARLO BERGONZI, tenor (Orchestra of Radio Italiana [RAI], Milano/ Alfredo Simonetto): GIOVANNA D'ARCO, Prologue: Sotto una quercia parvemi (Verdi) (I)
RAI broadcast, Milan, 26 Mar 1951

* 3. LUCIANO PAVAROTTI, tenor (Orchestra of the Teatro dell'Opera, Roma/Gianandrea Gavazzeni): I LOMBARDI, Act II: La mia letizia infondere (Verdi) (I)
Broadcast, Teatro dall'Opera, Rome, 20 Nov 1969

* 4. MIRTO PICCHI, tenor (Orchestra of the Teatro La Fenice/Tullio Serafin): I DUE FOSCARI, Act I: Dal più remoto esilio (Verdi) (I)
Broadcast, Teatro La Fenice, Venice, 26 Dec 1957

* 5. GIANFRANCO CECCHELE, tenor (Orchestra of the Teatro dell'Opera, Roma/Franco Capuana): ALZIRA, Prologue: Ed à nemici ancora . . . Un inca! eccesso orribile! (Verdi) (I)
Broadcast, Teatro dell'Opera, Rome, 12 Feb or 16 Mar 1967

6. GIANFRANCO CECCHELE, tenor (Orchestra of Radio Italiana [RAI], Roma/Riccardo Muti): ATTILA, Prologue: Qui, qui, sostiamo . . . Ella è in poter dei barbari (Verdi) (I)
RAI broadcast, Rome, 8 Dec 1970

7. GASTONE LIMARILLI, tenor (Orchestra of Radio Italiana [RAI], Turino/Franco Mannino): I MASNADIERI, Act I: Son gli ebbri inverecondi . . . O mio castel paterno (Verdi) (I)
RAI broadcast, Turin, 29 May 1971

SIDE 2 (575 B):

1. FRANCO CORELLI, tenor (Orchestra of the Teatro alla Scala/ Gianandrea Gavazzeni): LA BATTAGLIA DI LEGNANO, Act I: O magnanima e prima . . . La pia materna mano (Verdi) (I)
Broadcast, Teatro alla Scala, Rome, 7 Dec 1961

* 2. SIMON VAN DER GEEST, tenor (orch/?): UN GIORNO DI REGNO, Act II: Pietoso al lungo pianto (Verdi) (I)
Broadcast, Holland Festival, ?Amsterdam, 1966

3. GIORGIO CASELLATO LAMBERTI, tenor (Orchestra and Chorus of the Teatro La Fenice/Jesus Lopez-Cobos): IL CORSARO, Act I: Ah, si, ben dite . . . Tutto parea sorridere (Verdi) (I)
Broadcast, Frankfurt-Höchst, Frankfurt, 2 Oct 1971

4. GIUSEPPE DI STEFANO, tenor (Orchestra of the Teatro Massimo, Palermo/Nino Sanzogno): LUISA MILLER, Act III: Che ascolto . . . L'ara o l'avello apprestami (Verdi) (I)
Broadcast, Teatro Massimo, Palermo, 14 Jan 1963

* 5. GASTONE LIMARILLI, tenor; ANGELES GULIN, soprano, and WALTER ALBERTI, baritone (Orchestra of the Teatro Regio, Parma/Peter Maag): STIFFELIO, Act I: Vidi dovunque gemere (Verdi) (I)
Broadcast, Teatro Regio, Parma, 29 Dec 1968

6. MARIO FILIPPESCHI, tenor (Orchestra of the Teatro Massimo, Palermo/Tullio Serafin): LES VÊPRES SICILIENNES, Act IV: E di Monforte il cenno . . . Giorno di pianto (Verdi) (I)
Broadcast, Teatro Massimo, Palermo, 18 Jan 1957

* 7. VASCO COMPAGNANO, tenor, and MARIA VITALE, soprano (Orchestra of Radio Italiana [RAI], Torino/Arturo Basile): AROLDO, Act I: Sotto il sol di Siria ardente (Verdi) (I)
RAI broadcast, Turin, 24 Oct 1951

NOTES: EJS 575

Band 1 of the first side is given as band 7 on the label of EJS 575; the label numbers of side two (left), with their equivalent band-order numbers (right) are as follows:
1 = 3, 2 = 4, 3 = 5, 4 = 6, 5 = 7, 6 = 1, 7 = 2.

Excerpts from a majority of these performances also appeared the same month on EJS 576.

Side 1 (575 A):

Band 1: Labeled as tenor Gianni Poggi (it sounds like Poggi), this is from the complete 26 April, 1951 RAI OBERTO issued as EJS 146 (February, 1959). That issue gives the cast as Maria Caniglia, Elena Nicolai, Poggi, and Tancredi Pasero, where the RAI chronology lists Maria Vitale, Nicolai, Bonelli, and Giuseppe Modesti. See the note on Gino Bonelli for EJS 146.

Band 3: From the complete performance issued as EJS 503 (March, 1970).

Band 4: Leyla Gencer's first-act *scena* with soprano Marisa Salinbeni was included on EJS 421 (January, 1968).

Band 5: From the complete performance issued as EJS 396 (May, 1967). See the endnote for that release regarding the conflict of performance dates.

Side 2 (575 B):

Band 2: Soprano Jeanette Van Dijck's first-act *scena* from this performance appeared the same month on EJS 576.

Band 5: From the complete performance issued as EJS 461 (March, 1969).

Band 7: From the complete performance issued as EJS 156 (June, 1959).

EJS 576: "The Golden Age of Opera" (1 LP)
Issued November, 1971
MATRIX P-2745

"SOPRANO SOLOS (GIUSEPPE VERDI)"

SIDE 1 (576 A):

1. JEANNETTE VAN DIJCK, soprano (orch/?): UN GIORNO DI REGNO, Act I: Ah! non m'hanno ingannato . . . Grave a core innamorato (Verdi) (I)
Broadcast, Holland Festival, ?Amsterdam, 1966

2. RENATA TEBALDI, soprano (Orchestra and Chorus of Radio Italiana [RAI], Milano/Alfredo Simonetto): GIOVANNA D'ARCO, Prologue: Sempre all'alba (Verdi) (I)
   RAI broadcast, Milan, 26 Mar 1951

* 3. RENATA SCOTTO, soprano (Orchestra and Chorus of the Teatro dell'Opera, Roma/Gianandrea Gavazzeni): I LOMBARDI, Act IV: Vergin Santa, invoco . . . Salve Maria (Verdi) (I)
   Broadcast, Teatro dell'Opera, Rome, 20 Nov 1969

4. RENATA SCOTTO, soprano (Orchestra and Chorus of the Teatro dell'Opera, Roma/Gianandrea Gavazzeni): I LOMBARDI, Act IV: Qual prodigio . . . Non fu sogno (Verdi) (I)
   Broadcast, Teatro dell'Opera, Rome, 20 Nov 1969

5. LEYLA GENCER, soprano (Orchestra of the Teatro la Fenice, Venezia/Tullio Serafin): I DUE FOSCARI, Act I: Tu al cui sguardo onnipossente (Verdi) (I)
   Broadcast, Teatro la Fenice, Venice, 31 Dec 1951

* 6. VIRGINIA ZEANI, soprano (Orchestra and Chorus of the Teatro dell'Opera, Roma/Franco Capuana): ALZIRA, Act I: Da Gusman su fragil barca (Verdi) (I)
   Broadcast, Teatro dell'Opera, Rome, 12 Feb or 16 Mar 1967

* 7. RITA ORLANDI MALASPINA, soprano (Orchestra and Chorus of Radio Italiana [RAI], Torino/Franco Mannino): I MASNADIERI, Act I: Venerabile, o padre . . . Lo sguardo avea degli angeli (Verdi) (I)
   RAI broadcast, Turin, 29 May 1971

* 8. RITA ORLANDI MALASPINA, soprano (Orchestra and Chorus of Radio Italiana [RAI], Torino/Franco Mannino): I MASNADIERI, Act II: Oh! ma la pace . . . Tu del mio Carlo al seno (Verdi) (I)
   RAI broadcast, Turin, 29 May 1971

SIDE 2 (576 B):

* 1. MARIA VITALE, soprano (Orchestra and Chorus of Radio Italiana [RAI], Torino/Alfredo Simonetto): OBERTO, CONTE DI SAN BONIFACIO, Act I: Ah, sgombro è il loco alfin . . . Sotto il paterno tetto (Verdi) (I)
   RAI broadcast, Turin, 26 Apr 1951

2. RITA TALARICO, soprano (orch/?): IL CORSARO, Act I: Egli non riede ancora! . . . Non so le tetre immagini (Verdi) (I)
   Source and date unknown

* 3. ELENA SULIOTIS, soprano (Orchestra of the Teatro Comunale, Firenze/Nino Sanzogno): LUISA MILLER, Act I: Non temer . . . Lo vidi e'l primo palpito (Verdi) (I)
   Broadcast, Teatro Comunale, Florence, May 1966

* 4. ANGELES GULIN, soprano (Orchestra of the Teatro Regio di Parma/Peter Maag): STIFFELIO, Act I: [Tosto ei disse] . . . A te ascenda, O Dio clemente (Verdi) (I)
   Broadcast, Teatro Regio, Parma, 29 Dec 1968

5. ANTONIETTA STELLA, soprano (Orchestra and Chorus of the Teatro Massimo, Palermo/Tullio Serafin): LES VÊPRES SICILIENNE, Act I: Si, canterò . . . In alto mare [Oui, je chanterai . . . Au sein des mers] (Verdi) (I)
   Broadcast, Teatro Massimo, Palermo, 18 Jan 1957

* 6. MARIA VITALE, soprano (Orchestra of Radio Italiana [RAI], Torino/Arturo Basile): AROLDO, Act I: Ciel, ch'io respiri . . . Salvami, Tu, gran Dio (Verdi) (I)
   RAI broadcast, Turin, 24 Oct 1951

7. MARIA VITALE, soprano (Orchestra of Radio Italiana [RAI], Torino/Arturo Basile): AROLDO, Act II: O cielo! . . . Ah, dagli scanni eterei (Verdi) (I)
   RAI broadcast, Turin, 24 Oct 1951

NOTES: EJS 576

The contents listing on both labels of this LP are unusually chaotic: not one of the selections is given in its proper place. Below is a concordance, with the label numbers given at the left, alligned with their correct band number at the right:

Side 1:		Side 2:	
1 = 2	4 = 6	1 = 2	4 = 5
2 = 3 & 4	5 = 7	2 = 3	5 = 6
3 = 5	6 = 8	3 = 4	6 = 7
7 = 1		7 = 1	

Because there were no further "Golden Age of Opera" bulletins, Smith was unable to call this to the attention of subscribers.

Excerpts from a majority of these performances also appeared the same month on EJS 575.

Side 1 (576 A):

Band 3: This I LOMBARDI was issued complete as EJS 503 (March, 1970).

Band 6: This ALZIRA was issued complete as EJS 396 (May, 1967). See the endnote for that release regarding the conflict of performance dates.

Bands 7-8: Taken from a complete studio performance.

Side 2 (576 B):

Band 1: This OBERTO was issued complete as EJS 146 (February, 1959). See the endnote for that issue on cast attribution: Maria Caniglia sang in the 1952 Scala production of OBERTO, Vitale, heard here, in the RAI broadcast of 1951.

Band 4: This STIFFELIO was issued complete as EJS 461 (March, 1969).

Band 6: This AROLDO was issued complete as EJS 156 (June, 1959).

EJS 577: "The Golden Age of Opera" (1 LP)
Issued November, 1971
MATRIX P-2738

"TENOR SOLOS (VINCENZO BELLINI)"

SIDE 1 (577 A):

* 1. FLAVIANO LABÒ, tenor (Orchestra and Chorus of the Teatro Comunale, Firenze/Franco Capuana or Erasmo Ghiglia): IL PIRATA, Act I: Di mia vendetta ho pieno il mondo . . . Nel furor delle tempeste . . . Dal disastro di questi infelici (Bellini) (I)
   Broadcast, Teatro Comunale, Florence, ?13 Jun 1967

* 2. RENATO CIONI (Orchestra and Chorus of the Teatro Massimo, Palermo/Nino Sanzogno): LA STRANIERA, Act I: Che mai penso? . . . Rio presagio! Il ciel si oscura (Bellini) (I)
   Broadcast, Teatro Massimo, Palermo, 10 Dec 1968

* 3. LUCIANO PAVAROTTI, tenor, MARIO PETRI, bass-baritone, and WALTER MONACHESI, baritone (Orchestra and Chorus of the Teatro alla Scala/Claudio Abbado): I CAPULETTI ED I MONTECCHI, Act I: Rinvenirlo io saprò . . . E serbato, è serbato a questa acciaro (Bellini) (I)
   Broadcast, Teatro alla Scala, Milan, 26 Mar 1966

* 4. GIACOMO ARAGALL, tenor, MARIO PETRI, bass-baritone, and LUCIANO PAVAROTTI, tenor (Orchestra and Chorus of the Teatro alla Scala/ Claudio Abbado): I CAPULETTI ED I MONTECCHI, Act I: Ascolta . . . Se Romeo t'uccise un figlio . . . La tremenda ultrice spada (Bellini) (I)
   Broadcast, Teatro alla Scala, Milan, 26 Mar 1966

SIDE 2 (577 B):

* 1. PIERRE DUVAL, tenor, and RENATA SCOTTO, soprano (Philadelphia Opera Orchestra/Fausto Cleva): LA SONNAMBULA, Act II: Vedi, o madre . . . Tutto è sciolto (Bellini) (I)
   Broadcast, Philadelphia Lyric Opera, Philadelphia, 10 Jan 1967

* 2. GIOVANNI MARTINELLI, tenor (Metropolitan Opera House Orchestra and Chorus/Ettore Panizza): NORMA, Act I: Meco all'altar di Venere . . . Me protegge, me difende (Bellini) (I)
   Metropolitan Opera broadcast, NYC, 20 Feb 1937

* 3. ALFREDO KRAUS, tenor (orch/?): I PURITANI, Act I: A te, o cara (Bellini) (I)
   Source and date uncertain

* 4. GIANNI RAIMONDI, tenor, JOAN SUTHERLAND, soprano, MARIO ZANASI, baritone, and FERRUCCIO MAZZOLI, bass (Orchestra and Chorus of the Teatro Massimo, Palermo/Tullio Serafin): I PURITANI, Act III: La mia canzon d'amore . . . A una fonte afflitto e solo . . . Corre a valle, corre a monte (Bellini) (I)
   In-house recording, Teatro Massimo, Palermo, 12 Jan 1961

* 5. GIANNI RAIMONDI, tenor, JOAN SUTHERLAND, soprano, MARIO ZANASI, baritone, and FERRUCCIO MAZZOLI, bass (Orchestra and Chorus of the Teatro Massimo, Palermo/Tullio Serafin): I PURITANI, Act III: Cavaliere ti colse il Dio punitor . . . Credeasi misera (Bellini) (I)
In-house recording, Teatro Massimo, Palermo, 12 Jan 1961

NOTES: EJS 577

As if the labeling problems on EJS 575 and 576 were not enough, all of side 1 and the first two bands of side 2 on this Bellini recital contain some sort of tape "crosstalk"--especially irritating in the soft passages.

Side 1 (577 A):

Bands 1: Taken from the complete performance, with Montserrat Caballé as *Imogene* and Piero Cappucilli as *Ernesto*. This production went up on 13 June, 1967, but it is not known which performance was actually broadcast. The date quoted for other abridged and complete issues of the opera varies, one giving a precise *15* June. Both Capuana and Ghiglia have been cited as the conductor of the production.

Band 2: This LA STRANIERA, with Scotto as *Alaide*, was issued complete on EJS 454 (January, 1969): three Scotto excerpts appeared on EJS 578 as well.

Bands 3-4: Taken from a complete performance, the premier of conductor Abbado's controversial adaptation of I CAPULETTI ED I MONTECCHI, which recast *Romeo* as a tenor and severely rearranged Bellini's music. One of Scotto's arias also appears on EJS 578.

Side 2 (577 B):

Band 1: Taken from a complete performance.

Band 2: This 20 February, 1937 Martinelli NORMA was issued complete as EJS 113 (1957). The "Meco all'altar" and "In mia man" have appeared on various Smith issues.

Band 3: This Kraus aria appears to be from a broadcast recital: there are no other principals present in the scene, nor is there applause. Kraus did appear as *Arturo* at the Teatro São Carlos, Lisbon, in 1961, with Gianna D'Angelo as *Elvira*, and Dino Dondi as *Riccardo* Tullio Serafin conducting, but it is not known whether portions of this recording survive.

EJS 578: "The Golden Age of Opera" (1 LP)
Issued November, 1971
MATRIX P-2739

"SOPRANO SOLOS (VINCENZO BELLINI)"

SIDE 1 (578 A):

* 1. MONTSERRAT CABALLÉ, soprano, BERNABÉ MARTÌ, tenor, [] HELTON, mezzo-soprano, and JOHN REARDON, baritone (Orchestra and Chorus of the Philadelphia Lyric Opera/Anton Guadagno): IL PIRATA, Act I: Il duce lor? . . . Lo sognai ferito . . . to the end of the scene (Bellini) (I)
   In-house recording, Philadelphia Lyric Opera, Philadelphia, 8 Mar 1968

* 2. RENATA SCOTTO, soprano (Orchestra and Chorus of the Teatro Massimo, Palermo/Nino Sanzogno): LA STRANIERA, Act I: Tacete! un grido io sento (Bellini) (I)
   Broadcast, Teatro Massimo, Palermo, 10 Dec 1968

* 3. RENATA SCOTTO, soprano (Orchestra and Chorus of the Teatro Massimo, Palermo/Nino Sanzogno): LA STRANIERA, Act II: Sono all'ara . . . Barriera tremenda fra noi sorge (Bellini) (I)
   Broadcast, Teatro Massimo, Palermo, 10 Dec 1968

* 4. RENATA SCOTTO, soprano (Orchestra and Chorus of the Teatro Massimo, Palermo/Nino Sanzogno): LA STRANIERA, Act II: Or sei pago, o ciel tremendo (Bellini) (I)
   Broadcast, Teatro Massimo, Palermo, 10 Dec 1968

* 5. RENATA SCOTTO, soprano (Orchestra and Chorus of the Teatro alla Scala, Milano/Claudio Abbado): I CAPULETTI ED I MONTECCHI, Act I: Eccomi in lieta vesta . . . Oh! quante volte (Bellini) (I)
   Broadcast, Teatro alla Scala, Milan, 26 Mar 1966

SIDE 2 (578 B):

1. LINA PAGLIUGHI, soprano (Orchestra and Chorus of Radio Italiana [RAI], Roma/Ferruccio Scaglia): LA SONNAMBULA, Act II: Ah! non credea mirarti (Bellini) (I)
   Broadcast, *CONCERTO MARTINI E ROSSI*, Rome, 22 Nov 1954

* 2. RENATA SCOTTO, soprano (orch/Ottavio Ziino): LA SONNAMBULA, Act II: Ah! non giunge (Bellini) (I)
   In-house concert recording, ?Teatro Massimo Bellini, Catania, Sicily, 3 Jun 1961

* 3. ?CRISTINA DEUTEKOM, soprano (orch/?): NORMA, Act II: Ah, padre, un prego ancor . . . Deh! non volerli vittime (Bellini) (I)
   In-house recording, Open-Air Theater, Bregenz, Austria, August, 1970, or Dallas, 30 Oct 1971

* 4. LEYLA GENCER, soprano, and ANTIGONE SGOURDA, soprano (Orchestra and Chorus of the Teatro la Fenice, Venezia/Vittorio Gui): BEATRICE DI TENDA, Act I: O mie fedeli . . . Ah! la pena in lor piombò (Bellini) (I)
Broadcast, Teatro la Fenice, Venice, 10 Jan 1964

* 5. LEYLA GENCER, soprano, and ANTIGONE SGOURDA, soprano (Orchestra and Chorus of the Teatro la Fenice, Venezia/Vittorio Gui): BEATRICE DI TENDA, Act II: Chi giunge? . . . Ah! se un'urna (Bellini) (I)
Broadcast, Teatro la Fenice, Venice, 10 Jan 1964

* 6. VIRGINIA ZEANI, soprano; MARIO FILIPPESCHI, tenor; ANDREA MONGELLI, bass, and unknown soprano (Orchestra of the Teatro Verdi, Trieste/Francesco Molinari-Pradelli): I PURITANI, Act I: E la vergine adorata . . . Son vergin vezzosa (Bellini) (I)
Broadcast, ?Teatro Verdi, Trieste, 1957

* 7. LINA PAGLIUGHI, sopramo (Orchestra and Chorus of Radio Italiana [RAI], Roma/Fernando Previtali): I PURITANI, Act II: Qui la voce soave . . . Vien diletto (Bellini) (I)
RAI broadcast, Rome, 5 Jan 1952

NOTES: EJS 578

EJS 578 was the final issue of Edward J. Smith's "The Golden Age of Opera" series. In all, there were 479 regular entries and a host of "special" issues released over a period of fifteen years. As he did so many times before, Smith closed this final bulletin with a familiar message to his subscribers: "God Bless and Keep You All." The next issues, under the banner of the "Unique Opera Records Corporation," was announced in January, 1972.

Side 1 (578 A):

Band 1: Helton's first name could not be found. This excerpt was taken from an in-house recording of the complete opera. Caballé and Martì recorded the opera commercially with the RAI Orchestra and Chorus conducted by Gavazzeni (HMV SLS 953, issued in the U.S. as Angel S3772).

Bands 2-4: These excerpts were taken from a complete performance originally issued as EJS 454 in January, 1969. Excerpts also appeared on EJS 577 (November, 1971).

Band 5: Taken from a complete performance. Two ensembles appeared on EJS 577: see the endnote for that issue regarding the production itself. Scotto also appeared in a Montreal World's Fair production of CAPULETTI on 7 October, 1967, but the EJS 577-578 excerpts appear to come from the 1966 Scala production.

Side 2 (578 B):

Band 2: Scotto sings the concert ending here, without chorus. The location of this concert could not be traced, but it may well have been the Teatro Massimo Bellini in Sicily.

Band 3: Two Deutekom NORMAs were in circulation at the time EJS 578 was being prepared: an August, 1970 production in Bregenz's open-air theater, and a 30 October, 1971 Dallas concert performance conducted by Nicola Rescigno.

Bands 4-5: These excerpts were taken from a complete performance. 9 January has also been reported as the performance date, but 10 January appears to be correct.

Band 6: The *Enrichetta* has not been identified. Zeani undertook *Elvira* in a well-known production of PURITANI at the Teatro dell'Opera, Roma, in March, 1956, with Di Stefano as *Arturo*, Paolo Silveri as *Riccardo*, and Giulio Neri as *Sir Giorgio*, but it is not known whether this performance has survived. No other details of the Trieste performance could be found, but excerpts were subsequently reissued on Rococo 1006.

Band 7: The Pagliughi PURITANI was a complete studio recording produced on 4 January, 1952 (Pagliughi claimed that it was recorded on 1 January). Extensive excerpts appeared as EJS 272 in June, 1963.

APPENDIX

CONCORDANCE OF LABEL AND BULLETIN MISNUMBERINGS

The September, 1967 bulletin (GAO 404-407) was the first to include the catalog numbers of the LPs. Prior to this, only the titles of each release were given. However, even after the catalog numbers were added, the bulletins often ordered the LPs incorrectly, thus, misnumbering them, just as the 1970s "Golden Age of Opera" checklist, distributed after the demise of the "Golden Age of Opera" series (discussed further in the INTRODUCTION TO THE DISCOGRAPHY), assigned its own set of incorrect catalog numbers to large blocks of LPs. Even the LPs themselves were mismarked on a few ocassions--though they were usually *mislabeled* (that is, with labels carrying incorrect catalog numbers) rather than misstamped.

The following concordance is offered to bring the content of the misnumbered GAO LPs in line with their correct catalog numbers. The *incorrect* catalog numbers are at the far left, followed by the LP title, and the *correct* catalog number preceded by an equavalent sign: thus, a copy of the 1960 RAI OTELLO bearing the catalog number GAO 103 is in fact GAO 203, and will be found listed as such, with mention in the endnotes of both EJS 103 and 203 of the numbering error.

GAO 103: OTELLO
= **GAO 203**
GAO 113: POTPOURRI NO. 12
= **GAO 213**
GAO 116: LES HUGUENOTS
= **GAO 117**
GAO 117: CARMEN
= **GAO 116**
GAO 166: GÖTTERDÄMMERUNG
= **GAO 167**
GAO 175: GUGLIELMO RATCLIFF
= **GAO 275**
GAO 176: LA BETULA LIBERATA
= **GAO 276**
GAO 177: L'INCANTESIMO
= **GAO 277**
GAO 178: MIGNON
= **GAO 179**
GAO 179: DIE WALKÜRE
= **GAO 178**
GAO 187: RIENZI
= **GAO 189**
GAO 197: KIRSTEN FLAGSTAD, SOPRANO
= **GAO 198**
GAO 198: KIRSTEN FLAGSTAD / THIRTEEN UNPUBLISHED LIEDER
= **GAO 197**
GAO 214: BORIS GODUNOV
= **GAO 215**
GAO 215: POTPOURRI NO. XIII
= **GAO 214**
GAO 238: KIRSTEN FLAGSTAD 70TH BIRTHDAY DISC
= **GAO 338**

GAO 239: ZELMIRA
= **GAO 339**
GAO 240: IL GUARANY
= **GAO 340**
GAO 241: LUCIA DI LAMMERMOOR
= **GAO 341**
GAO 242: GÖTTERDÄMMERUNG
= **GAO 342**
GAO 243: GIACOMO LAURI-VOLPI
= **GAO 343**
GAO 244: INTERMEZZO
= **GAO 344**
GAO 245 IL GIUDIZIO UNIVERSALE
= **GAO 345**
GAO 246: CAVALLERIA RUSTICANA
= **GAO 346**
GAO 261: DIE TOTE STADT
= **GAO 263**
GAO 262: KHOVANSHCHINA
= **GAO 261**
GAO 263: POTPOURRI NO. 17
= **GAO 262**
GAO 375: I CAVALIERI DI EKEBÙ
= **GAO 376**
GAO 387: LE MÉDECIN MALGRÉ LUI
= **GAO 388**
GAO 388: LES BRIGANDS
= **GAO 387**
GAO 413: PIA DE TOLOMEI
= **GAO 412**
GAO 414: OBERON
= **GAO 413**

Index of Artists

Entries identify the series (the "GAO" prefix designating the "Golden Age of Opera") and the LP catalog number.

A lower-case "n" following a catalog number indicates that a performer is mentioned *only* in an endnote, not in the discography listing, while "+n" indicates a significant endnote *in addition* to mention in the listing. All performers are indexed, including conductors, accompanists, and those given in the cast listings who are not actually heard in the performance(s) cited. Artists who are listed in error on EJS labels, or are not really present in composites or forgeries (i.e. the EJS 267 "Mapleson Cylinders" issue), are not given in the index unless a substantial note about them is appended to a specific LP. Neither are accompanying orchestras indexed unless they are featured in significant passages of a score.

Strict alphabetical order has been observed for ease of access. Surname prefixes ("D'," "De," "Del," "Della," "Delle," "De Los," "Di," and "Lo") are used as filing elements and will fall in their proper alphabetical place. "Mc" is filed as "Mac" and "St." as "Saint." The German "Von" and "Vom" are *not* used as filing elements (Anny Von Stosch will be found under "Stosch"), where the generally-Dutch "Van" *is* (Mimi Van Aarden will be found under "Van Aarden"). The German umlaut designating the letter "e" will be filed in its proper place: "ö" as oe, "ü" as ue, etc. As a precaution, all hyphenated or otherwise troublesome names ("van," "von," etc.) will be cross-referenced where appropriate, along with those which no longer conform to common usage (e.g. Maurice *de* Abravanel).

In addition to voice type and profession (conductor, accompanist, pianist, etc.), dates will be supplied for artists where available, using the most reliable current sources (see bibliographic note in the INTRODUCTION).

In the case of *comprimarii* and singers whose careers did not allow for comparative verification, we have assigned voice ranges consonant with the score designation of the role(s) they sing in the performances under scrutiny. Certain roles, moreover, can and often are sung by more than one voice type. Similarly, basses and bass-baritones, like mezzo-sopranos and contraltos, become a source of bewildering confusion when attempting to fix a voice type to a given part.

INDEX ABBREVIATIONS

ac = actor/actress
au = author
b = baritone
bb = bass-baritone
bs = bass
c = contralto
cl = violoncellist
ch = chorus master
cd = conductor
cm = (radio) commentator
cp = composer
fd = film director
i = interviewer
md = musical director (films)
ms = mezzo-soprano
o = organist
pf = pianist
po = politician
ra = radio announcer
s = soprano
sp = speaker
t = tenor
v = violinist
vc = vocalist (popular)

A few less-common descriptions and accompaniments will be given in full.

AARDEN, MIMI VAN (see VAN AARDEN, MIMI)
ABBADO, CLAUDIO, cd (1933-
GAO: 577+n, 578
ABBATI, VALERIO DEGLI, sp
GAO: 413+n
ABBOTT, GREGORY, newsreel announcer
GAO: 512n
ABRAVANEL, MAURICE, pf/cd (1903-)
GAO: ?140, 170, 181, 183, 184, 186, 212, 213, 258, 270, 516, 557
ACAMPORA, IRENE, c
GAO: 350, 355
ACHSEL, WANDA, s (1886-1977)
GAO: 460
ACHORD, MARCEL, fd (1899-1974)
GAO: 420
ADANI, MARIELLA, s (1934-)
GAO: 293, 294, 296
ADLER, KURT HERBERT, cd (1905-1988)
GAO: 214, 470
ADONIS, PAULO, bs
GAO: 437
AGRELLI, ANDREAS CAMILLO
GAO: 273
AHLERSMEYER, MATHIEU, b (1896-1979)
GAO: 387
AKED, MURIEL, ac
GAO: 456
ALAN, HERVEY, bs (1910-1982)
GAO: 161, 553
ALARIE, PIERETTE, s (1921-)
GAO: 365
ALBANESE, FRANCESCO, t (1912-)
GAO: 467
ALBANESE, LICIA, s (1909 or 1913-)
GAO: 169, 172, 193, 212, 214, 228, 237, 240, 250, 265, 282, 321, 329, 448
ALBERT, HERBERT, cd (1903-)
GAO: 372
ALBERTI, WALTER, b
GAO: 412, 461, 575
ALBERTINI, SERGIO, t
GAO: 437, 505
ALDA, FRANCES, s (1883-1952)
GAO: 122 (speech), 141, 142, 513, 532, 566
ALDENHOFF, BERND, t (1908-1959)
GAO: 268
ALEMANNO, OSVALDO, t
GAO: 522
ALEXANDER, CARLOS, bb (1915-)
GAO: 558
ALGORTA, JORGE [GIORGIO], bs
GAO: 408, 467, 565
ALLAIN, RAYMONDE, ac
GAO: 420
ALLARD, GÖTA, c
GAO: 349, 406
ALLEN, BETTY, ms (1930-)
GAO: 473
ALLPRESS, ROBERT, cd
GAO: 304, 435
ALME, WALDEMAR, pf
GAO: 197, 199, 338, 390
ALNAES, EYVIND, pf (1872-1932)
GAO: 198
ALONSO, FRANCISCO, bb
GAO: 374, 559
ALSEN, ELSA, ms (1880-1975)
GAO: 444
ALSEN HERBERT, bs (1906-1978)
GAO: 334, 574
ALSTERGARD, BERTIL, b
GAO: 402, 406
ALTGLASS, MAX, t (1890-1952)
GAO: 111, 114, 134, 149, 186, 187, 224, 262, 489, 492, 496, 506, 509, 516
ALTHOUSE, PAUL, t (1889-1954)
GAO: 167, 169, 200, 444, 501
ALTMAN, THELMA, ms
GAO: 209, 241, 374, 561
ALTMANN, HANS, cd
GAO: 298
ALVA, LUIGI, t (1927-)
GAO: 459
ALVARY, LORENZO, b (1909-)
GAO: 164, 168, 169, 211, 217, 250, 266, 288n, 374, 462, 550, 558, 561
ALWIN, KARL, cd (1891-1945)
GAO: 336, 337
AMADE, RAYMOND, t (1915-1969)
GAO: 443, 449, 494
AMADINI, MARIA, ms
GAO: 376
AMARA, LUCINE, s (1925 or 1927-)
GAO: 208
AMATO, ALBERT CARLO, pf
GAO: 563
AMATO, PASQUALE, b (1878-1942)
GAO: 403n
AMEDEO, EDY, s (1935-)
GAO: 117, 323
AMFITEATROFF, MASSIMO, cl
GAO: 558

BURKE, HILDA, s
GAO: 103/4, 116, 484, 523
BURKSTEN, JOSEPH, b
GAO: 245
BURR, JOHN, bs
GAO: 221
BURZI, AURELIO, bs
GAO: 439
BYLES, EDWARD, t
GAO: 400

CABALLÉ, MONTSERRAT, s (1933-)
GAO: 577n, 578
CADET, RIVERS, ac
GAO: 456
CADONI, FERNANDA, s (1923-)
GAO: 222, 370, 413
CALABRESE, FRANCO, bb (1923-1992)
GAO: 138, 280, 299, 458, 459
CALIL, JOAO, t
GAO: 437
CALLAS, MARIA [MENEGHINI], s (1923-1977)
GAO: 166n, 360, 518n
CALLAWAY, IRENE, s
GAO: 394
CALUSIO, FERRUCCIO, cd (1889-?)
GAO: 105, 207, 212, 405
CAMBON, CHARLES, b (1892-1966)
GAO: 245, 377, 378
CAMERON, JOHN, b (1920-)
GAO: 257
CAMOZZO, ADOLFO, cd
GAO: 381
CAMPAGNANO, VASCO, t (1910-1976)
GAO: 156, 333, 575
CAMPANARI, GIUSEPPE, b (1855-1927)
GAO: 141
CAMPI, ADELINA, s
GAO: 350
CAMPI, ENRICO, bs
GAO: 286, 339, 454, 477
CAMPORA, GIUSEPPE, t (1923-)
GAO: 133, 194, 218, 316
CANALI, ANNA MARIA, c (1921-)
GAO: 380
CANEPA, LORENZA, s
GAO: 486
CANIGLIA, MARIA, s (1905-1979)
GAO: 142, 146n, 213, 281, 306, 308, 325, 329, 359, 360, 414, 575n, 576n
CANNARILE, ANTONIETTA, s
GAO: 507
CANTELO, APRIL, s (1928-)
GAO: 161
CAPDEROU, JANINE, s
GAO: 474, 495
CAPECCHI, RENATO, b (1923-)
GAO: 204, 216, 280, 287, 296, 370n, 373, 471
CAPNIST, RENATA HEREDIA, s
GAO: 174, 389
CAPOUL, VICTOR, t (1839-1924)
GAO: 563
CAPELLMAN, RICHARD, bs
GAO: 387
CAPPUCILLI, PIERO, b (1929-)
GAO: 307, 340, 577n
CAPRISTI, RENATA (see CAPNIST, RENATA HEREDIA)
CAPSIR, MERCEDES, s (1897-1969)
GAO: 493
CAPUANA, FRANCO, cd (1894-1969)
GAO: 254, 286, 311, 330, 396, 404, 575, 576, ?577
CARAVITA, CARLA
GAO: 514
CARBONE, MARIA LUISA, s
GAO: 569
CARBONARI, VIRGILIO, bs
GAO: 246, 284, 381, 391, 393
CARILLO, ROMAN, bs
GAO: 505
CARIVEN, MARCEL, cd
GAO: 494
CARLI, ANGELO, bb
GAO: 162
CARLIN, MARIO, t (1917-)
GAO: 133, 166, 194, 216, 370n, 376, 461
CARMELI, BORIS, bs (?1932-)
GAO: 522
CARMODY, HUDSON, bs
GAO: 167
CARNEVALI, VITO, cd & pf (1888-?)
GAO: 111, ?464+n, 529
CAROLI, PAOLO, t
GAO: 308
CARON, ROSE, s (1857-1930)
GAO: 242
CAROSIO, MARGHERITA, s (1908-)
GAO: 151, 311, 360, 441, 483
CAROSSI, O., ms
GAO: 421
CARRACCIOLO, FRANCO, cd
GAO: 335, 401
CARRENO, MANUEL, bs
GAO: 374
CARROLI, SILVANO, b (?1938-)
GAO: 305, 333, 552

CHARLES-PAUL bb (1903-1985)
GAO: 377, 378, 385
CHARON, JACQUES, ac
GAO: 420
CHARPENTIER, GUSTAVE, cp (1860-1956)
GAO: 456+n
CHIAPPI, MARIO, bs
GAO: 522
CHIARA, MARIA, s (1942-)
GAO: 528
CHICHAGOV, IGOR, pf
GAO: 191, 243, 247
CHIOCCA, GENNARO, bs
GAO: 254
CHRIST, RUDOLPH, t (1916-1982)
GAO: 517
CHRISTIAN, HANS, bs
GAO: 521
CHRISTOFF, BORIS, bs (1914 or 1918-1993)
GAO: 163, 206, 276, 295, 331, 360, 371, 422, 424, 436
CIABATTINI, GIUSEPPE, bs
GAO: 549
CIAFFI RICAGNO, LUISELLA
GAO: 388
CIAPARELLI, GINA (see VIAFORA, GINA CIAPARELLI)
CIAVOLA, GIOVANNI, bs
GAO: 518, 535
CIGNA, GINA, s (1900-)
GAO: 113, 147, 171n, 366
CILLA, LUIGI, t (?1885-?)
GAO: 144
CILLARIO, CARLO FELICE, cd (1915-)
GAO: 233, 360, 370
CIMARA, PIETRO, pf and cd (1887-1967)
GAO: 270, 306, 341, 566n
CIMINELLI, GIOVANNI, b
GAO: 275, 507
CIMINI, PIETRO, cd
GAO: ?262
CINIKA, LUDWIG, bs
GAO: 428
CIONI, BRUNO, bs (1918-1973)
GAO: 373, 376
CIONI, RENATO, t (1929-)
GAO: 317, 360, 454, 577
CLABASSI, PLINIO, bs (?1914-1984)
GAO: 166, 254, 286, 311, 312, 360, 391
CLARK, LILLIAN, c
GAO: 134, 504
CLAUDIA, ANTEA, s
GAO: 205
CLEMENS, HANS, t (1890-1958)
GAO: 109, 157, 221, 249, 492, 496, 499, 502, 504, 506
CLEVA, FAUSTO, cd (1902-1971)
GAO: 252, 341, 367, 426, 577
COATES, EDITH, c (1906 or 1908-1983)
GAO: 450, 546
COBOS, JESUS LOPEZ (see LOPEZ-COBOS, JESUS)
COCCHIERI, VINICIO, b
GAO: 323
CODA, ERALDO, bs (1903-)
GAO: 375
COERTSE, MIMI, s (1932-)
GAO: 521
COHEN, ELIE, cd
GAO: 563
COLELLA, ALFREDO, bs
GAO: 201, 308, 368, 503, 552
COLISIMO, ALFREDO, t
GAO: 205
COLLART, CLAUDINE, s (1923-)
GAO: 443, 474, 495
COLLIER, FREDERICK, b (1885-1964)
GAO: 127
COLLIER, MARIE, s (1926-1971)
GAO: 313
?COLLINGWOOD, ----?, an
GAO: 247
?COLLINGWORTH, ---?, an
GAO: 247
COLOMBO, SCIPIO, b (1910 or 1913-)
GAO: 388, 483
COLOSIMO, ROSELLA
GAO: 401
COLZANI, ANSELMO, b (1918-)
GAO: 138, 162, 408, 467
COMBE, LEON, bar
GAO: 361
COMPAÑEZ, IRENE, ms
GAO: 253, 253
CONNER, NADINE, s (1914-)
GAO: 292, 462, 559
CONRAD, PAUL, t
GAO: 428
CONSTANTINI, CONSTANTINO, ch
GAO: 359
CONTI, GINO, b
GAO: 308
COOLEMAN, GEORGETTE, s
GAO: 442
COOPER [KUPER], EMIL, cd (1877-1960)
GAO: 154+n, 217, 261, 288n, 477

GOOSSENS, [SIR] EUGENE, cd (1893-1962)
GAO: 226, 322+n, 452, 541+n
GORDON, JEANNE, c (1893-1952)
GAO: 102, 403, 470
GOSTIC, JOSEF, t (1900-1963)
GAO: 314
GOURAUD, COL., recordist
GAO: 267n
GRAARUD, GUNNAR, t (1886-1960)
GAO: 460
GRACIS, ETTORE, cd (1915-)
GAO: 162, 392, 554
GRANCHER, MICHELINE, s
GAO: 573
GRANDI, MARGHERITA, s (1894-)
GAO: 383
GRANFORTE, APOLLO, b (1886-1975)
GAO: 144, 325
GRAYSON, KATHRYN, s (1922-)
GAO: 457
GRECO, NORINA, s
GAO: 105, 141, 207, 405n, 562
GREER, FRANCES, s
GAO: 220, 236, 500
GREINDL, JOSEF, bs (1912-1993)
GAO: 318, 419, 572
GRELLA, BRUNO, b
GAO: 307
GRESSE, ANDRÉ, bs (1868-1937)
GAO: 143n
GREVILLIUS, NILS, cd (1893-1970)
GAO: 154n, 252, 337, 347, 384, 530
GRILLI, UMBERTO, t (1934-)
GAO: 476, 503
GRIMALDI, GIORGIO, t (1936-)
GAO: 305, 554
GROB-PRANDL, GERTRUD, s (1917-)
GAO: 572
GROOTE, MAURICE DE
(see DE GROOTE, MAURICE)
GROVE, ISAAC VAN
(see VAN GROVE, ISAAC)
GRUBER, FERRY, t (1926-)
GAO: 344
GRUHN [GRÜHN], NORA, s (1905-)
GAO: 447n
GUADAGNO, ANTON, cd (1925-)
GAO: 578
GUAGNI, ENZO, t
GAO: 138, 436
GUAJARDO, LUZ VERDAD, s
GAO: 302
GUALTIERI, ORAZIO, b
GAO: 430
GUARNERA, GUIDO, b (1929-)
GAO: 343, 570
GÜDEN, HILDE, s (1917-1988)
GAO: 171, 331, 365, 367, 371
GUELFI, GIAN GIACOMO, b (1924-)
GAO: 132, 137, 155, 254, 284, 467, 542, 552, 555
GUELFI, PIERO, b (1914-1989)
GAO: 350
GUENTER, PAUL, bs
GAO: 169
GUERRA, SANTIAGO, cd (1902-)
GAO: 205
GUERRINI, ADRIANA, s (1907-1970)
GAO: 204, 309, 320, 329
GUGGIA, MARIO, t
GAO: 305, 368, 392, 404
GUI, HENRI, t (1926-)
GAO: 498
GUI, VITTORIO, cd (1885-1975)
GAO: 171, 214, 366, 403, 413, 421, 458, 467, 553, 578
GUICHANDUT, CARLOS [CARLO MARIA], t (1915 or 1919-1990)
GAO: 325
GUIDOTTA, MARIELLA, i
GAO: 513
GUIOT, ANDREA, s (1928-)
GAO: 245, 435
GULIN, ANGELES (aka ANGELES GULIN DOMINGUEZ), s (1943-)
GAO: 461+n, 575, 576
GULLINO, WALTER, t (1933-)
GAO: 218, 246
GURNEY, JOHN, bs (1902-)
GAO: 126, 145, 164, 211, 215, 220, 224, 237, 516, 523, 527, 550, 556, 561
GUTHRIE, FREDERICK, bs (1924-)
GAO: 521
GUTSTEIN, ERNST, b (1924-)
GAO: 491

HAAS-KELLY, JUNE, s
GAO: 409
HABICH, EDUARD, b (1880-1960)
GAO: 167, 173, 249, 288, 489, 492
HACKETT, CHARLES, t (1889-1942)
GAO: 150, 262, 513
HADLEY, HENRY, cd (1871-1937)
GAO: 512n
HADRABOVÁ, EVA, s (1902-1973)
GAO: 332+n, 460
HÄFLIGER, ERNST, t (1919-)
GAO: 572
HAGE, ROBERT AMIS EL
(see EL HAGE, ROBERT AMIS)

MANTOVANI, DINO, b
GAO: 296
MANUEL, ROBERT, ac
GAO: 420
MARACCI, LIVIA, s
GAO: 470
MARCANGELI, ANNA, s (1910-)
GAO: 222
MARCHAL, ARLETTE, ac
GAO: 143
MARCHESI, BLANCHE, s (1863-1940)
GAO: 563
MARDONES, JOSE, bs (1869-1932)
GAO: 185, 493
MARGHINOTTI, FRANCA, ms
GAO: 535, 565
MARHERR-WAGNER, ELFRIEDE, s (1888-1973)
GAO: 548
MARICONDA, VALERIA, s (1939-)
GAO: 453
MARINI, PALMIRA VITALI, ms
GAO: 312
MARINUZZI, GINO, cd (1882-1945)
GAO: 329
MARIO, QUEENA, s (1896-1951)
GAO: 121, 213, 260, 270, 539
MARIOTTI, ALFREDO, bs (1935-)
GAO: 330
MARKWORT, EMIL, t
GAO: 390
MARLOWE [MARLOW], ANTHONY, t (1909-1962)
GAO: 154, 193
MARS, JACQUES, bs (1926-)
GAO: 304
MARSCHNER, KURT, t (1913-)
GAO: 387
MARSHALL, HELEN, s
GAO: 291
MARTÌ, BERNABÉ, t (1934-)
GAO: 578
MARTIGNONI, M., cd
GAO: 498
MARTIN, BENJAMIN, b
GAO: 169
MARTIN, MARIE-THERESE, ms
GAO: 433
MARTIN, MICHEL, t
GAO: 443
MARTIN, RICCARDO, t (1874-1952)
GAO: 100
MARTIN, RUTH, translator
GAO: 171n
MARTIN, THOMAS P., translator
GAO: 171n
MARTINELLI, C., ac
GAO: 143
MARTINELLI, GIOVANNI, t (1885-1969)
GAO: 101, 102, 105, 106, 108, 113, 121, 122½, 128, 130, 136, 147, 169, 170, 177, 181, 186, 213, 221, 225, 236, 240, 260, 264, 270, 281, 288, 409, 448, 470, 475, 481, 500, 512, 563, 566, 577
SPECIAL RELEASE: STE 100 (following GAO 495)
MARTINEZ-PATTI, GINO, t (1866-1925)
GAO: 242
MARTINI, NINO, t (1905-1976)
GAO: 171, 172, 176, 212, 477, 513
MARTINIS, CARLA, s (1924-)
GAO: ?508
MARTINOTTI, BRUNO, cd (1937-1986)
GAO: 528
MARTZ, WOLFRAM
GAO: 273
MARWICK, DUDLEY, bs
GAO: 492
MASCAGNI, PIETRO, cd (1863-1945)
GAO: 310, 360, 483
MASCHERINI, ENZO, b (1911-1981)
GAO: 302, 319, 380, 467
MASCITTI, CONSTANZO, b
GAO: 437, 505
MASINI, GALLIANO, t (1896 or 1902-1986)
GAO: 425
MASINI, MAFALDA, ms
GAO: 165, 421
MASSARD, ROBERT, b (1925-)
GAO: 324, 326
MASSARIA, ANTONIO, t
GAO: 125, 216
MASSUE, NICHOLAS (Nicola), t (1910-)
GAO: 112, 153, 181, 215, 224, 231, 496, 524, 527
MATAČIČ, LOVRO VON, cd (1899-)
GAO: 158n, 395
MATHIAS, MARIA, s
GAO: 332
MATRANGA, CARMINE, b
GAO: 472
MATTEINI, GIULIANA, ms
GAO: 555
MATTIOLI, RENATA, s
GAO: 275, 459
MATTIUCCI, FRANCA, ms
GAO: 404

PAGGI, TINA, ms
GAO: 477
PAGLIUCA, SILVANO, b
GAO: 307
PAGLIUGHI, LINA, s (1907-1980)
GAO: 111, 133, 214, 272, 370, 391, 407, 452, 578
PALLINI, RINA, s
GAO: 476
PALMER, GLADYS, ms (?1898-?)
GAO: 111, 306
PALOMBINI, VITTORIA, c (1906-1971)
GAO: 389
PALTRINIERI, GIORDANO, t (1890-?)
GAO: 103/4, 106, 108, 109, 113, 118, 121, 128, 130, 131, 134, 142, 145, 147, 177, 181, 187, 215, 224, 225, 232, 270, 484, 485, 492, 504, 506, 551
PALUMBO, LIA, ms
GAO: 401
PAMPANINI, ROSETTA, s (1896-1973)
GAO: 329
PANDANO, VITTORIO, t (1919-)
GAO: 286
PANERAI, ROLANDO, b (1924-)
GAO: 125, 156, 204n, 272, 311, 333, 565
PANIZZA, ETTORE, cd (1875-1967)
GAO: 101, 106, 107, 118, 128, 136, 147, 170, 171, 177, 181, 212, 213, 215, 225, 228, 230, 239, 264, 270, 281, 325, 384n, 414, 485, 488, 512, 531, 540, 545, 551, 577
PANNI, NICOLETTA, s (1933-)
GAO: 376, 455, 480+n, 558
PANTSCHEFF, LJUBOMIR, bb (1913-)
GAO: 521
PAOLILLO, LUIGI, b
GAO: 369
PAPAGNI, ROSSANA, s
GAO: 391
PAPANTONIU, VASSO, s
GAO: 554
PAPPAS, GEORGIO, bs (1938-)
GAO: 315, 554
PAPPI, GENNARO, cd (1886-1941)
GAO: 103/4, 121, 130, 131, 139, 142, 152, 168, 169, 170, 172, 176, 212, 232, 237, 239, 248, 509, 524, 512
PAPUET, MARGUERITE
GAO: 573
PARADA, CLAUDIA, s (1933-)
GAO: 554
PARODI, ARMANDO LA ROSA, cd
GAO: 275, 408
PARRAT, GERMAINE, s
GAO: 449
PARRO, MANUELA BIANCHI, s
GAO: 235
PARUTTO, MIRELLA, ms
GAO: 455
PASELLA, GUIDO, bs
GAO: 486
PASEROTTI, PIETRO, b
GAO: 552
PASERO, TANCREDI, bs (1892-1983)
GAO: 146n, 359, 434, 575n
PASINI-VITALE, LINA, s (1872-1959)
GAO: 144+n
PASQUALI, NINO, bs
GAO: 320
PASQUALI, RENATO, bs
GAO: 309
PASQUIERO, ENZO, boy soprano
GAO: 479
PASTERNACK, JOSEF, cd (1881-1940)
GAO: 100, 191, 192, 214, 292n, 397, 452, 470, ?481+n, 566
PASTORI, ANTONIETTA, s (1929-)
GAO: 117, 159
PATAKY, KOLOMAN, VON, t (1896-1964)
GAO: 332
PATANÈ, FRANCO, cd (1908-1968)
GAO: 350, 351
PATANÈ, GIUSEPPE, cd (1932-1989)
GAO: 566
PATCH, WALTER (WALLY), ac (1888-1970)
GAO: 143
PATTI, ADELINA, s (1843-1919)
GAO: 100, 185, 532, 563
PATZAK, JULIUS, t (1898-1974)
GAO: 298, 463
PAULEE, MONA, s
GAO: 164
PAUL, CHARLES (see CHARLES-PAUL)
PAULL, JARNA, ms
GAO: 527
PAULY, ROSE (ROSE PAULY-DREESEN) s (1894-1975)
GAO: 145, 425
PAVAROTTI, LUCIANO, t (1935-)
GAO: 503, 518, 575, 577
PECHNER, GERHARD, b (1903-1969)
GAO: 164, 186, 301, 302, 374, 548, 561

RESCIGNO, NICOLA, pf and cd
GAO: 169, 186+n, 270, 470, 566, 578n
RESNIK, REGINA, s/c (1922-)
GAO: 227, 250
RETTORE, AURORA, s (1903-?)
GAO: 127
RETHBERG, ELISABETH, s (1894-1976)
GAO: 106, 108, 114, 115, 118, 121, 122n, 122½, 130, 135, 148, 168, 177, 181, 184, 221, 233, 239, 247, 255, 256, 288, 289, 301, 331, 425, 492, 504, 512, 532
RETHY, ESTER [ESTHER], s (1912-)
GAO: 314, 337
REY, GASTON, t
GAO: 443, 449, 498
REYNOLDS, ANNA, c (1936-)
GAO: 203, 446
RIBETTI, ELDA, s (1920-)
GAO: 358
RIBLA, GERTRUDE, s (1919-1980)
GAO: 214
RICAGNO, LUISELLA CIAFFI, s (see CIAFFI RICAGNO, LUISELLA)
RICCI, LUIGI, cd and pf
GAO: 141, 169, 233, 464, 469
RICCIARDI, FRANCO, t
GAO: 162, 368, 421
RICCO, IGINIO, bs
GAO: 355, 424
RICHTER, KARL, b (1885-1940)
GAO: 384
RICO, ROGER, bs (1910-1964)
GAO: 385
RIEDEL, KARL, cd
GAO: 213, 539
RIEGLER, FRIEDL, s
GAO: 189
RIGACCI, BRUNO, cd (1921-)
GAO: 293, 296, 317+n, 412, 453
RIGAL, DELIA, s
GAO: 208
RIGAUX, LUCIEN, b
GAO: 140n
RIGIRI, GUERRANDO, b
GAO: 436
RILLE. PETER, boy soprano
GAO: 344
RIMINI, GIACOMO, b (1888-1952)
GAO: 513
RINALDI, ALBERTO, b (1939-)
GAO: 416, 455
RINALDI, MARGHERITA, s (?1935-)
GAO: 286, 348, 522
RINAUDO, MARIO, bs (1936-)
GAO: 396, 503, 505, 555
RIPLEY, GLADYS, c (1908-1955)
GAO: 450
RIPPON, MICHAEL, bb (1938-)
GAO: 400
RISTORI, GABRIELLE, s
GAO: 449
RITCHIE, MARGARET, s (1903-1969)
GAO: 385
RITTER, MARGARET, ms
GAO: 227
RIZZIERI, ELENA, s (1922-)
GAO: 392, 490
RIZZOLI, BRUNA, s (1925-)
GAO: 271
RIZZOTTI, ELVIRA, ms
GAO: 542
ROAN, LYDIA, ms
GAO: 146, 299
ROBERT, FRANCIS, ac
GAO: 511
ROBERTI, MARGHERITA, s (1930-)
GAO: 381, 477
ROBERTSON, JAMES, cd (1904-1991)
GAO: 553
ROBEY, (Sir) GEORGE, ac (1869-1954)
GAO: 143
ROBIN, NICOLE, s
GAO: 324
ROBINSON, STANFORD, cd (1904-1984)
GAO: 329, 336, 357, 379, 447, 464, 469
ROBOVSKY, ABRASHA, bs
GAO: 145
ROBSON, ANN, ms
GAO: 386
ROCCA BRUNA, EUGENIA, ms
GAO: 303, 547
ROCCO, ANGELA, ms
GAO: 486
RODRIGUEZ, ROSA, s
GAO: 319
RODZINSKI, ARTUR, cd (1894-1958)
GAO: 145, 426, 482
RÖSSL-MAJDAN, HILDE, ms (1921-)
GAO: 189, 521
ROGANI, MARCO, t
GAO: 552
ROGATSCHEWSKY, JOSEPH, t (1891-1985)
GAO: 227
ROGERS, WALTER B., cd (1865-1939)
GAO: 100, 141, 142, 452, 566
ROGGERO, MARGARET, c (?1921-)
GAO: 130+n

WEISSENBORN, GÜNTHER, cd
GAO: 429
WEISSMANN, FRIEDER, cd (1893 or 1898-1984)
GAO: 100, 279, 322n, 337
WEITER, GEORG, bs
GAO: 298
WELBERS, KARL-HEINZ, boy soprano
GAO: 244, 567
WELITSCH, LJUBA, s (1913-)
GAO: 158, 288n, 508n, 553
WELLS, PHRADIE, s (?-1980)
GAO: 187, 200, 452, 501
WELTER, LUDWIG, bs (1917-1965)
GAO: 344, 521
WERNIGK, WILLIAM, t (1894-1973)
GAO: 332, 444
WESTI, KURT, t
GAO: 429
WETH-FALKE, MARGRET, c (1908-)
GAO: 318, 327, 534, 538
WETTERGREN, GERTRUDE, c (1896-)
GAO: 170, 186, 213, 258, 288, 366, 516
WICKS, DENNIS, bs (1928-)
GAO: 293
WIEDEMANN, HERMANN, b (1879-1944)
GAO: 332, 460
WIENER, OTTO, b (1913-)
GAO: 189, 521
WIERZBICKI, TADEUSZ, bs
GAO: 439
WILDE, OSCAR, au/sp (1854-1900)
GAO: ?267
WILHELM II, Kaiser, po/sp (1859-1941)
GAO: 267
WILLE, STEWART, pf
GAO: 124n, 397
WILLIAMS, BEN, t
GAO: 123 , 515
WILLIAMS, EMLYN, ac (1905-1987)
GAO: 456
WILLIAMS, TOM, b
GAO: 390
WILLIS, CONSTANCE, c, (1894-1940)
GAO: 167, 342, 431
WILLS, JOHN, pf,
GAO: 532
WILSON, CORINNE, pf (possibly "Williston")
GAO: 466
WINDHEIM, MAREK, t (1895-1960)
GAO: 116, 129, 219, 463, 492, 506
WINKLEHOFER, LEOPOLD
GAO: 362
WINKLER, BRUNO SEIDLER
(see SEIDLER-WINKLER, BRUNO)
WISSMANN, LORE, s (1922-)
GAO: 298
WITT, JOSEF, t (1910-)
GAO: 158n, 463
WITTE, ERICH, t (1911-)
GAO: 550
WOLANSKY, RAYMOND, b (1926-)
GAO: 537
WOLFE, JAMES, bb
GAO: 109, 134, 157, 224, 492, 499, 502, 504, 506
WOLFES, FELIX, pf (1892-1971)
GAO: 533
WOLFF, ALBERT, cd (1884-1970)
GAO: 245, 361
WOLLNY, VICTOR, cd
GAO: 305
WOLOCH, IRENE, ac
GAO: 344
WRAY, JOSEPHINE, s (?1903-1964)
GAO:
WULF, MARTINA s (1909-1982)
GAO: 574
WUNDERLICH, FRITZ, t (1930-1966)
GAO: 365, 521, 537
WURMSER, LEO, cd
GAO: 274, 386
WYZANOWSKY, OLOF DE, b
GAO: 315

YEEND, FRANCES, s (1918-)
GAO: 457
YON, PIETRO (ALESSANDRO), organ (1886-1943)
GAO: 122½
YOUNG, ALEXANDER, t (1920-)
GAO: 438
YOUNG, VICTOR, cd (1900-1956)
GAO: 531

ZACCARIA, NICOLA, bs (1923-)
GAO: 117, 340, 376, 476, 518n, 542
ZAGONARA, ADELIO, t (?1905-)
GAO: 306, 308, 469, 552
ZALLINGER, MEINHARD VON, cd (1897-)
GAO: 273
ZAMBELLI, CORRADO, bs (1897-1974)
GAO: 111, 366, 403
ZAMBON, AMEDEO, t (1934-)
GAO: 554

Index of Works Performed

Major works are given in strict alphabetical order. Excerpts are given in their proper score order. Numerical titles precede the rest of the alphabet (e.g."20" will come before "ta"). Titles are given in their original language (except for those in Russian and Slavic languages) with cross-references furnished where appropriate. Familiar translations, in brackets, will be given selectively.

Because so many songs seem to inhabit the repertory outside of the context of their original *cycle* or collection (how many of us can recall off-hand that Richard Strauss' "Morgen" is drawn from his VIER LIEDER, Op. 27 of 1894?), they are listed under the title of the full cycle (Schubert's "Ständchen," for example, will be found under SCHWANENGESANG) but cross-referenced under their individual titles. Exceptions have been made in those instances where the name of a song collection or cycle is improbably generic (e.g. Brahms and Wolf), in which case the song is listed independently without a cross-reference. Opus numbers will be used generally, but modern catalog numbers (Köchel numbers for Mozart, Deutsch numbers for Schubert, etc.) will be given where appropriate, or when opus numbers no longer seem to apply.

Well-known operatic excerpts are listed specifically by title, while more obscure passages from the score (usually longer excerpts containing no well-known arias and ensembles) are given under the subheading "Excerpts." "Complete" performances, "abridgements," "adaptations", and "excerpts" are designated as they appear in the discography.

Lyricists for songs are not given in this index, but are found in the listing.

The *non-literary* spoken passages on EJS 267 are listed collectively in this index under SPOKEN WORD; such literary excerpts as "The Charge of the Light Brigade" are arranged by title. Brief spoken passages from musical concerts (Gigli, De Luca, etc.) are not indexed, as they are unclassifiable by title.

A lower-case "n" following a citation designates mention *only* in an endnote, while "+n" designates an endnote *in addition* to mention in the discography.

Index of Live Performances

All live performances, whether recorded in-house or off-the-air, are defined here as *public performances* played to a live (non-studio) audience in a live concert setting. Excluded are Metropolitan Opera broadcasts (see the **INDEX OF METROPOLITAN OPERA BROADCASTS AND TELECASTS**), and EIAR/RAI broadcasts and telecasts (see the **INDEX OF EIAR AND RAI BROADCASTS AND TELECASTS**).

Operatic stage performances are designated complete (c), abridged (a), or excerpted (e). As in the other indices, a lower-case "n" (or "+n") following a catalog number indicates an endnote. Abridged "concert versions," when given on an LP complete as performed, will be noted below as *complete*, but will be described fully in the endnote for that individual LP.

When the precise location of a performance (the theater, radio studio facility, concert hall, etc.) has not been determined, only the country or city is given as a heading in the index, reflecting the incomplete information cited in the discography. *Question marks* preceding LP catalog numbers designate an uncertainty about either the house or the date given, which will be discussed in the endnotes accompanying those issues.

Broadcast speeches and other non-musical performances are listed in the **INDEX OF STUDIO BROADCASTS AND TELECASTS**. Private recordings (given with or without an audience of any kind) are not included here.

For ease of access, and where appropriate, the broadcast indexes will occasionally overlap with this index of live performances.

CENTRO SPERIMENTALE, VENICE
1965: GAO: 333e

CHICAGO [CIVIC] OPERA HOUSE, CHICAGO
1 Nov 30: GAO: 444e
27 Nov 39: GAO: 169e
11 Nov 40: GAO: 270e
9 Dec 40: GAO: 282e
1 Dec 41: GAO: 220e
8 Dec 41: GAO: 477e

CHIESA DELL'ASSUNZIONE, L'ARRICCA
25 Jul 65: GAO: 343e

CINCINNATI MAY FESTIVAL, CINCINNATI
5 May 37: GAO: 226c

CITY HALL, SHEFFIELD, ENGLAND
30 Mar 49: GAO: 529c

COVENT GARDEN (see *ROYAL OPERA HOUSE*, *COVENT GARDEN*)

DALLAS, TEXAS
30 Oct 71: GAO: 578e

THE DOME, BRIGHTON, ENGLAND
13 Oct 49: GAO: 529c

EDINBURGH FESTIVAL, EDINBURGH
27 Aug 47: GAO: 383c
Sep 49: GAO: 553c

5th REGIMENT AMORY, BALTIMORE, MARYLAND ["EISENHOWER FOR PRESIDENT" RALLY]
25 Sep 52: GAO 531

FORT WORTH OPERA HOUSE, FORT WORTH, TEXAS
30 Nov 62: GAO: 563e

FRANKFURT-HÖCHST (see *TEATRO LA FENICE*, VENICE)

GÖTEBORG CONCERT HALL, GOTHENBURG
5 Aug 60: GAO: 252e

GOTHENBURG CONCERT HALL (see *GÖTEBORG CONCERT HALL*)

GRANT PARK, CHICAGO
21 Aug 41: GAO: 470e

HAMMERSMITH OPERA, FULHAM, ENGLAND
6 Apr 67: GAO: 400c

HAVANA [SYMPHONY] CONCERTS, HAVANA
24 Oct 48: GAO: 285e

HOLLAND FESTIVAL, ?AMSTERDAM
1966: GAO: 575e, 576e

HOLLYWOOD BOWL, LOS ANGELES
24 May 36: GAO: 103/104e, 190e, 191e
28 Aug 47: GAO 457e
13 Jul 48: GAO: 531e, 564e
24 Jul 48: GAO: ?457e
28 Jul 48: GAO: ?457e

INTERNATIONAL FESTIVAL OF MELODRAMMA (see *TEATRO DELL'OPERA DE CASINO*)

ISTITUZIONE UNIVERSITARIA DEI CONCERTI DI ROMA [see *VACANZE MUSICALI*]

KONINGLIJKE OPER, GHENT
1964: GAO: 439c
1968: GAO: 442c

JORDAN HALL (see *NEW ENGLAND CONSERVATORY OF MUSIC*

KURHAUS, *WALDFRIEDEN* (see *MUSIKTAGE HITZACKER*)

LANDESTHEATER, LINZ
?: GAO: 428c

LA SCALA, MILAN (see TEATRO ALLA SCALA)

LA SCALA OPERA, PHILADELPHIA
16 Apr 48: GAO: 270e, 409e

LEWISOHN STADIUM, NEW YORK CITY
22 Jul 37: GAO: 167e

MAGGIO MUSICALE FIORENTINO, FLORENCE
9 May 54: GAO: 467c
May 57: GAO: 514c
14 Jun 57: GAO: 422e
9 May 58: GAO: 253c
10 May 59: GAO: 421e
2 May 68: GAO: 421e

Index of Studio Broadcasts and Telecasts

All studio broadcasts (as distinguished from radio and television *shows*) are indexed below. Broadcasts of the BBC, Norwegian and Swedish Radio, WDR, etc., though mounted as broadcast performances, were not *regularly-scheduled*, sponsored radio shows: most were simply single-event broadcasts, such as the BBC concerts of Schumann, Flagstad and Gigli. Live theatrical performances emanating from an opera house or concert hall rather than from a radio studio are included in the **INDEX OF LIVE PERFORMANCES** and the **INDEX OF METROPOLITAN OPERA BROADCASTS AND TELECASTS**, just as the studio productions of Italian Radio will be found in the **INDEX OF EIAR AND RAI BROADCASTS AND TELECASTS**.

Though relatively few studio broadcasts appeared complete on any of the EJS labels, individual entries will nonetheless be designated complete or complete-as-broadcast (c), abridged (a), or excerpted (e). Abridged "concert versions," when given on an LP complete as performed, will be noted as *complete*, but will be fully described in the endnote for that individual LP. As in the other indices, a lower-case "n" (or "+n") following a catalog number indicates an endnote.

Special, one-time broadcasts from the United States which were given unique titles (*SWEDEN IN MUSIC*, for example) will be cited in the **INDEX OF RADIO AND TELEVISION PROGRAMS**, as these were most frequently heard as part of, or as a substitute for, a continuing series, though there were exceptions.

When the precise location of a performance (the theater, radio facility, concert hall, etc.) has not been determined, only the country or city is given as a heading in the index, reflecting the incomplete information cited in the actual discography.

Broadcast speeches and other non-musical live performances are also indexed here as appropriate, while private recordings are not.

ACRONYMS FOR CROSS-REFERENCE:

AFRS Armed Forces Radio Service (U.S.A.)
AVRO Algemeene Vereniging Radio Omroep [aka *Algemene Omroepvereniging] Hilversum*, Holland (Netherlands)
BBC British Broadcasting Corporation, London (U.K.)
CORSI Società Cooperative per la Radiotelevisione nella Svizzera Italiana [*Radio Svizzera Italiana*]
NBC National Broadcasting Company (U.S.A.)
NDR Norddeutschen Rundfunk, Hamburg (Germany)
NRK Norsk Rikskringkasting [*Norwegian Radio*], Oslo (Norway)
ORF Österreichischer Rundfunk [*Austrian Broadcasting Corporation*] (Austria)
ORTF Office de Radiodiffusion Télévision Française, Paris (France)
RAVAG Radio Verkehers AG [*Austrian Broadcasting Corporation*] (Austria)
RDF Office de Radiodiffusion (see ORTF)
SSR Office Suisse de Radiodiffusion et Télévision [*Radio Bern*], Bern (Switzerland)
VARA Omroepvereniging, Hilversum, Holland (Netherlands)
WDR Westdeutscher Rundfunk, Köln (Germany)

Index of Radio and Television Programs

Following is a brief summary of the most prominent regularly-scheduled radio and television programs excerpted throughout "The Golden Age of Opera" series.

AMERICA PREFERRED: Originating over station WOR, New York City (Bamberger Broadcasting Service), this show featured foreign-born and naturalized American artists performing on behalf of defense bonds. Lotte Lehmann, Ezio Pinza, Suzanne Sten, Kerstin Thorborg, Greta Stückgold, Salvatore Baccaloni, Lauritz Melchior, and Bidú Sayão were among the singers who appeared, but Elisabeth Schumann's 1942 broadcast was the only one excerpted in the GAO series (EJS 213). The show began in the autumn of 1941: Alfred Wallenstein was the conductor, Deems Taylor the narrator. Heard variously on Saturday and Thursday evenings, the repertory was primarily classical and also featured a number of important instrumentalists--Heifetz, Zimbalist, Rubinstein, Piatigorsky, and Casadesus among them.

AMERICAN RADIATOR HOUR (aka ***FIRESIDE RECITALS***): Sponsored by the American Radiator Company from 16 September, 1934 to 2 January, 1938 over station WEAF, New York City (NBC Red). The regular conductors were Frank Black and Frank St. Leger. See the endnote for EJS 397 (I/1j) for further details.

ATWATER KENT [RADIO] HOUR: One of the earliest concert music programs on commercial network radio, the ***ATWATER KENT HOUR*** began in the early 1920 and ran through the 1930-1931 season. It was heard over NBC on Sunday evenings beginning at 9:15 pm EST. The resident musical director was Donald Voorhees, though conductors varied. Soprano Frances Alda was the last featured soloist.

BELL TELEPHONE HOUR: This long-running Monday evening program began over WEAF, New York City (NBC Red) on 29 April, 1940. After the war it was produced in the studios of WNBC, Rockefeller Center, New York City. For twenty-eight years, on radio and television, Donald Voorhees was the regular conductor of the fifty-seven piece Bell Telephone Orchestra. A popular band leader in the mid 1920s, Voorhees had earlier directed ***THE ATWATER KENT HOUR***, also at NBC. For the first two seasons, tenor James Melton and soprano Francia White were the featured soloists, but Jascha Heifetz's ground-breaking appearance on 27 April, 1942 initiated the series of "Great Artists" broadcasts that resulted in many of the performances featured throughout "The Golden Age of Opera" series. ***THE BELL TELEPHONE HOUR*** was so popular that several short films were made depicting rehearsals and broadcasts with such artists as Ezio Pinza, Blanche Thebom, and Josef Hofmann. Released under the series title, "Rehearsal," they appear to have been advertisements for the sponsor, not a commercial theatrical product. After nearly twenty years on the air, ***THE BELL TELEPHONE HOUR*** moved to television on 9 October, 1959, where it survived on NBC until 26 April, 1968--with Voorhees steadfastly at the podium.

BLANCHE ARRAL: For details of this short-lived program, see the endnote for EJS 466.

BONINO: See the endnote for EJS 120 (II/3).

BRITISH BROADCASTING CORPORATION (BBC): Regular concert programming included the ***BBC HOME SERVICE***, ***FRIDAY RECITAL***, ***GENERAL OVERSEAS SERVICE***, ***LIGHT PROGRAMME CONCERT***, ***MUSIC FOR YOU***, ***REGIONAL PROGRAMME***, ***RADIO-CORRIERE DELLA LIBERTÀ*** (for broadcast to Italy during the War), ***ROYAL PHILHARMONIC CONCERT***, ***SUNDAY CONCERT***, and ***THIRD PROGRAMME***.

CHASE AND SANBORN HOUR (aka ***CHASE AND SANBORN PROGRAM***): One of the stable of Standard Brands programs, sponsored by Chase and Sanborn Coffee, a subsidiary of Standard Brands, Inc., it originated in Hollywood with a well-known cast that included Nelson Eddy, Don Ameche, Dorothy Lamour, and Edgar Bergen. Robert Armbruster was the regular conductor. The show was first aired in September, 1928, with a new series beginning 9 May, 1937, originating over KFI, Los Angeles (NBC Red). See also the ***GLADYS SWARTHOUT PROGRAM***.

A special series of fourteen opera adaptations apparently produced in New York, was heard between 2 December, 1934 and 17 March, 1935 as the ***STANDARD BRANDS HOUR***: see the endnotes for EJS 289-291.

CHESTERFIELD HOUR (aka ***CHESTERFIELD PRESENTS***): Sponsored by Liggett & Meyers Tobacco Company, this show began in the late 1920s. The earliest broadcasts represented in "The Golden Age of Opera" series are Ponselle's from 1934. The show originated in New York from station WABC (CBS) and was conducted (three nights a week from 9:00-9:30 pm EST) in the auditorium of the Manhattan Theater. Regular hosts included Deems Taylor and actor Paul Douglas. André Kostelanetz was the featured conductor of his own orchestra. The series that included regular guest appearances by Lawrence Tibbett (29 December, 1937 to 23 March, 1938) and Grace Moore (beginning on 30 March, 1938) was inaugurated on 6 July, 1937.

The ***CHESTERFIELD PROGRAM***, a CBS series begun on 31 December, 1937 and hosted by Paul Whiteman, was the popular music equivalent of ***CHESTERFIELD HOUR***. Similarly, NBC's ***CHESTERFIELD TIME***, first heard in 1939, was a popular show with Fred Waring and His Orchestra. See also the endnote for EJS 445 regarding Richard Bonelli's regular appearances on the show.

CHRISTOPHER PROGRAM: An Italian show in English produced in Rome in early 1957, evidently by the Catholic group, the Christophers. It is not entirely clear whether it was actually telecast in this country, but it may have been seen in syndication. Little else is known, but see the endnote for EJS 457 (II/6-8) for further details.

COCA-COLA SHOW (aka ***THE PAUSE THAT REFRESHES***): A long-running New York program sponsored by the Coca-Cola Bottling Company beginning in the 1934-1935 season over NBC, with Frank Black conducting a sixty-five piece orchestra and twenty-five vocalists. The show moved to CBS on 1 December, 1940, originating over WABC-AM and -FM. André Kostelanetz was the musical director and conductor, violinist Albert Spalding the narrator, and baritone John Charles Thomas the featured soloist. The show ran on Sunday afternoons from 4:30-5:00 pm EST until 1944. A solitary excerpt from a 1943 appearance by Jarmila Novotna (EJS 532) appeared in "The Golden Age of Opera" series.

CONCERTO MARTINI E ROSSI: This showcase for major musicians was first broadcast over Ente Italiano Audizioni Radiofoniche (EIAR), predecessor of RAI, on 1 January, 1936 and only expired with the passing of sponsored programming on RAI in the 1960s.

CONCERTO PER LE FORZE ARMATI: Produced by EIAR, this wartime broadcast series was offered to Italian troops.

EDGAR BERGEN AND CHARLIE McCARTHY SHOW: Bergen's lengthy career as a radio star began on Rudy Vallee's ***ROYAL GELATIN HOUR*** on 17 December, 1936, leading to his own NBC show, ***THE CHASE AND SANBORN PROGRAM*** (aka ***THE CHARLIE McCARTHY SHOW***), sponsored by Standard Brands, which premiered on 9 May, 1937 as a 60-minute variety show. Ray Noble's Orchestra served as the resident ensemble. After January, 1940 the show was reduced to 30 minutes, but remained in its established Sunday evening slot at 8:00 pm EST. The Standard Brands show ended on 26 December, 1948, but by 1949, Coca-Cola took over sponsorship, and the show, produced in Hollywood, moved to CBS. Only three broadcasts have been traced to "The Golden Age of Opera" series: a 1948 Dallas broadcast over NBC (EJS 457) and two 1951 CBS shows from Hollywood (EJS 252).

ED SULLIVAN SHOW: This American television institution was first seen on the CBS television network on 20 June, 1948 and ended its lengthy run on 6 June, 1971. It originated in New York (though it often featured filmed appearances of artists from elsewhere around the world) and was seen on Sunday evenings from 8:00-9:00 pm beginning in March, 1949. Sponsors varied. The original title of the show, "Toast of the Town," was replaced by "The Ed Sullivan Show" on 18 September, 1955. A number of important singers appeared on Sullivan's show, though only one segment, from a 17 February, 1957 telecast featuring Jussi Bjoerling, Hilde Güden, and Thelma Votipka (EJS 367) appeared on "The Golden Age of Opera" series.

ELIZABETH RETHBERG: From WOR, New York City, with Rethberg accompanied by Alfred Wallenstein, either on piano or conducting "Wallenstein's Orchestra." This was a ten-show series, broadcast, except for the last installment, on Thursday evenings beginning on 11 July, 1941 at 9:30 pm. The final show aired on Friday evening, 11 September, 1941.

FIRESTONE CONCERT: Originating out of Station WEAF (NBC Red), New York City, and sponsored by the Firestone Tire and Rubber Company, this was the predecessor of the long-running ***VOICE OF FIRESTONE***, q.v. See the endnote for EJS 482 (II/5-8). William Daly's Orchestra provided the accompaniment until 1936. The change of name to ***THE VOICE OF FIRESTONE*** came during the 1937-1938 season. Tibbett made several appearances on the ***FIRESTONE CONCERT***, but only a few Swarthout excerpts (three of the four with baritone Frank Chapman), circa 1934, were included in "The Golden Age of Opera" series (EJS 482).

FIRESIDE RECITALS **(see *AMERICAN RADIATOR HOUR*)**

FORD SUNDAY EVENING HOUR: Detroit broadcasts, produced by William Reddick and sponsored by the Ford Motor & Lincoln Motor Company beginning in 1934. The "Ford Symphony Orchestra" consisted of members of the Detroit Symphony Orchestra. The broadcasts originated in the Masonic Temple Auditorium in Detroit and were broadcast from WJR, Detroit--originally a CBS affiliate--on Sunday evenings from 9:00-10:00 pm EST. W. J. Cameron was the regular conductor, but the items included on EJS included guest conductors John Barbirolli, Fritz Reiner, José Iturbi, and Eugene Ormandy. Singers regularly affiliated with the show included Gladys Swarthout, Richard Bonelli, Helen Jepson, and John Charles Thomas. The show remained on CBS until 1 March, 1942, returning for the 1945-1946 season on ABC.

GENERAL MOTORS HOUR (aka ***GENERAL MOTORS CONCERTS***): Sponsored by General Motors Company, first out of Detroit, presumably from station WWJ (NBC Red), and by 1936, out of New York City over station WEAF. Erno Rapee was the featured conductor, Milton Cross the announcer. The Ponselle and Swarthout broadcasts from Detroit extend back to at least 1935. A Hollywood Bowl series from station KECA, Los Angeles, featuring Lucrezia Bori, Joseph Bentonelli and the Los Angeles Philharmonic Orchestra under Otto Klemperer, was heard in the spring of 1937 under the title ***GENERAL MOTORS PROMENADE CONCERT***. Another series of broadcasts excerpted in "The Golden Age of Opera" featured Helen Jepson, Jussi Bjoerling, Grace Moore, Richard Tauber, and Erna Sack, and ran over WEAF from 6 October to 26 December, 1937.

THE GLADYS SWARTHOUT PROGRAM: See the endnote for EJS 247 (I/8). This appears to have been an occasional program (the 31 March, 1937 broadcast being the sole example in "The Golden Age of Opera" series) sponsored by the National Ice Advertising, Inc. and originating over WEAF, New York City (NBC Red). Swarthout was appearing on a number of other shows the same year, including the ***CHASE AND SANBORN HOUR*** and ***FORD SUNDAY EVENING HOUR***.

GREAT MOMENTS IN MUSIC (aka ***CELANESE HOUR***): Sponsored by the Celanese Corporation of America, manufacturers of fabrics and textiles, this program ran for two seasons between 1945 and 1947. The conductor was Sylvan Levin. Each broadcast was usually built around some unifying theme--the music of a specific composer, highlights of a particular opera, etc., and featured a stock company of performers that came to include Jan Peerce, Robert Weede, Frances Yeend, Mario Lanza and Marie Rogndahl. It was heard Wednesday evenings from 10:00-10:30 pm EST over station WABC (CBS), New York City.

JOHN CHARLES THOMAS PROGRAM: See the endnote for EJS 531. Thomas' Westinghouse-sponsored show went on the air over NBC on 10 January, 1943. Originally assisted by the Lyn Murray Chorus and a studio orchestra directed by Mark Warnow, the musical direction for the show was eventually taken over by Victor Young. John Nesbitt, of "Passing Parade" fame, was also featured as a story teller, along with the Ken Darby Singers. The show was essentially popular in repertory: Thomas rarely performed serious music on the broadcasts.

KRAFT MUSIC HALL: From 2 January, 1936, when Bing Crosby became its host, this long-running program was produced in Hollywood, originating over station KFI, Los Angeles (NBC Red). The sponsor was the Kraft-Phenix Cheese Corporation. The program was first aired as a local New York City show on 26 June, 1933 with regulars Jack Fulton, Roy Bargy, master of ceremonies Deems Taylor, and the Paul Whiteman Orchestra. Al Jolson became the host later that year. The Crosby years yielded performances by a number of major artists, including Kirsten Flagstad in August, 1938 (EJS 183). Crosby left in the spring of 1946, apparently because Kraft would not consent to his pre-recording the shows. Al Jolson once again became the host beginning in the fall of 1947. Under the subsequent sponsorship of Philco (1946-1949), Chesterfield Cigarettes (1949-1952), and General Electric (1952-1956), Crosby went on to host his own long-running ***BING CROSBY SHOW***.

LÉON ROTHIER: An irregularly-scheduled local New York City show featuring Rothier and his guests over station WQXR (Interstate Broadcasting Company) during the 1938-1941 seasons (approximate). See the endnote for EJS 140. WQXR was one of the first stations to run shows specifically aimed at vocal record collectors: the famous Emma Eames broadcast of Thursday, 2 February, 1939 (transcribed as IRCC 3142, issued in January, 1954) appeared on the WQXR show, ***GREAT SINGERS***.

LOS ANGELES PHILHARMONIC: The earliest broadcasts found under this name were in fact ***GENERAL MOTORS HOUR*** broadcasts (q.v.) with Ponselle and Swarthout dating from 1935 and 1936. Excerpts from a group of 1950 Stella Roman broadcasts conducted by Artur Rodzinski, also from the Hollywood Bowl, appeared on EJS 426. The orchestra appeared frequently on ***THE STANDARD HOUR*** (q.v.), broadcasting from the Los Angeles Shrine Auditorium and suburban sites such as Whittier and San Bernadino.

THE MAGIC KEY OF RCA: Sponsored by the Radio Corporation of America (RCA) beginning on 29 September, 1935. [Dr.] Frank Black, erstwhile musical director of the Brunswick studios was the resident conductor of the NBC Symphony Orchestra. ***THE MAGIC KEY OF RCA*** originated from Studio 8-H, Radio City, New York, and was broadcast over WJZ (NBC Blue). By the 1938-1939 season, its last, the show was heard on over 100 affiliate stations across the U.S., with worldwide pickups. Milton Cross and Ben Grauer were the announcers (Grauer was the announcer for a host of NBC classical music shows, including the ***NBC SYMPHONY ORCHESTRA***). Prior to the merger of the Victor Talking Machine Company and RCA, the former had sponsored its own broadcast series in the mid 1920s over WEAF (NBC Red), New York City, featuring Victor artists almost exclusively, accompanied by the Victor Concert Orchestra under the direction of Victor's studio conductors of the period, Josef Pasternack and Rosario Bourdon.

METROPOLITAN OPERA AUDITIONS OF THE AIR: Originating from WJZ (NBC Blue), New York City. The broadcasts began on 18 October, 1935, and continued, with significant interruptions, through the 1950s. With the forced break-up of the NBC Red and Blue networks in 1942-1943, the show was subsequently heard over the newly-formed ABC network (the former NBC Blue) but still in its traditional time slot on Sunday afternoon at 5:00 pm EST. Wilfred Pelletier was the conductor, leading the credited "Wilfred Pelletier Orchestra," presumably a faction of the Met's house orchestra. Excerpts from only one 1948 show were featured in "The Golden Age of Opera" series (EJS 214).

METROPOLITAN OPERA FUND: The Metropolitan Opera Guild's pleas for financial support began on radio during Henry Souvaine's fund raisers in the 1939-1940 season and probably continue to this day. Giuseppe De Luca's spoken appeal from the 10 February, 1940 BOHÈME matinee is preserved complete on EJS 248. The 10 March, 1940 telecast over W2XBS (NBC), New York City, featuring Bruna Castagna (EJS 247) was an extraordinary extension of the concept, considering the date.

METROPOLITAN OPERA GUILD BROADCAST: see ***OPERA GUILD BROADCAST***.

METROPOLITAN OPERA: INTERMISSION FEATURES: These were intermission programs heard during the Saturday afternoon NBC Met broadcasts. Geraldine Farrar's 1934-1935 shows were featured on EJS 107 and 397 and a rare appearance by Margaret Matzenauer in 1942 was included on EJS 186.

THE METROPOLITAN OPERA PRESENTS: Special Sunday broadcasts from the Met during the mid 1940s featuring a variety of Met artists and conductors. These originated from station WJZ, New York City, by then part of the ABC network.

THE [METROPOLITAN] PRE-OPERA CONCERT: Annual Saturday matinee broadcast features originating from Cleveland's Municipal Auditorium over WHK, Cleveland [NBC Blue], to inaugurate the Met's 1939 and 1940 seasonal appearances in that city.

MUSIC OF THE NEW WORLD: A wartime (1943) series heard over station WEAF (NBC) on Thursday evenings, 11:30-12:00 pm EST, with the NBC Symphony Orchestra conducted by Frank Black, highlighting music of the American continents.

MUTUAL'S OPERA CONCERT: A syndicated Mutual network series that began in about 1949 and ended on 23 November, 1951. The half-hour show was hosted by conductor Sylvan Levin, formerly an associate of Stokowski in Philadelphia, and featured singers from the New York City Opera, Metropolitan Opera *comprimarii*, and an occasional "star" such as Jerome Hines, Herva Nelli, or Alexander Sved. Only one excerpt appeared in the GAO series (EJS 169), but Smith featured several on later labels.

NBC SYMPHONY ORCHESTRA: David Sarnoff, head of the Radio Corporation of America, created this celebrated orchestra for Arturo Toscanini in 1937. The ninety-two piece radio ensemble consisted of musicians lured away from some of the finest orchestras in the world. The broadcasts, which began in November, 1937 under conductors Artur Rodzinski and Pierre Monteux, originated from NBC's Studio 8H (capacity 1,200) in Rockefeller Center, New York City, and were heard over both the NBC Blue and Red networks on Saturday evenings at 10:00 pm EST. Toscanini (who was paid a reported $4,000 per broadcast) began his long association with the program on Christmas night, 1937. Until the 1950-1951 season, the show was *sustained* by the network, not sponsored. The last regularly-scheduled broadcast, under conductor Roy Shield, was on 29 August, 1954. Dr. Frank Black was the staff director of the orchestra, but guest conductors were frequent. Ben Grauer was the most prominent announcer.

NEW YORK PHILHARMONIC: The New York Philharmonic began its series of regular weekly broadcasts during the 1927-1928 season. Originating from Carnegie Hall over station WABC, New York City, the show was heard nationally over the CBS network on Sunday afternoons (Thursday evenings during its maiden seasons). From 1931 to 1940 it occupied a two-hour time slot, reduced to 90 minutes the following season. The program was still on the air in the late 1950s and was, for most of its run, *sustained* without sponsorship (between 1944 and 1950 it was underwritten variously by U.S. Rubber and Socony Oil). Conductors varied.

OPERA GUILD BROADCAST: Sponsored by Chase and Sanborn, this may have been an early Metropolitan Opera Guild program. It originated over station WJZ (NBC Blue), New York City. Only excerpts from a single Bori broadcast of 30 December, 1934 were featured on GAO (EJS 541).

PACKARD HOUR: Sponsored by the Packard Motor Car Company. Lawrence Tibbett's ***PACKARD HOUR*** broadcasts were featured prominently throughout "The Golden Age of Opera" series (EJS 110, 124, and 397), though Smith also issued appearances by Geraldine Farrar (1931), Giovanni Martinelli (1935), and Joseph Bentonelli (1936). A lengthy endnote about Tibbett's regular 1934 and 1935 appearances will be found for EJS 110. The show began on NBC Blue and by 1935 had moved to CBS. A later Packard series, ***HOLLYWOOD MARDI GRAS***, originating over KFI, Los Angeles (NBC Red) on 7 September, 1937, ended on 1 March, 1938 and featured only popular entertainment, including baritone Lanny Ross.

PERFORMANCE: An early National Educational Television [NET] production from WGBH-Radio and WGBH-Television, Boston. See the extensive endnote for EJS 533.

PHILCO MUSIC HALL (aka ***PHILCO RADIO TIME***): Bing Crosby's second long-running show, following the ***KRAFT MUSIC HALL***, q.v., the ***PHILCO MUSIC HALL*** began over NBC on 16 October, 1946 and was the first major network show to be pre-recorded for presentation on-the-air in edited form. From 1946 until 1 June, 1949, the show was heard on Wednesday evenings, 10:00-10:30 pm EST. Later that year, Crosby's show came under the sponsorship of Chesterfield Cigarettes (Liggett and Meyers Tobacco Company).

PRODUCER'S SHOWCASE: An NBC-TV anthology show, running on Monday evenings from 8:00-9:30 pm EST from 18 October, 1954 to 27 May, 1957. Some of American television's most famous dramas, as well as musicals (Mary Martin's legendary 7 March, 1955 "Peter Pan" was an original ***PRODUCER'S SHOWCASE*** presentation) were produced for the show. Only one excerpt (EJS 168) appeared in "The Golden Age of Opera" series: see the endnote for that issue (II/3).

PRUDENTIAL FAMILY HOUR: A CBS presentation produced at station WABC, New York City beginning on 31 August, 1941. The show was heard on Sunday afternoons from 5:00-5:45 pm EST. From 1945 to 1947 it was scaled back to 30 minutes. In 1948, the concert format was dropped altogether: the show was cancelled during the 1949-1950 season. During Swarthout's long tenure on ***PRUDENTIAL FAMILY HOUR***, Al Goodman was the conductor. Patrice Munsel became the featured *prima donna* in 1945. A large number of Swarthout excerpts appeared on three GAO LPs: EJS 141, EJS 184, and EJS 482.

SCOTT MUSIC HALL: This short-lived NBC television series showcasing popular singer Patti Page ran over NBC from October, 1952 to August, 1953 on Wednesday evenings, 8:30-9:00 pm EST. The 8 April, 1953 broadcast (EJS 120) featured Ezio Pinza.

SHOWER OF STARS: A monthly musical variety *substitute* for the dramatic anthology series, "Climax" on CBS-TV. ***SHOWER OF STARS*** was telecast from 1954-1955 on Thursday evenings, 8:30-9:30 pm EST. David Rose was the conductor, Jack Barry the host.

SONG TREASURY (aka *TREASURE HOUR OF SONG*): Sponsored by Conti Castle shampoo and heard, except in its first season (1942-1943) on Thursday evenings from 9:30-10:00 pm EST over station WOR (Mutual Broadcasting System), New York City. Alfredo Antonini was the conductor. Soprano Licia Albanese and Met baritone Francesco Valentino were heard most frequently, although Dorothy Kirsten and Vivian Della Chiesa made occasional appearances throughout the show's five-year run (1943-1947).

STANDARD BRANDS HOUR: See ***CHASE AND SANBORN HOUR***.

STANDARD HOUR (originally ***THE STANDARD SYMPHONY***): San Francisco broadcasts, sponsored by Standard Oil Company of California. Among the earliest regular Pacific Coast Network broadcasts, the show began about 1925 as a vehicle for Walter Damrosch. By September, 1927 it had apparently been assumed by NBC's Pacific Coast Network, though neither KGO (NBC Blue) or KPO (NBC Red) in San Francisco became official network affiliates until 1929 and 1932, respectively. By the early 1930s it had evolved into a one-hour broadcast, alternating between the 8:30 to 9:30 and 9:30 to 10:30 pm time slots, PST and featuring, variously, the San Francisco Symphony and the Los Angeles Philharmonic. The Portland (Oregon) and Seattle (Washington) Symphonies also made occasional appearances. The earlier credited "Standard Symphony Orchestra" boasted Pierre Monteux as its resident conductor. Beginning in the Fall of 1944, the San Francisco Opera Orchestra (40 members culled from the 60-member San Francisco Symphony) were used to accompany singers from the San Francisco Opera in operatic abridgements and excerpts. For "pops" concerts in the late 1940s, smaller ensembles from the Los Angeles Philharmonic and San Francisco Symphony Orchestras appeared as "The Standard Symphony Orchestra" of whichever city was appropriate.

The show's San Francisco broadcasts usually originated in the San Francisco Civic Auditorium, but a few were made from the War Memorial Opera House and the Berkeley Community Theater. Most of the Los Angeles broadcasts originated from the downtown Shrine Auditorium. Often the San Francisco Opera traveled to Los Angeles after their regular season, appearing on the Los Angeles broadcasts.

From 1945 to 1953, the Standard Hour originated over KPO, San Francisco, and KFI, Los Angeles, both Pacific Coast Red (later Orange) affiliates of NBC. KPO changed its call letters to KNBC in early 1949.

VICK OPEN HOUSE: Sponsored by the Vick Chemical Company, makers of Vick's cough drops and VapoRub. The earliest shows with Grace Moore from the 1934-1935 and 1935-1936 seasons ran 30 minutes and originated from KFI (NBC Red), Los Angeles. The show was heard on Tuesday evenings at 9:00 pm, moving to Monday evenings at 9:30 pm in 1936. In September, 1937, Nelson Eddy was featured briefly as soloist and the show moved to CBS, originating from station KNX in Hollywood, airing on 51 stations on Sunday evenings at 7:00 pm PST. From 10 October, 1937 through the 1937-1938 season, Jeanette MacDonald and Wilbur Evans were the stars of the program. The Josef Pasternack Orchestra was the accompanying ensemble, Thomas Freebairn-Smith the announcer.

THE VOICE OF FIRESTONE: Along with ***THE BELL TELEPHONE HOUR***, the most prestigious classical music program on American radio. The show was sponsored by the Firestone Tire and Rubber Company over station WEAF, New York City and was broadcast throughout the country over the NBC Red network. Until the 1937-1938 season, its title was *FIRESTONE CONCERT* (q.v.). From the first broadcast on 3 December, 1928, *THE VOICE OF FIRESTONE* was heard on Monday evenings from 8:30-9:00 pm EST. William Daly was the conductor from 1928 to 1936, followed by Hugo Mariani (1936), Alfred Wallenstein (1936-1943), and finally, Howard Barlow (1943-1954). Barlow was still conducting when the show made its successful transition to television in September, 1949. It remained on NBC in its Monday evening spot until June, 1954, when it moved to the ABC television network. Barlow remained until the 1962-1963 season, at which point guest conductors were rotated, among them, Wilfred Pelletier. This season also marked a change from the Monday evening time slot to Sunday evening, 10:00-10:30 pm EST. The show left the air after nearly thirty-five years in June, 1963.

Richard Crooks was a featured soloist by 1935, alternating and appearing with soprano Margaret Speaks. The guests included some of the most distinguished performers active at the time, as can be seen from the many excerpts preserved in "The Golden Age of Opera" series.

WESTINGHOUSE PROGRAM: See *JOHN CHARLES THOMAS PROGRAM*.

* * * * * *

The index lists all sponsored and *sustained* shows heard on a more or less regular, continuing basis on commercial radio and television, as distinguished from network broadcast concerts (see the **INDEX OF STUDIO BROADCASTS AND TELECASTS**). Unlike live performances (see the **INDEX OF LIVE PERFORMANCES**), radio and television shows are defined here as studio productions which played to either a *studio* audience, or to no audience at all.

No single EJS LP ever contained the full contents of any show as broadcast, so it should be assumed that the citations given below are excerpts. However, *complete* shows were frequently represented over the course of several LPs, and this is discussed and cross-referenced throughout the discography in the appropriate endnotes. As in the other indices, a lower-case "n" (or "+n") following a catalog number indicates an endnote.

Titles in brackets are "special," one-time broadcasts that usually pre-empted regularly-scheduled shows.

Index of Metropolitan Opera Broadcasts and Telecasts

See also: *METROPOLITAN AUDITIONS OF THE AIR*, *METROPOLITAN OPERA FUND*, *METROPOLITAN OPERA: INTERMISSION FEATURES*, *METROPOLITAN OPERA PRESENTS*, and *[METROPOLITAN] PRE-OPERA CONCERT*, in the **INDEX OF RADIO AND TELEVISION PROGRAMS**.

Letter suffixes to the LP catalog numbers designate complete or complete-as-broadcast (c), abridged (a), or excerpted (e). As in the other indices, a lower-case "n" (or "+n") following a catalog number indicates an endnote.

Index of EIAR and RAI Operatic Broadcasts and Telecasts

EIAR and RAI broadcasts, as defined here, are complete, abridged, or excerpted performances of single operatic works, not excerpts that appeared on regular RAI shows like *CONCERTO MARTINI E ROSSI* (which will be found in the **INDEX OF RADIO AND TELEVISION PROGRAMS**). Similarly, the many live theatrical performances (Teatro alla Scala, for example) that were simply broadcast over RAI, rather than produced under their musical auspices, will be found in the **INDEX OF LIVE PERFORMANCES**.

Broadcast dates and recording dates (abbreviated "RD") for EIAR/RAI performances are given below, and are cross-referenced.

Most of the RAI operatic broadcasts issued on EJS were presented complete or complete-as-broadcast, so that only abridgements (a) and excerpts (e) will be indicated below as suffixes to the LP catalog numbers: unsuffixed EJS catalog numbers may be assumed to be *complete* performances. As in the other indices, a lower-case "n" (or "+n") following a catalog number indicates an endnote.

Index of Film Soundtracks

Films from which soundtrack excerpts have been taken are listed below by proper title or by copyright title: no complete *feature film* soundtracks were issued on any of Smith's labels, so it may be assumed that all of the LPs cited for these contain excerpts only.

As in the other indices, a lower-case "n" (or "+n") following a catalog number indicates an endnote.

PARAMOUNT [SOUND] NEWS (Paramount Prods./Publix newsreel series) ["Say it With Song"], New York, circa 1934
GAO: 512+n

DER SINGENDE TOR
(see CASA LONTANA)

TAXI DI NOTTE (Cinecittà, 1950
GAO: 469
THIS TIME FOR KEEPS (M-G-M, 1947)
GAO: 213
TRAGÔDIE EINER LIEBE
(see VERTIGINE)
TRE UOMINI IN FRAK
(Caesar Film, 1933)
GAO: 288, 331

TU SEI LA VITA MIA
(see DU BIST MEIN GLÜCK)

UNA VOCE NEL TUO CUORE
(Cinecittà, 1949)
GAO: 357
UNDER YOUR SPELL (20th-Century-Fox, 1936)
GAO: 124

LA VALSE DE PARIS
(Lux Films, 1949)
GAO: 420
VERGISS MEIN NICHT
(see NON TI SCORDAR DI ME)
VERTIGINE (Cinecittà, 1941)
GAO: 169
LA VITA DI GIUSEPPE VERDI
(see GIUSEPPE VERDI]

VITAPHONE SHORTS (Warner Brothers-Vitaphone Corporation)

BENIAMINO GIGLI AND GIUSEPPE DE DE LUCA IN DUET FROM ACT I OF "THE PEARL FISHERS" (PESCATORI DI PERLE) . . . BIZET (Vitaphone Varieties 518) (c1928)
GAO: 403
BENIAMINO GIGLI IN CAVALLERIA RUSTICANA SUPPORTED BY MILLO PICCO, MINNIE EGENER, AND CHORUS OF METROPOLITAN OPERA CO. . . . (Vitaphone Varieties 414) (c1927)
GAO: 464
BENIAMINO GIGLI OF THE METROPOLITAN OPERA COMPANY IN "A PROGRAM OF CONCERT FAVORITES" . . . (Vitaphone Varieties 498) (c1927)
GAO: 464
BENIAMINO GIGLI, TENOR OF THE METROPOLITAN OPERA COMPANY SINGING SELECTIONS FROM ACT II OF THE OPERA LA GIOCONDA (Vitaphone Varieties 517) (c1927)
GAO: 111
CHARLES HACKETT AND ROSA LOW / ROMÉO ET JULIETTE TOMB SCENE (Vitaphone Varieties 1143) (copyright date unknown)
GAO: 513
CHARLES HACKETT SINGING "IL MIO TESORO INTANTO" [and] "O PARADISO" Vitaphone Varieties 916 (c1929)
GAO: 513
GIOVANNI MARTINELLI, ASSISTED BY JEANNE GORDON IN SELECTIONS FROM CARMEN (Vitaphone Varieties 474) (c1927)
GAO: 102, 470
GIOVANNI MARTINELLI SINGING "COME BACK TO SORRENTO" [AND] "NINA" (Vitaphone Varieties 1213) (c1931)
GAO: 512
GIOVANNI MARTINELLI SINGING M'APPARI FROM MARTHA BY VON FLOTOW ASSISTED BY LIVIA MARRACCI (Vitaphone Varieties 932) (c1929
GAO: 470

Index/Concordance of LP Matrix Numbers

The "CO-P-" and "P-" prefix matrix numbers, which began appearing on the Smith LPs in October, 1966 with EJS 374, are listed below with their corresponding catalog numbers: the earlier and short-lived "CO-P" series is given first. See the INTRODUCTION TO THE DISCOGRAPHY for details of this numbering system.

Note that, beginning in the 2000 block of LP matrix numbers, *reissues* of some of the older GAO LPs began appearing, pressed during the UORC period of production. Sometimes distinguished by their blue print on white or off-white labels, these second editions exhibit signs of remastering and were often superior in sound and pitching. These *reissues* will be preceded by an asterisk in the listing below.

Matrix Number	*Catalog Numbers*
CO-P-902	GAO 374
CO-P-906	GAO 375
CO-P-913	GAO 376
CO-P-960	GAO 377
CO-P-965	GAO 378
CO-P-1004	GAO 380
CO-P-1007	GAO 379
CO-P-1040	GAO 384
CO-P-1042	GAO 382
CO-P-1071	GAO 386
CO-P-1078	GAO 389
CO-P-1079	GAO 390

Matrix Number	*Catalog Numbers*
P-1014	GAO 381
P-1039	GAO 383
P-1041	GAO 385
P-1072	GAO 387
P-1073	GAO 388
P-1137	GAO 392
P-1139	GAO 391
P-1140	GAO 393
P-1041	GAO 385
P-1072	GAO 387
P-1139	GAO 391
P-1176	GAO 394
P-1267	GAO 396
P-1268	GAO 398
P-1269	GAO 399
P-1270	GAO 397
P-1300	GAO 400
P-1301	GAO 402
P-1302	GAO 401
P-1303	GAO 403
P-1382	GAO 405

Matrix Number	*Catalog Numbers*
P-1383	GAO 407
P-1384	GAO 406
P-1385	GAO 404
P-1404	GAO 408
P-1401	GAO 409
P-1405	GAO 410
?P-1410	GAO 411
P-1447	GAO 412
P-1448	GAO 413
P-1449	GAO 414
P-1472	GAO 415
P-1473	GAO 416
P-1474	GAO 417
P-1475	GAO 418
P-1500	GAO 419
P-1501	GAO 421
P-1502	GAO 420
P-1535	GAO 425
P-1536	GAO 422
P-1537	GAO 423
P-1538	GAO 424
P-1558	GAO 426
P-1565	GAO 427
P-1570	GAO 429
P-1571	GAO 428
P-1584	GAO 430
P-1588	GAO 432
P-1590	GAO 431
P-1611	GAO 433
P-1612	GAO 434
P-1615	GAO 435
P-1638	GAO 436
P-1639	GAO 436
P-1640	GAO 436
P-1644	GAO 438
P-1645	GAO 437
P-1692	GAO 439

Matrix Number	*Catalog Numbers*
P-1696	GAO 440
P-1697	GAO 441
P-1712	GAO 443
P-1713	GAO 444
P-1717	GAO 442
P-1718	GAO 442
P-1719	GAO 445
P-1736	GAO 446
P-1738	GAO 447
P-1739	GAO 448
P-1740	GAO 449
P-1757	GAO 450
P-1759	GAO 451
P-1760	GAO 453
P-1762	GAO 452
P-1776	GAO 454
P-1777	GAO 454
P-1778	GAO 455
P-1780	GAO 456
P-1781	GAO 457
P-1791	GAO 458
P-1792	GAO 458
P-1793	GAO 459
P-1794	GAO 459
P-1795	GAO 460
P-1801	GAO 461
P-1802	GAO 461
P-1803	GAO 461
P-1803	GAO 462
P-1804	GAO 463
P-1805	GAO 464
P-1819	GAO 465
P-1820	GAO 465
P-1821	GAO 465
P-1822	GAO 465
P-1823	GAO 466
P-1844	GAO 467

Matrix Number	Catalog Numbers
P-1845	GAO 467
P-1846	GAO 468
P-1847	GAO 469
P-1848	GAO 470
P-1861	GAO 472
P-1862	GAO 471
P-1863	GAO 474
P-1864	GAO 475
P-1865	GAO 471
P-1866	GAO 471
P-1881	GAO 476
P-1882	GAO 476
P-1928	GAO 478
P-1929	GAO 477
P-1930	GAO 477
P-1946	GAO 479
P-1947	GAO 480
P-1948	GAO 481
P-1950	GAO 483
?P-1956	GAO 484
P-1957	GAO 484
P-1958	GAO 484
P-1959	GAO 484
P-1968	GAO 485
P-1978	GAO 486
P-1979	GAO 486
P-1980	GAO 487
P-1981	GAO 487
P-1982	GAO 487
P-1991	GAO 488
P-2001	GAO 490
P-2002	GAO 490
P-2004	GAO 491
P-2008	GAO 489
P-2009	GAO 489
P-2010	GAO 489
P-2011	GAO 489
P-2024	GAO 492
P-2025	GAO 493
P-2026	GAO 492
P-2027	GAO 492
P-2033	GAO 495
P-2052	GAO 494
P-2063	GAO 496
P-2064	GAO 496
P-2065	GAO 496
P-2070	GAO 497
P-2071	GAO 497
P-2072	GAO 498
P-2090	GAO 499
P-2091	GAO 499
P-2092	GAO 501
P-2097	GAO 501
P-2098	GAO 500
P-2100	GAO 502
P-2118	GAO 504
P-2119	GAO 504
P-2120	GAO 505
P-2121	GAO 505
P-2122	GAO 506
P-2123	GAO 507
P-2140	GAO 508
P-2141	GAO 509
P-2142	GAO 510
P-2143	GAO 511
P-2162	GAO 514
P-2163	GAO 514
P-2164	GAO 516
P-2165	GAO 517
P-2166	GAO 518
P-2172	GAO 515
P-2250	GAO 522
P-2251	GAO 522
P-2252	GAO 522
P-2253	GAO 523
P-2254	GAO 523
P-2255	GAO 524
?P-2171	GAO 515
P-2286	GAO 527
P-2287	GAO 527
P-2290	GAO 526
P-2291	GAO 526
P-2192	GAO 519
P-2209	GAO 520
P-2210	GAO 520
P-2211	GAO 520
P-2217	GAO 521
P-2218	GAO 521
P-2219	GAO 521
P-2293	GAO 525
P-2318	GAO 529
P-2319	GAO 530
P-2320	GAO 531
P-2321	GAO 532
P-2322	GAO 533
P-2327	GAO 528
P-2328	GAO 528
P-2352	GAO 534
P-2353	GAO 534
P-2354	GAO 534
P-2357	GAO 535
P-2358	GAO 536
P-2359	GAO 537
P-2364	GAO 540
P-2366	GAO 538
P-2367	GAO 538
P-2368	GAO 538
P-2369	GAO 538
P-2370	GAO 539
P-2371	GAO 541
P-2374	GAO 572
P-2397	GAO 542
P-2398	GAO 542
P-2399	GAO 543
P-2402	GAO 544
P-2403	GAO 545
P-2404	GAO 546
*P-2426	GAO 356
P-2435	GAO 549
P-2436	GAO 551
P-2439	GAO 547
P-2437	GAO 548
P-2438	GAO 548
P-2440	GAO 547
P-2441	GAO 550
P-2468	GAO 552
P-2469	GAO 552
P-2470	GAO 553
P-2471	GAO 553
P-2472	GAO 553
P-2473	GAO 554
P-2474	GAO 554
P-2475	GAO 554
P-2504	GAO 503
P-2505	GAO 503
P-2536	GAO 558
P-2537	GAO 562
P-2538	GAO 560
P-2539	GAO 559
P-2540	GAO 561
P-2541	GAO 564
P-2542	GAO 555
P-2543	GAO 555
P-2544	GAO 555
P-2549	GAO 566
P-2550	GAO 565
P-2551	GAO 563
P-2552	GAO 556
P-2553	GAO 556
P-2554	GAO 557
P-2698	GAO 567
P-2699	GAO 567
P-2707	GAO 568

About the Authors

WILLIAM SHAMAN is on the library faculty of Bemidji State University, Minnesota. He is the author of several journal and encyclopedia articles, numerous short articles and reviews, and co-author, with Susan Nelson, of a forthcoming discography of Marcel Moyse. His first book, *Giuseppe De Luca: A Discography*, was published in 1991.

WILLIAM J. COLLINS, an Assistant Professor of English at Kutztown University, teaches Americn Literature and Science Fiction courses. He has been an opera critic for Pacifica Radio and music critic for the *Davis Enterprise* in Northern California. He has published several discographies of opera singers, critical essays on many aspects of the opera, as well as on Mark Twain, Ernest Hemingway, and Phillip K. Dick. He is the co-author, with Bruce Levene, of the first biography of the nineteenth-century outlaw, Black Bart, entitled *Black Bart: The True Story of the West's Most Famous Stagecoach Robber* (1992).

CALVIN M. GOODWIN, a priest of the Society of Jesus, teaches classics in a Jesuit secondary school in Portland, Maine. He writes the annotations for the International Record Collectors' Club reissues of historical vocal recordings.

Recent Titles in Discographies

The Aladdin/Imperial Labels: A Discography
Michel Ruppli, compiler

Rockin' the Classics and Classicizin' the Rock: A Selectively Annotated Discography—First Supplement
Janell R. Duxbury, compiler

Igor Stravinsky—The Composer in the Recording Studio: A Comprehensive Discography
Philip Stuart, compiler

One Night Stand Series, 1-1001
Harry Mackenzie and Lothar Polomski, compilers

Antonín Dvořák on Records
John H. Yoell, compiler

Sarah Vaughan: A Discography
Denis Brown, compiler

PARSIFAL on Record: A Discography of Complete Recordings, Selections, and Excerpts of Wagner's Music Drama
Jonathan Brown, compiler

A Glenn Gould Catalog
Nancy Canning, compiler

Forty Years of Steel: An Annotated Discography of Steel Band and Pan Recordings, 1951-1991
Jeffrey Thomas, compiler

The Banjo on Record: A Bio-Discography
Uli Heier and Rainer E. Lotz, editors

The Mercury Labels: A Discography
Michel Ruppli and Ed Novitsky, compilers

Saxophone Recital Music: A Discography
Stanley L. Schleuter, compiler